ENCYCLOPEDIA
OF BIBLICAL THEOLOGY

ENCYCLOPEDIA OF BIBLICAL THEOLOGY

The Complete
Sacramentum Verbi

Edited by
Johannes B. Bauer

CROSSROAD · NEW YORK

1981
The Crossroad Publishing Company
18 East 41st Street, New York, NY 10017

Originally published as *Bibeltheologisches Wörterbuch*
by Verlag Styria, Graz-Vienna-Cologne, 1959
This translation copyright © 1970 by Sheed and Ward
from the third enlarged and revised edition of 1967.

Printed in the United States of America

Library of Congress Cataloging in Publication Data

Bibeltheologisches Wörterbuch. English.
  Encyclopedia of Biblical theology.

  Reprint of: Sacramentum verbi. New York: Herder
and Herder, 1970.
    Translation of: Bibeltheologisches Wörterbuch.
  Bibliography: p.
  Includes index.
    1. Bible—Dictionaries.   2. Bible—Theology—
Dictionaries.   I. Bauer, Johannes Baptist, 1927-
[BS440.B46713 1981]   230   81-626
ISBN 0-8245-0042-3   AACR2

CONTENTS

Volume 1

v

Contents

Volume 2

Contents

Volume 3

Contents

CONTRIBUTORS

Nikolaus Adler, Mainz-Gonsenheim

Paul Asveld, Graz

Albert Auer, Flüeli

Johannes B. Bauer, Graz

Wolfgang Beilner, Salzburg

Peter Bläser, Paderborn

Josef Blinzler, Passau

G. Johannes Botterweck, Bonn

Norbert Brox, Salzburg

Henri Cazelles, Paris

Jean Daniélou, Paris

Alfons Deissler, Freiburg

Josef Dey, Hofheim

Walter Dürig, Munich

Jean de Fr.aine†, Louvain

Johannes Gabriel†, Vienna

Johann Gamberoni, Brixen

Heinrich Gross, Trier

Odilo Kaiser, Freiburg

Robert Koch, Rome

Elisabeth Koffmahn, Vienna

Walter Kornfeld, Vienna

Johannes Kosnetter, Vienna

Elmar M. Kredel, Munich

Johannes Kürzinger, Eichstätt

Johann Michl, Munich

Georg Molin, Graz

Franz Mussner, Regensburg

Paul Neuenzeit, Würzburg

Friedrich Nötscher†, Bonn

Jakob Obersteiner, Gurk

Elpidius Pax, Jerusalem

Rudolf Pesch, Freiburg

Wilhelm Pesch, Hennef

Myriam Prager, Pertlstein

Karl Prümm, Rome

Josef Scharbert, Freising

Karl Hermann Schelkle, Tübingen

Johannes Schildenberger, Beuron

Othmar Schilling, Bochum

Josef Schmid, Munich

Ernst Schmitt, Bamberg

Rudolf Schnackenburg, Würzburg

Suitbert H. Siedl, Salzburg

Ceslaus Spicq, Fribourg

F. L. R. Stachowiak, Lodz

Meinrad Stenzel†, München-Freising

Alois Stöger, Rome

Gerhard Trenkler, Graz

Anton Vögtle, Freiburg

Viktor Warnach, Salzburg

Georg Ziener, Hünfeld bei Fulda

Heinrich Zimmermann, Bochum

xi

TRANSLATORS

Joseph Blenkinsopp

David J. Bourke

N. D. Smith

Walter P. van Stigt

ABBREVIATIONS

1. *Biblical: Old Testament, New Testament, and Apocrypha*

Acts	Acts of the Apostles	2 Kings	2 Kings
Amos	Amos	Lam	Lamentations
Bar	Baruch	Lev	Leviticus
1 Chron	1 Chronicles	Lk	Luke
2 Chron	2 Chronicles	1 Macc	1 Maccabees
Col	Colossians	2 Macc	2 Maccabees
1 Cor	1 Corinthians	Mal	Malachi
2 Cor	2 Corinthians	Mic	Micah
Dan	Daniel	Mk	Mark
Deut	Deuteronomy	Mt	Matthew
Eccles	Ecclesiastes	Nahum	Nahum
Eph	Ephesians	Neh	Nehemiah
Esther	Esther	Num	Numbers
Ex	Exodus	Obad	Obadiah
Ezek	Ezekiel	1 Pet	1 Peter
Ezra	Ezra	2 Pet	2 Peter
Gal	Galatians	Phil	Philippians
Gen	Genesis	Philem	Philemon
Hab	Habakkuk	Prov	Proverbs
Hag	Haggai	Ps	Psalms
Heb	Hebrews	Rev	Revelation
Hos	Hosea	Rom	Romans
Is	Isaiah	Ruth	Ruth
Jas	James	1 Sam	1 Samuel
Jer	Jeremiah	2 Sam	2 Samuel
Jn	John	Sir	Sirach (Ecclesiasticus)
1 Jn	1 John	Song	Song of Songs
2 Jn	2 John	1 Thess	1 Thessalonians
3 Jn	3 John	2 Thess	2 Thessalonians
Job	Job	1 Tim	1 Timothy
Joel	Joel	2 Tim	2 Timothy
Jon	Jonah	Tit	Titus
Josh	Joshua	Tob	Tobit
Jude	Jude	Wis	Wisdom
Judg	Judges	Zech	Zechariah
Judith	Judith	Zeph	Zephaniah
1 Kings	1 Kings		

2. *Non-biblical: Talmudic, apocalyptic, and other apocryphal writings*

ActAndr	Acts of Andrew	Keth	Kethuboth (Talm.)
ActJn	Acts of John	3 Macc	3 Maccabees
ActPaul	Acts of Paul	4 Macc	4 Maccabees
ActPet	Acts of Peter	MartIs	Martyrdom of Isaiah
ApocAbr	Apocalypse of	Men	Menahoth (Talm.)
	Abraham	MidrSong	Midrash to the Song of
ApocElij	Apocalypse of Elijah		Songs (etc.)
ApocMos	Apocalypse of Moses	PsSol	Psalms of Solomon
ApocPet	Apocalypse of Peter	Sib	Sibylline Oracles
AssMos	Assumption of Moses	TestXII	Testaments of the
Bar (Gr)	Apocalypse of Baruch		Twelve Patriarchs
	(Greek)	TestAsh	Testament of Asher,
(Syr)	(Syriac)		etc: Benj(amin);
Ber	Berakoth (Talm.)		Iss(achar); Jos(eph);
Did	Didache		Jud(ah); Levi;
EpBarn	Epistle of Barnabas		Naph(tali);
Enoch (Eth)	Enoch (Ethiopic)		Reub(en);
(Gr)	(Greek)		Sim(eon);
(Heb)	(Hebrew)		Zeb(ulun)
(Slav)	(Slavonic)	TestAbr	Testament of
GosPet	Gospel of Peter		Abraham
Jub	Book of Jubilees	Zeb	Zebahim (Talm.)

In abbreviations of the Qumran texts, the symbol Q (= Qumran) is preceded by a number indicating the cave of the find, and in the case of biblical books followed by the usual abbreviations (a, b, c, etc in smaller type is used when several copies of the same text have been found in the same cave). For other texts the accepted Hebrew abbreviation is used, and in the case of bible-commentaries this is preceded by p (=*peser*, explanation). Thus 1 QIs^a = the first Isaiah-scroll found in the first cave at Qumran; 1 QpHab = the commentary on the Book of Habbakkuk from the first cave; 1 QS = *Serek hayahad*, the Manual of Discipline, found in the first cave; QM = *Milhamoth bne or*, the War Rule; QH = *Hodayoth*, the Thanksgiving Psalms. The Damascus Rule is CD (= Cairo Document), the corresponding texts found in Qumran 4QD and 6QD. Translations of the Qumran writings are readily available in G. Vermes, *The Dead Sea Scrolls in English*, Harmondsworth 1962.

3. *Books and periodicals*

AA	*Alttestamentliche Abhandlungen*, ed. A. Schultz, Münster 1908ff
AAS	*Acta Apostolicae Sedis*, Rome 1909ff
AfO	*Archiv für Orientforschung*, Berlin 1926ff
Allmen	J.-J. von Allmen (ed.), *Vocabulary of the Bible*, London 1958 (translation of *Vocabulaire biblique*, Neuchatel 1956²)
ALW	*Archiv für Liturgiewissenschaft*, Regensburg 1950ff
AOT	*Altorientalische Texte zum AT*, ed. H. Gressmann, Berlin 1926²
ARW	*Archiv für Religionswissenschaft*, Leipzig 1898ff
ATR	*Anglican Theological Review*, Evanston (Ill.) 1918ff
AV	Authorised Version of the Bible
BASOR	*Bulletin of the American Schools of Oriental Research*, New Haven (Conn.) 1919ff
BBB	*Bonner Biblischer Beiträge*, Bonn 1950ff
Bbl	*Biblica*, Rome 1920ff
BHHW	*Biblisch-historisches Handwörterbuch*, ed. B. Reicke and L. Rost, Göttingen 1962
BJRL	*Bulletin of the John Rylands Library*, Manchester 1903ff
BK	*Bibel in Kirche*
BKW	*Bible Key Words* (fourteen volumes), London 1949–65 (translations of some major articles in *TWNT*, q.v.)
BL	*Bibel und Liturgie*
BM	*Benediktinische Monatshefte*, Beuron 1919ff
Bousset-Gressmann	W. Bousset and H. Gressmann, *Die Religion des Judentums im späthellenistischen Zeitalter*, Tübingen 1926³
BRL	*Biblisches Reallexikon*, ed. K. Galling, Tübingen 1937
BTHW	*Biblisch-theologisches Handwörterbuch*, ed. E. Osterloh and H. Engelland, Göttingen 1954
Bultmann	R. Bultmann, *Theology of the New Testament* I, London 1965²; and II, London 1965² (translation of *Theologie des NT* [one volume], Tübingen 1954²)
BWANT	*Beiträge zur Wissenschaft vom A (und N) T*, Leipzig 1908ff and Stuttgart 1926ff
BZ	*Biblische Zeitschrift*, Paderborn 1957ff (n.s.)
BZAW	*Beiheft zur ZAW* (q.v.)
BZF	*Biblische Zeitfragen*, ed. P. Heinisch and F. W. Maier, Münster 1908ff
BZNW	*Beiheft zur ZNW* (q.v.)
CBQ	*Catholic Biblical Quarterly*, Washington 1939ff
CC	*La Civiltà Cattolica*, Rome 1850ff

CCSL	*Corpus Christianorum, Series Latina*, ed. E. Dekkers, Turnhout 1953ff
CIC	*Codex Iuris Canonici*, Rome 1918
CIG	*Corpus Inscriptionum Graecarum*, ed. Boeckh and others
CSEL	*Corpus Scriptorum Ecclesiasticorum Latinorum*, Vienna 1866ff
Cullmann	O. Cullmann, *The Christology of the New Testament*, London 1962[2] (translation of *Christologie des[2] NT*, Tübingen 1957)
CV	*Communio Viatorum*
DACL	*Dictionnaire de l'Archéologie chrétienne et Liturgie*, ed. F. Cabrol and H. Leclerq, Paris 1924ff
DB, DB(S)	*Dictionnaire de la Bible (Supplément)*, ed. L. Pirot and others, Paris 1928ff
DB, DS	H. Denzinger, *Enchiridion Symbolorum, Definitionum, et Declarationum de Rebus Fidei et Morum*, ed. C. Bannwart and others, Freiburg 1908ff; ed. A. Schönmetzer, Freiburg 1963ff (with revised numeration)
DBT	*Dictionary of Biblical Theology*, ed. X. Léon-Dufour, London and New York 1967 (translation of *Vocabulaire de théologie biblique*, Paris 1962)
DEB	*Dictionnaire encyclopédique de la Bible*, Paris-Turnhout 1960
de Vaux	R. de Vaux, *Ancient Israel: Its Life and Institutions*, London and New York 1961 (translation of *Les Institutions de l'AT* [two volumes] Paris 1958-60)
Diels	H. Diels and W. Kranz (ed.), *Die Fragmente der Vorsokratiker* (three volumes), Berlin-Neukölln 1954[7]
DV	*Dieu Vivant*, Paris 1954ff
Eichrodt	W. Eichrodt, *Theology of the Old Testament* I, London and Philadelphia 1960; and II, London and Philadelphia 1967; and *Theologie des AT* III, Stuttgart and Göttingen 1939 (1961[2])
EKL	*Evangelisches Kirchenlexikon*, Göttingen 1958
ET	*Evangelische Theologie*, Munich 1934ff
ETL	*Ephemerides Theologicae Lovanienses*, Bruges 1924ff
Feine	P. Feine, *Theologie des NT*, Berlin 1951[8]
FRLANT	*Forschungen zur Religion und Literatur des A und NT*, Göttingen 1903ff
GL	*Geist und Leben*, Würzburg 1947ff
Greg	*Gregorianum*, Rome 1920ff
Haag	H. Haag (ed.), *Bibellexikon*, Einsiedeln 1951
Heinisch	P. Heinisch, *Theology of the Old Testament*, Collegeville (Minn.) 1955 (translation of *Theologie des AT*, Bonn 1940)

HTG	*Handbuch theologischer Grundbegriffe*, ed. H. Fries, Munich 1962–3
HTR	*Harvard Theological Review*, Cambridge (Mass.) 1908ff
HUCA	*Hebrew Union College Annual*, Cincinnati (Ohio) 1914ff
IEJ	*Israel Exploration Journal*, Jerusalem 1950ff
Imschoot	P. van Imschoot, *Theology of the Old Testament* I, New York 1965; and *Theologie de l'AT* II, Tournai 1956
ITQ	*Irish Theological Quarterly*, Dublin 1951ff (n.s.)
Jacob	E. Jacob, *Theology of the Old Testament*, New York 1958 (translation of *Théologie de l'AT*, Neuchatel 1956)
JBL	*Journal of Biblical Literature*, Boston (Mass.) 1881ff
JEH	*Journal of Ecclesiastical History*, London 1950ff
JPOS	*Journal of the Palestine Oriental Society*, Leipzig-Jerusalem 1920ff
JSS	*Journal of Semitic Studies*, 1956ff
JTS	*Journal of Theological Studies*, London 1899ff
KD	*Kerygma und Dogma*
Köhler	L. Köhler, *Old Testament Theology*, Philadelphia (Pa.) 1958 (translation of *Theologie des AT*, Tübingen 1953³)
LM	*Liturgie und Mönchtum*, Maria Laach 1948ff
LTK	*Lexikon für Theologie und Kirche* (ten volumes), ed. J. Höfer and K. Rahner, Freiburg 1957–65²
LV	*Lumière et Vie*, Lyons 1951ff
LXX	Septuagint
Mansi	J. Mansi and others (ed.), *Sacrorum Conciliorum Nova et Amplissima Collectio*, Florence 1759ff and Paris-Leipzig 1901–27
MAOG	*Mitteilungen der Altorientalischen Gesellschaft*, Leipzig 1925ff
MD	*La Maison-Dieu*, Paris 1945ff
Meinertz	M. Meinertz, *Theologie des NT* (two volumes), Bonn 1950
MTZ	*Münchener theologische Zeitschrift*, Munich 1950ff
MVAG	*Mitteilungen der vorderasiatisch(ägyptisch)en Gesellschaft*, Leipzig 1896ff
NA	*Neutestamentliche Abhandlungen*, ed. M. Meinertz, Münster 1909ff
NKS	*Nederlandse Katholieke Stemmen*, Zwolle 1901ff
NKZ	*Neue kirchliche Zeitschrift*, Leipzig 1890ff
NRT	*Nouvelle Revue théologique*, Tournai-Louvain 1879ff
NTS	*New Testament Studies*, Cambridge 1954ff
NTT	*Norsk Teologisk Tidsskrift*
NvT	*Novum Testamentum*, Leiden 1956ff

OS	*L'Orient Syrien*, Paris 1956ff
OTS	*Oudtestamentische Studien*, Leiden 1942ff
PG	*Patrologiae Cursus completus, Series Graeca*, ed. J. P. Migne, Paris 1857ff
PL	*Patrologiae Cursus completus, Series Latina*, ed. J. P. Migne, Paris 1844ff
Proksch	O. Proksch, *Theologie des AT*, Gütersloh 1950
RAC	*Reallexikon für Antike und Christentum*, ed. T. Klauser, Stuttgart 1950²ff
RB	*Revue biblique*, Paris 1892ff
RGG	*Religion in Geschichte und Gegenwart*, ed. K. Galling, Tübingen 1956³ff
RHE	*Revue d'Histoire ecclésiastique*, Louvain 1900ff
RHPR	*Revue d'Histoire et Philosophie religieuses*, Strasbourg-Paris 1921ff
RHR	*Revue de l'Histoire des Religions*, Paris 1880off
RNT	*Regensburger Neues Testament*, ed. A. Wikenhauser and O. Kuss, Regensburg 1956³ff
RQ	*Revue de Qumran*, Paris 1959ff
RSPT	*Revue des Sciences philosophiques et théologiques*, Paris 1907ff
RSR	*Recherches de Science religieuse*, Paris 1910ff
RSV	Revised Standard Version of the Bible
RT	*Revue thomiste*, Brussels 1893ff
RTP	*Revue de Théologie et Philosophie*, Lausanne 1951ff (n.s.)
SB	H. Strack and P. Billerbeck, *Kommentar zum NT aus Talmud und Midrasch* (five volumes), Munich 1922–8 and 1956²
Schnacken-burg	R. Schnackenburg, *The Moral Teaching of the New Testament*, London and New York 1968 (translation of *Die sittliche Bottschaft des NT*, Munich 1954)
SE	*Sciences ecclésiastiques*
SEA	*Svensk exegetisk årsbok*, Uppsala 1936ff
SJT	*Scottish Journal of Theology*, Edinburgh
SKZ	*Schweitzerische Kirchenzeitung*
SNTSB	*Studiorum NT Societas Bulletin*
SP	*Sacra Pagina*, Paris-Gembloux 1959ff
ST	*Studia Theologica*, Lund 1948ff
Stauffer	E. Stauffer, *Theology of the New Testament*, London 1963² (translation of *Theologie des NT*, Gütersloh 1948⁵)
SZ	*Stimmen der Zeit*, Freiburg 1871ff
TB	*Theologische Blätter*, Leipzig 1922ff

TDNT	*Theological Dictionary of the New Testament* I–VI, ed. G. Kittel and G. Friedrichs, Grand Rapids (Mich.), 1964–7 (translation of *TWNT* [q.v.] I–VI, Stuttgart 1930ff)
TG	*Theologie und Glaube*, Paderborn 1909ff
TLZ	*Theologische Literaturzeitung*, Leipzig 1878ff
TPQ	*Theologisch-praktische Quartalschrift*, Linz 1848ff
TQ	*Theologische Quartalschrift*, Tübingen 1819ff
TR	*Theologische Rundschau*, Tübingen 1897ff
TS	*Theological Studies*, Baltimore 1940ff
TSK	*Theologische Studien und Kritiken*, Gotha 1828ff
TT	*Tijdschrift voor Theologie*, Wageningen
TTK	*Tidsskrift for Teologi og Kirke*
TTZ	*Trierer theologische Zeitschrift*, Trier 1888ff
TU	*Texte und Untersuchungen zur Geschichte der altchristlichen Literatur*, Leipzig 1882ff
TWNT	*Theologisches Wörterbuch zum NT* VII–VIII, ed. G. Friedrich, Stuttgart 1954ff (earlier volumes translated as *TDNT*, q.v.)
TZ	*Theologische Zeitschrift*, Basle 1945ff
VC	*Vigiliae Christianae: A Review for Early Life and Language*, Amsterdam 1947ff
VD	*Verbum Domini*, Rome 1921ff
von Rad	G. von Rad, *Old Testament Theology* I, Edinburgh-London and New York 1962; and II, Edinburgh-London and New York 1965 (translation of *Theologie des AT* [two volumes], Munich 1957–60)
Vriezen	T. C. Vriezen, *Outline of Old Testament Theology*, Oxford and Newton Centre 1958 (translation of *Hoofdlijnen der Theologie van het OT*, Wageningen 1960²)
VS	*La Vie Spirituelle*, Paris 1869ff
VT	*Vetus Testamentum*, Leiden 1951ff
WW	*Wissenschaft und Weisheit*, Düsseldorf 1934ff
WZKM	*Wiener Zeitschrift für die Kunde des Morgenländes*, Vienna 1887ff
ZAW	*Zeitschrift für die alttestamentliche Wissenschaft*, Berlin 1881ff
ZDMG	*Zeitschrift der deutschen morgenländischen Gesellschaft*, Leipzig 1847ff
ZDPV	*Zeitschrift des deutschen Palästina-Vereins*, Leipzig 1878ff
ZEE	*Zeitschrift für evangelische Ethik*, Gütersloh 1957ff
ZKG	*Zeitschrift für Kirchengeschichte*, Gotha-Stuttgart 1876ff
ZKT	*Zeitschrift für katholische Theologie*, Innsbruck 1877ff
ZNW	*Zeitschrift für die neutestamentliche Wissenschaft und die Kunde der älteren Kirche*, Giessen-Berlin 1900ff

Abbreviations

ZRG	*Zeitschrift für Religions- und Geistesgeschichte*, Marburg 1948ff
ZST	*Zeitschrift für systematische Theologie*, Berlin 1923ff
ZTK	*Zeitschrift für Theologie und Kirche*, Tübingen 1891ff

TRANSLITERATION

1. *Transcription of Hebrew characters*

Aleph	ʾ	Pe	p
Beth	b	Tsade	ts
Gimel	g	Qoph	q
Daleth	d	Res	r
He	h	Sin	ś
Waw	w	Šin	š
Zayin	z	Taw	t (th)
Heth	ḥ	Qames	ā
Teth	ṭ	Pathah	a
Yod	y	Tsere	ê or ē
Kaph	k	Seghol	e
Lamed	l	Hireq	î, i
Mem	m	Holem	ô, ō
Nun	n	Sureq	û
Samech	s	Qibbuts	u
Ayin	ᶜ	Šᵉwas	ᵃ ᵉ ᵒ

2. *Transcription of Greek characters*

Alpha	a	Ksi	ks
Beta	b	Omicron	o
Gamma	g (n before g, or k)	Pi	p
Delta	d	Rho	r
Epsilon	e	Sigma	s
Zeta	z	Tau	t
Eta	ē	Upsilon	u
Theta	th	Phi	ph
Iota	i	Psi	ps
Iota subscript	(i)	Khi	kh
Kappa	k	Omega	ō
Lambda	l	Digamma	(w)
Mu	m	Aspirate (rough breathing)	h
Nu	n		

Biblical theology

The diversity of views about biblical theology makes it necessary to begin with a brief account of them. In this way, by seeing what biblical theology is not, we may more clearly see what it is, and what is its status, its nature, and its justification.

Biblical theology may, in the first place, be viewed as that part of theology which supplies all the many doctrinal theses with their bases in scripture. This may be useful, but it contains many dangers. In this view the usual starting point is from the classifications and categories of modern theology, and these can all too easily be imported back into scriptural revelation itself, thereby causing shifts of emphasis and changes of proportion. But of course, if the identity of the doctrinal structure is to be preserved, all that is essential must remain essential and all that is accidental merely accidental. For example, the resurrection of Christ does not play a prominent part in the soteriology of Anselm—but it does in the soteriologies of Paul or John. This should be borne in mind. Again, particular points of doctrine may disappear altogether because they are no longer fully or properly discussed in later theology and so are not found in our contemporary handbooks of dogmatics. Take, for example, the cosmic significance of the redemption—a theme which is certainly mentioned by Paul (in Rom 8 and in the captivity epistles) and which finds expression in the liturgy: 'Unda manat et cruor; terra, pontus, astra, mundus, quo lavantur flumine' (see Aquinas, *Summa contra Gentiles* IV, last chapter).[1]

The alternative method does not start from modern categories of thought but from the sacred texts themselves; nor is it concerned with apologetics or with proving or disproving theses. The aim is to reveal, where possible, the categories, the modes of thought, of the biblical writers themselves—to show the world in which Christ, the apostles, and the early christians lived, their views and ideas, the images they used. In this way biblical theology is an attempt to arrive at a complete understanding of christian doctrine; it does not proceed from some preconceived system or in terms alien to its subject-matter, but uses modes of thought peculiar to the scriptures, trying to go to the very heart and real background of revelation.[2]

We must bear in mind that, since the time of Christ and the apostles, further development has taken place in christian doctrine, and above all that christian

---

[1] S. Lyonnet, 'La valeur sotériologique de la résurrection du Christ selon S. Paul', *Greg* 39 (1958), 295–318; J. B. Bauer, 'Um die ganze Lehre', *Der Seelsorger* 24 (1954), 373–6; and J. B. Bauer, 'In doctrina integritatem', *Oberrhein. Pastoralblatt* 55 (1954), 214–16.
[2] V. Warnach, 'Gedanken zur ntl. Theologie', *Gloria Dei* 7 (1952), 72.

doctrine has been presented in terms of certain philosophical systems, so that our present concepts and views have necessarily been influenced by—and are dependent on—this development. No wonder that a marked difference can be seen between the concept of *caritas Dei*, of God's love, as employed by the Council of Trent[1] in referring to Rom 5:5 and Paul's views as actually expressed in this passage, where he speaks, not of sanctifying grace through which God dwells in us, but of God's love towards man. The Council has quoted this text rightly only if it can be proved from the text that man, supernaturally reborn, does indeed possess the new life, the divine life, of the blessed Trinity.

Moreover, revelation was completed with the death of the last apostle, but not before. Up until then there was, for a period of about half a century, not only a kind of further elaboration—as afterwards—but a real development. It is evident from the writings of the evangelists that even Christ revealed himself by stages and still left a great deal to the Holy Spirit who was to teach his disciples—not because there was no more for him to reveal, but because the disciples were incapable of grasping any more at the time (see Irenaeus, *Adv. Haer.* IV, 38, 1ff). That is the reason why even the New Testament authors differ and diverge from each other in certain respects: eg Mark's christology is not necessarily identical with John's or Paul's. This may strike non-catholic readers as a contradiction, but anyone who really believes in the divine inspiration of the whole of the bible cannot view this development within revelation as anything but homogeneous. Indeed, in virtue of this homogeneity, a deeper understanding of Christ's own words may be obtained in the light of later revelation (as in the case of Paul)—an even deeper understanding than can be ascribed to the evangelist who actually heard these words and wrote them down. These different stages must always be in the foreground of our minds. It is the task of biblical theology to map out this 'history of revelation'.[2]

The significance of biblical theology

Dogmatic theology cannot be reduced to biblical theology. It arises out of tradition, although tradition can never be considered independently of the bible, any more than the bible can be fully understood independently of tradition. All the same, the importance of biblical theology for dogmatic theology can hardly be overestimated. It assists dogmatic theologians in their work and acts as a safeguard against the losing sight of those truths which receive less emphasis—a safeguard, too, against the shifting of emphasis and the change of relative importance as between the various different elements. Biblical theology will be of special use in the business of providing biblical proof which will no longer consist, like some fleshless skeleton, of texts taken out of their contexts. Rather, it will exhibit the development of a given doctrine in relation to other doctrines; it will enable us to form an idea of the place one particular truth occupies within the whole framework of revelation, and of the different forms in which this truth has been repre-

[1] *Decretum de justificatione* (DS 1530 [=DB 800]).
[2] P. Benoit, *RB* 54 (1947), 611f.

sented during the different periods of revelation—and this in turn will bring about a better preparation for the 'ministry of the word', the preaching of the faith.[1] Experience has shown that biblical theology is exactly what appeals to our contemporaries, and this alone should be enough to evoke our interest in it. It is not mere coincidence that the theology of the apostolic fathers had and still has such vital influence—our predigested, systematised handbooks, weighed down with speculation, were not available to them. They had to build up their own theology, and in their preaching they had to draw on their own resources. Their theology was always the result of personal study of the original sources—of the scriptures and the living tradition of teaching in the church. 'That is why the study of these hallowed sources gives the sacred sciences a kind of perpetual youth: evade the labour of probing deeper and deeper yet into the sacred deposit, and your speculations—experience shows it—grow barren', as Pope Pius XII put it, and one feels that he must have had some bitter experience in the matter himself.[2]

The study of biblical theology also demands collaboration with our separated brethren. Biblical theology is to them what dogmatic theology is to us Roman Catholics, since the bible is their only norm and they have to consult it to a correspondingly greater degree. One of the most prominent protestant scholars remarked a few years ago: 'Let us state once and for all what is really needed if we are to ascertain the facts about the early church: a merciless attitude towards one's own dogmatics. In the study of biblical theology one has to be prepared to cut one's own dogmatics to the bone without hesitation.'[3]

Moreover, biblical theology clearly shows the independence of catholic dogma from any system of philosophy. Provided the substantial identity of the various dogmas is preserved, no harm can be done by an explanation in terms of Platonism, Aristotelianism, or Indian and Chinese systems of philosophy. On the contrary, such attempts are to be desired since, if this is the case, the pearl of the gospel will always preserve its supernatural and manifest splendour and never be mistaken for the setting in which man has enclosed it—which will always be cramping, however beautiful it may be.[4]

The question remains whether biblical theology deserves the name 'theology'. Is it not really a history of christian doctrine? By no means. Unlike the historian, the biblical theologian does not approach pauline or johannine teaching with a purely historical interest, but because of the extent to which it reveals what the teaching of the Catholic Church was at that time. He regards this doctrine as a phase, an aspect, of the present teaching of the church, not independent of its present state. Such a view, which takes account of the later explication of revelation, enables us to assume what has not yet been fully worked out—without,

[1] A. Bea, *Greg* 33 (1952), 85–105; see also *BL* 19 (1952), 262ff.
[2] *Humani Generis*, 21: 'Quapropter sacrorum fontium studio sacrae doctrinae semper iuvenescunt, dum contra speculatio, quae ulteriorem sacri depositi inquisitionem neglegit, ut experiundo novimus sterilis evadit'.
[3] A. Oepke, *TLZ* 79 (1954), 103.
[4] P. Benoit, *RB* 54 (1947), 543–72.

however, importing our modern categories of thought into our interpretation. In this way the function of faith will be made clearer. Biblical theology, in fact, is simply 'the teaching of the New Testament or of one of the authors of the biblical books as shown in the light of faith' (Braun).[1]

The purpose of the Encyclopedia of Biblical Theology

In French there are about five different expressions corresponding to the English word *speech* (viz. *parole, discours, langage, langue, propos*): that is, the English word *speech* has such a wide range of meanings that it can be used to express any of these French words. We find something similar in translating Hebrew expressions in the bible. A word in one particular context can very often only be rendered by an entirely different word in our modern languages, although people have tried to construct new and unusual words and sum up in them all the meanings included in the Hebrew stem (eg the AV rendering 'loving kindness' and RSV rendering 'steadfast love' for the Hebrew *ḥeśed*). But when, as is usually the case, a comprehensive Hebrew term is translated by a much more restricted English word or phrase—however justified this may be in the particular case—it will inevitably lose some of its original vigour and depth. Moreover, the wide span of the one comprehensive word has been broken. Instead of one comprehensive idea we have several more restricted ideas without the obvious underlying coherence which existed in the original text. Another drawback is the fact that our modern expressions, apart from being narrower than their Hebrew equivalents, are often saddled with other more or less clear-cut concepts or nuances. Take, for example, words like *justice, truth, peace*, etc. And what can be said of the Hebrew words of the Old Testament applies equally to the Greek words of the New Testament. There is a strong temptation, here more than anywhere else, to take these Greek words and expressions simply in their Greek sense. But again, recent investigations have shown how very much more the Greek New Testament is rooted in Old Testament judaism than in hellenism. True to the tradition of the LXX translation, the Greek expressions in the New Testament frequently have the same wide range of meanings and nuances as their Hebrew-Aramaic equivalents, and have to be interpreted accordingly.

Needless to say, in this encyclopedia it is mainly the theologically important words that are discussed, though no claim is made for completeness. Nevertheless, the encyclopedia offers much more than a mere dictionary: as far as possible, we have tried to indicate the essential lines of development of any given concept. Only occasionally is an attempt made to explain non-biblical words by reference to the bible (eg 'asceticism'). Anything purely historical, biographical, or archaeological had, of course, to be omitted altogether.

[1] For general reading, see the introductions to the various biblical theologies. See also: C. Spicq, *RSPT* (1951), 561–74; F. M. Braun, *RT* (1953), 221–53; W. Hillmann, *WW* 14 (1951), 56–67 and 200–11; V. Warnach, *Gloria Dei* 7 (1952); S. Lyonnet, *VD* 34 (1956), 142–53; H. Schlier, *BZ* 1 (1957), 6–23; J. Michl, *BZ* 2 (1958), 1–14; M. Meinertz, *Theol. Rev.* 54 (1958), 1ff; V. Hamp and H. Schlier, *LTK* II², 439–49; R. Schnackenburg, *Neutestamentliche Theologie*, Munich 1963, 11–24; W. Beilner, *Dienst an der Lehre* (Festschrift F. König), Vienna 1965, 145–65.

This encyclopedia does not present a general survey of the whole field of biblical theology. The biblical texts themselves would admit of more than one opinion about how to make such a survey and more than one attempt at doing it. Rather, this work has been designed to provide one clear and straightforward service: wherever an approach is made towards God's word in the bible, whenever people begin to read the bible (prompted, often, by the liturgy), there is need of a companion such as this to explain and reveal in its full splendour each expression replete with meaning and with God's Spirit.

In order to encourage private reading of the scriptures and to help enrich the preaching of the word of God, in order to help reveal the source of divine revelation more purely and clearly, the contributors to this encyclopedia have unanimously and generously given their services, sparing themselves no efforts, in the hope that many may drink of the water given by the Lord, which shall quench their thirst and 'become in them a spring of water welling up to eternal life' (Jn 4:14).

Johannes B. Bauer

FOREWORD TO THE ENGLISH EDITION

It is fair to say that Prof J. B. Bauer's encyclopedia represents one of the finest fruits of the renewal in Roman Catholic biblical scholarship, comprising as it does important original articles by the outstanding German, Austrian, Swiss, and French biblical theologians of the present day. In the German-speaking world this fact was immediately recognised, and the first two German editions quickly sold out. In preparing the third German edition—from which this English translation has been made—Prof Bauer took the opportunity to add a further thirty-four articles and to revise many of the earlier articles and bibliographies, so that the English-speaking world first meets the encyclopedia in a thoroughly up-to-date and more comprehensive form.

As Prof Bauer's preface makes clear, the encyclopedia was conceived, written, and edited to provide a service to professional and amateur students of the bible alike—to act as a companion and aid to biblical scholars in their work, to parochial clergy in the preparation of sermons and addresses, and indeed to all christians who regard serious and regular scripture study as an essential part of their own spiritual growth. Both these concerns, the 'academic' and the 'pastoral', have been kept very much in mind throughout the preparation of this English edition, and the manner in which we have attempted to maintain a proper balance between them calls for additional comment in four particular respects:

1. *Translation.* The greater part of the translation has been carried out by the English biblical scholars, Mr Joseph Blenkinsopp and Mr David J. Bourke, though Mr N. D. Smith and Mr Walter P. van Stigt have also each translated a number of articles. Bible references and quotations are according to the Revised Standard Version (RSV). Its advantages are well known. Originally sponsored by the National Council of the Churches of Christ in the USA, it has been subsequently officially approved—in its complete form, including the deuterocanonical as well as canonical books—by the Roman Catholic Church. It is familiar to both British and American christians, and has won general acceptance among scholars. One further point on translation: for the benefit of readers who do not know Hebrew or Greek, all words and phrases quoted in the original apparent from the co̶n̶t̶e̶x̶t̶. ranslated into english wherever their meaning is

2. *Bibliographies.* The bibli̶o̶g̶r̶a̶p̶h̶i̶e̶s̶ which appear at the end of each article have been transferred in their entirety from the third German edition, despite the fact that German-language books and articles predominate. (This preponderance reflects, of course, not merely the German authorship of the majority of articles and bibliographies here, but the general pre-eminence of German scholarship in the fields of biblical exegesis and theology.) The retention of these

bibliographies is, we believe, essential if the encyclopedia is to be of real service to professional scholars and students: often they will have cause to follow up the references given, but in any case they will always need to know what secondary sources were available to or used by the author of a particular article. Nevertheless, every effort has been made to ensure that the bibliographies are also of the greatest possible use to readers who either have no knowledge of German or have no ready access to German books and periodicals. For these last we would point out that: (a) after German-language works, English-language books and periodicals are the most frequently cited in the German edition of the encyclopedia, and all these are of course retained in the English edition; (b) wherever they are available, English translations of German (or other foreign) works are substituted for the original works in the bibliographies here (in these cases, page references are to the English editions); (c) we have added recent English-language titles to some of the bibliographies where they seemed appropriate (such additions are marked by an asterisk); and (d) many more English-language works are included in the supplementary bibliography at the end of volume 2, which has been specially provided by Prof Bauer for this English edition. Above all, it should be noted that no less than thirteen major works frequently cited in the bibliographies are now wholly or substantially available in the following English translations:

ALLMEN, J.-J. VON (ed.), *Vocabulary of the Bible,* London, Lutterworth Press, 1958; and *Companion to the Bible,* New York, OUP, 1958.

BULTMANN, Rudolf, *Theology of the New Testament* I and II, London, SCM Press, 1952 (1965²); and New York, Scribner, 1951.

CULLMANN, Oscar, *The Christology of the New Testament,* London, SCM Press, 1959 (1962²); and Philadelphia, Westminster Press, 1959.

DE VAUX, Roland, *Ancient Israel: Its Life and Institutions,* London, Darton, Longman and Todd, 1961; and New York, McGraw-Hill, 1961.

EICHRODT, Walther, *Theology of the Old Testament* I and II, London, SCM Press, 1961 and 1967; and Philadelphia, Westminster Press, 1961 and 1967.

HEINISCH, Paul, *Theology of the Old Testament,* Collegeville, Liturgical Press, 1955.

IMSCHOOT, Paul van, *Theology of the Old Testament* I, New York, Desclee, 1965.

JACOB, Edmund, *Theology of the Old Testament,* London, Hodder and Stoughton, 1958; and New York, Harper and Row, 1958.

KITTEL, Gerhard, and G. Friedrich (eds.), *Theological Dictionary of the New Testament* I–X, Grand Rapids (Mich.), Wm. B. Eerdmans, 1964-76.

LEON-DUFOUR, Xavier (ed.), *Dictionary of Biblical Theology,* London, Geoffrey Chapman, 1967.

SCHNACKENBURG, Rudolf, *The Moral Teaching of the New Testament,* Burns and Oates, 1968; and New York, Herder and Herder, 1968.

STAUFFER, Ethelbert, *Theology of the New Testament,* London, SCM Press, 1955 (1963²).

VON RAD, Gerhard, *Old Testament Theology* I and II, Edinburgh and London, Oliver and Boyd, 1962 and 1965; and New York, Harper and Row, 1962 and 1965.

3. *Tables and indexes.* Several tables and indexes have been specially compiled or adapted for the English edition. Thus, the analytical index of articles and cross-references not only incorporates all the cross-references between articles of the German edition, but also includes many additional references to articles from synonyms and from theological themes which, though not given separate treatment, are covered in one or more of the articles. This table should provide readers with quick access to the subject in which they are currently interested, as well as enabling them to make the fullest possible use of the encyclopedia. The index of biblical references—an innovation in the English edition—is designed to serve two purposes. First, it will provide readers who are using the encyclopedia as a companion to their study of the bible or of a bible commentary with direct access to what the encyclopedia has to say about any given scriptural (or apocryphal) passage. Secondly, it will provide priests with a handy tool for using the encyclopedia in the preparation of their sermons, and it is for their especial benefit that parallel passages in the synoptic gospels—which in the text are referred to in the form 'Mt 3:1-12 and parallels'—are listed under Mark and Luke as well as Matthew.

4. *Transliteration.* The decision to transliterate Hebrew and Greek words by Roman characters was not taken lightly. We are well aware that readers who understand Hebrew or Greek will find this irritating, but we ask their indulgence for the sake of the far greater number who do not understand these classical languages. Hebrew and Greek words are invariably quoted in this encyclopedia for theological rather than for philological reasons, and so the transliteration makes it possible for readers who do not understand Hebrew or Greek to follow fully the theological argument of the writer.

ENCYCLOPEDIA
OF BIBLICAL THEOLOGY

Volume 1

Abraham – Hour

Abraham

A. *Old Testament.* Abraham's name may have a different etymological explanation from the one which occurs in Gen 17:5, and the short form *'abrām* and the longer form *'abrāhām* may in fact be identical (that is, 'the father is exalted', or 'he is exalted with regard to his father'). In either case, the interpretation of the name cannot diminish its theological significance, since P (the priestly source) posits assonance with the word *hamon* (=surging multitude) in order to express, in the name itself, the position Abraham occupies in the history of salvation. 'Father of the multitude' implies not only a great number of descendants, but also an abundance of blessings on those descendants (see Gen 12:2f).

Abraham's position is based on the call he received from God (Gen 12:1–3) and on the covenant established between him and God (Gen 17:7). His role is accomplished in the faith and obedience with which he responded to God and which was counted as justice in his favour (Gen 15:6). As a result of this Abraham was regarded, in the whole of the biblical tradition, and in a very real sense, as the bearer of revelation and of salvation, and was given the titles 'prophet' (Gen 20:7), 'friend of God' (Is 41:8), and 'servant of God' (Ps 105:6). Yahweh is the God of Abraham (Gen 26:24, etc) and Abraham is the father of Israel, the rock from which the people is hewn (Is 51:1f).

While it is necessary for us to avoid looking on revelation as a process similar to that of a *deus ex machina*—as taking place without the concurrence of the viewpoints of people living in a determined period of history—at the same time, revelation must not be confused with a process of development conceived as, for example, the building of a house or the crystallisation of a chemical element, a process which comes about inexorably following a geometrical pattern. We have, moreover, to think of Abraham as a real human being who lived in the full light of history and in an age of spiritual awareness — whether we date him around 1800 BC with Professor A. Parrot or follow C. Gordon's more recent suggestion of a date around 1400 BC. This is shown by the testimony of archaeology with reference to either the early civilisation of Sumer-Akkad (the city of Ur) or that of the kingdom of Mari (the city of Haran).

Particularly revealing is the 'object' of his faith. God did not ask Abraham either to square the circle or to come to grips with towering speculations in the realm of the supernatural. What he promised him was pasture land and a posterity—precisely what any other Bedouin sheik longed for—and expected him to accept this in faith and be convinced that in this way the foundation for the salvation of the nations was being laid. The simplicity of this agreement (↗ Covenant), the form in which it was given, so perfectly consonant with contemporary conditions, the rich promise which at the same time

3

it held out for the future, could not have been invented but must have been copied from reality.

The alliance with Abraham is the immediate prerequisite for the Sinaitic alliance. In addition, however, this latter must be understood against the background of the account of original sin and the *protoevangelium*. This is, in fact, 'the meaning of the first chapters of the bible: it is impossible to understand Israel correctly . . . unless everything is seen with God's creation of the world in the background' (Von Rad). It is thus obvious that Abraham represents the final stage in the ideal historical sequence which extends back by way of the lists of the descendants of Shem and Adam to Adam himself, and which can show clearly the divine work of selection within the history of salvation which leads up to the Semites and to Israel. The figures given for Abraham's age—his migration at 75, the birth of his promised son at 100, his death at 175—are ideal rather than chronological, and, with Isaac's birth in Abraham's hundredth year, conclude the remarkable interchange of generation-numbers between 100, 70, and 30 which appear in the genealogy of Shem.

It must therefore be stated plainly that the history of religion would have taken a very different course if Abraham had not believed. His faith was a condition *sine qua non* for the history of salvation, both in its factual origins in Israel and in its fulfilment in Jesus of Nazareth. The condition is, admittedly, not an absolute one, but it is certainly applicable within the limits of that human freedom which is recognised by God.

The key position which Abraham held introduces for the first time into the history of salvation ($\nearrow$ mediation) both the fact and the potentiality of God's saving ways; in other words, that it is not God's method to reveal himself to each individual man, but only to one who is to pass on what is revealed to the rest of the community and who, in this manner, assumes responsibility for all members of the community.

One further law in the history of salvation can be clearly recognised in the life of Abraham. His position is not entirely free from a certain dialectic. On the one hand, the numerous offspring promised to him (Gen 13:16) can be taken in the literal sense to signify that the means of salvation and the results of those who bring salvation are to be seen as closely related to Abraham's biological lineage. On the other hand, the exclusion of Ishmael from the line of salvation and the continued preferment of Isaac, the promised son, show that Abraham's vocation did not come about because of racial considerations, but that God left himself freedom of choice in the biological issue, and further that the basis, extent, and significance of Abraham's vocation are not to be understood in a biological but in a theological sense. In Hagar-Ishmael, as the representative of the merely biological element, and Sarah-Isaac, representing God's free choice, the points were already changed which would lead the Pauline interpretation of salvation away from that of the Pharisees. In this manner, 'justification by faith', as treated in the New Testament (Rom 3:28), finds its basis in the Old Testament.

B. *New Testament*. From the New

4

Testament we can discover one possible outcome of the attitude of the Jewish people towards Abraham, and from that we can deduce the teaching of Christ and the apostles concerning him. The Jewish people saw the basis of salvation in Abraham's biological lineage, and even though his 'merit' was not entirely disregarded, it was interpreted in many different ways (see Mt 3:8f and PsSol 9:17; 3 Macc 6:3; also Philo, *De Abr.*). From the theological point of view, the apocryphal books presented the writers of the New Testament with no material for a representation of Abraham; the Book of Jubilees simply provides a repetition of the story contained in Genesis, while the ApocAbr and TestAbr get hopelessly lost in fantasy and heavenly journeyings.

The Jewish obsession with the biological lineage of Abraham was bound to provoke the opposition of Christ and the apostles, and thus the figure of Abraham makes the essential law of redemption and salvation all the more intelligible: in the eyes of God the descendants of Abraham are worthless unless they also follow in his footsteps (Jn 8:39; Jas 2:21). God is thus able to bring forth children of Abraham 'from the stones' (Mt 3:9), that is, without recourse to the normal biological process, so that the spiritual children of Abraham as well as his physical children will sit down with him at table (Mt 8:11f). 'Father Abraham' cannot, then, even save 'his son', the rich glutton, from Gehenna (Lk 16:25f), whereas Lazarus, the poor beggar, is able to rest in 'Abraham's bosom' (Lk 16:22)—that is, Lazarus is permitted to recline with Abraham on the couch at the feast of the blessed (see Jn 13:25).

In accordance with his normal theological method of meditation and presentation, Paul made the figure of Abraham his criterion in his dispute with the Jews. Paul appreciated the meaning of the antithesis between Hagar/Ishmael and Sarah/Isaac, and fully exploited all the aspects of the question of justification; in this way he succeeded in exposing the underlying significance of this episode, namely, that the origins of the history of salvation in Abraham are, despite their association with Abraham's lineage in the purely biological sense, directly traceable to the freedom of God's grace. (Gal 4:28ff; Rom 9:7.)

Just as God's freedom of choice within sacred history was delineated in the figures of the ancestral women taken as types, so Paul illustrates, in the light of Abraham's attitude to faith, the 'works' of Abraham, which are an indispensible qualification for redemption, both for Abraham himself and for everyone. Abraham lived in the time before the proclamation of the law and he was not dependent on the law for his justification (Rom 4:3f). In his case, faith alone was sufficient (Rom 4:13).

As a consequence of this we find in Paul that, although the fact that Abraham is also the 'father of the circumcised' is clearly recognised (Rom 4:12), he is considered as 'father of the multitude' only with regard to his descendants in the faith (Rom 4:16ff). Just as each one of us is bound to prove himself by means of his faith before Abraham who is the 'father of our faith', so Abraham, in his turn assumed responsibility for all of us. That is why Abraham's faith is counted in his favour, not only out of personal consideration to him, but also—and even more particularly—with regard to the many who were to find faith through him (Rom 4:22ff).

Paul also interprets the blessing that was to pass, so to speak, in a kind of chain-reaction of salvation through Abraham to the nations. Paul regards the promise of Christ, which had been held out to Abraham for his offspring (Gal 3:16f; see Jn 8:56), as fulfilled in its true messianic perspective, even if the grammatical implication of collectivity in the statement 'thy seed' is discounted (Gen 12:7 and elsewhere).

Bibliography: H. H. Rowley, 'Discovery and the Patriarchal Age', *BJRL* 32 (1949); N. S. Schneider, 'Patriarchennamen in zeitgenössischen Keilschrifturkunden', *Bbl* 33 (1952), 516–22; H. Gordon, *Geschichtliche Grundlage des Alten Testaments*, Einsiedeln 1956; S. Moscati, *I Predecessori d'Israele*, Rome 1956; A. Parrot, *Babylon and the Old Testament*, London 1958; O. Schmitz, 'Abraham im Spätjudentum und im Christentum', *Festschrift A. Schlatter* 1922, 99–123; J. Jeremias, *TDNT* I, 8–9; M. Colacci, 'Il Semen Abrahae alla luce del V e NT', *Bbl* 21 (1940), 1–27; O. Kuss, *Der Römerbrief* I, Regensburg 1957, 178–95.

Othmar Schilling

Adam

A. *Old Testament*. 'Adam' is the generic name for 'man'—its etymology is uncertain—and also the name of the first man (in J, Gen 4:5 and elsewhere; 1 Chron 1:1). Although the use of the article renders it grammatically quite unambiguous, the representation underlying the concept is fluid in the chapters dealing with the creation.

(Is it 'man' or 'Adam' who calls his wife the 'mother of the living'?) The usually accepted connection with '*adāmâh*' (=field) (Gen 2:5 etc) would point to the meaning of 'human existence' in the name itself (see Gen 3:19).

The history of the first man in Gen 1–5 serves, in accordance with the salvation-theology presentation of the bible and within the framework of the selected traditions related to the history of salvation, like a splendid theological aetiology, in that everything of importance in the theological sense, for all mankind in general and also for Israel in particular, is exemplified in the first man. It was not uncommitted speculation which determined the narratives about Adam, but uniquely an interpretation of his being viewed from the standpoint of his relationship with God. In view of this, details of the natural sciences were considered of secondary importance, and so were omitted from the biblical record, thus being left open as far as revelation is concerned. The two essential aspects of Adam which emerge most clearly are his relationship with God and his relationship with himself and his environment.

1. *Adam's relationship with God*. The bible recognises the evidence in this connection as among the most decisive and important of all. Adam's development is traced back to God's creation (Gen 1:26ff; 2:7). It can be affirmed that, apart from the basic human state of being a creature, the first man became a living being only by the inbreathing of the divine spirit. His exceptional position in creation is a visible expression of the doctrine that

6

man is made in God's image (according to P, Gen 1:26; 5:1).

Corresponding to man's origin in God, there should be a communion with God lasting for the whole of life. The essential characteristic of the state of living in paradise is an intimate acquaintanceship with God. If it is affirmed (in P, Gen 5:1) that the quality of being made in God's image was transmitted to Seth and was, over the generations, passed on through Noah and Shem to Abraham, it becomes apparent how Israel saw itself from its very origins to be in a close alliance with God.

In the other documents which give an account of the creation, this succession of 'being made in the same image' (deriving from P) has, however, taken on another precise shade of meaning. The negative aspect of the first man's relationship with God is also brought into prominence with particular clarity and meaning in the form of an aetiology of salvation, in Adam's sin, his punishment, culminating in the threat of death, and God's curse on the land (Gen 3:17ff). Adam's wife nonetheless remains the 'mother of all living' (Gen 3:20), and the curse on the serpent offers to both of them the hope of salvation.

In this way it becomes evident that the position of Israel is the result of election, since Adam's sin was carried on in his sons and in the generation which perished in the flood. God's call to Israel to become one in his ↗ covenant is therefore a further call to mankind to fellowship with him.

2. *Adam's relationship with himself and his environment.* Adam's essential characteristics are expressed quite clearly,

although only incidentally, as a result of this interpretation of his personality, which can be understood in the sense that God's covenant with Israel is ever present in the history of salvation. Two distinct elements which go to make up his being may be deduced from Adam's formation from the dust and the divine breath. That man is powerless to exist and that he is, in his substance, worthless, is typified above all by the dust, which forms the material part of his being. The divine breath, on the other hand, is not a part, but is in fact the element of perfection in man and of his vivification through God. Life is grace! In connection with the subject of creation and man's likeness to God, Jesus, the son of Sirach, speaks in clear terms of Adam's spiritual and volitional endowments (Sir 17:1–7), just as in the Book of Wisdom creation and man's likeness to God are regarded as the basis of the first man's immortality (Wis 2:23).

Adam's relationship with his environment is in the same way outlined quite clearly. Adam was given a counterpart, Eve, who was in substance equal to himself and to whom he was bound in a monogamous union (↗ Marriage). Thus he became the progenitor of the entire human race.

Adam's position of authority, which is derived from his having been made in God's image, and the superiority he demonstrates over the animals in giving them their names, that is to say, in interpreting their nature, indicate that he has been placed only 'a little less than God' (Ps 8).

And so the Old Testament, though in an awkward literary style, expresses itself on the subject of the formation and worth, the nature and dignity of the first man so uniquely that, in the whole of the world's literature, there exists nothing which can be placed on the same level.

A biblical expression of this presentation of Adam living in communion with God as we read in Genesis can be found in the final sentence of Ben Sirach's song in praise of the great men of the past: 'Shem and Seth were honoured among men, and Adam above every living being in the creation' (Sir 49:16).

B. *New Testament*. That Adam was the first man for the New Testament writers emerges clearly from the genealogy of Christ (Lk 3:38) and from the fact that Paul establishes the position of man and woman in the community by means of a scriptural argument drawn from the original creation of Adam and the original seduction by Eve (1 Tim 2:13f).

The genealogy given in Luke is the christological continuation of a line which began in Gen 5:1ff, and thus places Christ in a striking relationship with Adam, who was 'of God'.

Paul, who designates Adam as *tupos mellontos* (Rom 5:14), completes in various ways this already suggestive Adam typology. As in the passages first quoted, it is the Old Testament, in the light of advanced christological studies, which might have provided the point of departure for the further development of this typology, and not the speculation of later judaism on the subject of the primordial Man, who was identified with the Messiah (thus *TDNT* 1, 142f). An example of this is that the 'Son of Man' in Enoch 1 (48:6; 62:7) is not called Adam, and

Paul's 'Son of Man' applies neither to Adam nor to Christ, though both would have come very close to this title, both from the point of view of linguistic usage and from Christ's own custom of referring to himself as the 'Son of Man'. The 'firstborn of all creation', who is the 'image of the invisible God' (Col 1:15), is without doubt an allusion to Wis 7:26 (↗ Likeness). In addition, the conception of the 'first' and the 'second' Adam in Philo (*Leg. All.* 1, 31; 2, 13; *De Conf. Ling.* 146) does not correspond to that of Paul; if it did, the 'second' or 'last' Adam would have to be identical with the Adam of Genesis. For Paul, even though he calls him 'the firstborn', Christ is the 'second' Adam. Paul has at least transformed the principal elements in the light of the christological data, since what is of first importance for him is not lengthy speculation on pre-existence, but the divine ascendancy of the second Adam over the first, on which the work of salvation of the new covenant is based, and the fact that it was precisely this work which was made necessary by the history of the first Adam. There does not seem to have been any speculation on Adam in Qumran, apart from occasional allusions to the first men (*CD* 4:21–5:1).

In accordance with the custom of employing the conceptual distinctions of *nepheš/rûah* and *psukhē/pneuma* in antithesis for earthly/natural and heavenly/supernatural (1 Cor 2:14) Paul sees in the assertion that Adam was created to become a 'living soul' (as the over-literal translation of Gen 2:7 reads) an expression of the first Adam's earthly, 'natural' state, which was to be over-

8

come and exalted by the 'life-giving *pneuma*' of the second Adam, so that thereby the condition was established, among other things, for the christian hope of resurrection (1 Cor 15:45ff).

The Adam/Christ typology has been set out in classic terms by Paul for the new 'hereditary succession' in the history of salvation: 'For as by one man's disobedience many were made sinners, so by one man's obedience, many will be made righteous' (Rom 5:19). This statement 'evidently means that mankind in the line of Adam as well as mankind in the line of Christ "was placed in a certain situation" as a result of the action of our first parents, by reason of God's judgement.... Many were in fact made "sinners" by Adam's deed, and through Christ many were made "righteous"' (Kuss). Paul has thus made use of typology in order to clarify the doctrine of original sin and grace which so deeply affects the history of our salvation.

In accordance with this doctrine, Paul also refers to a matter of which the Jews were not ignorant—that of the existence of an inherited death since Adam (↗ Original Sin). He sets against this, however, the efficacy of Christ's resurrection for all men (1 Cor. 15:21)

The church as the new mother of the living is to some extent on the same footing as Christ, the progenitor of the new life, so that not only is a new line of inheritance established in the history of salvation, but also a new depth is achieved in the relationship between man and woman, which goes beyond that indicated in Gen 2:23ff (Eph 5:21–33).

Bibliography: J. Jeremias, *TDNT* 1, 141–3; Haag 27; *LTK* I², 125–30; J. Feldmann, *Paradies und Sündenfall (AA* 4), Münster 1913; J. Freundorfer, *Erbsünde und Erbtod beim Apostel Paulus*, Münster 1927; J. Daniélou, *From Shadows to Reality: Studies in the Biblical Typology of the Fathers*, London 1960; O. Kuss, *Der Römerbrief*, Regensburg 1957; H. Renckens, *Urgeschichte und Heilsgeschichte*, Mainz 1959; P. Morant, *Die Anfänge der Menschheit*, Lucerne 1960; J. de Fraine, *Adam und seine Nachkommen*, Cologne 1962; O. Schilling, *Das Mysterium lunae die Erschaffung der Frau nach Gen 2:21f*, Paderborn 1963; P. de Haes, *Die Schöpfung als Heilsmysterium*, Mainz 1964.

Othmar Schilling

Adoration

A. *Old Testament. Hištahawâh*, together with *sogud*, are the usual expressions to describe adoration or worship. In the first place they denote a physical bowing down, and this meaning is clarified by such additions as 'to the ground' (Gen 18:2; 33:3, etc). By *qādad*—always used in conjunction with *hištahawâh*—is meant casting oneself down on one's knees. In most places, this 'proskynesis' (the Greek bible translates the Hebrew by *proskunein*) implies not only a public act of worship, above all of the true God (Gen 22:5; Ex 4:31; Deut 26:10; Ps 5:7; etc), but also homage paid to idols and false gods (Ex 20:5; Deut 4:19; 1 Kings 22:53; 2 Kings 5:18; Is 2:8; etc). Proskynesis is clearly perceptible in a song of praise and homage such as Ps 99 (v 2): 'The Lord is great in Sion: and high [*rām*] above all people'. In order that God's high position should be acknowledged, the cry is made: 'Exalt ye [*rôm'mú*] the Lord our God, and "adore" at his footstool' (v 5; see also v 9: 'at his holy mountain'). The 'and' is explanatory in character, and might conceivably be translated 'while ye are adoring him'. Thus the 'exaltation' of the Lord in praise is carried out both outwardly and inwardly by bowing down in adoration and homage. Vv 6 and 8 connect petition and the certainty of a hearing directly with the paying of homage. This is not by accident: on the contrary, the petition takes place, especially if it is performed with particular emphasis, in the attitude of proskynesis. In this sense of making an urgent request, Elijah bows down on the summit of Mount Carmel and lays his head between his knees, in order to implore God to send the longed-for rain (1 Kings 18:42), and the Rabbi Hanina ben Dosa entreats God in the same attitude to cure the son of the Rabbi Johanan ben Zakkai (see J. B. Bauer, 'Inter Genua Deposito Capite', *Hermes* 87 [1959], 383f).

The act of 'homage' is often accompanied by sacrificial acts (Deut 26:10; 1 Sam 1:3), music and the singing of psalms (2 Chron 29:28; Sir 50:16–18) and by prophetic exhortations to ↗ conversion (Ps 95).

Whenever homage is rendered to men, as in the case of Abraham to the children of Heth (Gen 23:7, 12), it is seldom done in a purely orthodox manner, and it was in fact later expressly forbidden (Esther 3:2, 5). It is customary to give due honour and to pay due homage to kings (1 Sam 24:8; 1 Kings 1:16, 23, 31), prophets (1 Sam 28:14; 2 Kings 2:15; 4:37) and to God's angels (Num 22:31; Gen 18:2; 19:1), because the power and authority which these hold and exercise comes from God.

Viewed in the light of prophecy and eschatology, Yahweh's universal dominion and sovereignty will be recognised by all mankind. All nations will come and, falling down before him, will pay homage to him and adore him (Is 2:3f; 24:15; Ps 22:27; 66:4; 86:9).

Bibliography: see under B.

Johannes B. Bauer

B. *New Testament*. 1. In the New Testament, the expression used in LXX —*proskunein*—is generally employed for 'adore', and the New Testament range of meaning does not to any great extent exceed the limits of the Old Testament meaning. Devotion is due to God alone (Mt 4:10; Lk 4:8; see also 1 Cor 14:25; Heb 11:21; Rev 4:10; 5:14; 7:11; 11:1, 16; 14:7; 15:4; 19:4, 10; 22:9), although false claims to devotion are made by idols, false gods, and demons, and indeed by Satan himself. Conversely, men sacrilegiously accord devotion to them (Mt 4:9; Lk 4:7; see also Acts 7:43; Rev 13:4, 8, 12, 15; 14:11; 16:2; 19:20). That is why angels, such as the Angel of the Apocalypse (Rev 19:10; 22:9), and men, such as Peter (Acts 10:26), refuse adoration, which is due to God alone. The instance of the church at Philadelphia (Rev 3:9), to whom it is promised that the Jews who are persecuting them will fall down in adoration at their feet, is apparently inconsistent with this conclusion. It must be noted, however, that this harks back to Is 45:14; 49:23; 60:14. If it is promised in these passages that the heathens will render proskynesis to God's people of the old covenant, then the promise is also made that the Jews will fall at the feet of God's people of the new covenant. This promise further holds good in the eschatological sense for the entire community of those included in the work of salvation and, finally, for the exalted Christ himself.

2. *Proskunein* in the New Testament corresponds exactly to the Old Testament reading in that adoration is to be given to a God who is personal and actually present. That is why the physical movement of falling down always accompanies *proskunein*, as is shown by the frequent association of *piptein* (= fall) with *proskunein* (Mt 2:11; 4:9; 18:26; Acts 10:25; 1 Cor 14:25; Rev 4:10, 5:14; 7:11; 11:16; 19:4, 10; 22:8). It is also why the place in which God's presence is manifested in a particular way is also important for the act of true adoration (see MidrPs 91 § 7 [200b]: 'Whoever prays in Jerusalem is as one who prays before the throne of glory, for there is the gate of heaven and the open door for his prayer to enter' [SB II, 437]). In this way *proskunein* can be used in the New Testament simply as a technical term for the pilgrimage to Jerusalem (Jn 12:20; Acts 8:27; 24:11; see Jn 4:20ff). In the new covenant, christian public worship is the 'place' in which God's presence is manifested (1 Cor 14:25).

3. The reading of *proskunein* in the New Testament stands in contrast to that in the Old Testament, as well as to that found in later Jewish usage, in that it admits of adoration—in the sense of *latreia*—of Christ, who has been elevated to God's right hand, to the extent that what is applicable to God within the framework of the Old Testament is now taken to relate to

Christ too. This can be seen quite clearly in the hymn to Christ contained in the Letter to the Philippians (2:6–11). The words of Isaiah, which Paul uses at the conclusion of the hymn—'To me every knee shall bow, every tongue shall swear' (Is 45:23)—are found in Paul's epistle in the form: 'At the name of Jesus every knee should bow . . . and every tongue should confess' (Phil 2:10f). In Isaiah, as the content of an adoring confession, we find: 'only in the Lord . . . have I righteousness and strength' (Is 45:24); similarly, Paul has: 'Jesus Christ is Lord' (Phil 2:11). This is also the case in Heb 1:6, where Ps 97:7 (LXX) is referred to Christ. The passage in the psalm referring to God—'adore him, all you his angels'—may be compared with Heb 1:6, a passage referring to Christ: 'Let all God's angels worship him' (see also Deut 32:43). In the same way this 'proskynesis' applies also to the risen Lord (Mt 28:9, 17; see also Lk 24:52), and Thomas falls down in worship before him with the words: 'My Lord and my God' (Jn 20:28).

4. The distribution of the word *proskunein* between the various books of the New Testament is as follows: Mt, thirteen times; Mk, twice; Lk, twice; John, eleven times; Acts, four times; Paul, once only (1 Cor 14:25); Heb, twice; and Rev, twenty-four times. From this it is clear that the verb occurs with greater frequency in the gospels of Mt and Jn than in all but one other book of the New Testament, and that it occurs with entirely disproportionate frequency in Rev. For this reason it will be useful to discuss these last three books separately.

a. Matthew's gospel. *Proskunein* has a special connotation in Mt: it is 'obviously one of his favourite words' (H. J. Held, *Matthäus als Interpret der Wundergeschichten*, Neukirchen 1960, 217). This emerges clearly from a comparison of Mt with the other synoptic gospels.

(1) in comparison with Mk and Lk:

Mt 8:2 *lepros proselthōn prosekunei autō(i)*
Mk 1:40 *lepros parakalōn auton kai gonupetōn*
Lk 5:12 *pesōn epi prosōpon edeēthē autou*
Mt 9:18 (of Jairus) *prosekunei autō(i)*
Mk 5:22 *piptei pros tous podas autou*
Lk 8:41 *pesōn para tous podas Iēsou*

(2) in comparison with Mk:

Mt 14:33 *hoi de en tō(i) ploiō(i) prosekunēsan autō(i) legontes alēthōs theou huios ei*
Mk 6:51 *kai lian ek perissou en heautois existanto*
Mt 15:25 (of the Canaanite woman) *hē de elthousa prosekunei autō(i) legousa*
Mk 7:25 *elthousa prosepesen pros tous podas autou*
Mt 20:20 (of the mother of the sons of Zebedee) *prosekunousa kai aitousa ti par' autou*
Mk 10:35 *prosporeuontai autō(i) . . . legontes*

(3) in comparison with Lk:

Mt 4:9 *ean pesōn proskunēsēis moi*
Lk 4:7 *ean prokunēsēis enōpion emou*
Mt 4:10 *kurion ton theon sou proskunēseis kai autō(i) monō(i) latreuseis* (Deut 6:13)

Lk 4:8 *proskunēseis kurion ton theon sou kai autō(i) monō(i) latreuseis* (Deut 6:13)

With the exception of the last-mentioned, the account of the temptation in the desert, Luke uses the word only in 24:52, where, however, the reading is not certain. Here it is a question of adoring the ascended Lord. Matthew has, in no less than five places, altered or expanded the text of Mark, 'in order to describe the gesture of those who approach Jesus explicitly as proskynesis' (H. Greeven, *TDNT* VI, 763). On the other hand, he has cut the word out completely in the account of the mocking of Jesus, while Mark preserves it, because in this instance there is no expression of true proskynesis. This suggests a highly conscious use of the word on Matthew's part and leads to the assumption that *proskunein* is, for the writer of the first gospel, 'a theological concept' (W. Trilling, *Das wahre Israel: Studien zur Theologie des Matthäusevangeliums*, Leipzig 1959, 148) which he wants to be understood in the sense of a genuine adoration of Jesus. At the same time he realises himself to be tied so strongly to the tradition that has been passed on to him that he introduces the word only in places where Mark uses a phrase that can be interpreted in the sense of *proskunein*.

The use of *proskunein* in exceptional cases in Matthew's gospel is in line with these general conclusions. The case, in Mt 28:9, 17, of proskynesis of the risen Christ, can be accepted unhesitatingly as a reasonable one. Nor does Mt 18:26 constitute an exception, for, if in this parable of the wicked servant it is said: *pesōn oun ho doulos prosekunei autō(i) legōn*, then it is probable that, as the connection with the 'household of God' (Mt 18) suggests, the Lord of the community is to be seen behind the *kurios* of the parable, especially as the falling down of the 'fellow-servant' is not to be interpreted as proskynesis. Finally, the proskynesis of the Magi must also be interpreted, in Matthew's view, as an adoring homage paid to the new-born King (Mt 2:11; see 2:8). This does not contradict the fact that proskynesis can also be seen in this case as 'the oriental expression of respect and subjection (see Gen 19:1; 42:6), and especially of homage paid to a king' (J. Schmid, *Das Evangelium nach Matthäus*, Regensburg 1956, 48). There is also no reason to fear that the idea of the proskynesis of the Magi, in the sense previously indicated, should 'cause either the meaning of the account to be misconstrued or its historicity to be sacrificed' (Schmid, 48).

b. John's gospel. If we disregard the technical term for the pilgrimage to Jerusalem mentioned above (Jn 12:20), there is an occurrence of the verb *proskunein* in the episode recounted in Jn 9:38 where the man whose sight Jesus had restored fell down and adored Jesus after his self-revelation and confessed his faith. Apart from this, the occurrence of the word is concentrated in the conversation with the Samaritan woman at the well of Jacob (4:20–24). This conversation with the Samaritan woman about worship arises from the question of the proper place for the adoration of God, a controversial issue between the Jews and the Samaritans. Whereas the Samaritans regarded Gerizim as the place where God desired to be worshipped, the Jews

believed that the only place of worship was the temple in Jerusalem (4:20). This demonstrates, on the one hand, how strongly a people can regard adoration as being tied to a particular place and, on the other hand, how much value the old order places on the temple in Jerusalem as the proper place of worship. In v 23, however, a new kind of adoration is mentioned: 'But the hour cometh, and now is, when the true worshippers will worship the Father in spirit and in truth.' This adoration is new by reason of the fact that it corresponds to the new order which is to dawn with the eschatological hour. (It is to this dawning that the phrase 'the hour is coming, and now is', points [see 5:25].) But how is this new form of worship 'in spirit and truth' to be understood? Does it imply a spiritualised, inner adoration which, in contrast to the customary form of Jewish worship, is no longer tied to any particular posture or to any particular place? Or is the practice of worship to be transformed from an outward act on the part of the worshipper into something which happens within him, as Schlatter seems to imply:

Now the practice of worship no longer remains a mere gesture, but takes place interiorly, within the worshipper. It is not simply an outward appearance to impress the onlooker, but is something offered to God. [A. Schlatter, *Der Evangelist Johannes*, Stuttgart 1948, 126.]

But this is clearly incorrect. The true interpretation is, in fact, rather more subtle, for in this context ↗ 'spirit' does not mean the spirit or soul of man, nor does ↗ 'truth' mean the truthfulness of man. The 'true worshippers' are not, therefore, those who worship God in 'truthfulness' rather than in 'hypocrisy' (↗ Hypocrite), in which the only thing that counts is outward appearance:

> The prophets too demanded a spiritual worship of God (Is 1:11–20; 29:13; Joel 2:13; Amos 5:21–6; Mic 6:6–8; Ps 40:6; 50:7–23; 51:18f). Both the Jews and the heathens of that period recognised that the prophets transcended the purely formal aspect of worship. [A. Wikenhauser, *Das Evangelium nach Johannes*, Regensburg 1957, 109.]

In this context, the 'new' kind of adoration which is to dawn with the eschatological hour has no place; rather are the 'spirit' and 'truth' of the new adoration to take their character not from man but from God himself. That is also postulated in v 24: 'God is spirit; and [therefore] those who worship him must worship him in spirit and truth'. The sentence: 'God is spirit', is not intended to be in any way a definition of God, but sets out to paraphrase God's being as the sphere of the divine in contrast to the sphere of the *sarx* = ↗ flesh (see Jn 3:6–8; 'The term *pneuma* being appropriated to Deity as such', C. H. Dodd, *The Interpretation of the Fourth Gospel*, Cambridge 1963, 226). God's being is, however, revealed through Jesus Christ, and the divinity of God has become, through him, a visible reality. That is what John means when he speaks of the *alētheia* (= truth): if the 'place' of worship is, so to speak, designated by *en pneumati* (=in the spirit), then *en alētheiā(i)* (= in the truth) infers that this 'place' has become a present reality in Jesus Christ. Ador-

ation 'in spirit and truth' thus means adoring God in a manner which has become possible and real for men in the revelation of Jesus Christ in the eschatological hour. He is the 'new temple' (see Jn 2:19–22), in which God may be worshipped in the way which is fitting to him alone. It can thus be seen that neither the 'place' nor the 'posture' of *proskunein* is preserved in the designation 'spirit' and 'truth', and that the link between these is permanently maintained in the revealed person of God.

c. Revelation to John. In Revelation, the word *proskunein* frequently occurs in connection with descriptions of heavenly worship (4:10; 5:14; 7:11; 11:16; 19:4), and, wherever *proskunein* occurs, the gesture of falling down before God and the Lamb is always expressly mentioned, and at the same time associated with a hymn of praise. It has been pointed out with some justification that the description of heavenly worship in Revelation is to be understood as a reflection of christian public worship on earth. Just as the heavenly beings fall down in adoration before God and Christ with hymns and songs of praise, so the christians on earth should have adored God and their risen Lord with the same, or at least with similar, words in their acts of public worship (see 4:8; 5:9f; 7:12; 11:17; 15:3f; 19:1–3). But the fact that the visionary only describes heavenly proskynesis in this way must be taken, as it were, as an image set in contrast to the situation on earth. For there another kind of proskynesis exists, a perverted public worship, as adoration is offered to the Dragon and the Beast, and all men, with the exception of those whom God has chosen, fall down in adoration of the power of Satan (13:4, 8, 12, 15; see also 14:9, 11; 16:2; 19:20; 20:4). True, christians on earth are styled *proskunountes* = adorers (11:1), and indeed the church of Philadelphia is given the promise that the Jews will come and be made to adore before it (3:9); from the Angel the summons goes forth to all the inhabitants of the earth that they are to worship God (14:6, 7). In the strict sense, however, adoration exists only in heaven: it will not become a reality for all the elect in the new creation until 'the Lord God Almighty is the temple thereof and the Lamb' (21:22).

Bibliography: ⁊ Prayer; see further: A. Frövig, 'Die Anbetung Christi im NT' *Tidskr. for Teol. og Kirke* 1 (1930), 26–44; J. Horst, *Proskynein*, Gütersloh 1932 (with bibliography); H. Greeven, *TDNT* VI, 758–66; E. Mussner, *LTK* I², 498–500 (with bibliography).

Heinrich Zimmermann

Agapē

A. ⁊ Love.

B. *Love-feast*. Apart from the unlikely reading *agapais* in 2 Pet 2:13, there is in the New Testament only one instance (Jude 12) where *agapē* is used as 'brotherly feast' or 'love-feast'. In this epistle, written against the libertinistic heretics (gnostics?), it says: 'These are blemishes in your love-feasts, as they fare sumptuously at your side, shepherds that feed themselves without scruple'. From a certain, authentic custom (Tertullian, *Apologeticum* 39) dating from the end of the second century, we may infer that it was a liturgical, communal meal, during which the presiding bishop or elder spoke the words of blessing over the bread while the same was done over the wine by each member taking part. Otherwise nobody besides the bishop was allowed to speak unless he was called upon. It cannot be stated with absolute certainty whether the *agapē* was a feast independent from the Lord's Supper or, as implied in 1 Cor 11:17–34, was combined with it in one common action, or preceded it. It is also doubtful whether the breaking of bread in Acts 2:42–6; 20:7–11, refers to these feasts (⁊ Eucharist).

In spite of its liturgical character this love-feast does not seem to have obtained a real sacramental function. Its indisputable importance was to express and foster the brotherly union founded by baptism and eucharist, and also to help the needy members of the community (compare the daily ministration of the widows in Acts 6:1). In comparative theology, *agapē* may be related to the Jewish ritual meals, as they were common practice mainly among the late Jewish sects, the Essenes (Flavius Josephus, *Bell. Jud.* II 8, 5) and the congregation of Qumran (*Book of Laws* I QS CI 4). This custom, however, also corresponds with the general view among the ancient peoples and especially in the Hellenistic cultural world that ritual meals have the power of forming communal solidarity.

Bibliography: H. Leclercq, *DACL* I, 775–848; L. Thomas, *DB(S)* I, 134–53; P. Battifol, *Etudes d'Historie et de Théologie Positive*, Paris 1926², 283–325; E. Baumgartner, *Eucharistie und Agape im Urchristentum*, Solothurn 1909; R. L. Cole, *Love Feasts: A History of the Christian Agape*, London 1916; H. Lietzmann, *Mass and the Lord's Supper*, Leiden 1934; K. Völker, *Mysterium und Agape*, Gotha 1927; W. Goossens,

Les Origines de l'Eucharistie, Paris 1931, 127 46; D. Tombolleo, *Le Agapi*, Rome 1931; Bo Reicke, *Diakonie, Festfreude und Zelos in Verbindung mit altchristlichen Agapefeiern*, Uppsala-Wiesbaden 1951; J. A. Jungmann, 'Agape II', *LTK* i², 218f; F. Bammel, *Das heilige Mahl im Glauben der Völker*, Gütersloh 1950, 90–107; V. Warnach, *HTG* ii, 54–75.

Viktor Warnach

Almsgiving

The stipulations of the law at various levels in favour of widows, orphans, strangers, and levites with regard to the harvest, tithes, mortgages, years of remission, jubilee, and so on (see especially Ex 22:21–7; 23; Lev 25; Deut 15; Sir 29:1ff) concern various contributions and benefits. However, it is not possible to regulate individual acts of almsgiving along legal lines, since these consist of free, personal gifts bestowed without any claim to a return or to compensation from the one in need. Such stipulations can nevertheless foster and stimulate further voluntary material help, or alms, especially if the motives are religious and of a broad and even universal character—the will of Yahweh (eg Lev 19:15–18); an unmerited act of deliverance by God leading the people to exercise a similar generosity (Lev 19:34; 25:35–8; Deut 24:18, 22; 15:15); God as the true possessor of the land and the fruits of the land, for which reason those in need have an immediate claim on their brethren (Lev 25:23; Job 31:15–22).

Throughout the entire eastern world of those times, ↗ justice was, in contrast to that of the West, not simply a question of a relationship between man and his fellow-men, but between the powerful and the rich on the one hand and the weak and the poor on the other. *Ts'dāqâh* (righteousness) is almost identical with mercy (Prov 21:21; 29:7, 4; Jer 22:16). Doubtless under the influence of the Aramaic, and because of the alarming spread of want and distress during and after the Exile, it also incorporates the meaning of actual alms. In LXX it is translated, in an apparently arbitrary way, sometimes by *eleēmosunē* (= pity, mercy) and sometimes by *dikaiosunē* (= righteousness): both are frequently placed side by side (see especially Tobit 12:9 BA; 14:11 BA; 14:9 S; etc). Moreover, 'alms' is often expressed synonymously, and so it is hardly possible to define any clear boundary between almsgiving and other negative or positive demands of justice and charity. (Compare the similar lack of clear distinction between alms and wages or reward: Lk 10:7; Mt 10:10b; 1 Tim 5:17f; 1 Cor 9:1–14; 2 Cor 12:14f; Gal 6:6—Bolkestein, *Wohltätigkeit*, 420–30.)

Almsgiving became more important in proportion as prophets and sapiential writers pondered over it and preached about it. For them, true morality, piety, and justice in the widest sense are inconceivable without almsgiving (Ezek 18:7, 16; Tobit 14:2 BA. It is spoken of in the same breath as fasting and prayer (Tob 12:8 BA; compare Mt 6:2, 16; against this, the Coptic *Gospel of Thomas*, Logion 14 [Leipoldt]). It is meritorious and brings about forgiveness of sins (Prov 11:4; 19:17–22; Tob 4:7–11; 12:9; Ps 41:1ff; Dan 4:27; Sir 3:30). It is a condition of salvation (Is 58:6–12). It is considered to be on the same level as sacrifice (Tob 4:11; Sir 35:2; see Heb 13:16).

In the sapiential literature there is, among countless commendatory phrases, no lack of references to the advantages of almsgiving (Prov 28:27) and to the disadvantages and disgrace of 'wicked and foolish' conduct and avarice (Sir 14:3-10; 20:10-17; 41:21; Prov 28:8; Job 27:13-17). These books also abound in exhortations to prudence (Sir 12:1-6; see *Didache* 1, 5-6). Where the poor are concerned, God is involved, their champion (Prov 14:31; 17:5; 19:17; Sir 4:6, 10). So much attention has been paid to the ethical aspect that the friendly word which accompanies the giving is regarded as more important than the gift itself (Sir 18:15-18; 4:1-6). The Jewish people allowed usury to be practised by private initiative to such an extent that almsgiving eventually came to count as the fulfilment of the whole law (SB IV, 536-41; Eichrodt III³, 61 and 131).

In the *New Testament* the practice and high esteem of almsgiving still continue (Jn 13:29; Lk 16:19-31; Acts 3:2; 6:1-6; 10:2-31; 1 Cor 16:15-17; see also 1 Tim 5:16; 1 Cor 11:20-22)—a fact borne out by the frequent use of Old Testament texts. On the other hand, it is not possible to detect any influence of the hellenistic environment here (Bolkenstein, *RAC* I, 302). In the same way, the fact that Jesus bases this practice on ↗ love is not by any means entirely new: his commandment to love is undoubtedly linked to that of the Old Testament (Deut 6:4; Lev 19:18; see also Sir 4:2; 18:15ff;). But his chief commandment equates the love of God with the love of one's neighbour (Mt 22:34-40; Lk 10:25-8; Mk 12:28-31; see also 1 Jn 3:14-22; 4:7f). This love has exclusive claims over every other consideration (Mt 7:12; Lk 6:31). It transcends all barriers or bonds between individuals and groups (Lk 6:27; 10:29-37; Mt 5:43-8; Mk 7:27-8; Rom 12:20; Jas 2:1-4, 8f, 15f)—transcends, too, every restriction or calculation, since God has the only valid claim to consideration (Mk 6:33-7; Lk 6:34-8; Mt 18:33; Jas 2:13). The christian acts in the knowledge that what is done to the poor is done to the Master (Mt 25:31-46; see Mt 10:40; 18:5). Almsgiving serves as a standard at the judgement (see Mt 18:23-5), and Christ is the ultimate reason for true beneficence (Mt 25:40, 45; 10:40-42; Jn 12:44f). The only standard which matters is that set by God. It is not the calculable value of the gift which counts, but the unselfish love which occasions the act of giving. The decisive factor is not the outward performance of the deed but the sentiment behind it (Mk 12:41-4; Lk 18:9-14; 19:1-10; 21:1-4; 1 Cor 13:3; 2 Cor 8:12; see 12:15). Alms thus bestowed are a store laid up in heaven (Lk 12:33; see Mt 6:19-21; 2 Cor 9:9f). Jesus also commends almsgiving as a means of making oneself free to follow him and thus of becoming perfect (Mt 19:21; Mk 10:21; Lk 18:22). Almsgiving can overcome the danger of riches (1 Tim 6:17-19; see Mt 19:23f; Mk 10:25; Lk 16:1-13, 19-31; 18:25). Jesus, however, takes sides with the woman who is said to have 'wasted' a fortune of ointment on his feet, and against the apostles—who, it is true, are thinking of the poor, but not from equally unselfish love (Mt 26:6-13; Mk 14:3-9; Jn 12:1-8).

The disposition of the primitive

church in Jerusalem (Acts 2:44f; 4:32–5), and, even more strikingly, the collections of Paul (Gal 2:10; 1 Cor 16:1–3; Rom 15:15–27, 31; 2 Cor 8, 9; see 1 Cor 11:20–22) cater, among other things, for the organised collection of alms—that is to say, in a social setting and with a social aim in view, arising from the situation within the church at any given moment (see Allo, *RB* 45 [1936], 529–37). Paul is on his guard against everything extravagant (2 Cor 8:12–13). He upholds, in a particularly realistic way, the first, though by no means exclusive, claim of those who belong to the household of the faith (Gal 6:10), and aims to restrain abuses (1 Thes 4:11; 2 Thes 3:6–15; 1 Tim 5:16; see Jude 12–16). The act of giving can, and should, take into account certain physical, moral, or social limitations and regulations (see 2 Cor 8:13; *Didache* 1, 5–6; E. Peterson, *Frühkirche*, 147–8; for a different view, Audet, *La Didachè*, 275–80). It is not, however, possible to impose limitations on the disposition to give alms. The right disposition can be maintained even where personal sacrifice is involved (Eph 4:28; see 1 Thes 4:11; 1 Cor 4:12; 2 Cor 8:2; Acts 20:35). The act of giving should be made in simplicity (Rom 12:8; 2 Cor 8:2; 9:11–13), that is to say, it should be performed with God in mind (see Mt 6:21; Lk 12:14). For that reason, the act is of its nature liberal, impulsive, and cordial (2 Cor 9:5, 7–9; Rom 12:8; Bacht, *GL* 29 [1956], 424–6). Only what is given from the heart has any real value (2 Cor 9:7), not what is given out of covetousness (2 Cor 9:5, 7; see 1 Tim 6:10). There is, to be sure, an 'equality' (*isotēs* 2 Cor

8:13f), but not as an adjustment of relations here on earth, but rather as *koinōnia*, a solidarity in sharing and participation (Rom 15:26f; 2 Cor 8:4; 9:13) in everything which can be of service (*diakonia* Rom 15:25, 31; 2 Cor 8:4, 19, 20; 9:1, 12, 13) to others. This follows naturally from, and expresses in a concrete way, the religious fellowship founded by Christ (Hauck, *TDNT* III, 804–9). Everything is *kharis* (=love, charity), applied in different ways, beginning with the poverty of Christ which causes grace to operate (2 Cor 8:9) and ending with the money distributed by christians among each other for the love of Christ (1 Cor 16:3; see 2 Cor 8, 9). No word of thanks is due to men. Everything is done from God-given love, with the result that the recipients are fortified in faith and charity and give thanks and praise to God (2 Cor 9:8–15; see Phil 2:13–15; 2 Cor 8:5).

Christian almsgiving is not to be thought of as a continuous or general relief of a distress which is always present (Mt 26:11; Mk 14:7; see Deut 15:11), but as the affirmation of a charity which arises from the prevailing circumstances. That is why, in the New Testament, there is relatively little explicit or exclusive discussion of almsgiving as such. Whatever discussion one finds is aimed at an immediately attainable end, as in the case of Paul's collections. For Jesus, it is a question of the general prevalence of charity, whether it happens to be in polemics directed against a ritualistic scrupulosity that is devoid of love (Lk 11:39–42; see Mt 23:25f), or in the application or illustration of the consequences of charity (Lk 12:33f; Mt

6:1–4, 19–21). The giving of alms shares in the nobility of charity.

Bibliography: E. B. Allo, 'La portée de la collecte pour Jérusalem dans les plans de S. Paul', *RB* 45 (1936), 529–37; J.-P. Audet, *La Didachè, Instructions des Apôtres*, Paris 1958; H. Bacht sj, 'Einfalt des Herzens—eine vergessene Tugend?, *Geist und Leben* 29 (1956), 416–526; Bammel, *TDNT* vi, 885–915; J. Bauer, 'Ut quid perditio ista? Zu Mk 14:4f und parr.', *Novum Testamentum* 3 (1959), 54–6; Beyer, *TDNT* ii, 81–93; R. Bloch, 'Valeur religieuse de la Justice dans le Bible', *Cahiers Sioniens* (Paris) 6 (1952), 17–32; H. Bolkenstein and W. Schwer, *RAC* i, 301–07; H. Bolkenstein, *Wohltätigkeit und Armenpflege im vorchristlichen Altertum*, Utrecht 1939; R. Bultmann, *TDNT* ii, 477–87; A. Descamps, *Les Justes et la Justice dans les évangiles et le christianisme primitif hormis la doctrine proprement paulinienne*, Louvain 1950; A. Descamps, *DB(S)* iv, 1443–4; Hauck, *TDNT* iii, 804–9; J. Hempel, 'Das Ethos des AT', *BZAW* 67 (1938); J. Nikel, *Das Alte Testament und die Nächstenliebe*, Münster 1913; R. North, 'Sociology of the biblical Jubilee', *Analecta Biblica* 4 (1954); Erik Peterson, *Frühkirche, Judentum und Gnosis*, Freiburg and Rome 1959; SB iv, 536–610; A. Wikenhauser, 'Die Liebeswerke in dem Gerichtsgemälde Mat 25:31–46', *BZ* 20 (1932), 366–77; W. Nagel, 'Gerechtigkeit—oder Almosen? (Mt 6:1)', *VC* 15 (1961), 141–5; V. Balogh, '"Selig die Barmherzigen". Die christliche Barmherzigkeit bei Matthäus im allgemeinen und in der 5. Seligpreisung im besonderen im Lichte des AT', Rome 1959 (dissertation).

Johann Gamberoni

Amen

A. *Old Testament*. Derived from the root *'mn* (= to be secure, firm, valid, or certain; ↗ truth), *'āmēn* is generally rendered in LXX by *genoito* (= so be it). In the Old Testament and in later judaism the word was never used simply to endorse a statement, but exclusively as a sign of agreement with what another affirmed. In 1 Kings 1:36; Jer 11:5; 28:6, assent is given to a command; in Num 5:22; Deut 27:15–26; Neh 5:13, a curse or a threat is submitted to; in Ps 41:13; 72:19; 89:52; etc, *'āmēn* is pronounced after a benediction or a eulogy.

An acclamation with *'āmēn* is the usual way of concluding a previously expressed aspiration in prayer with a personal affirmation. This custom is to be found since time immemorial in the liturgy, and numerous examples from later Jewish public worship can be quoted in support of it. At Qumran, benedictions and maledictions are assented to in this way when a covenant is entered into (1 QS 1:20; 2:10, 18).

B. *Jesus* uses *'āmēn* in quite a singular sense at the beginning of his own utterances in order to reinforce them: 'Amen, I say to you'. In John's gospel the word is always repeated, as in liturgical usage. This usage of Jesus can be rendered in English with a fair degree of accuracy as: 'I say to you in all seriousness', 'I say to you once and for all'. In this fashion the Lord expresses his claim to authority and the fact that his words have power absolutely to bind the conscience. There is no example in later Jewish literature which can be compared with this application of the word *'āmēn* on the part of Jesus, and for this reason it can be regarded as a characteristic of the *ipsissima vox* of Jesus, his very own manner of speaking (see Mt 5:18, 26; 6:2, 5; etc; Jn 1:51; 3:3, 5; etc). This *'āmēn* is also occasionally translated by *nai* (= yes) (Mt 11:9; Lk 7:26; etc) or, in the case of Lk 9:27; 12:44; 21:3, by *alēthōs* (= truly), and in Lk 4:25 by *ep' alētheias* (= in truth).

Elsewhere in the New Testament, *'āmēn* occurs in the usual way as a liturgical acclamation (1 Cor 14:16; Rev 5:14; 7:12; etc), or in order to reinforce an aspiration made in prayer or a eulogy (Rom 15:33; Gal 6:18). In certain cases the use of *'āmēn* cannot, from the point of view of textual criticism, be satisfactorily testified, and is then generally the addition of a copyist. Such cases include the use of *'āmēn* at the end of epistles (1 Cor 16:24; 2 Cor 13:14; etc) and other books (Mt 28:20; Mk 16:20; Lk 24:53; Jn 21:25; Acts 28:31; 1 Jn 5:21; 2 Jn 13; 3 Jn 15; see also Tob 14:15 LXX).

In Rev 22:20 the church replies to the divine promise with *'āmēn*. In 2 Cor 1:20 the community gives the answer *'āmēn* to God's 'Yes' that he has uttered through Christ and in which all promises have been realised. In Rev 3:14 Christ himself is called 'Amen' as the 'faithful and true witness' of divine revelation.

Bibliography: J. Jeremias, 'Kennzeichen der ipsissima vox Jesu', *Festschrift A. Wikenhauser*, Munich 1953, 86–93; J. Schmid, *LTK*I² (1957), 432f; A. Stuiber, *Jahrbuch für Antike und Christentum* I (1958), 153–9.

Johannes B. Bauer

Angel

A. *Word and meaning*—The English word *angel*, like its equivalent in most modern languages, is derived through the Latin word *angelus* from the Greek word *angelos* (= messenger). In christian usage, developed during the Middle Ages after a start in early christian times, it stands for supernatural spirits; in the bible not so much because of their nature, as in present-day usage (in that sense they are usually referred to as 'spirits', 'powers', etc), but because of their function in the service of God or the devil (Augustine: 'Angelus enim officii nomen est non naturae' [*Sermo* VII 3]). Although the belief in spirits and angel-like intermediary beings between God and man may be found in many religions, the conception of 'angels' is characteristic of the Jewish and christian beliefs and of those religions that have been influenced by them (eg old Syncretism, Islam).

B. *Angels in the Old Testament*

a. *Early period*. There are beings between God and man which are sometimes called 'angels' according to their function (*mal'kîm* [originally: 'messengers'], *angeloi* [Gen 19:1; 28:12; 32:1; Ps 103:20]), in other places 'men' according to their outward appearance (Gen 18:2, 16; 19:10, 12), or according to their relation to God, 'host of Jahweh' (Jos 5:14), of 'the army of heaven' (1 Kings 22:19). God consequently is called 'God of hosts' (Hos 12:5; Amos 3:13; 6:14) or 'Yahweh of hosts' (1 Sam 1:3, 11; Ps 24:10; 46:7, 11). The angels very often have a warlike appearance (Gen 32:1ff; Jos 5:13; Judg 5:20). They are with God in heaven (Gen 21:17; 22:11) and there form his heavenly household (1 Kings 22:19), but, according to an old tradition, they also live on earth (Gen 32:2). The angels come to man as messengers of God (Gen 16:7ff; 19:1ff; 21:17; 22:15; Num 22:22ff; Judg 2:1; 6:11; 13:3; 1 Kings 13:18; 2 Kings 1:3); they protect man (Gen 24:7, 40; 48:16; Ex 23:20–23; Ps 91:11), but occasionally they also pass divine judgement on him (2 Sam 24:16; 19:35; Ps 78:49). People generally pictured angels as beings in human form, as is evident from many apparitions (cf the epithet 'men') and therefore without wings.

The Angel of Yahweh. Among the angels, special prominence is given to the 'Angel of Yahweh' (Gen 16:7, 9; 22:11, 15; 31:11; Ex 3:2, 4; Judg 2:1; 6:11ff; see Gen 18f; Acts 7:30–5) or the 'Angel of God' (Gen 21:17; Judg 13:6, 9). God reveals himself through him in such a way that the text speaks directly of God and not of his angel (Gen 16:10, 13; 22:10–18; 31:11–13; 48:15f; Ex 3:1ff); but on the other hand this angel appears quite distinct from God (Gen 24:7; Ex 33:1f; 2 Sam 24:16). The relation of this angel towards God, which up to today has never been satisfactorily explained, has given rise to different attempts at explanation. The 'Representation-theory' sees in the Angel of Yahweh an angel-like creature acting on the authority of God (Jerome, Augustine). According to the 'Identity-theory' he is God himself, who, though in himself invisible, shows himself as visibly present and active in certain situations. The 'Logos-theory' (now obsolete) regards him as a revelation of the Logos, ie, of the pre-existing Son of God (early christian writers). According to the 'Interpolation-theory' (many modern exegetes) it is an indication of later theological convictions; ever since the period of an absolutely transcendental concept of God, the old stories of God's direct intercourse with man had become objectionable and therefore 'God's Angel' took the place of God himself. The figure of the Angel of Yahweh comes very close to that of the 'Angel of the Covenant' (Mal 3:1).

Cherubim and Seraphim. Mention is made occasionally of 'Cherubim' (*kᵉrûbîm*: probably related to the Accadian word *karibu* or *kuribu*, a deity of lower order mediating between man and the higher gods originally represented in human form and later with wings and the characteristics of the eagle, the lion, or the bull. This may have been influenced by the usual representation of Egyptian goddesses or genii by the Assyrian winged Colossi with bodies of lions or bulls and human heads standing at the entrances of temples and palaces). They guard paradise beside the flaming sword so that the first human couple could not again enter this garden of Eden from which they had been expelled (Gen 3:24). They were furthermore thought of as 'Bearers of God' (2 Sam 22:11; Ps 18:10), and as such they had very realistically been placed on either side of the cover of the ark (Ex 25:19f; cp the cherubs in the Holy of Holies of Solomon's Temple, which were of a related but quite different form, 1 Kings 6:23–8; 2 Chron 3:10–13), so that God was said to be 'sitting upon the cherubim' (1 Sam 4:4; Ps 99:1). This idea found its full and impressive expression in Ezekiel's vision, where four cherubs of a fiery nature with the faces respectively of a man, a lion, a bull, and an eagle were drawing God's chariot with their hands, feet, and wings (Ezek 1:10). The Tabernacle (Ex 26:1, 31; 36:8, 35) and the Temple of Solomon (1 Kings 6:29, 32; 2 Chron 3:14) were decorated with the woven and carved figures of cherubs.

In the glorious vision of Isaiah

21

(6:2–6) mention is made of 'Seraphs', beings with six wings, with hands, feet, and human faces, standing before God's Throne (*s'rāphîm*, originally: 'the burning ones'; other meanings of the word are: 'poisonous serpent' [Num 21:6, 8] or 'flying serpent' [Is 14:29; 30:6], which suggests an original connection of seraphs with snakes).

Cherubs and seraphs are not angels in the original sense of the word and are, therefore, never referred to as such in earlier times. But during the later Jewish period they are classed under those beings which are now called 'angels', for which reason they can safely be indicated as angels in the modern sense of the word.

b. *Later period*. The Jewish conception of angel and its representation became increasingly more elaborate and rich during the Persian and Greco-Roman period, especially in the so-called Apocryphal writings (*Pseudepigrapha*), eg the Books of Henoch, the Book of Jubilees, the Syrian Apocalypse of Baruch, etc, and to a certain extent also in the canonical writings of this period, eg Job, Daniel, and Tobit. The main reason for this development is the stronger emphasis on God's transcendence during this time as opposed to the preceding period, which again gave greater prominence to the part played by angels as intermediaries between God and the world. Other factors may have contributed, although there is not sufficient certainty as to their details (introduction of popular conceptions into the Jewish religion, contact with the religious ideas of the pagan countries where the Jews stayed). An especially fertile ground for this development is the apocalyptic literature which was

coming into fashion with the Book of Daniel. From this time onwards, new names are chosen for the angels. According to their relation to God, they are called 'sons of God' in the sense of 'beings closely related to God' (Job 1:6; 2:1; 38:7; Wis 5:5; see also LXX-suppl. Deut 32:43); 'holy ones' (Job 5:1; 15:15; Ps 89:5, 7; Dan 4:13, 17,23; 8:13; Zech 14:5; Sir 42:17; Wis 5:5; Jub 17:11; 31:14; 33:12; Enoch [Eth] 1:9f; TestLev 3:3; 1 QS 11:8; 1 QM 12:1, 4; 1 QH 3:22; 4:25; 10:35); 'holy angels' (Tob 11:14; 12:15; Enoch [Eth] 71:8f; 1 QM 7:6); 'divine beings' (*'ēlîm*: 1 QM 1:10f; 14:15; 17:7; 1 QH 7:28; 10:8); or, according to their function, 'watchers' (Dan 4:13, 17, 23; 8:13; Jub 4:15, 22; 7:21; 8:3; 10:5; Enoch [Eth] 1:5 etc; Enoch [Slav] 18:1, 3; 35:2; TestRub 5:6; TestNaph 3:5; CD 2:18); 'they who never sleep' (Enoch [Eth] 39:12f; 40:2); 'princes' (Dan 10:13, 20f; 12:1; 1 QS 3:20; 1 QM 13:10, 14); and, according to their nature, 'spirits' (Jub 15:31; Enoch [Eth] 15:4, 6, 8, 10; 1 QM 12:9; 13:11f; 1 QH 1:11; 11:13; 13:8; see also 1 Kings 22:21; Wis 7:23); and 'majestic beings' (1 QH 10:8; Enoch [Slav] 21:1, 3). According to their nature all angels and angel-like beings are called 'spirits', so that God is then referred to as 'Lord of spirits' (LXX Num 16:22; 27:16; 2 Macc 3:24; the constant expression used in the similitudes of Enoch [Eth] 37:2, 4ff; see also Ps 104:4; Sir 39:33). He is 'Prince of divine beings, King of majestic beings, and Lord of all spirits' (1 QH 10:8).

LXX mentions an angel in many places where, according to the Hebrew text, God acts himself (eg Ex 4:24;

Job 20:15); also 'the angels' instead of God himself (Ps 8:5). Also the phrase 'Son of God' is replaced by 'Angel' (Job 1:6) and 'gods' by 'angels' (Ps 97:7; 138:1; see also Dan 2:11 Theodotion).

During this period God no longer speaks directly to the prophet or apocalyptist as in the older prophecies; rather, an angel is sent to him to present and explain God's revelations, first in Ezekiel (40:3f; 43:6; 47:3–6), where he is simply referred to as 'a man', later, in a particular way, in Zechariah (1:8–14; 2:1, 7; 4:1–6 etc), where 'the angel of Jahweh' performs this function; also in Daniel (8:16–26; 9:21–27), where it is seen to by Gabriel, and in the Apocrypha (eg, Uriel in Hen [Eth] 10:1; 19:1f; 2 Esdras 4:1f).

Angels are disembodied spirits (Hen [Eth] 15:6; Philo, *De Sacrificiis Abelis et Caini*, 5; ApocAbr 19:6), of fiery essence (Bar [Syr] 21:6; 59:11; Apoc-Abr 19:6; Enoch [Slav] 1:4f; 20:1; 29:1, 3; 30:1), whom God has created (Jub 2:2: 'on the first day'; Bar [Syr] 21:6: 'right from eternity')—created, however, as immortal beings (Enoch [Eth] 15:4, 6). In accordance with their nature their food was not of an earthly or material kind (Tob 12:19; see also Judg 13:16 and the older, opposite view in Gen 18:8); it was, on the contrary, a heavenly manna (LXX Ps 78:25; Wis 16:20; 4 Esdras 1:19; see also Tob 12:19). They are visible on earth only as apparitions, not in material bodies. (Tob 12:19.) The angel appears in the form of a man (Dan 8:15; 10:5, 16; Tob 5:4f; Enoch [Slav] 1:4; see also Gen 19:5), as a young man (2 Macc 3:26), in glory (Dan 10:5f; Enoch [Slav] 1:5); his

face is like lightning (Dan 10:6). He is clothed in linen (Ezek 9:2f, 11; 10:2, 6f; Dan 10:5; 12:6f), in a beautiful garment (2 Macc 3:26), in white (TestLevi 8:2; see also 2 Macc 11:8; Enoch [Eth] 87:2; 90:21, 31). His belongings are made of gold (2 Macc 3:25) or fire (Enoch [Slav] 29:3; Joseph and Asenath 17:8). In the vision he speaks with a loud voice (Dan 10:6). The apparition of an angel confounds a man (Dan 10:9 [strictly speaking, the confusion here is resolved by the words of the angel]; Tob 12:16; 3 Macc 6:18f; Enoch [Slav] 1:7; see also Esther 5:2a LXX [= 15:16 Vulg]), but the angel lifts him up again (Dan 10:10; Tob 12:17; Enoch [Slav] 1:8). Men hide themselves from the sight of an angel (1 Chron 21:20). The movement of angels is generally represented as flying, even when wings are not mentioned (Dan 9:21; Apoc-Abr 12:9; see also Dan 14:36, 38).

The number of angels is beyond reckoning (Job 33:23; Dan 7:10; Enoch [Eth] 1:9f; Enoch [Slav] 11:4; 18:1; 1 QM 12:1, 4; 4 Esdras 6:3; Bar [Syr] 21:6f; see also Deut 33:2; Ps 68:17). They form God's council, along the lines of similar bodies at earthly courts, although, of course, God's sole and exclusive dominion is always preserved and the angels do not share his supreme rule (Job 1:6–12; 2:1–7; 15:8; Ps 89:7; see also 1 Kings 22:19–21; Dan 4:17). They stand before God as he sits on his throne (Dan 7:10; Enoch [Eth] 71:8; Bar [Syr] 21:6; 48:10; 4 Esdras 8:21). They praise him for ever more (Enoch [Eth] 39:13; Enoch [Slav] 8:8; 17:22–3; 42:4; TestLevi 3:8 (here it is a question of the 'thrones' and 'powers'), with one voice (Enoch [Eth] 61:11; Enoch [Slav] 19:6), with beautiful song (Enoch [Slav] 8:8, 17), with soft and gentle voices (Enoch [Slav] 20:4; see also 21:1). They form the 'host of heaven' (Neh 9:6; for angels and hosts of heaven side by side see Ps 103:2Lf; 148:2), the 'eternal army' (1 QH 11:13), which is equipped to fight for God's cause (Enoch [Eth] 60:1; 61:10; TestLevi 3:3; 1 QM 12:1, 4; 1 QH 3:35f; 11:13 etc; see also 2 Macc 3:25f). They are the 'angels of heaven' (Enoch [Eth] 97:2; see also 71:8; 104:1), who have their station in the different zones of heaven (TestLevi 3:2f, 5–8).

Angels come to men as bearers of divine messages (Tob 3:17; Dan 14:34), give him an unparalleled insight (LXX Dan Susanna 45), give him orders (1 Chron 21:18), and make known what God wants him to do (Job 33:23). They speak to God on behalf of men. (Job 33:23f) and present their prayers to God (Tob 12:15; Enoch [Eth] 99:3; TestDan 6:2; see also TestLevi 3, 7). The angels protect men (Dan 3:23 (26, 28), 25; LXX Sus 45; Vulg Jud 13:20; 2 Macc 11:6; 15:22f; Enoch [Eth] 100:5; 1 QM 9, 15f; 13:10; TestJud 3:10; TestDan 6:5; TestJos 6:7 etc), rescue them from danger (Dan 3:23 (26), 25; 6:23; Tob 3:17; 2 Macc 15:23; see also 2 Kings 19:35; Is 37:36), and help them in various ways (Tob 5:6; 12:3, 14; 3 Macc 6:18f; 4 Macc 4:10; see also 2 Macc 3:25). They transport them through the air to places they have never seen before (Dan 14:34–39); they have power over demons (Tob 8:3; Jub 10:7, 11). Individual men are under the protection of particular

angels (1 QS 4:15f); two spirits, one of truth and the other of unrighteousness, are given to men (1 QS 3:18f; see also TestJud 20:1; 1 QH 1:17; 17:17). Each man has an angel allotted to him by God. (Bar [Greek] 12:3; 13:1; Enoch [Slav] 19:4.)

Holy men of God are occasionally called 'angels' when they act as mediators between God and man in a role similar to that of the angels (eg the priest in Mal 2:7 and Moses in AssMos 11:17). A similar parallel is sometimes drawn between the king and an angel (Esther 5:2a, LXX [=15:16 Vulg]; even earlier in 1 Sam 29:9; 2 Sam 14:17, 20; 19:27; see also Zech 12:8).

Every nation has its own angel (Dan 10:13, 20f; Jub 15:31f; Enoch [Eth] 89:59; 90:22, 25; see also LXX Deut 32:8; Dan 12:1; LXX Sir 17:17.) The angel of Israel is Michael (Dan 10:13, 21; 12:1; Enoch [Eth] 20:5); but according to another point of view Israel does not come under any angel, but directly under God (Jub 15:32; see also LXX Deut 32:8f).

There are angels in charge of created things, as an angel of the firmament (Esdras 6:41), of the stars (Enoch [Eth] 72:1, 3; 74:2f; Enoch [Slav] 4; 19:2, where the stars themselves are not regarded as animated, angelic beings: Enoch [Eth] 18:13–16; 21:3–6; Philo, *De Opificio Mundi*, 73; *De Gigantibus*, 8), of the natural elements such as the wind, thunder and lightning, rain, and the like (Jub 2:2; Enoch [Eth] 60:11–21); also of the seasons (Jub 2:2; Enoch [Slav] 19:4; see also Hen [Eth] 82:11–20); water (Enoch [Eth] 61:10; 66:2; 69:22; Enoch [Slav] 19:4); fruit (Enoch [Slav] 19:4); and metals (Enoch [Eth] 65:8).

24

God passes judgement on man through his angels. (1 Chron 21:12, 15f, 27; 1 Macc 7:41; Bar [Syr] 6:4ff; Joseph and Asenath 25:6; see also 2 Macc 3:24-6.)

Groups of angels are formed, eg, a group of seven angelic princes or archangels (Tob 12:15) Enoch [Greek] 20:2-7; Enoch [Eth] 81:5; 90:21; Jerusalem Targum I ad Gen 11:7; see also TestLevi 8:2-10). Elsewhere, however, only six are given (Enoch [Eth] 20:1; Jerusalem Targum I ad Deut 34:6), or four (Enoch [Eth] 9:1; 10; 40:2-10f; Sib II 215). Besides these, seven orders of angels are known (TestLevi 3:2-8), or also ten (Enoch [Eth] 61:10; Enoch [Slav] 20:1; including in both cases the cherubim and seraphim). Names are also given to certain angels, such as Michael (Dan 10:13; 12:1; Enoch [Eth] 9:1; 10:11; 20:5; 1 QM 9:15f; Bar [Gr] 11:8; ApocMos 1:40; Sib II 215; JerTargum I ad Deut 34:6, etc); Gabriel (Dan 8:16; 9:21; Enoch [Eth] 9:1; 10:9; 20:7; 1 QM 9:15f; ApocMos 40; Sib II 215; JerTargum *loc. cit.*, etc); Raphael (Tob 3:17; 5:4; 9:1, 5; 12:15; Enoch [Eth] 9:1; 10:4; 20:3; 1 QM 9:15; ApocMos 40; Sib II 215; JerTargum *loc. cit.* etc); as well as Uriel in extracanonical writings (Enoch [Eth] 9:1; 10:9; 20:2; ApocMos 40; 2 Esdras 4:1; 5:20; 10:28; Sib II 215; JerTargum *loc. cit.* etc) together with a great number of often fantastic names.

The angels are not represented as being free from the possibility of sin in the eyes of God (Job 4:18; 15:15), but the canonical books of the Old Testament do not speak of a given sin committed by the angels; nevertheless, they are subject to God's judgement (Job 21:22; see also Is 24:21-23). The extracanonical literature, on the other hand, infers such a sin from Gen 6:2, 4: a section of the angels—those, namely, who are referred to in that text as 'sons of God' at one time left heaven, took the daughters of men to wife and by them engendered giants; for which, as a punishment, these angels were, for a time, chained in the underworld, to be thence cast into eternal fire at the judgement (Jub 4:22; 5:1; 6:10; 7:21; 10:5; Enoch [Eth] 6f; 10:4-13; 12:4; 15; 54:3-6f; TestRub 5:6; TestNeph 3:5; Bar [Syr] 56:12f; Philo, *De Gigantibus*, 6; Josephus, *Ant. Iud.*, 1, 3, 1 [73]; see also CD 3, 4 (Riessler) (=2, 17f [Schechter]). See also ↗ Demon.

While the Essenes were greatly exercised with angels (see Josephus, *Bell. Iud.*, 2, 8, 7, 142), popular belief went no further than can be seen from the extant texts, while the Sadducees, according to Acts 23:8, refused to accept such representations (cf. Hippolytus, *Refutatio Omnium Haeresium*, 9, 30, 4). Rabbinical Judaism, which grew out of Pharisaism, left plenty of freedom in the matter of belief in angels, but opposed exaggerations and attempted to bring this belief into a right relationship with belief in God, in keeping with Old-Testament conceptions.

3. *Angels in the New Testament.* The conception of angel in the New Testament is based on that of the late Jewish period as found in the so-called late Jewish apocrypha and related writings, rather than on the earlier canonical books of the Old Testament. In the New Testament, however, this conception is more subdued. Angels function

as messengers sent from God to man (Mt 1:20; 2:13, 19; Lk 1:11, 26; 2:9f; Acts 8:26; 10:3; 27:23; see also Gal 1:8). They appear to him in dreams (Mt 1:20; 2:13, 19), but also when they are fully awake (Mk 16:5; Lk 24:4f; Jn 20:12); in a vision (Acts 10:3), and resembling young men in shining white robes (Mk 16:5; Mt 28:3; Lk 24:4; Jn 20:12; Acts 1:10; 10:30; Rev 15:6; 19:14). People are frightened at the sight of angels (Lk 1:12; 2:9; see also Mk 16:5, 8); but the angels sent them at ease (Lk 1:13; 2:10; see also Mk 16:6; Mt 28:5.

There are a great many angels (Mt 26:53; Heb 12:22; Rev 5:11); they are spirits (Heb 1:14; see also Rev 1:4); they have been created in Christ (Col 1:16) and, like all other things they have been reconciled with God through his blood (Col 1:20). They form the legions of God (Mt 26:53) and represent the heavenly world (Mt 22:30; Lk 12:8f; Eph 3:15; 1 Tim 5:21; Heb 12:22; 1 Pet 3:22). The New Testament mentions various groups of heavenly beings (similar to the Apocrypha of the late-Jewish periods: Hen [Eth] 61:10; Hen [Slav] 20:1; TestLev 3:2–8): eg 'virtues' (*dunameis* Rom 8:38; 1 Cor 15:24; Eph 1:21; 1 Pet 3:22; see also 2 Thess 1:7); 'powers' (*exousiai* 1 Cor 15:24; Eph 1:21; 3:10; 6:12; Col 1:16; 2:10, 15; 1 Pet 3:22); 'principalities' (*arkhai* Rom 8:38; 1 Cor 15:24; Eph 1:21; 3:10; 6:12; Col 1:16; 2:10, 15); 'dominations' (*kuriotētes* Eph 1:21; Col 1:16); 'thrones' (*thronoi* Col 1:16), although the difference between these choirs of blessed spirits is not disclosed. The law of the old covenant was given to man by angels (Acts 7:53; Gal 3:19;

Heb 2:2). They serve Christ (Mt 4:11; Lk 22:43) and his disciples (Acts 5:19; 12:7–10; Heb 1:14). They rejoice in the proven integrity of the just and in the conversion of the sinner (Lk 15:10; see also 15:7). Children have their angels in heaven (Mt 18:10), and—at least in popular belief—everybody has his own angel (resembling him) (Acts 12:15). Angels guide the dead into eternity (Lk 16:22). In the resurrection of the dead, men will be like angels (Mk 12:25 and parallel passages); but even now the face of a witness of Christ, full of the Holy Ghost, may resemble that of an angel (Acts 6:15). Christ will come for his last judgement with his angels (Mt 16:27; 24:31).

Being the Son of God, Christ is superior to all angels, both before his incarnation and when he will be the God-man raised to the right hand of God (Mk 13:27 and parallel passages; Eph 1:20f; Col 1:16f; 2:10; Heb 1:5–14; 2:1–9; 1 Pet 3:22). Through his death and resurrection Christ has despoiled the principalities and powers (Col 2:15). The faithful will share Christ's restoration to power and will even judge the angels in the last judgement (1 Cor 6:3). God's intentions regarding the salvation of man will be made known to the angels through the church (Eph 3:10; 1 Tim 3:16); and learning of God's wise doings will be a joy to the angels (1 Pet 1:12).

The New Testament also uses the expression 'the Angel of the Lord' corresponding to the old expression 'the Angel of Yahweh', or 'the Angel of God' (Mt 1:20; 2:13; 28:2; Lk 1:11; 2:9; Acts 5:19; 8:26; 12:7 and many other instances) when referring to the angel sent from God with a special message. Only two angels have been given names, Gabriel (Lk 1:19, 26) and Michael (Jude 9; Rev 12:7), the latter once (Jude 9) being referred to as 'archangel' (*arkhangelos*, a Jewish-hellenistic word formation first used in Enoch [Gr] 20:7). The worshipping of angels is rejected (Col 2:18; see also Rev 19:10; 22:8f). Beside the angels of God there are the angels of the devil (Mt 25:41; 2 Cor 12:7; Rev 12:7, 9). Occasionally (Jude 6; 2 Pet 2:4) mention is made of a fall of certain angels and their punishment (in accordance with a widespread late-Jewish legend, eg in the Book of Jubilees 4:22; 5:1; 7:21; 10:5; Enoch (Eth] 6f). Neither angels nor principalities nor virtues are able to separate the christian from the love of God (Rom 8:38f), but he has to struggle against these principalities and powers, these rulers of the world of darkness (Eph 6:12). But when the time of the eternal Kingdom of God has come, principalities, powers, and virtues will lose the power they wield in this present world (1 Cor 15:24). Consequently, many of these beings have something demoniacal about them, are in league with the devil and 'spirits of wickedness' (Eph 6:12; see also 6:11).

Angels are most frequently mentioned in the Revelation to John in whose visions angels perform various functions. An angel sent from God conveys the revelations to the Seer (1:1; see also 19:10; 22:6, 8f). The Seer writes to the 'angels' of seven churches in Asia (1:20; 2f; it is very clear that real angels are referred to, not bishops or other officials of these churches). The traditional cherubs and seraphs have merged into a group of four 'living creatures' (4:6–8 and other instances) round the throne of God. And also before him stand the equally traditional seven angel-princes (Rev 8f), also simply referred to as 'seven spirits' (1:4; 3:1; 4:5; 5:6). There also appear the angels of the four winds (7:1f), the angel-prince of the demoniac locusts of the bottomless pit called Abaddon (=Destroyer; 9:11), the angels of the malicious horsemen (9:14), an angel with power over fire (14:18), another with power over the waters (16:5), and seven angels with vials full of the wrath of God (Rev 15f). See also ⟋ Principalities and powers.

D. *Theological value of biblical statements concerning angels.* In the theological appreciation of biblical evidence concerning angels, we must above all be mindful of the literary nature of the text; whether we are confronted with a simple account of facts or a free narrative in which more popular notions have been assimilated (eg Tobit), whether they represent a view strongly connected with the ancient conception of the world (the classification of angels in Paul), or whether they must be regarded as symbolic visions whose real meaning can only be found after lifting the veil of symbolism (eg the Book of Revelation). The church holds in accordance with the bible that apart from our visible world God created a world of pure, invisible spirits, serving God and man; also that that part of this host of angels has turned from God and is pitted against him in eternal enmity (see IV Lateran Council, DS 800 [DB 428]). The doctrine of the guardian angel for every human being is based on the bible and has always been held in the church, although it has not been formally pronounced as a dogma.

Bibliography: W. Grundmann, G. von Rad, and G. Kittel, *TDNT* I, 74–87; K. Prümm, *Der christliche Glaube und die altheidnische Welt* I, Leipzig 1935, 137–56; L. S. Chafer, 'Angelology', *Bibliotheca Sacra* 98 (1941), 389–420; 99 (1942), 6–25; Haag, 390–98; M. Ziegler, *Engel und Dämon im Lichte der Bible*, Zürich 1957; A. Winklhofer, *Die Welt der Engel*, Ettal 1958; J. Michl and R. Haubst, *LTK* III², 863–72; J. Michl, *RAC* v, 53–258; J. Michl, 'Engel', *HTG* I, 269–81.
On Section B: S. Landersdorfer, 'Zur Lehre von den Schutzengeln im AT' *Katholik* 98 (1918), 2 and 114–20; J. Felten, *Neutestamentliche Zeitgeschichte*, II, Regensburg 1925³, 107–41; P. Dhorme and L. H. Vincent, 'Les Chérubins', *RB* 35 (1926), 328–58 and 481–95; W. Bousset and H. Gressmann, 320–31; G. H. Dix, 'The Seven Archangels and the Seven Spirits', *JTS* 28 (1927), 233–50; C. Kaplan, 'Angels in the Book of Enoch', *ATR* 12 (1930), 423–37; J. Rybinski, *Der Mal'akh Jahwe*, Paderborn 1930; F. Stier, *Gott und sein Engel im AT*, Münster 1934; P. Volz, *Die Eschatologie der jüdischen Gemeinde im ntl. Zeitalter*, Tübingen 1934² (under 'Engel'); F. König, *Die Amesha Spentas des Avesta und die Erzengel im AT*, Melk 1935; E. Langton, *The Ministries of the Angelic Powers according to the Old Testament and later Jewish Literature*, London 1937; B. Stein, 'Der Engel des Auszugs', *Bbl* 19 (1938), 286–307; H. B. Kuhn, 'The Angelology of the Non-Canonical Jewish Apocalypses', *JBL* 67 (1948), 217–232; G. Heidt, *Angelology of the Old Testament: A Study in Biblical Theology*, Washington 1949; A. Dupont-Sommer, 'L'Instruction sur les deux Esprits dans le "Manuel de Discipline"', *RHR* 142 (1952), 5–35; A. Kolaska, 'Gottessöhne und Engel in den vorexilischen Büchern des AT und in der Ras-Schamra-Mythologie im Lichte des biblischen Monotheismus', Vienna 1953 (dissertation); B. Otzen, 'Die neugefundenen hebräischen Sektenschriften und die Testamente der zwölf Patriarchen', *ST* 7 (1953/4), 125–57; F. Nötscher, *Geist und Geister in den Texten von Qumran*, Paris 1957, 305–15; V. Hamp, *LTK* III², 879; H. Gross, 'Der Engel im AT', *ALW* VI, I (1959), 28–42; W. Herrmann, 'Die Göttersöhne', *ZRG* 12 (1960), 242–51.
On section C: M. Dibelius, *Die Geisterwelt im Glauben des Paulus*, Göttingen 1909; G. Kurze, *Der Engels- und Teufelsglaube des Apostels Paulus*, Freiburg 1915; J. Michl, *Die Engel-vorstellungen in der Apokalypse des hl. Johannes* I, Munich 1937; E. Langton, *The Angel Teaching of the New Testament*, London 1937; K. L. Schmidt, 'Die Natur- und Geistkräfte im paulinischen Erkennen und Glauben', *Eranos-Jahrbuch 1946*, vol. 14 (1947), 87–143; H. Bietenhard, *Die himmlische Welt im Urchristentum und Spätjudentum*, Tübingen 1951; C. Spicq, *L'Épitre aux Hébreux* II, Paris 1953, 50–61; G. H. C. Macgregor, 'Principalities and Powers: The Cosmic Background of St Paul's Thought', *NTS* I (1954/5), 17–28; G. B. Caird, *Principalities and Powers: A Study of Pauline Theology*, Oxford 1956; H. Schlier, *Principalities and Powers in the New Testament*, London 1961; H. Schlier, 'Die Engel nach dem NT', *Arch. für Liturgiewissenschaft* VI, I (1959), 43–56.

Johann Michl

Antichrist

Antichrist (*antikhristos*) is a word-formation used for the first time in 1 and 2 Jn, and occurs only here in the whole of the New Testament—one which belongs certainly to Greek-speaking christians. It means 'against Christ', and thus stands for the antagonist, the rival of Christ (1 Jn 2:18; 4:3). Scripture contains no formal declaration about the Antichrist; there is only occasional reference to him from which, however, some characteristics of this figure may be known.

A. *Prehistory*. The expectation of an Antichrist to come has its roots in the late Jewish period. The so-called history-of-religion exegetical school (represented by W. Bousset, H. Gunkel, R. Reitzenstein, and others) thought in terms of a background which was originally mythological—namely, either the primordial or final struggle of a god against a being hostile to him which he conquers. Thus, in Babylonia, we have the primordial victory of Marduk over

Tiamat, dragon of Chaos, and, in Persia, the final annihilation of the evil spirit Ahra Manju by Ahura Mazda. It would, however, be better to seek an explanation much nearer at hand than such a remote and entirely foreign conception, the development of which cannot be traced through judaism down to the figure of the Antichrist. Painful experiences in the past and the present gave the Jews reason to fear that also in the future heathen nations and their rulers would oppress Israel. In particular, it was expected that there would come in the last days a potentate of unprecedented power and cruelty.

Ezekiel (38f) already knows of such a prince and gives him the enigmatic name 'Gog', evoking thoughts of terror and brutality (Ezek 38:2f, 14, 16, 18; 39:1, 11, 15). Daniel speaks in prophecy of the 'Contemptible One', whom he beheld as a small horn which blasphemed against God, oppressed his people and eradicated his worship (7:8, 11, 20f, 24–26; 8:9–12, 23–25; 11:21–45). This was Antiochus IV Epiphanes (176–164 BC). The mysterious description is, however, intended to lead one to look beyond this Syrian king to a terrible figure belonging to the last days, of whom Antiochus is but the precursor. In the Book of Judith (6:2) Nebuchadnezzar, king of Babylon, who is fighting against Israel, is characterised as an anti-Yahweh.

The compilers of the late-Jewish apocryphal writings were powerfully stimulated by such material in the Old Testament. In the Ethiopian Book of Enoch (90:16) it is the Hellenistic nations, in the Jewish Sibylline Oracles (III 663–668) the kings of the heathen nations, who make war upon Israel. In 2 Esdras (13:33–8) the nations of the earth make a concerted assault on the Messiah who punishes them on this account with annihilation. (Cf also 5:6.) More detailed descriptions can be found in the Syrian Apocalypse of Baruch (36–60) and in the Testament (Assumption) of Moses (8); a particularly powerful and dangerous ruler, who exceeds all his predecessors in evil, makes his appearance on the very threshold of the messianic age, in this case before the general judgement, and crushes and persecutes the religion of the true God. This future transgressor does not as yet bear any definite name indicative of his nature. He is known simply as 'ruler' (BarSyr 40, 1) or 'potentate' (AssMos 8, 1). In keeping with the politically coloured messianic expectation of late judaism this assault was seen in a predominantly political light, as a struggle waged by a hostile army under the command of several, or, in the last resort, one leader against the people of God. At the same time, it was also believed that definite religious persecution would take place, a belief which emerges most strongly in the Testament of Moses.

The spiritual world of Qumran may well have made some contribution to the idea of an Antichrist; we find there, at any rate, mention of 'the Man of Lies' (1 Qp Hab 2, 1f), 'the Wicked Priest' (idem 8, 8), 'the Mocker' who deceives Israel and leads her astray. (CD 1, 10 [Riessler] = 1, 14f [Schechter]; cf 9, 39 [Riessler] = 20, 15 [Schechter].)

B. *New Testament.* These expectations were given a decisive turn by primitive christianity, though the way had admittedly been prepared already in late judaism. As it is now no longer a question of a blood-relationship with the people of Israel, but of belief in Christ, the coming fiend is seen as a tempter who tries to make the faithful apostatise and to put obstacles in the way of those who have not yet come to believe. The picture conjured up is of a gigantic levy, with its own means of recruiting and political machinery, in the service of these ends.

1. *General considerations.* Jesus himself spoke of false christs and false prophets who were to come and who would perplex his church and lead his people away from the true faith (Mk 13:22; Mt 24:24). The fear for the future was that false teachers would appear (Acts 20:29f), with particular reference to the last days. (1 Tim 4:1–3; 2 Tim 3:1–8; Jude 18; 2 Pet 3:3f.) This is known through a communication of the spirit (1 Tim 4:1), or is referred back to the prediction of the apostles (Jude 17f) or, alternatively, the prophets and apostles (2 Pet 3:2). Finally, the 'abomination of desolation' (Mk 13:14; Mt 24:15) is mentioned in Jesus' eschatological discourse with reference to Daniel (9:27; 11:31; 12:11). Many commentators have, right from the earliest times (Irenaeus, *Adv. Haereses*, v, 25, 2,5; Origen, *Contra Celsum* vi, 46 etc) referred this to the Antichrist.

2. *Paul* knows of 'the Man of Sin', 'the Lawless One', 'the Son of Perdition who opposes and exalts himself against every so-called god or object of worship'. The 'mystery of lawlessness' is already at work, but the evildoer is not yet in full control, since his coming is, for the time being, prevented by a power which stands in his way. As soon as he does make his appearance, however, he will set himself up, in the strength of the devil, against God in an attitude of self-deification, spread false teaching and find an audience among those who refuse the christian message and embrace error. Christ will eventually destroy this adversary at his second coming (2 Thess 2:3–12).

3. *John* also knows of a fiend who is to come, whom he refers to simply as 'Antichrist'. (1 John 2:18.) This title, however, also covers the false teachers who are at work destroying the church's teaching about Christ by their divergent interpretations (1 John 2:18, 22; 2 Jn 7; see also 1 Jn 4:3). They are, in fact, heralds of the seducer who is to come. If John calls a false teacher 'Antichrist' and sees in him the spirit of the Antichrist at work (1 Jn 4:3), it follows that, just as all the hostility and violent opposition of Israel's adversaries added up, in earlier Jewish representations, to the one oppressor of the last days, so the Antichrist is the sum total of all the opposition to Christ, the denials of christian doctrine, the surrender of the christian life. The Antichrist is thus, quite simply, the false teacher who tempts people away from loyalty to the Lord. Although, however, John allows only this aspect to emerge in the passages in which he mentions the Antichrist, we need not limit his conception just to this. On this assumption, then, the Antichrist of 1 Jn appears as the same figure as that of 2 Thess, even if the two descriptions differ in many respects.

4. A relevant parallel to the fiend that was to come can be found in the two beasts of the *Revelation*, the beast that came up from the sea and its

companion, the beast that came out of the earth. The first (Rev 13) appears like a leopard with the feet of a bear and mouth like a lion, with ten horns crowned with diadems and seven heads inscribed with blasphemous names (vv 1f). It has the strength of the dragon, who is the devil, and possesses its throne (v 2), makes men adore it (vv 4, 8; cf emperor-worship), blasphemes God (vv 5f), and persecutes the christians (v 7; see also v 15). Its name, which is not given, corresponds to the number 666 (v 18). In Chapter 17 this beast that comes from the sea bears the Whore of Babylon on its back (vv 3–6), the 'great city' (v 18). The seven heads of the beast refer to seven mountains upon which the city is built, likewise to seven kings, the seventh of whom is ruling at the time of the apocalyptic vision (vv 9f). The beast itself will come as the eighth and last of the kings, and together with it ten other kings will reign for a short time; these are symbolised by the ten horns (v 12). In Rev 11:7 this same beast rises up out of the abyss and slays the two witnesses of God. In 19:19f it joins battle with Christ and his warriors, but is vanquished and cast into a sea of fire. The beast that comes out of the earth resembles a lamb, has two horns but talks like the dragon (or devil, Rev 13:11). It performs wonders and leads men astray, causing them to worship the first beast or its image (13:12–15). Whoever refuses to do this is slain (13:15). It is the 'false prophet' (Rev 16:13; 19:20; 20:10; see also Mk 13:22f and parallels) who, together with the other beast, is cast into the sea of fire (19:20). The figure of the first beast forms a clear link with Daniel 7

and can be taken to symbolise, if not a demon, certainly a very powerful, godless ruler of the last days who claims divine worship for himself and persecutes those christians who do not give him it. The second beast, who also can hardly be taken for a demon, is the symbolical figure, standing for the bearer of a false religion, which encourages the divine honours paid to that ruler.

C. *Post-biblical, early christian literature.* The idea of the Antichrist plays an important part here. In the *Didache* (16:4) we find the expectation that 'the Tempter of the world' will appear in the last days, will come like the Son of God, rule over the earth, perform miracles and perpetrate hitherto unheard-of atrocities. In the Apocalypse of Peter (2) he is also 'the Tempter' who performs miracles and slays those who do not follow him. In a christian section of the Sibylline Oracles (III 63–74), he is given the name 'Belial' (see 2 Cor 6:15), which is the usual name for the devil in late judaism, but is not yet attested for the Antichrist. This can probably be best understood with reference to the *Ascensio Isaiae* (4:1–16) in which Belial, that is, the devil, appears in person on the earth 'in human form' and goes about his unholy business. We find references to 'the Man of Lawlessness' as late as Justin (*Dialogue with Trypho*, 32,3f), but thereafter as from the time of Irenaeus (*Adv.Haereses*, 1, 13,1; 3, 6,5; 7,2; 23,7; 5, 30,3f; 35,1) and Tertullian (*Scorpiace*, 12,10; *De Praescriptione*, 4,5; *De Monogamia*, 16,5) the title 'Antichrist' takes the place of this expression with reference to the tyrant, evidently influenced by the Johannine usage.

31

D. *Theological weight of the biblical evidence.* The Antichrist is the great tempter away from Christ, the oppressor of christians and a tool of the devil, though never the devil himself, since he is clearly distinguished from him (we meet the opposite view of the identity of both for the first time in the *Ascensio Isaiae*). The 'Antichrist' in John and the corresponding figure in Paul can be understood, in accordance with the statements which both writers make and in the light of the messianic expectation of late judaism, hardly otherwise than as a person, a human being, not just as an embodiment of tendencies and forces hostile to God or a group of false teachers. At the same time, John does know of other antichrists already at work in his own day (namely, teachers of false doctrine) apart from the Antichrist to come. The seer of the Revelation distinguishes between the political potentate and the religious seducer, who both together bring about the period of oppression connected with 'Antichrist'. This means at least that the 'Antichrist-like' attitude of spirit is found in several men, not only in one determined individual of the last days, and that in consequence the 'Antichrist-like' movement must not be attributed to one single person.

Paul, moreover, depicts the evildoer to come in a way peculiar to his own day, so that we cannot expect his representation will be fulfilled in every detail—literally as it is. It is legitimate, therefore, to ask whether the figure of the evildoer himself (although he is presented as an individual according to the conceptions peculiar to a certain age) may not nevertheless be interpreted in a collective sense of those rulers and seducers who oppose Christ. This would involve the expectation, not just of one, but of many 'Antichrists'. This problem cannot be settled with full certainty, but the evidence of scripture, and not just of 2 Thess, but also of the Johannine epistles and Revelation (even if these latter speak less clearly) would seem rather to indicate a definite person corresponding to the single person who is Christ—therefore an 'Antichrist' in the strict sense of the word who, however, has his precursors as history draws to an end.

Bibliography: commentaries on 2 Thess, 1 and 2 Jn, and Revelation; B. Rigaux, *L'Antéchrist et l'opposition au royaume messianique dans L'Ancien et le Nouveau Testament*, Paris 1932; A. Arrighini, *L'Anticristo*, Turin 1945; E. Stauffer, *New Testament Theology*, London 1955, 213–15; J. Schmid, 'Die Antichrist und die hemmende Macht', *TQ* 129 (1949), 323–43; E. Lohmeyer, *RAC* I, 450–57; Haag 72–4; P. Althaus, *Die letzen Dinge*, Gütersloh 1955, 282–97; H. Schlier, *Vom Antichrist, Zum 13 Kapitel der Offenbarung Johannis: Die Zeit der Kirche*, Freiburg 1956, 16–29; R. Schnackenburg and K. Rahner, *LTK* I², 634–6; M. Brunec, 'De "Homine Peccati" in 2 Thess 2:1–12', *VD* 35 (1957), 3–33; B. Rigaux, '*bdelugma tēs erēmōseōs*', *Bbl* 40 (1959), 675–83; V. Maag, 'Der Antichrist als Symbol des Bösen', *Das Böse*, Zurich 1961, 63–89; O. Betz, 'Der Katechon', *NTS* 9 (1962/3), 276–91; L. Sirard, 'La Parousie de l'Antéchrist: 2 Thess 2:3–9', *Studiorum Paulinorum Congressus* II, Rome 1963, 89–100; F. Mussner, 'Das Buch Judith und die ntl. Antichristidee', *TTZ* 72 (1963), 242–4.

Johann Michl

Apostle

A. *The word 'apostle' in general.* Neither the Greek nor the Aramaic speaking world of early christianity knew the word 'apostle' in the sense of the New Testament. Christianity itself has created this idea and the institution itself for the first holders of this office.

The word *apostolos*, however, is already used in prechristian literature. In classical Greek it means 'naval expedition', and in the papyri 'receipt' or 'passport'. LXX does not know the word at all (the Codex Alexandrinus uses it once [1 Kings 14:6], but this may have been taken from Aquila). Only Herodotus uses it twice in a meaning related to that of the New Testament (messenger, ambassador). It is therefore quite possible that Herodotus has adopted a colloquial idiom which, although not found in literature, may have been familiar to the authors of the New Testament. Nevertheless, from the choice of the word in this—to say the least—very unusual meaning, we may conclude that the more usual Greek words of related meaning seemed unsuitable to the early christians to describe the office held by the Apostles.

Neither is it a matter of the word *apostolos* being a translation of a usual Aramaic word. The Semitic equivalent of the Greek *apostolos* is used for the first time in the second century, and it is hard to believe that there were Jewish apostles before AD 70.

Nevertheless, the word 'apostle' points in its meaning to the world of the Semitic languages. It is closely related to the Hebrew verb *šālaḥ*. The meaning of *šālaḥ* is not fully covered by the English verb 'to send'; it means *to send with authority, to delegate*. In the Jewish legal system after the Babylonian captivity there was a kind of delegation through which people could act legally by proxy (eg contract a marriage). The person so empowered (*šālûaḥ*) was by law the representative of the one commissioning. Here applies the old rabbinic principle deeply rooted in judaism; 'the representative is equal to the person who has sent him' (Ber 5:5; see also Jn 13:16). In this context we must also remember the old Semitic laws of delegation which in point of fact are closely related. The ambassador of the king was the lawful and personal representative of his distant master, which explains why the insult offered to David's ambassadors by the Ammonites was the immediate cause of a destructive war (2 Sam 10). This was also the reason why Abigail washed the feet of David's servants (1 Sam 25:40f). In spite of his high rank, the ambassador of the king remained, of course, the servant of his master as before (1 Sam 25:41).

But when Jesus sent some of his disciples on a similar mission (Mk 6:7) he did not send them simply as messengers or as missionaries (late-Jewish missionaries are never called *šelûḥîm*; Cynic-Stoic itinerant preachers are never called *apostoloi*) or as heralds who had only to announce messages officially. Neither were they prophets (even prophets in the late-Jewish period were never called *šeluḥim*); even the idea of eye-witness is absent in the original concept of an apostle. Apostles were rather his personal and lawful representatives. This much can be derived from linguistic data. The purpose and duration of the mission are not indicated in this conception.

B. *The apostolic mission before the resurrection.* The men in Jesus' company are referred to in the gospels in three

33

different ways. Jesus called ↗ *disciples* to follow him; from these he selected '*the twelve*' (↗ Disciple); he gave full powers to the *apostles*.

A future mission for the realisation and propagation of Christ's work is already mentioned in the individual call to the disciples. Christ was sent into the world to call all men to the kingdom of God. Simon and Andrew would one day undertake this task as 'fishers of men' (Mk 1:17). In the election of the twelve (Mk 3:13–19) the prospect of a future mission is even more clearly indicated. Certainly, Christ did not choose the twelve only in view of a future authorisation, 'He appointed twelve to be with him' (Mk 3:14). The very number *twelve* points to a quite different purpose (↗ Disciple). Nevertheless, it is also an election for the future function of apostle; 'He appointed twelve . . . to be sent out to preach [the joyful tidings] and have authority to cast out demons' (Mk 3:14). The proclamation of the kingdom of God (see Lk 4:18–21) and the defeat of the prince of this world (see Lk 11:20) were the object of Christ's mission, and it was Christ's will that his apostles should share this mission (compare also Mt 10:1 and Lk 9:1). Their task was to propagate his messianic mission especially where he could not go himself. Christ expressed very clearly how greatly he wanted the apostles to be his legal and personal representatives: 'He who receives me receives him who sent me' (Mt 10:40–11:1; compare also Jn 13:20), and: 'He who hears you hears me; and he who rejects you rejects me, and he who rejects me rejects him who sent me' (Lk 10:16; compare also Heb 3:1,

where Christ himself is called an apostle). The city which does not accept the apostles shall suffer a fate worse than that of Sodom and Gomorrha (Mt 10:15). The person authorised is equal to the one who conferred the authority. Therefore, the mission of the twelve before the resurrection remained within the limits set to Christ. Like Christ himself, who was sent only 'to the lost sheep of the house of Israel', his apostles were to go 'nowhere among the Gentiles and enter no town of the Samaritans' (Mt 10:5f). Returning from their temporary mission the apostles were once again disciples of Jesus as before (Mk 6:30f).

C. *The definitive authorisation.* As early as the period of Christ's public life, some disciples were at certain times entrusted with the mission to represent the Messiah. The careful and extensive training of the disciples for their apostolic mission, as well as certain promises (see Mt 16:19; 18:18) show clearly that these temporary apostolic activities could not be the full realisation of Christ's plans for the apostles. He did not want to leave his flock behind after his departure 'like sheep without a shepherd' (see Mt 9:36; Jn 21:15–17). He therefore promised his disciples the power to bind and loose. Their decisions in the church would be the decisions of the Lord in heaven (Mt 16:18; 18:18). This power, unlimited in time and space, was given by the risen Lord (Mt 28:18f). From this time forward, Christ is sent not only to the lost sheep of Israel, but to all nations, which are subject to his power; and therefore he entrusted his authorised representatives with the pastoral care of all nations. Only when the Lord comes again will this representation of the Good Shepherd become superfluous, and end. This leads inevitably to the conclusion that power of representing Christ must be propagated throughout the history of the church, for it would surely be unthinkable that certainty of forgiveness of sins was only given to the first generation of the church. This divine power, which so much astounded the Jews (see Mt 9:8), Christ delegated to his apostles (Jn 20:21), so that this gift of grace should remain in this world even after the day of his ascension, and until his second coming.

Finally, Jn 21:15–17 shows (as already in Mt 16:18f) the special position of Peter as the first among those endowed with authority. In creating this prerogative, Christ established the hierarchical principle and gave a certain inner structure to the group of apostles. Multiplicity itself necessarily demands some kind of subordination.

D. *The apostolate in the early church.* The election of Matthias in place of Judas, which took place before Pentecost, is an event unique in the history of the church (Acts 1:15–26). It indicates above all the significance of 'the twelve' and is less important to the concept of 'apostle'. Of far greater importance is the fact that the apostolate can by no means be regarded as identical with 'the twelve'. Apart from the twelve, other apostles are mentioned who did not have to fulfil the conditions required for membership of 'the twelve' (Acts 1:21f). First of all we might mention Barnabas, who is called an apostle in Acts and in order of enumeration is mentioned before

Paul (14:4, 14). He introduced Paul into the community of the early church (Acts 9:27) and brought him from Tarsus to Antioch to join the missionary work there (Acts 11:25f). After the laying on of hands at Antioch, they were both sent out on their missionary travels. It is not quite certain that Acts 13:3 refers to their full authorisation as apostles; but at all events, Barnabas was an apostle in name and in function just like Paul (compare also Gal 2:9, and especially 1 Cor 9:4–6). The greater degree of gratitude and reverence in the church which Paul was to experience later on was not due to high rank or office but to other reasons. Whether Andronicus and Junias (Rom 16:7) were apostles cannot be definitely ascertained, but we must take into account the possibility. The fact that Paul mentions 'great apostles' (2 Cor 11:5; 12:11) and 'pseudo-apostles' (2 Cor 11:13) in his second epistle to the Corinthians may point to a considerable number of apostles. On the other hand, 2 Cor 8:23 and Phil 2:25 seem to refer not to apostles of Jesus Christ, but to delegates of the congregations who represented their communities to Paul. It is quite possible that at the time these two epistles were written, the word 'apostle', though created to express representation of Christ, was also used to indicate different but related functions. However, there is certainly at this time no question of its hardening into a term of special distinction reserved for a few persons only.

. E. *The apostolate of Paul.* For the later church and especially for the western church, Paul became the apostle *par excellence.* This is understandable enough, since he rendered a prominent service to the western church through his missionary work, and he is the only one of whom we know details concerning his life and work. His epistles form the most extensive part of the canon of the New Testament. We should not, however, be tempted to derive our idea of what an apostle was solely from the apostolate of Paul. Paul worked as a missionary, but this does not imply that missionary work is an essential element in the conception of apostle: whether the apostle represented Christ in the metropolis or in the diaspora is of no importance in defining the essence of apostolate. Paul knew himself to be primarily intended for the ⁄ preaching of the gospel (1 Cor 1:17), but it does not necessarily follow that the apostle is essentially a preacher. Paul also set great store by the fact that the risen Lord was also seen by him (1 Cor 9:1; 15:8); but, again, it does not follow that it is essential that an apostle should have seen the risen Lord and be one of the eye-witnesses of his resurrection.

It is quite clear from the epistles of Paul that the function of an apostle is essentially a function of an ambassador: 'So we are ambassadors for Christ, God making his appeal through us. We beseech you, on behalf of Christ, be reconciled to God' (2 Cor 5:20). Paul's ambassadorial activities, however, are not restricted to entreating in Christ's name. This is apparent from 1 Cor 2:4 and especially 2 Cor 2:4. The apostle is fully aware of his solidarity with Christ. We can clearly perceive here the echo of Christ's words: 'He who hears you, hears me, and he who rejects you rejects him who sent me' (Lk 10:16).

But he also knows well that as an apostle he is even more a servant of the Lord who has sent him, and that he is nothing but an 'earthen vessel' which God has filled with the precious treasure of his grace (2 Cor 4:7) for the blessing of christendom.

F. *The twelve apostles.* Difficulties in the daily administration of charitable relief were undoubtedly only the immediate motive for the institution of the *seven* (Acts 6:1–7). Their solemn investiture and activities, fully recorded in Acts (Philip and Stephen), show the seven as the apostolic assistants of the twelve. Here we can see how the twelve communicated their apostolic power. At the same time it is quite clear that this power was not necessarily to be transferred wholly and completely, but that certain limitations are possible (see Acts 8:14–25). But although the seven had the apostolic mission of representing Christ, Acts never refers to them as 'apostles'. Philip is only referred to as 'the evangelist' (Acts 21:8). The same applied to those who assisted Paul in his missionary work. They were men entrusted with apostolic power (cf the pastoral epistles) but are never referred to as 'apostles'. Occasionally they are also called Evangelists (2 Tim 4:5). We can even go further: Paul passionately defended his title of 'apostle' in his Epistles to the Corinthians, which, however, did not prevent later periods from not regarding him any longer as an apostle. Luke calls him an apostle only once (Acts 14:14), and this only together with Barnabas (Luke obviously uses an old source here); elsewhere he speaks only of the twelve apostles. The same applies to Revelation (see 18:20; 21:14). We find the same tendency even in the Epistle to the Ephesians (see 2:20; 3:5). The office of apostle remained; the power to represent Christ has been handed down. Even by the time that the books of the New Testament were written the title of apostle had become restricted to the twelve. The twelve who, as such, held a unique and fundamental office in the church (⁊ Disciple) were certainly also representatives of Christ. These two functions, however, should be clearly distinguished. The one is limited to the twelve and cannot be handed down; the other will continue to exist till the second coming of the Good Shepherd, even though those who possess this apostolic authority later are no longer called apostles.

Bibliography: A. Verheul, 'De moderne exegese over *apostolos*', *Sacris Eruditi* (1948), 380–96; A. Wikenhauser, *RAC* I (1950), 553–5; P. Gaechter, 'Die Sieben', *ZKT* 74 (1952), 129–66; E. M. Kredel, 'Der Apostelbegriff in der neueren Exegese', *ZKT* 78 (1956), 169–93 and 257–305 (references to the older literature are also given); J. Dupont, 'Le nom d'apôtres a-t-il été donné aux Douze par Jésus?', *OS* I (1956), 266–90 and 425–44; H. Reisenfeld, *RGG* I (1957), 497–9; K. H. Schelkle, *Discipleship and Priesthood*, London and New York 1966; P. Gaechter, *Petrus und seine Zeit*, 1958; K. H. Rengstorf, *TDNT* I, 407–47 (=*Apostleship* [*BKW* VI], London 1952); K. H. Rengstorf, *Apostolat und Predigtamt*, 1954²; A. M. Farrer, *The Ministry in the New Testament: the Apostolic Ministry*, London 1947; H. von Campenhausen, 'Der urchristliche Apostelbegriff', *ST* I (1948), 96–130; H. von Campenhausen, *Kirchliches Amt und geistliche Vollmacht in den ersten drei Jahrhunderten*, 1953; A. Fridrichsen, *The Apostle and his Message*, Uppsala 1947; P. H. Menoud, *L'Eglise et les ministères*, 1949; H. Mosbech, '*Apostolos* in the New Testament', *ST* II (1950), 166–200; J. Munck, 'Paul, the Apostles, and the Twelve', *ST* III (1950), 96–110; O. Cullmann, *Peter: Disciple, Apostle, Martyr*, London 1962; E. Lohse, 'Ursprung und Prägung des christlichen Apostolats', *TZ* 9 (1953), 259–75; A. Ehrhardt, *The Apostolic Succession in the First Two Centuries of the Church*, 1953; G. Klein, *Die zwölf Apostel: Ursprung und Gehalt einer Idee*, 1961; W. Schmithals, *Das christliche Apostelamt: Einer historische Untersuchung*, 1961; B. Gerhardsson, 'Die Boten Gottes und die Apostel Christi', *SEA* 27 (1962), 89–131; E. M. Kredel, 'Apostel', *HTG* I, 61–7; P. Bläser, 'Zum Problem des urchristlichen Apostolats', *Unio Christianorum* (1962), 92–107; *S. Freyne, *The Twelve: Disciples and Apostles. A Study in the Theology of the First Three Gospels*, London 1968 (with extensive bibliography).

Elmar M. Kredel

Ascension

I. Textual findings. 1. Luke is the only evangelist who mentions the 'ascension' in the conventionally accepted sense—as an event in the history of salvation which occurred in a given place and at a given time. This reference is to be found at the end of his first book and at the beginning of his second. According to Lk 24:50f, it would appear that Jesus ascended into heaven on Easter Sunday; in the second narrative, which is connected without a break to Jesus' words of farewell to his apostles, Luke reiterates what he has already said (Acts 1:9–12; see 1:2f): after the 'last appearance', forty days after his resurrection (Acts 1:3), the Lord was 'taken up into heaven' (Acts 1:2, 11: the aorist passive of *analambanō* = 'take up' [lacking in the 'western' text]), and 'as they were looking on, he was lifted up' (Acts 1:9: aorist passive of *hupolambanō* = 'take up', 'lift up'). As in the instances where God appeared of old (see Ex 13:21f; 24:15–18; 40:34–8), and in Jesus' transfiguration before his disciples (Mt 17:5; Mk 9:7; Lk 9:34f), the 'cloud' appears as a sign of God's presence; 'A cloud took him out of their sight' (Acts 1:9). As two angels in shining apparel announce Jesus' resurrection in Lk 24:4, so here two *angeli interpretes* promise the glorious second coming of the Lord in the same manner—that is, 'in a cloud' (Acts 1;11: see also Dan 7:13; Mt 24:30; 1 Thess 4:17; Rev 1:7; 14:14–16). Following their Lord's example, the two witnesses will also ascend 'in a cloud' into heaven (Rev 11:12), and those who are still alive when the Lord comes again will be taken up 'in the clouds' (1 Thess 4:17). According to the account given in Acts, Jesus did not 'ascend into heaven' on his own initiative, but was taken up into heaven by the Father through the Holy Spirit (see also Rom 6:4).

The bodily ascension of Christ is also the subject-matter of the (canonical) 'long ending' of Mark's gospel (Mk 16:9–20), but this summarises the account given by Luke and cannot be considered as a valid independent testimony.

2. Side by side with this visible ascension of Christ, which is reported only by Luke, the various books of the New Testament invariably speak only of the resurrection and exaltation of Christ. We touch here on the very heart of the apostolic work of preaching the gospel: it is a striking feature of the early missionary sermons that the *apostles* bear witness exclusively to the resurrection (Acts 1:21f; 2:32; 3:15, 26; 4:10, 33; 10:40f; 13:30–37; 17:18–31; 22:15; 26:16); to Jesus' 'exaltation at the right hand of God' (Acts 2:33–6; 5:30–32; 7:55f; see also Mt 22:44; 26:64; Mk 12:36; 13:26; 16:19; Lk 20:42; 22:69); and, finally, to his glorious second coming (Acts 3:20f;

1:7, 11). The subject of an ascension which was perceptible to the senses played no further part in the early church's preaching of the work of God.

Paul uses the same manner of speaking in his epistles. He emphasises again and again the close connection between the resurrection and exaltation of the Lord, without troubling greatly about the way in which Christ penetrated into this world of heavenly transfiguration. After the Easter-event, Christ inhabits heaven, where he is seated 'at the right hand of God' (Rom 8:34; 1 Cor 15:25; Eph 1:20; Col 3:1–3; Heb 1:3, 13; 2:7–9; 8:1; 10:12; 12:2) until he comes again at the end of time in power and in glory (1 Thess 1:10; 4:16; 2 Thess 1:7; 1 Cor 4:5; Phil 3:20; Col 3:4; 1 Tim 6:14), to judge the living and the dead (2 Tim 4:1, 8; Tit 2:13) and to take the faithful up into the eternal paschal glory (1 Thess 4:16; 2 Cor 4:14; 5:1–10).

The *catholic epistles* also allude to the glorification of Christ inaugurated by his resurrection (1 Pet 1:3f, 21; 1 Jn 2:1) and in due course to be crowned by his glorious second coming (Jas 5:7f; 1 Pet 1:7, 13, 21; 4:13; 5:1, 4, 6, 10; 1 Jn 2:28; 3:2), and by the transformation of mankind and all creation (2 Pet 3). It is self-evident that this exaltation presupposes an 'ascension', but for the most part such an ascension is implied only.

True, several texts allude to an 'ascension', but without reference to a particular time or place. In Eph 4:8–10 the ascent of the Lord above all the heavens is contrasted in a very general way with his descent into the lower parts of the earth and the underworld. In this instance, as in the case of the liturgical hymn in 1 Tim 3:16, the 'taking up in glory' is clearly more a matter of theological assertion, or confession of faith, than of a statement of fact concerning an actual experience. In the Epistle to the Hebrews, the mysterious journey of Christ to the right hand of God is compared with the entry of the high priest into the Holy of Holies (Heb 4:14; 6:19f; 9:11f, 24): just as once every year the high priest took the blood of calves and goats, passed through the tabernacle, and entered the Holy of Holies to sprinkle the top of the ark of the covenant with the blood (Heb 4:14; 6:19f; 9:24), so, in the same way, Christ passed, with his own blood, through a more perfect tabernacle and entered the innermost sanctuary. In other words, after his death as a sacrificial offering of the flesh, Christ penetrated the tabernacle of his own body (see 2 Cor 5:4; 2 Pet 1:13) and entered once and for all the sanctuary, the Holy of Holies of the Godhead, when he entered into glory (Heb 2:9f), appeared before the face of God (Heb 9:24), and took his place at God's right hand. We could express this another way by saying that, through his sacrifice, Christ gained— in a very real sense—a joint share in the Godhead. Whenever the text goes on to allude to the body as well, the intention is not to describe an event which can be perceived by the senses, but merely to stress a particular theological doctrine such as that contained in Eph 4:8–10. According to 1 Pet 3:21f, 'Jesus Christ . . . has gone into heaven and is at the right hand of God, with angels, authorities, and powers subject to him': in this instance, too, his 'ascension' is doubtless conceived as a fact of dogma which eludes the experience of the senses.

John goes more deeply and thoroughly into the original proclamation of the apostles concerning Christ's exaltation. On the morning of Easter Sunday, the risen Christ appeared to the faithful disciple Mary Magdalene: 'Do not hold me, for I have not yet ascended to the Father; . . . to my Father and your Father, to my God and your God' (Jn 20:17). Here the text refers to the ascension of the Lord to his Father *on Easter Sunday itself*—an ascension which eludes all possibility of apprehension by the senses. This mysterious event, this 'Easter ascension', therefore preceded the various appearances accorded to the disciples (see Jn 14:28; Mk 16:9–14).

Revelation celebrates the heavenly Christ in his triumph (Rev 1:13–18), sitting at the right hand of the Father (3:21; 5:6–14; 7:17), on a cloud (14:14) and in the new Jerusalem (3:12). But we are not told how he came there.

II. *The twofold 'ascension'*. It is clear that the texts quoted so far cannot be harmonised with each other. They appear to envisage a twofold 'ascension'.

1. The oldest tradition places chief stress on the real and essential taking up of the Lord into glory at the right hand of God on Easter Sunday itself. According to the evidence given in *Acts*, the missionary sermons of Peter (Acts 2:14–39; 3:12–26; 4:8–12; 5:29–32; 10:34–43) and Paul (Acts 13:16–41; 17:22–31; 22:1–22; 26:1–29; 28:17–28)—which Luke presents in a highly stylised form—continue to proclaim only the risen Lord who sits at the right hand of the Father, without

mentioning a visible ascension. *Paul*, too, sees the resurrection from the tomb, and the exaltation to the right hand of God above all heavens and the thrones of angels, as being very closely related to each other. Resurrection and exaltation form one, single paschal mystery of Christ's victory over sin, death, and hell. Even in the texts where the word 'ascension' is used (Eph 4:8–10; 1 Tim 3:16; Heb 4:14; 6:19f; 9:24; 1 Pet 3:21f) it is largely a question of a theological assertion without intended narrative content. The evangelist *John* construes this paschal transfiguration of the Lord as a return to the Father (Jn 8:14, 21; 13:33; 14:2, 12, 28; 16:5, 16, 28) which took place before his visible ascension, on the morning of Easter Sunday itself. If this return to the Father in heaven had coincided with a visible taking up, John would probably not have neglected to mention this in his narrative.

It seems clear that this 'ascension' of the Lord to the Father on the morning of Easter Day must be taken to exist on a higher plane. No human eye witnessed this exaltation and transfiguration: it was only because of Christ's own revelation of this invisible glorification that the apostles learned of it. With his resurrection Jesus adopted a different physical mode of being, into which the existence of the 'heavenly Adam' (1 Cor 15:42–50), penetrated and dominated by the Holy Spirit, had been assumed. It is with this 'invisible ascension' that we come into contact with the innermost heart of the mystery of the ascension. The risen Christ has, with this incursion into the world of the divine, penetrated all at once into the central core of the mystery of salvation.

Even if Christ the Lord had not been taken up bodily into heaven while his disciples were looking on, their belief in this 'ascension' would have lost very little by it. Even if Mary Magdalene and the apostles did not actually see the risen Lord enter into glory, such an entry into glory did nevertheless take place, and all the ancient creeds containing the phrase: 'ascended into heaven', pick up from the various confessional formulae in the New Testament and refer to this 'essential ascension'.

2. The *visible ascension* from the Mount of Olives (Lk 24:51f; Acts 1:2f, 9–12) is mentioned only by Luke. The paschal sermons of the early christian period are silent on the matter; similarly, the apostolic fathers—such as Clement of Rome, Ignatius, and Polycarp—make no mention of it. Some who do mention it place it eighteen months or even twelve years after the first Easter. Certain fathers—eg Tertullian and Jerome—sometimes refer to Christ's ascension as taking place on the twelfth day of his resurrection, but at other times as taking place after forty days.

Some critics conclude from these facts, often taken together with an explicit or implicit denial of a physical resurrection of Jesus, that the story of his ascension is a 'later legend'. Their reasoning takes the following form: in the view of the early christians, it was only the soul of Jesus which was taken up immediately into heaven after the death on the cross, and this victory of the soul was from time to time referred to by the term 'ascension'. With the passage of time this triumph was made to serve the cause of christian apologetics and extended to the body. In this way, the legends of Christ's appearances and of the empty tomb, and finally of the visible ascension of Christ's body into heaven, are said to have originated. We can make the following comment on this theory: no one who was by birth a Jew would have been able to make anything of the idea of an ascension of Christ's soul without his body, for—in the Old Testament view—the soul was not freed from the 'shackles of the body' at the moment of death. That was a purely Greek conception. On the contrary, it was held in the Old Testament view that body and soul were torn violently apart as a punishment for sin (see Gen 3:19; Wis 1:13), and so the triumph over death began in Jesus' case with his *bodily* resurrection, and will be completed with the 'resurrection of the flesh' on our Lord's second coming (see 1 Cor 15:3-5). Hence, from the very beginning, the various accounts of the Easter events are always given with reference to Jesus' body as well as his soul. This explains why Luke is so precise in his statements regarding the place ('the mount called Olivet', Acts 1:12; 'as far as Bethany', Lk 24:50) and the time ('during forty days', Acts 1:3) of the ascension. In Acts 1:9-11 he mentions the ascension 'into heaven' four times (though the second reference in v 11 does not appear in D, it is demanded by BSA as well as by Nestlé and Merk), and this would seem to be because he wants to give an account of a historical occurrence. Moreover, it is not as if Christ 'goes up' into heaven of his own free will, like the heroes of certain myths: on the contrary, his transfigured body is 'taken up' into heaven.

Luke, who knows the main theme of the early christian *preaching* on the resurrection and exaltation of Jesus very well indeed, cannot, as a painstaking compiler of narrative (see Lk 1:1-3), prevent himself from including the ancient tradition of the visible ascension in his *account*. According to his testimony, Christ appeared after his resurrection in transfigured corporeality to the two pilgrims on the way to Emmaus on the afternoon of Easter Sunday (Lk 24:13-35; see also Mk 16:12f), and to the disciples assembled in the room the same evening (Lk 24:36-43; Mk 16:14; see also 1 Cor 15:5-7). The last time that he appeared to his disciples was on the Mount of Olives ('the mount called Olivet'), forty days after his resurrection (this is, of course, in round figures: compare Deut 9:18, 25; 1 Kings 19:8; Mt 4:2 and parallels), with the purpose of taking his final leave from them on this earth until he comes again on the clouds of heaven. This farewell appearance of Christ to his disciples on the Mount of Olives was a concession to the frailty of men, men who are tied to their senses. This visible ascension while they were looking on was, however, something enacted on the mere fringe—as it were—of the Easter mystery. For this reason no more than secondary importance can be attached to this 'last appearance' of the risen Christ. Luke, the only real historian in the New Testament, does not see in it any new glorification or exaltation of the Lord, but, when he reports it, he has in view the connection between the risen Lord and the disciples remaining behind on earth.

The church has always, and from the

41

earliest times, celebrated the festival of the risen and exalted Lord—the very centre of the Easter mystery, the invisible and as it were 'background' ascension (see section 1, above). The feast of the Lord's ascension as we understand it does not appear in the liturgy until the fourth century, and serves then to convey to us one aspect of the whole paschal mystery, namely, that of the 'essential ascension of Jesus' in the terms of Luke's account of the 'taking up of Jesus into heaven after forty days'. This feast ought not to be allowed to obscure the essential exaltation of Easter Sunday: on the contrary, it should underline this very exaltation yet once more and in a special respect, that of the Lord's being 'seated at the right hand of God'. This can only be grasped by faith, of course, but it gives the deepest and fullest meaning to the mystery of Easter, and its effects will be fully realised only when the Lord comes again in his glory.

Bibliography: among various commentaries on Acts, see in particular: A. Wikenhauser, *Die Apostelgeschichte* (*RNT* 5), 1956, 28–32; E. Haenchen, *Die Apostelgeschichte*, Göttingen 1959, 115–19. See further: E. Nestlé, 'Zu Acta 1:12', *ZNW* 3 (1902), 247–9; B. W. Bacon, 'The Ascension in Luke and Acts', *The Expositor* (1909), 254–61; F. X. Steinmetzer, *TPQ* 77 (1924), 82–92 and 224–41; W. Michaelis, *TB* 4 (1925), 101–09; E. Fascher, *ZNW* 27 (1926), 1–26; G. Bertram, in *Festgabe A. Deissmann*, Tübingen 1927, 187–217; A. Friedrichsen, *TB* 6 (1927), 337–41; M. S. Enslin, *JBL* 47 (1928), 60–73; D. Plooij, Amsterdam 1929; U. Holzmeister, *ZKT* 55 (1931), 44–82; K. Lake, 'The Ascension' and 'The Mount of Olives and Bethany', *The Beginnings of Christianity* v, ed. K. Lake and H. J. Cadbury, London 1933, 16–22 and 475f; M. Goguel, *La foi et la resurrection de Jesus dans le christianisme primitif*, Paris 1933; S. M. Creed, *JTS* 35 (1934), 176–82; V. Larrañaga, *L'Ascension de Notre-Seigneur dans le NT*, Rome 1938; A. Oepke, *Luthertum* (1939), 161–86; A. N. Wilder, *JBL* 62 (1943), 307–18; W. Michaelis, *Die Erscheinungen des Auferstandenen*, Basle 1944; E. Flicoteaux, *VS* 76 (1947), 664–75; J. Leclerc, *VS* 72 (1945), 289–300; P. Benoit, *RB* 55, (1949), 161–203; P. Benoit, in Haag, 714–19; A. M. Ramsay, *SNTSB* 2 (1951), 43–50; H. Bietenhard, *Die himmlische Welt im Urchristentum und Spätjudentum*, Tübingen 1951; J. Daniélou, *The Bible and the Liturgy*, London 1960; P. H. Menoud, *Ntl. Studien für R. Bultmann* (*BZNW* 21), Berlin 1954, 148–56; G. Kretschmar, *ZKG* 66 (1954/5), 209–53; J. A. M. Weterman, *NKS* 50 (1954), 129–37; A. W. Argyle, *Expository Times*, 66 (1955), 240–42; J. Haroutunian, *Interpretation* 10 (1956), 270–81; P. Bonnard, Allmen 25–6; O. Cullmann, *The Christology of the New Testament*, London 1959; H. Kremers, *EKL* ii, Göttingen 1958, 159–61; W. G. Kümmel, *RGG* iii³, Tübingen 1959, 335; P. A. van Stempvoort, *NTS* 5 (1958/9), 30–42; R. Koch, *SKZ* 127 (1959), 493–4; M. Brändle, *Der grosse Entschluss* 14 (1959), 345–7; H. Conzelmann, *The Theology of St Luke*, London 1960, 187–206; J. Heuschen, *DEB*, 143–9.

Robert Koch

Asceticism

Askēsis (= exercise) is usually understood as the systematic training of human passions for a moral and religious purpose. Since this is hardly possible without abstaining from worldly goods it often stands for abstinence itself. In catholic theology, however, *askēsis* has a wider and more positive meaning; it is the systematic striving after christian perfection as far as this depends on human endeavour. Asceticism is not a biblical idea, and the bible can therefore hardly be consulted on this particular point. An *askēsis* not motivated by religion (a mere training of the will or a purely natural pursuit of virtue) is unknown to the biblical writers. Neither do we find a unanimous answer to the question as to how far man should seek union with God and his holy will through his own endeavour and renunciation. Nevertheless, much can be learned from the bible, and Christ's words and example give us guidance for a sound and beneficial asceticism or *askēsis*.

There is no tendency towards *askēsis* in the religious practice of the Old Testament when God's blessing consisted in earthly goods, conjugal bliss, and a long life (see the promises made to Abraham, Gen 12:1–3; 13:14–17 etc; Jacob's blessing, Gen 49; Job's rehabilitation, Job 42:10–16), unless one wants to see a certain form of asceticism in the unquestioning obedience to God's will (see the sacrifice of Isaac, Gen 22). The Semitic conception of man was of one undivided being of which the body was no inconsiderable 'part'. The bodily impulses reason to resist the passions and bodily instincts; a sumptuous dish (Ps 23:5), enjoyment of wine (Ps 104:15), a happy married life and fertility (Ps 128) are highly valued. Only religious reverence and fear of the holy prescribes in certain conditions abstinence from sexual intercourse (the people at mount Sinai, Ex 19:15; over the eating of holy bread, 1 Sam. 21:5f; at the holy war, 2 Sam 11:11) and from wine (priests in the holy tent of meeting, Lev 10:9 ⟋ Wine). But a certain asceticism motivated by religion may be found in the penitential fasting practised by all the people on special occasions (1 Sam 7:6; Jer 36:6; Joel 1:13f; 2:12), on the Feast of Expiation (Lev 16:29f) and later too on the days of Phurim (Esther 9:31), and also by some people individually after a grave offence (David, 2 Sam 12:16f; Ahab, 1 Kings 21:27) in order to avert God's wrath. The Nazirites bound

themselves by a vow of abstinence to a special service of God (Num 6:1–7; see also Judg 13:4f; Amos 2:11; 1 Macc 3:49), and similar vows for religious reasons were not infrequent in Israel (Num 30). The Rechabites, in accordance with an ancestral law, did not grow vineyards and abstained from wine, and they were praised for their faithfulness (Jer 35). This, however, hardly alters the general picture of the religious practices in ancient Israel in which joy in created things played such a central part.

It is only in the *later Jewish periods*, when through suffering and exile people had become more conscious of their own guilt and that of their ancestors, that we find a growing sense of abstinence and penance. At the same time stronger emphasis on the moral law, good works, and merit advanced the development of religious practices such as prayers at certain times, almsgiving, and fasting (Tob 12:8; see also Mt 6:1–18). The righteous freely imposed chastisement on themselves even for their errors (Ps Sol 3:9), and there were pious people who did not hanker after gold, silver, exquisite food and worldly honour, but 'who valued heaven higher than life in this world' (1 Enoch 108:7–8; see also 4 Ezr 7:125). This attitude, however, never became widespread; by the time of the New Testament many of these pious men had again become prosperous and practised fasting (twice a week, Lk 18:12) and almsgiving only as meritorious works, often for their own glory rather than for the love of God or from a sense of true remorse and contrition, a sanctimonious attitude severely castigated by Christ. The

43

spirit of real asceticism was alive only among certain sections of the Jewish community (the Therapeutai in Egypt, the Essenes, the 'League of God' at Damascus, and the community of Qumran, all more or less related sects; see also the Testaments of the Twelve Patriarchs); voluntary poverty (community of goods), celibacy, severe labour, vigilance, and strict obedience were highly valued and to some extent realised, even in their absolute demands. The motive behind all this was the will to study intensively the law of God and put it into practice. Moreover, they were full of ardent eschatological expectation; the (Essene) community of Qumran wanted to be the 'holy remnant' of Israel at the end of time, priests as well as laymen 'who had been faithful to the covenant with God and had stood firm in the midst of general wickedness and had therefore propitiated for all the people' (*Supplement to the Manual of Discipline* [1 QSa], beginning). This resulted in their secession from the rest of the people and the foundation of monastic settlements in the desert, where the ideal of religion and moral purity could be fully realised.

A different form of asceticism is to be found in the New Testament, to a certain extent in the life and words of John the Baptist, the great preacher of penance, and even more in the life and words of Jesus himself. John the Baptist certainly lived a life of complete self-denial, but this mainly to add force to his prophetic message as the one crying 'in the wilderness' (Is 40:3). He does not demand flight from the world but an inner conversion and 'fruits that befits repentance' from everybody in every state of life or profession (see Mt 3:7-10; Lk 3:10-14). His baptism of repentance (as distinct from the immersion practised by the Essenes) was received only once and was intended for all Israel for the cleansing of sins against the coming day of judgement. Jesus proclaimed the happiness and joy of the messianic times and therefore waived special acts of penance (see Mk 2:19); he took part in banquets (Jn 2:1-11; Mk 2:15; Lk 7:36 etc; see also Mt 11:19), and allowed women of substance to provide for him (Lk 8:3). Nevertheless, his life, in accordance with his messianic mission, was hard and full of adversities (Lk 9:58). All those who wanted to 'follow' him and share his itinerant life had to adopt a similar attitude, a serene acceptance of what was offered to them as preachers, and yet frugality too (Lk 10:7; see also 22:35). But most fundamental was the renunciation of possessions, home, and family (cp Lk 9:57-62; 14:26-33). This form of asceticism founded by Christ demanded more than a few mere practical acts of temperance; it demanded, first from his immediate companions and apostles but fundamentally from all who believed in him, open profession of their belief in him and willingness to take up his cross and even give their lives for him (Mt 10:34-38 and parallels). The actual demand might be different for different individuals; not everyone was called to unrestricted renunciation of possession (eg the rich young man, Mk 10:21ff and parallels) or to celibacy 'for the kingdom of heaven' (Mt 19:12). The hard struggle, however, to enter the kingdom of heaven ('the narrow gate', Mt 7:13) was common to all.

The *early church* accepted Christ's

demands and, mindful of his cross, came to an even deeper understanding of these demands. Paul considers the christian after baptism as 'crucified with Christ' (Rom 6:6; Gal 2:20), not only free from the 'sinful body' but also called to do the works of the spirit: he should 'crucify the flesh with its passions and desires' (Gal 5:24), 'not yield [his] members to sin as instruments of wickedness' (Rom 6:13), and 'put to death what is earthly in him' (Col 3:5). This requires abstinence and discipline as it does of competitors who run in the stadium (1 Cor 9:24–27, the classic quotation for *askēsis* as a systematic training). But christian asceticism in its fullest and deepest sense is revealed only in 'the inward struggle in suffering' (Phil 1:27–30), the free and conscious acceptance of the sufferings in the service of Christ. For the sufferings of those in union with Christ are part of 'the present evil age', this still continuing but doomed world from which they have been freed in principle (Gal 1:4), but in which they are still held by their mortal existence. Those who have been baptised have already become 'a new creation [in Christ]' (2 Cor 5:17); they have become citizens of the heavenly city of God (Phil 3:20; see also Gal 4:26) and should therefore 'not be conformed to this world' (Rom 12:2), nor be utterly devoted to the world, 'for the form of this world is passing away' (see 1 Cor 7:29–31). In contrast with the riotous joys and pleasures of the heathen we hear Paul's advice 'to conduct ourselves becomingly as in the day' (Rom 13:11–14; 1 Thess 5:1–11; 1 Pet 1:13), 'as sons of light' (1 Thess. 5:5; Eph 5:8f), and 'pray constantly' (1 Thess. 5:17; 1 Pet 4:7;

5:8f; see also Mk 14:38). As is shown in all these passages, aversion from the world is designed not as an escape from the duties of this world: no, the world is rather to be shunned as something dangerous and seductive (see Jas 1:27; 4:4; 1 Jn 2:15–17; 2 Pet 1:4; 2:20), especially in the expectation of the coming 'day of the Lord' (↗ Parousia and ↗ Judgement) (1 Thess 5:2; see also Rom 13:12; Phil 4:4f) for which all shall be 'prepared and guiltless' (1 Cor 1:8; Phil 1:10; 1 Thess 5:23).

This struggle against the evil desires of the flesh (1 Pet 2:11; 2 Pet 2:18) and the warning against 'the lust of the flesh and the lust of the eyes and the pride of life' (1 Jn 2:16) are not to be mistaken for rigorism and false asceticism. The early church had soon to make a stand against certain (gnostic) views according to which all that is corporeal or material should be regarded as sinful in itself, and any contact with it as a pollution of the spirit (see Tit 1:15f). Paul defends christian freedom against those who through rigorous and petty legislation try to reintroduce the old slavery of the law (Col 2:21f; see also Gal 4:9f). He permits the use of meat and wine, contradicting the scruples of over-delicate minds, but demands consideration for the weaker brother—charity first! (Rom 14). The pastoral epistles condemn those heretics who forbid marriage and the use of certain kinds of food (1 Tim 4: 1–5; Tit 1:14f). Christian asceticism should be practised freely, in union with Christ and in accordance with his special call. The early church, and especially the Book of Revelation, regard martyrdom as the highest form of *askēsis*, designed only for those chosen by God. Whatever has been predestined, whether imprisonment or death, we have to accept in 'the endurance and faith of the saints' (Rev 13:10). But 'the new song before the throne' of God is the privilege of those 144,000 ransomed from the earth, those 'who have not defiled themselves with women, for they are chaste' (in the literal or the metaphorical sense?); 'it is these who follow the Lamb wherever he goes' (Rev 14:4).

Bibliography: F. Martinez, *L'ascétisme chrétien pendant les trois premiers siècles de l'église*, Paris 1913; F. Tillmann, *Der Idee der Nachfolge Christi*, Düsseldorf 1949², 227–41; R. Schnackenburg, *The Moral Teaching of the New Testament*, London 1965; C. Feckes, *Die Lehre vom christlichen Vollkommenheitsstreben*, Freiburg 1953²; K. Rahner, *Theological Investigations* III, London 1967; A. Steinmann, *St John the Baptist and the Desert Tradition*, London 1958; L. Bouvet, *L'ascèse de S. Paul*, Lyons 1936; A. Penna, 'L'ascetismo dei Qumranici', *Rivista Biblica* 6 (1958), 3–22; R. Völkl, *Christ und Welt nach dem NT*, Würzburg 1961; E. Neuhäusler, *Anspruch und Antwort Gottes*, Düsseldorf 1962; A.-M. Denis, 'Ascèse et vie chrétienne', *RSPT* 47 (1963), 606–18. See further: H. Strathmann, *Geschichte der frühchristl. Askese bis zur Entstehung des Mönschstums*, Leipzig 1914; H. Strathmann, *RAC* I, 749–53, 758–63, and 794f; A. Köberle, 'Der asket. Klang in der urchristl. Botschaft', *Festschrift für A. Wurm*, 1948, 67–82; H. von Campenhausen, *Die Askese im Urchristentum*, Tübingen 1949; H. Braun, *Spätjüdisch-häretischer und frühchristlicher Radikalismus* (two vols.), Tübingen 1957; G. Kretschmar, 'Ein Beitrag zur Frage nach dem Ursprung frühchristlicher Askese', *ZKT* 61 (1964), 27–67.

Rudolf Schnackenburg

Assurance of salvation

The question of the assurance of salvation—which has been discussed with special interest since the reformation in connection with the doctrine of justification—is essentially connected with the understanding of christian salvation in general. As presented in the New Testament this consists of that deliverance from sin and death and summons to the ↗ glory of God (Rom 3:23) which has been achieved by the redemptive work of Jesus Christ, and graciously offered to mankind. It finds a basis already in this present life in the bestowal of the Holy Spirit, and the 'sonship of God' thereby given (Rom 8:14) will only achieve its full effect at the ↗ *parousia* of the Lord. Man obtains access to this grace of salvation by being justified by faith in Christ Jesus (Rom 3:21ff; 5:2), and by ↗ baptism in him (Rom 6). Does the christian, then, receive this salvation already on this earth as his inalienable possession, so that he appropriates it to himself with the utmost certainty, and is able to look forward to the fullness of salvation with complete and unwavering certainty? According to the particular point of view which is adopted it is possible to speak not only of 'the assurance of salvation', but of 'the assurance of grace' or 'the certainty of faith' as well.

In discussing this question we shall abstract from the problem (always obscure) of how the election or rejection of men (see Rom 9:6–29) are based upon the absolute freedom of God. Doubtless this problem also has a connection with our question, but we shall focus our attention upon the christians who are admitted to the community of salvation in the sense intended by Paul in the situation he depicts in Rom 8:29ff.

The New Testament has no direct answer to give to the question of the assurance of salvation, unless we are prepared to take particular sentences in isolation and to interpret them without regard to their context. All that we can establish is that we have two contrasted groups of statements which can only be related theologically to each other by having regard to revelation as a whole.

The first and most significant statement is found in all the passages in which christian salvation is proclaimed as being purely the work of God revealing himself in an act of ineffable love; in this way it is asserted to be a grace in the fullest sense of the term. Evidently these statements, in which the optimistic attitude towards salvation is strongly emphasised throughout, can of their nature provide a basis for an assurance of salvation in a high degree. We may call to mind words of Jesus such as, for example, the beatitudes in the Sermon on the Mount (Mt 5:3-12; Lk 6:20-23), the promises that prayers offered in a spirit of trust will be answered (Mt 7:7-11; Lk 11:5-13), his revelations concerning the powerful support of the Holy Spirit (Mt 10:19; 28:20; Lk 24:49; Jn 14:15ff; 16:13ff; Acts 1:8), and above all the strong emphasis that is placed upon the power and invincibility of ↗faith (Mt 8:13, 26; 9:22, 29; 17:20; 21:21f; Mk 16:16; Jn 1:12; 3:16ff: '. . . that whoever believes in him should not perish but have eternal life . . . He who believes in him is not condemned'; (Jn 11:25: 'He who believes in me, though he die yet shall he live, and whoever lives and believes in me shall never die'; see also Jn 10:28: 'I give them eternal life and they shall never perish, and no one

shall snatch them out of my hand'). We find the same message in the farewell discourse in Jn 14-16, with its powerful themes of confident faith and the security of Christ's disciples which is based upon this faith.

Paul spoke with special emphasis of the assurance of salvation which is attained in faith. In the last analysis the underlying purpose of the first eight chapters of the Epistle to the Romans is simply to arouse an unshakeable consciousness of salvation—see Rom 5: 2ff: 'We rejoice in our hope of sharing the glory of God . . . and hope does not disappoint us, because God's love has been poured into our hearts through the Holy Spirit who has been given to us'. The ↗ Adam–Christ antithesis (Rom 5:12-21) is likewise intended to support and strengthen this confidence. Rom 6 shows, in the accumulation of terms which are formed in Greek with the prefix *sun*—(=with, together with), the special basis for this confidence of salvation in the oneness of life with the risen Lord which is achieved sacramentally in the christian through baptism. Rom 8 brings these themes to a climax which is movingly expressed in the passage beginning at 8:31: 'If God is for us who is against us? . . . Who shall separate us from the love of Christ? . . . Neither death nor life . . . will be able to separate us from the love of God in Christ Jesus'. Similar statements of how God graciously intervenes with his almighty power on behalf of those who believe in him are to be found also in the rest of the Pauline epistles: see 1 Cor 1:18, 21; 2:9, 12; 15:2; 2 Cor 2:15; 4:14; 5:1, 5 (with a phrase which has an important bearing upon our question, namely the

47

'guarantee of the Spirit'; see also 1:22; Rom 8:23); Gal 1:4; 3:9, 29; Eph 1:4, 14; 2:6, 18; Phil 1:6; Col 1:13; 3:4; 1 Thess 1:10; 2 Thess 2:13f; 2 Tim 1:14; Tit 3:4ff. We encounter the same great confidence in salvation in 1 Pet 1:3ff; 2 Pet 1:11; 1 Jn 5:4; Jude 24; Rev 7:15; 12:11; 21:3f; 22:4f, 17.

While these statements appear to provide an adequate basis for full certainty of salvation on the part of the christian, they stand in sharp contrast to the second group of passages—many of which are closely woven into the pattern of the text—which warn us against adopting such an attitude of certainty in any absolute sense. To this second group belong all those passages in which, in conformity with the basic law of redemption, salvation appears to be connected not only with the working of God's grace, but also, as is stated very plainly and emphatically, on the co-operation of man and his perseverance through testing circumstances. Moreover, even the man who has been received into the grace of Christ is still exposed to peril from the attacks of the powers of evil, and is called to watchfulness and care in defence of the ↗ salvation with which he is initially entrusted as the 'guarantee of the Spirit'. Only in this way can any understanding be achieved of the numerous exhortations and warnings which are addressed to the redeemed in all the New Testament writings. What we are confronted with here is that same law we encounter in the story of the first sin, the original cause of our fallen state, as set forth in the narrative of Gen 3, inasmuch as when man had been created by God and

endowed with his grace he lost his salvation by the misuse of the freewill which had been given to him. In the New Testament, however, this law is applied in an inverse manner. For all the pre-eminence of the element of grace in his election, the christian is called upon to stand prepared to contribute his personal decision to receive this grace, and to work out his own salvation.

In the *gospels*, therefore, the possibility of losing salvation even after having received it is made clear by means of various images. For example, the saying about the 'salt of the earth' (Mt 5:13; Mk 9:50; Lk 14:34f), the exhortation to inner faithfulness (Mt 7:21ff, 24ff). The relevant themes in the parable of the sower (Mt 13:1–23; Mk 4:1–20; Lk 8:4–15), the saying about the sinning 'brother' (Mt 18:15–20; Lk 17:3), the warning against being led astray and allowing one's love to grow cold (Mt 24:4, 10, 12f, 22), together with the exhortation to constant watchfulness (Mt 24:42–51; 25:1–13) and preparedness (Mt 25:14–30; Lk 19:11–27), and the solemn warning against all falling back into sin (Lk 11:24ff). Again the fate of the apostle who betrayed Jesus is an illustration of this idea. The farewell discourse in Jn 17 should also be noted, for here Jesus prays (referring explicitly to Judas) that his apostles may be guarded against sin, and prays likewise for all who believe in him. We encounter the same theme in Lk 22:32: 'But I have prayed for you that your faith may not fail'.

Again the idea that the grace of salvation once received has to be maintained through the testing conditions of life is implicit in the idea of men being judged according to their works, to which Jesus often explicitly adverts (Mt 25:31–46; Mk 8:34f; Lk 6:37f; 8:17f; 12:5, 48; 19:26; 21:34f).

From these statements in the gospel it can already be seen that one called by God to salvation has a contribution to make towards it, and that the ultimate achievement of salvation in its fullness is closely connected with the fulfilment of this responsibility. This impression, already gained from the gospels, does not, however, make its full impact upon us until we turn to *Paul*. It is precisely in the writings of Paul, the man who might be regarded as the preacher of the assurance of salvation in its full and uncompromising sense, that the requirement that man shall take some of the responsibility upon himself is impressed upon us with the greatest possible urgency. Hence the close connection between the indicative and the imperative of salvation in Paul. It must be observed, however, that this imperative is related to the indicative not as an external and concomitant factor, but rather follows as an integral consequence from the fact that the grace of salvation has been bestowed. For in this bestowal it is not merely the subject's awareness of having been raised to a state of salvation that is awakened, in the sense that he then feels himself obliged to act in conformity with that state; it is the actual state of salvation in itself that is presented as a prior condition, in that it makes it possible for man to act in this way. As a result, faith in the apostle's sense is the opposite of Jewish legalism in that it is, of its very nature, applicable also to the sphere of action and morality. Union of

life with the risen Lord in the *pneuma khristo* (= spirit of Christ, Rom 8:9) creates an essentially new prior condition for right action and for the process of testing and purifying which is necessary for salvation to achieve its fullness. On the basis of this, the concept of ⁄ hope, to which Paul accords such prominence and importance (see Rom 5:2ff; 8:16, 19–25) acquires a content which comes very near to the 'assurance of salvation', even though this is not to be understood in an absolute sense.

But for all his emphasis on this confidence of salvation we can see how vividly the apostle is aware of the possibility of not persisting to the end from passages such as Rom 2:6f; admittedly, he is thinking here primarily of the Jews, but so far as the idea of judgement according to works is concerned what he says has universal application; or again, there is 1 Cor 9:27: '. . . lest after preaching to others I myself should be disqualified'. The same solicitude for salvation is also expressed in Phil 3:12: 'Not that I have already obtained this or am already perfect; but I press on to make it my own, because Christ Jesus has made me his own'. On the basis of the insight which the apostle offers us here we can understand his exhortation: 'Work out your own salvation with ⁄ fear and trembling' (Phil 2:12), though here it must be admitted that the sentence immediately following is once more important for the Pauline understanding of salvation: 'For God is at work in you, both to will and to work for his good pleasure' (Phil 2:13). On this tension between the grace of and the responsibility for salvation

49

Rom 6 is extremely instructive, inasmuch as we find here a close interpenetration of the two ideas, that of consciousness of salvation on the one hand, and at the same time also the demand for 'the obedience leading to righteousness'—the two ideas being connected together and formulated in a manner strongly suggestive of juridical concepts.

It will be observed, too, that the apostle draws attention again and again in his epistles to the significance of entreaty (↗prayer) for salvation (Eph 1:17; 6:18; Phil 1:3 with the connected sentence in 1:6: 'I am sure that he who began a good work in you will bring it to completion at the day of Jesus Christ'; see also 1:9 with its similar theme; 4:6; Col 1:9f etc). The apostle's references to the seriousness with which we ought to regard our state of salvation, and the possibility of our losing it (see 1 Cor 10:1–13; 2 Cor 7:1; 13:5; Gal 5:4; 6:7f; Phil 2:16; 3:18f; Col 1:23; 1 Thess 4:8; Heb 3:12; 6:4; 10:26f) are also important for our question, as are the catholic epistles and the Book of Revelation, which abound with demands for perseverance and with concern lest perseverance should be wanting (see the Seven Letters, Rev 2:1–3:22 with their emphatic summons to stand firm).

To conclude, this interplay between the assurance of salvation and the presence of continual threats to salvation can only be explained on the basis of the eschatological situation in which man is placed, and of the basic law for the final fulfilment of salvation —that is, the law by which man with his active co-operation is subsumed into the work of the ↗grace of God. It should not be overlooked that in the message of salvation as presented in the gospels and Paul alike the main accent falls upon the redemptive work of Jesus Christ, and the assurance of salvation for the christian which is based upon him. From this we may conclude that it is possible to speak of an extremely high degree of assurance of salvation, amounting to certainty, which if not to be taken absolutely, is at any rate a moral and practical certainty, for the man who entrusts himself to this grace with a lively faith 'to the end' (Mt 10:22; Rev 2:26).

Bibliography: the articles on↗faith,↗grace,↗judgement,↗justification,↗salvation, etc are all relevant here. See in particular: R. Schnackenburg, *The Moral Teaching of the New Testament*, London 1965 ; R. Schnackenburg, *LTK* v², 157f; O. Kuss, *Der Römerbrief* (two parts), Regensburg 1959, 396–430 ('Heilsbesitz und Bewährung' with copious bibliography); L. Cerfaux, *The Christian in the Theology of St Paul*, London 1967.

J. Kürzinger

Atonement

A. *Old Testament*. The Hebrew verb *kippēr* means 'to purify', through a priest, from things which defile (Lev 16:16, 33, the sanctuary; Ezek 45:20, the temple); or, when the subject is God, 'to forgive sins' (Num 35:33; Deut 21:8; 1 Sam 3:14; Ps 65:3; 78:38; Ezek 16:63). The Greek *hilaskomai* renders, besides other underlying Hebrew words, the idea of 'purifying' (Ezek 43:20, 22), of 'forgiving', 'being merciful' (Ex 32:12, 14; 2 Kings 5:18; Dan 9:9; Sir 5:5f), and so throws some light on the meaning of *kipper*. *Hilaskomai* never has God for object: Mal 1:9 is an intended irony—as if God could be 'placated' like any heathen idol! Zech 7:2 speaks of heathens who want to apply their own religious practices to the God of Israel, and 8:21f is likewise spoken by heathens and probably uses *kipper/hilaskomai* in a different sense, namely, 'to pray', 'to beseech'. In Greek religion, as in that of the Assyrians, Hittites, and Canaanites, God is always 'placated'—with sacrifices and the like; but against this conception stand texts like Ps 50:9; 51:17 (↗ Sacrifice).

B. *New Testament. Hilaskomai* is in no way used in the New Testament in the hellenistic sense, but must be connected with the Old Testament usage (as is the case, for that matter, with the Qumran use of *kipper*. See 1 QM 2:5; 1 QS 3:4; 5:6. The community practised virtue in order to win atonement and forgiveness for all men of good will; they made atonement for the world polluted by transgressors, but could not do so for the transgressors themselves as these were destined to be annihilated: 1 QS 8:6; see also 1 QS 8:10; 1 QSa 1:3). In Heb 2:17 the true high priest blots out sin, as in the Old Testament; the same is said in 1 Jn 2:2 of Jesus the righteous, whom the Father has sent for the expiation of our sins (1 Jn 4:10). The same is true of Rom 3:25, where Paul evidently wants to bring to our mind the Old Testament rite of atonement which consisted in sprinkling ↗ blood on the 'mercy seat' and offering sacrifices for sins on the Day of Atonement.

In LXX *hilastērion* translates *kappōreth*, the golden cover of the ark of the covenant which supported the cherubim, or at other times *ᶜªzārâh*, the pedestal of the altar in Ezekiel's temple (Ex 25:17–22; 26:34; 30:6; 31:7; 35:12 etc; Ezek 43:14, 17, 20; 45:19; Sir 50:11). This 'mercy seat' or *propitiatorium* (Jerome's term—Luther calls it the 'throne of grace') is the really essential thing in the Holy of Holies (1 Chron 28:11), the throne of God (hence the phrase 'enthroned on the cherubim': 1 Sam 4:4; Ps 80:1; 99:1) where revelation and the word of God are made immediately present (Jerome has *oraculum*, Ex 25:19, 20; Num 7:89)—compare Heb 1:2: 'In these last days he has *spoken* to us by a Son'. It was here that the sin of the whole people—not that of any individual—was expiated through the sprinkling of blood (Lev 16:14f: on the great Day of Atonement, except on occasions when it was not permitted to enter before the 'mercy seat', in which case the seven-fold sprinkling took place before the veil [Lev 4:13–21]). In Rom 3:25 we have 'type' and 'antitype': Christ on the cross makes expiation 'by his own blood' (see also 1 Pet 1:18f), no longer in secret since the veil has been rent (Mt 27:51; Mk 15:38; Lk 23:45), but openly manifested (*proetheto* = put forward) to all, so that 'God was in Christ reconciling the world to himself, not counting their trespasses against them' (2 Cor 5:19). ↗ Reconciliation.

Bibliography: A. Médebielle, *DB(S)* 3, 1–262; J. Hermann and F. Büchsel, *TDNT* III, 300–23; F. Büchsel, *TDNT* I, 251–9; J. Dupont, *La Réconciliation dans la Théologie de S. Paul*, Louvain 1953; L. Moraldi, *Espiazione sacrificale e riti espiatori nell' ambiente biblico e nell'Antico Testamento*, Rome 1956; L. Moraldi, *Dict. de Spiritualité* 4 (1960), 2026–45; L. Moraldi, 'Espiazione nell'Antico e Nuovo Testamento', *Rivista Biblica* 9 (1961), 289–304 and 10 (1962), 3–17; Imschoot II, 314–38; S. Lyonnet, *Theologia Biblica Novi Testamenti*,

Rome 1954, 103ff; L. Morris, *NTS* 2 (1955), 33–43; O. Kuss, *Der Römerbrief* 1, Regensburg 1957, 155–61; L. De Lorenzi, *Rivista Biblica* 5 (1957), 237–43.↗ Redemption.

Johannes B. Bauer

Authority

The concept of 'authority' in the context of biblical theology (in Greek *exousia*, for which there is no term in Hebrew or Aramaic which corresponds exactly) is a complex one as indeed it is in extra-biblical usage where it can mean possibility, right, freedom, power to perform some specific task, even arbitrariness; also used of office and the one who holds it.

A. *The Old Testament.* The reality itself is of course there from the beginning (cf the expression 'to fall into someone's hands'—2 Sam 24:14; 1 Chron 29:12; 2 Chron 20:6; Job 10:7 etc), but as a well-defined concept 'authority' appears only in the later books, which is hardly surprising since the idea is connected with the Greek. It signifies the power and sovereignty of God (Esther 13:9, 'the universe is in thy power'; Dan 4:17, 'the most High rules the kingdom of men, and gives it to whom he will'; Sir 10:4, 'the government of the earth is in the hands of the Lord', etc; cf also Dan 2:21f; 4:25, 34f; 6:26f). But God has also given authority over the earth to men (Sir 17:2). Such authority befits the king but he can subdelegate it (Dan 5:7). Through the 'law' God gave to the Israelites authority to perform specific actions (Tob 2:13; 'We have no authority to eat anything stolen'). Everlasting authority will be given to the 'Son of Man' (Dan 7:13)—and much of what the New Testament has to say about the authority which appears in Christ rests on this consideration.

B. *The New Testament* contains the concept of 'authority' in the fullness of its meaning. As in the Old Testament, we find the idea expressed that authority belongs essentially to God himself. He has the power to cast into hell (Lk 12:5). The Father has placed in his own power the decisive *kairoi* (Acts 1:7). The potter has the right or authority to make what use he sees fit of his vessels (Rom 9:21). Authority is one of the most essential characteristics of God and is attributed to him in hymns of praise (Jude 25).

Similarly the New Testament knows, as does the Old, that God entrusts this power to others in different degrees. It is a general postulate that any kind of power or authority exists only because it has its origin in God (Jn 19:11; Rom 13:1).

Such power committed to men by God comes to light also in the New Testament in the state. This 'power' is an essential element in the state and is distributed among individual holders of office: eg, 'power over ten cities', Lk 19:17; Herod (Lk 23:7); Pilate (Jn 19:10f) have power but are themselves, like the centurion (Mt 8:9 and parallels), set under human power and authority. This power and authority can be used either for good or for evil (Acts 9:14; 26:10, 12); Saul has authority from the Supreme Council to persecute the christians; Pilate condemned Christ who was in his power—in fact Christ was to be maliciously handed over to this power even earlier, on the occasion of the question about the tribute money (Lk 20:20). Since, however, all power comes from God (Rom 13:1) it must be respected (Rom 13:2; see also Titus 3:1). To be sure, Paul is here evidently referring to the state which has come by its power by fair means and uses it well—see Rom 13:3! It is quite another question with the manifestations of power exercised for evil and which have to be endured, such as are indicated in the Book of Revelation (see below).

The veil a woman wears is a sign of the authority which a man has over her (1 Cor 11:10—taking account of all the uncertainty involved in the explanation of this text!). The authority of the man, given by Moses and reaching so far as to enable him even to leave his wife (Mt 19:3—'for any cause?') is, however, brought back again into line with the true purpose of God by the Lord (Mk 10:9 and parallels; 1 Cor 7:10f).

'Authority', however, does not just signify power over another—even over inanimate objects (see Acts 5:4)— but can also express *dominion over oneself*. He who has control over himself— meaning his sexual desires—may keep 'his virgin' as she is, intact (1 Cor 7:37). He does well to do so; for it is now the last days (1 Cor 7:29), so that man and woman can give their attention wholly to the Lord (1 Cor 7:32–34).

The special kind of authority which Jesus has can be seen in everything he does. The people recognise this unique authority in and from what he teaches (Mk 1:22, 27; Mt 7:29; Lk 4:32). Jesus shows his authority when he casts out demons (Mk 1:27; Lk 4:36). That he stakes the claim for himself even to be able to forgive sins on earth (Mt 9:6 and parallels) is only the other side of this inclusive power of Christ. Jesus gave continual offence to the influential circles of the scribes and Pharisees with his continually asserted particular and unique authority; a good example of which would be the discussion about his authority after the entry into the city on Palm Sunday and the cleansing of the Temple (Mt 21:23, 24, 27 and parallels). But this offence is present in the whole opposition of Christ to the religious leaders of his people. He does not conform to current interpretations of the law (see Mt 12:2 and parallels; Mt 9:14 and parallels; Lk 13:10–17; 14:1–6). His opponents notice this and know that with this attitude Jesus arrogates to himself a unique authority. He does not enquire whether he may perform a certain action as in accord with the law: his own will is the norm of law. When his opponents take offence at his conduct his only answer is to renew his claim to unique authority: with him God's appointed time of salvation and joy has broken into the present (Mt 9:15 and parallels). He is Lord of the sabbath, and therefore not just of a particular interpretation of the law (Mt 12:8 and parallels). His achievement signified that Satan had been bound (Mt 12:29) and that therefore the rule of God, his kingdom, had come (Mt 12:28).

In his usual way, John gives a presentation of the whole question in just a few texts which, however, are full of meaning. The Son of Man has authority to hold judgement (5:27). Christ has the power (=freedom) to lay down his life and to take it up

53

again (10:18). He has received from his Father authority over all flesh (17:2). We have to bear in mind both aspects of this: namely, that his authority is conferred on him by his Father and that it is, at the same time, a limitless authority. This is precisely what the risen Lord says to his disciples, according to Matthew: 'All authority in heaven and on earth has been given to me' (28:18).

The spirit world, too, participates in the divine authority. With the texts which speak of this participation we must also enumerate those others which speak of the powers which God makes use of in putting into operation his plan for the world. This motif is continually in evidence in Revelation: Death and Hades (6:8); the locusts (9:3, 10); the horses (9:19); in a certain sense also the two witnesses (11:6); the angel in charge of the fire (14:18); another angel (18:1). It is not just the spirits who submit themselves absolutely to God who are bearers of his power; God has entrusted, given over, such authority also to the fallen spirits. Consequently 'powers' is a specific proper name for a spiritual being in general which has received such authority from God. They, all together, have been created in Christ (Col 1:16); he is the Head (Col 2:10, see also 1 Pet 3:22). The powers must recognise the manifold wisdom of God (Eph 3:10) which operates in him whom it has raised above all powers (Eph 1:21). The battle against the prince of the power of the air (Eph 2:2), against the powers of darkness in general (Eph 6:12) is left to man, even man who has been redeemed. They have already really been overcome by him who has freed us from the power of darkness (Col 1:13), but it is also true that he has to win this victory first (1 Cor 15:24). Satan, who is able to pass on the authority left to him by God (see Rev 13:2, the dragon gives the beast great authority; 17:12f, the ten kings pass on their authority to the beast) tries by means of this authority conferred on him to tempt all the kingdoms of the world (see Jn 12:31) and even Christ himself (Lk 4:6). Christ, who is the Lord and Head, victor over the powers of darkness, himself at the appointed time falls into their power (Lk 22:53). The fearful strength of these powers of darkness (for which see Rev 13:7: 'to make war on the saints and to conquer them') is given to them by God for a determined time only (see also Rev 13:5: 'forty-two months') and must co-operate in its turn in bringing to fulfilment 'that which has to come about'.

The authority of the Redeemer is not restricted to his own person, for he passes it on, in some measure, to his disciples and the faithful in general. As an essential element, he transfers to his disciples power over demons (Mt 10:1; Mk 3:15; 6:7; 'over all demons', Lk 9:1) and their wiles (Lk 10:19: 'to tread upon serpents . . . and over all the power of the enemy'). Through the participated power of Christ, the apostles are able to communicate the Holy Spirit (Acts 8:19). The authority given to the apostles by the Lord must contribute to the 'edification' of the faithful (2 Cor 10:8; see also 13:10). But the apostolic authority is not just a means of serving the church; it also confers rights with regard to the members of the church, even of a material kind. The apostle has the 'authority' (=right) to eat and drink, to be accompanied by a 'sister' as a wife, to be exempt from working for a living (1 Cor 9:4–6; for the last see also 2 Thess 3:9). These rights, however, give way before the service of the Gospel (1 Cor 9:18).

Those who believe in Christ have the power to become children of God (Jn 1:12). As members of the church, they have the authority to partake of the altar from which the Jews who have not believed may not eat (Heb 13:10). The knowledge proper to a believer allows him to eat of the so-called meat offered to idols (1 Cor 8:9), although charity dictates consideration for the 'weak brethren' (see on this point 1 Cor 6:12: 'All things are lawful for me, but not all things are helpful'). In the case of the victor in the epistle to the church of Thyatira to whom is promised authority over the heathens (Rev 2:26) the reference is to a share in the authority of Christ over the demons hostile to God. He who will share in the 'first resurrection' will not be subject to the power (authority) of the 'second death' (Rev. 20:6). Finally, there stands as a great promise to the faithful the Word which assures fulfilment for the deepest longing of man right from the beginning: 'Blessed are they who wash their robes, that they may have the right [authority] to the tree of life!' (Rev 22:14).

Bibliography: W. Foerster, TDNT II, 560–75 with corresponding bibliography (down to 1935); Bultmann I, 230, 257, 337; II, 95ff; H. Schlier, Principalities and Powers in the New Testament, London and New York 1961; W. Beilner, Christus und die Pharisäer, Vienna 1959, esp. 242–5. On particular questions: W. F. Arndt and F. W. Gingrich, A Greek–English Lexikon of the New Testament and other Early Christian Literature, 1957; *R. Murray, 'Authority and the Spirit in the NT', Authority in a Changing Church, J. Dalrymple and others, London 1968. Among recent commentaries: R. Bultmann, Johannes-Evangelium, 1941, 36; V. Taylor, The Gospel according to St Mark, London 1955, 173 and 469.

Wolfgang Beilner

Ban

The corresponding Hebrew word *ḥērem* (from the verb *ḥāram* = separate, cf *ḥārem* = an enclosure set aside for women) signifies separation from the profane sphere and deliverance into the power of God. It can be translated either 'ban' or 'interdict'.

The ban is connected in the first place with the practice of war. The Assyrians also imposed the ban on their enemies (see 2 Kings 19:11 = Is 37:11), and Mesha king of Moab boasted that he had annihilated the city of Nebo with its 7,000 inhabitants, thus dedicating it to his god Kemosh (see the Moabite stone lines 14–17). In the Old Testament the ban is always regarded as a religious punishment. The religious motivation behind this idea of annihilating everything pagan can at least be clearly perceived in that the inheritance of the surrounding nations is made to serve the religion of Yahweh (cf Num 21:2; Josh 6:18f; 7:15ff; 10:28–42; Judg 21:11; 1 Sam 15:3; see also ↗ War).

The operation of the ban is not, however, limited to time of war. In Ex 22:20 we learn that 'whoever sacrifices to any god, save to the Lord only, shall be utterly destroyed', with which

55

can be compared the ordinances in Deut 13:12–19 threatening the ban against Israelites not against pagans. As can be seen by comparing Gen 38:24 with Lev 21:9 there was also a private curse comparable to the ban. The same seems to be presupposed by Lev 27:28f, which speaks of the punishment which had to be meted out to a member of a family for some flagrant violation of law. In this case the possessions of this person, his cattle for example, could not be redeemed with money but became the property of the sanctuary and the priests, though they could be made use of only after a ritual of purification. In keeping with this the gold, silver, and bronze instruments taken from the interdicted city of Jericho were 'consecrated' to the Israelite cult.

In 1 Sam 15:20–22 a clear distinction is drawn between the ban and sacrifice. The *ḥērem* of Jephthah, Judg 11:30ff, is not a sacrifice in the strict sense of the word.

In LXX *ḥērem* is generally translated by *anathema*. In the New Testament also *anathema* generally corresponds to *ḥērem*, with the exception of Lk 21:5, where it refers to consecrated offerings in keeping with Hellenistic usage. In later judaism *ḥērem* also applies to the ban imposed by the synagogue, a kind of excommunication. Something similar to this is found in 1 Cor 5:3–5 and 1 Tim 1:20. But there is really nothing in the New Testament comparable to the practice of the ban in later judaism with the well-defined degrees by which it was implemented, though it is worth while comparing this latter with the statements found in the Qumran community rule (1 QS VI, 24–VII, 25). In

the New Testament a curse is pronounced on anyone who preaches a different gospel (Gal 1:8f) or does not love the Lord (1 Cor 16:22). This can also be a self-imposed curse for those who do not fulfil a duty which is incumbent on them (Acts 23:14). Rom 9:3 provides a difficulty: 'I could wish that I myself [Paul] were accursed and cut off from Christ for the sake of my brethren'. It should be interpreted in much the same way as the prayer of Moses in Ex 32:32, and in line with Gal 3:13 (which follows the principle laid down in Gen 18:23–32): the unrighteous and guilty will be saved with the righteous and the innocent for the sake of the community as a whole. In all of these New Testament texts *anathema* can hardly refer exclusively to separation from the community of salvation. In keeping with the Old Testament use of the word *ḥērem* it must also mean to be subject to the anger of God and to be delivered over to divine judgement. Both of these elements are stressed in Ezra 10:8 which brings out clearly the transition from the first to the second sense.

According to Zech 14:11 and Rev 22:3 the ban will cease to exist after the eschatological victory and the definitive overthrow of the powers which are opposed to God, since by then it will have no more reason to exist.

Bibliography: SB IV, 293–333 on the practice of the synagogue with relation to the ban: J. Döller, *ZKT* 37 (1913), 1–24; A. Fernandez, *Bbl* 5 (1924), 3–25; J. Behm, *TDNT* I, 353–6; H. Junker, *TTZ* 75 (1950), 227–30; Haag 153f; S. Cavaletti, *Festschrift Millás Vallicrosa*, Barcelona 1954, 347–50; C. H. Hunzinger, *Die jüdische Bannpraxis im neutestamentliche Zeitalter*, Göttingen 1954 (dissertation in typescript); W. Doskocil, *Der Bann in der Urkirche*,

Munich 1957; H. Gross, *LTK* I², 1225–7; C. H. W. Brekelmans, *De cherem in het OT*, Nijmegen 1959.

Johannes B. Bauer

Baptism

A. *The origin of christian baptism.* From the middle of the second century BC until AD 300 there was in Palestine and Syria widespread practice of baptism among many sects of various beliefs (see J. Thomas, *Le mouvement baptiste en Palestine et Syrie*). A prominent place in this movement is held by John, the son of Zechariah during the period immediately preceding Christ's public appearance, so that his contemporaries gave him the significant title 'the Baptist'. His baptism, to which even Jesus submitted himself, is distinguished from the Jewish (and Essenic) baptismal immersion in various respects: 1. It is received *only once*. 2. It is designed *for all the Jewish people* (not for the 'unclean' and 'sinners' only, or for proselytes). 3. It is received in order *to escape the coming judgement through repentance* (confession of sins). 4. The recipients did not administer this baptism to themselves, but *were baptised by the Baptist*, the eschatological prophet sent by God, or by one of his disciples. 5. It therefore had an *eschatological significance*: the creation of a holy people for God at the end of time, for the 'one mightier', the Messiah is soon to come for his final judgement and salvation. The early church regarded this baptism of John as preliminary to its own baptism and claimed that its baptism as distinct from that of John was 'a Baptism with the Holy Ghost' (see Mk 1:8 and parallels; Acts 1:5; 11:16). Scientific criticism may consider John to be more than only 'the precursor' of Jesus and 'witness' of the Messiah (see Jn 1:7, 33–5), the more so since the later disciples of John formed an independent group and entered into competition with the christian community (see Acts 18:25; 19:1–7; Pseudo–Clementines), but the peculiar characteristics of his baptism are indisputable. Both christian baptism and that of John were administered by others and could not be repeated; they both shared the prospect of an eschatological salvation (although this was certainly different after the coming of Christ). Christian baptism can hardly be related to the Jewish baptism of proselytes, which, although an act of incorporation into a supernatural community and received only once, was only an initiatory ceremony producing effects of a purely liturgical (purification from 'uncleanness') and legal nature. Even its age has not been satisfactorily ascertained. If the primitive church has administered and demanded baptism from its very foundation (Acts 2:38), even though the eschatological gift of the Holy Spirit may seem to be communicated without the actual ceremony with water (Whitsun; see also Acts 10:44; 11:15ff), it can only be based on a special command of Christ himself. True, we first hear it from the lips of the risen Lord (Mt 28:19; see also Mk 16:16), but not until then did it obtain its full significance, for the Spirit would only be released after Christ's exaltation (see Jn 7:39) and fill, guide, and build up the congregation, orphaned through Christ's departure. The far-seeing conversation of Jesus with Nicodemus reveals the deep significance of the necessity of baptism and its full meaning. It is impossible to explain baptism as an institution introduced by the primitive church, as a kind ceremony of admission resembling the Jewish baptism of proselytes, or a means of forgiving sins before the receiving of the Holy Spirit. Neither can the baptism of Jesus administered by John, which has its own unique messianic-christological significance, have been the cause and prototype of the early christian baptism. The references in Acts bear no relation to Christ's baptism and death (O. Cullmann has interpreted Christ's death as a kind of 'general baptism' of all christians: see Mk 10:38; Lk 12:50).

B. *Baptism in the early christian community.* The baptism administered by the apostles after the coming of the Holy Spirit is explained in Acts in the following ways. 1. It is an expression of the inner ⤴ 'conversion' working (sacramentally) the *forgiveness of sins* (see 2:38; 3:19; 5:31; 11:18; 22:16; 26:20). 'Conversion' means a complete turning away from one's past life, detestation of ⤴ sin (see 5:31 referring to the Jews; 11:18; 17:30 referring to the Gentiles), but also abandonment of an adverse attitude towards the Messiah (see 3:17, 19). The conditions for baptism are faith in Christ as the divine bringer of salvation and acceptance of the christian message of salvation ('the word' or 'the word of God': see 2:41; 4:4; 8:4f, 12f; 10:43; 16:30-3; 18:8). The forgiveness of sins is the beginning of salvation, the first eschatological act of God leading up to life everlasting (see 11:18; 13:46, 8). 2. Baptism is administered '*in the name of the Lord Jesus Christ*' (see 22:16; also 9:14, 21), which

means surrender to Christ as the Lord and Saviour, the only mediator of salvation (4:12) and author of life (3:15). 3. Baptism is the (normal) occasion of the *pouring out of the Spirit*. Only those who have been baptised in the name of Jesus Christ (see 19:2-7) will receive 'this gift of the Holy Ghost' (2:38), the eschatological pledge of God (see 2:17-21, 33). Although the Holy Ghost is (usually) 'poured out' after baptism (through the imposition of hands 19:6), baptism is not merely an occasion but the real cause and medium of this communication. The dissociation of the receiving of the Holy Spirit from baptism is probably due to the extraordinary effects of the coming of the Holy Spirit at that time (gift of tongues, prophecy). 4. Baptism is the *incorporation into the community of Jesus Christ*. Through this baptism God adds new members to the primitive church, and so the church grows outwardly and visibly (see 2:41, 47; 5:14; 11:24-6:7; 9:31; 11:21). Outside this community of God there is no salvation, and the church is charged with the world wide mission to bring salvation to the whole world. Therefore, all the essential elements of the doctrine of baptism can already be found in the primitive church, although theological development and penetration was yet to come.

C. *Paul's doctrine of baptism.* Paul is the first to give real impetus to the development of the theology of baptism in the primitive church. Although in his theology he places ⤴ faith as the sole means of salvation, contrary to the Jewish doctrine of salvation and justification through the law, and although he regards the preaching of the gospel and not the administration of baptism as his own personal task (1 Cor 1:17), he accepts baptism as a matter of course and gives it a firm place in the construction of his theology. Faith and baptism are not mutually exclusive but stand in need of each other. There is no baptism without faith—not a purely spiritual faith, but a faith together with the external profession of faith in the act of baptism (see Rom 10:8–10). The ceremony of baptism, which consisted in an immersion in water, is explained by Paul in various ways: 1. Being a rite of washing in water, baptism is a *'washing off the stain of sin'* (see the remission of sins in Acts), and at the same time a sanctification and justification of the former sinner (1 Cor 6:11). 2. He who is baptised is baptised *in the name of Jesus Christ* and is therefore subordinate to his Lord and belongs to him (see 1 Cor 1:13; 3:23; 15:23; Gal 3:29; 5:24 and other instances where possession is indicated by the use of the genitive; see again Acts). This, however, is not a purely external subordination but a sharing in one common life (often expressed as 'being in Christ'). 3. Compared to the initiatory ceremony of the chosen people in the Old Testament, baptism is called a *'circumcision in Christ'*, which however does not consist in the removal of a small part of the human body but in a burial of the old man full of sin (Col 2:11; see Rom 6:6). 4. Positively speaking, baptism is *'putting on Christ'* (Gal 3:27), ie, he who is baptised is clothed with Christ, absorbed in him, so that he becomes 'a new man in Christ' (see Eph 4:24; Col 3:10), a 'rebirth' (2 Cor 5:17; Gal 6:15). This idea presupposes that Christ possesses a

new, glorified life since his resurrection and ascension, a 'pneumatic' existence, through which the closest conceivable union of Christ with those baptised was made possible ('mystical union with Christ'). They receive a *new existence* 'in Christ', in which all previously valid sexual, racial, and social characteristics are transcended (Gal 3:28; Col 3:11), an *eschatological* existence in as much as those baptised already participate in the life of the risen Lord ('the Spirit'; see 1 Cor 15:44f) and this infused life points towards a bodily resurrection as the ultimate object (see Rom 6:5, 8; 8:11). 5. The sacramental union with Christ can also be described as a 'being crucified with him', 'buried with Christ', 'rising with him', and being 'restored to life' with him, so that those baptised will undergo all that happened to him (see Rom 6:4–8; Gal 2:19f; Eph 2:5f; Col 2:12–20; 3:1). These expressions are difficult to interpret and have in fact been interpreted in various ways but they have their main theological foundation in the Adam–Christ parallelism (Rom 5:12–21; 1 Cor 15: 20–2, 45–9): Christ is the progenitor of a new, redeemed human race and—as the first who is raised from the dead, 'the first fruits of those who have fallen asleep' (1 Cor 15:20; see Col 1:18), the 'first born among many brethren' (Rom 8:29)—continually incorporates new members through this baptism. On their behalf he accepted his cross and death (see 2 Cor 5:14–21; Gal 3:13), but they accept and share his fate in complete union with him, first of all sacramentally in receiving baptism in which they are 'buried . . . with him' (Rom 6:4, probably referring to the rite of immersion), then morally by 'dying to sin' and 'living for God' (Rom 6:4, 6; Gal 5:24; 6:14; Col 3:5, and other instances), but also by suffering and dying with him daily in the strength and hope of resurrection (mysterious significance of suffering; see Rom 8:17; 2 Cor 4:10–14; Phil 3:10f; 2 Tim 2:11f). 6. Since all christians in baptism experience the same and are filled with the same divine spirit (*pneuma*), baptism has another relation to the *community*: everybody, Jews and Greeks, slaves and freemen, men and women, will be 'all one in Christ Jesus' (Gal 3:28), one single body by the power of one Spirit (1 Cor 12:13; see Eph 4:4f); the body of Christ (1 Cor 12:27; Rom 12:5). Bearing this in mind one will certainly come to a better and deeper understanding of the ⁊ church (see Eph 1:23; 2:16–22; 4:12–16; 5:23, 30; Col 1:18; 2:19; 3:11, 15). 7. Starting from this view of baptism, Paul built up his moral theology stating the serious effects that baptism should have on the christian way of life in this world. A clear understanding of baptism precludes abuse of God's abundant grace (Rom 6), demands a continuous and hard struggle against our sinful desires and passions (Rom 6:12–14, 19; Gal 5:24; and other instances), requires that the community should be kept pure (1 Cor 5:6–8), and supplies many motives for a moral struggle in this world surrounded by evil (Eph 5:6–14; Phil 2:15f; Col 3:12–17; 1 Thess 4:3–8; and other instances).

D. *Other views on baptism in the New Testament.* It is hardly possible to improve on Paul's theology of baptism, which was centred on Christ. But in his later Epistle to Titus he used an expression which would be of great influence in the period that followed: 'the washing of regeneration' (Tit 3:5; see ⁊ Rebirth). This is reminiscent of an idea which formed the final object of the initiation in the Greek mysteries (⁊ Mystery) and in Hellenistic mysticism (see the 'Mithraic Liturgy', *Corpus Herm.* xiii), a kind of transformation through contemplation, a deification of man. But the idea of being raised to a divine level, a deification and ecstatic vision of God in the fashion of the Greek mysteries, is completely absent in the pastoral epistle. Paul speaks in a biblical way of a pouring forth of the Holy Spirit (Tit 3:6) and of a 'renewal' being worked in us by the recreating Holy Spirit (see also the texts of Qumran). This eschatological promise is fulfilled sacramentally in the communication of grace worked by the baptismal washing, which therefore becomes a source of life, recreating us and enabling us to participate in eternal life. A similar idea is to be found in our Lord's conversation with Nicodemus (Jn 3); the 'old man', bodily and earthborn, cannot see the kingdom of God unless he is born anew (Jn 3:3), without a re-conception and re-birth in water and the Holy Ghost (v 5). Nicodemus' misinterpretation of this rebirth (v 4) made Christ expound his analogy with natural human conception and birth. This can also be found in 1 Pet, an epistle full of references to baptism, regarded by many as a sermon for newly baptised and by others even as an early christian baptismal liturgy. By God's 'great mercy we have been born anew to a living hope' (1 Pet 1:3); christians are reconceived (or 'reborn'), 'not of perishable seed but of imperishable, through the living and abiding word of God' (1:23). The analogy of baptism and our 'first birth' (ie, our natural birth) and their difference was even further extended in the second century by Justin (*Apol.* 6:10). Other expressions of Paul, 'God . . . has put his seal upon us and given us his Spirit' (2 Cor 1:22; Eph 1:13; 4:30) and 'seeing the light' (see 2 Cor 4:4, 6; Eph 1:18—and even stronger in Heb 6:4; 10:32) have gradually since the second century been interpreted as references to baptism.

Other texts complete and confirm this doctrine of baptism in the New Testament. It is referred to as the cleansing and sanctifying laver prepared by Christ for his church, so that it may be presented to him, a glorious church, not having spot or wrinkle or any such thing (Eph 5:26—often thought of as a kind of ritual bridal bath). It is the great means of salvation through which we, like Noah in his ark, are saved by passing through the water, and which does not wash off any external contamination but gives us the assurance of a good conscience (1 Pet 3:20f—several themes converge here). There is also a deep relationship between the baptismal water and the ↗ blood of Christ, for the former derives its power from the latter. Through the blood of Christ we enter the heavenly sanctuary; this way lies open to us by having 'our hearts sprinkled clean from an evil conscience and our bodies washed with pure water' (Heb 10:22; see 19). Also the stream of water and blood flowing from Christ's side (Jn 19:34) has, in the eyes of the fourth evangelist, a deeper meaning and refers to the sacraments of the eucharist and baptism. A similar reference is almost certain in 1 Jn 5:7ff where 'the Spirit, the water, and the blood' are the three who give testimony, because in this passage the author does not only look back on Christ's historical coming into this world for our redemption but sees his continued presence in the present dispensation of grace: Christ's redeeming actions are also effective for later periods through the sacraments and the co-operation of the Holy Spirit—a profound view of John on the relation of the sacraments and Christ's work of salvation and his continued activity in the Holy Ghost.

To many questions concerning the external aspect of baptism there is no clear answer in the New Testament; we know little about the rite except that it was an immersion. The administration of baptism with the words 'in the name of our Lord Jesus Christ' (Acts) seems to contradict the traditional trinitarian formula as given in Mt 28:19; but both versions can be found side by side in the *Didache* (7:1–3 [trinitarian formula], 9:5 'those baptised in the name of our Lord') and need not be mutually exclusive. The question of the baptism of children in the primitive church, which has been passionately discussed for the last few years among protestants, cannot be answered from the New Testament with absolute certainty. As in many other cases, the New Testament finds complementary clarification in the teaching tradition and practice of the church in the following period, but the fundamental theology of baptism in the New Testament is an inexhaustible source which can inspire theology and devotion of any time.

Bibliography: *General*. J. Coppens, 'Baptême', *DB(S)* 1, 852–924; A. Oepke, *TDNT* 1, 529–46; H. Schlier, 'Zur kirchlichen Lehre von der Taufe', *TLZ* 72 (1947), 321–36; B. Neunheuser, *Taufe und Firmung*, Freiburg 1956; J. Crehan, 'Ten Years' Work on Baptism and Confirmation', *TS* 17 (1956), 494–515; J. Duplacy, J. Giblet, Y. B. Tremel, and M. E. Boismard, *LV* 27 (1956); J. Ysebaert, *Greek Baptismal Terminology*, Nijmegen 1962. See also: H. G. Marsh, *The Origin and Significance of NT Baptism*, Manchester 1941; F. J. Leenhardt, *Le bapteme chretien, son origine, sa signification*, Neuchatel-Paris 1946; W. F. Flemington, *The NT Doctrine of Baptism*, London 1948; O. Cullman, *Baptism in the New Testament*, London 1950; J. H. Crehan, *Early Christian Baptism and the Creed*, London 1950; G. W. K. Lampe, *The Seal of the Spirit*, London 1951; M. Barth, *Die Taufe ein Sakrament?*, Zollikon-Zurich 1951; J. Schneider, *Die Taufe im NT*, Stuttgart 1952; G. Delling, *Die Zueignung des Heils in der Taufe*, Berlin 1961; G. Delling, *Die Taufe im NT*, Berlin 1963; G. R. Beasley-Murray, *Baptism in the New Testament*, London 1962.

On A. J. Thomas, *Le mouvement baptiste en Palestine et Syrie*, Gembloux 1935; O. Kuss, 'Zur Frage einer vorpaulinischen Todestaufe', *MTZ* 4 (1953), 1–17; O. Betz, 'Die Proselytentaufe der Qumran-Sekte und die Taufe im NT', *Revue de Qumran* 1 (1958/9), 123–234; J. Gnilka, 'Die essenischen Tauchbäder und die Johannestaufe', *Revue de Qumran* 3 (1961), 187–207. See also: J. Leipoldt, *Die urchristliche Taufe im Lichte der Religionsgeschichte*, Leipzig 1928; R. Reitzenstein, *Die Vorgeschichte der christlichen Taufe*, Leipzig 1929; N. A. Dahl, 'The Origin of Baptism', *Festschrift for S. Mowinckel*, Oslo 1955, 36–52.

On B. J. Gewiess, *Die urapostolische Heilsverkündigung nach der Apg.*, Breslau 1939; N. Adler, *Taufe und Handauflegung*, Münster 1951; O. Heggelbacher, *Die christl. Taufe als Rechtsakt nach dem Zeugnis der frühen Christenheit*, Fribourg 1953. See also: H. Mentz, *Taufe und Kirche in ihrem ursprüngl. Zusammenhang*, Munich 1960; D. G. Molenaar, *De doop met de Heil. Geest*, Kampen 1963.

On C. R. Schnackenburg, *Baptism in the Thought of St Paul*, Oxford 1964 (with bibliography); R. Schnackenburg, 'Todes- und Lebensgemeinschaft mit Christus—Neue Studien zu Rom 6:1–11', *MTZ* 6 (1955), 32–53; V. Warnach, 'Taufe und Christusgeschehen nach Rom 6', *ALW* 3 (1954), 284–366; V. Warnach, 'Die Tauflehre des Römer-briefes in der neueren theologischen Diskussion', *ALW* 5 (1958), 274–332; H. Schlier, *Die Taufe nach Rom 6: Die Zeit der Kirche*, Freiburg 1956, 47–56; O. Kuss, *Der Römerbrief* 1, Regensburg 1957, 307–19; V. Warnach, *Taufwirklichkeit und Taufbewusstsein im Eph*, V. Warnach, 'Taufwirklichkeit und Taufbewusstsein im Eph', *LM* 33 (1963), 49–74. See also: G. Bornkamm, *Das Ende des Gesetzes*, Munich 1961³, 34–50; G. Braumann, *Vorpaulinische christl. Taufverkündigung bei Paulus*, Stuttgart 1961; G. Wagner, *Das religionsgeschichtl. Problem von Rom 6:1–11*, Zurich 1962.

On D. J. Dey, *Palingenesia*, Münster 1937; F. M. Braun, 'Le baptême d'après le quatrième év.', *RT* 48 (1948), 358ff; I. de la Potterie, '"Naître de l'eau et naître de l'Esprit"', *SE* 14 (1962), 417–43; M. E. Boismard, 'Une Liturgie baptismale dans la Prima Petri', *RB* 63 (1956), 182–208 and 64 (1957), 161–83; M. E. Boismard, *Quatres hymnes baptismales dans la première Ep. de Pierre*, Paris 1961. See also: W. Nauck, *Die Tradition und der Charakter des 1 Jn*, Tübingen 1957.—On infant baptism: K. Barth, *The Teaching of the Church regarding Baptism*, London 1948; J. Jeremias, *Infant Baptism in the First Four Centuries*, London 1960 (with bibliography); K. Aland, *Did the Early Church Baptise Infants?*, London 1963; J. Jeremias, *Nochmals: Die Anfänge der Kindertaufe*, Munich 1962; G. R. Beasley-Murray, *Baptism in the NT*, London 1962, 306–86; *C. Davis, *The Making of a Christian*, London 1964.

Rudolf Schnackenburg

Baptism of Jesus

All three of the synoptic gospels contain accounts of the baptism of Jesus (Mk 1:9–11; Mt 3:13–17; Lk 3:21f), whereas John contains only a brief mention of the episode (1:32–34), and Acts contains a bare reference to it (10:38). A fuller apocryphal account is to be found in the Gospel of the Ebionites (preserved by Epiphanius, *Haer*. 30, 13, 7f), while a shorter one is to be found in the Gospel according to the Hebrews (in Jerome, *Commentary on Isaiah* IV, on Is 11:2). A distinction must be drawn between the baptism of Jesus itself and the theophanic episode which follows it.

A. *It can be accounted historically certain that Jesus was baptised by John the Baptist*, for already in the early church the difficulties which this episode raises were being felt. The fact that Jesus took over the 'baptism of repentance for the forgiveness of sins' (Mk 1:4) seemed difficult to reconcile with his personal sinlessness (cf the omission of the words 'For the forgiveness of sins' by Matthew). In the Gospel according to the Hebrews Jesus explicitly puts the question: 'What sin have I committed that I should go and be baptised by him?'

Moreover such a proceeding could be interpreted as implying that Jesus was subordinate to John the Baptist. In the fourth gospel the difficulties are circumvented by omitting any real account of the episode of Jesus' baptism as such. With regard to the second point of difficulty, Luke mitigates this by omitting any reference to the Baptist in his narrative, which only touches in passing on the baptism of Jesus, while Matthew achieves a similar effect by interpolating the dialogue between John and Jesus in 3:14f (elaborated upon in the Gospel of the Ebionites: 'John fell at his feet and said: I beseech thee, Lord, do thou baptise me'). We should probably regard this dialogue as representing the answer of early christian apologetics to objections which had actually been put, although this is not to rule out the fact that the saying contained in v 15 represents a genuine saying of Jesus uttered on some other occasion (Descamps). If Jesus was aware of his role as Servant of God even before his baptism, then his motive in undergoing it would have been to manifest himself as him who was to take the sins of the 'many' upon himself (Mk 10:45 and parallels; 14:24 and parallels; Jn 1:29), and to make himself one with the sinners (see Mk 2:5, 16f etc). In any case we must assume that Jesus was conscious of the fact that when he took over the rite of baptism he was fulfilling the will of God. Mk 1:9 and parallels (together with Mt 11:7–15 = Lk 7:24–8 and Mt 21:32) bears witness to the fact that Jesus recognised the Baptist as a prophet, and his baptism and preaching of repentance as coming 'from heaven' (Mk 11:30); in other words his mission constituted a fulfilment of God's will and more immediately in the concrete a preparation for his own messianic work.

B. *The motive of the synoptic writers in including an account of the baptism of Jesus at all is to be found in the ensuing theophanic scene.* All of them agree in including three phenomena in their accounts: the opening of the heavens, the descent of the Spirit, and the voice issuing from heaven. The Gospel of the Ebionites and other witnesses also refer to an illumination (on this see W. Bauer, *Leben Jesu im Zeitalter der neutestamentliche Apokryphen*, Tübingen 1909, 110–41; A. d'Alès, *SDB* 1, col 855f).

1. The opening of the heavens is primarily a prelude to the second phenomenon, but at the same time it has a significance of its own as a sign of the inauguration of the eschatological age of grace (see Is 64:1). The descent of the (Holy) Spirit in the form of a dove upon Jesus is likewise an eschatological sign (see also Jn 1:32f) by which visible expression is given to the

fact that Jesus is now equipped with the power of the Spirit (his 'anointing' by God 'with the Holy Spirit and with power', Acts 10:38) so that he can take upon himself the task imposed by God (see Judg 3:10; 6:34; 11:29; 1 Sam 10:6; 11:6). There is an unmistakable reference here to Is 11:2 ('The Spirit of the Lord shall rest upon him'; see also Jn 1:32f), and also to Is 42:1. This indicates that it is the role of the messianic servant of God that Jesus is here assuming (on the messiah as the bearer of the Spirit, see also PsSol 17:37; Enoch [Eth] 49:3; 62:2; TestLev 18:7; TestJud 24:2). The dove as a symbol of the Spirit only appears at a late date in Jewish writings (Targum on Song 2:8). But the Spirit is not infrequently compared with a dove (instances in *TDNT* vi, 67f). The original form of the message uttered by the voice from heaven is that recorded in Mark and Luke. In other words it is couched in the second person singular. The suggestion that the words 'My Son' are derived from *pais mon* in Is 42:1 is hardly tenable, for already in the Q version of the temptation narrative reference is made to the designation of Jesus as 'Son of God' *huios tou theou* in the voice from heaven at the baptism (Mt 4:3, 6; Lk 4:3, 9: 'If you are the Son of God . . .'). The words 'beloved' (=only) and 'in thee I am well pleased' refer back to the opening words of the first Servant poem (Is 42:1; see also Mt 12:18). The latter words have the force of 'I have chosen you' (see 1 Macc 10:47; Ps 151:5 LXX), that is as messianic Servant of God. Even if, in accordance with apocalyptic and rabbinical ideas, we take these words as referring to a decree of election already formulated before the world began, in their existing context they are equivalent to a directive to execute that decree by assuming the role of the messianic Servant of God. In Lk 3:22 D these words are amplified by the phrase 'today I have begotten thee'. This would have been tantamount to saying that Jesus has now been exalted to the position of Son of God. But this reading is certainly secondary, formulated with the aim of completing what was assumed to be an incomplete quotation from Ps 2:7. In reality Ps 2:7 is not being quoted here at all, and even if there were any allusion to this verse, one would have to conclude from the fact that the closing words of the verse have been omitted that the idea of adoption and initiation into sonship now taking place for the first time is quite foreign to the author's intention. 'Sonship' as predicated of Jesus here was certainly understood by the community from whom the tradition derives in the same sense as in those other passages in which Jesus speaks of himself as Son of God and of God as his Father (Mt 11:27=Lk 10:22; Mt 17:25f; Mk 13:32; see also Mt 7:21 etc). In other words it was understood, not as a messianic title, but rather as the expression of the unique personal 'Father-Son' relationship between Jesus and God. It is to this relationship that the voice from heaven refers, because it constitutes the basis for the election of Jesus and for the fact that he is entrusted with the role of messiah.

2. On the character and meaning of the theophanic scene opinions have been, and still continue to be widely

64

divided. According to the earliest account, that of Mark, it is an experience personal to Jesus himself that is in question: Mk 1:10 (=Mt 3:16): 'He [Jesus] saw . . .'; Mk 1:11 (=Lk 3:22): 'You are . . .'. It is only in the other two synoptic authors that a tendency manifests itself to give the episode the character of a formal theophany (Mt 3:17: 'This is . . .' =17:5 parallel; Lk 3:22: 'In bodily form'). According to Jn 1:32-4 the Baptist at any rate witnessed the descent of the Spirit, though admittedly here it is clearly implied that others were excluded from the vision. It is nowhere stated that he actually heard the voice from heaven. (For an appraisal of Jn 1:32-4 see A. Vögtle, 631.) Whether the experience of Jesus consisted in an objective vision and audition, as most interpreters have assumed, or in a purely interior experience, as is sometimes concluded nowadays, can hardly be determined on the basis of the narratives alone. Probably the most unforced interpretation of the theophanic scene is that which envisages a divine directive to Jesus to commence his mission as messianic Servant of God. The descent of the Spirit is not merely a sign that this eschatological role has been laid upon him, but at the same time a sign that he is equipped for that role (Acts 10:38; Mk 1:8 and parallels; 1:12 and parallels; Lk 4:14, 18; 10:21; Mt 12:18, 28). The divine utterance solemnly recognises Jesus and confirms him in his role, just as Jesus himself has declared his submission to God's will by his gesture in undergoing baptism. The words uttered by God constitute an acknowledgment of Jesus as his Son, and characterise his status as Son as the basis of his election for the role of messianic Servant of God. Hence the solemn 'You are my Son' instead of the mere form of address 'My Son' (see, for instance, Mt 21:28). It has sometimes been suggested that it was not until this point that Jesus became aware either of his status as Son of God or of his messianic mission. But there are no real grounds for supposing this. This interpretation, and probably every other one which, like it, is based on the assumption that the account of the baptismal theophany is historical, is fraught with difficulties. For this reason the question has recently been raised of whether this account does not simply have the purpose of conveying to the early christian hearer or reader of the gospel in clear and vivid terms 'Who and what Jesus really is despite the fact that he was baptised by John and therefore seemed to be subordinate to him' (Vögtle, 664f). Another theory is that this account constitutes a mere didactic poem, the author of which has taken as his model Is 63:7-19 and/or TestJud 24 or TestLevi 18 (see Maurer, *TWNT* VII, 962 A. 17). But this theory too does not provide any convincing basis for our understanding of the account, although it is evident that numerous parallel motifs are to be found in these passages (Is 64:1; the dividing of the heavens; v 8, the voice of God and the acknowledging of his sons; vv 11, 14, the promise of the Spirit. TestJud 24:2: 'The heavens open over him and pour down the Spirit, the holy blessing of the Father'; v 4: 'This is the shoot of the most high God' [this verse, however, is probably a gloss]; TestLevi 18:6: 'The heavens open and holiness descends upon him from the shrine of glory, together with the voice of the Father like that of Abraham to Isaac'; v 7: 'The glory of the Most High is surely promised to him, and a Spirit of understanding will rest upon him, as also the Spirit of holiness [in the water]'; v 11: 'Then the Spirit of holiness rests upon them'; v 13: 'The Lord rejoices in his children, and has been well pleased in his loved ones for ever').

Bibliography: J. Kosnetter, *Die Taufe Jesu*, Vienna 1936 (with bibliography); J. Dupont, '"Filius meus es tu": l'interprétation de Ps. II, 7 dans le N.T.', *RSR* 35 (1948), 522–43; W. F. Flemington, *The NT Doctrine of Baptism*, London 1948; C. K. Barrett, *The Holy Spirit and the Gospel Tradition*, London 1948; H. Sahlin, *Studien zum dritten Kapitel des Lk-Ev*, Uppsala 1949; J. Dupont, 'Jésus, Messie et Seigneur dans la foi des premiers chrétiens', *VS* 83 (1950), 385–416; A. Descamps, *Les justes et la justice dans les évangiles*, Louvain 1950; G. W. H. Lampe, *The Seal of the Spirit*, London 1951; J. Bieneck, *Sohn Gottes als Christusbezeichnung des Synoptiker*, Zurich 1951; A. Robert, 'Considérations sur le Messianisme du Ps. II', *RSR* 39 (1951/2), 88–98; J. Schneider, *Die Taufe im NT*, Berlin 1952; J. A. T. Robinson, 'The Baptism as a Category of NT Soteriology', *SJT* 6 (1953), 257–74; V. Subilia, *Gésu nella più antica tradizione cristiana*, Torre Pellice 1954; C. E. B. Cranfield, 'The Baptism of our Lord', *SJT* 8 (1955), 53–63; M. E. Boismard, 'La révélation de l'Ésprit Saint', *RT* 63 (1955), 5–21; M. Dutheil, 'Le baptême de Jésus', *Stud. Bibl. Franc. Liver Annuus* 6 (1955/6), 85–124; M. E. Boismard, *Du baptême à Cana*, Paris 1956; J. M. Robinson, *The Problem of History in Mark*, London, 1962; M. Karnetzki, 'Textgeschichte als Überlieferungsgeschichte', *ZNW* 47 (1956), 170–80; E. E. Fabbri, 'El bautismo de Jesús en el Evangelio de los Hebreos y en el de los Ebionites', *Rev. de Teologia* 22 (La Plata 1956), 36–56; I. Buse, 'The Markan Account of the Baptism of Jesus and Is. LXIII', *JTS* 7 (1956), 74f; H. Bouman, 'The Baptism of Christ with Special Reference to the Gift of the Spirit', *Concordia Theol. Monthly* 28 (1957), 1–14; J. E. Menard, '"Pais Theou" as Messianic Title in the Book of Acts', *CBQ* 19 (1957), 83–92; F. Gils, *Jésus prophète d'après les évangiles synoptiques*, Louvain, 1957; Cullmann, *The Christology of the New Testament*, London 1959; J. A. T. Robinson, 'The Baptism of John and the Qumran Community', *HTR* 50 (1957), 183–87; G. W. H. Lampe, 'The Holy Spirit in the Writings of St Luke', *Studies in the Gospels (Essays in Memory of R. H. Lightfoot)*, ed. D. E. Nineham, Oxford 1957, 159–200; I. de la Potterie, 'L'onction du Christ', *NRT* 80 (1958), 225–52; M. A. Chevallier, *L'Ésprit et le Messie dans le Bas-Judaïsme et le NT*, Paris 1958; A. Feuillet, 'Le symbolisme de la colombe dans les récits évangéliques du Baptême', *RSR* 32 (1958), 524–44; A. Feuillet, 'Le baptême de Jésus d'après l'évangile selon Saint Marc', *CBQ* 21 (1959), 468–90; M. Smith, '"God's Begetting the Messiah" in 1 QSa', *NTS* 5 (1959), 218–24; J. Lamarié, 'Le baptême du Seigneur dans le Jourdain d'après les textes scripturaires en usage dans les églises', *MD* 59 (1959), 85–102; G. H. P. Thompson, 'Called-Proved-Obedient: a Study in the Baptism and Temptation Narratives of Mt and Lk', *JTS* 11 (1960), 1–12; J. Knackstedt, 'Manifestatio SS. Trinitatis in Baptismo Domini?', *VD* 38 (1960), 76–91; A. Nisin, *Histoire de Jésus*, Paris 1960; E. Lövestam, *Son and Saviour*, Lund/Copenhagen 1961; R. Siebeneck, 'The Dove as Epiphany', *Worship* 35 (1961), 97–102; J. Dutheil, *Le baptême de Jésus au Jourdain* Strasbourg 1961 (dissertation); A. Legault, 'Le baptême de Jésus et la doctrine du Serviteur souffrant', *SE* 12 (1961), 160–6; B. M. F. van Iersel, '*Der Sohn*' in den synopt. *Jesusworten*, Leiden 1961; T. de Kruijf, *Der Sohn des Lebendigen Gottes*, Rome 1962; H. Braun, 'Entscheidende Motive in den Berichten über die Taufe Jesu von Mk bis Justin', *Gesamm. Studien zum NT und seiner Umwelt*, Tübingen 1962, 168–72; M. Sabbe, 'Het verhaal va n Jezus' doopsel', *Coll. Brug. et Gand.* 8 (1962), 456–74, 9 (1963), 211–30, 333–65; J. H. Eybers, 'Die doop van Johannes die Doper', *Nederduitse Geref. Teol. Tydskrif* 4 (1963), 184–92; M. E. Boismard, 'Les traditions johanniques concernant le baptiste', *RB* 70 (1963), 5–42; F. Hahn, *Christologische Hoheitstitel*, Göttingen 1963; O. Kuss, 'Zur vorpaulin. Tauflehre im NT', *Auslegung und Verkündigung* I, Regensburg 1963, 98–120; A. Vögtle, 'Exegetische Erwägungen über das Wissen und Selbstbewusstsein Jesu', *Gott in Welt (Festg. K. Rahner)*, Freiburg i. Br. 1964, 608–67; C. H. Lindijer, 'Jezus' doop in de Jordan', *TT* 18 (1963/4), 177–92; A. Feuillet, 'Le Baptême de Jésus', *RB* 71 (1964), 321–52.

Josef Blinzler

Binding and loosing

Besides 'to bind' (*deō*) in its literal sense ('bind', 'bind together', 'fetter') there is also a figurative sense which refers to the marriage bond (Rom 7:2; 1 Cor 7:27, 39) and to a supernatural bond (with Satan, Luke 13:16; Satan being 'bound', Rev 20:2).

'To loose' (*luō*) in its figurative sense, either with or without the analogy of the demolition of a building (Jn 2:19; Eph 2:14), denotes the abrogation of a law, a repeal (Mt 5:19; Jn 7:23; 10:35; Jn 5:18 with reference to the Sabbath).

'To bind' and 'to loose' are the usual translations of the Hebrew *ᵓāsar* and *pittah* respectively, or the Aramaic *asar* and *sera*, as used by the rabbis; here they mean 'to declare a thing either forbidden or licit by means of a scholastic pronouncement, removal or imposition of an obligation'. Occasionally these two words refer to the infliction or removal of a ban. It is not certain whether Mt 16:19 and 18:18 use these words in one of these two meanings (a third meaning, based on Greek and rabbinical parallels, 'a binding and loosing by means of magic', certainly need not be considered). There exists in the semitic languages— and also in others—the peculiarity of expressing a totality by means of two contrary concepts (as heaven and hell, old and young, great and small, good and evil, etc). One must go to the context in order to know what the totality is which is so expressed. Peter is given the power of the keys (Mt 16:19) and this without restriction, as a totality! It appears from the change from singular to plural that Mt 18:18 is an addition to the original text which makes an exact interpretation rather difficult. The most obvious one, in view of the context as we have it, would be the above-mentioned *power of admitting into and excluding from the community which is the church in a way valid in the eyes of God*. This interpretation is generally accepted in defining the powers given to Peter (Mt 16:19).

Bibliography: SB I, 738–47; F. Büchsel, *TDNT* II, 60–61; IV, 335–7; G. Lambert, 'Lier—Délier', *Vivre et Penser* 3 (1943/4), 91–103; see also for expression by contraries: A. M. Honeyman, *JBL* 71 (1952), 11–18; P. Boccaccio, *Bbl* 33 (1952), 173–90; A. Massart, *Mélanges Robert*, Paris (1957), 38–46; O. Michel, *RAC* II, 374–80; C. H. Dodd, *NTS* 2 (1955/6), 85f; A. Vögtle, *LTK* II (1958²), 480–2.

Johannes B. Bauer

Blasphemy

A. *Terminology.* There are several terms in Hebrew for 'slander': *gādap*, *nāᵓats* (in Piel), *ḥārap*, *lāᶜag*, *qillēl* (in Piel), *qābab*, *nāqab*. The object of these verbs can be either men or God. In LXX and the New Testament the corresponding terms are *oneidizein*, *paroxunein*, and *blasphēmein*; this last has only God, persons chosen by God, or holy things or institutions for object.

B. *Old Testament.* 1. In the Old Testament blasphemy is a contempt of, an insulting of God or his name. (↗ Curse.) He blasphemes against God who makes use of the name of God for evil ends (magic, unlawful cursing of his fellow-men; Ex 20:7; Deut 5:11); who, being one of God's chosen (king or priest) commits a transgression, thus bringing his sacred office into discredit

(1 Sam 3:13; 2 Sam 12:14); who opposes one of God's chosen (Num 16:30); who breaks the covenant with Yahweh (Deut 31:20; Is 1:4); who despises the word of God (Jer 23:17) or doubts of the power of Yahweh to punish (Is 5:24) or to help (Num 14:11, 23; 20:10, 12). Job, stricken with suffering, is expected by Satan and by his own wife to 'curse God to his face' (in the Hebrew we find the euphemism 'to bless God to his face')— meaning, to doubt his help and thus to blaspheme against him. (Job 1:11; 2:5, 9.) The worst form of blasphemy is when a man, by comparing him with the mighty gods of the heathens, represents the God of Israel as a pitiable, helpless figure from whom nothing can be expected. (2 Kings 18:30–35; 19:4, 6, 22; 2 Chron 32:13ff; Is 10:8–11; 36:18ff; 37:10–13; Judith 6:1–4; probably also Lev 24:11, 14f, 23.) But also anyone who mocks at or opposes Israel as Yahweh's own people blasphemes against God. (Is 52:5; Ezek 35:12f; 1 Macc 2:6; 2 Macc 8:4; 10:34; 12:14; 15:24.) In general, the heathens are considered as blasphemers (2 Macc 10:4).

2. Blasphemy is a transgression which deserves death, and is punished either by human judges (Lev 24:10–16; 1 Kings 21:13) or by God himself with the most severe penalties (burning, extermination) (see Ex 20:7; Num 16:30; Deut 5:11; 1 Sam 4:11; 2 Kings 19:7; 2 Chron 32:21; Is 37:36ff; 2 Macc 9:4, 12, 28).

3. Though the self-righteous friends of Job consider objections against God as blasphemy (Job 15:2–6; 34:35ff), in fact God reacts against the at times daring reproaches of the just against

him in a strikingly mild way or even does not object at all (eg, Ex 5:22; Num 11:11ff; Josh 7:7; Is 38:13; Jer 12:1–5; 15:16–21; 20:7–10; Lam 3:10f; Job 9:12–20; 19:6–21; 30:18–23; 38:2; 40:2, 8). In these cases, there is no question of what the Old Testament means by blasphemy, that is, there is no 'making small' of Yahweh, no mockery. Quite the contrary: God appears here to these just men tried by suffering as incomparably mighty, as the Lord who rules with absolute freedom, whom man cannot call to account.

C. *New Testament.* 1. The Jews in Jesus' day, in accordance with the Old Testament, regarded as blasphemers those who claimed rights and powers which can be ascribed to God only (see SB I, 1007–19); in particular, the power to forgive sins (Mt 9:3; Mk 2:7; Lk 5:21; Jn 5:18f; 10:33–36). It was on this score that Jesus was accused of blasphemy (Mt 26:64ff; Mk 14:62ff).

2. The New Testament considers as blasphemy words and ways of acting which injure the holiness, majesty and honour of God. These can be directed either immediately against God (Acts 6:11; Rev 13:6; 16:11, 21), against his name (Rom 2:24; 1 Tim 6:1; Rev 16:9), his word (Tit 2:5), his law (Acts 6:11) or his angels (2 Pet 2:10ff; cf Jude 8–10).

3. They also commit blasphemy who deride Jesus' claim to messianic status and divine sonship (Mt 27:39; Mk 15:29; Lk 22:64f; 23:39). He also is guilty of blasphemy who falls away from his faith (Acts 26:11; 1 Tim 1:20) and spreads erroneous teaching (Rom 3:8; 2 Pet 2:2). The whole emergence of the apocalyptic enemies of God who

oppose him is one great blasphemy (Rev 13:1, 5f; 17:3, 5f). But christians also, through lack of charity and by leading a bad life, can be the occasions of others blaspheming (Rom 2:24; 1 Tim 6:1; Tit 2:5; Jas 2:7).

4. Just as the Jews and heathens have blasphemed against Christ, so will they against the disciples of Christ; therefore, it is the lot of the Church and its members to be the object of blasphemous talk (1 Cor 4:13; 1 Pet 4:4, 14; Rev 2:9). It is blasphemy when the Jews mock at and oppose Paul and his teaching (Acts 13:45; 18:6); Paul himself had been at one time a blasphemer, when he persecuted the christians (1 Tim 1:13). Even christians themselves can be guilty of 'blasphemy' when they hate and are angry with one another (Mt 15:19; Mk 7:22; Eph 4:31; Col 3:8; 1 Tim 6:4; 2 Tim 3:2; Tit 3:2).

5. According to Mt 12:31f; Mk 3:28f; Lk 12:10, any blasphemy can be forgiven except 'blasphemy against the Holy Spirit'. The exact meaning of this expression is disputed. Perhaps we should understand it this way: to blaspheme against the Holy Spirit means, maliciously and against one's better judgement, to ascribe the miracles of Jesus worked through the power of the Holy Spirit to the devil (Mt 12:24–28; Lk 11:19f); an attitude of this kind reveals a hardness and blindness of heart which stands in the way of conversion, which is a necessary condition for forgiveness.

Bibliography: H. W. Beyer, *TDNT* 1, 621–5; SB 1, 1006–20; J. Blinzler, *LTK* iv², 1117ff; J. Blinzler, *Der Prozess Jesu*, Regensburg 1960³, 108–15 and 129–37; J. Scharbert, '"Fluchen" und "Segnen" im AT', *Bbl* 39 (1958), 1–26

(esp. 8f and 13f); S. H. Blank, 'Men against God', *JBL* 72 (1953), 1–13; S. H. Blank, 'The Curse, the Blasphemy, the Spell, and the Oath', *HUCA* 23 (1950/1), 73–95.

Josef Scharbert

Blessing

A. *Terminology.* The Hebrew root *bārak* with its verbal and substantival formations has a far wider meaning than the English 'blessing'. The Arabic *baraka* is the innate gift of good fortune which some people have, which enables them to be successful in every enterprise, and which they can pass on to others; but it also stands for fertility, abundance, wealth of camels, water which is so longed for in the desert. Also in the Old Testament we can detect a connection between *bārak* and fertility of human beings, animals, and the fields. (See Gen 1:22, 28; 9:1; 12:2; 22:17; 24:60; 49:25; Ex 23:25ff; Deut 7:13f; 28:3ff; Ezek 34:26; Ps 84:4; 107:38; Prov 5:18.)

In Piel, *barak* means the opposite of *qillēl* (see↗ Curse A), therefore 'to praise someone as great, successful, mighty, happy'; when the king is the object, 'to honour' or the like (Gen 47:7–10; 2 Sam 14:22; 1 Kings 1:47); when it is God or his name, 'to praise' (Gen 24:48; Deut 8:10; Judges 5:2–9; Neh 8:6; 9:5; very often in the Psalms; the passive participle *bārūk* means therefore 'praised', Gen 9:26; 14:20; 24:27; Ps 41:13; 89:52; etc); when it is any person of merit 'to praise (with thanks)' or the like (Deut 24:13; Judg 5:24; Ruth 2:19f; 2 Sam 2:5; Neh 11:2; Job 31:20; Ps 72:15; Prov 10:7). When it is a question of one who has won a battle, *b'rākāh* refers to the recognition of his might and claims (2 Kings 18:31; Is 36:16). The godless, of course, do not bless their wickedness, but 'boast' of it (Deut 29:19; Ps 10:3; 49:6; Is 66:3).

As with a ⟋ curse, so with a blessing people were convinced that it really brought about the good fortune of which it spoke. This explains why in Babylonian 'blessing' is simply called 'the good word'. With such a 'good word' Ps 45:2 addresses the royal bride and bridegroom convinced that the effect will follow. Whence the real meaning of *bārak* (in Piel) is 'to address a good word to someone' or, at times, 'to speak well of someone'. It thus acquires the meaning of 'to wish well', 'to bless'. Good wishes, which imply at the same time blessing, are addressed to the king when he ascends the throne (1 Kings 1:47), to a friendly ruler on the occasion of a victory (2 Sam 8:10; 1 Chron 18:10), to the owner of a flock on the occasion of sheep-shearing (1 Sam 25:5f; 2 Sam 13:23-5), to newly-weds (Gen 24:60; Ruth 4:11f; Tob 8:17; 11:16f), to one who is departing before beginning his journey (Gen 28:1; 31:55; Tob 5:16). Since in Israel every greeting was a form of blessing, however, *bārak* in Piel can mean also simply 'to greet' (1 Sam 13:10; 2 Kings 4:29; 10:15; Ps 129:8). A present which is given on such an occasion is called *b'rākāh*, namely, a 'blessing' in visible form; we might say 'a greetings present' (Gen 33:11; 1 Sam 25:27; 30:26), a 'wedding present' (Josh 15:19; Judg 1:15), an honorarium (2 Kings 5:15). The meaning 'to bless', 'blessing' occurs particularly when it is a question of fathers blessing their sons, priests blessing those taking part in the service and the promises of God in favour of mankind (see B below). In the ritual instructions of Num 6:22–27; Deut 11:26–30 it is a question of well-established liturgical formulae.

There are certain turns of phrase the meaning of which is not at once apparent: *bārak* in Piel with *b'* referring to things means evidently 'to bless with goods' or the like (Gen 24:1; Deut 16:15; 23:20; 24:19; Ps 29:11)— which, however, is precisely the same as the granting of the goods in question. When used in Piel, Niphal, or Hithpael with *b'* referring to persons the meaning is very disputed. Gen 48:20 could give us a clue to the meaning: when other people pronounce a blessing they will say 'God make you as Ephraim and as Manasseh!' Gen 12:3; 18:18; 22:18; 26:4; 28:14 could be made to give a similar meaning, namely, 'to bless one-self with reference to the happiness of a certain person'. We must give the same meaning to the phrase 'to be a blessing', 'to be made a blessing', that is, the person named is a blessing insofar as his happiness, good estate, has become proverbial, and as such is mentioned in wishing a blessing when another person desires for the one to be blessed a similar great happiness (Gen 12:2; Is 19:24; Ezek 34:26; Zech 8:13; Ps 37:26). Many commentators prefer to translate *bārak* in Niphal or Hithpael when followed by *b'* referring to persons as 'to be blessed by means of a certain person', but this interpretation hardly corresponds to the Old Testament way of thinking. As far as the sense is concerned, this meaning is in any case contained in the interpretation given above; the naming of the person in question implies an avowal to him, a recognition of his happiness as God-given, and—since the pronouncing of a blessing was regarded as efficacious —the blessing comes about indirectly through the person named. Finally, the combination Piel with *b'* referring to God means 'to bless with the invocation of God's name' (Ps 129:8; Is 65:16).

Corresponding to the Hebrew *barak* in LXX and the New Testament we usually find the Greek *eulogein* (=to bless) and *eulogia* (=a blessing), with much the same meanings.

B. *Blessing in the Old Testament.* Both blessing and⁄ curse are forces which bring about what the words signify. One possesses a blessing (Gen 27:38), but it can be taken away (Gen 27:35f). One can be 'filled with' a blessing (Deut 33:23); a blessing can be 'set before' a person (Deut 11:26; 30:19), can be 'on a house' (Ezek 44:30) or 'laid on a place' (Deut 11:29) or can be 'poured out' (Is 44:3). The power of the blessing is transferred through the laying on of hands (Gen 48:14–17) or pronunciation of the formula of blessing (Gen 27:27ff; 49:28) to the one to be blessed. The blessing of the pious man benefits the town where he lives (Prov 11:11) and 'establishes its roots' (Sir 3:9). The blessing, once pronounced, releases a force which is no longer under the control of the one who has said it (Gen 27:33–5; see Num 22:6).

The source of all blessings in the Old Testament is always God himself even if he is not actually mentioned. God 'puts forth his blessing' (Lev 25:21; Deut 28:8; Ps 133:3); he blesses his creatures (Gen 1:22), the first human

beings (Gen 1:28; 5:2; 9:1), the patriarchs and their wives (Gen 12:2; 17:16; 22:17; 24:1, 34f; 25:11; 26:12– 24; 35:9; 48:3; Is 51:2), that they may be fruitful and multiply. Yahweh also blesses individuals who play a part in salvation history (Judg 13:24; 2 Sam 6:11f; 1 Chron 26:5) and the pious in general (Ps 5:12; 67:1; 115:13; 134:3; Is 61:9; Jer 17:7) together with their children and their 'house', namely, their whole offspring (Gen 17:20; Deut 7:13; 2 Sam 6:11; 7:29; Ps 112:2; 147:13; see also Ps 128:2ff). The object of the divine blessing is, in the first place, the people of Israel, as long as they keep the covenant with Yahweh (Ex 20:24; Deut 2:7; 7:13; 14:24, 29; 15:4–18; 16:10; 26:15; 30:16; 2 Chron 31:10; Ps 28:9; 29:11; 115:12). In the messianic age, however, the heathens too would receive a blessing from Yahweh (Is 19:25). The man who is chosen to serve Yahweh in a special capacity or on whom he showers his special gifts of good fortune is called 'blessed of Yahweh' (Gen 14:19; 24:31; 26:29; Judg 17:2; 1 Sam 15:13; 23:21; 2 Sam 2:5; Ruth 2:20; 3:10; Ps 115:15; Is 65:23).

Not just persons but things too can be the object of the divine blessing insofar as they belong to people who are worthy of a blessing. Thus fields (Gen 27:27; Jer 31:23; Ps 65:10), the produce of labour and the undertakings of the pious (Deut 28:12; 33:11; Job 1:10), food (Ex 23:25), 'the fruit of the womb and of the ground' (Deut 7:13), and, in general, all the possessions of the pious man (Ex 23:25; Deut 28:3–6; Prov 3:33).

From the point of view of theology and the history of salvation, it is particularly significant that Yahweh will bless all those who unite in friendship with his friends and chosen ones and give proof of their solidarity with them (Gen 12:3; Num 24:9). He who gives a friend of Yahweh hospitality will meet with his blessing. (Gen 30:27–30; 39:5.) Those who are blessed by Yahweh cannot be harmed by the curse of man. (Ps 109:28.)

God also dispenses his blessing through the medium of man. Certain men, in a particular way, receive a call to bestow blessing and are given power to do so. Such a blessing which is spoken by or mediated through a man will be all the more powerful in proportion as the one blessing has a closer relation to Yahweh, for which the fact of belonging to Israel is not an indispensable prerequisite. Thus Yahweh orders the heathen seer Balaam to bless Israel, although he had in fact been called on by his human overlord to curse her (Num 22–4). According to the Old Testament view, not everyone is *ipso facto* able to bless—if we prescind from the greeting which is, in point of fact, also a form of blessing (see above, under A). In the Old Testament, people who enjoy special authority pronounce a blessing in the real sense of the word: the patriarchs over their sons and descendants (Gen 9:26f; 27:23–9; 48:9–20; 49); fathers over their children (Sir 3:9); the great mediators of the covenant—Moses, Aaron, Joshua—over the people (Ex 39:43; Lev 9:23; Deut 33; Josh 14:13; 22:7). Also in liturgy the giving of blessing is the duty of particular persons. Thus, the king blesses the people at the dedication of the Temple or at the conclusion of a liturgical

reform (2 Sam 6:18; 1 Kings 8:14, 55f; 1 Chron 16:2; 2 Chron 6:3). The priests bless individual people who come to the sanctuary with their particular petitions (1 Sam 2:20; cf also Gen 14:19), pilgrims just arrived or about to depart (Ps 118:26; 134:3), the whole people gathered together for a liturgical celebration (Lev 9:22; 2 Chron 30:27). A particularly festive blessing is that reserved to the priests alone and called 'the blessing of Aaron' (Num 6:23–6). According to Deut 21:5 (see also 1 Chron 23:13) it would appear that only the priests are able to bless, but in Deut 10:8 the Levites may too. Only in a very special case do the people, gathered together as a unity, bless the king after the latter has blessed them (1 Kings 8:66). According to Ex 12:32, the Pharaoh asks Moses and Aaron for a blessing when they carry out their liturgical celebration in the wilderness which they were planning to do, but this is certainly not to be conceived of as a blessing which the people will pronounce but a prayer of intercession; apart from this case the Old Testament is familiar with sacrifices and prayers for the high kings of the heathens (Ezra 6:10). Whereas we today are familiar with liturgical blessings of devotional objects, cattle, houses, and other things, it does not appear that Israelite liturgy used blessings for things. Only in 1 Sam 9:13 do we find the isolated case of Samuel blessing the sacrificial victim.

As with the curse on the breakers of the law, so the blessing on those who observe it was the sanction of the great legal corpora (Lev 26; Deut 28). On the occasion of covenant renewal the Levites pronounced curse and blessing formulae and the assembled people confirmed them by their 'Amen' (Deut 11:26–30; 27:12–26; Josh 8:33). Curse and blessing were two juxtaposed powers laid upon the whole land and brought into effect in accordance with the people's attitude to the covenant of Yahweh.

The fact that *barak* in Piel often has God for its object has led many exegetes to the . conclusion, on the grounds of parallels taken from the history of religions among primitive peoples, that Yahweh also could be blessed. This blessing would have the purpose of increasing the power, might, and happiness of God. This interpretation, however, is certainly false since *barak* (Piel) here means nothing more than 'to glorify', 'to praise' or the like (see above, under A). A case which requires a similar interpretation would be '. . . who do not bless their mothers' parallel with '. . . who curse their fathers' (Prov 30:11), where *barak* (Piel) is used over against all (Piel), since in no other case do subordinates pronounce a real blessing over people in authority, or children over their parents; and so here it is not a case of a blessing on the mother but only of speaking respectfully of her.

Even if the unusual constructions with Niphal and Hithpael as well as the phrase 'to be a blessing' are interpreted differently, as we have already noticed under A, the texts in question still tell us that the patriarchs and their 'seed' (Gen 12:2f; 18:18; 22:18; 26:4; 28:14), meaning the whole people of Israel (Jer 4:2; Zech 8:13) and even, in the messianic age, the converted heathen nations of Assyria and Egypt together with Israel (Is 19:24), and

finally the Messiah as representative of the messianic people of God (Ps 72:17), will be the means of blessing for all peoples and races. This is to be understood in the sense that they will induce all nations, by means of the gift of salvation which Yahweh has given them, to acknowledge them and their God and to desire this same gift for themselves.

The net result of all this is that blessing in the Old Testament has nothing to do with magic. It is always either a petition addressed to Yahweh or an avowal to those chosen by Yahweh or a decision arrived at by Yahweh himself. It has its effect only when the person in question, in whose benefit the blessing is pronounced, is worthy of it by reason of his fidelity to God and his law or when, in spite of his unworthiness, Yahweh grants him a blessing purely out of his grace. As with a curse, a blessing is not irrevocable; for even if man cannot take it back (Gen 27:33, 35; Num 22:6) God can render it null and void; he can change a blessing into a curse (Mal 2:2; see also 1 Sam 2:30).

C. *Blessing in the New Testament.* In the Jewish temple liturgy at the time of Christ the officiating priests pronounced the blessing of Aaron (Num 6:22ff) at the daily morning service. This blessing was also in use in the synagogues and was there likewise reserved to the priests. Apart from this, the rabbinical writings know of the blessing of children by those learned in the law (Sopherim 18:5), of pupils by their teachers (Ber 28b, Meg 28a), of children by their fathers (GnR 16d ad Gen 26; *Siddur Sephat Emet*, ed. Rodelsheim, 1886, 44). The tractate Berakoth in the Mishna,

Tosefta, and the Talmud regulate the various blessing formulae in which it is a question of the praise of God. In Qumran, blessings as well as curses play a part in the covenant renewal and the ceremony of admission (1 QS II, 1–4). In the text 1 Q 28b there is contained a whole ritual for a blessing on the faithful, on the high-priest, on other priests, and on the head of the community.

The New Testament takes over, for the most part, the Old Testament and Jewish views on blessing as well as the practice. The Epistle to the Hebrews mentions the blessing of Melchizedek on Abraham (7:6f) and that of Isaac on Jacob (11:20; cf 12:17); these blessings were fulfilled because those blessed trusted in the divine promises. According to Gal 3:8f (cf Heb 6:14) faith is a necessary condition for the blessing of Abraham to be fulfilled in regard to those who believe, and this irrespective of descent by blood. Thoroughly in accord with the Old Testament where, as a rule, the formal blessing belongs to those who exercise authority over others, the author of the Epistle to the Hebrews deduces the superiority of Melchizedek over Levi, who was as yet 'in Abraham's loins', from the fact that Melchizedek blessed Abraham and not vice versa, since 'it is beyond dispute that the inferior is blessed by the superior' (Heb 7:6f).

Jesus blesses children as do those learned in the law (Mk 10:16); he also blesses his disciples (Lk 24:50). Peter sums up the mission of Jesus in the words: God has sent his son 'to bless you' (Acts 3:26). In contrast, however, to the old law, where the blessing had for its object material goods, the blessing which goes out from Jesus is a *eulogia pneumatikē* (='spiritual blessing', Eph 1:3) which will be fully realised only when the Lord at his second coming will say to his faithful: 'Come O blessed of my Father, inherit the kingdom prepared for you from the foundation of the world' (Mt 25:34).

Natural man curses as easily as he blesses (Jas 3:9f); but the supernatural man, the christian who has been called to inherit a blessing, does not curse but blesses only (1 Pet 3:9). Jesus demands from his disciples: 'Bless those who curse you' (Lk 6:28). Paul demands the same from those to whom he writes (Rom 12:14) and himself acts accordingly (1 Cor 4:12).

In the New Testament the following only are mentioned as 'blessed'= *eulogēmenoi*: the Messiah (Mt 21:9; 23:39; Mk 11:9; Lk 13:35; 19:38; Jn 12:13); his kingdom (Mk 11:10); his mother (Lk 1:42); and his redeemed disciples, when he welcomes them into the kingdom of his Father (Mt 25:34).

Whereas in LXX there are men who are called *eulogētoi* (eg, Gen 12:2; 26:29; Judg 17:2), in the New Testament *eulogētos* refers only to God (Mk 14:61; Lk 1:68; Rom 1:25; 9:5; 2 Cor 1:3; 11:31; Eph 1:3; 1 Pet 1:3).

In connection with meals *eulogein* or *eulogia*, in accordance with Jewish usage, do not mean 'to bless', 'a blessing', but rather refers to the prayer said at table in which thanksgiving and praise is offered to God (Mk 6:41; 8:7; 14:22; Mt 26:26). Only in 1 Cor 10:16 do we hear of 'the cup of blessing which we bless' in connection with the eucharist. Here the praise and thanksgiving concern the eucharistic meal itself as the pledge of our fellowship with Christ.

Bibliography: B. Landsberger, 'Das "gute Wort"', *MAOG* 4 (1929), 294–321; F. Horst, 'Segen und Segenshandlungen in der Bibel', *ET* (1947), 23–37; H. Junker, 'Segen als heilsgeschichtliches Motivwort', *SP* I (Gembloux 1959), 548–58; A. Murtonen, 'The Use and Meaning of the Words *lebarek* and *berakah* in the OT', *VT* 9 (1959), 158–77 and 330; T. Schäfer, 'Eucharistia', *BM* 36 (1960), 251–8; S. H. Blank, 'Some Observations concerning Biblical Prayer', *HUCA* 32 (1961), 75–90; E. J. Bickerman, 'Bénédiction et prière', *RB* 69 (1962), 524–32; J. Schreiner, 'Segen für die Völker', *BZ* 6 (1962), 1–31; H. W. Beyer, *TDNT* II, 754–65.↗ Curse.

Josef Scharbert

Blood

A. *Terminology*. The Hebrew term for 'blood' is *dām* in the Old Testament; in the plural it refers to a deed of blood or blood-guilt. An *'is dāmîm* is a man who has burdened himself with blood-guilt on account of having committed a murder or been guilty of some other transgression punishable by death. The *gō'ēl haddām* is the blood-avenger (Num 35:19, 21, 24f; Deut 19:6, 12; Josh 20:3, 5, 9; 2 Sam 14:11). LXX translates *dam* by *haima*, but also uses *phonos* (=murder, bloodshed) when it is a question of blood-guilt (Ex 22:3; Deut 22:8; etc); *aitia phonou* (=cause of bloodshed, Prov 28:17) and other expressions are also found. The 'man of blood' is *anēr haimatōn metokhos* (Prov 29:10).

The Israelites, in common with neighbouring peoples, regarded blood as the bearer of life (Lev 17:11) even to the extent of identifying the two (Gen 9:5; Lev 17:14; Deut 12:23).

'To shed blood' and 'to seek after a person's blood' meant the same as to take someone's life or to seek after someone's life respectively (Lev 19:16; Deut 27:25; Prov 1:16; Sir 11:32; Acts 22:20; Rom 3:15). David refused to drink the blood of his heroes, namely, he refused to drink the water which they had obtained at the risk of their lives (2 Sam 23:17). According to Lk 22:44 great fear can force blood with sweat out of the pores.

Only in the hellenistic period does 'blood' together with 'flesh' become a plastic expression for all that is transitory and mortal (Sir 14:18; 17:31; Enoch 14:4; for rabbinical usage see SB I, 730f). In the New Testament 'flesh and blood' is synonymous with the material and natural element in man in contrast with the supernatural (Mt 16:17; Jn 1:13; 1 Cor 15:50 etc). The Hebrew language has no term corresponding to 'blood-relationship', but expresses this idea by the phrase 'to be one bone and one flesh', etc (Gen 29:14; Judg 9:2; 2 Sam 5:1). Blood is used for the first time to express relationship in Judith 9:4. According to Wis 7:2 life in the maternal womb comes about through the semen causing the mother's blood to clot, but Jn 1:13 implies that the blood of the father mixes with that of the mother. The idea that the blood of the father of the race flows on through his descendents is testified only in some important manuscript readings of Acts 17:26, but elsewhere in this kind of context it is always a question of semen.

B. *Human blood in biblical theology*. Since life is located in the blood according to the Israelite view, or even is regarded as identical with it and both as the property of God alone, God protects human life insofar as he forbids the shedding of innocent blood (Gen 9:6). God defends the life of the just since 'precious is their blood in his sight' (Ps 72:14). He who sheds innocent blood encroaches on God's supreme rights and is therefore guilty of a monstrous crime especially should it happen in the precincts of the sanctuary (Gen 37:22; 2 Sam 12:5–12; 1 Macc 1:37; 7:17; 2 Macc 1:8; Mt 23:30, 35; 27:4). This crime can be expiated only with the blood of the murderer (Gen 9:5f; Ex 21:12, 23; Lev 24:17, 21; Num 35:19ff; Deut 19:11ff). The blood of a murdered person 'cries' for vengeance (Gen 4:10; 2 Macc 8:3; Rev 6:10; see also Heb 12:24), especially when it has not been covered up with earth (Is 26:21; Ezek 24:7f; Job 16:18). The murderer is 'a man of blood' (2 Sam 16:7f; Ps 5:6; 26:9; 55:23); he is defiled with blood (Jer 2:34; Lam 4:14), has blood 'on his hands' that he cannot thereafter wash off (Is 1:15; 59:3; Ezek 23:37, 45) and that gives him no rest (Gen 4:12–16; Prov 28:17; Lam 4:14f). The shedding of innocent blood represents a constant threat that it will come back upon the murderer, 'upon his head', thus destroying him (Deut 19:10; Joshua 2:19; Judges 9:24; 1 Sam 25:26, 33; 2 Sam 1:16; 1 Kings 2:33; Jer 26:15; Ezek 35:6; Hos 12:14). The blood of murdered prophets and martyrs brings judgement upon their persecutors (Mt 23:30–5; Lk 11:50f; Rev 6:10f; 16:5f; 18:21–4). The enemies of Jesus in their blindness go so far as to call down upon themselves and their descendants the blood of him who though innocent was condemned

to death, thus bringing down divine judgement upon themselves (Mt 27:25; see also Acts 5:28).

The blood of the murdered man threatens not only his murderer but also the murderer's family (Deut 22:8; 2 Sam 21:1) and even him who is responsible for the vengeance of blood if he does not do his duty (1 Kings 2:31). It can pollute a city and the whole land and bring them disaster (2 Sam 21:2; Ps 106:38; Jer 26:15; Ezek 7:23; 22:3; 24:6ff; Mic 3:10; Nahum 3:1; Hab 2:12). The soil which has received the blood of a murdered man remains sterile (Gen 4:11f) and has to be freed from this condition by the blood of the murderer (Num 35:33; Deut 19:13). If the murderer is not found, it is the duty of the community to dissociate itself from the deed of blood by a rite of purification (Deut 21:1–9).

Vengeance of blood was considered as a normal legal procedure and even enjoyed divine sanction in the Old Testament during the period when the maintenance of law was still very deficient and before a centralised political authority had taken over (↗ Vengeance). For this reason God himself sometimes interfered by inflicting a national catastrophe in order to encourage those responsible for avenging blood, whenever circumstances permitted, to carry out their duty (2 Sam 21). Even down to the monarchy, the actual execution of the murderer was not the competence of the public authority but was reserved for the next of kin of the murdered man. The king or other public authorities limited themselves to conducting an enquiry and handing over the murderer to the 'avenger of blood' (Num 35:19, 21; Deut 19:11f; 2 Sam 21:8f). If no human avenger could be found God himself took over the duty of the blood-avenger (Deut 32:43; 2 Kings 9:7; Ps 9:12; 79:10). In war it is allowed and even, all things being equal, commanded to shed blood, but even then the stain of blood attaches to the king so that he is not capable of certain religious functions (1 Kings 5:3; 1 Chron 22:8; 28:3).

There are other crimes apart from murder which can burden the guilty one with 'blood' and which, in the same way, can be atoned for only with the blood of the offender (Lev 17:4; 20:9–27). God demands the blood of those warriors who, through a too hasty surrender, jeopardise the very existence of the people (Judith 8:21), and of those guards who do not warn the population in time of a danger which threatens. This last image is also applied to prophets who do not warn the people of the divine judgement which threatens (Ezek 3:18, 20; 33:4–8). Paul, too, fears to make himself guilty of the blood of his hearers by not preaching repentance and conversion to them (Acts 20:26).

In this way blood becomes *a symbol of divine judgement*. Thus, the changing of water into blood throughout the land stood as a warning for the Egyptians (Ex 4:9; 7:14–21; Ps 78:44; 105:29). On the Day of Judgement the blood of God's enemies will flow in streams (Is 15:9; Ezek 14:19; 21:32; 32:6; Zeph 1:17; Ps 58:10; 68:23), like the blood of animals in a sacrificial feast, a feast of the slaughter (Is 34:3, 6; Ezek 39:17). It will stain the garments of the divine Judge and his assistants like the

juice of grapes that stains the clothes of him that treads the winepress (Is 63:1–6; Lam 1:15; Rev 14:19f; 19:13ff). On that day the moon will turn to blood (Joel 2:31f; Acts 2:20; Rev 6:12).

C. *Blood in the cult or sacrificial system.* Since blood is the bearer of life, and God is the only lord of life, the eating of meat with the blood was forbidden in the Old Testament under pain of exclusion from the community (Gen 9:4; Lev 3:17; 7:26f; 17:10–14; Deut 12:16, 23ff; 15:23; Ezek 18:11). This prohibition was taken and continues to be taken very seriously in judaism, and its observance was accepted as a sign of belonging to the people of the covenant (see SB II 734–9). According to Lev 17:11, God has reserved the blood to himself, but has presented it to his people in another form, namely, as the means of expiation.

The New Testament repealed this prohibition of the eating of flesh with the blood as it did other stipulations of the Old Testament cultic legislation. The profoundly modified view of ↗ life which we owe to New Testament revelation superseded this identification of blood and life, and, in the same way, the statement about what blood is for in Lev 17:11 is surpassed through the atoning death of Christ. Thus, the whole purpose of the prohibition collapsed. Only in the apostolic decree, Acts 15:20–29; 21:25, does it have value as a disciplinary regulation, with the purpose of facilitating the living together of Jewish christians and those converted from paganism; and, in any case, the prohibition of eating flesh with the blood seems to have had hardly

77

any place in practice in the communities founded by Paul.

Blood plays a great part in the *sacrificial liturgy* of the Old Testament. According to Lev 17:11 God, in his mercy, has put into the hands of his people Israel a means of freeing themselves from the guilt of sin. Life is in the blood, and therefore it contains a force which opposes death, a force which has its origin in God. According to God's disposition, therefore, blood produces its effect in the sacrificial liturgy by opposing sin and the forces hostile to salvation in general. It is from this point that we can understand the Old Testament expiation rites. But that blood itself was ever considered as an offering or that the blood of animals was ever considered as a substitute for human blood cannot be proved from the Old Testament.

In the *consecration of persons* (priests) *and things* (altar, sanctuary) daubing with blood had a consecratory significance. It removed the person or thing in question from the sphere of the profane and furnished them with a consecration which brought them into a close relationship with God (Ex 29:15-26; Lev 8; Ezek 43:20-7).

The blood which was sometimes sprinkled, sometimes daubed, on men, the altar, the curtain, or the ark of the covenant on the occasion of a *sacrifice of purification* or *guilt-offering*, as well as on the Day of Atonement, removed the pollution incurred by sin, purified persons, the community, the temple, altar, and land, and established once again the fellowship between God and man which had been destroyed by sin (Lev 4:5; 14:16; Num 19:4).

The *blood of the paschal lamb* (Ex 12:13-27) and perhaps also *the blood of circumcision* in Ex 4:24ff marks out the friends and chosen ones of God and exempts them from the effects of God's anger.

The ritual of the sprinkling of blood on the altar and people on the occasion of the making of the covenant is not quite clear (Ex 24:4-8). At any rate, the covenant came into force in this way and the contracting parties (God and the people) were bound together in fellowship. The blood ritual could, however, be similar to what we find at the conclusion of other contracts in the ancient Near East, a kind of oath-taking ceremony which says in effect: if the covenant is broken, the blood of the guilty party will be shed just as the blood of this animal here. Since the Sinaitic Covenant came into force through blood, Yahweh remembers the 'blood of the covenant' while Israel was in exile and has mercy on his people 'because of the blood of my covenant' (Zech 9:11).

At the time of Christ, judaism understood by the 'blood of the covenant' either the blood shed at the covenant-making on Sinai according to Ex 24:4-8 (Targum Onkelos and Jerusalem Targum *ad loc.*) or the blood of circumcision (pJeb 8:9a, 5). The rabbinical axiom 'without blood no expiation' (Zeb 6a; Joma 5a; Men 93b) implies at least that Jewish theology knows of no expiation without blood-rites, but this maxim probably refers only to expiation by means of a sacrificial rite—meaning that a sacrifice can have expiatory force only when the liturgical action includes the shedding of blood. At any rate, the rabbis know of other means of expiating: intercession, penance, 'chastisement'. This has to be taken into account in the interpretation of Heb 9:22.

In the New Testament only the Epistle to the Hebrews comments on the blood-rites of the Old Testament. The author does not deny that these rites have a deep meaning; they have sanctified such as are defiled 'for the purification of the flesh', that is, they have enabled these to take part in the cult and thus to approach God (9:13), and have 'purified almost everything' (9:22) (↗Clean and unclean). The Sinaitic Covenant came into force through blood (9:18ff) and the blood of the paschal lamb prevented the entry of 'the Destroyer of the first-born' (11:28). But these rites brought about a purely cultic purity; they did not purify on the moral and existential plane. Sin remained and its power was not broken; on the contrary, these rites even made man's consciousness of sin stronger and showed up the hopelessness of his position, for 'it is impossible that the blood of bulls and goats should take away sins' (10:3f).

The Old Testament knows already of an expiatory death of the just for the salvation of God's people (Is 53; Zech 12:10–14; 2 Macc 7:38; ↗Sin; ↗People of God), but it is in the extra-canonical texts that, for the first time, the salvation of Israel is ascribed in particular to *the blood of the martyrs* (4 Macc 17:21f). The New Testament teaches that such *expiatory force can be ascribed only to the ↗ blood of Christ*, and that this is for the benefit of all mankind (Rom 3:25; 5:9; Heb 9:14; 10:19, 29; 13:12; 1 Pet 1:19; 1 Jn 1:7; Rev 1:5).

Bibliography: J. Behm, *TDNT* I, 172–7; SB II, 734–9; *LTK* II², 538–41; O. Schmitz, *Die Opferanschauungen des späteren Judentums und die Opferaussagen des NT*, Tübingen 1910; E. Bischof, *Das Blut im jüdischen Brauch*, Leipzig 1929; C. Vriezen, 'Hizza: Lustration and Consecration', *OTS* 7 (1950), 201–35; L. Morris, 'The Biblical Use of the Term "Blood"', *JTS* 3 (1952), 216–27 and 6 (1955/6), 77–82; T. L. Dewar, 'The Biblical Use of the Term "Blood"', *JTS* 4 (1953), 204–8; L. Moraldi, *Espiazione sacrificale e riti espiatori*, Rome 1956; A. Charbel, 'Virtus sanguinis non expiatoria in sacrificio šelamîm', *SP* I (Gembloux 1959), 366–76; J. E. Steinmueller, 'Sacrificial Blood in the Bible', *Bbl* 40 (1959), 556–67; H. Graf Reventlow, '"Sein Blut komme über sein Haupt"', *VT* 10 (1960), 310–27; S. Lyonnet, 'De munere sacrificali sanguinis', *VD* 39 (1961), 18–38; K. Koch, 'Der Spruch "Sein Blut bleibe auf seinem Haupt"', *VT* 12 (1962), 396–416; T. Canaan, 'Das Blut in den Sitten und im Aberglauben der palästinens. Araber', *ZDPV* 79 (1963), 8–23; N. Füglister, *Die Heilsbedeutung des Pascha*, Munich 1963, 77–105; L. Sabourin, 'Nefesh, sang et expiation', *SE* 18 (1966), 25–46.

Josef Scharbert

Blood of Christ

The blood of Christ is frequently (more than thirty times) mentioned in the New Testament. This was not a mere emphasis on the bloody character of Christ's death. Neither was the blood of Christ ever thought of as an entity separate from the person of Christ from which a new 'blood-theory' developed. It is rather a phrase which is used to refer to Christ's death in relation to our salvation, and this in a comprehensive manner. In the background lies the Old Testament idea that ↗ blood is the principle of life and that giving up life works expiation (Lev 17:11) and also that Christ is the 'servant of the Lord' who has given his life for many (Mk 10:45). That this phrase was used before Paul can be proved not only from his account of the institution of the eucharist where he cites from tradition (1 Cor 11:25 = Lk 22:20; Mk 14:20): those passages where Paul mentions the blood of Christ sound rather formal, and may therefore not have been coined by him. Christ through his blood has made propitiation for the sins of man (Rom 3:24f; Rev 1:5), and we being now justified by his blood shall be saved from wrath through him (Rom 5:9); 'in him we have redemption through his blood, the forgiveness of our trespasses' (Eph 1:7). God has reconciled all things through the blood of Christ's cross (Col 1:20). Christ has redeemed us through his blood (1 Pet 1:19; see also 1 Cor 6:11; 7:23); he has redeemed all christians out of every tribe and nation (Rev 5:9), and won for himself the congregation of God (Acts 20:28). Even the heathens who, far from Israel's *politeia* (= state), were once without hope in the world ' have been brought near' (Eph 2:13). This blood cleanses us from all sin (1 Jn 1:7), its force enables all christians to conquer the satanic accuser (Rev 12:11) and the martyrs to complete their martyrdom (Rev 7:14). As the old covenant became operative through blood (Ex 24:8) so the new, eternal covenant, the perfect covenant promised in Jer 31:31f, the new divine dispensation has been founded by Christ's blood (Lk 22:20 = 1 Cor 11:25). This blood is therefore called 'the blood of the [new] covenant' (Mk 14:24; Heb 9:18-22; 10:29; 13:20). What could not be effected by the sacrifices of the Old Testament— the remission of sins, the purification of conscience from the works of death, and the entry into the heavenly sanctuary—

this was worked by Christ, the true eternal High Priest, through shedding his own blood (Heb 10). The sanctifying power of this blood is applied in the Supper of the Lord (1 Cor 10:16). Redemption through his blood imposes on the christians the obligation of a renewed way of life (1 Pet 1:13ff; Heb 10:19ff). The idea of Christ's blood working salvation is almost completely absent in the Johannine writings (see 1 Jn 1:7; 2:2; 4:10). John presents Christ's death more as the beginning of his exaltation ('being lifted up': see the double meaning of *hupsōthēnai* = 'exalt', 'lifts up [on the cross]', 3:14; 8:28; 12:32, 34) and of his glory (7:39; 12:16-23; 13:31ff; 17:1-5). When the Baptist refers to Christ as the Lamb that takes away the sins of the world, the word *airei* (= take away) is used (as in 1 Jn 3:5), which means 'carry away' and not 'take upon oneself' or 'shoulder'. Even if he uses the image of the Lamb of God when referring to Christ as the 'servant of the Lord' of Is 53, the evangelist was not necessarily thinking of Christ's death rather than of the whole of his life-work. Neither is there any reference (at least not expressly mentioned) to his death on the cross in 6:53-6 where Jesus offers his own flesh and blood as a food for man which gives eternal life. In 1 Jn 5:6 ('came by water and blood') water and blood in the antignostic polemic only refer to the beginning and the end (Baptism and Death) of Christ's life-work.

Bibliography: H. Windisch, *Hebräerbrief*, 1931², 82-92; C. Spicq, *L'Épître aux Hébreux*, Paris 1953, 271-85; E. Lohse, *Märtyrer und Gottesknecht*, Göttingen 1964²; L. Morris, *JTS* (1952), 216-27 and (1953) 204-08; E. H. Withley,

JTS (1957), 240–55; *RGG* I³, 1329; R. Schnackenburg, *The Gospel of St. John*, London 1968; P. Neuenzeit, *Das Herrenmahl*, Munich 1960.

Josef Schmid

Body

A. *In the Old Testament and judaism.* Just as God fashioned Adam's body out of earth and transformed it into a living human being by means of his breath (Gen 2:7), so, in the same way, he co-operates in the formation of each human body (Gen 2:21f; Ps 103:14; 139:13ff; Wis 7:1f). Historical and biological theories and hypotheses of modern science ought not to be inconsistent with these theological statements in the Old Testament, as they exist on different levels. According to the Old Testament, the body returns to dust at death (Gen 3:19; Ps 90:3; 146:4; Job 4:19f; 10:9; Eccles 3:19f; Wis 2:3; cf 1 Sam 17:44), whereas the living spirit returns to God (Ps 146:4; Job 34:14; Eccles 12:7). A life which followed after death was an unfamiliar notion in the Old Testament. Any anxiety about such a life was for the most part left without a second thought in God's hands, or else life after death was lamented as a shadowy existence, as an end or a downfall (↗ Death). It is only more recent texts which refer to a continuation of life after death (↗ Life), and in these texts mention is frequently made of a resurrection, which betokens a 'reanimation of the body' (↗ Resurrection; see Is 25:8; 26:19; Dan 12:1–3; 2 Macc 7:9, 11, 14, 36; Ezek 37:1–14).

The body, in the Old Testament view, is an essential part of man and the vehicle of his personality (Job 14:22; Ps 44:25), and as such also pertains essentially to the true image or likeness of God (↗ Likeness; Gen 1:26f; 9:6). All expressions of human life, including those which are spiritual, are at the same time inevitably 'bodily'.

Such an evaluation of the role of the body has exerted a great influence in the Old Testament over the answers given to many questions about life. With this in mind it becomes easier to understand why happiness and good fortune in this world, and especially good health (Sir 30:14–16), the blessing of many children (Ps 128) and of long life (Prov 3:16; Eccles 9:4) are valued so highly in the world of the Old Testament (↗ Blessing, ↗ Riches). This is also the reason why those phenomena which were later known as self-denial and ascesis were absent in those days. The Old Testament takes a positive view of physical impulses and desires and demands that they should be satisfied (↗ Asceticism). The feelings of affection that each individual had for those related to him—that is, for his family, tribe and race—gained powerful stimuli from this evaluation of the part played by the body. Genealogies were in this case more than mere proofs of birth and descent. Sometimes they offered prospects of happiness and good fortune, at other times they made it easier to accept and understand ill fortune (↗ People of God). The participation of the individual in religious services or in the liturgy was unthinkable without physical attendance (↗ Prayer, ↗ Sacrifice). There was also an important connection between the body and sin. Although sin admittedly does not reside in man's body, but in his ↗ heart (Gen 6:5; Sir 9:9), it is nevertheless committed with the body and leaves its effects behind in the body. Illness and disease were for this reason given a theological rather than a medical explanation, and the merciful God was regarded as the only reliable physician (2 Kings 20:2, 5; Sir 38:9–11). Every time any physical harm was caused to a pious man, the question of theodicy was raised (but see also Is 50:6; 52:13–53:12; ↗ Suffering). Finally, the concern expressed in the Old Testament for a fitting interment of the body (Gen 23 etc; Deut 32:50; Judg 2:9; 1 Kings 2:10), and that there should be no desecration of the dead, must be borne in mind, as these things were of great consequence (Is 14:19f; Jer 8:1ff; 22:19; Ezek 32:23). 'To bury the dead' developed into a very important work of mercy and thereby into a special application of the Old Testament idea of wisdom (Tob 1:17ff; 2:3–9; 4:3f; 12:13; Sir 38:16; 44:14).

It is not until the last period of the Old Testament and in late judaism that a dichotomy or even a trichotomy seems to arise under the influence of various trends, in particular hellenistic and perhaps also Parsee. In 2 Macc and in Wis, the soul can be regarded as a life-spirit dwelling in man, and the body is correspondingly the house of the soul (Wis 8:19f; see also Sir 47:19; Wis 1:4; 2:22f; 3:1f; 4:14f) or even the prison of the soul (Wis 9:15).

In 4 Macc and in Philo of Alexandria, such thoughts are modelled on the lines of Plato and the Platonic school and are brought into harmony with biblical data. In this respect, Gen 6:3

and Job 10:4 had an important part to play. The members of the Qumran Community taught in theory and in practice that the body and its influence were evil and opposed to God and that it stood, as a result of this, in need of discipline and was the cause of constant temptation to man (see also Test Dan 1; Test Gad 4). The Palestinian rabbis, however, attributed wickedness to the evil inclination which dwelt in man's heart (↗ Concupiscence) and thus remained faithful to the ancient inheritance. They seldom regarded the body as inferior and never subscribed to the harsh hellenistic view.

B. *New Testament.* In contrast to the contemporary spirit of judaism, and to that of later theologians, the New Testament never concerns itself with a precise determination of the essence and functions of the body. The Greek word *sōma* (=body) has in the New Testament, besides the meaning of 'corpse' (Mk 15:43ff and parallels; Lk 17:37; Acts 9:40; Jn 19:38; 20:12; Rev 11:8f), that of 'a body visible, tangible and entire' (Mt 5:29f; 6:22; Mk 5:29; 14:8 and parallels; Lk 11:34; Jn 2:21; Rom 1:24; 1 Cor 6:18). It is frequently found in conjunction with *pneuma* (=spirit; Rom 8:10, 13; 1 Cor 5:3; 7:34; Jas 2:26) and with *psukhē* (=soul; Mt 6:25; 10:28; Lk 12:22f) or even in conjunction with both together (1 Thess 5:23). This 'body' is systematically constructed and has organs and members (Mt 5:29f; Rom 12:4f; 1 Cor 12:12, 14–26; Jas 3:6) as well as possessing various physiological functions (Rom 12:1; 1 Cor 6:20; 2 Cor 4:10; Gal 6:17; Phil 1:20), among which Paul, for topical reasons, stresses sexual activity in particular

(Rom 1:24; 4:19; 1 Cor 6:12–20; 7:4).

Because of the controversies of the period, several passages in the New Testament sound an almost dualistic note, especially in those places where the body appears as a garment or as a tabernacle for man (2 Cor 5:1–10; 2 Pet 1:13f; cf 2 Cor 12:2–4; Phil 1:23). Other passages contain suggestions that the body and its functions are inferior (1 Pet 2:11; 2 Pet 2:18; 1 John 2:16) and the ↗ asceticism which was gradually beginning to gain importance and has been accounted for in various ways also played a part in this view. In Paul this comes especially to the fore in his treatment of ↗ marriage, which he designated as a necessary evil (1 Cor 7:1–11). It would, however, be wrong to lift these isolated passages, whose interpretation is the subject of much controversy, out of the whole doctrine of the New Testament, or to infer any exact anthropology from such observations made in passing (↗ Man). The conclusion of the speech on the Areopagus and the negative response of the Greeks to the doctrine of the resurrection gives a clear proof of how consciously the christians of the time would have felt this to be diametrically opposed to the Greek way of thinking (Acts 17:32). It cannot be denied that the concept of the 'body' which is found in the New Testament is equivocal, but it is clear that the origins of this concept are in the Old Testament.

This evaluation which places the soul on a higher plane than the body is not found in the synoptic texts (according to Schmid). The call to conversion, the conclusion that everyone is sinful and thus dependent upon God, and the message that salvation has been conferred upon sinful man, are all applicable to the body also, since the body is nothing else but man himself in one aspect of human existence. Even in Mk 14:38 ('The spirit indeed is willing, but the flesh is weak') it is not a question of the body being more sinful than the soul, but of man himself being prone to weakness. 'The evil in man is not the body, as a kind of inferior ego which somehow drags the superior part down to its level. It is, on the contrary, man's will which is evil. It is man's heart which makes him good or bad and not his body' (Schmid on Mk 7:20–23). The demand is made of the christian that he should have absolute trust in the Father (Mt 6:25–34), follow Jesus without looking back (Lk 9:57–62), and lead a new life of faith and charity (Mk 9:43–8). This demand means that all considerations of physical wellbeing must take second place, whatever the consequences may be (Mk 8:34–8). The early church reiterated this demand in many different forms (see 1 Cor 9:27; 13:3; Phil 1:20).

The teaching of Paul is of especial significance here, as being, in all essential points, a culmination of the teachings of the Old Testament. In Paul the word 'body' expresses the more popular concept already mentioned, but is also used as a precise term for the whole person, the man himself (↗ Man). It would be wrong, in such cases, to place any special emphasis on the use of the word 'body', as though it were only the body which christians present as a living sacrifice (Rom 12:1), the body over which man and wife have reciprocal control (1 Cor 7:4) and in which Christ is to be glorified (Phil 1:20).

The idea of the body as an influence which is hostile to God and prone to sin (↗ Flesh) is also found in Paul (see Rom 6:6 and 8:3), in particular where he refers to the body of unredeemed man (Rom 7:14–24). Such a man's deeds (Rom 8:13) and desires (Rom 6:12) are bad, since man himself, and not only his body, comes under the influence of the flesh, which is hostile to God and prone to sin. The language which Paul uses in many cases also serves the purpose of determining the existence of the christian between the infinitive of salvation itself and the imperative of the working out of his salvation. The body of the christian remains weak and is never proof against temptation. The christian's heart is, in other words, inclined towards evil (1 Cor 2:14; 2 Cor 4:7–18; 12:7–10; 1 Thess 5:23). That is why the christian must subject himself voluntarily, or be subjected against his will, to sacrifice (1 Cor 9:27; Gal 6:17; see also 1 Cor 13:3).

Paul draws a distinction between the body on this earth and the body after the resurrection. Elsewhere his ideas of the body and the flesh merge into one another, but here the distinction is precise. The flesh is the old man who will perish (see Gal 5:24; Col 3:9f) by virtue of the grace of ↗ baptism (Rom 8:9f), and finally pass away for ever at the ↗ resurrection (1 Cor 15:50). Christians must, however, possess the body in sanctification and honour (1 Thess 4:4; 1 Cor 6:13), since baptism has made it a temple of the Holy Ghost (1 Cor 3:16f; 6:19). At the resurrection of the dead it will be completely transformed and made into a 'heavenly body' (1 Cor 15:44–9), refashioned by the glory of God (Phil 3:21; see also 2 Cor 3:18) on the model and in the power of the reanimated and glorified body of Jesus (Col 1:18; cf Acts 3:15; 5:31; 26:23; Rev 1:5).

The New Testament contains several different references to the body of Jesus and to the reality of his incarnation (Rom 8:3; Phil 2:7; Col 1:22; Eph 2:15; 1 Tim 3:16; and especially Jn 1:13; 1 Jn 4:2; 2 Jn 7), in particular in connection with his vicarious death (Mk 15:43–5 and parallels; Mt 26:12; Jn 19:38ff; Rom 7:4; Heb 10:5, 10; 1 Pet 2:24), the resurrection (Lk 24:3, 23; Jn 20:12; see also Jn 2:21) and the Last Supper (↗ Eucharist; Mk 14:22 and parallels; 1 Cor 10:16; 11:24, 27, 29). In the figurative sense the christian community is characterised as the body of Christ (↗ Church).

Bibliography: ↗ Concupiscence, ↗ Death, ↗ Flesh, ↗ Life, ↗ Man.—Bultmann I, 192–203; Jacob, Mehl, and Koehnlein, Allmen 247–53; J. Schmid, *LTK* I², 603–15; Schweitzer, Baumgärtel, and Meyer, *TWNT* VII, 98–151 (with bibliography); W. G. Kümmel, *Das Bild des Menschen im NT*, Zurich 1948; W. Eichrodt, *Das Menschverständnis des AT*, Basle 1951²; J. A. T. Robinson, *The Body*, London 1952; J. Jerwell, *Imago Dei*, Göttingen 1960 (with bibliography). See also: E. Dhorme, *L'emploi métaphorique des noms de corps en hébreu et en akkadien*, Paris 1923; E. Käsemann, *Leib und Leib Christi*, Tübingen 1933; W. Gutbrod, *Die paulinische Anthropologie*, Stuttgart and Berlin 1934; W. L. Knox, 'Parallels to the NT use of *sōma*', *JTS* 39 (1938), 243–6; O. Kuss, 'Das Fleisch', *Der Römerbrief* II, Regensburg 1959, 506–40.

Wilhelm Pesch

Book

The idea that there are heavenly books was widespread and is of theological importance. In this connection it is possible to divide such books into three types: a. the so-called 'Book of Destiny'; b. 'books of judgement', in which men's works as well as their sins are recorded; and c. the 'Book of Life'.

a. According to the Babylonian view, 'tablets of destiny' were already in existence at the time of creation. Acting on the instructions of Marduk, in whose power destiny lies, Nebo noted down before all else the destinies of men. 'Records of human destiny' are to be found in Egypt, and are not unknown even in the Greco-Roman world (an Athenian epitaph refers to the Fates as writers, *CIG* 3, 2, 1337; see also Ovid, *Metam.* 15, 809ff; Martial 10, 44, 5f; etc).

The notion of a book of fate is met with here and there in the biblical and apocryphal writings (↗ Predestination): 'Thy eyes beheld my unformed substance; in thy book were written, every one of them, the days that were formed for me' (Ps 139:16).

In Jude 4 and similarly in Enoch 106:19; 108:7, evil-doers already have sentence passed on them by virtue of God's fore-knowledge, and this is set down in writing. The book with the seven seals may also possibly belong here (Rev 5:1ff). In this book are contained God's hidden decrees and judgements which powerfully determine the destinies of men and penetrate to the very end of history: see 1 QH 1, 23f: 'Everything is engraved for you with the stylus of memory for the duration of all time'—that is to say, engraved on heavenly tablets. (See also SB II, 173–6).

b. In Egypt the works of men were recorded for the judgement of souls by the God Thoth. In the Old Testament it is in Dan 7:10 that reference to such books of judgement is found, see Is 65:6; Jer 22:30, or Mal 3:16 and CD 20, 19, where a 'note-book' is referred to. In Bar (Syr) 24, 1, the writer recognises that sins are recorded in this book, and this idea is taken for granted when the suppliant prays for his sins to be rubbed out (as in Ps 51:1, 9 etc). The prayer *Abinu Malkenu*, which was used by Rabbi Akiba, contains the petition: 'In thy great mercy obliterate all [written] records of our debts', and the *kheirographōn* (= hand-writing) of Col 2:14 can also be understood in this light as a setting down in writing of our sins. In Rev 20:12, 'the books [are] opened' and the dead are judged 'according to their works' (see also Rev 14:13; Ps 56:8) and these works are recorded in the books. (But note that the dead are also judged according to their good works and not only according to their sins— in this the spirit of the New Testament is discernible.)

c. A 'Book of Life' is referred to only in biblical writings. The first mention is in Ex 32:32f, in which Moses offers the Lord his life for his people (as Paul does later, Rom 9:3), and God replies that he will erase only the name of the sinner from this book. For the 'blotting out' of the name of the evildoer from the 'Book of Life', see also Ps 69:28, Rev 3:5 and Enoch 108, 3. Further references are found in Ps 56:8; 87:6; 139:16; Is 4:3; 56:5; Ezek 13:9; Dan 12:1; Lk 10:20; Phil 4:3; Heb 12:23; and especially Rev 3:5; 13:8; 17:8; 20:12, 15; 21:27 and the many texts in the apocryphal books, such as Enoch 47:3; 104:1; Jub 19:9, etc. The 'Book of Life' does not appear in the Dead Sea texts.

A similar idea emerges from the 'bundle of the living' found in 1 Sam 25:29; 1 QH 2:20. A. Marmorstein (*ZAW* 43 [1925], 119–24) is inclined to think of this as a magic spell, but it is possible to draw a parallel between this and the 'Book of Life', and to regard *ts'rôr* (=bundle) as the linen or leather outer cover in which the book, that is to say, the scroll, is placed, bound with cords and possibly even sealed (see also Job 14:17).↗ Assurance of salvation,↗ Seal. Eissfeldt shows, with reference to the Nuzi texts, that a herd of cattle was counted and a tally made by putting pebbles into a bag.

Bibliography: G. Schrenk, *TDNT* 1, 615–20; L. Koep, 'Das himmlische Buch in Antike und Christentum', *Theophaneia* 8 (1952); L. Koep, *RAC* 2, 725–31; J. Leipoldt and S. Morenz, *Heilige Schriften*, Leipzig 1953; G. Rinaldi, *Bbl* 40 (1959), 282ff; O. Eissfeldt, 'Der Beutel der Lebendigen', *Verh. Sächs. Akad. Phil. Hist.* 105/6 (Berlin 1960); T. Holtz, 'Die Christologie der Apokalypse des Johannes', *TU* 85 (Berlin 1962), 31–6.

Johannes B. Bauer

Brethren of Jesus

Brothers and sisters of Jesus are referred to in the New Testament (Jn 2:12; Mk 3:31–5; Mt 12:26–50; Lk 8:19–21; Mk 6:3; Mt 13:55f; Jn 7:3–5, 9f; Acts 1:14; Gal 1:19; 1 Cor 9:5). Four brothers are mentioned, in fact, and their names are given as James, Joses (a form existing side by side with Joseph, see Mt 13:55), Judas, and Simon. We are not told the number or the names of Jesus' sisters, though we may infer from Mt 13:56, where 'all his sisters' are referred to, that there are at least three.

It is of some importance to examine the word *adelphos* (=brother) and ascertain the full extent of its meaning, in order to establish the precise degree of relationship in which these 'brethren' stood to Jesus. In Greek the word is generally used to denote one's full brother or at least one's half-brother. There are, however, many exceptions to this (Marcus Aurelius, 1, 14, 1, as well as numerous Egyptian papyrus texts). In LXX, too, first cousins and even second, third, and more distant cousins are referred to as 'brothers' and 'sisters'. LXX arrived at this extension of the original meaning of the Greek word as a consequence of the lack of any native Hebrew or Aramaic word for 'cousin'. In these languages, 'cousin' is simply known as 'brother' (*'āḥ*) in order to avoid more lengthy circumlocutions. The carelessness of the writers of the New Testament in the use of the Greek word *adelphos* can be explained on the one hand by this usage in LXX and on the other hand by the fact that they are themselves Semites and do not correct the inexactitudes of their native language even in the Greek version, although they would have had the chance to do so here, by using the word *anepsios* (=cousin). An analogous case is found in Latin, where the very precise terms *avunculus/patruus* and *amita/matertera* clearly differentiate between uncles and aunts as, on the one hand, brothers or sisters of the father and, on the other, as brothers or sisters of the mother: this precision of meaning was lost in the Romance languages, in which the words *patruus* and *matertera* failed to survive.

The following evidence shows that the term 'brother' must have had this wider meaning in the New Testament passages under question. Two of Jesus' brethren were certainly sons of a Mary different from Mary the mother of Jesus. According to Mk 15:40 (see Mt 27:56), 'Mary the mother of James the younger and of Joses' was at Golgotha beside Mary Magdalen, Salome, and the other women. The evangelist has hitherto not named this Mary, although he has already (Mk 6:3) introduced her sons as the Lord's brethren, and the unusual form of the name Joses (for Joseph) in both places proves that Mark has the same brothers in mind in 15:40. Mark calls this Mary in 16:1 (see Lk 24:10) simply 'Mary, the mother of James', whereas Matthew in both instances refers to 'the other Mary' (27:61; 28:1). The mother of Jesus is named as 'his mother' in addition to the above, once in Mk (3:31), eight times in Matthew and John, five times in Luke, and once in Acts.

Similarly, Jesus' act, when he was at the point of death, of giving his mother into the beloved disciple's keeping, must remain inexplicable if Jesus had had brothers or sisters. It emerges clearly from the emphatic use of the article in the designation of Jesus as '*the* son of Mary' (Mk 6:3) that he is Mary's only child, and this is borne out by the fact that Jesus is named as the son of Mary and Joseph (Lk 3:23) and that in the whole of the New Testament sons, daughters, or children of Mary or Joseph never appear. Furthermore, according to Lk 2:7, Jesus was Mary's firstborn. According to Lk 2:41–52, Mary takes part in the pilgrimage to Jerusalem at the time of the Passover, and this would be difficult to understand if she had left little children at home for the fourteen days of the pilgrimage. If Mary had had other children after this pilgrimage, these would not have reached the age of twenty by the time Jesus began his public life and would never have been able to behave towards their elder brother in such a free and easy manner as is outlined in Mk 3:21, 31–5 and Jn 7:2–5, in which texts they appear to treat him almost as a guardian treats his ward.

What emerges from all this is that Mary had no other children apart from Jesus.

This fact is not contradicted by the naming of Jesus in Lk 2:7 as the 'firstborn', as every firstborn child bore this title in the Jewish world, whether succeeded by other brothers or sisters or not (Ex 13:2; Num 3:12). It is probable, moreover, that Luke used this expression to emphasise the virgin birth, and certainly not to contrast Jesus with any other children Mary might have had later (see W. Michaelis, *TWNT* VI, 877, 14ff). Again, we cannot understand Mt 1:25 to mean that Joseph lived a normal married life with Mary after the birth of Jesus, for the translation (RSV and others): 'but [he] knew her not until she had borne a son', is philologically wrong. The true meaning of this passage must be: 'but although he knew her not, behold, nonetheless she bore him a son' (on this point, and on the general tendency of Mt, see M. Krämer, *Bbl* 45 [1964], 1–50).

Any attempt at a more accurate definition of the various degrees of relationship is bound to fail because of the paucity of information given by the New Testament and ancient tradition. It is possible to regard the Lord's brothers as cousins (Blinzler), yet the possibility must also remain that they were Joseph's sons as a result of a previous marriage (Stauffer). This view is supported by the fact that in the oldest christian tradition they are never given the name of 'nephews' (*anepsioi*)—it is even possible that the phrase 'Lord's brother' may very well have been used as a mark of distinction—and that whenever they appear it is almost always in close association with Mary (see Mk 3:31ff; the family list in Mk 6:3; Jn 2:12; Acts 1:14), and finally that the position of authority over Jesus to which they presume as older half-brothers can thus quite easily be justified.

Bibliography: Abundant material and a detailed bibliography in J. Blinzler, 'Simon der Apostel, Simon der Herrenbruder, und Bischof Symeon von Jerusalem', *Passauer Studien* (*Festschrift Bischof Simon Landersdorfer*) 1953, 25-55; J. Blinzler. 'Zum Problem der Brüder des Herrn', *TTZ* 67 (1958), 129-45 and 224-46; J. Blinzler, *LTK* II², 714-17 and *Lexikon der Marienkunde*, pts 5 and 6, Regensburg 1960, 959-69; E. Stauffer, 'Begegnung der Christen', *Festschrift Otto Karrer*, Frankfurt 1960², 367f (esp. n 46).

Johannes B. Bauer

Brother

A. The Hebrew word *ʾāḥ* means in the first place 'brother', but it is also used for other male relatives, like its Akkadian and Ugaritic equivalents. The Greek word *adelphos*, used to translate *ʾaḥ*, has sometimes, under the influence of the more flexible Semitic usage, acquired the wider meaning of this latter, although etymologically it means 'son of the same mother' (*a*-copulative; *delphus* = womb).

In the Old Testament, 'brother' is the word used for those who are of the same race (Lev 10:4; Deut 15:3, 12 etc). Especially in Lev 19:18 (↗ Neighbour) it is contrasted with the alien who happens to live in the land (*gêr*, Deut 1:16) and foreigners just passing through (*nākrî*, Deut 15:3).

For the rest *ʾāḥ* divides up the field of meaning in relationship with *rēʿa* (↗ Neighbour A), extending not only to fellow countryman but even further, eg, friend (2 Sam 1:26; Prov 17:17), colleague (2 Chron 31:15; Ezra 3:8; 6:20 etc), one who shares the same ideas or the same fate (Gen 49:5; Job 30:29; Prov 18:9) or just any other person at all (see Jer 9:4; Ps 49:7; Ezek 4:17; etc). While in the later history of Israel only *rēʿa* is used in the wider sense, *ʾāḥ*, on the other hand, is used in the strict sense (or is even further narrowed down, as with the members of the Qumran sect, who called themselves 'brothers'). The common brotherhood of Israelites is founded in their father Abraham (Jn 8:39) who was 'called' by God. Thus brother has a double meaning: 'fellow countryman' and 'fellow believer'; and the double commandment of love—of God and of the neighbour, that is, the brother—has its correspondents in the worshipping community and the civic community. The whole history of Israel is played out within these two concentric circles. Brotherhood in Israel is confined by nation and worship; in the New Testament, however, brotherhood is limited but is at the same time universal.

B. The distinction in the later period of Israel's history between a civic and religious community became fully manifest in the New Testament: 'Do not presume to say to yourselves, "We have Abraham as our father"; for I tell you, God is able from these stones to raise up children to Abraham' (Mt 3:9). Instead of a brotherhood based on *natural birth* there appears one which has its origin in a *rebirth*. Natural brotherhood had, literally, received its death-blow in the history of Cain and Abel; true brotherly love is therefore a sure sign that we are children of God (1 Jn 3:11ff). The brotherhood founded in Jesus Christ is the fulfilment and completion of that founded in Abraham; the true sons of Abraham are those who believe in Christ (Gal 3:7, 29; Rom 4:11f). The beginnings of this usage can already be found in the synoptic tradition, as Mk 3:31–5 shows. In Mk 10:30, the 'brothers and sisters and mothers' clearly refers to the christian brotherhood of the community. The distinction in Acts 14:2 is unmistakable: 'Jews . . . Gentiles . . . brethren'. This true brotherhood, however, was not founded and made possible by Christ's teaching and example, but only by his atoning death (Eph 2:11–18).

This christian brotherhood, therefore, does not come about as the result of an idealist theory of unity among men of good will nor just through the imitation of Christ's example, but through membership of a visible redeemed community. Christ is the first cause and the last end of this brotherhood; but its essence and its outward manifestation are ↗ love, for it is by our love for the brethren that we know we

are reborn (1 Pet 1:22ff). This love unites the brother not to another man but to God. The adjective most frequently attached to *adelphos* is *agapētos* or *ēgapēmenos* (=beloved), which is further defined in 1 Thess 1:4 as 'brethren beloved by God'.

We must bear with the weakness of our brethren (Rom 15:1) if we are not to sin against Christ (1 Cor 8:12). There are, however, limits, and the division can run through the visible community: there are false brethren (Gal 2:4; 2 Cor 11:26) and brethren only in name (1 Cor 5:11). Brotherhood is the privilege of those who are reborn, to such an extent that it does not necessarily apply to all the organised community, not even to all the Twelve (Jn 6:70).

Characteristics of the brotherhood. The brotherhood is never impersonal; it is always realised in some concrete form. It is a personal fellowship with the brethren in Christ; it flourishes wherever visible and tangible relations with the brethren are possible (Acts 28:15); it is life in communion with the children of God (the daily assembly of the faithful). This brotherhood is universal and yet circumscribed in time and place—the unity of the church as the body of Christ, the mystery of unity in diversity and diversity in unity (Groenewald). Scherffig is of the opinion that brotherhood is not to be identified with just unity of mind and spirit since it is founded in Christ only, that it does not depend on the extent to which it has been put into practice, and that it is not a community based on tradition and confined within the limits of a certain creed ('that which can have its origin only in Christ would be mistaken for the acceptance of specific theological propositions'). But reading Mt 18:15–17; Tit 3:10ff; 2 Tim 2:25ff, we are led to the conclusion that this view can be accepted only with the strongest reservations. There are 'false teachers' among the brethren according to 2 Pet 2:1, and if there are brethren in the visible community of God who are not true brothers the question arises whether, according to the New Testament, true brotherhood could be realised outside the church. This question in all its implications was never actually dealt with in the New Testament, any more than were the questions of schism and heresy (see M. Meinertz, *BZ* [1957], 114–8).

The relationship between 'brother' and 'neighbour' is almost like that of two circles, a smaller enclosed in a larger. The 'neighbour', as is clear from the parable of the Good Samaritan (↗ Neighbour B), is not only our brother in faith but anyone whom we 'assist' or help because we happen to be on the spot. Paul speaks of the smaller circle (Gal 6:10), and 2 Pet 1:7 (see also 1 Thess 3:12) shows clearly that love of the brotherhood (*philadelphia*) is a special and privileged form of love (*agapē*) in general (see Spicq).

Bibliography: H. von Soden, *TDNT* I, 144–6; F. Zorell, *Lexikon hebraicum*, 29f; W. Bauer, *A Greek–English Lexikon of the NT and other Early Christian Literature*, ed. W. F. Arndt and F. W. Gingrich, Cambridge and Chicago 1957; Bartelink, 75f; D. J. Georgacas, *Glotta* 36 (1957), 106–8 (etymology); K. H. Schelkle, *RAC* II, 631–40; W. Scherffig, *ET* 9 (1949/50), 49–65; E. P. Groenewald, 'Die christelike Broederskap volgens die Heilige Skrif', *Arcana Revelata*, Kampen 1951, 23–32; C. Spicq, 'La charité fraternelle selon 1 Thess 4:9', *Festschrift A. Robert*, Paris 1957, 507–11; H. Schürmann, *Gemeinde als Bruderschaft im Lichte des NT, Diaspora, Gabe, und Ausgabe*, Paderborn 1955, 21–31; J. Ratzinger, *Christian Brotherhood*, London and New York 1966; A. Andrewes, 'Phratries in Homer', *Hermes* 89 (1961), 129–40; C. Brady, *Brotherly Love: A Study of the Word 'Philadelphia' and its Contribution to the Biblical Theology of Brotherly Love*, Fribourg 1961 (dissertation); J. Gonda, *Mnemosyne* 15 (1962), 290ff; B. Lifshitz, *Aegyptus* 42 (1962), 241–56.

Johannes B. Bauer

Building up

The Greek word under consideration here is *oikodomein*, the Hebrew *bānâh*. In secular writing, besides its obvious literal meaning of 'build',' construct' (walls, houses, temples, etc), the word often has a figurative sense: eg, Cicero, *De Orat.* III, 152: 'quid ipse aedificet orator, ... id esse nobis quaerendum atque explicandum' ('the question we have to ask and answer is: What does the orator "construct"?'); Seneca, *Ep.* 88, 23: 'mathematica ... in alieno aedificat' ('mathematics "builds" on other things'); Xenophon, *Kyrop.* VIII, 7, 15: '*epi tauta euthus oikodomeite alla philika erga*' ('on these friendly actions at once "build" more'). (Further examples can be found in Vielhauer, *Oikodome*, 25f; Schelkle, *RAC* I, 1265f.)

In the *Old Testament*, God himself 'built' Eve out of Adam's rib (Gen 2:22); the restless fugitive Cain built a city in order to have a settled abode (Gen 4:17); Noah built an altar of sacrifice (Gen 8:20) for the worship of God, and similarly Solomon built his splendid temple (1 Kings 6:1–6). He built a throne-room for himself, in which he sat to pronounce judgement (1 Kings 7:7), and a palace or house for his wife (7:8). Later, unfortunately, he also built places of sacrifice for the idols Chemosh and Molech (1 Kings 11:7). Ahab built a Temple of Baal in Samaria (1 Kings 16:32) and allowed Jericho to be rebuilt (16:34). While still in captivity, Tobit blessed those who were to rebuild the destroyed city of Jerusalem, and even dreamed that the gates of the city would be built of sapphire and emerald (Tob 13:16). This splendid vision is mentioned again in the description of the heavenly Jerusalem (Rev 21:19ff; see also Is 54:11f).

God gives 'commissions to build', in the best sense of the word, to many prophets, and one of the most noteworthy of these is Jeremiah, whose task is first and foremost to uproot and pull down, but then to build up and plant again (Jer 1:10; Sir 49:7).

A difficult problem is always raised when sinful men wish to erect a shrine to the infinite God; hence the question which Yahweh puts to the Jews in Is 66:1f: 'Heaven is my throne, and the earth is my footstool; What is the house which you would build for me, ... But this is the man to whom I will look, he that is contrite and humble in spirit'. The builder is also often Yahweh himself. According to Jer 33:7, he will build up the house of Israel again, and in Jer 31:4, the 'virgin' of Israel. The ruined tabernacle of David (Amos 9:11) and the shrine on Mount Sion (Ps 102:16) are also to be reconstructed. In all this God does not, however, dispense with the cooperation of man. When the Jews spent their time exclusively on the reconstruction of their own houses after their return from the Babylonian captivity, God had to send bad harvests and drought to compel

them eventually to set about the rebuilding of the temple (see Hag 1:2–15). Even the 'wicked neighbouring peoples' were incorporated into this work of reconstruction—that is to say, they were able to share in the benefits of salvation, provided that they were converted to the worship of the true God (see Jer 12:14ff). God spoke, through Jeremiah, to the disheartened Jewish warriors who were afraid of the vengeance of Babylon and wished to flee: 'If you will remain in this land, then I will build you up and not pull you down; I will plant you, and not pluck you up' (Jer 42:10). God also comforted the Jews in their Babylonian captivity with the assurance that their homeland that had been laid waste would one day again be made as beautiful as the Garden of Eden (Ezek 36:35), and went on to promise them: 'The nations that are left round about you shall know that I, the Lord, have rebuilt the ruined places and replanted that which was desolate'. Wisdom, which can be interpreted as divine wisdom, has also built a house for herself and repeatedly invites men to her banquet (Prov 9:1ff). A perfectly ideal transition to the New Testament and the spiritual rebuilding of the temple by the Messiah (see Jn 2:19) is to be found in Zech 6:12: 'Behold the man whose name is the Branch [LXX: *anatolē* =rise, rising]: for he shall grow up in his place, and he shall build the Temple of the Lord'.

In the *Rabbinical writings*, the image of 'building' also occurs quite frequently. Here it is God who is the masterbuilder of the world (see SB 1, 732). The 'architect's plan' from which he constructs his edifice is often the

Torah (SB II, 357: 'Who advised him when he created the world? It was only the Torah that he consulted)'. The pupils of the Hebrew scholars or rabbis are occasionally named as builders (SB I, 876; III, 379), since, by studying the Torah (b. Schabb. 144a) they build the world and add to the peace of the world (see Ber 64a, with reference to Is 54:13). A similar comparison made by Elisha ben Abuja automatically calls to mind the conclusion of the Sermon on the Mount: 'A man who has performed many good works and has learnt much of the Torah, with whom can he be compared? With a man who ... builds with stones and then with bricks' (SB I, 469). In one midrash it is expected that the heavenly city will be completely rebuilt in the last days for the coming of the Messiah: 'Then Jerusalem, perfectly rebuilt, will come down from heaven with 72 pearls which will gleam from one end of the world to the other' (SB III, 796). In 4 Esdras 10:27, too, there is a vision of the rebuilt Jerusalem which aims to console the Jews of AD 70 and later.

There is an interesting example of the figurative use of the word under consideration in Ber 63a (Goldschmidt, 1, 286f). In the passage in question, the high priest has been reviling two scribes and accusing them of lying, after having bestowed high praise on them only a short while before. Their reply to him is: 'Thou hast already built up and canst not pull down again. Thou has already fenced in and canst no more break through that fence.'

According to Philo, *Leg. Alleg.* II, 3, 6, the heart of a man is created first and the rest of the human body is built on the heart (*oikodomeitai to allo sōma* = the rest of the body is built [on it]), just as a ship is built up on the keel. Implanting virtues in the soul and building them up is, of course, a concern of God himself: *prepei tōi theōi phuteuein kai oikodomein en psukhēi tas aretas* ('it belongs to God to implant and build up virtues in the soul'; *Leg. Alleg.* I, 15, 48). Philo, the philosopher, must naturally regret the way fools build their doctrine without foundation, like a tower: *dogma adokimon oikodomountes eis hupsos hoia purgon* ('building bad doctrine up on high like a tower'; *De Somn.* II, 284)—a tower which God is bound to destroy as he once destroyed the Tower of Babel. (Further references in *TDNT* v, 137f and in H. Leisegang, *Philo-Index.*)

The idea of a building or construction, the foundation of a wall, a tower, and so on, which stand for God's protection and powerful aid, is found in the Qumran texts and denotes both the entire community and the individual pious man. One example of this usage is: 'Thou settest me up as a strong tower, as a lofty wall; thou placest my building firmly on a rock and givest me eternal foundations' (1 QH VIII, 8f). In QH VII, 4, the fear of wicked men is clearly expressed by the author of the hymn: 'The foundations of my building [ie, body] are breaking to pieces, my frame is collapsing, my innermost heart is pitching and tossing like a ship in a raging storm'. The Community Rule of the Dead Sea sect has this to say with regard to the approaching judgement: 'Then, with his truth, God will sift and examine all the works of man and clear out his building [ie, body], so as to drive all evil spirits out of his flesh (1 QS IV, 20). In the Damascus text which follows, it is not certain whether the word 'house' refers to the Temple or perhaps to the community of the faithful (by analogy with Enoch 53:6; 89:36; 1 Tim 3:15; Heb 3:6; 1 Pet 4:17): 'He built them a safe house in Israel, like none other than has ever existed from times of old until the present' (CD III, 19). In QS VIII, the latter is certainly the case, for the 'men of the community' are described as 'a holy house for Israel and a dwelling of the Most Holy One for Aaron'. In the fragment of a commentary on Ps 37, the teacher (is this the Teacher of Righteousness?) has been appointed by God to build a community for him (4 Qp Ps 37, II, 16). (For these passages and further examples of the same kind, reference can be made to G. Vermes, *The Dead Sea Scrolls in English*, London 1962.)

The well known phrase 'builder of walls' (*bōnê haḥayits*) has no commendatory connotation but is, on the contrary, equated in CD VIII 2 with housepainters who cover all (moral) damage with a coat of limewash (see also Ezek 13:10). The name is applied to those half-hearted and impenitent members of the chosen people who are hated by God (CD VIII, 18). According to Nötscher 57, the word refers to the adherents of the preacher of lies and probably to the Pharisees as well, who, acting against God's express command (Gen 1:27; 2:24), permitted polygamy (see *CD* IV, 19ff). A. S. van der Woude, among others, is of the opinion that the word refers to the Pharisees (*Die messianische Vorstellungen der Gemeinde von Qumran*, Assen 1957, 240). The bitter allusion to Mic 7:11: 'The wall is built, but the law is remote. In all

these years Belial will be let loose against Israel' (CD III, 12), confirms the unfavourable meaning mentioned above.

In the *New Testament*, the word 'build' is mainly used in its literal sense. A man builds a house (Mt 7:24 and parallels) or a tower (Mk 12:1 and parallels) in order to have a better view over his vineyard, although the expenditure must be carefully calculated in advance (Lk 14:28). The stupid farmer wishes to build new and bigger barns (Lk 12:18), the Jews build tombs and memorials for the prophets (Lk 11:47), and the centurion, who was a gentile, even built a synagogue (Lk 7:5). There are many other examples. Buying and selling, planting and building, have formed an essential part of the ordinary language of human civilisation since the time of Lot (see Lk 17:28).

Those who build, or, in the figurative sense, 'edify', include God himself (Acts 20:32); Christ (Mt 16:18); the apostles, acting in Christ's name and receiving their commission from him (Rom 15:20), and—among the apostles —especially Paul (1 Cor 3:10, 12; 2 Cor 10:8; 13:10); many men who have been liberally endowed with grace (1 Cor 14:3-5); and, finally, every christian (Rom 15:2), either by his kind words of comfort (1 Thess 5:11; Eph 4:29) or else by foregoing some pleasure, which is in itself permitted, for his 'weaker' brother's sake (1 Cor 8:1; 10:23). Above all, fitting communal worship contributes a great deal to the edification of those who take part in it (1 Cor 14:26). The use of 'build up', in Gal 2:18, is completely out of place in this connection, as it refers to the old law and the 'wall of partition' which Christ fortunately did away with. It is in this instance 'quite unusual and not at all characteristic' of Paul (Vielhauer, 89).

If there are many different builders, there can be many different buildings too: a. The basis of our redemption and our faith must always be the Easter event, when *Christ's dead body*, the temple 'not made with hands', was 'built up' again 'in three days' (Mk 14:28: *oikodomēsō* ['I will build'] = Jn 2:19 *egerō* ['I will wake up, raise up']). b. Furthermore, the church was built on the rock of Peter (Mt 16:18), and this did not come about by an 'eschatological act on the part of Christ' on the Lord's day, as O. Michel (*TDNT* v, 139, 5f and 12f) seems to regard as possible. This building of the church is, on the contrary, clearly an immediate consequence of the resurrection of Jesus. The same Peter was solemnly entrusted with the duty of feeding Christ's entire flock only a short time after the resurrection (Jn 21:15ff). Despite the controversy surrounding the authorship of Chap. 21, R. Bultmann (*Johannes-Evangelium*, 1964, 552) maintains along with others that these three verses are derived from ancient tradition, since the risen Christ must somehow or other have adopted a definite attitude towards Peter's 'fall', as ultimately he had to keep his solemn promise to build his church on the rock of Peter. Vielhauer (76) calls the passage in Mt 16:18 an 'erratic block', by which he means that this is the only place in the New Testament in which Christ is named as a builder of the community. But it is permissible, in this connection to ask, with Karl Barth (716), who would then have built the church other than the one whom the church always calls her 'Lord'. After many setbacks, such as the death of Stephen, for example, a new era of peaceful 'construction' or 'edification' dawned when Paul, now converted to christianity, had left Palestine (Acts 9:31).

Paul brings a new vision and fresh points of interest to bear on the character of this mysterious building up of the church. It is built up on the foundation of the apostles and the New Testament prophets, and its cornerstone is Jesus Christ (Eph 2:20), who had already described himself as such in Ps 118:22f (Mk 12:10 and parallels). It stands to reason that the gentiles and the heathen who had recently been converted are incorporated into this building (Eph 2:22). But just as the ancient temples and, in the course of time, also the Gothic cathedrals of a later age, were in constant need of 'building', that is, of restoration and preservation (see A. Deissmann, *Paul: A Study in Social and Religious History*, New York 1957[2], 212), so also was the church itself. Indeed, the structure 'grows into a holy temple in the Lord' (Eph 2:21) and 'upbuilds itself in love' (Eph 4:16), since it is not a dead body but—in a mysterious way—the living body of Christ (Col 1:18, 24; Eph 1:22). 'It is precisely this complex picture of the "growing edifice" which does full justice to the historical character of the church in all its many aspects' (V. Warnach, *Die Kirche im Epheserbrief*, 1949, 34). The ↗ head of this body is Christ (Eph 4:16; Col 1:18). The baptised, however, are the 'body of Christ' (1 Cor 12:27), or the 'mem-

94

bers of his body' (Eph 5:30). Every-one, including the apostles, the prophets, and the evangelists, must assist in the 'edification' of this body of Christ (Eph 4:12), until the time when perfect unity in faith—'the measure of the stature of the fullness of Christ' (Eph 4:13)—is attained.

H. Schlier claims that 'this inter-mingling of body and building is also a kind of gnostic building-allegory' (*Der Brief an die Epheser*, 1963, 143). Today there are other catholic exegetes, too, who regard it as quite possible that Paul was influenced by (prechristian) gnos-ticism at least as far as the precise wording and linguistic imagery of his thought was concerned (see Pfam-matter, 107–14). However, this double image of body and building can be clearly traced back to Christ himself. Mention has already been made of the fact that Christ refers to himself as the cornerstone which the builders (ie, the powers-that-be in Israel) have rejected (Mt 21:42 and parallels). Jn 2:21 would seem to be decisive in this respect: 'But he spoke of the temple of his body'. This must certainly have been familiar to the oldest synoptic tradition (on this see A. Wikenhauser, *Johannes-Evangelium*, 1957, 81). In this connection, too, 1 Pet 2:5 invites christians to be 'like living stones . . . built into a spiritual house'. Paul, needless to say, is concerned not only with the church as a whole, but also with the 'edification' of each individual community, as, for example, the church at Corinth (2 Cor 12:19). Out of loyalty, he certainly does not wish to build up on foundations laid by others (Rom 15:20), despite the constant appeal that a preaching mission to the

christians in Rome must have had for him, anxious as he was to evangelise the populations of the great cities (Rom 1:13ff).

One last question remains to be answered: c. Is it possible, in accord-ance with New Testament teaching, for the individual christian as such to be 'edified', or is edification intended only for the christian community as a whole? Karl Barth (*Church Dogmatics* IV/2, Edinburgh 1958, sections 67f) comes down very strongly in support of the latter thesis, but F. Niebergall takes the opposite view and claims (*RGG* II [1928], 213): 'The first and foremost aim is not the edification of the christian community as a whole, but . . . of the individual in his christian life.' Both these views are onesided and fail to take all the scriptural data into consideration. If a christian who has the gift of tongues (which, after all, is meant to be a means of religious stimulation and advancement for all) 'edifies himself' only (1 Cor 14:4), then that is a result which the apostle certainly represents as of small account. Apart, however, from worship in com-mon, the christian is recommended to 'build [himself] up' by prayer (Jude 20). This is made explicit in 1 Thess 5:11: 'Therefore encourage one an-other [*allēlous*] and build one another [*heis ton hena*] up'; and in Rom 15:2 Paul exhorts every christian to serve his neighbour 'to edify him'. It is also possible for the individual conscience to be edified (1 Cor 8:1). For these reasons the claim is made, in *TDNT* v, 144, 4f, that the notion of 'building' or 'edification' is applicable both to the christian community or church and to the spiritual growth of the individual christian. With this can be compared Schoenen's statement ('Aedificatio', 21): all building up of the church, both as a whole and in its individual members, can therefore be regarded as the essential fructification of Christ's ↗ cross. This condition occurs when grace and faith come into contact with each other.

Although Luther translated the word in question, wherever it is used in the figurative sense (Rom 15:2; 1 Cor 8:1; 10:23; 2 Cor 10:8; 12:19 etc), by 'reform' or 'reformation' and thus succeeded in emphasising the 'grave, temperate quality and the vigorous ethical tone of the word' (Laasch, 1113), at the same time he deprived it of a great deal of its particular and venerable lustre. The word later acquired, with the pietists, a strong flavour of sentimentality and a meaning charged with a cheap emotionalism. Some indication of the depths to which this word—used so often by the Old Testament writers and by Paul—has sunk in the protestant church, is given by Doerne (*RGG* 2 [1958], 539): 'The word is worn out beyond repair. It has become alien to the linguistic and conceptual terminology of the christian religion and is an annoying, even blasphemous, word. It could hardly now be restored to its original dignity.' And yet, as we have seen, 'build' is used on the first pages of the bible, to describe a divine activity, and the church which has stood until the present day can thus stand only because she is, in fact, 'God's building' (1 Cor 3:9). This is why the christian must regain an understanding of the full import of this word, so full of meaning, as it is used in the bible, as

there can surely be no more worthwhile and important task for the christian than to 'build up' or 'edify'—in other words, to strengthen in faith—both the church, caught up as she is today in such a desperate struggle, and each one of his hard-pressed fellow christians. Above all, the pastor will feel himself, more than ever nowadays, bound to the principle of the Good Shepherd (Mt 12:20; Lk 15:4), which was so clearly formulated by Paul in the statement: *eis oikodomēn humōn kai ouk eis kathairesin humōn* ('for building you up and not for destroying you' 2 Cor 10:8; see also 13:10).

Bibliography: H. Bassermann, 'Über den Begriff "Erbauung"', *Zt. prot. Theol.* 4 (1882), 1–22; H. M. Scott, 'The Place of *oikodomē* in NT Worship', *The Princeton Theol. Rev.* 2 (1904), 402–24; P. C. Trossen, 'Erbauen', *TG* (1914), 804–12; W. Straub, *Die Bildersprache des Apostels Paulus*, 1937, 36, 85ff, and 93f; P. Vielhauer, *Oikodome. Das Bild vom Bau in der christl. Lit. vom NT bis Clem. Alex.*, 1939; K. L. Schmidt, *Die Erbauung der Kirche mit ihren Gliedern als den Fremdlingen und Beisassen auf Erden*, 1947; P. Bonnard, *Jésus-Christ édifiant son Eglise*, Neuchâtel-Paris 1948; T. Schneider (K. H. Schelkle), *RAC* 1 (1950), 1265–78; K. Barth, *Church Dogmatics* IV/2, Edinburgh 1958, 614–76; T. Laasch, *Evang. Kirchenlexikon* 1 (1956), 1112–3; A. Schoenen, 'Aedificatio. Zum Verständnis eines Glaubenswortes in Kult und Schrift', *Enkainia*, ed. H. Edmonds 1956, 14–29; W. Bauer, *A Greek–English Lexikon of the NT and other Early Christian Literature*, ed. W. F. Arndt and F. W. Gingrich, Cambridge and Chicago 1957, 560–62; M. Doerne, *RGG* 2 (1958), 538–40; H. Schlier, *LTK* III² (1959), 959–61; H. Kosmala, *Hebräer-Essener-Christen*, Leiden 1959, 363–78; J. Pfammatter, *Die Kirche als Bau*, Rome 1960; H. Pohlmann, *RAC* v (1962), 1043–70.

Johannes Kosnetter

Charisma

The Greek word *kharisma* (= free gift of grace) was coined by Paul in order to reduce a whole series of striking manifestations of the emotive state induced by faith in the first christian communities founded by him (especially in Corinth) to a common denominator. He laid down specific rules to govern these manifestations.

A. *Meaning of the term.* By 'charisma' we are to understand, in the majority of cases, a *supernatural and actual grace* which is given for the advancement of the mystical body of Christ and which comes from the Holy Spirit. Three conclusions can be drawn from this:

a. A charisma is a gift which has its origin in the *kharis* (= ↗ Grace), the favour or goodwill of God. Of his own free will (1 Cor 12:11) God portions out these 'gifts' or 'services' or 'manifestations' of power (1 Cor 12:4–6), but in doing so takes into account the needs of the church as a whole and the talents and capacities of the individual.

b. These gifts are such that the whole community may profit by them, that is, they are allotted, in the first place, 'for the common good' (1 Cor 12:7), and not for the spiritual benefit of the person so endowed. Scholasticism expresses this as *gratia gratis data* as distinct from a *gratia gratum faciens.* They are embodied in the most manifold 'services' or 'functions' which God raises up and presides over for the advancement and growth of the church, for the preservation of unity of faith and purity of doctrine (see Eph 4:7–16).

c. They are to be attributed to the Holy Spirit who was given to the disciples after the resurrection and ascension of Christ (see Eph 4:7–11 and Jn 7:39). Already during the lifetime of Jesus we meet with some extraordinary manifestations of the Spirit,

but these are not described as 'charismatic gifts' but as 'miraculous signs' (Mt 17:19; Mk 16:17f; Lk 21:15). The chosen people had witnessed, especially in times of need, mighty miracles such as the display of supernatural forces, heroic courage in war, the predictions of the prophets, and ecstasy. These same were foreseen as a part of the messianic age (Deut 28:49; Is 29:11f; Joel 3:1–3; ↗ Spirit A).

B. *Different kinds of charisma.* Paul enumerates a series of charismatic gifts without pretending to be exhaustive. Some of these are a constant feature of the life of the church, while others are conditioned by particular circumstances at a given time, as, for example, 'the gift of tongues' in the communities founded by the apostle of the gentiles. They are embodied in various 'services' connected with the life of the church (see 1 Cor 12:14; Rom 12:3–8; Eph 4:7–16; 1 Pet 4:10f).

1. *Charismata and the service of teaching.* Most 'gifts of the Spirit' play a major role in the worship and liturgy of the early church (see Acts 2:42).

a. The charismatic 'gift of tongues', otherwise known as 'glossolalia' or—better—'ecstatic utterance', was held in the highest honour at the liturgical gatherings of the faithful of Corinth (1 Cor 12:10; 14:1, 5, 6, 18; see also 13:1; 2 Cor 12:4). This gift was connected with the service of the word of God which was a preparation for the celebration of the eucharistic sacrifice. On the first occasion, the apostles probably spoke, as a result of the coming down of the Holy Spirit, 'in strange tongues' (not 'in foreign tongues'—compare the distinction in French between *langues étranges* and *langues étrangères*), implying that they were quite beside themselves with the exultation and joy of the Holy Spirit (Acts 2:4, 11, 15; see also 10:46; 11:15; 19:6). Those who had been seized by the Spirit emitted inarticulate, unintelligible sounds and expressions, disjointed and meaningless, which 'no one understands' (1 Cor 14:2, 6, 7–12, 16). They should therefore pray for the grace (14:13) to understand this 'ecstatic utterance' themselves or to be able to do so through someone else (12:10; 14:5, 27f). Only in this way can those who take part in the liturgical service draw spiritual profit (14:16, 26).

b. Paul gives a higher place to the service of teaching than to 'the gift of tongues'. The Holy Spirit takes part with power in the instruction of converted Jews and heathens by means of numerous charismatic manifestations which it is not always possible for us to distinguish and differentiate exactly. Particularly in 1 Cor 12:14 the apostle deals with these *ex professo*. The gift of *wisdom* endows the charismatic person with an amazing knowledge and a masterly command of the art of exposition with regard to the christian mystery in all its height and depth (see 1 Cor 2:6–16; Eph 1:2–23; Heb 6:1). The '*utterance of knowledge*' is shown in an intelligent presentation of the common, indispensable truths, 'the elementary doctrines of Christ' (Heb 6:1). The gift of '*prophecy*' has a foremost place (see Acts 11:27; 13:1; 15:32; 21:9f); it bestows the gift of reading the secrets of the heart (1 Cor 14:24f; see also 1 Tim 1:18; 4:14), predicting the future (Acts 11:28; 21:10f), and serves for 'upbuilding and encourage-

ment and consolation' (1 Cor 14:3; see also Acts 4:36; 11:23f). The most important task of the 'prophets' is, however, to interpret under the influence of the Holy Spirit the messianic oracles in a christological sense (1 Pet 1:10–12), and so to reveal the 'mystery' of the divine economy of salvation in Christ (1 Cor 13:2; Eph 3:5 Rom 16:25). The gift of *the discernment of spirits* permits the identity of a 'prophet' to be established beyond the possibility of doubt—whether he is such according to the Spirit of God or according to a 'lying spirit' (1 Cor 14:29; 1 Tim 4:1; 1 Jn 4:1). Distinct from the 'prophets' who give utterance during the liturgical celebration as a result of spontaneous inspiration, the '*teachers*' speak *ex officio* (Rom 12:7; 1 Cor 12:2–28; Acts 13:1; Eph 4:11–14). They are entrusted with the task of expounding the Holy Scriptures, that is, the Old Testament, and of giving moral instruction. The charismatic gift of *exhortation* puts in the mouth of the pastor of souls the admonishing and consoling word.

All the charismatic gifts so far named refer to teaching and instruction addressed to brethren in the faith in the context of the church, a teaching which, endorsed as it is by the Holy Spirit, is endowed with irresistible force.

2. *Charismata and the service of the missions*. When we read, in 1 Cor 12, that God had designated some as apostles (vv 28, 30; see also Eph 4:11–14), we have to take it in a fairly wide sense. They are *sent* to the heathens in order to bring them the word of God about Jesus Christ which has power to win them over. The charismatic gift of *apostolate*, which includes both ministers

and laypeople, will continue until the end of the world (Mt 28:20).

a. This gift of the Spirit equips its bearers with supernatural strength in order to proclaim to the nations the glad tidings of the glorified Lord and of his return with all confidence (↗ Word, ↗ Witness). Paul does not base the preaching of the message of salvation on human wisdom, but on the Holy Spirit and the strength which comes from him (1 Cor 2:4-5, 13; see also Rom 1:9; 1 Thess 1:5). This charismatic gift of proclamation has never been absent in the church's history. Thus, to take just one example, right in the middle of the shallow period of the Enlightenment, Blessed Clement Maria Hofbauer, the apostle of Vienna, raised the challenge: 'Today the Gospel must be proclaimed anew!' The return to the fountainhead in the bible, the liturgy and ancient tradition can be taken, to use an expression of Pius XII, as 'a sign of God's providence in regard to the present age, the breath of the Holy Spirit in his Church'. This providential return gives to missionary preaching a more biblical, liturgical, paschal and eschatological accent.

b. The Holy Spirit inspires and directs also the manifold *apostolic undertakings* which gave to life in the church at that time the kind of stamp which comes in our day from Catholic Action, the apostolate of the laity, the Legion of Mary, the Mission de France, the worker priests, etc.

The function of teaching and of missionary work in the early church was given firm support by the *gift of healing* and the *power of working miracles*, which made a great impression on 'those without' and provided a spec-

tacular proof of the truth of the christian message (1 Cor 12:9f, 28ff; see also Acts 4:30). Paul exults of 'what Christ has wrought through me to win obedience from the Gentiles, by word and deed, by the power of signs and wonders, by the power of the Holy Spirit' (Rom 15:18f; see also Gal 3:5).

3. *Charisma and the service of love.* The Spirit of God leads on irresistibly to deeds of charity. He gives the grace of 'solicitous charity' (*diakonia*), of loving service (Rom 12:7), so that this can stand as a shining sign of the love of Christ among men (see Jn 21:15-17; 1 Pet 5:1, 4).

a. At the birth of every great charitable work of the church there is present the charismatic gift of *assistance*. The Holy Spirit himself *appoints* certain people for the foundation of charitable institutions suited to the needs of the church at different times. The apostles appointed for the service of tables 'seven men of good repute, full of the Spirit and of wisdom' by means of the laying on of hands and of prayer (Acts 6:1-6; see also Rom 16:11). This gift of *diakonia* has never been extinguished in the church of God, and today it is as strong as ever: we have only to think of the ragpickers of Emmaus of Abbé Pierre, of Père Pire's villages for displaced persons, of the large-scale work of assistance organised by Fr van Straaten, etc.

b. Under the influence of this gift which comes from the Spirit, its bearers laid down with a sure touch the norms and the rhythm for an orderly development of this service of love.

c. This charismatic gift makes fruitful the labour of love of christian men and women who do not shrink back from the colossal difficulties and do not lay down their arms in view of the miserable means at their disposal. Just as the word of God possesses irresistible power, so is the work of God fruitful to an unsuspected, a supernatural degree.

4. *Charisma and hierarchy.* How are the charismatic gifts and the hierarchy related? Those who possess the gift of the Spirit go to work, as a rule, with great energy in every sector of church life, for the establishment of the kingship of Jesus Christ, while ecclesiastical rulers prefer to bide their time and weigh everything carefully. From this situation there arise tensions which sometimes deeply affect the parties concerned, but which are resolved in due time through the Holy Spirit. For, in the last analysis, it is the Holy Spirit who appoints to positions of leadership in the church (see the gift of 'administration', 1 Cor 12:28) and who governs the church through his representatives (see Acts 10:19; 11:28; 20:23; 21:4). It is the Holy Spirit who in particular gives to those in authority in the church the gift of 'differentiating' so that they can separate the weeds from the good wheat. It is the Holy Spirit who equips the successors of Peter with the charismatic gift of infallibility (according to the first Vatican Council; DS 3074), and by so doing unites in one person office and Spirit-given gift. These precious Spirit-given gifts can enrich the church as a blessing only when their bearers submit to the final decision of ecclesiastical authority.

C. *Order of importance of the charismata.* The charismatic gifts are not all of equal value. Paul admonishes his christians to strive after the most

perfect gifts of the Spirit, by which he meant the offices of apostle, prophet, and teacher (1 Cor 12:28, 30), since it is these which most advance the good of the church (1 Cor 14:4, 6).

But even the greatest and the most precious gifts of the Spirit are eclipsed by love. It is for this reason that the hymn to charity (love) (1 Cor 13) has such a dominant position between Chaps. 12 and 14, which contain an exposition of the charismatic gifts. In the Epistle to the Romans, the explanation of the gifts of the Spirit is crowned by the commandment of love (Rom 12). Even if the charismatic gifts do not belong to the essence of the church, they make a valuable contribution as building material for the construction of the mystical body of the Lord; and so the words of Peter still have their value today: 'As each has received a gift (*kharisma*), employ it for one another, as good stewards of God's varied grace: whoever speaks, as one who utters oracles of God; whoever renders service, as one who renders it by the strength which God supplies; in order that in everything God may be glorified through Jesus Christ. To him belong glory and dominion for ever and ever. Amen' (1 Pet 4:10–11).

Bibliography: F. Grau, *Der ntl. Begriff 'charisma', seine Geschichte und seine Theologie*, Tübingen 1947 (dissertation); E. Schweitzer, *Das Leben des Herrn in der Gemeinde und in ihren Diensten*, Basle-Zurich 1946; J. Brosch, *Charismen und Ämter in der Urkirche*, Bonn 1951; H. von Campenhausen, *Kirchliches Amt und geistliche Vollmacht in den ersten drei Jahrhunderten*, Tübingen 1953; G. von Rad I, 93–102; A. Lemmonyer, *DB(S)* I, 1233–43; J. V. M. Pollet, *Catholicisme* 2 (1949), 956–9; X. Ducros, *Dict. de Spiritualité* 2 (1953), 503–7; *LTK* II², 1025–36; J. Behm, *TDNT* I, 719–26; Haag, 540f; *BTHW*, 1631; E. Käsemann, *RGG* II², 1272–9; A. George and P. Grelot, *DBT*, 55–7. See also the commentaries on 1 Cor and other NT epistles mentioned, in particular E. B. Allo, *Première Epître aux Corinthiens*, Paris 1934, 317–86; K. Rahner, *The Dynamic Element in the Church*, London 1969; *K. Rahner, *Mission and Grace* II, London 1964, 26–34; G. Murphy, *Charisma and Church Renewal*, Rome 1965.

Robert Koch

Church

In opposition to the institutional vision of the church which up to now has been dominant, recent exegesis is bringing more strongly to the foreground a view of the church seen within the context of salvation history. This does not of course imply that the former view has become marginal or even superfluous; but when compared with the question of the foundation and structure of the church as a socio-religious corporation, the more important question of its position and function in the whole context of the redemptive operation brought to its completion by God through Christ is seen as more urgent. That this view corresponds with New Testament findings is established by a review of this material under the relevant headings.

A. *Terminology and concept.* What we mean by 'church' (derived from the late Greek *kuriakon* [*dōma*] = [house] of the Lord) can be established from the New Testament chiefly by means of the term *ekklēsia* (= assembly called together), which is derived from the verb *ek-kalein* (= to call [someone] out of). The word is also found in the New Testament with the secular meaning, which goes back to the period of classical Greek, of 'popular assembly' (Acts 19:39; see also 19:32, 41—'a gathering of men'), but in general it has a specifically religious or theological range of meaning. This is also the case in LXX, where it occurs almost a hundred times, mostly (seventy-two times) as translating the Hebrew *qāhāl* (= assembly), but sometimes with the more specific meaning of *qāhāl Yahweh* (= *ekklēsia kuriou* = assembly of the Lord: Deut 23:1–3, 8; 1 Chron 28:8; see also Num 16:3: *sunagōgē kuriou* = assembly, congregation of the Lord) or *ekklēsia theou* (= assembly of God: Neh 13:1), indicating the people of Israel as the gathered cultic or redeemed community of Yahweh. In the same way, in the New Testament writings—particularly in Acts and Paul—*ekklēsia* refers to the redeemed community of the new covenant or, at times, is used to characterise the sum total of men redeemed through Christ (eg, Mt 16:18; 1 Cor 12:28; Eph 1:22; 3:10, 21; 5:23–7, 29, 32; Phil 3:6; Col 1:18, 24), occurring quite often as *ekklēsia tou theou* (1 Cor 10:32; 11:16; 15:9; Gal 1:13; 1 Tim 3:15; in the plural: 1 Thess 2:14; 2 Thess 1:4; 1 Tim 3:5) or *ekklēsia tou khristou* (Rom 16:16). Very often *ekklēsia* means the particular community in a specified place (apart from references in the opening address of the epistles: see, eg, Acts 8:1; 11:22; 14:27; 15:41; 1 Cor 7:17; Gal 1:22; Phil 4:15; Rev 2:1, 8 etc) or also the 'house–church' (Rom 16:5; Col 4:15; Philem 2), in particular, however, the community gathered together for worship (1 Cor 11:18; 14:4f, 19, 28, 34f; see also Acts 15:22). The distinction between the local community and the church as a whole accepted by most exegetes is not, however, carried through with any great emphasis in the terminology used in the New Testament (eg, Acts 5:11; 8:3; 9:31; 12:1; 1 Cor 4:17; 6:4; 1 Tim 5:16), which fits in well with the idea of the universal church as realised in a concrete way in the local community (see under C2).

There is another distinction in the use of *ekklēsia* which is more relevant theologically. In many texts this term possesses a greater depth of meaning which is not exhaustively expressed in terms such as 'the church as a whole', or 'the universal church'; this is especially true in the epistles of the captivity (we might quote Eph 1:22f; 3:10, 21; Col 1:18). It can hardly be a question simply of the empirical church as realised here below in history; rather does it assume in these expressions a dimension which takes us beyond history and indeed beyond the cosmos. In this sense we could justly designate it as 'mystery' in the pauline sense, a point we shall establish more exactly under C1. In this sense it refers to the work of God with regard to men within history leading either to salvation or to judgement. We have now to distinguish (but not separate!) from this concept of the church in terms of mystery the more historical and concrete view according to which the church is the community of those who believe in Christ, a community at one and the same time visible and invisible since supernatural, whether used in the universal or local sense. The church as a redeemed community (*congregatio fidelium*) is in one sense the result, the historical manifestation or incarnation, of the church as mystery. Both concepts refer to the one and the same existent

reality of the church as seen from different points of view.

Apart from the term *ekklēsia*, the New Testament uses other expressions for the existing reality which we call 'the church'. Significantly, *sunagōgē* is used only once of the christian community (Jas 2:2, but see also 5:14), since this word was then applied to Jewish communities (eg, Acts 17:1). More frequently the church is referred to as *laos* (=people: Tit 2:14; Heb 2:17; 13:12; 1 Pet 2:9 [Ex 19:6]), more specifically as *laos theou* (=people of God: Rom 9:24ff [Hos 2:23; 1:10]; 2 Cor 6:16 [Lev 26:12]; Heb 4:9; 8:10 [Jer 31:33]; 1 Pet 2:10; Rev 18:4; 21:3). Numerous other expressions have a more or less plastic character, and can only be explained in terms of typological interpretation of the Old Testament, which means that we have to look into this first, since the New Testament—and not just Hebrews and Revelation, but also the synoptic gospels, John, and by no means least Paul (Gal 4:21-31; 1 Cor 10:1-11; Eph 5:31f)—make clear and explicit use of these figures.

B. *The church in Old Testament typology and New Testament imagery.* We find traces of such figures from the very first pages of the Old Testament writings; their deep roots and the wide-ranging ramifications of their prehistory takes us back to the time of the patriarchs and even as far as the Garden of Eden, since, according to Eph 5:31f, the mystery of Christ and the church is already announced in the matrimonial community of our first parents. The various covenants which we meet with in the course of Old Testament salvation history are likewise so many stages in the preparation for the new and eternal covenant which takes on living form in the church. In particular, the Old Testament people of the covenant, which passed under Moses' leadership through the Red Sea and the desert into the land of promise is, in its concrete destiny, a 'type' (1 Cor 10:6; cf 10:1–11) of the true 'Israel of God' (Gal 6:16; cf Rom 9:6), and even of the whole of mankind which is set free from the slavery of sin and death through the blood of Christ and which has already entered into the 'Sabbath rest' of God (Heb 4:9f) on the strength of rebirth by the water of baptism and may taste of 'the heavenly gift' (Heb 6:4). On the grounds of the contrast with 'the Israel according to the flesh' (Gal 4:22ff) we may conclude that the christian people is 'the Israel according to the Spirit' (see Eph 2:12; Heb 8:8–10; Rev 7:4; 21:12) to whom the promises first made to the patriarchs are transferred (Eph 3:6; see also Gal 3:22f, 29). Likewise, in contrast with the *politeia tou Israēl* (=commonwealth of Israel) from which the heathens were excluded there stands the church as the true theocratic commonwealth to which all heathens as well as Jews are admitted, thus forming *sumpolitai tōn hagiōn* (=fellow citizens of the saints) and even *oikeioi tou theou* (=members of God's household)—in short, the intimate community and family of God (Eph 2:12–19).

The metaphor of a 'flock' is often tied up in the Old Testament with the concept of a 'people', as in Ps 95:7; 100:3; etc. Just as Israel was the flock pastured by Yahweh (Ps 80:1; Is 40:11; Jer 13:17; 23:1–4; 31:10; Ezek 34; Mic 7:14; Zech 10:2f)—a metaphor which is used at times particularly of the 'remnant' of the people of God (Mic 2:12f), but at others admits of a certain universality (Sir 18:13)—so is the church, as the new people of God, compared with a flock (Mt 26:31; Lk 12:32; Acts 20:28f; 1 Pet 5:2f; Jn 10:1–16; see also 21:15–17), whose 'true shepherd' is Christ (Jn 10:11–16; Heb 13:20; 1 Pet 2:25; 5:4), but Christ as Messiah (Jer 23:4; Ezek 34:23f; see also Mt 25:32; 26:31). And just as Israel is described as the *vineyard* of Jahweh (Ps 80:8ff; Is 5:1–7; Jer 2:21; 12:10), so our Lord himself describes the plan of salvation and therefore the church as a vineyard into which the workers, that is, the prophets and apostles (and in reality all christians) are sent in order to cultivate it (Mt 20:1–16; see also Mk 12:1–12 and parallels; Rev 14:17–20). Further, he describes himself as the 'true Vine' from which we as the vine-branches take into ourselves the life of grace and love (Jn 15:1–6; see also Sir 24:17).

From another point of view the *city of God*, Sion (=Jerusalem), despite its dignity and glory, is only a shadowy model for the Jerusalem which is 'above' or which comes 'from above', and which is no longer a simple maiden but a lady and mother of the free, that is, of those who have been set free through Christ who gives true freedom (Gal 4:21–31 referring to Is 54:1; see also Is 26:1ff; 27:13; 40:1f, 9–11; 51:17; 52:1–10; 60; 62:10–12). This is seen in that we 'have come to Mount Sion and to the city of the living God, the heavenly Jerusalem, and to innumerable angels in festal gathering, and to the assembly of the first-born' (Heb 12:22f). The church is therefore the 'new' city of God (Rev 3:12) which the author of Revelation sees in a vision coming down from heaven as the 'holy city, the new Jerusalem, prepared as a bride adorned for her husband' (21:2). She is 'the dwelling of God with men' in which he himself dwells among them so that they may be truly 'his people' (21:3). She is also 'the Bride, the wife of the Lamb' (21:9) adorned with divine glory (21:11). In the last resort, these are all eschatological expressions; but they refer to the church on earth which is, in essence, one with that in heaven, which can be shown—to quote but one example—by the use of the perfect tense *proseléluthate* (=you have come [already]) in Heb 12:22.

The metaphor of a *city* is closely allied with that of a *house* or the 'house of God' (*oikos tou theou*); this is how the 'church of the living God' is designated in 1 Tim 3:15 (see Heb 3:6; 8:8ff [quoting Jer 31:31ff]; 10:21; 1 Pet 4:17). This metaphor is likewise rooted in Old Testament representations, such as 'the house of Jacob' (Is 2:2-6) or 'the house of Israel' (Is 5:7 and *passim*) or also 'the house of Wisdom' (Prov 9:1; see also 'the house of the Thorah' in the Damascus Document, 20:13). That it is a question of a 'spiritual edifice' is expressly stated and emphasised in 1 Pet 2:5. Its foundation-stone or corner-stone is Christ (1 Pet 2:6 [Is 28:16]; see also Mk 12:10 and parallels [Ps 118:22]; Acts 4:11; Eph 2:20), upon whom the faithful are built up 'like living stones' (1 Pet 2:4f; see also Eph 2:19-22). In 1 Tim 3:15 the church is further described as 'pillar and bulwark of the truth', by which is indicated one of her most

important functions, namely, the preservation of true or 'sound' doctrine (Tit 1:9). What is most specific in the idea of the church is represented even more forcefully in the metaphor of 'temple' (*naos*). Thus, according to Paul, the faithful are referred to as 'God's temple' in which 'God's Spirit dwells' (1 Cor 3:16f; see also 2 Cor 6:16f; Rev 11:1ff; 21:3).

If, as we have seen, the new Jerusalem, the church, is identified in Rev 21:2 and even more clearly in 21:9 as 'the bride, the wife of the Lamb' (see also 19:7ff; 22:17), this is explained by and corresponds to the common oriental way of designating a city as female. It is on this basis that we have to understand some typical Old Testament motifs. It was in fact precisely in this way that the prophets conceived of the relation between Yahweh and Israel: of bridegroom and bride (Jer 2:2, 32; see also 31:1-6; Is 49:18; 61:10); husband and wife (Hos 2:16-22; Is 50:1; 54:5f; 62:4f; Ezek 16:1-14; see also 23:4); even as lover and courtesan (Hos 2:4-15; Jer 2:20-25; see also 3:12f; 9:1; Ezek 16:15-63). The image of the community as the bride of Christ occurs in Paul at all events, for example 2 Cor 11:2, and particularly in the passage on matrimony in Eph 5:22-33 in which the relation between the Lord and the church, which he has made holy and cleansed from all stain through his living self-offering (5:25-7) and which he nourishes and cherishes as the bride entrusted to his care (5:29 —referring to the eucharist), stands as a type of christian matrimony which, in its turn, becomes the actualisation of the 'great mystery' of the community of love between Christ and the *ekklēsia*

(5:32). How far, both here and in general in the later writings of the New Testament, we have to take into account gnostic speculations about the 'union' of the Saviour with the 'Wisdom-assembly' (*Sophia-Ekklēsia*) is not quite clear or unambiguous according to the latest research, though the possibility of some such connection cannot be absolutely excluded.

Of greater importance for the Pauline concept of the church is the motif of the *body* as a community, which is already suggested in the Old Testament (eg, 2 Sam 19:13f; 1 Chron 11:1) and which is connected with the image of the church as a bride insofar as the woman is, as it were the 'body' of the man (Eph 5:28f). Behind this idea there stands the ancient understanding of the body as an element making for community, not just a means of intercourse, and, above all, the ancient semitic principle of solidarity. It cannot now be called into doubt that when Paul uses expressions with *sōma* (= body) the reference is first and foremost to a metaphor by means of which the church is described as a living organism in which a great variety of different kinds of members and organs (which, however, are related one to the other) are bound together in an organic and functional unity—as, for example, in 1 Cor 12:12, 14–26; Rom 12:4f; see also Eph 4:16. This is patterned on the 'diatribe' of popular philosophy, in particular of the Stoics. It would appear from the context that the use of this figure had the purpose of inculcating church unity despite the manifold nature of the several gifts given to each and in opposition to different schismatic groups and charismatic excesses.

There are, however, certain texts, beginning in the major epistles, which cannot be understood in a purely metaphorical sense. For instance, 1 Cor 10:16f reads 'The bread which we break, is it not a participation in the body of Christ (*koinōnia tou sōmatos tou khristou*)? Because there is one bread, we who are many are one body, for we all partake of the one bread'—here it is hardly adequate to take the collective *sōma* of v 17 in a purely metaphysical sense if we at the same time interpret *sōma* in v 16 realistically, since there is an internal (and originally intended) connection between the two phrases. There should be no reason for doubting that *sōma tou khristou* in v 16 is not metaphorical, whether one refers it directly to the eucharistic body of Christ (with the majority of exegetes) or to the crucified but now glorified body which is present to us sacramentally in the eucharist and socially in the church. No more is it possible to interpret 1 Cor 12:12f in a purely metaphorical or figurative sense.

While in the major epistles Paul has in view in a special way the relation of the members one to another and their unity in Christ (Rom 12:5: *hen sōma en khristō(i)* = one body in Christ), in the captivity epistles the relation of Christ as 'head' to the church as 'body' (ie, the 'body of Christ' *sōma tou khristou*; Eph 1:22f; 4:15f; Col 1:18) occupies the foreground, a fact which emphasises the 'bride' motif (Eph 5:23–33) closely related to it. In the passages which predicate *sōma* of the church, the purely metaphorical (as distinct from the realistic) content falls more and more into the background. Thus it cannot be just metaphor when Paul says that Christ has reconciled both Jew and heathen 'to God in one body (*en heni sōmati*)' (Eph 2:16; see also 4:4; Col 1:22). The statement about the church in Eph 1:22f sounds like a definition: *tē(i) ekklēsiā(i), hētis estin to sōma autou* (=for the church, which is his, ie Christ's, body). The expression in Col 1:24 has a similar function—in it Paul speaks of his sufferings for the sake of Christ's body *ho estin hē ekklēsia* (=that is the church). Similarly, in Col 1:18 the words 'the church' (*tēs ekklēsias*) appear in apposition to the phrase 'he [ie, Christ] is the head of the body' (*autos estin hē kephalē tou sōmatos*) (see also Eph 4:12). The context of these formulations within the history of religions, and in particular against the background of gnosticism, has not yet been sufficiently elucidated, but they are certainly statements about realities, and so they bring us at once into the field—indeed, into the centre—of biblical theology.

Before we go any further one general comprehensive point should be made: the metaphors which we have been reviewing can be divided into two groups according to the point of view which prevails in each. The one group refers to the church rather as redeemed community, the other more in its relation to Christ (the church as mystery):

Church as redeemed community:
Flock—shepherd
People, political entity
City, new Jerusalem
House, temple of God

Church as Mystery:
Vineyard or vine—vine branches
Covenant (marriage)—partner

Bride—bridegroom
Body—head

In the last resort, however, both aspects are mutually inclusive; thus, for example, the image of the city implies its spiritual origin 'from above', and therefore from Christ, and the image of the body illustrates the mutual belonging together of the members. It is a question here rather of a difference in the incidence of emphasis or of perspective.

C. *The theology of the church in the New Testament.* While the biblical images teach us much about the nature of the church, there are a good number of positive statements which speak directly of this even more clearly, though of course we shall never be able to grasp in its entirety what is, after all, a divine mystery.

1. *The church as mystery.* If we approach the question from the angle of the history of salvation, we have first to discuss, among the many deep and complex aspects of the idea of the church in the New Testament, the concept of the church as mystery in the sense explained above (see under A). That the church is in the real sense of the word *mustērion* can be deduced from the great parenthesis in Eph 3; for here the 'mystery of Christ' (3:4) is described as coextensive with the community of Jew and gentile in the one church, since in it the gentiles 'are fellow heirs, members of the same body [*sussōma*], and partakers of the promise [to the Jews] in Christ Jesus through the gospel' (3:6). Hence the *ekklēsia* belongs essentially to the mystery of Christ; indeed she is herself, as being in community with the Lord her bridegroom, a true 'mystery' (5:32),

and therefore a reality which originates in God. Since in Pauline usage *mustērion* refers principally to the eternal counsel and decision of God and the concrete revelation and actualisation of this counsel in the history of created reality as a whole and salvation history in particular, the church in its character as mystery is characterised as an essential factor in the carrying out of this counsel and decision which is itself the primordial mystery. The church is therefore related to the total history of the world and consequently to the work of creation and exists in view of 'the final restoration of all things in Christ as head' at the end of the world. In this *oikonomia* (=plan; Eph 1:10; 3:2, 9) the church has an inalienable and indeed a cosmic function. This is proved by Eph 1:22f, where Paul says that God has made Christ 'the head over all things for the church which is his body, the fullness of him who fills all in all' (see also Col 1:15–20 especially 1:18). The cosmic task of the church appears precisely in this, that here she is characterised not just as the body but also as the 'fullness' (*plērōma*) of Christ —and this *plērōma*, as we have shown elsewhere ('Die Kirche im Epheserbrief', 12–14, see bibliog.) is used with the twofold meaning of 'fulfilled' and 'fulfilling'.

This comes through even more forcefully in Eph 3:9–11, insofar as it is precisely by means of the church that 'the manifold wisdom of God might now be made known to the principalities and powers in the heavenly places' who have their part to play through Christ and the church in the working out of the primordial mystery which is 'the design prepared for the ages'. In view of this one can very well speak, with *Didache* 11:11, of the *mustērion kosmikon ekklēsias* (=universal mystery of the church). Nevertheless, the soteriological function of the church remains for Paul in the foreground, as it is presented, for example, in Eph 2:13–22; 3:12; 4:12–16; Col 1:18–23. The church is, first and foremost, the 'mystery of salvation'. It is its essential purpose to transform mankind split into two hostile groups (Jew and gentile) and man himself divided within himself (*sarx/pneuma* = flesh/spirit) into the 'one new man' through the body of Christ on the cross immolated for the atonement of all (see Eph 2:15f with 4:23 and Col 1:20–2 with 3:9–15).

Considered as mystery, the church is a reality which is beyond history, eschatological and supernatural or 'pneumatic'. According to Eph 3:9f, the church—together with the 'principalities and powers' (*tais arkhais kai tais exousiais*), is 'in the heavenly places' (*en tois epouraniois*); she is the 'heavenly Jerusalem' (Heb 12:22) or 'the Jerusalem above (*anō*)' (Gal 4:26), and so in herself a reality from 'beyond' which nevertheless 'comes down' into this world (Rev 21:2, 10) and is 'incarnated' in space and time. This follows from the essence of the mystery, according to Paul, by which God and man, eternity and temporality, come together in a concrete symbol. On the basis of its spiritual ('pneumatic') existence, the church is therefore 'from above', a reality which has its origin in God and therefore, like everything spiritual, is in a certain sense preexistent. This pre-existence implies that the church existed before the world (Eph 1:22f; see also 5:25), an understanding which is attested in an impressive way by ancient christian tradition starting from 2 Clement 14 and the *Shepherd* of Hermas, 2nd Vision, 4, 1 (see my 'Die Kirche im Epheserbrief' 33; 75–7) and does not in any way deny its created character. One must view it in relation to the created *sóphia* (= wisdom) of the sapiential literature (Prov 8:22–31; Wis 7:22–8; Sir 1:1–10; 24:3–22) when thinking of its cosmic function. The *origin* of the church in the context of salvation history, however, has to be sought without a doubt in the sacrificial death of Christ (Col 1:20–2; Eph 2:13–16; 5:25ff; cf Jn 19:26f), since she originated as the 'new' or 'true' Eve out of the side of the second Adam asleep on the cross, as theologians since Tertullian (*De Anima*, 43), with reference to Jn 19:34, have almost unanimously taught. Finally, her historical manifestation before the peoples of the world took place in the Pentecost event, when the Lord, exalted to the Father, sent down the Holy Spirit on the primitive community gathered together around the apostles and the mother of Jesus (Acts 2:1–5, 33).

The intimate connection existing between the church and the Spirit (*pneuma*) is expressed by Paul by means of the co-ordination of *hen sōma* (= one body) with *hen pneuma* (= one Spirit) (Eph 4:4; see also 2:16: *en heni sōmati* = 'in one body' alongside 2:18: *en heni pneumati* = 'in one Spirit'). The *pneuma* of Christ is the intrinsic, organic principle which gives growth and structure to the church considered as the 'pneumatic' body of the Lord (1 Cor 12:3–11; Eph 2:22; see also Rom 8:4–16, 27; etc).

It is by bearing in mind the origin of the church in the mystery of the cross that we can have an exact understanding of Paul's statements about the church as *body* in their peculiar theological connotation, statements which are of such central importance for Paul's ecclesiology. The church is certainly not identical with the physical body of Jesus in his earthly sojourn, since he has once and for all renounced his 'body of flesh' (*sōma tēs sarkos*: Col 1:22; 2:11) on the cross. And yet it is with particular emphasis that Paul calls the church to *sōma tou khristou* or *to sōma autou* (1 Cor 12:27; Eph 1:23; 4:12; 5:30; see also Rom 7:4; Col 2:17; Heb 10:10, 19f). For him the church is, in a mysterious way, 'the [true] body of *Christ*', understood certainly in a particular mode of existence or presentation. According to the New Testament, and in particular Paul, the body cannot simply be identified with the material body (*sarx* = flesh)—on the contrary, the visible here-and-now phenomenon taken normally as connected with a body corresponds to an inner, hidden, mostly personal reality. For this reason the church as the body of Christ is the social (collective?) modality of existence of the spiritual Lord living on and operative here below, somewhat similar to the way Christ takes on a sacramental modality of existence in the eucharist. For just as we cannot suppose—assuming the doctrine of the real presence—that the 'bread which we bless' at the Lord's Supper is a different 'body of Christ' from his crucified body now glorified in heaven (1 Cor 10:16; see also 11:27), so the church, if she is really to be the 'body of Christ', cannot be any other than this, the more so because it is precisely here (10:17) that the underlying unity of the eucharistic and ecclesiological body of the Lord is expressly stated. That the ecclesiological or 'mystical' body of Christ is in some way one with his material body can be deduced by comparing Col 1:22 with Eph 2:16, where both the crucified 'body of flesh' of the Lord and the 'one body' of the church are given as means of reconciliation with God. We might also refer to Rom 7:4 and to the Lord's word about his body as a 'temple' which he would build up again in three days (Jn 2:19–21; also Mk 14:58 and parallels). The one body of Christ, therefore, has several different forms and modalities of existence: physical and material during the historical life of Jesus, heavenly and glorified after his 'passing over' to the Father, sacramental — eucharistic — and social-ecclesiological. Behind these different modalities of existence there exists, however, a unity analogous to and based on the real unity of the personal body of Christ.

By means of the Pauline *sōma*-terminology the relation between *Christ and the church* in particular is illustrated. As mystery or, more precisely, as the 'body of Christ', the church is an objective, supra-personal reality in relation to different individual men but united in the most intrinsic way with Christ. She is the 'one new man' *to* (*eis*!) whom Christ through his creative activity had reduced a divided humanity (Eph 2:15), and this 'one new man' is in its turn none other than Christ himself, but 'the whole Christ' with head and body (see 1 Cor 12:12: *ho khristos*) or 'the complete man' into

whom we all have to grow up (Eph 4:13) just as we all, through baptism, 'put on Christ' so becoming 'one person [*heis*!] in Christ' (Gal 3:27f).

Christ and the church, therefore, are together one 'person', not of course in the individual sense, but in a higher 'mystical' but real unity through which the personal independence of the individual members of this body and of the head is in no way attacked, since it is not a question of a material fusion but of spiritual liberation and fulfilment. In any case, Christ remains as the 'head' in whom the 'whole *plērōma*' or the 'fullness of the Godhead' dwells (Col 1:18f; 2:9), established before and above the church. He is the source as he is the last end of all our being and existence; the *gratia corporis* is always a participation in the *gratia capitis*. There goes out from him who is the head that *pneuma* which gives life to all the members (see 1 Cor 15:45; 2 Cor 3:17f), producing in them an abundance of services and gifts of the Spirit (1 Cor 12:4–11; Eph 4:7–12, 16; Col 2:19; see under C 2). The whole body 'grows up' into him in order to fulfil itself in him 'the perfect man', 'to the measure of the stature of the fullness of Christ' (Eph 4:13, 15).

2. *The church as redeemed community.* As we saw, the church considered as mystery and even more as 'body' has also an external, visible, and concrete aspect and, indeed, the spiritual body of the Lord takes on in her the form of the community of men redeemed through the saving deed of Christ, which has to be brought into existence within history and which has, in fact, already been partially realised. She is not a pure 'church of the spirit'; on

the contrary, she has a particular sociological structure peculiar to herself which on the one hand puts her in relation with other human social structures and on the other distinguishes her from them.

In the church there are Jews and gentiles who, having accepted faith in the crucified Christ, are one in the true *people of God*, the 'Israel according to the Spirit'. It is of this new people of God that 1 Pet 2:9f speaks: 'But you are a chosen race, a royal priesthood, a holy nation, God's own people, that you may declare the wonderful deeds of him who called you out of darkness into his marvellous light. Once you were no people but now you are God's people; once you had not received mercy but now you have received mercy.' This text refers to practically all the stages which are relevant for the constitution of the church. In the first place, only election and call from God's side can lead to the church (1 Thess 1:4; Eph 1:4; 4:1, 4; 2 Pet 1:10; see also Rom 8:29f; 11:28). Consequently christians are known as *eklektoi* (= those who are chosen, the elect; Rom 8:33) and *klētoi* (= those who are called; Rom 1:6). The community finds its highest fulfilment and greatest honour in priestly service (1 Pet 2:5; Rev 1:6; 5:10), that is, in the liturgical worship; and so the church is conscious of itself as a cultic community (Eph 3:21; Heb 12:22f), since she is a 'holy' people, one, namely, set aside by God and consecrated to him—precisely that people which he acquired for himself in his merciful love by snatching it from the power of darkness and transferring it into the kingdom of light, the kingdom of his Son (Col 1:13).

Through this predominant history of salvation perspective the church is brought into close relationship with the ↗ *kingdom of God*. There is, however, no straightforward identity between the two realities, especially if we look at the church as a social and historical-contingent structure to which sinners also belong. Rather should we consider her as the *basileia* of Christ, the rule of *Christ* and the area where that rule obtains (Eph 5:5; see also 2 Pet 1:11; Jn 18:36; Rev 11:15), being, as it were, the prelude and preparation for the kingdom of God which is realised only at the end of time (1 Cor 15:24). The earthly church is still on the way towards the eternal 'kingdom of Heaven', yet the kingdom is in her by anticipation, it has already broken in (Rom 14:17; 1 Cor 4:20; see also 2 Tim 4:1; 2 Pet 1:11f; Rev 1:9; 5:10; also Mk 1:15 and parallels; Mt 12:28 and parallels; Lk 17:20f; etc). At the ↗ parousia of the Lord the church will be made one with the completed *basileia tou theou* (= kingdom of God) and, in consequence, her character as mystery will be annulled or 'fulfilled'.

As a community of the redeemed, the church is the new *politeia* (= commonwealth), that is, the 'state' and even the 'family' of God to which also the converted gentiles belong as 'members of the household' (Eph 2:19). The bond of ↗ *love* (*agapē*) unites all in the 'unity of the Spirit' (Col 3:14f; Eph 4:2f, 15f) as a true ↗ brotherhood (*adelphotēs*, 1 Pet 2:17; 5:9) in which no difference of race, social condition, or even sex is of decisive importance (Gal 3:28; 1 Cor 12:13; Rom 10:12; Col 3:11), since here all are fundamentally the same in the eyes of God (Acts 10:34;

Rom 2:11; see also 2 Cor 5:10; Eph 6:9). At the same time, it should not be considered merely as church bound together by love; it also has a juridical structure proper to itself. As a community actualised in the course of history, the church cannot exist without a social arrangement and a hierarchical order. Whence, according to 1 Cor 12:4–11, the Spirit effects in her the differentiated functions and charisms (see 12:14–25; Rom 12:3–8), though these are to be attributed to the glorified Christ, according to Eph 4:7–11, which really comes to the same thing, since the Spirit which is operative in the church is the divine power mediated through the Lord (Acts 2:33). Among those who serve the church under God or Christ, the ↗ apostles take the first place (1 Cor 12:28: *prōton* = first); then follow the ↗ prophets and teachers (*didaskaloi*) or the evangelists and pastors of the community (1 Cor 12:28; see also Eph 4:11), and finally the different 'ministries' among which we are to consider as not least in importance the various works of mercy (1 Cor 12:4–11; see also Acts 6:1). Already, therefore, in the New Testament period, the principal grades of the hierarchy had been set up, in particular the office of community leader (*prebuteros* = 'elder', Acts 11:30; 14:23; etc; or *episkopos* = 'overseer, bishop', Phil 1:1; 1 Tim 3:2; both identical in Acts 20:17, 28; Tit 1:5–7). The hierarchical (juridical) primacy of Peter (and his successors) can be deduced from the Lord's words in Mt 16:18f and is corroborated by other texts (eg, Lk 22:31f; Jn 21:15–17). The infallible power of the keys and of teaching possessed by the church

is referred to in Mt 18:17f and Lk 10:16 (see also 1 Cor 5:3–13; Jn 20:23; 1 Jn 2:24; 4:6).

The most important ministry entrusted to the church is the ministry of the word (*diakonia tou logou*, Acts 6:4) and the administration of the sacraments.↗ Preaching (*kērugma*, eg 1 Cor 2:4) constitutes a decisive ecclesiological function which has the purpose of awakening the faith (Rom 10:14f) which leads to conversion (*metanoia*) and *baptism* (Acts 2:38). Through baptism the individual believers are 'aggregated' (*prostithenai* = 'add', Acts 2:41, 47; 5:14; 11:24; see also 13:36) to the community of God—that is, are made members of or 'one body with' the church as the 'body of Christ' (see 1 Cor 12:13; Gal 3:27f). In the Lord's Supper, on the other hand, the church experiences itself as a sacrificial and living fellowship with and in Christ, since all those who eat 'of one bread' share in the one (immolated) body of the Lord and are therefore also in the deepest possible way united with one another (1 Cor 10:16f), a fact expressed in a particularly striking way in the ↗ *agapē* or love-feast, the celebration of which was often connected with the eucharist.

Church and sacrament have, therefore, a real relation one to the other, a fact already apparent in our consideration of the church as the body of Christ. Baptism has more the function of establishing (1 Cor 12:13), while the other sacraments, in particular the eucharist, have rather the function of building up and deepening (in addition to 1 Cor 10:16f, see Eph 5:29 with 2:20–22 and 4:15f). In the sacramental mystery which, like every true symbol, includes the outward sign and the reality indicated by the sign (*res*), the inner unity of the church as mystery of salvation and of fellowship is realised and experienced in a concrete way.

In this respect, moreover, the biblical *principle of solidarity* is of particular relevance and can be applied in two ways. The church is not just the body of the 'last Adam' (see 1 Cor 15:45); rather, she comes into existence and grows in proportion as the faithful, who are made members of this body, really co-operate in fulfilling the redemptive destiny of Christ. This ontological fellowship in destiny with the Lord is now made possible principally through the sacraments. Thus, we die with Christ in baptism, are 'crucified with him' in it and are 'buried with him into death' so that, rising with him, we may be able to walk in 'newness of life' (Rom 6:3–6; Col 2:12). When, however, we celebrate the Lord's Supper, which according to 1 Cor 10:16–21 (see also 11:24f) possesses a sacrificial character, by uniting our oblation to his we enter into the once-and-for-all sacrificial death of Christ and, in this way, 'proclaim', through the cultic commemoration implied in the action, this one saving death until the Lord comes again (11:26). Also in the everyday living of this mystical life of christians, the sacramental action in union with Christ is continued in the form of the following of Christ by carrying one's cross (Mk 8:34 and parallels; Rom 8:17; etc). It will reach its complete fulfilment one day in our physical death—the 'last mystery'—as the most real participation in the 'passing over' of Christ (see 1 Thess

4:14; 1 Cor 15:12–22, 51–57). The church is therefore, in its essential nature, a fellowship of destiny or an existential fellowship with Christ and of each member with the others in Christ (1 Cor 12:26; Rom 12:13, 15f), as is demonstrated by the relation existing between the apostle Paul and his communities, with whom he knew himself to be united 'in dying together and in living together' (2 Cor 7:3; see also 6:11–13; 11:28; 1 Pet 5:1, 9).

As regards the relationship of the *church as a whole*, in which the mystery of the church is primarily embodied, to the *local communities*, the latter can be considered as concrete reproductions or configurations derived from the former, as, for example, when it is a question of the church 'which is in Jerusalem' (Acts 11:22; see also 8:1; 13:1; 1 Cor 1:2; 14:23 (in the singular!); 1 Cor 10:32; 11:22; 1 Tim 3:15). These local communities, however, retain the ability to express this truth only as long as they remain in union with the church as a whole and the doctrine it believes, for there can be *only one legitimate historical collective embodiment* of the church of Jesus Christ considered as mystery, and the signs of this legitimate status are in the first place unity of teaching and continuity of function (the apostolic succession).

Unity is therefore the first mark of the church. This is by nature a spiritual thing (Eph 4:3f; see also 4:13), but in her outward aspect too she admits of no divisions (*skhismata*), as Paul in particular emphasises (1 Cor 12:25; see also 1:10; 11:18). The *holiness* of the church (Eph 5:26f; Heb 13:12; see also 2:11; 10:10, 14; 1 Thess 5:23; 1 Cor 1:2; 6:11; Acts 20:32; 26:18) does not just mean in the negative sense a separation from the profane, but a positive dedication to God (see Jn 17:19). Its *catholicity* leaves no room for racial or class distinction (*diastolē*, Rom 10:12; see also 3:22; Gal 3:28; 1 Cor 12:13), on account of the 'one Lord' whom she serves. Its *apostolicity* (Eph 2:20; 3:5) rests above all on the preservation of the apostolic tradition (*paradosis*, 2 Thess 2:15; 3:6; 1 Cor 11:2; see also 2 Pet 3:2; Jude 17) and succession imparted through the laying on of hands (Acts 13:3; 1 Tim 4:14; 5:22; 2 Tim 1:6; see also Acts 14:23).

The *eschatological* orientation which was brought to our attention in dealing with the relation between the church and the kingdom of God is especially important for the 'pilgrim' church (1 Pet 2:11; see also Heb 11:13–16; 13:14), but for the most part here, as elsewhere in the New Testament, it is a question of a 'realised eschatology'. Certainly, the church understands herself as the redeemed 'remnant' of the last days (Rom 9:24–9; 11:5; see also 1 Cor 10:11; 1 Pet 4:7; 1 Jn 2:18), but certainly not as an esoteric community like the Essene sects or that of Qumran. She knows that she has been 'called out' from the world (see Jn 15:19) and that her true 'commonwealth' (*politeuma*) is in heaven (Phil 3:20), and that therefore she is not 'of' this world (Jn 17:14, 16). But she retains the consciousness that she has been placed 'in' this world in order to be tested through faith and in patience (Jn 16:33; 17:11, 15, 18; see also Phil 2:15; 1 Pet 5:9).

The church consequently has a *task in the world*, not a profane and merely cultural one but religious, namely, the proclamation of the gospel (*euangelion*, Mt 28:19; Mk 16:15) and the rescue of the things of the world from the demonic powers by a consecration to God accompanied by thanksgiving through the powerful grace which Christ gives (sacramentals; see 1 Cor 10:23–33 and, especially, 1 Tim 4:4f). She therefore cannot indulge in a spiritualism which does not take seriously God's creation and the incarnation of Christ, but at the same time cannot conform to the world in the manner of the false messianic expectation of the Jews who wanted to set up the kingdom of God on this earth and therefore thought of the cross as a 'scandal' (1 Cor 1:23; see also Gal 6:12; Phil 3:18). Rather would the church's slogan be: 'Freedom from the world and freedom for God' (1 Cor 2:12; 7:29–34; Jas 1:27; 4:4; 1 Jn 2:15–17; see also Gal 6:14; Col 2:8; 2 Tim 2:4). The real mission of the church in the world is to co-operate in the redemption and return of the creation to God, the last end and native home of all being, by means of the grace measured out to her (Rom 8:19–22; 1 Cor 3:21ff; 2 Cor 10:5). Thus, in addition to her more urgent soteriological task, the church has also a *cosmological* one which will be completed only in the eschatological transformation and fulfilment, when the church on earth, united with the church in heaven and with the cosmos renewed through Christ, enters into the eternal kingdom of God. Then will she be in truth, as the perfected body of Christ, 'the fullness of him who fills all in all' (Eph 1:22f).

Bibliography: Older studies in O. Linton, *Das Problem der Urkirche in der neueren Forschung,*

Frankfurt 1957[2]; and A. Médebielle, *DB(S)* II (1934), 687–91.

Terminology and concept: H. Koehnlein, 'La Notion de l'Eglise chez l'Apôtre Paul', *RHPR* 17 (1937), 357–77; K. L. Schmidt, *TDNT* III, 501–36; N. A. Dahl, *Das Volk Gottes. Eine Untersuchung zum Kirchenbewusstsein des Urchristentums*, Oslo 1941; J. C. Fenton, 'NT Designations of the Catholic Church and of its Members', *CBQ* 9 (1947), 127–46 and 275–306; S. Giuliani, 'La nomenclatura paolina interno alla Chiesa', *Sap.* 3 (1950), 195–219; O. Moe, 'Um den ntl. Ekklesia-Begriff', *TTK* 23 (1952), 26–30; E. Schweitzer, 'The NT Idea of the Church', *Theology Today* 13 (1956), 471–83; P. Alonso, 'Idea de comunidad del pueblo de Dios en la Biblia', *Liturgia* 13 (1958), 76–89; P. S. Minear, *Images of the Church in the NT*, Philadelphia 1960; H. Schlier, 'Zu den Namen der Kirche in den paulinischen Briefen', *Besinnung auf das NT*, Freiburg 1964, 294–306; L. Cerfaux, 'Die Bilder für die Kirche im NT', *De Ecclesia* I, ed. G. Baraúna, Freiburg 1966, 220–35.

Church and OT: L. Rost, *Die Vorstufen von Kirche und Synagoge im AT*, Stuttgart 1938; H. W. Herzberg, *Werdende Kirche im AT*, Munich 1950; P. H. Menoud, *L'Eglise naissante et le Judaisme*, Montpellier 1952; J. D. W. Kritzinger, *Qehal Jahwe. Wat dit is en wie daaraan mag behoort*, Kampen 1957 (with a summary in English); Q. Linton, 'Ecclesia I', *RAC* 4 (1959), 905–21; K. Thieme, 'Das Mysterium der Kirche in der christlichen Sicht des Alten Bundesvolkes', *Mysterium Kirche* I, Salzburg 1962, 37–87; H. Gross, 'Der Sinai-Bund als Lebensform des auserwählten Volkes im AT', *Ekklesia*, Trier 1962, 1–15; H. Junker, 'Sancta Civitas, Jerusalem Nova (Is 2)', *Ekklesia*, 17–33; J. Schreiner, *Sion-Jerusalem, Jahwes Königssitz*, Munich 1963.

Jesus and the church: K. Pieper, *Jesus und die Kirche*, Paderborn 1932; R. N. Flew, *Jesus and his Church*, London 1938; P. Nepper-Christensen, *Wer hat die Kirche gestiftet?*, Lund 1950; R. L. Hicks, 'Jesus and His Church', *ATR* 34 (1952), 85–93; W. G. Kümmel, 'Jesus und die Anfänge der Kirche', *ST* 7 (1953), 1–27; A. Nygren, *Christus und seine Kirche*, Göttingen 1955; O. Kuss, 'Bemerkungen zu dem Fragenkreis: Jesus und die Kirche', *TQ* 135 (1955), 28–55 and 150–83; E. Finke and A. Vögtle, 'Jesus und die Kirche', *Begegnung der Christen*, ed. M. Roesle and O. Cullmann, Frankfurt-Stuttgart 1960[2], 35–54 and 54–81.

The church in the individual NT writings: S. Cipriani, 'La dottrina della Chiesa in S. Matteo', *Riv. bibl. it.* 3 (1955), 1–31; W. Trilling, *Das wahre Israel*, Leipzig 1949; J. Gnilka, 'Die Kirche des Matthäus und die

Gemeinde von Qumran', *BZ* 7 (1963), 43–63; E. Schweizer, *Der Kirchengedanke im Evangelium und den Briefen des Johannes*, Berlin 1959, 363–81; A. Corell, *Consummatum est: Eschatology and Church in the Gospel of John*, New York 1959; L. Cerfaux, *La communauté apostolique*, Paris 1953[2]; J. Schmitt, 'L'Eglise de Jérusalem ou la "Restauration" d'Israel d'apres Actes 1–5', *RSR* 27 (1953), 209–18; C. Charlier, 'De la communauté de Jérusalem aux églises pauliniennes (Actes 1–12)', *Bibl. et Vie chrét.* 1 (1953), 72–93; F. Mussner, 'Die Bedeutung des Apostelkonzils für die Kirche', *Ekklesia*, 35–46; H. Schürmann, 'Das Testament des Paulus für die Kirche (Acts 20:18–35)', *Unio Christianorum*, Paderborn 1962, 108–46; K. Pieper, *Paulus und die Kirche*, Paderborn 1932; W. L. Knox, *St Paul and the Church of the Gentiles*, Cambridge 1939; G. Sciaretta, *La Croce e la Chiesa nella Teologia di S. Paolo*, Rome 1952; C. T. Craig, 'The Church in Paul', *Rel. in Life* 22 (1953), 538–50; G. Bornkamm, 'Herrenmahl und Kirche bei Paulus', *ZTK* 53 (1956), 312–48; L. Cerfaux, *L'Eglise des Corinthiens*, Paris 1946; H. Schlier and V. Warnach, *Die Kirche im Epheserbrief*, Münster 1949; F. Mussner, *Christus, das All und die Kirche. Studien zur Theologie des Epheserbriefes*, Trier 1955; A. Feuillet, 'L'Eglise plérôme du Christ d'après Eph 1:23', *NRT* 78 (1956), 449–72 and 593–610; H. Schlier, 'Die Kirche als das Geheimnis Christi nach dem Eph', *Zeit der Kirche*, Freiburg 1962[3], 293–307; N. A. Dahl, 'Das Geheimnis der Kirche nach Eph 3:8–10', *Zur Auferbauung des Leibes Christi*, Kassel 1965, 63–75; T. da Castel S. Pietro, *La Chiesa nella lettera agli Ebrei*, Turin-Rome 1945; A. Kassing, *Die Kirche und Maria. Ihr Verhältnis im 12 Kapitel der Apokalypse*, Düsseldorf 1958; K. Stendhal, 'Kirche im Urchristentum', *RGG* III[3] (1959), 1297–1304; *Y. Congar, 'The Council as an Assembly and the Church as Essentially Conciliar', *One, Holy, Catholic, and Apostolic*, ed. H. Vorgrimler, London 1968, 44–88 (with an anthology of texts based on Mt 18:20).

Theology of the church: A. Médebielle, *DB(S)* II, 487–687; O. Michel, *Das Zeugnis des NT von der Gemeinde*, Göttingen 1941; Y. Congar, *The Mystery of the Church*, London 1960; F. M. Braun, *Aspects nouveaux du problème de L'Eglise*, Fribourg 1941; J. Daniélou, *Le signe du Temple ou la Présence de Dieu*, Paris 1942; G. Johnston, *The Doctrine of the Church in the NT*, Cambridge 1943; L. Cerfaux, *The Church in the Theology of St Paul*, London 1959; H. de Lubac, *The Splendour of the Church*, London 1956; W. H. Robinson, *The Biblical Doctrine of the Church*, St Louis 1949; T. W. Manson, 'The NT Basis of the Doctrine of the Church', *JEH* 1 (1950), 1–11; E. Sjöberg, 'Kirche und Kultus im NT',

Ein Buch von der Kirche, Berlin 1950, 85–109; Meinertz I, 69–79 and 231–7; II, 155–84, 254, 260, 309–12, and 326–9; V. Warnach, *Agape*, Düsseldorf 1951, 550–81; E. Schweizer, *Geist und Gemeinde im NT*, Munich 1952; K. L. Schmidt, 'The Church', *Theol. Today* 9 (1952), 39–54; E. Peterson, 'L'Eglise', *DV* 25 (1953), 99–112; J. F. Walvoord, 'Premillenarianism and the Church as a Mystery', *Bibl Sacr.* 111 (1954), 1–10 and 97–104; J. Lonke, 'Credo Ecclesiam Christi Apostolicam', *Coll. Brug.* 50 (1954), 23–32 and 318–27 (against Cullmann); A. Orbe, 'Cristo y la Iglesia', *Est. Ecl.* 29 (1955), 299–344; O. Cullmann, *The Early Church, Historical and Theological Studies*, London 1956; N. A. Dahl, 'Christ, Creation and the Church', *The Background of the NT and its Eschatology*, Cambridge 1956, 422–43; J. Schneider, *Taufe und Gemeinde im NT*, Kassel 1956; H. Schlier, *Die Zeit der Kirche*, Freiburg 1958²; R. Grosche, *Et intra et extra*, Düsseldorf 1958; P. Carrington, *The Early Christian Church*, Cambridge 1958; E. Peterson, *Il mistero degli Ebrei e dei Gentili nella Chiesa*, Milan 1960²; J. Pfammatter, *Die Kirche als Bau*, Rome 1960; R. Schnackenburg, *LTK* vi² (1961), 167–72; R. Schnackenburg, *The Church in the New Testament*, London 1965; E. Heible, 'Die Kirche als Wirklichkeit Christi im NT', *TTZ* 72 (1963), 65–83; F. Mussner, '"Volk Gottes" im NT', *TTZ* 72 (1963), 169–78; B. Rigaux, 'Das Mysterium der Kirche im Lichte der Schrift', *De Ecclesia* I, ed. G. Baraúna, Freiburg 1966, 197–219; *R. Schnackenburg, 'Church and Parousia', *One, Holy, Catholic, and Apostolic*, ed. H. Vorgrimler, London 1968, 91–134.

The church as the body of Christ: E. Mersch, *The Whole Christ*, London 1949; E. Käsemann, *Leib und Leib Christi*, Tübingen 1933; E. Mura, *Le corps mystique du Christ. Sa nature et sa vie divine d'après S. Paul et la théologie*, Paris 1937² (two vols.); S. Tromp, *Corpus Christi quod est Ecclesia*, Rome 1946²; A. Wikenhauser, *Die Kirche als der mystische Leib Christi nach dem Apostel Paulus*, Münster 1940²; E. Percy, *Der Leib Christi in den paulin. homologumena und Antilegomena*, Lund-Leipzig 1942; E. Mersch, *La théologie du Corps mystique*, Paris-Bruges 1944; L. Malevez, 'L'Eglise, corps du Christ. Sens et provenance de l'expression chez S. Paul', *RSR* 30 (1944,) 27–94; W. Goossens, *L'Eglise, corps du Christ d'après S. Paul*, Paris 1949; T. Soiron, *Die Kirche als der Leib Christi*, Düsseldorf 1951; P. Michalon, 'Eglise, Corps mystique du Christ glorieux', *NRT* 74 (1952), 673–87; E. Sauras, *El cuerpo mistico de Cristo*, Madrid 1952; E. L. Mascall, *Corpus Christi: Essays on the Church and the Eucharist*, London 1953; H. Holstein and D. Boumard, *L'Eglise, Corps vivant du Christ*, Paris 1953; A. Oepke, 'Leib

Christi oder Volk Gottes bei Paulus', *TLZ* 79 (1954), 363–8; E. Best, *One Body in Christ: A Study in the Relationship of the Church to Christ in the Epistles of the Apostle Paul*, London 1955; P. Benoit, 'Corps, Tête et Plérome dans les épîtres de la Captivité', *RB* 63 (1956), 5–44; J. I. Meuzelaar, *Der Leib des Messias*, Assen 1961.

Church unity: S. Hanson, *The Unity of the Church in the NT: Colossians and Ephesians*, Uppsala-Copenhagen 1946; F. Puzo, 'La unidad de la Iglesia en función de la Eucaristía', *Greg* 34 (1953), 145–86; C. T. Craig, *The One Church in the Light of the NT*, New York 1951 and London 1953; P. A. van Stempvoort, 'Paulus und die Spaltungen zu Korinth', *Begegnung der Christen*, 83–98; H. Schlier, 'Die Einheit der Kirche nach dem Apostel Paulus', *Begegnung der Christen*, 98–113; H. Schlier, 'Die Einheit der Kirche nach dem NT', *Besinnung auf das NT*, Freiburg 1964, 176–92; P. Benoit, 'L'unité de l'église selon l'épître aux Ephésiens', *Anal. bibl.* (Rome 1963), 57–77.

The church and the kingdom of God: E. Sommerlath, 'Kirche und Reich Gottes', *ZST* 16 (1940), 562–575; O. Cullmann, *Königsherrschaft Christi und Kirche im NT*, Zollikon-Zurich 1950³; D. M. Stanley, 'Kingdom to Church: The Structural Development of Apostolic Christianity in the NT', *TS* 16 (1955), 1–21; T. F. Torrance, *Kingdom and Church*, London 1956; J. Bright, *The Kingdom of God in the Bible and the Church*, London 1956; R. Schnackenburg, *God's Rule and Kingdom*, London 1963.

Church and world: M. A. Wagenführer, *Die Bedeutung Christi für Welt und Kirche*, Leipzig 1941; V. Warnach, 'Kirche und Kosmos', *Enkainia*, Düsseldorf 1956, 170–205; I. J. du Plessis, *Christus als Hoof van Kerk en Kosmos*, Groningen 1962.

Church and state: K. L. Schmidt, *Die Polis in Kirche und Welt*, Basle 1939; W. Bieder, *Ekklesia und Polis im NT und in der alten Kirche*, 1941; K. H. Schelkle, 'Staat und Kirche in der patrist. Auslegung von Rom 13:1–7', *ZNW* 44 (1953), 223–36; O. Kuss, 'Paulus über die staatl. Gewalt', *TG* 45 (1955), 321–34; A. Weithaas, 'Kirche und Staat in paulin. Sicht', *TG* 45 (1955), 433–41.

Life and constitution of the early church: G. Sass, *Apostelamt und Kirche*, Munich 1939; C. Journet, *L'Eglise du Verbe Incarné*, Paris 1942/51 (two vols.); P. H. Menoud, *L'Eglise et les ministères selon le NT*, Neuchâtel-Paris 1948; P. H. Menoud, *La vie de l'église naissante*, Neuchâtel-Paris 1952; J. Schniewind, 'Aufbau und Ordnung der Ekklesia nach dem NT', *Festschrift R. Bultmann*, Stuttgart-Cologne 1949, 202–8; H. von Campenhausen, *Kirchliche Amt* *und geistliche Vollmacht in der ersten drei Jahrhunderten*, Tübingen 1953; J. Gewiess, 'Die ntl. Grundlagen der kirchllichen Hierarchie', *Hist. Jahrb.* 72 (1953), 1–24; B. Reicke, *Glaube und Leben der Urgemeinde*, Zurich 1957; R. V. Clearwaters, *The Local Church of the NT*, Chicago 1954; B. C. Butler, *The Church and Infallibility*, London 1969²; F. W. Beare, 'The Ministry in the NT Church: Practice and Theory', *ATR* 37 (1955), 3–18; G. Dix, *Le ministère dans l'église ancienne*, Neuchâtel 1955; J. Daniélou, 'La communauté de Qumrân et l'organisation de l'église ancienne', *RHPR* 35 (1955), 104–15; J. Colson, *Les fonctions ecclésiales aux deux premiers siècles*, Bruges 1956; K. H. Schelkle, *Discipleship and Priesthood*, New York 1965 and London 1966; E. Schweitzer, *Church Order in the NT*, London 1962; K. H. Schelkle, 'Kirche als Elite und Elite in der Kirche nach dem NT', *TQ* 142 (1962), 257–82; O. Kuss, 'Kirchliches Amt und freie geistliche Vollmacht', *Auslegung und Verkündigung* i, Regensburg 1963, 271–80; *J.-P. Audet, *Structures of Christian Priesthood: Home, Marriage, and Celibacy in the Pastoral Service of the Church*, London and New York 1967.

Viktor Warnach

Circumcision

Circumcision refers to the removal of the foreskin and took place on the eighth day after birth (Gen 17:12; 21:4; Lev 12:3). The fact that circumcision was first carried out with a flint (Ex 4:25; Josh 5:2f) is indicative of the antiquity of this custom. In more remote times it was carried out by the father of the child (Gen 21:4)—there is only one case where the mother does it (Ex 4:25)—and later by a specialist (1 Macc 1:61), but never by a priest in a sanctuary. In order to take part in the passover, which was *the* Israelite community festival, non-Israelite slaves and aliens also had to be circumcised (Ex 12:43–9). According to the view found in the most recent strand of the Pentateuch, which comes from priestly circles, circumcision was imposed on Abraham's family by God as a sign of the covenant (Gen 17:9ff; ↗ covenant). It was practised by the patriarchs and probably kept up during the sojourn in Egypt (Gen 34:13ff; Josh 5:4f). From the fact that Moses was uncircumcised (Ex 4:24–6) we may suppose that it gradually fell into desuetude and was taken up once again after the conquest of Canaan (Josh 5:4–9).

Ethnological studies have shown us that circumcision was practised by many African tribes, but we cannot be certain that it was widespread in the ancient Near East. It seems that priests had to be circumcised in ancient Egypt. As far back as the third millennium BC we find representations of circumcision being carried out on stone reliefs. Ancient texts refer to it, as does Herodotus, yet on the other hand there are mummies which show no trace of circumcision. Nor does the Old Testament provide unambiguous evidence for the widespread practice of circumcision by the mere fact that it describes Egyptians, Edomites, Ammonites, Moabites, and Arabs as uncircumcised (Jer 9:25f), and places the uncircumcised Egyptians, Assyrians, Elamites, Edomites, and Sidonians in Sheol (Ezek 32). According to the testimony of Herodotus the Phoenicians and Syrians were circumcised. The Arabs of antiquity were too, since the Romans attempted to prohibit circumcision in Arabia. After the conquest the Israelites came into immediate contact with the Philistines who were certainly uncircumcised (Judg 14:3; 15:18; 1 Sam 14:6; 17:26, 36; 18:25–7; 31:4) and with the Canaanites whom they never branded as uncircumcised. We must conclude, then, that circumcision could never have been a unique individuating factor of the Israelites *vis-à-vis* other groups in Palestine. On the contrary, the people of Old Testament times must have learned of this practice for the first time in Canaan and begun to practise it there (Gen 17:9–14, 23–27; Josh 5: 2ff). But as was the case with so many other practices taken over by Yahwism, circumcision in Israel was given an entirely new and specifically religious sense.

Among the customs most widespread among the peoples of the world belong what are called *rites de passage*, that is, rites which are connected with birth, arrival at sexual maturity, marriage, and death. The initiation rituals which qualified a candidate for married life and life as a full member of the community demanded of him some proof of valour and courage (eg killing a man, chopping off a finger, pulling out an incisor, etc). Circumcision took place at the time of puberty as an initiation ritual—as it does among primitive tribes today—and this significance probably attached to it also in the ancient Near East. The Arabic verb *ḥatana* (to circumcise) corresponds to the Hebrew *ḥōtēn* (father-in-law, see Ex 3:1), *ḥᵃtan* (son-in-law, see Gen 19:12) and *ḥᵃtunnâh* (marriage, see Song 3:11). The story of the Shechemites (Gen 34) and of the 'bridegroom of blood' (Ex 4:24–6) associate circumcision expressly with marriage. Even the metaphorical reference to circumcision points to its original character as an initiation ritual. An 'uncircumcised heart' cannot understand (Jer 9:25; Deut 10:16;

30:6), an 'uncircumcised ear' cannot hear (Jer 6:10), and 'uncircumcised lips' cannot speak (Ex 6:12, 30).

When circumcision began to be practised shortly after birth its significance as a ritual of initiation naturally ceased and it acquired a new meaning as a necessary qualification for life as a member of the chosen people (Gen 34:14–16; Ex 12:47f). It also became a sign of the covenant which God had made with Abraham and his descendants (Gen 17:9–14, from P). But this religious view of circumcision took a long time to establish itself. It is given only incidental mention in the law in connection with the stipulations concerning the passover (Ex 12:44, 48), the purification of a woman who has just given birth (Lev 12:3), and in comparison with the first-fruits of trees (Lev 19:23↗ Firstfruits). It was only during the Exile that circumcision became the characteristic of one who belonged to the covenant-people, since the peoples of Mesopotamia were uncircumcised and those of Palestine had already given it up (cf Ezek 32:19ff; Judg 14:3). At all events, Flavius Josephus notes that in his day—that is, in the first century AD—the Jews were the only people living in Palestine who practised circumcision. It was therefore demanded of those gentiles who wished to embrace the Jewish faith, since it was the sign of the covenant (Esther 8:17). With the advance of hellenism Antiochus Epiphanes, then ruler of Palestine, prohibited circumcision under the most severe penalties (1 Macc 1:60f; 2 Macc 6:10). Jews who were weak in faith attempted to remove any sign of circumcision (1 Macc 1:15; cf 1 Cor 7:18).

As we know from Jn 7:22f, circumcision was carried out at the time of Jesus on the sabbath. But for those who were part of the new covenant it had lost its significance since it was a sign of the old covenant (Acts 15; Rom 4; Gal 2).

Bibliography: A. van Gennep, *Les Rites de passage*, 1909; A. E. Jensen, *Beschneidung und Reife-zeremonien bei Naturvölkern*, 1933; J. G. Schur, *Wesen und Motive der Beschneidung im Lichte der alttestamentlichen Quellen und der Völkerkunde*, 1937; A. Allwohn, 'Die Interpretation der religiösen Symbole erläutern an der Beschneidung', *ZRGG* VIII (1956), 32–40; F. R. Lehmann, 'Bemerkungen zu einer neuen Begrundung der Beschneidung', *Sociologus* VII (1957), 57–74; de Vaux, 46–8.

Walter Kornfeld

Clean and unclean

A. *Concept and Terminology*. The idea of *cultic* (as distinct from moral) cleanness and uncleanness is found both in the primitive religions and among the Greeks, and also in the world of the ancient Near East in general which constitutes the background to the bible. Intercourse with the divinity requires that man shall be free from everything which is hostile to that divinity: from contamination by 'common' or everyday things, which were regarded as causing uncleanness. Examples of this are manifestations of the sexual functions, birth, sickness, death. All these entail cultic uncleanness. The biblical terms covering this department are *ṭāhôr* or *katharos* (=clean), and *ṭāmēʾ* and *ṭumʾāh*, or *akathartos* (=unclean).

B. In the *Old Testament*, where special emphasis seems to be laid upon the holiness of God, the contrast between clean and unclean is drawn particularly sharply. The category of the unclean applies *above all* to everything which is in any way associated with *pagan cults*. It is prohibited to eat various kinds of 'unclean' animals. Now on closer examination it turns out that the animals covered by this prohibition are those which have some sort of cultic or religious significance in the religions of Israel's neighbours (Lev 11, Deut 14). Again land belonging to Gentile peoples is 'unclean land' (Amos 7:17). Palestine alone, as belonging to Yahweh himself, is clean. A further factor, associated with this uncleanness of the territory of the Gentiles, is the ↗ban which is pronounced upon it (Josh 6:24–7:26). These ideas are carried so far that it is even prohibited to partake of the fruits of the land of Canaan in the first three harvests after the conquest. Those of the fourth year have to be offered to Yahweh, and it is not until the fifth year comes that the Israelites are allowed to take the fruits of the harvest for their own use, 'For I, Yahweh, am your God' (Lev 19:23). For similar reasons it was also prohibited to partake of meat offered to idols (1 Macc 1:62f).

For the rest an idea which Israel had in common with the surrounding peoples of her world was that contact with corpses or with the phenomena connected with sex brought about uncleanness (for examples of this see Num 19:11 or Lev 12:5; 1 Sam 21:5; 2 Sam 11:4). The same applies to blood and diseases (probably the so-called 'leprosy' referred to is in reality a curable skin-disease, and not leprosy in the modern sense: see L. Köhler, *ZAW* 67 [1955/1956], 290f). The case of uncleanness incurred through contact with corpses enables us to realise how little the concept of uncleanness here has to do with *morality*. To bury the dead is actually a duty, or at least a praiseworthy deed (Lev 21:1–3; Tob 1:18; 2:9; 12:12).

Nevertheless—and this is characteristic for the Old Testament—uncleanness of this cultic kind does exclude the subject in some sense from communion with Yahweh. The priest who has incurred uncleanness is thereby disqualified from the normal priestly activities (Lev 21f), while the layman who is in this condition must not partake of sacred meals or enter the temple or take part in the holy war (Lev 7:20f; 12:4; Deut 23:9–14 etc).

The means of cleansing which is employed is water (or less frequently blood as well) applied in the form of sprinkling, washing, or bathing. In addition certain prescribed periods have to be observed during which the state of uncleanness continues.

The specialists are divided in their opinions as to what precisely constitutes the original basis for believing that corpses, various kinds of animals, blood, etc, cause uncleanness. We do not possess any texts which could throw light upon this problem for us. In the case of the Old Testament at least all these matters have been brought under a common heading by acquiring a specific reference to Yahweh. The religion of Yahweh has taken over the heritage of earlier times and customs, and placed it at its own service. Whatever the earlier significance of these purificatory rites may have been, henceforward their function is to protect Israel from believing in idols and idolatrous practices, or to rid them of

such practices where they are already in existence. Admittedly, when the idea of cleanness is over-emphasised it does lead, in the last analysis, to a ludicrous degree of formalism, and this had in fact already taken place even before the time of Jesus.

It is against this kind of formalism that the prophets inveigh when they urge the claims of interior purity of mind and heart. For many had come to neglect this in favour of a wholly external and ritual purity (Hos 6:6; Amos 4:1–5; 5:21–5; Is 1:10–17; above all Is 6:5, Jer 13:27 etc). Morals, and not an externalist idea of purity, must be accorded the first place, a morals consisting in acknowledgement of God, obedience to his will, and especially practical love of one's neighbour. It is this that is truly demanded (see also Ps 15; 40:7–9; 50:16; etc).

C. In the *New Testament* the idea of ritual cleanness or uncleanness is presented as inadequate and destined to disappear. In its place, and in continuation of the message of the prophets, *inner purity* is demanded. In his controversies with his opponents on the subject of clean and unclean (Mk 7:1–23; Mt 15:1–20) Jesus has spoken the last word on this subject. In these controversies Jesus first defines his position with regard to the concept of the tradition of the elders, and then goes on to treat of various particular cases. In Mk 7:14ff and Mt 15:19f he touches upon our subject in particular. He provides a definition of the idea of cleanness which is fundamentally new. The death blow is dealt to the old view of ritual cleanness and uncleanness, but in its place the basic principle of all morality, of morality as such, is defined: it is on the basis of what comes from the ↗ heart of man (ie, from his disposition, his attitude), his words, therefore, and his deeds, that he can be pronounced truly clean or unclean. The primitive church had, of course, still much to do before this radical decision could be put into effect with all its implications. Something which had been rooted so deeply and so long in the customs and habits of men could not be abolished overnight. Jesus himself was fully aware of this, if we may take Mt 23:23ff as representative in this sense (see also Acts 10:10–16; ↗ Three A; 15:20f, 28f; Gal 2:11ff etc). The procedure of the early church was, in fact, comprehensible not only from the standpoint of Jewish Old Testament tradition, but also from that of its own teaching. So long as the observance of the prescriptions of purity did not constitute an obstacle to that which was essential in the christian message there was no need to insist upon its abolition. But whenever this did become desirable the church did not hesitate so to insist.

The effect of this was that attention came to be concentrated exclusively upon one particular aspect of cleanness, one which was certainly also present in contemporary Judaism (under the influence of the prophets), namely cleanness in the inner man (R. Meyer, 426f). Jesus declares that those who are 'clean of heart' are blessed, and promises them that they will ↗ see God and share in the ↗ kingdom of God (Mt 5:8; see also Ps 24:4; 73:1). Again in 1 Tim 1:5; 3:9 and 2 Tim 1:3; 2:22 we find references in the same sense to the 'pure heart' and 'clear conscience' (the two are syn-

onymous). Again in John strong emphasis is laid upon purity. The disciples of Jesus are 'clean' through his word (15:3). The betrayer is 'unclean' (13:11). It can be deduced from this that uncleanness is sin in all its aspects (see 1 Jn 1:7, 9). According to 1 Pet 1:22 purification is achieved through obedience to the ↗ truth. In Eph 5:26 (see Heb 9:13f) it is the blood of Christ which 'cleanses' us through the conferring of baptism. It is always a question of purification, a liberation from sin of every kind. This purification is achieved essentially through the sacramental act of ↗ baptism, in which the salvific work of Christ is applied to the individual. But the obedience of man in faith is also an indispensable contributory factor (as Jn 15:3 and 1 Pet 1:22 likewise show).

D. The *restriction* of 'cleanness' in the moral sense (inner purity) to the *sexual sphere* is foreign to the New Testament. Uncleanness as conceived of among pagans, on the other hand, consists primarily in avarice and unchastity. It is precisely uncleanness and excesses in the sexual sphere, 'burning the candle at both ends', which is felt as 'uncleanness' (*akatharsia*: see Gal 5:19; Rom 1:24–32; 2 Cor 12:21; etc). The idea that relationships *even in marriage* may cause uncleanness in the moral sense (ie, may have an element of sinfulness in them) is utterly foreign to the bible. Ideas of this sort, remotely derived from those of the bible, were put forward by certain fathers of the church. But they are the outcome of, and at the same time characterised by, a certain intermingling of the two originally distinct concepts of 'cultic' and 'moral' uncleanness, and at the same time of a fresh incursion of the ancient Jewish ceremonial law as an influence upon the theology of the church. Thus the prohibition of servile works (*opera servilia*) as an act of sanctification of the sabbath entered once more into christian moral theology on the basis of the principle: 'Si Judaei quanto magis Christiani' ('if the Jews did it, how much more should christians do it too'). In the same way too the church's concept of celibacy was arrived at on the basis of the same principle (see Lev 22:2ff and 15:18; and, on the principle itself, see Ex 19:15). Further examples are that it was forbidden to come to church or receive communion after married intercourse or *pollutio nocturna* (= 'nocturnal emission of semen': thus, *ne polluantur corpora* = 'that [our] bodies may not be defiled' in the hymn of compline). Further examples still might be adduced. Not the least important result of all this was that it paved the way for the disastrous process by which all the emphasis in moral teaching was exaggeratedly laid on sexual morality.

Bibliography: F. Hauck and R. Meyer, *TDNT* III, 413–31; P. van Imschoot in Haag, cols 1420–3; Imschoot II, 204–16; von Rad I, 272–9; D. Lys and M. Carrez in Allmen, 59–63; J. Schmid, *RNT* on Mk 7:1–23 with Excursus; Schnackenburg, 35f; W. H. Gipsen, *OTS* I (1948), 190–6; A. Penna, *Riv. Bibl. It.* 6 (1958), 15f; a thorough treatment of the individual passages is provided especially by J. Döller, 'Die Reinheits- und Speisegesetze des At', *AA* 7/2f (1917). On D: F. Pettirsch, *ZKT* 69 (1947), 257–327, 417–44 (esp. 430, n. 196, and 439); H. Doms, *Vom & Sinn des Zölibats*, Regensberg-Münster 1954; A. Adam, *Der Primat der Liebe*, Kevelaer 1954[6]; L. Moulinier, *Le pur et l'impur dans la pensée des Grecqs*, Paris 1952; O. W. Buchanan, 'The Role of Purity in the Structure of the Essene Sect', *RQ* 15/4/3, 397–406.

Johannes B. Bauer

Confession

Confession or avowal corresponds to ↗ preaching, as can be seen from Rom 10:8–9: 'The word is near you . . . the word of faith which we preach (*kērussein*); because, if you confess (*homologein*) with your lips that Jesus is Lord and believe in your heart that God raised him from the dead, you will be saved'. In other words, if what you say with your lips agrees with what you say in your heart, if the *same word* comes from both in agreement with the word of the preacher (*homo-* = the same, *logos* = word) you will reach salvation. The original sense of the word, therefore, implies expressing what the heart receives in faith. Faith and avowal are intimately associated; both together they constitute the response to the preached word or kerygma. In this way the kerygma is enlarged through the confession or avowal of faith—an idea which, though rooted in the Old Testament, only reaches its complete development in the New.

A. *The Old Testament*. The verb 'to avow' occurs thirteen times in LXX with the sense of acknowledging, being in agreement, confessing. The texts are as follows: Job 40:9[14] corresponding to Hebrew *yāda[c]*; Wis 18:13; 2 Macc 6:6; 4 Macc 6:34; 9:16; 13:5; Esther 1:10; in 1 Macc 6:61; Jer 51(44):25 the sense is 'to swear by' or 'vow' ('avow') corresponding to Hebrew *nādar*; the phrase 'confess (avow) one's sins' occurs in Sir 4:26; Dan 13:14 (Vulg: with which see 1 QS 1, 18–III); in Ezra 4:60; 5:58 (see also 1 QH) it occurs with the sense of 'praise'.

The noun *homologia* (= confession, avowal) occurs seven times. It can refer to a vow (Hebrew: *nēder*) in Lev 22:18; Jer 51(44):25; a 'goodwill offering' in Dt 12:6, 17; Ezek 46:12; Am 4:5; and in one case (Ezra 9:8) has the meaning 'praise'.

As in classical Greek the compound verb *exhomologeisthai*, more rarely *anthomologeisthai*, can have the meaning 'to make open profession or confession' (eg of sins). In LXX the connotation 'praise, thank' is original, a genuinely new sense which has no doubt been influenced by the Hebrew verb *yādaᶜ* meaning 'know' or 'confess openly'.

In this connection we have to take into account the old Testament liturgy of thanksgiving sacrifices (*tôdâh*) which included a series of short, hymnic utterances dealing with the high deeds of Yahweh in leading his people. The greatest of these was of course his taking them out of Egypt, usually expressed in the classical formula: 'Yahweh who has led Israel out of Egypt' (eg Ex 20:2; Lev 11:45; 25:38; Num 15:41; 23:22; 24:8; Dt 5:6; 8:14; Mic 6:4; Ps 81:10; 136:11 etc), 'with a mighty hand' (Dt 6:21; 7:8) or 'with a mighty hand and an outstretched arm' (Dt 4:34; 26:8; Ps 136:12; see also Ex 6:6).

This is the primitive confession of faith and all others are in some way connected with it: the promise to the fathers, the leading of the people through the wilderness, the revelation on Sinai, 'the entry into the cultivated land of Canaan' (M. Noth). The *Sitz im Leben* of all these individual confessions is to be sought in the cult.

The confessional character of the Old Testament also finds expression in the wider historical presentations as, for example, in Josh 24:2–15, Jud 5:6–21 and Ps 105, 136; etc.

In the last resort all of these confessional formulations, whether short or long (as Dt 26:5–9), are to be understood on the basis of covenant theology. They constitute the response of the people to the wondrous movement of God in their direction. This comes through in the classical covenant formula: 'Yahweh is our God' (eg Ex 6:7; 24:3, 7; 29:46; Dt 4:7, 35) which is expressed with greater theological profundity in Dt 5–6; 10:17; Josh 3:10; 24:24; 1 Kings 18:21; 2 Kings 19:15; and elsewhere.

All of these confessional forms in the Old Testament refer not to abstract truths but always to events which have taken place within the history of salvation or, more precisely, to the God who guides this history, the God who is acknowledged and praised in the 'historical credo' (von Rad) of Dt 26:6–9; 6:21–5 and Josh 24.

B. *The New Testament*. In the New Testament the verb *homologein* occurs twenty-six times. In most cases it has the meaning 'to acknowledge': Mt 7:23; 10:32 (twice) = Lk 12:8 (twice); Jn 1:20 (twice); 9:22; 12:42; Acts 23:8; 24:14; Rom 10:9, 10; 1 Tim 6:12; Tit 1:16; Heb 11:13; 13:15; 1 Jn 2:23; 4:2, 3, 15; 2 Jn 7; Rev 3:5. In addition to these twenty-three texts we find the verb once with the meaning 'to confess sins' (1 Jn 1:9) and twice with the meaning 'to swear, to promise with an oath' (Mt 14:7; Acts 7:17). The noun *homologia* is used six times and refers rather to the content of what is professed in faith than the act of confessing or avowing (2 Cor 9:13; 1 Tim 6:12–13; Heb 3:1; 4:14; 10:23).

The compound verb *exhomologein* which occurs ten times, means 'to confess' (Phil 2:11) and more especially 'to praise', the latter under the influence of LXX usage Mt 11:25 = Lk 10:21; Rom 14:11; 15:9. The meaning 'to confess sins' is also found (Mt 3:6 = Mk 1:5; Acts 19:18; Jas 5:16), and in one case 'to promise, agree' (Lk 22:6).

Homologein and *homologia*, as well as other forms which do not use this technical expression, always refer to a confession or avowal by which one makes a public decision for Christ. The New Testament use of this term always therefore contains strongly christological connotations (Rom 10:8–10; Phil 2:11; 1 Tim 6:12, 13; 1 Jn 4:2, 3).

I. *The form of confession or acknowledgement.* 1. *The synoptic gospels.* a. Peter was no doubt the first to give public expression to his faith: 'You are the Messiah (the Christ)' (Mk 8:29). Matthew enlarged this by the addition of 'the Son of God' (Mt 16:16), while Luke has 'the Messiah of God' (Lk 9:20). The title 'Christ' has a striking part to play throughout the passion narratives. So, for example, the high priest asks Jesus: 'Are you the Christ, the Son of the Blessed?' (Mk 14:61; Mt 26:63; Lk 22:67 cf Mt 27:17, 22; Mk 15:32; Lk 23:35, 39).

b. 'Son of God' is also found as a confessional formula in the synoptics. It occurs at the baptism of Jesus (Mt 3:17; Mk 1:11; Lk 3:22), in the temptation scene (Mt 4:3, 6; Lk 4:3, 9), the transfiguration (Mt 17:5; Mk 9:7; Lk 9:35); is used by the unclean spirits (Mk 3:11; 5:7; Lk 4:41), by Peter after the storm at sea in the Matthean tradition (Mt 14:33) and at Caesarea Philippi (only in Mt 16:16), during the hearing before the Sanhedrin (Mt 26:63; Mk 14:61), and the mocking on the cross (Mt 27:40, 43), and by the Roman centurion (Mt 27:54; Mk 15:39).

c. The three earliest gospels have also handed down another title, that of Son of David. This was attributed to Jesus by the people (Mt 12:23; 21:9 cf Mk 11:10; Mt 22:41–5 = Mk 12:35–7; Lk 20:41–4) and by the unclean spirits speaking through the mouths of the sick: 'have mercy on us (me), Son of David' (Mt 9:27; 15:22; Mt 20:30, 31 = Mk 10:47, 48; Lk 18:38, 39).

2. In *Acts* the word *homologia* does not occur and *homologein* only in the sense of 'promising' (7:17) and 'acknowledging' something (23:8; 24:14). But in the preaching of the apostles we meet with a whole series of christological titles.

a. The most common of these is 'Jesus is the Messiah' as, for example, on the lips of the apostles in Jerusalem (5:42: *euangelizomenoi ton khriston Iēsoun* = 'preaching Jesus as the Christ'. Taking in the preceding *didaskontes* = 'teaching' we should translate: 'teaching and preaching that Jesus is the Messiah'). It is also used by Paul in the synagogues of Damascus (9:20, 22), Thessalonika (17:2–3), and Corinth (18:5, 28), and by Apollos in Ephesus (18:28).

b. The classical formula 'Jesus is the Lord' occurs several times. The Hellenistic Christians from Cyprus and Cyrenaica preach the good news (*euangelizomenoi*) of the Lord Jesus or, paraphrasing, 'they preach: Jesus is the Lord' (11:20). The Lord-ship of Jesus is the nucleus of the message as presented to the Gentiles, as is clear from Pauline theology. It is grounded on the resurrection of Jesus: 'God has made both Lord and Christ this Jesus whom you crucified' (2:36). Peter puts it the same way to the Gentile Cornelius: 'He [Christ] is lord of all' (10:36), of Jews and Gentiles. Although the Kyrios-formula seldom occurs expressly in Acts and almost always as addressed to Gentiles, it reflects the faith in the exalted Lord as held and expressed at the time the book was written.

c. Acts also testifies to Jesus under another confessional title as 'judge of the living and the dead' (10:42) whom God has appointed 'to judge the world' (17:31). That this is really a confessional formula can be seen in the use of the introductory particle *hoti* (= [to the effect] that); see also (17:31; 9:20, 22) or the infinitive with indirect speech (18:28).

d. In addition to these christological formulae made up of one clause or member there are also others with two which refer to the death and resurrection of Christ. In these cases the formulaic character of the confessional statements is apparent in the use of the *hoti* which introduces the formula (4:10). In the first half of Acts we find many different ways of avoiding a dichotomy between crucifixion and resurrection, as can be seen in 2:22–4; 2:36; 3:15; 5:30–1 cf 10:39–40; 17:2–3; 26:23 (*ei* = 'whether' instead of *hoti*).

3. *The Pauline epistles.* Just as the formula 'Jesus is the Messiah' predominates in the synoptics and Acts, so does 'Jesus is the Lord' in Paul. Both confessional formulae reflect the different spatial and temporal situations of Jewish and Gentile christianity respectively.

a. The short form of this formula is introduced by *homologein* in Rom 10:9 (with introductory *hoti* in Codex B) and by *exhomologein* in Phil 2:11. We have here a formula in current use at the time of Paul and one which must have made a deep impression on the communities to which he writes. In most cases, however, it does not occur with the verb *homologein*, eg 1 Cor 8:6; 12:3; Heb 13:20.

b. At a slightly later stage a two-part formula developed from this: Jesus is the Lord whom God has raised from the dead. Here the verb occurs twelve times in the active voice (Rom 4:24; 8:11, 11; 10:9; 1 Cor 6:14; 15:15, 15; 2 Cor 4:14; Gal 1:1; Eph 1:20; Col 2:12; 1 Thess 1:10) and thirteen times in the passive (he who has been raised by God) Rom 4:25; 6:4, 9; 7:4; 8:34; 1 Cor 15:4, 12, 13, 14, 16, 17, 20; 2 Cor 5:15).

When the emphasis is on *God* who has raised Jesus the direct object is *Jesus* (Rom 8:11; 1 Thess 1:10), *the Lord* (1 Cor 6:14), *the Christ* (1 Cor 15:15; Eph 1:20; Col 2:12), *Jesus the Lord*, or *the Lord Jesus* (Rom 4:24; 10:9; 2 Cor 4:14). When, however, the verb is in the passive, *Christ* is always the subject (except Rom 4:25), even in Rom 8:34 (following B, D, Koine and Syr.). We may therefore conclude that even if in the christology of Paul the emphasis has passed from Messiah to Lord the original Messiah-motif appears still in the titles 'Jesus Christ' (sixty-five times) or 'Christ Jesus' (sixty-three times).

c. As a result of theological reflection these christological formulae are given a deeper and broader connotation and expressed dialectically in the opposites: 'died—raised from the dead' (Rom 8:34; see also Rom 4:24, 25; 1 Cor 15:3–5; 2 Cor 13:4; 1 Thess. 4:14; Rom. 14:9), 'descended—ascended' (Eph 4:8–10; see also Rom 10:6–13; Phil 2:6–11), 'descended from David according to the flesh—designated Son of God' (Rom 1:3, 4 and, dependent on this, 2 Tim 2:8), 'according to the flesh—according to the Spirit' (Rom 1:3, 4; compare 'crucified in weakness —living by the power of God', 2 Cor 13:4), 'put to death in the flesh—made alive in the Spirit' (1 Pet 3:18).

d. In the pastoral epistles Jesus himself is represented as the exemplar of confession or avowal during his trial before Pilate. In the presence of the Roman ruler he made 'the good confession' (1 Tim 6:13) by stating that he was the Messiah (cf Mk 15:2).

4. *The Johannine writings.* The confessional character of these writings can be clearly discerned in the frequent use of *hoti* as an introductory formula (Jn 1:20; 1 Jn 4:15), the double accusative (Jn 9:22; 1 Jn 4:2; 2 Jn 7; see also Rom. 10:9), and the infinitive (Jn 9:22 in D and e; 1 Jn 4:2 in B; see also Tit 1:16).

a. The primitive confessional formula 'Jesus is the Christ' is found also in the Johannine writings (Jn 1:20, 41; 3:28; 4:25, 29; 7:26, 27, 41; 9:22; 10:24; 11:27; 12:34; 20:31; 1 Jn 2:22; cf v 23; 4:15; 5:1; 2 Jn 7).

b. The closely related form 'Jesus is the Son of God' is often met with in the fourth gospel and the Johannine epistles (eg Jn 1:34, 49; 6:69; 10:36; 1 Jn 4:15; 5:5) and is practically identical with 'Jesus is Christ (Messiah)' (see

1 Jn 2:22 with v 23; 1 Jn 4:15 with 5:1; 5:5 with v 6). Reference to Jesus as Christ and as Son can also be found together, as in Jn 11:27 and 20:31: 'Jesus is the Christ, the Son of God'.

c. The expression: 'Jesus Christ has come in the flesh' (1 Jn 4:2; 2 Jn 7 cf 1 Jn 5:6) provides a further interpretation of the original confession of faith: 'Every spirit which confesses (*homologein*) that Jesus Christ has come in the flesh' (1 Jn 4:2 and 2 Jn 7). Referring back to 1 Jn 4:3 and Johannine christology as a whole, Jesus and Christ are put together to form one accusative. In 1 Jn 5:6 the author spells out further the christological formula: 'Jesus Christ . . . is he who came by water and blood'. His intention in putting it this way is to stress the humanity of Jesus.

II. *The Word.* Jesus stands at the centre of the confession of faith as we find it in the New Testament. It is he who, through the mouth of the apostles, announces the good news of eschatological salvation and demands the response of faith and confession of his name. Faith and confession or avowal are therefore intimately related. The *proclaimed word* awakens *faith* in the heart and *confession* on the lips (see Rom 10:8–9; 2 Cor 4:13). All of the christological formulae found in the New Testament are not only doctrinal but confessional—above all, confessional. They are originally and remain preponderantly of a pure christological character. The whole thought-world of the early church centres on Jesus Christ whose incomparable prerogatives are expressed compendiously by the sacred writers, interpreted and deepened by theological reflection, and then acknowledged and praised openly before the world by the early Christian communities.

1. According to the witness of *the synoptic gospels and Acts*, the expression 'Jesus is the Christ' forms the most original and basic confession of faith first proclaimed by Peter at Caesarea Philippi (Mk 8:29). The *Sitz im Leben* of this confession has to be sought in the earthly life of Jesus and in that of the early church at a time when the messianic question played a prominent part in the polemic with official judaism. The decisive question for the contemporaries of Jesus and convert judaeo-christians in Palestine and in the diaspora was precisely this: is Jesus really the promised Messiah who has come as king of Israel to free his chosen people from their enemies? (See Jn 1:41; 4:29; 7:26f, 41f; 9:22; 12:34; 20:31; Mk 14:61; 15:2; Acts 1:6.) The significance which Jesus attached to the messianic idea after the confession of Peter (Mk 8:29), according to which the Son of Man was to suffer, die, and be raised from the dead (Mk 8:31 cf 9:31; 10:33f), was filled out after Pentecost by the inspired writers with reference to the relevant Old Testament texts. The intention of the apostles in their preaching was to show that, in accordance with the scriptures, Jesus had to die and be raised and thus establish himself as the promised messiah (see Lk 24:25-7; Acts 2:22-4; 3:15; 4:10; 5:30; 10:40; 13:29f, 34; 17:2f; 18:28).

The belief that Jesus had appeared as the promised Messiah (see Acts 4:10; Rom 8:34) entered so deeply into Paul that he made a proper name out of the christological formula: Jesus Christ or Christ Jesus.

For the early church the title 'Christ' was not a jaded formula as it has come to be for so many today. It awakened in their minds the figure of the suffering, dying, and risen Jesus in keeping with the representation of the Son of Man in the way Jesus himself had interpreted it. In its liturgy the early church acknowledged and praised Jesus the 'Christ' as the one who suffered, died, and was raised for the salvation of the world.

We conclude therefore that the formula 'Jesus is the Christ' preceded the avowal of his sonship and lordship both logically and chronologically.

2. The formula 'Jesus is the Lord' forms the kernel of *Pauline* christology. For the first christian communities it at once recalled the easter-event. Jesus, who had lived and died in a given place and at a given point of history, had been designated by God as *lord* (*kurios*) by the resurrection from the dead. This brief confessional formula was in use principally in the gentile-christian communities (see Acts 11:20 with 11:19). It evoked the figure of Jesus Christ as raised to the right hand of God (Rom 10:9; 1 Cor 12:3) at the resurrection (1 Cor 15:3-8), having subdued the powers and principalities (Phil 2:10f; 1 Pet 3:22), as present in the community and one day to return in glory (1 Cor 16:22: *marana tha*—our lord, come!).

Here we come to the very centre of the early church's life. Dedicated entirely as it was to the risen and glorified lord, it could not start out with the enunciation of timeless truths. Hearing the title *kurios*, christians of Jewish extraction would think automatically of Yahweh the God of the fathers, translated *kurios* in LXX. Gentile christians would praise Jesus as the one and only *kurios* as against the official cult of Caesar and the gods. *All* Christians would acknowledge him as the risen and glorified lord, the *kurios* of the life and death of his followers and servants, the lord of the church and of the entire creation.

In the two-part christological formulae the avowal 'Jesus is the Lord' is expanded by reference to God the Father who had raised Jesus from the dead; but the reference to Jesus as *kurios* is antecedent to mention of God the Father (as in Eph 4:5f; 1 Jn 2:23f; 4:15), not vice versa (as in 1 Cor 8:6; 1 Pet 1:3).

In the three-part formulae a reference to the Holy Spirit is added (Rom 15:30; 2 Cor 13:14).

In this way the reference to Jesus as *kurios* is expanded by a confession of faith in God the Father who had glorified Jesus and strengthened by reference to the Holy Spirit through whom he is present to his community.

3. The christological title 'Son of God' is encountered chiefly in the *gospel and epistles of John*, but we find it also in the Pauline epistles and in the synoptics (see above).

We should take note of the fact that, according to the synoptic tradition, Jesus never refers to himself expressly as 'Son of God', despite the fact that he was conscious of being such in a unique manner, as can be seen from the way he addressed God as father and spoke of him as *his* father in a way different from other people. It is quite another question, however, whether the apostles arrived at an understanding of this title in all its significance during the

lifetime of Jesus. If we take in the various stages of the gospel tradition it will be clear that they understood it in full significance only after the resurrection and *in the light of* the resurrection. After the descent of the Holy Spirit they were able to recognise that Ps 2:7 (see Acts 13:33; Rom 1:3f; Heb 1:5) and the promise to David in particular (Mt 22:41–6) had been fulfilled in Jesus. He was truly the messianic king and Son of God.

This post-resurrection acknowledgement of the unique and inalienable divine sonship of Jesus is confirmed in the christology of Paul. In such important, and in some cases, ancient confessional formulae as 1 Cor 15:3–8, 1 Tim 3:16, 2 Tim 4:1, and 1 Pet 3:18–22 the resurrection is mentioned but Jesus is not referred to as 'Son of God' as is the case elsewhere (eg Rom 1:3; Heb 1:5). We may conclude from this that the resurrection and exaltation of Jesus were not deduced as consequences of the divine sonship of Jesus previously recognised and accepted. On the contrary, the great event of the resurrection and glorification of Jesus led directly to belief in his divine origin and nature.

By using this most recent of the christological formulae 'Jesus is Son of God', therefore, the early church expressed and professed its unshakeable faith in the divine sonship of Jesus and read it back into his earthly life, his birth and miraculous conception (Mt 1:20–23; Lk 1:34f), and from it deduced his pre-existence (Phil 2:6–11; Col 2:9; Rom 9:5; Tit 2:13).

Nowhere more strongly does this title appear than in the Johannine gospel and epistles which represent Jesus in the light of his 'glory as of the only Son from the Father' (Jn 1:14 cf 1:34, 49; 5:25; 10:36; 11:27; 17:1; 19:7; 20:31; etc).

The christological formulae in the Johannine epistles: 'to confess Jesus *Christ* [who has] come in the flesh' (1 Jn 4:2; 2 Jn 7 cf 1 Jn 2:22), '[to confess] *the Son*' (1 Jn 2:23), 'to confess that Jesus is *the Son of God*' (1 Jn 4:15), have a marked confessional character. John's intention in using these brief and concise christological confessions is not so much to arm his readers against the attacks of an emergent gnosticism which questioned the truth of the incarnation and the universality of redemption but rather to warn them against those 'antichrists' (1 Jn 2:18, 22; 4:3; 2 Jn 7) who, influenced by the pagan milieu, indulged in an insidious materialism, had given way to religious indifference, no longer took their christian calling seriously, and had turned their backs on Jesus Christ. Here as in the fourth gospel we cannot fail to notice the marked christocentricity of the writer.

III. *The Locus.* Though the literary evidence no longer permits us to determine exactly in each case the original situation in which these forms of christological confession arose, we can in a general way designate their *Sitz im Leben* as *the worship of the early church*, the celebration of the eucharist and early christian preaching in particular. This gives these christological statements a distinctly *confessional* character.

In the ordinary divine service of the early church, especially in the *celebration of the eucharist*, the community confessed its faith in Jesus Christ with 'psalms and hymns and spiritual songs'

(Eph 5:19; see also Acts 2:47). In Phil 2:6–11 Paul has preserved for us in rhythmic form one of the most ancient confessions of faith. This is a composition which can with reason be called a christian psalm. Its climax comes in the avowal (*exhomologeisthai*, see too Is 45:23) that 'Jesus is the Lord', Lord, that is, over the whole cosmos. We find ancient christological hymns also in 1 Tim 3:16 and, in a fragmentary state, 1 Pet 2: 21–4; perhaps also in the opening verses of Eph, Col, and 1 Pet (see Col 1:15–20).

The many formulae in the Johannine writings which speak of Jesus as Christ and Son of God, as also the post-resurrection formulae 'my lord and my God' (Jn 20:28) and 'it is the lord' (Jn 21:7, 12) reflect the confession of faith in Christ in early christian liturgy.

Praise of Christ in the liturgy probably took on at an early stage the fixed form of a cultic *homologia* (see Heb 3:1; 4:14; 10:23).

In Heb 13:15 the community 'confesses' the name of God, doubtless in the context of a liturgical celebration.

The well-known resurrection confession of 1 Cor 15:3–7 was probably recited and explained in early Christian *preaching* and *catechesis*. As he tells us himself, Paul had taken it from the primitive church and explained it in his preaching to the Corinthians. It held a position of primary importance in his missionary preaching ('as of first importance', v 3): the expiatory death of Jesus, his burial and resurrection according to the scriptures, his appearances after his resurrection. The confession of faith in the risen and exalted lord was the centre of his preaching against the cult of Caesar and the gods (1 Cor 12:3; 2 Cor 4:5) and as such aroused in his hearers both faith and ·the open confession of faith (Rom 10:8f).

From the earliest times the administration of baptism provided the occasion for confession of faith in Jesus Christ. Even if v 37 in Acts 8:36–8 is generally considered inauthentic, it can still be taken as a very ancient witness to the fact that a confession of faith in Christ followed baptismal catechesis— 'I believe that Jesus Christ is the Son of God' (see Mt 28:19; Mk 16:16). Rom 10:9 refers in all probability to a confession of faith in the resurrection which preceded baptism. 1 Pet 3:18–22 has also preserved a confession of faith which was made during baptism, faith in Christ who died for our sins, who 'went and preached to the spirits in prison . . . who has gone into heaven and is at the right hand of God'. This christological confession is interrupted by the parenthesis of vv 20–1 which form a short baptismal instruction.

According to New Testament tradition the christological confession of faith also contains the idea of *judgement*, the context of which is to be sought during the time of persecution when the faithful had to decide clearly either for or against Christ.

According to the entire context of 1 Tim 6:12–16, Timothy is represented as standing at the bar of judgement where he has already made 'the good confession' (of faith) in the presence of many witnesses (v 12). He still has to 'fight the good fight', that is, confess Jesus openly before his judges in imitation of the testimony which Jesus himself gave during his trial. In other words, just as Jesus made 'the good confession' during his trial in the hearing before Pilate by solemnly declaring himself to be the messianic king, so must Timothy testify to the messianic kingdom of Jesus. Perhaps the christological confession 'Jesus is the *kurios*' (Rom 10:9) is referred to indirectly here, in the sense that Timothy boldly declares before the Roman judgement seat for the *kurios* Jesus rather than for the *kurios* Caesar. 1 Cor 12:3; 'No one can say, "Jesus is lord" except by the Holy Spirit', has nothing to do with speaking with tongues but reflects, in the same way, a time of persecution. According to Mt 10:17–20 (see also Lk 12:11–12) Jesus promises his disciples the gift of the Spirit when they are brought to judgement by the synagogue and stand before earthly governors and rulers. This points in the same direction.

The same can be said of the saying of Jesus about confessing him before human judges. This judgement is paralleled by the confessing of the 'Son of Man' at the final judgement (Mt 10:32: *homologein en tini* = 'to confess *in* someone' is an Aramaism for the more normal accusative; Lk 12:8; see too Mk 8:38 = Lk 9:26; 2 Tim 2:12; Rev 3:5). In their difficult confrontation with a hostile world the disciples can count on the assistance of the Holy Spirit (Mk 13:11; Lk 12:11f). The avowal of faith in Christ is therefore given the greatest possible importance since it already decides the ultimate fate of the individual here and now. The primitive form this confession took is continually developed and expanded as time goes on.

The opposite of confession or avowal is *denial* (*arneisthai*: Mt 10:33; Lk 12:9 cf Mk 8:38; Lk 9:26). The opposite of confessing Jesus as Messiah and *Kurios* is quite simply apostasy (1 Cor 12:3).

According to the synoptics and Acts, the form 'Jesus is the Christ' expresses the personal faith of the apostles. This, however, very soon became a kind of slogan or watchword in the struggle against judaism and a confession of public faith appropriate to certain specific occasions in the life of the christian community as, for example, at baptism and in time of persecution (see 1 Tim 6:13).

These christological confessions of faith could also have a polemical tone, for example in the struggle against false teachers (eg 1 Jn 2:23; 4:2–3; 4:15; 2 Jn 7). The formula in 1 Cor 8:6 directed against pagan polytheism also no doubt conceals a polemical note: '*One* God, the Father, from whom are all things and for whom we exist, and *one* lord Jesus Christ, through whom are all things and through whom we exist'. The reference to meat offered to idols in the first verse of the same chapter shows us how polemic against many gods and the many lesser 'lords' could have led to the expansion of the primitive form 'Jesus is lord' into the dual formula we find here which refers also to the Father.

The publicly proclaimed faith of the community gives its answer to the kerygma or gospel by declaring in unison: 'Jesus is the Christ', 'Jesus is the *Kurios*', 'Jesus is the Son of God'. In these brief christological formulae we feel the heartbeat of the early church which on more than one occasion took its witness to the point of martyrdom. It was on the basis of these christological confessions that the great statements of faith were gradually built up.

Bibliography: F. Kattenbusch, *Das apostolische Symbol* (2 vols), Leipzig 1894 and 1900; W. Foerster, *Herr ist Jesus*, Gütersloh 1924; E. Lohmeyer, *Kyrios-Jesus: eine Untersuchung zu Phil 2:5–11*, Heidelberg 1928; F. J. Babcock, *The History of the Creeds*, New York 1930; O. Michel, 'Biblisches Bekennen und Bezeugen', *ET* 2 (1935), 231–45; O. Proksch, *Das Bekenntnis im AT*, Leipzig 1936; G. Bornkamm, 'Homologia', *Hermes* 71 (1938), 377–93; W. Fiedler, *Bekennen und Bekenntnis*, Berne 1943; C. H. Dodd, *The Apostolic Preaching and its Developments*, London 1944²; H. Dörries, *Das Bekenntnis in der Geschichte der Kirche*, Göttingen 1947²; M. Noth, *Überlieferungsgeschichte des Pentateuch*, Stuttgart 1948, 48–67; O. Cullmann, *The Earliest Christian Confessions*, London 1949; J. Jeremias, 'Zwischen Karfreitag und Ostern', *ZNW* 42 (1949), 194–201; C. Crehan, *Early Christian Baptism and the Creed*, London 1949; J. N. D. Kelly, *Early Christian Creeds*, London 1950; O. Cullmann, *Early Christian Worship*, London 1956; O. Michel, *TDNT* v, 199–220; H. A. Blair, *A Creed before the Creeds*, London 1955; E. Schweitzer, *Erhöhung und Erniedrigung bei Jesus und seinen Nachfolgern*, Basle 1955; E. Lichtenstein, 'Die älteste christliche Glaubensformel', *ZKG* 63 (1950/1), 1–74; E. Schweitzer, 'Discipleship and Belief in Jesus as Lord from Jesus to the Hellenistic Church', *NTS* 2 (1955/6), 87–99; C. Westermann, 'Bekenntnis II. Im AT und Judentum', *RGG* I, Tübingen 1957³, 989–91; E. Kamlah, 'Bekenntnis III. Im NT', *RGG* I, 991–3; E. Schweitzer, 'Der Glaube an Jesus den Herrn in seiner Entwicklung von den ersten Nachfolgern bis zur hellenistischen Gemeinde', *ETL* 17 (1957), 7–21; H. Braun, 'Der Sinn der ntl. Christologie', *ZTK* 54 (1957), 341–77; R. Schnackenburg, 'Bekenntnis II. Biblisch', *LTK* II², 143–4; H. Schlier, *Die Verkündigung im Gottesdienst der Kirche*, Cologne 1958²; R. P. Martin, *An Early Christian Confession: Phil 2:5–11 in Recent Interpretation*, London 1960; J. Schreiner, 'Führung—ein Thema der Heilsgeschichte im AT', *BZ* 5 (1961), 2–18; N. Brox, 'Bekenntnis I. Biblisch', *HTG* I, Munich 1962, 151–5; P. Sandevoir, 'Confession', *DBT*, London 1967, 71–2; H. Ott, *Glaube und Bekennen*, Basle 1963; V. H. Neufeld, *The Earliest Christian Confessions*, Leiden 1963 (bibliography 147–54); F. Hahn, *Christologische Hoheitstitel. Ihre Geschichte im fruhen Christentum*, Göttingen 1964².

Robert Koch

Conscience

The ancient world was not ignorant of the idea of conscience and of man's responsibility with regard to good and evil, but the word *suneidēsis* (= consciousness, conscience), of Ionian origin, which occurs for the first time in Democritus (fl. c. 430 BC: see frag. 297, H. Diels, *Fragmente der Vorsokratiker*), is very rare in the inscriptions and papyri (W. H. Buckler, W. M. Calder, and W. K. C. Guthrie, *Monumenta Asiae minoris antiqua* IV, Manchester 1933, 648, 10f; *Pap. Osl.* XVII, 10; *Pap. Ryl.* 116, 9; and others, all after the first century AD) and is found only twice in the Old Testament (Sir 10:20; Wis 17:11; see the variants of the Codex Sinaiticus on Sir 42:18). Although the word is not found at all in the gospels—Jn 8:9 is inauthentic—it is used by Paul, Hebrews, and Peter surprisingly often (some thirty times in all), and usually with a qualifying adjective such as 'good', 'bad', 'defiled', or 'pure'. It is just possible that the apostle's use of the word 'conscience' is derived from his compatriot, the Stoic Athenodorus of Canana (near Tarsus), who lived from 74 BC to AD 7 and instructed the Emperor Augustus (see Seneca, *De Tranqu. Anim.* III, 4). It is, however, an established fact that the hellenistic philosophers, and especially the Romans (Cicero, Seneca, and Lucretius), influenced by the teaching of Zeno and the Stoa on *sunkatathesis* (= assent given by the mind to its perceptions), tackled the study of this power of discernment and free choice insofar as it applied to rational human beings (see Philo, *De Spec. Leg.* I, 203; II, 49; *De Virt.* 206). But when it is realised that the word does not appear in Epictetus, Plutarch, Marcus Aurelius, or in the *Onomasticon* of Pollux, and that it occurs only once in Von Arnim's *Stoicorum Veterorum Fragmenta* (Chrysipp., III, 43, 2–5), one is bound to come to the conclusion that Paul's use of the word is not in fact derived from the Stoic philosophers—nor did he borrow it from literary sources, but, coming across the word in everyday speech and in hellenistic moral teaching, he took it and made out of it his detailed and elaborate moral and religious conception of conscience, placing special stress on its autonomy of judgement and its powers of moral responsibility.

It is no longer a question of mythological deities whether of a terrifying or a benevolent kind, such as the Greek Fates or Graces, who personify the moral law and its sanctions, or of the *daimōn*, the individual intellect, which is implanted in each man as a share in the godhead. Nor is it a question of the voice of wisdom which fortifies each individual man in his response to the ideal of the good life. It is, on the contrary, a capacity, situated in the ⟋ heart, or, one might almost say, in the interior of the soul, which each man, even the heathen, has at his disposal (Rom 2:15), and which spreads its light so that it can act as a guide to practical conduct or as a law-giver, and sanction such action as a judge. This is above all a judgement based on reflection, which puts man in the position to take stock of the way he is living his life, so that he is able to pass a favourable or unfavourable judgement upon it. The *suneidēsis* distinguishes between right and wrong, good and evil, and in doing so metes out praise or blame (1 Cor 10:28f; Tit 3:11) as an impartial, sovereign judge who pronounces a verdict (2 Cor 1:12). The conscience has authority, as its verdict is guaranteed by Christ (1 Cor 8:12), and is produced in collaboration with the Holy Spirit (Rom 9:1) and by means of divine illumination (2 Cor 1:12; 4:2; Acts 23:1; 24:16). This distinct and well-justified evaluation extends to all basic attitudes and to all good intentions as well as to their translation into action (2 Cor 4:2). This accounts for the summons to examine the conscience (1 Cor 11:28; Gal 6:4; see also 2 Cor 13:5), the chief element of which must be the love of one's neighbour, as this is God's chief commandment to his children. No one is without blame, but whatever other errors he has committed, he can have an easy conscience so long as he can prove that he has loved his neighbour in deed and in truth (1 Jn 3:20–3).

This notion of the conscience which follows the act (*conscientia consequens*) incorporates those elements of Paul's contemporaries with which he was quite familiar. But Paul's great innovation in the history of morals is that he elaborated the idea of an imperative conscience which precedes the act and does not simply state what should be done and what should not be done, but speaks with the authority of God himself, and obliges man to act in a certain way. It is a guide or controlling agent of which man, in his ⁊ freedom, has the use. (Philo mentions the reins of conscience, *Quod Deter.*, 23; see also *Decal.*, 87). Hence the phrase 'for conscience's sake', which denotes the individual motive and the immediate moral precept for action (1 Cor 10, 25–9; Rom 13, 5). This subjective orientation is to some extent in contradiction to the directives of an external law, as it is determined by the love of what is good and true, knowing this to be the definite will of God, and is not determined by ⁊ fear of any possible sanctions. This notion of conscience presupposes a distinction between speculative knowledge and an evaluation of definite action under given circumstances. In the case of the second, a conscience that is 'weak' or 'sickly' (*asthenēs*, which appears for the first time here with a moral, religious meaning, can be said to correspond more or less to 'immature' or 'undeveloped' in the modern classification) can be deceived in the determination of a duty—as, for example, in the question whether it is permissible to eat flesh sacrificed to a false god or an idol. The conscience is in such cases not sufficiently well informed as to the principles of the new religion and the order of priorities within that religion. It is above all not firm or secure enough to apply these principles in every situation, and it also lacks the powers of discretion and prudence to put them to use in particular and complex situations. This conscience, which is so prone to error, is binding in every contingency, even if, under the impression of doing good, its decision is in favour of wrong. It would be a sin to reverse this decision (1 Cor 8:7, 10, 12). Another kind of pathological weakness is the 'scrupulous' conscience, which is hesitant and doubt-ridden, uncertain and easily swayed, and can never come to a decision—as, for instance, in the case of a man who cannot trust himself to take anything other than a vegetarian diet (Rom 14:2). Everyone must act from personal, independent faith and conviction (Rom 14:5), for 'whatever does not proceed from faith is sin' (14:23).

A 'good conscience' (1 Tim 1:5; 1 Pet 3:21) is one, the intention of which, illuminated by God (1 Tim 1:19; 3:9), is direct—that is to say, fixed upon God and the service of God (see Rom 12:2)—and which is secure and firm enough to carry out its decisions (Acts 23:1; 1 Pet 3:16). A 'pure' (*kathara*, 2 Tim 1:3), 'blameless' (*aproskopos*, Acts 24:16), 'good' (*kalē*, Heb 13:18), or 'perfect' (see Heb 9:9) conscience considers God's will and is intent on good behaviour 'in all things' (Heb 13:18). In contrast to this, a bad or 'defiled' conscience (Tit 1:15) is not capable of making morally right decisions (Tit 1:15) or of putting decisions into action. It is also branded by man's hypocrisy and malevolence (1 Tim 4:2), and at the same time afflicted by the stain of guilt and sin which can be washed away only by the ↗ blood of Christ (Heb 10:2, 22; 9:14). In ↗ baptism the conscience is cleaned and at the same time dedicated to God (Heb 10:22; 1 Pet 3:21). This is why it is so intimately connected with worship (Heb 9:9, 14; 10:2) and with the theological virtues, especially that of brotherly love (1 Cor 8), for, unlike the good heathen, the child of God does not confine himself to ascertaining the rule of the intellect, as far as his emotions and attitude are concerned,

and simply to behaving decently and correctly. He is, on the contrary, mindful of his neighbour and intent on what will be profitable and edifying to him (1 Cor 10:23f). A conscience which is properly guided by the demands of faith will also be in a position to relate personal freedom with duty to one's neighbour, and to subordinate the permission to perform mutual acts of brotherly love which are neither good nor bad. Paul leaves delicate decisions of this kind to the conscience, and gives it primary importance in his moral teaching on ↗ love. Peter appeals to integrity of conscience as the most effective defence of christian communities (1 Pet 3:16).

Put in another way, merit is commensurate with the degree of goodness which the conscience has, as the conscience is the source and fountain of morality. The objective will of God is translated by the conscience into the subjective rule applicable to man. The christian is either good or bad, only to the extent that he obeys the promptings of his conscience, bearer of the divine law. This is what the Jew meant when he spoke of the 'inclination of the ↗ heart'. Paul, who denounced the Jewish ↗ law and so roundly condemned a purely preceptive morality, was obliged to replace the directions which were engraved on stone tablets by an 'autonomous' ordinance written in men's hearts (Jer 31:33 was a herald of this; see also Heb 8:10). This interior and personal norm of concrete behaviour is the spirit, not the letter, numbered among the finest things which the New Testament ascribes to the child of God, together with freedom, pride, candour, and frankness. On the ethical plane, the step from the old covenant to the new is made in this way—that is, from the written law to personal conscience.

Bibliography: See especially the bibliography in C. Spicq, *RB* 47 (1938), 50–80; C. Spicq, *Jahresbericht über die Fortschritte der klass. Altertumswissenschaft*, 1943, 169f. See further: R. D. Congdon, 'The Doctrine of Conscience', *Bibliotheca Sacra* (1945), 26–232 and 474–89; B. Reicke, *The Disobedient Spirits and Christian Baptism*, Copenhagen 1946, 174–91; J. Dupont, *Studia Hellenistica* 5 (Louvain 1948), 119–53; Haag, 467–653; H. Clavier, 'Hē Suneidēsis: Une pierre de touche de l'Héllénisme paulïnien', *Symposium*, Athens 1953; O. Seel, 'Zur Vorgeschichte des Gewissensbegriffes im altgriechischen Denken', *Festschrift F. Dornseiff*, Leipzig 1953, 291–319; G. Rudberg, 'Cicero und das Gewissen', *Symbolae Osloenses* (1955), 96–104; C. A. Pierce, *Conscience in the NT*, London 1955; B. Reicke, 'Syneidesis in Rom 2:15', *TZ* (1956), 157–61; W. D. Stacey, *The Pauline View of Man*, London 1956, 206f; J. Stelzenberger, *Syneidesis im NT*, Paderborn 1961; G. Bornkamm, *Studien zu Antike und Christentum* II, Munich 1962, 111–18.

Ceslaus Spicq

Consolation

Though the ancient world spoke and wrote much on the subject of consolation and the art of consoling, it remained, in the deepest sense, characterised by lack of consolation. Indicative of this is the fact that the same epoch which recognised a deity, a *numen*, for each and every thing in the world had no god whose function was to console. Once we enter the world of the bible, however, we find it full of divine consolation.

The bible recognises the multiplicity of earthly needs which make men feel so much the necessity of consolation. It recognises too the human means of achieving this end: friendship (Sir 6:16), a visit from friends (Gen 37:35; Job 2:11; 42:11), embassies (2 Sam 10:1–2; 2 Chron 19:1–2), and letters (Jer 29:1–23; Bar 4:5–9; 6 [= Letter of Jeremiah]; 2 Macc 1:1–2, 18; 2 Cor 1:1–7). It knows too of the consolation which food and drink can bring (Gen 14:18) and which comes from ↗ wine, 'the consoler' (Gen 5:29: the name Noah based on word-play with the vine as a consoling agent; Prov 31:6).

It knows also, of the consolation afforded in sorrow and old age by well-disposed children and posterity (Gen 5:29; Ps 128).

But it knows, too, how soon a merely human consolation can risk being an idle expenditure of energy or turning into the empty social custom of 'consoling'—regarded as a disagreeable task (Job 16:2; Jer 6:14; Zech 10:2; Mk 5:38; Lk 7:12; Jn 11:19, 31). So it is that men are advised to mourn but briefly and then 'to console themselves', since uncontrolled sorrow consumes one's life (Sir 30:21–3; 38:17–23). On the other hand, the bible is not ignorant of the dangers of false consolation (Is 28:14–22; Jer 7:4; Zech 10:2; Job 21:34; 31:24; Lk 6:24).

Over against all this there stands, as the true and, in the last analysis, the only consoler, the Lord God. He consoles the individual in trouble (relevant texts are to be found, in particular, among the psalms where they are too numerous to be noted separately), just as he does the people fallen under the sentence of history. (We find this, for example, in Second Isaiah, eg, Is 40:1; 51:3, 12; 66:11–13, and Ezek 33–48; Jer 14:8 [quoted in Lk 2:25]; 31:9; etc.) This divine consolation comes through God's word and his law (see, for example, Ps 119), but in a special way through the 'scriptures' (1 Macc 12:9; 2 Macc 15:9; Rom 15:4) and the ↗ prophets (2 Pet 1:19) who, despite all the warnings of judgement, have as their dearest task that of consoling. They remain in the memory of later generations above all as consolers (Sir 48:24; 49:10).

A special form of this prophetic consolation is their indication of the one who is to come—messianic and eschatological consolation. This line is taken up by the New Testament (Lk 2:25, 38) and attached to the consolation of God manifest in the person of the redeemer Jesus Christ, in the proclamation of salvation, in the Good News. Also, for the New Testament, every genuine consolation comes in the last resort only from God (Rom 15:5; 2 Cor 1:3–5; 2 Thess 2:16–17), and is ordered to eschatological salvation ('Take heart, your sins are forgiven' [Mt 9:2]; 'Blessed are those who mourn, for they shall be comforted' [Mt 5:4]). Conversely, the absence of consolation consists in the last resort in eschatological ruin (Wis 3:18; Lk 6:24).

At the same time, the New Testament does not in any way deny the need which man feels for consolation even in earthly necessities, and so among those who can in particular hope to obtain consolation it numbers the sick and imprisoned (Mt 25:36, 43), orphans and widows (Lk 1:27; 4:25; 7:12; 1 Tim 5:5; Jas 1:27), the poor (Mt 11:5; Lk 4:18; 7:22), the fainthearted (1 Thess 5:14), and the apostle himself, then in prison (Col 4:11). Here, too, the divine 'christian' consolation is achieved through human means.

These are the apostles and the other preachers of the good news of salvation, church leaders and, indeed, all christians with respect to one another (1 Thess 2:11; 2 Cor 1:3; 2:1; 7:2, 6, 13; Acts 20:20; 1 Thess 5:14; Col 1:28; 2:2; 4:8; Eph 6:22; Philem 7).

All this consolation goes back in every case to God who shapes all human destinies and consoles the humble (2 Cor 1:3; 7:6, 13). And so the New Testament stands in the same line as the Old-Testament teaching on human and divine consolation, but adds for the consolation of man in his greatest needs, namely, sorrow and death, two forms which come through Jesus Christ: the reference to the ↗ resurrection—'just as Christ has risen' (1 Cor 15; Jn 11:21–7)—and the encouragement to suffer (↗ suffering) in union with the passion of Christ (2 Cor 1:5; 4:17; 1 Pet 4:13), since man can reach his eschatological salvation only by following this road.

Bibliography: O. Schmitz and G. Stählin, *TDNT* v, 771–98; G. Stählin, *TDNT* v, 815–22; G. M. Behler OP, *Die Abschiedsworte des Herrn (Jn 13–17)*, Salzburg 1962, esp. B 1 3b (143–54), III 2a (233–40), and III 3 (245–54); W. Klaas, *Anfechtung und Trost*, Neukirchen 1963.

Suitbert H. Siedl

Contest

Starting out from the experience of human life and human history, of which contest and strife, quarrelling and ↗ war, and even rivalry in sport form a part, the bible attempts to elucidate sacred history in terms of struggle and contest. This sacred history is not something other than or apart from human history, but is essentially part of it, and therefore of the many struggles which go to make it what it is.

A. The *Old Testament* speaks not just of the holy war which Yahweh fought on behalf of his people but also of a contest which God undertakes on behalf of men, together with his anointed and his angels, against the political, cosmic, and demonic powers which are opposed to him (eg, Gen 3:15; Is 24:21; Ps 2:1; 5:6; 83:6–9; 89:10). The contest in which God has been engaged against the powers of evil since the beginning of time (Ps 74:13; 89:11; see also Is 51:9f; Job 27:7f) takes on visible form in the struggle against the enemies of his people (Ex 3:20; 11:4; 14:18; Josh 5:13f; Judg 5:4, 20; 2 Sam 5:24; Ps 2; 20; 21; 83:6–9), as also against the people themselves, who sin by breaking the covenant and therefore must be opposed (Num 14:39–44; Josh 7:1; 1 Sam 2:31; Is 1:4–9; 5:26–30; Jer 4:5–5:17; 6; 25:14–38). For their own eventual salvation Yahweh holds a lawsuit with his people who have fallen away from him (Is 1:18; Mic 6:2).

Under the influence of dualistic tendencies—though there is no genuine dualism in the Old Testament, since Yahweh is always the only sovereign lord (Ps 18:4–20)—the apocalyptic writers understand the war waged by the gentiles against 'the saints' (Dan 7:19–25; 11:40–5) as the final powerful attack of the evil powers (Ezek 38; Zech 14:1–3; Judg 1–7). In this they are the heirs of the great prophets of the earlier period. These powers will be finally destroyed by God in the final ⁊judgement (Dan 8:25; 11:45), when God will put an end to all evil (Wis 5:17–23). Men are also involved in the struggle which rages between the angels of God on the one side and the hostile spirits on the other (Ass Moses 10:2; Jub 15:26, 31f).

An important role is given in the Qumran writings to the contest between light and darkness, the angels of light and the demons of darkness (1 QS III; 18–IV:1). The members of the community are set up for battle against the unrighteousness and also against their own weaknesses and temptations (1 QS IV: 15–26). This struggle is an anticipation of the eschatological contest of God against his enemies (1 QH III: 29–36). In this final struggle the righteous men of the congregation form the army of God against sinners and sin. The War Scroll (1 QM) has the purpose precisely of preparing and ordering the eschatological struggle of the community against the gentiles. The very existence of the community forces the individual to decide whether he wishes to fight for or against God. The confidence of the community in ultimate victory is rooted in trust in God and in its unique consciousness of election.

B. According to the witness of the *New Testament*, the christian community is also conscious of being heavily engaged in a cosmic struggle—a struggle, however, which through the contest and ⁊victory of Christ (Jn 16:33 etc) has already been decided favourably in advance. Unlike the attitude of hatred characteristic of the Qumran community in its warlike preparations (1 QS 1:9–11), the christian community follows Christ in fighting not *against* those who do not belong to it but rather goes out in missionary enterprise into 'the world' (Eph 6:15, 17b; 1 Thess 2:2) on their behalf (Lk 23:34; Acts 7:60). In the following of Christ there is no longer any room for war and fighting with the weapons of this world (Lk 22:50f; Jn 18:36f)—any kind of *makhesthai* (=fight, do battle) receives a negative verdict in the New Testament and is rejected (Jn 6:52; Acts 7:26; 2 Cor 7:5; 2 Tim 2:23f; Tit 3:9; Jas 4:1f). He who wishes to fight for God as a member of the christian community puts on the armour of God (Eph 6:10ff; see also Rom 6:13; 13:12, 2 Cor 6:7; 1 Thess 5:8; 1 Pet 4:1) and fights in the strength of God which has already overcome all powers and principalities in the resurrection and exaltation of Jesus (1 Cor 15:55-7 etc). The contest of the christian is against sin (2 Pet 2:16; see also 1 Tim 3:16; Heb 12:4) and against Satan and the demons, the rulers of this world. Jesus himself engaged in conflict against these powers (Mt 4:1-11; 12:27ff; Lk 11:18ff) which strove to destroy him (Lk 22:3; Jn 13:2, 27; 14:30; Acts 4:25-8; Rev 12:1-5) but which through the death and resurrection of Jesus were finally overcome (Jn 12:31; Col 2:15). Whoever becomes a follower of Jesus is committed to the struggle against the evil powers, a rearguard action which is fought out with extraordinary ferocity (Rev 12:7). These evil powers launch their attacks from every side. The power of this world is manifested both in temptation to apostasy and disobedience and in the persecutions and sufferings which the christian is called upon to endure (Rom 7:23; 8:35-9;

1 Cor 9:27; 2 Tim 2:3; Heb 10:32; Jas 4:1).

By taking over the Jewish apocalyptic tradition and allying it with the diatribe of the Cynics and Stoics, Paul was able to represent the contest in which the christian is engaged as an *agōn* (=contest, 1 Thess. 2:2) which requires the deployment of all one's powers (1 Cor 9:25f; Phil 1:27; Col 1:29; see also Lk 13:24), has to be sustained by prayer in common (Rom 15:30; Col 4:12) and is put to the extreme test by suffering and martyrdom (1 Tim 6:11; 2 Tim 4:6; see also Heb 10:10ff; 12:1ff). The struggle in which the follower of Christ is engaged is represented by Paul in terms of *strateuesthai*, of undertaking a military campaign for the salvation of men through the preaching of the gospel (1 Tim 1:18; 1 Thess 2:2; 2 Cor 10:3f; Phil 4:3; Col 2:1; 2 Tim 2:3-5; see also 1 Cor 9:7). Relying on the victory which Christ has already obtained, the christian enters the contest for the salvation of the world and for the prize which is set before him, the imperishable crown which is eternal life (Rom 8:18; 1 Cor 9:25; 1 Tim 6:12; 2 Tim 2:5; 4:7f; Heb 9:15).

The Revelation of John, which speaks so much of struggle and contest, stands in the tradition of Jewish apocalyptic. It sets out the drama of the final struggle in symbolic images as the victory of the Lamb which has already been won. In view of this victory which is now being celebrated in heaven, it seeks to encourage the christian reader and hearer and exhort him to steadfastness and faithfulness in the fierce attacks which he still has to endure from the evil Power (12:12) here on earth in the period before the end. The message of the glorified Lord to his community on earth is: 'Be faithful unto death, and I will give you the crown of life' (2:10).

Bibliography: *TDNT* I, 135–40; IV, 533f; *TWNT* VII, 701–13; *BHHW* II, 925f; *DBT*, 560–63; R. Völkl, *Christ und Welt nach dem NT*, Würzburg 1961, 315f, 333, 359, 430, and 451f; H. W. Huppenbauer, *Der Mensch zwischen zwei Welten*, Zurich 1959; H. Schlier, *Der Brief an die Galater*, Düsseldorf 1962³, 288–300; H. Schlier, *Principalities and Powers in the NT*, London and New York 1961; R. Leivestad, *Christ the Conqueror: Ideas of Conflict and Victory in the NT*, London 1954; A. von Harnack, *Militia Christi*, Tübingen 1905; Schnackenburg, 223–30; G. Richter, *Deutsches Wörterbuch zum NT*, Regensburg 1962, 492–6.

Rudolf Pesch

Conversion

The *Old Testament* knows of a cultic-ritual repentance (↗Atonement) which, to be sure, drew upon itself frequently the criticism of the prophets, since the most important element in it, the interior change of heart and correction, was for the most part left on one side. This *interior* conversion is necessarily implied in the word *šûb* (=to turn about, 'to return to Yahweh'). There is here supposed a deep understanding of the nature of ↗ sin. Such a conversion implies obedience with regard to the will of God (Hos 6:1–6), and trust in God even in the absence of earthly or human help (Hos 14:4; Jer 3:22f; Is 30:15). From the negative point of view, conversion implies a turning away from everything evil, an aspect stressed especially by Jeremiah and Ezekiel. In the post-exilic period there comes to the foreground the turning to the Law and its complete fulfilment (Deut 30:2, 10; 2 Kings 23:25; Neh 9:29; 2 Chron 30:6ff). We find a similar legalistic understanding of conversion at Qumran: a man turns away from sin and separates himself radically from sinners in order to observe the Law in its purest form.

Basic for the *New Testament* is the demand of Jesus: 'Be converted!' (*metanoeite*, Mk 1:15). Before this, the preaching of John the Baptist had linked up with the prophetic insistence on conversion: turning away from sin with baptism and confession (Mk 1:4f) and observance of the commandments of God, together with works of love for a neighbour (Lk 3:8, 10–14). Jesus' call to conversion had, however, a yet more decisive and deeper meaning: he demands ↗ faith as the basic condition for forgiveness and salvation: the wedding garment that had to be brought to the heavenly banquet is nothing other than this interior conversion (Mt 22:11–13). The parables of Jesus illustrate at every turn how ready God is to forgive (Lk 15) and what are the necessary conditions on man's part (Lk 18:10–14; see also 17:10). We can trace a definite development in the preaching of repentance and conversion. Whereas the prophets threatened those who did not accept conversion with a judgement of condemnation within time (see also Is 5:25ff; 8:1ff; 9:8ff etc), John the Baptist speaks of a final judgement which is imminent and which will coincide with the coming of the kingdom of Heaven. The Baptist announces that the axe is laid to the roots of the trees and that he who is to consummate human history in judgement is near (Mt 3:10; Lk 3:9). Jesus, on the other hand, does not hurl condemnations but explains that the rule of God, the ↗ Kingdom of God, has already come (Mk 1:15). The condition for entering this kingdom, however, is conversion. Jesus' call goes out to everyone, sinners and the just alike, but especially to sinners (Lk 5:32).

In order to be able to describe what is essential in conversion we have to bear in mind the Lord's word about being converted and becoming like little children (Mt 18:3). It is not just turning away from evil and from ↗ sin; it is not just ↗ asceticism or ↗ fasting and the like that constitute the essence of conversion, but, first and foremost, the turning of the ↗ heart to God, in the manner of little children who allow themselves to be led without guile and with unlimited trust. There is genuine conversion in the sense in which Jesus understood it, when we no longer try to bring about our salvation relying on ourselves and our own powers, but rather, forgetful of self, look for salvation to God and trust courageously in him.

Different from the Baptist, whose preaching is stamped with sombre earnestness, Jesus speaks constantly of ↗ joy in connection with conversion (Lk 15:7, 10, 32). It is, of course, true that Jesus also announces an unmitigated, hard judgement on those who reject this call to conversion (Mt 11:20–4; 12:41). Nevertheless God comes half way to meet the repentant sinner of good will, as Jesus shows by the example of the rich ruler who had attached his heart to property and possessions: 'For it is easier for a camel to go through the eye of a needle than for a rich man to enter the kingdom of God' (Lk 18:25). The question of the disciples, as to who then could be saved, receives its answer: 'What is impossible with men is possible with God' (v 27). ↗ Grace has a decisive part to play in the conversion of the sinner to God.

The apostles continue the preaching of the Lord on conversion, as can be seen from Acts (2:38; 3:19; 5:31; 8:22; 11:18; 17:30; 20:21; 26:20; see also Heb 6:1). Paul uses the words *metanoia* and *metanoein* seldom (2 Cor 7:9f; 12:21; Rom 2:24), but he puts conversion at the beginning of the christian life which has detached itself from sin (1 Cor 6:11; Rom 6:19ff etc) and crucified the flesh (Gal 5:24).

The word does not appear at all in the Johannine gospel and epistles, since the believer (for whom these were written) has already accepted this call to be converted. Basically, conversion is a unique and decisive event. Falling back into the former state is worse than the primitive, unaltered state of unbelief (Lk 11:24–6 and parallels). Heb 6:4–6 expresses the same point: 'It is impossible to restore again to repentance those who have once been enlightened . . . if they then commit apostasy, since they crucify the Son of God on their own account'. The author is speaking, as a pastor, with a severity destined to drive home the lesson—quite apart from the fact that a second conversion is a rarer and more difficult occurrence than a first—and does not intend to take up a position with regard to a dogmatic problem, namely, whether a second conversion is in fact possible.

In Revelation the call to conversion has to do directly with grievances in the communities. (Cf 2:14f; 2:20ff; 3:1f, 14ff.) Tribulations inflicted by God are meant to induce even the most hardened evildoers to conversion and make possible salvation for them (2:22f). Thus, the communities of Philadelphia and Smyrna, often purified by afflictions, no longer required censure and an invitation to be converted, since poverty and oppression are always a good defence for faith and love.

Bibliography: Behm and Würthwein, *TDNT* IV, 975–1003; W. L. Holladay, *The root šûbh in the OT*, Leiden 1958; Schnackenburg, 10ff (with bibliography and index); B. Poschmann, 'Busse und letzte Ölung', *Handbuch der Dogmengeschichte* IV/3, Freiburg 1951, 3–10; J. Schmid, *RNT* 3 (1955³), 150–5; A. Kirchgässner, *Erlösung und Sünde im NT*, Freiburg 1950, 130–5; A. van den Born, Haag 278–80; L. de Lorenzi, *Riv. Bibl. It.* 5 (1957), 243–9; R. Koch, 'Die religiöse-sittliche Umkehr nach den drei ältesten Evangelien unter der Apostelgeschichte', *Anima* 14 (1959), 296–307 (with bibliography); J. Kosnetter, 'Die Busspredigt in der Verkündigung Jesu', *Der Seelsorger* 29 (1959), 200–5; O. Garcia de la Fuente, 'Sobre la idea de contrición en el AT', *SP* 1 (1959), 559–79; M. F. Lacan, J. Dupont, M. E. Boismard, and D. Mollat, *LV* 9/47 (1960), 1–114; R. Joly, 'Note sur metanoia', *RHR* 160 (1961), 148–56; W. Pesch, *Der Ruf zur Entscheidung. Die Bekehrungspredigt des NT*, Freiburg 1964.

Johannes B. Bauer

Covenant

In the covenant of God with his people there is resumed the essence of the religion of the Old and the New Testament, so that in Dan 11:28, 30 'the holy covenant' comes to mean the same thing as the religion of Israel. Although the etymology of the Hebrew word for covenant, *b'rîth*, is disputed (compare the Akkadian *birîtu*=chain, and *birît*=between) it derives from the domain of human law. *B'rîth* implies the strongest possible mutual pledge, but the ensuing relationship can be of different kinds. The word *covenant* is therefore an inadequate rendering of *b'rîth*. When a *b'rîth* is made between partners of unequal strength it is natural that the stronger accedes to a *b'rîth* for which he can be petitioned by the less powerful (as the Israelites are petitioned by the Gibeonites [Josh 9], and Nahash, King of the Ammonites, by the Jabeshites [1 Sam 11, 1f]). The relation, however, is only apparently unilateral; for the less powerful must observe the conditions under which he petitioned the *b'rîth* in the first place (in the case of Josh 9 and 1 Sam 11:1f, a position of servitude), or at any rate maintain loyalty in respect to the granter of the *b'rîth*; in other words, he must maintain *hesed*, the covenant-obligation, and be guilty of no lack of faith in regard of the other; otherwise the preponderant party is no longer bound by his promise.

When two equal partners enter into a *b'rîth*, it is evident that they contract on equal terms—for example, Hiram and Solomon (1 Kings 5:12). Also the covenant-making that we hear of in Gen 21:23–32 (Abimelek and Abraham) and 31:44–54 (Laban and Jacob) is bilateral. Abner petitions David, already King of Juda, for a *b'rîth*, but he is evidently thinking of mutual obligations (2 Sam 3:12). In the case of the *b'rîth* between Jonathan and David, it would appear that at the outset it is the king's son who gives and the poor shepherd who receives (1 Sam 18:3f);

but later (20:8) it demands *chesed* from David's side in respect of Jonathan and his posterity (20:14f). Then the *b'rîth* entered into (that is, renewed) in 1 Sam 23:18 is quite clearly reciprocal, in view of the prevision that David will become king.

The agreement is voluntary on both sides even though the request for a *b'rîth* comes from one side (Gen 31:44), or a party finds itself obliged to enter into one under unfavourable circumstances (1 Sam 11:1ff). The particular stipulations can be of different kinds (see Gen 21:30; 31:50, 52; 1 Kings 5:7–11; 20:34), though in one way or another *šālôm* must always result (Gen 26:31; 1 Sam 20:42; 2 Sam 3:21ff). 1 Kings 5:12: 'And there was *šālôm* between Hiram and Solomon; and the two of them made a *b'rîth*', shows that *šālôm* must mean more than 'peace', which is the word commonly used to translate it, for Hiram had already had friendly relations with David which Solomon continued right from the start. By means of the *b'rîth* the two partners were bound together in a unity which could not be broken, the kind of unity which can imply anything from the guarantee of life (1 Sam 11:1f) to the most intimate personal relationships (as friendship, 1 Sam 18:3f; marriage, Mal 2:14). There can, at any rate, come into existence as a result of the *b'rîth* a relationship which comes the closest possible to blood-relationship and can sometimes even substitute for it. Thus, partners who are to some extent of equal social standing are called brothers, as David and Jonathan (2 Sam 1:26), Hiram and Solomon (1 Kings 9:13), Ahab—by anticipation —and Benhadad (1 Kings 20:32).

By nature, the *b'rîth* is of limitless duration (1 Sam 20:15). The ceremonies accompanying the making of the covenant witness eloquently to the indissoluble nature of the bond. The swearing of an oath (Gen 21:31; 26:31; 31:53; 1 Sam 20:17, 42) or, alternatively, the pronouncement of a ↗ curse, sometimes mentioned expressly at the making of a covenant (Gen 26:28; Ezek 17:13, 16, 18f)—the Hebrew oath-formula is already an abbreviated or implicit form of self-curse—is symbolised by one or both partners passing in the midst of animals which had been quartered (Jer 34:18f; cf Gen 15:9f, 17f—where God perhaps appears also as the fire which consumes the sacrifice, in the opinion of Henninger). This could be the origin of the usual term used for making a covenant, namely, *kārath b'rîth*, literally, 'to cut a covenant'. In the event of breaking the covenant, the contracting parties take upon themselves the same lot which befell the quartered animals—namely, to suffer death. By means of these oaths the covenant is sealed in the eyes of God (see 1 Sam 23:18), and the deity is solemnly invoked as guardian and avenger of the covenant (Gen 31:49f, 53; cf Mal 2:14). In this way a covenant between two human parties is considered as a 'covenant of Yahweh' (1 Sam 20:8; see also Ezek 17:19). The indissoluble fellowship resulting can also be strengthened by the shaking of hands (Ezek 17:18), even more so by both partners dipping the hand together in a bowl filled with blood or some other liquid (for the custom of the ancient Arabs see Karge, 236f), and especially by means of a meal taken in common (Gen 26:30; 31:54; Josh 9:14; 2 Sam 3:20; Ps 41:9), or the tasting together of salt, the great preservative (a 'covenant of salt', Num 18:19; 2 Chron 13:5; see also Lev 2:13).

The line of conduct corresponding to such an ensuing unity goes by the name of *ḥesed*, namely, 'conduct towards others with regard to whom one stands in a relation of kinship, friendship, hospitality or service; the duty arising out of close bonds with another; community; solidarity (L. Köhler, *Lexikon in VT libros*; see also the basic article by N. Glück, 'Das Wort *chesed*', *BZAW* 47 [1927]; and see 1 Sam 20:14; 2 Sam 9:1, 3, 7; 1 Kings 20:31, 34). Renderings such as 'love', 'favour', 'grace', 'goodwill', or 'mercy' (LXX, Vulgate) are inadequate.

At the heart of the Old Testament there stands the Sinai covenant. This however is preceded by two other covenants, that with Noah (Gen 9:8–17) and that with Abraham (Gen 15 and 17). The spiritual relationship of God with our first parents in paradise is never called a covenant (Hos 6:7 refers to the town of Adam and Sir 17:12 to the Sinaitic covenant), since the relationship existed from the beginning and did not need to come into existence through a covenant. In the covenant with Noah, which applied to all living things on the earth, God pledged himself to the continuation of life on the earth without any corresponding stipulation on man's part, though the making of the covenant is preceded by commandments (Gen 9:4ff). According to Is 24:5f, the breaking of this covenant would have as its effect the eschatological catastrophe.

The covenant with Abraham (which comes to us in two traditions, Gen 15 and 17) guarantees to the latter a numerous posterity, beginning with the birth of Isaac (Gen 17:19) and, for this posterity, the land of Canaan (Gen 15:18ff). The condition for this is faith (15:6); and in 17:1 the covenant is preceded by a general commandment to walk before God and be blameless (as is said in reference to Noah in Gen 6:9). One entered into the covenant by means of the practice of circumcision, which was the sign of the covenant (17:10–14, 23–7).

As with the covenants with Noah and Abraham, so in the Sinaitic covenant the initiative came from God's side. In view of the exalted nature of the divine partner the granting of a *b'rîth* is an unheard-of grace, in particular in the covenant with Abraham and on Sinai, since, as a result of these, an interior union comes into existence: Abraham is the friend of God (Is 41:8; 2 Chron 20:7; Jas 2:23) and Yahweh is his guest (Gen 18); Israel is the People of Yahweh, and he is their God (see Ex 6:7; Lev 26:12; Deut 26:17f; Jer 7:23; 11:4; Ezek 14:11). Israel is attached to him in the closest possible way, more than all other peoples, as his personal possession, a people belonging to him, set aside, a kingdom of priests in which Yahweh is King, and in which all Israelites together assume the office of priesthood on behalf of all other nations, by fulfilling the statutes of the covenant (Ex 19:5f).

This relationship appears as even more intimate when represented as one of father to son (Ex 4:22f; Deut 14:1; 32:6; Is 1:2; Jer 31:20; Hos 2:1; 11:1), or of husband to wife (for the first time in Hos 1–3; then Jer 2:2; 3:4, 12; Ezek 16; Is 50:1; 54:4–10; 62:5; in a particularly frank way in the Song of Solomon). *The foundation of the covenant is in the freely-bestowed divine love* (Deut 7:7f; Jer 31:2f), and it represents the sealing of the divine election (see also Deut 14:2; Ps 33:12; Amos 3:2). As a result of this, Yahweh and Israel do not enter into a covenant in the way human partners do (Gen 21:27, 32), but it is Yahweh who makes the covenant with Israel (Ex 24:8—see Köhler, p. 45; when we read, in Josh 24:25; 2 Kings 23:3; 2 Chron 15:12; 29:10; 34:31, of men making the *b'rîth*, it is merely a question of solemn promises and an undertaking to fulfil a covenant which is already in existence; there enters at this point a human agency in mediating the covenant between God and the people—here Joshua, elsewhere the king, which is the way of mediating a covenant which we find in one of the Mari texts; see also Hos 2:20). Even more expressive are the phrases 'to establish a covenant' (Gen 9:9; 17:7; Ex 6:4; Ezek 16:60), 'to make' (Gen 9:12; 17:2; Num 25:12) or 'set up' a covenant (2 Sam 23:5), since the covenant is God's doing and God's gift. The LXX rendering of *b'rîth* as *diathēkē* = 'covenant' (not *sunthēkē* = 'agreement', 'compact') also presupposes that the covenant is a divine institution. (The Latin *testamentum* = 'last will and testament' is too one-sided a translation.)

The ceremony of making the covenant is symbolical of Yahweh's inner union with Israel. In this ceremony Moses sprinkles the altar, which represents Yahweh, with half the blood of the sacrificial victim and the people with the other half (Exod 24:6, 8). The revelation of his name, Yahweh, which precedes the granting of a covenant, is a sign that God enters into a truly personal union with Israel in the Sinaitic covenant (Ex 3:14f). It is in this name that the covenant is sealed (Ex 6:2–8) and which corresponds in a concrete way to the reality and proximity of God ('I am he, yes, I am he!'), which are manifested in actions of assistance and salvation. Another way of representing this is by God's dwelling among his people in the holy place above the ark of the covenant (Ex 25:8, 22; 29:45f; Lev 26:11f; Deut 4:7; 12:5). All the earthly gifts which Yahweh gives to the Israelites who remain true to the covenant (in particular, their prosperous existence in Canaan) are the outcome and the expression of his love (Deut 7:13ff). The grateful *hesed* of the human partner, which must also be a *personal devotion to Yahweh*, should correspond to the *hesed* of Yahweh himself (see Deut 7:9, 12; 1 Kings 8:23 = 2 Chron 6:14; Neh 1:5; 9:32; Dan 9:4 where we find the phrase: '. . . who keepest covenant and *hesed*'), which is essentially unmerited grace and mercy. This human attitude is included in the commandment of love (Deut 6:4f; 11:1), though already the Song of Deborah had referred to love of Yahweh (Judg 5:31). In this way the Israelite shows that he is not observing God's commandments through compulsion and slavish fear, since he too has entered into the covenant of his own free decision (Ex 19:8; 24:3, 7; Deut 26:17f; Josh 24:15–24).

The whole institution of ↗ law, which developed in the course of time, has an essential relation to the Sinaitic covenant. Its purpose is to actualise in the human partner of the covenant this loving, personal devotion. Even though the external deed required by God is limited and proportioned to human capabilities, yet considered as an expression of the interior homage of obedience it is reckoned to the Israelite as 'righteousness' in the eyes of God (Deut 6:25). On the other hand, God turns away from the external offering when it does not correspond to the conduct required by God, in particular with respect to a neighbour. Hence the war waged by the prophets against a purely external cult (see Is 1:10–20; Jer 7:21–8; Amos 5:4f, 14f, 21–7). In the practice of ⁄ justice and charity towards a ⁄ neighbour—especially those who are socially handicapped (see Ex 22:24ff; Lev 19:33f; 25:35–43; Deut 12:12; Ezek 18:7) — the Israelite shows the genuineness of his love for God and how much store he puts by his belonging to the covenant, which is, in any case, a privilege he shares with the poor.

It is also within the context of the covenant that we can understand the nature of sin—namely, as infidelity, apostasy. Hence also the heavy punishments inflicted for violation of the covenant (Lev 26:14–39; Deut 28:15–68), which are, however, intended in the first place as a warning against such an apostasy, which also explains the awe-inspiring appearance of Yahweh on Sinai (Ex 20:20). The fear of God, so often praised in the Old Testament, is in reality awe filled with humility, faith, trust and obedience (see Ps 34:10–15; 112:1; Prov 14:26f; Sir 1:11–21; 2:7–11). To be sure, the

punishments threatened for the breaking of the covenant are in fact inflicted, in particular, in the ruin of both the kingdoms of Israel and Judah. Yet God maintains his *chesed* (Jer 31:3; Lev 26:44f), and through Jeremiah (31:31–4) he promises a 'new covenant' which brings forgiveness of sins, and by means of which Yahweh writes his law in the heart of each individual. Ezekiel expresses this even more clearly: Yahweh will give the Israelites a new heart in the innermost part of which he will place his Spirit (Ezek 36:26f). This will be an 'everlasting covenant of peace' (37:26), by means of which all will be taught directly by God (Is 54:10, 12). The songs of the Servant of Yahweh widen the circle beyond Israel to take in all peoples and reveal that the ⁄ Servant of the Lord will be made by God 'a covenant to the people' (Is 42:6; 49:8)—that is, to all the peoples of the earth (42:5). He is a light for the nations, and through him the salvation of Yahweh reaches the farthest parts of the earth (42:6; 49:6); yet at the same time he will justify 'the many' through his atoning death (53:10ff).

This 'new covenant' will be sealed in the ⁄ blood of Christ, as he himself said when instituting the holy eucharist, with reference to Ex 24:8 and Is 53:11; 'This is my blood of the covenant which is poured out for the many' (Mt 26:28; Mk 14:24; Lk 22:20; see also 1 Cor 11:25). Christ is therefore, in an incomparably higher sense, ⁄ 'mediator of a new covenant' (Heb 12:24), as Moses was of the Sinaitic covenant. The new covenant is also 'better', since it assures better promises (Heb 7:22; 8:6). It promises and bestows not material gifts, gifts of this earth, but 'eternal redemption' and 'eternal inheritance' (Heb 9:12, 15), and a share in the eternal life of God as is expressed in the somewhat modified ancient covenant-formula in Rev 21:3 and 6f. At the end of time the tabernacle of God will not be with just one people, from whom in any case he is divided by the double curtain (Ex 26:33, 36; Lev 16:2; Heb 9:6ff), but 'with men'; and he will take up his dwelling with them so that they will be his people and God himself will be among them (Rev 21:3). The union with God is at the same time broader and more interior. In addition, it has passed—as already in Jer 31 and Ezek 36—from the collective to the individual plane: 'He who conquers shall have this heritage, and I will be his God and he shall be my son' (21:7). This is actualised in the highest gift which God can give to a human person: 'They will see [my] face' (22:4) in a way represented in Ex 24:10, 17 only as an anticipatory glimmer. Finally, since already in the old covenant God had entered into a personal relationship, we have in the progressive divine self-revelation, culminating in its most exalted and immanent form, an organic process.

History of the covenant. The covenant with Noah can be understood as a theological interpretation of a real historical datum. The covenant with Abraham fits into the religious genre described by Alt (*Der Gott der Väter*, 1929: now *Kleine Schriften zur Geschichte des Volkes Israel* I, 1–78), according to which the deity appears as connected, not with a locality, but with a social group, represented by the ancestral father. In Yahweh the people of Israel see the God of their fathers (Ex 3:6,

13ff), to whom he has revealed and committed himself. The Sinaitic covenant is deeply anchored in the traditions of Israel and corresponds to his nature, since it does not represent him as united to Israel in the nature of things. The covenant is already presupposed in the ancient Song of Deborah (Judg 5:3, 8, 11). There are references to ceremonies in which the Sinaitic covenant was continually renewed: the account of the renewal by Moses before the entry into Canaan (Deut 29:1), under Joshua (Josh 8:30–5, especially 34); the stipulation that this renewal should take place every seven years at the Feast of the Tabernacles (Deut 31:10–13; see also 29:9–14); the coming together in a common sanctuary before the ark of the Covenant (see Judg 21:19; 1 Sam 1:3); the lapidary formulae of the Ten Commandments (Ex 20:2–17; Deut 5:6–21) with their historical framework of the covenant-making (see Deut 5:1–5); or those of the twelve commandments preserved in the form of a curse (Deut 27:15–26), which were certainly not promulgated solemnly only on *one* occasion; the allusions in the Psalms, as in Ps 50 and Ps 81.

In speaking against the abuse of the covenant-idea—proud reliance on their election and false security in this reliance (see Amos 3:1f; 5:14, 18; 6:1; 9:7)—Amos, Isaiah and Micah do not name the covenant expressly, but presume it; but their contemporary, Hosea, names it expressly (6:7; 8:1). The reforms of Hezekiah (2 Chron 29:10; cf 2 Kings 18:4ff, 22), of Josiah (2 Kings 23:3; 2 Chron 34:31), and of Ezra, provided the occasion for an extraordinary renewal of the covenant. After the Exile, Pentecost became the commemorative day of the making of the covenant (see Kutsch). In the Book of Jubilees all the covenants of the Old Testament are dated from Pentecost, even that made between Jacob and Laban. The connection between the Book of Jubilees and Qumran permits us to place their festival of covenant-renewal at Pentecost. This sect referred to itself as 'the Community [Union] of the New Covenant', since it believed that the predictions of the prophets were fulfilled in it. In reality, the new covenant did come while this sect was still in existence; not with the teacher of righteousness, but in Jesus Christ.

Bibliography: P. Karge, *Geschichte des Bundesgedankens im AT*, Münster 1910; J. Pedersen, *Der Eid bei den Semiten*, Strasburg 1914; J. Pedersen, *Israel* i–ii, Oxford 1954², 263–310; L. G. de Fonseca, *Bbl* 8 (1927), 31–50, 161–81, 290–319, 418–41; and 9 (1928), 26–40 and 143–60; A. Alt, *Die Ursprünge der israelitischen Rechts*, 1934 (now *Kleine Schriften* i, Münster 1953, 278–332 esp. 322–32); Quell and Behm in *TDNT* ii, 104–34; J. Begrich, *ZAW* 60 (1944), 1–11; P. van Imschoot, Haag 267–74; J. Schildenberger, 'Die Religion des AT', *Christus und die Religionen der Erde*, ed. F. König, Vienna 1951, 439–521; Imschoot i, 237–59; J. Henninger, *Bbl* 34 (1953), 344–53; M. Noth, 'Das atl. Berith-schliessen im Lichte eines Mari-Textes', *Geschichtliche Studien zum AT*, 1957, 142–54; L. Arnaldich, 'La Alianza con Dios, Ideal de la Restauración del Orden religioso destruído según la secta del Mar Muerto', *Secc. de Estudios* i (Barcelona 1954), 341–4; P. E. Mendenhall, *Law and Covenant in Israel and the Ancient Near East*, Pittsburgh 1955; E. Vogt, *Bbl* 36 (1955), 565f; E. Kutsch, 'Das Herbstfest in Israel', *TLZ* 81 (1956), 493ff; H. W. Wolf, 'Jahwe als Bundesvermittler', *VT* 6 (1956), 316–20; M. Buber, *The Kingdom of God*, London 1958; Eichrodt i, 36–69; von Rad i, 129–35, 192ff, and 338ff; T. C. Vriezen, *An Outline of Old Testament Theology*, Oxford 1958, 139–43; Hempel and Goppelt, *RGG* i (1957³), 1512–18; V. Hamp and J. Schmid, 'Bund', *LTK* ii², 770–78; H. Wildberger, 'Jahwes Eigentumsvolk', *Abh. z. Theol. d. AT u. NT* 37 (Zurich 1960); K. Baltzer, 'Das Bundesformular', *Wiss. Monographien z. AT u. NT* 4 (Neukirchen 1960); W. Beyerlin, *Herkunft und Geschichte der ältesten Sinaitraditionen*, Tübingen 1961; J. Haspecker, 'Bund', *HTG* i, 197–204; N. Lohfink, 'Das Hauptgebot', *Analecta Biblica* 20 (Rome 1963); N. Lohfink, *Das Siegeslied am Schilfmeer*, Frankfurt 1964, 129–50; W. L. Moran, 'Moses und der Bundesschluss am Sinai', *SZ* 170 (1961/2), 120–33; W. L. Moran, 'The Ancient Near Eastern Background of the Love of God in Deuteronomy', *CBQ* 25 (1963), 77–87; L. Krinetzki, 'Der Bund Gottes mit den Menschen nach dem AT u. NT', *WB* 15 (Düsseldorf 1963).

Johannes Schildenberger

Covetousness

The term *pleonexia*, which Paul so often employs, signifies 'covetousness', not 'avarice' (which would be *philarguria*). In the LXX renderings of the Hebrew *betsaᶜ* or *bātsaᶜ*, the word-group signifies 'ill-gotten gains', 'rapacity', and is never employed when the profits referred to are come by honestly. This covetousness, is, according to Paul, 'uncleanness' (Eph 4:19; 5:3), and 'idolatry' (Col 3:5; see also the epistle of Polycarp 11:2), just as 'impurity' is 'uncleanness' and 'idolatry'. While we do not feel compelled to conclude with Trench and Klaar that *pleonexia*, since it is mentioned in connection with sins of impurity, must likewise signify illegitimate *sexual* desire, it is nevertheless clear that a single basic *concept* underlies Paul's use of the term. The ideas of covetousness and impurity serve to define the basic attitude of materialism which is characteristic of the pagan world, and in this sense they are equivalent to idolatry. Christian living in the kingdom of God is diametrically opposed to such an attitude (see Eph 5:3ff). The state of holiness which the redeemed christian receives through the sacraments as a member of Christ and as the temple of God must be made manifest in an existential sense; in other words it must be made real in the actual practice of his life.

Bibliography: J. C. Trench, *Synonyms of the New Testament*, London 1901, 51–3; E. Klaar, *TZ* 10 (1954), 395–7; P. Rossano, *VD* 32 (1954), 257–65; R. Beauvery, *VD* 33 (1955), 78–85; G. Delling, *TDNT* VI, 266–74; H. Schlier, *Der Brief an die Epheser*, Düsseldorf 1957, 41f and 233–6; Maurer, *TDNT* VI, 636f.

Johannes B. Bauer

Creation

A. *In the Old Testament. Introduction.* It is in the light of the concept of *doxa* that the significance of creation in the Old Testament becomes apparent. It is concerned with the manifestation of God in his deeds rather than with the proof of his existence, with the *gesta et facta* of God, the *mirabilia Dei*, rather than with his *esse*. For this reason the Old Testament presents the idea of creation not in the sense, or with the logical precision, of a statement of a philosophical thesis, but rather in the form of a historical narrative. When we encounter the term *creation* we moderns think immediately of the idea of 'creation out of nothing'. But if we enquire of the scriptures for this notion of *creatio ex nihilo* then we encounter it there not as the principal factor in a logically structured argument, but rather as an effect of the ↗ glory and dominion of God, who has revealed himself to his chosen people in a manner that manifests his power.

The Terminology. To describe the activity of the creator the Old Testament employs several terms: *ʿāśâh*, the range of meaning of which is roughly equivalent to that of the German term *machen* (= to make) (Gen 1:7, 31; 2:4; Is 43:7); *qānāh*, to found, to form (Gen 14:19, 22); *yātsar* (= to fashion, shape, form: Gen 2:7, 8, 19; Jer 1:5), and above all *bārāʾ* (Gen 1:1; Num 16:30; Ps 51:12). Further terms, borrowed from the world of ideas of the ancient Near East conjure up vivid images. Such are *nāṭâh* (= to stretch out), *yāsad* (= to found) and *kônēn* (= to set up). Of these terms *bārāʾ* is the one which is richest in meaning to the extent that it is predicated exclusively of God. Admittedly it is not in any sense a specialist term belonging to 'ecclesiology', but it does designate the divine activity in the creation, with man and in the miracles performed by God. The very fact that this range of usage is attached to the word *bārʾā* in itself suggests that we should regard creation and fashioning as conceived of in the Old Testament as belonging to the broader category of divine deeds of power. Apart from this chief characteristic of being used exclusively with God as subject *bārāʾ* is characterised especially by the fact that what results from it is new, unprecedented (eg, Is 41:20; Jer 31:22) and extraordinary (eg, Ex 34:10; Num 16:30), as well as by the fact that the manner in which it takes effect is totally free and uncircumscribed.

The distinctive term which the LXX employs to characterise God's creative activity is *ktizō* and not—though this would have been equally conceivable—*dēmiourgeō*. In the case of this latter term it is the element of manufacturing in the sense of actual craftsmanship that is uppermost. *Ktizō*, on the other hand, denotes the original act of a being endowed with intelligence and will. In its original meaning it is used of the founding of cities and other permanent landmarks. By their choice of the term *ktizō*, LXX authors have to a large extent excluded the idea of creation out of pre-existing matter.

The Idea of Creation in the Old Testament. In order to obtain a correct understanding of the Old Testament idea of creation let us first put the question of what the relationship is between God as he appears in the bible and other being apart from himself. How is he related to the dimension of space and time? In the process of explaining what this relationship consists in a quite definite image emerges, on the basis of which the specific character and the origin of the idea of creation can be unambiguously defined without ascribing any undue primacy of importance to any one passage of scripture.

1. *God is the Absolute Lord.* a. *Matter* belongs inalienably to him. Nothing is impossible to him (Jer 32:17). Viewed from his standpoint the cosmos shrinks to the dimensions of a mere toy. He measures the oceans in the hollow of his hand and marks off the heavens with a span (Is 40:12). Men are as minute as grasshoppers in his sight (Is 40:22). He sets Leviathan, the monster, swimming about in the sea like a goldfish in an aquarium (Ps 104:26). All nature belongs to him: he overthrows mountains, shakes the earth out of its place, commands the sun (Job 9:5–7), and so on.

b. A further characteristic, corresponding to this transcendence of his over material things, is his dominion over *history*. He who fashions light and creates the darkness is the bringer of peace and also of woe (Is 45:7). He it is who brings princes to nought, and makes the rulers of the earth as nothing (Is 40:23). He has formed his people for himself (Is 43:21), and led them down the ages with a mighty hand. From him come riches and honour. Light and power are in his hand, and it lies with him to make great and mighty whomsoever he will (1 Chron 29:11–12).

c. This *omnipotence* is not only confined to factors outside the natural order. Without God things *could not exist*. The song lives by the breath of the singer. As soon as he withdraws his breath the song falls away into silence. 'When thou hidest thy face, they are dismayed; when thou takest away their breath, they die' (Ps 104:29). Natural things cannot even claim the support of permanency, for they are changed like a garment while he remains (Ps 102:27).

2. *God is the creator.* The fact that God is totally and completely transcendent over all beings apart from himself is emphasised again and again in the Old Testament, and it excludes the possibility that any non-divine being can be supported in existence independently of God himself. Pressed to its ultimate logical conclusion the omnipotence of God implies his activity as creator, or more precisely the idea of creation out of nothing.

a. *The fact of the creation.* The creation is the deed of God's power, and created things, by their very existence, proclaim the immensity of that power. The bible contains no reference to any conflict between a power which creates order on the one hand and chaos on the other. No trace whatever is to be discerned in the biblical account of the establishment of the world of the idea of some resistance being offered to God as creator. God himself commands the primordial *tōhúwābōhú*, and this is not capable of setting any obstacle to his will. 'In the beginning God created the heavens and the earth'. Thus Genesis intones that powerful hymn of praise which is carried on and developed in the mighty deeds of God throughout the whole of history. The planets which were objects of adoration to the ancients are set in the firmament to act as lanterns (Gen 1:14ff). God has created the earth itself and men and beast upon the earth by his mighty power and his outstretched arm, and he gives them to whomsoever he wills (Jer 27:5).

b. *Creation by the word.* The scriptures do unquestionably contain images ultimately based on anthropomorphic conceptions. But mythology properly so called plays no part in the biblical narrative. At most it serves to provide embellishment. God utters his word and things exist. It is here that the biblical accounts of creation are, theologically speaking, at their most profound: God creates by his word. 'By the word of the Lord the heavens were made, and all their host by the breath of his mouth' (Ps 33:6). He has created all things by his word, and fashioned man by his wisdom (Wis 9:1). He spoke, and it came to be; he commanded, and it stood forth (Ps 33:9). There was no instrument and no mediator, no compulsion and no process of emanation. As St Ephraem Syrus puts it in his *Discourse Upon Faith* 25 (BKV II., 37, 24). 'His will is his treasure-house. For everything came to be out of nothing.'

c. *Creation out of nothing.* This relationship between total impotence on the one hand and total omnipotence on the other finds its only possible counterpart in terms of philosophy in the idea of *creatio ex nihilo*. In 2 Macc 7:28 we find the mother of the Maccabees saying to her son: '. . . Look at the heavens and the earth and see everything that is in them, and recognize that God did not make them out of things that existed'. We should not regard this as an expresson of a later theological development which should be considered as secondary and as representing a different mentality from scripture as a whole. Rather it is the ultimate logical conclusion and at the same time the intrinsic and inevitable point of departure for what the Old Testament has to tell us about creation. Whether what is recorded in the first book of scripture is *genesis* in the true and strict sense, or merely the imposition of basic order on things is a matter of dispute. But in any case this would make no difference to the statements about creation in the Old Testament as a whole.

3. *The further implications of the idea of creation.* From this basic conception certain consequences follow with regard to the relationship of the creature to his creator. Of these the following, which in our opinion are the most important, may be mentioned at this point: praise, trust and the solidarity of all created things.

a. *Praise.* The ultimate purpose of creation is the glory of God. 'The heavens are telling the glory of God, and the firmament proclaims his handiwork' (Ps 19:1–2). From its contemplation of the work of creation the Old Testament rises again and again to praise of the Creator, and exhorts its readers to share in this praise: 'All thy works shall give thanks to thee, O Lord, and all thy saints shall bless thee' (Ps 145:10). Man in particular, as an intelligent being, has the duty of responding with words of thanksgiving to the word of God in the creation.

b. *Trust.* God is solicitous for the work of his hands. Man is not left to the mercy of conflicting cosmic powers. The creator lovingly upholds his creatures in existence. He distributes while they gather. He opens his hand, they are abundantly satisfied (Ps 104:27). It is on the basis of this elemental trust that Job can actually call God to justice with the words: 'Thy hands fashioned and made me; and now thou dost turn about and destroy me' (Job 10:8–9). And to this question he will obtain the answer of life.

c. *The solidarity of all creatures.* All men are created by God, and in this fact lies the ultimate and inalienable basis of their equality and their value. 'Have we not all one Father? Has not one God created us? Why then are we faithless to one another, profaning the covenant of our fathers?' (Mal 2:10). An offence against one's brother is accounted a sin against one's creator; service of one's brother is service of one's creator. 'He who oppresses a poor man insults his maker, but he who is kind to the needy honours him' (Prov 14:31). In the New Testament this idea attains its full development. It is an idea which has transformed the whole world and continues to transform it right to the present day, while the underlying truth of it which we seek to suppress is knocking at our door with a hostile fist.

B. *In the New Testament. Introduction.* The theocentric approach of the Old Testament remains in force in the New. Knowledge of the creation is not acquired as the outcome of an increasingly advanced process of speculation, but has its basis rather in God as he manifests his omnipotence and reveals himself to us. The word of the fathers is confirmed, but still more, it is seen in a fresh light and achieves its ultimate depths in the God-man. The basic orientation is the same. We do not start from a multiplicity of geometrical points and so conclude where the central point lies. Rather this central point has acquired a fresh clarity beyond all possibility of confusion, and thereby the whole system of co-ordinates falls under the same illumination. The word which God spoke 'last of all' through his own Son (Heb 1:2) contains within it a further word concerning the essence of creation.

Terminology. The terms most frequently used are *ktizō* (= to create: Mk 13:19; Eph 2:10; Col 1:16; etc) and its derivatives: *ktistēs* (= creator: 1 Pet 4:19), *ktisma* (= creature: 1 Tim 4:4; Jas 1:18; Rev 5:13; 8:9), and *ktisis* (= creation: Mk 10:6; Rom 1:20; 2 Cor 5:17). But in addition to these we also have *poieō* (lit. = to make, do: Acts 4:24; Heb 1:2; 3:2), *poiēma* (lit. = a thing made: Rom 1:20; Eph 2:10), *plassō* (lit. = to form, shape: Rom 9:20; 1 Tim 2:13) together with *plasma* (lit. = a thing formed: Rom 9:20), and *kataskeuazō* (lit. = to prepare, build: Heb 3:4). *Ktizō* is used here only of divine creative activity, while *ktisis* can refer to the act of creation or the result of this act—namely, the created order or the creature. Although everything, including even angels and powers (Col 1:16) has been created, *ktisis* is only applied to that part of creation which is visible and transient, of which man is the representative and the spokesman. In considering the whole range of expressions relating to the creation we ought also to include a number of prepositional usages. For the words *ek*, *pro*, *dia* or *eis* are also used to express the origin and the ultimate purpose of all that exists.

The idea of creation in the New Testament. 1. The taking over and the further development of the Old Testament witness to the creation: a. In the New Testament too the creation is regarded in the context of *the manifestations of God's power.* When the apostles Peter and John were acquitted at the end of their judicial examination by the high priests the early christian community praised their Lord as he who made 'the heaven and the earth and the sea and everything in them', and it entreats the all-powerful God to continue his mighty deeds in the preaching of the gospel (Acts 4:24-30). Creation is the first—and that too in a logical, not merely in a psychological sense—and fundamental deed of power on God's part. It is the paradigm, as it were, on which all else is based, when it is a question of convincing one's self or others that with God nothing is impossible.

In the confrontation between christianity and the pagan world the fact of the divine origin of the creation is more strongly emphasised, and is sometimes made the central point in the whole discussion. It must be remembered, however, that in this controversy the disputants can no longer find a common basis in the Old Testament. In their reaction against the divinisation of the created order and its forces the relevant doctrinal statements in the New Testament acquire a polemical note. When the inhabitants of Lystra react to a miraculous cure on the part of the missionaries of the gospel by attempting to offer sacrifices to them Paul has to use his utmost resources to turn their minds to the living God 'who made the heaven and the earth and the sea and all that is in them' (Acts 14:15). At the Areopagus the controversy about the cult of idols provides a starting-point for the preaching of Christ: 'The God who made the world and everything in it, being Lord of heaven and earth, does not live in shrines made by man' (Acts 17:24). The inversion of the creator-creature relationship, is in fact, *the* sin and *the* reproach of the pagan world (Rom 1:25), in which every evil has its roots. Paul, therefore, constantly renews his insistence upon the divine origin of the creation (Rom 1:25; 11:26; 1 Cor 8:6; 10:26; Eph 3:9; Col 1:16), although admittedly here, in accordance with the theocentric standpoint which he adopts, it is always God and not the creation as such which occupies the central point in his argument.

b. Similarly we encounter in the New Testament the conception of *creation by the will and the word of God.* God calls into being that which does not exist (Rom 4:17), and upholds all things by the word of his power (Heb 1:3). It is by his word that the ages of the world were established (Heb 11:3), and all that exists had, and still continues to have, existence through the word of God alone. As it was and is, so shall it always be from eternity to eternity, and the twenty-four elders of Revelation lay down their crowns before the omnipotent Lord and acknowledge: 'Worthy art thou, our Lord and God, to receive glory and honour and power, for thou didst create all things, and by thy *will* they existed and were created' (Rev 4:11). It was the will of God that ordained the beginning of being, and it is his will that will bring about its ultimate consummation. In scripture we do not find any speculations about anything taking place prior to the creation, or about how the cosmos came to acquire its form, after the manner of the various mythologies. The 'beginning of the creation' constitutes the absolute horizon of all arguments from tradition, whether these are adduced by Jesus himself (Mt 19:4; Mk 10:6; Mt 24:21; Mk 13:19) or by those who scoff at christian teaching (2 Pet 3:4). There can be no reaching back beyond the beginning. That which was established at the beginning has an absolute quality. The fact that emphasis is so often laid upon the beginning in various connections (Mt 19:8; Rom 1:20; Heb 1:10; see also the combinations so frequently employed of *apo* and *pro katabolēs kosmou* = 'from' and 'before the foundation of the world'—Mt 13:35; 25:34; Lk 11:50; Jn 17:24; Eph 1:4; Heb 4:3; 9:26; 1 Pet 1:20; Rev 13:8; 17:8) ultimately goes back to the idea of creation as a *creatio ex nihilo*, and this in turn is to be understood on the basis of the Old Testament.

c. The New Testament insists in season and out of season on the fact that creation as a whole derives its existence and its meaning utterly from God. 'From him and through him and to him are all things' (Rom 11:36; see also Jn 1:3, 10; 1 Cor 8:6; Heb 2:10). There could be no more concise or more exact way of expressing the fact that God is the source, the maintainer and the ultimate goal of creation. These three points of reference, 'from him, to him, and through him' exclude any kind of intermediary, whether this is conceived of as a demiurge, or as pre-existing matter. In all respects and from first to last creation is something that is God-willed and immediate to God. Hence there is no creature which could be concealed from God (Heb 4:13). Hence too there is no creature which could ever separate us from his love (Rom 8:39), and for the same reason there is no food which man has to abstain from. The very fact that it is the gift of God is enough to make it good (1 Tim 4:3). The creation bears the imprint of God's hand, and for this reason it is possible for man to gain knowledge of God from it: 'Ever since the creation of the world his invisible nature . . . has been clearly perceived in the things that have been made' (Rom 1:20; see also Heb 3:4).

Creation in Christ. The New Testament, however, is not only an interpretation of the Old; it extends beyond it in its message and is its fulfilment. 'In these last days he has spoken to us by a Son' (Heb 1:2). And in this word of his a further message about the creation is contained, one which could not hitherto have been deduced. The more the idea of God becomes clarified the more the idea of the creation is freed from the obscurities surrounding it. The *new factor* is that what has been said about God as the creator and the sacred author of all things is now applied to Christ—often, indeed, in the same words. The result is that we can now speak of a christocentric specification of the creation over and above the theocentric aspect in it which was all that we had hitherto perceived. In the relationship between God and creaturehood the name of Christ can now appear where before there was simply the name of God. Christ is the beginning of the creation (Rev 3:14), the first-born of all creation (Col 1:15), but at the same time he is heir to all things (Heb 1:2). Through him all things were made (Jn 1:3); through him the world came to be (Jn 1:10); in him all things were created, through him and for him (Col 1:15, 16). All things have been made subject to him (Heb 2:8). Passages of the Old Testament which speak of the creation are applied directly to Christ (Heb 1:10), and in setting Christ above Moses Paul gives as his reason that the builder of the house is greater than the house itself, and that God is the builder of all things (Heb 3:4–6). In 1 Cor we encounter two statements set in parallelism (8:6): 'Yet for us there is one God, the Father, from whom are all things and for whom we exist, and one Lord, Jesus Christ, through whom are all things and through whom we exist'. What is the significance of this parallelism which is carried through consistently, and which extends to form and content alike? First Paul's intention is certainly to bring out the fact that Christ is on an equal footing with God. This was necessary precisely in view of the tenets of the Jews. But over and above this, the creation is unreservedly and totally orientated to

Christ. The nature and history of the creation can find its ultimate explanation only in its relationship to him. It is the function of creation undeviatingly and irresistibly to make manifest the glory of God through the will of every creature, and that too not at random but precisely through the incarnate love and grace of our Lord Jesus Christ. The plan of creation depends for its meaning upon the plan of salvation or, to put it better, on the plan for the manifestation of God's glory. The one is incomprehensible without the other. 'The order laid down in that mystery which has been hidden throughout the ages of the world in God, who has created all things' contains at its kernel the revelation of God in Christ, and embraces both creation and redemption. 'For he has made known to us . . . the mystery of his will, according to his purpose *which he set forth in Christ*, as a plan for the fullness of time, to unite all things in him, things in heaven and things on earth' (Eph 1:9–10). This is the goal of creation, and this goal is achieved with the resurrection, even though its achievement is visible only to the eye of faith. Viewed in this perspective our conception of man's fall and subsequent redemption is no longer hopelessly distorted, as it is when we envisage it as a catastrophic failure of God's plan followed by a repairing of the damage. Creation as a whole is conceived of in view of Christ, in view of the God-man, and what leads up to him in historical terms is the way to its ultimate consummation. ⁊ Rebirth, Restoration.

3. *The New Creation.* Admittedly it is not yet possible to perceive the consummation ushered in by Christ in the

present state of the created order. Man stands in a certain mysterious solidarity with creation in that all creation has an inherent connection with matter; and because his destiny is one with that of the created order as a whole, he has subjected the whole of this order, himself included, to the bondage of transience and eventual annihilation (Rom 8:20, 21) by rebelling against the claims of God. We may conceive of God's plan as a song that flows on uninterrupted, and it has been made manifest in Christ that this song does not end in a discord. But, to retain the terms of this simile, the present state of the creation is like a harmony in which a dominant note can be detected, this being open to its due development and, as it were, reaching out towards that development and, in a certain sense, already containing it. With the incarnation and resurrection of Christ the age of the new creation began in the world, an age in which the earlier discords are resolved into a new harmony: 'Neither circumcision counts for anything, nor uncircumcision, but a new creation' (Gal 6:15; see also Eph 2:15–16): 'If anyone is in Christ, he is a new creation', we are told in 2 Cor 5:17: 'the old has passed away, behold, the new has come'. Here again the concept of creation is most intimately connected with that of salvation. Creation is orientated to that which is 'new': the God-man and man as conformed to him by faith and the sacraments. In this connection it would be wrong to regard 'a new heaven and a new earth' (Rev 21:1) as a restoration of the order of paradise. The New Testament is aware that man originally existed in a state of bliss. But any con-

cept of a cyclic process in world history is foreign to it. Christ is not the restorer but the consummator, and we are told that when it is finally revealed the new creation will be something which 'no eye has seen, nor ear heard, nor the heart of man conceived', something which 'God has prepared for those who love him' (1 Cor 2:9). The creation endures until that point in time when the voice of him who is enthroned says: 'Behold I make all things new', and 'It is done' (Rev 21:5, 6).

A final conclusion may be drawn. Creation is the sphere in which *kharis* and *agapē* in Christ are developed to the praise and glory of his name. In temporal terms its total span is coextensive with that of saving history itself. Thus it is not only the basic manifestation of God's power and the reflection of his 'manifold' wisdom; it is also the work of his love, and hence man must be faithful to 'the faithful Creator', and put his trust in him (1 Pet 4:19). ↗ Grace.

Bibliography: H. Fruhstorfer, *Weltschöpfung und Paradies nach der Bibel*, Linz 1927; F. M. T. Böhl, 'Bara als Terminus der Weltschöpfung im altl. Sprachgebrauch', *Festschrift Kittel*, Stuttgart 1913, 42ff; A. Janssens, 'De scripturae doctrina de Creatione mundi', *Coll. Gandavienes* 30 (1947), 95–9; H. Lehmann, 'Schöpfergott und Heilsgott im Zeugnis der Bibel', *ET* 11 (1951), 97–112; G. Lindeskog, *Studien zum neutestamentlichen Schöpfungsgedanken*, Uppsala 1952; Gerhard Schneider, *Kaine Ktisis. Die Idee der Neuschöpfung beim Apostel Paulus und ihr religionsgeschichtliche Hintergrund*, Trier 1959 (see also *TTZ* 68 [1959], 257–70); V. Warnach, *Agape*, Düsseldorf 1951, 496–504; L. H. Taylor, *A Study of the Biblical Doctrine of 'Kaine Ktisis' in Pauline Theology*, Louisville 1955; P. Humbert, 'Emploi et portée du verbe bara (créer) dans l'AT', *TZ* 3 (1947), 401–22; *A. Hulsbosch, *God's Creation*, London and New York 1965; *P. Schoonenberg, *Covenant and Creation*, London and South Bend (Indiana) 1968; *H. McCabe, *The New Creation*, London and New York 1964.

Gerhard Trenkler

Cross

From the historical point of view the cross is the instrument of the *passion of Christ*. It consisted of a beam driven into the ground on which the condemned man was hanged, nailed, or bound, to a cross-beam. The historical connection with the death of Christ introduced the word *stauros* (= cross) into the field of theological language. This usage is exclusive to the New Testament and is in a special way Pauline. The gospels use the word in the material sense only, with but one exception, to which we shall return. In Paul, the cross stands for the passion of Christ, both as showing forth his humiliation and death, and as an expression of his obedience to the father, reaching as far as absolute self-emptying (Phil 2:8). The cross also expresses the mysterious way of salvation which goes against ordinary human wisdom (1 Cor 1:17f; Gal 5:11). The life of the christian must be conformed to the cross (Phil 3:18; Gal 2:19; 6:14)—in presenting which view Paul follows Is 53.

In addition, we also find the idea of the *cross of↗glory* as the sign of the victory of the Son of Man which will appear with him at the↗*parousia*. Mt 24:30 already presents this sense and it occurs in Judaeo–Christian literature (*Did.*, 16, 6; *Epist. Apost.* 27; *Sib.*, 8, 224; ApocPti). It is in this same sense that we have to interpret the custom of drawing a cross on the eastern wall of houses. Another theme allied to that of the cross of glory is that of the cross which accompanied Christ in his descent into the underworld. (EvPti 42), or his ascent into heaven (Sib 6, 26); in these texts the cross appears as a living person. It stands, in fact, for Christ himself, a point which emerges in particular in the gnostic Acts of Apostles (ActJo 98). The cross stands less for the humiliation of Christ than for his victorious power.

It was not long before people began to look for *types* of the cross in the Old Testament, the most ancient of these being the serpent raised up in the wilderness (Jn 3:14) and Moses praying with uplifted arms (Barn 12, 2). In the oldest collections of *Testimonia* we also find Is 65:2 and Deut 33:3. The apologists look for symbols of the cross also in the natural order. Thus mast and plough point to the cross (Justin, *I Apol*, 55, 1–6). The wood of the cross, as distinct from the shape, brings to mind types such as the Tree of Life and the staff of Moses. The mention of the wood is even given a place in an ancient judaeo–christian *targum* on Ps 96:10.

The cross admits of different *symbolical interpretations*. In the first place, its four dimensions can stand for the universality of redemption, which unites the heavenly and the earthly spheres and bridges the gap between Jew and gentile. This symbolism already appears in Eph 2:16 and Jn 12:32, but not in Eph 3:18. It is also found in PsSol 22, 1f and ActPti 38, and Irenaeus often uses it (*Dem*, 34). Again, the cross is presented as strengthening (*stērizōn*) and upholding the world (Melito, *Hom. Pasch.*, 16, 15; ActAnd 14), which would appear to provide a relationship between the 'word' as creating agent and the redeeming cross (1 Clem 33, 3), emphasises the *dunamis* of the cross. Finally, the cross is interpreted as something which divides (*merizōn*), a view which is developed especially in the Valentinian *gnosis*, in which *stauros* and *horos* (=boundary, border) are more or less identified. But the fundamental idea is evidently the identification of the function of the cross with that of the 'Word'.

What, in conclusion, is the meaning of *the cross signed on the forehead (sphragis)*? It is usually connected with the cross of Christ, but this reference is secondary. Its origin must be sought in the letter Tau, with which the members of the eschatological community would, according to Ezek 9:4, be signed on their forehead. The LXX translation is *sēmeion* (=sign). The Sadokite community were acquainted with this sign (*CD*, 19, 19) and Revelation speaks of the seal (7:3, *sphragis*) with which the servants of God would be signed on the forehead. This sign stands for the name of Yahweh, since Tau was the last letter of the alphabet. Thus Revelation speaks indifferently of 'signing with the seal' (7:3) and 'signing with the Name' (14:1). Now, we know that at the beginning of the christian era Tau was written either + or ×.

In judaeo–christian texts the cruciform sign made on the forehead still stands in relation to 'the Name'. The *Shepherd* of Hermas (in Parable 8, 10, 3) speaks in this sense of 'those who bear [*bastazein*] the Name', in which connection we must bear in mind that for Hermas 'name' and 'word' are used as synonymns.

Very soon, however, the interpretation of the cross as the instrument of Christ's passion prevailed—it is present, in fact, already in the New Testament.

We have so far prescinded from: 'He who does not take [*lambanein*] his cross and follow me is not worthy of me' (Mt 10:38); in Lk (14:27) we read: 'Whoever does not bear [*bastazein*] his own cross . . .' The similarity to Hermas suggests that it is a question here of a play on the idea of Tau on the forehead. One could also compare Gal 6:17: 'I bear [*bastazein*] on my body the marks [*stigmata*] of Jesus.' Shortly before, the cross had been mentioned in the context of circumcision (Gal 6:12), which would appear to indicate that it was considered the sign of belonging to the new Israel. In these texts, then, the Tau, signed on the forehead and signifying the 'Name', is brought into relation with the cross of Christ's passion.

Bibliography: A. Grillmeier, *Der Logos am Kreuz*, Munich 1956; M. Sulzberger, 'Le symbole de la croix', *Byzantion* 2 (1925), 356–83; H. Rahner, 'Das mystische Tau', *ZKT* 85 (1953), 385–410; E. Peterson, *Das Kreuz und das Gebet nach Osten: Frühkirche, Judentum, und Gnosis*, Freiburg 1959, 15–35; E. Dinkler, 'Zur Geschichte des Kreuzsymbols', *ZTK* 48 (1951), 148–72; E. Dinkler, 'Jesu Worte vom Kreuztragen', *Ntl. Studien für R. Bultmann*, Berlin 1954; 117–23; E. Dinkler, 'Kreuzzeichen und Kreuz', *Jahrbuch für Antike und Christentum* 5 (1962), 93–112; J. Daniélou, *Les symboles chrétiens promitifs*, Paris 1961, 143–51; J. Daniélou, 'La charrue, symbole de la croix', *RSR* 42 (1954), 193–204; J. Daniélou, *Théologei du judéo-christianisme*, Paris 1958, 204–8 and 384–6; W. Michaelis, 'Zeichen, Siegel, Kreuz', *TZ* 12 (1956), 505–26; J. L. Teicher, 'The Christian Interpretation of the Sign X in the Isaiah Scroll', *VT* 5 (1955), 189–98.

Jean Daniélou

Cult

A. *Basic data (cult in general)*. Cult (compare Latin *colere*) refers to an encounter with the divine generally within the framework of determined forms. The connotation given to the word *encounter* here covers the widest possible range of meaning and the forms which the encounter takes change according to the meaning given to the encounter. The encounter can be realised in different places (either natural such as mountains or man-made such as temples), or at different times (either determined by the natural cycle or by history), by a community or by the individual. The intentions which are brought to the encounter can be of different kinds, as also the results which accrue from it such as reassurance, increase of power, defence against demonic powers, expiation, union with the deity. The functionaries who mediate the encounter can be different though they are generally priests, as can the circle of participants (family, clan, community), and also the degree of *intensity* with which one participates or to which one is committed, which will generally be higher for cultically qualified personnel than for others.

B. *The Old Testament (basic characteristics)*. Even on the level of vocabulary the Old Testament idea of cult is seen to consist above all in *service* (it contains no word which corresponds exactly to *cult* or *worship*). In keeping with this, cultic actions themselves (eg, Ex 40:15ff), together with everything which leads up to and prepares for them (Num 3:31) and everything related to the place of cult and to cultic functions (Num 3:25f), are described in terms of service.

The Old Testament informs us that the patriarchs frequented Canaanite sanctuaries such as Shechem, Bethel, Mamre, Hebron, and Beersheba. They built altars (Gen 12:6ff; etc), sacrificed (Gen 46:1), and called on the name of Yahweh (Gen 13:4). The most impressive expressions of Old Testament cult can be seen in passover (⁄ Easter) and the covenant festival (⁄ Covenant), and it is characterised by an exclusive attachment to Yahweh, the absence of images, the building of the temple and concentration of worship in the ⁄ temple organised by the priesthood. As a result of the cultic reforms of Josiah the temple was to be the only place of worship. In the post-exilic period the sacrificial system became predominant, and the place of prayer in worship was greatly developed as a result of what had happened during the Exile. It was from this latter that the synagogue service as we know it grew.

C. *Qumran*. It is quite impossible to maintain that the Qumran community was opposed to cult. The liturgy of the temple was not rejected in itself. What was objected to was the current practice of cult which was then in the hands of a (high) priesthood which was regarded as illegitimate and unworthy. The Qumran sectarians awaited the re-establishment of legitimate temple liturgy, one which would be fully in accord with the Torah, in the eschatological age. While, therefore, they maintained the necessity of offering sacrifices at the future eschatological temple as the only legitimate place of worship, in the meantime they practised other forms of worship as, for example, ritual lustrations which were in principle reserved to the priests with reference to similar rites prescribed for temple worship. According to 1 QS 3:4–12 these rites had an expiatory effect and therefore could take the place of sacrifice. We should also mention in this respect the daily cultic meal under the presidency of priests which was associated in their thinking with the cultic meals taken by the priests in Jerusalem. These meals called for a high degree of cultic purity on the part both of the participants (only full members who were in a state of purity could attend them) and of the food which was eaten (1 QS 6:4–6; 1 QSa 2:17–22). Finally, sexual abstinence, either in the form of complete celibacy (1 QS) or in that of occasional abstention from marital relations (CD), has to be understood in terms of the striving for absolute purity of the priestly-cultic kind. With regard to the absence of sacrifice at Qumran which, as we have seen, must be explained in terms of the contemporary situation, we can understand how the community opposed its perfect fulfilment of the law to the sacrificial routine of normative judaism. The superiority of their chosen way of law-observance was supported by the use of cultic terms transferred to their own situation as, for example, when the community describes itself as the true temple (1 QS 8:5–10; 9:3–5). We should not, however, overlook the fact that this spiritualisation of the cultic is obviously limited by the fact that cultic actions carried out outside the Jerusalem temple and apart from the priesthood which served it were considered as a way of observing the law.

D. *The New Testament*. I. *Jesus and Old Testament worship*. 1. *Basic principles*. It must be understood in the first place that we can only approach the question of Jesus' position with regard to Old Testament cult through the witness of New Testament writers and the traditions on which they depended and which they incorporated and edited into their work. Insofar as we are able to identify them, these traditions are to be emphasised with respect to the different contribution which each makes. But we can say of all of them that, despite their distinct qualities, they are characterised by the post-resurrection insight into the understanding of the Christ-event in whatever way we choose to define it. This is also true of those elements in the tradition which betray a historical or quasi-historical interest and which demand, or at least allow for, an interpretation based on this premiss. The historical Jesus can be attained by following the course of his life on earth and the identity of this figure engaged in a saving mission with the exalted Christ can be grasped by faith. This identity entails the necessary conclusion that the earthly life of Jesus is represented for the most part as a reflection backwards of the church's image of the exalted Christ. Moreover, the post-resurrection proclamation of Christ took place in a milieu where various influences were at work on the process of preaching, maintaining, strengthening, forming, and deepening faith in Christ, influences which we cannot discuss in detail here and which are not in every case easy to assess. If in carrying out our investigation we bear in mind the presuppositions necessary for understanding the material which the New

Testament offers on our subject, we will be able to recognise without difficulty that the answer to our question about the *historical* Jesus implies the attempt to identify what Jesus really did and said insofar as the New Testament writings and the traditions which we can perceive behind these writings allow us to do so.

2. *A glance at the relevant texts.* a. Mk 1:40–5 and parallels record the healing of a leper. The text reveals an inner tension, not just between the imposition of silence on the healed man by Jesus and his subsequent conduct (vv 44, 45), but in the very demand of Jesus itself (v 44a, 44b). If no one ever hears about the healing it would be impossible for the man to present himself before the priest as healed, therefore his return into society would be dangerous and difficult to accomplish. He would not be able to avoid answering the question as to *how* he had been healed. This tension or contradiction within the text is open to various solutions. For example, one could suppose that two traditions have been incorporated into the account, in one of which (to take one of the main differences) the healed man is commanded to say nothing about it (v 44a), whereas in the other he is commanded to show himself to the priest (v 44b). A solution might also be attempted by taking account of the editorial work of the evangelist as in the addition of the command to keep silent on what had happened. However we attempt to justify the presence in the narrative of the command to show himself to the priest, the question at issue is whether it can be used to show a respect, however conditional, on the part of Jesus for

the priesthood, the office which it represented, and the functions which it fulfilled.

We should note in the first place that the whole point of the command is explained by the phrase 'for a proof to the people'. Even if we suppose that this is an editorial addition of the evangelist we would hardly be wrong in seeing here the explanation why the command was given. In this latter case the phrase could hardly be taken as an explanation of what had already been said. If the phrase *eis marturion autois* (= 'for a proof to them') does not simply indicate the intention to prove that a miracle has taken place, with even less reason can it be taken as justification for the return of the healed man to life in society. *Rather does it presuppose a definite attitude on the part of the priesthood to what had taken place and to the one responsible, namely, to Jesus himself,* and in the view of the underlying tradition and certainly of the evangelist himself this attitude had taken shape long before this point in the narrative. Viewed from this angle, the main centre of interest which determines the thrust of the narrative and focusses on one point becomes clear. Certainly neither the tradition on which the evangelist drew for his information nor the evangelist himself had any intention of depicting Jesus as taking his inspiration from or being directed by the temple and its functionaries; from which it may be concluded that Jesus himself had never given occasion to anyone to think that he had.

b. The critical position which Jesus took with regard to the cultic prescriptions of the Old Testament can be clearly seen in the dispute-saying about what is ↗ 'clean and unclean', which has to be understood against the background of current views on the law and the traditions of the fathers (Mk 7:1–23; see also Mt 15:1–20). This passage is composed as follows: introduction to the general theme and question of the Pharisees (vv 1–5), Jesus' answer to the question (vv 6–13), instruction of the people (vv 14–15), instruction of the disciples (vv 17–23). With regard to the question of ritual purity the attitude of Jesus was clearly one of *rejection* (vv 1–5; see also 15a, 18). Ritual or apparent impurity is contrasted with what really makes a man impure (vv 15b, 20–3), implying that in the conflict between the duty to love one's parents and that of making a gift to the temple the latter must quite definitely be relativised. It is not, however, easy to determine what the phrase *korban* (= 'given to God') really refers to (v 11). Does it signify the sacrificial offering for the temple worship and does the saying affect the requirement in the law to make such an offering and, if so, in what sense? Or is it in part or entirely here a question of correcting those abuses which had crept in with the practice of vowing property to the temple? If we take the text as it stands it would seem arbitrary and even perverse to limit the criticism of Jesus to this kind of abuse. The text speaks in a general and unspecified way about ritual purity and impurity. The main point at issue is clearly the highly significant one that any kind of cultic prescription must take second place to the law of love; in the fulfilment of the will of God there can be no conflict of duties! To help one's parents is a sacred duty prescribed by God's law. They must not be left to suffer want. God himself can say: 'Every beast of the forest is mine . . . if I were hungry I would not tell you, for the world and all that is in it is mine' (Ps 50:10, 12). That God does not *need* anything from man is a well-established datum of Old Testament revelation.

c. The purification of the temple (Mk 11:15–17 and parallels; Jn 2:13–17). From the point of view of our theme in general this incident seems to the modern reader to have a very special importance; and the meaning seems to be quite simply that to purify means to make holy, to restore an original holiness which had been lost. Yet this text raises a whole series of very difficult questions which have to be faced, two of which may be mentioned here. The first concerns the historical character of the narrative. How could Jesus, acting alone and a stranger in Jerusalem, have cleared the forecourt of the gentiles of merchants and money-changers without interference from the authorities and the temple police or interruption by these people whose concessions to trade there were guaranteed by the authorities? Then there is the theological difficulty: why should Jesus have objected to what after all was meant to be at the service of the sacrificial liturgy of the temple? The difficulty is even greater if the expression 'house of prayer' taken from the Isaian quotation (56:7) refers in general to 'the house where God is worshipped' and therefore presupposes a positive assessment of the temple and its sacrificial liturgy, as all agree is the case, rather than referring merely to synagogue worship. The original connection between this scene and the question of

Jesus' authority (Mk 11:27–33 and parallels) does not offer a solution to the difficulties raised by this passage, especially since it is redacted in such a way as to reveal no interest in providing an answer to these difficulties but rather raises questions of its own similar to these. But if we cannot get any help towards understanding the episode from this quarter other possibilities lie open. Traditions and evangelists which have influenced the formation of the text and given it the form it now has (the difference is important!) leave us in no doubt as to the real meaning of the event. They understand it as a symbolic anticipation of the judgement which threatens the temple as the centre of cult, a judgement which is soon to come upon it or—seen from a later perspective—which has already been passed on it and, at the same time, as pointing to the theological outcome of this judgement which is that the temple is no longer of any significance as a place of cult and its liturgy no longer represents the true worship of God as God himself wills it. At the same time, the character of the event as implying an eschatological promise for the gentiles has also been built into it. Suffice it to think of where the action takes place (the forecourt of the gentiles) and the phrase 'for all the nations' in Mark. It should be added that we cannot exclude the possibility that for some groups at some stage of the formation of the tradition the event may have been understood in a less progressive way within the context of contemporary Jewish eschatology—a new material temple in which a perfect form of divine worship would be carried out.

d. Those texts require a thorough examination which appear to express a direct and forceful rejection of and enmity towards the temple and its worship on the part of Jesus. Mk 13:1f and parallels relate that Jesus replied to one of his disciples who referred to the architectural glories of the temple with a saying predicting its total destruction. This implies that, *in the view of the evangelists, Jesus attributed little value to the temple and its worship*. On this point at least there can be no doubt at all. At the same time, however, this text has been so over-interpreted that we have to insist that nothing more than the above can be extracted from it as it stands. All connections which have been supposed to exist between Mk 13:2 and 14:58; 15:29; Mt 26:61; 27:40 in order to give sharper edge to Jesus' hostility to the temple expressed in this saying must be deemed hypothetical. No matter how much one may be tempted to accept any of these attempts, one thing can be said against them all, namely, that both the tradition and the evangelists insist on branding as false witness (Mk 14:57) brought by false witnesses (Mt 26:6of) the claim that Jesus' own attitude to the temple was one of personal hostility.

The announcement of Jesus that the herodian temple then standing would be destroyed and the severe relativisation of its cult implied in this must be seen against the background of Old Testament and rabbinical tradition. Passages such as 1 Sam 15:21f; Ps 40:6; 50:9–14; 51:16ff; Is 1:11; Jer 7:21–3; Hos 6:6; Mic 6:6–8 speak out very clearly and unambiguously on the sacrificial system. 1 Kings 8:27 presupposes that the temple as the house of

God has no absolute value in itself; Enoch (Eth) 90:28f refers to the old temple as having been set aside; the talmudic tractate Joma 39b (the Babylonian recension, see JerJoma 43c) knows that the temple will be destroyed and in fact presupposes the expectation that in the eschatological age a more glorious temple would take the place of the present building.

e. Mk 12:41–4 (see also Lk 21:1–4): the two coins of the widow. This narrative is always being used to make room in the evangelists' sketch of the earthly life of Jesus for the importance of temple piety. Taken by itself, however, it gives no support to this view; the interest is focussed on the poor widow who shamed the rich by giving all that she had, little though it was. Her exemplary conduct in doing so has really nothing to do with the temple as a place of worship. Her action which provoked Jesus to say what he did could have taken place elsewhere and have been otherwise motivated. It is conceivable that the place where her good action was performed was named to show the greatness of the gifts being made and introduce a variety of givers in order the more clearly to emphasise the poverty of the widow and the smallness of her gift. The episode is not concerned with the significance of the temple and its worship or whether participation in the temple services was necessary and desirable. We hear no instruction on this occasion from Jesus on this subject nor does the narrative as a whole betray any tendency to express a view on the significance of the temple. These are clear indications that this episode has nothing to do with the theme we are discussing.

f. It is generally taken for granted that the saying in Mt 5:23f was associated in the mind of the evangelist with the text just discussed, though the reasons for affirming this differ in each case. If we accept this supposition, the unity of the saying can be better understood. As is generally admitted, its meaning has to be sought on the level of a general statement prescinding from particularities such as the nature of the gift, the identity of the 'brother', what the nature of the disagreement was and the question of guilt. It is reminiscent of Mk 11:25 in that both can be characterised as general statements from the point of view of both form and content.

As far as our present theme is concerned one thing is clear. *The relationship of each one to his 'brother' is the touchstone of genuine worship of God.* There is nothing here about the intrinsic value or lack of value of sacrifice as such. It is therefore illegitimate to interpret the saying in terms of either sympathy for or hostility towards cult; this would represent in either case imposing on the text a weight which it cannot bear. It does not fit at all into this kind of category.

g. We find an abrogation of Old Testament cultic prescriptions expressed in the account of the calling of Matthew, the descriptions of Jesus' dealings with publicans and sinners (Mt 9:9–13 and parallels) and the account of the disciples picking the ears of wheat on the sabbath (Mt 12:1–8 and parallels) which is supported in Matthew by a quotation from Hosea— 'I will have mercy and not sacrifice' (Mt 9:13 = 12:7; see Hos 6:6). The frequent dealings of Jesus with publicans and sinners speak for themselves; anyone associating or eating with them could not possibly observe the prescriptions concerning ritual purity. There is, however, more to it than that. The call of Jesus goes out not to the just but to sinners. In calling sinners (it was understandable that occasion was later taken to add 'to repentance') he fulfilled the prophetic oracle or, to put it more strongly and precisely, *the saying of the Lord in Hos 6:6 is fulfilled in the activity of Jesus* (for the character and content of Hos 6:6 as a 'doctrinal clarification' see H. W. Wolff, *Dodekapropheten* I, *Hosea, Biblische Kommentar zum Alten Testament* 14/I, Neukirchen 1961, 131–67 esp. 132, 152–4, 164–7). Even if we do not accept the supposition that the meaning of the Hosean text is conveyed in all its depth in the quotation in Matthew, we have sufficient grounds for believing that here the old cultic ordinances have been voided of significance. This comes about not so much as the result of any direct statement but indirectly, by reason of the new interpretation of the law which Jesus offers in Matthew.

The account of the disciples eating the ears of corn on the sabbath also raises many problems. We shall refer here only to one or two of these. The disciples violate the law of the sabbath, not just by eating the ears of corn, but also by walking through the cornfields. At the least, we must suppose that this brings them very near to a violation—though if a strict interpretation of the law is presupposed, the violation was complete and unambiguous. According to the way the story is told, we might suppose that the Pharisees also were involved in this violation, but the

interest is focussed above all on Jesus. We can see here already how strongly the purpose which inspired the composition of this story has influenced and determined the way it is told. The text makes it impossible for us to think of this walking through the fields as the equivalent of a stroll through the park on Sunday. Yet it is clear that the emphasis is elswhere and hence the walking through the fields does not really constitute a serious problem. In this case Jesus and the Pharisees are not considered to have violated the law if the primary intention of the writer is taken into account, and this is a point which has to be borne in mind. And so Jesus is taken to task by the Pharisees not on account of his own but of his disciples' violation of the law.

If, therefore, the story is concerned only with the eating of the ears of corn and not with the walking, it would appear that a simpler answer would have sufficed and indeed been more effective; but in fact the answer of Jesus is on a different plane from the objection made by the Pharisees. He does not reproach them with having themselves violated one or other of the more important stipulations of the law. Nor can his answer be understood in the context of the contemporary discussion carried on by the scribes with regard to the law of sabbath observance. We have to bear all this in mind in order to realise how inadequate the answer of Jesus is seen in the context of the actual situation. His answer goes well beyond this context in a variety of different ways. The disciples are absolved from any guilt (Mt 12:7c); the reason why the judgement of the Pharisees is declared false is, in the circumstances, couched in the most general of terms: they do not know the true will of God as to how he is to be honoured since they have not grasped the fact, long ago proclaimed through the prophets (v 7a–b), that the Son of Man is also lord of the sabbath and makes a claim which goes far beyond anything that had been expected (v 8). The same was true of the claim made by Jesus that in him there had appeared 'something greater than the temple' (v 6).

There remain the examples adduced by Jesus in vv 3–5. These fit in perfectly to the episode as here interpreted. Jesus approves of the conduct of David with which many of the scribal interpreters of the Scriptures were decidedly uneasy. We must not, of course, regard the two cases—the eating of the Bread of the Presence and the plucking of the ears of grain—as parallel and then set up a discussion on the resulting similarity or dissimilarity. There is not even a remote resemblance between the two cases with regard either to the action or the situation. By taking not a similar case but one which was one of the most extreme possible—and yet one guaranteed by the scriptures—Jesus replied in effect that since even eating the holy bread could be permitted when it was a question of saving life (even though this was the only reason), provided that nothing was done contrary to the holiness of God and his true worship, *a fortiori* could the disciples pluck ears of grain on the sabbath. There is no special emphasis here on the degree of hunger which they suffered (despite v 1b) as if this were the decisive factor on which the justification of their conduct depended.

One final point concerning priestly worship in the temple. The example adduced by Jesus fails in its purpose if we suppose that its only object was to provide a sharp and decisive justification of the disciples. Cultic actions are contemplated by the law itself and cannot be set in opposition to it. Even if we are to regard the action of the priest in giving the holy bread to David and his men in a casuistic way, as objectively an infraction of the law but one which in the circumstances was free of guilt, it would certainly not provide any justification for what the disciples did. The example would only make sense if it presupposed either that the action was deprived of its cultic character and therefore of its privileged position, or that the disciples had the right, justified on religious (cultic) grounds, to make this kind of exception in the conduct of their (profane) existence. In the final analysis both interpretations of the situation come down to the same thing.

h. Mt 17:24–7: the temple tax. The point made in this episode retains its force irrespective of its historicity in the context of the life of Jesus. According to the information provided by Matthew, Jesus instructs Peter to pay the temple tax but the reasons given are not very encouraging for those who wish to make use of this incident to build up a picture of Jesus as spiritually attached to the temple. Not just Jesus himself as *the Son* but *the sons* are basically free with regard to the payment of this tax, and even though the tax is in fact paid the only reason given is to avoid giving offence (v 27a). There is nothing here about the temple being the house of the Father (Lk 2:49), no distinction made between the temple as the house of God and the unworthiness of those who served it. That from a whole series of possible reasons for paying the tax the only one which is given refers to the temple not as the dwelling of God and the place of cult but only to how others thought of it shows clearly enough how far removed from this episode is the whole idea of temple piety.

i. The parable of the Pharisee and the publican points in the same direction (Lk 18:9–14). The place chosen for the confrontation is the temple as a place of prayer (this, we should note, is how it is considered in Luke) and it is as such that it is important in the context of this parable. But the point which the parable makes has really nothing at all to do with the temple nor does its meaning depend on it being understood as the place of worship; in fact the contrary would be nearer the truth. Drawing on Ps 51:3 the publican represents himself as a sinner. His attitude which, according to what Jesus says (Lk 18:14), leads to his being justified by God, is also stated with reference to this psalm (vv 18–19).

j. Other texts could be adduced which, far from weakening the results of our enquiry so far, would in fact further support them. In Mk 12:33, for example, a scribe declares (with indirect reference to 1 Sam 15:22) that an all-embracing love of God and the neighbour is superior to any kind of sacrifice and is acknowledged by Jesus as not being far from the kingdom of God. Mt 23:16–22 refers to the swearing of oaths but in a very different way from the strong expressions found in Mt 5:34. Distinctions made publicly when vowing are brushed aside as invalid; whoever swears by anything which is considered to belong to God is bound by his vow. Lk 17:14 cannot be adduced as a counter-argument to what we have said so far, much less the first two chapters of this gospel which are stamped with such a strongly original literary and theological character. The question asked in Jn 4:20–4 by the Samaritan woman about the legitimate place of worship is very clearly expressed and so is the answer: *the locus of cult is now 'in the spirit and in truth'*. (We cannot go on to discuss here the theological riches contained in this expression.)

3. *The attitude of Jesus to Old Testament cult.* How then can we characterise the situation of the historical Jesus— insofar as we are able to determine it— with respect to Old Testament cult? The picture which the evangelists give us of Jesus while on earth shows that he regarded the cultic ordinances of the Old Testament as nothing more or less than historical data. It is on this neutral basis that Jesus directs his strong criticism against the cultic ordinances of the Old Testament, relativises them in a radical way, predicts in threatening terms their abrogation, and all this in prophetic words, images, expressions, and actions which take up, intensify, and go beyond the prophets of the Old Testament in their condemnation of contemporary cultic practices. In this respect the picture of Jesus given us by the evangelists is as historically well-founded as we could wish, though we should add that, precisely because the emphasis and interest in the gospels is often centred on the theological elaboration and reproduction of the Christ-event, it is often impossible to

reconstruct historically in any useful way what actually happened.

If this last point is neglected we end up in serious difficulties. We would find it impossible to explain, for example, how the hellenistic christians associated with Stephen (Acts 6–7), Paul, and others in the early church period stand in absolute contradiction to a historical reconstruction of Jesus as a Jew full of reverence and respect for the temple (and also to the view that the gospels describe him as such). It is not a question either of a finely balanced harmony or reconciliation between seemingly irreconcilable differences comparable to those which existed between christians of Jewish and hellenistic backgrounds. But it would not be appropriate to leave in abeyance the solution to the vast range of problems concerning Old Testament cult (and also the law) and simply represent Jesus as protesting against certain abuses and aberrant tendencies in temple worship.

The position of Jesus with regard to the cultic regulations of the Old Testament should not be viewed or investigated apart from his preaching as a whole. To characterise these cultic regulations merely as data implies that they only merit consideration insofar as they come in contact in some way with the aims and intentions of Jesus. And insofar as the evangelists intend to represent the Jesus of history, these points of contact are strengthened by the addition of theological reflection pointing to the deeper meaning of the words or the actions. Unfortunately the attitude of Jesus cannot always be discovered and stated clearly and unambiguously, but some points at least can be stated confidently. It will at least follow from what has been said so far that Jesus is not described (in the purification of the temple scene) as attacking and occupying the temple. This is not in accord with what we know of the historical Jesus and cannot be deduced from what the gospels say. It is equally clear that Jesus was not a reformer of the cult. As with the prophets, his chief concern was with the heart of man. What difference would it have made to the aims which Jesus had in his preaching that he drove a few merchants a couple of yards further away from the temple? If Jesus was concerned at all with the merchants as such it would most probably have been with their rather shady way of doing business.

Once we renounce an 'objective' understanding of the texts which is too little subject to critical control and which often is the result of a false attempt at historical reconstruction, we are able to solve the otherwise insoluble problem of an inner contradiction which affects the person of Jesus and shows itself in his actions: devotion to the temple on the one hand, rejection of the temple on the other.

The prophetic criticism of Jesus directed against the cultic institutions of the Old Testament is part of the picture of the earthly Jesus presented by the gospels, a picture which appears to be firmly grounded in history even though the formulation of the traditions which can be found in the gospels or which lie behind them can be shown to come from communities which already believed in Jesus. This prophetic criticism of Jesus may be taken as one of the essential starting points for the development and elaboration of a new cultic reality proper to the New Testament. Yet the connection between the two cannot simply be represented as a continuum; what we have here is a possible line of development which makes sense but which also contains considerable gaps. In this process we also have to leave room for various tendencies of a more or less judaising nature and can accommodate also those texts which paint an idealistic picture (eg, Acts 2:46; 3:1; 5:12) insofar as they can lay claim to historicity.

That Paul in his theological reasoning did not appeal to the earthly Jesus, Jesus during his life on earth, can be understood from the whole context of the question of *complete* freedom from the law and also, of course, from the fact that in his letters he never refers to the earthly life of Jesus.

II. *Cult in the New Testament.* According to the New Testament there is only only one cultic reality, which is the Christ-event. By means of this the way has been opened to the Father (Eph 2:18).

The Christ-event as the new cultic reality proper to the New Testament is expressed in forms which are ever new, which cannot be contained in any kind of framework, elude any attempt to circumscribe them and can often be subsequently harmonised and systematised only in a purely arbitrary way. Any description of what is implied in these ways of expressing the Christ-event, this continual deepening of insight into the faith, will only be able to touch on one aspect of this complex reality and therefore can never be fully satisfactory. They may, perhaps, best be understood as comprehensive ex-

pressions set against the background and the changing horizon of a Christian mission of preaching which was forever moving forward into new milieux. It would be quite irrelevant and inappropriate to make comparisons between the various writings of the New Testament—Mark, John, the Letter to the Hebrews, for example—with respect to the excellence of their presentation of the Christ-event. Each one is in its way unique and evades any such classification. Each one has its own unique way of expressing itself. In this respect no one can take the place of another. In keeping with their different approaches to the understanding of the Christ-event, any one New Testament author can communicate to the right kind of reader all that the Christ-event means to him. Moreover, it would be difficult to think of a more impressive witness to the inner dynamic and the ability to fit every situation characteristic of early Christian preaching than the process we have been describing.

The New Testament cult takes up the Jesus of history into the now exalted Christ who is the high priest (Heb 5; 7; and 8), the mediator of the covenant (Heb 8:6; 9:15; 12:24), who offered himself for a sacrifice and that 'once for all' (Heb 7:27; 9:28; 10:12, 14). In this way the thinking and imagery associated with Old Testament cult are put to use in the service of the Christ-event and New Testament cult is seen to be the eschatological fulfilment of the expectation implicit in that of the Old Testament. The total self-giving of Jesus unto death is the object of continuing theological reflection which works out the universal significance of the Christ-event and emphasises its unique and definitive character. The universal significance of the event is seen above all in connection with the idea of vicarious expiation (Rom 4:25; 8:32; Eph 5:2; 1 Tim 2:6) and in dependence on Is 53. And if the self-offering of Jesus is the true, final, and all-surpassing sacrifice of atonement and of the new covenant, whereas the former sacrifices appear now only as shadows and types, then it must follow that Jesus is himself the true lamb of sacrifice (Jn 1:29, 36; 1 Pet 1:19).

III. *The various forms of New Testament worship.* Seen from our point of view, the Christ-event is an event for *us*, not just an event in itself—it is something in which we participate. This participation is brought about and manifested in the various forms of worship which must, however, in being directed to the totality of human life, lay claim to different dimensions which neither require nor allow for any facile harmonisation. We must therefore beware of schematising New Testament worship in a light-hearted kind of way and of a too easy appraisal of the quality of the various forms it takes.

The 'place' in which this worship is carried out is basically and incontrovertibly the entire life of the believing christian. Leaving aside other purposes which the author may have had in mind, this fact is set out in a doctrinal and programmatic way in the Letter to the Romans which, to judge by the salutation, was addressed to the community in the capital of the Roman Empire. The fact that the Roman community was not founded by Paul gives added strength to the claim of teaching a *doctrine* which had binding force rather than a mere series of edifying admonitions. Also, Paul uses the strongest means at his disposal, both stylistically and theologically, this is most apparent in those passages (Rom 12; 14; and 15) where we find a transposition of the terminology and representations associated with sacrifice and cult to the totality of the life of the believer.

On the basis of this radicalisation of Old Testament cultic ideas we are to understand that the only temple is now the community of those who believe (1 Cor 3:16f; 6:19; 2 Cor 6:16; Eph 2:20-2). The community offers sacrifices and is itself a sacrificial offering (Rom 12:1; 15:16; see also the offering of the firstfruits, 2 Thess 2:13; 1 Cor 16:15; Rom 16:5) and is a holy and royal priesthood (1 Pet 2:5, 9). Paul understands his work of spreading the gospel as sacrificial (Rom 15:15f). Within these comprehensive statements which indicate the end of the old cultic order and nothing less than the complete dissolution of the cultic thinking which was determined by it, there is room for a whole series of actions, attitudes, and points of view which can be regarded as genuine acts of cult, such as acts of love (which is true piety, Jas 1:27) and internal detachment from the world which does not think and act in accord with the divine will (also thought of in terms of piety in Jas 1:27). Finally we arrive at the point of the total offering of one's life (Phil 2:17; Rev 6:9). Prayer may also be regarded as an act of true worship (Acts 13:3; Heb 13:15).

We should not make the mistake of wanting to build up a fixed system of these different forms and acts of christian worship; their number remains open and can be augmented in response to new requirements which may arise. Only one thing remains constant, and that is love (1 Cor 13), for the property of love is to guarantee openness to all possible needs and insights. Finally, the community was consoled at a time when persecution threatened by the thought of the heavenly liturgy (Rev 5; 7; 11; 12; 14; 19).

The fact that the locus of the New Testament cultic reality is the entire life of the believing christian corresponds to a basic datum of the experience of man who lives as an individual in the human community to the extent that the existential reality of community is the locus of the cultic reality of the New Testament. However we may look at it, individual and community are inseparably related, and this is true also for the theme which we are discussing.

That the community is the locus where this new cultic reality is realised is seen clearly in the christian cultic assembly which takes shape around the service of the word and the common meal. The gradual development of these forms of worship arises from an inner necessity of human togetherness and corresponds to the requirement of love and care for the neighbour, the brother. In itself, therefore, it in no way implies a concession to superseded forms of cult which tend to re-emerge, even though it is not immune to a relapse into such forms in its understanding of what it is doing. Initiation into the community takes place in baptism and follows on the faith of the one to be baptised (Acts 8:37 is a later and demonstrably stylised interpretation of baptism while recording faithfully one actual case of baptism).

Baptism was already *there* before Paul came on the scene: in his letters it is self-evident that all who believe must be baptised (1 Cor 12:13; Rom 6:3). But even though the sacramental character of baptism is presupposed, there is an emphatic attempt to get rid of false interpretations of baptism as merely a cultic and ritual action (1 Cor 10:1-13).

In the context of the history of the early church, the service of the word—which it is practically impossible for us to reconstruct—must be seen as taking different forms according to the circumstances and must not be separated from the celebration of the eucharist. It was thought of as having its distinct quality through the presence of the Spirit of the risen and exalted Lord. It was composed of scripture reading and interpretation, confessional formulae, the singing or reciting of psalms, hymns, and canticles. It also could include speaking with tongues, acclamations, prayers, and intercession (see 1 Cor 14).

In addition to the service of the word the celebration of the eucharist was also the 'locus' of this new cult-reality of the New Testament. In fact this was true of the eucharist in a unique way in so far as the Christ-event was made present in it in a more palpable way by the proclamation of the salvific death of Jesus, the confirmation of the eternal covenant and the participation of those present in the eschatological meal of fellowship. Understood in this way, it was an invitation and an appeal to the believing community to realise this new cultic reality in practice. In all of this the determinative character of the word was not lost. In terms of the New

Testament understanding of cult it would be the height of folly to set the service of the word over against the eucharist, to play off one against the other or to suppose that the Christ-event was *more* present and active in one than in the other. Basic to both is the one whole and entire Christ-event. Having said this, however, we must add that it is entirely legitimate to attempt to grasp the unique dimension of the eucharistic meal as opening up to man in the totality of his existential reality the experience of the pledge implicit in saving history in terms of objective and bodily reality.

From this understanding of the Christ-event as the new cultic reality and the ways in which it is realised are derived the different ministries mentioned in the New Testament. These are always understood primarily in view of the event-character of the word (apostles, prophets, teachers, but also church leaders) and also comprise the sacramental event insofar as this calls for human ministry. Yet the idea of a distinct personnel qualified only for cultic actions has always been alien to New Testament thinking; it belongs rather to the cultic order of paganism or that of the Old Testament which had now been superseded. This is not contradicted by the understanding of the eucharist as a sacrificial meal which is attested in the New Testament (Mk 14:24; Mt 26:28).

The inadequacy of any attempt to describe what is implied in the new experience of the cultic in the New Testament comes through with particular clarity in the fact that it is practically impossible to give a satisfactory account of the fundamental difference between the content of this new cultic reality and other ways of understanding the cultic, while at the same time doing justice to the concepts which we have at our disposal and preserving the distinct and unique element in New Testament cult. The clear and unambiguous uniqueness and apartness of the reality which constitutes New Testament worship must be established not only with regard to the past, that is, to the cultural and spiritual environment of the New Testament, but also to the present, since here too it must be protected as far as possible from misunderstandings. If we remain insufficiently conscious of the impossibility of fitting New Testament cult into any general pattern it will be very difficult to avoid the danger of thinking of it as simply a new experience and form of worship which supersedes others. And once it is thought of in this way, it could easily happen that a wrongly understood idea and practice of worship supposedly based on New Testament principles could produce once again just those accretions against which Jesus and Paul, to mention no others, had so radically protested.

It would certainly be wrong to overlook the fact that we find in the New Testament writings a primitive christian experience and consciousness with regard to worship which set them apart from other areas of living as, for example, from the experience of living with non-believers. Yet acts of cult, in particular the 'sacraments' of baptism and the eucharist, could not, in New Testament thinking, become independent entities, and therefore there could not be a serious conflict of duties between worship and other aspects of life since cultic duties of a kind which could conflict with other duties simply did not exist. This is a conclusion which is presupposed in all the New Testament writings without exception, despite their great diversity, and one the significance of which it is still impossible to exaggerate. (↗ Prayer ↗ Sacrifice ↗ Priesthood).

Bibliography: H. Menschkewitz, *Die Spiritualisierung der Kultusbegriffe Tempel, Priester und Opfer im Neuen Testament*, Leipzig 1932; J. M. Nielen, *Gebet und Gottesdienst im Neuen Testament*, Freiburg im Br., 1937; E. Lohmeyer, *Kultus und Evangelium*, Göttingen 1942; P. Seidensticker, *Lebendiges Opfer*, Münster 1954; Y. Congar, *The Mystery of the Temple*, London 1960; H. Schlier, 'Die Verkündigung im Gottesdienst der Kirche', *Die Zeit der Kirche*, Freiburg 1959², 244–64; A. Vögtle, 'Der Einzelne und die Gemeinschaft in der Stufenfolge der Christusoffenbarung', *Sentire Ecclesiam* (Hugo Rahner Vol.), Freiburg 1961, 50–91; G. Lanczkowski, H. Haag, H. Schurmann, 'Kult', *LTK* vi², 659–65; L. Bouyer, *Rite and Man*, South Bend (Indiana) 1963; O. Cullmann, *Early Christian Worship*, London 1956; R. de Vaux, *Les Sacrifices de l'Ancien Testament*, Paris 1964; *J. Smith, *A Priest for Ever: A Study of Typology and Eschatology in Hebrews*, London 1969.

Odilo Kaiser

Cup

The Greek *potērion*, which in LXX translates the Hebrew *khôs*, means a drinking vessel made out of stone, earth or metal. We find earthenware drinking vessels (bowl-shaped with stands) as early as the Middle Bronze period (*BRL*, 316f) and a chalice in the true sense of the term, together with its stand, on Maccabean coins.

The word is used in different ways in the New Testament. We refer first of all to the relevant texts:

A. *Cup in the proper sense of the term*, as the drinking vessel in daily use among the people, is mentioned in Mk 9:41 (see also Mt 10:42) and Mt 23:25f (see also Lk 11:39–41).

B. *In the metaphorical sense* it refers either to the cup of suffering or the cup of wrath.

1. *The cup of suffering.* The Saviour refers to this in his question addressed to the sons of Zebedee (Mk 10:38–9; see also Mt 20:22–3): 'Are you able to drink the cup that I drink?'. He is asking in effect whether these apostles are prepared to take on themselves the destiny of suffering, namely martyrdom, which he had proclaimed in advance. The cup of suffering appears as a symbol of martyrdom also in early christian writing outside the New Testament, eg, in the Martyrdom of Polycarp (14:2).

In the prayer of Jesus in the garden of Gethsemane the cup which he asks will pass from him or be taken from him (Mk 14:36; see also Mt 26:39, 42; Lk 22:42) refers to the suffering and death for which he is destined. The metaphor of the chalice offered by God symbolises elsewhere in the bible the happy (Ps 16:5; 23:5) or bitter (Ps 11:6; 75:8) destiny reserved for the individual or the people as a whole. It derives no doubt from the Jewish custom of each guest being handed a cup filled with wine by the head of the family (sharing in the cup).

2. *The chalice of wrath.* The image of the chalice in the hand of God which is filled with his anger or the wine of his wrath and which is given to the nations to drink occurs frequently over a long period of time in the Old Testament. We find it most often in the prophetic oracles of doom, as in Jer 25:1'f;

Hab 2:15; Is 51:17; Ps 75:8; see also
Ezek 23:33. On account of its intoxi-
cating effect it is sometimes called 'the
bowl of staggering' (Is 51:17; Ps 60:3).
This highly poetical figure could also
derive ultimately from the idea of
sharing in the cup passed round at a
banquet. Some, however, think in
terms of a mythological origin, and
refer to Babylonian representations of a
cup or bowl held by the gods from
which is poured the water of life. In
this case the cup would symbolise the
fact that the determination of human
destiny pertains to them (Goppelt, 152
n. 32). In the Old Testament the
determination of destiny is associated
with the will of a personal God; hence
the cup of destiny becomes the cup of
judgement, a symbol of 'the power of
God as judge in human history, his
right to judge'. Whether the agent is
God himself or someone commissioned
to act for him, the offering of this cup
signifies condemnation, and drinking
from it subjection to the judgement and
punishment of God.

In the *New Testament* we come upon
this metaphor of the chalice of wrath
only in the Book of Revelation, which
is here clearly influenced by the Old
Testament. The whore of Babylon
holds in her hand a golden chalice full
of abominations and the impurities of
her fornications (Rev 17:4; see also
Jer 51:7). The reference is to the power
of perversion exercised on the nations
by the world-wide empire of Rome.
Blinded by the allure of its power,
riches and luxury they are led to take
up the idolatry and immorality current
in 'Babylon' and so drink 'the wine of
her impure passion', as the contents of
the cup are elsewhere described (Rev

18:3; see also 14:8). In reality it is God
himself who offers the peoples this cup
of wrath since it is he who has given
Babylon the power to deceive them
(13:5). The cup in the hand of the
scarlet woman makes it quite clear that
the Roman Empire is the means by
which God's anger is visited upon the
world.

Yet this same world-power which has
intoxicated the nations with the wine of
its fornication (14:8) will suffer retribution and be paid back in kind for
what it has visited upon others. Now it
will be the nations themselves who will
act as instruments of the divine wrath
and mix a double draught for Babylon
in the cup she mixed (18:6). A particularly hard punishment is often
represented in the bible as a double
punishment (see Jer 16:18; 17:18; Is
40:2); it is in this way that the cup of
the divine anger will be offered to the
great city of Babylon (Rev 16:19).

Finally, every single person who
allows himself to be led into idolatry by
worshipping the anti-Christian world-
power as if it were divine will have to
drink of the wine of God's wrath which
is prepared unmixed in the cup (Rev
14:9f). This will be when God will
proceed to the final judgement and his
anger will consign all idolaters to
eternal damnation (14:11).

C. *The chalice at the last supper.* 1. *The
first cup.* At the outset of the last supper,
which—according to the view of most
exegetes—must be understood in the
context of a passover meal, Jesus took a
cup filled with wine, recited the prayer
of thanksgiving over it, and gave it to
his disciples to drink (Mk 14:25; see
also Lk 22:17b). This is not the
eucharistic cup over which Jesus spoke

the words of institution but the first of the four cups of wine drunk at the passover meal. This emerges clearly from the words which accompany the action as found in the following verse of Luke: 'from now on I shall not drink of the fruit of the vine until the kingdom of God comes' (Lk 22:18; see also Mt 26:29; Mk 14:25).* In the kingdom of God the passover, which Jesus was celebrating for the last time with his disciples, would find its fulfilment and completion. This eschatological saying of Jesus is based on the prayer of praise and thanksgiving which the father of the family pronounced over the first cup before the breaking of bread. This prayer runs as follows: 'blessed art thou Lord our God, king of the universe, thou who hast created the fruit of the vine' (SB IV, 61f). The Lukan account which puts vv 15–18 before the actual words of institution (which are spoken by Christ over the third cup) is clearer and fuller than that of Mark, in which the eschatological saying and the words of consecration are not clearly distinguished.

2. *The eucharistic cup* (Mk 14:23; see also Mt 26:27; Lk 22:20; 1 Cor 10:16). Paul calls this cup 'the cup of blessing' (1 Cor 10:16), a technical term taken from the usage governing Jewish meals. At every meal during which wine was drunk the head of the family pronounced in the name of all present the prayer of thanksgiving over the cup filled with wine which he raised in his hands. This took place after the main course was finished. On the occasion of the Lord's passover, this was the third of the four cups of wine commonly drunk during this meal. The account found in the synoptics and in Paul of the consecration of the chalice at the last supper is connected with this custom. After the meal was over (Lk 22:20; 1 Cor 11:25) Jesus took the chalice, 'gave thanks' (*eukharistēsas*, Mk 14:23; see also Mt 26:27), spoke over it the words of institution and passed it around the company of the disciples without tasting it himself—as would normally be the case.

D. *The chalice of the Lord and of demons.* In 1 Cor 10:16–22 Paul speaks of the eucharistic cup of blessing: 'The cup of blessing which *we* bless, is it not a participation on the blood of Christ?' By using this emphatic language he wishes to contrast the eucharistic christian cup with the cup of blessing in use during a Jewish meal. His statement presupposes that this cup gives to those who drink of it a share in the blood of Christ and brings them into a living communion with him. It is 'the cup of the Lord' (1 Cor 10:21) which is contrasted in what follows with the chalice of demons. What Paul means is that it is impossible for the christian to drink from both chalices. By saying this he is showing himself to be decisively opposed to christians taking part in pagan cultic meals involving the worship of false gods. On these occasions a drink-offering was made to the deity from the cup. In opposing these practices Paul follows the Old Testament view that any sacrifice which was not offered to Yahweh must be offered to demons (see Deut 32:17, 37f); hence any cup in pagan sacrificial meals could be called the chalice of demons. This by no means implies that he is contradicting his earlier statement about the non-existence of idols (1 Cor 8:4);

he is only emphasising that in reality pagans do offer sacrifice to demons (1 Cor 10:20). He thereby expresses a belief in the existence not of gods but of demons. Who therefore drinks of this chalice of the pagans places himself in the power of demons and cuts himself off from communion with the Lord. For it is impossible to be at the same time in table-fellowship with Christ and with demons.

Bibliography: Haag, 168; E. Kalt, *BRL* I, Paderborn 1937, 207; D. Forstner OSB, *Die Welt der Symbole*, Innsbruck 1961, 552f; F. J. Dölger, 'Der Kelch der Dämonen', *Antike und Christentum* IV, 266–70; L. Goppelt, *TDNT* VI, 148–58 and Büchsel III, 168, 13f; Stählin V, 438, 17f.

Jakob Obersteiner

Curse

A. *Terminology*. The Hebrew language has several expressions which correspond, more or less, to the English *to curse* or *a curse*.

1. *'Alâh* is (a) a curse which the owner pronounces aloud and publicly, when he finds he has lost something, against the thief, dishonest finder, or receiver of the property, with the purpose of inducing the person responsible to give the lost object back (Lev 5:1; Judg 17:2; Prov 29:24); (b) a conditional curse upon oneself to corroborate a promise or an agreement, sometimes to back up an oath (Num 5:21; 1 Kings 8:31; 2 Chron 6:22; Gen 24:41; 1 Sam 14:24; Neh 10:29; Gen 26:28; Ezek 17:13, 16, 18; perjury, therefore, is known simply as *'alâh*: Ps 10:7; 59:12; Job 31:30; Hos 4:2, or *'alôth šâw*: Hos 10:4); (c) a curse added by a human or divine legislator to a legal code, also to the Code of the Alliance, as a sanction in the case of infraction of the law (Deut 29:19f; Is 24:6; Jer 23:10; Ezek 16:59; 17:19; 2 Chron 34:24). An *'alâh* can be directed only against equals, inferiors or one's own person, never against superiors or against God.

2. Formations from the root *'ārar*: in *qal, piel,* and the noun *me'ērâh.* A curse indicated in this way arises from a specific formula, is connected with certain rites, and serves to render enemies and the wicked powerless to harm. The shortest of these curse-formulae goes: *'ārûr* [cursed] be N.N.!' As a result, according to the idea of the ancient Near East, happiness and blessing would be destroyed in the one so cursed and evil released upon him. At the same time, the person who pronounces the curse announces that he is breaking off all association with the one cursed. Even inanimate objects can be cursed in this way, and will henceforth bring disaster and bad fortune on those who use them. Such curse formulae could also be abused by people for magical ends since sinister powers were attributed to them (Num 22:6; 23:7; Job 3:8). But they could also be used by those who were legitimately members or functionaries within the community, in order to dissociate themselves from evildoers. Thus a father could cast a curse-formula of this kind upon a badly-disposed son (Gen 9:25; 49:7), or the divinely appointed leader of the people against lawbreakers and evildoers (Deut 28:16–19; Josh 6:26; 9:23; 1 Sam 14:24, 28); or the whole people gathered together against members who had ignored a decision made in

common or violated the Covenant law, which was incumbent on the whole people (Judg 21:18; Deut 27:15–26); or God himself against seducers (Gen 3:14), murderers (Gen 4:11), adversaries of the one chosen by him (Gen 12:3; 27:29; Num 24:9) and the land on account of sinners who live in it or cultivate it (Gen 3:17; 5:29). The destructive power emanating from such a curse burdens the one so cursed with an evil fate and finally brings him to utter ruin, unless its course is checked by God. It is called *me̅ērâh* (Deut 28:20; Mal 2:2; Prov 3:33; 28:27).

As a means of imposing trial by ordeal on a woman suspected of marital infidelity, a curse was written on the surface of some writing material; this was washed off with water and the water given to the woman to drink. In the event of her being guilty the curse would produce fatal illness in her, but if innocent it would remain without effect. This water was called 'the water that brings the curse' (Num 5:18–27). A curse-formula with *ᵓārar* can never be directed against God.

3. The most common expression for 'curse' is the root *qll*, usually in *piel* or in the form of a noun, *qᵉlālâh*. According to its etymology, its real meaning in *piel* would be 'to make small of', 'to deal with contemptuously' and therefore also 'to mock', 'to make ridiculous'. Since people in antiquity attributed a very real efficacy to the spoken word, they believed that scoffing at any given person really aroused destructive powers and could diminish his happiness. Hence David calls the mocking directed against him by Shimei a *qᵉlālâh nimretseth* = 'dangerous mocking' (1 Kings 2:8). It is for this reason that

qallēl can have the meaning 'to curse', though it is a question here not of a curse with determined formulae and rites but rather of an indeterminate execration, mocking, cursing or slandering. It is therefore not always possible to translate *qll* and its derivates as 'to curse', 'a curse', etc. In order to determine the meaning, we have to note the following contexts: (a) Against the king. Here *qallēl* refers not so much to a curse as to the act of condemning, slighting the king, therefore an act of *lèse-majesté* which comes near to rebellion (Judg 9:27; 2 Sam 16:5, 7, 9–13; 19:22; 1 Kings 2:8). (b) Against parents. *Qallēl* refers here to the refusal of obedience and the undermining of parental authority; this threatens the structure of patriarchal society and so is punishable by death (Ex 21:17; Lev 20:9; Prov 20:20; 30:11). (c) Against God. In this case *qallēl* refers to the attitude of a person who has become disillusioned with God, who no longer takes him seriously, abuses him and tries his luck with other gods—therefore blasphemy (Lev 24:11, 14f, 23; in 1 Kings 21:10, 13 and Job 1:5, 11; 2:5, 9, we have also to read *qll* instead of the euphemism ↗ 'bless'). The sons of Eli by their unworthy conduct incurred the guilt of 'making light' of God (1 Sam 3:13), and we have a good example of how such a *qᵉlālâh* works out in practice in the abusive language used by the Rabshakeh against Yahweh (2 Kings 18:30–5) and in Is 10:8–11. (d) Against other given persons. Here, too, we can easily recognise the basic meaning of 'making light' of someone. Just like the heroes of the Homeric poems with regard to their opponents, Goliath sets out to 'make light' of the

Israelites, and in particular David, by means of wordy and high sounding insults (1 Sam 17:43f). When this kind of slighting of an opponent takes the form of execration we have a form similar to the curse (Gen 8:21; Deut 23:5; Josh 24:9; Jer 15:10; Ps 37:22; 62:4; Prov 30:10; Neh 13:2, 25 etc).

4. *qbb* and *nqb* also have the primary meaning of insulting, abusing, and therefore blaspheming when they have God for object (Lev 24:11, 16). When persons or things are object there can be present here also the idea of a 'curse' (Num 22:11, 17; 23:8, 11, 13, 25, 27; 24:10; Job 3:8; 5:3; Prov 11:26; 24:24).

5. The Hebrew verb *zāʿam* really means 'to threaten' or the like (Is 10:5, 25; Jer 10:10; Ps 7:12 etc). But a threat can be equivalent to a curse, especially when pronounced by God (Num 23:7f; Mal 1:4; Prov 24:24).

6. The nouns *ʾālâh* and *qelālâh*, as used in the expressions 'to make cursed', 'to become a curse'. When a curse has had devastating effect on a person, a city or a country, then these same are said to be 'a curse' (Num 5:21-7; Deut 21:23; 2 Kings 22:19; Jer 24:9; 25:18; 26:6; 29:18, 22; 42:18; 44:8, 12, 22; 49:13; Zech 8:13; similarly Is 65:15, 'an imprecation'). The precise meaning of this type of expression is disputed, but, on the basis of Is 65:15 and Jer 29:22, the most likely interpretation would be that the person or thing in question is in such a fearful condition that his or its fate is taken proverbially for a curse—that is, when anyone desires to curse another person or pronounce a conditional curse upon himself when making an oath he says, 'May you [I] become as that person!'

or 'May it happen to you [to me] as to that person or city!'

In the LXX and New Testament *ara* with its derivatives generally corresponds to the Hebrew terms in 1-4, and sometimes to 5. There occurs also *orismos* for 1, and for 3 *katalogein* or, when God is the object, *blasphēmein*.

B. *The curse in the Old Testament.* As with other peoples in antiquity, so in Israel the curse is connected with the belief in the power of the spoken word. In the ancient Near East curses serve as a defence against enemies, to prevent inscriptions and documents from being falsified, or sacred buildings and graves from being profaned, and as a sanction for contracts and laws. The belief was that the evildoer or the person acting in defiance of the curse would be totally ruined, and with him his whole family and descendants.

Since in Israel God was the guardian of order and supreme lawgiver, the Old Testament ascribes the efficacy of a curse inflicted by him or in his name directly to him, and looks to him also to bring to pass the adversity mentioned in the curse. The degree of efficacy of the curse depends on the proximity of the one cursing to God, the heinousness of the outrage, or the importance of what is defended by the curse. Formal curses or threats of ruin which are equivalent to a curse can be found in the Old Testament in the mouth of patriarchs (Gen 9:25; 49:3-7), men of God (Josh 6:26; 1 Sam 15:26; 2 Sam 12:11f; 2 Kings 5:27), kings (1 Sam 14:24; 2 Sam 3:29f), but also of ordinary pious people in their clashes with their own personal adversaries (in the cursing psalms: 5:10; 6:10; 7:10-16; 10:15; 28:4; 31:17f; 35:4ff; 40:15;

54:7; 58:7–11; 69:23–9; 109:6–19; 139:19; 140:9–12; 141:10; 143:12), or of the community as against the national enemies (Ps 79:6, 12; 83:10–19; 129:5–8; 137:7ff). Cursing the king is expressly forbidden (Ex 22:28).

We ought not to judge the curse in the Old Testament according to our present-day moral and religious sensitivity, but rather attempt to understand it within the context of the situation which then prevailed. The rule of law was not yet guaranteed by the existence of a system of justice which really worked, or of a police force, so that it was possible only in a few cases to discover the criminal and make good the damage done. Rulers and conquerors in battle were not in any way bound by law; but even the transgressor, the warrior, the conqueror and the ruler lived in fear of the hostility of numinous powers and of the curse. And so Israel could not dispense with the curse as a means of defence against evildoers and enemies. God made use of this means in favour of his people and his faithful servants, as a sanction for the law of the alliance which he had granted to them, and as a punishment for evildoers (Gen 3:14, 17; 4:11; 12:3; 27:29; Lev 26; Num 24:9; Deut 28:15–68; 1 Sam 2:30–6; etc). The people of the alliance and its functionaries act in a corresponding way when they dissociate themselves from evildoers (Deut 27:15–26). The vision of the flying scroll inscribed with curses against all kinds of evildoers (Zech 5:2ff) expresses the manner in which the Old Testament believes in the immanent sanction of the moral law: God has so instituted the moral order that any infringement of it works out ill for the transgressor in the form of a curse.

When a good man pronounces a curse against an ↗ enemy or a reprobate he thereby calls on God as defender of the right and prays him to apply the sanctions which he has assigned. The curse in the Old Testament, in distinction to the rest of the ancient Near East, is not a magical tool which can be used to compel the deity to intervene, but rather a prayer addressed to God. An irregular curse recoils on the one making it (Ps 10:7–15; 109:16–19). God can turn an irregular curse into a blessing (2 Sam 16:12; Ps 109:28; cf the Oracles of Balaam and Deut 23:5; Neh 13:2). A pointless or irregular curse is 'like a sparrow in its flitting, like a swallow in its flying' (Prov 26:2), namely, without effect. The blessing, too, is no magical force which brings about good fortune necessarily and in all circumstances. If a person does not deserve it God can also turn it into a curse (Mal 2:2; see also 1 Sam 2:30).

We must be careful not to take the individual expressions, which we usually understand as curses, out of their context. At the same time certain curses here and there do appear to be unalterable and to exercise a fateful influence also on the posterity of the one cursed. But here it is not a question of punishing the innocent posterity but the evildoer in question against whom the curse is directed, understood according to the basic concept of a 'punishment on the father'. In other words, the evildoer in such cases is affected in a particularly hard way, insofar as his family is ruined and his 'name and seed' is taken from him (Ps 109:6–14; 2 Sam 3:29f; 1 Kings

14:8–11; 16:2ff; 21:19–24). This idea was based on the fact of general experience that the children are generally no better than the father. As can be easily understood, the one who cast a curse on his enemy in a highly emotional state would not have reckoned with the possibility of the conversion, either of the one he cursed, or his descendants; but the Old Testament historical outlook does take this possibility into consideration, and so Yahweh removes the curse when the person cursed repents (Deut 4:29ff; 30:1–10; Zech 8:13ff).

Judaism at the time of Christ was familiar with the curse, above all in the form of an anathema which accompanied the expulsion of a transgressor of the Law from the Jewish cultic community (SB IV, 293–333). The rabbis freely resort to curse-formulae if they hear of such a transgressor (SB III, 446). In Qumran, the curse pronounced on the godless takes place within the ritual of the Renewal of the Covenant and at the reception of candidates (I QS II, 4–18).

C. *The curse in the New Testament.* The New Testament is familiar with the conditional self-curse pronounced on the occasion of making a promise confirmed by an oath (Acts 23:12, 14, 21: Jewish fanatics who bound themselves in this way to take Paul's life), or accompanying an oath by which one clears oneself (Mt 26:74; Mk 14:71: Peter protests that he had had nothing to do with Jesus). It is apparent, however, that the curse had to appear in a new light because of the deepened and modified understanding of retribution brought about by the teaching on an after-life and the christian love of neighbour. A curse against one's personal enemies is incompatible with love; the disciples of Jesus bless their enemies instead of cursing them (Lk 6:28; Rom 12:14; see also Jas 3:9–12). At the same time, the New Testament is familiar with the curse retained as a sanction of the divine law and as a means of promoting justice (Mt 25:41; 2 Peter 2:14). The Law of Moses was guaranteed by the sanction of a curse and really brought the curse into effect (Gal 3:10, 13). If the evangelist narrates in Mt 27:25 that those who took part in the condemnation of Jesus called down a curse upon themselves it is evident that he was convinced that the curse was fulfilled in the history of the Jewish people. By means of the cursing of the fig tree (Mt 21:18f; Mk 11:12ff) Jesus showed his determination to pass irrevocable judgement on all those who do not bear 'fruit'. By means of the authority which they had from God, the apostles and the christian community also had the power to deliver over apostate church members and false teachers to a curse (I Cor 5:3ff; 16:22; Gal 1:8), thereby excluding them from the community. Such a curse, however, did not imply eternal damnation; the demonic forces of destruction would have their effect on the one concerned until he was moved through suffering to contrition and conversion and so regained salvation (I Cor 5:5). The only irrevocable curse will be the one Jesus will cast at sinners in the Last Judgement (Mt 25:41).

The meaning of the expression 'Christ having become a curse' (Gal 3:13) is disputed. It certainly does not imply that Christ has become the object of the Father's curse (see O. Kuss, *RNT ad loc*), but rather that Christ has taken upon himself the fate of one who is cursed. According to Is 65:15 and Jer 29:22, one could also give it this explanation: Christ has been overtaken by a terrible affliction similar to that which a man would desire for the one he wanted to curse (see A6 above).

Bibliography: J. Behm, *TDNT* I, 354f; F. Büchsel, *TDNT* I, 448–51; F. Steinmetzer, 'Babylon: Parallelen zu d. Fluchpsalmen', *BZ* 10 (1912), 133–42 and 363–9; J. Pedersen, *Der Eid bei den Semiten*, Strassburg 1914; P. Heinisch, *Das Wort im AT u. im Alten Orient*, Münster 1922; S. Mowinckel, *Segen und Fluch in Israels Kult and Psalmendichtung*, Kristiania 1924; J. Hempel, 'Die israelit. Anschauungen von Segen u. Fluch im Lichte oriental. Parallelen', *ZDMG* 79 (1925), 20–110; T. Canaan, 'The Curse in Palestinian Folklore', *JPOS* 15 (1935), 235–79; S. H. Blank, 'The Curse, the Blasphemy, the Spell, and the Oath', *HUCA* 23 (1950/1), 73–95; J. Scharbert, '"Fluchen" und "Segnen" im AT', *Bbl* 39 (1958), 1–26; J. Scharbert, *Solidarität in Segen und Fluch im AT und in seiner Umwelt*, Bonn 1958; M. Noth, 'Die mit des Gesetzes Werken umgehen, die sind unter dem Fluch', *Gesammelte Studien zum AT*, Munich 1960², 155–71; F. C. Fensham, 'Malediction and Benediction in Ancient Near Eastern Vassal-Treaties and the OT', *ZAW* 74 (1962), 1–9; F. C. Fensham, 'Common Trends in Curses of the Near Eastern Treaties and Kudurru-Inscriptions', *ZAW* 75 (1963), 155–75; H. C. Brichto, *The Problem of 'Curse' in the Hebrew Bible*, Philadelphia 1963; H. A. Brongers, 'Die Rache- und Fluchpsalmen im AT', *OTS* 13 (1963), 21–42; D. R. Hillers, *Treaty Curses and the OT Prophets*, Rome 1964; J. Kiss, 'Der Begriff "Fluch" im NT', *CV* 7 (1964), 87–92.

Josef Scharbert

Day of Yahweh

The form criticism and history-of-tradition methods of investigation require that we do not view the idea of the Day of the Lord in isolation on the basis of the relevant texts taken singly, but rather within the framework of the related field of ideas. Hence, it is not correct to exclude the concept from Amos 5:18–20, as is usually done, on the grounds that it is not present there expressly but is rather presented as a familiar reality—as a result of which this text lends itself to different and even conflicting interpretations. Apart from this, we meet the idea of the Day of the Lord in Is 2:12; 13:6–9; 22:5; 34:8; Jer 46:10; Ezek 7:10; 13:5; 30:3; Joel 1:15; 2:1f, 11, 31; 3:14; Obad, 15; Zeph 1:7f, 14–18; Zech 14:1.

On the basis of Is 13:4; Ezek 7; Joel 2, it follows that the idea of the Day of the Lord stands in relationship with the institution of the holy war, revived in the prophets—an institution which goes back to the early days in Israel (see especially Deut, Josh, Judg, Sam) with reference to the conquest of the Holy Land, brought about by God. In it Yahweh himself takes part in the battle, musters his army, leads it into battle against the enemy who at once lose heart. In accordance with this, the Day of the Lord, in the texts referred to, takes on the character of a battle and a complete victory for Yahweh which is achieved under the dreadful signs of darkness and earthquake. Even the metaphor of the plague of locusts on the Day of the Lord which we find in Joel 2—an accessible image taken from the actual experience of Israel—is part of this tradition and refers to the battle of Yahweh. Zeph 1 has to be understood in a similar way. It follows from this that the Day of the Lord refers first and foremost to a warlike episode in which Yahweh breaks the resistance of his enemies in battle and overcomes them. It should be said further that this idea was not borrowed from the surrounding milieu but is of israelitic origin, from the epoch of the holy war, many episodes of which reach their climax in a theophany.

It is a question, then, in the prophetic texts which speak of the Day of the Lord, of an actualization of old revelational material. The holy war dealt originally with a saving deed of God on behalf of his people. The original element in the prophetic preaching consists in this, that instead of salvation Israel can and will encounter judgement and merited punishment on the Day of the Lord—see Amos 5:18–20. (This text, we might add, should not be interpreted on the basis of a supposed but undemonstrable festival of Yahweh's accession to the throne, as maintained by Mowinckel; in general, Amos gives no grounds for thinking of the Day of the Lord in terms of a festival which was already in existence in his day.) Looked at in this way, the fall of Jerusalem, 586 BC, and also of Samaria, 721 BC, would represent, being historical events, the Day of the Lord actualised in the course of human affairs.

Gradually, however, the representation of the Day of the Lord takes on in the prophetic preaching meta-historical and eschatological characteristics. It belongs, as a basic concept, to the essential elements introduced in the process of eschatologising which went on within the Old Testament development of revelation. This can be recognised above all in the use of the idea in both parts of Joel. If the plague of locusts in Joel 1f is a description of the inexorable judgement of God on an historical enemy, Joel 3f would appear

to be transposed on to an eschatological level, since there the Day of the Lord takes on the characteristics of the final day of judgement, an event of cosmic proportions concerning all nations. The prophets of the post-exilic period announce that the holy remnant will be saved from judgement (see Obad, 15–21; Joel 3:20f). In accordance with this, the Day of the Lord does not imply a total and definitive annihilation but rather, for the holy remnant at least, a passage through to a new eschatological future in which God will cherish Israel in a special way.

The idea of the Day of the Lord passed into Jewish apocalyptic as the day of judgement. Bar (Syr) 48, 47; 49:2 calls it 'thy day' (=the Day of God); 2 Eschas 13:52 'the day of my son'; Enoch (Eth) 61:5 'the day of the Chosen One [the Servant]'.

It has an even more significant role in the New Testament than in the apocalyptic literature. 2 Pet 3:12 and Rev 16:14 depend, in content and terminology, on the Old-Testament presentation. The announcement in Lk 17:24 of the final appearance of the Son of Man in his glory derives from the same presentation. In Jn 8:56 Christ speaks of his day as the day of the ultimate revelation of his glory.

It is above all in Paul that the Day of the Lord, now changed to the Day of Jesus Christ, stands for the day of the judgement of the world in which Christ appears and acts as judge, eg, 1 Cor 1:8; 2 Cor 1:14; 1 Thess 5:2; 2 Thess 2:2; Phil 1:6, 10; 2:16; Heb 10:25.

The concept of the Day of the Lord is therefore one of the leading ideas in the Old and the New Testament which express and embody the eschatological tension and expectation of the future within revelation. It signifies, at different stages of the development of revelation, a decisive incision in the course of history made by God in order to bring his plan of salvation to a more compact and intense reality, while, on the day itself, he both holds judgement according to merit and inflicts punishment where it has been incurred, and at the same time confers on his own the salvation reserved for them. Understood in this way, the Day of the Lord has enough depth of meaning and elasticity both to express the final judgement and to indicate the inauguration of the eschatological age of salvation which coincides with the definite appearance of the kingdom of God.

Bibliography: G. von Rad and Delling, *TDNT* II, 943–53; L. Černy, *The Day of Yahweh and some Relevant Problems*, Prague 1948; R. Pautrel, *DB(S)* IV, 1321–44; B. J. Alfrink, Haag 1580–82; H. H. Rowley, 'The Day of the Lord', *The Faith of Israel*, London 1956, 177–201; S. Mowinckel, 'Jahves dag', *NTT* 59 (1958), 1–56; J. Bourke, 'Le Jour de Yahvé dans Joël', *RB* 66 (1959), 5–31 and 191–212; G. von Rad II, 119–25; G. von Rad, 'The Origin of the Concept of the Day of Yahweh', *JSS* 4 (1959), 77–108.

Heinrich Gross

Death

Death is the common lot of men (Josh 23:14; 1 Kings 2:2; Eccles 9:5; 12:7). All men must die (Sir 14:17), 'We must all die, we are like water spilt on the ground' (2 Sam 14:14)—this is the basic attitude of the Old Testament. Death was taken as an inevitable

necessity, and people considered themselves fortunate if they could die 'old and full of days' (Gen 25:8; 2 Chron 24:15) 'at a good old age' (Gen 15:15; Judg 8:32). In the New Testament, likewise, the fact that men were destined to die was taken for granted (Heb 9:27; Jn 6:49, 58; 8:52f; Heb 7:8). Only the living God is immortal (Deut 5:23; 1 Tim 6:16). Man lives in the fear of death (Sir 40:2; Heb 2:15), which would be thought of as desirable, at the most, only in the last age (Lk 23:30). Death is never glorified, not even by Christ and the apostles (2 Cor 4:11f; Rev 2:10; 12:11).

The scriptures do not contain reflections on the details of death as a physiological process. The separation of soul and body (in the modern sense) is never clearly presented as *the cause* of death, even if it is commonly stated, in accord with external appearances, that 'God takes back the breath of life' (Job 34:14; Ps 104:29; Eccles 12:7; see also Gen 2:7). In a similar way, the New Testament speaks of giving up the spirit (Mt 27:50; Lk 23:46; Jn 19:30), or the soul (Jn 10:11, 15, 17; 13:37; 15:13). As one gets older one sees death as something in the nature of things (Ps 90:10). A sudden or premature death is the result of the divine anger (Job 15:32; Ps 55:23; 90:7; Eccles 7:17.) No-one knows the hour of his death (Lk 12:16ff).

God is the absolute lord over ↗ life and death. 'He has established the number of his [man's] months and the bounds which he cannot pass' (1 Sam 2:6; Job 14:5). Death evidently had no part in God's original plan of creation (Gen 2:17)—on the contrary, death even appears as an evil power in opposition to God (1 Cor 15:26; Rev 6:8; 20:12f) which is subject to the empire of Satan (Heb 2:14).

Already in Wis 2:24 the necessity of death is ascribed to the envy of the devil, with reference certainly to the history of the Fall, in which death was threatened as a punishment for neglecting the divine command (Gen 2:17; cf Sir 25:24). The idea that death was a punishment must also be the reason why it rendered unclean (Num 9:6; 19:16; Deut 21:23). Apart from this, death is simply taken in the Old Testament as the inevitable destiny of mankind. An early or sudden death was often taken as a punishment for personal sins (Num 27:3; Ps 55:23; Prov 2:18; Sir 21:2f; Jer 6:11), but was not necessarily this (Is 57:1f; Wis 4:7–15). Before man 'are death and life and whichever he chooses will be given to him' (Sir 15:17). Life and death are in parallelism with good and evil, blessing and curse (Deut 28:15–20; Jer 21:8). In Paul the causal relationship existing between sin and death is quite clear; the latter is the result of, and punishment for, the former; it is 'the wages of sin' (Rom 6:23; 1 Cor 15:56). Death came into the world through Adam's sin (Rom 5:15; 1 Cor 15:21f).

Existence after death, as described in the Old Testament, is a comfortless affair. There is no doubt about the fate of the body: it falls away into dust and will be food for worms (Job 34:15; Sir 19:3). The burial of the dead is a sacred duty (2 Sam 21:12ff; 1 Kings 13:29f), and it is a terrible thing not to be buried (1 Kings 14:11; 16:4; 21:19ff). Pagan rites in connection with the dead were ruled out (Lev 19:28;

Deut 14:1f), and there was no attempt to get in touch with the dead (Lev 19:31; 20:6, 27; Deut 18:11; 1 Sam 28). Sadness reigned in the world of the dead (Deut 34:8). Apart from 2 Macc 12:38–46 there is no mention of prayers or sacrifices on their behalf. Cremation was considered as dishonourable (Josh 7:25; 1 Kings 13:2).

For the religious man of the Old Testament, however, *death was not the end of all* (↗ Resurrection). If Job complains (7:8): 'while thy eyes are upon me, I shall be gone', this does not imply the end of existence but the end of life conceived of as activity, for he continues: 'as the cloud fades and vanishes, so he who goes down to the Sheol does not come up' (7:9). The dead man is gathered to his fathers (Gen 15:15; 49:33), an expression which can best be explained with reference to the family grave (1 Kings 13:22; Gen 49:29; 2 Sam 21:14). He arrives at the place where the dead are gathered together (Job 30:23), which is in a dark pit (10:21) beneath the waters (26:5). In the description of this underworld, *š^{e}ôl,* (↗ Hell) sombre representations of little comfort predominate. It is referred to, flatly, as destruction (Job 26:6; 28:22; Prov 15:11). It would appear also, according to the original representation, that the dead man was separated from God (Ps 88:5). At any rate, the tongue of the dead can no longer praise God. (Ps 6:5; 88:10ff; 115:17; Sir 17:27f). It is difficult to determine how Yahweh is connected with *š^{e}ôl* (see Is 38:11, 18f), but it is subjected to him in the end, since the reach of his power knows no limits (Amos 9:2; Ps 139:8).

The Old Testament speaks only very

obscurely of survival after death, full assurance of which came only with the Easter-event. The Israelite could, however, already find some consolation in survival in his descendants (Deut 25:6), since the important thing for him was the continued existence of the people, depositary of the promise (Gen 12:1ff). In the taking up of Enoch (Gen 5:24) and of Elijah (2 Kings 2:11), there appear momentary glimpses of a possible overcoming of death. The hope of the just man remained, even 'in his death' (Prov 14:32), without an explanation if looked at from a this-worldly point of view. The faithful Israelite trusted in God his defender (Job 19:25) that he would not be abandoned, and that the grave would not claim him irrevocably. He already knew that God could, in his omnipotence, snatch him from death (Ps 73:23ff), that he forces death to give up its booty (Is 26:19), that it is he who brings down to the underworld and raises up (1 Sam 2:6). In Daniel we come finally to explicit mention of the general↗ resurrection of the body (Dan 12:2).

The strongest impulse to revise the gloomy picture of death in the Old Testament came from the problem of ↗ retribution (Ps 73:11f, 26). We must be careful, of course, neither to underestimate nor overestimate these texts.

The whole situation changed with the coming of Christ. Through Christ God had destroyed death (Heb 2:14); his victory over death is the great news which the gospel brings (2 Tim 1:10). The belief in the resurrection is a vital part of the New Testament (1 Cor 15). Death is no longer master in his own house, for ever since Christ went down into the underworld (1 Pet 3:19; 4:6) he has in his hands the keys of the kingdom of death (Rev 1:18). As he was dead so is he now living (Rom 8:34; 14:9; 1 Thess 4:14). Christ is the first that death has not been able to detain (Acts 2:24); freely he takes his life back again (Jn 10:18). Death must give up its booty to him (Mt 9:25; Lk 7:14; Jn 11:44), and even has to give way before his disciples (Mt 10:8; Acts 9:40; 20:7–12).

Since Christ himself has died for us (Rom 5:6, 8; 2 Cor 5:14f; Gal 3:13) he has overcome death, that death from which no man is exempt. His death is the model for our dying (Jn 21:19; Acts 21:13; Phil 1:20; 3:10). The faithful christian lives and dies in the Lord (Rom 14:7f); death for him has been overcome in Christ, the firstborn from among the dead (Col 1:18; Rev 1:5; see also Rom 8:38f).

At the same time, death remains the last enemy which must finally be overcome (1 Cor 15:25f; Rev 20:14), for death as the common lot of mankind has not been removed. The three raisings from the dead in the gospels happen as a result of special circumstances (Mk 5:41f; Lk 7:14; Jn 11:44). Describing death as sleep was understood as a euphemism (Mt 9:24; Mk 5:39; Lk 8:52; Jn 11:11f; 1 Cor 15:18)—only, after sleep one wakes up again!

There will be no more death in the consummated↗ Kingdom of God (Is 25:8; Rev 21:4), but our true life is as yet hidden (Col 3:3). For the christian, however, death is no longer a frightening reality (Rom 14:7f) and has lost its sting (1 Cor 15:55ff), since the christian possesses the living hope (1 Pet 1:3f).

Those who die in the Lord (1 Cor 15:18; 1 Thess 4:16), and in particular the martyrs (Rev 14:13), are not thereby separated from him (Rom 8:38f).

Through↗ baptism, which is a copy of the death of Christ (Rom 6:5), the christian unites himself with the death of Christ with whom he is buried but only to rise again (Rom 6:3–11; Col 2:11ff, 20; 2 Tim 2:11; 1 Pet 2:24).

Through the↗ Law sin was aroused and with sin death. The letter of the law kills (2 Cor 3:6); whence the believer is dead to the law (Rom 7:7; Gal 2:19; Col 2:20), and anyone trying to bring the law back into force nullifies the effects of Christ's death (Gal 2:19–21).

Through the imitation of Christ, the life of the christian becomes a *daily dying* (2 Cor 4:7–12; 6:9; 11:23), and he must each day mortify his flesh and its works (Rom 6:11ff; Rom 14). This being dead to sin (Rom 8:10) is carried through by a change of life. In this new life the christian must take part in all seriousness in the proclamation of the Lord's death in the eucharist (1 Cor 11:20ff). He who is living in sin is as good as dead (Lk 15:32); but the world which is not in Christ is in sin and therefore in death (Jn 1:4; 8:21–4, 34–7). For those who reject it, the gospel deals out death (2 Cor 2:16; 4:3f; Phil 1:28). Outside of the sphere of the gospel even the living are really dead (Mt 8:22; Jn 5:21–5; Col 2:13; 1 Tim 5:6), whereas in Christ even he who is dead lives and cannot be subject to death (Jn 11:25f; 6:50), since he has passed over into life (Jn 5:24, 1 Jn 3:14).

In these texts we are well past the idea of natural dying when death is mentioned. We can perhaps already find allusions to death, understood *in the spiritual sense*, in the Book of Proverbs (7:27; 13:14; 14:27; 23:13). From this death one is rescued by↗ righteousness and almsgiving (Prov 10:2; 11:4; Tob 4:10; 12:9). In the New Testament this death is the result of infidelity and sin (Rom 7:10; 8:6; Jas 1:15; 1 Jn 5:16). Hence we have the reference to the second death, the only one which has to be feared (Rev 2:11; 20:6; 21:8), which is the lot of sinners after the judgement which follows the death of the body (Heb 9:27). He who does not love, abides in death (1 Jn 3:14).

Bibliography: G. von Rad and R. Bultmann, *TDNT* II, 846–9 and III, 7–21 (= *Life and Death* [*BKW* XIV], London 1965, 8–14 and 85–107); H. Alswede, *BTHW* 585f; Allmen, 79–83; J. B. Alfrink, Haag 1625–7; A. Schulz, *Der Sinn des Todes im AT*, Braunsberg 1919; G. Quell, *Die Auffassung des Todes in Israel*, Leipzig 1925; H. M. Feret, *Das Mysterium des Todes*, Frankfurt 1955, 13–126; J. Guillet, *Leitgedanken der Bibel*, Lucerne 1954, 168–92; Imschoot II, 48–82; Heinisch 244–9; A. Kassing, 'Der Tod im Leben des Christen nach dem Apostel Paulus', *Pro veritate*, Münster-Kassel 1963, 7–21; F. Hoffmann, *HTG* II, 661–70; *K. Rahner, *On the Theology of Death*, London and New York 1961.

Ernst Schmitt

Decalogue

A. *The Decalogue in the Old Testament.*
1. *Form and arrangement of the Decalogue.* The division into sections of this short set of laws depends largely on the translation of the LXX, which renders the Hebrew *ᵃśereth hadd°bārim* (Ex 34:28) as *tous deka logous*. In both languages this phrase means 'the ten

words', and it is usually expressed in English by 'the ten commandments'. Three facts are thus already established in the original text: the exceptional position and the unity of this set of laws within the body of the Torah as a whole, the fact that the commandments number ten, and that they have been moulded into a formula.

The fact that there are *ten* commandments is not quite so certain as might first be thought, for the first commandments exist on a far greater number of different levels than they do in the catechism form which has been adapted for our purposes, and, what is more, they are not in fact numbered at all. Another factor is that the wording has been handed down in two different forms (in Ex 20:1–17 and in Deut 5:6–21), as well as a third version which is derived from the later Jewish period and has been passed on to us in the so-called Nash papyrus, which, like the Phylacterus in Qumran, contains the decalogue and the so-called šemaᶜ with the commandment concerning the love of God (Deut 6:4f).

According to Ex 20, the text is worded in the following way:

I am Yahweh your God, who brought you out of the land of Egypt, out of the house of bondage.

You shall have no other gods before me. You shall not make for yourself a graven image, or any likeness of anything that is in heaven above, or that is in the earth beneath, or that is in the water under the earth; you shall not bow down to them or serve them; for I Yahweh your God am a jealous God, visiting the iniquity of the fathers upon the

children to the third and the fourth generation of those who hate me, but showing steadfast love to thousands of those who love me and keep my commandments.

You shall not take the name of Yahweh your God in vain; for Yahweh will not hold him guiltless who takes his name in vain.

Remember the sabbath day, to keep it holy. Six days you shall labour, and do all your work; but the seventh day is a sabbath to Yahweh your God; in it you shall not do any work, you, or your son, or your daughter, your manservant, or your maidservant, or your cattle, or the sojourner who is within your gates; for in six days Yahweh made heaven and earth, the sea, and all that is in them, and rested the seventh day; therefore Yahweh blessed the sabbath day and hallowed it.

Honour your father and your mother, that your days may be long in the land which Yahweh your God gives you.

You shall not kill.

You shall not commit adultery.

You shall not steal.

You shall not bear false witness against your neighbour.

You shall not covet your neighbour's house; you shall not covet your neighbour's wife, or his manservant, or his maidservant, or his ox, or his ass, or anything that is your neighbour's.

Apart from variants in the text due to transcription, differences of expression etc, the text of Deuteronomy has two essential differences which are of interest to us in our examination of this subject. The commandment to observe the sabbath has this substantiating reason—'You shall remember that you were a servant in the land of Egypt, and Yahweh your God brought you thence with a mighty hand and an outstretched arm'. This addition ought to make the social significance of the sabbath even clearer and more emphatic than the version of the commandment in Exodus. That is why, in Deuteronomy, less stress is placed on the day of creation as the day on which man should rest from his labours, and far more is placed on the servitude of the people and their consequent liberation by God.

The second important difference is that the penultimate commandment reads: 'You shall not covet your neighbour's wife', to which are appended the commandments not to covet the house etc, of one's neighbour. It has not been established how this difference might possibly have come about, though Norbert Peters surmises that the transcriber of Exodus might, in error, have copied out the wrong lines here, while Steuernagel tends to the view that in a later period it was considered desirable to recognise the higher status of woman in society. The only certain thing is that the coveting of one's neighbour's wife as such was soon given considerable emphasis and regarded as definitely taboo.

The arrangement of the decalogue is uniform in both Exodus and Deuteronomy. It is the fundamental norm of the Torah which was made known when God manifested himself on Mount Sinai and which was taken as a basis for the setting up of the Covenant.

2. *The origin and purport of the Decalogue*

and its importance within the framework of the Old Testament. These three elements, the origin and purport of the Decalogue and its importance within the framework of the Old Testament, must be considered systematically in relation to one another, as both the purport and the importance of the Decalogue throw light on the period of its formation. The controversy concerning the *origin* of the Decalogue is well known. Wellhausen's verdict on the entire tradition regarding the law is that 'such a living law, which at every point reflects real conditions . . . cannot be the whim or fancy of an idle mind, but has arisen out of historical conditions and is destined to intervene effectively in the course of historical evolution' (in his *Prolegomena*).

The theory that the Decalogue was composed by Moses has, all the same, often found champions among non-Catholic scholars such as A. Alt, and, more recently, E. Auerbach, W. Kessler, and G. von Rad among others. The early origin of the Decalogue is, however, supported by archaeology. The 'two tablets' (Ex 32:15) have not, of course, been discovered. As it is only possible to date these by palaeographical methods, based on comparisons with similar material, there is scarcely a single compelling argument in support of the belief that the decalogue was in fact composed by Moses, since the commandments certainly did not bear Moses' signature. On the other hand, although archaeologists have made numerous finds of images of Canaanite gods and goddesses, they have still not brought a single image of Yahweh or of a female partner to Yahweh to light.

The dictum: 'Apart from me there is no God', must therefore have dominated the entire history of Israel from its very beginning. The commandment which forbids images had accordingly an importance in itself, and was not only a negative complement to the first commandment made simply to secure Yahweh's pre-eminence over all false gods and idols. It was, on the contrary, a true ban on images of false gods, in that even an image of Yahweh was regarded as a contradiction of his spiritual being. There were thus four commandments in the original version which related to God, and the second of the 'two tablets' contained the commandment against coveting one's neighbour's wife and his home in an undivided form.

Certain 'parallel' instances which exist outside the sphere of the bible can be quoted to support the great age of the decalogue. One section of the Assyrio-Babylonian tablets of exorcisms of the Shurpu series establishes definite points of contact with the decalogue. This ritual was applied when a sick man wished to be cured. A list was read aloud, giving a record of the sick man's innocence, and it was hoped thereby that he would be 'delivered from the spell which had previously bound him', as the final sentence reads. The formula consists of a series of rhetorical questions to which the answer 'No' is expected:

May N. be delivered, you great gods, from the sickness, fear, care, and affliction which troubles him!

Has he consumed what is atrocious to his God, what is atrocious to his goddess . . .?

Has he despised his father and mother or scorned his elder sister? Has he indulged in small matters and neglected great matters?

Has he said 'it is' instead of 'it is not'?

Has he said 'it is not' instead of 'it is'?

Has he uttered impurities or acted recklessly?

Has he uttered calumny?

Has he used false scales?

Has he broken into his neighbour's house?

Has he offended against his neighbour's wife?

Has he shed his neighbour's blood?

Has he ever let a man go in nakedness?

Has he taken away his neighbour's garments?

Has he abducted a good man away from his family?

Has he disrupted the unity of a tribe?

Has he ever opposed the chief of his tribe?

Was his mouth ever honest while his heart was dishonest?

Did his mouth give consent while his heart dissented?

[*AOT* 324f.]

There are further similarities between the Decalogue and Chapter 125 of the so-called *Book of the Dead* which provide a protestation of innocence, which is in fact the protestation of a man who is already dead and who must testify to his innocence in order to enter the hall in which Osiris is enthroned and where the heart is to be 'weighed in the balance'. The most important sections are as follows:

187

I have not dealt unfairly with men;

I have not slaughtered cattle set aside for sacrifice . . .

I have done nothing abominable in God's sight;

I have not slandered any servant in his master's hearing;

I have let no man go hungry;

I have brought no man to tears;

I have not killed;

I have given no command to kill;

I have not acted badly towards anyone;

I have not taken away from the sacrificial meals in the temples . . .

I have not committed adultery . . .

I have neither taken away from nor added to the corn-measure;

I have not cheated with the measure of arable land . . .

I have not robbed;

I have not been avaricious;

I have not stolen;

I have not killed men;

I have not uttered lies . . .

I have satisfied God with the things that he loves;

I have given bread to the hungry and water to the thirsty and clothes to the naked and a ferry-boat to those who lack a ship . . .

Only save me and protect me and do not testify against me before the great God!

I have clean lips and clean hands and am one to whom 'welcome' is said by those who see me.

[*AOT* 9ff.]

Neither of these two chapters is the expression of a serious moral decision, but both are connected with the practice of magic and aim either to exorcise sickness or to pave the way to the next world (in this respect, the Babylonian text provides the clearer example). They are thus very clearly distinguished in their spiritual content from the Decalogue. Their purpose is self-assertion and compulsion of the gods, whereas the Decalogue is based, in its essential elements, on obedience to God's command and was made known as a moral imperative demanded by God who had manifested himself expressly as the Lord of morality. The unsystematic arrangement which is not ordered according to the degree of guilt, and in which matters pertaining both to worship and to morals are quite mixed up, is striking from the point of view of the form of the Decalogue. On the other hand, the extra-biblical texts do show that there was in existence, distinct from and independent of the biblical revelation, a moral consciousness which had already achieved a literary expression and had had some influence on the conscience.

Thus the Decalogue is in no way an isolated case in its period, though even this fact tends to prove that its author was Moses. The decisive factor was, however, the close link with the cult of Yahweh. In changing the old order, Moses fashioned a new one which was to reshape the world.

It is now necessary to take a look at *the Decalogue within the framework of the history of the people of the Old Testament.* That it was valid in the spiritual sense is indisputable, but the principal question is: Was it known in its literary form? There is no word-for-word quotation of the 'ten commandments' apart from the versions given in Exodus and Deuteronomy. Many scholars regard this fact as a strong argument in support of the view that it was not Moses but the prophets who were the originators of ethical monotheism. In contradiction to this theory, however, it must be affirmed that once the decalogue was well known an exact quotation was hardly necessary, when one wished to refer to the 'statute of God'. A straightforward memorising of the Decalogue would not have succeeded in establishing the relationship between God's law and the actual sins which the prophets were intent on denouncing. The task of the prophets consisted in showing the people that their conduct, despite their apparent piety, nonetheless contradicted the law of God (Jer 8:8). If, on the other hand, one places too great an emphasis on the tension between the Decalogue and the message of the prophets, it is easy to fall into self-contradiction holding the view that the Decalogue is a result of the prophetic mission.

The two oldest writing prophets provide evidence that they are acquainted with the Book of Exodus. Amos mentions the forty years in the desert (5:25). He knows too of the taking out of Egypt and the closely allied fact that the Hebrews were God's chosen people (3:1f), and he draws certain moral conclusions from these data. Hosea would appear to be quoting the introduction to the Decalogue when he twice emphasises the words of God with the sentence: 'I am the Lord your God from the Land of Egypt' (12:9; 13:4). Furthermore, he gives a list of vices which has certain points of contact with the ten commandments: 'Swearing, lying, killing, stealing and committing adultery' (4:2). Jeremiah has a similar list: 'Will you

steal, murder, commit adultery, swear falsely, burn incense to Baal, and go after other gods?' (Jer 7:9). The Hebrew word for 'to murder' or 'to kill' is identical in these instances quoted from Jeremiah and Hosea with the word used in the Decalogue. As for any variation in the order in which the sins are listed, the order in the Nash papyrus, from the fifth commandment onwards, also reads: 'commit adultery, murder, steal, bear false witness'. The order is thus, as far as our problem is concerned, not important. The fact that the oldest prophets were also familiar with the written law of God is stated unambiguously in Hosea (8:12), and all the other prophets know about God's 'precepts' (Amos 2:4; Jer 6:19).

Jeremiah also bears witness to the fact that the commandment regarding the sabbath had already been given to the fathers (22:17), just as it was already regarded at the time of Amos as an obligation under law (8:5). The formulaic principle with which Tamar confronted her half-brother Amnon on the point of raping her, 'such a thing is not done in Israel' (2 Sam 13:12), should be seen as a consequence and an application of the unusual fact that the commandments of the Decalogue are in the indicative: 'Thou shalt not kill, thou shalt not commit adultery' etc. There are features of Psalm 15 and 24 which have certain similarities with the Decalogue, namely, the 'examination of conscience' when a visit is made to the temple.

The sequence, numbering and additions vary from one version of the Decalogue to another. This tends to show that the *original version* is no longer extant and that this must have been much simpler in form and more closely approximating to an apodictic form, which may have had the following wording:

I am the Lord thy God.

1. Thou shalt have no other gods beside me.

2. Thou shalt not make to thyself any graven image in order to worship it.

3. Thou shalt not take the name of God in vain.

4. Remember that thou keep holy the sabbath day.

5. Honour thy father and thy mother.

6. Thou shalt not kill.

7. Thou shalt not commit adultery.

8. Thou shalt not steal.

9. Thou shalt not bear false witness.

10. Thou shalt not be covetous.

B. *The Decalogue in the New Testament.* Christ has also instituted his new order by changing the old. Christ's ethics are therefore not the same as those of Moses, yet despite this he formulates his ethical demands—for example, in what he says to the rich young man (Mt 19:17–19)—in the words of the Decalogue. In this connection it should not be forgotten that in Deuteronomy too the commandments of the 'first tablet' are simplified and dominated by the demand: 'Hear, O Israel: the Lord our God is one Lord; and you shall love the Lord your God with all your heart . . .' (Deut 6:4f). There is also another extant version in which the 'second tablet' might have been worded in another way: 'You shall love your neighbour as yourself' (Lev 19:18). Christ himself has, with deliberate

emphasis, pronounced the love of God and one's neighbour to be the root, the measure and the consummation of all moral conduct (Mt 22:36–40). He has also given greater depth and intensity to the positive demands of the Decalogue which he has personally assimilated and has thus made them sound afresh with a new note. They have not been abolished but 'fulfilled' (Mt 5:17–32). If one result of this is that it is impossible to conceive of this 'law of liberty' as existing without any moral content, then both James (2:8–13) and Paul (1 Cor 5:1f) have, for a particular reason in every case, cleared up these and similar misunderstandings (↗ Law NT).

In contrast to those commandments which were assimilated by Christ himself, the commandment to observe the sabbath was so closely bound up with the Old Testament that it had to be replaced when the Old Testament was replaced, and in fact no longer obtained. It is not to be expected, however, that any analogous Christian commandments should come from Christ himself, so long as the saving events in the course of salvation had not been accomplished. In this case it is only the tradition of the apostles and the early church which can give us any idea as to what strictly pertains to the New Testament in this respect, unless Christ's words 'do this in remembrance of me' (Lk 22:19) are regarded as capable of being construed as a commandment. Christian tradition can also assure us that the commandment against the making of images no longer holds force, for Christ certainly had no reason to take any definite attitude with regard to this. It is, however, an established fact, despite the lack of explicit references, that Christ did not wish the commandment that God alone should be worshipped, and that his name should be sanctified, to be overlooked. (It should be noted that the clause 'hallowed be thy name' of the Our Father is different in substance from this.)

Bibliography: A. van den Born and H. Cazelles, Haag 316–20; P. Volz, *Mose und sein Werk*, Tübingen 1932; A. Alt, 'Die Ursprünge des israelitischen Rects', *Kleine Schriften*, Munich 1953, 278–332; H. Reiner, 'Zur Frage "Sittlichkeit und Religion"', *Die Sammlung* II, 1947; A. Schüler, *Werantwortung*, Munich 1948; H. H. Rowley, *Moses and the Decalogue*, Manchester 1951; E. Auerbach, *Moses*, Amsterdam 1953; W. Kessler, 'Die literarische, historische und theologische Problematik des Dekalogs', *VT* 7 (1957); H. Schneider, 'Der Dekalog in den Phylakterien von Qumran', *BZ* 3 (1959), 18–31; G. E. Mendenhall, 'Recht und Bund in Israel und dem vorderen Orient', *TS* 64 (1960).

Othmar Schilling

Demon

A. *In the Old Testament*. The idea of demon, *daimōn* began as a Greek name for gods and beings with divine powers, and especially for unfriendly beings against whom it is necessary to seek protection by means of magic spells and invocations. There are traces too, in the Old Testament, of a similar popular belief in such spirits. Although there is no single, comprehensive name for such beings in the Hebrew version of the bible, the LXX Daimonion invariably has *daimonion* (the adjective derived from *daimōn*) and the New Testament, following LXX, has this also in most cases.

An 'evil spirit', which troubles men or throws them into confusion, is referred to several times, but it is a spirit which comes from God (1 Sam 16:14–16, 23; 18:10; 19:9; see also 1 Kings 22:21). There are also spirits of the dead, which can be conjured up (1 Sam 28:13—here denoted by *ʾlōhîm*, 'God', 'divine being'). It is true that Saul had driven all the magicians and necromancers from the land (1 Sam 28:9). Such people ought not to be tolerated among the Jews (Lev 19:31; 20:6, 27; Deut 18:11). The *šēdîm* (Deut 32:17; Ps 106:37)—the word is connected with the Akkadian *šedu*, meaning deities—are also true demonic figures, and this is translated in the LXX by *daimonia*, while the *śəʿîrim* (Lev 17:7; 2 Chron 11:15; Is 13:21; 34:14—the description, as 'hairy ones' is to be understood in the sense of their having the form of a goat) are translated in the LXX by *mataia* (nothingness, nothing: Lev, 2 Chron, as above), or else rendered by *daimonia* (Is, as above). These *śəʿîrim* inhabit ruins (Is, as above—here mentioned only to describe in popular fashion the destruction in store for the people). The Israelites also offered sacrifices to them (Lev, 2 Chron, as above), as well as to the *šedim* (Deut, Ps, as above), although it is questionable whether the sacrifice is really offered to such beings or whether these names do not in fact apply to some strange gods thus described out of scorn (see LXX Is 65:3; Bar 4:7). The Lilith (corresponding to the Assyrian demon of the storm *lilitu*) is one spirit which is the object of popular belief and lives in the ruins (Is 34:14). Azazel is the demon which inhabits the desert and which, on the Day of Atonement, is presented with a goat, to which the high priest has transferred all the sins of the people (Lev 16:8, 10, 26). On one occasion, at least according to the LXX, the just man refers to the need of protection from the noonday demon— although it should be noted that the Hebrew text has 'the plague at noon' here (Ps 91:6). Jewish belief in demons is most strikingly encountered in the popular account which forms the Book of Tobit. The demon Asmodeus (*Asmodaus* or *Asmodaios*, presumably derived from the Iranian *aĕsma daĕva*, or 'evil demon') slays the seven husbands of Sarah (Tob 3:8). Any demon or evil spirit (*daimonion ē pneuma ponēron*) which haunts a man or woman can only be banished if the heart and the liver of a fish is burnt before that man or woman (6:8). Tobit does this on the advice of the angel Gabriel, when he goes into Sarah's bridal chamber, and, with that, Asmodeus is driven away by the smoke and flees into the desert of upper Egypt where Raphael binds him (6:17f; 8:2f).

B. *In the extra-canonical, later Jewish literature.* There are very many references here to fallen angels who have, as is generally believed to be the case in connection with Gen 6:2, 4, sinned by having sexual intercourse with human women (Jub 4:22; 5:1; 7:21; 10:5; Enoch [Eth] 6f; 12:4; 15; 69:2–4; 84:4; 86:1–6; Test Rub 5:6; Test Naph 3:5; Bar [Syr] 56:12; CD 17f; Josephus, *Antiquitates Judaicae* I, 3, 1 [73]). These angels are, however, different from demons, though Philo equates the 'angels' of the bible with the 'demons' of the world of Greek mythology (*De Gigantibus*, 6). Elsewhere the demons are considered as the fruit of that union between angels and human beings, as spirits who animated the 'giants' who were the children of those unions and who, after their death, cause mischief among human beings as demons (Jub 10:5f; Enoch [Eth] 15:8–12; 16:1; 19:1; Enoch [Slav] 18:5). Although the name 'demon' occurs relatively infrequently (eg, Enoch [Eth] 19:1; Bar [Gr] 16:3; *Test. Adae* 1:1), these fiends are often simply called 'spirits' (Jub 10:5, 8; 11:5; 19:28; Enoch [Eth] 15:10–12; 19:1; 1 QS 3, 24); also 'evil spirits' (Jub 10:3, 13; 11:4; 12:20; Enoch [Eth] 15:8f; 1 QM 15, 14; 'malicious spirits'); 'unclean spirits' (Enoch [Eth] 99:7; see also Jub 10:1); the spirits of Mastema (Jub 19:28), or Beliar (Test, Iss 7:7; Test Dan 1:7; Test Jos 7:4; 1 QM 13, 2, 4, 11f; CD 12:2; see also Test Rub 2:2). Their prince is Mastema (Jub 10:8; 11:5; 19:28). But, like Beliar (Belial), Mastema is a name for the devil, who thus rules over the evil spirits.

The demons do grievous harm to human beings (Jub 10:1–3, 5, 8; 11:5; Enoch [Eth] 15:11; 16:1; Bar [Gr] 16:3; Test Adae 1:1; 2:10 [Greek fragments in M. R. James, *Apocrypha Anecdota*, Cambridge 1893, 141 (frag 10a) and 142 (frags 1a and 4a)]; *Lives of the Prophets* 16 [P. Riessler, *Altjüdisches Schrifttum ausserhalb der Bibel*, Augsburg 1928, 878]). In particular, they tempt men to bad actions (Jub 7:27; 10:1f, 8; 11:4f; 12:20; Test Dan 5:5; Test Benj 3:3; 1 QS 3, 24; see also 1 QH 14, 11), such as bloodshed (Jub 7:27; 11:5) and sacrifices to demons (Enoch [Eth] 19:1), or to false gods or idols (Jub 11:4). The worship of false gods or idols is nothing but the worship of demons, as false gods and demons are similar (*Jerusalem Targum* I; see also Deut 32:17). It is [the same as] adoring demons (Jub 22; 17; Enoch [Eth] 99:7).

It was not only feared that demons can do harm to men and tempt them, but it was also believed that they can take possession of men. The belief arose that there was such a thing as demonic ↗ possession, in a form which was not mentioned in the Old Testament (Josephus, *Antiqu Jud* VIII 2, 5 [45–8]; see also many examples in the New Testament and in the rabbinical texts). There are also references to fallen angels who tempt human beings (Enoch [Eth] 9:6–8; 10:8; 64:2).

There is one angel of darkness, apparently Belial, the devil, who reigns over the unjust and makes the just fall into error (1 QS 3, 20–2). This angel has subordinate 'spirits' who attempt to make the 'sons of light' fall (1 QS 3, 24). Whoever does not live according to the law of Moses comes under the sway of an angel of Mastema (*CD* 16:5).

The Satans (Enoch [Eth] 40:7; 65:6) are a group of evil beings on their own and must not be confused with the being who is specifically known as Satan, that is, the devil (Enoch [Eth] 53:3; 54:6).

No more than a tenth of the entire number of demons still remains on earth to the detriment of mankind. The rest are already in the place of damnation (Jub 10:9). The demons lose their power in the messianic age (Test Sim 6:6; Test Lev 18:12; see also Jub 23:29; 50:5), and men rule over them. (Test Sim 6:6; Test Lev 18:12; see also under C). Eventually the demons incur eternal punishment (Test Jud 25:3 [Armenian translation]; see also Enoch [Eth] 16:1), which is also the lot of the evil angels (Enoch [Eth] 21:10; 90:22–5; see also 18:13–16; 21:3–6).

In cases such as these, many primitive beliefs are revived and perpetuated (eg, demons as spirits of the dead). What is of theological importance is, however, that Jewish monotheism avoided an absolute dualism, of which many rudiments might have existed. As far back as our knowledge goes of the history of evil angels and demons, God is always thought of as the creator of all spirits, both those of light and those of darkness (1 QS 3:25).

C. *In the New Testament.* Beside 'demons' (*daimonion*, but in one instance [Mt 8:31] *daimōn*), the New Testament also has the name 'spirit' (Mt 8:16; 9:33; Mk 9:20; Lk 9:39; 10:20; Acts 16:18), 'unclean spirit' (Mk 1:23, 26f; 3:11, 30; 5:2, 8, 13; 6:7; 7:25; 9:25; Mt 10:1; 12:43; Lk 4:36; 6:18; 8:29; 9:42; 11:24; Acts 5:16; 8:7; Rev 16:13; 18:2; cf Lk 4:33), 'evil spirit' (Lk 7:21; 8:2; Acts 19:12f, 15f), 'spirit of a demon' (Lk 4:33; Rev 16:14) and various other names. Though there is one instance of possession of animals (Mk 5:12f and parallels), the most frequent references are to the ↗ possession of men by demons (Mk 1:23–6, 32, 34; 5:2–13 and parallels; 9:17–26 and parallels; Mt 4:24; 8:16; 9:32f; 12:22; Lk 4:33–5, 41; 7:21; 8:2; 11:14; Acts 5:16; 8:7; 16:16–18; 19:12). Such spirits can cause a person to become dumb (Mk 9:17, 25; Mt 9:32); deaf (Mk 9:25; Mt 12:22; Lk 11:14); blind (Mt 12:22); insane (see Lk 7:33; Jn 7:20; 8:48f, 52; 10:20); or diseased

(Lk 13:11). They can also cause a person to prophesy (Acts 16:16). By no means all diseases or physical infirmities can be traced to the influence of demons, even though they are in the last resort the work of the devil (Acts 10:38). It is possible for many demons to dwell in one human being (Mk 5:9; Lk 8:2, 30; see also Mt 12:45; Lk 11:26). Such spirits are able to impart an extraordinary strength to those whom they possess (Mk 5:3f; Lk 8:29; Acts 19:16). They torment those whom they attack (Mk 5:5; 9:18 and parallels), and treat them as tools with no power to resist (Mk 1:26; 5:3-7; 9:18-26 and parallels; Lk 4:35; 8:29). There is, however, no single instance of demons leading the men whom they possess so far astray that they commit morally reprehensible deeds, nor do they ever attempt to lead them into eternal perdition, as Satan does. Satan is the one who rules over the demons (Mk 3:26 and parallels; Eph 6:11f; see also Lk 13:11, 16). The devil is also apparently given the name of Beelzebul (*Beelzeboul*; in the Vulgate and the Syrian the form is Beelzebub [the origin and meaning of the name are uncertain]; Mk 3:22 and parallels; Mt 12:27; Lk 11:18f; see also Mt 9:34). It is above all Jesus who drives demons out of men with his simple but powerful words (Mk 1:25f, 34 and parallels; 5:2-13 and parallels; 7:29; 9:25f and parallels; Mt 4:24; 9:32f; 12:22, 28; 15:28; Lk 4:35; 6:18; 11:14, 20). It is this fact which tells us that the kingdom of God is at hand (Mt 12:28; Lk 11:20 and that the power of Satan is collapsing (Mk 3:27 and parallels; Lk 10:18). When Jesus exorcises them, the demons acknowledge him to be the Messiah (Mk 1:24, 34; 3:11; 5:7 and parallels; Lk 4:34), and this means torment and destruction for them (Mk 1:24; 5:7 and parallels; Lk 4:34). But the disciples of Jesus also have the power to exorcise demons (Mk 6:7 and parallels; 6:13; Lk 10:17-20; Acts 5:16; 8:7; 16:16-18; 19:12). Even Jews who have not joined Jesus's disciples have this power (Mt 12:27; Lk 11:19), although success is sometimes denied to them (Acts 19:13-16). Once having been driven out of a man, the demon seeks rest in the desert (Mt 12:43; Lk 11:24), or enters animals' bodies (Mk 5:12f and parallels). Demons also inhabit ruins (Rev 18:2). Heathen worship is due to demons (1 Cor 10:20f; Rev 9:20), and those who take part in such practices are brought into close association with the demons (1 Cor 10:20f). There are spirits of error who lead men away from the true faith (1 Tim 4:1; 1 Jn 4:6), and there are also the false doctrines of demons (1 Tim 4:1). There is a wisdom which is demonic (Jas 3:15), and the christian has to resist all demonic spirits (Eph 6:12). These spirits will exert a particular influence in the last days, and try to make men forsake the true doctrine of Christ (1 Tim 4:1; see also 1 Jn 4:1-6; Rev 16:13f). But there is a judgement in store for the demons which will punish them with torments (Mt 8:29; see also Jas 2:19).

Certain beings are to be found in the New Testament which are in fact angels of the devil (↗ Angel, C) but these are never formally equated with demons, despite their similarity to them. The one was clearly distinguished from the other in the early christian period, and it was only after this that they gradually came to be grouped together, as the conception of 'angel' began to change and demonology began to be developed as a branch of theology. For the demonic aspect of principalities and powers and similar beings, see↗ Angel C and↗ Principalities and Powers.

D. *Theological importance of the biblical evidence concerning demons.* In judging the importance of the biblical evidence in this respect, two extremes should be avoided. It would be wrong to accept everything that is in the bible concerning demons as factual, as a great deal that merely pertains to the ancient world has been done away with today. But, recognising this fact and bearing in mind that much that was formerly attributed to demons can today be explained by natural or psychical causes, it is still not possible simply to deny the existence and the efficacy of the powers of demonic spirits. It stands to reason that an Azazel, a Lilith, or an Asmodeus have never existed. It is also certain that the Jews saw evil spirits at work when in reality this was due to nervous or psychological disorders. The literary style of the specific text in question must also be borne in mind in any examination of the biblical evidence concerning demons or, for that matter, angels as well. There are, for example, poetical descriptions of the destruction of a town (Is 13:21; 34:14; Rev 18:2), and Tobit contains a good deal of pleasant, free narrative. Even when popular views of the ancient world are quite obviously contained in those statements in the bible that concern demons, it is nonetheless striking, taken as a whole, how reserved these statements are in comparison with those of the later Jewish and extra-canonical writings, the rabbinical texts, and the literature of the early christian period.

Since the eighteenth century, the practice has found increasing favour in protestant exegesis to regard the fairly frequent instances of↗ possession in the New Testament as various manifestations of nervous or psychological disturbances or illnesses, and especially as epilepsy, delirium, schizophrenia, and so on. Apart from the fact that the different accounts cannot be satisfactorily interpreted in this way, the whole problem—and it is admittedly a difficult one—can only be solved if it is seen against the background of Jesus's personality and his work directed against Satan and his kingdom; and thus, in this case, as in all cases of demonology, it is necessary to adhere to the view that there are demonic beings who wish to cause harm to men, but who can be entirely deprived of their power by Jesus. Taken as a whole, the references in the bible to demons do present a real problem which has not yet been satisfactorily settled, and there is a strong case for a more searching and detailed examination.

Bibliography: J. Smit, *De daemoniacis in historia evangelica*, Rome 1913; SB IV, 501–35; H. Kaupel, *Die Dämonen im AT*, Augsburg 1930; K. Prümm, *Der christl. Glaube u. die altheidnische Welt* I, Leipzig 1935, 137–56; W. Foerster, *TDNT* II, 1–20; P. Samain, 'L'Accusation de Magie contre le Christ dans les Evangiles', *ETL* 15 (1938), 449–90; B. Noack, *Satanás und Soteria: Untersuchungen zur ntl. Dämonologie*, Copenhagen 1948; Bruno de J.-M., ODC (ed.), *Satan*, London 1951; E. Langton, *Essentials of Demonology: A Study of Jewish and Christian Doctrine—Its Origin and Development*, London 1949; S. Eitrem, *Some Notes on the Demonology in the New Testament*, Oslo 1950; Haag 305–7;

M. F. Unger, *Biblical Demonology: A Study of the Spiritual Forces behind the present World Unrest*, Wheaton (Ill.) 1952; B. J. Bamberger, *Fallen Angels*, Philadelphia 1952; A. Dupont-Sommer, 'L'Instruction sur les deux Esprits dans le "Manual de Discipline"', *RHR* 142 (1952), 5–35; B. Otzen, 'Die neugefundenen hebräischen Sektenschriften und die Testamente der zwölf Patriarchen', *ST* 7 (1953/4), 125–57; C. H. C. Macgregor, 'Principalities and Powers: the Cosmic Background of St Paul's Thought', *NTS* 1 (1954/5), 17–28; E. von Petersdorff, *Dämonologie: I. Dämonen im Weltplan*, Munich 1956; G. B. Caird, *Principalities and Powers: A Study in Pauline Theology*, Oxford 1956; J. Hempel, *TLZ* 82 (1957), 815–20; M. Ziegler, *Engel und Dämon im Lichte der Bibel*, Zurich 1957; F. Nötscher, 'Geist und Geister in den Texten von Qumran', *Mélanges bibliques A. Robert*, Paris 1957, 305–15; H. Schlier, *Principalities and Powers*, London and New York 1961; J. Henninger, R. Schnackenburg, and A. Darlapp, *LTK* III², 139–43; H. W. M. de Jong, *Demonische ziekten in Babylon en Bijbel*, Leiden 1959; E. Dhorme, 'La démonologie biblique', *Hommage W. Fischer*, Montpellier 1960, 46–54; H. Wohlstein, 'Zu den altisraelitischen Vorstellungen von Toten- und Ahnengeistern', *BZ* 5 (1961), 30–8; A. Winklhofer, *Traktat über den Teufel*, Frankfurt 1961; F. J. Schirse and J. Michl, 'Satan', *HTG* II, 465–78.

Johann Michl

Demythologising

The word *demythologising* must be reckoned among the most important keywords in use in recent theoretical writing and discussion. Moreover, its use has spread from biblical theology to philosophy, and from a small circle of specialists to a much wider public— witness the great success of J. A. T. Robinson's book *Honest to God* (London 1963).

By *demythologising* is meant a problem or programme, namely, that of 'abolishing' (*aufheben*) myth. This 'abolition' should, of course, be understood in the Hegelian sense: far from being a completely negative process, it examines mythical modes of thought for their positive truth content.

Theologians currently engaged on the question of demythologising are not usually very much interested in a detailed historical or systematic examination of the *concept* of myth. For some years now philosophers, anthropologists, sociologists, and psychologists who have gone into the matter have been concerned with the *meaning and significance* of mythical modes of thought. There are still problems unsolved, even today. What exactly is myth? What is its role in human life and thought? What is its value? Clearly the answer to these large questions is determined by the programme of demythologisation.

This article could not possibly pretend to provide a survey of the many different aspects and levels of contemporary views on myth, or of the corresponding interpretations of demythologising. Still less could it venture to pass judgement on contemporary research into myth. In an encyclopedia of biblical theology it seems appropriate to confine discussion to an exposition of Rudolf Bultmann's celebrated demythologising of the message of revelation.

In the seventh issue of *Beiträge zur Evangelischen Theologie* (1941) appeared two contributions by Bultmann, the second of which—entitled 'Neues Testament und Mythologie' (quotations will be taken from *Kerygma and Myth: A Theological Debate*, London 1953)—has since given rise to one of the most thorough-going and most passionate theological controversies of modern times. Bultmann attempted to take up a position with regard to the difficulties which bar the way to the acceptance of faith to modern man, formed as he is in the image of science and technology. One of the chief difficulties, as he saw it, was that the churches demand from modern man an unnecessary *sacrificium intellectus*.

According to Bultmann, the New Testament presents the divine kerygma in the form of myth. Bultmann understands myth 'in the sense popularised by the "History of Religions" school. Mythology is the use of imagery to express the otherworldly in terms of this world and the divine in terms of human life, the other side in terms of this side' (*Kerygma and Myth* I, 10, *n* 2).

The cosmology of the New Testament is essentially mythical in character. The world is viewed as a three-storied structure, with the earth in the centre, the heaven above, and the underworld beneath. Heaven is the abode of God and of celestial beings—the angels. The underworld is hell, the place of torment. Even the earth is more than the scene of natural, everyday events, of the trivial round and common task. It is the scene of the supernatural activity of God and his angels on the one hand, and of Satan and his demons on the other. These supernatural forces intervene in the course of nature and in all that men think and will and do. Miracles are by no means rare. Man is not in control of his own life. Evil spirits may take possession of him. Satan may inspire him with evil thoughts. Alternatively, God may inspire his thought and guide his purposes. He may grant him heavenly visions. He may give him the supernatural power of his Spirit.

History does not follow a smooth, unbroken course; it is set in motion and controlled by these supernatural powers. This aeon is held in bondage by Satan, sin, and death (for 'powers' is precisely what they are), and hastens towards its end. That end will come very soon, and will take the form of a cosmic catastrophe. It will be inaugurated by the 'woes' of the last time. Then the Judge will come from heaven, the dead will rise, the Last Judgement will take place, and men will enter into eternal salvation or damnation.

[*Kerygma and Myth*, 1–2.]

The representation of the events of salvation is equated with the mythological view of the world.

It proclaims in the language of mythology that the last time has now come. 'In the fullness of time' God sent forth his Son, a pre-existent divine Being, who appears on earth as a man. He dies the death of a sinner on the cross and makes atonement for the sins of men. His resurrection marks the beginning of the cosmic catastrophe. Death, the consequence of Adam's sin is abolished, and the daemonic forces are deprived of their power. The risen Christ is exalted to the right hand of God in heaven and made 'Lord' and 'King'. He will come again on the clouds of heaven to complete the work of redemption, and the resurrection and judgement of men will follow. Sin, suffering and death will then be finally abolished. All this is to happen very soon; indeed, St Paul thinks that he himself will live to see it.

All who belong to Christ's church and are joined to the Lord by baptism and the eucharist are certain of resurrection to salvation, unless they forfeit it by unworthy behaviour. Christian believers already enjoy the first instalment of salvation, for the Spirit is at work within them, bearing witness to their adoption as sons of God, and guaranteeing their final resurrection.

[*Kerygma and Myth*, 2 (textual references omitted).]

'All this is the mythological way of expressing things,' Bultmann goes on, 'and the individual motives for it can easily be traced back to the contemporary mythology of the Jewish apocalyptic period and the gnostic myth of the redemption' (p. 2). But, insofar as it is the language of mythology, then it becomes quite impossible for men of today to believe in it. This is affirmed again and again by Bultmann in various places. For example, he comments on the resurrection:

It is impossible for modern man to comprehend the *resurrection of Jesus* as an event in history by virtue of which there is set free a life-power which man is able to appropriate for himself by means of the sacraments. This type of language is completely meaningless to the man who has been trained to think in terms of the biological sciences because, for him, the problematic aspect of death does not exist. The idealist too, although he can grasp the significance of a life which is subordinated to death, finds it quite inconceivable that a man who has died may be awakened once again to physical life. . . . But a

miraculous natural event such as the revivification of one who is already dead, quite apart from the fact that it is in the first place unworthy of belief, cannot be viewed by him as a divine act which concerns him personally.

[*Kerygma and Myth*, 8.]

Further on (in *Kerygma und Mythos* III, 51—quoted from 'The Case for Demythologising: A Reply to Karl Jaspers', *Myth and Christianity: An Inquiry into the Possibility of Religion without Myth*, New York 1958, 57–71) Bultmann sets out his own position regarding this difficulty of belief in the revivification of the dead: 'He [ie, Jaspers] is as firmly convinced as I am that a body cannot return to life and rise from the grave'.

Thus the New Testament message is presented in a mythical form, and is as such unacceptable to modern man. If this message is to retain its validity, the only course remaining is to demythologise it, not by a process of selection, nor by making deletions, but by interpreting the myth. The question is, however, whether the demythologising would not, if it were in fact carried out under such circumstances, be based on a postulate which is alien to the spirit of the New Testament. Bultmann, speaking both as a historian of comparative religion and as an exegete, is of the opinion that such a demythologising would not go contrary to the spirit of the New Testament.

He has created his theory of myth from the history of religion, and, as a scholar of comparative religion, he includes the New Testament among the mythical modes of thought. Now, in the study of comparative religion, the general laws which are applicable to this type of literature, its significance and the way in which it must be interpreted, have all been carefully worked out.

> The true significance of myth is not to be found in its ability to provide an objective cosmology, but tends rather to be expressed in the sense in which man understands himself in his world. Myth ought not to be interpreted in the cosmological sense, but rather in the anthropological or, even better, in the existential sense. . . . That is why the mythology of the New Testament ought not to be examined with an eye to its objective conceptual content, but rather to the existential perception which is expressed in these concepts. It deals with the question of the truth of this perception and its truth affirms a belief which may not be bound to the conceptual world of the New Testament.
>
> [*Kerygma and Myth*, 8.]

But Bultmann is also an exegete, and as such he points out that the New Testament itself invites criticism by reason of the fact that within its own conceptual world there are individual concepts which cannot be reconciled intellectually with each other, and that indeed concepts which are mutually contradictory are often found in juxtaposition—and that, furthermore, demythologising within the New Testament has in certain places already been carried out.

Bultmann thus attempts to present an existential interpretation of the mythological abstract world in its principal characteristics and by means of a number of examples. Using language which is strongly influenced by that of Heidegger, he outlines the christian apprehension of reality, both external to and within faith. He strives above all to present, in a non-mythological manner, the essential core of the christian message, that is, that Christ's appearance has occurred only once and has not been repeated in the course of history, that God's act in the person of Christ was decisive and that the christian is of necessity closely bound up with this single, unrepeated and unrepeatable, appearance of Christ.

His article 'Heilsgeschehen und Mythologie' has given rise to a spate of books, a great deal of passionate argument, and a veritable storm of indignation within the various protestant communions of the German-speaking countries, and this has all been a matter of considerable surprise to Bultmann himself, who had certainly said nothing more in this single essay than could be extracted quite easily from his exegetical writings, from *The History of the Synoptic Tradition* (1921; English translation, Oxford 1963) and *Jesus and the Word* (1926; ET London 1962).

The controversy over demythologising presents in general a very confused picture, because the struggle to gain an insight into the New Testament message is weighed down by such laborious efforts to understand Bultmann properly. Apart from a general lack of familiarity with Bultmann's historical writings, the main cause of many misunderstandings may have been the literary form of the 1941 article, by means of which the author attempted to give his interpretation of the divine kerygma a more powerful impact, by representing it as the only possible interpretation acceptable to modern man. This pastoral aim, however, conceals the real foundations of Bultmann's attitude to belief. It is probably only in this way that Jaspers' verdict, and other similar judgements, can be explained:

> Bultmann's demand that the New Testament should be demythologised is based on two suppositions, firstly on a view of modern science and of modern man in his world which causes him to deny so many objects of christian belief, and secondly on his view of philosophy itself, which makes it possible for him to adopt those attitudes towards faith which, in his opinion, still hold good, by means of an existential interpretation, the conceptuality of which should be available in a scientific philosophy. These two suppositions form the twin pillars upon which Bultmann has built his thesis. Neither seems to be capable of bearing its weight.
>
> [K. Jaspers, 'The Issues Clarified', *Myth and Christianity*, New York 1958, 72–116.]

Bultmann has, with justice, repeatedly stated his objections to this type of interpretation of his thought. As a protestant and a dialectical theologian, he does not judge faith from the viewpoint of secular science or philosophy. If he came to the question of demythologising already armed with presuppositions, he came also with the experience of an exegete and historian of comparative religion. New Testament exegesis, viewed in the light of comparative religion, does not of itself lead, in Bultmann's opinion, to an acceptance of the power of God to intervene miraculously in the normal course of events in Christ and his church, as is generally taught by the various christian bodies. As a historian, he puts the form of the New Testament message in the same category as the mode of thought which is so well known in the sphere of comparative religion. Bultmann the historian can, it is true, carry out his work of interpretation with a far easier conscience when this is seen as a rationalisation of the views of Bultmann the protestant believer on those aspects of God which are not within our range, and on the principle of *sola fides*, and when it is harmonised with the views of Bultmann the philosopher on the process of understanding in general, and on the value of the concepts contained in the statements concerning God in particular, and when it is regarded as raising Bultmann the pastoral theologian above the level of that clash with the narrow philosophy of man and the world which is considered by so many scientists as their ultimate triumph and achievement. In this sense Bultmann may well be called a systematic thinker, in that such differing elements do not conflict with each other, but rather tend to cohere mutually in his philosophy. He is not, however, a systematic thinker in the sense that he approaches his study of the New Testament with ready-made solutions.

In Bultmann's view, God's act in Christ is decisive in that it makes possible authentic existence, the concept of which is not inaccessible to philosophy, since this existence consists in a willing render to a God, who is invisible and who is not at man's disposal, and in the inner freedom of the world. It is then true to say that Bultmann experiences his greatest difficulties when he strives to preserve the innermost core of the New Testament— in other words, the fact that Christ's appearance has taken place once only and that the christian is of necessity tied in the closest alliance to this single, unrepeated and unrepeatable act of God in Christ. Christ's incarnation and passion remain as little more than an occurrence which, emerging in the person of Jesus and in the earliest christian period, does not become an *event* until the word of grace is actually spoken personally, at a given time, to a man (see *Kerygma und Mythos* III, 57f):

> That words of grace are spoken in this way, and that not the God-idea but God himself appears as *my* God, and speaks personally to *me* here and now, and, what is more, speaks through the mouths of men—this is the 'demythologised' sense of *ho logos sarx egeneto* (= the word became flesh) of the church's doctrine of the incarnation. Moreover, the christian message is to this extent tied to a tradition and looks back to a historical form and an existence in history, insofar as it sees the proof of the identity of these personal words spoken to men in this historical form and existence.
>
> [*Kerygma und Mythos* III, 58.]

In order to form a true assessment of Bultmann's theology, it is important to make a clear distinction between philo-sophical problems and those of comparative religion. However important they may be in practice, philosophical problems, which concern the fact that God is not available to us and the confusion of our concepts in the evidence that we have of God and the problems concerning the narrow view of man and the world today, remain questions of a purely preliminary nature, or, in Newman's phrase, of antecedent probability. They are, however, the problems with which those catholics who have taken part in the discussion of Bultmann's theology are best acquainted, and it is towards these problems that they have defined their attitude in the most satisfactory manner and in the greatest detail. It would perhaps be as well to give some warning of the risk that is inherent in a certain tendency to use the words 'mythology' and 'mythological' merely in order to stress the transcendence of God and the purely analogous value of human discussion about God, and to represent our statements concerning the existence and ordinances of God as being of necessity mythological.

In any discussion of Bultmann's theology it is not enough, in an attempt to ascertain the orthodox view of the truths of faith, to establish their compatibility with modern scientific thought and a sound philosophy. The problem of demythologisation is essentially a historical problem. To what extent may Holy Scripture, and above all the New Testament, be placed in the category of myth as found in comparative religion, and to what extent, too, should the words of God, spoken personally to men, be interpreted in a purely existential way? The answer to these questions depends on the history of the origins of the New Testament tradition. Before any fruitful discussion of Bultmann's position can take place, it is necessary to make a very careful study of the genesis of this tradition.

Bibliography: The most important contributions to the discussion of the problem of demythologisation have been collected by H. W. Bartsch in the series *Theologische Forschung: Wissenschaftliche Beiträge zur kirklichevangelischen Lehre*, under the general title *Kerygma und Mythos* (five volumes, two of which have been translated into English: *Kerygma and Myth: A Theological Debate*, ed. H. W. Bartsch, London 1953 [vol. I] and 1962 [vol. II]). The most detailed bibliography on Bultmann and the demythologisation debate is to be found in G. Hasenhüttl, *Der Glaubensvollzug: Eine Begegnung mit Rudolf Bultmann aus katholischem Verständnis*, Essen 1963. (There is also a short but useful bibliography of Bultmann's works available in English, and of other books in English dealing with Bultmann's theology, in *Existence and Faith: Shorter Writings of Rudolf Bultmann*, ed. and trans. Schubert M. Ogden, London 1961.) Among recently published works not cited by Hasenhüttl are: R. Bultmann, *Glauben und Verstehen* IV, Tübingen 1965; R. Bultmann, *Jesus Christ and Mythology*, New York 1958 and New York 1960; G. Bornkamm, 'Die Theologie Rudolf Bultmanns in der neueren Diskussion', *TR* 29 (1963), 33–141; R. Marlé, 'Mythos', *HTG* II, 193–201; G. Lanczkowski and H. Fries, 'Mythos', *LTK* VII², 746–52; J. Slok, J. Haekel, S. Mowinckel, R. Bultmann, and H. Meyer, 'Mythus und Mythologie', *RGG* IV³, 1263–84; H. Cazelles, 'Le mythe et l'Ancien Testament', *DB(S)* 1957, 246–61; J. Henninger, 'Le mythe en ethnologie', *DB(S)* 1957, 225–46; R. Marlé, 'Le mythe et le Nouveau Testament', *DB(S)* 1957, 261–8; G. van Riet, *Mythe et Vérité: Problèmes d'Epistémologie*, Paris 1960, 345–422; J. Pépin, *Mythe et Allégorie: Les origines grecques et les contestations judéo-chrétiennes*, Paris 1958. The proceedings of the conferences which, since 1961, have been held annually on the subject of demythologisation by the International Centre for Humane Studies and the Rome Institute for Philosophical Studies, are as follows: 1. *Il problema della demittizzazione*, 1961 (= *Kerygma und Mythos* VI/1, Hamburg 1963); 2. *Demittizzazione e imagine*, 1962 (= *Kerygma und Mythos* VI/2, Hamburg 1964); 3. *Ermeneutica e Tradizione*, 1963 (= *Hermé-* *neutique et Tradition*, Paris 1964); 4. *Tecnical Escatologia, e Casuistica*, Rome 1964; 5. *Démythisation et Morale*, Paris 1965.

Paul Asveld

Descent into hell

The concept of the descent into hell (journey to the underworld), with which important christological and soteriological speculations have been associated from the earliest times (Ignatius of Antioch (?), Justin, Hermas, Irenaeus etc; see also especially the descent into hell which occurs in the apocryphal gospel of Nicodemus), calls to mind at once the time that Jesus spent in the kingdom of the dead between his death and his resurrection. The chief elements which go to build up the idea of what hell or the underworld is like as a place and as a state, are drawn from the contemporary view of the nature of the underworld, and from the way in which late judaism regarded the survival of the soul. Quite apart from numerous Old-Testament references to the underworld or hell itself (1 Sam 2:6; 2 Sam 22:6; Tob 13:2; Job 11:8; 14:13; Ps 49:15f; 86:13; 139:8; Prov 1:12; Sir 21:10; Is 14:11; 38:10, 18 etc), there are also passages which describe a descent into hell, as in the case of the descent into hell of the King of Babylon (Is 14:9–15) and that of Pharaoh and his people (Ezek 32:17–32).

In the New Testament, those passages which indicate or presuppose a descent into hell on the part of Christ are of a predominantly christological interest, since the factual basis of Jesus's death and the reality and the magnitude of his resurrection are illustrated and placed on a firmer footing by his sojourn in hell, which is to be understood in the very widest sense here, as underworld, Hades, or *Sheol*. This resurrection, however, is of great importance in connection with the whole matter of salvation, and Christ's descent into hell must, even from this christological point of view, also have a marked soteriological significance, which will naturally be all the more profound if, in addition to the descent itself, any particular activity on the part of Christ in the underworld can be established. Some evidence of such activity does seem to be provided by the New Testament.

The christological importance of the descent into hell has been expressed since the fourth century in the formula *descendit ad inferos* (var: *infernos, inferna*) which occurs between *mortuus et sepultus est* and *tertia die resurrexit* in the Apostles' Creed. It is also apparent in all the passages in the New Testament in which the resurrection of Jesus is described as an *anastasis ek nekrōn* (=resurrection from the dead). The plural form is doubtless intended to denote the kingdom of the dead or the underworld, which is, in accordance with the cosmology of those times, situated in the lower regions of the earth, and where, according to the earliest ideas about hell, the dead dwelt together in a shadowy existence, but where, in the later view which is set out clearly—for example, in Lk 16:19–31—there were separate regions for the just and the unjust. In the remark of the dead rich man (Lk 16:30), Luke already implies that it is possible for someone 'from the dead' (*apo nekrōn*)

to be sent back to earth. It is also interesting to note that Herod expresses the view, in Mk 6:14, 17 (see also Mt 14:2; Lk 9:8) that John the Baptist had been raised 'from the dead' (*ek [apo] nekrōn*). In this way, all similar expressions dealing with Jesus' resurrection presuppose that he had previously spent some time in the kingdom of the dead: see Mt 17:9 (Mk 9:9); 27:64; Lk 24:46; Jn 2:22 (see also 12:1; 9:17, with its reference to the resurrection of Lazarus *ek nekrōn*); 20:9; 21:14. In Acts 2:14–36, where in fact the expression *ek nekrōn* does not occur, the same ideas are stated very clearly when Peter, making use of and interpreting Ps 16:10 in a messianic sense, refers to Jesus' sojourn in Hades (*Sheol*) in the phrase *oute enkataleiphthē eis ha(i)dēn* (='he was not abandoned to Hades'), and to his body placed in the grave but preserved from corruption in the phrase *oute hē sarx autou eiden diaphthoran* (='nor did his flesh see corruption'). The separate existence of the dead person, in terms of his body and soul, is here vividly represented in the anthropological language of the period and the concept of life after death. Further passages which refer to a resurrection *ek nekrōn* based on the same suppositions are: Acts 3:15; 4:10; 10:41; 13:30, 34, 37; 17:3, 31; Rom 1:4; 4:24; 6:4, 9; 7:4; 8:11; 10:7, 9; 1 Cor 15:12, 20; Gal 1:1; Eph 1:20; Col 1:18 (*prōtotokos ek tōn nekrōn* ='first-born from among the dead'; see also Acts 26:23); 2:12; 1 Thess 1:10; 4:13ff; 2 Thess 2:8; Heb 11:19; 13:20; 1 Pet 1:3, 21.

All these passages—and the list could be augmented by others which do not contain the phrase *ek nekrōn*, though referring strictly to the resurrection of Jesus—provide evidence that Jesus spent some time in the underworld, and thus that he must previously have descended into hell. The formula *ek nekrōn*, therefore, does not mean simply that Jesus' body was raised from the sepulchre. Above all, it means that he was also recalled from *Sheol*. The resurrection, furthermore, does not appear only as a personal mark of distinction for Jesus, but also has considerable importance with regard to the salvation of the redeemed. This is illustrated in the description of Jesus as *prōtotokos ek nekrōn* and in evidence such as that provided by Rom 6:4; 1 Cor 15:20–8.

Further evidence of the descent of Jesus into the kingdom of the dead can be drawn from the comparison between the resurrection of Jesus (Mt 12:39ff) and the experience of Jonah, but this is really of no more than secondary importance in this particular passage, as in the case of Mt 16:4 and Lk 11:29, where the principal intention is to call attention to the resurrection as a sign, and the descent into hell is mentioned, as it were, only in parenthesis. It is certainly not necessary to assume that because the peace of the grave is expressed periphrastically by the words 'in the heart of the earth' that this must refer to *Sheol*, as being situated in the interior of the earth (see Jon 2:2f, in which Jonah's prayer is represented as having been uttered 'from the belly of the fish', despite the fact that Jonah 'cried out of the belly of *Sheol*'). A further indirect reference to Christ's descent into hell is also contained in Mt 27:52.

The most obvious instance of the soteriological significance of the descent into hell, or at least the one which is most closely related to Jesus's resurrection, is to be found in Rev 1:18; 'I died, and behold I am alive for evermore, and I have the keys of Death and Hades' (Rev 20:12–15).

From 1 Pet 3:18ff, and possibly also from the evidence in 1 Pet 4:6, which is so difficult to interpret, there emerges a feature which was later developed with the growth of christian tradition and theological speculation. It cannot be established beyond all doubt whether the words: 'being put to death in the flesh but made alive in the spirit; in which he went and preached to the spirits in prison (*en hō[i]* [ie, *pneumati*] *kai tois en phulakē[i] pneumasin poreutheis ekēruxen*), who formerly did not obey, when God's patience waited in the days of Noah, during the building of the ark, . . .'; are to be taken to refer to the descent of Jesus into hell in the sense outlined above, or whether, as many believe to be the case, this is a reference to Jesus's resurrection and exaltation to the right hand of God. It is also not certain whether the 'spirits' who are addressed by Christ refer to the souls of the dead who are waiting in the underworld, either together with, or separated from, their bodies, or angelic beings, rather in the sense of those referred to in Jude 6. In the same way, the intention and the content of the 'sermon' referred to in 1 Pet 3:19 remain obscure.

What stands in the closest relationship to this is the preceding passage in 3:18, which deals with the descent of Jesus after his death, and it is stressed that this death was 'for sins' and 'the righteous for the unrighteous'. For it is particularly striking that what immediately follows the mention of the sermon addressed 'to the spirits in prison' is the reference to the resurrection and exaltation of Jesus to 'the right hand of God ... swallowing down death [Vulgate], being gone into heaven, the angels and powers and virtues being made subject to him.' In 1 Pet 1:3, 21, the resurrection *ek nekrōn* has already been mentioned. It is therefore permissible to regard the passage in question (1 Pet 3:18ff) as a fairly close representation of the time Jesus spent in the underworld and the 'sermon' may be regarded, not as a severe admonition, but rather as a message of salvation (*ekēruxen*, 'he preached'). True, it is especially the people 'in the days of Noah' who are said to be the recipients of Jesus' sermon, but the particular reason for this may well be that Peter at once leads up to the baptism of Christ which confers salvation and is here symbolised by the flood. The generation of Noah is moreover to be taken as representative of those who are already dead and in the underworld (or perhaps merely of heathens?) and this sermon in Hades is possibly intended to proclaim to them the redemption which the death of Jesus on the cross has brought about, and the incipient dominion of God.

Viewed in this way, 1 Pet 3:18ff is in a direct line with the later controversy and speculation which grew up around the soteriological significance of the descent into hell. In addition, similar themes in the apocryphal tradition of late judaism can readily be called to mind, as, for example, in the first book of Enoch (Eth), after the apocalyptic journey of Enoch through the prisons of the fallen angels (17–20), a visit is made to the 'caves' in which the 'ghosts of the dead are gathered' and 'which are so made that all the souls of human beings can be assembled here' (22:4) in separate chambers or compartments, one of which is reserved for the 'spirits of the just', another for 'sinners', one for the 'souls of mourners', and another for those who are absolutely depraved.

As far as comparative religion is concerned, there is a definite connection between Christ's descent into hell and comparable notions in the ancient Near East and Egypt, as well as in the hellenistic civilisation of Greece and Rome. It is certainly possible to establish many parallels in this respect between the usual external forms of representation and the various ideas of the underworld and the fate of man after death which are common to all. Similarly, the idea of a kingdom of death, inhabited by the dead, and the urgent desire and longing to overcome this power of evil, which gained expression in the form of myth and its related types of worship, is firmly founded in the natural and practical experience of the human race. A close analogy is to be found in the Babylonian myth of the descent of the goddess Inana into the underworld and her consequent re-ascent, the epic of Gilgamesh of Akkad and his unsuccessful attempt to liberate the spirits of the underworld, and the warlike assault on the underworld by Ishtar and Nergal, who conquered the ruler of the kingdom of the dead. The mythology concerning the growth of plants and the phases in the sun's and moon's course play an important part in fashioning man's concept of the next world. Varying examples of this are to be found in the worship of Attis, and of Isis and Osiris, and in the Eleusinian cult. Within hellenistic civilisation, although the descent of Theseus, Orpheus, and Heracles into the underworld are to a certain extent analogous to Christ's descent into hell, it is however not possible to trace any direct influence of an essential kind in this case. Christ's descent into hell is, in fact, unique and distinctive, and the vital truth which lies at the heart of this descent can only be fully understood if it is related to Jesus' incarnation as God-man and his participation in the ordinary lot of mortal man. This implies that the Redeemer had to go down into the realms of death after he had died. But, even more than this, it stood at the time for redemption from death through the power of Christ's resurrection, brought about by God who rules absolutely over life and death, and this power was the condition by means of which all those who have been redeemed in Christ might overcome death.

Bibliography: A. Grillmeier, 'Der Gottessohn im Totenreich', *ZKT* 71 (1949), 1–53 and 184–203; A. Grillmeier, *LTK* v², 450–5, with a full bibliography which includes: K. Gschwind, *Die Niederfahrt Christi in die Unterwelt*, Munich 1911; J. A. MacCulloch, *The Harrowing of Hell*, Edinburgh 1930; B. Reicke, *The Disobedient Spirits and Christian Baptism*, Copenhagen 1946; W. Bieder, *Die Vorstellung von der H.J.Chr.*, Zurich 1949; P. Benoit, 'La descente aux Enfers selon W. Bieder', *RB* (1951). See also: Haag 1206f and the commentaries on 1 Pet, esp. the excursus by J. Michl in his *Der Brief an die Hebr. und die kath. Briefe* (*RNT* 8), Regensburg 1953, 224–6; and K. H. Schelkle, *Die Petrusbriefe, der Judasbrief*, Freiburg 1964², 104–8.

Johannes Kürzinger

Desire

The various words used in the bible to denote the sphere of human striving are, in the main, formations from ᵓāwâh, ḥāmad, epithumos—see *TDNT* III, 168–70—and cover all shades of meaning—that is, striving which is good, bad, or indifferent. The English word 'desire' can refer to either good or evil striving, and it is in the latter sense that it is discussed here.

Desire can be a sin, and in the form of covetousness it is expressly forbidden in the Decalogue (Ex 20:17; Deut 5:21). Compliance with this commandment is the basis of the more perfect justice demanded by Jesus (Mt 5:27–8).

In the Old Testament the 'wicked man', who is the enemy of the religious man, is characterised in a general way by means of evil desires, wishes, and intentions which are harmful to himself and to others (eg, Prov 11:6; 21:25, 26) but which, however, God is able to thwart (Prov 10:3; Ps 140:9)—though no exact distinction is made here between temptation and sin and between striving in the sexual, sensitive, and spiritual spheres. The piety of a later age, more concerned with the individual's own ethical achievement, will experience all the more painfully this opposition which works in the depth of the soul against the performance of duty. The religious man is acutely conscious of this apparently innate predisposition to sin (Ps 51:7; 130:3; 143:2). The Old Testament contains frequent complaints of man's hardness of heart and obduracy (Ezek 36:26; Ps 81:13), and his lascivious running after evil (Jer 2:23; see also Prov 1:22), and there are also many pleas for self-control and many ad-monitions and pieces of advice (Prov 23:3; Sir 22:27–23:27). In such cases there is often no clear distinction drawn between the general character of the actual sin committed and the cause which is to be found in man himself, an interior disposition to personal sin (see Ezek 11:19; Zech 7:12; Jer 4:4; Ps 143:2), and there are many references to categories of sins other than those pertaining to desire. It is, however, possible to see, in the later view, that the commandment forbidding evil de-sire embraces the entire law (4 Macc 2:6; *Vita Adae*, 19; cf Rom 7:7; 13:9), and in the rabbinical doctrine of the 'evil impulse' (see Gen 6:5; 8:21; SB IV 466f) the intersection of the various ideas and terms for one and the same reality, all of which were later grouped by theologians under the common heading of concupiscence (not, in-cidentally, to be thought of in its exclusively sexual connotation).

In the gospels and the catholic epistles, very much the same picture may be found. Man is defiled by his evil desires (Mt 15:18–20; Mk 7:20–3; see also Gal 5:16–21). They give rise to temptations and sins (Jas 1:13–15; 4:1–4). Man is made a slave to the world by his evil desires, which in any case must perish with the world. Man's evil desires thus exclude him from eternal salvation (1 Jn 2:15–17; see also 1 Tim 5:6; Tit 2:12; Jude 18). In Christ's own interpretation of his parable of the sower, the failure of the word of God to take effect among the third group of people is traceable to the 'cares of the world, and the delight in riches, and the desire for other things' (Mk 4:19; see also Mt 13:22; Lk 8:14).

In reality, the same effect is attributed to Satan in the case of the first group of people (Mk 4:15; see also Mt 13:19; Lk 8:12). Thus, it can be assumed that some kind of co-operation exists be-tween the external evil power and man's interior concupiscence. This is quite apparent in 1 Cor 7:5 (see also Jn 8:41–4; Wis 2:24).

In Rom 7:7–8:4, the relationship between desire and salvation is pre-sented with considerable emphasis, although this is merely incidental to the main theme of the passage. Paul devises a whole scheme of salvation-history (see Rom 5:12–17) with un-avoidable generalisations and rough outlines, in the form of a drama in which 'sin', 'flesh', 'death', and 'law' enter as personified powers (see R. Benoit, *RB* 47 [1938], 483–5). The 'I' of the narrative is not to be understood as playing an empirically personal or generally human role, but as gathering the unredeemed situation up into a comprehensive entity. Kuhn (*ZTK* 49 [1952], 204–26) points out that an analogous 'I', as narrator, exists in Qumran (1 *QS* 11, 7–6). Although it is certainly difficult to keep 'sin' distinct from evil desire, because the close relationship that exists between them tends to make them appear to be used almost as interchangeable ideas, it would nonetheless be wrong to identify the one completely with the other (Schauf, *Sarx*, 29–32). The desires appear as the object, result, aim or means of the 'sin' which is regarded as the power behind them (Rom 7:8, 11; 6:12, 13). They control the 'flesh'—that is to say, not only the material part of man (see 2 Cor 2:12; Col 2:18), but the entire 'old' man who has not yet become a 'new' man in Christ. The innate tendency of the old man is to oppose God and to incline towards sin (Rom 1:24–5; 6:12–13; 8:6–7; Gal 5:16–24; Eph 2:3), and even to oppose the 'inner', better man, namely his reasoning faculty (Rom 7:22, 23, 25).

The real malice of desire of the 'flesh' is most apparent where it comes into conflict with the Law. The Law is indeed good and holy (Rom 7:12). It certainly does not arouse concupiscence for the first time (Rom 1:24; 2:12, 15), but the very commandment which forbids concupiscence in fact gives it further stimulus (Rom 7:7) and provides occasion for transgression. The Law brings the evil quality of the sin to the forefront and makes the sinner fully responsible for his transgression. The emphasis is thus placed less on the immediate psychological occasion of desire (Rom 7:8, 11; Benoit 487f), than on the fact that desire, acting, as it were, as a kind of fifth column, makes man a slave to sin (Rom 7:14–23; 8:12; Gal 5:17; 1 Pet 2:11; Jas 4:1ff). This is not to say that the law can prevent the tyranny which desire exercises over the flesh from mastering man. In itself the situation is indeed hopeless. (Rom 7:13–25.)

God's intervention in man's affairs through Christ redeems him from sin and death. Salvation consists in the victory of the 'spirit' over the 'flesh' (Rom 8:1–4; see also Gal 5:24; Eph 4:23; Tit 3:3–7; Benoit, 492–502). The situation in which redemption can occur is presented in several contrasting ways—man's one-time evil inclination towards the flesh and its desires and his present inclination towards the life of the spirit; the old man

and the new man; death and life; flesh and spirit; the heathen and the redeemed man, and so on. None of these antitheses is purely empirical, but they are valid *de jure*. All these illustrations are accompanied by warnings to christians not to let sins and desires become habitual, and that each individual must develop for himself what has been established as a fundamental principle of redemption (Gal 5:16–24; Eph 4:17–24; Col 3:5–11; Rom 6:11–23; 2 Tim 2:22). Although the Spirit of God has delivered the redeemed from the slavery of their evil desires and sins (Rom 8:1–14), these evil desires have not been physically destroyed. They have, however, certainly been deprived of their power, and the christian is thereby able to renounce sin (Col 3:5; Gal 5:24; 6:14; Rom 8:13). In this way it can be seen that redemption is not simply the realisation of a stoic ideal (see the Coptic Gospel of St Thomas, logion 38 [Leipoldt]: cessation of the sense of shame). For this reason, christians are urged to continue to discipline the flesh (Rom 13:14; see also Sir 22:27–23:27; Behm, *TDNT* IV, 1004).

Only the most obscure indications and hints concerning the origins of evil desire are to be found in indirect references in the bible, which is of course concerned with man in the whole of his afflicted and sinful condition. From a state of general sinfulness which exists from his earliest youth (Ps 51:7; Gen 6:5; 8:21; Deut 31:21; Prov 22:15) it is no more than a step to the acceptance of the idea of his inborn perversity. His condition as a whole is in fact traceable to the original sin of his first parents, but what the bible has

in mind is the general state of degenerate man, and here and there this is
referred to explicitly (Sir 25:24; Wis
2:23–4; Rom 5:12–21; cf 1 Tim
2:14). It is not possible, however, to
gather any unequivocal evidence, as
the relative importance of the part
played by evil desire as such is nowhere
made explicit, though it is indisputable
that it was fatally instrumental in
preparing the way for the Fall (Gen
3:6).

Bibliography: B. Bartmann, 'Die Konkupiszenz, Herkunft und Wesen', *TG* 24 (1932), 405–46; P. Benoit, 'La Loi et la Croix d'après Saint Paul', *RB* 47 (1938), 481–509; Büchsel, *TDNT* III, 167–72; A. M. Dubarle, 'La condition humaine dans l'Ancien Testament', *RB* 63 (1956), 321–45; A. M. Dubarle, 'Le péché originel dans la Genèse', *RB* 64 (1957), 5–34; A. M. Dubarle, 'Le péché originel dans les suggestions de l'Evangile', *RSPT* 40 (1956), 213–54; K. G. Kuhn, '*Peirasmos-hamartia-sarx* im NT und die damit zusammenhängenden Vorstellungen', *ZTK* 49 (1952), 200–22; R. E. Murphy, '*Bsr* in the Qumran Literature and *Sarx* in the Epistle to the Romans', *SP* II, Paris 1959, 60–76; W. Schauf, '*Sarx*: Der Begriff "Fleisch" beim Apostel Paulus unter bes. Berücksichtigung seiner Erlösungslehre', *NA* 11 (1924), 1–2; Stählin, *TDNT* II, 909–26; R. Storr, 'Das Frömmig keitsideal der Propheten', *BZF* 12/3–4, Münster 1926; SB IV, 466–83; P. Wilpert, *RAC* II, 62–78; S. Lyonnet, '"Tu ne convoiteras pas" (Rom 7:7)', *Neotestamentica et patristica: Eine Freundesgabe, Herrn Professor Dr Oscar Cullman zu sienem 60 Geburtstag überreicht*, Leiden 1962, 157–65; S. Lyonnet, 'Questiones as Rom 7:7–13', *VD* 40 (1962), 163–83.

Johann Gamberoni

Disciple

A. *The Talmid*. The teacher of the
Law, or rabbi, was a common sight
during the time of our Lord, and he
was generally followed at a respectful
distance by his pupils, or *talmidim*. At
the very commencement of his public
life, Jesus gathered disciples round him
and these followed him (Mk 1:16f;
Jn 1:37–51). At least as far as external
appearances are concerned, he re-
sembled a Jewish teacher of the Law,
accompanied by his pupils. This is also
illustrated by the comparison between
the disciples of our Lord and those of
John the Baptist and of the pharisees
(Mk 2:18; see also Jn 9:28f).

Although the Hebrew verb *lāmad*
means in the first place 'to learn a
trade', it is in most cases used in the
specific sense of being engaged in the
study of the Torah. Correctly speaking,
the entire people of Israel ought to be,
as it were, apprenticed to the Torah
and thus be *talmidim*. Even the Messiah
was expected to come as pupil and
teacher of the Torah. Yet, in practice,
it was only comparatively few who
could be fully and intensely engaged in
the study of the Torah, and those who
did specialize in this way became the
teachers of the people and, first and
foremost, of those specially chosen to be
their pupils. These in their turn were
also destined, like them, to become
teachers of the Law.

The pupil acquired a knowledge of
the Law by listening and in debate. He
received his initiation in the life-
according-to-the-Law by keeping constant company with his teacher. But,
although the pupil of the Law was a
person who commanded great respect
among the more ignorant sections of the
community, especially if he was well
advanced in his studies, he had a slave-
like relationship with the rabbi, who
had dedicated his entire life to the study
of the Law, and he performed menial
duties for him. The attitude of the

talmid towards his teacher, the rabbi, was expressed in the respectful distance at which he followed him.

B. *The call of Jesus.* It must be stressed, however, that the resemblance which exists between the pupils of the rabbi and our Lord's disciples is purely external. An important difference was apparent from the very beginning of this discipleship. The pious Jew who wished to become a rabbi singled out one man from among the many who were scholars in the Law and made every attempt, from that time onwards, to be accepted by that teacher as a talmud. Jesus, on the other hand, issued a supreme call to his disciples: 'Follow me!' (Mk 1:17; Jn 1:43), whereas he sent men who tried to force their attentions on him away (Lk 9:61f; Mk 5:18). There was no particular or standard qualification for the vocation of this discipleship. The prophets of the old covenant were not made fit to carry out their task because of certain human facts or data which were already known in advance, but because God himself had made them fit for their work (Ex 3:11f; Is 6:5ff; Jer 1:6ff; Ezek 2:8ff). In just the same way, Jesus called those 'whom he desired' (Mk 3:13) and 'made' them (Mk 3:13; cf Mk 1:17) into what he wanted them to be. He even included the 'sinful man' Peter (Lk 5:8) and Matthew the tax-collector (Mt 9:9).

C. *Those who followed Jesus.* The supreme call of Jesus evoked a corresponding answer from those who were called and they left everything—their parents and their nets or, in the case of Matthew, the custom-house—and at once followed Jesus. There is no parallel between the relationship of the rabbi towards his talmidim and this unreserved obedience in response to Jesus's call, for it is a question of obedience to a master who has the right to demand everything. Jesus is not merely a rabbi. He is the Messiah. It is not a question of choosing between one teacher and another, but of deciding for or against the Messiah— and that is why Jesus did not tolerate consent given to him being qualified in any way at all (see Lk 9:59–62). The Messiah is inseparable from his mission and must give himself to it wholeheartedly and without reserve (see Mk 3:31–5). What applies to the Messiah also applies to his disciples: 'He who loves father or mother more than me is not worthy of me' (Mt 10:37), and, even more pointedly: 'If any one comes to me, and does not hate his own father and mother and wife and children and brothers and sisters, yes, and even his own life, he cannot be my disciple. Whoever does not bear his own cross and come after me, cannot be my disciple' (Lk 14:26f). The pupils of the Hebrew scholars followed their rabbi like servants, out of respect for him and his knowledge of the Hebrew texts, but the disciple of Jesus, in following the Messiah, put his entire existence, his life itself, at the disposal of the Messiah: 'Thomas, called the Twin, said to his fellow disciples, "Let us also go, that we may die with him"' (Jn 11:16).

D. *The Twelve.* Jesus chose twelve from a much larger number of disciples (Mk 3:13–19). These twelve formed what was above all a smaller circle of disciples within the larger circle. From the time of the crisis in Galilee onwards, however, it is more than likely that these two circles overlapped and the 'disciples' and the 'twelve' meant the same thing (compare Mk 14:12ff with 14:17).

What did Jesus intend to do with the Twelve? Mk 3:14 supplies the answer to this question in a nutshell: 'And he appointed twelve, to be [always] with him, and to be sent out [as deputies or plenipotentiaries] to preach.' They were also to be with him and to be initiated into the 'secret of the kingdom of God' (Mk 4:11). They were, however, to be sent out as plenipotentiaries, with full authority. All the twelve disciples whom Jesus had chosen as his ↗ apostles were granted such powers, which were conferred upon them provisionally during his public ministry (Mk 6:7) and definitively—with the exception of Judas Iscariot—after his resurrection (Mt 28:16–20). All twelve —or eleven—were thus apostles, though apostleship was not restricted exclusively to the Twelve, for there were other apostles apart from the Twelve, as for example, Barnabas and Paul. The actual number twelve has nothing to do with the apostolate, although it is not purely coincidental — a fact which emerges clearly from the addition of Matthias to the number of apostles after the defection of Judas (Acts 1:15–26). After its lapse, it was imperative to restore the number twelve, which corresponds to the number of the twelve sons of Israel who formed the basis of God's chosen people. As apostles, it was the function of the Twelve to represent the Messiah (↗ Apostle), but as the Twelve, they represented the New Israel. 'The people of the saints of the Most High' (Dan 7:27) belong to the Son of Man (Dan 7:13ff). The 'kingdom and the

dominion and the greatness of the kingdoms under the whole heaven' which is given to the 'people of the saints of the Most High' can be compared with Mt 19:28: 'When the Son of man shall sit on his glorious throne' the Twelve will likewise 'also sit on twelve thrones, judging the twelve tribes of Israel'. Although it would be possible for any arbitrary number of disciples to embody the new people of God, the exact number twelve does unmistakably draw attention to this particular function of Jesus's disciples and at the same time implies a certain compactness. When Jesus 'made' the Twelve (see Mk 3:14: 'He appointed twelve . . .'), he established the basis of the eschatological people of God. This unique and basic function (see also Eph 2:20) is in fact exercised exclusively by the Twelve (among them, Peter has a special role to play [Mt 16:18]), and, what is more, they carry out this function independently from their apostolic mission, as the Twelve. The embodiment of the eschatological people of God is, however, only one part of this basic function that the Twelve have to perform, for they had a particularly active task to fulfil in addition to this more passive one. They accompanied Jesus from the moment that he began his public life to the time of his death. They heard everything that he taught the people and were given special instruction and tuition by him. They shared in the experience of all his miracles and heard all his prophecies. They were eye-witnesses of his passion, death and resurrection and were thus the guarantors of an unbroken continuity between the risen Lord and the Jesus of history. The faith of the church is dependent upon the testimony of these men, who did not happen by chance to be Jesus's witnesses, but were appointed, as authorised witnesses, to exercise this unique function for the church of all ages (see Acts 1:21f). This is why he called upon them to accompany him and to attend upon him constantly and why he appeared to them immediately after his resurrection: 'But God raised him [Jesus] from the dead [on the third day]; and for many days he appeared to those who came up with him from Galilee to Jerusalem, who are now his witnesses to the people' (Paul in Antioch of Pisidia: Acts 13:30f; see also 1 Cor 15:3ff). This double function, then, bestows a unique and supreme importance on the Twelve and puts them in a position of unrivalled distinction with regard to all other members of the embryonic church. It also explains why the death of the last of the Twelve is such a significant date in the history of the church and of revelation.

E. *Discipleship in the widest sense of the word.* The two words *disciple* and *follow* are very closely connected with each other. Used in its fullest sense, and not merely to denote walking aimlessly along behind, 'following' in the New Testament always signifies following Jesus, treading in his footsteps, and implies his physical presence. Thus, apart from the use of the word in Rev 14:4 ('These who follow the Lamb wherever he goes'), it is met with only in the gospels. All the same, it is not always easy to distinguish, in the synoptic gospels, whether the demands which are made on the disciples who follow Jesus are meant to apply only

to those disciples who have 'left everything' in obedience to Jesus's call and have given themselves without reserve to the service of the Messiah, or to all men who believe in Jesus. In Jn 8:31, a far wider concept of discipleship comes to light: 'Jesus then said to the Jews who had believed him, 'If you continue in my word, you are my disciples . . .' This concept of discipleship in the wider sense is frequently met with in Acts (Chapters 6–21), but is unknown in the writings of Paul, where a different concept of discipleship, which is only incidental to the text of the synoptic gospels, is to be found. This is the imitation of Jesus. Though the germ of this idea of imitation is contained in the original concept of following Jesus (see Mk 10:45), it does not come into prominence until the time after Easter—that is, subsequent to the Lord's resurrection (1 Cor 11:1; 1 Thess 1:6; see also 1 Jn 2:6; 3:16). These various extensions of the original meaning go to show how the early church strove to preserve, after Easter, the practical significance of the words which Jesus had spoken in connection with discipleship and the need to follow him. It is also possible to perceive in the life of the apostle Paul how he had accepted without any reservation all the demands which Jesus made of his disciples.

Bibliography: G. Kittel, *TDNT* I, 210–16; K. H. Rengstorf, *TDNT* IV, 415–61; P. Gaechter, 'Die Wahl des Matthias', *ZKT* 71 (1949), 318–46; T. Süss, 'Nachfolge Jesu', *TLZ* 78 (1953), 129–40; R. Schnackenburg, *The Moral Teaching of the New Testament*, London and New York 1964; J. Schmid, *Das Evangelium nach Markus* (*RNT*), Regensburg 1954³, 76–9; J. Schmid, *Das Evangelium nach Lukas* (*RNT*), Regensburg ·1955³, 178–82; K. H. Schelkle, *Discipleship and Priesthood*, London and New York 1966; P. Gaechter, *Petrus und seine Zeit*, 1958; B. Rigaux, 'Die "Zwölf" in Geschichte und Kerygma', *Der historische Jesus und der kerygmatische Christus*, ed. H. Ristow and K. Matthias, 1960, 468–86; A. Schulz, *Nachfolgen und Nachahmen*, 1962; E. Neuhäusler, *Anspruch und Antwort Gottes*, 1962; H. Kahlefeld, *Der Jünger*, 1962²; A. Schulz, 'Nachfolge', *HTG* II, 202–7; *S. Freyne, *The Twelve: Disciples and Apostles. A Study in the Theology of the First Three Gospels*, London 1968. On the imitation of Christ: W. Michaelis, *TDNT* IV, 659–74.

Elmar M. Kredel

Discipline

A. *The Old Testament*. The Hebrew word *mûsār* (from the root *ysr*) stands indifferently for two distinct concepts, those namely of *discipline* and *chastisement*. The reason for this is that it is through chastisement that one who has neglected the law and tradition, one therefore who is deficient in discipline, must be brought back to a due awareness of them. The concept of discipline carries with it the further connotation of forming one's understanding (see Prov 4:1ff), and for this reason *mûsār* can also signify *education (paideia), training*. Hebrew contains no term which exactly hits off these ideas. Often it is not easy to distinguish precisely between the various meanings in individual cases. Neither *mûsār* nor the verb *yāsar* is ever used in connection with animals.

The responsibility of maintaining discipline in daily life belonged to the father of the family. He was responsible for bringing up the younger generation in the spirit of the law and of tradition (see Gen 18:19; Ex 12:26; 13:14; Deut 6:7, 20ff). In bringing up his children the father must not spare the rod of chastisement (Prov 13:24;

19:18; 23:13f). It was legitimate for masters to chastise their slaves to a certain limited extent (see Ex 21:20f, 26f; Prov 29:19, 21). In the case of certain specific crimes the judge or the elders of the city had to have the perpetrators chastised (Deut 22:13–19: 25:1–3). In 1 Kings 12:11, 14; 2 Chron 10:11–14 chastisement is mentioned as a method of coercion exercised against subordinates.

Just as a father keeps his son to the right path by chastising him, not in spite of the fact that he loves him but rather because of it, so too the Lord chastises him whom he favours (Prov 3:11f). And just as he acts towards the individual so too he acts towards his people as a whole (Deut 8:5). The whole record of Old Testament history is written from this basic standpoint of the people being educated by God. Disobedience and apostasy from God bring down punishment upon the people (Lev 26:14–33; Jer 2:19), though admittedly these were often unwilling to accept the chastisement (Jer 32:33; Zeph 3:2–7).

Bibliography: L. Dürr, *Das Erziehungswesen im AT und im Antiken Orient*, MVAG 36/2, Leipzig 1932; G. Bertram, *TDNT* v, 596ff.

Johannes Gabriel

B. *The New Testament*. The law is the disciplinarian, *paidagōgos*. But when the pupil comes of age there is no further room for this function of the law (Gal 3:24). Christians are no longer under the law, but under grace (Rom 6:14). With Paul the early church took over the ideas of education belonging to the Old Testament, reinterpreting them and developing them further in a christological sense.

The idea of education by God is treated of in Heb 12. When they are chastised christians must take this as a clear sign that they are children of God (12:7f). Sufferings must be regarded as chastisement and so endured, for they admit the sufferer to a share in God's holiness (12:10), and bring him peace and righteousness (12:11).

In Rev 3:19 it is laid down as a principle that God imposes punishments on those men whom he loves in order to educate them and to bring them to ↗ conversion. In Tit 2:12 grace itself 'educates' the community, teaching them to renounce all that is hostile to God, and to live in hope—although in this passage we are told nothing of what means of education are used for the attainment of this. He who does not act as judge towards himself will be judged by the Lord and sentenced to chastisement in order not to be condemned together with the world that is hostile to God (1 Cor 11:32). Sometimes even those who are endowed with grace are chastised in order to make sure that they do not lose it (2 Cor 12:7-9).

In the list of moral precepts in Eph 6:4 the elders are admonished to bring up their children 'in the discipline of the Lord', that is in the discipline which the Lord himself (subjective genitive) exercises through the father, and all the means which are recognised as useful for the purpose in the non-christian world are to be applied here also. The phrase *en paideia(i) kai nouthesia(i)* (='in discipline and instruction') can be taken as a hendiadys, but it is equally possible to find two distinct meanings here, ie, 'discipline' and 'exhortation', and to regard the former as standing for education by means of deeds, while the latter refers to education by means of words.

In the pastoral epistles this basic principle is applied to the community. Scripture itself has an educative value (2 Tim 3:16; see also 1 Cor 10:11). The leaders of the community are responsible for the religious education of their fellow christians (Rom 2:20; 2 Tim 2:25; Heb 12:9). They are also authorised to impose ecclesiastical disciplines (Acts 5:1-11; 13:6-12), and even to deliver individuals over to Satan as a means of chastisement (1 Tim 1:20; see also 1 Cor 5:5 and 2 Cor 12:7).

Bibliography: G. Bertram, *TDNT* v, 619-25; W. Jentsch, *Urchristliches Erziehungsdenken*, Gütersloh 1951; O. Leclerq, *Dict. de la Spiritualité* 3, 1291ff; J. Campos, 'Concepto de la "Disciplina" biblica', *Revista Calasancia*, Madrid 6 (1960), 47-73.

Johannes B. Bauer

Dream

A. *In the Old Testament.* The belief in the significance of dreams was widespread throughout the ancient world. It took a long time to arrive at the rational explanation that in dreaming one's psyche is concerned with the same things which occupy one during the waking hours. This finds expression in the Letter of Aristeas 16 and even earlier in Sir 34:3 'the likeness of a face confronting a face' (see also Ps 126:1). This universal belief in dreams made it possible for God to use the dream as a medium of revelation. This does not imply that the dream as such has any intrinsic capacity for revelation but that it is considered merely as a means whereby God communicates. Hence it is stressed, on the one hand, how transient and ephemeral is what is seen in dream (Is 29:7f; Job 20:8) and, on the other, that God can use even the dreams of pagans as a means of revelation (Gen 20:6; 28:10ff; Dan 2:1ff; 7:1ff). This is shown most clearly by those dreams which require an interpretation since it is only God who can give to whom he pleases the ability to interpret (Gen 40:8; 41:16, 39; Dan 2:17ff).

Both in the ancient world as a whole and in the Old Testament we can distinguish between cultic (Gen 28:11ff), political (Judg 7:13ff), and purely personal dreams (Gen 40:8ff; Job 33:15f). In the early sources of the Pentateuch, the Yahwist is reserved as regards dreams, while the Elohist has—we may say—a strong faith in dreams, even though the latter seems to preserve the distance between man and God much better than the former. In Deut 13:2ff we find a critical position taken up with regard to dream visitations. The criterion for discerning the genuineness of a dream-revelation is whether it confirms fidelity to the God of the covenant. This critical note finds its strongest expression in Jer 23:16ff. Even here, however, it is not dictated by lack of faith. On the contrary, it springs from a genuine faith in Yahweh. Zech 10:2 speaks to much the same effect. It is not until we come to the Wisdom literature that we find a genuinely rational explanation of dreams of the kind referred to earlier (Eccles 5:3, 7; Sir 34:3ff).

B. *In the New Testament.* The line which starts in the Old Testament is continued in the New, and the limits within which one can speak of meaningful dreams are even further restricted. The early christians did not positively disbelieve in dreams but took up a very critical attitude towards them. The dream constituted a marginal phenomenon and there is no case of any central theme of the gospel being based on a dream-revelation. Its significance was restricted to particular cases when God chose this way to guide a certain individual. Paul never refers in his letters to any of the dreams mentioned in Acts (16:9f; 18:9; 23:11; 27:23f), even though they at times touched on decisive points in the life of the church and the apostles. We find accounts of dreams only in Mt (1:20f; 2:12, 13, 19, 22; 27:19), where they clearly are meant to serve an apologetic purpose.

None of the dreams mentioned in the New Testament requires an interpretation. Moreover, biblical dreams in general manifest a striking economy of description and soberness in contrast with the kind of thing found in the cultural milieu of that time. In dreams which we read of in antiquity superstition, idle curiosity and the baser passions generally play a large part. The New Testament dream-narratives, on the other hand, are centred on Christ. God guides those who belong to him (Mt 1:20; 2:13; Acts 16:9) and the Lord consoles and strengthens his disciples (Acts 18:9; 23:11; 27:23f) *even* by means of dreams.

It is only in a later period that we find people reverting to a quite unbiblical propensity to dreams and the interpretation of dreams.

Bibliography: T. Hopfner, *RE* 2/VI (1937), 2233–45; A. Oepke, *TDNT* v (1954), 220–38; E. L. Ehrlich, *Der Traum im Alten Testament*, Berlin 1953; A. Oepke, *ZAW* 67 (1955), 127; A. Caquot, 'Les songes et leur interprétation selon Canaan et Israel', *Les Songes et Leur Interprétation*, Paris 1959; L. Oppenheim, *The Interpretation of Dreams in the Ancient Near East*, Philadelphia 1956; W. Richter, 'Traum und Traumdeutung im Alten Testament', *BZ* 7 (1963), 202–19; A. Resch, *Der Traum im Heilsplan Gottes, Deutung und Bedeutung des Traums im AT*, Freiburg 1964; A. Finkel, 'The pesher of Dreams and Scriptures', *Revue de Qumran*, 15, IV fasc. 3, 357–70; A. Wikenhauser, 'Die Traumgesichte des Neuen Testaments in religionsgeschichtliche Sicht', *Ant. und Christentum* I, Münster 1939, 320–33; A. Wikenhauser, 'Doppelträume', *Bbl* 29 (1948), 100–11.

Johannes B. Bauer

Emotion

A. *Old Testament and judaism*. In the bible no concept is to be found precisely corresponding to what the scholastics called *passio* and *concupiscentia*, and what in the German of the seventeenth century was called *Leidenschaft* (passion). Old Testament man, oriental as he was, and strongly emotional by disposition, was well aware of the reality of passion. Violent desires and sudden changes of mood (Jon 4:2f; see also Gen 30:1; Judg 16:16; 2 Sam 13:2; Prov 17:22) are recorded, and, no less prominently than these, the fear which degenerates into panic. A further phenomenon known to Israel was a kind of uncanny mass excitement which threw whole peoples into enthusiasm, fear, or uproar (Deut 20:8; Ex 23:27; 1 Sam 10:5; 19:20–4; 2 Sam 21f). According to the Old Testament the passions are located not exactly in the body, but in the heart of men (Gen 6:5; 8:21; 1 Kings 3:11f; Hos 4:11; cf Rom 2:29).

All the accounts of ↗ sin and guilt from the sin of paradise (Gen 3:6), the sin of Cain (4:5) and the sin of the generation of Noah (6:5) onwards, and right through the bible to the hatred of the enemies of the Maccabees (1 Macc 7:26; 11:21) either mention passion explicitly, or at any rate presuppose it as an existing fact. Such passion is especially emphasised in the case of two kinds of sin, namely offences against God (Lev 26:19; 2 Kings 19:28; Amos 6:8) especially through idolatry (Ex 32:1–6; Num 25:1–5; 1 Kings 18:26ff; Wis 14:28), and offences against human rights, especially murder and oppression (Gen 4:8, 23f; Job 24:14; see also Is 1:21; Jer 7:9; Hos 4:2) and sexual vices (Gen 39; 2 Kings 13:1f; Dan 13). Instinctive desires of every kind (see Gen 31:30; Deut 12:20f) were considered as in themselves the starting-point and root of every sin (Num 11:4, 34; Deut 9:22; Ps 106:14). Later the formula 'You shall not covet (lust after)' (see Ex 20:17f) came to be regarded, without further qualification, as a summary of all the prohibitions of the Old Testament (4 Macc 2:6; see also Rom 7:7; 13:9).

In the bible Cain is the type of the impulsive and violent man. His passionate nature is explicitly mentioned (Gen 4:5). It is also manifested in the episode in which he builds a city (4:17), which is reminiscent of the Tower of Babel (11:1–9). Most of all it is manifested in his unscrupulous descendant Lamech (4:19, 23f), whose song of victory is a piece of unbridled boasting over his own sense power, and in which he pretends to outdo the power of God without regard to the value of human life (see Judg 11; 1 Jn 3:12).

Passion which is hostile to God in the Old Testament is called drunkenness (Is 29:9). It seals the eyes (29:10f), stops the ears, and makes the heart fat (Is 6:10) or stony (Ezek 11:19). The Old Testament theology of history, unsystematic in character as it is, often represents the effects of passion as coming directly from God and from his Spirit (Judg 9:23; 1 Sam 19:9), without thereby intending to derogate from the ⁄ freedom and responsibility of men (Deut 2:30; Josh 11:20; Is 44:18; Jer 7:22ff; Ezek 2:3–7; cf Ezek 12:2 with Is 6:9f; ⁄ hardening of heart). It is only in the eschatological age, when God will blot out all the sins of those who are his own, that the vital emotions of the heart will also be cleansed and purified, but not obliterated (Is 57:14–19; Ezek 11:19).

It is not only in excessive sensuality or in a multiplicity of sins that the passionate nature finds expression. On the contrary it is also the prior condition of, and the quality from which proceed many good actions. This is already apparent in natural love; the special intimacy between father and child (Judg 11:35; 2 Sam 19:1), husband and wife (Gen 29:20, 30; 34:2f; Judg 16:4; 1 Sam 1:8; 2 Sam 3:16; esp Song 8:6f), and between two friends (1 Sam 16:21; 18:1, 3; 20:17; 2 Sam 1:26). Again the love of Old Testament man for his God is unrestricted and vehement (Deut 6:5; 30:6; Jer 4:4) because it is based upon an experience of God as Father (Is 1:4; 30:1, 9; Hos 11:1–4) and bridegroom (Hos 1–3; Jer 12:7–9; Is 54:5–8) of his people

(⁄ love). This love of Old Testament man looks to the end in which God will write another law once and for all in the hearts of men, namely the law of love, and will thereby instill in them an inalienable instinct for God, a purified passion (Jer 31:33; cf Is 57:14–19; Ezek 11:19). In anticipation of this event the devout are already dominated by a passionate hatred of all that is hostile to God. The examples of Phinehas (Num 25:11, 13f; Sir 45:23; 1 Macc 2:26, 54), of Elijah (1 Kings 19:10, 14; 1 Macc 2:58), of Jehu (2 Kings 10:16) and of Mattathias (1 Macc 2:24, 26f, 50) find their echo in prayers and canticles (Ps 69:10; 119:139; ⁄ curse), and the good Israelite models his life upon them.

This passion in man is in emulation of the passion of God. Yahweh's ⁄ joy is represented as an exuberant rejoicing (Zeph 3:17), Yahweh's aversion as disgust and loathing (Lev 20:23; Ps 106:40), as hatred and ⁄ wrath (Deut 12:31; 29:20; 2 Sam 24:1). Conversely Yahweh's love is depicted as boundless jealousy (Ex 20:5; Deut 5:9), and his disappointment as bitter regret (Gen 6:6; Jon 3:10). This anthropomorphism, in which human passions are ascribed to ⁄ God is proof of the fact that Yahweh was thought of as existing and reacting as a personal God, that as a holy God he removes all that is unholy far from him, that as a powerful God he intervenes again and again in the course of events. At the same time such anthropomorphisms are used by the preacher to convey a message of penance to sinners, and an exhortation to those who fear God to seek him with a passionate ardour corresponding to his own. Thus the ⁄ Spirit of God becomes effective. He comes upon his own and produces effects of incredible power in them (Ex 31:3; Judg 6:34; 13:25; Is 63:11; Ezek 36:27), even to the point of transports and ecstasies (Num 11:25-9; 1 Sam 11:6, 13; 19:20; Joel 2:28f; etc).

In the Wisdom literature of the Old Testament the exhortation to conduct that is without passion, that is without sin, and to moderation in every department of life (↗ wisdom) acquires special significance (Prov 27:4; Wisdom 4:12; see also Job 5:2f). Not the least of the motives adduced for such an exercise of self-discipline are natural ones (Sir 18:33; 30:24; 40:5-7) and specific examples of self-command are held up for emulation (Sir 44:1) as a major element in this moral teaching. This particular kind of moral teaching is in conformity with a Hellenistic influence which was making itself felt at the period in question, although it was at no time absolutely dependent upon this influence. In it a particularly prominent feature is the emphasis on self-restraint in sexual matters (Wis 7:2; Sir 9:1-9; Job 31:1; Dan 13). It finds its finest expression in the prayer for cleanness of heart and for protection from lust and passion (Sir 22:27; 23:6).

Rabbinical judaism evolved the doctrine of the 'evil impulse' by developing earlier sayings (see Sir 15:14; 21:11; TestJud 20), and on the basis of Gen 6:5; 8:21. This impulse, which God inserts afresh into each man, is the cause, so it is held, of all lustful desires and vices, especially unchastity and idolatry. At the same time it impels men to eat, to beget and to strive for happiness. Without the help of God, that is without prayer and fulfilment of the law, no man can bring this impulse under control. This doctrine has nothing to do with the doctrine of the ↗ sin of the first parents as set forth by the apostle Paul (see J. Schmid, *LTK* II [1958²], 618-20). It is rather a systematic 'doctrine of the passions external to the bible itself, which is intended to digest theologically and to render comprehensible the statements of scripture and of experienced men.'

B. *New Testament.* The New Testament recognises passion that is holy, and anger that is just (cf Rev 14:10; 16:19; 18:3; 19:15). Of Jesus it records that he was very sorrowful (Lk 19:41-4; Jn 11:33), that he was greatly distressed (Mk 14:33 and parallels) and was stirred up into a holy zeal for God (Mk 11:15-17 and parallels, esp Jn 2:17). The message of the New Testament demands the greatest zeal from all disciples. A passionate ↗ joy shall come upon them (Mt 13:44), so that in a moment, at a sudden inward prompting (↗ vocation) they can abandon all things without a single backward glance to earthly ties and earthly necessities (Mk 8:34-8 parallels; Lk 9:57-62). Their engagement for the Lord is not tempered by any spirit of calculation and human wisdom (2 Cor 11-12), and is to go far beyond the zeal of the Jews, great as this is (see Rom 10:2; Gal 1:14; Phil 3:6; Acts 21:20; 22:3). To be a christian means to become dedicated body and soul to the service of the Lord (Phil 3:12ff), and to remain utterly and unreservedly true to him (2 Cor 8:11f; 9:2; Gal 4:18; Tit 2:14) even to the point of martyrdom (↗ witness). For christians the service of love requires most of all heartfelt compassion (Lk 10:33, 37).

The judgement as described by Jesus (Mt 25:31–46) shows that impulsive acts of compassion are not of little worth, but on the contrary are highly prized (see 2 Cor 7:8–11). The teaching of the New Testament, on this point is stronger than that of the Old. Every good passion, especially if it takes effect in a manner too powerful to be explained in purely human terms (↗charism) is an act of the Spirit (1 Cor 12–14;↗Spirit).

The formula 'Thou shalt not covet' can be taken as a summary of all the particular commandments (Rom 7:7; 13:9). Passion, therefore, is also the root of all sins. In a certain sphere, that namely of the physical in its unconsecrated and 'fleshly' aspect, it takes disastrous effect. It is in such a sphere of unholiness that men who are still unbaptised and men who are heathens live and act (Rom 1:18–32; Tit 3:3; see also Eph 2:3; 1 Pet 1:14). Again in christians who are tepid and not fully committed, men of 'double mind' (Jas 4:8), the passions live on as evil desires, so that the preaching of the sanctifying word has no effect upon them (Mk 4:19 parallels). Teachers of error in particular are often branded in the New Testament as servants of diabolical passions (Phil 3:18f; 2 Tim 3:2–9; 2 Pet 2:12–22). In this connection two powerful expressions of the Old Testament are taken up and repeated. Such teachers of error are like dogs that turn back to their own vomit, and like swine who wallow in the mire (2 Pet 2:22). In the desire for sexual pleasure, which Paul compares to a firebrand (1 Cor 7:9), proneness to passion is a major factor (Rom 1:24–7; 6:13, 19; Jas 4:3f). But in every other kind of

sin (catalogue of vices), and above all in apostasy from God and Jesus Christ (↗blasphemy, sin) a passionate disposition plays a major part.

In the imagery of the New Testament we are clearly told how disastrous passion can be. In the image of the contest it is depicted as the adversary of God (1 Pet 4:2) who tries to kindle the spirit of rebellion against the Lord in man (1 Cor 3:3; 2 Cor 10:4f; Jas 4:1; 1 Pet 2:11), and deprives him of every joy (Gal 5:16ff) and peace (Rom 7:23; 1 Cor 3:3; see Is 57:20f). By means of the image of slavery passion is unveiled as the dangerous enemy of man and of his freedom (Rom 6:17f). He who does not struggle against her, or who submits to her she binds with chains (1 Cor 6:20; 7:23; Tit 3:3). The men thus in bondage are those whose 'God is the belly' (Rom 16:18; Phil 3:19). A third image represents passion as a murderess (1 Jn 3:15), who hands over her slaves to death (Rom 1:32; 6:23; Phil 3:19; Jas 1:15; cf Lk 8:14).

In Paul the essential holiness of believers is emphasised as the opposite to sinful passion (1 Thess 4:3ff). Corresponding to his teaching on this point we find in the later writings of the New Testament that a special emphasis is laid upon one virtue in particular, namely temperance (↗discipline). Because of the need to strive against the passions (1 Pet 1:13; 5:8) all are bound to practise this virtue, especially the leaders (1 Tim 3:3; Tit 1:7), both men (Tit 2:2) and women (1 Tim 3:11). This virtue is a gift of God (2 Tim 1:7). With its help man subdues his passions for the things of this world (2 Pet 1:4ff) and becomes fruitful in good works (Jas 1:19ff, 26f).

In many passages what the New Testament has to say on the subject of passion corresponds to what it says on ⟋ flesh and ⟋ sin. Passion too, like these, drives man into a veritable sphere of the devil, and makes his life a lie (compare Jas 4:1 with 4:2f). Only through the ⟋ grace of the Lord, and by resolutely becoming the disciple of Jesus (Jas 4:7ff) can he break out of this sphere. His task in this is to belong to Christ, and to crucify the flesh together with its passions and lusts (Gal 5:24; see also Rom 8:13). 'For all that is in the world, the lust of the flesh and the lust of the eyes and the pride of life, is not of the Father but is of the ⟋ world. And the world passes away, and the lust of it; but he who does the will of God abides for ever' (1 Jn 2:16f).

Bibliography: ⟋ Asceticism, Body, Joy, Wrath. Bultmann I, 232–43; A. Stumpff, *TDNT* II, 877–88; G. Stählin, *TDNT* II, 909–26; F. Büchsel, *TDNT* III, 167–72; see also L. Köhler. *Der Hebräische Mensch*, Tübingen 1953, 101–10,

Wilhelm Pesch

Enemy

A. *Terminology.* The Hebrew words *'ôyêb, tsar, śônê'*, mean 'enemy', both in the personal and in the national sense. Frequent references are to be found in the Old Testament, and above all in the Psalms, to the enemy of the religious man. Precisely who is meant by this individual enemy has caused lively controversy among exegetes, and the various suggestions which have been put forward as to who the enemy or enemies may be include a personal adversary, an opponent in a lawsuit, a political opponent, rival religious sects, godless fellow-countrymen who have allowed their religion to lapse, Israelite or foreign oppressors, pagans, the enemies of God, or even sorcerers. The question has still not been finally resolved. The notion of this enemy in any case always has a definitely religious flavour, since the enemy of Israel as well as the enemy of the religious man is regarded as the enemy of God. Both in LXX and in the New Testament the enemy is generally rendered by *ekhthros*. The word *polemios*, which is used in Greek for a national enemy or an opponent in war, appears more frequently in 2 Macc (seventeen times in all). In LXX it appears only thirteen times and it is not used at all in the New Testament.

B. *The Enemy in the Old Testament.* 1. *Hostile people.* Alien races living among the Israelites enjoy the protection of the law under the covenant (Lev 19:34; Deut 10:18f; 23:8; 27:19). But races who have severely oppressed Israel in the course of her history or who have tempted her to worship false gods are considered as enemies. The Israelites not only refuse to have anything to do with them (Deut 23:3–6), but also try to exterminate them (Ex 23:31ff; Num 25:1ff, 16ff; Deut 7:1–5; 20:17f; Ps 137; Wis 11:5–20; 16:1–19, 17; Is 34:1–17; Ezek 35). The prophets threaten the enemies of Israel with destruction (Is 13–21; 23; Jer 46–51; Ezek 25–32; 38f; Amos 1:3–2:3). Both individually and collectively Israelites implore God to show no mercy and to take vengeance on their adversaries (Ps 68:22ff; 83:10–19; 129:5–8; Lam 3:64ff), and those who slay the children of the enemy are blessed (Ps 137:9).

To arrive at any understanding or judgement of this attitude towards heathen nations it is necessary to take into account the outlook, still untempered by christian ethics, of a people struggling for its bare existence in a pitiless environment. The Israelites cherished a particular hatred for their semitic neighbours because they had been perfidiously attacked by them again and again despite their blood-ties with each other (Jer 49; Ezek 25:12; Amos 1:11; Obad 8–14; Ps 137:7ff). As each attack on Israel was an attack on Yahweh, the enemies of Israel came to be regarded as the Lord's enemies (Ex 23:22; Num 10:35; Judg 5:31). God was in honour bound to humiliate his enemies (Josh 7:7ff; Jer 46:10; Zeph 2:8; Zech 1:15; Ps 2:1–9; 74; 79; 83; 1 Macc 4:30–3; 2 Macc 14:35ff; 15:22ff). The enemies of Israel will be made to pay in the same coin for the atrocities they have committed, in accordance with the principles of justice expressed in the *Lex Talionis* (Is 13:16; 14:22; Joel 3:4–8; Nahum 3:10; Ps 137:9).

It must not be forgotten, however, in view of the natural temptation to judge Israel's invective against her enemies too harshly, that the prophets were just as harsh in their condemnation of their own people if they broke the covenant which bound them to the Lord (Is 3–5; Jer 18f; Ezek 9; Amos 2:4–8; 4:1–5:3 and many other instances). This desire for judgement to be passed on the heathen nations is in sharp contrast to the confident expectation of Israel that the pagans too will achieve some share in the salvation promised to Israel (Is 19:22ff; Jer 18:7–10; 48:47; 49:6, 39; Zech 8:23;

14:16). Intercession for pagans is a familiar feature of the Old Testament (Gen 18:20–32; 1 Kings 8:41ff; 2 Chron 6:32f; Jer 29:7). It is possible for those who belong to alien races to be considered worthy enough to participate with Israel in the worship of the true God (Ex 18:7–12), to be accepted as members of God's people (Num 10:29–32; Judith 14:10), and to experience special proofs of God's grace (2 Kings 5).

2. *Personal Enemies.* In the Old Testament, the religious man does not hesitate to give frank expression to his hatred of his personal enemies, and he fully expects Yahweh to humiliate or even to destroy them (Ps 5:10; 6:10; 7:9, 16; 10:15; 28:4; 31:19; 35:4ff; 109; 139:19 etc). He wants his opponents to be judged without mercy (Ps 55:15, 23; 140:9ff), and curses them together with their families (Amos 7:17; Jer 17:18; 18:21ff; Ps 17:13; 109:6–14; ↗ Curse). The religious man's joy over the salvation which he receives from the Lord is all the greater if his enemies are witnesses of his good fortune (Ps 5:8; 23:5; 27, 11–14). He gloats over the downfall of his adversaries (Jer 11:20; Ps 37:34; 54:7; 112:8), and most of all wishes to have personal vengeance on them (Ps 41:10). The wise man, however, does not become too upset about the world's injustice, and his attitude towards his enemies is therefore less passionate. All the same, he deems it advisable not to trust his enemies too far, even if they approach him in a friendly and sociable way (Prov 26:24f; Sir 6:13; 12:8–18).

Man in the Old Testament is like every emotional man of the East, and lets his mood or passion of the moment run away with him. Nevertheless, he is inspired with a perfectly fanatical sense of justice which demands that God himself should be relentless in his punishment of injustice. Whoever does an injustice to a pious man must suffer the same evil himself, in accordance with the principles of the *Lex Talionis*. Personal enemies, too, count as enemies of the Lord. This is because the religious man is under Yahweh's protection (Ps 9:3f; 55:22; 139:21), and because the Lord has sanctioned the regulation of justice (Ps 17:6–12; 40:15; 54:5; 55:22f; 59:5). If God were simply to watch the activities of his enemies without taking any action, he would damage his own prestige and strengthen the wicked in their godless deeds (Ps 10:4, 11; 35:25; 64:6; 94:7). Triumph over the enemy is thus the triumph of justice and right, and rejoicing over the downfall of the enemy is rejoicing over the victory of justice (Ps 35:27; 40:14ff).

This attitude towards enemies shows clearly how imperfect the Old Testament is in comparison with the New. Nevertheless, prayers that the enemies should be punished, and the violent outbursts of emotion directed against both national and personal adversaries, do testify to faithfulness to religion, to the constant war which both the individual and the entire race had to wage in order to keep their faith in Yahweh, and to the unshakable trust they had in his justice.

In spite of this hatred of one's enemy which strikes the christian as so strange, the Old Testament is also familiar with the love of enemies, although this love is generally restricted to those of the same race and religion. Joseph forgives his brethren (Gen 45:5, 15). Moses makes

intercession on behalf of his people, even though they oppose him (Num 14:10, 13–19). David spares the life of Saul, who is his deadly enemy (1 Sam 24:10), and the wise man advises against taking revenge on one's enemies (Prov 20:22; 24:29).

In Lev 19:17f, the people of Israel are forbidden to entertain feelings of hatred towards their enemies, and are commanded to admonish their adversaries as brothers. The religious man ought not to rejoice over his enemy's misfortune (Prov 24:17), and his enemy should be helped if he gets into difficulties or is in distress (Ex 23:4f; Prov 25:21f). The man who refuses to let God avenge him, but takes his own revenge, will himself be judged (Sir 28:1).

The religious man, knowing that he is a sinner, has therefore to rely on God's mercy. That is why he forgives his enemies (Sir 28:1–9). Not to have rejoiced over the misfortune of an adversary counts as a great merit and is the sign of great piety (Jer 15:11; Job 31:29f).

C. *The Enemy in the Jewish World at the time of Christ.* There was, of course, no formal commandment in the Jewish world to hate one's enemy. Jesus's saying: 'You have heard that it was said: You shall love your neighbour and hate your enemy' (Mt 5:43f) is thus not to be interpreted as referring to one. All the curses in the Old Testament, and especially those contained in the Psalms, the various rabbinical maxims and the utterances in the Qumran texts which sanction the hatred of one's enemy, are sufficient to account for the existence of this saying of Jesus.

Although, generally speaking, the

rabbis condemn hatred of one's enemies (Ab 2:11; SLev 352a; Lev 19:17), they do frequently permit it, when it is directed against the godless (Taan 7b) and pagans (SLev 19:18) and sometimes even command it (Pes 113b). In the Qumran texts, hatred and vengeance against other members of the community are condemned (1 QS 6:25ff; 7:2–9), though, on the other hand, an inexorable hatred is expressly demanded for the 'Sons of Darkness', by whom are probably meant all outsiders (1 QS 1:4, 10; 8:6f; 9:21f). This does not necessarily mean that the godless are to be attacked by force, but rather that they are to be completely ostracised. The 'Sons of Light' will not wage their merciless war of annihilation on the 'Sons of Darkness' until the eschatological time, the messianic age (1 QM).

In the apocryphal writings, the enemy of the human race is quite simply the devil (ApocMos 2; 7; 25; 28; Life of Adam and Eve 17; Bar (Gr) 13; 2).

D. *The Enemy in the New Testament.* Christ's message removes the differences between compatriots and aliens. The disciples of Jesus regard a Samaritan who is, for the Jews, a deadly enemy, as a 'neighbour' (Lk 10:29–37). The only real enemy is the devil, who sows cockle among the wheat in God's field (Mt 13:25ff). The disciples will, however, triumph over him (Lk 10:19). Paul sees death as the enemy which will be conquered by Christ (1 Cor 15:26).

It is, however, true to say that human enemies can be found in the New Testament. These include in particular those who, as allies and instruments of the devil, lie in wait for God's people (Lk 1:71, 74) and his witnesses (Rev 11:5, 12). In this sense even the members of his own family may become the religious man's enemies, if they try to tempt him, as Jesus' disciple, to betray his master or to lose faith in his gospel (Mt 10:36). The man who opposes God or his anointed Son is an enemy of the kingdom of God (Lk 19:27; Acts 13:10; Phil 3:18). But even the man who merely thinks and acts in accordance with the natural law and is continually coming into conflict with God's will is an enemy as well (Rom 5:10; 8:7; 11:28; Col 1:21; Jas 4:4). Jesus too is drastic in his attitude towards his opponents and calls them a brood of vipers (Mt 12:34; 23:33) and sons of the devil (Jn 8:44).

On the other hand, Jesus does realise that his opponents are men who are in need of his mercy and forgives from the cross even those who have condemned him to death (Lk 23:34), in this way making the love of one's enemies a law for christians, not only by his example, but also by means of his explicit commandment (Mt 5:43ff; Mk 11:25; Lk 6:27ff, 35f). His disciples accept this law and follow it in their lives. Stephen, for example, forgives his executioners just as his master forgave his (Acts 7:58ff). The disciples look upon the love of one's enemies as the mark which distinguishes the christian from his heathen counterpart. The christian goes contrary to the custom of the heathen by doing good to those who hate him and by extending his love even to his enemies (1 Thess 5:15; 1 Pet 3:9). He blesses those who persecute him (1 Cor 4:12), and leaves retribution in God's hands (Rom 12:19ff). Because he knows that he is in need of God's pardon, he himself forgives his adversaries (Mt 6:14; 18:13; see also Rom 5:10; Col 1:21f).

Bibliography: J. Nikel, *Das AT und die Nächstenliebe*, Münster 1913; P. Jedzink, *Das Gebot der Nächstenliebe im Evangelium*, Braunsberg 1916; S. Mowinckel, *Psalmenstudien* I, Kristiania 1921; H. Schmidt, *Das Gebet des Angeklagten*, Giessen 1928; W. Foerster, *TDNT* II, 811–16; A. F. Puukko, 'Der Feind in den Psalmen', *OTS* 8 (1950), 47–65; F. Mussner, 'Der Begriff des Nächsten in der Verkündigung Jesu', *TTZ* 64 (1955), 91–9; H. Birkeland, *The Evildoers in the Book of Psalms*, Oslo 1955; J. Ridderbos, *De Psalmen* I, Kampen 1955, 382–408; G. Castellino, *Libro dei Salmi*, Turin 1955, 254–63; J. Gewiess, *LTK* IV², 60–61; B. S. Childe, 'The Enemy from the North and the Chaos Tradition', *JBL* 78 (1959), 187–98; H.-J. Kraus, *Psalmen*, Neukirchen 1960, 40–3; SB I, 353–68.

Josef Scharbert

Epiphany

Apparition (= *epiphaneia*) is a central theme of biblical theology showing only occasional external points of contact with analogous pagan ideas. By this term we understand the intrusion of God into the world which is brought about unexpectedly before men's eyes, either with or without a specific form, which can be of a familiar or mysterious character, and which is withdrawn just as quickly. From the point of view of terminology, we read in the Old Testament of a *theophany*, in the New Testament of an *epiphany*. While there exist in pagan religions what we might call indirect 'epiphanies' by means of which the deity provides proof of its existence through deeds of power, there is in biblical theology a sharp distinction between apparition and miracle.

Such apparitions take place, basically, only at crucial points of human history. There are really, therefore, no private revelations since the apparitions granted to individuals are in view of the community as a whole (Gen 18:1ff; Is 6:1ff; Jn 20:11ff; 1 Cor 15:5ff).

We can trace them right back to the beginning of creation insofar as both inanimate and animate nature as well as man himself owe their existence to the apparition of God (Gen 1:1ff), though this belongs to the period of prehistory and can be grasped only in a speculative way. Within the historical period, we have to take account of the various vocation-narratives (of Moses [Ex 3]; of prophets [Is 6:1ff; Ezek 1:1ff]; of Peter near the Sea of Galilee [Jn 21:15ff]; the divine promises of posterity [Gen 18:1ff; Judg 13:3ff]; of a covenant [Gen 17:1ff]; of land [Gen 28:10ff]; of salvation [1 Kings 19:10ff]; the accompanying presence of God in the pillar of cloud and of fire during the wanderings of the Israelites [Ex 13:21f; 40:34ff], sometimes visible appearances during the occupation of the land, at the setting up of an altar [Gen 12:7ff], or the destruction of an enemy city [Josh 5:13ff]; etc). In the Old Testament the climax comes with the occurrence on Mount Sinai with thunder and lightning and other extraordinary phenomena (Ex 19:18ff), an event which lays the foundations of the human order and which, as is stressed throughout the whole of revelation, is unique. In the New Testament the apparitions of Christ are central. They are prepared for by the apparition of angels (Lk 1:11ff; 1:28ff; 2:9ff) which sometimes have the purpose of attesting to an appearance of Jesus (Mt 28:2;

Mk 16:5; Lk 24:4ff; Jn 20:12). In this connection we might mention the occasions when the apostles were miraculously set free from prison (Acts 5:19; 12:7). The theophanies, which are extremely reserved in character, serve the purpose of the divine proclamation of Jesus' messianic status (Mk 9:4). The tongues of fire at Pentecost are described as sent by the Lord (Jn 16:7).

As historical events, these apparitions have a fixed time and place (Ex 19:18ff; Is 6:1; Mk 16:2; Lk 24:1; Jn 20:1). Hence they can never be repeated in the same way—they are unique and isolated events, and there is a complete absence of apparition motifs. There are, at the same time, certain places which are favoured for revelations—mountains (Ex 3; 19:18ff; Mk 9:2); lakes (Mk 6:48); the Ark of the Covenant (Ex 40:34)—these are considered as particularly apt on account of the natural advantages they offer—in particular, solitude.

The apparition, considered in itself, is a complex phenomenon. It is perceptible to the senses, in particular to the eyes and the hearing—assisted in some cases even by the sense of touch (Gen 32:24; Jn 20:27). In the Old Testament the accent is on hearing while in the New Testament sight or vision plays an equally important part, especially in proving the reality of the resurrection. Since the word of God is the essential element, there can be no silent apparitions; it follows that the bearer of the word occupies the centre, and that though he may be hidden it is always a question of a person. His voice can also be heard—from out of the burning thorn bush (Ex 3), in the sighing of the wind (1 Kings 19:13), and in the cloud (Mk 9:7). Every apparition is, therefore, first and foremost an announcement. The divine pronouncements in the Old Testament are promises, in the New Testament they are decisive witnesses of the resurrection, and provide at the same time guidance for the further progress of the kingdom of God, in particular through the confirmation of the office of 'shepherd' (Jn 21:15ff), and the command to baptise and evangelise (Mt 28:16ff).

Thus the biblical apparitions are at the service of the history of salvation and therefore eschatological, unlike their pagan counterparts which serve a momentary purpose only. One can detect already in the historical apparitions characteristics which point to the final goal (Ex 3)—something which comes through even more strongly in the eschatological and prophetic apparition of the day of Yahweh (Amos 5:18; Is 40:3ff), and shines out briefly in the Transfiguration (Mk 9:4ff), reaching its full development in the ↗ parousia. One result of this is that in the pastoral epistles the word *epiphaneia* is used to stand for the second coming of Christ (1 Tim 6:14; 2 Tim 4:1, 8; Tit 2:13). Satanic apparitions (Rev 6; 12:3; 13:1, 11; 2 Thess 2:9) are crude imitations of the parousia of Christ and have the purpose of deceiving the faithful.

Considered as an announcement, the apparition is always addressed to a particular person who has to keep a respectful distance from the holy one who comes to him (delimitation of a place, Ex 19:21; 34:3; of a person, Jn 20:17; taking off one's shoes, Ex 3:5; covering one's face, Ex 3:6;

33:22; 1 Kings 19:13), or to whom God manifests himself but in a hidden way. Smoke, a cloud, also the 'angel of the Lord' (Gen 16:7; 31:11; Judg 6:11; 13:3; accompanied by two others, Gen 18:1ff) and the human form of Christ conceal the true divine being, which, as ⌐ glory, will shine forth in its visible splendour only at the end of the world (Is 60:1ff; 62:1f etc; Mk 13:26; Lk 17:24), while in the meantime it is only occasionally discernible (Ex 33:22; Mk 9:3; Acts 9:3). In this connection, angels often appear as messengers of light (Lk 2:9; Acts 12:7), also expressed by their wearing white garments (Lk 9:29; Jn 20:12).

Many obscure points occurring in individual apparition-accounts can be explained by the attempt to conceal the real identity of the person in the apparition (Gen 32:24; Mk 9:2), or as comparisons used as a stylistic procedure (Ezek 1:26; Mt 17:2). This also explains why there were no witnesses present at the ⌐ resurrection. The human reaction to the apparition can take different forms. The person concerned can be completely overcome when God lays his hand on him (Is 8:11; Jer 20:7) or, like Paul, be cast to the ground. He can be seized by fear (Gen 28:17; Is 6:4; Mk 6:50; 9:6; Lk 2:9), which explains the frequently used phrase: 'Fear not!' (Mt 28:10; Mk 6:50; Lk 24:38; Jn 6:20). When he is unable to pierce the surrounding obscurity he can be restless and uncertain (Gen 18:12; Jn 20:15), though, on the other hand, once he has understood the profound significance of the experience he can enter fully into it (Gen 32:29f; Mk 9:6f).

In its character of revelation—and to this category the 'It is I' sayings also belong (Mk 6:50; Jn 6:20)—the apparition compels man to a decision and gives him the choice between doubt and faith, refusal or acknowledgement (Jn 20:24ff). It is never just for its own sake, but is an appeal which requires an answer which must show itself in action. The function of the ⌐ apostle is, like the mission of the prophets (Is 61:1), intimately bound up with apparition. Thus, only a witness of the resurrection can be chosen to take the place of Judas (Acts 1:22), and Paul explicitly appeals to what happened on the road to Damascus in self-authentication (1 Cor 15:8). In consequence of the close link existing between the members and the head which is Christ, the New Testament apparition has a social character as reflecting the inner and absolute *epiphaneia* of Father, Son, and Holy Spirit (Jn 12:44). That is why apparitions to individuals are less prominent (1 Cor 15:5ff). So Thomas had to learn that the Lord would come to him, not when he was by himself, but only in the company of the brethren (Jn 20:24ff), and it is precisely when they are at table that he allows himself to be recognised (Lk 24:30–41ff; Jn 21:12).

The deepest significance of every apparition is, however, the imparting of salvation in peace and joy (Gen 32:29; Jn 20:19f). This is denied to the unbeliever only if he positively conjures up for himself condemnation and judgement which stand at the opposite pole (Is 2:10ff; 4:4ff; 30:27ff; 2 Thess 1:8); he is then given to see not light but the fire which destroys. He cannot hope to enjoy the final apparition so graphically described in the apocalyptic books (Enoch; Testament of the Twelve Apostles).

The theology of John takes up a special position in this regard, insofar as it views the whole earthly life of the Lord in one broad sweep as *theophaneia* and praises God for it, in hymn form, in the prologue to the gospel (Jn 1:1–18) and in 1 Jn 1:1ff, since from its surrounding mystery the ⁄ glory shines forth continually. No certain trace has yet been discovered of a cultic *epiphaneia*, such as some scholars believe they can detect in the Psalms and even in certain texts of the New Testament.

We have to consider this question not just from the religious but also from the *literary* angle. In Ps 29 Ugaritic representations go to make up the outward form only which, however, has been filled with a new substance, since Baal-Hadad, the storm-god as manifested in the elements, is used as a symbol for the showing forth of Yahweh's holiness. In the historical and prophetic books of the Old Testament, the sections in the first person manifest more strongly-emphasised individual characteristics than those in the third person. In the New Testament, Matthew is sober and logical (Mt 17:2), in contrast with the greater originality of Mark, while Luke, bearing in mind the needs of his hellenistic–christian readers, gives prominence to the description of apparitions (Lk 3:21ff; Acts 5:19; 12:7). In Paul the ⁄ parousia, the bright rays of which already reach the earth occupies the central position. In the Letter to the Hebrews, there takes place a strong spiritualisation which sees in Sinai and Sion a powerful revelation by word of mouth constituting a divine proclamation. The Apocrypha contain numerous cases of the expansion of the biblical narrative in the form of apparitions (*Protoevangelium Jacobi* 18/20).

The oldest artistic representations of biblical apparitions are to be found in the Museum of Antiquities at Brescia, on the pilgrim bottles of Monza and Bobbio, and in the mosaics at San Vitale and Sant' Apollinare Nuovo in Ravenna. The apparitions of the Risen Christ have been treated by Rembrandt among others.

Bibliography: O. Casel, 'Die Epiphanie im Lichte der Religionsgeschichte', *Benedikt. Monatsschrift* 4 (1922), 13–20; R. Guardini, *Jesus Christus: Das Christusbild in den johanneischen Schriften*, Würzburg 1940; W. Michaelis, *Die Erscheinungen des Auferstandenen*, Basle 1946; C. Mohrmann, *Epiphaneia*, Nijmegen 1953; E. Pax, *Epiphaneia: Ein religionsgeschichtlicher Beitrag zur biblischen Theologie*, Munich 1955; Stauffer 298 n. 709; C. Westermann, *Das Leben Gottes in den Psalmen*, Göttingen 1961; H.-P. Müller, 'Die kultische Darstellung der Theophanie', *VT* 14 (1954), 183–91.

Elpidius Pax

Eucharist

A. *Sources*. Three different kinds of text referring to the eucharist are to be found in the New Testament. 1. *Accounts of the institution of the eucharist:* Mt 26:26–9; Mk 14:22–5; Lk 22:15–20; 1 Cor 11:23–5. Luke's account has been handed down in several different forms, but these can be traced back to two original sources—the shorter text of the gospel (15–19a, without 19b–20 in the 'Western' text), and the longer text (15–20), which is generally regarded by present-day scholars as the authentic version, though opinions differ with regard to how it originated. It is possible to look upon Lk 22:15–18 as the fragment of an old account of the feast of the Passover in which the paschal lamb is replaced by the eucharistic offering, as represented by the chalice (this is well brought out in *MTZ* 4 [1953] 223–31). (See H. Schürmann.) The two types which underlie these four accounts are those of Matthew/Mark—that is, Matthew's work of editing, based on Mark's account—and Luke/Paul. It is not that Luke's account depends on 1 Cor, but that both go back to a common tradition. Mark, on the other hard, represents a different line of tradition. The Luke/Paul tradition can be regarded as older than that of Mark's version (H. Schürmann, as against J. Jeremias). Certain features of Luke's version do seem to show that it is closer to the original tradition than Paul's (H. Schürmann, as against J. Betz and others).

These accounts of the institution of the eucharist have been handed down as the standard forms for its celebration in the early christian communities, and their character was to a great extent determined by the current form of worship of the community. (This character bears an imprint which is unchangeable; the liturgical acclamation 'for you' shows a tendency towards parallelism). These accounts are also incomplete—the event taking on a timeless quality in the liturgy. They are concerned first and foremost, not with providing a historical report on what occurred at the last supper, but with setting out the celebration of the eucharist on a basis of Christ's own actions. This is why the words of consecration, as pronounced by Jesus, have not been handed down verbatim, but have been allowed to evolve quite

legitimately—without undergoing any essential change or alteration in their meaning.

Paul classes the various accounts of the institution of the eucharist as *paradosis* ('For I received from the Lord what I also delivered to you', 1 Cor 11:23; the rabbis used this term to denote the reception or the passing on of a tradition: see 1 Cor 15:1–3). At the beginning of this chain of tradition is the 'Lord', the historical Jesus, who, having been exalted to the right hand of the Father, directs the life of his church and stands behind the Apostles, who pass on this tradition. The language of the pauline account of the institution of the eucharist is quite uncharacteristic of the writer, and this does tend to confirm the view that the account is 'recitative' and thus traditional. Paul's understanding of the eucharist is thus not due to a revelation which was received direct from God. The form of the words of consecration, which Paul passed on to the Corinthians in the year 49 or 50 AD, was probably received by him in Antioch, round about 40 AD. Whenever he visited Jerusalem, he must have had the opportunity to compare his preaching on the subject of the Eucharist with that of St Peter (Gal 1:18; Acts 9:27; 11:30; Acts 15; Gal 2:1–10). The Semitic influence perceptible in all the accounts of the institution of the eucharist and the peculiar form, found in the Paul/Luke version, of the words spoken over the chalice—due to the fact that the taking of blood was particularly offensive to the Jews—refer to the primitive christian communities as far back as approximately AD 30. These words of consecration contain the 'primeval rock of tradition' (J. Jeremias). As a result of the kerygma of the first apostles, Christ's message is not to be found in its exact form in the various accounts of the institution of the eucharist, but rather in a fragmentary form according to the particular view of each apostle. These, as 'witnesses', passed on the words of Jesus in accordance with their sense and meaning and not with word-for-word accuracy. Any attempt to go behind the words of consecration as they have been handed down to us, and to arrive at the original form which Jesus himself used when he spoke them, can only be in the nature of a reconstruction and can never be based on verifiable historical knowledge. Jesus certainly never merely said: 'This is my body', and: 'This is my blood' (despite what is contained in Justin, *Apol.*, 1, 66, which, contrary to the opinion of R. Bultmann, only hints at this). Jesus undoubtedly gave a much closer interpretation of his gift of the eucharist and of his death (cf the interpretation of the elements in the ritual of the Passover). Thus he would at least have said: 'This is my body (*den bisri*: see J. Bonsirven, *Règne de Dieu*, Paris 1957, *n* 60) which is given for you' (see Mk 10:45; Is 53:12). He must have related the blood to the covenant, for by his death the new people of God were granted a new relationship with regard to the covenant. This may be compared with the eschatological expectation connected with the meals of the Qumran sects (*BZ* and ↗ Mediator).

2. *The promise of the eucharist.* There is no actual account of the institution of the eucharist in John's gospel, although the washing of the disciples' feet (Jn 13:1–17: see *GL* 31 [1958], 25–30) and the 'priestly prayer' of Jesus (Jn 17), neither of which can be said to refer primarily to the eucharist, are in a sense interpretations of Christ's death. Instead, there is a 'lesson on the eucharist' (the 'catechèse eucharistique' of J. Bonsirven, 175). This is composed of material which was handed down and thus already formed before it reached John, but which was arranged and adapted by him. It includes the account of the miraculous feeding of the five thousand and Jesus's walking on the sea (6:1–24). It also includes the discourse on the bread of life (6:25–59), in which two distinct parts stand out in sharp contrast—the sermon on the bread of life as a gift of the Father to men which is received through faith (25–51a), and the sermon on the bread of life as the gift of Jesus himself which will be bestowed only at some future time and will then be taken as food and drink (51b–58). Finally, it includes a repetition of this sermon addressed to the disciples alone (60–71). The individual parts of this lesson on the eucharist are held together by the common theme. Verses 51b–58 are generally understood nowadays of the eucharist, since 'the entire eucharistic terminology' can be found in them (see recently G. Bornkamm, 'Die eucharistische Rede im Johannes-Evangelium', *ZNW* 47 [1956], 161–9). These verses are not the outcome of 'ecclesiastical redaction' and interpolation (contrary to R. Bultmann and G. Bornkamm) since their stylistic quality shows clearly that John composed them on the basis of tradition and adapted them to fit into the gospel

(E. Ruckstuhl, *Die Literarische Einheit des Johannes-Evangelium*, 1951; J. Jeremias, 'Jn 6:51c–58 redaktionell?', *ZNW* 44 [1952/3], 256f). It can be taken as certain that the words about the eucharist were not spoken at the same time as the discourse on the bread of life (27–51a), contrary to the view of E. Ruckstuhl, but were first spoken only at a later period, after Christ had revealed himself as the suffering Messiah (Mk 8:31ff; see also Jn 6:51). This is also the view of M. J. Lagrange. It is quite likely that this is a case of a Johannine *midrash* based on an account of the institution of the eucharist (H. Schürmann, *LTK* iii², 1162).

3. *The early christian sacred meal.* Luke uses the expression 'the breaking of bread' (Acts 2:42) or 'breaking bread' (Acts 2:46; 20:7, 11) when, basing himself on early Palestinian sources and his own personal experience (the 'we-sections'), he refers to the communal meals of the early church. This term *the breaking of bread* signifies, in Jewish circles, the rite which inaugurates the meal—the blessing, breaking, and distribution of the bread—and it was regarded as a sacred action (Mk 8:19; though it is questionable whether Lk 24:35 can be viewed in this light: E. von Severus, *RAC²*, 620–26). Luke never uses the phrase *share in a meal* (J. Jeremias, *The Eucharistic Words of Jesus*, London 1966). The view is widely held by present-day scholars (eg, E. Haenchen, *Die Apostelgeschichte*, Göttingen 1956, 523ff; Behm, *TDNT* iii, 730) that Acts 20:7, 11 refers to the celebration of the 'Lord's Supper' within the context of Paul's mission. The passage in Acts 2:42–6 is clearly meant to refer to the eucharist, since a

distinction is made between the 'breaking of bread' and 'taking food'. 'Breaking bread' is, for Luke, a designation for the celebration of the eucharist, and it was, without any doubt, established as such at the beginning of the second century (*Didache* 9, 3f; Ignatius *ad Ephes.* 20:2; *Philad.* 4). Jesus performed the rite of the breaking of bread at the last supper with an unprecedented sense of purpose, as is borne out by his accompanying words of explanation. This new and deeper content is probably the reason for naming this new institution which was set up by Jesus the 'breaking of bread'. The Jewish usage in this christian context was 'narrowed down and made to refer specifically to the eucharistic breaking of bread' (*Bbl* 32 [1951], 526).

In 1 Cor 11:23–33; 10:1–13, 14–22 we find certain and abundant reference to the eucharist. The passage in Heb 13:9f may well be taken to refer to the eucharistic meal, although it is obscure (F. J. Schierse, *Verheissung und Heilsvollendung*, Munich 1955, 184–95). It has been suggested, though without foundation, that 1 Cor 12:13; 1 Pet 2:3; Rev 3:20; Jn 15:1 are closely related, in their subject-matter, to the eucharist.

B. *Setting.* In order to arrive at a true understanding of the eucharist, it is of some importance to consider in what kind of setting it was celebrated.

1. *The setting of the accounts of the institution.* Jesus instituted the eucharist at a festive farewell meal. That this had the character of a feast (see *SB* iv, 611–39) is shown by the fact that it was held in an upper room in Jerusalem Mk 14:15; Lk 22:12), that those present reclined at table according to

the hellenistic custom (Mk 14:18; Jn 13:23, 25), and that wine was used (Mk 14:23ff; Lk 22:17f). That it was also a farewell feast is borne out by the words of farewell (Lk 22:16, 18), the 'testament' of Jesus (Lk 22:28ff) and the parting gift which took the form of the 'institution' of the sacrament, which was bequeathed to the disciples (Lk 22:19; 1 Cor 11:24f).

No complete agreement exists as to whether this festive meal was in fact held on the ritual feast of the Passover (Mk 14:12–17; Lk 22:15 are in support of this; in Jn 18:28; 19:14—see also 19:35—it would appear to have taken place on the day preceding the official feast of the Passover). In the synoptics and in John there can be found numerous unintentional pointers to the fact that this festive meal bore the stamp of the Jewish Passover. In particular the interpretation of the elements of the meal, as expressed by Jesus over the bread and wine, was a stable element, referring to the part played by the head of the family in the Passover celebration (J. Jeremias, *TDNT* v, 896f). Even if Jesus did not celebrate a paschal meal, 'he must certainly have been considerably influenced by the idea of the Passover' (H. Schürmann, *LTK* I², 27f).

The eucharist was instituted within the setting of the paschal meal (for this rite see, for example, *RNT* 2, 260ff; A. Stöger, *Brot*, 103–6). The main part of the feast began with the blessing, breaking, and distribution of the soft, round, flat cake of unleavened bread. This was followed by the eating of the paschal lamb, and the feast concluded with what was, in effect, grace after meals, when the father of the family pronounced the prayer of thanksgiving over the cup. Jesus, then, made use of the bread at the beginning of the paschal feast and the wine at the end for the Eucharistic gift (hence the phrase 'after supper' Lk 22:20; 1 Cor 11:25). In the Mark/Matthew version, the two actions of the Eucharist, which are divided in Luke/Paul, are joined together and form a single unity ('while they were at supper' or 'while they were eating'). The celebration of the Eucharist is, as it were, freed from its bond with the Passover in the case of these two evangelists. In Luke's version, the Eucharist is regarded as the new paschal feast (Lk 22:15). Christ is the paschal lamb who has been slain for sacrifice (1 Cor 5:7). According to John's version, Jesus is 'slain' in the same way as the paschal lambs were slain, in the temple sacrifice, and no bone of his body was broken (19:36). This comparison between Jesus and the paschal lamb, which was current in the early church (1 Pet 1:19; Rev 5:6; etc), can indeed be traced directly back to our Lord (J. Jeremias, *TDNT* v, 899). Since 'body-blood' and 'pouring out' are part of sacrificial terminology, Jesus certainly referred to himself as the paschal lamb in the words of institution. The paschal meal was a sacrificial meal (see Deut 16:1–8; Mk 14:12; Lk 22:7). The ancient blood-rite (see Ex 12:7, 22–7), after the reforms which took place in the year 621 BC, under Josias, in the celebration of public worship consisted in the sprinkling of the blood on the altar of sacrifice where the victim was burnt (2 Chron 35:11; Jub 49:20; Pes 5:6). This blood-rite had the character of an atonement. In addition, the sacrificial paschal meal was an act of commemoration which brought both the past and the eschatological future vividly to mind. It was also a communal meal, shared by God's people, which had an exclusive character (Ex 12:43–9) and was binding on all Israelites (Ex 12:6, 43ff; Num 9:10–13). The entire people—in Christ's time no less than ten persons had to be present—was bound to celebrate the meal at the same hour in the square of the temple. From the first century before Christ onwards, the celebration took place within the walls of the temple in Jerusalem.

2. *The setting of the 'breaking of bread'*. It is probable that a picture of the celebration of public worship among the early christians is outlined in Acts 2:42. The faithful listened to the teaching of the apostles, brought their offerings (for the 'poor': see Rom 15:26; Phil 1:5), held a communal feast (the breaking of bread), and said communal prayers together. According to Acts 2:46, Christians continued to take part in the worship in the temple and celebrated the breaking of bread in the houses of their fellow-christians. There they took meals in common and praised God 'with gladness and simplicity of heart'. Although the celebration of the eucharist had been freed from its connection with the paschal feast, it was still associated closely with a meal which was imbued with the joyful hope of the return of the Lord, for he was held to be actually present (1 Cor 16:22: *Maranatha*—'Come, Lord' or 'The Lord is nigh'; see *TDNT* IV, 470f). In Troas, the breaking of bread took place within the setting of the Lord's Supper as celebrated by the Pauline communities.

The christian community assembled in the evening of the 'first day of every week' (1 Cor 16:2; Jn 20:19; Rev 1:10; *TDNT* III, 1096, 27f), Paul gave a discourse, broke the bread and ate some of it, not alone, of course, but with the others who were present. The celebration of the eucharist and the delivery of a sermon were inseparable. The place where the community assembled was an upper room, lit by many lamps. (Was this reference to lighting intended to allude to the suspicion that christian religious feasts lent themselves to lewdness?—see Minutius Felix, *Oct.*, 9; Tert., *Apol.*, 8f; E. Haenchen, *Apostelgeschichte*, 524.)

3. *The setting of the Pauline 'Lord's Supper' in Corinth* (1 Cor 11:17–34). The sacramental meal took place as part of a feast at which the participants satisfied their hunger, and Paul was constrained to reproach them on account of abusing this. His censure was not directed against the establishment of these meals as such, in imitation of the Jewish or pagan sacred meals (contrary to the opinion of L. Thomas, *DB[s]* I, 145–50 and J. Coppens, *DB[s]* II, 1174), since the celebration was already linked to the taking of a meal, but against the lack of fraternal charity which was apparent at such festive meals. This meal, which was later to become an *agapē* (Clem. Al, *Paed.* 2, 1, 4; Tert, *Apol.* 39; etc), was followed by the sacramental meal (1 Cor 11, 27, 34). This account of the setting of the celebration of the eucharist does serve to show that the eucharistic act was regarded as the essential part and was a sacred institution, and, although its setting varied, its essentials remained constant.

C. *Interpretation of the meaning of the eucharist.* 1. *According to the accounts of the institution of the sacrament.* A certain obscurity is bound to persist concerning the implication of the eucharist, as expressed in Jesus' own words, because of the difficulties of reconstructing, with complete accuracy, the original form of the words of consecration, and the fact that a certain amount of revision or consequent touching up must be taken into consideration.

The extant texts go to show that these revisions do not represent any fresh addition, but a development of what is already known from other utterances of Christ himself. The words of consecration constitute a simple and direct pronouncement of salvation.

a. *The meal* which Jesus gives for his own is both a farewell supper (Lk 22:15; 1 Cor 11:23; see also Jn 13:1) and a new paschal meal (Lk 22:15). It anticipates the eschatological meal: that is to say, it looks forward to the feast which will take place in the kingdom of God (Lk 22:16; Mk 14:25; 1 Cor 11:26; see also Lk 22:30).

b. *The presence of Jesus.* Jesus interprets the gifts which he offers. That which is offered (the subject) is identical with his body (the predicate) or blood. (It should be noted that the copula *is* linking subject and predicate is not expressed in Aramaic; that *cup* is a figure of speech by which the contents are represented by the container; and that *covenant* represents the cause by its effect.) It is not the act or actions of the offering, but the gifts themselves, which Jesus interprets, just as the father of the Jewish family interpreted the gifts in the paschal Haggadah. These gifts are not, however, interpreted by Jesus'

words merely as symbols, for there is an essential difference between the way in which Jesus interprets the gifts and the way in which this is expressed in the Haggadah. Jesus says, in the case of the bread: 'This is my body', whereas in the Haggadah the words are: 'See the bread of sorrow which our fathers ate when they left the land of Egypt'. Whichever solution to the problem of the originality of either the Luke/Paul or the Matthew/Mark version is accepted (J. Betz, 26–35), the words spoken over the chalice are expressed in discreet and highly individual form which without doubt takes into consideration the Jewish—and pagan—aversion to the taking of blood (Gen 9:3f; Lev 17:10–14; Acts 15:29). The original form of the offering and the emphatic description which accompanies it, as an invitation to eat and drink (Lk 22:17; Mt 26:26; Mk 14:22; Mt 26:27) all serve to stress the unprecedented nature of Christ's gift. It is evident that, in leaving behind a parting gift which is in close harmony with the whole of his mission, Jesus is bound to leave *himself* behind, as the revelation of both the Old and the New Testaments is not a revelation by word alone, but also by deed. All these observations demand a realistic understanding of the words of consecration. They do not simply express a likeness, though a comparison can certainly be drawn between the broken wafer of bread and Jesus' body, the red juice of the grape and his shed blood, and so on. The words are also not just a 'pledge of a spiritual presence' (Behm), nor do they merely imply an activity on the part of Christ within his own community. They are, contrary to the opinion of E. Schweizer, the handing over of a substance. The food and drink which Jesus offers are his 'body' (flesh) and 'blood'. The 'flesh' (body) is the living person of Christ in accordance with his bodily existence. The ⟋ blood, as the vehicle of life (Lev 17:11, 14; Deut 12:23), thus denotes the living person of Christ in such a way that attention is drawn first and foremost to the blood. In his body and blood, then, Jesus himself is offered. He presents himself as a gift for salvation (the offering of the chalice is an effective benediction: SB IV, 60). A new depth is thus given to the fellowship at the feast which Jesus keeps with his disciples and which he only succeeds in uniting in a true bond by means of the celebration of the paschal meal, when he offers himself to this company as a saving gift.

c. *Memorial of Christ's death.* In the Luke/Paul version the words: 'which is given [shall be delivered] for you', are added to the words of consecration of the bread. In the Matthew/Mark version, the consecration of the wine contains the phrase: 'which shall be shed for many', and to this Matthew adds, by way of elucidation: 'unto remission of sins' (see Mt 1:21).

All these additions interpret Christ's body and blood in accordance with Is 53:12. Jesus himself represented his death as the propitiatory death of the servant of God (*TDNT* v, 709–13). His is a martyr's death and as such has a propitiatory value. The atonement benefits 'many', which means 'everyone' (*TDNT* VI, 542: the words *for you* do not set a limit to the application, but extend it). Christ's death serves to atone for the world and as such is in a

vicarious sense a propitiatory death. His body is 'given' (or 'delivered') and his blood 'poured out' or 'shed'. The logical subject of these passive forms is, in the first place, God (Is 53:6, 10) and in the second, Jesus (Is 53:10b–12). Jesus was destined by God to atone for mankind in suffering and death (Phil 2:8), and he offered himself for this act (Is 53:7, 10). The phrase 'to shed blood' is applied particularly to martyrs (1 Macc 1:37; 7:17), but it also forms part of the accepted language of sacrifice (Ex 29:12; Lev 4:7, 18, 25; etc). In Is 53 too there is a suggestion of the idea of sacrifice (vv 7, 10). It is likely that the words 'flesh' and 'blood' are intended to designate Christ's body and blood as the sacrificial material. 'The life of the flesh is in the blood; and I have given it for you upon the altar to make atonement for your souls' (Lev 17:11). Christ offers himself as a sacrifice of atonement. It is possible that the participle also denotes an action taking place, relatively speaking, in the future (Blass and Debrunner, *Grammatik des neutestamentlichen Griechisch*, Göttingen [1913], 195), but what is more probable is that it has a timeless quality—that is to say, that Christ's blood is sacrificial blood.

d. *The renewal of the covenant.* The words spoken over the chalice refer to the 'covenant' in the Matthew/Mark version and to the 'new covenant' in the Luke/Paul version. The servant of God is the mediator of this covenant (Is 42:6). The Luke/Paul version refers to Jer 31:31–4 (see also Is 54:10; 55:3; 61:8; Ezek 16:60–3; 34:25; 37:21–8). This eschatological promise is, by virtue of the sacrifice of Christ's blood, offered and actually present as a saving possession. The form of the words spoken over the chalice in the Matthew/Mark version are in accordance with the conclusion of the covenant on Mount Sinai (Ex 24:8), while the eucharistic meal is the fulfilment of the meal of the covenant (Ex 24:11). Christ not only announces the eschatological era of salvation, he also inaugurates it, and the kingdom of God is not merely proclaimed by him as a state which is imminent, but is actually inaugurated by his presence and his activity. For this reason it is easy to understand why he does not simply refer to an eschatological meal, but actually anticipates this meal. The contemporary existence of a 'community of the new covenant' (see Qumran and the Damascus Document) helps us to understand this hope and fulfilment. The Eucharistic meal, at the centre of which is Christ himself, contains the fulfilment of all the Old Testament expectations and the dawn of the eschatological hope.

e. *The charge to perpetuate the eucharist.* Both Luke and Paul add, to the words of consecration, the charge: 'Do this for a commemoration of me'. In the case of Luke, these words follow the consecration of the bread. In 1 Cor 11:24, 25, they follow the consecration both of the bread and of the wine. To the latter are also added the words: 'as often as you shall drink'. The Matthew/Mark version does not include this charge, which clearly follows the normal tendency of the traditional Jewish feast, or annual commemoration, especially that of the Passover. It is not in the line of the hellenistic commemoration of death, since Jesus was not regarded as dead by the early church, but as her eternally living *Kyrios*. There is no period in the existence of the church at which this charge to perpetuate the eucharist was not fulfilled. The reason why it is omitted in the Matthew/Mark version is because it is in fact continually put into practice in the celebration of the eucharist. Paul repeats it twice in order to impress forcibly upon the Corinthians that the Lord's supper was instituted by Jesus himself and that it must in fact be treated by them as such. The words of consecration contain Christ's own legacy as well as his charge, and constitute a handing over of his power. 'Commemoration' (*anamnēsis*) must not be regarded as merely a memorial in thought and words alone. The Lord himself is present in the celebration of the eucharistic meal, just as God's act of salvation in the exodus from Egypt is present for each generation of Jews in the feast of the Passover.

All the essential concepts of the Old Testament are gathered up in Christ's words of consecration—the Covenant, the supreme authority of God, atonement and martyrdom, worship and the eschatological message. Everything is centred in Christ and through him God's activity in the matter of salvation is consummated and perfected. Everything that God has done in the past and everything that he wishes to accomplish in the future regarding man's salvation is incorporated in the Eucharist.

2. *The interpretation of the meaning of the eucharist according to Paul* (1 Cor 10:1–4, 14–22; 11:17–23; also Heb 13:9f).

a. *The celebration of the eucharist is the 'Table of the Lord'* (Mal 1:7, 12). In the Greek terminology of worship, the

235

'table' of a god is a sacrificial table and one on which ritual meals are consumed. The eucharistic celebration is, in striking contrast to the ritual meals of the pagan gods (*TDNT* II, 34f), the Lord's supper (1 Cor 11:20)—a ritual meal which was appointed by the Lord Jesus. For Paul, the celebration of the eucharist incorporates both a sacrifice and a sacrificial meal, and it is the second aspect which predominates. The heathens' sacrifices and sacrificial meals are intended for demons (10:20) and the gods are worthless (Jer 2:5), and demons lie in wait behind them. The sacrifices of the Jews are intended, not for God (1 Cor 10:20) but only for the 'altar'. The 'third race', that is, the Christians, possess the true sacrifice and the true sacrificial meal. The eucharist is the only true form of worship for the new era.

The Lord's supper proclaims the death of the Lord (11:26: note that this is expressed as 'you proclaim . . .'). This is a solemn proclamation to the effect that the death of the Lord is actually happening at the present moment (*TDNT* I, 72). The death of the Lord is actually present because Christ's body, sacrificed for his own in death, and his blood, shed for them in death, are both present (see 11:23f). This commemoration of Christ's death must on no account be understood in the sense of the *dromenon* of the mystery-cults (R. Bultmann, *Mysterientheologie*). Christ's death is given prominence in order to arouse awe, but it is also in complete conformity with the whole of Pauline theology, at the centre of which is Christ's death. The consequence of this death, with all its implications for our salvation, is the

glorification, and Paul shows his awareness of this eschatological prospect in the words 'until he come (again)'.

b. *The eucharist is 'food' and 'drink'* (10:1-4). The manna or 'spiritual food' is the type of the eucharistic food. The water out of the rock (Ex 17:1-7) or 'spiritual drink' is the type of the eucharistic drink. Both foreshadow the eucharistic food and drink. The pre-existent Christ—the 'spiritual rock' was Christ (1 Cor 10:4)—was present for the people of God and gave them spiritual or 'pneumatological' drink. Similarly the transfigured Christ, who is present in his church, gives a new food and a new drink for the salvation of its members. They, God's people in exile, are provided for by their Lord. It emerges clearly from Paul's christological appreciation of scripture and of history that he views the eucharist as the nourishment of God's people of the New Testament—as the food for their journey.

A participation or 'communion' (*koinōnia*) in the body and blood of Christ (10:16) is effected by the eating and drinking of the eucharist. This may be contrasted with the sacrificial meals of the heathens, which brought about a communion with demons (10:20) and with the Jewish sacrificial meals, producing a communion 'with the altar'. A communion 'with God' might have been expected in this context (10:13), but this is not expressed, possibly to avoid mentioning the name of God, but more probably because the Old Testament form of worship had already fallen into disuse. There are essential differences between each of these three instances of 'communion'. The communion established by the reception of the eucharist is not merely moral or ecstatic, dependent upon the personal feeling or experience of the recipient, but is a real communion in the sense that it exists independently.

This communion unites those who partake of the eucharistic meal not only with Christ but also with each other (10:17). 'The many are one body'—that is, Christ himself (see Gal 3:27). 'The many—one body' is Paul's definition of the church (Rom 12:5). The concepts of the Covenant, of the servant of God (Is 53:10–12), and of the paschal meal all contain the germ of the idea that it is the eucharist which forms and constitutes the church.

Though the reception of the eucharist brings about man's salvation—his deliverance from God's displeasure (1 Cor 10:5) and from condemnation and destruction (11:32; 10:10f)—it does not do so in every case. To eat and drink 'unworthily' results in 'judgement', which in the first place takes the form of punishment in this world, either by sickness or premature death (11:29f). These, however, can and should lead to a change of heart (see 11:32). The recipient of the Lord's supper partakes 'unworthily' if his moral attitude does not conform to what the eucharist is, in its essence and in its operation. In this context, 'communion' with the Lord and with the other members of his church in mutual charity and sharing of possessions can be contrasted with participation in the sacrificial meals offered to false gods and the complete absence of any sense of communion.

c. It is generally conceded that *Paul conceived the eucharist as a 'sacrament'* and was quite convinced of the real presence of Christ in the eucharist. In his view an essential difference exists between ordinary food and the eucharistic food (11:27, 29). In his teaching, communion with Christ is to be regarded as the effect of reception of the eucharist and this is furthermore an objective occurrence which is fixed in time (*ex opere operato*). At the same time, however, he links this up with an appeal to the will, in order to draw an inference from this effect—namely, to participate in the Lord's supper in the right moral condition, so as not to debar the effect of the sacrament. The effect of reception of the eucharist does not come about in any magical or material way, but is personal and ethical (see 10:1–11).

Paul is at pains to strengthen the attitude of reverence which ought to be present before receiving 'communion', and this is why he stresses that it is 'my' body (cf Luke) and 'my' blood in the words of consecration. This probably also accounts for the interpolation of the phrase: 'as often as you drink' (11:25b), in the commandment to perpetuate the eucharist. Furthermore, he insists that the eucharistic chalice used at the Lord's supper should be the sole wine-cup (11:21; Eph 5:18).

The account which Paul gives of the last supper in his exposition of the abuses which were taking place in Corinth concerning its celebration provides for the regulation ('agenda') of the form of public worship, and the ordering of moral life and of the community (*agapē*). This is even more pronounced in Luke's account of the last supper (22:7–38). The celebration of the eucharist is depicted as an event which is integrally woven into the fabric of the life of the community, and must be completely impenetrated by the moral life of the faithful, so that both the religious worship and the moral life of each individual forms a single entity within the community (H. Schürmann).

d. *Paul takes tradition as his authority for his conception of the eucharist* (11:23). His account of the institution of the sacrament is based firmly on tradition and his conception of the eucharist is derived from the interpretation given by Jesus himself in his words of consecration. Paul brings certain aspects into sharp relief and puts others more into the background, according to his own theological outlook and as a result of coming to grips with the world in which he moved. It is not necessary to resort to the hellenistic communities to understand Paul's view of the eucharist. He remains firmly by the tradition which goes back to the Palestinian communities. The feasts of the hellenistic communities which were 'not properly speaking ritual celebrations, but the expression of a bond of communion in accordance with the tradition of the Jewish world and of the historical Jesus himself' (E. Schweizer, *Gemeinschaftsmahl mit dem Dienen Jesu und eschatologischen Ausblick*) were not remodelled by the Greeks into the form of sacramental feasts, in the manner of mystery-cults (contrary to the claims of Bultmann and others). Rather, they passed on what they too had received and what was already inherited from Jesus himself. All the accounts of the last supper go back to the year 40, and refer to an even earlier period (see above). Is it however possible for such a radical transformation to come about in such a short space of time, a change which was to be such a stumbling-block for the Jews especially? Is it possible that this could have happened under the eyes of the last of the apostles? Can it be that all this escaped his notice, that the hellenistic communities deviated, in a particular matter which St Paul considered essential, from the ancient tradition which he recognised and to which he appealed so strongly, and that these communities consequently drew closer towards the heathen world? (With reference to the question of mystery cults and the eucharist, see *DBs* II, 1194–1210; K. Prümm, *Der christliche Glaube und die altheidnische Welt* II, Leipzig 1935, 81–98.)

Although the Letter to the Hebrews contains no explicit reference to the last supper or to the eucharist, the entire language in which Jesus's mission and work, his high priesthood and his unique sacrifice, is described in the epistle, is derived from eucharistic terminology. In this context, the heavenly gift (Heb 6:4), reminder or *anamnēsis* (10:3), the blood of Jesus (10:19), and Christ's flesh (10:20) should be especially noted, also the particular emphasis placed on the blood of Christ in the work of redemption (C. Spicq, *L'épitre aux Hébreux*, Paris 1952, 316f). Finally, Heb 13:7–16, and in particular v 9, must surely be considered together with these references which emerge from the theology of the Epistle to the Hebrews as pointers to the eucharist. A new type of doctrine was arising in the society to which the epistle was addressed, and this doctrine misconstrued the nature of the life of the Christian community. The balance of christian piety had been shifted to the act of eating the sacrificial food, and 'strengthening of the heart' was expected from this act of eating alone. Anyone expecting grace and salvation —'the strengthening of the heart'— just from the act of eating had fallen back into the old order of salvation which was concerned only with what was imperfect and belonged to this world and had, in fact, been finally done away with. Christians, however, have an 'altar', which is to be thought of in the sense of the heavenly altar of the epistle, namely, as the cross and the eucharistic table in one. Those who continue to serve the things of this world and what is imperfect are not permitted to eat from this table. But eating does not of itself alone lead to communion with Christ. The christian does not achieve this by natural or temporal means, through eating alone, but as the result of a spiritual decision to follow Christ in suffering and death. There are three practical consequences resulting from this: the christian ritual meal should stimulate hunger for the future City of God—in this sense it is an eschatological meal; God must be praised and thanked in connection with it—in this sense it is *eu-kharistia*; lastly, the result of participation in this meal must be works of love—in this sense it is *agapē*. Its validity is not lost 'despite the excesses, abuses and misinterpretations of the religious attitude of each age towards the sacramental and liturgical life of the church' (F. J. Schierse).

3. *Interpretation of the meaning of the eucharist according to John.* John's conception of the eucharist bears the stamp of the peculiar quality of his theology.

a. He brings out *the realism of Christ's presence* in the sacrament with even greater emphasis than the other evangelists and Paul, almost going so far as to cause scandal, as for example in the use of the word *chew* for eat (6:54, 56, 58) and *flesh* for body. E. Schweizer calls this his 'rough sacramentalism', countering the misconceived spirituality of the Docetic gnosis. On the other hand, it was imperative to overcome any possible scandal of anthropophagy (the 'Capharnaite' or 'Thyestean' meal) and the suggestion, which gave such offence to the gnostics, that 'flesh' and 'blood' were the vehicle of divine life. It was neither dead matter nor matter that was grossly sensual that was consumed in the sacrament, but the flesh and blood of the exalted and transfigured Lord (6:62). Flesh which lacks the life-giving spirit is incapable of leading men to eternal life (6:63). The eucharistic words of promise have to do with flesh and blood, insofar as they contain life which is given by the spirit (see the commentaries on John).

b. John uses the words *flesh* (and not *body*, which is used in the accounts of the institution) and *blood* when he refers to the giving of the eucharist. By using the word *flesh* he portrays the incarnation (1:14). Contrary to the views of the gnostics, the reality of the 'flesh' and the godhead of the *Logos* (=Word) which is latent in it belong to one another. John, who is the 'preeminent theologian of the incarnation', succeeds in establishing an intimate connection between the incarnation and the eucharist (see Phil 2:7; 1 Tim 3:16; for a further development of this subject, see also J. Betz, 260–342).

The idea of atonement contained in the sacrifice, as outlined by John (6:51b), harks back to Isaiah (53:12).

The 'many' are replaced by the 'world' and the saving gift of forgiveness of sins is replaced by the Johannine conception of ↗ life. The gift that is offered is the flesh and blood of the 'Son of man' (6:27, 53). The title 'Son of man' is used by John in association with Christ's death and with the glorification so closely connected with it (3:14; 12:34; 12:23; 13:31), with his heavenly origin and his return to heaven (1:51; 3:13; 6:62), and with his office as judge (5:27). Christ's expiatory death recedes into the background as his glorification overshadows it. The effect of the eucharist in atoning for sins, and the idea of sacrifice which goes with this, pale beside the life-giving effects and the resurrection made possible by it. There is clearly a very close connection between 1 Jn 5:8, with its emphasis on the 'water and blood' and the remarkable account given in Jn 19:34 of how 'water and blood' flowed from the wound in Jesus's side. In 1 Jn 5:8, the water and blood point to baptism and the eucharist, and both have a suprahistorical function and testify to later generations (1 Jn 5:7). 'God's work of salvation, which can be said to be the result of the mission and death of his Son, is continued uninterruptedly by his church, which makes the divine life available to each and every one of the faithful even in later ages, by means of Christ's message and the sacraments' (R. Schnackenburg, *Die Johannesbriefe*, Freiburg 1954, 234f). Thus it can be seen that the closest possible association exists between the eucharist on the one hand, and the incarnation, death, and glorification (or second coming) of Christ and the descent of the Holy Spirit on the other. The eucharist is the 'representation and application of the whole of christological activity concerning man's salvation' (H. Schürmann). The spirit bears witness to the important role of Jesus in the matter of salvation in the sacraments of baptism and holy eucharist.

c. *The eucharist is food and drink* for the preservation of eternal 'life'. The distinctive quality of the eucharist as food is secondary to its quality as a meal and attention is directed more to the individual than to the community in this respect (R. Schnackenburg, 'Herrenmahl und Lebensbrot', *Amt und Sendung*, Freiburg 1950, 136–60). John's arguments are directed principally against those who are individualistically seeking a purely personal communion with God and eternal life for themselves alone, thus completely disregarding the commandment to love one's brother (1 Jn 2:9–11; 3:10, 14f; 4:8, 20; 5:2).

John emphasises most strongly that reception of the sacrament is necessary to salvation (Jn 6:53f). In the view of the gnostics, with whom John is in conflict, it is possible to make contact with God, to have communion with him, without the aid of any intermediary, whereas the christian faith insists that this communion with God can only be achieved through the unique humanity of Jesus Christ (6:37ff; 1 Jn 1:1–13).

The effect of the eucharistic food and drink is, according to John, a communion with Christ, a sharing in his life (6:56), and this state is expressed by the evangelist in his own characteristic manner—his 'reciprocal expression of Christ's immanence': 'he . . . abides in me and I in him' (15:4–7; 17:1ff; 1 Jn 2:24; 3:24; 4:16). He avoids any expression of identification such as that common to hellenistic mysticism and takes care to keep the individual personalities distinct ('I in him, he in me'). Communion with Christ is a permanent communion and not merely a passing experience. Although an enduring possession, it can, however, be lost, hence the moral admonition which underlies the emphasis on its 'abiding' quality (R. Schnackenburg, *Die Johannesbriefe*, 91–5). Reception of the eucharist makes it possible for the communicant to enter the tide of life which flows from the Father to the Son (6:57). The unity of being and the activity of the Father and the Son form the ideal for the close relationship between Christ and the recipient of the eucharist (Jn 17:20ff). The eucharist bestows life and, at the last judgement, will bring about a resurrection from the dead. Through the eucharist, this eschatological possession becomes the christian's property here and now. The eucharist is superior to manna, because it bestows eternal life and the overriding importance of the messianic age over the Old Testament finds its true expression in the eucharist. The 'peak point' of the call to salvation, which occurred at the time of Moses, is reached and surpassed in the present era. To put it in gnostic terms, the eucharist is 'true' food and 'true' drink (6:56) and fulfils all that is included in the concept of food and drink. It bestows 'everlasting' (divine) life and is the fulfilment of mankind's most powerful desire. The food of the eucharist is not acquired in any mechanically magical way. It is the 'medicine of immortality' (Ignatius on Eph 20:2), but it must be received with faith. (This is particularly stressed in the sermon on the Bread of Life.) It is Christ himself who raises the participant in the sacrament to eternal life (6:54, 57).

An interpretation of the meaning of the eucharist based on the bible alone gives some idea of the inexhaustible profundity of this 'mystery of Faith'. The eucharist appears in a new light in every period of man's history and every generation can illuminate some fresh aspect of this great mystery.

Bibliography: *DB(S)* II, 1164–215 (with bibliography); H. Schürmann, *Der Paschalmahlbericht Lk 22:(7–14,) 15–18* (*NA* XIX, 5), Münster 1953 (with bibliography); E. Ruckstuhl, 'Wesen und Kraft der Eucharistie in der Sicht des Johannesevangeliums', *Opfer der Kirche*, Lucerne 1954, 47–90; H. Schürmann, *Der Einsetzungsbericht Lk 22:19–20* (*NA* XX, 4), Münster 1955; H. Schürmann, 'Die Gestalt der urchristlichen Eucharistiefeier', *MTZ* 6 (1955), 107–31; J. Betz, *Die Eucharistie in der Zeit der griechischen Väter* I/1, Freiburg 1955; A. Stöger, *Brot des Lebens*, Munich 1955; H. Schürmann, *Jesu Abschiedsrede Lk 22:21–38* (*NA* XX, 5), Münster 1957 (with bibliography); H. Schürmann, *Die Abendmahlsbericht Lk 22:7–38*, Paderborn 1957; J. Bonsirven, *Le règne de Dieu*, Paris 1957, 174–81. See also: F. F. J. Leenhardt, *Ceci est mon Corps*, Neuchatel-Paris 1955; 'L'Eucharistie dans le Nouveau Testament', *LV* 31 (1957); W. Marxsen, *Ev. Kirchenlex.* I, 3–6; E. Schweitzer, *RGG* I³, 10–21 (with bibliography); *BTHW* 1–9; J. Jeremias, *The Eucharistic Words of Jesus*, London 1966; H. Schürmann, 'Die Eucharistie als Repräsention und Applikation nach Jn 6:53–8', *TTZ* 68 (1959), 30–45 and 108–18; R. Schnackenburg, 'Die Sakramente im Johannesevangelium', *SP* 2 (Paris 1959), 239–43; A. Stöger, 'Die Eucharistiefeier des NT', *Eucharistiefeiern in der Christenheit*, 1960, 10–19; J. Betz, *LTK* III², 1143–7; H. Schürmann, *LTK* III², 1159–62; P. Neuenzeit, *Das Herrenmahl*, Munich 1960; J. Betz, *HTG* I, 336–42; *N. Lash, *His Presence in the World: A Study of Eucharistic Worship and Theology*, London and Dayton (Ohio) 1968.

Alois Stöger

Exaltation

According to Mk 14:62, Jesus foresaw and spoke of his exaltation as the Son of Man sitting at the right hand of God and coming with the clouds of heaven. After Easter and Pentecost, christian preaching testified to the fact that this exaltation had taken place and explained it in all the fullness of its significance.

According to Acts 2:33-6 and 5:31, both the term and the concept of the exaltation of Christ are a further stage of the kerygma of his resurrection and ascension (Acts 1:9f). By means of the exaltation, this event is completed insofar as he who rose from the dead is appointed 'Lord and Christ' and enthroned 'at the right hand of God' (Mk 16:19; Rom 8:34; Eph 1:20; Col 3:1; Heb 1:3; 1 Pet 3:22). The hymn in Phil 2:9f, which is probably pre-Pauline, also speaks of the exaltation 'above all'. This implies that Christ receives a new name, which is above all names, namely, the name of Lord. His sovereign power is distinguished as power over heavenly, earthly and infernal beings. At the present and at all times the church experiences the efficacy of this name and the power of the exalted Lord. It is in this name that it receives the Spirit (Acts 2:38), forgiveness of sins (Acts 10:43), and salvation in general (Acts 4:12). It is in this name also that signs and wonders are worked (Acts 4:30).

According to Rom 1:3f, the exaltation means that Jesus, who was already in possession of the divine sonship which had been hidden all along in his human existence, was proclaimed as the Son of God in all the fullness of his power and was established, according to the spirit of holiness and sanctification, in other words, according to his spiritual and divine being. In this sense he is now the Lord of the Church. In another hymn too, the exaltation is described (1 Tim 3:16). Christ is taken up out of the earthly sphere of the flesh into that of the divine and spiritual. He is shown to be justified by means of this, as God acknowledges his faith in him and reveals him who was rejected by the world as the one who is justified (Jn 16:10); so he is invested with divine glory. The canticle goes on to say that the exalted Christ was 'seen by angels' and thus he sees the heavenly triumph over the subjected powers, who pay homage to the one who is exalted (see Phil 2:10; Eph 3:10; Col 2:15; 1 Pet 3:22). It should be noted that Asc Is 11:23 indicates that the New Testament has here taken over certain apocalyptic ideas from the later Jewish world.

On earth too, his dominion is recognised, in that he is 'proclaimed to the heathen and is believed in the world'. In the letter to the Hebrews, the author speaks of the exaltation, using words and images which are both new and old. Jesus is 'crowned with glory and honour' for 'the suffering of death' (Heb 2:9). He was given a new name, that is, the name of Son, which denotes that he has become 'much superior to the angels' (Heb 1:4). He has passed through into the heavens (Heb 4:14) and has received the dignity of high priests for all eternity (Heb 5:5f). He has taken his place at the right hand of God (Heb 1:13). In this way the Epistle declares (as already in Acts

2:34f and elsewhere) that the ancient psalm of coronation (Ps 109:1) has been fulfilled in Christ, following the veiled claim already made for him in Mt 22:44.

The exalted Christ is, however, also the Christ who is to come again. Very often, expressions concerning the exaltation are closely linked with others on the subject of the Second Coming (see Mt 26:64; also Acts 1:2f; Phil 3:20; Col 3:1).

In St John's Gospel, we find statements relating to the exaltation used in the characteristic manner of the evangelist, full of associations and references to other contexts (see John 3:14; 8:28; 12:32-4). Christ's exaltation on the Cross fulfils the foreshadowing of the exaltation in the raising up of the bronze serpent by Moses, and is in itself a foreshadowing and indeed the commencement of his exaltation to divine glory. Since, according to St John's conception, Jesus lives on earth in the closest possible unity with the Father and is always both the Word of God and his Son, the exaltation is simply a return to the glory which he has always possessed and a revelation of this glory which is now, on the occasion of his return to the Father, manifested to the whole world. The christological statement of Jesus's exaltation thus sets out, in figurative and graphic terms, the consummation of God's action and plan for his Christ. In addition, it depicts the eventful beginning, the permanent duration and the awaited consummation of the sovereignty of Christ over the church and the world.

Bibliography: *DB[S]* IV, 1068-71; E. Schweizer, *Erniedrigung und Erhöhung bei Jesus und seinen Nachfolgern*, Zurich 1955; A. Vergote, *L'exalta-tion du Christ en croix selon le 4 évangile*, ETL 28 (1952), 5-23; H. Bleienstein, *Der erhöhte Christus*, GL 27 (1954), 84-90; G. Bertram, *Der religionsgeschichtliche Hintergrund der Erhöhung in der Septuaginta*, ZAW 68 (1956), 57-71; J. Daniélou, *La session à la droite du Père*, Studia evangelica = *TU* 73 (1959), 689-98; W. Thüsing, *Die Erhöhung und Verherrlichung Jesu im Johannesevangelium* (*NA* XXI, 1), Münster 1960.

Karl Hermann Schelkle

Faith

A. *Faith in the Old Testament*. According to the bible, God stands at the midpoint of all history. It is he who directs and guides everything. In the last analysis, everything can be traced back to him; evil itself has no existence if God does not permit it or, in biblical language, 'bring it about'. Faith is, therefore, the attitude which seeks to encounter *him* in all things and in all events, which alone in the last resort can make sense of everything and which shows a way out of present tribulation for a man whose life is based on the bible and who stands in the presence of God and says 'yes' to his summons.

In the Old Testament faith is grounded upon a historical religion—that of the covenant. Faith is, therefore, in the first place, the response of the people to the covenant. Every year, on the occasion of the offering of the firstfruits, the Israelite made his profession of faith: 'A wandering Aramaean was my father; and he went down into Egypt and sojourned there, few in number; and there he became a nation, great, mighty, and populous. And the Egyptians treated us harshly, and afflicted us, and laid upon us hard bondage. Then we cried to the Lord, the God of our fathers, and the Lord heard our voice, and saw our affliction, our toil, and our oppression; and the Lord brought us out of Egypt with a mighty hand and an outstretched arm, with great terror, with signs and wonders; and he brought us into this place and gave us this land, a land flowing with milk and honey. And behold, now I bring the first of the fruit of the ground which thou, O Lord, hast given me' (Deut 26:5-10). This ancient creed praises the freedom, power, fidelity, and love manifest in the gracious choice of God as something which is always new and which must be both recognised and acknowledged anew by each generation. Faith is, then, man's response to this attitude on the part of God.

This faith also expresses the fact that God presides over events and the course of history. What has come to pass in the beginning has been brought about by God and this bestows certainty and assurance on faith and the hope that God will continue his intervention on behalf of his people.

Two Hebrew roots in particular are used to express faith. One (*'āman*) stresses the idea of certainty, strength and firmness; the other (*bātaḥ*) expresses the energy of faith and trust. The Hebrew word for truth, authenticity is *'meth*; the Hebrew mind does not contrast truth with error but with nothingness, which is known as vanity or futility (*šeqer*). Thus God is also called the God of *'meth*, of truth, or more accurately, the God of faithfulness or of trustworthiness. Yahweh is a God *ne'mān*, that is to say, a sure God who can be relied upon and trusted (Deut 7:9). Christ himself is called the

'Amen' in this sense (Rev 3:14). It is necessary to go back to Deut 27:15-26, in order to gain some impression of the true significance of the term Amen—the knowledge that one is committed to and involved in the covenant with God. *He'emin* therefore refers to that attitude which comprises a complete reliance on what is incapable of disappointing and is absolutely certain and dependable. Indeed, it goes further than this and implies that the believer leaves himself entirely in the hands of the one who on his own merits deserves this unlimited self-commitment.

The other root—*bataḥ*—expresses above all the energy of faith, showing that there is no place in it for any kind of passivity. There is also a certain element of hope and expectation contained in the meaning, and in this way the word occurs about a hundred times in the Psalms and is rendered as 'believe' and frequently also as 'trust' or 'hope'. In Ps 4:5, for example, we find: 'trust in Yahweh'; in Ps 25:2; 'O my God, in thee I trust'; and in Ps 55:23; 'But I will trust in thee'.

The first model for this unlimited faith, this believing and faithful self-abandonment to God based on the covenant, is *Abraham*, the father of those who believe. 'He believed in Yahweh; and he reckoned it to him as righteousness' (Gen 15:6). Literally, everything was demanded of him, so that his faith was tested to the utmost limit (Gen 22:1: 'God tested Abraham'). In the first place, he had to exchange his homeland and family, well-being and security, for the uncertain and unsettled life of a nomad. Then he was obliged to have a son, despite his great age, and finally he had to sacrifice this son, the heir to God's promise. Again and again, these various situations in which he finds himself and which affect him in his inmost being are intended to confront the man as he is, and make him into a 'believer' or an 'unbeliever'. Nonetheless, we read in Heb 11:8f: 'By faith Abraham obeyed when he was called to go out to a place which he was to receive as an inheritance; and he went out, not knowing where he was to go. By faith he sojourned in the land of promise, as in a foreign land, living in tents with Isaac and Jacob, heirs with him of the same promise ... By faith Sara herself received power to conceive, even when she was past the age'. Paul had also to go into the meaning of this faith in Rom 4, as faith is as essential to the New Covenant as it was to the Old.

The *prophetic period* brought these still latent characteristics of such sublime personalities into full relief, in accordance with the religious tendencies which were peculiar to them—Abraham (Gen 20:7) and Moses (Hos 12:13) were explicitly associated with the prophets.

A similar theme of the pre-prophetic period can, however, be found in an ancient royal psalm, and this theme, that the king in Israel, if he wishes to live up to his calling, must acknowledge no other support or source of strength than God, is later even further developed: 'Now I know that the Lord will help his anointed; he will answer him from his holy heaven with mighty victories by his right hand. Some boast of chariots, and some of horses; but we boast of the name of the Lord our God. They will collapse and fall; but we

shall rise and stand upright' (Ps 20:6-8).

The extraordinarily graphic and vivid quality of the allegorical language of Israel can often be traced back to concrete historical origins. The horse cannot have originated until the beginning of the second millennium or thereabouts, at the time of the *Hurrite* invasions in the Near East. The Israelites first discovered it when it was used by their enemies and did not know how to defend themselves against it. The Lord had to give them help and instructions as to how they might save themselves (Josh 11:6-9). This gave rise to the theme of 'fallax equus ad salutem'—a theme which recurs frequently, as for example in Hos 14:3; Ps 33:17; 147:10; Deut 17:16. In Zech 9:9f, we read: 'Rejoice greatly, O daughter of Zion ... Lo, your king comes to you; triumphant and victorious is he, humble and riding on an ass, on a colt ... I will cut off the chariot from Ephraim and the war horse from Jerusalem ...' For the messianic king arrays himself again in the archaic uniform and equipment of a desert chieftain; he has appointed a day of judgement over all that is proud and arrogant (see Is 2:12ff). The power of men is to be destroyed and the weakness of man saved. Again in Zech (4:6) we read: 'Not by might, nor by power, but by my Spirit, says Yahweh of hosts'. Ezra (8:21ff) prefers to ask God (for a good journey) after proclaiming a general fast, although he might have asked the king to provide a protective escort. In his revision of the material, the chronicler transforms the hosts of Jehoshaphat into spectators who sing praises to God and at the same time watch while God deals with their enemies (2 Chron 20).

It is *the prophet Isaiah* who teaches and himself fully embodies heroic faith. No more than an indication of this can be given here. On looking at Chapter 7, for example, we find that King Ahaz wants to provide human safeguards, such as the construction of fortifications and alliance with the Assyrians, because he fears the enemy who wishes to overthrow him (Is 7:6). His people too are in a state of panic (7:2). Only Isaiah remains calm and proclaims the word of the Lord: 'It [ie, the sack of Jerusalem] shall not stand, and it shall not come to pass . . . If you will not believe, surely you shall not be established' (Is 7:7, 9). The sign which the Lord gives is none other than the continued existence of the dynasty and this is given at a time and in circumstances which seem to be humanly impossible. The royal house and capital are the tangible signs which guarantee the continued existence of the Covenant (see 2 Sam 7:15f). It is possible to follow the proclamation of the prophet and the reaction of the king in this way throughout the entire book, and Isaiah's utterance is one which again and again demands faith.

A hundred years later Habakkuk preaches on exactly the same theme in his attempt to give support to the hopelessly wavering people at the time of the Babylonian invasion. The prophet listens to God, who commands him: 'Write the vision; make it plain upon tablets, so he may run who reads it. For still the vision awaits its time; it hastens to the end—it will not lie. If it seem slow, wait for it; it will surely come, it will not delay. Behold, he whose soul is not upright in him shall fail, but the righteous shall live by his faith' (Hab 2:2–4). Habakkuk addresses what he says to the whole nation, yet the final sentences could easily refer to the content of the book of Job. The task of the individual is thus the same as that of the nation. If the history of the chosen people is viewed as a movement between these two opposite attitudes—that of believing against all human calculation that God's help will not fail and that of relying on one's own strength, not trusting in God, not believing God since he at times lets his people down—then the life of the individual must also be considered in this light.

The Book of Job sets forth the situation of the believer in the most moving manner. Satan is presented as one of the angels in God's presence and is asked whether he has seen Job on earth and has observed how pious and godfearing he is. Satan answering said to the Lord: 'Doth Job fear God *for naught*?' (Job 1:9). This is the question which is central to the book. If it were to be proved that the pious man does serve God 'for naught', Satan would have to admit defeat. Job has no idea of this prelude in heaven. His sons and daughters are suddenly taken from him in an accident, he himself is stricken with leprosy and has to withdraw from the town. He is completely misunderstood by his wife and his friends. He is ground down and tormented to the limits of his endurance, all human support is taken away from him and his friends, instead of comforting him, reason thus: 'if you are so afflicted, then you must have offended God in some way'. Satan too speaks through his wife: 'Curse God and die!'

But, in spite of everything, Job cleaves to God. He knows that he is bound to God in faith and even when he has been deprived of everything, including the ultimate guarantees of this faith, he refuses to allow himself to be argued out of it (see 13:15; 16:19f; 19:25).

Thus, in its religious usage, the word *he'emîn* (in LXX and in the New Testament most frequently translated as *pisteuein*), carried on by its use in the prophets and employed in the vocabulary of individual piety, has come to occupy a prominent place than other roots of similar meaning as the word which best describes the relationship which exists between the people of the covenant and God.

Bibliography: O. S. Virgulin, *Bbl* 31 (1950), 346–64 and 483–503 (on Isaiah); J. C. C. van Drossen, *De derivata van dem staam "mn" in het Hebreeuwsch van het OT*, Amsterdam 1951; A. Weiser, *TDNT* VI, 182–96; P. van Imschoot, Haag 578f; Jacob 148–63; A. Gelin, *LV* 22 (1955), 431–42; J. B. Bauer, *BL* 23 (1955/6), 226–30; E. Pfeiffer, 'Glaube im AT', *ZAW* 71 (1959), 151–64; O. S. Virgulin, *La fede nella profezia d'Isaia*, Milan 1961.

Johannes B. Bauer

B. *Faith in the New Testament*. I. *Belief in the Message of Jesus*. In Mk 1:15, Jesus's message is summarised thus: 'The time is fulfilled, and the kingdom of God is at hand; repent, and believe in the gospel'. 'Faith' can accordingly be described as the acceptance of the kingdom of God as it has been brought about by Jesus's proclamation.

1. *Contrast between the idea of faith in the Old Testament and that contained in the New*. In contrast to the Old Testament, two fresh impulses are given to the idea of faith in the New Testament:

a. 'The time is accomplished', which means that what has been promised in the Old Covenant is fulfilled in the person and in the work of Jesus of Nazareth. That is why the synoptic account is moulded on the life and work of Jesus in accordance with the message of the Old Testament (see especially the story of the Passion) and why the evangelists themselves repeatedly stress that such and such has come to pass 'in order that the Scriptures might be fulfilled'. This evidence of faith occupies a particularly important place in Matthew's gospel (Mt 1:22f; 2:15, 17f, 23; 4:14ff; 8:17; 12:17ff; 13:14f, 35; 21:4f; [26:54]; 26:56; 27:9f).

b. Conversion as a condition of faith now implies—as in the message of St John the Baptist (see Mt 3:2)—not only a turning away from everything that is contrary to God, but also a turning towards God as he has become manifest in Christ, and a radical preparation for the kingdom of God as it has dawned in Christ. 'The conversion and penitence to which he urges the Jews implies at the same time belief in him' (Schmid, *RNT* 2:117). This is why Jesus condemns the cities of Galilee which have failed to believe in him in spite of all the miracles which had taken place in them (Mt 11:20–4; Lk 10:13–15).

2. *Faith and Christ*. What emerges from this is that Christ claims for himself the faith which had been directed to God. It makes no real difference whether this is regarded as belief in God or belief in Christ (cf Mk 9:42 and Mt

18:6), since faith in God is contained in the latter.

a. His miracles demand faith, so that we find many cases where Jesus ascribes his saving acts of curing disease to the power of faith (Mt 9:2, 22, 29; Mk 2:5; 5:34; 10:52; Lk 5:20; 7:50; 8:48; 18:42). Everything is possible to him who believes; he can obtain from God even what is impossible (Mk 9:23; 11:23; cf Mt 17:20; Lk 17:6). If faith is absent, no miracle is possible (Mk 6:5, 6; cf Mt 13:58). Nevertheless, it is not faith which works miracles, but the divine power of Jesus, who makes his working of miracles dependent on the faith of men. It is for this reason that Jesus reproaches his disciples for their unbelief or 'little faith' (Mt 17:20). When he is with them on the boat nothing can happen to them, however violently the storm may rage (Mt 8:23–7; Mk 4:35–41; Lk 8:22–5). Peter is able to walk on the waves in perfect safety at Jesus's command, although he sinks at first because fear overcomes him and he begins to doubt (Mt 14:28–31). Since faith is a condition for the working of a miracle, Jesus rejects the demands of his demonic enemy and his earthly opponents who clamour for 'signs', that is to say, proofs of his power which compel recognition of his messianic mission and his divinity and leave no place for faith (Mt 4:1–11; Lk 4:1–13; Mt 12:38, 39; Lk 11:29, 30; Mt 16:1–4; Mk 8:11–13; Lk 11:16; Mt 27:42; Mk 15:32). It is true that Jesus's miracles have the object of authenticating his messianic mission and his claim to divinity. There is, however, no contradiction here, since Jesus demands of those who wish to experience his power no immediate, complete faith, but rather only a firm trust in his power and his desire to help them; his miracles do not compel faith, but always leave the way open for man to decide of his own free will.

b. *His words demand faith.* It is possible only for the believer to penetrate the secret of Jesus's doctrine and to make it his own. Mk 4:10–12 demonstrates this with frightening clarity (see also Mt 13:10–15; Lk 8:9f). This passage originally referred, probably in an all-embracing sense, to Jesus' activity as a teacher, and its meaning has thus been narrowed down by the evangelist to refer to the sermon on parables. In it, Jesus makes a clear dividing line between 'you'—that is, the apostles—and 'those that are without'. To the latter, everything that he says is mysterious, whereas the secret of the kingdom of God is revealed to the apostles. It is faith, however, which draws this dividing line and causes God to reveal himself to the former and harden the hearts of the latter (passive phrases are used to express periphrastically the activity of God). The outcome of Jesus's message, which offers grace and passes judgement, bestows salvation and life and brings ruin and death, is powerfully exemplified in this Logion (see Lk 2:34; J. Jeremias, *The Parables of Jesus*, London 1954, 11ff). It is faith which brings about grace, salvation and life, and this faith must not be regarded as the meritorious action of man, but as a free gift on the part of God. Since faith implies a distinction between the apostles and those who are outside, this will apply also to the parables— this is, at any rate, how Mark has understood it. Although it is the apostles who are, in accordance with their special position, entrusted with the task of clarifying the teaching of Jesus and making it comprehensible to men, the result of their activity is in fact that only those who believe can be led by them into the mystery of the kingdom of God. Only the believer is able to assimilate the absolute and authoritative claims which Jesus's words make, as in the 'I say to you' of the sermon on the mount (Mt 5:22, 32, 34, 39, 44) or in his full power to forgive sins (Mk 2:1–12; see also Mk 1:27). For the rest this is a stumbling block.

c. *Faith as a decision for Christ.* What emerges from all this is that man is called upon by Christ to make a decision, either for him or against him: 'He who is not with me is against me; and he who does not gather with me scattereth' (Mt 12:30; cf Mk 9:40). This decision takes place in the profession of faith as Peter pronounces it in the name of the disciples (Mk 8:29 and parallels). It is not by chance that Mark places Peter's profession of faith precisely in the middle of his gospel. What is evident here is that the people as a whole do not acknowledge Jesus as the Messiah and that only the small band of his disciples believes in him. The declaration of faith in Jesus, however, decides the attitude of man towards God: 'So every one who acknowledges me before men, I also will acknowledge before my Father who is in heaven; but who ever denies me before men, I also will deny before my Father who is in heaven' (Mt 10:32, 33; Lk 12:8, 9; see also Mk 8:38).

3. *Faith and the kingdom of God.* a. *Faith as grace.* A faith which implies complete self-surrender to God and opens up the kingdom of God must be brought about by God himself. Thus Jesus pronounces Peter to be blessed after he has made his profession of faith: for flesh and blood has not revealed this to you, but my Father who is in heaven' (Mt 16:17). Thus he praises his Father, in his prayer of rejoicing, for hiding his revelation from the 'wise and prudent' and bestowing it upon the 'little ones' (Mt 11:25). It is clear from this that Jesus ascribes both the unbelief to the 'wise and prudent' and the belief of the 'little ones' to the dispensation of his heavenly Father.

b. *Faith is necessary to salvation.* If unbelief precludes salvation (Lk 8:12; Mk 16:14, 16), then belief is necessary to salvation. That is why the worst thing that can be done to the 'little ones who believe' is to cause them scandal, that is to say, lead them astray in their faith. It would be better for any man who does such a thing, if 'a great millstone were hung round his neck and he were thrown into the sea', rather than that he should undergo the punishment which threatens him at the Last Judgement (Mk 9:42).

c. *The new condition.* Faith is the prerequisite for the new condition of being into which the disciple of the Lord enters when he leaves everything behind in order to follow Jesus (Mk 1:18; Lk 5:11; cf Mk 10:28). By this is meant that the believer separates himself from everything and everybody (Mt 10:34–7; Lk 14:26; cf Lk 18:29) in order to unite himself with Jesus in a lifelong communion. He participates in the destiny of his Lord, shares his poverty (Mt 8:19f), takes up his cross with Jesus (Mk 8:34), is scorned and abused, hated and persecuted with him (Mt 10:17–22). 'It is enough for the disciple to be like his teacher, and the servant like his master' (Mt 10:25). But he also has a share in his life, he is permitted to enter the kingdom of God which has dawned with Christ (see Lk 9:61f) and partake of his glory, since the Beatitudes of the sermon on the mount (Mt 5:3–12) and the acknowledgement by the Son of Man when he comes in his glory (Mk 8:38; 9:1) can be referred to him.

II. *Faith in the preaching of Paul.* With 'faith', we are dealing with an idea that springs from the very centre of Paul's theology and message. This can be observed even from a superficial examination of the Pauline epistles, in that the basic noun *pistis* and the verb *pisteuein* not only occur very frequently in all the epistles, but also occupy a central place in them, and especially in those to the Romans and the Galatians. It is an idea which, however, has different levels of meaning. The range of meaning of *pistis* extends from that of 'fidelity' (Rom 3:3; Gal 5:22; 2 Thess 1:4; 2 Tim 4:7) to certainty of belief and conscience (see Rom 14:23) and finally to the idea of faith in the truly religious sense.

1. *The exposition of faith according to Rom 10:4–17.* It would not be too wide of the mark to assume that Rom 10:4–17 is the passage in which the apostle sets out in general terms his view of faith. Faith presupposes revelation, and this is brought about by the word, either directly, as Paul himself experienced it on the way to Damascus (1 Cor 9:1; 15:7; 2 Cor 4:6; Gal 1:15, 16; Eph 3:3; see also Acts 9:1–19; 22:5–11; 26:12–18), or indirectly, by means of

the proclamation of the word of God to men: 'Faith comes from what is heard, and what is heard comes by the preaching of Christ' (Rom 10:17). The proclaimed word, in Paul's view, places Christ firmly in the centre, and, what is more, Christ crucified (1 Cor 1:18, 23; Gal 3:1). By belief is meant— and here Paul explains by means of the example of Abraham, Rom 4—that as Abraham considered his body which was 'as good as dead' and yet remained, despite all human considerations, firmly convinced of the truth of the word of God which had established him as 'father of many nations' (4:18), so should we consider the body of the dead Christ on the cross and remain, here too despite all human considerations to the contrary, firmly convinced that God has established him as 'father of many nations', that is to say, that he was 'raised for our justification' (Rom 4:25). *Hupakoē* comes from *akoē*, 'obeying' comes from 'listening' (see Rom 10:16); and indeed, in Paul 'faith' and 'obedience' are very closely related. In Rom 1:5 and 16:26, he speaks of the 'obedience of faith', which means in all probability the faith which consists in obedience, recognition and acknowledgement of the christian message and subjection to the will of God which is revealed in it. In this way the apostle is able to employ the words 'faith' and 'obedience' almost reciprocally. What is designated in Rom 1:8 as 'your faith' can be called, in Rom 16:19, 'your obedience'.

What occurs in man's inmost heart concerning the complete renunciation of self and subjection to the will of God for the purpose of salvation, is made external in the oral profession of faith.

In Rom 10:9, 10, basing his reasoning on Deut 30:11–14, Paul makes a distinction between 'belief in the heart' and 'belief confessed with the mouth'. Faith 'in the heart' has its counterpart in the statement made in Rom 4:24; 'that God has raised him from the dead' (Rom 10:9; cf 1 Cor 15:12ff), whereas the essence of the external profession of faith is to be found in the primitive christian credo: 'Jesus is the Lord' (Rom 10:9; cf 1 Cor 12:3; Phil 2:11; Acts 18:28). Similarly, the apostle speaks of the *fides qua creditur* and of the *fides quae creditur*. It is possible to assume with complete certainty that he makes use of formal professions of faith which have been handed down to him (see Rom 10:9; 1 Cor 15:3, 4; 1 Tim 3:16). Faith is thus indispensable and must remain indispensable (see 1 Cor 13:13) because it forms the basis of the new existence for the christian and represents the first step towards 'existence in Christ' which is ultimately brought about through ↗ baptism, when the believer receives Christ's act of redemption, his death and resurrection (Rom 6:4, 6, 8; Gal 2:19; 5:24; 6:14; Col 2:12; 2 Tim 2:11).

2. *Faith and justification.* Over and above these general features which characterise the Pauline conception of faith, it is also particularly distinguished by the fact that it stands in complete contrast to the pharasaical and judaistic idea of man's ↗ justification through the operation of the law. The great emphasis on faith which we find in the theology of Paul is doubtless occasioned by his early passionate defence of the ↗ law as the only means to salvation, sustained until he was overcome by the power of grace (see Gal 1:13–16).

Christ's atoning death, becomes effective for the individual human being through faith (Rom 3:25), and by faith the individual is justified (Rom 3:28). His justification does not take place by means of the works of the law, but by means of faith. The various arguments of the Letter to the Romans move, as it were, around this central idea. The law has shown itself to be incapable of leading men to salvation. This inability does not arise from the law itself, but from man's failure to fulfil its demands in their entirety. It is true that 'the doers of the law . . . will be justified' (Rom 2:13), but man is incapable of becoming a 'doer' in the fullest sense of the word. Paul recognises the deceptive external lustre that typifies the proud self-confidence of the Jew who strictly obeys the law and who imagines himself to be 'a guide of the blind', 'a light of them that are in darkness', 'an instructor of the foolish', 'a teacher of infants' and who supposes that he possesses 'the form of knowledge and of truth in the law'. The apostle, however, points out to such a man the fatal dichotomy that exists between the demands made by the law and their fulfilment, between the desire to fulfil them and their accomplishment (Rom 2:19ff) and shows that all are 'under the power of sin' (Rom 3:9) and that no human being is justified before God through the works of the law (see Rom 3:20). Sin has indeed made use of the law in order to show up in its true colours, for sin is only imputed where the law is (Rom 5:13). Paul is able to make this idea all the more pointed and precise in his statement: 'Law came in, to increase the trespass' (Rom 5:20). What has been enacted in the whole of the history of salvation is reiterated in the life of the individual, as experienced personally by Paul himself. At first he lived without the law. Then the law came and he experienced a revival of sin and he himself died. The law, then, forces man into a situation from which there is no way out and no rescue, except through Christ. 'For God has done what the law, weakened by the flesh, could not do', namely sending his Son into the world (Rom 8:3). God's justice has thus been revealed without the law (Rom 3:21). God has brought about, by a free act of grace, what man would never have dared to anticipate, and man cannot attain salvation by his own actions, but has to be given it by God through grace. Now he is 'justified by his grace as a gift', by virtue of the redemption in Christ Jesus (Rom 3:24). Thus the provisional disposition of salvation under the law is contrasted with its final disposition according to grace. Grace has taken the place of the law: 'for Christ is the end of the law' (Rom 10:4). Whereas the law demands works, the indispensable condition for grace is faith: 'for we hold that a man is justified by faith apart from works of law' (Rom 3:28). What the apostle has in mind is the following antithesis:

Without Christ	With Christ
Law	*Grace*
Works	*Faith*

What is contained in this distinction is a clear choice: either with Christ or without him, either grace or the law, either faith or the works of the law. As a way to salvation, the one excludes the other: the way of faith has replaced that of the works of the law.

This is shown with great clarity in Gal 3:23–6. The law is the taskmaster or 'pedagogue', under whose authority men used to stand: 'but now that faith has come, we are no longer under a custodian' (Gal 3:25). 'Faith' is to be understood here simply as the new disposition or order of salvation which has been brought about through Christ and is so closely connected with him that it can in fact almost be identified with him, for the passage, 'now that faith has come . . .' could be read as 'now that Christ has come . . .' After it has been revealed by Christ, faith has become the only way to salvation.

3. *Faith in Christ.* Paul's statements on the matter of faith are imprinted with his own particular individuality and not only where they point to this antithesis to judaism. The apostle also develops a view of faith which is entirely his own, derived from his passionate 'intimacy with Christ' and for which he has coined the formula 'in Christ'.

Phrases such as *pistis in Khristō(i) Iēsou* (lit = 'faith in Jesus Christ': Gal 3:26; 5:6; Col 1:4; 2:5 [*eis Khriston*]; Eph 1:15; 1 Tim 1:14; 3:13; 2 Tim 1:13; 3:15) or *pisteuein eis Khriston Iēsoun* (lit = 'believe in Jesus Christ': Gal 2:16; Phil 1:29; see also Eph 1:13) occur quite often in Paul's letters, and these can indeed be rendered quite correctly by the literal translations given. Nevertheless, it is possible to assume that the phrases *en Khristō(i)* and *eis Khriston* are not used here in the technical sense of the pauline formula. The new existence 'in Christ' in fact grows out of faith (Gal 2:20; 3:26; 2 Cor 4:18; 5:7; 13:5) and faith and communion with Christ belong so closely together that it is possible to say that faith in Christ means that faith is brought about through a life-relationship with Christ.

In addition to this, the word *faith* is frequently met with—as is the case with other important ideas connected with christian existence—in the genitive construction *pistis Khristou* (lit = 'faith of Christ': Rom 3:22, 26; Gal 2:16, 20; 3:22; Eph 3:12; Phil 3:9; 1 Tim 3:13; 2 Tim 3:15). Just as we find references in Paul to 'Christ's afflictions' (Col 1:24), the 'marks of Jesus' (Gal 6:17), the 'steadfastness of Christ' (2 Thess 3:5) and the 'love of Christ' (2 Cor 5:14; Eph 3:19; Phil 1:8), so do we find him speaking of the 'faith of Christ' (see O. Schmitz, *Die Christusgemeinschaft des Paulus im Lichte seines Genetivgebrauches*, Gütersloh 1924, 268; A. Deissmann calls this genitive construction 'genetivus mysticus' in his *Paul*, New York 1957, 161ff; see also E. Wissman, *Das Verhältnis von 'pistis' und Christusfrömmigkeit bei Paulus* (*FRLANT* 40), Göttingen 1926, 68ff; see also Meinertz 2, 136). The apostle is referring here to his own faith which he has in communion with Christ.

4. *Faith in the Letter to the Hebrews.* Important statements are made concerning faith (in the Epistle to the Hebrews) especially in the eleventh chapter. Nevertheless, in considering Heb 11:1, we should guard against thinking in terms of a 'definition' of faith, as the writer's intention here is, strictly speaking, only to give the distinguishing marks of the attitude of faith which he would like to recommend to his readers. In his view, this attitude is characterised by two aspects: 'assurance (*hupostasis*) of things to be

hoped for' and 'conviction (*elegkhos*) of things not seen'. The first links faith in the most intimate way with hope and calls it a confident and optimistic approach to what is hoped for, an attitude for which there are countless examples in the history of salvation (Chap. 11), by far the most outstanding being that of Christ himself (12:1–11). The second of these aspects extends the meaning of the first insofar as it sees in faith, the 'proof' for what is of its nature invisible, and recognises in it the essential reality from which the visible reality has emerged (see 11:3). In this way faith has for its object the existence of God and the fact that he is the rewarder of good works (v 6). Without this attitude of faith, which includes confident trust and conviction, it is impossible to please God or to come to him (v 6: cf 6:12; 10:22).

If faith, in accordance with the particular stress which the author here places on it, is the attitude of firm confidence with regard to what is hoped for, then it is scarcely to be wondered at that the word *pistis* is frequently used in the sense of 'constancy in faith'. Thus, the examples of faith mentioned in Chap. 11 are at the same time examples of constancy in faith as well. As Christ himself proved his faithfulness (3:1–6; cf 10:23), so is it necessary for christians to preserve this attitude of commitment and not to betray this trust (10:32–9), so that, after all that God has bestowed upon them, they do not go astray through lack of trust and so apostasise (3:7–4:11). Two things stand in very close relationship to each other here. On the one hand, faith must be demonstrated in patience (10:36; 12:1).

On the other hand, however, it is also coupled with a victorious frankness (*parrhēsia*) with which the christian has confident access to God (4:16; 10:19) and is able to endure all that the world may inflict upon him (10:32–6).

III. *Faith in the Letter of James.* At first sight the comments made on faith in the Letter of James appear to contradict completely Paul's statements on the same subject. In particular, the basic expositions contained in the Letter to the Romans seem to stand in formal contrast to what is stated in Jas 2:14–26 (cf especially Jas 2:24 with Rom 3:28; see also Gal 2:16). It must, however, be taken into account that James envisages a different antithesis from Paul (see above). With him there is no question of discussing the relationship between faith and works in the matter of justification, but of giving practical guidance and impressing on christians that their faith should be a living faith which has a positive result in everyday life (1:3, 6, 21; 2:1–5; 4:7; 5:8–11, 15). The demons believe in the one God and shudder (2:19); a faith without works is dead and barren (2:17, 20). A living faith is shown in patience (1:3), in the love of one's neighbour (2:15–17), in hospitality (see 2:25), in trusting prayer (1:6; 5:15) and, above all, in piety (1:27; 2:22).

Paul's letters demonstrate clearly that such a conception is in no way opposed to the pauline view of faith, and Paul too fundamentally insists on the practical working out of faith in everyday life (Gal 5:6).

IV. *Faith in the writings of John.* When John writes, towards the end of his gospel: 'But these are written that you may believe that Jesus is the Christ, the Son of God, and that believing you may have life in his name' (20:31; see also 1 Jn 5:13), he acknowledges that his entire message is aimed at faith, and it is true to say that 'faith' plays a very important part in his writings, especially in his gospel and in 1 Jn.

He frequently expresses the idea, as is shown in the passage quoted above, in accordance with the general use of the word in the New Testament, that it is necessary to 'believe' in Christ, the Son of God, in order to achieve salvation, or, more simply, that the acceptance of the message of Christ makes one a 'believer' (Jn 3:15, 18; 4:53; 6:47; 8:24; 1 Jn 5:1, 5; see also Acts 2:44; 9:42; 11:17; 14:23; 16:31; 18:8; 19:4; 1 Cor 15:2; Gal 2:16; Phil 1:29). As is the case with other books of the New Testament, the object of faith is often expressed in John in a *hoti*-clause (Jn 8:24; 11:42; 13:19; 14:10f; 16:27, 30; 17:8, 21; see also Rom 10:9; 1 Thess 4:14; Heb 11:6; Jas 2:19).

A rapid examination of John's writings will reveal the particular quality of the Johannine conception of faith, and it is remarkable that whereas the verb *pisteuein* occurs frequently (ninety-six times in the gospel and nine times in 1 Jn), the noun *pistis*, with the exception of 1 Jn 5:4 and Rev 2:19; 13:10, does not appear at all. What undoubtedly seems to emerge from this is that John is more concerned with the reality of faith than with any abstract discussion of a conception of faith.

Another peculiarity of John's writings is that *pisteuein* occurs more frequently with the dative than as *pisteuein eis.* Thus, in John, men believe the word which Jesus says (4:50; cf 2:22), or simply his words (5:47); they believe him (8:31, 45, 46; 10:37, 38; 14:11) or they believe the Father who has sent him (5:24; cf 5:38). A further characteristic of John's texts is that 'to believe' is replaced by various other words and can thus be elucidated to a considerable degree. 'To believe' means 'to hear' (5:25; 6:60; 8:43, 47; 18:37); 'to believe in him' means 'to come to him' (5:40; 6:35, 37, 44f, 65; 7:37); 'to receive him' (1:12; 5:43) or 'to love him' (8:42; 14:15, 21, 23f, 28; 16:27).

1. *The essence of faith.* The manner in which faith is brought about in man, how it originates and is consummated, is set out in many different ways in the writings of John. The faith of the ruler who asks Jesus to cure his son resides in the first place merely in a trust in Jesus's power to work miracles. The Lord says to him: 'Go; your son will live'. The man places his faith in the word of the Lord and makes the long journey home, with nothing more than this word in his possession. Then, when the news is brought to him by his servants that his son is alive, he experiences the truth and the divine power of the word of Christ. It is not until that moment that faith in its fullest sense comes to him: 'And he himself believed, and all his household' (4:46–54). The course of events is similar in the case of the healing of the man who was born blind (Chap. 9). The blind man who has begun to see attains, through the miracle of his cure, a generic faith and believes that Jesus is a prophet (v 17). This faith emerges successfully from the test of the debate with the pharisees which even leads to the man's expulsion from the synagogue, and eventually reaches its culmination through Christ's personal revelation (v

37). The healed man says: 'Lord, I believe', and falls down before Jesus in adoration (v 38). At the marriage in Cana (2:1–11), what is revealed by Jesus's miracle of the transformation of water into wine is 'his glory' and, as a result, 'his disciples believed in him' (2:11). When he meets the risen Christ, Thomas falls down before him with the words 'My Lord and my God!' (20:26–8). If the aim of this event of faith—the personal encounter with Christ and the falling down in adoration of his *doxa* or 'glory'—is achieved, then there is no further need of any external sign, whether this takes the form of a miracle or of a word. In this way, the Samaritans believe in the first place on account of the testimony of the woman, but after their personal encounter with Christ they say: 'It is no longer because of your words that we believe, for we have heard for ourselves and we know that this is indeed the Saviour of the world' (4:42). The following factors come together at the same time when the act of faith takes place: on the basis of an external sign—a miracle or a word—there is an encounter, either direct or indirect, with Christ. The outcome of this is that the initial faith reaches its perfection and the man falls down in worship of Christ as the one who reveals the 'glory' of God. Faith must however be able to do without the external sign as well, and be strong enough to be dependent upon Christ alone. The latter emerges from Peter's confession of faith (see 6:68, 69) and from what the Lord says with regard to Thomas's act of faith: 'Blessed are those who have not seen and yet believe' (20:29; see also 4:48).

2. *The effects of faith.* John describes

the effects of faith in various passages: 'He who believes in him is not condemned' (3:18); 'He has eternal life; he does not come into judgement, but has passed from death to life' (5:24); 'He who believes in the Son has eternal life' (3:36; 6:40, 47; 20:31; 1 Jn 5:13; see also 6:35; 11:25ff; 12:36, 46; 1 Jn 5:1, 5). What is common to all these references is the conviction that faith is the means to salvation and that unbelief leads to perdition. It is a particular attribute of John's conception of faith that both faith and unbelief anticipate the end—judgement on lack of faith is already effective and where faith is present everlasting life has already dawned (3:14-21; see also 5:24).

Faith in Christ is thus decisive in the matter of man's salvation, since his relationship with Christ determines his relationship with God: Whoever believes in Christ believes in the Father (12:44); whoever does not believe in Christ neither sees nor hears the Father (5:37, 38). 'To see God' means, in effect, to believe that Christ is in the Father and the Father is in him (10:38; 14:10, 11, 20).

It is clear from this that man cannot produce faith of his own accord. Faith must be bestowed upon him by God: 'No man can come to me unless the Father who sent me draws him' (6:44; cf 6:65; 17:6-8). On the other hand, however, it is man's own fault if he does not come to believe (15:22: cf 40).

3. *Faith and knowledge.* We have noted that other verbs can, in John's writings, be allied with 'to believe'—for example, the verb 'hear' (4:42) or 'see' (20:8, 25). There is, however, a particularly strong link between 'believe' and 'know', and these two verbs are so closely connected that they are almost indistinguishable one from the other. Both have the same object, for it is stated, with reference to the same fact, that it can be 'believed' and 'known' (6:69; 1 Jn 4:16; see also Jn 17:8; 8:24, 28). This does not mean, however, that 'to know' or knowledge is intended to describe a higher status of christian being, the achievement of which leads to the abolition of 'faith'. If this were so, the two expressions would not be so closely related in the text and interchanged so frequently in order of sequence. For example, in Jn 6:69 we read 'We have believed, and have come to know', but in 1 Jn 4:16 'We know and believe'. There is, however, a difference between the two words, and this is clearly expressed in the relationship between the Son and the Father, which can certainly be rendered by 'knowledge', but never by 'faith' (10:14f; 17:25). If, in this instance, 'knowledge' denotes what is usually rendered in the johannine gospel as 'I and the Father are one' (10:30; cf 17:11) or 'the Father is in me and I am in the Father' (10:38; cf 14:20), then it becomes apparent that 'to know' implies the utter self-abandonment of the Son to the Father and the perfect communion between the Father and the Son. A state of 'knowing' is thus possible for the man who believes that God is in Christ and that Christ lives in the most intimate communion with the Father, that is to say, he can also be included in this life-communion as this is expressed in Christ's prayer, as 'high priest' for his apostles (17:21; cf 17:3, 11). All the same, there can be no 'knowing' without 'believing' and this

is why we find the demand: 'Believe the works, that you may know' (10:38). 'Knowing' is thus the result and the aim of 'believing'.

4. *Faith and conduct.* If John holds that faith must be orientated towards God, and that this orientation reaches its objective in 'knowing', then it follows that this orientation must be closely related to the conduct of the christian in the world. It is true that the christian is not 'of the world' (15:19; 17:14, 16; cf 17:6), but he is 'in the world' (13:1; 17:11, 15; 1 Jn 4:17) and his faith is that very power which triumphs over the world (1 Jn 5:4f). The faith of one who is 'in the world' is demonstrated in keeping the commandments (15:10; 1 Jn 2:3f; 3:22ff; 5:2) and especially the commandment to love one another (13:34; 15:12; 1 Jn 2:7f; 4:21). This 'new commandment' of love of one's neighbour arises from the new relationship between man and God which is based on faith (13:34; 15:12). John stresses again and again, especially in 1 Jn, that the love of God which the believer receives must be effective in the love of one's neighbour. This injunction at the same time points out clearly the task of the christian with regard to the 'world'—the 'world' will know christians as the disciples of Christ by their love for each other (13:35).

Bibliography: J. Huby, 'La connaissance de foi dans St Jean', *RSR* 21 (1931), 385–421; T. Soiron, *Glaube, Hoffnung, Liebe*, Regensburg 1934; R. Schnackenburg, *Der Glaube im vierten Evangelium*, Breslau 1937 (dissertation); E. Walter, *Glaube, Hoffnung und Liebe im NT*, Freiburg 1940; O. Kuss, 'Der Glaube nach den paulinischen Hauptbriefen, *TG* 46 (1956), 1–26; P. Morant, 'Der Glaube in der ntl. Theologie, *Anima* 13 (1958), 5–14; A. Schlatter, *Der Glaube im NT*, Stuttgart 1927⁴; E. Grässer, *Der Glaube im Hebräerbrief*, Marburg 1965; P. Valloton, *Le Christ et la foi: Etude de théologie biblique*, 1960; W. G. Kummel, 'Der Glaube im NT', *TG* 16 (1938), 209–21; P. Antoine, *DB[S]* III, 276–310; A. Weiser and R. Bultmann, *TDNT* VI, 174–228; P. van Imschoot, Haag 578–83; Meinertz II.

Heinrich Zimmermann

Fasting

The law commands a fast only on the great Day of Atonement (Lev 16:29–30; 23:27, 32; Num 29:7). The practice of fasting, on the other hand, is very common and takes many different forms, even if the special food laws of the Levites and the abstinence practised by priests, Nazarites, and Rechabites, which are outside the scope of this article, are not taken into consideration.

Those who fast include men of every class in society, both individuals and the whole people, and even beasts (Jon 3:7). Fasting is carried out either on one's own account or on official instructions and lasts from one to three or seven days, three weeks, fourteen days or even one's entire life (Judith 8:6). Annually repeated and prescribed fasts became more numerous after the exile (Zech 7:3, 5; 8:19) and special fasts, which were not unknown before, were more frequently proclaimed (Ezra 6:16; Neh 9:1). The pious fasted twice a week (Lk 18:12).

In the Old Testament, fasting is scarcely ever practised purely for its own sake. It forms a conspicuous part of the religious life and worship of the individual or of a group within the nation, requiring serious external application, when it is necessary to turn to God in a time of distress. The following are often closely connected with the essential abstinence from food and drink, or the voluntary limitation of these (as, for example, in Dan 10:3): lamentation, wailing, the use of sackcloth and ashes, dust, the rending of garments, abstinence from marital relationships, neglect of the care of the body such as anointing and bathing, going barefoot, neglect of normal greetings, sleeping on the ground (as in 2 Sam 12:16) and, in the case of public fasts, religious meetings and abstinence from work (Joel 1:14; 2:14–16; 1 Kings 21:9–10, 12; Jer 36:6, 9). Prayer is never out of place during a fast (eg, Neh 1:4), nor are external works of mercy (Is 58:3–7). Fasting is often called, together with these acts, the essence of piety (eg, Tob 12:8). See Fruhstorfer, *TPQ* 69 (1916), 59–72.

The external peculiarities associated with fasting are, in their natural environment, the normal expression of deep sorrow (as with fasting as a means of lamenting for the dead, [1 Sam 31:13; 2 Sam 1:11, 12]; fasting among widows in mourning, [Judith 8:5, 6]). This is why fasting is always incompatible with joy (Judith 8:6; Joel 2:18–27; Zech 7:3; 8:19). The word *tsôm* (=fasting) is often substituted or elucidated by "*innâh napšô*" (='to humiliate one's soul', that is, 'oneself': Lev 16:29, 31; 23:27, 29, 32; Num 29:7; 30:13; Is 58:3, 5; Ps 35:13: see also 1 Kings 21:27, 29; Sir 2:17). It is the external expression of a conscious desire to escape from the threatened punishment of God's might, and an inner dissociation from the sin which calls forth this power (see Sir 2:17ff). Even where no sin is involved, fasting is the expression

of the same mental attitude or a reminder of it or a means towards achieving it. The man who is conscious of his guilt and his dependence upon God does all within his power to remove the possible cause of God's severe intervention and in a plain and straightforward human way seeks to move God to pity. Fasting is a form of prayer which hopes for everything from God (Is 58:3; Jer 14:2; Mt 6:18). In the Old Testament we find little to remind us of the ascetic aspect of our 'mortification of the flesh'. Any magical conception of fasting is also quite unknown in the bible. The outward aims of fasting are many: remorse for sins (1 Sam 7:6; Sir 34:25–6), the desire to avert misfortune or punishment (1 Kings 21:27, 29; Esther 4:1–3, 16; 9:31), or to appease God's anger (Joel 2:14–17); fasting forms a part of or reinforces vows and adds support to petitions (1 Sam 14:24; 2 Sam 12:15–23; Joel 1:13ff; 2:17; Ezra 8:21; Tob 7:11; see also Acts 23:12, 14), it serves as a reminder of national catastrophes (Zech 7:3; 8:18–20; Esther 9:31), and prepares the way for special encounters with God, for example, revelations (Ex 34:28; Deut 9:9; Judg 20:26, 27; Dan 9:3; 10:2; Acts 13:2; Lk 2:37; 1:80) and other manifestations (Acts 14:22; see also Mt 4:2 and parallels; 9:29). In the case of official acts of public worship, fasting takes the form of a ceremonial penitential preparation (1 Sam 7:6; Judg 20:26). Atonement is peculiar to the ritual actions of the priest (Lev 16:32–4; Num 29:11).

Neither the prophets, the sages nor Jesus himself are opposed to fasting as such, but to fasting which is devoid of true spirit and represents pride and a demanding attitude rather than humility towards God (Zech 7:5–6; Lk 18:12, 14; Mt 6:16–17). What is important is that the essential duties of outward and inner morality, and especially those of justice and charity, are fulfilled (Is 58:3–5; Jer 14:12; Sir 34:25–6; Joel 2:12, 13). Isaiah gives to fasting which is hopeful and pleasing to God the figurative meaning of the practice of justice and active charity (Is 58:6–12). The prophets and sages maintain the ideal of true piety in opposition to the tendency towards spectacular and ostentatious practices which become more and more pronounced with the passage of time (see Mt 6:16–18; StB IV 105–7).

We find two important statements in Zech 7:1–8:23; a negative one to the effect that the fasts undertaken up to that time were worthless, because they have not been related to God (Zech 7:1–3, 4–5; cf 7–14), and at the same time a series of passages which contain promises of salvation in contemporary form (8:1–23) and give an affirmative answer (8:18–19) to the query (7:3) whether or not the periods of fast should be occasions of joy. It is not a question here of material fasting; the author is referring rather to the true sense and meaning of all striving— namely, 'truth and peace', that is, true morality. Thus the real point at issue (that is, fasting) is passed over and attention is directed to a point beyond it, as the interrogators had expected. There is no rejection of contemporary practice in the text; this has already been kept up at least partially for a long time. But this transition is intended to stimulate the people, who have become enslaved to ritual, to intensify

their inner life and to reflect about the meaning of fasting.

Jesus's answer to the question put by the pharisees and the disciples of John on the matter of fasting (see especially Mk 2:18–20, 21–2; also Mt 9:14–17; Lk 5:33–9) should be seen in a similar light. Jesus completely dismisses the unreasonable twofold suggestion which is contained in the question, that he includes himself and his disciples among those who are recognised as 'pious' and that fasting according to their particular manner is therefore necessary (Mk 2:19). He bases his answer in the parable of the bridegroom and the 'children of the marriage' on his presence as the Messiah. What emerges from the text and context of both the parables which follow, concerning the fundamental newness of the christian reality and the necessity of new categories in the philosophical sense (Mk 2:21–2), is at least the strong probability that Jesus is not referring to special periods of fast and is neither approving these nor condemning them (Mk 2:20), but is dealing with something more profound which must first be grasped by his interrogators. Their narrow and ritualistic philosophy completely misses the single, decisive fact that Jesus, who is salvation itself, is present. If they could understand that, the irrelevance of their misguided anxiety would dawn on them. Another kind of 'fasting', not self-imposed, is in store for the disciples. They will, after Jesus's death and ascension into heaven, be in a state of mourning, deprived of his visible presence (Mk 2:20; see also Mt 9:15; 2 Cor 5:6–8; Phil 1:23). 'Fasting' is thus, in Mk 2:20, depicted figuratively and symbolically in the allegory of the 'bridegroom'. In this way, Jesus directs attention to salvation. Zechariah (8:18–19) points to the joy of the consummation; Jesus on the other hand points to the distress of man's period of transition on earth. Both make use of 'fasting' to typify different situations within salvation, Zechariah by abolishing it and Jesus by giving it a new and more perfect meaning. Both transcend the normal bounds of authority in respect of the details which had come to the fore in ritual practice (see Logion 28 in the Coptic Gospel of Thomas [Leipoldt] where 'fasting' = to abstain from the world.

Nothing either in favour of or in opposition to the christian practice of fasting can be deduced from Jesus's answer to his questioners; and, in fact, this text has never been seen as providing a valid argument either then or later (Schäfer, *Synoptische Studien*, 124–47).

The ritual decrees concerning 'meat and drink', being but 'shadows of things to come', are in themselves neutral in the 'kingdom of God' (Col 2:16–17; Rom 14:17; 1 Cor 8:8). Jesus does not introduce any new external norms, but the fullness of salvation and of piety. The christian has to fashion such norms in freedom from his own upright mental attitude. In certain circles there was a very keen interest in such matters as fasting which had in earlier times frequently been systematised by the law and various customs. The keenness of this interest and the uncertainty which prevailed are demonstrated by the numerous difficulties associated with the question concerning fasting in Mk 2:18–20 as found in the apocryphal writings and

in the works of christian writers (see Arbesmann, 32–3) and at a later stage in practically all the obscure Logia in the Coptic Gospel of Thomas (Log 5; 14; 28; 101 [Leipoldt]) which are concerned in a passive sense with fasting. Some textually uncertain New Testament passages in which the mention of fasting may not be original are, by their very existence, proof of the esteem in which fasting was held in certain circles (Mk 9:29 = Mt 17:21; Acts 10:30; 1 Cor 7:5). Both Jesus's personal example and his teaching positively commend genuine fasting and persevere with what is valuable and lasting in the Jewish practice. When he dismisses prearranged regulations concerning external fasts and in so doing describes the life of christians on earth as 'fasting', he indirectly implies that bodily fasting, correctly conceived, has a place in the new order as well.

Bibliography: R. Arbesmann, 'Fasting and Prophecy in Pagan and Christian Antiquity', *Traditio* 7 (1949–51), 1–72; K. Fruhstorfer, 'Fastenvorschriften und Fastenlehren der Heiligen Schrift des Alten Bundes', *TPQ* 69 (1916), 59–72; K. T. Schaeffer, '. . . und dann werden sie fasten an jenem Tage' (Mk 2:20), *Synoptische Studien: Festschrift A. Wikenhauser*, Munich 1953, 124–47; Behm, *TDNT* IV, 924–35; D. E. Briggs, *Bible Teaching on Fasting*, Dallas 1953; A. Guillaumont, '*Nēsteuein ton kosmon* (P Oxy 1, verso, 1:5–6)', *Bulletin de l'Institut Français d'Archéologie Orientale: Le Caire* 61 (1962), 15–23.

Johann Gamberoni

Father

The Hebrew word for father (*ʾāb*, Aramaic *ʾabba*) is onomatopoeic (compare *pappa*). The concept of father in the bible is determined by the structure of patriarchal society which gives the primacy in the family (or the larger structures based on the family) to the father. He has jurisdiction over the children (Ex 21:7, 9; Gen 38:24 limited by Ex 21:7–11, 26ff; son = servant in 2 Kings 16:7), the son also is dependent on the father's will with regard to marriage (Gen 24:31; 28:1ff; 34:4; 38:6–8; Judg 14:1–2), a daughter's vow has no validity apart from the father's consent (Num 30:4–6), it is the father who decides with regard to legacies (Lk 15:11–32), he even exercises sacerdotal rights (cf Judg 17ff: the ↗ priest is called 'father'; according to Ex 12:1–14, 21–8 the paschal lamb was slaughtered in the family, therefore by the father).

The earthly father. The authority of the father (and the mother) is guaranteed in the ↗ decalogue (Ex 20:12; Deut 5:16; cf Lev 19:3). Rebellion against the father, or the act of cursing or striking him are transgressions punishable by death (Ex 21:15, 17; Deut 21:18–21). The Wisdom literature in particular is concerned to a great extent with the piety of children towards their father (and mother). We find a summary of this teaching in Sir 3:1–16 (cf Prov 1:8; 4:1; 6:20; 10:1; 13:1; 15:20; 19:26; 20:20; 23:22, 24, 25; 28:24; 29:3; 30:11, 17; Sir 7:27; 23:14; Tob 4:3–5).

Jesus confirms the fourth commandment (Mk 10:19 and parallels) and establishes its original meaning as against contemporary rabbinical casuistry (Mk 7:10–13; Mt 15:4–7). He has a tender regard for the relations between father and child (Mk 5:40; Lk 8:51; Mk 9:14–29; Mt 17:14–21; Lk 9:37–43). Moreover, the words of

Jesus which seem to go against the duties of filial piety do not in fact oppose piety with regard to one's father but rather express the urgency of the decision which a follower of Christ has to make with relation to the kingdom of God (Mt 8:21ff; Lk 9:59ff; 14:26 where 'to hate' means 'to give second place to' cf Gen 29:31, 33—Mt 10:37; 19:29). In these logia Christ demands from those who wish to share in the kingdom of God nothing more than that implied in contracting ↗ marriage, namely, separation from one's parents (Gen 2:24).

The moral rules which Paul lays down for families (Col 3:18–4:1; Eph 5:22–6:9) include also warnings for both father and son (Eph 6:4; Col 3:21; Eph 6:1–3; Col 3:20). The 'honouring' enjoined in the decalogue is defined as 'obedience', the promise contained in the fourth commandment is spiritualised and the *patria potestas* limited through religious (Eph 6:4) and psychological (Col 3:21) considerations.

In a broader sense, the *ancestors* of the people of Israel are called 'fathers' (Acts 5:30; 13:17, 32; 15:10; 28:25; Heb 1:1). The scribes and pharisees wish to avoid the offences committed by the fathers in going against the prophets sent by God, nevertheless Jesus must reproach them with having, by their attitude towards him, filled up 'the measure of the fathers' (Mt 23:30, 32; cf Lk 6:23, 26; 11:47ff; Acts 7:11–52). The term 'fathers' is used in a special way for the generation which passed through the desert and had experienced the decisive event in the history of salvation in the Old Testament, thus becoming a 'type' for the last age (Jn 6:31, 49, 58; Acts 7:19;

13:17; 1 Cor 10:1; Heb 3:9). All the outstanding men of days gone by are commemorated in Sir 44:1–50:26 under the heading 'Praise of the fathers'.

The period of late judaism refers to ↗ Abraham, Isaac and Jacob as fathers. The God who presides over sacred history is the God of these fathers (Acts 3:13; 5:30; 7:32; 22:14). It was to them that the promises and the ↗ covenant had been given. The promises made to them are fulfilled in Jesus (Lk 1:55, 72ff; Acts 3:25). The ↗ fulfilment and completion of all the promises, namely, the kingdom of God, is described as sharing a meal with these fathers (Mt 8:11; Lk 13:28). The history of salvation begins with father Abraham (Acts 7:2); the promises are directed to him, those promises by which he was to become the ancestor of many peoples (Gen 12:2; 15:5; 17:5). The Jews regard themselves with pride as free sons of Abraham (Jn 8:33, 37, 39) and think that, since they have Abraham as father, they do not stand in need of the ↗ conversion demanded by the Baptist (Mt 3:9; Lk 3:8). Their father Abraham rejoiced that he was to see the day of Christ; he saw it and was glad (Jn 8:56). The promise directed to him finds its fulfilment in Christ (Gal 3:16). Christ and with him all christians are the descendance of Abraham (Gal 3:29)—he is in fact father of all those who believe in Christ (Jn 8:56; Gal 3:7). All christians, of both Jewish and pagan origin, venerate Abraham as their father since they follow him in his faith (Rom 4).

Persons in authority are also known as fathers: priestly officials (Judg 17:10), ↗ prophets (2 Kings 2:12; 6:21), persons holding office (Gen 45:8; Is 22:21; 1 Macc 11:31ff), benefactors (Job 29:16). Rabbis also accept this name as a title of honour (SB 1, 287, 919). Jesus forbade his disciples to accept this title on the grounds that there was only one father, their father in heaven (Mt 23:9). Paul refers to himself as father of the communities which he had founded—but in a metaphorical sense, not as a title, insofar as through his preaching the ↗ gospel the faithful had been given ↗ life (1 Cor 4:15; cf Gal 4:19; Philem 10). He admonishes and consoles his children like a father (1 Thess 2:11). He says of Timothy that he had served him as a child a father in announcing the gospel (Phil 2:22).

↗ *God as Father.* Only rarely is the word *father* used in the Old Testament to describe the relationship between God and ↗ man. This reticence seems to have been imposed through the fear of being misunderstood in a mythological sense. God is not the father of men through procreation or physical descent; the name *father* is thought of and expressed in a metaphorical sense. It is used to represent the idea of election and of the covenant and expresses Israel's belonging to God and his care and ↗ love for his people. God is the father of his chosen people because he made them, gave them their very essence and existence (Deut 32:6ff), is their saviour (Is 63:16ff) and creator (Mal 2:10) and has shown them every sign of his love (Jer 3:19; 31:9; cf 31:18–20). God is father of the offspring of David; God will be his father and he will be God's son (2 Sam 7:14; cf Ps 89:27; 2:7). He is called father of the ↗ poor since he takes care of all the lowly and helpless with solicitous love (Ps 68:5f; cf 27:10; 103:13). Later on, with the advent of a more individualistic way of thinking, he is also called father of the individual religious person (Sir 23:1, 4; 51:10), though this title is used in connection with ↗ 'Lord'.

Jesus often refers in his preaching to 'your father', 'your father in heaven', and addresses God simply as 'father'. He uses the word when he announces the new saving deed of God: the dawn of the rule of God (↗ kingdom of God, Mt 13:43; 20:23; 25:34; Lk 12:32), the mission of the ↗ Spirit (Mt 10:20), the confession of Christ (Mt 16:17), hearing the unanimous ↗ prayer of the disciples (Mt 18:19), ↗ reward (Mt 6:1). The God who sets up his kingdom is also the father. Above all there is contained in the idea of father the thought of God's care for men (Mt 6:26, 32; Lk 12:30; Mt 6:8; 10: 29), his generous love that delights to give (Mt 5:45; 7:9–11; Lk 11:11–13) and forgiveness (Mt 6:12, 15; Lk 15). According to Jesus' proclamation, God is therefore father, a fact expressed in an absolute way by the use of this title for God (Mt 11:25; Lk 10:22; Mt 24:36; Mk 13:32; Lk 9:26; 11:2, 13; Mt 5:16). Jesus demands that men fulfil the will of the father (Mt 7:21; 5:45) and that they be perfect (Mt 5:48), merciful (Lk 6:36) and ready to forgive (Mt 6:14) as their father is. He desires that the father mean more to them than anything else and that they seek him in all things (Mt 5:16; 6:14, 18). This preaching about God as father is intimately bound up with the idea of the kingdom of God. Jesus gives great importance to his relation to the father—his knowledge of (that is,

association with) the father (Mt 11:27; Lk 10:22) and his invocation of him (Abba, Mt 6:9; Lk 11:2; cf Rom 8:15; Gal 4:6).

According to *Paul*, God is 'our God and Father' (Gal 1:1; Phil 4:2; 1 Thess 1:3; 3:13; 2 Thess 2:16). He speaks almost always of salvation (1 Cor 6:14) and ↗ judgement (1 Thess 3:13) in connection with God the father. God is the father from whom is everything and for whom we exist (1 Cor 8:6)—he is the father of all (Eph 4:6). As father, God is the giver of salvation—the salutation formulae at the beginning of the epistles describe peace as a gift of 'God our father' (1 Cor 1:3; 2 Cor 1:2; Gal 1:3; Eph 1:2; Phil 1:2; Col 1:2; 2 Thess 1:1; 1 Tim 1:2). It is the father who qualifies us to share in the ↗ inheritance of his saints in ↗ light (Col 1:12ff). It is reserved for those who believe to experience what the Old Testament promised, namely, that God will be to them a father and that they will be his sons and daughters (2 Cor 6:18; cf Ezek 37:27). Through the gift of the spirit of adoption (↗ sonship) believers are enabled to invoke God full of confidence with the title abba ('dear father'—Rom 8:15; Gal 4:6).

John deepens this idea of the fathership of God for men in that he speaks of 'being born of God' (or, 'from above'). This is a necessary condition in order to be able to share in the good things of salvation (Jn 3:3), in freedom from sin (1 Jn 3:9) and victory over the ↗ world (1 Jn 5:4). Being born of God is not understood literally but rather in an eschatological sense (1 Jn 3:1, 2). It is given through ↗ baptism (Jn 3:3), through ↗ faith in the ↗ revelation of

Christ (Jn 1:13; 1 Jn 5:1; cf 2:23; 2 Jn 9) and through a morally good life consisting in ↗ justice (1 Jn 2:29; 5:18), ↗ love (1 Jn 4:7) and separation from the world (1 Jn 2:16).

Jesus's revelation of God as his father. In all his prayers which have come down to us Jesus prays to God as his father (Mt 11:25, 26; Lk 10:21; Mk 14:36; Mt 26:39; Lk 22:42; Lk 23:34, 46; Jn 11:41; 12:27, 28; 17:1, 5, 11, 21, 24, 25). Mk 14:36 has also preserved the *ipsissima verba Christi* of this prayer which consists in abba ('dear father'). Judaism did not presume to use this simple, trustful and intimate form of address; even in the popular way of speaking in aramaic the solemn, liturgical Hebrew form ᵓab was used when it came to addressing God as father.

When Jesus speaks of God as his father, the word takes on a wholly particular tone. He asks that the will of his father be done (Mt 7:21), has it at heart that his father's house be honoured (Jn 2:16), knows the decisions of his father (Mt 15:13; 16:17; 18:35; 20:23; 24:36; Mk 13:32; Mt 25:34; Lk 11:13; 24:49). He must be about his father's business (Lk 2:49), he submits himself to the will of his father (Mt 26:39; Mk 14:36). The father has delivered all things to him (Mt 11:27; Lk 10:21); he has bequeathed his kingdom to him and Jesus now disposes fully of it (Lk 22:29); he acknowledges his own (Mt 10:32; 26:53) and hears the prayers which are addressed to him in the name of Jesus (Mt 18:19). The Son of Man comes in the ↗ glory of his father (Mt 16:27; Mk 8:38; Lk 9:26). Jesus' relation to the father consists in a unique and exclusive knowledge (in the

sense of association with him; Mt 11:27; Lk 10:22; cf Jn 10:15). He speaks of God as father and of himself as son. When he speaks of the father, either in prayer or conversation, he does not put himself in the same category with his disciples (Jn 20:17). His consciousness of divine sonship and of a special relationship to the father is not the result of his eschatological ↗ hope but rises rather from his eschatological proclamation; he announces not only the coming of the kingdom of God but also this relationship to his father.

Of the *synoptics* Matthew in particular represents God as father. In *John* 'father' is the common designation for God (115 times); the fatherhood of God in relation to Jesus illustrates for him the whole idea of revelation. The father is the dispenser of revelation, the son is the revealer who lives in intimate union with the dispenser. The union between father and son comes about through love (3:35; 10:17; 15:9; 17:23, 26), ↗ obedience (6:40, 49; 10:18, 37; 14:31; 18:11), knowledge (10:15), unity in work (5:17, 21; 10:25), being in one another—what we can call reciprocal immanence (10:38; 14:10, 11; 16:32; 17:21), being *one* (8:19; 10:30; 14:9; 15:23; 16:3). The father gives everything into his hands (13:3), gives him all (3:35), shows him all (5:20: cf 8:28; 12:50), places a seal upon him (6:27), gives him mankind (10:29), life (6:57), his ↗ name (17:11), and glory (17:22). Jesus is the 'only son' (1:14; 3:16, 18; 1 Jn 4:9); who is in the bosom of the father (Jn 1:18), the only-begotten of God (1:18; cf v 1). This divine sonship is not understood in a merely functional sense (that is, as the perfect revelation of God) but also metaphysically.

Paul, in his solemn formulae of blessing or confession of faith, speaks of 'the God and Father of our Lord Jesus Christ' or 'God the Father of our Lord Jesus Christ' (2 Cor 1:3; Eph 1:3; Col 1:3; Eph 1:17; Rom 15:6; Gal 1:1). The Book of *Revelation* demonstrates the greatness of Christ by referring to God as his father. Christ has made the faithful to be priests for his God and father (1:6), he has received power from his father (2:27), he will confess the name of the victor before his father and the angels (3:5) and grant him to sit on his throne just as his father had placed him upon his throne after his victory (3:21). The chosen ones bear the name of the ⁊ Lamb and the name of his father written on their foreheads (14:1).

In *the trinitarian formulae* the father is the 'first person', as can be seen in the baptismal form (Mt 28:19). Such a formula is surely behind the phrase: 'Through Jesus we both have access in one Spirit to the Father' (Eph 2:18). The father is the final goal of sacred history (1 Cor 15:24) and of the confession of Christ in which sacred history is implied (Phil 2:11). In cases like this, the name 'father' can also simply be substituted by 'God' (2 Cor 13:14—a trinitarian formula).

Bibliography: G. Quell and G. Schrenk, *TDNT* v, 945–1014; R. Gyllenberg, 'Gott der Vater im AT und in der Predigt Jesu', *Studia Orientalia* 1 (1926), 3–140; E. Lohmeyer, *Das Vaterunser*, Göttingen 1952³, ch. 2; H. Schürmann, *Das Gebet des Herrn*, 1957, 17–26; W. Marchel, *Abba, Père*, Rome 1964. For further bibliography ⁊ Sonship.

Alois Stöger

Fear

A. *The Old Testament*. The beginning of man's fear of God coincides with the first sin committed in Paradise. The consequence of this original sin is the loss of intimate and childlike communion with God (Gen 3:10: Adam is afraid because he realises that he is naked). As soon as this communion with God is restored, man may safely forget all his fear. God is always calling upon those who are dear to him to do this (Abraham in Gen 15:1; Isaac in Gen 26:24; Jacob in Gen 28:13; Hagar in Gen 21:17; Jeremiah in Jer 1:8, 17). All the manifestations of religious fear and fearlessness which occur in scripture lie between these two extremities. Any appearance of God arouses fear, and a striking example of this is the theophany on Mount Sinai (Ex 20:18). Exactly the same phenomenon occurs in the case of any miraculous act on God's part, as for example the destruction of the Egyptians in the Red Sea (Ex 14:31). So long as God is with Israel, his people have nothing to fear from their enemies (eg Num 14:9; Deut 1:29; Josh 1:9, etc). Any reference in ancient times to the fear of God almost always implies a concrete and literal fear, based on the fact of God's prodigious and sovereign might or a reverent awe of the *Mysterium Tremendum* (eg Jacob's fearful awakening with the memory of the heavenly ladder, Gen 28:17). God's intention, in inspiring this fear which is his due, is to provide a motive for moral behaviour (eg Lev 19:32; 25:17). As the man who acknowledges God must of necessity also fear him, the way was open for the term 'to fear God' to develop by abstraction from its proper and original meaning into the generally accepted and widely used sense of religious awe. In the psalter especially this extended meaning is almost always consistently adhered to (to mention a few of the many examples: Ps 22:23; 23:4; 25:12; 61:5, etc). A parallel case is to be found in the sapiential literature. On the one hand, the 'fear of God' is called the 'beginning of wisdom' (eg Prov 1:7; 9:10; Sir 1:13, 14, 16), and in this usage the original meaning is still discernible; on the other hand, however, those who fear God certainly appear to be equated with the 'pious' (eg Sir 1:13; 2:7, 8, 9, 15, 16, 17 etc). The use of the phrase 'those who fear God' in the New Testament (see Acts 13:16, 26) for pagans who are sympathetically inclined towards judaism and its culture, provides a partial view of the line of development of this conception which was already beginning to appear clearly in the Old Testament.

B. *The New Testament.* Here, too, there is frequent reference to the fear of God in the ordinary sense of the word. Christ himself requires that we fear God on account of his fearful punishments (Mt 10:28 and pars.—note the reference to hell; see also Heb 10:27, 31). Man in the New Testament also experiences fear with regard to the *Mysterium Tremendum.* Fear is experienced, for example, in the case of the angelic apparition (to Zachary in Lk 1:12f; to Mary in 1:29f; to the shepherds in 2:9); in the case of extraordinary occurrences which reveal the hand of God (the healing of the man sick of the palsy, Mt 9:8 and pars; the expulsion of the demons from the swine, Lk 8:37 and pars; the healing of

the woman with an issue of blood, Mk 5:33 and pars; possibly also Joseph's fear, Mt 1:20; the events which take place at the time of Jesus's death, Mt 27:54; the resurrection of the young man at Naim, Lk 7:16). A sensation of fear was also often present in connection with Christ, not only among those who had to reckon with his superior might when they attacked him (the Synedrium, Mt 21:26, 46 and parallels; Mk 11:18; 12:12 and parallels; a similar case is that of Herod's fear of putting John the Baptist to death, Mt 14:5 and parallels). This fear is also experienced as a religious awe (by Christ's most intimate friends) on account of the mysterious power which is active in him, as, for example, in the case of the Transfiguration in Mt 17:6 and pars, his walking on the lake in Mt 14:27, the miraculous catch of fish in Lk 5:9ff and his foretelling of his own passion in Mk 9:32 and pars, when the apostles do not dare to ask him what this means.

Again and again Christ exhorts his own to fear no more. Many terrifying experiences may be in store for the disciples, as, for example, persecution (Mt 10:26) and physical death (Mt 10:28). There is, however, still no cause for fear, as the soul is incomparably more valuable than the body and is in God's hands (Lk 12:4). They have, moreover, his promise of intercession with the Father (Mt 10:29–31 and pars) and the promised inheritance of the 'kingdom' as his 'little flock' (Lk 12:32). In the case of the miraculous walking on the waters, the disciples ought to have felt no fear as it was Christ himself who performed this miracle (Mt 14:27; Jn 6:20). Peter would not have feared and thus would not have sunk beneath the surface of the lake if he had trusted and believed in the Lord (Mt 14:30). Jairus too ought to have believed, in which case he would have been able to overcome all fear for his daughter's well-being (Mk 16:8; Mt 28:10). It is hardly surprising that the risen Christ inspires fear in the women and in the apostles (Mk 16:8; Mt 28:10), but there is also no cause for them to go on fearing, as he has truly arisen (the message of the angel, Mt 28:5; Christ himself 28:10). In John's gospel we find Christ's own reason for urging his disciples to be fearless: 'Have confidence; I have overcome the world' (Jn 16:33). Christ is simply the fulfilment of the message of the prophets: 'Fear not, daughter of Zion; behold thy king cometh sitting on an ass's colt' (Zech 9:9; Jn 12:15; see Is 40:9). He and he alone provides the reason for our complete fearlessness.

The most significant and characteristic admonition to christians concerning the necessary interrelationship between fear and fearlessness comes from *St Paul*. The redeemed christian who possesses the Spirit of God has the duty to forsake fear (Rom 8:15). All the same, he must work out his salvation in fear and trembling (Phil 2:12). This, then, is the characteristic situation of the christian—he has already attained his salvation, but this salvation must nevertheless be worked out continually during his life in this world. What is interesting here is the reason for this affirmation of St Paul, namely that it is God himself who both conceives and carries out the work of salvation. Thus, here too, there is a close connection

between God inspiring fear and taking it away.

The fearlessness which is required of the christian makes no difference to the fact that even the Apostle himself experiences both human fear and apprehensions and misgivings. He was filled with fear when he came to Corinth (1 Cor 2:3). Inner fear, as well as external conflicts, is the constant companion of all apostolic activity (2 Cor 7:5). St Paul too fears the one before whom we must all appear (2 Cor 5:11).

In his teaching, the apostle frequently enjoins fear for human masters and human authority. This injunction holds good for the state as the servant of God (Rom 13:3f) in respect of those who have cause to fear punishment on account of their evildoings, for the masters of servants or slaves, whether these are well disposed or not (1 Pet 2:18; Eph 6:5; slaves are here enjoined to be subject to their masters 'as to Christ') and finally for husbands (Eph 5:33: the husband-wife relationship refers here also to the relationship between Christ and his church). But in all these instances, legitimate fear can be aroused and respect claimed only because those in question have received their authority for the time being from God.

St Paul's own personal example in this respect applies also to the various communities within the church of God which have been entrusted to his care. The christian who has been moved by God's elective grace to forsake heathenism must guard against presumption with regard to the fate of Israel whose people were called upon to believe in the first place; he must have salutary fear (Rom 11:20). The sanctification of the christian will be perfected in the fear of God (2 Cor 7:1). Timothy is to admonish sinners publicly so that the others may feel fear as a motive for prudence and improvement (1 Tim 5:20). Christians are to be subject one to another in the fear of Christ (Eph 5:21).

In his first Letter, Peter lays great stress on fear as the necessary basis for a proper mental attitude on the part of the christian. Christians are exhorted time and again to fear God (1 Pet 2:17) and to conduct themselves in fear so long as they are here on earth (1 Pet 1:17). The chaste and holy conduct of wives is to be grounded on fear (1 Pet 3:2) and the servants of the house are to be subject to their masters in fear (1 Pet 2:18). As a general rule, christians are urged to conduct themselves with modesty and fear (1 Pet 3:16), but, on the other hand, St Peter's first Epistle also recognises the other side of the christian message concerning fear. The christian is not to fear those who act evilly towards him (the state may be implied in this instance: 1 Pet 3:14 = Is 8:12). Similarly, wives who, like Sarah, are upright in their actions (Sarah obeyed Abraham: 1 Pet 3:6), have no cause for fear.

In John's gospel we find many passages in which Christ especially encourages his disciples to be fearless. Though this exhortation is prominent also in all the teaching of Christ in the rest of the johannine writings, we find it said here too that God is to be praised by those who fear him (Rev 19:5 = Ps 115:13). The other angel calls upon the people to fear God and give him the honour that is due to him (Rev 14:7). God will reward those who fear him (Rev 11:18). The way in which this fear which is demanded of men is to be understood is demonstrated in the Book of Revelation itself by the comforting assurance which the Son of Man gives to John: 'Fear not, I am the first and the last, and the living one; I died, and behold I am alive for evermore' (1:17-18). This statement leads directly to the great, and genuinely johannine statement concerning the reason why we should not fear: 'There is no fear in love, but perfect love casts out fear. For fear has to do with punishment, and he who fears is not perfected in love' (1 Jn 4:18). Thus it can be seen that St John has also reached the point where he accepts, as St Paul did before him in his conception of the spirit of adoption, that God has saved us from fear because he wished to make us brothers of his dearly beloved Son.

The biblical pronouncement on the subject of fear can be briefly summarised thus: the man who is completely united with God knows no fear. Separation from God leads to the development of fear as an important element in man's life, and he is then bound to fear his fellows, the principalities and powers of this world and even God himself, who wishes, as far as we are concerned, to be nothing but love. Christ appeared in order to liberate us from the bonds of fear through his presence. And even if fear is still the lot of man who has already been redeemed, so long as he has not reached the point of sharing in a complete and undivided way in God's love, nevertheless he can at the same time already put aside every vestige of servile fear.

Bibliography: W. Lütgert, 'Die Furcht Gottes', *Festschrift für M. Kähler*, 1905, 165ff; S. F. H. J. Berkelbach van der Sprenkel, *Vrees en Religie*, 1920; R. Sander, *Furcht und Liebe im paläs-tinensischen Judentum*, 1935; Köhler 36ff; E. Boularand, *Dict. de la Spiritualité* II, Paris 1953, 2464–775; D. Lys and E. Diserens, Allmen 51–5; R. Borchert, *Ev. Kirchenlex.* I (1956), 1408f; G. van der Leeuw (C. M. Edsman), *RGG* II³, 1180ff (on the comparative religion aspect, with relevant bibliography); Bultmann I, 320ff and II, 213f; Haag 607f; L. Nieder, *LTK* IV², 1107f; K. Romaniuk, 'La crainte de Dieu à Qumran et dans le NT', *RQ* 4 (1963), 3–10; Eichrodt III, 1964, 184–90; P. Auvray and P. Grelot, *DBT* 149–51.

Wolfgang Beilner

Fire

A. *The Old Testament*. The word *fire*—in Hebrew *ʾēš* and in Greek *pur*—often occurs in the bible in its normal meaning and is particularly used in connection with ↗ sacrifice (Lev 1:7ff; 6:9, 15; 10:1 with the appropriate instructions).

Fire, with its consuming power, is used as a symbol or image of calumny (Prov 26:20ff), anger (Sir 28:10ff), bloody deeds and murder (Sir 11:32; 22:24), physical passion and lust (Sir 9:8; 23:16; see also 1 Cor 7:9), adultery (Job 31:12; Prov 6:27f) and sin (Sir 3:30; 8:10). Very often we find the image of fire used with reference to the ↗ law and to the anger or ↗ wrath of God (Jer 4:4; 5:14; Ezek 21:31; Ps 79:5; and elsewhere in the Psalms). Fire also accompanies God's appearances to man (theophanies)—good examples of this are Ex 19; 3:2 and Judg 6:21—and is occa-sionally a sign of a favourable ↗ visitation, as, for example, when God wishes to show his satisfaction with a sacrifice (Gen 15:17; Lev 9:23f; Judg 6:21, etc), to lead the people in a pillar of fire (Ex 13:21f; 14:24; Num 14:14) or to protect his people by encircling them with a wall of fire (Zech 2:5). Whenever God himself is called a 'consuming fire', it is not really that he wishes to be represented in the form of personified fire, but rather that he seeks to give expression to his just and merciful majesty.

B. In *later judaism* and in the *Qumran texts* we find fire used especially in the eschatological sense, that is, in connection with God's justice (1 QpHab 10:5; 10:13). In 1 QS 2:8 we find reference to the everlasting fire of ↗ hell, and in 1 QH 3:29–33 to the idea of the universal conflagration (as in the Jewish Sibylline Oracles, 2:186ff; 3:83ff; 4:172ff; 5:158ff, etc).

C. *The New Testament*. As in the Old Testament, fire is often used here to symbolise God's judgement, together with representations taken from the everyday language of a rural society, such as trees which no longer yield fruit (Mt 3:10), chaff (Mt 3:12), cockle and other weeds (Mt 13:40)—these are all to be burnt. In the Apocalypse in particular, fire appears as an omen of the judgement of God (8:7, 8; 11:5; 13:13; 14:18). In the main, however, fire is used in the New Testament in the eschatological sense, as the fire of God's judgement. The baptism by fire is foretold in the sermon of John the Baptist (Mt 3:11; Lk 3:16). The most probable inter-pretation of the passage in Mk 9:49, 'everyone shall be salted with fire', is that everyone who wishes to enter the Kingdom of God has to pass through the judgement of God. Lang (*TDNT* VI, 944, *n* 82) compares this with 2 Cor 5:17 and Jn 3:3, 4, 7 (which are in a different theological setting). Jn 3:18 has also to be taken into consideration in this connection. Lang gives this striking explanation: for everyone, 'the way to fellowship with God is by judgement of the old man' (*TDNT* VI, 944). In Lk 12:49ff, we find the following comment on the promise of John the Baptist which was brought to fulfilment through Jesus: Jesus himself must also go through the fire, that is to say, through his ↗ passion; he himself has cast fire on the earth (v 49) and with his coming the eschatological judgement has dawned. A remarkable and johannine passage occurs in the Coptic Gospel of Thomas: 'I have cast fire on the *cosmos* and will *maintain* it until the (= the fire?) burns' (Logion 10). In this context we must also include the agraphon (a saying of Jesus that has not been handed down through the medium of the Bible): 'Whoever is close to me is close to the fire; whoever is far from me is far from the kingdom' (in another version, 'far from life'). This passage occurs in the Gospel of Thomas, Logion 82, and should be compared with Origen, Hom lat in Jer 3:3, etc. What is very clearly expressed here is that closeness to Jesus implies closeness to the judgement, and at the same time closeness to the ↗ kingdom of God and to ↗ life, and that life and access to the Kingdom are to be gained through this judgement (see J. B. Bauer, *TZ* 15 [1959], 446–50).

Paul speaks in three places about fire and in each case refers to the eschatological fire of the judgement. In 1 Cor 3:13–15, we read that the fire will try every man's work. The man who works with little success to achieve the kingdom of God will be able to survive only by the skin of his teeth when the Lord comes—this is what is meant by the passage 'he himself will be saved, but only as through fire' (v 15). Paul depicts, in 2 Thess 1:7f, the ↗ parousia of the Lord as the revelation of his miraculous power to all those who believe in him (v 10) and as the ↗ judgement and ↗ retribution he will exact from those who do not acknowledge God. Jesus will reveal himself here 'in flames of fire'. The quotation from Prov 25:21f, which Paul uses in Rom 12:20, is not easy to understand in itself (see O. Michel, *Der Brief an die Römer*, Göttingen 1955, 278f), but it would appear to be associated by Paul himself with God's judgement (see verse 19). The coals heaped upon the head of one's enemy symbolise his humiliation, which will either lead him to conversion or condemn him in the end to perish in God's judgement by fire.

The eschatological fire of God's judgement is also alluded to in Heb 10:27; 12:29, as well as in Rev 20:9 and in 2 Pet 3:7, where it is connected with the wider teaching on the universal conflagration. The fire of ↗ hell (see that article for examples) is mentioned both in the Book of Revelation and in the rest of the New Testament.

Finally, fire and brightness occur frequently as symbols of heavenly glory. The Book of Revelation gives many examples of this usage: the description of Christ triumphant (Rev 1:14f; see also 2:18; 19:12), the description of the angel (10:1), that of the seven spirits who appear before the throne in the form of torches or lamps of fire (4:5), and the description of the 'sea of glass mingled with fire' (15:2). Fire marks out the angels and spirits as important elements of the heavenly world of light. In this connection, rather than in the Stoical sense in which spirit and fire are equated, the fire which appears in the account (given in Acts 2:3) of the descent of the Holy Spirit at Pentecost can be regarded as a sign of the miraculous and heavenly origin of the Holy Spirit—a visible sign of God's invisible revelation.

Bibliography: F. Lang, *Das Feuer im Sprachgebrauch der Bibel, dargestellt auf dem Hintergrund der Feuervorstellungen in der Umwelt*, Tübingen 1950; F. Lang, *TDNT* VI, 928–52 (full bibliography); F. Lang, *Ev. Kirchenlex.* I, 1282f; H. Eising, *LTK* IV², 107f; J. Gaillard, *Catholicisme* IV, 1227–9: on the subject of purgatory, not implied in 1 Cor 3:12–15, see J. Gnilka, *LTK* IV², 50f (bibliography included); S. Cipriani, *Rivista Biblica* 7 (1959), 25–43; G. Rinaldi, 'La preparazione dell'argento e il fuoco purificatore', *Bibbia e Oriente* 5 (1963), 53–9; J. Michl, 'Gerichtsfeuer und Purgatorium, zu 1 Cor 3:12–15', *Stud. Paul.* (Rome 1963), 395–401; P. D. Miller Jr, 'Fire in the Mythology of Canaan and Israel', *CBQ* 17 (1965), 256–61.

Johannes B. Bauer

Firstfruits (firstborn)

Religious ethnology is familiar with the institution of the offering of firstfruits in very many ancient and primitive religions. By means of this practice the deity was acknowledged and thanked as the lord and preserver of life. It could also constitute a recognition of the deity's right to the object in question in that it could be made use of only after payment of an appropriate levy. So, for example, hunting tribes offered the first animal taken at the beginning of the hunting season and shepherds and farmers offered the first produce of the herd or the fields. The Old Testament is no exception to this practice; we find there the terms *beĸôr* (the firstborn of men and cattle: Gen 25:13; Ex 11:5; 12:29) and *bikkûrîm* (the first produce of the grain and the fruit trees: Ex 23:16; Lev 23:20; Num 18:13) and to these Yahweh laid special claim. During the first three years the produce of the fruit trees was considered 'uncircumcised' (↗ circumcision), namely, not to be put to common use; it was consecrated to Yahweh in the fourth year and was thus not to be enjoyed until the fifth year (Lev 19:23–5). Similarly one could not eat of the corn harvest until the first sheaf had been offered to Yahweh (Lev 23:14). This offering was associated in the first place with the three great agrarian festivals (see Lev 23:9f; 15ff). In Deut 16:1ff we find preserved the prayer to be recited at the offering of the firstfruit of the land which reveals the deep significance of this act performed at the sanctuary; it was first and foremost the fulfilment of Israel's duty of gratitude to her divine lord for his gracious gift of the land of Canaan.

The firstborn of men had to be offered to Yahweh. The firstborn of unclean domestic animals (the ass) had to be substituted for by the offering of a clean animal (the lamb, Ex 13:2, 12f; 34:19f; Num 3:12f), since they belonged to Yahweh. If they had not already been sacrificed on the eighth day after birth at a local sanctuary

(Ex 22:29) the firstborn of animals were used in the sacrificial meal. This idea seems to be associated with the Passover and the offering of the Passover animal which occurred at the beginning of the year (see Ex 13; 34:19ff; Num 3:13). The fact that the laws concerning firstfruits speak of animals and men together may constitute something of a difficulty, and some have tried to explain it by applying an hypothesis taken from the history of religions to the Old Testament according to which an original practice of human sacrifice was later replaced by the sacrifice of animals. Human sacrifices certainly took place in the ancient Near East—for example, the Phoenician practice of sacrificing children at the dedication of a building —but these were extremely rare. The sacrifice of Isaac (Gen 22:1–19) has always been understood as an exceptional testing of faith rewarded by the renewal of the divine promise to the descendents of Abraham. Its relevance for Israel was that it showed her that she owed her existence to the divine mercy and to the obedience of her ancestors. The sacrifice of Jephthah (Judg 11:30–40) must be thought of as an exceptional case analogous to the sacrifice carried out later by the king of Moab (2 Kings 3:27). The sacrifice carried out at the consecration of a building under king Ahab (1 Kings 16:34) was due doubtless to Phoenician influence. The Israelites never sacrificed children to Yahweh, though some sacrifices to Moloch took place in the eighth and seventh centuries BC. Old Testament religion rejected human sacrifice right from the beginning, it was expressly forbidden in the Law

(Deut 12:31; 18:10; Lev 18:21; 20:2–5), and the prophets denounced it as an idolatrous practice (Hos 13:2). The redemption of the firstborn of men found in the oldest sources of the Pentateuch together with the injunction to sacrifice the firstborn of animals (Ex 22:28f; 34:19f) does not by any means imply a mitigation of the cruel practice of child-sacrifice current at an earlier period. All it implies is that the firstborn of both men and animals belong to Yahweh and that the former had to be redeemed and the latter sacrificed. Ezekiel, who condemned child-sacrifice, certainly never thought that this practice was ever positively inculcated by Yahweh (Ezek 16:20; 20:31). He does indeed say on one occasion (20:25f) that Yahweh gave his people, as punishment for their idolatry, ordinances which must have been objectionable to them in so far as they would be rendered unclean by the sacrifice of children. But this only implies that on account of the sin of the people, what had been originally meant as a blessing turned into a curse for them. The stipulation about the consecration of the firstborn could be interpreted by a people whose mind was far from God as if child-sacrifice was required by Yahweh. Moreover Jer 7:31 denies clearly and explicitly that Yahweh had ever commanded the sacrifice of children.

The levites were consecrated to Yahweh in a special manner as a substitute for the firstborn of the people (Num 3:12f; 8:16–18). They certainly received part of their living from the sacrificial offering of firstfruits brought to the sanctuary (Ex 23:19 E; Ex 34:26 J; Deut 12:6f, 11f, 17–19). The first produce of the fields, the trees and the herds was considered as of special value. The firstborn son enjoyed special privileges over the other children during the lifetime of the father (Gen 43:33), received a double portion of inheritance after his death (Deut 21:17) and became head of the family. These privileges could, however, be lost as the result of punishment (Gen 35:22) or waived in favour of another (Gen 25:29–34). ↗ Sacrifice.

Bibliography: A. George, 'Le Sacrifice d'Abraham', *Mélanges Vaganay*, Lyon 1948, 99–110; W. Kornfeld, 'Der Moloch', *WZKM* 51 (1952), 287–313; J. Henninger, 'Menschenopfer bei den Araben', *Anthropos* 53 (1958), 721f and 776f; de Vaux, 490–91.

Walter Kornfeld

Flesh

Flesh may mean simply meat (Rom 14:21; 1 Cor 8:13), but in most places in the bible it is used, together with various other words, in a different sense, to convey a theological meaning.

1. *Flesh and man.* Flesh is the animate substance, the carnal matter which is fashioned into human or animal form. It is man's external substance (Gen 2:21; Ex 4:7; 1 Sam 17:44; 2 Kings 5:10, 14; 9:36; Ezek 37:6; Job 2:5; Lk 24:39—the risen Christ is not a 'spirit' because he has flesh and blood: 1 Cor 15:39). Flesh is also the body, in which usage the idea of an organic unity is disregarded, as this is contained in the term 'body'. Here the idea of vitality is brought more closely into focus. Flesh is used for body in Ex 30:32; Num 8:7; 1 Kings 21:27, and the 'thorn' in the flesh (2 Cor 12:7) and the 'bodily ailment' (Gal 4:13f)

are physical frailty, not sexual temptation. 'Tribulation of the flesh' is an abject distress (1 Cor 7:28; see also Col 1:24; 2 Cor 7:5; 1 Pet 4:2). When Paul refers to others seeing his 'face in the flesh' (Col 2:1), he is referring to his physical countenance. The 'destruction of the flesh' (1 Cor 5:5) is of course death. By his flesh, that is to say, by his passion and death, Christ has made peace (Eph 2:14; Col 1:22). Circumcision is performed in the flesh (ie body) (Rom 2:28; Gal 6:12f; Eph 2:11; Col 2:13). Presence in the flesh is physical presence (Col 2:5). The bread of the Eucharist is called flesh (John 6:51–6; it is called 'body' in the synoptic gospels) and it is the living body, the whole of Jesus's being in his physical existence. The phrase 'my flesh' replaces the personal pronoun 'I' in Ps 16:9; 63:1; Acts 2:26; 2 Cor 7:5; Rom 7:18. 'All flesh' is creation as a whole (Gen 6:17; Ps 65:2; 136:25; Sir 40:8), mankind (Is 40:5 = Lk 3:6; Joel 2:28 = Acts 2:17; Jn 17:2). Flesh is the human person, the living man, and the logos, or preexistent Christ, has become flesh (Jn 1:14; 1 Jn 4:2; 2 Jn 7; 1 Tim 3:16). The boundary which exists between the man as body and the personal 'I' is not always clearly determined, but often remains fluid. Flesh is the living creature, the human person, similar to the 'soul' (cf 1 Cor 2:14 with 3:3; 1 Cor 15:44–6; 'natural' is the same as 'carnal'). According to the Hebrew mode of thought, the elements which comprise the human being are not viewed as static, but as dynamic, not as anatomical units, but as a complete entity and as a living unity. This conception of man remained unchanged until the influence of Greek philosophy began to be felt (Wis 8:19f; 9:15; in 1 Pet 3:21 flesh is contrasted with the conscience and possibly with the soul already touched by grace).

Flesh also expresses the community of man and his relationship with his fellow-men. Eve, because she is taken from Adam and is part of the same essential being, is 'flesh of his flesh' (Gen 2:23). They are joined to each other in marriage and are thus 'one flesh' (Gen 2:24; quoted in Mt 19:5; Mk 10:7f; 1 Cor 6:16; Eph 5:31; see also 5:29). Blood-relations are (one bone) and one flesh (Gen 29:14; 37:27; Judg 9:2). Fellow citizens are also one flesh (2 Sam 5:1; 19:12; Is 58:7). 'Eating the flesh of my people' (Mic 3:2f) means to destroy the entire people. Physical genealogy is characterised by 'flesh' (Rom 4:1; 9:3, 5; 11:14; 1 Cor 10:18). This is also the probable reason why the genital organs are called 'flesh' (Lev 15:2; Ezek 16:26; 23:20).

The expression 'all flesh' is also used with a collective meaning, in the sense of the unity of mankind. This meaning is to be found in the second part of the book of Isaiah, in which the mode of thought is universal in application (Is 40:5; 49:26; 66:23), as well as in Jer 25:31; Joel 2:28. The promises of salvation are to be extended to the whole of mankind. These ideas are taken up in the New Testament with reference to the Old (Lk 3:6, with reference to Is 40:5; Acts 2:17, with reference to Joel 2:28; Jn 17:2, in which Jesus, in the prayer of the high priest, praises the Father for giving him power over 'all flesh'). The whole of mankind stands in need of salvation,

since 'all flesh' is infirm (1 Pet 1:24 = Is 40:6), prone to sinfulness (Rom 3:20; Gal 2:16 = Ps 143:2), unable to glory in itself (1 Cor 1:29) and is subject to pain and tribulation at the end of time (Mt 24:22; Mk 13:20). In certain places, flesh represents the whole of creation, both men and animals (Gen 6:12f; 7:21; 9:11; possibly also Jer 32:27). Man is closely associated with the whole of creation (Rom 8:20f).

2. *Flesh as man's frailty and infirmity.* Flesh is man specifically in his humanity. The bible views man throughout in his relationship with God, and flesh portrays man's situation with regard to God. In the light of God's truth man can discover what he really is—a being that is shortlived (Gen 6:3; Is 40:6), weak (Ps 55:5; Is 31:3), and doomed to death (Ps 78:39; cf Ps 90:5ff: Sir 14:17f). No trust can be placed in the flesh (Jer 17:5). 'Flesh and blood' cannot penetrate the mysteries of the revelation without God's help (Mt 16:17), nor can it resist temptation (Mt 26:41; Mk 14:38). This idea of weakness is generally discernible in the phrase 'flesh and blood'. As examples of this we find that flesh and blood cannot inherit the Kingdom of God (Sir 14:18; cf 17; 17:31; 1 Cor 15:50), that our conflict is not against flesh and blood, but . . . against the evil spirits in high places (Eph 6:12; see Gal 1:16). A further reference to flesh and blood is to be found in Heb 2:14. Flesh and blood are not separate parts of man. The bible views man as an indivisible whole.

Flesh represents the sphere of the earthly and natural, of the purely human in contrast to that of the supramundane, the supernatural and the divine. This contrast is not always explicit but it is always suggested. Above all, no ethical judgement is implied in it. A contrast is made between circumcision of the flesh and that of the heart (Rom 2:28f), earthly (or carnal) things and supernatural (or spiritual) things (1 Cor 9:11), the purely natural mode of thinking and faith (2 Cor 5:16), the wisdom of this world (represented by those who are wise according to the flesh) and that which has been revealed and given to us by the Spirit (1 Cor 2:1–16). To live in the flesh (Gal 2:20; Phil 1:22, 24) or to walk according to the flesh (Rom 8:9) means to live one's life, as a human being, on the purely material and earthly plane, as opposed to living it in the spirit (Rom 8:9), with Christ (Phil 1:23) and in faith (Gal 2:20). Onesimus is to be treated as a brother both in the flesh and in the Lord (Philem 16), as a human being and as a christian. 'According to the flesh' expresses a natural relationship (eg genealogy), in implicit or explicit contrast to a relationship which has been brought about supernaturally by God. Jesus is descended according to the flesh from David (Rom 1:3; cf 9:5), Abraham is the father of the Jews according to the flesh (Rom 4:1), St Paul himself is a brother of the Jews according to the flesh (Rom 9:3). Israel according to the flesh (1 Cor 10:18) is contrasted with the Israel of God (Gal 6:16), Ishmael was Abraham's son according to the flesh (that is, as a result of natural, human procreation), whereas Isaac was his son according to the spirit (that is, he was

begotten in a miraculous manner). Similar examples of this usage are to be found in the rest of the New Testament. Flesh and spirit are contrasted in Jn 3:6—a man cannot enter the Kingdom of God purely as a result of his having been born in this world; he must be born again supernaturally (of the spirit, according to Jn 3:7f; according to 1 Pet 1:23, of the word of God). In 1 Pet 3:18 the human body is contrasted with the spirit (as divine essence).

3. *Flesh in contradiction to God.* Whenever man presumes exclusively on the flesh, his purely human status, this attitude would appear to disqualify him (Is 31:3; Jer 17:5). He cannot attain salvation when he places his hopes solely in the flesh, that is, in his descent from the people of Israel (Phil 3:3f), in exclusively human privileges or qualities (2 Cor 11:18), in personal asceticism (Col 2:18, 23) or in his fulfilment of the mosaic law (Gal 3:3). 'Flesh and blood', that is, man alone acting without grace, cannot inherit the kingdom of God (1 Cor 15:50). Flesh is thus man in isolation, seeking his salvation merely by the exercise of his own powers. The Jew does this by fulfilling the law, the Greek by means of his philosophy. Man is always eager to work out his own salvation without God, by his own efforts alone, and this is basically the original sin of man, that he wishes to achieve perfection—to be as God—without God (Gal 3:5). Man's illusion is that he, who is flesh, can be God despite his condition.

Flesh is man in hostility to God and represents that part of man which is not just physically but also morally weak and infirm. St Paul in particular states this with great insistence, particularly in Rom 7–8 and Gal 5. Before Christ, unredeemed man is carnal and sold under sin (Rom 7:14): 'The mind that is set on the flesh is hostile to God' (Rom 8:7), and 'those who are in the flesh cannot please God' (8:8). It is sinful conduct to walk according to the flesh (Rom 8:4; 2 Cor 10:2), to live according to the flesh (Rom 8:12), or to exist according to the flesh (Rom 8:5). Christians are to live no longer according to the flesh (Rom 8:9) but according to the spirit (Rom 8:4f), according to God (2 Cor 11:17) and according to love. Flesh and spirit are completely opposed to each other, as sin and obedience to God, as selfishness and love, or as death and eternal life (Gal 5:17). 'Sarx' is a power or principle to which man is subject and against which he is scarcely able to defend himself successfully (Rom 8:7).

The works of the flesh are the so-called sins of the senses, such as lewdness, impurity, debauchery, drunkenness and gluttony. Among these sins, however, are those which more or less belong to the sphere of spirituality, such as idolatry and sorcery, animosity, enmities and contention, jealousy, quarrels and dissension, selfishness, envy and arrogant pride (Gal 5:19ff; Col 2:18). Only 2 Pet 2:10 calls unchastity the 'licentious passions of the flesh' (see 2:18). In Jude 7f, 'going after other flesh' is called leading an unchaste life. The 'works of the flesh' are evoked by the desires which urge man towards what is morally bad (Rom 7:14; 7:5—here the 'sinful passions' are those passions which lead to the committing of sin: Gal 5:16, 24; Eph 2:3; 2 Pet 2:18; 1 Jn 2:16). These desires are the wisdom of the flesh (Gal 5:24) and are situated in the flesh (Rom 7:5—'nothing good dwells in me, that is, in my flesh').

4. *Flesh and redemption.* According to the theology of St Paul sin (regarded as a personified force) makes use of the Mosaic law to stimulate the desires which are situated in the flesh, law to goad men on to commit sin and to establish all the more firmly the mastery of sin (Rom 7:7–13). The law cannot be fulfilled on account of the 'weakness of the flesh' (Rom 8:3). Unredeemed man serves the law of sin with the flesh (Rom 7:25). He who lives according to the flesh must die. 'While we were living in the flesh (ie unredeemed), our sinful passions, aroused by the law, were at work in our members to bear fruit for death' (Rom 7:5; cf 8:3). Flesh, the ↗ Law (see also ↗ Justification), ↗ sin, and ↗ death are very closely associated. What lies behind Rom 7 is man's proneness to sin. Paul does not really mean here that man's *nous* (=mind) is a power which can, after the manner of the Greek philosophers, master his *sarx* (=flesh), but rather that pre-christian man could only act, despite the best of intentions, in a manner which contradicted God.

Yet God uses this very flesh, which has the ability to lead man to sin and destruction, as his means to save man, by sending his own Son 'in the likeness of sinful flesh' (Rom 8:3). The Son of God accepted and took on the infirm nature of man, which, in our case, is under the sway of sin. Paul refers especially to the 'likeness of sinful flesh' because he is anxious to forestall any possible idea that Christ also might have been subject to sin or have actually sinned, since Jesus 'knew no sin' (2 Cor 5:21). In the death of the flesh God condemned the tyrant Sin and deprived him of his power (Rom 8:3). By means of baptism, christians have crucified the flesh with its passions and desires (Gal 5:24; no asceticism is implied here in the use of the word 'crucify'). Similarly they have put off the old man together with his works (Col 3:9). God has given christians, who were dead by reasons of their sins and their uncircumcised and unredeemed flesh, life together with Christ, by the forgiveness of sins (Col 2:13). Flesh is, as we have already seen, not a part of man which can be put off or 'mortified'. It is man himself. The christian, then, does not live according to the flesh but according to the spirit (Rom 8:4, 9). The sacramental act of baptism calls for a corresponding moral response. Even when the baptised christian has put aside his sinful flesh, the weakness of the flesh remains and continues to exert its influence (Rom 6:12ff; cf 8:9). The flesh is still in revolt against the spirit (Gal 5:17), and this is why the admonition against living according to the flesh is still necessary (Rom 8:5, 12f; 13:14; Col 3:5). It is not until the resurrection that the flesh will be finally and completely overcome (see Rom 8:10f). Paul does not call the transfigured body 'flesh', but 'a spiritual body' (1 Cor 15:44). Flesh and blood cannot possess the Kingdom of God, just as corruption cannot possess incorruption (1 Cor 15:50).

5. *Interpretation of the pauline doctrine of the flesh.* The synoptics tend to use the language of the Old Testament (see Mt 26:41; Mk 14:38). This applies also to James and to the Rabbinical writers and Qumran. In the case of St Paul, St John and St Jude, as well as in 1 and 2 Pet, this Old Testament linguistic usage is overlaid by the new way of thinking, although there are few relevant texts apart from St Paul. The characteristically pauline use of the word 'flesh' to designate a power which can completely control man cannot be traced back to the Old Testament. St Paul views flesh as a personal force, similar to sin—it has its own way of thinking, its own aims (Rom 8:5ff; 13:4; Col 2:18), it is constantly in revolt against the spirit (Gal 5:17, 24), performs works (Gal 5:19) and even appears as a believer (Rom 8:12). This view of the flesh is not based on mythological ideas, but is firmly established in his own thought patterns. St Paul does not think of flesh in the dualistic sense of the Greek philosophers or the gnostics, as something which is directly opposed to the soul—though it is of course possible that he may have been influenced by their terminology. We find, for example, that even the man who is justified and sanctified (1 Cor 6:11) lives in the flesh. He lives in the flesh, but does not fight according to the flesh (2 Cor 10:3; Gal 2:19f). Even Christ himself, who is without sin, lives in the flesh (2 Cor 5:16; Rom 8:3). The association of flesh and sin is neither necessary nor essential. It is not possible to detect any latent traces of the strictly dualistic conception of the antithesis between flesh/body and spirit/soul in the pauline antithesis between sarx and pneuma. St Paul is not hostile to the body and the antithesis between the 'flesh' and the spirit is not physical but ethical. Man is

flesh insofar as he is in a state of disorder as a result of original sin (see Rom 5:1–12) and insofar as he is in the bondage of sin. This condition, in which he is afflicted by original sin, expresses itself in selfish activity. Outwardly man, with his desires and the physical organs which serve them, is given over to the service of these false activities. The disorder in his life can only be overcome by the Spirit of God, by charity and by a new life in Christ. The germs of the church's teaching on original sin and concupiscence can be found in the doctrine of the flesh.

Bibliography: W. Schauf, *Sarx* (*NA* xi), 1–2 (Münster 1924); E. Käsemann, *Leib und Leib Christi*, Tübingen 1933, 100–18; Prat ii 1941[28], 59–65 and 487–9; W. Gutbrod, *Die paulinische Anthropologie*, Stuttgart-Berlin 1934; N. Krautwik, 'Der Leib im Kampf des "pneuma" wider die "sarx"', *TG* 39 (1949), 296–311; Bultmann i, 227–46; *BTHW* 139–42; Nötscher, 85f; O. Kuss, *Der Römerbrief*, 1959, 506–40; E. Schweizer, 'Die hellenistische Komponente im neutestamentlichen *Sarx*-Begriff', *ZNW* 48 (1957), 237–53; E. Schweizer, '*Sarx*', *TWNT* vii, 98–151.

Alois Stöger

Foolishness

The concept of foolishness is opposed to wisdom; which means that what is said about foolishness in the scriptures will be the contrary of the descriptions found there of ↗ wisdom (or prudence).

A. The *Old Testament* has a number of words which stand for fool, foolishness, foolish. What constitutes a foolish person as such is the refusal and even the inability to accept instruction or to learn from experience and to regulate his behaviour in accordance with the laws in force in the community.

The fool despises wisdom and discipline (Prov 1:7); he derides warnings (Prov 15:5) and hates reproof (Prov 12:1). He does not listen to good advice (Prov 12:15) and despises instruction (Prov 23:9). It is practically impossible to instruct a foolish person: 'A rebuke goes deeper into a man of understanding than a hundred blows into a fool' (Prov 17:10, cf Sir 21:14). Nor does experience make a fool any the wiser: 'Like a dog that returns to his vomit is a fool that repeats his folly' (Prov 26:11).

Instruction in Israel included religious and moral teaching as well as general rules of prudence. The kind of foolishness that despises instruction is therefore a religious or moral fault though it can also be merely a violation of ordinary worldly wisdom. Israel also is called foolish when she does not live according to the commandments of the Lord her Father and Creator (Deut 32:6) and turns to strange gods (Jer 5:21ff). This also applies to the Samaritans who were considered as fools for having separated themselves from Israel (Sir 50:26). Anyone who has no care for God, who gives the lie to God in his practical, everyday life, is also a fool (Ps 14:1). Sin, therefore, is always foolishness (see Prov 15:21), and sins such as reviling God (Ps 74:18, 22), hardness of heart (1 Sam 25:25), the violation of a virgin (2 Sam 13:12) and adultery (Deut 22:21) are expressly referred to as foolishness.

In his dealings with his fellow-men the fool lacks in prudence. He speaks without deliberation (Prov 10:14; 12:23; 13:16; 14:3) and at the wrong time (Prov 20:19); he gives an answer before he has time to hear the question

(Prov 18:13), and even any infraction against good manners is considered as foolishness (Sir 21:22–4).

Scripture warns against the company of fools since there can come of it only provocation (Prov 27:3; Sir 22:13) and harm (Prov 13:20). There is no real prospect that a fool will correct his ways (Prov 27:22) since his folly sooner or later gets the better of him (Job 5:3–7; Prov 1:32; 5:23). God himself punishes the foolish who, through their immoral conduct, provoke his power to punish (Wis 5:4–14). They will acknowledge their foolishness at the final judgement (Wis 5:4–14).

B. In the *New Testament* there are only a few cases where foolishness refers to ordinary lack of intelligence. Thus, in comparison with the Greeks, the culturally backward barbarians are fools (Rom 1:14). Christians have to avoid giving foolish men (among the heathens) any occasion for slanderous talk (1 Pet 2:15). In his parables, Jesus speaks of the foolish man who built his house upon sand (Mt 7:26ff) and of the foolish virgins who did not prepare themselves for the coming of the bridegroom (Mt 25:1–13). Both parables demand that the believer base his conduct upon the last judgement (cf here the parable of the rich and foolish farmer, Lk 12:16–21; the saying about salt 'becoming foolish'—ie insipid, Mt 5:13; Lk 14:34, and the use of 'fool' as an expression of abuse, Mt 5:22—see the commentaries).

In the remaining cases foolishness gets its meaning with reference to revelation. Thus, the heathens are foolish since they do not know the true God, worship false gods and do not observe God's law (Rom 1:21, 22, 31;

2:20; 10:19; Tit 3:3). Hair-splitting theological speculations which do not help towards salvation (Mt 23:17; Lk 11:40), and indeed all empty talk (Eph 5:4) are described as foolish. Jesus refers to the disciples as without understanding since they do not know how to explain his parables (Mt 15:16; Mk 7:18) and have not grasped the meaning of his death on the cross (Lk 24:25). Christians are foolish who do not know the will of the Lord (Eph (5:17), who wish to observe the Jewish law (Gal 3:1, 3) or who quite simply lack the necessary knowledge of the faith (1 Cor 15:36). Paul describes his self-praise as foolish since it is not done with the Lord's authority (2 Cor 11:17; cf 11:1, 16, 23).

Paul confronts in a most forceful way the christians of Corinth, who consider themselves wise and strong (1 Cor 4:10), with the foolishness of the cross (1 Cor 1:18). God redeemed the world in a way quite different from what they had expected. A crucified Messiah was for Jews quite unacceptable and indeed a stumbling-block, while for Greeks it seemed sheer folly to believe in a crucified man. Hence the preaching of the cross must appear as foolishness to the world (1 Cor 1:23). But since God himself was active in the event of the crucifixion, the wisdom and power of God were revealed precisely in the foolishness and weakness of the cross (1 Cor 1:18ff). The man who is confronted with the word of the cross has to make a decision: either to hold on to his own criteria and expectations, in which case he must reject the word of the cross as foolishness, shut out the wisdom and the power of God ready to help and thus be lost; or give up his natural ideas about God and the divine activity, becoming foolish and believing in the apparently foolish message of the cross, and thus be saved.

Just as Christ is revealed as the crucified wisdom and power of God (1 Cor 1:24), this divine wisdom and power is only communicated to christians when they recognise themselves as foolish and weak, when they realise that they are radically dependent upon God (1 Cor 1:26–31). Hence Paul's warning to the 'wise' Corinthians: 'If any one among you thinks he is wise in this age, let him become a fool that he may become wise. For the wisdom of this world is folly with God' (1 Cor 3:18, 19a).

Bibliography: E. Kalt, *Bibl Reallexikon* II, Paderborn 1939², 882–4; W. Caspari, 'Über den bibl. Begriff der Torheit', *NKZ* 39 (1928), 668–95; *TDNT* IV, 832–47; U. Wilckens, *Weisheit und Torheit: Eine exeget-religionsgeschichtliche Untersuchung zu 1 Kor 1 and 2*, Tübingen 1959; A. Caquot, 'Sur une désignation vétérotestamentaire de "l'insensé"', *RHR* 155 (1959), 1–16.

Georg Ziener

Freedom

A. *External freedom*, that is, the freedom which gives man the opportunity to lead his life according to his own discretion, was regarded by the Greeks as 'a fine and splendid possession, both for the individual and for the state' (Socrates, cited by Xenophon, *Memor.* IV, 5, 2; further references are to be found in *TDNT* II, 487ff, and in Otto Michel, 2–12). A conspicuous mark of this essential freedom is the right of free speech, *parrhēsia*, which the Greeks found by experience could most easily develop in a democracy (see *TDNT* II, 490 and V, 870ff). Almost an earlier form of Jesus' words: 'The truth will make you free' (Jn 8:32), is to be found in one of the truly classic sayings of Anaxagoras (d. 427 BC): *Anaxagoran . . . tēn theōrian phanai tou biou telos einai kai tēn apo tautēs eleutherian legousin* = 'they say Anaxagoras maintained that philosophical contemplation, and the freedom which comes from it, is the purpose and goal of human life' (cited by Clem. Alex, *Str* II, 130, 2 [Diels II, *Anaxagoras* A 29]).

In the Old Testament too, freedom is held in very high esteem. Moses defended a Jew against oppression by his Egyptian overseer (Ex 2:12) and later—although it must be admitted that he did this as a result of God's repeated exhortation (Ex 3:7–4:17)—led the entire people of Israel out of Egypt, the 'house of bondage' (Deut 7:8), to a freedom which was however, to begin with, associated with uncertainty, distress and hunger, with the result that the Hebrews longed to go back to the flesh-pots of Egypt (Ex 16:3). But, in Yahweh's view, it was more important for the people of his Covenant to be free than to be economically secure in Egypt, as he had their future tasks in mind. The people of Israel were certainly permitted to own slaves (see Lev 25:44), but, both socially and legally, their position was essentially better than that of slaves owned by other races. This was laid down in the 'Slavery Decalogue' (Ex 21:2–11). According to these laws, Hebrew slaves or servants had to be set free again after six years, though this regulation was certainly not always followed (see Jer 34:14–18).

When Jerusalem was destroyed in the year 586 BC and the majority of the people led away into captivity in Babylon (2 Kings 25; 2 Chron 36:17–21), this loss of national freedom was powerfully expressed in the Lamentations of Jeremiah. Later, the political independence of Palestine was defended again and again by the Maccabees in heroic battles, as it was feared that if political freedom were lost, religious freedom would be sacrificed also (see 1 Macc 1:41–9; 2:19ff; 14:29; 2 Macc 3:1ff; 6:1ff, etc).

In the New Testament, the political freedom of the Jewish people, or their attempt to regain it, no longer plays any important part. Jesus had made it abundantly clear by his admonition: 'Render to Caesar the things that are Caesar's', that he had no intention of being a political Messiah or one who would liberate them from the political yoke of Rome, but that he had come as the redeemer of the world (Mt 28:19; Lk 24:47; Jn 4:21; 11:52). He was able to admonish the Jews to do this with an easy mind, since they had possessed a great measure of religious freedom and many special privileges since the time of Caesar (see Jos., *Ant.* 14, 10, 5–8) and were thus able to give to God the things that were God's without hindrance. Mere external freedom is moreover not the highest possession, nor the one which the christian should strive at all costs to gain, for he has no lasting dwelling-place here on earth, but should seek the one that is to come (Heb 13:14). 1 Cor 7:21 has probably to be understood in this sense too, on account of the statement made in v 24 (see J. Michl, *Freiheit* 30f; C. Biber 158, No. 3; and

H. D. Wendland, *Die Briefe an die Korinther*, 1954, 54: 'religious freedom in Christ is more than civil liberty'). At the same time, Paul himself laid heavy stress on the need for personal freedom to be respected by and among christians. He sent the baptised slave Onesimus back to his master Philemon 'no longer as a slave but . . . as a beloved brother' (Philem 16).

B. Man's *freedom of will* is the basis of all moral responsibility and the prerequisite for all punishment or reward. The very first human beings in paradise, who were created in God's likeness—God's absolute freedom here is stressed in the well-known simile of the potter shaping his vessel (Jer 18:6; Wis 15:7; Rom 9:21)—possessed this freedom of will (Gen 2:7; Sir 15:14ff; 'It was he [God] who created man in the beginning, and he left him in the power of his own inclination. If you will, you can keep the commandments, and to act faithfully is a matter of your own choice'). On Mount Sinai, life and death, blessing and malediction are presented to the people of Israel, with the admonition 'therefore choose life!' (Deut 30:19). Later, the prophets remind the people again and again that they should not abuse this freedom of will (Is 1:19; Jer 11:8, etc) and according to Sir 31:10 praise and glory is assured for the man who might have transgressed but who in fact did not. In Eccles too we find no fundamental denial of man's freedom of will, although many passages (Eccles 2:26; 7:13; 8:10, etc) do give this impression (see Nötscher, *Schicksal*, 460ff).

In the Qumran texts divine predestination is occasionally quite emphatically stressed (eg Hymn Scroll

15:12–20), but this should on no account be taken to mean absolute predestination. The 'elect' had to make their own personal decision to enter the covenant. That is why they were also called 'the Chosen Ones' (*hammith-nadbim*—see 1 QS v, 1, 6, 8, 10, etc). The relatively severe punishments for any transgression of the rules of the community also, without any doubt, imply the possibility of the exercise of free will and personal decision, but precisely how this can be aligned with divine predestination is not yet clear from the Qumran texts which have so far been edited. The compilers of the texts were, generally speaking, not scholarly theologians, but men who were intent on the practice of asceticism (see, in this connection, K. Schubert, *Die Gemeinde vom Toten Meer*, 1958, 55ff; and Nötscher, *Schicksalsglaube* 218).

The heathen philosophers too are convinced of the need for freedom of will and regard victory over desire and passion as possible and worth striving for. Epictetus (*Ench.* 15) compares life to a banquet at which one can and may take part in a civilised way: 'But if of yourself you do not take what is proffered ... you are not merely a worthy guest of the gods; you will also reign with them' (*TDNT* II, 494, 45ff).

Naturally, Philo too never tires of praising this higher, inner freedom as the greatest good of man. No intelligent man, in his view, is ever enslaved, even when others have bought him; and no irrational man is free, be he Craoesus, Midas, or the King of Persia (*Quod omn. prob*, lib. c XIX, sec. 136). God and the natural law are the final guarantees of this freedom (*Quod omn. prob*. x, 62). Simply being able to live as one wants

is not in itself freedom; only the man who is pleasing (to God) is prudent in all he does, and so only he is free (*Quod. omn. prob.* IX, 59: *panta phronimōs poiei ho asteios; monos ara estin eleutheros*). Of course, the only one who is in the fullest and truest sense free, and able to make others free, is God himself (*Quis rer. div.* 38, 186: *ho monos apseudōs eleutheros kai eleutheropoios theos*. Further references in H. Leisegang, *Philo-Index*, under 'eleutheros'.)

The New Testament also takes freedom of will for granted and expresses it clearly: 'How often would I have gathered your children together ... and you would not' (Mt 23:37). So great a respect did Christ have, during the time he spent on earth, for the free will of his people, that he preferred to submit himself to death on the cross, rather than to force Israel to accept his saving message, 'and so freedom became a stumbling block' (Schmaus 83), because the danger exists at all times that man will misuse it for evil purposes. Nevertheless, the decision to accept the new doctrine of salvation is for Paul essentially an act of man's free will ('We beseech you on behalf of Christ, be reconciled to God!' [2 Cor 5:20]). The evangelists may not compel this act (Acts 13:46; 18:6; Tit 3:10), but God is able to bring it about by means of his grace (Acts 9:15; 22:18; Gal 1:19; Phil 1:29) and indeed is even obliged to do so, if conversion is really to take place (Rom 9:16; Phil 2:13). In every case the freedom of the human will is preserved, though how this act is achieved remains a mystery which we should not, according to the admonitions of many of the Fathers of the Church, try to penetrate in our curiosity and presumption (see Schelkle, 195–9).

In the case of fallen men, who are thus 'sold' under sin (Rom 7:14), there are however also many *obstacles*, some more formidable than others, in the way of freedom of will. These may take the form of the ↗ world which is hostile to God (1 Jn 2:15), personal weakness (Mt 26:41), the desires and longings of the ↗ flesh (Rom 8:7; Eph 2:3) and many other obstacles which can thwart the carrying out of any good intention (Rom 7:19). This was as clearly recognised in the Jewish as in the heathen world (Ovid, *Metam.* 7:19: *aliudque cupido, mens aliud suadet: video meliora . . . deteriora sequor.* Further examples of both can be found in SB III, 234ff; H. Lietzmann, *An die Römer*, 1933, 77; and *TDNT* III, 167ff). All the same, these obstacles are generally surmountable with the help of God's grace (2 Cor 3:5; Phil 2:13; 4:13) and the christian remains in any case responsible for his actions both before and afterwards, and will also be judged according to his works (Mt 7:21; 25:34–46; Rom 2:6; 2 Cor 5:10; Gal 6:7; Heb 6:10; Jas 2:14ff; Rev 22:12). Luther, unlike Melanchthon and Erasmus, tried, as is well known, to escape this extremely serious responsibility by a denial of free-will (see Veit 148). Even modern, post-christian man obviously labours under the difficulty that he has to rely entirely on his own strength for the responsibility of his actions and decisions, as is well expressed by J. P. Sartre: 'L'homme est condamné à être libre' (more on this in Grässer 333).

C. *Christian freedom* is something quite new and unknown before Christ. The necessary condition for christian freedom is faith in Jesus Christ as the Son of God: 'If you continue in my word, . . . you will know the ↗ truth, and the truth will make you free . . . so if the Son makes you free, you will be free indeed' (Jn 8:31–6). 'Where the Spirit of the Lord is, there is freedom' (2 Cor 3:17). This freedom is received objectively through baptism—its seed is implanted by the sacrament (see Rom 8:23: *aparkhē*, 2 Cor 1:22; 5:5: *arrabōn*)—and it gradually becomes a personal possession of the child of God in the subjective sense (Rom 8:21). Its effects on the different departments of christian life are many and various.

1. He is *freed from sin*, which had fallen to his share since Adam (Rom 5:12ff; 1 Cor 15:21; Eph 2:3) and to which he had been a slave because of personal transgression as well (Rom 6:17–20)—literally 'sold' under sin (Rom 7:14). The apostle, however, triumphantly proclaims: 'Sin will have no dominion over you' (Rom 6:14) and we are 'freed from sin' (6:18). The result of this is:

2. *Freedom from eternal (the 'second') death* (Rev 2:11; 20:6; 21:8), since death is the wages of sin (Rom 6:23) and its inevitable consequence (Rom 7:11) and indeed its child: '. . . and sin when it is full-grown, brings forth death' (Jas 1:15). This applied to Adam's sin (Gen 2:17) and it still applies to ours. The resurrection of the Lord did not only free him from physical death—it also freed us from eternal death (Col 2:12–14). This everlasting death has certainly 'not been conquered once and for all by means of a mark of the Covenant like baptism. On the contrary, it hangs like a

constant threat of danger above the baptised man's head' (O. Michel, *An die Römer*, 1963, 135). The Christian too can be lost, if his faith remains 'without works' (Jas 2:14ff). Death (both in the physical and in the spiritual sense) will only be completely destroyed by God at the end of time (1 Cor 15:26: see also Rev 21:4). God also bestows on the christian:

3. *Freedom from the rule of Satan*, who, although he had already tempted Christ three times without success (Mt 4:1–11 and pars) and was thereby deprived of much of his influence over men (satanic possession, Mt 8:28ff; 12:22; 17:18; Lk 13:16; Jn 12:31), tries again and again to gain mastery over him and thus to regain his dwindling influence in human affairs (Eph 6:12; 1 Pet 5:8). An outstanding example of Satan's success is that of Judas (Jn 13:27). Satan must be overcome by prayer and fasting (Mt 17:21). Before the end of the world he will be first of all bound for 'a thousand years' (Rev 20:3) and then, after a short interval, he will be damned for all eternity (Rev 20:10). A further consequence of the redemption is:

4. *Freedom from the mastery of the ↗ flesh*, which fights in us against the spirit (Rom 8:5–9; Gal 5:17ff), which is synonymous with the 'old self' in us (Rom 6:6; Eph 4:22; Col 3:9) and the activity of which, aiming as it does at our ruin, must be mortified by the spirit (Rom 8:13), so that our mortal body, which is in itself good—a temple of the Holy Spirit (1 Cor 9:27)—may at last share in the resurrection (Rom 8:11). Last, but not least, Christ has brought us:

5. *Freedom from the ↗ law of the Old*

Testament: 'You are not under the law, but under grace' (Rom 6:14; see also Gal 5:18). Christ is the 'end of the law' (Rom 10:4), which was in itself holy, just (Rom 7:12) and good (1 Tim 1:8), because it aimed to preserve men from sin (Gal 3:24). Because of the increasingly strict application of the 'tradition of the elders' (Mk 7:3) however, it developed with the passage of time into an unbearable yoke (Acts 15:10; Gal 2:4), a dungeon in which the Jews were shut up (Gal 3:23), a bondage, from which Christ has liberated us (Rom 7:6). It should be noted, however, that the rabbis also warned that the 'fence around the Torah' should not be built too high in case it should collapse and crush the plants inside; this type of warning did not, however, appear until the second century AD (see H. J. Schoeps, *Paulus* [1959] 302). Man was certainly quite unable, purely on his own account and without the help of grace, to fulfil the Law and thus to achieve ↗ justification (Rom 3:28; Gal 2:16).

The christian has been 'called to freedom' (Gal 5:13) by reason of Christ's work of redemption, but the apostle gives the warning in the same sentence that this liberty is not to be conceived as an unbridled licence. Christian freedom from ritual and dietary laws (↗ pure), which were imposed in Old Testament times, was not to be abused as a 'pretext for evil' (1 Pet 2:16). Though it is true that the baptised man is a 'freedman of the Lord', he remains at the same time a 'slave of Christ' (1 Cor 7:22) who has purchased him with his blood, and is thus bound to the law of Christ (1 Cor 9:21). This law has loosened our previous bonds and is truly the 'perfect law of liberty' (Jas 1:25). In this way, christian freedom clearly bears the imprint of a 'dialectical character' (in the phrase of Bultmann) and must be conceived as a 'freedom of service' (J. Michl 26) which not only has a regard for the conscience of each individual among the 'weaker brethren' (1 Cor 8:9; 9:19ff), but also willingly complies with the requirements of public law and order and the demands of the communal good (Rom 13:1–7; Tit 3:1; 1 Pet 2:13). It is thus a freedom in charity, as is proper to the children of God. On the other hand, it is, in the last analysis, all to the advantage of those in authority in the church when they respect the freedom of individuals to express their opinion— even when contrary—in established cases and in the appropriate manner (see Gal 2:11–14; and further, Hirschmann 88ff). Pius XII once drew attention to the fact that there must be a 'public opinion' in the church entitled to scope and tolerance. It is 'the birthright of any normal human society' (*Osservatore Romano*, 18 February 1950). Details in Rahner, *Free Speech in the Church*, 5f.

D. *Religious liberty*, freedom of conscience, or freedom of belief is the right (and duty) of a man to adhere to whatever religion or world-view he in conscience firmly believes to be right (even when, objectively speaking, he may be wrong). Consideration for the misguided consciences of the weak is to be found as early as Paul (1 Cor 10:28ff), in the case of those who regarded eating the food offered to idols as wrong for a christian in any circumstances—provided, that is, that

they are fully convinced of their view (Rom 14:5). Tit 3:10 may certainly be regarded as the first christian 'edict of toleration': 'As for a man who is factious (*hairētikos*), after admonishing him once or twice (ie, to no effect), have nothing more to do with him'; he will henceforward have to take on himself the responsibility for his actions. Admittedly, in later times a church which was too often hand-in-glove with the state (*une foi, une loi, un roi*; further references in Heinzel, 9) frequently forgot the early christian maxim: 'not force but persuasion' (*mē anaḡkazein, alla peithein*: Athanasius, *Hist. Arian.* 67 [*PG* 25, 773A]). The same is true of the Reformers, who unquestioningly accepted *cuius regio, eius religio*, with the result that Henry VIII, Calvin, and others could equally lightly allow the execution of 'heretics'.

Only with Leo XIII did the early christian attitude to this range of problems really make itself felt once more. Its authoritative echo remains in Canon 1351 of *CIC*: *Ad amplexandam fidem catholicam nemo invitus cogatur* ('no-one is to be compelled to embrace the catholic faith against his will'). But simple tolerance is not adequate for our modern pluralist society, particularly insofar as it is a-catholic. If tolerance were not to lead to indifferentism, it could only be 'relative tolerance' (see Ebneter, 202); that is to say, erroneous consciences, even when in good faith, cannot be given the same status as a religious conviction which corresponds to objective truth, since truth and error of their very nature cannot claim equal protection. On the same grounds E. Melichar has recently explained (*LTK* VIII [1963], 1177) that religious liberty is only 'to be tolerated'—a view which now, however, seems superseded by *Pacem in Terris*. John XXIII was not concerned to protect error as such, but the man in error, since 'he does not cease to be a man and never loses his personal value, which must always be taken into account' (*AAS* 55 [1963], 299).

This view has finally prevailed. In its *Declaration on Religious Liberty* the second Vatican Council declared— after long and heated debates—that religious liberty is an authentic right of the person, rooted in his human dignity, which civil society is obliged to recognise.

Bibliography: H. Schlier, *TDNT* II, 487–502; E. Kalt, *Bibl. Reallexikon* I, 1937, 556f; E. G. Gulin, 'Die Freiheit in der Verkündigung des Paulus', *ZST* 18 (1941), 458–81; O. Michel, *Universitas* I (1946), 1–17; O. Veit, *Die Flucht vor der Freiheit*, Frankfurt 1947; R. Egenter, *Von der Freiheit der Kinder Gottes*, 1949; E. Wolf, *ET* 9 (1949/50), 127–42; J. Michl, *Freiheit und Bindung: Eine zeitgemässe Frage im Lichte des NT*, Munich 1950; K. H. Schelkle, 'Erwählung und Freiheit im Römerbrief nach der Auslegung der Väter', *TQ* 131 (1951), 17–31 and 189–207; H. Ridderbos, 'Vrijheid en wet volgens Paulusbrief aan de Galaten', *Arcana revelata* (Festschrift F. W. Grosheide), Kampen 1951, 89–103; Bultmann I, 330–40; S. Lyonnet, *Liberté chrétienne et loi nouvelle selon S. Paul*, Rome 1954; E. Grässer, *ET* 15 (1955), 333–42; G. Harbsmeier, *ET* 15 (1955), 469–86; C. Biber, Allmen 129ff; M. Schmaus, 'Kirche und Freiheit', *MTZ* 8 (1957), 81–92; R. Guardini, *Freedom, Grace and Destiny*, London 1961; J. B. Hirschmann, 'Die Freiheit in der Kirche', *SZ* (1957), 81–92; B. Ramazzotti, *Riv. bibl. it.* 6 (1958), 50–82; G. Heinzel, 'Kirche und Toleranz' (rectorial address 1958); Campenhausen and Bornkamm, *Bindung und Freiheit in der Ordnung der Kirche*, 1959; F. Nötscher, 'Schicksal und Freiheit', *Bbl* 40 (1959), 446–62; F. Nötscher, 'Schicksals glaube in Qumran und Umwelt', *BZ* 3 (1959), 205–34; P. Bläser, *LTK* IV², 328–31; J. Gnilka, *LTK* IV², 338–40; C. Spicq, *Charité et liberté dans le NT*, Paris 1961; O. Betz, *Gefährliche Freiheit*, Munich 1961; C. Maurer, 'Glaubensbindung und Gewissenfreiheit im NT', *TZ* 17 (1961), 107–17; K. Rahner, 'Freedom in the Church', *Theological Investigations* II, London and Baltimore 1963, 89–107; *K. Rahner, *Free Speech in the Church*, London and New York 1959; L. Roy, *DBT* 532–7; A. Güemes, *El Descubrimiento de la Libertad por san Pablo*, Madrid 1963; B. Häring, 'Die religiöse Freiheit', *Theologie d. Gegenwart* 7 (1964), 187–93; A. Ebneter, 'Von der Toleranz zur religiösen Freiheit', *Orientierung* 28 (1964), 202f; H. Küng, *The Church and Freedom*, 1965; *H. Küng, *Freedom in the World: St Thomas More*, London 1965; *H. Küng, *The Theologian and the Church*, London 1965; J. Leclerq, *Kirche und Freiheit*, 1964; J. C. Murray, *The Problem of Religious Freedom*, London 1965; C. Spicq, *La liberté chrétienne: Théologie morale du NT* II, Paris 1965, 623–64; K. Niederwimmer, *Der Begriff der Freiheit im NT*, 1966.

Johannes Kosnetter

Freedom of speech

Freedom of speech and frankness are terms used to render the Greek *parrhēsia*. This derives originally from the political sphere, and it is only secondarily that it has been transferred from that into the sphere of private life, where it is applied to friends who tell each other everything. It is related to the concept of ↗ freedom. In LXX God endows the people with freedom of speech (Lev 26:13), and wisdom is said to show frankness in this sense (Prov 1:20). In this the biblical term is still wider in its range of meaning than the Hellenistic one, as appears in passages such as Job 27:9f, where frankness means the free and joyful attitude in God's presence of one who has unhindered access to him. In Wis 5:1 we read that the just man will show great frankness or boldness in his dealings with those who have oppressed him (see 5:5, 15f). Such frankness presupposes ↗ righteousness. Only the righteous man, not the sinner, possesses frankness (see Prov 13:5f). This frankness is expressed in prayer (Job 27:9; 22:21-7). The philosopher prays in a similar manner (see Epictetus, *Diacr.* 2, 17, 29: as a free man looking up to heaven, as a friend of God who has nothing to fear). The actual idea of friendship with God is mentioned in Job 22:21 (not in LX, where the passage has been brought into conformity with Job 9:4, whereas MT rightly translates: 'Become friends with him').

In Ps 93:1 LXX and 11:6 LXX the verb *parrhēsiazesthai* is used with God as subject. The original Hebrew word which lies behind this is commonly translated: 'to radiate light', 'to appear illumined with light'. There is no doubt that the reference here is to God emerging from his silence and appearing in radiant glory as judge of the wicked and as deliverer of the just.

The *New Testament*. In the Acts of the Apostles *free speaking* (*showing frankness*) is used only in relation to men, and is frequently found in parallelism to terms signifying 'to teach' and 'to speak' (4:29, 31; 9:27f, etc), so that here it is actually possible to translate *parrhēsiazesthai* as 'to preach'. Often it is the Jews (2:29; 13:46 etc), the Jewish authorities (4:13; 26:26), but also Jews and Gentiles together with their authorities (4:29, 31; 14:2f) in whose presence the apostles speak. Here it is always some specific utterance based upon the ↗ confession of faith; it has a force which does not derive from rhetorical training but which the Lord imparts to his ministers (see 4:13, and 14:3), and which is

made possible through the ↗ Spirit (see 4:8, 31; 18:25f). In this way this frankness or free speaking attains the status of a ↗ charism.

The *Pauline literature* yields a similar picture. Free speaking here is no less relevant when applied to the preaching of the gospel (Eph 6:19f) than as used in the sense of openness in relation to God (2 Cor 3:12 and esp Eph 3:12). The freedom of speech which the apostle exercises in his dealings with men (Eph 6:19f; 1 Thess 2:2 etc) is based on his frankness in his relations with God, and is a reflection of the divine ↗ authority. The comparison with Moses in 2 Cor 3:12ff makes this clear (On this point van Unnik has rightly pointed out that the words corresponding to *parrhēsia*, in Aramaic and Syrian signify 'unveiled countenance' and 'uncovered head'. This conclusion, moreover, enables us to understand the association of ideas in the mind of the apostle to the gentiles). Eph 3:11f provides a still clearer expression of the idea: in Christ man shows frankness and (what amounts to the same thing) trustful access (to God) through faith in Christ.

In Col 2:15 the *parrhēsia* of Christ himself is spoken of. He has disarmed the principalities and powers, and triumphed over them in his coming in boldness and frankness, that is in power and without fear.

There are four occurrences of the term 'freedom of speech' or 'frankness' in the Letter to the Hebrews. In 3:6 it is associated with the hope which we may truly take pride in, in holding firm to which christianity consists. The same thing is expressed in another way in 3:14, where it is said that we share in Christ if only we hold firm to the end to the position which we adopted in the beginning (*hupostasis* never means confidence, but refers to the state of soul), and avoid being made obdurate by the deceitfulness of sins (3:13). This frankness, like ↗ hope in and expectation of Christ, consists not merely in an interior attitude, but also in the reality to which that attitude is directed, namely the actual fact that we have freedom of access to God. Since however it is always possible to forfeit this (10:35), an exhortation to hold fast to this attitude of frankness and boldness is included. Taken together vv 4:14 and 10:19 tell us how Christ our high priest has opened this new way to us, namely through his blood, through his death. But it is only when our conscience is pure, and when we have been washed in the waters of baptism and are sure in our faith (10:22), that we can follow this way of free speaking and boldness.

The *Johannine Usages*. In Mk 8:32 (the sole occurrence in the synoptics) *parrhēsia* is already used as the opposite of teaching in parables. And in the passage concerned this mode of speaking, precisely in its openness, veils the Messiah from the disciples, as the episode with Peter which follows makes clear. Thus according to Mark also Jesus can appear in 'openness' only to the eyes of faith. It is only in following the way of the Cross that we can understand him (see E. Schweizer, *ZNW* 56, 1965, 7). For John, Jesus' works are indeed performed in public before the eyes of the world (18:20f; cf 7:25f). Yet this openness of Jesus' work is not to be confused with an openness as to his actual nature, a

mistake into which the disciples fall because they fail to understand the character of his works as signs (7:4f). As the evangelist understands it, on the other hand, Jesus went up to Jerusalem 'in secret' (7:10). The openness of Jesus' work which is immediately visible for all to see is not the *parrhēsia* of the revealer himself (10:24f). It is the same in 11:11 ('Lazarus *sleeps*') and, by contrast with this, 11:14 ('Then Jesus said to them *openly*, "Lazarus is *dead*"'). The disciples do not understand that the presence of Jesus makes death into a mere sleep from which one arises! Only at his return in the power of the Paraclete is this veil removed. Only in his ↗ glorification will his *parrhēsia* appear. Admittedly the believer can see through the veil, as is shown by 16:29ff as following upon 16:25ff.

The first Letter of John recognizes that man can take up a frank or bold attitude in God's presence by reason of his good conscience (3:21). Those who keep his commandments are assured that this frankness will obtain them the hearing of their ↗ prayers (5:14f), 'if we ask according to his will'.

This attitude of (eschatological) frankness or freedom of speech is the opposite of ↗ fear in that it is maintained in the presence of the judge (2:28; 4:17), cf the adumbration of this in Wis 5:1. The attitude of frankness excludes the possibility that at the end we must be overcome by shame and fear. In fact this attitude of frankness and free speaking is in the last analysis based upon the fact that God loves us and brings his love for us to its perfection. The attitude of abiding in that love that knows no fear because it keeps the commandments manifests itself at the judgement precisely in the fact that man can have access to God freely and without fear.

Bibliography: M. Radin, 'Freedom of Speech in ancient Athens', *Am. Journ. of Philology* 48 (1927), 215–20; E. Peterson, 'Zur Bedeutungsgeschichte von parrhesia', *Festschrift für R. Seeberg* I, 1929, 283–97; P. De Ambroggi, *VD* 9 (1929), 269–76; P. Joüon, 'Divers sens de parrhesia dans le NT', *RSR* 30 (1940), 239–41; C. Spicq, *L'Epître aux Hébreux* II, Paris 1953, 69f; H. Schlier, *TDNT* v, 871–86; H. Jäger, 'Parrhesia et fiducia, Etude spirituelle des mots', *Studia Patristica* I (TU 63) Berlin 1957, 221–39; W. C. Van Unnik, 'De semitische achtergrond von parrhesia in het NT', *Mededelingen Kon. Nederl. Akad. van Wet., Letterk.* 25 (1962); W. C. van Unnik, 'The Christian's Freedom of Speech in the NT', *BSRL* 44 (1961/2), 466–88; H. Holstein, 'La parrhesia dans le NT', *Bible et Vie Chrétienne* 53 (1963), 45–54; G. Scarpat, *Parrhesia. Storia del termine e delle sue traduzioni in latino*, Brescia 1964; L. Engels, 'Fiducia dans la Vulgate', *Graecitas et Latinitas Christianorum primaeva* (Suppl. I), Nijmegen 1964, 97–141.

Johannes B. Bauer

Fulfilment

1. The original meaning of the word 'fill' (see Ex 8:17: to fill a space) is extended to denote the universal presence of God (Jer 23:24) and of his spirit (Wis 1:7). This should not be taken to mean that God is enclosed by the universe (see 1 Kings 8:27), but that he embraces the universe in his creative power, rules it and preserves it in existence (see Wis 1:7; 7:24, 8:1). In Ex 40:34f, it is Yahweh's presence in the midst of his people (Ex 25:8, 22; 29:45f), which is represented by his glory (*kābôd*) in the cloud filling the tabernacle. In Is 6:3, where we read that all the earth is filled with Yahweh's

glory, what is implied is the revelation of God, who is holy (ie, exalted above the earth) and who shows his power in acts of punishment and salvation. This is to be understood within the total context of Isaiah's prophecy (see Num 14:21; Ps 72:19; see also B. Stein, *Der Begriff Kebod Jahweh*, Emsdetten 1939, 171–96).

According to Eph 4:10, Christ has ascended above all the heavens 'that he might fill all things (*ta panta*)', that is, rule them as a sovereign (the opinion of Gewiess, Mussner, Schlier, Schnackenburg). Paul is referring in particular to the beings that are 'in heaven and on earth' who have received the spirit (Eph 1:10; Col 1:16), for with his ascension Christ has 'put all things under his feet', especially the spiritual powers which are hostile to God (Eph 1:21ff; Col 2:15). It is also possible to understand Eph 1:23: 'the fullness of him who fills all in all' (=who fills everything in all parts, universally and intensively) in the light of Eph 1:10, 20ff as well as Eph 4:10. Although it is possible to think of *plēroumenou*, in the middle voice in Greek, as having an active meaning, *plērousthai* is never used in this way in the New Testament. In the Vulgate and in the writings of Origen and St John Chrystostom the sense is always passive. In any case, the meaning that Christ, as Head, receives his fullness through his mystical body, the Church, in all its parts (*ta panta*, in the adverbial sense) and members, is not really appropriate within the context. However suitable the idea is in itself, it is certainly not to be found anywhere in Paul. He does not regard the church as making up what is lacking in Christ, as a fulfilment of Christ (for *plērōma* in this sense, see Mt 9:16; Mk 2:21). According to him, the faithful, therefore the church, are filled by Christ, who is the head of every principality and power (Col 2:10). The parallel with Eph 1:21ff, in which Christ is also seen to appear elevated above all these various powers, is quite clear and is made even clearer when Col 2:9 is taken into consideration. Here the entire pleroma of divinity is seen to dwell corporeally in Christ, that is to say, 'the whole fullness of diety dwells bodily' in Christ and not simply as a shadow of what is to come (see Col 2:17: A. Wikenhauser, *Die Kirche als der mystische Leib Christi nach dem Apostel Paulus*, Münster 1937, 188). The interpretation that this fullness took flesh in Christ is less probable here, although it is grammatically feasible. In Col 2:9f, we find also that christians are filled by Christ in whom the entire fullness of divinity dwells. Col 1:19 should also be considered in connection with Eph 1:23: 'For in him all the fullness of God was pleased to dwell'. According to the usual interpretation, the same is meant here as in Col 2:9, but more correctly, it refers to the fullness of divine and created being (Benoit). But Paul, unlike the Stoics, nevers calls the cosmos *plerōma*. What he is using in this case is a conception taken up by the judaeognostic heretics of Colossae, but he uses it against them. What he is in fact saying is that it is not the angelic powers to which they give worship who represent the *plērōma*, but that the fullness of all power and everything that exists which is great and good is in Christ, with the result that he takes precedence in everything (Col 1:15–18). Thus Eph 1:23 may be understood in the sense of Col 1:19: Christ is filled by everything in every possible way (Benoit and Feuillet, for example, accept the passive meaning here), and may be matched with what is expressed in Eph 1:10: everything (= the universe, *ta panta*) that is in heaven and on earth (the heavenly and terrestrial world which has been disrupted by Adam's sin) will, by God's ordination, in the fullness of time, be gathered up into one (*anakephalaiōsasthai*) in Christ as into one short and ordered heading, an epitomised compendium (*kephalaion*: see also Heb 8:1), so that all things may once again be brought into that peaceful unity through him—the unity that is already present in him by reason of the union of his divine and human nature. The Christ who is filled in this way fills the universe (Eph 4:10), which means that he keeps it together by his power as ruler as he does the church which is his *plērōma* (Eph 1:23) and which is filled by him (Col 2:10) through his being and the power of his grace. Accordingly, christians are to attain the 'measure of the stature (in the Vulgate, measure of the age) of the fullness of Christ' (Eph 4:13), and 'existing truly in charity' ('speaking the truth', see Gal 4:16: 'doing the truth', Vulgate), they may 'in all things (*ta panta*) grow up in him who is the head, even Christ' (4:15). According to the traditional interpretation, *auxēsōmen* is taken here to be intransitive, thus meaning simply to grow, in the same sense as *auxei* in Eph 2:21 (see Eph 4:16; Col 2:19). The transitive meaning used by Schlier, to make grow (see 1 Cor 3:6; 2 Cor 9:10): 'to make everything grow up to him' tends to result in an unusual sense and one which is not strictly appropriate to Eph 4:16 (see Schnackenburg). According to Eph 4:10, Christ fills the universe as a result of his ascension, ruling directly over it (see 1:21f) and not through his church. The faithful, filled with the fullness of Christ (Eph 4:13), are also 'filled with all the fullness of God' (Eph 3:19), for the 'fullness of deity' or divinity 'dwells bodily' in Christ (Col 2:9). It is possible to take *plēroumenou* (Eph 1:23) here either in the sense of the passive or the middle voice, but in either case what is expressed is Christ's fullness of power which he allows to penetrate his church by filling her, his mystical body, with himself. Paul refers to this fullness of power which the church shares with Christ in order to demonstrate to the faithful in Colossae, in opposition to the teaching of the heretics there, that they had no need to worship angels (Col 2:18) and also no need to fear those powers which were hostile to God (Col 2:15), but that they could successfully hold out against them in the power of Christ (Eph 6:10–17). He had already told the Corinthians that they had become rich in all things in Christ and thus lacked none of the gifts of grace, and that Christ would so strengthen them to the end that they might be found without blame on the day of his coming.

When Paul says that he vicariously fills up (*antanaplērō*) for the faithful what is lacking in the suffering of Christ by his own suffering and tribulation (Col 1:24), he does not intend to imply that anything is essentially lacking in the work of redemption on Christ's part—

Christ has indeed brought a perfect reconciliation by his death on the cross (Col 1:20). What he is referring to here are the 'sufferings of Christ' which continue to take place, and must thus continue within his mystical body (see also 2 Cor 1:5; 4:10; Gal 6:17). All the members of this body have the task of contributing towards its building up or edification (Eph 4:12, 16) and the first and foremost must be the apostles (Eph 4:11), especially by means of their sufferings (2 Cor 4:12; Eph 3:13; Acts 9:16; 1 Cor 4:9ff; 2 Cor 11:23ff).

Other examples of the verb *to fill*, used in its wider meaning, present few difficulties. Among these we can include the following references: ↗ wisdom (Lk 2:40),↗ joy (Acts 2:28), sorrow (Jn 16:6), the fruit of↗ justice (Phil 1:11), the↗ knowledge of the will of God (Col 1:9). When he refers to the 'fullness' of Israel (Rom 11:12) or the fullness of the gentiles (Rom 11:25), Paul implies their completion with the 'fullness of time' (Gal 4:4; Eph 1:10) and the full measure that has been prepared for them by God and which they will receive with the coming of Christ (cf Mk 1:15: 'the time is fulfilled'). The 'times' will acquire their full meaning in Christ. The 'fullness of the blessing' of Christ's teaching (Rom 15:29) is, similarly, blessing in full measure. The incarnate Son of the Father is 'full of grace' to such an extent that we receive 'from his fullness . . . grace upon grace' (Jn 1:14, 16).

2. *Fill* is also used in the sense of *fulfil*, as for example, fulfilling the law (Rom 8:4; 13:8; Gal 5:14). Christ has to 'fulfil all↗ righteousness', that is to say, what is right in God's sight and

what he demands (Mt 3:15; cf 6:1; 1 Jn 2:29; Rev 22:11).

3. *Fill* or *fulfil* is moreover used, for example, in Mt 5:17, according to the context (see especially 5:20–48) and, taking into consideration the fact that Christ is here exercising his function as a teacher, with the sense of accomplish. He has, in any case, already fulfilled the law of the Old Testament in the sense that he has adhered to it (see Rom 15:8; Gal 4:4). But in this instance he is referring to his messianic mission to accomplish and perfect everything. This is brought about in the case of the ↗ law by his making the will of God which is proclaimed in the law effective in its total purity. Thus he transcends the letter of the ancient law by forbidding the evil motive which leads to evil action as strictly as he forbids the action itself, by prohibiting all temporary concessions in connection with the law (see 'hardness of heart' Mt 19:8) and by assigning to the law the place that is due to it (the commandment to love one's neighbour takes precedence over that concerning the Sabbath). The accomplishment which has come about through Christ also includes the complete abolition of the Old Testament form of worship and the ceremonial laws which are appropriate to the provisional and temporary nature of the Old Testament, since these have lost their sense and purpose with Christ, for whom they were a preparation (see J. Schmid, 1959[4], 87 and 90–94). Since fulfilment is reached with Christ, the 'time is fulfilled' with his appearance (Mk 1:15; Gal 4:4), has acquired its full measure and is brought to a conclusion. Further examples of *fill* or *fulfil* used in the sense of

accomplish or bring to an end are: Lk 7:1; 22:16; Jn 3:29; 15:11; 16:24; 17:13; Acts 12:25; 13:25; Rom 15:19 (what is meant here is that Paul's sermon on the gospel is at an end): Col 1:25 (cf 1:28f): 2 Thess 1:11; Rev 3:2.

4. *Fill* or *fulfil* is also found with the sense of realise. This usage is found particularly in connection with the messianic prophecies of the Old Testament, which are fulfilled or realised in Christ and his church. After his resurrection, Christ is at pains to point out to the apostles that everything that was written about him in the Mosaic Law, the Prophets and the Psalms is to be fulfilled (Lk 24:25ff, 44ff). But he does this even before his resurrection: see Mt 11:3ff; Lk 4:17ff; 7:22 and Is 35:5f; 61:1f—Mt 11:10, 14; 17:12f and Mal 3:1; 4:5—Mk 9:12; 14:49; Lk 22:37 and Is 53—Mk 10:45; 14:24 and Is 53:10ff—Jn 10:14, 16 and Ezek 34:23f; 37:24. The apostles and evangelists also point to the fulfilment or realisation of the Old Testament prophecies in Christ, in a general way in Mt 26:56; Acts 3:18, 24; 10:43; 13:27, 29; 17:3, 11; 20:27; 28:23; Rom 1:2; 15:8; 1 Cor 15:3f; 2 Cor 1:20, and with reference to more precise details in the following instances: Christ is the son of Abraham and David (Mt 1:1; cf Gen 22:18; 2 Sam 7:16; Jer 23:5); he is to be born of a virgin (Mt 1:22f; Is 7:14); further examples of this fulfilment are: Is 9:1, 2 (Mt 4:14ff); 11:10 (Rom 15:12); 42:1–4 (Mt 12:17ff); 53:7f (Acts 8:32ff); Jer 31:31–4 (Heb 8:8ff); Mic 5:2 (Mt 2:6); Zech 9:9 (Mt 21:4f); 12:10 (Jn 19:37; Rev 1:7); Ps 2:1 (Acts 4:25f); 2:7 (Acts 13:33;

Heb 5:5); 16:8ff (Acts 2:25ff; 13:35 ff); Ps 22:18 (Mt 27:35; Jn 19:24); 22:22 (Heb 2:12); 45:7f (Heb 1:8f); 110:1 (Acts 2:34f; Heb 1:13); 110:4 (Heb 5:6; 7:1–28). The fulfilment of the Old Testament prophecies in Christ is in particular clearly demonstrated by a review of the relevant texts (↗ messianism). The most sublime and purely religious features of the image of the Messiah, those features which transcend national and political considerations and which are the least easy to explain on the purely natural level, all come together in Christ and his work to form an inner unity which is even less easily explained on the natural level. As early as Gen 3:15 we find reference to the expectation that the disorder brought about by the original sin of man's first parents is to be remedied not simply by God, but by a man who represents the whole of sinful mankind. This man is depicted in the ↗ Servant of God (especially in Is 53) and Jesus has fulfilled this prophecy completely in his atoning death and fulfilled it for all mankind (see Is 49:6; 53:12). The spread of the religion of Israel over the whole world (see Is 2:2ff; 45:22f) is accomplished by Christ and his church. The high quality of this atonement and reconciliation which includes the whole world is based on the union of the human and the divine in Christ's nature which is indicated in Is 9:6; Ps 2:7; 45:7; 110:1, 3; Dan 7:13. Furthermore, the representation of divine ↗ wisdom as a person who proceeds from God and dwells with him in the most intimate communion of life and activity (Prov 8; Wis 7f) provides a preliminary insight into the true relationship which exists between the

Father and the Son. What is also demonstrated in Christ is the truthfulness of the promises that God will come to redeem his people and dwell in their midst (see Is 40:3ff; 42:13ff; Ezek 34:11ff; 43:1ff; 48:35; Zeph 3:15; Zech 2:10ff; Mal 3:1ff). As the divine Messiah, Christ is the son of a virgin (Is 7:14) and a 'priest for ever' (Ps 110:4). Even the features of the messianic image which caused the Jewish commentators such difficulties and were so often misinterpreted or falsely understood by them are to be found in Jesus Christ in a state of harmonious unity. One of the basic principles of the plan of salvation, namely, that God is to bring about the salvation of mankind by means which are humanly inadequate (Is 9:3f—the day of Midian; see also Judg 7:2ff) is put into effect in Christ's death on the cross (see 1 Cor 1:23ff). It is, of course, true that the promise concerning the miraculous fertility and transformation of nature, Israel's victory and supremacy over the other races, Jerusalem's glory and the royal sway of the Messiah was not fulfilled in the way in which these things were described, or at least has not yet been fulfilled in this way. But it must be borne in mind in any consideration of these promises, that God had to allow his prophets to present his future kingdom in the various forms which were familiar to them and which they had encountered in the present and in the past, so that what they were promising would both be understood by their contemporaries and be attractive to them, with the result that their religious and moral attitude would be fashioned by their view of the messianic future (see Is

2:5). All this conformed to the way in which God wished to bring about his people's gradual religious development. Thus the messianic period is described as a complete reversal of the present unhappy state of bondage (see Is 14:2; 60:9ff; 61:5f) or as a return to the ideal time of David (Is 11:13f) or to the exodus from Egypt (Is 11:15f; 40:3ff; 41:17ff; 43:16ff). Indeed, everything is depicted as being far more splendid than these happy times of the past. It is in fact the task of the prophets to bring the importance and the happiness of the messianic future powerfully home to the people, and descriptions which attempt to approximate to the truth are sufficient to give a general but vivid picture of this supremely important future. In every consideration of this problem it is necessary to remember the essential and ultimate task of the prophets. When, for example, Jeremiah (33:20ff) or Zechariah (6:13) proclaim the eternal preservation of David's kingdom or the priesthood of the levites, they are not ruling out the possibility that this may be realised in a more sublime form. It is also permissible for the ⁄ church of Christ to claim that those passages which deal with Israel and Jerusalem are applicable to herself, since she rightfully inherits these ancient promises because she is incorporated, by means of her faith and sacraments, into Christ, who inherits them (Gal 3:29). The church has in fact grown organically from the ancient people of God and it is she who perpetuates its life (⁄ people of God). The prophecies, moreoever, leave the way clear for the possibility of a gradual fulfilment which can unfold in stages. The first stage in the fulfilment of the prophecies is completed in the return from exile. The first glimpse that the prophets give provides the outlines of the picture, but the prophecies penetrate beyond this and envisage the following stages: the redemption from ⁄ sin through Christ, and the glorious consummation with the transfiguration of the whole of nature. The resplendent colours of the picture are provided by this final accomplishment. The intervals of time between the stages generally remain obscure to the prophets. Whenever they speak of an imminent realisation of the prophecies (see Joel 1:15; 2:1; Hag 2:6) it is possible that they are referring to the first stage, though in any case they always have a practical purpose in mind, to exhort the people to a state of constant watchfulness, intense expectation and trusting ⁄ hope which will not result in disappointment, even if this 'soon', this imminent coming, is something which has been determined by and is known to God alone (see 2 Pet 3:8ff). It should also be noted that it is possible for the prophecies to imply certain conditions which are not expressly stated (see Jer 18:7ff); thus Jerusalem did not know the day of her visitation (Lk 19:42). And yet the day of mercy is still to come for Israel (Rom 11:23–32; cf Mt 23:39). Whenever words from the Old Testament, which in their immediate context refer to persons or things *of* the Old Testament, are quoted in the New as having been fulfilled or as to be fulfilled in Christ (see Mt 2:15 and Hos 11:1; Jn 13:18 and Ps 41:9; Jn 19:36 and Ex 12:46; Num 9:12), then what we have here are types of Christ and examples of the many ways in which the Old Testament foreshadows the New.

This particular type also shows how Christ fulfilled the Old Testament. He accomplished all the good beginnings that were made by the great and pious figures of the Old Testament, but he had to endure as well all the sorrow, misunderstanding and ingratitude that they suffered and to an even greater degree, and he had to embrace the entire history of Israel and make it his own in order to be the faithful Servant of God and to make up for the debt incurred by the blind and deaf servant of God—Israel (see Is 42:19) and indeed by the whole of mankind, and to fulfil what they had not fulfilled.

Bibliography: G. Delling, *TDNT* VI, 238–309; J. Gewiess, *Festschrift Meinertz: Vom Wort des Lebens*, Münster 1951, 128–41; F. Mussner, *Christus, das All und die Kirche*, Trier 1955; P. Benoit, 'Corps tête et plérôme dans les épîtres de la captivité', *RB* 63 (1956), 5–44; A. Feuillet, 'L'Eglise plérôme du Christ d'après Eph 1:23', *NRT* 78 (1956), 449–72 and 593–610; H. Schlier, *Der Brief an die Epheser*, Düsseldorf 1958²; K. Staab, *Die Gefangenschaftbriefe* (*RNT* 7), 1959; R. Schnackenburg, *God's Rule and Kingdom*, Edinburgh, London and New York 1963; J. Schildenberger, 'Weissagung und Erfüllung', *Bbl* 24 (1943), 107–24 and 205–30; J. Schildenberger, *Vom Geheimnis des Gotteswortes*, Heidelberg 1950, 181–204; P. Bläser, 'Erfüllung der Schrift', *LTK* III², 983f; Baumgärtel and Kümmel, 'Weissagung und Erfüllung im AT und NT', *RGG* VI³, 1584–8; H. Gross, 'Zum Problem Verheissung und Erfüllung', *BZ* 3 (1959), 3–17; Eichrodt I, 381–7; von Rad II, 357–87; P. Grelot, *Sens chrétien de l'AT*, Tournai 1962, 388–403; C. Westermann, *Probleme atl. Hermeneutik*, Munich 1960, 28–53; W. Zimmerli, *Verheissung und Erfüllung*.

Johannes Schildenberger

Glory

The Hebrew word *kābôd* is rendered as *doxa* in the Greek bible. Our usual translation is 'glory'.

A. *Extra-biblical usage.* Among ancient writers *doxa*, which is of course connected with the verb *dokeō* (lit = to think), is used with two meanings: 1. 'the opinion which I have', and 2. 'the opinion which others have of me'. In the first case, the meaning is extended to include expectation, perception, doctrine, dogma, axiom, imagination, outward appearance, etc, and in the second to include good reputation. In conjunction with an appropriate adjective, however, it can also mean 'bad reputation'.

Philo also uses the word with the above meanings. In all the two hundred and fifty instances in which it is found in his works, only once does it mean 'brightness', and then obviously as a result of biblical influence. In Josephus, it means splendour or magnificence.

B. *Biblical usage in general.* In the Septuagint and the New Testament, *doxa* is never found with the first meaning, that is, opinion, but can mean (a) fame, reputation or honour, (b) brightness, brilliance or splendour, (c) reflected splendour and (d) when referring to God, heavenly brilliance, sublimity or magnificence. In the last meaning, *doxa* can even be used in parallelism with the name of God, and elsewhere as a substitute for God. This arises from the fact that in LXX *doxa* is equivalent to *kābôd*, and is in fact even used to translate other Hebrew words closely related, in their context, with the idea of *kābôd*.

C. *Old Testament usage.* 1. In the *Masorah*, *kābôd* has the secular Hebrew meaning of 'honour', *what adds to a person's standing, what increases a person's position and influence.* (The basic meaning of the root *kbd* is 'to be heavy'.) In the

295

concrete sense, it means 'wealth' or 'position of honour' (see Gen 31:1; 45:13; Nahum 2:9; Ps 49:17). When it refers to peoples and racial groups, *kābôd* means the prestige or the standing of a given race among others in the world (Is 16:14; 17:4; 21:16). Splendour or glory is the meaning of *kābôd* in Is 10:18; 60:13, used in conjunction with a wood or a hill. *Kābôd* may also be used as parallel with *nepheš* and *ḥayyîm*, with the meaning of 'soul' or 'I', in many of the psalms. This usage is, however, questionable, as the reading may be *kābēd* (liver).

Whenever *kābôd* is used in connection with God—this occurs frequently in the phrase *kᵉbôd Yahweh*—it means the 'impact of the divine appearance'. The transcendent God reveals himself on earth in meteorological phenomena, as for example in a dark thunder-cloud (Ex 24:15; Ezek 1:4; Ps 29; 50:2f). In Ex and Num particularly, the *kᵉbôd Yahweh* appears in conjunction with *ᵓānān* (cloud). This is also the case in 1 Kings 8:10. This cloud, however, only serves to conceal the real apparition of God—the all-consuming fire and light—which would destroy men if it were fully revealed to them (Ex 24:17; 33:18ff). God reveals himself in this way only at important points in the history of salvation, and it is possible to define the *kᵉbôd Yahweh* as 'God himself, whenever he reveals himself in a solemn theophany, accompanied by thunder and lightning, storm and earthquake' (Steinheimer, 6). The *kᵉbôd Yahweh* is therefore not God himself in his true and unrecognisable essence, but *God insofar as he allows men to recognise him*. What *kᵉbôd Yahweh* means in substance, then, is the power, majesty,

magnificence, and *glory of God* (Ex 24:16f; Num 16:9ff) and, at the same time, his appearance and heavenly substance of light (Ex 24:15ff; 40:34ff; Ps 50:2; 104:2: and, less obviously, in 1 Kings 8:11). In the vision of Ezekiel, the cloud is replaced by cherubs (eg Ezek 1:4ff; 43:2). In both Ezekiel and Psalms, the *kᵉbôd Yahweh* is associated with the temple, the tabernacle or the holy mountain, Sinai—all places which are intimately connected with God's earthly appearances. In Ps 66:2 and 79:9, *kābôd* is used in parallel with *šēm* (name), and stands for the name of God. *Kābôd* is also frequently used in the psalms, with the meaning of greatness and honour, in conjunction with verbs, to imply that man is bound to give this honour to God. 'Giving honour' in this case adds nothing to God's majesty; it is simply a recognition of it (Ps 19:1; 24:7; 66:2; 96:3, 7; 138:5; 145:5, 11). In Is 42:8; 48:11, God makes it clear that he will not share this honour with others. In the case of Ps 57:5, 11; 72:19; Is 40:5, *kābôd* implies the kingdom of God which will appear at the end of time.

2. In LXX, *doxa* occurs 445 times, including 280 times in the proto-canonical books. Generally speaking, it translates the Hebrew *kābôd*. As Kittel quite rightly claims, the two words *doxa* and *kābôd* have become identical in meaning. The classical meaning of 'opinion' is completely absent from LXX, whereas that of glory is to be found when it refers to splendour, power, reputation, or honour in the human sense or to power, glory, honour, brightness or, as in the case of *kābôd*, self-revelation in the divine sense.

Doxan didonai tō(i) theō(i) (lit. = to give *doxa* to God) has the same meaning—that is, 'recognition of the glory of God'—as the Hebrew phrase 'to give *kābôd*' (to sing or tell of the glory of God).

3. *Kābôd* in *later Jewish* usage. In the Targums, *kābôd* is usually rendered by *yᵉqār* (honour). The rabbis tend to use *kābôd* in the sense of human honour, with which God, however, frequently identifies himself. They regard the divine *kābôd* as a foreboding of the advent of the *šekinâ*. Man has no share in this divine *kābôd*, although according to Ex 34:29f Moses, and according to Gen rabba 11, the *ʾādām qādmôn*, who lost this share in the divine *kābôd* through the fall, are apparent exceptions. The rabbis infer from Dan 12:3 that the pious will have a share in the divine *kābôd* at the end of time, though according to Num 3:15 it is only the Messiah who will have a real share in this *kābôd*. Blessedness for the others consists merely in being permitted to behold the divine *kābôd* (b Ber. 34a). The apocryphal books (Apoc Mos 20f; 4 Ezr 7:91–7; Bar (Syr) 51:10; 1 Hen 38:4) reveal a similar attitude towards the *kābôd*.

D. The *New Testament usage* is in accordance with that of LXX: the usual meanings are 'renown', 'power', 'honour', and 'divine revelation'. The brightness which accompanies God's appearance is sometimes stressed; at other times it is little emphasised (Lk 2:9; 9:31ff; 2 Pet 1:17; Acts 22:11; Rev 15:8; 21:23). In the New Testament, too, *doxan didonai* means a recognition of the divine majesty (Acts 12:23; Rom 4:20; Rev 14:7). In the doxologies of the New Testament, the word needed to complete the sense is not *eiē(i)* (lit. = let [it] be), but *esti(n)* (lit. = [it] is)—this is shown very clearly by 1 Pet 4:11: 'To him *belong* glory and dominion for ever and ever. Amen'. The *doxa theou* (= glory of God) of the New Testament is associated with revelations which are of importance in the matter of salvation, as is the case with the *kābôd Yahweh* of the Old Testament. As, however, these New Testament revelations are always intimately bound up with the person of Jesus, the New Testament goes beyond the Old and makes the *doxa* appear as something new, referring to Jesus as the Christ. It is only in John that such statements are made with reference to Jesus in this world. John is, however, perfectly in accord with the writers of the synoptic gospels, in maintaining that this *doxa* is veiled, and can be recognised only in *pistis* (= ↗ faith; see Jn 1:14). The man who has faith is able to recognise the *doxa* in the *dunameis* (powers) of Jesus (Jn 2:11; 11:4, 40). In Lk 2:9, it shines forth as a final greeting from the heavenly world. In the Transfiguration on Mount Tabor, the presence of *doxa* is clearly indicated in the substance of all three synoptic accounts, although it is only Luke who explicitly refers to it (9:31f). In John, however, Jesus frequently prays for the coming of the *doxa* (Jn 12–17). It is personally revealed in him on the occasion of his passion, death and resurrection. On his ascension, Jesus returns to his heavenly *doxa* (Acts 1:9; Phil 2:9; 1 Tim 3:16). Stephen is permitted to see him in this heavenly glory (Acts 7:55). At his parousia, Jesus will appear in his *doxa* and with his *dunamis* (Mt 19:28; 25:31; Mk

8:38; 10:37; 13:26; Lk 21:27; Tit 2:13; 1 Pet 5:4, 10).

The New Testament presents a far more hopeful picture of the *doxa* of the faithful than the Old. Not only does the New Testament state that the faithful will behold the *doxa* of God (1 Cor 13:12)—it also promises that they are to be led, through their sharing with Christ in suffering, to a share in his *doxa* (Mt 13:43; Phil 3:21; Col 3:4; 1:27; Rom 5:2; 8:17; 2 Thess 2:14). *Aiōnios doxa* (eternal glory) is the aim which they are called to achieve in Christ and the goal to which he is leading them, as members of his body (2 Cor 4:17; 1 Thess 2:12; 2 Tim 2:10; 1 Pet 5:4, 10). The faithful already have, in this life, a share in the *doxa mellousa* (coming glory), in a hidden sense, in the *pneuma* (Spirit). It is the *aparkhē* (=firstfruit: Rom 8:23; 2 Cor 3:7f; 1 Pet 4:14) which will eventually be accomplished. There is no real contradiction here with Jn 17:22, in which Jesus gives the *doxa* to his disciples. The *pneuma* belongs so intimately to him that it can, in fact, be completely identified with him. In the New Testament, the angels too possess this glory, because they are constantly in the company of God (Heb 9:5; Rev 18:1; Jude 8; 2 Pet 2:10).

E. Usage in the *Latin bible*. In the pre-Vulgate Latin translations, *claritas* was used when the emphasis was on the light or brilliance of the apparition (African translation), *gloria* when the idea of light or glory was predominant (Itala), and *maiestas* when God's power was to be stressed. In the Vulgate, which is based upon the Itala, *claritas* does not appear at all in Matthew, Mark, or the catholic epistles, and very rarely in Luke, Revelation, or the letters of Paul. *Maiestas* appears very rarely in the Vulgate translation of Matthew, Luke, Jude, and the Apocalypse. In most cases, the Vulgate translates *doxa* by *gloria*. The church fathers follow the biblical usage, seeing in the *doxa* the divine essence of the Blessed Trinity and also the divine essence of Christ. They tend to speak very often of the *gloria crucis, gloria passionis,* and *gloria resurrectionis.* The fact that the divine *Logos* (Word) retained the *gloria* in becoming man was regarded by the fathers as the first step in the incorporation of human nature in the glory of the Father. The Roman meaning of 'renown' or 'honour' is perpetuated in *gloria*, in patristic references to the glory of the martyrs.

Finally, the liturgy continues this biblical usage—in the case of the Roman (Latin) liturgy, that of the Latin translations.

Bibliography: G. Kittel and G. von Rad, *TDNT* II, 232–55; J. Schneider, *Doxa* (Ntl. Forschungen III/3), Gütersloh 1932; G. Kittel, *Der Herrlichkeit Gottes*, Giessen 1934; B. Stein, *Der Begriff kebod Jahwe und seine Bedeutung für die atl. Gotteserkenntnis*, Emsdetten 1939; M. Steinheimer, *Die 'Doxa tou Theou' in der römischen Liturgie*, Munich 1951 (with bibliography). See also: Z. Alszeghy and M. Flick, *Greg* 36 (1955), 361–90; C. Mohrmann, *Festschrift A. Debrunner*, Berne 1954, 321–8; P. de Haes, *Collectanea Mechlinensia* 27 (1957), 485–590; E. Pax, 'Ex Parmenide as Setuaginta: De notione vocabuli *doxa*', *VD* 38 (1960), 92–102; *J. Bourke, 'Encounter with God', *Life of the Spirit* xv (1961), 398–405 and 490–7.

Georg Molin

God

A. *The image of God in the Old Testament.* Not only does the Old Testament recognise no image of Yahweh in the form of a statue or any kind of visual representation, it also contains no fully developed, systematic doctrine in the form of a 'spiritual' image of God. What occupies the most prominent place in Old Testament revelation is not the divine being, but divine activity, although there is no lack of statements in which God is used predicatively with the verb to be. What is more, the activity of God as it appears in the Old Testament provides a good deal of information about his being. Before attempting, however, to fit together the individual details of what we may call the image of God in the Old Testament, it should be noted that Old Testament revelation is intrinsically a 'revelation in process of development' (*revelatio in fieri*). Although Yahwism can scarcely be traced back to any generally accepted form of historical religious development, it is certainly subject, at its own particular level, to certain laws of growth which are ultimately to be found in the teaching concerning the God of revelation. The ebb and flow of time plays an important part in this process, as well as Israel's contact with various spheres of tradition and proximity to various kinds of written and oral testimony and traditions. In any attempt to systematise the Old Testament statements concerning God, different factors such as these must of necessity overlap, but all must be borne in mind.

I. *The one and unique God.* In striking contrast to the other religions of the Ancient East, Israel's monotheism is the crystallisation and the universal postulate determining the structure of all religious teaching. This monotheism has its own historical development in Israel, a development towards greater explicitness and clarity. In the patriarchal age, what is stressed is Israel's commitment to the one God of revelation, without any clear statement being made concerning the non-existence of other divine beings. The God of Moses reveals himself as the God of the Patriarchs (Ex 3:6). He will not tolerate any form of worship for other gods (Ex 20:3). What is more, the question of the existence of any other gods is not raised. The God of the Covenant is, for Moses, without any doubt the God of the whole world, even if the statement 'All the earth is mine' is accepted as a later gloss (Ex 19:5). It is thus possible for us to speak with complete certainty of a monotheism in practice with regard to those who were witnesses to divine revelation even in the early history of Israel. The ordinary people would for a long time also have taken the existence of other gods in foreign lands and among strange people for granted. Evidence of this is to be found in Judg 11:24; 1 Sam 26:19; 2 Kings 3:27. A formal and theoretical monotheism was evidently less important to the God of revelation, at least in the early stages, than the achievement of a single-minded obligation on the part of the people of his Covenant towards him alone. His purpose was to lead them by a progressive enlightenment. It was only later, through the prophets, that he allowed the full truth to be disclosed in all its clarity, that no other associations were possible because no other gods in fact existed. According to the evidence of 1 Kings 18:39, Elijah was able to stir the people to the expression of monotheistic belief: 'The Lord, he is God! The Lord, he is God!' This is the one great theme which is common to all the prophets, however variously they express their message, and it eventually emerges in the sixth century in Deutero–Isaiah in hymn form, as for example in 43:10ff; 'I, I am the Lord, and besides me there is no saviour.' With such an absolute monotheism as the sure foundation of its official religion, Israel stands out on a lonely and isolated prominence in the Ancient Near East, although from the political and cultural point of view it was an insignificant and second-rate people compared with the other peoples of that period. Various finds made in the Middle East indicate, it is true, that monotheistic tendencies existed in individual and private devotion in Egypt and Mesopotamia, but these had no influence on the official religion of the people. The attempt made by the Pharaoh Achnaton in the fourteenth century to establish monotheism failed completely. The religion of Zarathustra is the only phenomenon which is even remotely analogous to the monotheism of Israel, but both spatially and temporally there could have been no contact between the two before 500 BC. Furthermore, the monotheism of Zarathustra was weakened by dualistic elements, which were unknown in the religion of Israel.

II. *The transcendent God.* In the sun-worship of Achnaton, divinity belongs completely to this world and is regarded as immanent. Its being is essentially a 'being in the world', which is a basic conviction common to all the religions of the Ancient East and is in particular the distinguishing feature of all the western Semitic fertility religions against which Yahwism had to try to make headway. Yahweh, on the other hand, appears (despite his close personal relationship with man and his bearing on the world) as the transcendent God who is in his true being and essence raised above all worldly affairs. This transcendence is manifested in many different ways.

1. *Yahweh is transcendent.* Whereas divinity was in the first place always conceived in the ancient Near East as a regional numen or Lord of a particular locality (as an example of this, see 2 Kings 5), the God of the Patriarchs is proved to be one who is in no way limited to a particular land, people or empire. His sovereign power extends over the whole of the so-called 'fertile crescent'—therefore from the estuary of the Euphrates to Egypt. He has control over the land of Baal, that is, Canaan, in the first place by virtue of the promise and later by virtue of the fulfilment of the promise. Although it is true that he appears, at the time of Moses, to be the God of Mount Sinai and, during the period of the monarchy, the God of the city of Jerusalem, this 'localisation' does not imply that his presence was limited to a particular place, but that he had appeared there. The people themselves certainly never thought that they would be able to find him only on Sinai or in Jerusalem. They endeavoured to worship him everywhere in the country where the so-called 'high-places' were to be found. Even Elijah repaired the altar on Mount Carmel (1 Kings 18:30). According to the view of those appointed to bear the revealed word of God, Yahweh could not be contained within the walls of the temple of Jerusalem. In Isaiah's well-known vision of the temple (Is 6), the whole space above the

throne is empty, there is room in the temple only for the royal train of Yahweh, and the Seraphim testify that the whole is filled with the overwhelming glory of the king of the world. The author of Solomon's prayer of dedication of the Temple, belonging to a prophetical movement, puts these words into the mouth of the builder (1 Kings 8:27): 'Behold, heaven and the highest heaven cannot contain thee; how much less this house which I have built?' According to Jer 7:12, Yahweh can thus also allow the Temple to be destroyed. Yahweh's supraspatial aspect is further indicated in Amos in the eighth century: 'Not one of them shall flee away, not one of them shall escape. Though they dig into Sheol, from there shall my hand take them; though they climb up to heaven, from there I will bring them down. Though they hide themselves on the top of Carmel, from there I will search out and take them; and though they hide from my sight at the bottom of the sea, there will I command the serpent, and it shall bite them' (Amos 9:1ff). The author of Ps 139 has taken up this theme and explains the idea of God's action and influence as transcending space with reference to the transcendant nature of his being and essence: 'Whither shall I go from thy Spirit? Or whither shall I flee from thy presence? If I ascend to heaven, thou art there! If I make my bed in Sheol, thou art there! If I take the wings of the morning and dwell in the uttermost parts of the sea, even there thy hand shall lead me, and thy right hand shall hold me' (Ps 139:7–10). Yahweh is in fact Lord of nature and of all space. He is, however, in no way a part of nature. Even the heavenly

powers of the cosmos which produce the movement of the stars and planets are not of the same being as he is. According to Genesis 1, the sun and the moon are merely 'lamps', thus material things—mere material elements of the cosmos in the most matter-of-fact sense of the word. All great human powers too are insignificant before him. Considering the mighty empires of the ancient world, whose extent and power impress us so much today, and faced with the presence of the Mediterranean civilisations of Europe, Africa and Asia, Deutero–Isaiah nevertheless says: 'Behold, the nations are like a drop from a bucket, and are accounted as the dust on the scales; behold, he takes up the isles like fine dust. Lebanon would not suffice for fuel, nor are its beasts enough for a burnt offering. All the nations are as nothing before him, they are accounted by him as less than nothing and emptiness. To whom then will you liken God, or what likeness compare with him?' (Is 40:15ff). This transcendence of Yahweh above everything that is visible is firmly rooted in his absolute creativeness concerning everything that is in the process of being. This creativeness did not flow or proceed from his being by emanation, but was brought into existence out of the original power of his creative will, as his word which, so to speak, takes on concrete form (Gen 1:1ff; Is 42:5; 45:18; Ps 33:6, 9; 148:5, etc.).

2. *Yahweh is universal.* Evidence of Yahweh's transcendence is also to be found in his attitude towards the people of God as presented in the Bible. He is not simply the God of the people of Israel, to be thought of in the same way as the other peoples regarded the chief

god of their pantheistic system. In the Ancient Near East, the relationship between a god and his people was conceived in purely natural terms. In Israel too, there was always a tendency to regard the union between Yahweh and Israel as a kind of natural bond—as a mutual dependence upon each other. In contrast to this, the Mosaic tradition testifies from the very beginning that the relationship of the covenant must of necessity be conceived as a relationship based upon free election, with the result that it contains the inherent possibility of rejection. This became a fundamental aspect of the teaching of the prophets. They emphasise again and again that the Covenant depends upon grace and in this way direct attention to the fact that it is possible for Yahweh and Israel to exist at a distance from each other. Amos assumes the role of spokesman for Israel when he proclaims the verdict of God: 'Are you not like the Ethiopians to me, O people of Israel? . . . Did I not bring up Israel from the land of Egypt, and the Philistines from Caphtor and the Syrians from Kir?' (Amos 9:7). Here Yahweh disavows the purely practical use which Israel has made of him, as a God of the people. His special Covenant with Israel is a free one, and can therefore be broken. Indeed, Jeremiah is bound to announce the restoration of Israel by the promise of a 'new Covenant' (Jer 31).

3. *Yahweh is the Lord of time*, though he is not in any way subject to any temporal laws or to any diminution of his being. The Hebrew does not think of eternity simply as another mode of existence, but in his imagination lengthens the line of time both forwards and backwards into the vast obscurity where nothing is visible. Everything that is coming into being or passing out of existence occurs along this imaginary line, with the exception of what is divine. In this way the Old Testament stands in complete contradiction to all the mythological theogonies of neighbouring civilisations. Existence is such an essential part of Yahweh's being that even what we find in the introductory verse of the Johannine gospel (= in the beginning *was* God) is left out of Gen 1:1. Only in Ps 90:2 do we find 'Before the mountains were brought forth, or ever thou hadst formed the earth and the world, from everlasting to everlasting thou art God'. God is thus the fulness of life itself, to which transience is completely unknown. This is why, according to Ps 90:4, a thousand years are as a single day to him, and why Deutero–Isaiah calls him 'the first and last' (44:6; 48:12), and why, according to Hab 1:12, the death referred to in the myths of the vegetation-gods is unknown to him. He is simply the living one in whom every generation can have absolute confidence (Judg 8:19; 1 Sam 14:39, etc.). Nothing is capable of diminishing his life. It can also not be diminished by sin. Job exclaims (7:20; cf 35:6): 'If I sin, what do I do to thee, thou watcher of men?' Yahweh's life is at the same time so abundant that it is incapable of being increased, either by justice (Job 35:7), purity (22:2f), fasting (Zech 7:5) or sacrifice (Is 1:11ff, etc.). The God of Israel has no need of anything from man to sustain his life, as this is far removed from everything that is temporal or in any way tied to the world.

4. *Yahweh transcends every type of sexual*

dimorphism. Sexuality is a phenomenon which pervades the whole of terrestrial life, and which contains the source of life in the animal and human sphere. Life and the origin of life is a divine mystery for the people of the Ancient Near East. They look for the source of all fertility in the womb of divinity and do not think of this in the metaphorical but in the concrete sense, and thus their idea of human sexuality is transferred to the divine sphere. It even takes the form of sexual dualism, and god and goddess are worshipped as a divine couple. In direct contrast to this, Yahweh appears in the Old Testament as a single divine being. The Hebrew word for goddess has not even been handed down to us. Yahweh has no female counterpart, although he is regarded as the source of all life and has been endowed with human characteristics and is always represented as possessing the fullness of life and serene happiness. Even the conception of Yahweh as a Father does not have an exclusively male application in his case (see Is 49:15; 66:13). Indeed, whenever the Covenant is, for the purpose of elucidation, likened to a matrimonial covenant or union, Yahweh appears in the role of bridegroom or husband, although this is always in the form of an allegory and refers to his activity rather than to his being. This transcendent quality with regard to sexuality distinguishes Yahweh from the deities of all the other religions of the period, and it is not possible to find an adequate explanation for it—even if Israel's alleged fear of sex is taken into consideration—on the purely natural level.

5. *Yahweh is intrinsically holy.* The adjective ↗ holy, used predicatively (*qādôš*) has the strictly etymological and objective meaning of being separate and completely different and has a close affinity with the 'taboo' of comparative religion. The notion of holiness is also closely connected with a particular place, as, for example, in Gen 28:17 (Jacob at Bethel) and Ex 3:5 (Moses and the burning bush). But what is behind this is the experience of the 'mysterium tremendum', which is God's way of manifesting himself. God's 'jealousy' and the theophany in the form of fire (Ex 20:5; 34:4) clearly indicate this. That holiness is, from the ontological and the ethical point of view, the essence of Yahweh, is borne out not only by the theology of the priests and levites (see Lev 19:2), but also, even more emphatically, by the prophets. According to Amos 4:2, Yahweh swears by his holiness, which is for him the most sublime and ultimate ideal. In his prophetic vision (Chap. 6), Isaiah sees Yahweh as a king of terrifying sublimity, blinding purity and overwhelming splendour. The only possible reaction that man can experience in the face of such holiness is to feel himself a sinner and the lowest of creatures, and the power of Yahweh's holiness thus forms the principal theme of Isaiah's message (see 10:7 and the constant reference to Yahweh as the 'Holy One of Israel', Is 1:4; 5:19; 10:20; 12:6, etc.). According to Deutero-Isaiah, the mark of Yahweh's holiness is that it bears no comparison with anything belonging to man or the world (see Is 40:13ff, 25; 55:8, etc.). But this quality of being absolutely other also contains the idea that Yahweh is quite different from man in his love (see Hos 11:8 and Is 55:8).

6. *Yahweh is the God who must be worshipped 'differently'*. In all the religions of the ancient civilisations, divinity is visibly apparent in the form of a statue or statues. From the earliest times, the only object or place which visibly represents God for Israel was the sacred Ark of the covenant. The commandment forbidding images, handed down to Israel in the Sinaitic tradition, applied in the first place originally to the making and worshipping of images of other gods, and it was therefore possible for cases of a popular image-worship of Yahweh to crop up occasionally (see Judg 17:4f; 1 Kings 12:28ff). But the true tradition of Israel was, from the very beginning, a worship of Yahweh without images (see Ex 34:17) and this became more and more marked with the passage of time (see Deut 4:15ff) and even more firmly established on the basis of the conception that Yahweh could not be compared with any creature or wordly object (Is 40:12ff). In the matter of sacrifice, however, the worship of Yahweh does appear to approximate very closely to the other religions of Israel's neighbours. It is not difficult to find phenomenological and terminological support for this comparison, but the significance and the spirit of Israel's sacrificial worship are quite different from those of other religions. All magical tendencies are dismissed forthwith (see Ex 20:7 [and the commandment in 20:2]; 22:18; Deut 18:10ff). In this way, sacrifice is conceived as the fruit and the expression of a fundamental moral choice on the part of the people, who share in the covenant. Thus, even at the conclusion of the Covenant on Mount Sinai, what is central to the sacrificial ceremonies is ethical and personal commitment to the will of Yahweh (Ex 24:6ff). The prophets repeatedly point out the overriding importance of moral and personal commitment in the religion of revelation and reject any sacrifice which is not accompanied by the 'spirit' which God desires (Amos 5:21ff; Hos 6:6; Is 1:10ff; Mic 6:6ff; Jer 7:21ff).

It is in the transcendence of God that the religion of Israel differs so completely from all other religions which are known to have existed in that region at that time, and it is this which makes it simply impossible to derive Yahwism from other sources. There are no satisfactory, natural reasons which can explain how it was that the small, politically and culturally insignificant people of Israel arrived at this idea of God, and from this point of view Israel's idea of a transcendent God is quite simply the miracle of the Old Testament. What, nonetheless, is remarkable about this idea is that, despite the transcendence of the divine being and essence, the immanence of the divine activity and influence is demonstrated again and again. In what he does Yahweh is, as it were, present at every single point of time and space. Natural phenomena are all traceable back to him, though no particular notice is taken of what might be termed intermediate causes (see Ps 147:15-18; Job 38:28ff). The principal theme of the Old Testament is that Yahweh is truly the Lord of history. It is true to say that not only does the Old Testament contain, in an unparalleled manner, a fully developed theology of history, but that it is in fact a theology of history in itself, according to which Yahweh, with a definite plan and object in view, yet 'reacting' specifically to human 'action', intervenes in man's history with mercy and justice and is indeed himself the central and leading factor in the history of the chosen people and of mankind in general. The most striking attestation of Yahweh's influence and control over everything that happens is to be found in the practice of giving him the title of king (see Num 23:21; Is 6:5; 24:23; 33:22; 41:21; 43:15; 44:6; 52:7; Jer 10:7, 10; Mal 1:14; Ps 24:7; 47:6; 93:1; 96:10; 97:1, etc). This conception of the kingship of Yahweh incorporates and gradually develops the idea that he is directing the history of the cosmos and of mankind towards the eventual revelation of his royal majesty and glory in a restored world. Thus nature and history do not come into being and evolve as independent and self-contained consequences of what is and what happens. What we could call the established laws of nature or even of history appear in the Old Testament as divine action taking place according to a regular pattern, which is controlled by its own laws but which is always open to God's free intervention. Thus the transcendence of God's essential being is attested in the free immanence of his activity. It must be admitted, however, that the consistent employment of a markedly anthropomorphic mode of expression, which appears throughout the whole of the Old Testament with very few variations from the earliest to the latest texts, seems to be diametrically opposed to this conception of God's transcendence. The main reason for such an anthropomorphic form of writing with regard to divine matters is generally speaking to be found in the innate limitations and the finite quality of the human mind, but it must also be borne in mind that this pronounced anthropomorphism of the Old Testament is intimately connected with the extremely figurative and metaphorical oriental mode of thought and speech. These frequent examples of anthropomorphism do not, however, expose the basic Old Testament image of God's transcendence to any real danger of compromise or diminution, for what they aim to portray is not God's being which is withdrawn from the world, but his activity which is immediately effective within it. It is, in fact, only possible for them to appear in precisely this form and in such abundance against the background of the fundamental transcendence of God. They do, however, fulfil a very important and positive function in enabling the Hebrews to comprehend and to depict Yahweh in the fullness of his total personality.

III. *The personal God*. It should be clearly recognised at the very outset that, contrary to some modern objections concerning the personality of God, the authentic conception of personality does not imply any essential modification or limitation of being as it presupposes any essential independence, in the sense of a relationship with itself, and this applies equally whether this relationship is, in its being, finite or infinite. The Jews, like other oriental people of antiquity did not develop the idea of spirit and spirituality into a philosophy, but they did firmly grasp the essence of the spirit and conceived it as an element that relates strictly to itself and intimately possesses itself, and succeeded in delineating it in the most sublime manner in their own image of God, which was stamped through and through with the mark of their personal conception of the nature of the spirit. Divinity is thus not represented simply as the creative first cause and the source of all being in the aspect of an indeterminable and all-embracing 'it', nor is it seen merely as being itself (*ipsum esse*). God is quite simply viewed as 'he' or 'I', or as a 'self'. This is most strikingly evident in the principal statements made about him in the Old Testament, that is, in those places where God 'speaks'. In these passages his knowledge and wisdom, his will and his freedom are expressed, not only in the subject-matter, but also in the fact of his speaking. Hence very often this speaking by God takes place after the manner of a dialogue in which God is the subject, the 'I' who is speaking and, in the majority of cases, man is the object, the 'thou' who is addressed by God. It is hardly necessary to quote particular instances of this phenomenon, since almost every page of Holy Scripture provides at least one. Furthermore, what is contained in the representation of man as the 'image of God' (↗ Likeness) is the fundamental statement that God is personality, and the divine elucidation of the name of Yahweh ('I am who I am': Ex 3:14ff) incorporates the personal element as a component of the divine essence. God also makes direct allusions to the fact that he is a person, and in a manner which could not be more directly personal. This is found in books which are principally concerned with the law, in the sapiential literature and above

all in the prophetic books. The following two examples have been selected from many: 'I will be gracious to whom I will be gracious and will show mercy on whom I will show mercy." (Ex 33:19) and 'I say: my counsel shall stand, and I will accomplish all my purpose' (Is 46:10). In these two examples alone, God's spirit and freedom appear with unmistakable clarity as essential elements of absolute personality. Finally, the divine being as a person is most conspicuously in evidence in God's freedom and autonomy with regard to his love for man within the Covenant. This love of Yahweh within the Covenant forms the main theme, not just of New Testament revelation, but also of that of the Old Testament (↗ Covenant). Everything that forms part of God's rule [and the government of man] revolves around this axis: ↗ love and ↗ judgement (see also ↗ justification), ↗ wisdom, guidance and faithfulness, promise and threat, admonition and warning. The God of the Covenant shows himself as the Father of the people (Ex 4:22f; Hos 11:1; Is 64:8; Mal 2:10, etc), as a Father in whom the paternal and the maternal elements are intimately interwoven (see Hos 11:1ff; Jer 31:9–20; Is 49:15; 66:13), as the Father of kings (2 Sam 7:13f; Ps 89:26f), as the Father of orphans (Ps 68:5), as the Father of those who fear him (Ps 103:13) and of the just (Wis 2:16). He also reveals himself as a provident shepherd (Mic 4:6; Zeph 3:19; Jer 31:10; Ezek 34; Ps 23:1ff), and as bridegroom and husband (see Hos 2:16; Jer 2:2; Ezek 16:8; Is 54:5 and Song of Sol.). In the same way that the human person is characterised in particular by his heart and his face, the God of the Old Testament too has a heart (see Gen 6:6; 1 Sam 13:14; 1 Kings 9:3; Jer 3:15; Ps 33:11, etc.) and a face (Ex 33:14f, 20; Job 1:11; Ps 80:19, etc). All higher inward impulses can be predicated of him and, what is more, even those which seem to be particularly human, which has at times provided material for indictments against the Old Testament image of God. These human impulses which the Old Testament attributes to God should, however, be understood in relation to the rest of Scripture and in the context of the whole of divine revelation (see 3). Moreover, the very fact of their lack of perfection bears witness to Yahweh's vital personality whose inner decisions and motives are often obscure to man. With regard to the problem of natural theology concerning the existence of evil in the world, the book of Job alludes to the impenetrable mystery of the divine dispensation, but, at the same time, firmly precludes the idea of any form of solution in the nature of a blind or impersonal fate. In Job 38ff Yahweh reveals himself as a person of a unique kind. At the same time, his universal causality is also clearly demonstrated, as indeed it is in almost every book of the Old Testament. The Hebrew mind makes no clear distinction between what God causes to happen and what he permits to happen. Thus it is that the Hebrew is able to express dialectically the objectively identical fact of the Pharaoh's obduracy of heart in the two statements: 'The Lord hardened Pharaoh's heart' (Ex 9:12) and 'Pharaoh . . . sinned yet again . . . and his heart was hardened' (= Pharaoh hardened his heart, Ex 9:34–5).

God's personal causality and man's freedom of choice receive an equal emphasis and, as in the thomist formulation of their interrelationship, they are not regarded as antitheses which cancel each other out. In this way, it is possible for Yahweh to appear quite frequently to bring evil about, or for some seemingly demonic attribute to be present in the metaphorical and often hyperbolical delineation of his dispensation over man. In any attempt to arrive at a theological interpretation of passages of this kind, care should be taken not to divorce such texts from the context of the customary Hebrew manner of expression and the question of literary genre, particularly relevant here, and to bear in mind also the imperfection of Old Testament revelation relative to the New.

IV. *God as the source of abundant life.* Although God is transcendent, he is also the vital source of all ⁄ life in the human and animal kingdom. In Num 27:16, he is called the 'God of the spirits of all flesh'. Considered in its context, this refers particularly to man. According to the passage dealing with creation, man, unlike the animals, is also essentially constituted by God breathing the breath of life into his nostrils (Gen 2:7). On the other hand, however, according to Ps 104:29ff, animal life is also a form of divine breath. Thus all life on earth is a sharing in the divine life. But what strike us especially in this flowing of the living spirit of God into man are the extraordinary and unusual manifestations of life, such as the special strength of Samson (Judg 14:6), the creative inspiration of artists and craftsmen (Ex 28:3), the ecstasy of the prophets (see 1

Sam 10:5ff) and the understanding of the wise men (see Job 32:8). The more extraordinary and supernatural such phenomena become, the more powerfully is God's vital activity at work in them. Indeed, he manifests himself in them simply as life itself, and the believing Israelite freely acknowledges himself as one who has, at all levels of his existence, been given life by him. This is why the psalmists (and particularly the author of Ps 119) so willingly address the petition 'Give me life!' to Yahweh. What is sought first and foremost here, of course, is deliverance from mortal danger, but closely associated with this is a renewal of the inner life (see Ps 22:20f; 69:33), and finally a joyous experience of the spiritual treasures of life, such as the word of God (Ps 119) and has grace and friendship within the covenant. Thus we find in Ps 16:11: 'Thou dost show me the path of life; in thy presence there is fullness of joy, in thy right hand are pleasures for evermore'. This sentiment is expressed even more powerfully in Ps 36:7: 'How precious is thy steadfast love, O God! The children of men take refuge in the shadow of thy wings. They feast on the abundance of thy house, and thou givest them drink from the river of thy delights. For with thee is the fountain of life; in thy light do we see light.' It is precisely this knowledge of Yahweh's plenitude of light and life which made it possible for the believer to endure the tension which is inherent in his strictly monotheistic conception of God and which may be described by the phrase 'absolute solitude'. It is true that the Israelite knows that the 'heavenly ones', to whom he gives various names including even that of 'sons of God', are

with Yahweh, but he is bound to conclude from his knowledge of the transcendence of God that even these cannot, for Yahweh, be perfect associates. The post-exilic books which are concerned with speculation about wisdom certainly intimate that the life of God must, personally and in itself, be abundantly rich. This reflection about the nature of divine wisdom, which claims to rely upon the support of scriptural texts (see A. Robert, 'Les attaches littéraires bibliques de Prov 1–9', *RB* 43 [1934] 42ff) led, in Prov 8, to a personification of ⁊ wisdom, the significance of which goes beyond a merely poetical expression of the matter-of-fact truth that Yahweh is wise. What is in fact attained in this personification of God's wisdom is the first clear expression of an inspired knowledge of God's personal plenitude of life, even though there is no explicit indication yet of any kind of authentic plural personality in God. This particular passage has, however, been positively identified as one of the Old Testament bases of the New Testament teaching of the *Logos*. The divine ⁊ word was also personified in the Old Testament, though in this case the outline is always fainter and less clearly defined than that which appears in the case of divine wisdom. Nevertheless, we find in Ps 119:89: 'For ever, O Lord, thy word standeth firm in heaven' and the word 'stand' is used in this way in Hebrew with a characteristically personal connotation. The 'word' too is thought of here as a divine herald, standing above all heavenly beings, in which Yahweh's speaking—and at this period the whole of God's connection with the world and with man is contained within the category of divine 'speaking'—acquires precise form and powerful expression. A similar idea is to be found in the following texts: Is 9:7; 55:11; Ps 107:20; 147:15ff; Wis 16:12; 18:14ff. In certain passages, too, Yahweh's ⁄ spirit is personified: in Hag 2:5, his spirit dwells as a protector among the people of Israel; according to Neh 9:30, his spirit warns them through the prophets; in Is 63:10, his spirit is afflicted by the people and according to Wis 1:7, the spirit of the Lord which fills the entire world and embraces the universe has knowledge of every voice. These personifications of God's wisdom, word and spirit should on no account be regarded in the philosophical sense of hypostasisation, but they are, on the other hand, much more than poetic or merely exaggerated literary expressions. They demonstrate the wealth and abundance of the divine life and represent, from the point of view of sacred history, the first tentative and anticipatory movements in the direction of the revelation of the plural personality within the fullness of being of the single divine essence which emerges ultimately in the New Testament as the Trinity.

The Old Testament does not present a complete and self-contained reflected-image of the divine being. What St Paul says about the mysterious and fragmentary knowledge of the image of God (1 Cor 13:12) is applicable to that given in the Old Testament. It is, however, in every way greater than any image that could possibly have been achieved by any human process of intuition, reflection or contemplation in the history of the highest religions or philosophies. The Old Testament image not only

depicts, but also signifies the presence of the God of revelation himself and thus the direct encounter with the 'God of Abraham, Isaac and Jacob' as in Pascal's phrase and consequently with the God who is the Father of Jesus Christ.

Bibliography: H. Schrade, *Der verborgene Gott, Gottesbild und Gottesvorstellung in Israel und im Alten Orient*, Stuttgart 1949; M. Rehm, *Das Bild Gottes im AT*, Würzburg 1951; W. Eichrodt, *Das Gottesbild des AT*, Stuttgart 1956; A. Gelin, 'Le monthéisme d'Israel', *LV* 29 (1956), 9–26; V. Hamp, 'Montheismus im AT', *SP* 1 (1959), 44–56; M. Buber, 'Die Götter der Völker und Gott', *Festschrift O. Michel*, Cologne 1963, 44–57; O. Eissfeldt, 'Jahwe, der Gott der Väter', *TLZ* 88 (1963), 481–90; *H. Renckens, 'The God of Israel', *The Religion of Israel*, London and New York 1967, 97–139.

Alfons Deissler

B. *The Image of God in the New Testament. 1. Jesus and the Image of God in later Judaism*. Jesus and the primitive church did not announce a different God from the God of the Old Testament, but they did proclaim the old God in a new way and in an extended revelation. Nowhere in the New Testament is it possible to find an antithesis to the creator of the world and the God of the covenant (such as the evil demiurge and law-giver of Marcion and other gnostics). It also gives a false and unbalanced picture to portray Jesus's image of God in the soft colours of mildness and pity. Any attempt to tone down the strong and severe aspects of this image results only in a diminution of the background against which the message of God's mercy stands out in brilliant relief.

Jesus presupposes the image of the

God of the Old Testament and judaism in its fullest dimensions. For Jesus God is the creator (Mk 10:6ff; 13:19; see also Jn 17:5-24), the Lord of heaven and earth (Mt 11:25); he is also the God of the patriarchs who spoke to Moses in the burning bush (Mk 12:26; see also Mt 8:11; Lk 16:23ff) and who proclaimed the ten commandments on Mount Sinai (Mk 10:19). It is this same God who must be loved with one's whole heart and one's whole strength (Mk 12:29ff), just as the pious Jew remembered him in his daily recitation of the *šĕmaʾ* ('Hear, O Israel . . .' Deut 6:4ff). He must be served exclusively (Mt 6:24), with an undivided heart (Mt 6:21), in purity (see Mt 5:8; 6:23) and in sincerity (Mk 7:6ff). His commandments take precedence over human laws and institutions (Mk 7:8–13). In all this, Jesus is, in a sense, stricter than the Pharisees. A sublime and pure idea of God reigns in his soul and this conception cannot be tainted by human thought or dragged down to the human level (see Mk 8:33). In later judaism the notion of God's transcendence was greatly heightened by removing his heavenly dwelling place even farther away from earth into the 'third' or 'seventh' heaven and by surrounding his throne by countless heavenly beings and many categories of angels. The feeling of awe for God was also considerably enhanced not only by the strict avoidance of the use of the holy name of God in speech, but also by the employment of substitutes, such as 'the Name' and 'the Place', for the title 'Lord'. Jesus did not seek to lessen in any way this attitude of religious reverence and even makes use himself of this veiled manner of speaking of God by means of words such as 'heaven' (Mt 18:18; Lk 15:7-18, etc: cf the 'authority of heaven' with the 'authority of God'), or 'angels' (Lk 12:8f; 15:10); sometimes using a passive construction (Mt 5:5; 7:8, etc) or the third person plural (Lk 6:38; 12:20; 16:9, etc). But it should be noted that he avoided all scrupulous anxiety and aimed to teach a true reverence by stressing the absolute holiness of God and everything that is associated with him, as against the punctilious and hair-splitting attitude which characterised the pharasaical approach (see Mt 23:16–22). He goes much further than Moses, who proclaimed the laws of God, and the prophets, who emphasised morality in the worship of God, by giving radically new moral commandments in the authority of his messianic mission: 'But I say to you, do not swear at all, either by heaven, for it is the throne of God, or by the earth, for it is his footstool' (Mt 5:34ff). Thus he seizes upon one of the most sublime images for God's transcendent greatness (see Is 66:1) and draws grave moral inferences from it. By continuing: 'Or by Jerusalem, for it is the city of the great King' (cf Ps 48:2), he shows clearly that he also accepts the fact that God dwells among his people, and particularly in the Temple at Jerusalem, just as he does not hold himself personally aloof from the worship of the Temple (eg festivals connected with pilgrimages to Jerusalem, the Passover, etc). Elsewhere he enhances the true reverence for this place where God is particularly close to his people by refusing to tolerate the presence of buyers and sellers in the forecourt of the Temple, who turn the house of God into a 'den of robbers' (Mk 11:17; cf Jer 7:11). To be sure, he envisages the approach of the end of Jewish worship which was required by God for a definite period in the history of salvation, and indeed sees this end as having already come. He will himself build another Temple, 'not made with hands', thus hinting at the eschatological community of God (see Mk 14:58). This new temple is, according to the profound vision of St John, his own person (Jn 2:21ff). The true adoration of the Father 'in spirit and in truth' (Jn 4:23f) is in no way a devotion of a piously individualistic nature and it will surpass the old form of worship in universality, merit and spiritual content.

One of the most exalted features of Jesus's image of God is that of unlimited divine power, which can bring about salvation for mankind or show itself in the form of justice. What Jesus desires is a wholesome fear of the one who has the power to destroy both soul and body in hell (Mt 10:28) and who is able to claim the life of and call to account a rich man who, in his self-satisfaction and complacency, has forgotten God (Lk 12:20). God does whatever he wishes, but his will is exercised in the direction of salvation and mercy (see Mt 20:15). With him, everything is possible—this, indeed is the answer which Jesus gives to the fearful question of the disciples: 'Who then can be saved?' (Mk 10:27). The power of God is shown in his constant activity, but for Jesus the most urgent aspect of this activity is God's work in curing the most deeply concealed of all human maladies, sin. Jesus feels himself to be personally called to co-operate

with the Father in this work and to save man from sin and also from physical infirmities (Jn 5:17; see also 14; Mk 2:1–12 and pars). But God is also the Lord of history and guides it towards the end which he has ordained for it. He has appointed the times and fixed the hours (see Lk 12:56; Acts 1:6f). All that happens is subject to his decree—'This must take place' (Mk 13:7). All that is to happen at the end of time, too, is known only to him and is subject absolutely to his decree: the day and hour are known only to the Father (Mk 13:32). He will, however, shorten the days of eschatological tribulation for the sake of the elect (Mk 13:20). All that can be done is to pray for the coming of God's sovereignty in power and glory (Mt 6:10). It is God alone who bestows positions of honour (Mk 10:40). He has, from the very beginning of the world, 'prepared' the kingdom for his blessed (Mt 25:34) and everlasting fire for Satan and his angels (Mt 25:41). Even in later judaism, this sovereignty of God as the Lord of the world was recognised and humbly submitted to, though the people were still groaning under the rule of Belial (see the Qumran texts). Jesus certainly did not destroy the image of God which was in force at that time, but rather proclaimed the message that the time of God's sovereignty was at hand—the sovereignty which promised salvation and indeed had already brought it (Mk 1:15).

But only those who are converted and who believe in Jesus's saving message are saved. It is not possible to ignore the terrible fate which, according to Jesus's warning, will befall all those who refuse God's offer of grace and mercy in their last hour. With prophetic insight he pronounces judgement on the cities of Galilee that had witnessed so many of his miracles and yet have not been converted. It will be more tolerable for the heathen cities of Tyre and Sidon than for them in the day of judgement (Mt 11:22). Whatever city does not receive his disciples, when they bring his message of the coming of God's sovereignty, will hear the joyous tidings as a threatened judgement: 'I say to you, it shall be more tolerable at that day for Sodom than for that city' (Lk 10:12). The inhabitants of Nineveh will rise up as witnesses for the prosecution against this generation at the last judgement, for they did penance as a result of Jonah's preaching, 'and, behold, something greater than Jonah is here' (Mt 12:41). Indeed, the Son of Man himself will accuse those who did not confess him while he was still on earth (Mk 8:38 and pars).

What is more, the moral obligations of those who wish to participate in God's sovereign rule are related directly to their actions: 'Not every one who says to me, 'Lord, Lord', shall enter the kingdom of heaven; but he who does the will of my Father who is in heaven' (Mt 7:21). The most striking example of the close interrelationship in the New Testament between God's mercy and judgement is provided by the parable of the unforgiving servant (Mt 18:23–35). God is willing to forgive even the greatest debt that man can owe him, and he makes a start by showing boundless mercy. But he expects man to respond to this by showing equal love and pardon towards his fellowmen. Otherwise, his mildness is transformed into a terrible anger. With the same measure that we mete out, God will measure to us (Lk 6:38). In the great scene of judgement (Mt 25:31–46), the question which is asked concerns deeds of charity on behalf of 'the least of the brethren' and those who did not do these will be consigned to the everlasting fire.

All this forms the background to Jesus's message of salvation, but his own personal and essential message is that of a God who is gracious, forgiving and super-abundant in his gifts, and by virtue of this message, Jesus stands out in clear relief against judaism for the first time and presents us with an image of God that had not been revealed up to this point and was indeed almost beyond the understanding of his contemporaries.

2. *The special message of Jesus concerning God.* The word 'father' was frequently applied to God in judaism at the time of Jesus, but he was always thought of as the Father in heaven, or, as in the case of the Jewish prayer, the Eighteen Petitions, in close association with 'our King'. The intention here was to preserve a reverent distance and to avoid any confusion with one's purely physical father here on earth. Jesus, on the other hand, simply took over the word Abba, which was used colloquially by the Jewish child to address his father and 'sounded familiar and disrespectful to His [Jesus's] contemporaries' (G. Kittel), and instructed his disciples to pray to God with an attitude of childlike trust (cf also the form of the Our Father without the words 'in heaven' in Lk 11:2; see also Rom 8:15; Gal 4:6). Elsewhere, too, Jesus speaks in a completely

spontaneous and natural way of 'your' Father, frequently without any direct reference to his own personal relationship with God. These examples show how 'the language of the family circle has been extended to apply to God' (G. Dalman). What Jesus aims to bring home to us by this use of language is the goodness of God and his willingness to forgive us and to grant us a hearing, for in all these respects, God surpasses any human father. Jesus repeatedly makes use of a comparative way of speaking which proceeds from the lesser to the greater: 'If you then, who are evil, know how to give good gifts to your children, how much more will your Father who is in heaven give good things to those who ask him?' (Mt 7:11; see also Lk 11:13). Other examples are the parable of the man who is seeking a hearing with his friend (Lk 11:5-8; the point here is that a hearing is in fact granted) and that of the unjust judge (Lk 18:2-5, and the application of the parable to God, 6-8). Jesus consciously heightens the graphic quality of his parables by drawing boldly on everyday experience, in order to impress upon us the great goodness of God, which is at the same time both human and superhuman. But this father-image of God is not intended simply to help in a general way in religious instruction. It also serves to further Jesus's eschatological message and to clarify the special relationship between Jesus's disciples and God: since we have been called to seek first the kingdom of God, we may safely burden God with all our cares concerning our life and our body, for he knows all our needs (Lk 12:22-31 = Mt 6:25-33). In the Our Father, the petition for our daily bread is subordinate to that which seeks the coming of God's kingdom, and the ceaseless cries of the elect have an effect in bringing about their eventual deliverance from eschatological suffering. Jesus encourages his apostles by telling them that, when they are brought to trial the spirit of their Father will speak through them (Mt 10:20) and that they have no need to fear, for he without whose will not a single sparrow is permitted to fall to the ground, will protect them with his hand (see Mt 10:29-31 = Lk 12:6f).

This close relationship with God is so important for Jesus because it is only when it has been established that real attention will be paid to his message of grace and redemption. God is inconceivably rich in mercy and always ready to call all men, even sinners and 'lost' souls, through Jesus, into his kingdom. The mystery of God's sovereignty is that it is brought closer by Jesus's words and deeds, not in the form of justice, but as saving grace and mercy. To many people of the Jewish world of that time, and in particular to the pharisees, Jesus's message was so outrageous that he was obliged to justify it. Thus he defended his association with publicans and sinners (Mk 2:17 and pars) and, while proclaiming God's mercy in the parables of the Prodigal Son, of the Workers in the Vineyard and of the Pharisee and the Publican, he spoke out against narrow-minded piety. There is a double climax in the parable of the Prodigal Son. In the first part of the parable, Jesus draws a striking and unforgettable picture of the forgiving heavenly Father, who reinstates the son who was 'lost' but who has returned, penitent and converted, to his previous position of privilege. In the second part, the elder son is taught not to criticise his father's attitude (Lk 15:11–24, 25–32). Jesus similarly justifies the goodness of the owner of the vineyard in doing exactly what he likes with regard to the dissatisfied labourers who have toiled throughout the day (Mt 20:1–15). In the parable of the Pharisee and the Publican, he goes even further and launches an attack, and we are told that the penitent publican 'went down . . . justified rather than the other' who bragged so loudly about his works (Lk 18:14; see also Mt 21:31). Jesus is also deliberately harsh in the contrast he makes between the characteristically Jewish attention to literal detail and the approach of the Gentiles who will share in the kingdom of God. Many will come from all over the world and recline at table with the Jewish patriarchs, whereas those who were originally called—the 'sons of the kingdom' —will be cast out into the exterior darkness—excluded, in other words, from the kingdom (Mt 8:11–12 = Lk 13:28ff). The parable of the Marriage Feast too (Mt 22:1–10; cf Lk 14:16–24) contains a polemical climax (the originally intended contrast may have been between the pious and the sinners) which both evangelists who have handed this parable down to us have made clear, each in a different way. In Matthew, we find an allusion to the judgement which will be passed on the Jewish leaders and on Jerusalem (Mt 22:7), whereas St Luke refers to God's call to the Gentiles (Lk 14:23). Jesus's deeds, and especially his forgiveness of sins (see Mk 2:1–12; Lk 7:36–50; Jn 5:14; 8:3–11; also Lk 19:1–10; 23:43),

reaffirm his message of salvation and firmly establish as the central teaching of the Gospel God's offer of unlimited grace and his desire to save the whole universe.

Finally, an essential part of God's goodness and magnanimity is the super-abundant reward which he promises to those who believe his Son's message and who follow him with perseverance. It is a recompense (see Lk 17:7–10) which exceeds all expectations (see Mt 20:1–15). God will, in St Luke's image of the corn-measure, pour a good measure, pressed down, shaken together and running over, into the lap of anyone who follows the commandment to love his neighbour and freely gives what he has to others (Lk 6:38). The disciples who have left everything for Jesus's sake will receive a hundred-fold reward (Mk 10:29ff). The fitting summit to the work of redemption of the God of love is the matchless eschatological reward in which he finally gives himself to the blessed in a state of perfect communion (see Mt 5:8–9).

3. *The image of God of the early church deepened through belief in Christ.* The early church received Jesus's image of God and was also able to work it out more fully after he had fully revealed himself and they had begun to believe in him as their risen and exalted Lord. The early christians followed his teaching on the subject of the Father and his instructions concerning prayer in the spirit of adoption, crying Abba, and were thus able to experience the freedom of the sons of God (Gal 4:6ff; Rom 8:15ff). They became joyously sure of the God whom Jesus had proclaimed as merciful and desirous of man's

redemption through their faith in the blood of Christ and by the power of their new life in the Holy Spirit. They praised him at once as 'God the Father' or as 'God the Father of our Lord Jesus Christ', since he had raised Jesus to the state of Kyrios (see Acts 2:34–36) and every hymn to the Lord Jesus Christ ended (as in Phil 2:11) in the praise of God the Father. God's eternal plan of salvation, which was realised in the temporal sphere by Christ's redemption, was now fully disclosed to the christian community and visibly displayed before its members as a testimony of God's incomprehensible wisdom and goodness, and they praised him in splendid eulogies (Eph 1:3–12), doxologies (Rom 16:25–7; Eph 3:20ff; Jude 24f) and hymns of praise (see especially the Apocalypse). With deep emotion Paul speaks of the unsearchable ways of God's salvation (Rom 11:33–6) and John acknowledges God's perfect love, which conforms essentially to his nature and his alone, and which sent the son to a world enslaved by sin, to be the fundamental principle motivating all his actions (Jn 3:16; 1 Jn 4:8–11; 16). This same God gave 'repentance unto life' (Acts 11:18) to the heathens as well, and his saving grace appeared to all men (Tit 2:11). More than any of the contemporary rulers or emperors, God merits the title of *Sōtēr* ('Saviour'), since his goodness and kindness appeared in Jesus Christ (Tit 3:4). This same God also satisfied the profound longing felt in the Greek world for the need to overcome the transience of the world and to become 'partakers of the divine nature' (2 Pet 1:4). Thus, though it was possible for many gods and many lords to be worshipped at that time, there was, for the christian, 'but one God, the Father, from whom are all things and for whom we exist [are created], and one Lord Jesus Christ, through whom are all things and through whom we exist' (1 Cor 8:6).

The cosmic dimensions of this image of God, however, in no way prevent the primitive church from being loved, guided and heard by the Father of Jesus Christ and of being conscious of this love and guidance and of the hearing which God the Father grants her. Jesus' promise that prayer will be heard by the Father (see Mk 11:23ff and pars), a promise which is, according to Jn 16:26ff, founded on the love of the Father for the disciples of Jesus, was a powerful incentive to the early community to ardent prayer for protection and freedom of action (see the oldest prayer of the christian community: Acts 4:24–30). The triumphant spread of the gospel from Jerusalem to Rome, which was at that time the centre of the known world, forms the principle theme of Acts. From it emerges the deep conviction that God is directing the mission and the history of the church according to a carefully prepared plan. The Apocalypse is only one document which testifies to the great confidence which the church in Asia Minor, already shaken by the first storms of persecution, felt that God nonetheless remained all-powerful and would soon grant victory to the oppressed christian community on earth and give the church power to rule in such a way that the violence and might of evil would be destroyed and God's perfect kingdom would be established.

Faith in God the Father, in Jesus

315

Christ, the Messiah and the Son of God, and in the Paraclete, whom Jesus sent to his own when he had returned to the Father (Jn 16:7) must have finally opened men's eyes to the mystery of the Trinity. There are many indications of the gradual emergence and development of this final divine revelation in the New Testament. The New Testament writers did not define the doctrine of the three persons in one God as such, nor did they reduce it to a doctrinal formula, but they did, however, describe quite clearly the efficacy of the united activity of the three divine persons in the matter of salvation, sometimes in parallel passages (1 Cor 12:4–6; 2 Cor 13:14). Frequently, however, they showed their close cooperation (Jn 14:16ff, 26; 15:26; 16:7–11, 13f) in acts which were directed towards man's salvation and would be realised in the course of the history of salvation: the Father's eternal predestination, the Son's redemption by his blood, the Spirit's gift of life and sanctification (see Eph 1:3–14; 1 Pet 1:2). The Holy Ghost, who is the first fruit of salvation in the eschatological sense and the pledge of the full redemption which is to come (see Rom 8:23; 2 Cor 1:22; 5:5; Eph 1:13ff), is always regarded as the gift of the Father and the life spirit of the risen Son (see Rom 8:9–11; 1 Cor 15:45; 2 Cor 3:17f). Even though the New Testament may lack conceptual clarity, it makes up for this by its remarkable portrayal of the triune God's dynamic action for our salvation. The aim and result of this view of God is a personal, living and constantly developing communion with God and with all those who similarly confess him and are closely associated

with him in love (see Eph 3:14–19; 1 Jn 1:3; 3:24; 4:13).

Bibliography: T. Paffrath, *Gott, Herr und Vater*, Paderborn 1930; W. Koester, 'Der Vater-Gott in Jesu Leben und Lehre', *Scholastik* 16 (1941), 481–95; W. G. Kümmel, 'Der Gottesverkündigung Jesu und der Gottesgedanke des Spätjudentums', *Judaica* 1 (1945), 40–68; V. Warnach, *Agape*, Düsseldorf 1951; E. Lohmeyer, *Das Vaterunser*, Göttingen 1952³; K. Rahner, *Theological Investigations* 1, London and New York 1961, 79–148; J. Jeremias, *Synoptische Studien* (Festschrift A. Wikenhauser), Munich 1954, 86–9; G. Kittel, *TDNT* 1, 5–6; E. Stauffer *TDNT* 111, 90–119; G. Schrenk, *TDNT* v, 978–1014; F. J. Schierse, *LTK* iv², 1078–80; E. Neuhäusler, *Anspruch und Antwort Gottes*, Düsseldorf 1962, 17–36; G. Delling, 'Partizipiale Gottesprädikationen in den Briefen des NT', *ST* 17 (1963), 1–59; W. Marchel, *Abba, Vater!*, Düsseldorf 1963. See also: J. Leipoldt, *Das Gotteserlebnis Jesu im Lichte der vergleichenden Religionsgeschichte* (Angelos-Beiheft 2), 1927; R. A. Hoffmann, *Das Gottesbild Jesu*, Hamburg 1934; T. W. Manson, *The Teaching of Jesus*, Cambridge 1935² (reprinted 1951), 89–170; H. F. D. Sparks, *The Doctrine of the Divine Fatherhood in the Gospels: Studies in the Gospels*, Oxford 1955, 241–62; W. Grundmann, *Die Geschichte Jesu Christi*, Berlin 1957, 65–86.

Rudolf Schnackenburg

Good and evil

The combination 'good and evil' (*tôb warāᶜ*) is often used in the Old Testament, generally in connection with a verb, rarely alone.

We find phrases such as: 'to know good and evil' (with the verb *yādaᶜ*, Gen 2:9–17; 3:5–22; Deut 1:39); 'to distinguish between good and evil' (2 Sam 19:36 with *yādaᶜ*; 1 Kings 3:9 with *bîn*; 2 Sam 14:6 cf Deut 1:16 with *šāmēaᶜ*); 'to refuse the evil and choose the good' (Is 7:15–16); 'to depart from evil and do good' (Ps 34:14; 37:27); 'seek (*dāraš*) good and not evil' (Amos

5:14); 'to hate evil and love good (Amos 5:15; Mic 3:2 the other way round); to do 'good and not harm' (Prov 31:12); to speak neither good nor evil (Gen 24:50); 'to do good or bad' (Num 24:13); 'to speak neither good nor evil' (Gen 31:24–9: 2 Sam 13:22); 'to substitute a good for a bad' (Lev 27:10); 'to value as either good or bad' (Lev 27:12, 14); 'to inquire whether it is good or bad' (Lev 27:33); to return 'evil for good' (1 Sam 25:21; Prov 17:13; see also Jer 18:20; Ps 35:12; 38:20). The two words can also stand by themselves: 'good or evil' (Num 13:19; Jer 42:6); 'not good but evil' (1 Kings 22:8, 18; cf Ps 52:5); 'good and evil' (Deut 30:15; Is 5:20; Jer 39:16; 44:27; Lam 3:38; Job 30:26).

Perhaps the most important use of the combination 'good and evil' occurs in the theological etiology of sin and fallenness where it plays a fundamental and decisive role. The whole account is centred on 'the tree of the knowledge of good and evil' (Gen 2:9–17; 'of good and evil' as object of the infinitive used substantively is syntactically awkward and therefore probably an addition which anticipates the *dénouement*; see also 3:5–22). The fruit of this tree is forbidden under pain of death (Gen 2:17; 3:5–11, 13); 'the knowledge of good and evil' is a rather protean phrase; its purpose is, as Quell puts it, 'rather to conceal than to reveal'. It derives from the theological and psychological reflection of the teachers of wisdom in Israel who had given long thought to the enigma of sin. The cunning serpent dangled before the woman the prospect of a godlike knowledge: 'God knows that when you eat of it your eyes will be opened, and you will be like God, knowing good and evil' (Gen 3:5). After the sin had been committed God exclaimed: 'Behold, the man has become like one of us, *knowing good and evil*' (3:22). By knowing good and evil, therefore, man becomes godlike. This raises a twofold question: (a) what is meant here by *knowledge*; and (b) what are we to understand by 'good and evil?' In order to answer these difficult questions we shall have to refer to the relevant texts which are susceptible of more than one explanation. Hence the difficulty and ambiguity in interpreting the meaning of this combination.

a. *The kind of knowledge implied*. As can be seen from the name of the tree and the context as a whole, eating of its fruit gives knowledge which our first parents actually acquired as a result of their sin (Gen 3:11–13, 22). As is clear from what the Serpent, Eve and God say, it is a divine kind of knowledge. The Serpent tempts them by saying 'you will be like God' (3:5). The beauty of the tree seduces the woman's heart: 'the tree was good for food and a delight to the eyes and to be desired to make one wise (*lehaśkîl*)' (3:6). This verb in the causative means 'to make wise or clever' (cf Deut 32:29; Is 41:20; Jer 9:23; 23:5; Ps 119:98) and is more often than not used in parallelism with the noun *da'ath* (knowledge). So, for example, Jeremiah promises for the messianic age: 'I will give you shepherds after my own heart, who will feed you with knowledge (*da'ath* and understanding (*haśkêl*)' (Jer 3:15; cf Dan 1:17; Job 34:35). It follows therefore that 'knowledge' in Gen 2-3 refers first and foremost to an *interior and spiritual process*. This is confirmed in the words spoken by God: 'Behold, the man has become *like one of us*' (3:22). This kind of knowledge is the exclusive privilege of the elohim, those within the divine sphere. By taking of the forbidden fruit man hoped to attain to this higher knowledge and so become like the elohim.

But if the main emphasis is on intellectual knowledge the experiential aspect could hardly be absent for men of that time living in the ancient Near East. Hence it refers also to an experience which irrupted into human life after the fall ('their eyes were opened', 3:5–7) and was to be characteristic of the existential distress in which man now lives. It was this dark aspect of the preferred knowledge which the Serpent withheld from the woman.

It was a rather perverted aberration on the part of liberal exegesis to interpret this knowledge as the awakening of sexual desire and awareness of sexual differentiation which our first parents achieved by having intercourse either in defiance of a divine prohibition (Clement of Alexandria) or before arriving at sexual maturity (H. Gunkel and J. Guitton). The sexual interpretation is excluded purely on the grounds of vocabulary: the verb 'to know' is of course used in some texts as a euphemism for sexual congress (Gen 4:1–17; Judg 11:39; 1 Sam 1:19 etc) but there is all the difference in the world between the man 'knowing' the woman or knowing good and evil. There are no grounds in the text for identifying the two; in fact, there is no specification at all with regard to the object of knowledge.

The attempt was also made to prove the same thing on the basis of inter-

preting 'good and evil' in terms of the experience of sexual passion (H. Schmidt). Against this is the fact that *tôb* (good) never has a sexual connotation in the Old Testament. Such an interpretation, which held the field for a long time, has 'a far too strong dash of sentimentality about it' (G. Quell in *TDNT* I, 284). The kind of knowledge referred to here is on the spiritual level. Through these chapters there blows the clean air of faith in Yahweh and we hear a note reminiscent of the Song of Songs and the love between the bridegroom and the spouse.

Whether the internal and spiritual sin was externalised in some sexual way is of purely marginal importance and in any case can no longer be determined. The essence of the first sin is not touched at all by this possibility.

b. '*Good and evil*'. The phrase 'good and evil' points in a different direction from the views discussed above; it points upwards not downwards. Since according to Old Testament usage the combination is susceptible of more than one interpretation we find different views on the kind of spiritual activity referred to. We cannot solve the problem purely on the basis of vocabulary and the meaning of the words; we have to look at the context and at parallel passages in the Old Testament. In any case these differing interpretations have at least one good thing in common, that unlike the sexual interpretation they all start out from specifically scriptural data.

1. According to some exegetes the Yahwist understood 'the knowledge of good and evil' as the awakening of the intellect or of moral consciousness (P. Humbert). These exegetes refer to

certain texts which speak of children arriving at 'the knowledge of good and evil' explained as the ability to differentiate between what is sweet and bitter, pleasant and unpleasant, useful and harmful and above all between what is morally good and evil (cf Deut 1:39; Is 7:15f). The old man, on the contrary, is no longer able to distinguish between good and evil or, in other words, 'taste what he eats and what he drinks' (2 Sam 19:35; cf Lev 27:10, 12, 14, 33 where the reference is to the good and bad qualities of the sacrificial animals).

On the basis of these texts the same meaning is given to the phrase 'good and evil' in Gen 2–3. But this conclusion is quite clearly false. From the fact that the phrase has this meaning in the texts adduced it does not follow at all that it must have the same meaning in Gen 2–3. On the contrary, the immediate and wider context does not support this interpretation. The power of reason and moral consciousness were not first acquired by Adam and Eve after they had eaten the fruit since both are presupposed necessarily for the responsible action which they performed. It would hardly have been reasonable of God to impose on them a prohibition under pain of the most severe penalties if they had been incapable of acting as responsible beings. If they could only grasp the meaning and import of the prohibition *after the fall* he would have been the most cruel of tyrants to impose it in the first place.

The entire narrative reveals that the first parents are represented as anything but immature and innocent children. God put man in the garden so that he might cultivate it (2:15). The

man gave to each animal a name corresponding to its properties (2:20a). The bringing together of the animals to the man did not, however, produce the desired result; only in the woman did he recognise a helper fit for him (2:23–4). God then laid upon him the prohibition of eating of the tree of knowledge (2:17). It is clear from all this that the Yahwist is thinking of a grown man in the full possession of his spiritual and moral capacities.

Further, in these two chapters ʾadam is correctly translated by 'man' (2:7, 8, 15, 16, 19–23, 25; 3:8, 9, 12, 20–2, 24) and the aetiological explanation of the narrative has recognised correctly that the Yahwist is here expressing something of permanent validity on the nature of man, the close relation between man and woman, sin, evil tendencies, sorrow, the burden of work and the inescapable fact of death. Hence it is clear that in speaking of 'the knowledge of good and evil' he cannot be referring to the development of reason or moral consciousness but rather to sinful knowledge possessed by a grown man.

2. For this reason other exegetes explain 'good and evil' as universal knowledge (eg H. Junker, G. von Rad, P. van Imschoot). They appeal to certain texts where the two opposite terms found in combination refer to a totality in either a positive or negative sense, either 'all' or 'nothing'. So, for example, David seems to the wise woman of Tekoa to be 'like the angel of God to discern good and evil' (2 Sam 14:17) which is further explained in v 20 in that she attributes to David a wisdom 'like the wisdom of the angel of God to know all things that are on

the earth'. The expression: 'to speak neither good nor evil' means to say nothing at all (Gen 24:50) as also 'to say nothing of either good or evil' (Gen 31:24–9; 2 Sam 13:22).

Purely on the grounds of vocabulary one could attribute this meaning of universal knowledge to the expression as used in Gen 2–3. But we must not overlook the fact that the man after his sin really did not attain to such knowledge which the exclamation of God in 3:22 would have led us to expect. Further, the knowledge of good and evil understood as universal knowledge is too exclusively intellectual. The Hebrew verb 'to know' always has the idea of concrete experience of some kind or other. He who knows something or gives a name to something has gained power over it and can exert influence on it. This means that the man did not achieve any effectual knowledge of 'good and evil' since, according to the narrative, nature and the animal kingdom turn against him (3:15, 17–19). Finally, according to the context as a whole, it is not so much a question of universal knowledge as of a knowledge which enables one to distinguish and differentiate.

Other exegetes have taken account of the experiential character of this 'knowledge'. They restrict 'knowledge of good and evil' to what is either useful or harmful, sweet or bitter, healthy or unhealthy or even in a general way to cultural progress (J. Wellhausen and G. Quell). But the general feel of the narrative is quite alien to the question of the progress of civilisation and intends only to describe in dark colours the irruption of evil into the lives of the first parents and the escalation of sin

in their descendants. And quite apart from this the expression always takes in the idea of a moral dichotomy especially in those texts which speak of a distinction between good and evil (eg Deut 1:39; 30:15; 2 Sam 19:35; 1 Kings 3:9; Is 7:15f; Amos 5:14f; Mic 3:2; Eccles 12:14). Though it is not stated explicitly, this also applies to Gen 2–3. The man is confronted with a choice between obedience and disobedience, paying attention to the divine prohibition of eating from the tree or neglecting it. The expression 'good and evil' fits this situation very well.

3. This is the direction in which we are to look for a solution. What is at issue is not the gift or talent for differentiating or discernment but the *ability* to do so. The man strives for a *divine* knowledge as the serpent promised the woman: 'you will be like God' (3:5) and as God himself states: 'Behold, the man has become like one of us' (3:22). He was no longer happy to live under the moral guidance of God but wanted to decide autonomously what was for him morally good and morally evil. What he aimed at therefore was *moral autonomy*. Certainly, the man had to decide freely between good and evil but this decision was to be made under divine guidance. When a judge has to make a decision between two parties in a question of law he too decides between good and evil according to the norms of law. He does not make the decision autonomously but in dependence on basic principles laid down by God; he does not act purely on his own initiative, at his own good pleasure, but in accordance with the will of God (see 1 Kings 3:9). By his sinful deed the man

turns the basic principles of good and evil upside down. What is good he calls evil and what is evil he calls good according to his own good pleasure (cf Is 5:20; Amos 5:14–15). Sin is the reversal of basic values. R. de Vaux remarks appositely: 'En se prenant eux-mêmes pour mesure, ils ont commis une faute de démesure' (*RB* 56 [1949], 340), and the same view is expressed in other words by H. Renckens, A-M Dubarle, and other authors.

The striving for moral independence really implies arrogating to oneself a prerogative which is superhuman and divine, one that belongs to God alone. By so striving man usurps to himself a 'knowledge' which lies at the root of all sin. In each evil deed that he commits he grasps at the forbidden fruit *sub specie boni*; but as with the first man bitter disappointment is quick to follow.

The sin of 'knowing good and evil' took place deep in the soul of the first parents. It was an internal and original experience. Instigated by the serpent they attempted to be 'like God' (3:5–22) in a limitless autonomy. They were guilty of the sin of pride, of arrogance beyond measure, of *hubris* as were, later on in the narrative, those who began to build the tower of Babel (11:1–9).

In keeping with the literary genre of this narrative, psychologically perceptive and theologically profound as it is, this teacher of genius presents 'the tree of the knowledge of good and evil' as figurative of a spiritual reality, as we have attempted to demonstrate above. How did he come by this symbol? Though this tree of life is in some respects reminiscent of the 'plant of life' or 'tree of life' found in Mesopotamian mythology (for example, in

the Gilgamesh epic) it is really without parallel. We must attribute it to the creative power of the Yahwist himself.

The texts do not allow us to arrive at any certain conclusion as to the external form which this spiritual sin took. We are only told that it was committed by both the man and the woman (3:6b).

Bibliography: H. D. A. Major, 'The Tree of the Knowledge of Good and Evil', *Expository Times* 20 (1909), 427–8; H. Gunkel, *Genesis*, Göttingen 1964[6]; H. Schmidt, *Die Erzählung von Paradies und Sündenfall*, Tübingen 1931; H. Junker, *Die biblische Urgeschichte*, Bonn 1932; P. Humbert, *Etudes sur le récit du Paradis et de la chute dans la Genèse*, Neuchatel 1940, 82–116 (see the review of A. Bea, *Bbl* 25 [1944], 81f); L. J. Kuyper, 'To Know Good and Evil', *Interpr.* 1 (1947), 490–2; J. Coppens, *La Connaissance du bien et du mal et le Péché du Paradis*, Bruges-Paris-Louvain 1948; J. Guitton, *Le Développement des Idées dans l'Ancient Testament*, Aix-en-Provence 1947; M. Buber, *Good and Evil, two Interpretations*, New York 1953: J. Engnell, '"Knowledge" and "Life" in the Creation Story', Suppl. *VT* 3 (1955), 103–19; W. Buchanan, 'The Old Testament Meaning of the Knowledge of Good and Evil', *JBL* 75 (1956), 114–20; Bo Reicke, 'The Knowledge hidden in the Tree of Paradise', *JSS* 1 (1956), 193–201; R. Gordis, 'The Knowledge of Good and Evil in the Old Testament and the Qumran Scrolls', *JBL* 76 (1957), 123–38; I. de Fraine, 'Jeux de mots dans le récit de la chute', *Mélanges Bibliques A. Robert*, Paris 1957, 47–59; H. S. Stern, 'The Knowledge of Good and Evil', *VT* 8 (1958), 407f; H. Renckens, *Urgeschichte und Heilsgeschichte: Israels Schau in die Vergangenheit nach Gen 1–3*, Mainz 1961[2], 240–4; A-M. Dubarle, 'La Tentation dans le jardin d'Eden. Genèse 3:1–6', *LV* 53 (1961), 13–20; Haag 412–13; *DEB* 342–4 (H. Renckens); *DBT* 101–5 (H. de Vaux); G. von Rad I, 154ff; Imschoot II, 288–90.

Robert Koch

Goodness

A. *In the general sense*, Yahweh's goodness was a fact which was always strikingly evident in the history of the Israelites. Whether it goes back to the original revelation made to the Hebrews, or whether its source is to be found in the powerful divine acts which were manifested in the Exodus, what is certain is that all the biblical texts refer to God's goodness, either directly or by implication. Yahweh is the good, kind and benign one who shows his favour and benevolence to his people, and does this by virtue of their election and of the covenant. The full revelation of God's goodness is certainly not finally established in the earliest books—these merely mark the end of the first, pre-literary stage in the progressive revelation of the divine nature and the gradual intensification of the collective and individual relationship which was growing up between the people of Israel and their God. In the course of this gradual development, fresh aspects of goodness in the biblical sense are all the time being brought to light, providing an essential contribution towards progress in man's relation to God.

B. *The concept of divine goodness.* No clear or theologically well developed concept of divine goodness can be found in the earliest books of the bible. The word which is most commonly used to include all aspects of goodness is the Hebrew *tôb.* In its original meaning, it was probably used mainly to denote sense perceptions and then, in an extension of meaning, to include higher perceptions. In the historical books of the Old Testament, however, *tôb* is found especially in connection with ethical judgements and aesthetic assessments—even in the account of the creation, God's work is described as *tôb* (see *Mélanges Bibliques A. Robert*, Paris

1957, 22–6). On the one hand, this predicative use of *tôb* usually implies God's beneficent acts, leading to the well-being of the people, while, on the other hand, it can apply to anything which is fitting or morally good (here it is synonymous with the Hebrew *yāsār:* 1 Sam 12:23 etc). The idea of essential goodness underlies all these different shades of meaning, and this basic idea is contrasted with that of evil (ra^c). *Tôb*—in the sense of a state of absolute goodness—is, of course, applied exclusively to God, and, in the New Testament too, it is to him alone that this absolute quality of goodness can be truthfully applied (Mt 19:17; Mk 10:18; Lk 18:19; see also W. Wagner, *ZNW* 8 [1907], 143–61). The Hebrew word *ḥesed* expresses goodness in a more concrete form, in the sense of divine favour and God's loyal readiness to give help, particularly in connection with the covenant made on Mount Sinai. Whenever Yahweh is powerfully affected by his people's distress—or by the distress of a single individual—he exercises his *raḥ^{a}mîm* (*raḥûm*), or mercy, and this appears as his divine favour and finds expression in concrete acts of beneficence. Even when the Israelites are forgetful of God's goodwill (*ḥēn*) and turn away from their benefactor, God does not resort to judgement and punishment, but waits with patient forbearing (*'erek appîm*) until they are converted.

The earliest Greek translators of the Old Testament seem to have set themselves the special task of determining the many shades of meaning contained in the generalised use of the word *tôb,* and they must take the credit for having established the bases of a real theology of goodness by employing the word *khrēstotēs* (goodness) in the context of revelation. *Khrēstos* (good) is derived from *khraomai* (to use, to be of use, to refer to, to have relations with), and its original meaning was certainly that of usefulness or sociability. But, from the very beginning, the word also conveyed the sense of moral excellence, with the result that *khrēstotēs*, which was coined at a later stage and had a meaning which was distinct from that of the original *khrēstos*, managed to combine the idea of moral perfection and sublimity with that of friendliness and loving kindness. As an honorary title and as an epithet used to describe a sovereign ruler—though probably never in the profane sense—*khrēstotēs* was particularly suitable for the purpose of conveying the fullness of divine *tôb* towards men. To convey God's absolute state of goodness, however, the early Greek translators naturally had recourse to the word *agathos*. In addition, however, they also introduced a second, purely biblical word, *agathōsunē*. This word contains the same subtle shades of meaning as *khrēstotēs*, but points rather more clearly in the direction of God's quality of goodness and uprightness (see Jerome, *PL* 26,420). In contrast to this, *philanthrōpia* (human kindness in general) and *epieikeia*, which signifies a lenient and forbearing attitude of mind, were introduced into the bible, but played only an insignificant part in it, because of their close associations with the whole heathen way of life.

Although *benignitas* as used in the Vetus Latina corresponds exactly to the Greek *khrēstotēs*, the Latin tradition nevertheless preferred 'sweetness' (*dul-cedo* or *suavitas*: see Jerome's definition, *PL* 26,420) to emphasise the intimate nature of man's experience of God's goodness (perhaps with reference to Ps 34:8; see also 1 Pet 2:2-3). Nowadays we tend to think of *khrēstotēs* as having lost much of its original and deeply theological significance, and as having become to some extent debased in meaning—this false conception of a sweet and sentimental bearing on the part of God can be traced back to the use, in the Vulgate and elsewhere, of the word *sweetness*. Jerome's later translation of the psalms—'Versio Piana'—was far more sober in this respect and, going back to the original Hebrew, has replaced these traditional shades of meaning by the more consistent use of the words *bonus* (good) and *bonitas* (goodness) and, in a few instances, by *benignus* (kind) and *benefaciens* (beneficent).

C. *The theology of goodness.* 1. *In the Old Testament and in later judaism.* Theological speculation concerning the nature of Yahweh's goodness began at a very early date. This is demonstrated, for example, in the formula used in the worship of Yahweh in Ex 34:6: 'The Lord, the Lord, a God merciful and gracious, slow to anger, and abounding in steadfast love and faithfulness' (see also *Bbl* 38 [1957], 130–50). Frequent use is made of technical formulae of this kind in later texts (see Ps 86:15; 103:8; 145:8; Joel 2:13; Jonah 4:2; Neh 9:17). God's mercy and his faithful readiness to help his people are, however, forcefully stressed in the earlier biblical texts, and are regarded as that particular form of goodness which the people of God clearly remembered from the time of the Exodus and the birth of the nation of Israel. The historical books of the Old Testament, with their particular literary form, were also, of course, less well suited to the function of detailed theological speculation on the subject of Yahweh's goodness.

It is in the *Psalms* that the first true theology of divine goodness appears. It is possible to make a general statement to the effect that divine goodness is present in the psalms as a *basic law of God's providence*. At the one extreme, it appears in the most general form, promising mercy to all creatures (Ps 145:9), while at the other extreme it appears in a more concrete form, giving an assurance of positive help in every necessity. When God shows his goodness, all living creatures are overwhelmed with gifts, but when he turns his face away from them, their well-being is transformed into affliction and even into ruin (Ps 104:28–9). It is, however, the proofs of God's goodness towards men which provide the most common motive for thanksgiving in the psalms. With the passage of time, an appropriate formula was perfected, and this may have played a very important part in the worship of the people: 'Give thanks to the Lord, for he is good; for his steadfast love endures for ever' (Ps 106:1; 107:1; 136:1, etc). These proofs of Yahweh's goodness were, of course, shown particularly to the chosen people. The fullness of divine goodness was reserved for them, even though, in Ps 100:1–5, all the earth is called upon to praise God for his goodness.

It is in Yahweh's glorious acts, during his people's wanderings in the desert, in which he showed his great power, that we find the essence of divine good-

ness in the Old Testament and, at the same time, the most frequent motive for his people's praise of him. These divine acts reveal the superabundance of Yahweh's goodness. He shows his omnipotence, together with his goodness, in preserving his chosen people. Divine goodness is often portrayed as the favour and compassion of a king or ruler—in Ps 65:11, Yahweh is seen as a king who travels throughout the land in his chariot, dispensing blessings upon it. Divine goodness has this special attribute—it cares particularly for the weak and the persecuted, and, in so doing, it assumes the quality of a protective grace which first of all delivers the subject from a desperate situation and then grants protection from further persecution (Ps 31:20). An angel of God pitches his camp round about those who fear the Lord in order to protect them from danger of any kind. This causes the psalmist to cry out enthusiastically: 'O taste, and see that the Lord is good!' (Ps 34:8–9). The religious man is so certain of God's goodness that his thanksgiving follows directly upon his prayer of petition, as if he had already experienced the effects of divine goodness (Ps 31:18–20, and elsewhere).

Even the *sinner* is not excluded from God's goodness, so long as he is ready to repent and places his trust in God's mercy. Because of his goodness, God is not only willing to forget the sins and misdeeds committed earlier in life (Ps 25:6f); he is also ready to set the sinner, by means of the Law, which is a particular gift of divine goodness, on the right path (Ps 119:41–72).

In the psalms, the two poles between which the goodness of God is operative are his immense mercy and his justice, though no tension exists between these two divine attributes, nor are they placed in antithesis. Despite Yahweh's goodwill towards man, it is always upright, and would seem, in fact, to be a special work of divine ↗ justice, through which God fulfils his promise, made under the covenant, in so magnanimous a way.

It is in the *later books of the Old Testament*, however, that a *change of mood with regard to divine goodness* is, for the first time, clearly perceptible. Captivity and the loss of independence led to a tension between God's power and his goodness which was previously quite unknown. What is expressed with increasing frequency in these last books is the inaccessibility of God: 'O Lord God, Creator of all things, dreadful and strong, just and merciful, who alone art the good king' (2 Macc 1:24). Divine goodness is also praised indirectly as ↗ wisdom (Wis 7:30).

If we leave on one side the biblical texts which were influenced by hellenistic thought, it becomes obvious that the idea of *human goodness*, as opposed to divine goodness, is relatively little developed in the Old Testament. Yahweh is essentially good. Man, on the other hand, is good only in a very limited sense. Ps 14:3 expresses this conviction clearly: 'They are all alike corrupt; there is none that does good, no, not one'. The same thought is even more clearly expressed in the apocryphal Psalms of Solomon: 'the goodness of man is grudging and is shown only for the sake of reward and it is an admirable thing when man shows his goodness again and again without murmuring' (Ps Sol 5:13 [15]).

Human goodness is, in fact, overshadowed by the all-embracing favour and compassion of God, which is too sublime for man to imitate. It calls for recognition—and this plays a decisive part in man's moral formation. The Qumran texts provide a fairly well-developed theology of goodness, in the form of instructions concerning human conduct, and the whole bears a striking resemblance to the Pauline notion of *khrēstotēs*. In the list of the attributes of the Spirit of Light, which is part of the teaching on the Two Spirits, in addition to mercy (*raḥªmîm*) and patience (*ʾerek ʾappayîm*), there is also 'eternal goodness' (*tôb ʿôlāmîm*) (1 QS IV, 3), which is closely connected with a humble attitude. The communal life of the sect obviously also required this of its members. This 'eternal goodness' should also be compared with the frequently recurring phrase 'merciful love' (*ʾâhābat ḥesed*). But the feeling of 'eternal hatred' for the sons of injustice (1 QS 4:17) certainly indicates that the spiritual delineation of goodness given in the Qumran texts shows distinctly Old Testament features and a colouring which is peculiar to later judaism.

2. *The New Testament.* The great advance in the concept of goodness shown in the New Testament is intimately connected with the deeper penetration into the nature and essence of God given us in Jesus Christ. In the New Testament, the effects of divine goodness are no longer to be found in good actions, blessings or as protective graces—God's goodness is entirely concentrated upon man's salvation and the events connected with it. The gospels outline the close relationship between divine goodness and the new

325

life in Christ, whereas the letters of Peter and Paul tend rather to portray the part played by God's goodness in the history of salvation.

It is almost possible to state that divine goodness can now be applied to those who were excluded from God's love in the Old Testament. Those who are hostile to God, those who are ungrateful, hardened sinners—all such people have a special, prior claim to God's goodness in the New Testament. The commandment to hate, which was clearly formulated in the law of the Qumran sect (1 QS 1:9ff, and elsewhere), and which is continually inculcated in the Old Testament, is finally overcome in the New Testament by the Father's *khrēstotēs* and the new relation of *agapē* (love: Lk 6:35). The 'easy' yoke of Christ, which Jesus calls upon all who are weary from the burden of the law to bear (Mt 11:30) expresses the same idea. Only one condition is imposed upon those who wish to be able to experience the full goodness of this new yoke, and that is that they must take it up in the same attitude of humility and gentleness as Jesus, when he took it from his father.

The *crowning biblical-theological definition of goodness is to be found in Paul's letters.* The Old Testament conception of God's goodness is still clearly perceptible in the Letter to the Romans, although it appears in quite new proportions, in view of the now completed work of redemption. In a vigorous diatribe, Paul strikes out at the typical Jew who, in his self-righteousness, mistakenly interprets the most shining examples of God's goodness as a reluctance to punish. A similar attitude arising from a wrong way of thinking

about divine goodness or a scornful attitude towards it is a basic sin against goodness (Rom 2:4). The consequences of such an attitude may well be disastrous for the sinner—in his severity, God may ultimately reject him (Rom 11:22).

It is only in his later epistles that Paul has fully embodied goodness into the organic whole of the plan of salvation, and he achieves this by presenting the entire plan of divine redemption in function of God's goodness. The two most important historical moments in this plan are the manifestation of divine goodness (Tit 3:4), that is, the moment of Christ's birth, and the perfection of divine goodness in the time which is to come (Eph 2:7). Human life flows between these two points of time and undergoes a process of maturation within the context of the goodness which is revealed in Jesus Christ.

A harmonious relationship has already been established between God and man in the preaching of Jesus, in that the new man seeks to imitate the goodness of God. Paul is obviously convinced that it is quite within the reach of every christian, by virtue of his union with his Lord and Master, to realise this goodness to a high degree in his own life. This idea underlies all Paul's lists of virtues in which he recommends goodness, although the contexts, in which occur also humility, gentleness, mercy and patience, are still reminiscent of what we find in the Old Testament, and, above all, in later judaism. This goodness is frequently given a more concrete form by being placed in close proximity to agape; the clearest example is to be found in Paul's hymn to love, in which goodness appears as an essential attribute of charity (1 Cor 13:4; cf Eph 4:32; Col 3:12). The position of goodness among the fruits of the Spirit testifies to the importance which Paul attaches to it (Gal 5:22; see also 1 QS IV, 2f—although, from the theological point of view, there are basic differences here). It is the new vital principle, brought about by the Holy Spirit.

In Paul's view, then, goodness is an essential part of the christian way of life. It provides the new man, the man of Christ, with the sensitivity and delicacy of feeling with which he is able to enter into the mind and spirit of others. Its possession of course presupposes a high degree of moral maturity in man. While the Greek and gentile world held that this quality was apparent above all in rulers and outstanding personalities, it is clear from the New Testament that from this time onwards all men were called to share in the sublimity of the divine life and thus to practise goodness in the full, christian sense. It is possible to do full justice to the quality of goodness only when its chief function is regarded as a radiation of charity. Viewed in this way, not only does the active and utterly spontaneous nature of goodness become at once apparent—it is also possible to perceive its intimate relationship with ↗ agape.

D. *Systematic theology of goodness.* In the bible, the theology of goodness is developed progressively. This line of development can be traced without a break from the earliest stages of divine revelation, through the culminating point of Christ's revelation and onwards to its effects on the whole of human life. In the first place, God's paternal goodness was responsible for the creation of the universe. Man himself, and all the gifts with which he was endowed in his original state, resulted from this goodness, and God's plan of salvation was carried out, after man's first fall, above all as a direct consequence of God's goodness. It is to God's initial impulse to save mankind and to all the various concrete forms of his goodness which subsequently came into being—the law, the mission of the prophets, his assistance in every kind of distress—that we owe his mercy, which constitutes the principal form of divine goodness towards fallen man. Even in the Old Testament, goodness, although it reveals itself only gradually, already points clearly to Christ—the fullness of time coincides with that moment in history when divine goodness is bestowed upon mankind in its most perfect form. Christ undertook to offer the sacrifice of goodness to the Father in order to set a seal upon the new covenant of love. The way of Christ's goodness leads from the mystery of the Incarnation—that vital decision of the Trinity—through the goodness of his earthly life up to his death on the Cross and his glorification. In his act of salvation, Christ has revealed the meaning of goodness, as it is progressively revealed in the bible, by realising in his own life its every single feature, both divine and human. Furthermore, the fact that goodness prevails within the Trinity is disclosed in the person of Jesus Christ. That Christ's goodness is the mark of his communion with the Father is forcibly demonstrated in the theology of Paul, who points out how this goodness is derived from the Father who is its source and how it was realised in history, so that it might be conferred on men by the Holy Spirit. The spirit of Christ's goodness guides the life of the church and is renewed in her members. This will continue until the mystery of salvation is consummated at the end of time.

Bibliography: R. C. Trench, *Synonyms of the New Testament*, London 1901; A. Vögtle, *Die Tugend- und Laster-Kataloge im Neuen Testament* (*NA* xvi, 4/5), Münster 1936; J. Ziegler, *Dulcedo Dei* (*AA* xiii/2), Münster 1937; C. Spicq, 'Bénignité, mansuétude, douceur, clémence', *RB* 54 (1947), 321–39; C. L. Mitton, 'Motives for goodness in the New Testament', *Expository Times* 63 (1951/2), 360–4; J. B. Bauer, *BL* 19 (1951/2), 73–5; L. R. Stachowiak, *Chrestotes, ihre biblisch-theologische Entwicklung und Eigenart* (Studia Friburgensia NF 17), Freiburg/Schwaben 1957; A. I. Mennessier, 'Douceur', *Dictionnaire de la Spiritualité* iii, 1674–85 (Volume xxiv, 1957); J. Chatillon, 'Dulcedo', *Dictionnaire de la Spiritualité*, iii, 1777–95 (Volume xxiv, 1957); Eichrodt 232ff; S. Wibbing, *Die Tugend- und Laste-kataloge im NT* (*ZNW* 25), Berlin 1959, esp. 46–105; C. Spicq, *Agape* ii, Paris 1959, 379–91; W. Barclay, *Flesh and Spirit*, London 1962, 97–102; K. Winkler, 'Clementia', *RAC* iii, 206–31; Suitbert H. Siedl, *Qumran—eine Mönchsgemeinde im Alten Bund*, Rome 1963, 195–209.

F. L. R. Stachowiak

Gospel

A. *The meaning of the word.* In classical Greek, *euangelion* signified everything connected with a *euangelos*, or bearer of good news (Aeschylus, *Agamemnon*, 646ff), whose *euangelion* could apply both to the glad tidings which he carried to other people or to the reward which he received for performing his task (Homer, *Odyssey* 14, 152ff; 166ff). The word was especially used to denote a message announcing a victory. Its religious connotation was derived from its oracular usage, in which connection it signified a divine utterance (Plutarch, *Sert* 11), and from its use in emperor-worship. As the emperor was regarded as a divine being and the bearer of salvation (*sōtēr*), everything which referred in any way to him was included in the category of *euangelion*. The news of his birth, of his ascension to the throne and even of his imperial decrees were all joyous messages.

Hellenistic Jewish writers such as Philo and Josephus, also used the word in this sense (Schniewind 78–112) and it is even found in the Septuagint with the same profane meaning (2 Sam 18:20, 25, 27; 2 Kings 7:9; Jer 20:15, and elsewhere). Whenever it is found in the New Testament, however, it is used neither in the pagan, hellenistic sense, nor with the meaning with which it is associated in lxx. The New Testament uses the word in the sense in which it, or its Hebrew equivalent (*bāśar*, and the noun *b'śôrâh*), is employed in Deutero–Isaiah and texts depending on him (Nahum 1:15; Ps 68:11; 96:2; Ps Sol 11:2)—thus signifying the news that the time of salvation is at hand. The bearer of glad tidings is the herald who speeds on ahead of Yahweh's triumphal procession, proclaiming his victory and announcing to Sion: 'Your God reigns' (Is 52:7). The time of salvation is actually made present by the very fact of its proclamation. This conception of the bearer of good tidings and his message of salvation persisted as a vital reality also in Palestinian judaism (see the targum on Is 40:9; SB iii, 8–11).

B. *The gospel as an eschatological message of joy in the New Testament.* Jesus claimed for himself the office of bearer of the eschatological message of joy when he replied to John the Baptist's question: 'Art you he who is to come?' (Mt 11:3; see also Lk 1:22) and when he preached in the synagogue in Nazareth (Lk 4:16–21). Whereas in the case of emperor-worship in the Greco-Roman world the joyous tidings look back to an event which has already taken place, the gospel looks forward to something which is still to come. The message of Jesus is of this type (see Mk 1:14ff). The underlying theme of his preaching is the coming of the ⁄ kingdom of God (see Lk 4:43; Mk 1:38; Mt 4:23; 9:35; 24:14). In the rest of the New Testament, however, the word 'gospel' is generally not used in this original, 'biblical' sense (one exception is Acts 8:12; the word does not occur at all in John). This may be attributed to the fact that the early christians were fully conversant with the idea of Jesus not simply as the herald of the kingdom of God, but also as the embodiment of the gospel itself. This idea was, of course, based on their knowledge of his manifest work of salvation, and the word itself underwent a change of meaning—'gospel' no longer implied a proclamation of salvation to come, but an announcement of salvation already present. The central theme, then, of the preaching of the apostles is Jesus himself and his work of redemption (Acts 5:42; 8:35; 11:20). This is particularly so in the case of Paul, who uses the word far more frequently than any of the other New Testament writers (eg Rom 1:9; 15:20; 1 Cor 9:12, 18; 2 Cor 2:12; Gal 1:6, 7). That the 'gospel' concept has become by this time quite firmly established is shown by the fact that Paul uses the word in an absolute sense

and usually without any qualifying adjective (see Rom 1:16; 11:28; 1 Cor 9:14 and elsewhere; similarly Mk 8:35; 10:29; 13:10; 14:9). In Paul, the word has the double meaning of the act of proclamation, preaching activity (Rom 1:1; 2 Cor 2:12; Phil 4:3, 15) and of the content of this preaching (1 Cor 15:1; 2 Cor 11:4; Gal 1:6, 11f; Col 1:23 and elsewhere). The actual content of the gospel is found in Rom 1:3f; 1 Cor 15:3–11; 2:16. Paul sometimes calls it the 'gospel of God', because it proceeds from God (Rom 1:1; 15:16; 2 Cor 11:7, etc), and sometimes the 'gospel of Christ', both because it is derived from Christ and because it deals with him (1 Cor 9:12; 2 Cor 2:12; 9:13; 10:14; Gal 1:7, etc). He also calls it 'my' or 'our' gospel (Rom 2:16; 16:25; 2 Cor 4:3; 1 Thess 1:5; 2 Thess 2:14), not in order to contrast it with the gospel of Peter, but because he has received it himself from Christ (Gal 1:12; 1 Cor 15:3) and because he, as the 'minister' of the gospel (Col 1:23), has the task of proclaiming it. Since the gospel is the gospel of God, the 'power of God' is given to everyone who accepts it in faith (Rom 1:16; Eph 1:13). The meaning of the gospel is not 'reasonable' to man, but 'hidden' (2 Cor 4:3)—it is a stumbling block and foolishness for many, but for those who are called it is the power of God and the wisdom of God (1 Cor 1:18–25). At the judgement, the fate of man depends upon his acceptance or his rejection of the gospel (2 Thess 2:14). Paul also calls it the word of God, precisely because it is the gospel of God (Col 1:5). When the apostle proclaims the gospel, the words which are heard are those of God, who speaks through the mouth of the preacher (1 Thess 2:13). It is the 'word of truth' (2 Cor 6:7; Eph 1:13) and cannot be 'bound' by men because it comes from God (2 Tim 2:9). The essential meaning and content of the gospel is, for Paul, always Christ's death and resurrection. He passes over the preaching and miracles of Jesus, not, however, simply due to the fact that he himself was never personally acquainted with the 'historical' Jesus, but because Christ's work of redemption, rather than any historical account of his earthly life formed the real theme of the message of salvation. Obedience to the faith is not the only demand made by the gospel (Rom 1:5; 16:26)—it also supplies the norm for all moral behaviour (Phil 1:27). The proclamation of the gospel message initiates a new order in the history of salvation.

Throughout the New Testament, 'gospel' means the *living, spoken word of Christ's saving message*, and is thus never a literary concept. Also, since there is only *one* saving message, the word is consistently used only in the singular. Even in the second century, this primary meaning predominates (Polycarp, *Philad* 9:2; *Did* 15:3, 4). The individual gospels, too, are referred to as *to euangelion kata Matthaion, kata Markon*, etc (= 'the gospel according to Matthew, according to Mark', etc). In the second century, however, it is also used for the titles of books (Justinian, *Apol* 1, 66; *Dial* 10:2; 2 Clem 8:5; Theophilus, *Ad Autol* 3:14). Used thus, it may also refer to the *whole* of the New Testament, with the result that its content and meaning are brought to mind (Iren, *Adv Haer* 11, 27:2).

C. *The gospels of the New Testament.* The transference of the name 'gospel', originally referring to the oral missionary preaching of the joyous message, to the *written* gospels bears witness to the important fact that these texts were recognised as having the same missionary value as oral preaching, and as serving the same purpose, namely, that of awakening men to faith and of confirming them in that faith (Jn 20:31). In their content and meaning, therefore, the gospels refer back to the *euangelion* in its original sense, since, in handing down the words and acts of Jesus Christ, they clearly reveal his mission and his absolute power, including that over human disease and demons. In this way, they visibly demonstrate who he is—the Messiah, the Son of God and the Saviour of mankind, who proclaims in his preaching the will of God and the moral demands which God makes upon man. This, and not the history of Christ's life on earth in the biographical sense, forms the basic content of the gospels. The material of the gospels is derived from that tradition which goes back directly to the oral preaching of the apostles who were eye-witnesses and the first 'ministers of the word' (Lk 1:2). The apostles certainly never intended to provide their hearers with a complete, coherent and fully rounded picture either of the life of Jesus or simply of his public ministry. Their 'proclamation' consisted rather of the sayings and parables of Jesus and of his various controversies. Above all, however, they were concerned to proclaim his death and resurrection. All these various details were gathered up into a whole within a single framework—which is nevertheless strikingly different in the case of each individual evangelist—and, when this was done, the total result was a written record vividly illustrating the message of Jesus Christ. The origin of the gospels is quite clearly discernible in the form in which they have been handed down to us. Their literary style, which cannot be placed in the same category as any of the Jewish or Greek writings of the same period, was determined by the manner in which they originated. The historical and biographical interest of the gospels is completely subordinated to their religious and kerygmatic content. It is clear that little attempt was made either to produce a complete account, or to set out the events in chronological order. Generally speaking, the gospel events are strung together very loosely—this is especially evident in Mark, which is the earliest of the gospels—or according to purely practical criteria, and the order varies widely in the case of each evangelist. The only exception to this is the account of the Passion, but even here the gospels differ markedly from every other historical account, for they view the events of the Passion not as the result of human will, but as the outcome of the expression of God's will. In the gospel accounts of the Passion, it is not the Jewish opponents of Jesus who are at work, but God. When the apocryphal writers attempted to fill in the gaps left by the canonical gospels, they evinced an interest in the person of Jesus which was different from and alien to that of the evangelists. But since the canonical gospels are, to all intents and purposes, the only real sources of the knowledge we have of the life of Jesus, we can safely say that a

modern 'life of Jesus', offering only what has been historically handed down to us, can in fact never be written. Not only would such an undertaking be impracticable, but it would be without religious significance from the point of view which the evangelists themselves intended to present, namely, the significance of the person of Jesus within the context of salvation history.

The written gospels originate in the preaching or kerygma of the first christian community. They also reflect the situation of the communities in which and for which they were written. Finally, there is the literary and—most important—theological purpose of each individual evangelist. These various factors allow us to understand the many, often significant differences between the texts, and even in the renderings of the words of Christ. Examples of the tendency at work in such cases to rearrange, or sometimes even to rewrite, are the interpretations added to the parables of the sower (Mk 4:1–9, 13–20) and of the weeds (Mt 13:24–30, 36–43). Matthew in chapter 18 has put together various sayings of Christ to make a 'community code' aimed at the situation of a community and its problems, and passages such as Mt 7:15–23 (parallel Lk 6:43–6) and Mt 24:10–12 reflect the unsatisfactory state of such communities. The conversation between John the Baptist and Jesus which precedes the account of the baptism of Jesus in Matthew (3:13–15) clearly betrays an apologetic purpose. It was a puzzling question for early christian circles how Jesus, the sinless one, could come to the Baptist to receive the baptism of repentence—and by doing so subordinate himself to the

Baptist. It is Matthew's intention to answer this question. The more radical reorganisation of the parousia speech in Lk 21:5–36 (contrast Mk 13:1–33) becomes intelligible once one takes into account the way the expectation of an imminent second coming recedes in the third gospel, and once one notes in addition that Luke clearly looks back to the destruction of Jerusalem as an event in the past. It is only a careful consideration of the obvious differences between the gospels and the individual tendencies they bring to light which enables us to appreciate the true character of the gospels, and also to see how the fourth gospel, so different not simply in literary form but also in theological content, can occupy a place beside the synoptics. The question of how far the picture of Jesus given by the gospels draws on the characteristics of the historical Jesus is, however, the central problem of contemporary gospel studies.

Bibliography: J. Schniewind, *Euangelion*, Gütersloh 1937–41; E. Molland, *Das paulinische Euangelion*, Oslo 1934; K. L. Schmidt, 'Die Stellung der Evangelien in der allgemeinen Literaturgeschichte', *Eucharisterion* II (dedicated to H. Gunkel), Göttingen 1925, 50–134; R. Asting, *Die Verkündigung des Wortes im Urchristentum*, Stuttgart 1939; M. Albertz, *Die Botschaft des NT* I/1, Zurich 1947; J. Huby, *L'Evangile et les Evangiles*, Paris 1954³; Bultmann I, 87–92; *TDNT* II, 707–37; H. Ristow and K. Matthiae (edd.), *Der historische Jesus und der kerygmatische Christus*, Berlin 1961²; X. Léon-Dufour, *Les évangiles et l'histoire de Jésus*, Paris 1963.

Josef Schmid

Government

The Greek word *exousia*, can signify 'controlling power' (eg Rev 17:12f) and 'area of jurisdiction' (eg Lk 23:7), but is normally applied to those *persons* who, or *institutions* which, are vested with such controlling power. The bible has no fixed term for what we call 'the state'. To express the reality underlying this term it not only speaks of 'controlling power' or 'authority' but uses such terms as 'king', 'kingdom', 'caesar', 'ruler', 'potentate', etc. Moreover in questions connected with authority its interest is restricted almost entirely to the aspect of man's practical attitude to authority. Even such expressions as do appear to carry more fundamental implications normally envisage the concrete situation, so that in themselves they do not admit of any universally applicable rules being deduced from them. At the same time the New Testament does contain certain fundamental statements of principle, which can serve as starting-points for the working out of a theory in terms of natural law.

A. *Old Testament and judaism*. To understand the attitude of the Old Testament to political authority it must be noticed that Yahweh was accounted the Creator and Lord of Israel his people, and also as their sole king: 'I am the Lord, your Holy One, the Creator of Israel, your King' (Is 43:15; see also 33:22; Num 23:21; Deut 33:5; Judg 8:23; 1 Sam 12:12). Hence the demand of the people for a king was at first considered as a rejection of Yahweh (1 Sam 8:6f; 10:19; 12:12, 17, 19). But when the people had overcome all opposition and obtained a king, those who had opposed them came to terms with the altered situation by explaining that the king was Yahweh's representative or vizier

(1 Chron 28:5; 29:11f, 23; 2 Chron 9:8; Ps 72:1), that he had been chosen by him (1 Sam 10:24; 16:12; Wis 9:7), instituted by him (1 Sam 12:12; 15:17, 28, 35), and guided by him (Prov 21:1) as his anointed one (1 Sam 15:17; 24:6, 10; 16:6; 26:9, 11, 23). And if the king depended for his position upon God, this meant that men could not institute and depose kings at their own discretion (Hos 7:3; 8:4, 10), and it also meant that those who opposed him were in a real sense opposing Yahweh himself (2 Chron 13:8). By reason of his close connection with Yahweh, a closeness which finds its most pregnant expression in the description 'son of God' (2 Sam 7:14; Ps 89:27; 2:7), the king was also considered to be, in a special sense, the bestower of blessings (2 Sam 6:18; 1 Kings 8:14, 55f; 1 Chron 16:2; 2 Chron 6:3), and a powerful intercessor on his people's behalf (1 Kings 8:22–53; 2 Kings 19:15–19; 2 Chron 6:12–33; 30:18f). And this in turn was one of the reasons why he was particularly remembered in the prayers of the cultic community (1 Kings 8:66; Ps 20:9; 61:6–9; 84:9). But however exalted a conception of the king men might entertain they never forgot the fact that the power of God sets a limit to all political power (Ps 33:16–18; see also Rev 17:12f). Thus in Israel we never find a divine status ascribed to the king, as it is in writings emanating from other royal courts of the ancient Near East. Nor was there any lack of criticism of the monarchy as experienced in concrete fact (Hos 10:3; Jer 10:21; 21:11–23, 8; Ezek 34:5). It is significant how easily the people dispensed with any return to the monarchical form of government after the exile. The rebellion instigated in certain pious circles against Alexander Jannaeus (Josephus, *Ant* 13:372, 376; *Bell* 1:70, 88) probably originated from the fact that this potentate, like Aristobulus (*Ant* 13:301; 14:41), had laid claim to the title of king. Now precisely in a community which—to use a formulation first coined by Josephus—wished to be a 'theocracy' there was no lawful place for a king: 'The government of states had been entrusted here to monarchs, there to a few powerful families, elsewhere to the people; our lawgiver, on the contrary, refused to entertain any such form of government, but—to sum the matter up in a single pregnant word—made the state into a theocracy in that he submitted it to the power and dominion of God.' [*Apol* 2:164.] Now if God is the head of his people it follows that its leaders are by vocation the priests. 'Where could a more sublime or a wiser dispensation be found than that which makes God the director of the universe, the head, and makes over the whole administration of government in the state to the priests?' [Josephus, *Apol* 2:185]. According to Josephus the authority of the high priest is, in a certain sense, quasi-divine: 'He who does not hearken to the high priest must do penance in exactly the same way as if he had sinned against God himself (*Apol* 2:194). But if in spite of this a king ever rules in the land he may not do this without the priests: 'The king shall undertake nothing without the high priest and the council of the elders' (*Ant* 4:224). In his letter to Caligula, Agrippa I maintains that his forebears would have thought of themselves first as priests and only

secondarily as kings because the dignity of the high priest is greater than that of the king, just as God is greater than man (Philo, *Leg ad Caium*, 278). Yahweh, however, is Creator and Lord not only of Israel but of the whole earth (Jer 27:5; see also Ex 15:18; 19:5; Josephus, *Ant* 14:24), and as such 'king of the nations' too (Jer 10:7, 10f; Ps 22:28; 99:1) and over their rulers, 'Lord of kings' (Dan 2:47) or 'king of kings' (3 Macc 5:35; Enoch [Eth] 9:4; Jub 8:26; 23:1), in fact 'king of the kings of kings' (Sir 51:14). He institutes and deposes the kings of the peoples at will (Dan 2:21; 4:22; cf 2:37; 2 Kings 19:15; Jer 27:5–11; Is 37:16; 45:1; Sir 10:4). All kings, even gentile ones, have received their power from God (Wis 6:3; Enoch [Eth] 46:5; Barn [Syr] 82:9; Letter of Aristeas, 219, 224), and are therefore merely vassals of God, 'ministers of his kingdom' (Wis 6:4). Among the rabbis too there were hardly any differences of opinion on this point (instances in SB III, 303f). The Essenes had to swear an oath that they would keep faith with everyone, and especially with the rulers, for it fell to no-one to have dominion except by God's will (Josephus, *Bell* 2:140). Therefore the people were exhorted to pray for the ruling body in power at the time even when these were gentiles as in Babylon (Jer 29:14; Bar 1:11). According to Ezra 6:9f Darius provided the materials for public sacrifices in Jerusalem, directing that at these sacrifices prayers should be offered 'for the life of the king and his sons'. Again sacrifices seem regularly to have been offered in the temple at Jerusalem for Antiochus the Great, for he made notable provisions for the sacrificial

cult at Jerusalem (Josephus, *Ant* 12:140) and there is reliable evidence of a sacrifice at least being offered for him from the time of the Maccabee wars (1 Macc 7:33). In the Letter of Aristeas forty-five sacrifices and prayers offered by the Jews for the Egyptian king and his family are spoken of. From the time of Augustus two lambs and an ox were offered daily in the temple at Jerusalem 'for Caesar and the Roman people' (Philo, *Leg ad Caium*, 157, 317; Josephus, *Bell* 2:197; *Apol* 2:77), and these sacrifices, paid for according to Philo by Caesar, according to Josephus by the Jewish people, but in reality probably out of Jewish taxes, were continued up to the outbreak of the revolution in the year AD 66 (Josephus, *Bell* 2:409f, 415f). In addition to these, supplementary sacrifices for Caesar were also offered on special occasions: thus under Caligula at his accession to power (Philo, *Leg ad Caium*, 232), at his recovery from a serious illness and before the beginning of his campaign against the Teutons (*ibid*, 356; see also *In Flaccum*, 48f). The fact that the Roman authority could be valued as a regulating force is attested by the following statement of Rabbi Ḥananiah from the period of about AD 70: 'Pray for the wellbeing of the [gentile] government. For if it were not for the fear of this we would already have swallowed one another up alive' (Mischna, Abot 3:2). When the demands of the ruling body are in conflict with the law then admittedly one must refuse to obey them. As early a ruler as Saul was forced to experience the fact that his people were 'more afraid of offending God than of refusing to obey the king' (Josephus, *Ant* 6:259).

The reply of the priest Mathias to the emissaries of the Syrian king was: 'Far be it from us to desert the law and the ordinances. We will not obey the king's words by turning aside from our religion to the right or to the left' (1 Macc 2:21f). Similarly the youngest of the Maccabee brothers said: 'I will not obey the king's command but I will obey the commandment of the law which was given to our fathers from Moses' (2 Macc 7:30). A tendency is apparent in the apocalyptic writings to discern behind the great empires of the world powers hostile to God which are to be annihilated in the final age (Is 27:1; Dan 7:2–12; Hen eth 89:59–90, 25; see also 1 QM 15:2f), and cut off from the eternal kingdom of God (Dan 7:13–18). The authority of Rome was rejected root and branch by the Zealots, who recognised no-one save Yahweh alone as king and Lord (Josephus, *Ant* 18:23f; *Bell* 2:118, 433; 7:323, 410, 418), and hence proclaimed and unleashed the holy war against Rome.

B. *New Testament.* We may commence with the saying of Jesus which runs: 'Render to Caesar the things that are Caesar's and to God the things that are God's' (Mk 12:17 and parallels). Manifestly this is quite different from the demand of the Zealots that their compatriots should refuse to pay taxes to Caesar. At the same time, however, it does not in any sense set Caesar on an equal footing with God, but rather throws all the emphasis upon the exhortation to render to God the things that are God's. The will of God is the sole standard for Jesus, and in cases of conflict the will of the earthly lord goes unheeded, as is shown from Jesus' reply

to the veiled attempt to banish him from the territory of Herod Antipas (Lk 13:31f). He is aware of how in concrete fact the ruling body tends to misuse its power (Mk 10:42f; 13:9–11 etc), but he still refuses to rebel against it (though not to speak against it, Jn 18:22f; see also Acts 23:3) even when he has to endure injustice at its hands. This appears from the manner in which he bore himself in the passion (see especially Mk 14:48f; Mt 26:52–4; Jn 18:11). He has no political aims to pursue (Mt 4:8–10 and parallels). His kingdom is not of this world (Jn 18:36), and anyone who denies this will be disappointed in his expectations (Jn 6:14f; see also Lk 19:11; 24:21; Acts 1:6). The primitive church is in accord with the Old Testament and judaism in adopting a fundamentally positive attitude towards the ruling authorities, if, indeed, we may not go so far as to maintain that in 2 Thess 2:6f an actual function in salvific history is ascribed to the Roman government. The existing order derives its power from God (Rom 13:1; Jesus's answer to Pilate in Jn 19:11 has a different meaning). It must protect and reward the good and punish the wicked (Rom 13:3f; 1 Pet 2:13f). All have to give it their obedience (Rom 13:1; Tit 3:1; 1 Pet 2:13), and that too not under compulsion but on grounds of conscience (Rom 13:5) or for the sake of God (1 Pet 2:13). So true is this that any disobedience would actually amount to a resisting of what God has appointed (Rom 13:2). The way of the christian is not to reject the authority of the pagan ruling body, but to pray for it (1 Tim 2:1f; see also Lk 23:34; Acts 7:60; 1 Clem 6of; Polyc

12:3; Justinus, *Apol*, 1, 17:3; Theophilus, *Ad Autol*, 1, 11; Tertullian, *Apol* 30:39). Just as the secular authority has its source in the will of God, so too it has its limits there: 'We must obey God rather than men' (Acts 5:29; see also 4:19). The exhortation in 1 Pet 2:17: 'Fear God. Honour the emperor' is perhaps an intentional corrective to the Old Testament exhortation: 'My son, fear the Lord and the king' (Prov 24:21). Paul's attitude towards the Roman authorities, which is on the whole (in spite of 1 Cor 6:1-6) an affirmative one, is to be explained primarily by his Jewish origins (see above under A), but his basic eschatological orientation (see Rom 13:11-13; Phil 3:20; also 1 Pet 2:11) and his relatively favourable experiences of the workings of Roman authority are also factors which have to be taken into account. In the case of the Book of Revelation the situation is quite different. Here the Roman authority, claiming divine honour for Caesar as it does, figures explicitly as a Satanic power (13:2-4), against which the church summons its members, not indeed to rebellion, but certainly to a refusal of obedience even at the cost of martyrdom. Lk 4:6 might represent an anomaly if we do not follow Irenaeus (*Haer* 5, 22:2; 24:1) in taking this saying of Satan as empty boasting. The idea that the world as a whole is under the dominion of Satan might represent, to some extent, a parallel to this (Jn 12:31; 13:2, 27; 14:30 etc).

Bibliography: General: F. G. Dölger, 'Zur antiken und frühchristl. Auffassung der Herrschergewalt von Gottes Gnaden', *Antike und Christ*, 3 (1932), 117-27; 5 (1936), 142ff; K. L. Schmidt, *TDNT* 1, 564-93; *TDNT* vi,

516-35 (see *Basileia* [*BKW* vii], London 1957); C. H. Powell, *The Biblical Concept of Power*, London 1963. On A: K. Galling, *Die israelitische Staatsverfassung in ihrer vorderorientalischen Umwelt*, Leipzig 1929; C. R. North, 'The OT Estimate of the Monarchy', *Am. Journ. of Semitic Languages* 48 (1931/2), 1-19; O. Procksch, *Der Staatsgedanke in der Prophetie*, Gütersloh 1933; W. Rudolph, 'Volk und Staat im AT', *Volk, Staat, Kirche. Ein Lehrgang der theol. Fak. Giessen*, Giessen 1933, 21-33; E. R. Goodenough, *The Politics of Philo Judaeus*, New Haven 1938; B. Balscheit, *Gottesbund und Staat. Der Staat im AT*, Zürich 1940; M. Noth, 'Gott, König, Volk im AT', *ZTK* 47 (1950), 157-91; A. Seeger, *Staatsgott oder Gottesstaat im alten Israel und Hellas*, Göttingen 1951; H. J. Kraus, *Die Königsherrschaft Gottes im AT*, Tübingen 1951; H. J. Kraus, *Prophetie und Politik*, Munich 1952; A. Alt, 'Das Königtum in den Reichen Israel und Juda', *VT* 1 (1951), 2-22; A. Alt, 'Die Staatenbildung der Israeliten in Palästina', *Kleine Schriften* II, Munich 1953, 1-65; H. Gross, *Weltherrschaft als religiöse Idee im AT*, Bonn 1953; I. Mendelsohn, 'Samuel's Denunciation of Kingship', *BASOR* 143 (1956), 17-22; A. Weiser, 'Samuel und die Vorgeschichte des israelit. Königtums', *ZTK* 57 (1960), 141-61; L. Rost, 'Königsherrschaft Jahwes in vorköniglicher Zeit?', *TLZ* 85 (1960), 721-4; W. Schmidt, *Königtum Gottes in Ugarit und Israel*, Berlin 1961; T. Blatter, *Macht und Herrschaft Gottes*, Fribourg 1962; G. Wallis, 'Die Anfänge des Königtums in Israel', *Wiss. Zschr. d. M. Luther- Univ. Halle-Wittenberg* 12 (1963), Gesellsch. und sprachwiss. Reihe, 239-47; E. Lipinsky, 'Jahwe malakh', *Bbl* 44 (1963), 405-60; H. Donner, *Israel unter den Völkern*, Leiden 1964. On B: W. Stählin, 'Das Reich Gottes und der Staat', *TB* 6 (1927), 141f; H. Windisch, *Imperium und Evangelium im NT*, Kiel 1931; F. Delekat, *Die Kirche Jesu Christi und der Staat*, Berlin 1933, G. Bertram, 'Volk und Staat im NT', *Volk, Staat, Kirche. Ein Lehrgang der theol. Fak. Giesse*, Giessen 1933, 35-52; K. Pieper, *Urkirche und Staat*, Paderborn 1935; E. Stauffer, *Gott und Kaiser im NT*, Bonn 1935; G. Kittel, 'Das Urteil des NT über den Staat', *ZST* 14 (1937), 651-80; K. L. Schmidt, *Die Polis in Kirche und Staat*, Basle 1939; F. J. Leenhardt, *Le chrétien doit-il servir l'État?*, Geneva 1939; G. Kittel, *Christus und Imperator*, Stuttgart 1939; W. Bieder, *Ecclesia und Polis im NT*, Zürich 1941; W. G. Kümmel, *Theol. Rundschau* 17 (1948), 133-42; W. Schweitzer, *Die Herrschaft Christi und der Staat im NT*, Zürich 1948; L. Hick, *Die Staatsgewalt im Lichte des NT*, Aachen 1948; K. H. Schelkle, 'Jerusalem und

Rom im NT', *TG* 41 (1950), 77–119; E. Gaugler, 'Der Christ und die staatlichen Gewalten nach dem NT', *Intern. Kirchl. Zschr.* 40 (1950), 133–53; J. Hering, *A Good and a Bad Government according to the NT*, Springfield (Illinois) 1954; R. Schnackenburg, *The Moral Teaching of the New Testament*, London 1964; M. Dibelius, 'Rom und die Christen im 1 Jh.', *Botschaft und Geschichte* II, Tübingen 1956, 177–228; H. Schlier, 'Die Beurteilung des Staates im NT', *Die Zeit der Kirche*, Freiburg 1956, 1–16. See also *Catholica* 13 (1959), 241–59; L. Goppelt, *Der Staat im NT*, Tübingen 1961²; O. Michel, 'Das Problem des Staates in ntl. Sicht', *TLZ* 83 (1958), 161–6; W. Schmauch and E. Wolf, *Königsherrschaft Christi. Der Christ im Staat*, Munich 1959; H. W. Bartsch, 'Die ntl. Aussagen über den Staat', *ET* 19 (1959), 375–90; A. Penner, *The Christian, the State and the NT*, Scottdale (Penn.) 1959; R. Völkl, *Christ und Welt nach dem NT*, Würzburg 1961; H. von Campenhausen, 'Die Christen und das bürgerliche Leben nach den Aussagen des NT', *Tradition und Leben*, Tübingen 1961, 180–202; C. E. B. Cranfield, 'The Christian's Political Responsibility according to the NT', *SJT* 15 (1962), 176–92; W. Böld, *Obrigkeit vor Gott?*, Hamburg 1962; H. U. Instinsky, *Die Alte Kirche und das Heil des Staates*, Munich 1963; C. J. Mans, 'De owerheid in die NT en by die reformatore', *Hervormde Teologiese Studiese* (Pretoria) 18 (1962), 90–115; H. R. Schlette, 'Die Aussagen des NT über "den Staat"', *Der Anspruch der Freiheit*, Munich 1963, 21–52; H. R. Schlette, 'Staat', *HTG* II, 551–5; A. M. Ferrando, *Christianisme et Pouvoir civil* (dissertation), Fribourg 1961; M. L. Ricketts, 'Christians and the State—the New Testament View', *Religion and Life* 33 (1963/4), 74–9. On Mk 12:17: E. Stauffer, *Christus und die Cäsaren*, Hamburg 1954⁴, 121–49; E. Stauffer, *Die Botschaft Jesu*, Bern 1959, 95–118; A. Bea, *CC* 109 (1958), 572–83; P. Vanbergen, *LV* 50 (1960), 12–22; L. Goppelt, *Ecclesia und Respublica*, Göttingen 1961, 40ff; J. W. Doeve, *Vox Theol.* 32 (1961/2), 69–83; J. N. Sevenster, *Nederl. Theol. Tijdschr.* 17 (1962), 21–31. On Jn 19:11. H. von Campenhausen, *TLZ* 73 (1948), 387–92. On Rom 13: W. Bauer, *Jedermann sei untertan der Ordnung, Gött. Universitätsreden*, Göttingen 1930; L. Gaugusch, *TG* 26 (1934), 529–50; G. Dehn, *Festschr. K. Barth*, Munich 1936, 90–109; J. E. Uitman, *Onder Eig. Vaandel* 15 (1940), 102–21; W. Parsons, *Theol. Studies* 1 (1940), 337–64; 2 (1941), 325–46; J. Koch-Mehrin, *ET* 7 (1947/8), 378–401; H. von Campenhausen, *Festschr. A. Bertholet*, Tübingen 1950, 97–112; K. H.

Schelkle, *ZNW* 44 (1952/3), 223–36; A. Weithaas, *TG* 45 (1955), 433–41; A. Strobel. *ZNW* 47 (1956), 67–93; R. Morgenthaler, *TZ* 12 (1956), 289–304; E. Käsemann, *ZTK* 56 (1959), 316–76; C. E. B. Cranfield, *NTS* 6 (1960), 241–9; P. Meinhold, *Römer 13*, Stuttgart 1960; E. Bemmel, *TLZ* 85 (1960), 837–40; C. D. Morrison, *The Powers that Be*, London 1960; E. Käsemann, *Beitrag z. EvT* 32 (1961), 37–55; E. Barnikol, *Studien z. NT und z. Patristik* (=*TU* 77), Berlin 1961, 65–134; F. Neugebauer, *Kerygma und Dogma* 8 (1962), 151–72; G. Delling, *Römer 13:1–7 innerhalb der Briefe des NT*, Berlin 1962; O. Kuss, *Auslegung und Verkündigung* I, Regensburg 1963, 246–59; J. Kosnetter, *Sud. Paulin. Congr. Intern. Cath.* I, Rome 1963, 347–55; G. Hillerdahl, *Luth, Rundschau* 13 (1963), 17–34; A. Strobel, *ZNW* 55 (1964), 58–62; V. Zsifkovits, *Der Staatsgedanke nach Paulus in Röm 13*, Vienna 1964. On 1 Tim 2:1f. A. Bludau, *Der katholische Seelsorger* (Vienna) 18 (1906), 295–300, 349–55, and 391–5; L. Biehl, *Das liturgische Gebet für Kaiser und Reich*, Paderborn 1937. On Rev 13. P. Ketter, *TTZ* I (1941), 70–93; H. Schlier, *Die Zeit der Kirche*, Freiburg 1956, 16–29; L. Cerfaux, *The Sacral Kingship*, (=*Studies in the History of Religion* IV), Leiden 1959, 459–70.

Josef Blinzler

Grace

A. *In the Old Testament*. No special word is used in the Old Testament to convey what is understood by grace in the christian, and particularly in the Pauline sense. The Old Testament did, however, prepare the way for an understanding of the nature of grace, and displays an inherent recognition of it. *Kharis* is the usual translation in LXX of the Hebrew *ḥēn*, which in the first place means affection, goodwill, favour, or friendliness (particularly on the part of someone in a high place) (see Ps 45:2). The meaning of *ḥēn* is extended to the object of this special goodwill or favour, to imply charm, graciousness, comeliness or beauty (see Prov 4:9; 5:19; 11:16; 31:30; Nahum 3:4). Thus *ḥēn* and *kharis* have basically the same meanings, though the meaning of *kharis* developed from that of charm, beauty, etc, to that of goodwill or favour. The meaning of *ḥēn* is to be found especially in the phrase: 'to find favour in the sight of God, or of man' (in the sight of God, see Gen 6:8; 18:3; 19:19; Ex 33:12f, 16f; 34:9; in the sight of man, see Gen 39:4; 47:29; Ex 3:21; 12:36). The adverb *ḥinnām*, in vain, which is formed from the same root as *ḥēn*, and the two instances of the use of the word in Gen 18:3 and Ex 33:12, suggest a favour which the recipient does not deserve. The word *ḥesed*—translated by *kharis* in LXX (Esther 2:9, 17), but elsewhere generally by *eleos* (=pity: *misericordia* in the Vulgate translations of Psalms) means the attitude of mind and individual behaviour appropriate to life in the community, and in particular the mutual loyalty of those who share in the covenant (see 1 Sam 20:8, 14ff; 2 Sam 9:1, 3:8) and their duty towards one another within the community. The↗ covenant, which God entered into with man, proceeded from his freely-given love, and was therefore grace. For this reason, his attitude towards the covenant (*ḥesed*) was also grace, and in a very special sense, his attitude towards his people when they broke the covenant. The translation of *ḥesed* as 'mercy' is thus factually correct. (For *ḥesed* in connection with the covenant, see Deut 7:9; 1 Kings 8:23; Neh 9:32; Dan 9:4; Ps 89:28; Is 55:3.)

The Old Testament certainly foreshadows the idea of grace which helps men—again and again we find explicit references to the need for Yahweh's help. Israel was freed from bondage in Egypt, led through the wilderness and given the land of Canaan (see Ex 6:6ff; 13:21f; Deut 7:17–24; 8:2ff, 7–18; Josh 21:43f). The land was, indeed, always under the special care of God (Deut 11:10ff, 14ff). The Israelites had always to remember that they could do nothing of their own accord (Deut 8:17f; Judg 7:2; Ps 44:3–9). The prophets constantly censured the people for relying arrogantly upon themselves and neglecting to trust in God, and for presuming upon worldly means to gain power (see Is 2:7–17; 28:15; 30:16; 39:2–7; Amos 6:8, 13; see also 2 Sam 24), as well as for allowing themselves to be deluded into thinking that the fruits of the land came from the fertility gods or goddesses (Hos 2:5, 8, 12). God's way of making his people realise that they owed everything to him was invariably to withdraw his gifts and his help (see the schematic outline in Judg 3:7ff, 12ff; 4:1ff; also Hos 2:9, 12; 5:13ff; 13:9ff; 14:4–9; Mic 5:9f; Zeph 3:11f). The strength of Israel is completely dependent upon the people's trust in Yahweh (see Ps 20:7ff: Is 7:9; 30:15). No man was to glory in his wisdom, his strength or his riches, but in his understanding and knowledge of Yahweh, who exercises mercy and↗ goodness (*ḥesed*), judgement, and↗ justice on earth (Jer 9:24; cf 1 Cor 1:31). The prosperity of every single person depends upon the↗ blessing of Yahweh (see Num 6:22–7). This conviction is at the heart of the faith of every religious Israelite. Whenever Yahweh turns away his face, every being is confounded and destroyed and all security is lost (see Ps 30:7; 31:15ff; 104:27–30; 121; 127; 145:15ff; 146; 147:9ff). It should be noted, in this context, that the word of blessing which comes from Yahweh is efficacious and accomplishes that which he purposes (Is 55:11), as, indeed, is true of his ⁄ word in general. This confident faith and trust in Yahweh (see also Prov 18:10f) corresponds closely to the belief that he was the creator of the universe and its first mover (see Prov 16:1, 4, 7, 9; 19:14; 20:24; 21:1; Sir 11:14).

The Old Testament also recognises that divine grace, in the form either of goodwill or of a gift, is both *freely bestowed* on God's part and *undeserved* on man's part. This is clearly so in the case of man's state of original blessedness in Paradise. The name *hā᾿âdâm* (man) indicates that man is destined, by his very nature, to cultivate the soil (*hā᾿adâmâh*: see Gen 2:5). God, however, assigns a much more pleasant task to him by putting him in a garden full of splendid trees (Gen 2:8–15). Man, fashioned from clay, is by nature mortal, but God ordained not only that he should labour at tilling the soil, but also that he should die only as a punishment for his transgression of the divine commandment (Gen 2:17; 3:17ff). In this context, man's intimate relationship with God in Paradise (see Gen 2:19, 22; 3:8f) is shown to be a grace which is quite independent of any merit on his part. But an even more striking example is that of God's treatment of fallen man within his plan of salvation. He does not carry out the sentence of death on the day of his sin, as he had threatened to do, but rather makes it possible for the human race to perpetuate itself and eventually to triumph over the seducer, the serpent, whose head will be crushed underfoot

(Gen 3:15). Adam, in grateful recognition of this action, calls his wife Eve, mother of all the living, that is, *life* (Gen 3:20). Moreover, as the further history of man's salvation clearly shows, God did not forsake man after the fall (see Wis 10:1). Another instance of his grace is the covenant which he made with Noah—although he recognised that man was incorrigible, he nevertheless guaranteed his continued existence (Gen 8:21). By far the most striking example of this grace, however, is God's Covenant with Israel. It is impressed upon the minds of the Israelites that Yahweh has chosen them and has entered into the covenant with them from motives of pure love, and without any merit at all on their part (Deut 7:6ff; see also Ezek 16:4–14). God's predestination is made especially clear in his choice of Isaac (Gen 17:18–21; 21:12f) and of Jacob (Gen 25:23) for the continuity of the patriarchal line and the furtherance of the covenant. (Paul has a penetrating comment on this in Rom 9:7–13.) God himself is emphatic about the absolute nature of his choice—he will have mercy on whom he will (Ex 33:19; see also Rom 9:15). The fact that God's grace is not dependent upon human merit emerges very clearly in the attitude of Yahweh towards his people when they have not been faithful to the covenant (see Ex 34:6–10; Lev 26:44f; Is 43:22–44:5; Jer 31:3, 20; Hos 11:8f; Mic 7:18ff). There are, furthermore, two culminating points within the whole of the messianic prophecy which indicate the *necessity* of divine grace as new nature and as the present help of God. In Jer 31:31–4, a distinction is made between the 'new covenant' and that made on

Mount Sinai. Under this 'new covenant', Yahweh will not simply present his law externally to his people on stone tablets or in his word, but will rather present it interiorly to each individual man, writing it in his heart, with the result that it will become, as it were, his second nature. God will give to each man an inner understanding of himself, and to the Hebrew mind, which sees everything as a single whole, this would imply a corresponding attitude and moral behaviour on the part of the recipient (see Jer 22:15ff; 1 Jn 2:4). The negative aspect of this transformation is the overcoming of sin through God's forgiveness. Ezek 36:25–28 gives clear evidence of this change, and shows even more strikingly how God's grace is both habitual and actual. Yahweh will cleanse those from their sins who have been delivered from exile, give them a new heart and a new↗ spirit by putting his own spirit into them, thus causing them to keep his commandments. But Yahweh does not do this for their sakes—he does it for the sake of his holy name (Ezek 36:22, 32; see also Is 48:9, 11). It is thus evident that there is no question at all of any merit on the part of Israel. A close parallel exists between Ezek 36:25ff and Ps 51:9–14—the psalmist speaks of being cleansed of his sins, of being given a clean heart and a new, firm and willing spirit and of being informed by the holy, divine spirit. It is clearly stated in this psalm that this transformation can only come about by means of God's creative power. Is 6:7f shows too that the↗justification of a sinner really implies the eradication of his sin and grants him a new life which may enable him to become God's

herald or prophet. The justification of Israel, as expressed, for example, in Is 45:25, does not imply that Israel has an automatic claim to justification, which would be in direct contradiction to what is stated in Is 43:22ff and elsewhere. On the other hand, however, it should be noted that this is not simply a declaration of God's justice, as Is 44:22 shows (see also, for example, Mic 7:19).

Finally, the fact that divine grace, in its choice of persons for special purposes and offices, is not dependent upon the merit of the man chosen, is exemplified in Num 16:3–11; 18:7 (the gift of priesthood): 1 Sam 9:21; 15:17; 2 Sam 7:18ff, etc.

Bibliography: J. Ziegler, *Die Liebe Gottes bei den Propheten* (*AA* 11, 3), Münster 1930; J. Köberle, *Sünde und Gnade im religiösen Leben des Volkes Israel*, Munich 1905; J. Hempel, *Gott und Mensch im Alten Testament*, Stuttgart 1936²; W. F. Lofthouse, 'Chen and Chesed in the Old Testament', *ZAW* 51 (1933), 29–35; N. Glueck, 'Das Wort chesed im alttestamentlichen Sprachgebrauch' (*BZAW* 47), Giessen 1927; F. Asensio, *Misericordia et Veritas: E, Hèsed y 'Emet Divinos*, Rome 1949; R. Bultmann, *TDNT* II, 477–82; P. van Imschoot, Haag, 589f; J. Guillet, *Leitgedanken der Bibel*, Lucerne 1954, 29–111; D. R. Ap-Thomas, 'Some Aspects of the Root "chen" in the OT', *JSS* 2 (1957), 128–48; G. Farr, 'The Concept of Grace in the Book of Hosea', *ZAW* 70 (1958), 98–107; J. Haspecker, 'Gnade', *LTK* IV², 977–80; I. Hermann, *HTG* I, 548–53; H. J. Stoebe, 'Die Bedeutung des Worted ḥäsäd im AT', *VT* 2 (1952), 244–54; A. Jepsen, 'Gnade und Barmherzigkeit im AT', *KD* 7 (1961), 261–71; E. Würthwein, 'Gnade im AT und Judentum', *RGG* II³, 1632ff.

Johannes Schildenberger

B. 'Kharis' in the Greek-speaking world. 1. In the Greek-speaking world, *kharis* (grace) was a commonly used word, and one with very many shades of meaning. On the one hand, it was used to denote certain aesthetic qualities and had the meaning of charm, loveliness, or graciousness; in the sphere of personal relationships, on the other hand, it was used in the sense of favour, goodwill, beneficence, gift, thanks and gratitude. In the language of hellenistic Emperor-worship it expressed condescension on the part of the ruler. At a lower level, in the spells and charms of the religion of the people, it implied secret power. Aristotle defines the word according to the sense in which it was used in the New Testament, that is to say, something which was bestowed, not as wages or as a reward, but as a freely offered gift, without any implication of debt (see *Ars Rhet.*, lib. B, cap. 7, 1385a).

2. In the writings of Philo, the word *kharis* has a decidedly theological significance. The original divine powers or moving forces are designated by Philo as the *kharistikē dunamis* (lit.=gracious power) and the *kolastikē kharis* (lit.= chastising power) (*Quis rerum div.* 34, 166). Not-being attains to being by means of the *kharites* (graces: *De migr. Abr.* 32, 183), and it is only by virtue of *kharis* that it is possible 'to leave the kingdom of mortals or to remain immortal' (*De ebrietate* 36, 145–6).

3. LXX translates the Hebrew *ḥēn* fairly adequately by *kharis*, but does not use it in the strictly religious sense. The Hebrew *ḥesed* better conveys the idea of grace in the New Testament sense, though this is only translated twice in LXX by *kharis* (Esther 2:9, 17). (See ⁊ Grace in the Old Testament.)

C. *In the New Testament*. In the New Testament *kharis* still bears distinct traces of the original meaning with which it was used in secular Greek literature—Luke employs it quite frequently in the current sense—but in general it is certainly not possible to claim that the New Testament has preserved the word according to its original linguistic usage. Although a number of overtones, traceable to its original secular usage, are certainly present in the theological concept of *kharis* in the New Testament, its application to man's salvation gives the word a unique quality which has no etymological derivation. An entirely new meaning is added to *kharis* by its use in a soteriological sense.

The unique position which this word occupies in the New Testament and the supreme importance of the concept of *kharis* in the theology of the New Testament is due above all to Paul. It is, in fact, a Pauline concept. The word occurs most frequently in his writings and in those texts which were written under his influence (Luke and the Petrine letters).

1. *God's will to save.* The translation of *kharis* as 'favour' or 'goodwill' (*favor, benevolentia*) certainly has its merits, though grace does not mean the divine goodwill which God, as creator, bestows upon all his creatures. In the New Testament, the word grace has a definitely soteriological connotation. With the exception of a few passages, grace always refers to the redemption. 'According to his grace'—a phrase which occurs frequently in Paul— implies the absolute supremacy of God in the work of redemption. We are saved according to his free will and by his free choice. In theological controversy with the Jews, grace goes beyond the meaning of the origin of the

redemption, or God's will and decision, to save man, and takes on the meaning of a principle which permeates the whole history of man's salvation. It is not used to imply that a display of leniency on the part of the judge will make up for any deficiency in divine justice in the judgement of man. (The phrase 'to show mercy rather than justice' is not to be found.) It means rather that justification according to works is cancelled out by a spontaneous act of will on the part of God, in other words, that the law is invalidated by divine grace. It is 'according to grace' that we have been called before the origin of the world (2 Tim 1:9) and that the promise was made (Rom 4:16). It is 'according to the riches of his grace' that we have redemption (Eph 1:7) and 'according to the election of grace' that there was, at the time of Paul, a remnant of Jews who were saved (Rom 11:5).

2. *God's decision to save and the fact of salvation.* God's will to save did not, however, remain an abstract entity. His decision was taken once and for all time in Christ (see 2 Tim 1:9). It is possible to state that all references to grace are ultimately references to Christ. *Kharis* is thus *hē kharis hē en Khristō(i) Iēsou* ('the grace that is in Christ Jesus': 2 Tim 2:1) and *kharis hē tou henos anthrōpou Iēsou Khristou* ('the grace of that one man Jesus Christ: Rom 5:15). Grace came by Christ (Jn 1:17). The passion appointed for Christ and the glory which was to follow this passion are the grace of which the prophets spoke (1 Pet 1:10–11). The work of redemption itself is sometimes referred to as grace (2 Cor 8:9). In Gal 2:21, grace and Christ's sacrificial death

are understood as interchangeable terms.

3. *The gift of salvation.* The grace which was revealed in Christ is in no sense a historically isolated manifestation of God's attitude towards salvation. On the contrary, this grace brings the christian into communion with God. The benedictions at the beginning and the end of most of the epistles must be considered with this in mind. God has bestowed his beloved Son upon us with his grace (Eph 1:6). The christian 'stands' in this grace (Rom 5:2; 1 Pet 5:12) and must continue in it (Acts 13:43).

This communion which the christian shares with God is certainly not an abstract or intellectual relationship. It is a soteriological gift. The word *kharis* has the unique quality of being able to stand both for gift and for mental attitude, but whereas these are two separate entities at the human level, they are, in God's eyes, identical. Divine grace is not simply effective in bringing about man's salvation by means of the redemption through Christ's death on the cross—it is at the same time salvation itself and causes a new reality to come into existence. Grace and ↗ justice are often found together in the epistles and are clearly complementary terms. To be made 'void of Christ', that is, to be separated from him, means that the Christian is outside of grace (Gal 5:4). The 'abundance of grace' and the 'free gift of righteousness' (Rom 5:17) are two aspects of the same reality seen, in the case of the first, from the point of view of the giver, and in the case of the second, from the point of view of the recipient. Grace 'reigns' now (Rom

5:21), having broken the power of sin (Rom 6:14). We are instructed by grace (Tit 2:11f) and if we are lacking in grace, evil may grow and flourish in us (Heb 12:15). We should feed our hearts with grace (Heb 13:9) and strengthen ourselves with it (2 Tim 2:1). Grace is also the origin of the various gifts of the Spirit which are given to every christian (Rom 12:6; 1 Cor 1:4-7). It is in fact impossible to grasp the full meaning of grace so long as it is regarded simply as an intention to save upon which man can confidently rely; it is rather *the* sustaining power in the life of the Christian, as will be brought out more clearly in what follows.

4. *The power of grace.* Grace is very closely associated with the idea of 'power' and that of the 'apostolate'. To think of the recipient of grace as being simply brought into intimate contact with God, as being in communion with him in a purely static way, is to underestimate the vital importance of grace in the christian life. Grace is an active agent, and as such is not simply effective in the interior life of the christian as a power which overcomes the sins of the recipient; it goes further than this and has a powerful external effect. We learn that Stephen was 'full of grace and power'—the power of the grace that was in him enabled him to lead a most effective christian life among the people (Acts 6:8). Barnabas rejoiced to see the effects of divine grace—the conversion of a great number of gentiles (Acts 11:23). This dynamic aspect of grace is especially noticeable in Paul's references to himself. When he asked God to take away the cause of his temptation,

he received the answer: 'My grace is sufficient for you', and further, 'for my power is made perfect in weakness' (2 Cor 12:9). This divine strength which was given to Paul was not without fruit (1 Cor 15:10)—its outcome was his apostolate among the gentiles. He was made a minister of the gospel 'according to the gift of God's grace which was given' him (Eph 3:7). Also 'according to the commission of God given' to him he was the wise architect who laid the foundations (1 Cor 3:10). It should be noted in this context that *sophia* (wisdom) and *kharis* are closely related concepts (see also, for example, 2 Cor 1:12; 2 Pet 3:18). But grace is not a gift or endowment, which can be separated from the giver—it is most important not to lose sight of the fact that grace means essentially that God is at work. In the case of the free gifts of the Spirit (see ⁊ Charisma), we read that 'all these are inspired by one and the same Spirit' (1 Cor 12:11). There is, in fact, no such thing as a power which is separate from God. Paul says, in Gal 2:8f: *ho gar energēsas Petrō(i) eis apostolēn tēs peritomēs energēsen kai eis ta ethnē* ('for he who worked through Peter for the mission to the circumcised worked through me also for the gentiles'), and continues thus: *kai gnontes tēn kharin tēn dotheisan moi . . . dexias edōkan emoi . . . koinōnias* ('and when they perceived the grace that was given to me . . . [they] gave to me . . . the right hand of fellowship'). What is meant by 'they perceived the grace that was given' to him is that they recognised that the one who had been at work in Peter was also at work in Paul. *Grace thus is a name for the activity of God with and through men, for the purpose of salvation.*

We may conclude this very brief examination of the concept of grace in the New Testament by summarising it as follows: grace is the soteriological activity of God, decreed from eternity, which is made manifest to man and effective in his salvation in Christ's act of redemption and which continues and perfects the work of redemption in us and in the world. The New Testament does not acknowledge two separate concepts of grace—that of a divine gift and that of a disposition on the part of God, though it does happen that at times the one aspect of grace and at other times the other emerges more clearly. They are, however, integrally part of each other—God's benevolence and goodwill towards man is a gift, and whenever God gives, he gives himself. Grace includes the redeeming God and redeemed man. In connection with the subject of grace, see also ↗ justification, ↗ goodness, ↗ love.

Bibliography: P. Bonnetain, *DB(S)* III, 701–1319; O. Loew, *Kharis*, Marburg 1908 (this work is concerned only with an examination of the word in its secular Greek sense); J. Moffat, *Grace in the New Testament*, London 1931; J. Morson, *The Gift of God*, Cork 1952; A. Pujol, 'De salutatione Apostolica "Gratia vobis et Pax"', *VD* 12 (1932), 38–40, and 76–82; H. Rondet, *Gratia Christi*, Paris 1948; T. Torrance, *The Doctrine of Grace in the Apostolic Fathers*, London 1948; R. Vömel, *Der Begriff der Gnade im NT*, Leipzig 1913; G. P. Wetter, *Charis*, Leipzig 1913; R. Winkler, 'Die Gnade im Neuen Testament', *ZST* 10 (1933), 642–80; J. Wobbe, *Der Charisgedanke bei Paulus*, Münster 1932.

Gerhard Trenkler

Hardness of heart

1. *The concept.* Hardness of heart can be defined as 'persistent refusal when faced with the divine call' (see Hesse, 6). The subject can be either an individual or the people of Israel. God's call can take the form of either an invitation or a demand.

2. *Hardness of heart in the New Testament.* In the New Testament hardness of heart refers particularly to the persistent refusal when faced with the divine reality which has appeared on earth in the person of Jesus Christ. The New Testament is not, however, familiar with a relevant term which is immediately recognisable. It uses rather metaphorical expressions such as the verbs *pōroun* (to harden), *sklērunein*, which has roughly the same meaning, and *pakhunein* (to 'make fat'); the nouns *pērōsis* (hardening) and *sklērotēs* (hardness, stubbornness); and their derivatives *sklērokardia* (hardness of heart) and *sklērotrakhēlos* (obstinate). The centre of all this is the *kardia* (heart) regarded as the source of the moral and religious life of a person. Hence unbelief can occur as parallel with hardness of heart (Mt 16:14). We also read, however, of eyes and ears being hardened (or blinded), that is, disturbed in their function of perceiving and recognising. The recognition in question here is not just an act of the intellect but an obedient and thankful acceptance of the activity of God and his demands upon us. In every case hardness of heart is presented as a condition which has become so far advanced through long duration that only God can take it away.

The disciples are censured for this characteristic of *sklērokardia* in Mt 16:14 while Mk 6:4–6 = Mt 19:8 attributes it to the people of Israel and traces it back to the time of Moses. In

Acts 7:51 Stephen characterises Israel and its leaders right back to the time of the prophets as *sklērotrakhēloi* in parallelism with *aperitmētoi tē(i) kardia(i)* (uncircumcised in heart). Paul sees *sklērotēs*, used in parallelism with *ametanoētos kardia* (impenitent heart, Rom 2:5), as in general a recognisable characteristic of human existence, as can be seen from v 9. Mk 3:5 uses *pōrōsis tēs kardias* (hardness of heart) as characteristic of the attitude of those in the synagogue confronted with a healing on the sabbath carried out by Jesus, while Paul in Rom 11:25 uses the same expression for the relation of Israel to Jesus, and finally, in Eph 4:18, for the obtuseness of the heathens in their relations with God. With regard to the verbs, *sklērunō* is used in Heb 3:8, 13, 15; 4:7 in a quotation from Ps 95:7-11; in Acts 19:9 with reference to the Jews of Ephesus and in Rom 9:18 as a reminiscence of its use in the story of the Exodus. This is particularly significant since Paul here wishes to testify to the sovereignty of God which stands out with special clarity in the Exodus, the God who has mercy upon whomever he wills and hardens the heart of whomever he wills.

Pōroun is used in Mk 6:52 of the disciples (passive participle) as in Mk 8:17. Rom 11:7f takes us back to the Old Testament (Deut 29:4; Is 29:10) as well as to 2 Cor 3:14 and Acts 28:27 (*pakhunō*). Is 6:9f is explicitly quoted in this last text. This quotation takes on a very particular significance in the mouth of Jesus—see Mt 13:15 (see Mk 4:12; Lk 8:10). Since the quotation in the Marcan version corresponds to the form it has in the Palestinian Targum we certainly have here an actual saying

of Jesus which goes straight back to Is 6:9ff. According to J. Jeremias (*The Parables of Jesus*, London 1954, 11ff) it did not originally belong to the context of the question about the reason for speaking in parables but was meant to provide an explanation of why Jesus gave esoteric teaching to his disciples which had to be withheld from those who, through hardness of heart, refused his message. In this respect, *mēpote* presents a problem since it can mean not only 'lest' (I should heal them) but also 'so that' (I might heal them). Jeremias suggests translating 'so that' in Mark, as corresponding to *dilema* in the targum, and, on the other hand, 'lest' in Matthew as corresponding to *pen* in the Massoretic text. This would be in agreement with the fact that the use of the imperative in Matthew gives his version a more peremptory form than Mark. There would, therefore, according to this explanation, be quite a different point of view as regards the real nature of the hardness of hearts referred to in the Isaian text as interpreted on the one hand as a hardening brought about positively by God (in Matthew) and on the other as brought about by man himself for which he alone is responsible (in Mark) and after which he can still do penance, though indeed this might be considered an improbable eventuality. Both viewpoints can be found in the Old Testament. In Lk 8:10 and Jn 12:40 God seems to be clearly considered as the original agent of this hardening of hearts.

J. Gnilka, however (*Die Verstockung Israels*), comes to quite different conclusions. He would prefer also to translate the *mēpote* of Mk 4:12 as 'lest' (cf the *dilema* of the targum). Therefore, according to Mark's point of view, Jesus would be speaking to the people in parables *so that* their hearts might be hardened, and according to Matthew, *since* they were already hardened. Therefore the point of view represented by Jeremias would be completely reversed. According to Gnilka, the Lukan version expresses in the strongest possible form the idea of predestination. In Acts 28:26ff Luke uses the Isaian quotation in order to provide a justification for the changeover to the mission of the gentiles. The connection of the logion in Mark 4:11 with the parable of the sower, Gnilka continues, is not original but comes from a different synoptic source; but he takes it to be an authentic saying of Jesus the original form of which is best preserved in Mark despite later editing and which in the Markan setting shows clear evidence of its antiquity. The connection with the Isaian context also goes back to Jesus, for he sees this text fulfilled in the attitude of the people in his regard and reads it as an expression of the will of God. He does not seek to mitigate this divine decision to punish, as is the case with the form adapted in the targum, but sees in it a pinpoint of light in the surrounding darkness, namely, that the 'holy Remnant', now constituted by the community of his disciples, would become the nucleus of a new People of God.

3. *Hardness of heart in the Old Testament.* The fact that the New Testament texts which refer to the hardening of hearts are found, in the great majority of cases, connected with Old Testament quotations or allusions, shows clearly that the New Testament seizes on Old Testament lines of thought—whether it is a question of the sayings of Jesus or a text in Paul or an occurrence elsewhere. The idea of the hardening of hearts in the Old Testament is closely allied with the theology of the covenant, and only against this background does it become fully intelligible.

We can state at once that the terms used in the New Testament are taken from the Old since the verbs, adjectives and nouns used there (to harden, hardening, to be stubborn, stubbornness, 'to make fat') go back to the literary usage of LXX. What is common to them all, as also to the Hebrew words from which they derive, is a strong graphic character capable of representing and objectivising an inner event of the human heart. This, together with the ability of the Hebrew to express a wide range of shades of meaning, really proves to be necessary since the Old Testament shows concern to present the idea according to its different aspects, while the New Testament takes over the expressions of the Old.

As regards verbs, the Old Testament uses: *kābēd* in Qal occurring only in Exodus; in Hiphil in Exodus, Isaiah, and Zecharias; and in Piel in 1 Samuel; *ḥāsaq* in Qal only in Exodus; in Piel in Exodus and Joshua; and in Hiphil in Jeremiah 5:3; *qāšâh* occurs only twice without an object, but elsewhere with *lēb* (heart), *rûaḥ* (breath, spirit), *pānîm* (face), *ʿorep* (neck), and once with *derek* (way). In Hiphil it occurs twice, and the relative adjective *qāšeh* six times, with *ʿorep. šāʿaʿ* (cry out) occurs only seldom —twice in Isaiah, in Qal and Hithpalpel; *šāman* (make fat)—once in Hiphil, with *lēb* (Is 6:10); *ʾāmats*

346

(strengthen) thirty-three times with *lēbāb* (heart) or *lēb*; and, finally, *qāšāḥ* (harden) in Is 63:17. The idea of hardness, stubbornness, and heaviness therefore predominates. As one can see from the frequent connection with *leb*, the Old Testament has already laid down the essential lines for the New. The heart, seat of the moral and religious life, is hardened, made obdurate, made 'fat', namely, insensitive and unwilling to act. Side by side with this usage, we also find as objects of this process, the eyes, ears, face, forehead and neck. The end-result of the hardening can be a 'stiff-necked people', an uncircumcised (*ʿārēl*) heart, a heart of stone (Ezek 11:19; 36:26), dullness of heart (*mᵉginnath lēb*, Lam 3:65) or obstinacy of heart (*šerirûth lēb*), which latter is frequent in Jeremiah and Deuteronomy.

This usage continues in post-biblical terminology and occurs frequently in 1 QS and 1 QH. It is striking how often the Old Testament causative usage (Hiphil of *kābēd* and Piel of *ḥāzaq*) occurs, expressing the idea that this condition of hardness is the result of an action freely willed. In the J strata of the Pentateuch and in Jeremiah, Ezekiel, and Deutero-Isaiah the subject is often a human agent or Israel itself. In a particular case, this subject refuses to pay attention to the word of God and hardens his (its) heart. While on the one hand Deutero-Isaiah and as far as can be seen also Jeremiah and Deuteronomy contemplate the possibility that a man can remove this condition of a hardened heart and turn to God again, it would appear on the other hand that in Ezekiel and the J strata of the Pentateuch the hardening is so deeply implanted and so far progressed that the one concerned is irretrievably lost, for he has passed from a personal decision to a permanent state, a habit which no conversion can get rid of and which in fact excludes the idea of conversion. It is quite different in Isaiah, Trito-Isaiah, and the P strata of the Pentateuch. In this last God hardens the heart of the Pharaoh in order to place him in a state of guilt and therefore to punish him, just as is the case in Joshua 11:17 with the kings of Canaan. In Isaiah this applies to Israel as a whole and in Trito-Isaiah to the sum total of the godless within Israel. We should not suppose that it is a question here of demonic characteristics in the nature of Yahweh; rather what is implied in these hard expressions which savour of predestination is that, in the last resort, no other will has any force except the will of God, that God's designs are to be fulfilled when the kingdom of God, the final end of all history, becomes a reality. The God whom the prophets encounter is the God whose will is omnipotent, while the priestly tradition knows a God who unfolds his plan for the world in spite of the opposition of the enemies of Israel and the godless. This priestly tradition is continued in the thinking of the Qumran community, characterised as it is by predestination and dualism (1 QS, 1 QH).

As for the object of the hardening of hearts, it is in the first place Israel on which God has a special claim as a result of the Covenant. Israel repudiates this claim and consequently its heart is hardened by God and it becomes liable to be punished by him. It becomes ripe for judgement, only beyond this

347

judgement it is possible for it once more to receive the covenant-gift of salvation. This view is expressed most clearly in Is 6:9ff where the prophet receives the mission from God to harden the heart of the people through his announcing the judgement merited by the continual repudiation of the divine claim upon her. This fate can, however, also overtake the individual Israelite insofar as he refuses God's call expressed in the law and the preaching of the prophets. According to Jeremiah, Deuteronomy, and Deutero-Isaiah, hardening of the heart is simply the result of a wrong decision which is at the same time sinful in itself and brings other sins in its wake. If this chain of sin is not broken in time through conversion to God (*šûb*) it will become a vicious circle from which there is no escape. In this case, judgement is not left over to an eschatological event even if represented as imminent, but comes in the course of historical events, so that there is still at times room for the saving action of God. Isaiah seems to represent the hardening itself as judgement, while in Trito-Isaiah it is a sign of the divine anger which the evildoer brings upon himself. The emphasis placed on the guilt of the individual confronted with the divine will permits of no mitigation of the teaching on predestination and therefore of no exoneration of the evildoer.

When the Old Testament mentions foreigners (non-Israelites) as the objects of this process of hardening of the heart, they are defeated by God after being presented with a concrete demand on the part of God—as, for example, the Pharaoh who must allow the people of Israel to leave—a demand which they refuse to recognise and so, through their hearts being hardened, are led on to judgement. They must encounter this judgement because they stand in the way of the saving action of God on behalf of his people and so obstruct the coming of the Kingdom of God. In this respect the New Testament goes even further. In his epistle to the Romans, Paul places the pagans also under the obligation of knowing God in which respect he refers to the possibility of arriving at a knowledge of God starting from created things.

Throughout the different statements on the hardening of hearts in the Old and the New Testaments there is present a certain strange and almost unnatural element which can be detected very strongly in Is 6:9ff. No wonder, then, that this text has had such considerable influence on both Old and New Testaments. This element alluded to is, however, softened somewhat by the references to the fidelity of God in keeping his promise so that even the most severe expressions of the prophets undergo a certain correction of perspective through this hope that God himself will resolve the vicious circle and that, on the other side of judgement, the redeemed 'holy remnant' will be able to experience the grace of God. By means of this grace God will change the dispositions of the heart and lead it to such a joyful and voluntary obedience that any hardness of heart will be unknown in this new world. Sometimes however, judgement and hope stand in unreconcilable opposition—a sign that God is not rationally comprehensible and free of mystery for us, that he is not at our disposal but at all times his will remains sovereign.

Harvest

Bibliography: J. Jeremias, The Parables of Jesus, London 1954; K. L. Schmidt, 'Die Verstockung der Menschen durch Gott', TZ 1 (1945), 1ff; F. Hesse, Das Verstockungsproblem im AT (BZAW 74), Berlin 1955; J. Gnilka, Die Verstockung Israels, Munich 1961; Eichrodt II/III⁴ (Index); Hesse and Gnilka give further bibliography.

Georg Molin

Harvest

A. *In the literal sense.* 1. Every harvest comes from God who gave vitality to the seed and fruitfulness to the earth (Gen 1:11), who gave the fruits of the earth to man, for his sustenance (Gen 1:29; 9:3) and solemnly guaranteed that the cycle of seed-time and harvest would not cease (Gen 8:22; Jer 5:24). God also gives a fruitful land to his people, as their inheritance (Ex 3:8; Num 13:17–27, etc). To those whom he loves, he gives to reap a hundredfold (Gen 26:12; Ps 128:2), but to those who disobey him and are hostile, he sends bad harvests and famine (2 Sam 21:1; 1 Kings 17:1; 2 Kings 8:1; Mic 6:15; Amos 4:7; Jer 5:17; 12:10–13; Joel 1, etc). The pronouncement of a blessing or a curse upon the harvest was an important form of parenesis in the Old Testament (Deut 28; Lev 26, etc). One of the most frequently occurring elements constituting the hope of Israel was an abundant yield in the harvest (Mic 4:4; Zech 3:10; see also 1 Kings 42:5). This element is also to be found in the prophetic and apocalyptic promises (see below). In the New Testament period too, there are references to God's blessing on (Mt 6:26) and his care for the seed (Mk 4:27f; 1 Cor 15:36ff) and the fruit of the earth (Jas 5:18).

2. The harvest was always an occasion for great joy (Is 9:3; Ps 4:7; 126:5; Hos 9:1), for charitable actions (Lev 19:9f; 23:22; Deut 24:19–21; see also Deut 25:4) and also to praise God, especially at the great harvest feasts of the year—Easter, Whitsun and the Feast of the Tabernacles (Ex 23:16–19; 34:22; Lev 23:9–21). These feasts were marked by an offering of the first fruits, the first loaves (Num 15:17–21; Deut 26:1–11) and various other gifts. The seventh year, when the land was to lie fallow, was designated as a sabbatical year in honour of Yahweh (Lev 25:2–5). There are frequent references in later Jewish writings and in the New Testament to such festivals of the harvest accompanied by the payment of honour to God and charitable works, and to such offerings of the first fruits and of tithes.

B. *In the figurative sense.* 1. The image of the harvest is used in a proverbial saying to denote literary activity (Sir 33:16f) and man's death (Job 5:26). The seed and the harvest, sowing and reaping, are images which occur frequently in many different proverbial sayings, especially of course in the sapiential literature (Prov 6:8; 10:5; 22:8; Job 4:8; Sir 7:3) and in the prophets (Hos 8:7; 10:12f). The same image is used by Philo to illustrate his ethic of immanence (*Conf. Ling.* 152); it can be used also in strictly legalistic teaching (4 Esdras 2:28–39; 7:17–19), as a figure of eschatological promise (Midrash on the Song of Songs 8:14), and finally in the New Testament message. Paul also applies the image of the harvest to the spiritual seed of the preaching of the gospel, from which he expects to receive the fruit, for his

349

own sustenance (1 Cor 9:7–11; Phil 4:17) and for Jerusalem (Rom 15:28; 2 Cor 9:6). He uses the image too in his teaching on the resurrection (1 Cor 15:35–58) and in terse, aphoristic form in the phrase: 'Whatever a man sows, that he will also reap' (Gal 6:7). Closely related to the image of the seed and the harvest, sowing, and reaping, is that of the tree and its fruit (SB 1, 466f, 638f; Mt 7:16–20; 12:33). The bible makes frequent use of such proverbial utterances to stress a law which is of great importance in the doctrine of retribution, namely that man's actions are closely connected with his salvation, both in time and in eternity.

2. *God's judgement* is often described in the bible by the image of the harvest. This takes three forms:

The chastisement of God. There are biblical references to the harvest as God's judgement on the enemies of the people (Is 24:13; Jer 51:33), on his people themselves in times of national calamities (Hos 13:3; Amos 8:2; Is 17:5f; Jer 6:9) and at the final, eschatological judgement (Is 63:1–6; Joel 3:13). John the Baptist refers to the one who is to come as him who will gather in the harvest (Mt 3:12). John, in the Book of Revelation, speaks of the harvest of the earth as the judgement on the world. Christ's allegorical interpretation of the parable of the cockle is also distinctly apocalyptic in manner (Mt 13:37–43).

The *beginning of the time of salvation.* The image of the harvest, based on the pattern of the ancient sayings on the subject of abundant harvests, is found in the promises occurring in contexts probably dating from after the Exile (Amos 9:13–15; Mic 4:4). The day of God's judgement on the enemies of his people will be one of great joy for Israel (Joel 2:19–24; Is 27:12f). On that day the eternal harvest will begin (Joel 3:18), and Israel will be comparable to a luxuriant plantation (Is 60:21; 61:3; cf 5:1–7). This image of the rich eschatological harvest was developed in great detail by the Jews (P. Volz, *Die Eschatologie der jüdischen Gemeinde*, Tübingen 1934, 387f), and the idea of the eschatological community as God's plantation plays a very important part in rabbinical teaching (SB 1, 666; see also 4 Esdras 6:41), in the literature of Qumran (1 QS 8, 5:12f; 11:8; see also 1 QH 6:25; 8:6) and in the New Testament (Mt 15:13; 1 Cor 3:6f; Heb 12:15; Rev 22:2).

The *individual retribution imposed by God.* The Old Testament seldom refers to the retribution which God demands from man, according to his 'fruit' (see Sir 27:6), but there is frequent mention of it in later judaism (SB 1, 466f, 638f). At the last judgement God will 'harvest' the deeds of every man (Volz, 305f)—both John the Baptist (Mt 3:8–10) and Jesus (Mt 7:16–20) also refer to this harvest. The same idea is further developed in the missionary preaching of the New Testament, often in the form of lists of virtues and vices, accompanied by pointed references to God's judgement (Gal 5:19–23, etc). The same idea is also made available to the apostles in the missionary field (see Mk 4:14–20).

3. Two further important aspects of the image of the harvest are to be found in the New Testament:

The *kingdom of God* is a harvest. The parables of Jesus which speak in terms of contrasting situations do not emphasise the phase of development and ripening (this is alien to the biblical mode of thought), but rather draw a contrast between the beginning and the end. Thus, despite everything that happened to prevent it, the sower's harvest is plentiful (the parable of the sower: Mk 4:3-8); despite the smallness of the grain of mustard seed, the significance of the fully grown tree is world-wide (the parable of the mustard seed: Mk 4:30-32) and without any human assistance, the seed grows of its own accord and the harvest is suddenly there (the parable of the seed growing secretly: Mk 4:26-9). Finally, it is necessary for man to wait patiently for the day which God appoints for the harvest (the parable of the good seed and the cockle: Mt 13:24-30). But, in Jesus' opinion, it is already time for the harvest and for this reason he tells his disciples to pray for labourers to be sent to reap this great harvest of the kingdom of God (Mt 9:37f). Those who are to proclaim the gospel of Christ are not the sowers of the seed, but the reapers (Jn 4:35-8) and their mission is the beginning of the eschatological harvest (Rom 1:13). It is this which gives the 'harvest' its judicial and decisive aspect, as part of the final fulfilment.

The second important aspect of the harvest image in the New Testament is that *Jesus is both the sower and the seed.* This emerges from the allegorical interpretations which Jesus provides for the parables of the sower (Mk 4:14-20) and of the cockle in the field (Mt 13:37-43). What we have here is Jesus himself, his word and the christian message. Paul applies the image

to the christian message (1 Cor 3:6-9; Col 1:5f)—he who sows in the Lord and in the Spirit reaps everlasting life (Rom 6:21f; 7:4f; Gal 6:8). In the same way, John stresses the importance of communion with Christ in order to yield fruit (Jn 15:1-8). Most important of all in this context is the word of Jesus, when he compares himself to a grain of wheat (Jn 12:24f). By its death, this seed yields a rich harvest to the world.

Bibliography: F. Hauck, *TDNT* III, 132f and 614f; H. Traub, *BTHW* 120; J. P. Ramseyer, Allmen 182; H. Sahlin, 'Die Früchte der Umkehr', *Studia Theologica* I (1947, Lund 1948), 54-68. See also G. Dalman, *Arbeit und Sitte in Palästina* III; F. Nötscher, *Altertumskunde* 173-82.

Wilhelm Pesch

Hatred

One of the most striking manifestations of the inner division within man is mutual antipathy between individuals. Gen 4:2-8 represents hatred, which appears with the first descendants of Adam and Eve, as one of the direct consequences of the fall. Though this depends on the point of view of the Yahwist author in his survey of primitive history it corresponds to an understanding of human nature which is found throughout the bible. In the Old Testament hatred is above all a datum of experience in both public and private life. The earliest writings simply state it as a fact of experience without attempting to explain it by going more deeply into it.

In order to designate this whole complex process which goes on in the will and the feelings, biblical Hebrew disposes only of the one word *šānēʾ* which LXX translates almost invariably by *misein*. This must be explained not only by the fact that Hebrew has a limited vocabulary for expressing concepts but also by the unique characteristic of Hebrew in expressing reality in antithetical terms. In general the Semite prefers to express a relationship of sympathy or antipathy in polarized terms rather than distinguish with psychological nicety between different spiritual states. Thus the language of the Old Testament prefers to speak directly of love or hatred rather than of a preference for or antipathy towards a certain person or thing; hence the frequency with which we come across polarized concepts in relation to this theme. In divorce proceedings, for example, the texts refer to the man 'hating' the woman but this simply means that they failed to get along together (see Deut 21:15; 22:13–16 with Gen 29:33 where the 'hatred' of Jacob merely signifies that he was less pleased with her than previously).

This, however, does not at all imply that the existence of real hate testified to in the Old Testament is to be questioned; it merely implies that caution is in order in explaining the terms used. Hatred in the Old Testament takes in every degree of intensity of bad will from lack of love (Ex 20:5; Deut 7:10) or omission of friendly relations through occasional hostilities and speaking in hostile terms (Gen 26:27; Judg 11:7; 2 Sam 5:8; 13:22; 22:18, 41; 1 Kings 22:8) to a permanently hostile state which can end in murder (Gen 4:2–8; 27:41; 2 Sam 13:22, 28–9). The decisive factor in deciding punishment for a murderer is whether the killing resulted from hatred (Deut 19:4, 6, 11; Josh 20:5). Only in this case was the death penalty inflicted on the guilty party even when he had fled to a city of refuge (Deut 19:11ff).

Although hatred is essentially a human characteristic Yahweh is, by analogy, represented as harbouring feelings of hatred which find expression in opposition to the sinful deeds of men. This divine antipathy applies in the first case to any kind of idolatry (Deut 12:31; 16:22; Ps 31:6; Jer 44:4), to false oaths (Zech 8:17) and to a great number of moral lapses (Ps 5:5ff; 11:5; Prov 8:13; Sir 10:7; 27:24 etc). This way of speaking is, of course, metaphorical; it would be quite impossible in view of the loving assent of Yahweh to his creation to transfer to him human hatred in the real sense of the term (Wis 11:24). What is expressed in speaking of God hating is the incommensurability between his holiness and any kind of unrighteousness in which man remains obdurate. On account of its infidelity even the chosen people can provoke Yahweh to hatred (Hos 9:15; Jer 12:8) until such time as it finds again the way of truth.

The true Israelite must not hate his fellow-men but must, on the contrary, show them brotherly love (Lev 19:17f). Although the basis of the so-called Law of Holiness is clearly formulated it has in the course of time been interpreted and put into practice in very different ways. In practice, the law of love was restricted to Israelites; those outside the covenant merited hatred insofar as they proved themselves to be the enemies of Yahweh or of his people (Num 10:35; Ps 83:2ff). Within the community evil-doers, those who persecuted the righteous and pious devotees of Yahweh (Ps 34:21; 35:19; 38:19f; 86:17), were to be regarded as hating God (Ex 20:5; Deut 5:9; 7:10 etc). The hatred of the godless against those closely united with God is found throughout the whole length of salvation history. It reaches its climax in the crucifixion of Christ for which hate was responsible even though it was through the cross that the eternal enmity of the Evil One was overcome.

In the Old Testament it is expressly forbidden to the pious Israelite to enter into league with the evil-doer or show him love (2 Chron 19:2); on the contrary, he must be hated as Yahweh hates him (Ps 26:4f; 101:3f; 139:21 etc). This is closely connected with the demand of unconditional self-giving to Yahweh encumbent on every Israelite. According to the anthropomorphic way of speaking common in the Old Testament, God is jealous for the love of his people. Understandably hatred has for its first object evil and wickedness but for Old Testament man no real distinction was made between hating evil and hating the evil-doer.

The idea of the ⁄ covenant played a large part in emphasising the polarity between hatred and love. In connection with the feast of covenant-renewal formulae of cursing and blessing were developed which were applied respectively to the transgression and observance of the covenant stipulations. At any rate, by the inter-testamentary period we find stereotype liturgical formulae of curse and blessing as those, for example, in use in the Qumran community (1 QS 2:4–18; 1 QM 13:1–6). It we take these into account

we will be better able to interpret the law of love: not only was the neighbour to be loved but the evil-doer was to be hated. As is well known, the Old Testament not only does not contain such a commandment but several expressions appear to contradict it (Ex 23:4; Prov 25:21). Yet the words attributed to Jesus in Matthew's gospel (5:43) and those found in the Manual of Discipline of the Qumran sectarians (1 QS 1:9f; 9:16, 21f; cf 4:17) prove that this was in fact the practice in Old Testament times.

The Zadokite community of Qumran thought of itself as the only true people of God; hence it became more and more imbued with a sense of the distinction between its members and those who did not form part of it. But whether all of these latter were to be hated without distinction is not so certain. The stipulation in 1 QS 1:10 clearly speaks in a restrictive way: the true member of the community must hate 'the sons of darkness each one according to the extent that he has incurred the vengeance of God'. The basic criterion is here the same as in the Old Testament: in their dealings with one another men must follow the example of God himself. At the same time, however, the obligation to hate is expressed in even more precise and stringent terms than is the case in the Old Testament. Judgement is passed on the 'spirit' of each member, that is, on the degree of perfection which he has attained, with reference not only to how he loves but how he hates (1 QS 9:15–16). Yet the devout member of the community postpones the wrath of God on those to be hated until 'the day of visitation' (1 QS 10:17–18). This obligation to

353

hate expresses the radical demand made on the member to segregate himself from any kind of evil; an obligation made necessary by the imminence of the world-end. By keeping clear of unrighteousness (understood dualistically), expressed in terms of hatred, these sectarians hoped to make their contribution to the ultimate victory of God over the forces of evil.

It is quite another question, however, when we ask how this basic postulate of hating the enemy was worked out in the practical everyday living of Old Testament man and the member of the Qumran community. There was obviously the constant danger of identifying the enemy of God with one's personal enemies which could at least have the result of excluding these from the category of 'neighbour' to whom love was due. 'Who is my enemy?' was a question as obscure and ambiguous to Old Testament man as that other asked of the Lord: 'who is my neighbour?' (Lk 10:29).

Christ dissolved any possible misunderstanding by absolutely forbidding any kind of hatred. The Old Testament prohibition of hating one's brother (fellow-Israelite) was now applied universally and given a new meaning by being displaced by the command to love one's enemy (Mt 5:43-4; Lk 6:27f). The unconditional love of the Father is activated by acceptance of the neighbour and the putting aside of any kind of hostility towards him. By means of the saving activity of Christ those who had been re-created in him learned to overcome hate by love, even though the tension between these two opposing attitudes was not thereby removed. The authors of the most

recent books of the Old Testament are already beginning to reflect on the roots of hatred and traced its cause to Satan, the old enemy of the human race (Wis 2:24, cf Jn 8:44). According to the apocalyptic writers the present age was subordinate to him, and the world which had fallen prey to hatred lay in his power. By keeping clear of hatred which had been overcome in principle by Christ (Tit 3:3f) the Christian hastened the coming of the future age. But at the same time he continued to live in the world where hatred is an ever-present reality. He should therefore not be surprised if the world hates (Mt 10:22; Jn 15:19; 17:14; 1 Jn 3:13) or persecutes him (Mt 5:10; Lk 6:22). On the contrary, he has to rejoice that it is given him to follow in the footsteps of the Master (Lk 6:22f; Mt 27:18; Jn 5:18; 7:7; 15:24; Eph 2:14, 16).

In the fourth gospel hatred is presented within the context of the author's 'theology' of light. As the essence of darkness (1 Jn 2:9, 11), hate reveals itself as to all intents and purposes a satanic force which is violently active in opposition to the fulfilment of God's saving design. In the opposition between love and hate we recognise the definitive distinction between the kingdom of light and the kingdom of darkness (1 Jn 2:9-11) and the appearance of a judgement within history (cf Jn 3:19). Hatred of the brethren is likened to murder (1 Jn 3:15; cf Mt 5:22) and excludes the one who hates from eternal life (see Jn 15:23-5).

In addition to this we should note that Old Testament usage also lies behind much of what we find on the subject of hatred in the New Testament.

The admonition of Jesus addressed to the disciples to hate their relatives (Mt 10:37; Lk 14:26) or even themselves (Lk 14:26) signifies a radical rupture of natural ties which could compromise their absolute dedication to the Saviour and his saving mission (see Jude 23 on the need to keep away from those who are fickle and inconstant). To the same way of speaking belong what Paul has to say in Rom 7:15 where hatred is to be understood as the opposite of the will to do good in man delivered up to the power of sin; also Lk 19:14 (see Rev 17:16) which refers to political malice. ⊅ Vengeance. ⊅ Love.

Bibliography: A. Carr, 'The Meaning of "Hatred" in the New Testament', *The Expositor* VI, 12 (1905), 153–60; J. Denney, 'The word "Hate" in Lk 14:26', *Expository Times* 20 (1909), 41f; W. Bleibtreu, *Paradoxe Aussprüche Jesu*, 1926, 15–35; O. Michel, *TDNT* IV, 683–94; Haag 649–51; M. Smith, 'Mt V, 43. Hate thine enemy', *Harv. Theol. Review* 45 (1952), 71–3; R. Schnackenburg, *Die Johannesbriefe*, Freiburg 1953, 174–6; H. Braun, *Spätjüdisch-häretischer und frühchristlicher Radikalismus* II, Tübingen 1957, 57–9 (esp. *n.* 1); C. Spicq, *Agapè* I, Paris 1958, 17–20; E. F. Sutcliffe, 'Hatred at Qumran', *Revue de Qumran* 2 (1959/60), 345–56; J. Brière, 'Hate', *DBT* 198–200; M. Weise, *Kultzeiten und kultischer Bundesschluss in der Ordensregel vom Toten Meer*, Leiden 1961; B. Renaud, *Je suis un Dieu jaloux*, Paris 1963; A. Dihle, *Die goldene Regel*, Göttingen 1962, 114–16.

F. L. R. Stachowiak

Head

In the literal sense of the word, head stands of course for the head of a living creature, and especially for the head of a human being. Jesus's head is also mentioned occasionally (Mt 8:20 and pars; Jn 19:30). As the head is the most important part of the body, it is customary to swear by one's head (Mt 5:36). Various movements of the head are used to express a person's thoughts, feelings, and reactions. An uplifted head expresses self-confidence and justifiable pride (Sir 11:1). It can also express haughtiness, arrogance, and boundless presumption (Ps 83:3; Job 20:6). On the other hand, it can also be the expression of justified hope and joy (Lk 21:28). The opposite movement—bowing of the head—may indicate either submission, humility, and reverence (Sir 4:7), or fear and timidity (Job 32:6 Vulg.). Jesus bowed his head when he died (Jn 19:30). Shaking the head is a gesture of incomprehension, disdain, scorn or mockery (Job 16:4f; Ps 22:7; Lam 2:15; Mt 27:39). Covering the head is a sign of affliction, disappointment or shame (2 Sam 15:30; Esther 6:12; Jer 14:3f; Mic 3:7). Paul regarded it as a disgrace for a man to cover his head while praying or at public worship, whereas for a woman it was disgraceful to pray with uncovered head (1 Cor 11:4–7). The hairs of the head are all numbered (Mt 10:30) because God's providence is concerned even with such relatively unimportant things as this. Even their colour is determined by God (Mt 5:36). The head was shaved after the Nazaritic vow had been taken (Acts 21:23f). The Israelite was bound by the law to honour those whose hair had become grey with age by standing up (Lev 19:32). Finally, baskets, are carried on the head (Gen 40:16).

Certain symbolic acts are associated with the head. Dust or ashes are put on the head as a sign of affliction or grief (Josh 7:6; Lam 2:10). Hands are placed upon the head to bestow a blessing (Gen 48:14; Mk 10:16) or to transfer responsibility to another person (↗ laying on of Hands). In the consecration of priests or kings, the head is anointed with oil (Ex 29:7; 1 Sam 10:1). The expression 'to heap hot coals of fire upon the head of an enemy' by doing good to him (Prov 25:21f; Rom 12:20) undoubtedly means that good actions will result in causing the recipient to feel shame and humiliation.

The head is the noblest part of the human body and as such it frequently stands for the whole person and in particular for the individual as against a large number of people (see Ex 16:16). In this way, when people are numbered in the bible, they are counted by heads (see, for example, Num 1:18), that is to say, a count is made of individual persons. To raise up the head of a person means that this person is honoured (Gen 40:13) and the guardian of someone's head is the guardian of the whole person and of his life (1 Sam 28:2). A curse pronounced upon another person or upon other people, or the delegation of responsibility to another or to other persons is spoken of as being upon his head or upon their heads (2 Sam 1:16; Acts 18:6). But a person who wishes to take on himself a very heavy responsibility expresses this readiness by declaring that he is prepared that the blood of another be on his own head (Josh 2:19; cf Mt 27:25). In Ezek 17:19, however, God reserves for himself the right to take the appropriate action against the person who has failed him when he says: 'I will lay upon his head the oath he has despised and the covenant he has broken'.

The bible also contains references to the head of superterrestrial beings and to the head of God himself, since celestial beings and God are both described in human forms. In the Apocalypse, for example, the head and the hair of the Son of Man appear as snow-white wool (Rev 1:14). The Son of Man also has a golden crown on his head (14:14). The angel's head is adorned with a rainbow (10:1) and the twenty-four ancients also wear crowns of gold (4:4).

There are also frequent references to the heads of animals, as in their case, too, the head is the most important part of the body. The head of the serpent is to be crushed (Gen 3:15) and the head of the Paschal lamb is to be eaten (Ex 12:9). In the case of the 'dog's head' used as a term of abuse (2 Sam 3:8), it is clear that the head is, as with man, referred to as *pars pro toto*.

The word *head* is also frequently used in the *figurative sense*. The position of the head in relation to the rest of the human body results in an extension of meaning, in which the word is applied figuratively to denote, for example, a topographical or architectural feature which is elevated. In this sense, the Hebrew word head is used for the top of a mountain (Gen 8:5; Is 2:2) and elsewhere for a whole mountain range rising above a plain ('the head of the valley': Is 28:1, 4). In the same way, the Hebrew word for head is used to denote the top of a tree (Is 17:6) or the capital of a pillar (1 Kings 7:16). The highest stone forming the top of a building is also called its head (Zech 4:7) and the lintel of a gate is known as the head (Ps 24:7, 9). The word is also used figuratively in Hebrew for the upper end or top of an object such as Jacob's ladder (Gen 28:12), a sceptre (Esther 5:2) or an ear of corn (Job 24:24).

The meaning is further logically extended to denote what is qualitatively superior to everything else. The 'head' of balsam is the best and finest sort of this spice (Ezek 27:22) and the word for head is similarly used in Ex 30:23 and Song 4:14 to designate the best kinds of various spices. The greatest joy, superior to all other kinds of joy is the 'head', or summit of joy (Ps 137:6).

Since, in the case of animals, the head is the foremost part of the body, we have the extended meaning of 'head' as the first in time, the beginning. Thus we find the word *head* used to indicate the beginning of the night-watch (Judg 7:19), the first days of a month (Num 10:10; 28:11) or the first month of a year (Ex 12:2). It can also mean the beginning of a series of actions (1 Chron 16:7), the beginning of a road (Is 51:20; Ezek 16:25, 31) or the source of a river (Gen 2:10). The beginning of a paragraph or book is called its head (Ps 40:8 in LXX; Heb 10:7). It is also used for the capital in the sense of the first and main instalment of a payment due (Lev 6:5). The word is used also to convey the idea of primary or basic elements in nature (Prov 8:26).

The word is extended even further in meaning to include the idea of priority over others. Thus, the ruling classes of Israelite society are referred to as the 'head' of the people, in contrast to the 'tail'—the mass of the people which follows them and is subordinate to them (Is 9:14). This idea is, however, not restricted solely to Israel. The prophet Isaiah also calls Damascus the 'head' of the Syrian Empire (7:8). What is meant here is that Damascus is the leading city of Syria. According to Jer 31:7, a people which has gained ascendancy over other races is their 'head'.

The conception of priority, precedence or superiority conveyed by the word *head* and particularly the closely associated idea of gaining and retaining the ascendancy and hegemony over others led to the further meaning of authority, especially that of the head of a family, tribe and so on. Thus the family (Ex 6:14), the tribe (Num 30:1) and even the Galaadite army (Judg 11:8f) has its authoritative leader or head. In the same way, the Syrian king (Is 7:8) and the government of Juda and Israel (Hos 1:11) are called the 'head'. According to 1 Cor 11:3; Eph 5:23, the man is not only the head of the family, but also the head of his wife, that is, as head of the family, he has authority over his wife.

Finally, the New Testament also contains frequent references to *Christ as head*. Here, the various elements common to the figurative use of the word in the Bible come together to form a single, total image, though this image has a certain distinct colouring. As the Head of all things (Eph 1:22), Christ is not simply the uppermost part, the crown of all things, but at the same time the one who is in his very being and essence above the universe, since he himself created all things (Col 1:16) and is the source and origin of all being. As the creator of the universe, he is invested with supreme authority as its Lord right from the moment of his incarnation (Eph 1:20–22). As Head of the universe, the incarnate creator is also Head of every cosmic principality and power (Eph 1:21f; Col 2:10). For this reason the entire universe, including the demonic powers, is subject to the Son of Man since he is exalted to God's throne, that is, he shares in the sovereign supremacy of God's rule (Eph 1:20f). He fills all things—the entire universe which is at his feet (Eph 4:10). He is able to do this by allowing the universe to become entirely permeated by his sovereign power. The demonic powers which succeeded at least for a time in disturbing the unity of the universe, are no exceptions to Christ's sway (Eph 2:2; 6:11f). The original unity of the universe was, however, restored by the exalted God-man, who conferred upon it a new, single principle of government which re-established unity and brought about the subjugation of the demonic powers (Eph 1:21f). The entire universe was gathered up into a single whole under Christ as its Head (Eph 1:10). The first step was taken in establishing this universal unity when the Son of Man was exalted to the right hand of the Father so that he might share in the Father's sovereign rule (Eph 1:20). This single universal unity under one Head will not, however, be finally consummated until the end of time, when the demonic powers will also ultimately be subdued and at the same time completely eliminated (1 Cor 15:24f). This does not imply that these demonic powers are included in the atonement. They are unredeemable (see Rev 20:10). It is only through their submission to the exalted Christ (Eph 1:22) that they are made to realise that the original plan of creation, which was thrown into disorder by them, has ultimately been restored throughout the universe (Mussner).

In a very special sense Christ is also the *head of the church* as his Body (Eph 5:23; Col 1:18, 24). What is new in this aspect of Paul's christology, in contrast to the theology of his earlier epistles, is due principally to his controversy with those who taught false doctrine in Colossae. He realised that what the situation demanded was that he should lay particular emphasis on Christ's sovereignty. In the church too, Christ occupies a sovereign position, as the church is his body. He is also, in a very special sense, the head of the church. The head belongs essentially to the human body, it guides and directs the body and conditions its growth within the essential unity existing between the head and the body. In the same way and with similar functions, Christ as head belongs essentially to the church as his body. The church is subject in obedience to its head, since Christ is also its Lord, just as a wife is bound in obedience to her husband as her head (Eph 5:22-4). This subjection of the church to Christ as its head is complete, total, and unconditional (Eph 5:24). The entire human body is joined and held together by its various muscles and ligaments which proceed from and are controlled by the head—Christ is similarly, as head of his church, the unifying and central principle of the church (Eph 4:15ff). As its head, Christ is also the source from which the church gains sustenance and the means by which it continues to grow (Eph 4:16; Col 2:19). He nourishes and cherishes it (Eph 5:29). Christ is also the ultimate goal to which the church is moving, until all its members achieve full maturity and perfect manhood—'to the measure of the stature of the fullness of Christ' (Eph 4:13). It is in this way that the body of Christ is built up and this process of growth is accomplished in charity (Eph 4:16). It is through this building up of the church, as a result of its growth which proceeds from Christ, that the ultimate stage is reached when Christ becomes, in the fullest and most perfect sense, the head of the universe (Eph 1:10). The entire universe grows, in the church, with and through it, towards Christ as its head (Eph 1:23).

This does not, however, mean (even according to Col 1:20) that the cosmic principalities and powers are for this reason included in the church as the body of Christ. The church is the community of the redeemed (↗ church). The good angels have no need of redemption and the demonic powers cannot be redeemed (see Rev 20:10f). Christ is undeniably their head, but his headship of the demonic powers is totally different from his headship of the church. He is the head of the church in that it is his body, kept alive and nourished by him (Eph 5:29) and enabled to grow by him (Eph 4:13). Christ, the head, and the church, his body, form one single living organism. This does not apply to the demonic powers, which explains why they are never referred to in the New Testament as the body of Christ or as members of that body (cf Eph 1:22a with 22b). Christ is their head only by virtue of the fact that they are—either voluntarily or reluctantly—subject to him as

the exalted Son of Man, raised up into heaven and sharing in the sovereign rule of the eternal Father (Eph 1:20–22; Col 2:10).

This truth, that Christ is the head of the church his body, marks the highest stage in the development of the concept of 'head' and, as such, has no parallel in any non-christian religion. Even the Qumran sect can offer nothing which is even remotely comparable to this.

Bibliography: *DB* v, 2100f; E. Kalt, *Bibl. Reallex.* I², 761f; *TDNT* III, 673–82; Haag 651f; W. Bauer, *Wörterbuch zum Neuen Testament*, 1958⁵, 850f; T. Schmidt, *Der Leib Christi*, Leipzig 1919, 166–91; P. Dhorme, 'L'emploi métaphorique des noms de parties du corps en hébreu et en akkadien', *RB* 29 (1920), 465–506; H. Schlier, *Christus und die Kirche im Epheserbrief*, Tübingen 1930; J. Gewiess, *Christus und das Heil nach dem Kolosserbrief*, Breslau 1932 (dissertation); E. Käsemann, *Leib und Leib Christi*, Tübingen 1933; P. Benoit, 'L'horizon paulinien de l'Epître aux Ephésiens', *RB* 46 (1937), 342–61 and 506–25; A. Wikenhauser, *Die Kirche als der mystische Leib Christi nach dem Apostel Paulus*, Münster 1940², 197–224; E. Percy, *Der Leib Christi* ('*sōma Khristou*') *in den paulinischen Homologumena und Antilogumena*, Lund 1942; J. Michl, 'Die "Versöhnung" (Col 1:20)', *TQ* 128 (1948), 442–62; B. N. Wambacq, '"*Per eum reconciliare . . . quae in caelis sunt*" (Col 1:20)', *RB* 55 (1948), 35–42; H. Schlier and V. Warnach, *Die Kirche im Epheserbrief*, Münster 1949; O. Cullmann, *Königsherrschaft Christi und Kirche im NT*, Zollikon-Zürich 1950; T. Soiron, *Die Kirche als der Leib Christi*, Düsseldorf 1951; J. Gewiess, 'Die Begriffe *plēroun* und *plērōma* im Kolosser- und Epheserbrief', *Vom Wort des Lebens* (Festschrift Max Meinertz), ed. N. Adler, Münster 1951, 128–41; J. M. Gonzalez Ruiz, 'Sentido soteriológico de "Kefalé" en la cristologia de S. Pablo', *Anthologia Annua*, Rome 1953, 185–225; S. Bedale, 'The Meaning of *kephalē* in the Pauline Epistles', *JTS* 5 (1954), 211–15; C. Maurer, 'Die Begründung der Herrschaft Christi über die Mächte nach Col 1:15–20', *Wort und Dienst* 4 (1955), 79–93; F. Mussner, *Christus, das All und die Kirche*, Trier 1955; J. A. T. Robinson, *The Body: A Study in Pauline Theology*, London 1952; P. Benoit, 'Corps, tête et plérôme dans les épîtres de la captivité', *RB* 63 (1956), 5–44; H. Schlier,

Die Zeit der Kirche, Freiburg 1956, 159–86; E. Schweizer, 'Jesus Christus, Herr über Kirche und Welt', *Libertas christiana* (Festschrift F. Delekat), Munich 1957, 175–87; G. Rinaldi, 'Capo', *Bibbia e Oriente* 1 (1959), 14; E. Schweizer, 'Die Kirche als Leib Christi in den paulinischen Antilogumena', *TLZ* 86 (1961), 241–56.

Nikolaus Adler

Heart

The primary meaning of the Hebrew *lēb* and *lēbāb* and of the Greek *kardia* is heart in the purely physical sense. In the figurative sense, however, these words have a theological significance (see also ↗ conscience, ↗ life, ↗ man).

A. *In the Old Testament.* The heart is the inward, spiritual part of man, into which God is able to see (1 Sam 16:7; Jer 31:33; here 'heart' and 'bowels' are analogous). It is the seat of man's spiritual strength and faculties and of his intelligence.

The heart is also the seat of man's feelings, such as courage (2 Chron 17:6; 2 Sam 7:27; the Hebrew phrase corresponds to the English 'to take heart'), joy (Deut 28:47; Judg 19:9; Zech 10:7; Job 29:13; Ps 45:1), sorrow and grief (Jer 4:19; Is 65:14), arrogance and pride (Jer 48:29; 49:16, etc), goodwill (2 Sam 15:13; Ezra 6:22; Mal 4:6), care (1 Sam 9:20), sympathy or pity (Hos 11:8), excitement (Deut 19:6; Prov 23:17), composure (Prov 14:30), and desire (Ps 21:2; Job 31:7).

We find in the Old Testament a counterpart to the Latin *cordatus*, meaning literally 'man of heart', thus an intelligent, wise, and understanding man (cf Job 34:10 with 37:24; see also 1 Kings 5:7). The man who denies (Hebrew *ḥ*ᵃ*sar*) his heart, in this case his intelligence, is a fool (↗ foolishness: Prov 6:32; 10:21; Eccles 10:3). ↗ Wine takes away a man's heart, or intelligence (Hos 4:11). Men's thoughts dwell in the heart (Judg 5:15ff); to 'come into' the heart means to come to mind (Is 65:17).

It is in the heart that intentions and plans are formed (Jer 23:20; Is 10:7; 1 Chron 22:19; Dan 1:8, etc). The heart is the inward impulse causing man to act (Ex 36:2; Num 16:28). The phrase 'with all ones heart' is parallel to 'with all one's soul' (Josh 22:5). Thus it can be seen that the whole man is inwardly under the influence of his *leb*, and especially so where his will and actions are concerned, and from this point it is not difficult to understand how the word 'heart', through its connection with the human will and intelligence, came to have a religious and moral significance. The heart of the upright, pious man trusts in God (Ps 7:10) and accepts his teaching (Prov 7:3). The heart can also be faithless (Is 29:13; Ezek 6 9, etc) and harden itself against God (Ex 4:21; 9:7, etc: ↗ hardness of heart). The heart of the sinner is 'uncircumcised' (Jer 9:25) and must be circumcised, that is to say, it must be converted (↗ conversion) (see Deut 10:16; Joel 2:12). The religious man has a clean heart, meaning that his attitude of mind is pure (Ps 24:4; 51:10). The evil man, on the other hand, has a perverse heart (Prov 11:20, etc).

H. Brunner has drawn attention to the particular usage of the word 'heart' as the secret source of man's life, of his fate and destiny. In Judg 16:15ff, Samuel reveals his entire heart to Delilah—not simply his love for her, but also the ultimate secret of his inner life. We may interpret similarly the words of Samuel to Saul: 'I will tell you all that is on your mind (heart)' (1 Sam 9:19)—in other words, reveal what God has in mind for you, the secret of your life. In this context Dan 2:29ff should also be quoted, where we find the following correspondence: future thoughts = the mysteries of God = the thoughts of the heart, providing evidence for the interpretation in the sense of the secret of man's fate or destiny.

B. *The Qumran texts* reveal a similar picture in their use of the word 'heart'. It is most frequently used for 'courage', as the seat of man's feelings (1 QM 1:14; 8:10; 10:3; 16:14; 18:13; 1 QH 7:16). Those who are 'willing in heart' (1 QM 10:5) are contrasted with those who lose heart (1 QM 10:6; 11:9). In this sense, the heart, that is to say, courage, 'melts' (1 QM 14:6; 1 QH 2:6; 2:28; 4 QpIs^a 3:4), 'trembles' (1 QH 10:33), 'shudders' (1 QH 7:3) or is 'restless' (1 QH 7:5). On the other hand, the heart rejoices in the ↗ covenant and in the ↗ truth (1 QG 10:30) and is strong in this ↗ joy and superior to the children of the world (CD 20:33).

The rational aspect of the 'heart' (1 QS 11:3) and, even more particularly, the religious and moral aspect is very forcibly expressed in the Qumran texts. The 'integrity of heart' (1 QS 11:2) is contrasted with falsehood ('with a double heart', that is, duplicity, 'not in thy truth' 1 QH 4:14), pride (1 QS 4:9; 1 Q 22:2, 4; 1

QpHab 8:10), hardness of heart (1 QS 1:6; 2:3; 2:26; 3:3; 4:11; 5:4; 7:19, 24; 1 QM 14:7; CD 2:17f; 3:5; 3:11f; 8:8; 8:19; 19:20, 33; 20:10) and perversity of heart (1 QS 11:9; 1 QH 7:27; 17:19). Such a heart is 'foolish' (1 QH 1:37), 'stony' (1 QH 18:26), 'troubled' (1 QH 18:20) or uncircumcised (1 QpHab 11:13); it has idols and false gods (CD 20:9; 1 QS 2:11) and in following its inclinations man is led astray (1 QS 5:4). The members of the community are therefore constantly urged to be converted 'with their whole heart' (1 QS 5:8f; CD 15:9, 12; 1 QH 16:17), to seek God and to love him with their whole heart (1 QH 14:26; 15:10; CD 1:10) and to serve him with their whole heart (1 QH 16:7).

Man is, however, not alone in this struggle, for God opens his servant's heart (1 QS 11:15f; see also 1 QH 2:18; 4:10; 5:33; 7:13; 12:34; 14:8; 17:22, 26; 18:24, 27). Belial, too, holds council in the heart of man (1 QH 6:21f), and the 'spirits of truth and falsehood wage war in the heart of man' (1 QS 4:23; cf 4:2).

Even the 'heart of God' is referred to in the Qumran texts. It is clear from the parallelism in 1 QH 10:2 that what is meant by this is the divine plan, God's will. This use of the word also occurs in 1 Sam 13:14 (God sought 'a man according to his own heart': cf Jer 3:15). The plan of God's heart is established for ever (1 QH 4:18). Evildoers take no heed of God's deeds and do not hearken to his word, but rather say that these are not a revelation of knowledge and the way of his heart (1 QH 4:17f). But, on the contrary, there is no falsehood in God's works and no guile in the plan of his heart (1 QH 4:21) and those who walk in the way of his heart will live for ever, because they hearken to him (1 QH 4:24). The upright man walks without wickedness in the way of God's heart (1 QH 6:7). God leads him on this way by means of the teacher of righteousness (CD 1:11) and no uncircumcised, impure or violent man may walk in God's way with the purpose of tempting the upright man to stray from it (1 QH 6:20f).

C. *In the New Testament*, the Greek word *kardia* is used with the same wide range of meaning as in the Old Testament Greek translation, where it corresponds to leb or lebâb. The Hebrew *leb, lebâb* is, however, sometimes translated in LXX by *nous* (lit = mind), and this is of some significance. The essential difference between *kardia* and *nous* is that *nous* places emphasis on the idea of knowledge, whereas *kardia* does not stress this. In *kardia* the emphasis is rather on intention, endeavour and feeling.

The heart feels joy (Jn 16:22; Acts 2:26; 14:17), fear (Jn 14:1), sorrow (Jn 16:6; Rom 9:2; 2 Cor 2:4; Acts 2:37), love (2 Cor 7:3; 6:11; Phil 1:7), longing (Rom 10:1; Lk 24:32), desire (Rom 1:24; Jas 3:14; Mt 5:28; 6:21). Similarly, thoughts, understanding and the intellect are associated with the heart (Mk 7:21; Mt 12:34; Jn 12:40; Acts 8:22, etc). 'To say in one's heart' means to think (Mt 24:48) and 'to come into one's heart' means to come to mind (Acts 7:23).

Decisions have their origin in the heart (Lk 21:14; 2 Cor 9:7; Acts 11:23; sometimes it is God who puts this decision into man's heart, as in Rev 17:17, sometimes it is the devil, as in Jn 13:2). Sometimes the heart is synonymous with ⁊ conscience (1 Jn 3:20ff; Test Gad 5:3).

The heart is man's ego, his inward self, his personality (the 'hidden man' of 1 Pet 3:4), in contrast to the outward man (Mk 7:6; Rom 10:8). According to Paul, it is this inward, spiritual man who stands in need of circumcision. This is more important than the outward, visible circumcision of the foreskin (Rom 2:28f).

It is in the heart that God first approaches man, in order to influence him; he searches out man's heart and puts it to the test (Lk 16:15; Rom 8:27; 1 Thess 2:4). God writes his ⁊ law in the hearts of man (Rom 2:15; 2 Cor 3:2; Heb 8:10). There is either ⁊ faith in the heart (Mk 11:23; Acts 8:37; Rom 10:8–10; Heb 3:12), or else doubt (Lk 24:38; Mk 11:23) or ⁊ hardness (Mt 13:15; Rom 1:21; 2 Cor 3:14).

God opens the heart of man (Lk 24:45; Acts 16:14, cf 2 Macc 1:4). He shines into our hearts, to give us the light of the knowledge of his ⁊ glory (2 Cor 4:6). The eyes of the baptised christian's heart are enlightened so that he is able to know ⁊ hope and the ⁊ inheritance stored up for him (Eph 1:18; see also H. Schlier on this subject). The peace of God keeps our hearts and minds in Christ (Phil 4:7). The spirit of God is poured into our hearts (Rom 5:5; 2 Cor 1:22; Gal 4:6) and Christ dwells in our hearts and is active in them by means of ⁊ faith (Eph 4:17ff). The christian's heart is purified and sanctified through faith and ⁊ baptism (Acts 15:9; Heb 10:22); it is made clean (Mt 5:8);

it is blameless and strengthened by God (1 Thess 3:13). In such a heart it is possible for the christian virtues of ↗ humility, modelled on the example given to us by our Lord (Mt 11:29), simplicity and ↗ obedience (Eph 6:5; Col 3:22) and, above all love of God and of ones neighbour (↗ love: Mk 12:30; Lk 10:27; Mt 22:37) to grow to perfection.

Bibliography: P. Jouon, *Bbl* 5 (1924), 49–53; P. Dhorme, *RB* 31 (1922), 489–508; H. Cazelles, *Catholicisme* 2 (1949), 1280; F. H. van Meyenfeldt, *Het Hart in het Oud Testament*, Leiden 1950; F. Baumgärtel, *TDNT* III, 605–7; J. Behm, *TDNT* III, 608–14; H. Brunner, *Archiv für Orientforschung* 17 (1954/5), 140f; J. Doresse, *Etudes Carmélitaines* 29 (1950), 82–97; B. de Gerardon, 'Le coeur, la bouche, les mains. Essai sur un schème biblique', *Bible et Vie Chrétienne* 1/4 (1953), 7–24; Haag 704; Bultmann I, 220–27; Jacob, 132–5; C. Tresmontant, *Études de metaphysique biblique*, Paris 1955; F. Nötscher, *Gotteswege und Menschenwege in der Bibel und in Qumran* (*BBB* 15), 1958 (indexed under 'heart'); N. Adler, *LTK* v², 285f; N. Schmidt, 'Anthropologische Begriffe im AT', *ET* 24 (1964), 374–88; G. E. Closen, 'Das Herz des Erlösers in den heiligen Schriften des Alten Bundes', *Zeitschrift für Aszese und Mystik* 18 (1943), 17–30 (those passages in scripture which refer to the 'heart of the Redeemer' are mentioned here, as well as in the same author's book, *Wege in die Heilige Schrift*); J. M. Bover, 'Das Heilige Herz Jesu im NT', *Zeitschrift für Aszese und Mystik* 13 (1938), 285–301; J. B. Bauer, 'Das Herz des Erlösers in der Heiligen Schrift', *BL* 19 (1951/2), 291–4; H. Rahner, *Cor Salvatoris*, Freiburg 1954, 19–45; D. M. Stanley, '"From his heart will flow rivers of living water" (Jn 7:38)', *Cor Jesu* 1 (Rome 1959), 507–42; S. Garofalo, 'Il Cuore del Redentore in San Paolo,' *Cor Jesu* 1 (Rome 1959), 543–67; J. B. Bauer, *VD* 40 (1962), 27–32.

Johannes B. Bauer

Heathen (gentiles)

In modern usage the word *heathen* has no precise and objective connotation, but carries with it pejorative associations resulting from a tradition which can be traced back to the Old Testament. The pejorative connotation of the word has been further accentuated by the fact that what we have today is a new kind of paganism which really has no right to this name at all. This new paganism is made up to a very high degree of either atheism or pseudo-religious sentiment whereas genuine paganism, in the sense in which the term was used in antiquity, could take in a very deep sense of religious piety. The negative way in which the word is used springs from a christian sense of reality and of the insurmountable opposition between that reality and those who do not share it; and this no doubt contains an element of genuine biblical truth. Karl Barth characterises all non-christian religions as *Unglaube*, the absence of faith, since they represent attempts on man's part to effect his own salvation. Schlink holds that the pagans know that there is a God but do not know *who* he is. Aquinas contrasts christian revelation with the use of unaided reason on the part of pagans. The experience of this opposition between christian faith and paganism finds these and similar expressions in all christian confessions both in ancient and modern times. Behind all of these we find biblical statements which clearly and unequivocally express the distinction between the people of God and the pagans on the grounds that the latter are not within God's covenant.

Biblical usage supports this distinction. Though there are exceptions, the distinction between ʿām and gôyîm is clear-cut in the Old Testament and becomes even clearer with the passage of time. The *gôyîm* are the pagan peoples who are outside the covenant or the individuals who belong to such peoples. LXX translate these terms by *laos*, always in the singular, and *ethnē*.

The *gôyîm* have no part in the covenant and the law. They live in sin, the folly of idolatry (Is 44:9–20; Jer 16:18) and pride (Ps 2:1); hence they stand under the anger and judgement of God (Jer 10:25). Whoever makes light of or seeks to oppose God and his chosen people is subject to divine judgement (Ps 137; Is 14; Jer 51:64). Gen 11:1–9 and Deut 32:8 (also Jub 10:22 based on this last) express the idea that the world of the nations comes into existence as the result of a divine judgement for the arrogance of mankind. The judgement expected to come on the pagans is seen, in the first place, in concrete events following on particularly flagrant examples of pride and arrogance (eg Is 37:36ff). As time goes on, however, a more profoundly theological view is taken of this question. So, for example, Daniel (chapter 7) sees judgement coming on the proud and tyrannical world-empires which can have no share in God's kingdom. In keeping with this view it was understandable that the pagans or gentiles had to be avoided (Ex 34:15).

In addition to this line of thought, however, there is another which stresses that the pagan nations have also been created by God and that therefore they too are under his rule and providence (Amos 9:12; Jer 10:7). Their origin is not seen as the result of punishment by God but of the natural spread of humanity on the earth (2[4] Esd 37:12). And if they are created by God they must in the last resort come under his

dispensation of grace (Jn 4:10). Many of them acknowledge Yahweh's activity (Ps 126:2; Dan 2:47), he uses them as his instruments (Is 7:1; 45:1; 25:9) and they are promised a share in eschatological salvation (Is 2:2–4; 25: 6–8; 44:3; 51:4f; 55:5; 66:18ff; Mic 4:1ff; Zech 2:11; 8:20; 14:16). They too, therefore, have the duty of honouring and praising God (Ps 67:3; 117:1).

The LXX terms *laos* and *ethnē*, which in general correspond with *ʿam* and *gôyîm* respectively, are taken over and used in the New Testament. Here *ethnē* is often indeterminate and generalised in connotation (Mt 25:32; Mk 13:10) and can sometimes refer to Israel (Lk 7:5; 23:2; Jn 11:48; 18:35). On a few occasions it can be referred to gentile christians on account of their pagan origins. But for the most part it corresponds to the *gôyîm* of the Old Testament and the adjectival form— also used as a substantive—is *ethnikoi*. The most frequently attested paraphrase of *ethnē* is *Hellēnes* (lit. = Greeks) and, the Johannine writings, *kosmos* (lit. = world).

Despite all this, the situation in the New Testament is radically different from that in the Old. The church knows that Christ has died for all men (Rom 5:18; 2 Cor 5:14; 1 Cor 15:3ff; Rev 22:2f) even though he himself had very little contact with pagans (Mt 10:5; 15:24). Hence she preached the good news about Jesus not only to Israel but to all nations (Mt 24:14; 28:19) since Jesus is the light of the nations (Lk 2:32). How persuasive and convincing this preaching was can be seen from the account of the conversion and baptism of Cornelius in Acts 10–11. This was not a case of one of those who 'feared God', a proselyte who could in some way be considered as belonging to the people of God, but of a pious pagan, a pagan in the real sense of the term.

The line of division now runs not between those who belong by descent and faith to the community of Israel and those who do not, nor between those who observe the law and those who do not, those who belong to the old covenant and those who do not, but is determined with reference to Christ and membership of the new covenant. Rom 3:9, 27ff and 1:18f show clearly how those who belong to the old people of God can now be classed with the *ethnē*. Christ is necessary for all and all can through him receive redemption and aggregation to the 'household of God' (Eph 2:12, 19f; 3:6). Those who have not been baptised are, in spite of all their striving, without God and his justification, though Paul himself recognises the value of Israel's obedience to the law and contrasts it with the disobedience and immorality of the pagans (Rom 1:21; 1 Cor 6:9ff; 5:1; 12:2; Gal 2:15; Col 3:5; 1 Thess 1:9; 4:5). They still belong to the old creation which is given up to the things of this world (Mt 6:32) and is doomed to transitoriness, damnation and death. They are far distant from God or, in other words, in sin (Rom 6:1, 16; Eph 2:1ff; 4:17). On the other side of the dividing line constituted by baptism is the new creation initiated by the death and resurrection of Christ and to this belong life, salvation and grace. Baptism means a break with the past and conversion; in other words, dying in order to enter a new life (Acts 11:1, 18; 14:27; 17:30ff; Rom 6:3–11). The anger of God is no longer directed at those who have through Christ returned to the living God. In this state one can see the happy fulfilment of the prophetic utterances (Acts 4:25; Gal 3:8, 14; 1 Pet 2:9).

Paul is the chief representative in the New Testament of this theology of conversion. For him it is the foundation and justification of his life's work. His purpose is to recall the gentiles to Christ so that, together with those members of the old people of God who have believed in Christ, they may come together to form a new people of God and possess one Spirit, one baptism and one eucharist (1 Cor 12:13; Gal 3:27f; Col 3:11; Eph 4:4–6). On the basis of the old people of God there comes into existence, by the grace of God, a new people, the beginnings of a new humanity reconciled with God, all the members of which can now inherit the promise.

The need for such a theology and its outcome in the mission to the gentiles grew out of the universal significance of the death and resurrection of Christ. We know very little of the formation of gentile–christian communities before Paul. According to Acts 11:21 the mission to the gentiles started with individual christians speaking the word to those they met, following on the Jewish mission to the diaspora. In this process the Jewish proselytes (*phoboumenoi ton theon* = 'those who fear God') played an important part. It appears that very soon a great number of small communities came into existence (Acts 21:4ff; 21:13). The sending of Barnabas to Antioch (Acts 11:22) was in effect a legitimation of this mission by the primitive Jerusalem community which remained in contact with it (Acts 24:17;

Gal 2:10; 1 Cor 16:2; 2 Cor 8:4; 9:1, 12). The activity of the apostle Paul was of decisive importance in this movement not only because of its extent but also from the point of view of its theological significance. Only the substitution of Christ for the Torah as the one means of salvation (Rom 3:21f; 10:4; 15:8ff) made it possible to solve the problems raised by the mission to the gentiles (Acts 15:6; Gal 2:1ff) and freed the church from the hold of the synagogue. Now the way to the nations of the world was open and the ground prepared for a confrontation with their laws and way of life which was to be one of the principal tasks of the church fathers. This confrontation has continued throughout the history of the church and has in our day entered a new phase.

Bibliography: C. G. Diehl, *RGG* II³, 141ff (with a full bibliography); Bertram and K. L. Schmidt, *TDNT* +1, 364-72; T. W. Manson, *Jesus and the Non Jesus*, London 1955; J. Jeremias, *Jesus' Promise to the Nations*, London 1958.

Georg Molin

Heaven

The Hebrew word for heaven, *šāmayim*, is always found in the plural. The Greek word, *ouranos*, used in LXX and the New Testament, is found sometimes in the singular and sometimes in the plural.

A. *Heaven as part of the universe*. The phrase 'heaven and earth' is of very frequent occurrence, and is used to denote the world as a whole (Gen 1:1; 2:1; 14:19, 22; 24:3; Ps 102:25 [v 10 in the Hebrew]; 136:5ff; Is 1:2; 65:17; 66:22; Hag 2:6 [cf Heb 12:26]; Joel

3:16 [cf Acts 2:19]; Tob 7:18; Judith 9:17; 1 Macc 2:37; Mk 13:31; Mt 5:18; 6:10; 11:25; 28:18; Lk 10:21; 16:17; Acts 17:24; 1 Cor 8:5; Eph 1:10; 3:15; Col 1:16; Jas 5:12; 2 Pet 3:5, 7, 10, 13; Rev 20:11; 21:1). The tripartite formula 'heaven, earth, and sea' also occurs frequently (Ex 20:11; Acts 4:24; 14:15; Rev 10:6; 14:7; see also Ex 20:4; Judith 9:17; Rev 5:13). In this sense, heaven is very much the same as the so-called firmament (Gen 1:6-8), which was thought of as a hollow hemisphere above the earth, bearing above it the ocean of heaven, the 'waters above the heavens' (Ps 148:4; Dan 3:60). Heaven is 'stretched out' (Ps 104:2; Is 40:22; 44:24; 45:12; 48:13; 51:13, 16; Jer 10:12; 51:15; Zech 12:1); it has 'flood-gates' (Gen 7:11; Mal 3:10; see also 2 Kings 7:2, 19); it is supported by pillars (Job 26:11) or rests on foundations (2 Sam 22:8). The sun, the moon, and the stars move in this heaven (Gen 1:14-17; Mk 13:24f; Mt 24:29; Heb 11:12). Man cannot ascend to heaven (Deut 30:12; Prov 30:4; Jn 3:13). Thus by heaven is implied the space of air between the firmament and earth. The frequently used phrase 'birds (fowls) of the air' shows this clearly (Gen 1:26, 28, 30; 2:19ff; 6:7; 7:3, etc; Mk 4:32; Mt 6:26; 8:20; Lk 8:5; 9:58; Acts 10:12; 11:6).

Several *heavenly spheres* are recognised in ancient cosmology. The phrase 'the heaven of heavens' (Deut 10:14; 1 Kings 8:27; 2 Chron 2:6; 6:18; Neh 9:6; Ps 148:4) would certainly seem to reflect this view; it is, however, merely a rhetorical exaggeration, employed to express the sublimity of heaven. It was not until the later Jewish period that several heavens were referred to (Test Lev 2:7–9; 3:1–8; ApocMos 37; ApocAbr 19:5–9; Bar [Gr] 2:2; 3:1; 10:1; 11:1; Enoch [Slav] 3:1; 7:1; 8:1; 11:1; 18:1; 19:1; 20:1; SB III, 531–3; Traub 511f). Paul also refers to heaven in this way (2 Cor 12:2; Eph 4:10).

Heaven, as a part of the structure of the world, will be destroyed in God's judgement (Is 13:13; 34:4; 51:6; Job 14:12; Mk 13:24f; 2 Pet 3:7, 10, 12; Rev 20:11; see also Ps 102:26f; Jer 4:23–6; Joel 3:3f; Hag 2:7, 22; Mk 13:31; Mt 5:18; Lk 16:17; Heb 1:10–12; 12:26). In its place a new heaven will be created, together with a new earth (Is 65:17; 66:22; 2 Pet 3:13; Rev 21:1; see also Rom 8:21f).

B. *Heaven as a space above the world.* 1. *Heaven is the dwelling place of God* (1 Kings 8:30, 32, 34, 36, 39, etc; Ps 2:4; 14:2; 115:3; Mk 11:25; Mt 5:16, 45; 6:1, 9; 7:11, 21; 10:32f; 16:17; 23:9; Lk 11:13; Eph 6:9; Col 4:1; see also Gen 11:5, 7; 19:24; 24:3, 7; 28:12f; 1 Kings 22:19; Job 1:6–12; 22:12; Ps 29:10; Rom 1:18; Rev 21:2, 10). Heaven is also God's throne (Is 66:1; see also Acts 7:49; Mt 5:34; 23:22), in contrast to the earth, which is his footstool (Is 66:1; see also Acts 7:49; Mt 5:34). God's throne is, however, sometimes represented as being situated in heaven (Ps 11:4; 103:19; Wis 18:15; Heb 8:1; Rev 4:2; 5:1; 21:5). God, therefore, is frequently referred to as the God of heaven (Gen 24:7; 2 Chron 36:23; Ezra 1:2; Neh 1:4f; 2:4, 20; Ps 136:26; Jonah 1:9; Rev 11:13; 16:11). Sometimes the word 'heaven' is used for God (Dan 4:23; 1 Macc 3:18; 4:10, 24, 55; 12:15; 2 Macc 7:11; Lk 15:18, 21).

Similarly, 'in heaven' means very much the same as 'with God' (Mt 16:19; 18:18) and 'from heaven' means 'from God' (Mk 8:11; 11:30; Jn 3:27). Thus, in place of the 'Kingdom of God', we often find the 'Kingdom of heaven' in the New Testament, although only in the semitically coloured Gospel of Matthew (Mt 3:2; 4:17; 5:3, 10, 19f; 7:21; 8:11, etc). The nearness of God is frequently indicated by the heavens opening (Mk 1:10f; Jn 1:51; Acts 7:55f; 10:11; Rev 4:1; 19:11; see also Is 64:1; Ezek 1:1). The voice of God (Mk 1:11; Jn 12:28; 2 Pet 1:18) and the light which brings divine grace (Acts 9:3; 22:6; 26:13) also come from heaven.

2. *Heaven as the dwelling place of the angels* (Gen 21:17; 22:11; 1 Kings 22:19; Lk 2:15; Heb 12:22; Rev 1:4; 4:5f; 5:11; 7:11; 8:2, etc: see also Job 1:6–12; Ps 89:6f; Tob 12:15). Reference is made to the angels of heaven (Mt 24:36) or in heaven (Mk 12:25; 13:32; Mt 18:10; 22:30) who always see the face of God (Mt 18:10). The angels form the heavenly army (1 Kings 22:19; 2 Chron 18:18; Lk 2:13; Rev 19:14). It is even possible in the bible to use the term 'heaven' when 'the angels of heaven' is meant (Lk 15:7; cf 15:10). The angels call from heaven (Gen 21:17; 22:15) or actually come down from heaven to earth (Mt 28:2; Lk 22:43; Gal 1:8; Rev 10:1; 18:1; 20:1; see also Lk 1:19,26). There are also evil spirits in heaven (Eph 6:12; Rev 12:7f) and even Satan has access to God, and therefore clearly to heaven (Job 1:6–12; 2:1–7; see also Rev 12:8, 10). He falls from heaven, however, as a result of what Christ has done (Lk 10:18; Rev 12:8–10:13).

Many of these statements, it must be admitted, give us cause to ask what is really meant by 'heaven' (see Eph 2:2 with 6:12).

3. *Heaven as the dwelling place of Christ.* From the very beginning, Jesus was with God (Jn 1:1; 17:5). He came down from heaven to earth (Jn 1:9, 11; 3:13, 31; 6:38, 41f, 51; 16:28; 17:8; Eph 4:9; see also Dan 7:13f; Jn 6:33; 13:3; Rom 10:6) and, as the God-man, returned to God in heaven in his ascension (Mk 16:19; Acts 1:9-11; Eph 4:10; Heb 4:14; 7:26; see also Jn 6:62ff; 7:33; 13:3; 16:5, 28; 17:13f; Acts 2:33f; Heb 9:11f, 24). In heaven, Christ sits at the right hand of God (Mk 16:19; Acts 2:33f; 5:31; 7:55f; Rom 8:34; Eph 1:20; Col 3:1; Heb 1:3, 13; 8:1; 10:12; 12:2; 1 Pet 3:22; see also Mk 14:62; Rev 3:21; 5:6). He has once and for all entered into the Holy of Holies of heaven (Heb 9:11f, 24), where he is the intercessor, mediator, and advocate for his church (Rom 8:34; Heb 9:24; 12:24; 1 Jn 2:1). Heaven had to receive him until the time when the world is to be renewed (Acts 3:21); then, at the end of time, he will come again from heaven (Acts 1:11; Phil 3:20; 1 Thess 1:10; 4:16; 2 Thess 1:7; see also Dan 7:13; Mk 8:38; 13:26; 14:62; Mt 26:64; Acts 3:20; 1 Cor 15:47; Heb 9:28; Rev 1:7). At his second coming, he will take his disciples with him into heaven (see 1 Thess 4:16f).

4. *Heaven as the place of salvation.* Heaven is the source of God's blessing (Gen 49:25; Deut 33:13), and God's word stands firm for ever in heaven, because he is there (Ps 119:89). God's mercy and truth are established in heaven (Ps 89:2). It is from heaven that the Holy Ghost comes (Mk 1:10; Jn 1:32; Acts 2:2-4, 33; 1 Pet 1:12; see also Jn 14:16, 26; 15:26; 16:7; Acts 1:8). ⟋ Paradise (2 Cor 12:4; see also Lk 23:43; Rev 2:7) and the pattern of the tabernacle established on earth (Ex 25:9, 40; Heb 8:5; 9:23; see also Rev 15:5) are to be found in heaven. The temple of God (Rev 3:12; 11:19; 14:15, 17; 15:5f; 16:17), with the altar of incense (Rev 8:3, 5; 14:18) and the Ark of the Covenant (Rev 11:19) are also in heaven. It is in heaven too that the true Jerusalem is situated (Gal 4:26; Heb 12:22; Rev 3:12). This new Jerusalem will come down on earth when the world is renewed (Rev 21:2, 10). Salvation is preserved in heaven for christians (Col 1:5; 1 Pet 1:4; see also Col 1:12).

5. *Heaven as the abode of the blessed.* In the Old Testament we find occasional examples of men being taken up into heaven (2 Kings 2:11; see also Gen 5:24; Ps 73:24). It was the expectation of later judaism that the just would live for ever with God (Wis 5:15f; 6:18f; see also 3:1-9; Ps 49:15). In the New Testament, the pious store up treasures for themselves in heaven (Mk 10:21; Mt 6:20; Lk 12:33) and it is there that they receive their reward (Mt 5:12; Lk 6:23). The true home of christians who are still on earth is really in heaven (Phil 3:20; Heb 12:22-4; see also 2 Cor 5:6; Heb 13:14), and the names of Jesus' disciples are written in heaven (Lk 10:20; see also Ex 32:32; Ps 69:28; Dan 12:1; Heb 12:23; Rev 21:27). The souls of the just who have died are already in heaven (Heb 12:23), and Jesus' disciples will also eventually go to heaven (Jn 14:2f; 2 Cor 5:1)

immediately after their death (Phil 1:23; see also Lk 23:43; 2 Cor 5:1ff). They will sit with Christ in heaven (Eph 2:6; Rev 3:21), or stand before God's throne (Rev 7:9). They will no longer experience any earthly tribulation or hardship (Rev 7:16; 21:4), but will be protected by God and Christ (Rev 7:17; 21:3f; 22:1–5). In their resurrection, their new form of existence will be from heaven, in contrast to their previous form of existence, which is from earth (1 Cor 15:47–9).

C. *The theological importance of the biblical statements concerning heaven.* The cosmology of antiquity, now completely outdated by the advance of modern scientific knowledge, underlies all these biblical utterances concerning heaven. It is clear that there is no single passage in the bible referring to heaven which is aimed at providing scientific instruction. All these passages, however, do make use of the ancient view of the universe and the linguistic usage of the period to express religious ideas. To appreciate these ideas, it is necessary to peel away the surrounding husk of ancient language and concept—if this is done, the idea of heaven which emerges can be seen to have, in many cases, a definitely qualitative content which, even remaining within the text as it is, predominates over the purely local content. In this sense, then, heaven is seen as *the sphere of God, his angels and saints—the sphere of perfection and salvation.* The word *sphere* is, of course, quite inadequate in this context, and open to misinterpretation, but inadequate and easily misinterpreted language is all that we have when we need to speak of this absolute mystery. In the bible we find an attempt on the

part of men to depict heaven in its perfection, beauty and blessedness. The language used is, of necessity, figurative, and we must take this into account in our examination of the subject.

Bibliography: A. Klawek, 'Der Himmel als Wohnung der Seligen im ntl. Zeitalter', *Collecteana Theologica* 13 (1932), 111–24; T. Flügge, *Die Vorstellung über den Himmel im AT*, Borna-Leipzig 1937; H. Bietenhard, *Die himmlische Welt im Urchristentum und Spätjudentum*, Tübingen 1951; H. Traub and G. von Rad, *TDNT* v, 497–538; U. Simon, *Heaven in the Christian Tradition*, London 1958; J. Haecke, J. Schmid and J. Ratzinger, *LTK* v, 352–8.

Johann Michl

Hell

Hell (Old English *hel*, cognate with the Old High German *hêlan*, to conceal; Hel—in Norse mythology, the goddess of the underworld) is the name used in scripture, with various shades of meaning, to denote the place of punishment of the damned after death.

A. In the *Old Testament*, šᵉʾôl is the place, believed to be situated under the earth, to which both good and bad go after death (Gen 37:35; Deut 32:22; 1 Kings 2:6; Prov 9:18; 15:11; Job 10:21f; Ps 9:17; 31:17; 49:15; 55:15; 88:3–7, 11–13; 94:17; 115:17; Is 38:10, 18; Wis 1:14). The fate of the dead is, however, gradually seen in a different light in the Old Testament, and good and bad are judged according to their merits. The good are awakened after death to a new, eternal life (Dan 12:2; 2 Macc 7:9, 11, 14, 23; see also Is 26:19) and are received by God (Ps 49:15; Wis 5:15f; 6:18ff; see also 3:1–9). The wicked and godless, however, will be punished (Is 50:11; 66:24;

Judith 16:17; Wis 4:19; Sir 7:17f; see also Wis 3:10, 18) and will rise again to reproach and dishonour (Dan 12:2; see also 2 Macc 7:14). Their punishment will be by fire (Is 50:11; 66:24; Judith 16:21; Sir 7:17f) and worms (Is 66:24; Judith 16:17; Sir 7:17f). In this context, it is important not to overlook the element of imagery contained in these ideas—fire representing destruction and the worm corruption—although in themselves these two elements are scarcely reconcilable.

B. In the *New Testament*, hell is conceived according to the view prevalent in later judaism (with the exception of the canonical books, and especially Enoch [Eth] 22, etc). After death the sinner is taken to Hades (*ha(i)dēs* is the usual translation of *šᵉ°ôl* in LXX), where he is tormented by fire (Lk 16:23f). This place of punishment is often called Gehenna (Mk 9:42f; Mt 5:29f; 10:28; 23:15, 33; Lk 12:5; Jas 3:6), or Gehenna of fire—'hell fire' (Mt 5:22; 18:9). Sometimes it is described as an everlasting or inextinguishable fire (Mk 9:42f; see also Mt 18:8), where the worms and fire torment the damned (Mk 9:47f; cf Is 66:24). The word *Gehenna* (used thus in the Vulgate; in Greek *geenna*) is derived from the Hebrew *gê-hinnōm*, the 'valley of Hinnom' (Joshua 15:8b; 18:16b; Neh 11:30), which is an abbreviation of *gê-ben-hinnōm*, or the 'valley of the son of Hinnom' (Joshua 15:8a; 18:16a; 2 Chron 28:3; 33:6; Jer 7:31f; 19:2, 6). This was the valley or ravine to the south of Jerusalem where children were burnt as sacrifices during the reigns of Ahaz and Manasseh (2 Chron 28:3; 33:6;; Jer 7:31). It was in this valley too, that the Israelites would be punished (Jer 7:32; 19:6). It is in the New Testament and the texts of later judaism (4 Esdras 7:36; Bar [Syr] 59:10; 85:13) that the name first occurs with the meaning of a place of punishment after death. This place of punishment is already in existence, and the human body is corrupted by its influence (Jas 3:6). Other passages refer to various aspects of hell as a place of punishment—eternal fire (Mt 18:8; 25:41; see also Mt 3:12; Lk 3:17; Jude 7), the 'fury of fire' (Heb 10:27), the 'furnace of fire' (Mt 13:42, 50), the outer darkness (Mt 8:12; 22:13; 25:30; see also 2 Pet 2:17), where there is weeping and gnashing of teeth—thus signifying the most extreme agony and the greatest anger (Mt 8:12; 13:42, 50; 22:13; 24:51; 25:30; Lk 13:28) by which hypocrites are punished (Mt 24:51; see also Lk 12:46). This fire is prepared for the devil and his angels, and those who do not show mercy on others will be punished in it (Mt 25:41). In the Apocalypse, it is characterised as the 'lake of fire that burns with brimstone' (Rev 19:20; see also 14:10; 20:9, 14). Into this pool of fire are cast first of all the two beasts, representing the Antichrist (19:20; 20:9f), then the devil (20:9), the kingdom of Death (*ha[i]dēs*), Death itself (*thanatos*: 20:14) and finally all sinners (21:8). The punishment in this place of fire is final and everlasting (Mt 18:8; 25:41, 46; Rev 19:20; 20:9f; 21:8), but it varies according to the guilt of each individual sinner (Lk 12:47f; see also Mt 10:15; 11:22; Lk 10:12, 14).

In other passages of the New Testament, this ultimate punishment of sinners is not characterised in figurative language or in imagery, but simply as

God's wrath and anger (Rom 2:8; see also 2 Thess 1:8; Rev 16:19), as evil (2 Cor 5:10), as death (Jn 8:51f; Rom 6:21, 23; see also 5:21), as the second death (Rev 2:11; 20:6, 14; 21:8), as judgement (Jn 5:24, 29; see also 1 Cor 11:29), as destruction (Mt 7:13; Gal 6:8; Phil 3:19; Heb 10:39; see also Jn 17:12), as eternal destruction (2 Thess 1:9) or as exclusion from the kingdom of God (Lk 13:28; 1 Cor 6:9f; Gal 5:19–21; Eph 5:5; see also Mt 8:12; Lk 14:24; Col 3:5f). The wicked too will be resurrected (Jn 5:29; Acts 24:15; see also Mt 25:31–46), but to the resurrection of judgement (Jn 5:29; see also Mt 25:31–46).

The New Testament also recognises a temporary state of punishment, which corresponds to the ideas current in later judaism (Jub 5:6, 10; Hen [eth] 10:4–6, 11–14). Thus the sinful angels are kept in chains and in darkness until the last judgement (Jude 6), or in Tartarus, or the lowest part of hell (2 Pet 2:4). What is more, Hades is also regarded as a temporary place of punishment—hell will not only have to give up its dead for judgement at the resurrection (Rev 20:13), but will also be replaced by the everlasting Gehenna (Rev 20:14; hell, together with death, will be cast into the pool of fire). In Hades the sinner's soul is separated from his body. In Gehenna, on the other hand, he will be punished, after the resurrection, both in his body and his soul (Mk 9:43, 45, 47; Mt 5:29f; 18:8f).

C. *The theological importance of the biblical references to hell*. The bible uses words such as fire, worm, and darkness which, in their literal sense, are irreconcilable. Used figuratively, how-ever, such words aim to express, by their associations with terrible experiences undergone in this life, the inexpressible torments of the damned. 'Weeping', for example, is used to express the pain which the damned suffer, 'gnashing of teeth' their anger and despair. Language of this kind, wherever it is found in the New Testament, however, is always extremely restrained and sober, compared with the cruel and fantastic descriptions of hell in the apocryphal books. Its main purpose is, of course, to stir the conscience and to instil a healthy fear of God as heavenly judge. God's anger, which strikes the sinner and, excluding him from the kingdom of heaven, sentences him to eternal perdition, is expressed in the New Testament without recourse to imagery. It is true that certain words—fire, darkness, weeping and so on—are used in an attempt to convey something of the terrible nature of the punishment of the damned, but exactly what this punishment is really like remains a mystery which is not revealed anywhere in the bible. How-ever, any attempt to mitigate the grave and terrible implications of the reality of hell, by appealing, for example, to 1 Cor 15:29, or to some similar passage, is bound to fail, in view of the absolute clarity of scripture on this subject.

Bibliography: J. Felten, *Neutestamentliche Zeitgeschichte* II, Regensburg 1925³, 227–42 and 258–63; SB IV 2, 1016–118; J. Jeremias, *TDNT* I, 146–9 and 657–8; P. Volz, *Die Eschatologie der jüdische Gemeinde im ntl. Zeitalter*, Tübingen 1934, 256–72 and 309–32; C. Spicq, *Le révélation de l'enfer dans la sainte Ecriture: L'Enfer*, Paris 1950, 91–143; H. Bietenhard, *Die himmlische Welt im Urchristentum und Spätjudentum*, Tübingen 1951, 205–9; J. Gnilka and J. Ratzinger, *LTK* v², 445–9.

Johann Michl

Holy

Holiness is a primordial religious phenomenon which can be grasped in full only in objective experience (see Is 6:3ff). Any attempt to analyse holiness is bound to be piecemeal and there is always the danger that its homogeneous nature will be destroyed in the analytic process and that a one-sided interpretation may result from an overemphasis of certain elements at the expense of others. Another risk inherent in such analysis is that of regarding many aspects of holiness as the consequence of a tendency or development, when in fact these aspects are traceable to a gradual deepening of man's understanding of the nature of holiness. It is essentially something different from and alien to our normal empirical knowledge, something which intrudes into this known world and remains in it. No close parallel to the phenomenon of holiness can, in fact, be found.

Holiness is above all connected with material things in Old Testament worship. Certain places (Jerusalem, Is 52:1; Sion, Is 27:13; the tabernacle, Ex 28:43; the temple, 1 Kings 9:3; the Holy of Holies, Lev 16:2; the altar, Ex 29:37), certain objects (the Ark of the Covenant, 2 Chron 35:3), certain vestments (Ex 29:29), sacrifices (Ex 28:38), holy days (Gen 2:3)—all are called holy. Such things are, however, not static in themselves. Frequently they possess a strange dynamic force of their own. Examples of this are Uzzah's death as a result of touching the Ark (2 Sam 6:6f), what happened in Bethel (Gen 28:17) or in connection with the burning bush (Ex 3:5). These instances show quite clearly that a place is called holy when God reveals himself there. That the name of God is, at quite an early stage, used instead of the Ark (Deut 26:2)—it is preferable to regard this less as a spiritualisation than as the emergence of the reality concealed in the Ark itself—is evidence of the fact that holiness in the Old Testament is not abstract or connected purely with material things, as in the case of the pagan religions, but personal. God is, in fact, the three times Holy One (Is 6:3), the Holy One, quite different from men, who is in the midst of men (Hos 11:9). He is the one to whom no man can compare himself (Is 40:25), since he cannot be either approached or touched and thus is able even to swear by his own holiness (Ps 89:35). Although he is unique, he is nonetheless not isolated. In him there is a vital force which is constantly directed outwards and wishes to possess everything in the world by invoking his name upon his people (Amos 9:12), by revealing himself as the Holy One (Ezek 20:41) or by glorifying himself (Ex 14:18). He claims the whole of history as his own (Ezek 20:41; 38:16), until the whole earth is ultimately filled with his glory and fulfilled in him (Num 14:21). On that day every sacrificial vessel in Jerusalem and Judea will be sanctified to the Lord of hosts (Zech 14:21). Ps 29 provides a most impressive description of this dynamic power of God, symbolised here as a thunderstorm which will overcome everything that attempts to stand up against it. His zeal is directed especially towards men, who are to be holy because he is holy (Lev 11:44). From this no one is exempt. The entire people has been chosen by him, the Holy One of Israel (Is 1:4) and is consequently incorporated into his process of sanctification (Lev 20:26). Everyone whose name is written in the book of life forms a part of this plan (Is 4:3). Special leaders are chosen to prepare the way for this sanctification (Ex 19:14; Joshua 7:13), and among these the priests play a very special part (Lev 21:7). Among these consecrated priests, the high priest is to bear the visible mark of dedication to God on his forehead (Ex 28:36).

God's intrusion into the world causes a marked division between what is holy and what is profane. The completely distinct character of holiness prevents any fusion here. The profane element even attempts to protect itself from the power of holiness as it draws near (Ex 3:5; 19:12). Correspondingly, man's reaction to the holiness of God is amazement at its magnitude (Ex 15:11; 1 Sam 2:2), awe which prevents man from uttering the name of God, fear, and even terror (Gen 28:17; Ex 3:6). Together with this goes a feeling of surrender, a sense of dependence, which causes the man who is faced with God's holiness to feel impotent (Gen 18:27) and guilty (Is 6:5). This gulf can be bridged only by God (Is 6:3). The distance does not, however, imply a separation. On the contrary, it serves rather as a bond, as it enables holiness to be recognised as such. The special quality of holiness and its particular relationship with the creature are brought out by this distance.

It is impossible for man to escape God's holiness. He has to come to grips with it in every sphere of his daily life. The giving of a law of holiness (Lev 17–26), which contains so many elements which appear so strange to us and which covered every detail of human life, must be seen in this light. It cannot, in itself, be related to any form of theoretical casuistry. It has to do rather with the requirements of a concrete, but constantly changing situation (see Num 9:15ff). As the individual, however, has not yet reached a sufficiently mature stage to be able to deal with the complications of this situation, he has need of the authority of the priest, whose position consequently becomes increasingly more powerful. Since holiness reveals itself with such incomparable force in the bible, too little serious attention has been paid to the origin and nature of the opposite element, the profane. The tendency has been to see this as the purely negative aspect—the unholy and unclean—and the result has been that the laws concerning public worship were restricted principally to the sphere of consecration and atonement. But since holiness lays a claim to the whole of man, it must at the same time be the moral norm, as expressed in various ways in the decalogue (Ex 19:5f) and in the prophetic books. There is bound to be a sharp clash whenever man sets himself up against what is holy and is thereby exposed to God's justice and punishment (Is 5:16), which descends upon him in judgement (Gen 19:24; 1 Sam 6:19; Ps 18:8f). This was the experience of Adam and Eve when they were banished by the cherubim from the holy Garden of Eden (Gen 3:23f). Here, however, God reveals himself as the one who is completely different and who shows mercy and grace and gives protection (or asylum,

373

Obad 1:17) to his people, despite their unworthiness and their persistence in sin. What is more, he does not begin to do this just at a later stage, in Israel's history, but from the very beginning (Gen 3:15-21). Similarly, he is the saviour and redeemer of the 'holy remnant' (Is 41:14; 43:5; 45:22), because he is God and not man (Hos 11:9). Thus we see that in the last resort it is God's love which bridges the gulf between the sacred and the profane and at the same time reveals the innermost heart of holiness, before which man can only fall down in worship, as he does in the presence of the angels (1 Sam 2:2; Is 6:1ff).

The power of God's holiness impressed itself deeply upon all the thoughts and actions of Old Testament man. Nevertheless, the close connection with material things, which in themselves had a deeply religious significance, and the dominant position of the hereditary priesthood, whose members frequently acted as officials and sophisticated theologians rather than as ministers of God, led to a debasement of the idea of holiness. It was the prophets (Is 1:11f; Hos 6:6) who first took up the cudgels against this distortion of the meaning of holiness. The struggle was continued in the New Testament.

With the passage of time, God's holiness was to such an extent regarded as the normal expression of his inner being that it was not particularly emphasised in the New Testament, and, when it is mentioned it refers back for the most part, to the Old Testament (see Rev 4:8; cf Is 6:3). Christ is more often called holy, but always when the intention is to stress the contrast between the holy and the profane, as, for example, in the case of the casting out of the unclean spirits (Mk 1:24) or of Peter's confession (Jn 6:69), or else when Christ's hidden divinity is visible through the outer covering of his humanity, as his ↗ glory (Jn 2:11, etc). For the rest, the emphasis throughout is on the dynamic aspect of divine holiness. Christ expressed this aspect in the first Our Father (Mt 6:9). In its absolute formulation, this Our Father embodies in a most impressive way, without any explicit reference to the creature, this elemental power which will not come to rest until the end of time, as the close bond between the Our Father and the ensuing prayer demonstrates. A decisive part is played here by the Holy ↗ Spirit, who is closely associated with the Lord as the one who announces the glad message (Mt 3:11; Lk 1:35; Jn 20:22) and is sent down with tongues of fire (Acts 2:4) to confirm the new people of God (Rom 15:16; Eph 3:16) which, transcending all national boundaries, includes all men who are sanctified in Christ (1 Cor 1:2), the Lord himself preparing the way for this (Eph 3:5). Luke, in the Acts of the Apostles, has expressed the eschatological restlessness of the Holy Spirit (Acts 1:5, 8). Man, however, no longer feels himself to be exposed to holiness as an incalculable primordial force, but realises that the bridging of the gulf which exists between the holy and the profane is the ultimate aim of his life. It is even possible for him to pray for the fulfilment of this aim, as a child of the father who is holy (Jn 17:11). This does not, however, imply that he should lose sight of the distance between the holy and the profane—the name of God is, for example, avoided in Mt 6:9, and man's consciousness of sin is indicated in Lk 5:4ff. With very few exceptions (Lk 5:6f), the process of sanctification is accomplished essentially within man—in striking contrast to the externalism which prevailed in later judaism—by a deeper penetration into man's being. In this way, human sanctification progresses from the stage where man's sinfulness is expiated by the seraph's touching of his lips (Is 6:7) to the stage where this expiation is brought about by the circumcision of his heart (Rom 2:29). The 'holiness' of Mount Sinai (Lev 11:44) corresponds to the 'perfection' of the Sermon on the Mount (Mt 5:48), which finds its final expression in man's deliverance from ↗ sin, darkness, and the bondage of Satan (Acts 26:18)—in which the essence of unholiness is clearly manifest. The christian, however, is able by virtue of his faith to enter the sphere of holiness through the word of God and above all through ↗ baptism (Eph 5:26). He is thus a man who is set apart for God (Eph 1:1), whose glory shines in him (2 Cor 3:18). The holiness which he possesses in this way is, however, by no means static. It is, of necessity, dynamic, and the christian is above all concerned with the need to preserve it intact. So great is the danger of its loss through the unholy element that the help and power of God the Father himself is invoked (Jn 17:11). Christ's mission (Jn 10:36), culminating in his sacrificial death (Jn 17:18ff), is, however, intimately associated with this process of sanctification, as it is only he who is personally within the sphere of holiness who is able to 'sanctify' others (Heb 2:11). This gradual extension of the range and scope of holiness may, of course, lead to serious conflict with the profane element. Examples of this are Christ's expulsion of the money-lenders from the temple (Mt 21:12), his curse on the fig-tree (Mt 21:19) and his ↗ judgement passed on the 'goats' at his left hand (Mt 25:41). This judgement is firmly established on the principle of holiness (1 Cor 6:2), the marks of which are ↗ truth and ↗ justice (Rev 6:10). But all this is transcended by the love of God which is unique in that he did not spare his own Son in order to draw the whole world to himself. In this context, the 'foolishness' and 'weakness' of God clearly reveal his holiness as otherness, as being totally distinct (1 Cor 1:25).

The early church was unable to prevent a certain debasement of the concept of holiness. As soon as everyone who was touched by God or Christ became known as a 'saint', the word 'holy' was bound to lose its particular significance and become more general and universal in application, and thus to take on all too easily a commonplace and everyday meaning. Acts 3:21 and Eph 3:5 give an indication of the beginning of this process.

Bibliography: J. Dillerberger, *Das Heilige im NT*, Kufstein 1926; Eichrodt I, 107–77; Haag 674–80; B. Häring, *Das Heilige und das Gute*, Tübingen 1948; E. Lohmeyer, *Das Vaterunser*, Göttingen 1952², 41–59; O. Procksch and K. G. Kuhn, *TDNT* I, 88–115; von Rad I, 203–7 and 271–9; O. Schilling, *Das Heilige und Gute im AT*, Leipzig 1956; see also R. Otto, *The Idea of the Holy*, London 1923.

Elpidius Pax

Hope

A. *In the Old Testament.* Hope plays a less important part in the Old Testament than in the New. It is normally expressed by the root *qwh*, meaning to remain, to wait, to look forward, to hope, usually in the sense of waiting or hoping for, or looking forward to, something or someone. In the first place, it refers to something which is expected, but which does not materialise (Is 5:2, 4, 7; 59:9, 11, etc). Frequently, however, it expresses an expectation which is fulfilled (Job 7:2; 17:13, etc). God is often the object of hope (Ps 25:2, 4, 21; 27: 14; Is 8:17; Jer 14:22, etc). The noun *miqweh*, formed from the root *qwh*, also usually refers to God (Jer 14:8; 17:13; 50:7; see also 1 Chron 29:15), whereas the other noun formation, *tiqwâh*, which is found frequently in Job, Proverbs, and Sirach, tends to refer to worldly happiness and good fortune. In the religious sense, *qiweh* and *tiqwâh* refer especially to things which God bestows on man in this life and which the just expect to receive from him alone. (In the Psalms, *qiweh* is translated by *hupomenō* or by *menō* and its compounds and *thiqwah* as *hupomonē*; in Job and in Proverbs, however, they are translated by *elpis*.) *Elpizō* denotes a state of expectation in the soul of something either greatly desired or else greatly feared. *Hupomenō*, on the other hand, preserves the basic meaning of remaining behind, thus waiting, looking forward to. Both words are used to translate *qiweh*, with the same meaning. A verb which is less commonly used is *hâkâh* (Is 8:17; 30: 18; Dan 12:12; Ps 33:22; 106:13, etc). It implies especially an expectation of an event, a turning towards God, the idea that God will do something. The word *śābar* is used when something is expected of somebody (Ps 104:27; 119:116, 166, etc), *Yāhal*, and its noun derivative *tôheleth*, is used in a specifically religious sense, and refers to Yahweh and to his grace, favour, judgements, and word (Ps 33:18; 119:43, 74, 81, 114, 147; 130:5, etc). *Bāṭah* is a static verb, used to express a state of the soul. It means to have trust or confidence, to hope confidently (see various parallel passages with equivalent verbs, Judg 18:7, 27; Ps 78:22; Job 24:22). It is frequently found without an object and often refers to Yahweh (Ps 4:5; 9:10; 21:7, etc) or to his grace or mercy (Ps 13:6; 52:9). According to this sense man ought not to trust in his own justice (Ezek 33:13), in Egypt (Is 36:6, 9; Jer 46:25), in princes (Ps 146:3), in his own strength (Ps 10), in riches (Prov 11:28; Ps 52:7; Jer 48:7) or in vanities and lying words (Jer 7:4, 8; Is 59:4, etc). *Ḥāsāh*, meaning to seek refuge, to conceal oneself (Ps 2:13; 5:11; 7:1; 11:1; 16:1; 17:7, etc) always has God as its object, or the shadow of Yahweh's wings (Ps 36:6). The noun *maḥseh* is also used in many places. It denotes a refuge, a place of refuge or a fortress. God will save his own if they take refuge in him (Ps 7:1; 17:7, etc), since he is just (Ps 31:1f) and good (Ps 25:8) (in LXX this is translated by *elpis, elpizō*, etc). *ʾāman* can also be included under this head. In the Niphal and the Hiphil, LXX translates this word by *pisteuō* and *pistis* and occasionally by *alētheia* (↗ faith, ↗ truth). The root *ʾāman* tends here to approach the sphere of faith, although strictly speaking it belongs more closely to the verbs which have already been discussed, and bears a special affinity to *bāṭaḥ*.

The Old Testament idea of hope is, however, not so closely related to the conception we have of it. We tend more or less to think of hope as an attitude of the soul, a turning towards something, in itself difficult to attain, with the aim of possessing it. In the Old Testament, however, and particularly in LXX, hope is closely connected with trust; it clings, in its expectation, to Yahweh's faithfulness, although the element of uncertainty, which is part of this hope, is never absent, for the man who hopes submits himself utterly to the mysterious will of God, knowing that he may often be put to the test for a long time, and that God is not necessarily bound to act (see also ↗ resurrection, ↗ messianism, ↗ prophecy).

B. *In the New Testament*, hope is expressed especially by *elpis* and *elpizō*. In the secular Greek world, these words had the meaning of anticipation, expectation, apprehension, supposition, or conjecture. In the New Testament, this anticipation or expectation was always directed towards a good, and never towards an evil object, and, as in LXX, included an additional shade of meaning, which implies trust and taking refuge. In 1 Tim 4:10, the implication is not that the christian hopes to possess God (in the beatific vision), but that he should place his hope in him and expect his salvation from him—as in LXX, *elpizō* has come closer in meaning to *pepoitha* and *pisteuō*.

The formula 'faith, hope and charity' (1 Cor 13:13) is of the greatest significance here. It may have developed from a bipartite formula—'faith, charity'—to which the third virtue, hope, was added on account of its close proximity to and intimate association with faith (see 1 Thess 1:3; 5:8; Gal 5:5f; Col 1:4f; 2 Thess 1:3f; Tit 2:2; Rev 2:19). The words 'now there remain ...' (1 Cor 13:13) are not intended to affirm the continuation of the three theological virtues into the eschatological age; they serve rather as an introductory formula, in the sense of 'now what are important are ...' (see Plato, *Crit.* 48b).

Unshakable trust in God is expressed in those formulae, such as 'to hope in God' (Rom 15:12; 1 Cor 15:19, etc), which are derived from the Old Testament. The man who hopes is prevented from experiencing disgrace or ignominy (*aiskhunē*) (see Ps 22:6; 25:3, 20), which is not the same as shame or a sense of shame. 'To put to shame', or 'confound' (*kataiskhunein*) is more accurately an act of God which places man in a disgraceful or ignominious situation or leads him to judgement or destruction (see Ps 35:26, etc). When it is put to shame or confounded, hope is thus much more than just disappointment. It is not just that what was hoped for is not accomplished. Indeed the very opposite result is achieved, and this, what is more, is brought about by divine ordinance. Christian hope is, in this sense, not brought into disgrace or 'confounded' (Rom 5:5). The opposite situation is that of *doxazesthai* and *kaukhasthai* (see Ps 91:15; Is 45:24f), of 'glorification'.

Paul, in his contribution to the theology of hope, has made it clear that the object of hope is the *doxa*, or ↗ glory, of God and Christ. Man has been deprived of this glory (Rom 3:23). The christian, however, is able to 'rejoice in the hope of sharing the glory of God' (Rom 5:2; see also 8:18; Eph 1:18).

The same object of christian hope is also called ↗ salvation (Rom 5:9f; 1 Thess 2:13), ↗ life or life everlasting (Rom 5:17; 6:22; 1 Cor 15:22; Gal 6:8; Tit 1:2; 3:7), the resurrection (see 1 Cor 15:19; Phil 3:21), the redemption of our body (Rom 8:23), ultimate justification (Gal 5:5), the ↗ inheritance (Rom 8:17; Eph 1:18; Tit 3:7; 1 Pet 1:3f), the ↗ kingdom, or the kingdom of God (Rom 5:17; 1 Cor 6:19; 15:50; 2 Thess 1:5; 2 Tim 4:18), the things which 'no eye has seen' (1 Cor 2:9; see also 2 Cor 4:17f), and 'the hope laid up for you in heaven' (Col 1:5). *The expectation of 'what we do not see'* (Rom 8:24f) can be taken as a kind of popular and rough definition of hope, referring to things over which we have no control, and no doubt meant as an admonishment to perseverance. In 2 Cor 4:18 and Heb 11:1, however, the contrast is between what is visible and what is invisible in order to indicate the glory of Christ and of christians, at present still concealed, but to be revealed in the future. Thus it is clear that *christian hope is definitely eschatological* and refers to the final fulfilment of the already 'realised eschatology'.

The main motive of hope is *God's promise* (Gen 15:6; see also Rom 4; Gal 3), the *divine mystery*—God's plan of salvation (Col 1:25-7; see also Eph 1:3-14; 3:1-21). Closely connected with this are two other motives, namely that a beginning has already been made in the realisation of the

divine work of salvation in the first place through Christ—in his mission, death, and resurrection—and secondly through the gift of the ↗ Spirit (Rom 5:5). In this connection, the two important Pauline texts on hope (Rom 5:1–11; 8:17ff) should be consulted.

With regard to the *attitude of the soul* within christian existence, the relationship between *hope* and *faith* consists in the fact that hope arises from faith in the divine promises and, like faith, is directed towards the future (Gal 3:11; 5:5).

The relationship between *hope* and ↗ *love (agapē)* is to be found in the eschatological character of the latter. The work of God's 'love' has already begun; his charity has been poured out into our hearts to strengthen them in preparation for the ↗ parousia (see Rom 5:5; 1 Thess 3:12f; 2 Thess 2:16f; Phil 1:9f).

The relationship between *hope* and *patience (hupomonē)*: Stoic philosophy excludes hope and is sufficient in itself (see Boethius, *Cons.* 1, m. 7:25ff; 'gaudia pelle, pelle timorem, spemque fugato nec dolor adsit!'). The patience of the Stoic is not expectation. It is rather self-mastery with regard to the world and to destiny. In the New Testament, however, patience is an auxiliary virtue to hope. It is always used in an eschatological context (Rom 5:3f; 2 Tim 2:12; see also Mk 13:13). If hope is always directed towards the aim of eschatological perfection, patience consists in putting up with ↗ suffering. This attitude of patience, perseverance and endurance enables man to share not only in the Lord's patient and persevering attitude, but also in the fruits of his suffering (Rom 8:17; 2 Cor 4:7ff; Col 1:24).

Finally, there is a close relationship between *hope and fear*. Like patience, fear is an essential characteristic of christian hope, since it is possible that, in great tribulation, a christian may not persevere to the very end (1 Cor 10:12). So long as the christian hopes, in faith, for the ↗ grace of God, he is safe (1 Cor 2:5; 1 Pet 1:21). If, however, he lives in the ↗ flesh, he is exposed to ↗ temptations and must 'fear', not with anxious fear, but with a salutary fear which is inseparably bound up with christian existence—an existence which remains constantly in faith and hope and can never depend upon itself (Rom 11:20–22). What is of importance concerning the attitude of hope in the individual soul is not necessarily of importance with regard to the hope of the christian community as a whole. The church awaits the parousia of the Lord and the revelation of his glory with unerring certainty, whereas each individual christian is not necessarily justified (1 Cor 4:4; Phil 3:12). This is why hope is always accompanied by trust—the basic meaning of *pistis* and *elpis* shows this, and Paul also mentions this fact (2 Cor 3:12f; Eph 3:12).

According to Paul, then, christian existence is characterised by hope. In contrast, the pagan world is marked by an existence without hope (Eph 2:12; see also 1 Thess 4:13; Marcus Aurelius, *De Seipso* 3:14).

Bibliography: J. de Guibert, *RSR* 4 (1913), 565–96; A. Pott, *Das Hoffen im NT*, Leipzig 1915; A. Lesky, *Gnomon* 9 (1933), 173ff; R. Bultmann and K. H. Rengstorff, *TDNT* II, 517–35 (=*BKW* XII); T. C. Vriezen, *TLZ* 78 (1953), 577–86; C. Westerman, *Theologia Viatorum* 4 (Berlin 1952), 19–70; E. Wolf, *ET* 13 (1953), 157–69. See especially: J. van der Ploeg, *RB* 61 (1954), 481–507; W. Grossouw, *RB* 61 (1954), 508–32; W. Grossouw, *NKS* 51 (1955) 265–76; S. Pinckaers, *NRT* 77 (1955), 785–99; F. Urtiz de Urtaran, 'Esperanza y Caridad en el NT', *Scriptorium Victorense* I (Vitoria 1954), 1–50; E. Schweizer, *Studies C. H. Dodd*, Cambridge 1956, 482–508; J. P. Ramseyer, *Allmen* 172–4; Bultmann I, 319–23 and 344–7; P. A. H. de Boer, 'Études sur le sens de la racine QWH', *OTS* 10 (1954), 225–46; H. Haag, *Anima* 12 (1958), 111–18; G. Bertram, *ZNW* 49 (1958), 264–70; A. Gelin, *LV* 8 (1959), 3–16; E. Neuhäusler, *LTK* v², 416–18; H. Schlier, 'Über die Hoffnung', *GL* 33 (1960), 16–24; L. Fedele, 'La speranza cristiana nelle lettere di S. Paolo', *Aloisiana* I (Naples 1960), 21–67; J.-H. Nicolas, 'Valeur de l'espérance enseignée par l'Ecriture', *Dict. de la Spiritualité*, 1960, 1209–16; G. Bornkamm, 'Die Hoffnung in Col', *TU* 77 (1961), 56–64; C. F. D. Moule, *The Meaning of Hope*, Philadelphia 1963.

Johannes B. Bauer

Hour

In the bible *hour* does not simply refer to a unit of time into which the day (see Jn 11:9; the day has twelve hours) or the night is divided (the Jews divided the night into three watches of four hours each: Judg 7:19; Lk 12:38; the Romans into four watches of three hours each: Mk 13:35). Corresponding to the Hebrew *ʿēth* it also commonly stands for the period of time during which an action takes place (eg the phrase 'in that hour'). The Semitic experience of time is less of the spatial-temporal order than dynamic, determined by the experience of the event which fills or takes up time (eg 'in a single hour', Rev 18:10, 17–19 = very quickly; and phrases such as 'the hour of the harvest, of temptation, for taking a meal', etc). Hence there are special 'hours' in which, following on the divine decision, some specific event will take place which will have significance for the salvation of the world.

1. *Jewish apocalyptic.* Jewish apocalyptic writers refer to particular 'hours' in a way which is of special theological significance. In Old Testament prophecy 'the day of Yahweh' or 'that day' played an important part, sometimes referring to an event within history, sometimes having an eschatological connotation. But this way of speaking did not imply that the last age was thought of as divided into discrete periods, into 'hours'. This tendency is peculiar to apocalyptic writing and we find it for the first time in Daniel (chapter 9: the seventy weeks of years). In this chapter LXX translates 'the final age' (Hebrew: *'ēth qes*) by 'an hour of the fixed time' (for the end, that is = *hōra kairou*; 8:17, 19; cf 11:40, 45). The 'fixed times' determined by God which the apocalyptic writers refer to are called 'hours' in the Apocrypha: 'but now your time is passing quickly and your hours are upon you' (Bar [Syr] 36:9); 'he has measured the hours by measure and numbered the times by number' (4 Esd 4:37); 'he governs the hours and whatever things come to pass in the hours' (4 Esdras 13:58). We also find reference to 'the twelve hours of the age of the world' Apoc Abr 29:1f) and especially to 'the twelfth hour of the godless age of the world' (ApocAbr 29:8; cf 13). Attempts were made to calculate the time of 'the end' by means of various signs and it was believed that God would, for the sake of the righteous, shorten the last terrible age (see Volz, *Eschatologie* 137f; 141–6).

2. *In early christianity.* Jesus had nothing to do with such apocalyptic speculations and attempts to predict the end of the world (see Lk 17:20; Mk 13:32). His eschatological message concerned the time of fulfilment, the approaching kingdom of God (Mk 1:15), the time of God's gracious visitation (Lk 19:44). To express all of this another concept was used, that of the *kairos* or appointed time. The *kairos* is the eschatological time of salvation determined by God and inaugurated by Jesus. It is a time when salvation is offered to men, a time of decision and crisis in which men must acknowledge the power of God and decide to accept the offer in conversion and faith (cf Lk 12:56). This *kairos* which brings on a state of crisis is not at all to be understood as an 'hour' in the sense of a discrete unit of time measured along a line of temporal succession. It is determined uniquely by the events which take place, events which are brought about by God and impinge on the life of men. The apocalyptic writers speak not only of 'times or seasons' (*kairoi*; Acts 1:7; see also 1 Thess 5:1) but also of 'the day' and 'the hour'. It is categorically denied in Mk 13:32 that anyone apart from the father knows anything about 'that day or the hour'. There are, indeed, comparable statements in the apocalyptic literature about God reserving such knowledge to himself, but here it is emphasised that even Jesus, who is 'the Son', can say nothing about the time of the end and that therefore such speculations are pointless and all that is demanded is vigilance (vv 33–7). In this logion it is not a question of determining a specific hour in a day which is deemed imminent; 'hour' is

just another way of expressing the same thing as 'that day'. The Son of Man will come 'at an hour you do not expect' (Lk 12:40; see also v 46 = Mt 24:44, 50).

Any attempt to calculate 'the hour' is therefore rejected (see Lk 12:38; Mk 13:35). Paul only appears to do this when he speaks metaphorically of 'the hour' to arise from sleep and states that the night is far gone and the day draws nigh (Rom 13:11f). Objectively considered, we have here an eschatological appeal and 'the hour' is nothing else but the *kairos* of salvation (see 2 Cor 6:2, and for this metaphor also 1 Thess 5:1–6). We have to interpret in much the same way the 'last hour' in 1 Jn 2:18, the coming of which can be recognised by the appearance of false teachers. This 'hour' is not to be understood as the last hour which strikes before the end but rather as a way of characterising the last age (that is, the period of time before the end) in general. The decisive factor, even for the Apocalyptics, is not the end of a temporal succession but the way in which fulfilment takes place. In spite of the proximity of the end (understood as the *kairos* of eschatological fulfilment; see 1:3 and 22:10) the community does not know at what hour the Lord will come (3:3: cf 16:15). There is 'the hour of judgement' and 'the hour of the harvest' (14:7, 15); the emphasis is on the fact of divine judgement rather than the time when it will take place (18:10, 17, 19).

In Mk 14:41 the 'dark hour' in which Jesus will be 'delivered up', the hour of the Messiah's death foreordained by God, corresponds to the 'hour' of the coming of the Son of Man in glory. In Gethsemani Jesus is afraid of this hour and prays that it may pass from him (14:35) even while accepting it from his Father's hand. This has to be understood within the 'Son of Man theology' of Mark's gospel. According to Lk 22:53 this is the hour of his enemies ('your hour') and of 'the powers of darkness'.

3. *The Gospel of John.* 'The hour' or 'the hour of Jesus' is given most importance theologically in John's gospel. Though its significance is expressed in different ways there is an underlying unity. This gospel makes use of eschatological terminology as when it speaks of the 'hour to come' when the dead in their graves will hear the voice of the Son of God (5:28), or when it refers to persecutions which will come upon the disciples (16:2, 4), or when it records Jesus as saying that he will speak to them no longer in figures (16:25). But the genuinely johannine view is that the hour which is to come has already come in Jesus, that the true worshippers of the Father worship him in spirit and truth (4:23) and that 'the dead' hear the voice of the Son of God and that they who hear it will live (5:25). The eschatological turning-point is already present in Jesus and therefore the eschatological 'hour' has already been accomplished.

In view of this context, which understands salvation as already present in Christ, hardly any difference is made between the time of Jesus's life on earth and that of his exaltation when he dispenses salvation to makind. It is another matter, however, when the author has in view his death and subsequent return to the glory which is his in heaven. Here he speaks of 'his hour' which is the hour of the decisive turning-point (13:1). This is the hour of his exaltation on the cross (3:14; 8:28; 12:32, 34) which is also the hour of his glorification (12:23; 17:1). According to the johannine point of view, the cross is no longer the nadir of the humiliation of Christ (see Phil 2:8) but rather a lifting up (symbolically of the lifting up of the cross: see 12:34), the beginning of his glorification and of the salvific activity of the exalted Christ (12:32; 17:1f). His 'hour' on the Mount of Olives (12:27f) must also be taken into account in this perspective. This decisive hour in the redemptive mission of Jesus is entirely dependent on the will and the power of the Father for its fulfilment. Hence we are told on more than one occasion that the Jews did not lay hands on him since 'his hour had not yet come' (7:30; 8:20). Immediately before the Passover of his death, at the Last Supper, Jesus knows that the hour of his return to the Father has come (13:1), and after the traitor has left the room he says that the Son of Man is 'now' glorified (13:31; cf also the 'now' in 12:31). The 'little while' which must pass before that hour is really at hand (16:16ff) disappears as far as Jesus is concerned (see the tenses in 12:23, 31; 13:31; 16:32; 17:1) but signifies for the disciples a time of tribulation (16:20ff—comparison with 'the hour' of the woman in travail) and temptation.

It is clear, therefore, that 'the hour of Jesus' has its meaning more from what happens than from its significance as a unit of time. What is decisive is that both as regards what happens and when it happens it is within the salvific design and the will of God. This is important for the interpretation of the most difficult passage which we have to consider, namely, the words of Jesus at the marriage feast of Cana (2:4). There are many catholic exegetes who attempt to interpret the hour of which Jesus speaks on this occasion ('my hour') as referring to the hour of his exaltation and glorification and therefore as revealing his glory of which the miracle of changing water into wine is a sign or symbol. Others recognise here only the expression of the messianic consciousness of Jesus whose entire activity, right from the beginning of his self-revelation on earth, results from the mission given him by the Father and is manifested by 'signs'. In this case 'the hour' cannot be understood in a purely temporal sense since Jesus goes on at once to work the miracle.

The attentive expectation of the Jesus of the fourth gospel for the striking of the eschatological hour of salvation in which the will of the Father is revealed serves as an admonition to his disciples to recognise the eschatological hour which has come with him and is still to be completed and, at the same time, to take cognizance of their situation within the history of salvation and the task which awaits them (see 16:1-4, suffering and persecution; 16:22-7, joy and confidence; 16:33, peace and the assurance of victory).

Bibliography: P. Volz, *Die Eschatologie der jüdischen Gemeinde*, Tübingen 1934²; G. Delling, *Das Zeitverständnis des NT*, Gütersloh 1940; O. Cullmann, *Christ and Time*, London 1951; J. Barr, *Biblical Words for Time*, London 1962; R. Motte, 'Hour', *DBT*, 439ff; P. Neuenzeit, '"Als die Fülle der Zeit gekommen war . . ."' (Gal 4:4): Gedanken zum biblischen Zeitverständnis', *Bibel und Leben* 4 (1963), 223-39.

Rudolf Schnackenburg

Volume 2

Humility – Righteousness

Humility

One of the positive contributions which Rudolf Bultmann's demythologising of the New Testament message has made is to focus attention on the central position of humility in biblical theology. According to Bultmann, the interpretation of what he calls 'myth' provides the clearest insight into the nature of christian existence. In his view, true human life is

> that which lives from what is invisible and not available to us, that which therefore surrenders all self-created security, . . . a radical submission to God, expecting everything from him and nothing from itself, implying a detachment from everything which is available to us in the world and thus an attitude of disentanglement from the world and of freedom. This attitude at the same time opens man to human relationships. Free from fear and from a clinging to what is present and available to him, man is thus open to others.
>
> ('The New Testament and Mythology', *Kerygma and Myth* 1, ed H. W. Bartsch, London 1953, 28ff.)

Elsewhere Bultmann writes of humility's opposite, 'worldliness', and how it is manifested in human 'care' and 'pride':

> This pride, whether it is based on national or social advantages, or on wisdom or works of the law, is rebellion against God, before whom no man may boast. The height of illusion is that man thinks he can separate himself from the 'world' and bring himself to a being beyond it.
>
> ('Paul', *Existence and Faith*, London 1961, 151f.)

A recognition of man's total dependence upon God and a readiness to serve God selflessly, together with one's fellow-men—these are essential to the idea of humility. Several words are used for humility in the Hebrew bible. In LXX, the idea of humility is expressed by various derivatives and formations from the adjective *tapeinos* (2 lowly, small, oppressed humble). The New Testament follows a similar linguistic usage. In secular Greek literature, *tapeinos* and its derivatives generally imply a servile attitude of mind, a blend of fear and obsequiousness. Many have consequently inferred that humility, as a virtue, was unknown in the Greek world (E. Kalt, *BRL* 1, 365; M. Meinertz, 185). This is, however, not the case—the Greeks understood the nature of humility very well (S. Rehrl).

In the Old Testament, their deliverance from base servitude, oppression and desolation in Egypt gave the Israelites an insight into God and an awareness of themselves which formed the central core of their religious thought, theological consciousness and eschatological message (Guillet, *Leitgedanken der Bibel*, 9–28).

The pre-exilic texts refer to humility (baseness, lowliness) as a condition rather than as an attitude of mind. The desolation of Israel in Egypt is described as abasement (*tapeinōsis*); the Israelites cried to the Lord, the God of their fathers, and he heard their cry and saw their affliction, their labour and their distress and brought them out of Egypt with a strong hand and an out-stretched arm, with dreadful power and with signs and wonders (Deut 26:7; see also Neh 9:9; Ps 89:10). This resulted in Israel's conviction that God always looked on the misery and desolation of his people and would help them when they cried to him (1 Sam 2:1–10; 9:16; 2 Sam 16:12; 2 Kings 14:26; Judith 6:21).

It was the poor and the oppressed who, so long as they placed their hopes in God, experienced God's readiness to help. This applied both to the individual and to the people. God's power is not to be found in the multitude or in proud men who boast of their strength – God is a God of the humble, a helper of the lowly, a support to the weak, a protector of the rejected, a saviour of those who are in desperate straits (Judith 9:11; see also Judg 7:1ff; 2 Sam 24; 1 Chron 21; Deut 8:17f; Amos 6:13). There is always the hope of help in distress (Job 5:11; Ps 9:13; 18:28; 107:12f; 119:50, 153; Is 2:10; 66:2). Childless women who have conceived claim especially that God has looked down on their misery (lowliness; Gen 16:11ff; 29:32; 31:42; 1 Sam 1:11; Lk 1:48).

It is a general law, often expressed in gnomic form, that God exalts the lowly and humbles the proud (1 Sam 2:7; Ps 147:6; Job 22:29; Prov 3:34; 29:23; Is 1:25; 2:11; Ezek 21:31). God 'humbles' the proud in this way by casting them down from their high positions in order to call them to conversion (1 Kings 8:35; 1 Chron 4:10; 2 Chron 6:26; Ps 90:15; 107:17; 119:75; Lam 3:32). Desolation and oppression are reasons for which man should praise God (Dan 3:23 [65]). Exaltation must always go hand in hand with humility (Sir 3:19f).

Whoever seeks God's mercy and help has to humble himself and perform penitential exercises such as fasting and the rending of his garments for God to look down upon his wretchedness and help him (Lev 16:29, 31; 23:27, 29, 32; Judith 4:8; Sir 2:17; 7:17). All fasting, mortification and self-castigation must, however, be accompanied by moral conversion and true repentance (Is 58:3, 5).

The person in distress who wishes to receive help from God must have confidence in God. He must also be conscious of his need and recognise his dependence on God. This inner, spiritual element became much more prominent during and after the Exile. From this period onwards, a distinction was made between the outward state of poverty and lowliness and the inward attitude of humility. God reigns as the Holy One in the highest, yet he is with the humble man who is contrite in spirit (*šefal rûah*), 'to revive the spirit of the humble, and to revive the heart of the contrite' (Is 57:15). In the words of the psalmist, 'Yahweh is near to the broken-hearted, and saves the crushed in spirit' (Ps 34:18). The terms *poor* and *humble* (*ʿānîîm*, *ʿānāwîm*) are often equated with one another: 'he leads the humble in what is right; and teaches the humble his way' (Ps 25:9). The 'Servant of the Lord' is portrayed as a figure combining outward lowliness with inward humility (Is 53:7f; see also other references to the ↗ Servant in Isaiah: 42:1–4; 49:1–6; 50:4–10; 52:13–53:12). The Messiah is not expected to come in the form of a proud warrior, riding on a horse, but in humility, riding on an ass (Zech 9:9).

The ideal religious figure is represented in the psalms as being a humble man who places all his hope not in worldly possessions but in God, and who acknowledges God alone to be his highest possession (Ps 10:17; 22:26; 25:9; 34:2; 37:11; 69:33; 76:9; 149:4). This religious shade of meaning is also usually present even when the word *poor* is used (Ps 10:2, 9; 14:6, etc). The authors of the Wisdom literature were particularly concerned with the question of humility (see especially Sir 10:7–34). Humility is the outcome of man's recognition of his own frailty—'How can he who is dust and ashes be proud? for even in life his bowels decay.' (Sir 10:9). The fear of God and humility are intimately associated with each other. True glory is to be found in the fear of God (Sir 10:23–27). 'The beginning of man's pride is to depart from the Lord; his heart has forsaken his Maker' (Sir 10:12). The humble man may and indeed should honour himself too (Sir 10:28). Humility implies an attitude of truthfulness towards oneself and honour is a possession which presupposes self-respect in man (Sir 10:27f). Humility is to be found in man's spiritual attitude, not in his outward behaviour (Sir 19:26f). The fruits of humility are recognition by God and men (Sir 3:19–21), the mercy and grace of God (Sir 3:20; Job 22:29; Ps 33:18–20), God's favour (Prov 16:19), wisdom (Prov 11:2), honour (Prov 15:33; 18:12; 29:23), and exaltation (Sir 10:14f). Humility is not held in high esteem by the proud, who regard it rather as an abomination (Sir 13:20).

In the New Testament. The transition from the Old Testament attitude towards humility to that of the New is most clearly shown in that part of Luke's gospel which deals with Christ's childhood and early life. The Jews who figure in this account are, like those of the post-exilic books, the humble who are waiting for the 'consolation of Israel' (Lk 2:25). The Magnificat (Lk 1:46–54) is imbued with the Old Testament idea of humility.

Jesus referred to himself as 'humble of heart' (Mt 11:29; cf Is 57:15). He urged his disciples to be the same, and encouraged them by his example of mildness and humility. He saw himself as the humble ↗ Servant of the Lord and viewed his life in this perspective (Acts 8:33). He took upon himself the ultimate humiliation of death (Phil 2:8) and was at the same time the ↗ Son of Man and the Servant of the Lord. He did not wish to be ministered to, but to serve and to offer his life as a ransom for many (Mk 10:45). All his activity is marked by humility (Mt 12:15f; cf Is 42:1–4). The same humility is apparent in his messianic entry into Jerusalem (Mt 21:5; cf Zech 9:9).

He directed his attention and his message above all to the poor and the oppressed and brought salvation to them. It was the poor, the hungry and the sorrowful (Lk 6:20f; 4:18; cf Is 61:1f), the little ones of this world (Mk 9:41; Mt 10:42; 18:10), those who are last (Mk 10:31), the children (Lk 10:21; Mk 10:14; Mt 19:13–15; Lk 18:15f) whom he came to save. 'But many that are first will be last, and the last first' (Mk 10:31; Mt 19:30; 20:16).

Humility is a necessary condition for entry into the ↗ kingdom of God. The beatitudes of the Sermon on the Mount promise the kingdom of God to the poor.

In Luke's account there is more emphasis upon the social aspect of this poverty. Matthew, on the other hand, is more concerned with man's spiritual attitude towards God (see Mt 5:3f with Lk 6:20f). Only those who are as small, weak and insignificant as children are by nature can enter God's kingdom (Mk 10:15; Mt 18:3; Lk 18:17); they must, by implication, be humble (Mt 18:14). The normal rule of modest deportment, by which a man should choose the lowest place at a festive occasion and not the highest (see Prov 25:6f), is taken by Jesus as an example of the need for humility in any man who wishes to enter the kingdom of God (Lk 14:10). Only those who do not boast of their own achievements but rather, in a spirit of humility, expect everything from him and acknowledge themselves to be 'unworthy servants', will be admitted into God's kingdom (Lk 17:7–10). The self-righteous cannot hope to find justification; it is only those who are contrite of heart and humble themselves before God who will be justified (Lk 18:9–14). God claims man's whole heart and will not tolerate vanity or ambition (Mt 6:2–6, 16–18; 23:5; Mk 10:35–40; Mt 20:20–23). Jesus also made use of the gnomic utterance of the Old Testament, namely that God humbles the proud and exalts the lowly, in his proclamation of the kingdom of God: 'What is exalted among men is an abomination in the sight of God' (Lk 16:15; see also Mt 5:20; 6:1), 'Whoever exalts himself will be humbled, and whoever humbles himself will be exalted' (Mt 23:12; 18:4; Lk 14:11; 18:14). Jesus not only demanded humility before God, he also expected men to serve each other in

humility, imitating God himself in his condescension (Lk 6:36; Mt 5:45). Jesus' service to men in life and death is intended for man's imitation (Lk 22:27; Mk 10:45): 'If any one would be first, he must be the last of all and servant of all' (Mk 9:35; Lk 9:48; Mk 10:42–4; Mt 20:25ff; Lk 22:25f; Mt 23:11).

The word *tapeinos* and its derivatives occur more frequently in *the Pauline letters* than anywhere else in the New Testament. Paul views the whole of Jesus' mission as a 'humiliation' (*tapeinōsis*). The humility of God in Christ consists in his taking flesh and assuming man's lowly condition without either sacrificing his divinity or in any way destroying his humanity (Phil 2:8). Jesus is the sublime and primordial example of humility. He has renounced the honour of being equal to God so that God might be glorified and mankind saved, and this process of humiliation has resulted in his exaltation (Phil 2:6–11). Paul makes use of an older eucharistic hymn, reminiscent of the Old Testament teaching on the subject of humility, especially with regard to the idea of poverty in relation to humility, to help him to interpret Christ's work in this connection: 'Though he was rich, yet for your sake he became poor, so that by his poverty you might become rich' (2 Cor 8:9).

In the light of Paul's doctrine of salvation, man is forbidden to boast of his own achievements or to glorify himself. Justification is due to grace and does not depend upon merit, with the result that no man is entitled to glory in his achievements (Rom 3:27). The christian must, on the contrary, recognise that he is a sinner who is completely dependent upon God (Rom 1:18–3:2). God chooses weak things that are of no value in the eyes of the world and exalts them so that he may be praised rather than that man should glorify himself (1 Cor 1:26–31). It is the humble man whom God consoles (2 Cor 7:6).

Paul insisted that christians should show humility towards one another, and that they should not strive, in a spirit of arrogance and vanity, for those things which they were not intended to possess, but should rather adapt themselves to the measure of grace which is accorded to every individual (Rom 12:3; 1 Cor 12:12–30). According to Paul, all offices and all natural aptitudes and charisma have their valid place in the building up of the body of Christ (Eph 4:11–16). An essential element in the unity of the christian community is that they should all have the same mind and the same way of thinking, and therefore it is necessary that no single man should try to raise himself on to a higher level than his fellows in the community or claim a great share of the honours or more prestige for himself (Rom 12:16). Christ did not live according to his own pleasure, but took upon himself the abuse of those who hated God. In the same way, Paul insists, christians ought not to consider their own satisfaction, but concentrate on the spiritual gain of their fellow christians (see Rom 12:2f). They should, in humility, 'count others better than' themselves rather than strive after vainglory, and be attentive to the well-being of others rather than consider their own personal advantage (Phil 2:3). Humility characterises the attitude and behaviour of the man who thinks more of others than of himself, and who does not do this in order to achieve an ultimate superiority over them, but because he recognises, in a spirit of genuine modesty, what God has in fact assigned both to him and to others. Humility plays a particularly important part in preserving the constantly threatened unity of the church. The demands of ambition within the church have to be renounced for the sake of unity, and this renunciation can only be achieved by a humble attitude of mind and when human endeavour is governed by humility. There is a constant interchange between and intermingling of unity, charity and humility. In the Pauline and Petrine lists of virtues (Col 3:12; Eph 4:2; 1 Pet 3:8; 5:5), humility appears as the first condition for ↗ love. Paul also calls fasting and mortification 'humility' (Phil 4:12); however, no significance should, in Paul's view, be attached to such penitential exercises if they should in any way tend to diminish the importance of the salvation wrought by Christ (Col 2:18, 23).

Paul himself lived in humility. Although he was conscious of being endowed with the grace of the apostolate, he felt himself to be unworthy of this high calling. He thought of himself as 'one untimely born' (1 Cor 15:8f), as the least and the unworthiest of the apostles (Eph 3:8), and as the greatest of sinners (1 Tim 1:15). He served the Lord in all humility (Acts 20:19; 2 Cor 6:4) and attributed all his abilities and all his success to the one God (2 Cor 3:5) or to his grace (1 Cor 15:10) or to his power to strengthen (Phil 4:13). It was from his very weakness that he formed the hope that

God would make him strong: 'When I am weak, then I am strong' (2 Cor 12:10; see also 1 Cor 3:5ff; Eph 2:8; 2 Tim 4:17). Carrying out his apostolate without any thought of recompense, and suffering humiliations on account of it, his hope was that his humiliation would bring about the exaltation of those to whom he preached the gospel (2 Cor 11:7). He regarded lack of success in his work as a humiliation imposed by God (2 Cor 12:21). Finally, Paul, like Christ who took upon himself every ignominy for the salvation of mankind, also took upon himself similar ignominy and disgrace (1 Cor 4:9–13; 2 Cor 6:8f) and even death, so that life should be really effective in those who listened to his preaching (2 Cor 4:12).

Neither the word *tapeinos* nor any of its derivatives occur in John, but humility has a place in his writings. Jesus was to such an extent the revealer of his Father to mankind that his mission and the accomplishment of his Father's will were all-important to him. What he sought was not his own glory, but his Father's honour (Jn 8:50ff; 7:18; see also 17:4). Men, on the other hand, seek their own glory (12:43). The glorification which Jesus asked the Father to give him was the glorification of God himself (17:1, 5). Death was viewed as a service of humility to men (as in the washing of the disciples' feet, 13:1–20). This lowly, servile duty was necessary for the establishment of the christian community united with Christ and the share which christians were to have in his glory (13:8). The man who is intent only upon himself and wrapped up in his own importance cannot begin to understand Jesus' way of humble

service (13:6, 8). It is impossible to have any share in Christ unless full assent is given to this way. Jesus' humility opened the minds of the disciples to the possibility of humility towards each other and indeed demanded humility on their part. Their sharing in him, achieved by means of his service of humility towards them, was to result in their service of humility towards others (13:12ff). Even more than in the case of Paul, there is, in John, an intermingling of charity, obedience and humility, and these, like the death of Christ, are viewed as glorification.

Bibliography: K. Thieme, *Die christliche Demut*, Giessen 1906; H. Rosman, 'In omni humilitate', *VD* 21 (1941), 272–80 and 311–20; R. North, '"Humilis corde" in luce Psalmorum', *VD* 28 (1950), 153–61; A. Gelin, *Les Pauvres de Jahvé*, Paris 1953; S. Rehrl, *Das Problem der Demut in der profanischen Literatur im Vergleich zu LXX und NT*, Münster 1961; A. Dihle, *RAC* iii, 735–78; J. Gewiess, *LTK* iii², 223–4; H. J. Kraus, *Psalmen*, Neukirchen 1960, 82f; W. Grundmann, *TWNT* viii, 1–27.

Alois Stöger

Hypocrite

The concept *hypocrisy* does not appear in the Old Testament. *ḥānep*, which also stands for 'to play the hypocrite' in later judaism, has, according to Old Testament usage, the meaning 'to corrupt'; and the corresponding adjective, 'profligate', 'godless'. By way of reproach of an enemy or adversary *within* the chosen community of the Jewish people are phrases such as 'flattering lips (tongue)' (Ps 12:2); 'to speak smooth things' (Is 30:10); and to speak seductive 'flatteries' (Dan 11:21,

34). The community of Qumran was itself clear that it was separated, cut off, from the *dāraš ḥelqâh* (= 'those who seek after smooth things': 1 QH 2:5, 32; 4 QpNah 1:2, 7; 2:2, 4; 3:3; 4 QpHos^c 10 (Erg); see also Dam 1:18; 1 QH 4:10).

The New Testament is familiar with the idea of hypocrisy in the sense of 'giving oneself the appearance of being good'. This is the meaning of the reproach of Christ addressed to the emissaries of the Pharisees and Herodians (Mt 22:18 and parallels). He who wishes to remove the splinter which is in his brother's eye and yet overlooks the beam which is in his own is a hypocrite. There is also a warning against hypocrisy for christians (1 Pet 2:1).

The Greek word *hupokritēs* is bound up with the idea of *play-acting*—one's outward attitude bears no relation to one's inner being. In this way almsgiving, prayer, and fasting can be just hypocritical play-acting rather than a service rendered to God (Mt 6:2, 5, 16).

Side by side with this, the New Testament attaches a radically theological meaning to the expression 'to play the hypocrite' which is peculiar to itself. When Peter and the Jewish christians who accompanied him separated themselves from the table fellowship of the hellenistic christians, Paul considered it *hypocrisy*, a watering down of the 'truth of the gospel' (Gal 2:13ff). The reason was that this attitude must have given the impression that the law was still in force while being, at the same time, an offence against the proclamation of the faith. The attitude of these christians attached to Peter did not agree with the assured knowledge

of the faith which they already possessed (Gal 2:16). Paul, therefore, felt obliged to condemn this since it was a question of something essential to the faith.

Apostates are reproached with the hypocrisy of their deceitful talk (1 Tim 4:2)—referring evidently to a falsification of the true faith. It is not surprising, therefore, that the sentence passed on the wicked servant, that his master will come and 'put him with the hypocrites' (Mt 24:51), is paraphrased and explained in Lk 12:46 as 'with the unfaithful'. The accusation of hypocrisy in the New Testament refers above all to *the rejection of faith*.

The Lord refers to those who know how to interpret the signs of good and bad weather but cannot recognise the presence of Christ calling out for faith as hypocrites (Lk 12:56). The ruler of the synagogue and his people were hypocrites because they did not recognise that Christ, in healing the woman who had been ill for eighteen years, had loosed the bonds put on her by Satan and had so fulfilled his messianic mission (Lk 13:15ff). The scribes and pharisees were hypocrites because they wanted to prevent people honouring their parents, a divine commandment of great binding force, by means of a purely human insistence on fulfilling certain vows to the letter (Mt 15:7). Since they do not recognise the divine will in this they are blind to the mission and identity of Jesus (Mt 15:14), they are not 'planted by the heavenly Father' (Mt 15:13) since they reproach the Lord on account of his disciples transgressing the traditions (Mt 15:2 and parallels).

Since the scribes and Pharisees have refused to believe in Christ (see Mt

22:41-5 and parallels) they draw upon themselves the fearful words of denunciation: 'Woe to you, scribes and Pharisees, hypocrites!' (Mt 23:13, 14, 15, 23, 25, 27, 29). In this case the Lord is not attacking the conscious attempt to give themselves the appearance of being good, as with his merciless denunciation of the 'hypocrites' in the Sermon on the Mount. Here he recognises what is good in the conduct of his adversaries—scrupulous fidelity in paying tithes is a good thing, but the lack of justice, mercy, and faith is bad; 'these you ought to have done, without neglecting the others' (Mt 23:23). The conversion of pagans (Mt 23:15), observance of the laws of ritual purity (Mt 23:25 and parallels), decoration of the graves of the murdered prophets (Mt 23:29 and parallels) are good—Christ in no way implies that his opponents perform these good works out of hypocrisy understood in the strict moral sense. What he condemns is their neglect of the weightier matters of the law, with the result that they make their proselytes twice as bad as themselves (Mt 23:15), that they are full of extortion and rapacity (Mt 23:25 and parallels), that they fill up the measure of their fathers who murdered the prophets (Mt 23:32) insofar as they kill those who are sent by Christ (Mt 23:34ff and parallels). They are like graves which are not seen (Lk 11:44) being inwardly full of 'hypocrisy' and the rejection of God (Mt 23:28). They themselves do not enter into the kingdom of heaven and prevent others from doing so (Mt 23:13 and parallels) since they oppose Christ and do not believe in him. Their 'hypocrisy' consists in this, that out- wardly they appear to put the will of God fully into practice and yet at the same time reject the Son of God and his appeal. This rejection of Christ's appeal for faith is the essential reason for their condemnation. This rejection works like leaven throughout the whole being of these opponents of Christ (Lk 12:1) and is the real cause also of their refusal to obey the moral demands of the law, for this law contained within itself the impossibility of perfect ful- filment on account of 'the flesh' (Rom 8:3). The law of the Spirit of life in Christ Jesus has brought freedom (Rom 8:2) so that now everyone who believes in him has eternal life (Jn 3:15). Those, however, who do not possess the Spirit of Christ through total submission in faith to the saving design of God abide in the death which consists in being far from God, and those who do not accept Christ through faith are, in the language of the New Testament, 'hypocrites' since, although they may outwardly appear good, they do not bear within themselves the true righteousness of God.

Bibliography: F. Heimsoeth, 'De voce hypo- crites commentariolus', *Index Scholarum*, Bonn 1873/4, I–XIV; P. Joüon, 'Hypocrites dans l'évangile et Hébreu Chânef', *RSR* 20 (1930), 312–16; W. Beilner, *Christus und die Pharisäer*, Vienna 1959, esp. 227–35; G. Bornkamm, *RGG* III[3], 305f; J. Maier, 'Weitere Stücke aus dem Nahumkommentar aus der Höhle 4 von Qumran', *Judaica* 18 (1962), 215–50; *DBT* 220f. For the Greek concept, see: G. F. Else, *Wiener Studien* 72 (1959), 75–107.

Wolfgang Beilner

Image

The following terms are found in the Hebrew Bible with the meaning 'image': *tselēm* (Num 33:52; 2 Kings 11:18; Ezek 7:20), *semel* (Deut 4:16; Ezek 8:3, 5: 2 Chron 33:7, 15), *matstēbâh* (Ex 32:4, 8), *pesel* (Ex 20:4; Deut 5:8; Is 21:9), *tabnîth* (Deut 4:16ff; Is 44:13), *temûnâh* (Deut 4:16, 23, 25; Ex 20:4).

For the most part the Septuagint translates the above terms by *eidōlon*, *agalma*, *eikōn*. The Vulgate has *imago*, *idolum*, *sculptile*, *simulacrum*, *statua*. As far as our knowledge goes at present, Israel is the only people known to history in the pre-christian period which practised a religion without images. As yet no representation of a deity has been found by the archaeologists in Palestine which can with certainty be identified with Yahweh. The representation of Yahweh as Dionysos on a coin from fifth-century Gaza is of non-israelitic origin. These negative results of the investigations of archaeologists would appear to confirm what we learn of the absence of images in Israel's official worship from all the different literary strata of Old Testament legislation (Ex 20:4f; 20:23; 34:17; Lev 19:4; Deut 4:15–25; 5:8f; etc) and from the polemic of the prophets against the worship of images (Hos 2:10; 8:4ff; 10:5; 11:2; Is 2:8; 10:10f; 17:7f; 40:12–26; 44:9–20; Jer 2:26–8; 10:1–16; Ezek 8; 14; 16; 20; 23). The orthodox worship of Yahweh was free of images both in the patriarchal period and during the time of the wandering in the desert; it was only at the time of the settlement in Canaan that the worship of images intruded, though even after that time the *official* divine worship of the israelitic tribal federation remained free of images. Canaanite influences were certainly at work behind the setting up of bull-worship by King Jeroboam in the northern kingdom. It is disputed whether the bull-figures set up in Bethel, Dan (1 Kings 12) and Samaria (Hos 8:5f) were meant to be theriomorphic divine images or merely pedestals or a means of conveyance for the deity which remained invisible. The blunt polemic of Hosea against the kissing and fondling of these animal-figures (13:2) and that found in the later history (1 Kings 13:34) against the sins of Jeroboam would seem to support the first hypothesis. The recent History of Religion school doubts whether the idea of the spirituality of God, and therefore the impossibility of representing him in images, is the real reason for the prohibition of images in Old Testament legislation and for the campaign of the prophets against the worship of images which began with Hosea and went down as far as Deutero–Isaiah and Ezekiel, that is, into the postexilic period. According to the oriental way of thinking, an image was not just a representation but a part or a reproduction of the one represented, and was considered on the one hand as an incarnation of the deity, on the other as giving the worshipper a certain power over it. Therefore the History of Religion school understands the Old Testament prohibition of images as blocking any attempt to control Yahweh, as represented in the image, by magical means. It follows that the various prohibitions of images and the struggle against the worship of images would, according to this view, be not so much a proof for the belief of Israel in the spirituality of Yahweh as rather an indication of the demand that his dynamic transcendence and unlimited sovereignty be recognised.

Beginning with the time of the Maccabees, in opposition to the hellenistic milieu, the prohibition of images found in the Pentateuch, originally concerned only with the setting up of sculptured representations of God, was interpreted more and more as a radical prohibition of any artistic representation of whatever kind it might be. This radical opposition to images did not, however, entirely prevail either in Palestine or in the Jewish diaspora, but it was strong enough, even as late as the period of the primitive church, to exclude any religious representation or even any merely artistic portrait of Christ or his apostles. Later, however, there came to prevail gradually in christendom a more liberal attitude to images, beginning with the *sumbola* (Christ as shepherd, teacher, fisherman, etc) and the *historiai* (biblical images). It should be noted, nevertheless, that according to the common teaching of the Western Church right down to the encyclical *Mediator Dei*, the principal value of religious images lies in the field of religious education, and that the decree of the Council of Trent dealing with the veneration of images in no wise teaches that there resides in any of these images either the Godhead itself or any divine power.

Bibliography: *DB(S)* IV (1949), 169ff and 199ff; W. Dürig, *Imago*, Munich 1952; J. B. Frey, 'La question des images chez les juifs à la lumière des récentes découvertes', *Bbl* 15 (1934), 265ff; *RAC* II (1954), 287ff; H. Schrade, *Der verborgene Gott*, Stuttgart 1949; *TDNT* II, 381–97; W. Vischer, 'Antwort', *Festschrift K. Barth*, Zürich 1956, 764–72; K. H. Bernhardt, *Gott und Bild*, Berlin 1956; J. Hempel, *Das Bild in Bibel und Gottesdienst*, Tübingen 1957; C. Westermann, *EKL* I, 518–24; Haag 242f; J. Haspecker, *LTK* II², 459f; F. W. Eltester, *Eikon im NT*, Berlin 1958; J. Jervell, 'Imago Dei: Gen 1:26f im Spätjudentum, in der Gnosis und in den paulinischen Briefen', *FRLANT* (*NF* 28), Göttingen 1960.

Walter Dürig

Inheritance

1. *The right of possession and succession in Israel* was based on the fact that all the land was the property of Yahweh (Lev 25:23; see also Is 14:2) which, however, he had presented to his people (Ps 44:3). It was concluded from this that property should be divided up by casting lots (Jos 18:1–10 etc), that the poor had a right to a share in the harvest and gleanings (Lev 19:9f; 23:22; Deut 24:19–22), that 'stealing' food when in need was legitimate (Deut 23:25f), that the buying up of property and the possession of large landed property (Is 5:8; Mic 2:2) as well as any kind of mortgage or charging with interest were illegitimate (Deut 23:20). The dividing up of property among many heirs does not occur, and according to the law of the Jubilee Year all alienated property had to return to its original owner, the one appointed by God, every fifty years (Lev 25:8–34). Even if such ideals were not often observed in practice (Is 5:8), they reveal nevertheless a deeply religious conception of property and inheritance.

2. '*Inheritance*' and '*share*' (*klēronomia* and *klēros*) will be dealt with together in what follows since they are closely related terms not only in Greek but also throughout the whole bible. Both can be used of the land of Canaan (Num 33:54; 36:3; Jos 17:4) and the parts allotted to the Levites (Num

18:20; Deut 10:9), both appear as interchangeable in similar proverbial expressions (Deut 18:1; Gen 31:14; 1 Kings 12:16, etc). 'Inheritance' has in this connection often acquired the meaning, foreign to that which it bore originally, of 'portion' (Is 17:14; Ps 16: 5f; Ps Sol 14:7), which shows that the juridical sense is secondary, since the reference to the promises and saving deeds of Yahweh always occupies the foreground. The Inheritance is a gift which comes from God which is assigned to Israel as her portion and which will belong to Israel irreversibly and perpetually.

3. *The land of Canaan* is often referred to as the inheritance of Israel (see G. von Rad, 'Verheissenes Land und Jahwes Land im Hexateuch', *ZDPV* [1943], 191–204).

a. *The Promised Land.* This inheritance of Israel is a gift from Yahweh (Deut 9:5f; 1 Kings 8:36; Ps 105:9–11) made to the homeless descendants of a wandering Aramaean (Deut 26:5–10). Side by side with the multiplying and blessing of the people appears the promise of this inheritance in a text which is programmatic (Gen 12:1–7), a promise renewed with each patriarch and present in all the Pentateuchal sources (Gen 13:14–16; 15:7, 18; 22:17; 26:3; 28:3f, 13–15; 35:9–12; 48:16) and which is repeated also for Moses (Ex 3:8, 17; 6:8; 23:20–33). It is also found in liturgical credal formulae (Deut 26:5–10) and is carried on in the preaching of Deuteronomy (4:21, 38; 12:9f; 15:4 etc). Historically considered, this inheritance of Israel is an extension of the landed property of the tribes and their families; theologically, it is the luxuriant (Deut 8:7–10), cultivated (11:10–12) gift of God similar to the Garden of Eden, the land which Moses was allowed to see before his death (Deut 34:1–5). This 'inheritance of Yahweh' (Jos 22:19; 1 Sam 26:19; 2 Sam 21:3; Ps 79:1; Is 47:6) becomes through the assistance of Yahweh (Jos 1:6; 21:43ff; Ps 44:2ff) and after division by casting lots (Jos 15:1–13; 18:1–10) the inheritance and portion of Israel and of individual Israelites. (See *H. Wildberger*, 'Israel und sein Land', *ET* [1956], 404–12.)

b. *The Holy Land.* This inheritance is holy as being the place of revelation and the possession of God (see Ex 3:5) and must be kept holy by means of obedience (Deut *passim*; Jer 5:19). Yahweh himself demands this holiness for his inheritance (2 Kings 21:8; 1 Chron 28:8; Neh 9:8; Jer 7:5–7; 25:5; Ps 37:18). Consequently Israel would be punished by the loss of her inheritance if her conduct was not holy thereby polluting the land (Deut 4:25f; 1 Kings 14:15; Jer 12:7–10; 17:4; Mic 2:4).

c. The concept *inheritance*, when used of the land of Canaan, therefore, is an indication of the concrete nature of the Old Testament expectation of salvation, of God's fidelity in keeping his promises, of the hope in their fulfilment, and of Israel's obligations with regard to Yahweh as the real owner of the land.

4. *Other meanings.* Yahweh himself is the inheritance of the Levites, who did not receive any specific share in the apportioning of the land (Num 18:20; Jos 13:14). This expression refers to the share which the Levites have in sacrifices (Deut 18:1–8; Ezek 44:28ff). The people of Israel is very often

designated as the inheritance of Yahweh (eg Ex 19:5; Deut 7:6) which serves to emphasise the special care which Yahweh has for his people and his fidelity to the covenant. Even the Law (Deut 33:4; Ps 119:57, 111; Sir 24:23) and a numerous offspring can be called an inheritance (Ps 127:3), as also man's destiny in general (see under 5c).

5. *The further development of the concept* came about as a result of national catastrophes and along three more or less parallel lines while, however, the former representations remained in force:

a. During the Exile, hope was aroused of a new allotting of the inheritance of Yahweh to a purified people, as can be demonstrated from the final redaction of Deuteronomy (see 4:25–31) and the words of Ezekiel (see Ezek 40–48). The 'Remnant' of the people saw themselves as once again poised between promise and fulfilment (notice the 'today' of Deut and Ezek 36:8–12; 37:21–8; Is 49:8f), though now any foreigner could share in this (Ezek 47:21ff), or better, *all peoples and countries* must belong to the inheritance of Yahweh and his anointed ones (Ps 2:8; see also Ps 82:8; Is 19:25). In later judaism this further development moved in the direction of a political world-empire (eg Jub 22:14; 32:19). In the New Testament these hopes are purged of their political character: all pagans are co-heirs of the promises of God (Eph 3:6) insofar as they have received the Spirit as a 'guarantee of our inheritance' (Eph 1:14). The full inheritance is *the universal rule of God* (see below).

b. Already in the later prophetic writings (see Is 57:1-2) and psalms

(73:23–6) the inheritance is no longer understood as something *belonging to this world*. This is certainly true, at any rate, of Dan 12:13 with its connection between inheritance and resurrection, and of the teaching on immortality which we find in the Book of Wisdom with its 'sharers in the inheritance of the saints' (3:1–3; 4:7–17; 5:5). The Book of Enoch (Eth) already paraphrases the term 'share' as 'eternal life' (37:4 etc). The expression 'inheritance of eternal life' becomes a fixed term used in opposition to hell, the inheritance of the godless (Ps Sol 14:7; 15:11f). The same is true of the Qumran texts (see Nötscher 172) which speak of an eternal curse and eternal life as the lot respectively of the wicked and the good and as an inheritance, which, however, must not be misunderstood in the sense of a rigid doctrine of predestination. This is continued in the New Testament (Heb 9:15; Col 1:12), which speaks of the inheritance of eternal life (Titus 3:7; cf Mk 10:17; Lk 10:25), the inheritance of glory and grace (1 Pet 3:7; Rom 8:17f; Eph 1:18), of incorruptibility (1 Cor 15:50–57), the *eschatological* fulfilment of hope (Heb 6:11), and the *transcendent* Kingdom of God (see below).

c. The expression 'Yahweh is my hope' as referring to the share which the Levites have in the sacrifices (see 4) was transposed into religious idiom under prophetical influence (cf Jer 10:16) and used of *each individual person* (Ps 16:5f; 73:26; 142:5), leading directly to the individualisation of the concept of inheritance (Job 20:29; 27:13). LXX and many modern versions often use 'to harvest' and 'to inherit' side by side (Prov 11:29; Sir 6:1; 20:25) since it can be observed that in many proverbial expressions there is a close relationship between inheritance and sayings about the harvest (and about trees and fruit). The idea of inheritance can be used in the service of the doctrine on individual retribution just as these can. The idea of an 'allotted share' plays a great part in the Qumran texts in connection with the judgement on the members of the community (Nötscher 169–73), thus emphasising this process of *individualisation* also on the basis of retribution 'according to each one's works' (1 QS 10:18). This is further developed in the New Testament with its teaching on being a child of God as the final stage of perfection (see below).

6. *What is peculiar in New Testament teaching* derives from the relation to this condition of being a child of God and the proclamation of the kingdom of God:

a. *Inheritance means being a child of God.* The Matthean and Lukan forms of the parable of the wicked tenants (Mt 21:33–43 and parallels) both understand by the inheritance the kingdom of God (see below), and by the heir the Son of God who is Jesus (Mt 21:38), according to the interpretation of their literary presentation. That they are here taking up an idea current in the preaching of the early church can be seen from Heb 1:2 (see Mt 28:18). Now all those who are baptised are considered as brothers of Jesus (Heb 2:11, 17 etc), children of God and also as heirs of God and co-heirs with Christ (Rom 8:17). Through the death of Jesus (Heb 9:15), his work of redemption, those who were slaves receive the rights of children, the Spirit of the Son as the guarantee of an inheritance (Eph 1:13f) and thus become heirs of God (Gal 3:26–4:7). Paul explains this doctrine more thoroughly by means of a detailed exegesis of the promises made to Abraham (Gal 3–4; see also Rom 4) as part of his polemic against the judaising heretics who appealed to their inheritance as children of Abraham. He derives this inheritance not from bodily descent (1 Cor 15:50) and the works of the law, but from the fact of being children of God, a condition which springs from faith and baptism (see 1 Pet 1:3–5) and knows no longer any distinction between Jew and pagan (Eph 3:6; Gal 3:28f).

b. *That the inheritance is the kingdom of God* is affirmed in Mt 21:38, 43 based on a statement of Jesus himself (Mt 25:34). Side by side with parallel meanings of inheritance as salvation (Heb 1:14), glory (Rom 8:18), grace (1 Pet 3:7), blessing (1 Pet 3:9) and eternal life (Titus 3:7) this occurs as another central concept (1 Cor 6:9f; 15:50; Gal 5:21; Eph 5:5). This inheritance which is the kingdom of God is the ↗ reward of the faithful (Col 3:24), the outcome of the good works which a man performs (1 Cor 6:9f etc), and is described in eschatological colours as land (Mt 5:5), the holy city (Heb 11:10, 16), the eternal Jerusalem (Rev 21:2), the new heaven and the new earth (2 Pet 3:13). There the faithful will have a share as 'co-heirs' in the kingdom of God (Rev 5:10; 20:4; 22:5; cf Rom 5:17) and in the inheritance of the saints in the kingdom of the Son (Col 1:12f). It is no longer a question of Canaan or of earthly hopes or a world empire, but of the final possession of salvation in the sense of

New Testament eschatology, a salvation which depends as an 'inheritance' on the promises of God and will be possessed as the 'share' of the children of God securely and for ever.

Bibliography: J. Herrmann and W. Foerster, *TDNT* III, 758–85 (esp. 767 for further bibliography); J. C. Margot, Allmen 181–5; F. Nötscher, *Biblische Altertumskunde*, Bonn 1940, 133–5; von Rad I, 296–306; F. Dreyfus, 'Le thème de l'héritage dans l'AT', *RSPT* 42 (1958), 3–49.

Wilhelm Pesch

Intercession

A. *Old Testament*. Side by side with the most common word for 'to intercede' (in hithpallel) there occur in particular, in the Yahwistic strand of the Pentateuch, *ʿāthar* (originally a word which must have been connected with the sacrificial system) and *pāgāʿ* the real meaning of which is 'to set upon someone' and which here has the meaning of 'annoying someone with importunate requests'. Then there are expressions such as 'to step into the breach for Israel' (Ezek 13:5; 22:30; Ps 106:23; Sir 45:23) and 'to build a wall round the people' (Ezek 13:5; 22:30). There are of course the usual words for ↗ prayer such as 'to call on Yahweh's name' (1 Kings 17:20; Ps 99:6), 'to turn to Yahweh' (Ex 5:22) in order to recommend his people to him in their dire need. Those in misfortune turn to a man of God that he might 'enquire of Yahweh' in their favour (2 Kings 22:13; Jer 21:2). The intercessor 'cries out to Yahweh on behalf of someone' (Ex 8:8; Num 12:13; Ezek 9:8); only then can he

succeed in 'conciliating the countenance' of Yahweh (Ex 32:11; Jer 26:19).

This way of speaking enables us to see at once that the prayer of intercession is not so much concerned with the pronunciation of a long series of prayers by the one interceding, as a wrestling with God in prayer on behalf of the people and of his fellowmen.

For the representation of the patriarchs, of Moses and the priests as intercessors and mediators, see under ↗ mediation and ↗ priest. In the ↗ prophets there is some evidence of the continuation of the office of covenant-mediator, and in this respect intercession is an essential part of the duties of a prophet. The oldest example is Amos: 'Yahweh, God, forgive, I beseech thee! How can Jacob stand? He is so small!' (7:2, 5) as a result of which 'Yahweh repented' (7:3, 6). The intercession performed in view of the impending judgement of God was therefore successful. Isaiah (6:1–13) had to be set apart from the 'people of unclean lips' and purified in order that he could fulfil his ministry as man of God. Micah also considered himself after his call as involved in condemnation on account of the guilt of the people (7:19f): 'He will again have compassion upon *us*, he will tread *our* iniquities under foot. Thou wilt cast all *their* sins into the depths of the sea!' The prophet hesitates in his choice of words; at first he includes himself with sinners but then goes on to speak of 'them', of the sins of the people.

Jeremiah is one of the greatest of intercessors in the Old Testament. Both the people and their kings go to him in order that he might represent them in the presence of Yahweh (21:2; 37:3;

Intercession

42:1-4), a duty which the prophet takes upon himself with fiery earnestness without getting any thanks for it (15:10f; 17:16; 18:20). It can even be taken as a sign of the *true* prophet that he intercedes for the people (27:18). Jeremiah's prayers of intercession are in the plural (14:7ff, 19-22)—it is natural for him to include himself among the sinners for whom he is praying. His intercession is different from that of Moses or Amos; in his case God expressly refuses to hear any prayer of intercession on behalf of the people as a whole (7:16; cf 11:14; 14:11f; 15:1), but though Jeremiah was unable to avoid the ruin of the kingdom of Juda, the destruction of the Temple and the Exile which followed, God left a holy⁊ remnant to provide a new beginning. And Jeremiah remained, as we can see from 2 Macc 15:12-16, as the unceasing intercessor for the people.

Ezekiel never includes himself in the number of sinners or speaks of 'our' but always of 'your' or 'their' sins, in the manner of the mediators of the early period. With the same insistence with which he emphasises the personal responsibility of the individual (14:12-23; 18:1-32; 33:10-20) he expresses his conviction that the false prophets have deeply incriminated themselves for not having plucked up courage to take on the demanding office of intercession (13:1ff; 22:28-31). The post-exilic prophets speak of intercession very seldom (see, however, Is 59:16; 62:6f; Joel 2:17). In Zech 1:12 an angel appears as heavenly intercessor.

The Psalms contain intercession for Jerusalem (51:18; 122:6-9), and the king (20; 61:7; 72; 84:9; 132:10).

The so-called public lamentations (also in the Book of Lamentations) plead for the averting of a national crisis and sometimes also for forgiveness of sins (44; 74; 79; 80; 83; 90; 137; Sir 36; Ps 106:6ff and 130:8 also contains a confession of sin). They are essentially prayers of the community pleading its own cause but could be used—and indeed were so used—as prayers of intercession for the people in the mouth of a particular religious individual.

The Wisdom literature speaks little of intercession (but see Job 42:8; Sir 45:23f); in Job 5:1; 33:23-6 it is a question of heavenly intercessors. Throughout the course of the history of revelation one can discern a certain development from the idea of intercession for others *alone* to that on behalf of oneself also *as one of* the group, and from the prayer for the averting of impending material disaster to that for salvation and for the preparation of the people for God's saving intervention. There remains, unchanged, however, the demand for a right intention on the part of those who are to profit by the intercession (this right from the time of the patriarchal narratives, Gen 18:22-32; 20:3-7, 17). At a later period we also find intercession on behalf of pagans (2 Macc 3:31-3) and of the dead (2 Macc 12:40-45).

Bibliography: N. Johansson, *Parakletoi: Vorstellungen von Fürsprechern vor Gott in der atl. Religion, im Spätjudentum und im Urchristentum,* Lund 1940; P. A. H. de Boer, *De voorbede in het OT,* Leiden 1943; F. Hesse, *Die Fürbitte im AT,* Erlangen 1951 (dissertation); above all, J. Scharbert, 'Die Fürbitte in der Theologie des AT', *TG* 50 (1960), 321-38.

Johannes B. Bauer

399

B. *New Testament.* Intercession, as it occurs in the New Testament, cannot simply be placed in the category of christian ↗ prayer. One can only speak of intercession as the prayer of the christian when one has explained what the New Testament has to say about Christ and the Holy Spirit as intercessors.

1. *Christ as intercessor.* The logion which is preserved only in Luke in a context which connects it with the Passion narrative, speaks of Jesus as intercessor on behalf of his own: 'Simon, Simon, behold, Satan demanded to have you, that he might sift you like wheat, but I have prayed for you that your faith might not fail' (Lk 22:31f). In the great temptation which the Passion of the Lord implied, Satan had asked God for the disciples of Jesus (see Job 1:6-12; 2:1-6) in order to shatter their faith. Jesus, however, has already confronted Satan as the accuser in the presence of God, appearing as counsel for the defence, and has obtained by means of his prayer that Peter's faith should not disappear altogether. The intercession of Jesus in the presence of God is not made on Peter's behalf just because the latter's faith has been placed in jeopardy but because he, once converted, must strengthen his brethren (Lk 22:32).

The same situation as intercessor is assigned to Jesus in the logion deriving from Q (the special Logia source) which has been preserved in Matthew and Luke in the following form:

Mt 10:32-3	Lk 12:8-9
Every one who acknowledges me before men, I also will acknowledge before my Father who is in heaven; but whoever denies me before men, I also will deny before my Father who is in heaven.	I tell you, every one who acknowledges me before men, the Son of man also will acknowledge before the angels of God. But he who denies me before men, he will be denied before the angels of God.

In spite of the modifications introduced which derive partly from Matthew ('I', 'before my father in heaven'), partly from Luke ('of God'), the basic form of the logion can still be clearly perceived. It is constructed in strict parallelism and betrays clear indications of its palestinian origin (*homologein en* is to be taken as an Aramaism just as *emprosthen*). *homologein* is used here in the forensic sense and means 'to depose testimony', 'to witness'. The logion, the meaning of which is not easy to elucidate, can be paraphrased more or less as follows: the attitude of the Son of Man to men in the final judgement depends on their relation to Jesus on earth. At the final judgement the Son of Man is the spokesman of those who have confessed him on earth; he will testify in their favour as a witness before God's judgement seat (Matthew) or, acting himself as judge, will reserve for them a share in an eternal association with God (Luke). He is, however, also the accuser of those who have denied him on earth; he will, acting as a witness before God's judgement seat, deny them (Matthew) or, acting himself as judge, he will exclude them from this association with God (Luke). The saying is significant because it makes the eternal salvation of a man dependent on his attitude to

Jesus; it is, however, also significant in that it makes the pronouncement of the Son of Man, spoken either in intercession or rebuttal, appear as final and definitive.

If the first half of the saying is interpreted as a hopeful promise for the future, the second must certainly be understood as a threat. The tradition represented by Mark has preserved only the second half of the saying containing the threat (Mk 8:38 = Lk 9:26), whereas the first half, containing the promise, is found also in Rev 3:5.

Whereas the so-called 'sacerdotal prayer' of Jn 17 shows how Jesus stands before the Father as interceding for his own on earth that they may be preserved, remain in unity and be completed in love (Jn 17:11–26), Jn 14:16 designates him directly as the *paraklētos* that is, as the counsel for the defence on behalf of his own before God. Hence it is easy to understand how 1 Jn 2:1 sees the exalted Christ as the intercessor before the Father.

The term *paraklētos*, in the sense of the exalted Lord as defendant of his own before God, does not occur in the New Testament apart from the Johannine writings, but the idea is certainly there. According to Rom 8:34, it is the priestly function of him who has been exalted to the right hand of God ($\nearrow$ exaltation) to intercede for us—this is a clear use of the paraclete motif which is also expressly put to use in Heb 7:25. According to this latter, Christ as high priest 'lives to make intercession' for his own. This function of intercession which he exercises constitutes his eternal high-priestly service in the presence of God.

2. *The Holy $\nearrow$ Spirit as intercessor.*

According to John's gospel, Christ is not the only paraclete; even more clearly we are told that after Christ's return to heaven, the Father will send 'another Counsellor' (paraclete) who is 'the Spirit of truth' (Jn 14:16, 17). To be sure, the function performed by the Holy Spirit as paraclete is different from that of Jesus while on earth (see Jn 17) or of the exalted Lord (see 1 Jn 2:1), but as *paraklētos* the *pneuma* exercises the office of intercession, and in this capacity fulfils the function of counsel for the defence of the disciples of Christ and of accuser of those who do not believe in Christ. As counsel for the defence of the disciples of Christ who will remain with them perpetually (Jn 14:17), the 'Spirit of truth' will take up and continue the message of Jesus insofar as he testifies in favour of Jesus and leads the disciples into all truth (Jn 14:26; 15:26; 16:13). As accuser of the 'world' which cannot receive him (Jn 14:17) he convinces the men who do not believe in Christ of sin, of unrighteousness, and of judgement (Jn 16:8).

The apostle Paul is also familiar with this idea of the Holy Spirit as intercessor. Although the word *paraklētos* itself does not occur in Rom 8:26, the function which Paul here ascribes to the *pneuma* resembles rather that of the exalted Lord than that which John ascribes to the paraclete. There is, however, mention of the Spirit interceding (*huperentunkhanein*), which certainly belongs to his function as assistant and intercessor. He comes to the help of our weakness when we do not know how, what is the right way (*katho dei*) to pray, and intercedes for us with sighs too deep for words (Rom 8:26; see also

2 Cor 12:4). He completes our prayer and brings it to its conclusion, a conclusion which our unaided human forces cannot reach since God's Spirit must be given to us in order that we may be able to say the word ↗ 'Father' in all its meaning (Rom 8:15; Gal 4:6).

3. *The intercession of Paul.* In the introduction to many of his letters the apostle Paul assures his readers that he remembers them in his intercessory prayer (Rom 1:9; Eph 1:16; Phil 1:4; Col 1:3; 1 Thess 1:2; 2 Tim 1:3; Philem 4). In this connection Paul makes use of a stereotyped formula common in the epistolary style of antiquity (for examples from Jewish epistolary literature see 1 Macc 12:11; Apoc Bar 86:1ff; for the hellenistic practice, see A. Deissmann, *Light from the Ancient East*, London 1927). Granted that such 'remembering' is in no way an unusual element in letter-writing in antiquity and that in taking it over the apostle is using a form elsewhere well attested, nevertheless in doing so he fills it out with a new content just as is the case with the introductory formulae of greeting. His 'remembering' consists in a ceaseless intercession (Rom 1:9; 1 Thess 1:2; see also Eph 1:16) for the christians whom he is addressing, which is what he asks for in their prayers for him (1 Thess 5:25; 2 Thess 3:1; Rom 15:30; 2 Cor 1:11; Eph 6:18f; Phil 1:19; Col 4:3).

The content of his intercessory prayer is determined as from God's point of view and is directed to him: 'May the Lord direct your hearts to the love of God and the steadfastness of Christ' (2 Thess 3:5); 'Now may the Lord of peace himself give you peace at all times in all ways' (2 Thess 3:16); 'May the God of steadfastness and encouragement grant you to live in such harmony with one another, that together you may with one voice glorify the God and Father of our Lord, Jesus Christ' (Rom 15:5–6); 'May the God of our Lord Jesus Christ, the Father of glory, give you a spirit of wisdom and of revelation in the knowledge of him' (Eph 1:17); 'According to the riches of his glory may he grant you to be strengthened with might through his spirit in the inner man, and that Christ may dwell in your hearts through faith' (Eph 3:16–17). These are only a a few examples to illustrate the intercessory prayer of Paul. They have the purpose of showing that his intercession, which he addresses to the 'God of our Lord Jesus Christ' (Eph 1:17) is only, as it were, the human expression of the intercession of the exalted Lord or of the Holy Spirit.

4. *The intercession of christians.* In what has been said about Christ or the Holy Spirit as intercessors everything is contained which can be said about the intercession of christians. The indispensable presuppositions of christian intercession are: a. that the exalted Lord on the throne of God be always 'living' to make intercession for us (see Heb 7:25); b. that the Holy Spirit come to the assistance of our own weak prayer and intercede for us (see Rom 8:26); and c. that christians pray 'in the name of Jesus' (see Jn 14:13f; 15:16; 16:23, 26) and, through the Holy Spirit, dare to call God 'Father' (see Rom 8:15; Gal 4:6)—we should note that Paul, in Rom 15:30, asks the christians of that city for their intercession on his behalf 'through our Lord

Jesus Christ and the love of the Spirit'.

The intercessory prayer of christians for one another can help their faith, strengthen their hope and make sure their love (see Eph 1:17–19; 3:16, 17). It can come to the assistance of the suffering, oppressed and persecuted brethren and bring them release (see Acts 12:5, 12; Jas 5:14–16). It gives an inner strength to the community and consolidates the unity of the church (see Rom 15:5).

The close union of christians in the Holy Spirit gives such power to their intercessory prayer that a christian by means of it can save his sinful brother and bring him back to a full living association with Christ (1 Jn 5:16)—as we read also in a similar context (Jas 5:16): 'The prayer of a righteous man has great power in its effects'. While, however, the piety of later judaism attached such powerful efficacy only to the prayer of the 'righteous man'— James adduces the example of Elijah (Jas 5:17–18)—it is a certain truth of faith that this is so of the prayer of any christian. According to both the word (Mt 5:44) and the example (Lk 23:34) of their Lord, christians should also intercede for their persecutors (↗ persecution) as Stephen did at the moment of his death (Acts 7:60). It is precisely in their intercession for their ↗ enemies, that is, for those people who oppose Christ, that their priestly service to the world is manifested.

Bibliography: ↗ Prayer; also: H. Sasse, 'Der Paraklet im Johannes-Evangelium', *ZNW* 24 (1925), 260–77; H. Windisch, 'Die fünf johannische Parakletsprüche', *Festschrift für A. Jülicher*, Tübingen 1927, 110–37; W. Michaelis, 'Zur Herkunft des joh. Paraklet-Titels', *Coniect. Neotest.* xi (Lund 1947), 147–62; G. Bornkamm, 'Der Paraklet im Johannes- Evangelium', *Festschrift für R. Bultmann*, Stuttgart 1949, 12–35; O. Bauernfeind, 'Die Fürbitte angesichts der Sünde zum Tode', *Festschrift fur V. Schultze*, 1931, 43–54; N. Johansson, *Parakletoi: Vorstellungen von Fürsprechern für die Menschen vor Gott in der atl. Religion, im Spätjudentum und Urchristentum*, Lund 1940 (dissertation); R. Schnackenburg, *LTK* II², 515–17; O. Betz, *Der Paraklet: Fürsprecher im häretischen Spätjudentum, im Johannesevangelium und in neu gefundenem gnostischen Schriften*, Leiden-Cologne 1963; J. Behm, *TDNT* v, 800–14.

Heinrich Zimmermann

Jealousy (zeal)

A. *Terminology.* The English 'jealousy', 'to be jealous' correspond to the Hebrew terms deriving from the root *qnʾ*. The verb occurs only in Piel and Hiphil. Piel is construed transitively with accusative of the person or intransitively with *lᵉ* or *bᵉ* governing an indirect object, which is likewise as a rule a person but can occasionally be Sion, Jerusalem, the land or the name (of) Yahweh. The following shades of meaning should also be noticed: 1. *qinnē* used with *ʾištô* = 'to suspect one's wife through jealousy' (Num 5:14–30; Sir 9:1). 2. *qinnē* with the name of a person or *bᵉ* with the name of a thing or sometimes *lᵉ* with a person signifying jealousy in the broad sense, that is, a hostile attitude against a fellow man arising from the groundless fear that one might be harmed by the position, authority, or prosperity of another whom one envies on account of these advantages. We could therefore translate: 'to be suspicious of a person through jealousy', 'to be jealous of another'—or the like (with the direct object: Gen 26:14; Is 11:13; Ezek

31:9; with *bᵉ*: Gen 30:1; Ps 37:1; Prov 3:31; Sir 9:11 etc; with *lᵉ*: Ps 106:16). According to this usage the participle has the sense of 'envious', 'jealous' (Sir 37:10). 3. *qinnê* with *lᵉ* and person = 'to be jealous *for* someone', 'to be zealous on behalf of someone' (eg Joshua on behalf of Moses: Num 11:29; Saul on behalf of Israel: 2 Sam 21:2; the religious man on behalf of God: Num 25:13; 1 Kings 19:10–14; Sir 45:23; God on behalf of Israel: Joel 2:18; Zech 1:14; 8:2; God in defence of his own Name: Ezek 39:25). 4. *qinnê* with *YHWH bᵉ* = 'to provoke Yahweh in some way' (eg by sin) so that he is 'jealous' for his honour or holiness (Deut 32:21; 1 Kings 14:22).

The meaning of the verb in Hiphil corresponds more or less to that in Piel as explained under 4 (Deut 32:16; Ps 78:58; cf Ezek 8:3). In Deut 32:21, however, God is subject and Israel object; by means of a hostile people God will 'provoke them to jealousy', that is, he will bring Israel to the point where they will have to defend themselves against their enemies with their last breath.

The noun *qinʾâh* corresponds to the shades of meaning discussed under Piel that is: 1. jealousy with regard to one's own wife (Num 5:14f, 18, 25, 29f; Song 8:6) or a rival (Prov 6:34); 2. 'jealousy' in the broader sense—ill-will, envy, and the like (Is 11:13; Ezek 35:11; used often in the Wisdom literature); 3. jealousy for God's cause or for his house (2 Kings 10:16; Ps 69:9; 119:139); 4. the 'zeal of Yahweh' is God's declared intention to carry through to its completion his claim to universal rule in opposition

to Israel which has broken his covenant (Num 25:11; Deut 29:19f; Zeph 1:18; 3:8; Ps 79:5), or on behalf of Israel against his and their enemies (2 Kings 19:31; Is 9:6 etc; Ezek 36:5f; 38:19; Zech 1:14; 8:2).

The adjective *qannāʾ* (Exod 20:5; 34:14; Deut 4:24; 5:9; 6:15), sometimes in the form *qannôʾ* (Jos 24:19; Nah 1:2), is used only as an attribute of Yahweh—'Yahweh is a jealous God', meaning a God who carries through to its fulfilment his claim to universal rule and absolute holiness in spite of anything to the contrary.

In LXX *qnʾ* and its derivatives correspond to *zēlos* and its related forms. LXX translates the Hebrew Piel in the meanings explained under 1–3 as *zēloun tina* with only few exceptions (*tini*: Num 5:14; 1 Kings 19:10, 14; 2 Kings 10:16; *epi tini*: Prov 3:31). Unlike the Hebrew, however, the Greek verb can have a direct or indirect object when it is not a case of a person—thus 'death' (Wis 1:12), 'goodness' (Sir 51:18), 'to strive zealously for something bad' (2 Macc 4:16), 'to be zealous for the Law' (1 Macc 2:26f, 50). In addition we find the phrase *zēloun zēlon theou* or *nomou* = 'to burn with zeal for God or for the Law' (Judith 9:4; 1 Macc 2:54, 58). LXX translates Piel in the meaning given under 4 as well as Hiphil by *parazēloun* with the exception of Deut 32:16 (which has *paroxunein*). As a rule *zēlos* corresponds to the Hebrew noun but when it is a question of jealousy in the narrower sense, the case of matrimony, we find only *zēlōsis* (Num 5:14, 30; as also in Wis 1:10). The 'offering of jealousy' is *thusia zēlotupias* (Num 5:15, 18, 25, 29). *zēlōtēs* and *zēlōtos* (the latter is found only in Ex 34:14 and Gen 49:22, in the latter text, however, without a Hebrew counterpart) translate the Hebrew *qannâ* or *qannô*.

We note in the New Testament a considerable shift in construction and meaning with regard to LXX. *zēloun tina* in the sense of 'being jealous with regard to someone' occurs only in an Old Testament quotation (Acts 7:9) whereas it otherwise means 'to take zealous care of someone' or 'to make much of someone' (2 Cor 11:2; Gal 4:17). *zēloun ti* is found occasionally, as in LXX, with the meaning 'to earnestly desire something' (1 Cor 12:31; 14:1, 39). More commonly *zēloun* is given its straight meaning, 'to burn with jealousy (or envy)' (Acts 17:5; 1 Cor 13:4; Jas 4:2). There are isolated occurrences of the passive (*zēlousthai en kalō[i]* = 'to have zeal to good purpose' Gal 4:18) and *zēleuein* = 'to show zeal' (Rev 3:19). *parazēloun*, as used in 1 Cor 10:22, corresponds to the Hebrew Piel or Hiphil in the sense of provoking God to anger, as is the case in LXX. It is clear that behind Rom 10:19 there is a quotation from Deut 32:21, but in Rom 11:11, 14 *parazēloun* has an entirely new sense, namely, 'to spur someone on to emulation'. The noun *zēlos*, as in LXX, sometimes has the meaning 'jealousy' in the broad sense of ill-will (Rom 13:13; 1 Cor 3:3; 2 Cor 12:20; Gal 5:20; Jas 3:14, 16) while elsewhere it refers to jealousy in the religious sense (Acts 5:17; 13:45; Rom 10:2; 2 Cor 7:7, 11; 9:2; Phil 3:6). In translating Heb 10:27 a paraphrase has to be used such as 'the blazing heat' (of the fire). Contrary to what we find in LXX, *zēlōtēs* is never used of God but refers always to a human

being who is zealous for God or for the Law, therefore a 'zealot' Lk 6:15; Acts 21:20 etc).

B. *Jealousy in Old Testament theology.* According to the Hebrew text, by jealousy the Old Testament understands the conduct or mentality of a person who tries by every means in his power to maintain and put into effect his legitimate claims (and even those which are illegitimate) to property, position and those connected with marriage in the face of competition from others. This striving will be morally justifiable or reprehensible according to the motives which inspire it.

Old Testament law, like law in general in the ancient Near East, gives the husband the exclusive right over his wife and provides him moreover with the means of implementing this right with regard to rivals (cf Prov 6:34). Whence in a case of justifiable suspicion of adultery on the wife's part the *rûᵃch qinᵓâh*, that is, 'jealousy', is legitimate and the man is authorised to clarify the issue by means of trial by ordeal (Num 5:15, 30). When this happens he has to present a *minḥath (ḥaq) qᵉnāᵓōth* = 'a cereal offering of jealousy' (Num 5:15, 18, 25). The proceedings are regulated by a 'jealousy law' (*tôrath ḥaqqᵉnāᵓōth*, 5:29). We find, however, a warning against unfounded jealousy in this matter in Sir 9:1.

Jealousy in the broad sense, envy of one's neighbours (e.g. the Philistines against Israel, Gen 26:14; Edom against Israel, Ezek 35:11), of one's relations (against Joseph, Gen 37:11), of one's fellow kinsmen (against Moses, Ps 106:16; Sir 45:18; the tribes among themselves, Is 11:13), against those appointed by Yahweh, arises from the wrong-minded idea that one can suffer loss with regard to property, privileges or freedom as a result of the good things which have fallen to the lot of others. Such an attitude goes clean contrary to Yahweh's saving plan and the working out of his design within history, and therefore is condemned to ruin. We find warnings in the Wisdom literature against a foolish 'jealousy' which springs from envy and is animated by the desire to see everyone on the same level irrespective of conditions (Job 5:2; Prov 14:30; 27:4; Eccles 4:4). The jealous man becomes bitter, burdens his life unnecessarily (Sir 30:24; 40:5) and when he comes to die is seen to be senseless (Eccles 9:6). Even with regard to *the apparent prosperity of sinners and the godless* the religious man should not become envious since this prosperity is deceptive and of short duration (Ps 37:1; 73:3; Prov 3:31; 23:17; 24:1, 19; Sir 9:11).

Reprehensible is *the godless jealousy* of wanting to be like the pagans (2 Macc 4:16)—this manifests itself as a death-dealing jealousy since it brings down upon one the divine judgement (Wis 1:12).

There is, however, also *a religious and praiseworthy jealousy* which has something good for its object (Sir 51:18); for the house of God (Ps 69:9), or the divine law (1 Macc 2:26f, 50; 2 Macc 4:2). If wise men warn against jealousy felt on account of the prosperity of sinners, it must nevertheless be remembered that jealousy against evildoers can be considered as a sacred duty when it leads to the defence of the sanctity of God or of the divine moral law (1 Kings 19:10, 14; 2 Kings 10:16;

Ps 119:139; Judith 9:4; 1 Macc 2:24). In this sense, the jealousy (that is, zeal) with which Pinehas carried out summary judgement on the transgressor of the Law was regarded as a specially meritorious action (Num 25:11, 13; Sir 45:23; 1 Macc 2:54, 58). On the other hand, the zeal of Saul for Israel against the Gibeonites was a false and reprehensible zeal since he thereby broke a covenant which had been sanctioned by Yahweh (2 Sam 21:2).

Of special theological interest are the Old Testament statements about the *jealousy of God*. It is always a question here of the putting into effect of Yahweh's absolute claim to unique lordship, honour and obedience in respect of both Israel which had broken his covenant and the Nations and their false gods. Yahweh had chosen Israel as his bride, as his spouse in matrimony; he therefore cannot tolerate that this people of his turn to other gods. The breaking of the Covenant is therefore similar to adultery. Israel conjures up the jealousy of Yahweh by worshipping false gods and by disobedience; that is, she compels him to defend his rights and legitimate claims by every means in his power even when it comes to passing a fearful judgement upon her (Deut 32:16, 21; 1 Kings 14:22; Ps 78:58). It is for this reason that an image of a false god is called 'an image provoking to jealousy' (Ezek 8:3). Yahweh's answer to such an attitude of his unfaithful people is to force upon Israel a life and death struggle with the heathen nations in which she is reduced to a fight for the very right to survive (*'aqni'ēm belō'—'ām*, Deut 32:21). Yahweh 'directs his jealousy against his people' (Ezek 23:25 and, according to an emended reading, 16:38). The jealousy of Yahweh must therefore be understood as inflicting in the same way as his anger and punishment a judgement on wrongdoers (Num 25:11; Deut 29:20; Ezek 16:42; Zeph 1:18; 3:8; Ps 79:5; Sir 48:2). According to Wis 1:10 there is also a 'jealous ear' (*ous zēlōseōs*) which hears the blasphemies of the godless and thus assures that they will be punished. The jealousy (that is, zeal) of God against Israel is not to be equated with that of a husband who has been betrayed by his unfaithful wife and delivers her over to the supreme penalty of death; it lasts only until Israel admits it has done wrong and acknowledges once again Yahweh's claim to lordship (Ezek 5:13).

Yahweh cannot allow this his people to be annihilated by other nations. He owes it to his own honour, to 'his holy Name', to save Israel from the heathen (Ezek 39:25). Hence in the last analysis the zeal of Yahweh has for its object the salvation of Israel and is therefore the expression of a boundless love for the people chosen by him (2 Kings 19:31; Is 9:6; 26:11; 37:32; Ezek 36:5f; Joel 2:18; Zech 1:14; 8:2). When the enemies of Israel threaten to exterminate her, Yahweh 'stirs up his fury' (=zeal: Is 42:13) or 'wraps himself in fury (zeal) as a mantle' (Is 59:17) or like 'armour' (Wis 5:17). It is significant that the Old Testament speaks of the 'zeal (jealousy) of Yahweh' only in connection with Israel, never in the context of his relations with the nations except when this refers directly to Israel. Yahweh is, with regard to Israel, a 'jealous God' in a twofold

sense: he will tolerate no liaison of Israel with other gods nor will he permit that the heathen nations or the forces of evil touch his people (Ex 20:5; 34:14; Deut 4:24; 5:9; 6:15; Jos 24:19; Nahum 1:2). The zeal of Yahweh against other gods, expressed in the prohibition of the cult of idols or of images (Ex 20:5; Deut 5:9), has nothing to do with a state of uncontrolled emotion or even with envy of other gods—since in fact these do not exist—much less with envy at the thought that men might grasp at divine powers; rather is it an expression of his very being. It corresponds to the relation between the one and absolute God and the creature, between the divine Lord of the covenant and the covenant people chosen by him by an act of grace.

C. *Jealousy in the theology of the New Testament.* Judaism in the time of Christ attempts to water down or paraphrase the Old Testament expressions on the jealousy of God in order to purify as much as possible their concept of God from anthropopathisms. The rabbis identify completely the jealousy of God with his judgement of punishment. According to MEx 6 (on Ex 20:5) Yahweh is called a 'jealous God' in the Old Testament since he has control over this emotion and does not allow it to master him. Philo speaks always of *zēlos* as a noble human striving for something good. The Qumran texts speak of a 'zeal for the (divine) judgements' (1 QS II, 15) and of a 'jealousy of striving' which has flared up between the Sons of Light and the Sons of Darkness (1 QS IV, 17f). The zeal for God and his Law was highly developed in the extreme nationalistic circles of Judaism for whom the zeal of Pinehas and the Maccabees against those who broke the Law served as an example leading them to a fanatical hatred of foreigners which was directed especially against the Romans. The Zealot movement arose in these circles, the history of which is still not very clear. It is uncertain whether the nickname of the apostle Simon—*zēlōtēs* (Lk 6:15)—is connected with the Zealots.

In the *New Testament* we come across expressions concerned with 'jealousy' especially in the epistles. *Jealousy against one's fellow men*, which is born of ill-will and envy, is classified with the reprehensible passions which are unworthy of a christian (Rom 13:13; 1 Cor 3:3; 2 Cor 12:20; Gal 5:20; Jas 3:14, 16; 4:2) and cannot be reconciled with love (1 Cor 13:4). Envy of this kind, even when it has the appearance of piety, redounds to the spiritual harm of the community.

Opposed to this there is the *upright, religious zeal* for the higher gifts of grace (1 Cor 12:31; 14:1, 12, 39) and for what is good (Gal 4:18; Titus 2:14; 1 Pet 3:13). This serves for the edification of the community since it spurs on the members to holy emulation. Paul praises especially the touching zeal of the Corinthian christians in the matter of the collection for the poor in Jerusalem (2 Cor 9:2). Zeal in loyalty to the apostles is especially valuable in the life of the community (2 Cor 7:7, 11). But woe to the community whose zeal has been extinguished; it can only save itself from the judgement which threatens by a complete renewal of its zeal (Rev 3:19).

The *zeal of the apostles* is compared with that of God in that it aims in particular to see that the community does not prove untrue to the gospel (2 Cor 11:2). This zeal has for its object not christians themselves but rather their loyalty to Christ and therefore redounds to their salvation (2 Cor 11:2). But there is also the zeal of the false apostle to be reckoned with (Gal 4:17f).

On the obverse side, there is also *the jealousy of the Jews in regard to the gospel*. In itself, their zeal for God is touching and praiseworthy (Acts 21:20; Rom 10:2). Paul himself had been animated by this zeal for the Law and he praises himself for it (Acts 22:3; Gal 1:14; Phil 3:6). But at the same time this zeal is the outcome of a tragic misunderstanding since it has led eventually to an unholy and reprehensible jealousy in regard to Jesus and his message (Acts 5:17; 13:45; 17:5; cf Phil 3:6). God has punished this rejection of the gospel by fulfilling what is said in Deut 32:21: *parazēlōsō humas ep' ouk ethnei* (= 'I will make you jealous of (those who are) not a nation': Rom 10:19). Salvation, to which they had laid such jealous claim to the exclusion of the pagans, has now come to these pagans, and all they can do is burn with envy against them (Rom 10:19; 11:11). Yet Paul sees precisely in this envy of the Jews the beginning of their salvation. He is never tired of praising his own successes among the pagans before his Jewish kinsfolk, his own 'flesh', in the hope that he might win at least some of them in this way for the gospel and so save them (Rom 11:14). The description of the saving deeds of God with regard to the heathen world had the object of arousing in the Jews the longing desire to obtain a share in this and therefore join with the pagans in the profession of faith in Christ. In this way the promise made in Zech 8:23 is completely reversed in what might appear a tragic way for the Jewish people: instead of the pagans hanging on to the robe of the Jews in order to come to God the Jews must join the ranks of the pagans if they wish to achieve salvation.

The idea of a *jealousy of God* is kept firmly in the background in the New Testament as it is also in contemporary judaism. It is referred to only in 2 Cor 11:2, where Paul compares his endeavours on behalf of the community with the 'jealousy' of God in relation to Israel, and in 1 Cor 10:22 which, however, is nothing more than a quotation from the Old Testament (Deut 32:21). It is significant for New Testament christology that *zēlos* is never attributed to Jesus, with just one exception, again in a quotation from the Old Testament (Jn 2:17 from Ps 69:9).

Bibliography: A. Stumpf, *TDNT* II, 877–88; Eichrodt I, 210, 216f and 260; von Rad I, 203–12; S. Lyonnet, 'De zelotypia Jahve', *VD* 35 (1957), 83–7; K. A. Brongers, 'Der Eifer des Heron Zebaoth', *VT* 13 (1963), 269–84; B. Renaud, *Je suis un Dieu jaloux*, Paris, 1963.

Josef Scharbert

Jerusalem

A. *History*. It is generally accepted that Jerusalem is mentioned in the Egyptian Execration texts of the nineteenth or eighteenth centuries BC as *aushamen* or *rus(h)alimum* and in the Amarna letters of the early fourteenth century as *urushalim* (= 'foundation of the god *salim*': see Ps 87:1). Excavations reveal a Semitic settlement going back to the fourth millenium. The south-eastern hill of what was to be later the city area, on which the Canaanite settlement stood, was called Zion (= 'mountain of defence'?). This name is applied to the whole city especially in Psalms and Lamentations. The south and east of the ancient hill on which the city stood still provide a strategically sound position for defence today. To the west the valley of Tyropoeon (= 'the cheese-maker') was formerly deeper than it is today, so that the only direction from which the city was open to attack was the north. In ancient times the city was considered impregnable ('You will not come in here, but the blind and the lame will ward you off'; 2 Sam 5:6). The most important cities of antiquity owed their origin and growth to a position on a river (Babylon), a sea (Tyre), or the intersection of great highways (Damascus). The significance and greatness of Jerusalem depended not on its natural position but on its history.

The city was already more than a thousand years old when it first became a part of Israel's history. It belonged to the 'lot' of the tribe of Benjamin (Josh 15:8; 18:16) but could not be captured from its inhabitants who were Jebusites (Josh 13:3, 6; Judg 1:21) of 'Hittite' (probably Hurrian) origin (see Ezek 16:3). David was the first to take it and that only by a ruse (2 Sam 5:6-8; 1 Chr 11:4ff). He made this fortress into his residence, called it the City of David and kept it as his own possession. His purpose in doing this was to make it a means of uniting the northern and southern tribes torn by rivalry. The process initiated by David was carried to its conclusion by Solomon who built the temple and the royal palace based on a Canaanite prototype and with the help of Phoenician workmen. By so doing he gave to the city the greatness and prestige of being the capital of a splendid kingdom. This together with its religious significance made it possible for Jerusalem to supersede the crisis of the division of the kingdoms even though it remained the capital only of the very much reduced southern kingdom of Judah. Two events are of special significance with regard to Jerusalem during the period of the monarchy down to the death of Josiah (609). The first was the siege by the apparently invincible Assyrians under Sennacherib during the reign of Hezekiah which ended in an unexpectedly sudden deliverance from danger (2 Kings 18f; 2 Chr 32; Is 36–7). The second was the reform of Josiah with the centralisation of worship in the Jerusalem temple (2 Kings 22–3). In 587 BC both city and temple were destroyed by the Babylonians (2 Kings 25:8–21; Jer 52:12–30; 2 Chr 36:17–20). During the exile religious aspirations and hopes centred on the rebuilding of the city (Ps 136; 137; Is 40–55; Zech 1:12–17; 2). In 538 BC Cyrus gave back to the Jews what had formerly been taken from the temple as booty and granted them permission to rebuild the temple (Ezra 1; 6:1–5) though political independence was not restored. This led to the constitution of a community in and around Jerusalem which was in the real sense of the term a cultic community later to be centred on the temple. After the dedication of the temple in 515 it became in fact the religious centre of the people. Nehemiah, the governor appointed by Cyrus (445–433), rebuilt the walls and made Jerusalem the capital of the reconstituted political community. Together with Ezra he carried through a religious and moral reform according to the norms of an uncompromising Yahwism, and this reform became the basis of later Judaism.

Under the rule of the Ptolemies (from 301) and the Seleucids (from 198) Jerusalem was able to preserve its historic character. Antiochus IV, called Epiphanes (175–164), attempted to hellenise the city by force. His purpose was 'that all should be one people, and that each should give up his customs' (1 Macc 1:41 cf Dan 11:21–45; 1 Macc 1–6; 2 Macc 3–9). 'Jerusalem was uninhabited like a wilderness, not one of her children went in or out. The sanctuary was trampled down and the sons of aliens held the citadel' (1 Macc 3:45). The struggle for independence was taken up under the leadership of the Maccabees, the desecrated sanctuary was re-consecrated (165/4 BC), worship resumed (1 Macc 4:36–59; 2 Macc 10:1–9) and Zion defended with walls (1 Macc 4:60). The city, now re-occupied, rebuilt and defended (1 Macc 10:10; 12:35f; 13:10), became the official residence of the Hesmenaeans. Their rule was brought to an end by Pompey who occupied Jerusalem by force in 63 BC and even set foot in the Holy of Holies (Ps Sol 2:1–25; 8:1–34). With the approval of Rome Herod the Idumaean ruled from 37 to 4 BC. He undertook a vast building operation and in 20 BC began to rebuild the temple. At the time of Jesus the city must have had a population of about 25,000. Here the famous scribes had their academies to which people came to study from far and wide. The supreme Jewish council was located in the city as were a great number of synagogues. The Roman procurators (from AD 6 to 41 and then again AD 41–66) moved their residence to Caesarea on the coast but kept a military garrison in the Antonia fortress in Jerusalem. During the revolt the Jews expelled the Romans from the city (AD 66) but soon after Jerusalem was besieged, conquered and destroyed by the legions of Vespasian and Titus. The temple went up in flames in AD 70. After the abortive revolt under Bar Koseba (132–5) the city was made into a Roman colonia with the name Aelia Capitolina.

B. *Theological aspects in the Old Testament.* 1. *Election.* We find a reference in the Abraham narratives to pre-Israelite Jerusalem. Just as Abraham the ancestor of Israel was blessed by Melchizedek the priest-king of Salem (meaning Jerusalem; see Ps 76) so the chosen people receive blessing from the Jerusalem sanctuary (Gen 14:18ff). At God's command Abraham offered Isaac on Mount Moriah (=Jerusalem) signifying that the mountain-temple has already been sanctified by the divine election and by sacrifice.

The deity El Elyon was worshipped in pre-Israelite Jerusalem. In Canaan and Syria he was the high god, king of heaven and prince of the earth (see Lev 18:21; 20:2f; 2 Kings 23:10; Mic 6:7; Ezek 20:26; Jer 7:18; 44:17). There would certainly have existed before the time of David a kind of city-theology which was taken over and transformed by the Yahwist faith though still reflecting the place of origin, as can be seen in references to the mountain in the north identified with the mountain of the gods (Ps 48:1–3; Is 14:13f), the river of the garden of the gods (=Paradise; Ps 46:4; 65:9; Is 33:21; Ezek 47; Joel 3:18; Zech 14:8), the struggle between Chaos and the creative power of God (Ps 46:6; 93:2; 96:10; 104:5–7), the gathering of the nations to Jerusalem in festive celebration (Ps 48). The mythological language used here expresses the historical experience of Israel and Jerusalem, for example, deliverance from the attack of Sennacherib.

God himself chose Jerusalem as the locus of his presence with his people (Ps 132:13) when David became the instrument of his will in bringing the ark of the covenant, the symbol of the presence of Yahweh of the hosts, to Jerusalem (2 Sam 6 cf 1 Sam 4–5). The basis of this choice was his love for the mountain of Zion (Ps 78:68; 87:1f). David wished to build a 'house' (a permanent abode) for the ark but it was not permitted him to do so. God will build David a 'house' in Jerusalem, referring to the permanence of the Davidic dynasty (2 Sam 7). The official role and status of the Davidic dynasty are determined with reference to Zion (ie Yahweh), as is clear from Ps 2:6; 20:2; 110:1–4; 132:13–17. Jerusalem is the locus of the divine presence but this is understood as the outcome of the free choice of God and of an act of grace which is constantly renewed throughout the history.

With the building of the temple by

Solomon God decided for a fixed abode in Jerusalem (1 Kings 5:2–8:13). The locus of the divine presence, which previously had no settled abode, either outside or inside Jerusalem, was now in the temple and, correspondingly, the chosen people were in peaceful possession of the promised land. The glory of God occupies the temple which is filled with his presence (1 Kings 8:10f). Yahweh causes his name to dwell there (1 Kings 8:29f; Deut 12:5, 11) and it is this name which brings salvation (1 Kings 8:29f; Ps 33:21; Ezek 20:9, 22).

2. *Grace.* God dwells in the temple and therefore also on the mountain fortress of Zion (Ps 43:3; Is 8:18; Ps 74:2) and in the city itself (Ps 76:2; Joel 3:21). The temple is the palace of Yahweh the king, the place of his throne and of his footstool (1 Kings 8:13; Ezek 43:7). Hence it can be said that God is enthroned on Zion (Ps 9:11) and that Jerusalem is the city of the great king (Ps 48:2f). It is not only the temple which is chosen to be God's own possession but also the city of Jerusalem (1 Kings 11:36; 14:21; 2 Chron 6:6; Ps 132:13). The holiness of God is transferred from the ark to the temple (1 Kings 9:3), thence to the mountain on which the temple stood (Zion, the holy mountain of Yahweh: Ps 2:6; 15:1; 24:3; 48:2; Joel 2:1) and thence to Jerusalem (Ezek 48:12; Neh 11:1). Jerusalem is the city of the temple (Ps 48), since it guards the temple in its midst (Ps 116:19) as the centre of the people of God even after the division of the kingdom (1 Kings 11:29–39; 12:1–20, 26–31; 13:1–6). It is also the mid-point of the world (Ps 48:2; Ezek 5:5) and the spiritual centre of the nations (Is 56:6–8; Ps 87:4ff).

The mystery of the city of God is the dwelling of Yahweh in its midst as the *deus praesens.* It is there that he appears, irradiates his presence and allows his Face to be seen (Ps 50:2; 97:3ff; 80:2, 3; 94:1). Under the shadow of his wings, under the outstretched wings of the cherubim, there reigns peace and unassailable security. The Psalms of Zion show us the faith and experience of the Israelite when he came to worship in Jerusalem (Ps 46; 48; 76; 84; 87; 122; 132). The hope which finds expression in these psalms was vindicated by the deliverance of Jerusalem from the attacks of Sennacherib in 701 BC. This event helps us to understand a great deal in the prophecies of Isaiah of Jerusalem who had a visionary experience of the presence of the holy God in the Jerusalem temple (Is 6). On Zion the Lord has a fire and a furnace (Is 31:9); Zion is the mountain of Yahweh (Ps 24:3; Is 2:3; Mic 4:2), a mountain of God like Sinai (Ex 19:18), a furnace in which the fire of the divine presence burns bright (Gen 15:17). Alliance with Egypt will not bring salvation but only Yahweh's sanctuary on Zion which is the mountain of the Lord and the rock of Israel (Is 30:29). Jerusalem is saved in spite of the besieging enemy (Is 29:1–3). Greedy as they are, and thinking themselves already in possession of the city, it befalls them as it befalls a hungry and thirsty man in his dreams: he thinks he is eating and drinking but when he wakes up he is still devoured by hunger (Is 29:8). The overweening arrogance of the Assyrian king is humbled when the Lord brings to fulfilment all his work on Mount Zion and in Jerusalem (Is 10:12). Jerusalem thus becomes a symbol of assurance of the saving power of Yahweh (Ps 125:1f: 'as the mountains are round about Jerusalem so the Lord is round about his people').

3. *Guilt and Judgement*. Zion-Jerusalem represents for Israel both a gift and a task. It is here that the people pray for God's salvation, his help and protection; but it is also here that the unchangeable divine law is promulgated, that law by which Israel has to live and which is the source of her life (Ps 24:3–6).

In the preaching and criticism of the prophets Jerusalem is represented as the city of sin. Their comminations and warnings are addressed more often than not to 'Judah and Jerusalem'. As the centre and focus of the land, the capital city has to bear the brunt of guilt since it is there that the national leaders and those who are responsible for the people live (Mic 1:5). The guilt of Jerusalem is even greater than that of Sodom (Lam 4:6). All classes of its population have rendered themselves guilty (Jer 17:19–27; 19:7, 13). Jerusalem therefore is despised and referred to laconically as 'this city' (Jer 21:4–10; Ezek 11:2, 6). The sin of Jerusalem consists in apostasy from God, infidelity, disobedience and arrogance in its relations with God (Is 1:10–17; 3:8, 24ff; 28:14; Jer 2:3ff; 5:1; 7:17; 8:1f; 11:12f; 13:27; Bar 3:15–22; Ezek 5:6: 'she has wickedly rebelled against my ordinances more than the nations, and against my statutes more than the countries round about her'; 8:1–16; 16:2–63: a history of her infidelity; 23:1–4, 11–49). To these religious transgressions there is added also social injustice (Mic 3:9f; Jer 5:1; 6:6f). Jerusalem is the city of blood-guilt (Ezek 22:2f; 24:6). All guilt is summed up in her (Is 2:6f).

Since the city does not change her ways despite the warnings of the prophets and their exhortation to conversion, punishment comes upon her (Jer 14:19). Jerusalem is therefore the city of judgement. Judgement overtakes her when she is captured by the Babylonians (Is 29:1–7; Jer 13:9f; 14:16; 15:5f; 18:11; 19:3; Ezek 10). The glory of God leaves the city and she is given over to the enemy (Ezek 11:9–12). Lamentations in particular, which was composed in the same literary milieu as Jeremiah and Ezekiel (Jer 42:18; 44:13; 51:17–23; 2 Kings 24:13, 20), looks back on the judgement which had already been visited on the city.

4. *Eschatological hope*. After judgement visited upon her Jerusalem will find mercy and salvation in the coming age of salvation. The guilt of Zion is expiated and she will no more be burned to the ground. Her accounts have been settled and now the loving mercy of God turns once more in her direction (Lam 4:21; Is 40:1–5; 49:14–17; 54:7–12). All the grace which the presence of God in Jerusalem has brought her will then be superseded; he will enter into her once more and dwell permanently in her midst (Is 52:7–12; Ezek 43:1–9; Is 4:5; 30:20; Zeph 3:14–17; Zech 2:13; 8:3; Joel 3:17). There he will exercise his everlasting and definitive rule (Ps 47; 93; 96; 98–9; Mic 2:13; 4:7; Zeph 3:15; Jer 3:17; 8:19; Ezek 20:33; Is 43:15; Obad 21; Zech 14:9) in glory, holiness,

and transcendence (Is 52:1; Joel 2:32; 3:17). Then the nations will make pilgrimage to her (Is 2:2–4; 45:14f; 49:14–21, 22f; 60; Hag 2:6ff; Zech 14:10–20; Tob 13:9ff; 14:5ff). The prophets of the exilic and post-exilic periods in particular described the coming salvation of Jerusalem in the glowing colours of Paradise and of the time of grace when Israel left Egypt. These visionary statements had a definite purpose in view which was actually fulfilled in history—the return from exile, the building of the temple and reconstitution of the state. But beyond these events their words take in a further horizon which lies at the end of human history. The era of eschatological salvation is the return to the lost paradise where God is present to man. The name given to this eschatological city is 'Yahweh is present', signifying that the kingdom of God has become a reality. What we find proclaimed in Is 2:2 and Mic 4:1 about the highest mountain on which stands the house of the Lord is taken by Ezekiel as the basis of the new temple-torah for the age to come (Ezek 40–48). These chapters also speak of the glory of Jerusalem (48:30–34). Deutero-Isaiah, whose writings reflect the events around 538 BC, announces the coming redemption (51:17–52:6), the joy occasioned by the homecoming (52:7–12), the glory of the new Zion (54:1–17), the gathering of the nations in the house of the Lord (56:3–8). Trito-Isaiah deserves to be called 'the bard of the new Jerusalem' (60:1–62:12). In his poems he represents Zion as the centre of the world (60:16). Faith in the new and eternal covenant (61:8), a new espousal between Israel and Yahweh

(62:4), the new land overflowing with blessings (62:8ff) confer a sense of invincible conviction to these poems. Zion becomes a symbol of faith. Starting from the presence of God in the Jerusalem temple the vision takes in the promised wonder that God some day will dwell on earth among men and reveal himself as he really is. Finally, we find the echo of all that the prophets had proclaimed and the psalmists sung in the hymn of praise of Tobiah to Mount Zion (Tob 13:8–17).

C. *Theological aspects in the New Testament. 1. At the time of Jesus.* Because of the temple, Jerusalem was the centre of both Palestinian and diaspora Judaism. It was towards Jerusalem that the pious Jew turned in prayer and that synagogues were orientated and it was to Jerusalem that pilgrims came on the great feast-days. This placed great responsibility on those who lived in Jerusalem. Since Jerusalem was the property of all Israelites pilgrims had to be given hospitality free of charge. Though the Qumran community had severed connections with the immoral priesthood of Jerusalem and gone into the desert, yet Jerusalem still remained for them the city chosen by God. They looked in hope from the dark present to the new Jerusalem of the future. Among the apocalyptic movements we find the idea of a heavenly pre-existent Jerusalem which God had established from the beginning of time and which would descend from heaven at the end of time (Eth Hen 19:20; Apoc Bar 4:2–6). According to the view found in the rabbinical writings this city was built either by God or the messiah. In the Eighteen Petitions the pious Jew prayed daily: 'have mercy on us, O

Lord our God, with the riches of thy mercy on Israel thy people, on Jerusalem thy city and on Zion where thy glory dwells and on thy temple where thou dwellest, and on the kingdom of the house of David thy righteous anointed one. Praised be thou, O Lord God of David, thou who buildest Jerusalem'.

2. *In the words of Jesus.* For Jesus as for any other Jew Jerusalem was the city in which the temple worship was celebrated. In the story of the man who fell among thieves the priest and levite are coming from Jerusalem, probably after they had celebrated the prescribed forms of divine worship (Lk 10:30). It was the city of the great king by whose name the Jews swore their oaths; which, however, Jesus prohibited as he did all forms of swearing (Mt 5:35; see also 23:29ff). The city on the mountain mentioned in Mt 5:14 is reminiscent of the holy city of God to which the nations were to come in pilgrimage (Is 2:2–4; Mic 4:1–3).

In his preaching of repentance he refers to the death of the eighteen people upon whom the tower in Siloe collapsed (Lk 13:4).

Jerusalem is the city outside which it is not fitting for a prophet to die (Lk 13:33; Mt 23:37f). It had become a general rule that a prophet had to suffer and undergo a violent death in the holy city; and Jesus himself shared the fate of the prophets in this respect. The guilt of Jerusalem consists in the faithless rejection of the one sent by God. Hence it is threatened with divine judgement (Lk 19:43; 21:20). There follows on the word of warning, however, the promise of eventual salvation (13:35). Jerusalem will be

left to its fate until the parousia but then Jesus will appear and be greeted as messiah. It is in Jerusalem that Jesus suffers, dies and is glorified (Mk 11:1; Mt 21:1, 10; Lk 19:28). The predictions of suffering, death and resurrection refer to Jerusalem (mentioned by Mark in the third: Mk 10:32; by Matthew in the first and third: Mt 16:21; 20:18; by Lk in the third: Lk 18:31).

3. *In the synoptics.* According to the outline in the Synoptic gospels, the public ministry of Jesus begins in Galilee and ends in Jerusalem where he died and rose again. Jerusalem is the city of the opponents of Jesus. Though his message was also received there (Mk 3:8; Mt 4:25), those who opposed him came into Galilee from Jerusalem (Mk 3:22 and par; 7:1–23; Mt 15:1–20). The disputation which took place in Jerusalem (Mk 11:1–12, 44) led directly to the trial of Jesus.

In Matthew, Jerusalem is the city of the king of the Jews (2:1), the holy city (4:5; 27:53); but it is also the city which kills the prophets (23:37). With Jesus the history of the city reaches its conclusion. It is in the holy city that he is tempted to abandon his chosen way of obedience (4:5). As king of the Jews it is in Jerusalem that he is condemned and dies on the cross, but not before his words threaten it with judgement (22:7; 23:38). At his death the veil of the temple was rent in two, the earth quaked, the rocks were split, the graves opened and the bodies of the saints arose and appeared to many in the city (27:52f). In other words, Jerusalem experienced the anticipatory signs of the end to come. The day is proclaimed on which the Lord, on his return, will be greeted with the words: 'blessed is he that comes in the name of the Lord' (23:39).

Jerusalem has a place of particular importance in the theological interpretation of the two-volume work of Luke. The Jerusalem temple appears at the beginning (1:8f) and the end (24:53) of the time of salvation inaugurated by Jesus. Luke narrates how the word went forth through Palestine to Jerusalem and from Jerusalem to the ends of the earth (Rome). According to the Infancy-gospel, the salvific event begins with the message brought to Nazareth by an angel: Jesus is conceived, born in Bethlehem and revealed in Jerusalem as the saviour of the world and a sign calling men to decision (2:22–38). It is in Jerusalem that the twelve-year-old child is revealed as he who 'must be concerned with the things of his Father' (2:49: referring to Jesus as Son of God, his obedience in suffering and the end of the temple). Mary is represented as the new Zion (see Lk 1:28 with Zeph 3:14–17). She is the city in whose midst (womb) the king and deliverer lives, he who vanquishes the enemies of the people of God. In Luke the geographical framework of the 'life of Jesus' is worked out more clearly and schematically than in the other Synoptics: his activity in Galilee, journey to Jerusalem, the 'taking up' in Jerusalem (ascension). The narrative of the journey (9:51–19:27), which comes from Luke himself, reminds us on four occasions (9:51, 53; 13:22; 17:11; 19:11) that Jesus is on the way to Jerusalem where his death and glorification (ie his ascension) are to take place. The words and deeds of Jesus which are narrated have the

purpose of showing the progress of the Word (the proclamation of the Christ-event) and at the same time of enlightening the way of the christian. When he enters the city Jesus goes at once to the temple (19:28–38, 45), takes possession of it and makes it once more a place of prayer (19:45f). It is there that he teaches the people (19:47; 20:1; 21:37) and prepares them to receive him in faith (cf 2:22ff). He only goes to the city for the feast of passover (22:10f; cf 2:41f). Jerusalem, however, refuses his offer of grace (19:42); it will therefore be destroyed since it has not recognised God's coming to it in grace (19:44). It is because of the Jews that Jerusalem has not fulfilled its destiny. The city will therefore be besieged by hostile armies, conquered and trodden down by the gentiles (21:20, 24; 23:28).

True to his design, according to which Jerusalem is the city of the glorification of Jesus, Luke represents the appearances of the risen Lord, and indeed the whole of the decisive phase of saving history in which passion and resurrection are indissolubly united, as taking place only in and near Jerusalem (24:13, 18, 33, 52). After the ascension the disciples of the risen Lord gather in the temple which they too can lay claim to as the place where the praise of God is sung (24:53). The purpose of Acts is to show how the saying of Jesus about the disciples witnessing to him from Jerusalem to the ends of the earth is fulfilled (Lk 24:47; Acts 1:8). Jerusalem serves to bind together the history of Jesus with that of the church traced from its beginnings (Acts 10:39; 13:27, 31). It is there that the apostles receive the Holy Spirit (24:49; Acts

2:1). The Jerusalem community was the centre from which went out christian missionaries (8:14; 11:22) and from which were sent prophets to the other churches (Acts 11:27; 15:32; 21:10). It was in Jerusalem that the whole church came together in plenary assembly (Acts 15:1–35; Gal 2:1–10). It was to Jerusalem that christian missionaries returned after the completion of their mission (11:2; 13:13; 19:21; 21:15). Jerusalem therefore was the centre and nucleus of the new people of God. It was in Jerusalem that the apostle Paul also began his mission. It was here that he came to study the Torah (26:4), that he persecuted the church (9:13, 21; 22:19f; 26:10) and whence he departed to continue his persecution of christians in the diaspora (9:2; 22:5; 26:12). He too is a witness to Jesus from Jerusalem to the ends of the earth (22:17f). Acts ends with his trial which is the last phase of his struggle for Jerusalem (Acts 21:15–25:12). But this attempt to save Jerusalem was no more successful than those of Jesus and Peter before him. His delivery into the hands of the Romans begins in Jerusalem (28:17). Jerusalem had refused salvation; Paul meanwhile who must continue on to the ends of the earth leaves the city to its fate.

4. *The fourth gospel* has a historical, chronological, and geographical framework which is quite different from that of the synoptics. It gives particular significance to the Jewish liturgical feasts which were celebrated in Jerusalem (three passovers are mentioned: 2:13; 6:4; 11:55; a feast which is unspecified: 5:1; a feast of Booths: 7:2; the dedication of the temple:

10:22. According to the theory of a one-year ministry 5:1 is also passover and 6:4 Pentecost; in which case the gospel follows a one-year liturgical cycle). Little space is given to the Galilean ministry; most of the gospel is given over to the ministry in Jerusalem where the temple was and the Jews lived who are represented in this gospel as the unbelieving opponents of Jesus or, in other words, as 'the world'. The first thing that Jesus does in Jerusalem is to cleanse the temple (2:13–22). As presented here, this event signifies the fulfilment and end of salvation history. In place of the temple desecrated by the Jews there comes the crucified and risen Lord. He is the new temple: 'the Word was made flesh and pitched his tent (dwelt) among us' (1:14), signifying the epiphany of God in our world (12:41). The new cult is carried out through him and in union with him. The question as to the place of cult has been decided: the worshippers whom the Father seeks are those who worship in spirit and truth, who believe in the truth revealed by Jesus and in consequence receive the Spirit (4:19–24). Jesus himself is the Passover meal (Chapter 6), the lamb of the Passover (19:33), the fountain of blessing which flows out from Jerusalem (7:37f; 9:11; see also Ezek 47:1–12), the presence of God in this world (20:28). Jerusalem is abandoned to its fate by Jesus since it did not believe in him (2:23f; 10:40; 11:54). The Jews hope to save 'this place' (referring either to Jerusalem or the temple) by handing Jesus over to the Romans but in so doing bring him to his death and thereby contribute to the fulfilment of the prophecies about Jerusalem and the temple (11:51f).

5. *In the early church.* The first
christians came together in Jerusalem
(Acts 1:13f). The number of those who
believed grew as a result of the sending
of the Spirit at Pentecost (2:1–13) and
the preaching of the apostles (2:41;
5:14; 6:7). The new people of God
was centred in Jerusalem. It was from
this primitive Jerusalem community
that the gospel was spread abroad
(8:4; 11:22; Gal 2:12). Paul acknowledges that the gospel has gone forth
from Jerusalem (Rom 15:19, 26–31).
The Jerusalem community regarded
itself as the mother-church with which
those newly converted to the faith were
in communion (8:14; 9:32; 11:22). It
was in Jerusalem that the decisively
important question of obliging christians to observe the Mosaic law was
deliberated (15:1–35; Gal 2:1–10).
Paul laid before the leading men of the
Jerusalem community the gospel which
he had received from God (Gal 1:11f;
16f, 18f) since he feared that otherwise
his work of building up the church
would be in vain (Gal 2:1f). As
H. Schlier in his commentary on
Galatians put it: 'It was therefore not
enough for him to be convinced that
he had received his gospel and apostolic
status by a revelation of Christ. Precisely because this was unmistakably
the case, unity between him and the
apostles before him had to be maintained with regard to both the gospel
and the apostolic office'. Grateful
dependence on and union with the
primitive Jerusalem community was
expressed by gentile christians in the
form of offerings and gifts (Gal 2:10;
1 Cor 16:1; 2 Cor 8:4; 9:1, 12; Rom
15:26f). The collection was not occasioned by the poverty of the Jerusalem
community but by the conviction that
the saints of Jerusalem had already
conferred spiritual gifts on the gentile
christians. It did not therefore have
a juridical character occasioned by
the claim of Jerusalem to hold the
primacy among the churches both
historically and by moral right. The
primacy of Jerusalem was not juridical
at all (Schlier, p. 81).

6. *The new Jerusalem.* In Gal 4:21–31
Paul speaks of the present Jerusalem
which is in bondage (represented by
the slave-woman Hagar who stands for
Judaism attached to the law of Moses)
and the Jerusalem above, which is the
mother of christians (represented by the
free woman Sarah standing for christians who are liberated from the Mosaic
law). In presenting this thought Paul
makes use of categories taken from
rabbinical theology. The Jerusalem of
the world to come is not like the
Jerusalem of this world. Anyone who
wants to enter the present Jerusalem
may do so; but only those who are
invited may enter the Jerusalem of the
age to come (Rabbi Johanan + 279).

The Epistle to the Hebrews represents christians as the people of God *en
route.* They have come to Mount Zion,
to the city of the living God, to the
heavenly Jerusalem ... to the community of the first-born who have been
taken into heaven and to the presence
of Jesus who is the mediator of the new
covenant, to the sprinkled blood that
speaks more loudly than the blood of
Abel (Heb 12:22ff). The path which
the people of God takes in its pilgrimage leads from the present Jerusalem to a heavenly goal which bears
the same name as the earthly city. The
heavenly church is the goal and model

of the church on earth. Here we find a combination of eschatological thinking and Alexandrian philosophy.

In the Book of Revelation the seer contemplates the new Jerusalem which at the end of history will come down from heaven (Rev 3:12; 21:2, 10). This is the city of God (3:12) which contains the glory of God (21:11), the holy city (21:2, 10; 22:19), the bride of the Lamb (21:9), a bride adorned for her bridegroom (21:2). The glory of this new Jerusalem is described in terms taken from Ezek 40–47 and Is 60, and with its coming we have a correspondence between the Paradise of the first age and the last age of the world. In this new Jerusalem there is no temple, for its temple is the Lord, the almighty God and the Lamb (21:22).

Bibliography: In general: Fohrer-Lohse in *TWNT* vii, 291–338 (Zion). On A: H. Vincent, *Jérusalem de l'Ancient Testament* i–ii, 1954/6; C. Kopp, *Die heiligen Stätten der Evangelien*, 1959, 339–465; H. Haag, 'Jerusalem', *LTK* v², 899–905; J. Jeremias, *Jerusalem zur Zeit Jesu*, 1963²; H. Kosmala, *BHHW* ii, 820–50. On B: H. Haag, *LTK* v², 367f; von Rad *passim*; J. Schneider, *Sion-Jerusalem. Jahwes Königssitz. Theologie der heiligen Stadt im AT*, 1963. On C: K. L. Schmidt, 'Jerusalem als Urbild und Abbild', *Eranos Jahrbuch* 18 (1950), 207–48; T. Maertens, *Jérusalem cité de Dieu*, 1954.

Alois Stöger

Jesus Christ

'Jesus Christ' or 'Christ Jesus' are the most frequently used designations for Jesus in the New Testament. With this title, which recapitulates the ancient confessional formula 'Jesus is the Christ', the church of the apostles proclaimed Jesus of Nazareth as the bearer of the eschatological event of salvation. From the point of view of biblical theology we have to expound: A. the history of the revelation of Christ; and B. the basic features of the New Testament representation of Christ.

A. *The history of the revelation of Christ.* An attempt to trace the development of the revelation of Christ and the post-resurrection preaching of Christ which is parallel to it have to contend with the fact that our sources including the gospels which are particularly relevant to our subject do not offer us a genuinely historiographical and pragmatic account of this development. But although we have to suspend judgement on numerous points of detail we can isolate the basic data, even with regard to the earthly ministry of Christ as revealer, especially on the basis of our three oldest gospels.

1. *Jesus' message of eschatological salvation.* According to the testimony of the oldest kerygmatic statements and of the gospels, the real activity of Jesus as revealer begins with his public ministry. Jesus recognised the Baptist's eschatological preaching of penance, which announced him as the 'stronger one' to come, as genuinely prophetic, as *the last and therefore the most significant message coming from God during the entire period of the promise* (Mt 11:7–13 and parallels). He received from him the baptism of penance which sealed the expectation of salvation to come (Mk 1:9) and later on associated his own mission with that of the Baptist (Mk 11:27–33 and parallels; Mt 11:18f). Whatever we may say of an initial ministry of Jesus similar to that of the Baptist (Jn 3:22–6; 4:1f), Jesus certainly appeared with *a new eschatological message* of a kind which the

prophetic figure of the Baptist did not anticipate (Mt 11:2–6 and parallels). Unlike the Baptist and other contemporary movements of renewal (especially the Pharisees and Essenes) Jesus did not begin with the preaching of imminent judgement or the call to repentance, to fulfil the will of God as already known. He spoke in the first place not of what men must do but of what God himself was then doing through him on behalf of mankind and would bring to fulfilment in the future. Hence Jesus gave primary emphasis to the term ⌐ the kingdom of God which, in accordance with its Semitic connotation, designated the activity of God as king, the 'rule of God'. For Jesus this term subsumed all that was essential in the expectation of salvation and the way it was to be realized. The complete manifestation of God's rule when he would be 'all in all' (1 Cor 15:28) signified the achievement of salvation and fullness of life. It is this future realisation of salvation which is implied in most of the sayings about the kingdom of God, especially where Jesus speaks of 'inheriting' or 'entering' the kingdom. *The alarmingly new element in this preaching of the kingdom of God* can however be seen in the proclamation of Jesus that this was no longer a purely future reality but had already been inaugurated by him, that through him it was already at work in the present age conferring blessing and making its demand upon men, giving them assurance and promise for the future. This activity of God leading to final redemption has its starting point in the revelation by Jesus of God's absolute will for man's salvation and sanctification. This emerges and makes its demand most clearly in the exorcisms carried out by the power of God (Lk 11:20 and parallels; Mk 3:23) and other 'deeds of power' which are presented as an essential element of the preaching of Jesus (Mt 11:4f, 20ff; ⌐ miracle). Since Jesus by word and deed reveals God as he really is, always was and will be, his appearance signified for his generation a unique divine visitation in grace which explains why he referred to those whom he addressed as blessed (Lk 6:20b–22; 10:23f). But it was also a moment of decision which allowed of no postponement or compromise (⌐ conversion).

2. *Jesus' claim to be revealer and bringer of salvation.* On the basis of his claim to this kind of mission Jesus was different from and more than a rabbi, a mere interpreter of the Mosaic law. He is also more than a prophet and can therefore contrast the present time of fulfilment inaugurated by him with the prophetic age of expectation which preceded him (Mt 11:11ff; Lk 10:23f; 11:31f). He himself forgives sins, which only God can do (Mk 2:5 and parallels). Though for Jesus the Word of God contained in the Old Testament is not only one of promise but also of absolute binding force (Mt 22:24–40; Lk 10:25–8; 16:29; etc), he makes the shocking claim to know perfectly the will of God revealed only imperfectly in the Old Testament and on this basis to impose an obligation by his own authority, in virtue of his own 'I say unto you . . .' (Mt 5:22ff; Mk 7:1ff). In accordance with this, he goes on to explain quite logically that the here and now reception or rejection of his message decides the final destiny of the individual addressed and anticipates the sentence

to be passed by the eschatological judge (paraphrased as 'the Son of Man') as to whether one will enter or be excluded from the kingdom of God (Lk 12:8f; Mt 8:38—for another view, see: E. Käsemann; P. Vielhauer; H. Conzelmann; and, most recently, H. M. Teeple, *JBL* 84 [1965], 213–15. According to these authors Jesus never spoke of the Son of Man not even with reference to the future or to a person distinct from himself). In keeping with this Jesus laid claim to a special mission *with regard to his person and his activity* which can only be described as that of *revealer and mediator of salvation*. This is true even if we hold that Jesus did not give adequate expression and legitimation to this claim by using any of the titles then available (Son of David, Messiah, Servant of the Lord, Son of God or even 'the Man'), or if he only accepted with reservation the title of Messiah used against him by his adversaries (Mk 8:29f; 14:61f) in order to avoid misunderstandings involved in disputing his claim to be the bearer of salvation. With regard both to the way he represented salvation as coming about (through the rule of God first announced and then breaking in irrespective of the political situation of Israel) and the unprecedented attribution of sovereignty to the revealer and mediator of salvation, the claim of Jesus broke decisively with and superseded all previous representations. Hence even the prophetic figure of the Baptist had to be told to resign himself to the fact that the one to come would be different from what he had represented him to be and that his activity would proceed along different lines (Mt 11:4–6 and pars).

The only satisfactory explanation of the evidence which the gospels offer is that which they themselves give, namely, *that Jesus really enjoyed the ultimately mysterious immediate relationship to God which he claimed to have* or, in other words, that he thought of himself as Son of God in an exclusive sense even though this cannot be taken as a primary theme of his preaching. This he does in the saying recorded in Mt 11:27, the wording of which shows it to be characteristic of his way of speaking. It was this immediacy of relationship to God which qualified Jesus and him alone to be the revealer of God. The entirely novel formula of asseveration used by Jesus: 'truly, I say to you' and his way of addressing God as 'abba' allow us to conclude that his authority as revealer stems from a unique and immediate knowledge of God and his saving design. This, however, demands neither an explicit and particularised omniscience, even as regards the divine plan of salvation (Mk 13:32), nor does it eliminate 'the loving, obedient submission of the Son of God sent into the world to bring about salvation among men'. This last quality is unmistakably emphasised in the Fourth Gospel (4:34; 6:38; 8:55; etc) which is at the same time so emphatic and explicit on Jesus' consciousness of divine sonship as the legitimation of his status as revealer (3:16, 18; 7:29; 8:14, 55; 10:15; 14:9f etc).

3. *The effect of the activity of Jesus as revealer on the historical people of God.* Jesus respected *the privilege of Israel*, guaranteed in the Old Testament, to be the heir and locus of the promised revelation of salvation, a privilege founded on the fact that Israel was the

covenant people. True, Jesus' preaching of the kingdom of God antecedently and in every respect left the way open for the Gentiles to share in the eschatological salvation. But it is not at all probable that Jesus addressed himself indiscriminately to Jews and gentiles or even to the half-pagan Samaritans since it was only towards the end of his public ministry that he carried his missionary activity outside Palestine (see Jeremias, *Verheissung* 28ff). In acknowledgement of the difference between Israel and the nations with regard to God's saving design, *Jesus' preaching of salvation concerned only the people of Israel* and sought to make all of them fit to receive salvation (Mk 7:27 and par; Mt 10:16; see also 15:24). Since all Israelites without exception were destined to enter on the new way of salvation and holiness now revealed through Jesus irrespective of the contemporary distinction between 'righteous' and 'sinners', it could not have occurred to him to separate those disposed to conversion from the rest of Israel and bring them together into a community of the saved. Moreover, Jesus promised the gentiles a share in salvation not primarily for their own sake but rather for the sake of his Israelite hearers. In order to make them conscious of the seriousness of the present moment of decision he even threatened them with exclusion from salvation (Lk 13:28f; 11:31f and parallels)—which for a Jew was something quite unheard of and intolerable. It is not at all easy to adduce clear, unambiguous and original sayings of Jesus in support of the view, in any case intrinsically improbable, that Jesus weakened, we might say annulled, the

impact of his demand for conversion and vigilance addressed to a Jewish public by speaking expressly of or even hinting at a mission to the gentiles which would precede the end (see especially Mk 13:10; 14:9). The same could be said of any other factors which would postpone indefinitely the end like, for example, proclaiming an action which would bring salvation quite apart from this demand for conversion (his redemptive death), or saying something which would lead them to understand that the kingdom of God would come only towards the end of the lifespan of the present generation (Mk 9:1 and parallels).

Jesus' preoccupation for the mission to Israel finds expression in two ways. The first is the creation around the nucleus of the Twelve of an ever-increasing *group of disciples* who would strengthen the message of salvation and appeal to repentance addressed to Israel by the personal testimony of men ready to leave everything and dedicate themselves to discipleship (Lk 9:57–62; Mk 10:21f and parallels). The second is the active participation of the disciples at a later stage in the preaching of the kingdom by means of which Jesus could address a wider circle of Israelites and seek with all urgency to win them over to this movement of eschatological conversion (Mk 6:7–12 and parallels; Lk 10:1–16). This most significant fact, significant also for the later development of Christ's revealing mission, that Jesus in the course of his earthly activity expressed the conviction of a mission fully authorised by God (Mt 10:40; see also Mk 9:37b; Jn 13:20; Lk 10:16; Mt 10:16a) and began to realise it by sending his disciples on the same mission to the Jews of Palestine, is also confirmed by missionary sayings like that in Mt 10:5f (see also Mk 1:19) which can hardly be explained as post-resurrection sayings. This quite apart from the secondary question as to how many disciples Jesus sent out, which we are no longer in a position to answer. We may at least suppose that there were more than twelve.

In spite of the urgency which Jesus showed in his mission the leading circles in judaism met his demand and his message as a whole with a rejection which hardened into deadly hatred. In stating that many of Jesus' disciples parted company with him—no doubt partly due to the fact that they had not experienced the hoped for coming of the Son of Man and the kingdom—the author of the Fourth Gospel may well have preserved a tradition of historic importance (6:66). Since the fact, if not the exact time and concrete circumstances, of the formation of the Twelve as an inner group within the company of disciples may be taken as genuine historical tradition (on Mk 3:13-19, see: W. Burgers, *ETL* 36 [1960], 626-54), we may without difficulty explain this formation by supposing that it represented the consolidation of a group of proven disciples chosen from a more numerous company which was beginning to break up. At a point of his mission when the meagre results of his activity seemed to tell against Jesus as the authoritative proclaimer of the kingdom to come, he could have purposed, by means of the Twelve who acknowledged and followed him, to give symbolic expression to the fact that, despite the lack of response in

faith to his message of salvation and repentance, he still maintained his claim to prepare the way for the Israel of the last days which was to inherit the promised salvation. The logion contained in Mt 19:28 = Lk 22:28-30, could point in this direction. Here it is promised to the Twelve that, on account of their fidelity in following Jesus, they would take part in judging Israel considered as the people of God which refuses to recognise the present moment as the time of God's visitation, offering them grace yet making a demand on them through Jesus (Lk 12:54-6 and parallels; 19:41-4). It remains true, of course, that the significance of the Twelve cannot be exhausted in terms of the mission to Israel during the earthly activity of Jesus. This can be seen from the further development of the revelatory activity of Christ.

4. *The suffering and death of Jesus as a new act mediating salvation.* The view is well founded that Jesus, as a result of maintaining his claim to a special mission—which he did not promulgate in Jerusalem for the first time towards the end of his ministry (Mt 23:37 and parallels; Mk 11:2f; 14:3f; Jn 2:13ff) —not only foresaw that he would die a violent death but took this to be the will of God for him. Having experienced throughout his whole life the unshakeable conviction that the kingdom of God would come and that God would complete the eschatological event of revelation and salvation inaugurated by him (Mk 14:25; Lk 22:16, 18), and having by virtue of this conviction laid upon Israel the duty of repentance for which it proved to be unprepared, he saw in the destiny of

violent death which pressed upon him *a divine imperative which had to be carried out if the mission of salvation which he had undertaken was to succeed.* Difficult though it is to reconstruct with any assurance the exact words spoken by Jesus at the Last Supper, as recorded in the different accounts, words which not only contain his own understanding of his death but reflect the post-resurrection celebration of the eucharist, it can at least be stated that the idea of expiation is present and is supported by other logia which are beyond suspicion. As the emissary of God it was the will of God that Jesus should die in Jerusalem (Lk 13:32f). He had to take upon himself the judgement of God, even though it could not apply to himself (Mk 10:38 and parallels; though it is certainly ancient, the connection between *polla pathein* [='suffer many things'] and *exoudenēthēnai* [='to be made nought', to be treated with contempt'] in Mk 9:12, and between the former and *apodokimasthēnai* [='to be rejected'] in Mk 8:31 and Lk 17:25, is disputed; though see J. Jeremias, *TDNT* v, 706f; W. Michaelis, *TDNT* v, 914ff). Even if, therefore, the explicit claim of founding a covenant in his death (as held by many against J. Jeremias, *TDNT* v, 678 and 712–17 and O. Cullmann 59–68) and the representation of the death as having the force of vicarious expiation, as in Mk 10:45 with reference to Is 53, are the result of Christian reflection after the resurrection (as held by F. Hahn, 54–66; M. Rese, *ZTK* 60 [1963], 21–41; and others), we must take it as certain *that Jesus understood his death to mediate salvation.* By means of his death understood in this way Jesus created *an* entirely new condition for entry into the kingdom of God, for belonging to the community of those who await salvation and, correspondingly, for a new approach to the proclamation and mediation of salvation.

On the basis of this understanding of his death we cannot exclude the possibility that Jesus reckoned with an interim period between his death and the final revelation and that therefore he prophesied suffering and persecution for his followers (Lk 6:22; Mk 8:34), commanded Simon to confirm his brethren (Lk 22:31f), promised the latter that in the future he would be known as 'the Rock'—with the explanation of this term that we find in Mt 16:18—and even foretold that his exaltation would lead to a continually active existence after death of the kind presupposed by the resurrection faith of the early church. On the basis of this understanding Jesus could even have gone beyond the original significance of the calling of the Twelve (see above A3) and considered them as founders of a newly constituted people of God, as representing symbolically the rebuilding of the community of salvation, to continue the metaphor of Mt 16:18. The disputed question whether at any time during his earthly career, at least in his trial before the Sanhedrin, Jesus stated that he himself was the Son of Man who was to come or even, in addition to this, claimed for himself the prerogative of continued activity after his death in a heavenly existence (which is even more subject to dispute, though see E. Schweizer, *ZNW* 50 [1959], 185–209) is not really of decisive significance if the history of Jesus is understood not to end with his death but as beginning anew after his death in a different dimension.

5. *The resurrection as revelatory act of God.* According to the unanimous testimony of the kerygma and the resurrection narratives in the gospels the disciples were firmly convinced, on the basis of the self-proclamation of the Risen One who appeared to them, that God had responded to the execution of Jesus with a new revelatory act, namely, the resurrection of Jesus understood quite simply as a miracle. As a result of this Jesus was raised from death and given a place of authority in heaven which assured him a decisive role in the coming of the eschatological age (*Marana tha!*). In view of the new formulation of the saving message which this new act of divine revelation necessitated, the outcome of the act can be seen as (a) *the apostolate* and (b) *the sending of the Spirit.* These two factors, which are intimately related, provide the basis for the proclamation and mediation of salvation which had a new beginning in what happened on Good Friday and Easter Sunday.

a. *The accounts of the resurrection appearances* in the gospels and the account given in Acts 1 betray very strong divergencies as regards place and time, to whom the Lord appeared, how he appeared and, not least, the form and content of what he said when he appeared. Quite apart from the question whether the Risen Lord spoke to his disciples in the same way as he had done during his life (this is disputed by A. Kolping, *HTG* i, 143), it is no longer possible to reconstruct the original words by applying critical methods (however, see the article 'Binden und Lösen' *LTK* ii², 480–82). It can be

proved that the texts dealing with the appearances of the risen Christ reflect to a greater or lesser extent developments which were going on in the post-resurrection church, christological, liturgical, exegetical etc. The resurrection narratives were composed with the purpose both of confirming faith in the event-character of the resurrection and the reality of the one who had appeared, and of explaining the significance of the resurrection for Jesus himself and for the church. They were therefore composed from several different points of view, theological, kerygmatic and not least apologetic. Having stated this, however, we should go on to note the following points of fundamental importance with regard to these narratives: (i) It is true that, with regard to the words attributed to the risen Christ, we have to do in the first place with the interpretative activity of the early church and its attempt to apply the meaning of the event to its own situation. It is even possible to regard these words as formulations having the purpose of explaining the specific revelational content of each of the appearances. Yet having said this we must note that *their central theme is the obligation and authorisation to mediate salvation by word and deed,* in other words, the apostolate which, as is also proved by the authentic testimony of Gal 2:7 (see also 1:17f), is authenticated by appeal to the risen Lord (see also Gal 1:8, 16f). Therefore just as Paul was conscious that he had been called by the risen Lord to be an apostle and to preach the gospel with authority among the gentiles, he took it for granted that 'the apostles who were before him' (Gal 1:17), and Peter in particular

(1:18f; 2:8), had been called apostles in the same way. That the appearances or, at any rate, some of them, provide the foundation for the apostolate, does not depend on the supposition that the risen Christ spoke in the same way as he did during his lifetime—the less so in view of the absolutely miraculous character of these appearances, as of the resurrection itself. We should recall that Paul appears to refer in some texts to special 'revelations' (Rom 11:25f; 1 Cor 15:21; 1 Thess 4:15; 2 Thess 2:3ff).

(ii) With regard to those appearances, which cannot easily be understood as establishing the apostolate (especially the one to 'more than five hundred brethren', 1 Cor 15:6), we should note that in 1 Cor 15:7 Paul speaks of an appearance to '*all* the apostles'. He clearly understood this to refer *to a fairly well defined group of those who had been called by the risen Lord to the apostolate*, to which he himself belonged (15:8f). In his case the special character of his apostolate as addressed to the gentiles (Gal 2:7f) gave it a decisive orientation towards the development of a gospel basically free of the Law and hence to the formation of a genuinely gentile church.

The view that Mt 16:18 and Jn 21:15-17 express by different metaphors the significance of the first appearance to Simon alone (1 Cor 15:5; Lk 24:34; see also Mk 16:7) is supported by the giving of a new name, the fact that Paul also witnesses to the primacy of Kephas (Gal 1:17f) and the significance of Peter for the whole church which comes through in several incidents. With regard to the new name, we should note however that 'Kepha' represented in the first place an object rather than a name as the Greek translation 'Petros' shows, but that already before Paul it was also being translated as a proper name (transcribed as 'Kephas') and for the most part replaced the original name Simon, though Paul never uses this name.

b. Paul, called to be an apostle by the risen Lord, understood the Holy Spirit soteriologically as 'the power of the divine life associated with the risen and living Lord and issuing from him' (see 1 Cor 15:45; 2 Cor 3:17) (Schnackenburg, *Theologie* 100). The Spirit also was the means by which God revealed himself, and Paul claimed that he too had access to this medium of revelation (1 Cor 2:10f; 7:40). The writings of Luke (Lk 24:48; Acts 1:4; see also 2:33), and the first (Mt 28:20) and fourth gospels (Jn 7:30; 14:15ff; 16:7, 13ff; 20:21f), testify in their own way to the same significant truth concerning the revelation of God's saving design, namely, that the sending of the Holy Spirit was a consequence of the resurrection understood by the early church as a decisive turning-point in the Christ event (Mk 9:9f; Lk 24:44ff; Jn 2:22; 12:16; 7:39), and that the exalted Christ is now efficaciously present through the Spirit sent by him. Whether the emphasis is on the operation of the Spirit or only the gracious presence of the exalted Christ (Mt 28:20), it is always the same mysterious reality which is referred to. The exalted Christ is active through the Spirit and the Holy Spirit is, at least functionally, 'the Spirit of the Lord' (2 Cor 3:17f). H. Schlier has boldly expressed the revelational significance of the sending of the Spirit as follows:

'God has revealed himself by the power of the Spirit in the Christ event which culminated in the appearance of the risen Lord. But it is only by the power of the Spirit that God discloses the Christ event in the interpretative word of those who experience the Spirit' (*Besinnung auf das NT*, 1964, 43).

B. *The Christ of New Testament preaching*. Corresponding to the progress of the revelation of Christ, the picture of Jesus which emerges from the preaching of the early church was fixed with reference to the turning-point of the resurrection. This picture is expressed essentially in statements concerning saving history and in categories which are determined functionally and soteriologically. Not the least of the factors determining this picture was the sum total of the questions arising out of the changing missionary and pastoral situation of the early church, to which can be added the personal, religious experience of early christians of the kind which was so important in the case of Paul. These factors would lead us to expect a development within the presentation of Christ in the early church period. In what follows we will attempt to isolate and identify *some of the more important lines and structures of christology* without claiming to give a complete account of its traditio-historical development which is obviously a highly complex and many-sided question.

1. Since the shameful death on the cross as an executed criminal of the one who was presumed to be the mediator of salvation constituted for the Jews an almost insurmountable 'scandal' and was later experienced by hellenistic gentiles as 'folly' (1 Cor 1:23), *the presentation of Jesus had to begin with the death on the cross and work onwards from that point*. The statement that 'God raised him [Jesus] from the dead' (1 Thess 1:10b; Rom 10:9; Acts 4:10; see also Gal 1:1; Rom 8:11) was therefore necessarily the starting point for preaching which aimed at providing a basis for faith. This is in fact what we find in the preaching of the apostles recorded in the first half of Acts. We must add that right from the time of the first apostles the resurrection was understood as *exaltation to a position of honour and authority in heaven, as a royal accession to the throne*, not just as the anticipation of an eschatological event corresponding to the taking up of Jesus into a heavenly existence thus anticipating the lot of all christians. This last representation cannot find support in the typically Lucan formulation of Acts 3:20, 21a which states that the delay in the parousia is the result of the divine will (this interpretation is accepted by Vielhauer 45ff and rejected by Hahn 106ff, 126ff, and 184ff). The traditional conviction that the exaltation of Jesus resulted from the resurrection must be regarded as 'an original datum of christian faith' (Vielhauer 52). This faith in Jesus who has received the power to be active in salvation, which is faith in his lordship, is presupposed by the cry of longing for the Lord's coming *marana tha!* (1 Cor 11:26; 16:22; Rev 22:20) heard in the eucharistic liturgy of the earliest Palestinian communities. It also witnesses to the close association between the exaltation and the coming of Christ in judgement which, according to the kerygma, will be the manifestation in power of Christ who has already won his throne in heaven and

427

completed his work of redemption. Although this prayer for the parousia of Jesus includes the promise or expectation of the coming Son of Man it does not, understandably, address the exalted Christ with the title 'Son of Man'. It is all the more worthy of note that the prayer makes use of the title *mari* or *marana* which in Aramaic is addressed principally to those in authority who exercise a judiciary function (S. Schulz 134ff) and also to God (as often in 1 QGen Apoc). The fact that both in these texts and elsewhere in the New Testament there is no mention of a '*second* coming' can be explained without difficulty by the fact that *marana* refers to the status of Jesus acquired as a result of the resurrection, a status which not only makes possible but requires his 'coming' or 'appearance' and which distinguishes the resurrection-existence from that of Jesus during his life on earth.

In both the most ancient and the more recent strata of the tradition the resurrection is interpreted with reference to messianic texts which speak of God's future government of his people (2 Sam 7:14; Ps 2:7; 110:1). These are used to prove that Jesus has been *designated Son of God* (Rom 1:4; Acts 13:33; see also Heb 1:5f; 5:5), *is now seated at the right hand of God* (Rom 8:34; Mk 14:62 and parallels; Acts 2:33–5; 5:31; 7:56; Col 3:1; Eph 1:20; 1 Pet 3:22; Heb 1:13f; 12:24) and finally—according to Phil 2:9–11 taken with Is 45:23—*has been exalted to the position of kyrios or universal ruler to whom divine honours are due* (see also Mt 28:18), he who disposes of the power of God himself (1 Cor 12:3; 8:5f) and will come in the power of God on the ⁊ 'day of

the Lord' (1 Thess 5:2; Acts 2:20). The *marana tha* of the primitive community, therefore, witnesses to the cultic veneration of the exalted Christ even though the title *mara = kurios* cannot claim to bear the same fullness of meaning as *kyrios* in LXX which was the name for God and was applied to the exalted Christ even before the time of Paul. The form which the confession of faith took in the areas of Greek christianity was 'Jesus is Lord' (1 Cor 12:3; Rom 10:9). For the history of this form and the attempt to distinguish between *mara = kurios* and the *kurios* of the royal acclamation see Kramer 95–103.) To this interpretation of the Easter experience with reference to the scriptures there corresponds the purpose, which is apparent in the oldest of the Passion narratives, to present the sufferings and death of Jesus not as the tragic outcome of chance, but rather as 'fulfilling and revealing the meaning of all the sufferings of the Servant of the Lord and the other holy men of the Old Testament period' (H. Schlier, 55). This is done by referring throughout to the Scriptures in a way which is generally indirect and allusive. This representation of the sufferings and death of Jesus made it possible to view them as the way chosen by God for his glorification. The thought of suffering and death was also closely associated with the title 'the just (one)' which was applied to Jesus by the early church (Acts 3:14; 7:52; 22:14; see E. Schweizer, 93–9).

2. A christology centred on the exaltation of Jesus, therefore, has in view to provide a firm foundation for the 'messianic' and authoritative status of the risen Christ which alone makes it

428

possible for salvation to be mediated (see Acts 2:33–6) and also for the divine judgement which, as early Christian preaching asserted, was to be carried out by the eschatological revealer. We should note, however, that the pre-pauline piece of kerygmatic tradition preserved in 1 Cor 15:3f looks beyond the resurrection from the dead conceived of in terms of exaltation to *the special significance for salvation which the death of Jesus taken by itself contained.* The preaching of the redemptive power of the death of Jesus in terms which speak expressly of expiation, as in the accounts of the Last Supper ('on behalf of many'), pervades the whole of the New Testament (Gal 1:4; 1 Cor 15:3; 2 Cor 5:14f, 21; Rom 4:25; 8:32; 1 Pet 3:18; 1 Jn 2:2 etc) and is implied in the use of other terms such as ↗ the blood of Christ, ↗ redemption, ↗ sacrifice (not so clearly in the very old description of Jesus as the ↗ 'Servant of God', Acts 3:13, 26; 4:27, 30, which was very common in judaeo-christian circles but later abandoned).

The title *Christ* which appears in 1 Cor 15:3 and which was soon to achieve a unique place among the titles predicated of Jesus seems, as is suggested by such short statements on the death of Jesus as Rom 5:6, 8 and 1 Pet 3:18 which contain the idea of expiation, to refer originally to the death and resurrection of Jesus. In this context the resurrection is presented as proof that the death was in fact willed by God and possessed redemptive value (see Kramer 34–6). Probably the early church intended in using this title to take up in a positive sense and proclaim the death of Jesus as the execution

of a messiah vindicated by God in the resurrection (see especially N. A. Dahl 160–3, 166–8; Hahn 210–18). Basing himself precisely on 'the cross of Christ' (1 Cor 1:17) and 'the scandal of the cross' (Gal 5:11), which put to shame the wisdom of the world (1 Cor 1:18ff), it was Paul's intention to develop the theme of God's saving design which showed up the powerlessness of both the gentile and Jewish world as under the sway of sin (Rom 1:18–3:20) and which, in the last analysis, could be explained only by the love of God which overcomes every obstacle—'they are justified by his grace as a gift, through the redemption which is in Christ Jesus' (Rom 3:24). This presentation enabled Paul to show how the saving acts of the death and resurrection of Christ affect the person who bears his name, how salvation is appropriated and what kind of existence is demanded by this appropriation (see the expressions which use the prepositions *dia-*, *sun-*, and *en-*, and the texts which deal with ↗ baptism, ↗ the Spirit, and ↗ the body of Christ; also Gal 2:19; Rom 6:3–11; Gal 3:18; 2 Cor 5:17; Gal 2:20; 6:2, 14f; etc).

The title of Messiah or Christ may have suggested itself as the subject of which statements about the death of Jesus could be predicated since it came from judaism and denoted an earthly leader who would bring salvation (unlike the title 'the Son of Man') and, at the same time, permitted an association with the idea of fulfilment 'according to the scriptures' since as a title it stood for the eschatological bringer of salvation, unlike non-eschatological designations such as *mara = kurios* and 'Son of God' which is hardly a title. On the other hand, the bearer of the title was thought of so much in christian terms as the bearer of salvation through the saving history which was acted out in him, namely, his death for our sins and resurrection by the power of God, that the various meanings attached arbitrarily to this title in judaism remained ineffectual. The title 'Christ' was thus able to become 'the point of crystallization for all the different christological points of view found in the New Testament' (N. A. Dahl). At the same time it lost its original meaning as a title in gentile christianity and became more and more a proper name even before the time of Paul. By the time of Paul 'Jesus' and 'Christ' could be combined (as in Rom 8:11b) or used interchangeably (as in Rom 8:9–11; ↗ Messiah).

3. The claim of messianic status for Jesus who, through his death and resurrection, brings to pass the decisive event of salvation, and even more so the application of 2 Sam 7:12ff to the resurrection of Jesus (in Acts 2:25–32 also connected with Ps 16:10f), may explain the early *inclusion of the Davidic genealogy in the preaching of Christ* (Rom 1:3f; 2 Tim 2:8). The Davidic descent and the designation as messianic Son of God were, according to the pre-Pauline formulation of Rom 1:3f, interpreted as the basis for the two different aspects of the existence of Christ: the earthly-human and the heavenly-spiritual, a distinction which is also found in the ancient kerygmatic formulations in 1 Pet 3:18 and 1 Tim 3:16a. Since it cannot simply be understood as a haggadic type of question, the Scripture proof presented in scholastic terms in Mk 12:35–7 and

parallels (understood differently by E. Lövestam, *SEA* 17 [1962], 79–82) aims at explaining the two aspects of the existence of Christ. It is aimed polemically against another kind of messianic concept resting on Davidic descent against which it puts forward, with the help of Ps 110:1, lordship resulting from exaltation by God as *the decisive status proper to the Messiah*. The emphasis is rather different in Acts 2:25–35 and 13:34–7 where a contrast is made between David who ended in death and corruption and Jesus exalted after his resurrection (in 2:34f Ps 110:1 is also referred to). The Davidic descent of the Messiah is here used in an ancient and very artistic way to show that *the resurrection of Jesus from the dead is the fulfilment of the promise made to David*. The same is clearly the case in the ancient judaeo-christian confessional formula in 2 Tim 2:8. Following on the account of the conception of Jesus as brought about by the power of God, Matthew and Luke connect the Davidic sonship of Jesus and his inheritance of the promise to David with the fact that the Davidite Joseph is his father, legally in Matthew (1:16, 18–25), putatively in Luke (3:23). The title 'son of David' which is completely messianic and nationalistic in meaning, only assumes some importance in the synoptic gospels in the messianic polemic found in Matthew (ten times; see also Rev 5:5; 22:16), and is never used by the disciples.

4. Starting out from the earthly life of Jesus which ended in death and his exaltation to divine lordship which contrasted so strongly with the earthly life, the early church worked backward. Its deepening reflection took it beyond

the birth of the Messiah and led it to ask what was the ultimate basis of the Christ-event. No doubt in reliance on the judaeo-hellenistic teaching about ↗ wisdom conceived of as pre-existent and the means by which the world was created, it arrived at a knowledge of *the pre-existence of Christ* (1 Cor 8:6; 10:4; Col 1:15ff; Jn 1:1ff; see E. Schweizer, *ET* 19 [1959], 65–70) and therefore of *the incarnation*. The christological hymn in Phil 2:6–11, which is almost universally recognised as pre-Pauline, does not appear to lead necessarily either to the anthropos myth or a representation of the Son of Man figure in terms of Adam, the first man. What it does is describe 'the succession of events in the history of salvation' (J. Geiselmann), the pre-existence, kenosis and final triumphant accession of Christ to the throne. The question is undecided whether the kenosis saying refers to the attitude of the Servant of the Lord in Is 53 which culminates in the sacrifice of his life (eg, J. Jeremias, *Novum Testamentum* 6 [1963], 182–8) or to the incarnation (2:6f) which is completed in the death of Christ (2:8; 'even death on a cross' is a secondary addition).

In contrast with the presentation of Christ in Phil 2:6 Paul himself attempts to give *more precise definition to the understanding of pre-existence by means of the designation 'Son of God'*. Jesus Christ whom God revealed to the Apostle of the gentiles as 'his son' (Gal 1:16) was Son of God, God's own son (Rom 8:32) when God sent him into the world and he became truly man (Gal 4:4; Rom 8:3). As the 'image of God' which has taken on visible form (2 Cor 4:4ff; Col 1:12ff) he is Son of God of his very nature (↗ image). *The theological importance of the designation 'Son of God'*, which indicates the original and unique relationship of Jesus to God presupposed by the incarnation, can be deduced from the way Paul refers to the life and activity of Jesus as a whole beginning with the incarnation (Rom 1:3a) and, in particular, to his decisive acts and his whole manner of existence. Its importance can further be gauged by Paul's reference to the incomprehensible love of God as revealed in the self-offering of Jesus in an atoning death (Rom 5:10; 8:3, 32; Gal 2:20), by the way he speaks of the risen Lord (Gal 1:16; 1 Cor 1:9) through whose Spirit we become 'sons' of God (Gal 4:5f), and of Christ who is to return in order to save us (1 Thess 1:10) and to whose image we are to be conformed (Rom 8:29; 1 Cor 15:49). Paul preaches 'the gospel of his [God's] Son' (Rom 1:9, cf 1:1–3). When we come to John and the author of Hebrews we find this Son of God christology associated with the use of the simple term 'the Son' (see R. Schnackenburg, *LTK*, ix², 852–3).

5. It is in keeping with the significance of the resurrection for the life of the individual christian and of the ↗ church in terms of the revelational and salvific design of God, as also of the glorified existence of Christ resulting from the resurrection, that in the confession of faith the title *kurios* (divine lord) is applied to Christ much more often than *Son of God*. This last is in fact not found at all in several New Testament writings including the Pastorals, Jas, and 1 and 2 Pet. The proclamation of 'the lord of glory' (1 Cor 2:8), the superior position of authority of the exalted Christ over all

principalities and powers (Phil 2:11; 1 Cor 15:25ff; Eph 1:20ff), his present activity in dispensing grace (1 Thess 3:8, 12; Rom 3:24; 10:12; etc) as well as a certain antithesis between the 'gods' and 'lords' worshipped in the hellenistic world and the 'one kyrios Jesus Christ' (1 Cor 8:5f), the 'Lord' celebrated in Christian liturgy (1 Cor 10:19–22; see also 1 Cor 2:2b; etc) who alone is awaited as the future *sōtēr* (Phil 3:20), 'our Lord Jesus Christ' as Paul generally designates him, no doubt in a liturgical formulation—all of this enables us to understand how LXX title of *kurios* occurs in the Pauline corpus alone (with the exception of Hebrews) 247 times. It is true, of course, that for Paul God remains the first cause and the last end of everything that is in the world (1 Cor 8:6; 15:28; Rom 11:36; Phil 2:11). Hence after the definitive annihilation of the last enemy, the power of death, the Son also will be subject to the Father so that finally God may be 'all in all' (1 Cor 15:24–8).

6. The threat presented to the absolutely unique position of Christ as mediator of salvation by false teachers from judaeo-gnostic circles who spoke of angelic demiurges who ruled the world and to whom adoration was due (Col 2:8, 18, 20) led to *the full development of the cosmological and ecclesiological significance of Christ* that we find in Colossians and Ephesians. Here is emphasised Christ's position as the unique means of the atonement and fulfilment of the cosmos (cf Eph 1:10), and as 'the firstborn of the dead' which corresponds entirely with the preeminent position as lord and ruler which has been accorded him as the

universal means of creation and 'the firstborn of all creatures' (Col 1:15–20). This arises from the fact that in him 'the whole fullness of deity dwells bodily' (2:9). The Epistle to the Hebrews also proclaims the absolutely unique position of Christ as mediator of both creation and salvation starting out from the scripturally well-founded datum of the unique excellence of the Son who 'reflects the glory of God and bears the very stamp of his nature' (1:2ff).

7. The following should be noted as *additional christological statements and categories of interpretation* taken from the New Testament epistles:

a. The function of Jesus as *the second Adam* developed on the basis of Paul's soteriological thinking, throws further light on the necessity, universality and superabundant richness of the redemption which Christ brings (Rom 5:12–21). It also provides a basis for the completion of redemption in the resurrection of the christian promised for the future (1 Cor 15:20–22, 44–9).

b. Christ as *he who makes peace* by bringing together the two divided parts of humanity (Jew and Gentile) to make of them 'one new man', so that 'he might reconcile us both to God *in one body* through the cross' (Eph 2:13–16).

c. Christ as *the lamb without spot or blemish* (1 Pet 1:19f with which compare the very strong soteriological connotation in the reference to 'the lamb of God' in Jn 1:29, 36). This figure refers to Christ as *the prototypal suffering and atoning* Servant of God, as 'the shepherd and guardian of souls' (1 Pet 2:21–5).

d. 'The Son' who is to bring 'many sons' to glory (Heb 2:10) and who is therefore like Moses who led the people of God in the wilderness (3:1–6). He has become 'like the brethren in all things', *a compassionate and sinless high priest* who, as a result of his unique self-offering valid for all time has become *mediator* (⁊ mediation) of a new ⁊ covenant and represents his disciples in heaven in order to lead them into the heavenly kingdom. He is the 'head' of the church and therefore is above all others, fulfils and nourishes the whole life of the church (see F. Mussner, *LTK* vi², 715; Heb 2:14–18; 4:14ff).

e. The divine status which belongs to Christ alone is expressed particularly in the Pastoral epistles by means of *titles taken from the hellenistic mystery religions and the kyrios-cult*. He is 'our Saviour' (Titus 1:4; 3:6; 2 Tim 1:10), 'our great God and Saviour' (Titus 2:13; see also 2 Pet 1:1).

f. As against a gnostic-type christology *the unity of the person of Christ as the source of our salvation* is emphasized. 'Jesus is the Christ' (1 Jn 2:22; 5:1), 'the son of God' (4:15; 5:5). Only he who 'has come in the flesh' (4:2f) and has died for us (5:6 etc) redeems the world from sin and gives eternal life. This truth is one of the basic motifs of the Fourth Gospel.

8. As witnesses to the message of Christ *the gospels* also have to be taken into account. As the tradition which they have made use of shows, the image of Christ which they present includes *the concrete 'historical' Jesus*, he who by his words and deeds throughout his earthly life reveals God's will for man's salvation and sanctification. This is obviously truer of the gospels than of the other 'occasional writings' in the New Testament (though with regard

to Paul, Hebrews, and 1 John see Léon-Dufour, *Les Evangiles*, 62–78, and on J. F. Mussner, *Der Jakobus-Brief*, Freiburg 1964, 47–52). We should not, however, overlook the fact that the preaching of Christ into which the points of detail found in the gospels fitted always looked to and was determined by the culmination of the whole event of revelation in the resurrection and exaltation of Christ. Whoever first created the literary genre of gospel, whose example was followed by the later evangelists down to John (see 20:21), understood the selections from the 'history of Jesus' which he included in his gospel, especially the words and 'mighty deeds' of Jesus, *as illustrating and corroborating 'the gospel of Jesus Christ the Son of God'* (Mk 1:1), or, in other words, the message concerning the unique status of Jesus as a person and as the bringer of salvation as it was proclaimed after the resurrection (and only after the resurrection) and at the time when the gospels were actually written. Hence the death and resurrection of the bearer of salvation stand not at the end but right at the centre of the gospel, as can be seen from a consideration of the second part of Mark's gospel (8:27ff), and in a particularly impressive manner the predictions of suffering and resurrection (8:31–3; 9:30f; 10:32–4), explicitly and kerygmatically formulated, including the reference which follows to the universally efficacious expiatory value of the passion which is stated explicitly in the saying about the Son of Man in Mk 10:45. Going beyond Mark, the two secondary sources of synoptic material contained in Matthew and Luke introduce, each in its own way, the proclamation of Jesus as the promised bearer of salvation and his divine status by presenting accounts of his birth and infancy each with its own particular theological point of view. The same can be said, *mutatis mutandis*, of the prologue to the fourth gospel dealing with the incarnation of the divine *Logos* (↗ word).

Since the tradition about Jesus is in the service of the post-resurrection proclamation and the forming of faith in Christ the synoptics betray evidence of ideas and forms of expression found in the older, pre-synoptic preaching of Christ. So, for example, the christological interpretation of many of the parables and the emphasis given to their christological significance; narratives about Christ which proclaim him against the background of prophecy to be the promised Messiah and miracle or epiphany narratives which represent him as God (Yahweh) become present, though indeed this has to be seen in the light of the claim which Jesus himself makes that God is eschatologically active in him. The early church has also throughout stressed the unity and continuity of the revelation of Christ by the translation, already accomplished before the composition of the synoptic gospels, of the exalted title 'Son of Man' (originally referring only to the eschatological judge who was to come) into statements dealing with the earthly life of Jesus and the manner in which it ended. We find examples of this in the didactic formulation of the claim of Jesus to be revealer and bringer of salvation in Mk 2:10 and parallels and 2:28 and parallels, and in the prophecies which are referred to his suffering, death and resurrection.

In keeping with the specifically 'evangelical' character of their writings on Jesus *the writers of the gospels themselves also stress certain characteristics of the presentation of Jesus* by the way in which they select and edit their material. *The Gospel of Mark* stresses the epiphany of God in him who proclaims the kingdom with full authority, who is the Son of God endowed with divine power (1:10f), whom the demons are obliged to acknowledge as such (1:34; 3:11; 5:7), whom God himself reveals to the three trusted witnesses (9:7)—though even here the messianic secret is preserved unbroken until the resurrection of the Son of Man—who reveals himself as Son of God at his trial (14:61f) and whom, finally, the representative of the gentiles proclaims as such to many as Jesus lies dying on the cross (15:39f). *The Gospel of Matthew* proclaims Jesus as the messianic founder of the true people of God who fulfils the prophetic words and realities of the scriptures, the sovereign and perfect teacher of the will of God who lays claim on all men to become his disciples, who is addressed by his followers as *Kurios* and recognised as the 'Son of God' (14:33; 16:16). *The Gospel of Luke* presents the picture of a merciful saviour of sinners, the poor, the sick and in fact of all mankind. He is, however, at the same time, the Kyrios who looks ahead to the completion of his mission in Jerusalem, from which city he as the Exalted Lord sends his apostles out in the power of the Spirit to spread the church, as is clear from the continuation of Luke's work in Acts.

In looking at these different emphases and characterisations of the figure of

Christ which are to be found in the synoptic gospels, we must not overlook one *basic conviction shared by all the evangelists which is essential for our understanding of the message of Christ.* On the one hand, this presentation of Christ combats any kind of dehistoricising and gnostic reduction of the revelation of Christ. On the other hand, the gospel-tradition about Jesus proclaims the resurrection as the decisive turning-point and end-point of the revelation of God, as an event which has already taken place, and it does this by means of a post-resurrection interpretation and actualisation of what Jesus did and said on earth but in a manner which is anything but arbitrary. The supposition behind the gospels is, therefore, that Jesus represented for the early church not just an event which happened once for all in the past but in the first place a mysterious present reality, the lord of his church who still lives on and is active. There is presupposed here the conviction of the early church that the Christ-event which began with the incarnation or the appearance of Jesus as revealer and culminated in the ascension and sending of the Spirit constitutes one divine operation which results from the design of God for human salvation and moves forward by phases to its conclusion which still lies in the future.

In the *Gospel of John* we find the strongest expression of the fact that he who was raised by the power of God is present in the cult, is actively associated with the church which receives grace from him and is still to complete his work of salvation, is one and the same as the Jesus whose earthly life ended on Good Friday. Going beyond what we find in the older gospels, but still holding firmly to the consciousness of sonship which these claim for him, this gospel presents Jesus himself as proclaiming his way as the descent of 'the Son' or 'the Son of Man'—the 'only-begotten of the Father' (3:16, 18; see also 1:14, 18) who reveals the Father completely (14:9ff), living and giving life from him as the Son (5:26; 6:57)—who will return to heaven into the glory which he antecedently enjoyed, after triumphing over death on the cross (3:13, 31; 6:62; 13:1; 14:28; 16:28; 17:5). This gospel, moreover, gives strongest expression to the role of Jesus in the divine plan of salvation, a role which was achieved and fulfilled only with the resurrection, by means of the words spoken by Jesus during his life on earth which take up and interpret this situation of Jesus after the resurrection. Hence in this gospel the present of the earthly ministry and the future of the risen Christ are mutually inclusive to a much greater extent than in the synoptics. Characteristic expressions of this self-revelation which in John's gospel takes in the entire history of Christ are the theophany formulations (8:24, 28, 58; 13:19) or the sayings introduced by the formula 'I am . . .' (6:41, 48, 51; 8:12, 28; 10:7, 11, 14; 11:25; 14:6; 15:5 etc) often expanded by means of metaphorical predications (as, for example, 'I am the resurrection and the life'), and even more clearly the formulae which expresses immanence (10:38; 14:9f, 20; 17:21).

9. Finally, the only prophetic book of the New Testament proves its claim to be a genuine christian *apocalypse* by concentrating on the revelation of

Christ which has already come about but still awaits completion. In numerous visions, acclamations and titles of different kinds, it develops an image of Christ by taking up imagery and motifs of the Old Testament and giving them a rich theological meaning. Right from the prologue the unity of the Christ-event is clearly and powerfully expressed, taking in the earthly ministry ('the true witness'—see also 3:7, 14; 19:11), the atoning death and the resurrection of Jesus as 'the firstborn from the dead'. Here too the exalted status of Christ receives major emphasis (1:5f), implied in the reference to the world which is hostile to God and Christ (he is 'ruler over the kings of the earth') and to the faithful who have a share in his kingdom and priesthood. This is in keeping with the situation which this book presupposes and the theme around which it is written. The Christ who has been raised to eternal life and is introduced in genuine apocalyptic manner as 'one like a Son of Man' in the guise of *king, judge, and priest*, the first cause and last end of the church, is proclaimed to the communities addressed (1:9–20). It is to these that Christ communicates his words of recognition and blame, his threat of punishment and promise of victory (Chapters 2–3).

The frequent reference (twenty-nine times) to the Lamb is used to bring together the idea of a redemptive death and the lordship which has passed to Christ after his resurrection. Only the Lamb knows the saving design of God and is able to bring it to completion (5:1ff). It is he who makes it possible by his redemptive death for the faithful christian to emerge victorious from the

battle with Satan and those in league with him (12:11; 14:1–5). He will annihilate the enemies of God (6:15ff; 17:14) and unite himself for ever with his bride the ↗church (19:7f; 21:9).

We find many other titles of honour in this book, some of them very probably of liturgical origin. There are several of these which have the purpose of underlining and giving substance to the universal divine power and exalted status of Christ. Examples would be 'the beginning of God's creation' (3:14), 'the first and the last', 'the living one' (1:17; 22:13), 'the beginning and the end' (22:13), 'the Alpha and Omega' (22:13)—even 'the Amen' (3:14). The power of the risen Christ expressed by these and other titles guarantees the completion of the victory of 'the anointed of God' (12:7–12) which has already been won in principle, the definitive establishment of the kingdom of God. Out of this confrontation of the Apocalypse with the cult of the emperor there emerges the vision of the victorious Christ who comes in judgement. He is not only 'the Word of God' (19:13 cf 1:16b; 19:15) but bears the title of absolute authority: 'king of kings and lord of lords' (19:16; 17:14; ↗kingdom).

Bibliography: On A: H. Conzelmann, *RGG* III³, 619–53; A. Vögtle, 'Jesus Christus', *LTK* v², 922–32; J. Leipoldt, *Vom Jesusbild der Gegenwart*, Leipzig 1925²; A. Reatz, *Jesus Christus*, Freiburg 1925²; J. Lebreton, *La Vie et L'Enseignement de Jésus-Christ*, Paris 1931; F. Prat, *Jésus-Christ, sa vie, sa doctrine, son oeuvre* (2 vols.), Paris 1933; J. R. Geiselmann, 'Der Glaube an Jesus Christus: Mythos oder Geschichte', *TR* 126 (1946), 257–77 and 418–39; K. Adam, *Christ our Brother*, London 1935; M. Dibellus, *Jesus*, Philadelphia 1949; J. Guitton, *Le Problème de Jésus et les fondements du témoignage chrétien*, II: *Le Problème de Jésus: Divinité et Résurrection*, Paris 1950/53; J. Guitton, *Jésus*, Paris 1956; F.-M. Braun OP, *Jesus Christus in Geschichte und Kritik*, Lucerne 1950; J. Bultmann, *Jesus and the Word*, London 1934; J. Klausner, *Jesus of Nazareth*, London 1925; W. Manson, *Jesus the Messiah*, London 1946; W. G. Kümmel, *Verheissung und Erfüllung*, Zürich 1956³; E. Percy, *Die Botschaft Jesu*, Lund 1953; V. Taylor, *The Life and Ministry of Jesus*, London 1954; E. Käsemann, 'Das Problem des historischen Jesus', *ZTK* 51 (1954), 125–43; E. Sjöberg, *Der verborgene Menschensohn in den Evangelien*, Lund 1955; N. A. Dahl, 'Der historische Jesus als geschichtswissenschaftliches und theologisches Problem', *KD* I (1955), 104–6; G. Bornkamm, *Jesus of Nazareth*, New York 1960; K. Schubert, *Der historische Jesus und der Christus unseres Glaubens*, Vienna 1962; E. Stauffer, *Jesus and his Story*, London 1960; H. Diem, *Der irdische Jesus und der Christus des Glaubens*, Tübingen 1957; J. A. T. Robinson, *Jesus and his Coming*, London 1957; W. Grundmann, *Die Geschichte Jesu Christi*, Berlin 1957; A. Vögtle, 'Das öffentliche Wirken Jesu auf dem Hintergrund der Qumranbewegung', *Freiburger Universitätsveden* 27 (1958), 13–20; R. Bultmann, *The History of the Synoptic Tradition*, New York 1963; B. Rigaux, 'L'Historicité de Jésus devant l'exégèse récente', *RB* 65 (1958), 481–522; F. Amiot, *Vie de Notre Seigneur Jésus-Christ*, Paris 1958; R. Schnackenburg, *God's Rule and Kingdom*, London and New York 1963; W. Beilner, *Christus und die Pharisäer*, Vienna 1959; H. E. Tödt, *Der Menschensohn in der synoptischen Uberlieferung*, Gütersloh 1963²; J. Jeremias, *Jesus' Promise to the Nations*, London 1958; A. Vögtle, 'Ekklesiologische Auftragswörte des Auferstandenen', *SP* II, Paris–Gembloux 1959, 280–94; E. Stauffer, *Die Botschaft Jesu—damals und heute*, Berne 1959; J. M. Robinson, *A New Quest of the Historical Jesus*, London 1959; A. Vögtle, 'Der Einzelne und die Gemeinschaft in der Stufenfolge der Christusoffenbarung', *Sentire Ecclesiam*, Freiburg 1961, 50–91; M. Kähler, *Der sogenannte historische Jesus und der geschichtliche Christus*, Munich 1961³; E. Lohse, 'Die frage nach dem historischen Jesus in der gegenwärtigen ntl. Forschung', *TLZ* 87 (1962), 162–74; P. Althaus, 'Das Evangelium und der historische Jesus', *Universitas* 13 (1962), 17–27; W. Marxsen, 'Zur Frage nach dem historischen Jesus', *TLZ* 87 (1962), 575–80; F. Hahn, *Das Verständnis der Mission im NT*, Neukirchen-Vluyn 1963; Léon-Dufour SJ, *Les Evangiles et l'Histoire de Jésus*, Paris 1963; A. Vögtle, 'Exegetische Erwägungen zum Wissen und Selbstbewusstsein Jesu', *Gott in Welt* II,

Freiburg 1964, 608–666; J. Jeremias, *Das Problem des historischen Jesus*, Stuttgart 1964; J. Blinzler, *The Trial of Jesus*, New York 1959; J. R. Geiselmann, *Jesus der Christus*, Munich 1965. — On B: G. Sevenster, *RGG* I³, 1745–62; Bell and Deissmann, *Mysterium Christi*, Berlin 1931; R. Bultmann, 'Zur Frage der Christologie', *Glauben und Verstehen* I, Tübingen 1954, 85–113; R. Bultmann, *Die Christologie des Neuen Testaments*, 245–67; W. Bousset, *Kyrios Christos*, Göttingen 1965⁵; K. L. Schmidt, *Jesus Christus im Zeugnis der Heiligen Schrift und der Kirche*, Munich 1936; R. Guardini, *Jesus Christus sein Bild in den Schriften des NT*, Würzburg 1940; A. E. Rawlinson, *The New Testament Doctrine of the Christ*, London 1949³; A. W. Argyle, *The Christ of the New Testament*, London 1952; F. Mussner, *Christus, das All und die Kirche*, Trier 1955; F. X. V. Filson, *Jesus Christ the Risen Lord*, New York–Nashville 1956; V. Taylor, *The Person of Christ in the New Testament Teaching*, London 1958; R. P. Casey, 'The Earliest Christologies', *JTS* 9 (1958), 253–77; E. Fuchs, 'Jesus und der Glaube', *ZTK* 55 (1958), 170–88; G. Ebeling, 'Jesus und der Glaube', *ZTK* 55 (1958), 64–110; G. Ebeling, *Die Frage nach dem historischen Jesus und das Problem der Christologie* I, 1959, 14–30; Ristow and Matthiae (edd.), *Der historische Jesus und der kerygmatische Christus*, Berlin 1960; J. M. Robinson, *A New Quest of the Historical Jesus*, London 1959; R. Schnackenburg, *LTK* v², 932–40; W. Marxsen, *Anfangsprobleme der Christologie*, Gütersloh 1960; W. Thüsing, *Die Erhöhung und Verherrlichkeit Jesu in Joh-Evangelium*, Münster 1960; R. Bultmann, *Das Verhältnis der urchristlichen Christusbotschaft zum historischen Jesus*, Heidelberg 1961²; L. Hejdanek and P. Pokorny, 'Jesus, Glaube, Christologie', *TZ* 18 (1962), 268–82; E. Schweitzer, *Erniedrigung und Erhöhung bei Jesus und seinen Nachfolgern*, Zürich 1962²; E. Fascher, 'Christologie oder Theologie? Bemerkungen zu O. Cullmans Christologie des NT', *TLZ* 87 (1962), 882–910; G. Lindeskog, 'Christuskerygma und Jesustradition', *Novum Testamentum* 5 (1962), 144–56; W. Kramer, *Christos Kyrios Gottessohn*, Zürich–Stuttgart 1963; L. Sabourin, *Les noms et les titres de Jésus*, Bruges 1963; R. Schnackenburg, *Ntl. Theologie: Der Stand der Forschung*, Munich 1963; F. Hahn, *Christologische Hoheitstitel*, Göttingen 1965²; B. van Iersel, 'Der Sohn' in den synoptischen Jesus worten, Leiden 1964²; P. Vielhauer, 'Ein Weg zur ntl. Christologie?', *ET* 25 (1965), 24–72.

Anton Vögtle

Joy

Joy, as a basic emotion, corresponds to the state of happiness. In the scriptures there is a gradual process which takes it beyond its terrestrial meaning, applying it to the salvation which approaches, becomes imminent and at length is present.

A. *In the Old Testament.* The Old Testament has not only an astonishing wealth of expressions for joy but can evoke the feeling of joy by a multitude of symbols (a countenance which lights up, light, clothing, matrimonial relations, wine, oil, the water of life). On every page of the Old Testament we read of *joy in earthly goods* (life cf Gen 25:8; posterity Ps 113:9; riches Ps 37:11; peace 1 Macc 14:11). The Wisdom literature in particular emphasises the limitations and the fleeting nature of these things ('the end of joy is grief' Prov 14:13). What, however, is decisive is *the religious context* of earthly joy (Deut 28:22–47: God withdraws the earthly good things which bring joy as a punishment for the refusal to serve him in joy). The Old Testament knows that all joy depends on God (Jer 7:34).

Orgiastic joy dominated *cult* in the pagan religion of Canaan, but Israel's joy had not to be of this kind (Hos 9:1–4). True joy, however, had its rightful place in the celebration of each of *the feasts of Yahweh* (the Passover, 2 Chron 30:21–5; Ezr 6:22; Pentecost, Deut 16:11; Tents, Neh 8:17; 14; Purim, Esther 9:17–22; the New Moon, Ps 81:2–4; transferring the Ark of the Covenant, 2 Sam 6:12 and parallels; dedication of the walls of Jerusalem, Neh 12:27; on offering a sacrifice, 1 Chron 29:22; 2 Chron 23:18; 29:30). Joy had special prominence on the occasion of *the sacrificial communion meal* (Deut 12:7; 28:47) since this was not just one of many occasions for joy but was a symbolical participation in the good things associated with salvation (see Ammermann, 36).

The piety of the psalmists strives always towards *spiritual joy.* Not only does God rejoice over his creation (Ps 104:31), man also finds his joy in it especially when at the same time he recalls to mind the course of sacred history (Ps 74:13–21; 92:5–12). The faithfulness of the alliance—God (for example, in Ps 31:8f; 145:7f) and the election of Israel (Ps 149:2–4) are frequent objects of joy. God's wisdom (Wis 8:16; Sir 4:12), his will expressed in his law (Ps 1:2; 19:9; 119:162), his word (Jer 15:16) and the forgiveness of sins (Ps 51:10, 14, 16) are sources of deep joy, a joy which has God himself for its object (Neh 8:10; Esther 14:18). It can even exist in the absence of the good things of the earth (Hab 3:16–19).

The decisive transformation in the content of this concept of joy in the New Testament consists in the proclamation of the *eschatological—messianic joy.* On several occasions the return of the people is taken as the type of the joyful eschatological epoch. Enemies will be destroyed (Is 25:9), and God will console his people (Is 49:13) so that all will rejoice at his mercy and his salvation (Is 44:23). The Lord brings into existence a new age (Is 44:22; 42:9) and enters into a new alliance (Jer 31:31). The king will come (Zech 9:9), God will be great among his people (Is 12:6), he himself will come to perform great wonders (Is 35:1–10) and to array Israel in the garments of salvation (Is 61:10) and thus bring his people joy (Is 62:5).

B. *In the New Testament.* Even though there are cases in the New Testament of *the joy of the 'world'* (the high priests rejoice over the betrayal of Judas, Mk 14:11 and parallels; Herod rejoices over the miraculous sign he expected to see, Lk 23:8; the 'world' has joy on account of the sorrow of the disciples, Jn 16:20; the inhabitants of the earth over the death of the witnesses, Rev 11:10), they are without consequence and are destined to come to nought (Jas 4:9). In fact, earthly joy remains generally in the background in the scriptures. Joy as a religious possession is in every respect bound up with the person of Jesus Christ and the salvation which is given through him. Zechariah and many others with him will rejoice at the birth of the precursor (Lk 1:14), John himself leaps with joy at the meeting with Jesus while yet in his mother's womb (Lk 1:44), Mary exults on account of the salvation which has now appeared (Lk 1:47), the joyful news of the birth is brought to the shepherds (Lk 2:10), the magi rejoice when once again they see the star (Mt 2:10). Long before, both Abraham and David had rejoiced to see the redeemer (Jn 8:56; Acts 2:26, 28). The precursor rejoices that he was able to bring the bride to Christ (Jn 3:29). Jesus himself exults over the revelation which the Father makes to 'little ones' (Lk 10:21) and rejoices for the disciples' sake when they were able to witness the sign of the resurrection of Lazarus (Jn 11:15). In the parable he avows his joy over sinners that do penance (Mt 18:13; Lk 15:5), together

with the joy of 'heaven' and of the angels (Lk 15:7, 10).

Christ is anointed with the oil of gladness on account of his righteousness (Heb 1:9 = Ps 45:7), sets joy before him on account of the cross so as to be able to communicate to his brethren a life of joy. The Lord *promises* joy to his own—as a *great reward* after persecution (Mt 5:12 and parallels), as the sure outcome of their sorrow since he himself will come and no one will take their joy from them (Jn 16:20, 22) and as joy caused by the success of the missionary harvest of the apostles (Jn 4:36). In this respect, joy as a way of life is even a *commandment of the Lord*: the disciples are told to rejoice that their names are written in heaven (Lk 10:20 and parallels), that Christ is going to the Father (Jn 14:28) and that they will remain in love (Jn 15:11). They have to pray in the name of the Lord so that they may be full of joy on account of their prayer being heard (Jn 16:24). The elder brother is told to rejoice over the homecoming of the prodigal (Lk 15:32).

The entire proclamation of the good news is presented in terms synonymous with joy: a marriage (Mt 9:15 and parallels); a joyful meal (Mt 22:1–14 and parallels; the banquet prepared by Levi is a type of this, Mt 9:10 and parallels; see also Mt 8:11 and parallels; the bridegroom is led in, Mt 25:10; the Lord himself will serve them at table, Lk 12:37; it is the Father who has issued the invitations to this meal, Lk 22:30; the pledge of the eternal banquet is already present here in the eucharistic meal cf Lk 14:15); also as a treasure, a pearl or a catch of fish (Mt 13:44–6), sitting on thrones of glory and judging the world (Mt 19:28; 20:20–28 and parallels; Lk 22:30), victory over Satan (Mt 12:24–9 and parallels; Lk 10:18). God, insofar as he is a father, is the source of joy (Mt 6:9 etc), his providence (Mt 6:25–33 and parallels; 16:8) which leads to salvation (Lk 12:32), the beatitudes (Mt 5:1–12), the great promises made to those who believe with confidence (see Mt 8:26 and parallels; 14:31—everything is possible to him who believes, Mt 9:24; he can even move mountains Mt 21:21; the efficacy of prayer accompanied by faith, Mt 6:5–8; 7:7–11 and parallels), freedom from many limitations of the law (to some extent from fasting, Mt 9:14f; the food laws are abrogated on principle, Mt 15:11 and parallels).

The proof of what Christ really means can be seen from the fact that he brings joy to those who are of good dispositions. Such occasions would be, in particular, the healing of the sick (Lk 5:25; 13:13, 17; 17:15; 18:43), the driving out of demons and raising from the dead (Lk 7:15) and the forgiveness of sins (Mt 9:1–8 and parallels; Lk 7:36–50). Christ speaks of the joy which is felt on hearing the word of God (Mt 13:20 and parallels), of the man who has found the treasure of the Kingdom of God (Mt 13:44), of the faithful steward whom the Lord welcomes into his joy (Mt 25:21, 23). This joy which is proclaimed and to which man is called really becomes present: the people praise God for all the mighty works they had seen (see Lk 19:37 during the entry into Jerusalem), Zacchaeus rejoices on account of the salvation which has come to him through the call received from the Lord (Lk 19:6), the 'seventy-two' rejoice

over the powers given to them (Lk 10:17). The women hasten away from the empty tomb with joy (Mt 28:8) and the highly emotional joy of the disciples even constitutes an obstacle to their believing in the resurrection (Lk 24:41). Joy flows from the presence of the Christ who could be seen and touched on Easter day (Jn 20:20) and remains even after the ascension into heaven (Lk 24:52).

The risen Christ is the real object of the joy of the church (joyful faith in Christ is mentioned in 1 Pet 1:8; 1 Jn 1:4; joy in the Lord, Phil 4:4). It is he who gives this joy (Jn 17:13). It comes through in the encounter with Christ in the sacraments (Acts 2:46). Joy fills those to whom the manifold gifts of God's grace have been confided and distributed (the Samaritans as a result of the miraculous deeds of Philip, Acts 8:8; the eunuch after his baptism, Acts 8:39; the pagans on hearing the word preached to them, Acts 13:48; the jailer after his baptism, Acts 16:34; those newly converted remain in this state of joy, Acts 13:52). Barnabas (Acts 11:23) and the communities founded during Paul's journeys (Acts 15:3) rejoice over the zeal of the Antioch community. John knows no greater joy than that his children should abide in the truth (2 Jn 4; 3 Jn 3f). The perfect conduct of the various communities (Rom 16:19), the strength of their faith (Col 2:5; 1 Thess 3:7, 9) and their harmony of mind (Phil 2:2) are sources of joy for St Paul. In this way the communities are his joy and his crown (Phil 4:1; 1 Thess 2:17) at the remembrance of which he rejoices (Phil 4:10). He rejoices over the grief which he has to inflict on them for their

correction (2 Cor 7:9) so that they—
the christians of Corinth—might prepare for him the joy which they owed
him when he should visit them (2:3).
Since he is strong when in their midst
(7:16), he can rejoice with them over
the good news which he receives and
share the joy of Titus (7:13). All
church leaders should be in a position
to rejoice in the same way (Heb 13:17).
As with Christ, the apostle calls on the
communities entrusted to him to rejoice (Phil 3:1; 4:4; 1 Thess 5:16) and
he himself contributes to this joy in the
faith (Phil 1:25). Human joys, too, are
not unknown to Paul (1 Cor 16:17; 2
Cor 7:6) and he desires them for others
(eg the joy of Epaphroditus arriving
home, Phil 2:28; rejoicing with those
who rejoice, Rom 12:15) even though
he sets a limit to the joys of this world
('as though not rejoicing' 1 Cor 7:30).

Paul says little explicitly about his
own joy over the possession of salvation
now at last available (note the victory
hymn in Rom 8:31-9; the praise of
the Lord Rom 5:2, 3, 11; 1 Cor 1:31).
On the other hand, he has something
profound to say about the joy of the
apostle's suffering with Christ. Thus
even though the trial itself does not
appear to have been a joyful experience
(Heb 12:11), yet the apostles left the
Synhedrium full of joy that they had
been able to bear opprobium for
Christ's sake (Acts 5:41). The faithful
also bore with joy the confiscation of
their earthly goods (Heb 10:34), the
churches of Macedonia rejoiced in the
trial of tribulation (2 Cor 8:2). The
faithful should not just rejoice *in* their
tribulations (1 Pet 1:6), they should
take the tribulation itself as a source of
joy (Jas 1:2). With all his afflictions

Paul was overjoyed (2 Cor 7:4); he
rejoiced in his weakness (2 Cor 13:9)
since he could thus offer himself as a
victim for the faith of his churches
(Phil 2:17). He rejoices so long as
Christ is being preached even though he
has to suffer because of the misrepresen-
tations and bad intentions of his adversaries (Phil 1:18). Above all, he
rejoices in his sufferings since in this
way he can 'make up for what is lacking' in the sufferings of Christ (Col
1:24). This paradoxical joy in suffering
is based not only on the expectation of
salvation which consists in a readiness
to suffer with Christ (1 Pet 4:13) or on
the hope of bringing closer the final
redemption in proportion as the sufferings become more intense (see for this
Bouttier and Allmen p. 144) but is the
expression of the definitive union with
Christ in love. Whence the apostle is
always full of joy even when he seems
most oppressed (2 Cor 6:10) since it is
no longer he who lives but Christ lives
in him through his suffering with Christ
(Gal 2:20).

God is not only the giver of each joy
(Jude 24)—even purely natural joys
(Acts 14:17)—but joy as such has a
very special relationship with the Holy
Spirit (Acts 13:52; Rom 14:17; 1
Thess 1:6). It is natural, therefore, that
joy should stand in close connection
with the Trinity (1 Cor 13:13). Joy
is therefore enumerated among the
fruits of the Holy Spirit immediately
after love (Gal 5:22), it appears to be
practically identical with faith (Phil
1:25), it arises and persists through
hope (Rom 12:12). It is also closely
connected with peace (Rom 14:17;
15:13; Gal 5:22), which is the condition
of the person who has been reconciled

Judgement

to God (see Lk 2:14; 7:50; Christ our peace, Eph 2:14; Rom 1:7 etc in closest connection with grace). Therefore joy is at the same time pledge, possession, and essential part of that day when the redeemed will praise God: 'Let us rejoice and exult . . ., for the marriage of the Lamb has come' (Rev 19:7).

Bibliography: E. G. Gulin, *Die Freude im NT* I, Helsinki 1932, II Helsinki 1936; R. Bultmann, *TDNT* I, 19–21; II, 772–75; M. Ammermann, *Die religiöse Freude in den Schriften des Altes Bundes*, Rome 1942; U. Holzmeister, '"Gaudete in Domino semper" et "Beati qui lugent"', *VD* 22 (1942), 257–62; P. Humbert, '*Laetari et exsultare* dans le vocabulaire religieux de l'AT', *RHPR* 22 (1942), 185–214; P. Humbert, *Opuscules d'un Hébraisant*, Neuchâtel 1958, 119–45; B. Reicke, *Diakonie, Festfreude und Zelos*, Uppsala 1951; W. Nauck, 'Freude im Leiden', *ZNW* 46 (1955), 68–80; Höpken, *BTHW* 146; Bouttier, Allmen 143f; E. Schick, *LTK* IV², 361; R. Voeltzel, *Das Lachen des Herrn*, Hamburg–Bergstedt 1961; H. von Campenhausen, 'Ein Witz des Apostels Paulus und die Anfänge des christlichen Humors', *Festschrift für R. Bultmann* (*BZNW* 21), 1957², 189–93; H. von Campenhausen, 'Christentum und Humor', *TR* 27 (1961), 65–82; J. Perrier, *La joie dans l'Evangile de Jésus*, Lausanne 1962; R. E. Backherms, *Religious Joy in general in the New Testament and its Sources in particular*, Fribourg 1963; G. Fitzer, *TWNT* VII, 403ff; H. Rusche, 'Die Freude: Ein biblischer Grundbegriff', *Bibel und Kirche* 5 (1964), 141–3; A. Ridonard and M. F. Lacan, *DBT* 237–40.

Wolfgang Beilner

Judgement

A. *Human Judgement.* 1. *Judging and ruling* are closely connected in the bible (see Judg 2:16; Hos 7:7; Amos 2:3; Wis 3:8). In the Ancient Near East, legislature and executive were united in the hands of the ruler who was considered as lord over life and death and whose will was aken as law. The supreme lord of Israel, however, was Yahweh and his laws, and judicial pronouncements signified the putting into practice of the divine saving will with regard to his people (↗ law). All human leaders were no more than representatives of God who, as 'judges', had the task of re-establishing the social order—an idea thematic in the Book of Judges (cf Ruth 1:1). In this sense the Old Testament also speaks of the 'judging' of Samuel and the kings (1 Sam 4:18; 8:20; 2 Sam 15:4; 1 Kings 3; Is 11:3–5; 61) and in this context the best king is always the most just judge (Ps 72). This meaning of *to judge* in the sense of *to rule* is used in a derivative sense in the New Testament where the throne of judgement is promised to the disciples as a figure of their share in the rule of God (Lk 22:30; cf Mt 19:28; Mk 10:37). In the same way, the activity of those who are mentioned in Rev 20:4 as sitting on thrones for judgement is paraphrased expressly as 'ruling'.

2. *Israelitic tribunals* are distinguished from those of the present day as they were from those in the Near East at that time by their special religious significance, namely, their relation to the God who had chosen his people in and through the Covenant. Judgement concerned with kinship (Gen 38:24ff), places (Ruth 4:1–11; 1 Kings 21:8; Is 28:6), the priests (Deut 17:8–13) and the kings (2 Sam 14:1–11) was, in Israel, subordinated to the supreme decision of Yahweh since 'the judgement is God's' (Deut 1:17). The influence of religion on judicial practice resulted in a repudiation of any foreign (Deut 14:21) or magical (Deut 24:16)

representations and brought about a greater severity in penalties inflicted for transgressions against God (Deut 13:2–19), a greater emphasis on the humane character and the moral foundations of the norms of law (1 Kings 3:9) and especially the reference of all the activity of judges, lawyers, and witnesses to Yahweh considered as the supreme judge, lawyer and witness (often in the Psalms; eg, 7:12; 18:26ff; 103:6). The judicial decisions of the law should assure to each one the position which was his among the people of God according to the will of God—hence the proceedings which were to be taken in the case of abuses committed by judges (Lev 19:15; Deut 1:17; Prov 24:23f etc) and the threatening language addressed to those judges who 'tear the skin from off my people and the flesh from off their bones' (Mic 3:1–4; see also Jer 5:28; Amos 6:12 etc).

3. *Pagan tribunals.* Pagan tribunals, which were to play an important part in Israelite history after the loss of national independence, had their own part to play side by side with Jewish tribunals especially in New Testament times (see Acts 23:3; Rom 13:1–5). They assume particular importance in the trial of Jesus and of Paul (see Acts 25:10ff) as well as during the persecution of christians who had been admonished by the word of the Lord to be courageous and trustful when brought before these tribunals (Mk 13:9–13), for the power which they wield comes from God (Jn 19:11; Rom 13:1). Paul expressly states that internal difficulties within the communities should not be settled before these pagan tribunals (1 Cor 6:1–6).

4. *Passing judgement on the moral value of another* is expressly forbidden in the New Testament (Mt 7:1f; Rom 14:4, 10; Jas 4:11f), not so much on account of it being impossible to look into the heart of another person as rather in view of the eschatological judgement of God which no man should anticipate (Mt 6:15; 1 Cor 4:1–5) and of the commandment of charity. The parable of the ungrateful debtor who was a believer but without mercy (Mt 18:23–35), condemns this human way of judging (see Jas 2:13) and emphasises the absolute precedence of the disposition to forgive above all merely formal right to pass judgement (see 1 Cor 6:7).

B. *Divine judgement.* 1. *The National Expectation.* a. According to texts coming from the earliest Old Testament period, the Israelites expected the humiliation of all their national enemies in the divine judgement (Ex 14:14; 23:22; Num 10:35), since Yahweh was conceived of as the friend of his chosen ones and the enemy of all others (Judg 5 etc). This Yahweh who judged his enemies went into battle on behalf of his people (Judg 3:9f) and a record was kept of these 'Wars of Yahweh' in certain books (Num 21:14). The whole history of Israel from the victory over the Egyptians (Ex 6:6; 7:4) to the conquests of David (1 Sam 18:17; 25:28) was seen as 'judgement' which would be fully manifested on behalf of Israel, full of light and the joy of victory, in a 'Day of Yahweh' which was drawing near (cf Amos 5:14, 18ff). Both the past and the future were explained in terms of the intervention of Yahweh who would pass judgement on behalf of his people.

b. A fairly strong nationalistic emphasis is found even later, especially in those violent images of judgement, the psalms of cursing and imprecation (68:22–4; 83:10–19; 129:5–8; 149:7f) and in certain expressions found in the Wisdom literature (Sir 50:25f; Wis 11:5–20; see also Deut 23:4–7). This often reaches the point of hatred against the enemies of the people and campaigns of extermination—at least in literature (Esther 8–9)—which are seen as a sharing in the divine judgement. In Jewish literature, and especially in popular piety, such characteristics remained very much in force together with many other ways of representing judgement (see Volz, 282f) so that we even find John the Baptist having to preach against this way of thinking (Mt 3:7–10).

2. *The Prophetic Preaching.* a. *The language of the prophets* is full of images of judgement of which the most original would appear to be that of a trial, probably deriving from liturgy (Hos 4:1; Is 1:2, 18; 3:13; Zeph 3:8; Joel 3:2). Yahweh also appears as a shepherd who sorts out the good and the bad in his flock (Ezek 34:17–22), as a labourer in the harvest (Is 27:12; Jer 15:7), as treading the wine press (Is 63:1–6), as the owner of a furnace for smelting and purifying (Ezek 22:18–22), as a warlike hero (Is 42:13), as a dangerous beast of prey (Hos 5:14; 13:7f). Yahweh's anger is vividly described: his trembling lips, his tongue like a devouring fire, his consuming breath, his snorting nostrils, his threatening voice, his punishing hand and arm lifted to strike (Is 30:27–30; cf Ex 15 etc). Yahweh whistles to him the instruments of his anger (Is 5:26).

Judgement appears in the form of a battle (Zech 14:3), as storm weather (Is 29:6), as the great ingathering of the ⌐ harvest, and as the final theophany (Is 24:21ff) accompanied by the shaking of the heaven and the earth (Joel 3:16), the stars losing their light (Is 13:10) and the heavens being rolled up (Is 34:4).

b. The prophets therefore proclaim *a divine judgement of punishment* against Israel's neighbours and against the great world powers of their time (Is 13–27; Jer 46–51 and passim). Even in Jeremiah such words are related more to an event or events within this world and of a political and military nature, described in language which is often hyperbolical and having a pedagogical intent (Is 3). But already in Zephaniah the representation of a catastrophic phenomenon resulting in annihilation and a judgement applying to the whole world is already assuming proportions which point to a final judgement on all peoples of the earth (Zeph 1–3; cf Is 24–6; 66:15–17; Joel 3:1–16; Obad 15f; Zech 14:12–21; see also Ps 2; 110; for Ezek see below).

In the case of Israel also, however, judgement did not remain just at the level of occasional divine visitations; on the contrary, they will experience a terrible judgement which will go against all their short-sighted nationalistic expectations. From the time of Amos (5:18ff) and Hosea (1–3; 9:15), all the prophets denounce 'a sinful nation, a people laden with iniquity, offspring of evildoers, sons who deal corruptly' and who 'have forsaken Yahweh' (Is 1:4). This is understood at first of national tragedy within history, above all, the ruin of both kingdoms (Jer

5:19; 16:11–13; Ezek 23) as well as of accompanying calamities such as pestilence, hunger, sword, desolation, and imprisonment (Jer 15:2ff). In this judgement God would use nature and other peoples as instruments (Is 10:5; Jer 25:9). Correspondingly, the term ↗ 'Day of the Lord' refers to a day of judgement (Hos 5:9) full of fury and the burning anger of God (Is 13:6–9), a day of terror for the whole world (Zeph 1:14–18; 3:8). Together with its frequent use in the prophets (cf Mal 3:2; Zech 14:1), this expression for a divine judgement of condemnation (though see below for another meaning) occurs also in the rest of the Old Testament (Lam 2:1, 22; Prov 11:4; etc).

c. *This divine judgement also makes for salvation* since the 'remnant of Israel' (Amos 5:15; Is 6:13) will be favoured by God as the beginnings of a new people (Amos 9:11–15; Is 10:20–3; Mic 4:6–8), the purified people, once the unfaithful spouse, will be taken back by her husband (Hos 2:9). This thought of salvation which is attained through judgement is presented under the image of a refining furnace (Is 1:25; Jer 9:7; Is 48:10) and of punishment (Ezek 14:21ff). With the development in eschatology, this salvation comes to be understood differently but there remains always the conviction that each divine act of judgement must be in the service of God's grace and that God will once again look upon his people with favour (Jer 24:5). Even in the case of judgement on the pagan nations this is seen to be true: Yahweh will heal Egypt (Is 19:22ff), lead the nations to repentance (Jer 18:7f) and allow a holy remnant of the nations to

to have a share in the salvation of his own people (Is 24:6, 13f). Since every proclamation of judgement therefore implied both punishment and salvation at the same time, it came to be recognised that the expression 'the Day of Yahweh' (see above) would not be just a day of anger but also of salvation (Amos 9:11; Hos 2:16f; Is 1:26; 11:9; Jer 30:23f; 31:31f; Zeph 3:8–20) and of the two, salvation is ever more strongly emphasised from the time of the Exile, particularly in Ezekiel and Deutero–Isaiah (the same is true of the judgement-metaphor of the ↗ harvest).

d. Of great importance is *the moral and religious foundation* of judgement which is found in the prophets. The pride of the nations (eg Is 10:13; 14:13f; Jer 48:42), their worship of idols (Is 2:18–20), their raging against Yahweh and his people (Joel 3:2–6) and also against other peoples (Is 10:7), together with a great number of moral faults (Amos 1:3, 13; 2:1f; Nahum 3:1), call down punishment upon them. The prophets confront their own people with the worship of idols and other sins (Amos 2:4)—even in the temple itself (Ezek 8:3–16)—together with sacral prostitution (Hos 4:13f), the neglect of all the commandments of the decalogue and other community laws—faults brought about particularly through oppression, fraud and egotism. Hence Yahweh himself must intervene and bring low this overweening pride (Is 2:11–17). At the bottom of all this, there is the zeal or jealousy of Yahweh as the foundation of all judgement, Yahweh who is vitally concerned with his honour and the hallowing of his name in his ↗ inheritance (Is 48:11). It is for this reason that he punishes (Ezek

445

39:21, 23), shows favour (Ezek 39:25, 27), and will hold the universal judgement on the world and bring into existence the eternal order of salvation (Zech 14:9; cf Sir 36:1–5).

3. *Theological developments.* a. *The application to the individual of the idea of judgement* was formed in close connection with the prophetic teaching on the moral foundations of punishment (Amos 5:14; Is 5:8–24) and the teaching on individual retribution (Jer 31:29; Ezek 18:2), and is found particularly in the Psalms and Wisdom literature where it betrays certain foreign influence (see Wis 2:21–3, 12; 2 Macc 12:43–5). In this connection, the typical ways of expressing judgement as found in the prophets are often used of the destiny of individual men (see Prov 11:4; 16:4; Wis 3:18). For the most part, it is a question here of a judgement of God taking the form of earthly happiness or unhappiness or some particular kind of death (Sir 11:26ff). Continuing the line of development of the Wisdom literature (Wis 4:20–5:23), the apocryphal writings describe an other-worldly judgement for the individual (Enoch 22:9–13; 39:4; 2[4] Esd 5:75–101 and other texts). By the time of Jesus this way of thinking had a predominant part in the representation of divine judgement (see SB IV, 1036f; Volz 270f; cf Lk 19:22f; 23:43).

b. *The apocalyptic descriptions* of divine judgement have their starting-point in the various representations found in the prophets and their systematisation in Ezekiel. This latter distinguished in the first place the judgement on Israel in which there emerges as a distinct element the sacred remnant of Israel (23; 36); secondly, judgement on the

pagans from which a remnant would be saved (25:7, 11, 14, 17; see also Jer 48:47; 49:6); thirdly, after a period of peace, there would be judgement on Gog king of Magog (38:1–39:22) in which God would manifest his glory (38:19–23); fourthly, the great age of salvation (39:23–9). Already here we find numbers which have to be calculated (29:12f) and apocalyptic terms (38:8). The apocalyptic writings, which are all linked up with one another, are no longer made up of exhortation which has conversion as its aim but are works of edification of a different kind. Their purpose is not to arouse fear by reference to the divine judge but rather to console by their teaching on *the nature* of the judgement to come (Joel 2:28–3:21; Zech 12ff). Thus their horizon both as regards space and time is often without limit and even transcendent while at the same time not excluding a marked nationalistic prominence for the Jews. Dan 7–11 contains technical terms, contemporary calculations and interpretations, symbolical statements and descriptions of scenes and action connected with judgement. Wis 4:20–5:23 describes judgement on men who have immortal souls and are therefore familiar with eternal sanctions. In extrabiblical literature there is a richly-coloured assortment of representations in which different judicial acts, places, characters, procedures, books, scales and forms of torture have their part to play (see especially in Enoch and 4 Esdras). By this time even angels and demons are judged and the pious may have the part of judges. In most cases there is a distinction between a messianic judgement followed by a period of peace and an eschatological

final judgement (see Volz; SB references as above; *DB(S)* IV, 1262–5). The
Qumran community was familiar with
and provides a description of these two
judgements (Nötscher, see below). At
all events, the description and expectation of a divine judgement is an
essential characteristic of later judaism
and explains on the one hand how
national pride was taken for granted
(see Mt 3:9), on the other the feeling of
helplessness as presented by Paul in
Rom 7.

c. *The development of this tradition in the
New Testament.* We should mention in
the first place some important limitations. The New Testament does not
refer explicitly to the so-called 'particular judgement'. It is very likely
possible to deduce this indirectly from
the teaching on ↗ retribution for good
works (not, however, on the basis of
Sir 11:26 and Heb 9:27f!) and the
various indications of a state after death
(Lk 16:19–31; 23:43; see also Phil
1:23; 2 Cor 5:6–8). Moreover, the
New Testament stands opposed to any
scholastic presentation or description of
the apocalyptic event; even in texts
where the traditional and contemporary
images of judgement are used (see Mt
3:7–12; Mk 13 and parallels; also Mt
13:37–43; 25:31–46; 2 Pet 3:7–13;
Rev 19:11–20, 15; Jas 5:5, refers to
'fattening your hearts in a day of
slaughter' with reference to the rich)
it is only in a very subdued kind of way
in contrast to what we find in contemporary literature, and contributes
to the appeal to conversion by emphasising the proximity of judgement.
There are no apocalyptic calculations
in the New Testament either with
reference to a fixed date for the end

(Rom 13:11–14; 1 Thess 5:1–11;
Rev 3:3) or the time of judgement (Lk
13:1–5); this can be seen also from the
doctrine on ↗ retribution. At the same
time, however, there are cases where the
intervention of God in the course of
existence is seen as judgement (Acts
5:1–10; 12:23; 13:11; Rom 1:18–32;
1 Cor 11:27–32; Rev 2:5), but in these
cases the impossibility of calculating is
emphasised. For the rest, the whole
gamut of representations is widely
attested in the New Testament as is
shown by the use of corresponding
terms such as a ↗ harvest, fruits, the
shepherd and his flock. In the centre
there is the expectation of a final
judgement to take place on a certain
day (Mt 10:15; 12:36; 2 Pet 2:9;
1 Jn 4:17) fixed by God (Acts
17:30f). This day will bring salvation
for those who believe (Lk 18:1–8; 2
Thess 1:5–10) but damnation for the
enemies of the divine will whether they
are spirits (1 Cor 6:2f; 15:26; Rev
12:7–9 etc) or men (Rom 2:5; 12:19;
2 Pet 2:9). This judgement will include
all men without exception (Mt 11:20–
24; 25:31–45; Lk 12:17–21; Rom
2:12–16). It will have effects on a
cosmic scale (Mk 13:24; Lk 21:25f; 2
Pet 3:7–13). The criterion for this
judgement will not be national (Mt
3:9; Jn 8:33–40; cf Mt 8:11f) but of a
purely religious and moral nature: the
'Law' (Mt 5:17–20; Mk 10:19), the
conduct of each one (Rom 2:6; 2
Cor 5:10; cf Mt 12:33–7; Rom
13:8ff; Jas 2:14–26) and finally his
position in relation to Jesus (see below).
The result of the judgement is described
as, on the one hand, eternal joy,
blessing, honour, good estate, peace,
happiness, and the blessed company of

God; on the other, as darkness, weeping, gnashing of teeth, punishment by fire, fear and terror, torture and ruin, eternal separation from God (↗ heaven, ↗ hell, ↗ retribution). The sentence is eternal (Heb 9:15; 2 Pet 1:11), as also the judgement itself is described as eternal in its consequences (Heb 6:2), but that is not meant in the sense of without end but rather as *timeless, transcendent.*

4. *Elements peculiar to the New Testament.* a. *Jesus himself announces the coming judgement.* This is shown in every phase of his activity, speaking to the disciples, to the Pharisees, and the people; it occurs in all the sources at our disposal and in all the synoptic summaries of his teaching, for example in the Sermon on the Mount (Mt 5:22, 26, 29f; 7:1f, 21ff, 24–7), in the discourse to the disciples (Mt 10:28, 33), in the eschatological discourse (Mk 13 and parallels), his words to the Pharisees (Mt 23:13–35), and finally in some of the more important of the parables (eg Lk 16:1–8, 19–31; Mt 22:11ff; 24:37ff; 25). According to the teaching of Jesus, man can only attain to a share in the eschatological Kingdom of God and free himself from the eschatological judgement when he listens to the word of Jesus and puts it into practice (Mt 7:24–7). Hence the whole of this message points to an approaching judgement (see Mk 1:15; 9:1 and, related to this, Rom 13:12; Jas 5:8) with the cry 'Take heed!' and 'Watch!' (Mk 13:5, 9, 23, 33, 35, 37). The teaching on the forgiveness of sins belongs also assuredly to this message of judgement (Mk 2:5, 10), as also the saying about the Son of Man giving his life as a 'ransom' (Mk 10:45), whereby Jesus

explained the meaning of his death and at the same time solved the great problem inherent in the theology of judgement in late judaism, namely, by what means man could survive this judgement.

b. *Jesus Christ is judge in the final judgement.* This is emphasised by the New Testament side by side with the traditional presentation of the judgement of God (Mt 18:35; Rom 14:10; 1 Pet 1:17). Jesus' consciousness of his own identity and his self-proclamation (cf Mk 14:62) show that here it is not just any prophet of doom who is speaking and whose word awaits confirmation (cf Mt 11:7–15) but rather the 'one who is mightier' indicated by the Baptist (Mt 3:11f). Jesus himself states that he will one day appear in judgement (Mt 7:22f; 13:41ff; 16:27; 25:31–46; cf Jn 5:22; Rom 2:16; 2 Cor 5:11 etc). As a consequence, the Old Testament 'Day of Yahweh' or 'Day of Judgement' (Mt 10:15; 1 Jn 4:17) is transformed into the 'Day of the Lord' (1 Cor 1:8; 1 Thess 5:2; Heb 10:25). God has given over all judgement to the Son, and the angels (Mk 8:38; 2 Thess 1:7) and the holy community (1 Cor 6:2f) will stand by his side and take part in the judgement (cf Mt 16:19; 18:18; Jn 20:23). Side by side with fear and terror at the thought of this day (Phil 2:12), there is also the appeal to the Lord for a judgement of salvation (Phil 3:20). The identity of the one who announces the judgement and the one who judges gives the New Testament proclamation of judgement a sense of profound seriousness and calls for decisive action (Mk 1:15; Mt 11:20–24; Lk 13:1–9; Acts 2:38; 3:19 etc), a state of readiness

(Mt 24:43–25:13), patience and stead-fastness (2 Thess 1:4; Heb 12:1 etc).

c. *The sentence is decided by one's attitude to Jesus Christ.* This is true in the first place of the future judgement (Mk 8:38; Mt 10:32f). To all those who are not acknowledged by Jesus in the decisive moment will the formula of rejection— 'I know you not!' be addressed (Mt 7:22f; see also Mt 25:11f; Lk 13:25). He on the other hand who follows Jesus will attain to salvation in the final judgement (Lk 22:28ff). This stands out most clearly in the metaphorical presentation of the judgement on the whole world (Mt 25:31–46). All the good actions which had been performed or omitted were, even if the person doing them was unconscious of it, performed for or refused to the Lord, and this hidden relationship is a decisive factor in the sentence pronounced (Mt 25:40, 45). In a similar way, Paul teaches (see Rom 5:9f; 8:33f) that the decisive criterion is the law of faith (Rom 3:27; cf 8:2), the 'law of Christ' (1 Cor 9:21; Gal 6:2). Therefore the eschatological appearance of the Judge will spell salvation for all those who acknowledge him in faith (Lk 21:28; 1 Thess 1:9f; Phil 3:20f). This implies at the same time that the all-important decisions are taken in this life (↗ justification).

John takes this further. Judgement is already present in the decision which a man takes (3:18f; 9:39). Hence the hostile forces are already drawn up against one another in this world: Sons of ↗ Light against Sons of Darkness, ↗ truth against falsehood, God against the Devil (1 Jn 3:13f). The judgement is already carried out once a man takes up a definite attitude to Christ (Jn 8:24). Whole sections of the fourth gospel are dedicated to this doctrine (3:1–21, 31–6; 6:22–59; 7:14–30; 8:12–20; see also the concrete case in 6:60–71). The world is blind to the genuine reality which lies behind the appearances and this blindness is a proof that it has already been judged, especially in its moment of triumph represented by the Cross (12:31; 16:8–11). The future judgement (Jn 5:28f; see also 1 Jn 4:17) is not, however, unknown to the Johannine writings since according to this theological presentation it will be the great revelation of a judgement which is already present.

Bibliography: Pautrel and Mollat, *DB(S)* IV, 1321–94 (with detailed bibliography); Herntrich and Büchsel, *TDNT* III, 921–54; Schmid, *LTK* IV², 727–31; Burnier, Allmenn 146–50; Heinisch 262–74; Köhler, 209–18; Eichrodt, I, 381–4; Jacob 255–63; Bultmann I, 74, 79; II, 37–40. See also Bousset-Gressmann, 202–301; P. Volz, *Eschatologie der jüd. Gemeinde*, 1934², 89–97 and 272–309; SB IV, 1119–212; S. Mowinckel, *He that Cometh*, Oxford 1956; de Vaux, 143–63 and 353–5 (with critical bibliography); F. Nötscher, *Altertumskunde*, 123–33; Nötscher, 158–67; F. Horst, 'Recht und Religion im Bereich des AT', *ET* 16 (1956), 49–75.

Wilhelm Pesch

Justification

A. *Justification in Paul.* Although the substantive *justification* occurs only twice (Rom 4:25; 5:18; see also Rom 5:16), the verb *to justify* is met with very often in the writings of the apostle Paul (26 times). As with the word *righteousness*, the references occur, for the greater part, in Romans and Galatians, that is to say, in letters in which Paul opposes the Jewish teaching on salvation and with it that which governed his own past. This means that, in order to determine exactly the pauline concept of justification, it is in the first place necessary to take a closer look at *the Jewish concept.*

The *Jewish doctrine of salvation*, even though differing sharply within itself on particular points, is based on the fundamental assumption that man has within himself the possibility of fulfilling the law, and *he who has fulfilled the law is righteous.* Justification is therefore the work of man himself and is, in the strictest sense of the term, his own merit. Whence the fulfilling of the law is not seen as a general attitude *vis-à-vis* the law, but in the sense of the fulfilling of the individual prescriptions, of works of the law as opposed to transgressions of individual legal points. The sum total of the individual compliances with or transgressions of the law determines whether a man is righteous or not. The judgement on this final condition is reserved to God and passed at death or at the final judgement. He who has a credit balance is justified by God, that is, he is reckoned as righteous and has a claim to share in the life of the world to come. He who has not will be condemned. Exactly how mechanically this system was conceived to be is shown in the well-known discussion between the schools of Shammai and Hillel on the destiny of those whose works were exactly balanced between good and evil. While the former believed that a person in this position would be condemned by God, the latter held that God would justify such a one in consideration of the merits of the patriarchs, so that the scales might be tipped in his favour. Judaism is certainly familiar with the idea of *grace and the forgiveness of sins*, but these play no part in the doctrine of justification. This is conceived of as a purely *external act consisting in acknowledging a reality which is already there.* Man is not for the first time made righteous through justification, nor does justification arise out of this act of acknowledgement, nor is it constituted by it; rather, justification is the recognition of a righteousness which has already been brought about and which is therefore already in existence. The Jewish teaching on justification could be summed up objectively in a phrase: *man is righteous because declared so by God.* This implies that justification is not a grace but strictly a merit of man, something that God owes to man and to which man, in the strictest sense, has a claim.

Paul's teaching shows itself to be *in radical opposition* to this Jewish concept both in the way he formulates it and in its content. In this respect there appear some essential differences in his teaching on justification in respect to that which had gone before. Paul agrees with the Jewish idea only in the one point that only those who fulfil the law will be justified in the final judgement (Rom 2:13). In this text the term *justify* evidently has the same meaning as in judaism, namely, to be declared and acknowledged as righteous. This meaning also occurs in Paul's statement: 'I am not aware of anything against myself, but I am not thereby justified' (1 Cor 4:4); or where he says, in Rom 8:33; 'It is God who justifies', meaning at the final judgement—for it is significant that the term which is used as the opposite of this is 'to condemn'.

In general, however, Paul understands justification as an *act taking place within history*. This is clear in particular from the fact that he can speak of it in the past tense as when he says 'We have been justified' (Rom 5:1, 9), or 'those whom he [God] called he also justified' (Rom 8:30). The process of coming to believe—including also baptism—is the beginning and the cause of justification (Gal 2:16; Rom 3:21–6; 2 Cor 5:18–21). This justification which we have described as taking place *within history* is not identical with that which takes place *at the end of time*. Even for those who have been justified, there is still reserved a judgement according to their works (as can be deduced from numerous texts, cf Rom 2:16; 14:10ff; 1 Cor 9:23–7; 2 Cor 5:10; Gal 6:7–10; Phil 2:12).

However, it is not only from the point of view of its relation to time but also from that of its content that Paul's idea of justification differs from that of judaism. While according to the Jewish concept a man is justified because declared so, Paul adopts the opposite thesis, namely, that God justifies those who were previously sinners (Rom 4:5). It is at this point that there enters an entirely new element in the pauline concept of justification, and it is obvious that the structure of the concept itself cannot remain uninfluenced by it. Since Paul employs the same verbal form *to justify* (*dikaioō*) both for the final and the historical process of justification, and since his thesis is the antithesis of that of late judaism, it must be assumed that he uses this word throughout in the same sense, that of *pronouncing a person justified*. This means that even when referring to a process

within history Paul understands justification as a judicial pronouncement made by God with regard to man. But this pronouncement is not the recognition of a reality which is already in existence but brings this reality into existence for the first time. Sinful man becomes righteous through this divine pronouncement. Just as truly as men were constituted sinners through the original sin of Adam they are made righteous through the obedience of Christ (Rom 5:19). So in the same way that the parallelism in the history of salvation between Adam and sinners leaves no room for an 'as if' explanation, the same is true of that between Christ and the righteous. *To be justified* and *to achieve justification* are really, therefore, one and the same thing for Paul; viewing it from God's point of view we should speak of *justifying* and *reckoning righteousness to someone* in the sense of giving it to him (Rom 4:2–5). We can explain in a similar way how the expression *God's righteousness*, which includes also the idea of this righteousness as a gift given to men, is to some extent just a paraphrase of what Paul designates as justification. It would therefore be in accord with the essential content of the pauline concept of justification to understand it as *making a person righteous*, even if strictly speaking this concept is taken from the forensic area and given a judicial meaning.

We have not yet, however, said the last word or the decisive word about this concept. The decisive question concerns what Paul means by 'making a person just'. If we start from the often quoted text of Rom 4:8, it could appear as if, for him to make a person just were the same as 'not to reckon his sins to a person' ('blessed is the man against whom the Lord will not reckon his sin'). In this event we should once again have a clearly forensic meaning given to justification. It would be a pronouncement of absolution from sin, and righteousness would be identical with being declared absolved. This interpretation might appear to be supported by the fact that Paul is actually giving a definition of the concept *justification* in this context, and that he has already, in the preceding v 7, paraphrased justification with the quotation: 'Blessed are those whose iniquities are forgiven and whose sins are covered'. It should, however, be noted as against this view that Paul is here quoting from Ps 32:1ff, and using a text which was not meant to include the whole radius of meaning contained in the concept of justification. One must rather take in the whole body of material which the pauline epistles offer for the elucidation of the word *justification*, and above all the series of parallels which Paul uses to describe in different ways the reality of redemption. From this would emerge that justification is not just an absolution from guilt and forgiveness of sins but includes much more. Just as righteousness implies an intrinsic freeing from sin (Rom 6:18), the same would be true also of justification. It is significant in this respect that Paul speaks only on three occasions of the forgiveness of sins (Rom 4:7; Col 1:14; Eph 1:7), once in a quotation from the Old Testament, and uses a formulaic expression much in use in early christian preaching. This evidently is due to the fact that the expression 'forgiveness of sins' appears rather to contain absolution *in foro*

externo, whereas Paul is more concerned with the inner freeing from sin and the power of sin. In Paul, sin is not just guilt; the whole essence of sin lies in an inner perverted attitude of man—it means turning away from God and at the same time the self-glorification of man ($\nearrow$ sin). Therefore being freed from sin, and the justification which goes with it, imply an inner reconstitution of man, bringing him round to a new attitude which is pleasing to God. In 1 Cor 6:11 Paul appeals to the community: 'But you were washed, you were sanctified, you were justified in the name of the Lord Jesus Christ and in the Spirit of our God'. Here one term explains another, although it is not possible to divide them off precisely and objectively. It is important to note in this connection that *sanctified* is mentioned before *justified*. As the formula 'in the name of the Lord Jesus Christ and in the Spirit of our God' shows, this word has to do with the effects of baptism. As a result of this, it is possible and even necessary in the context of Paul's teaching to think of the statements which he makes in Rom 6, about the death to sin of the baptised person, characterised as they are by an unmistakeable realism, as a further illustration and consequence of his teaching on justification. It would hardly be possible to express in a stronger and more realistic way than we find here the meaning of the intrinsic liberation from sin, a fact which is now generally recognised by all exegetes. Therefore any attempt to distinguish in Paul two quite distinct and independent doctrines of salvation—one (juridical) implying a merely forensic justification based on faith as the central point, and the other (mystical) which has as its starting-point the sacraments and the life in Christ and which teaches a real blotting out of sin and an inner sanctification—founders on 1 Cor 6:11 (see also Gal 3:23f). On the contrary, *the doctrine of justification* and that on the *sacraments* form an *original and indivisible unity* in Paul, even if the elaborated synthesis of the two elements is carried through only under the second heading.

Since, for Paul, justification and the reception of righteousness are one and the same thing, it follows that the concept of justification also must have a moral content which can be recognised as an essential component of his idea of righteousness (↗ righteousness). Since righteousness includes within itself moral integrity, a basic holiness, and the possibility of a sinless life, it follows that for Paul justification also must be *brought about by God who gives man the possibility of an interior conversion to a new life*. This is what he means when he characterises justification as 'leading to life' (Rom 5:18).

The verb *dikaioō* which Paul uses when speaking of justification is taken from the vocabulary of law. Whereas in classical Greek it has the meaning 'to declare a person innocent', 'to judge', 'to pass sentence', it is used in LXX to translate very varied Hebrew terms which also express quite different realities. These are chiefly in the passive: 'to be in the right', 'to be just', 'to be pure'. It is used very often with the meaning: 'to clear a person of guilt by means of a judicial decision'. In this case the reference is always to persons who are really just and therefore really deserve this favourable decision as being just before the decision

was made. There is no question of anyone being made just by such a process. Paul also uses this word with the meaning of a sentence which God passes with regard to men, but from the point of view of the content of the term it acquires the meaning of making someone just since the pronouncement of the omniscient and omnipotent God really gives something to man which frees him from sin and elevates him to a condition of righteousness which has been brought about by God himself.

Paul sets down the antithesis to the Jewish thesis that man is justified on the basis of works of the law, and that means on the basis of his own unaided efforts, namely, that man is justified or made righteous (↗ righteousness) *not on the basis of works of the law but on the basis of faith*, and that means purely from the grace of God. Chiefly by means of the example of Abraham (Rom 4:1–8; Gal 3:6) he shows that it is also a scriptural datum that the justification of a man reposes not on works but on faith (see also Rom 1:17; Gal 3:11). An 'as if' interpretation is excluded here, too, since faith and works of the law are realities belonging to two quite different orders and are diametrically opposed one to the other (Gal 3:12; 5:4). The decisive basis of the apostle's teaching on justification, however, is his understanding of the atoning death of Christ as the revelation of the salvific action of God, and the ensuing recognition of the hopelessness of the human situation before Christ and outside of Christ as a predicament from which man, by himself, cannot escape. No man, not even the Jew with his works of the law, has the intrinsic possibility of overcoming sin and being justified in the eyes of God but is rather dependent on the grace of God which alone justifies, that grace which has become objective reality in the death and resurrection of Christ (Rom 4:25) and which is distributed to man through faith (Rom 3:24–6). Only by means of this justification does man receive the basic possibility, the power to fulfil the law, namely, to live in righteousness (Rom 8:1–13).

B. *Justification in the Letter of James*. In 2:14–26 this letter deals with the question of justification. The problem of this text consists in the fact that it seems to express a formal contradiction of the view of Paul. We read in Rom 3:20 and Gal 2:16: 'No man can be justified through works of the Law'; and in Rom 3:28: 'We hold that a man is justified by faith apart from works of the Law'—but Jas 2:24 has: 'You see that a man is justified by works and not by faith alone'. This impression is strengthened even more by the fact that both Paul and James adduce the example of Abraham as a scriptural proof (see Gen 15:6), but give it two mutually contradictory interpretations: Paul uses it in favour of the thesis that justification reposes on faith without works of the law, James in favour of the apparently opposite view that it is precisely works which furnish the basis for justification.

It is well known that Luther in his struggle against justification by works and in favour of the 'pure', that is, the pauline gospel, for the reason stated above refused to admit the canonicity of the Letter of James. Nowadays protestant exegesis speaks with a more sober tone on this point and recognises, even if with some hesitation, that there

is no question here of a formal and irreconcilable opposition between the teaching of the two apostles. The apparent contradiction disappears at once as soon as it is recognised that James cannot be interpreted from a pauline point of departure, but that rather the two expositions have an essentially different point of departure and object and that the terms which are of decisive importance in this matter— *justification, faith, works*—have quite a different sense in the two writings. Whereas Paul is speaking as a theologian and wishes to offer a doctrinal presentation of the way of salvation in opposition to that current in judaism, James is concerned only with christian life in practice, that is, with the actualisation of the christian law of morality, the highest norm and perfection of which is, for him as for the gospel, the commandment of loving one's neighbour (2:8). While justification is for Paul the basic reality in the order of salvation which elevates man to the condition of righteousness, for James it has the meaning of the moral life of the person who has already in principle been made righteous in the pauline sense and the consequent acceptance of this moral life on the part of God. The works which Paul refuses to acknowledge as the foundation of justification are those referred to in the law of the Old Testament, understood in the sense of an action accomplished by man's unaided power by which he himself merits justification. The works of which James speaks are, on the other hand, the good works arising out of love for the neighbour (2:8–16) and piety 1:27; 2:21f) which have to be exercised by the christian, that is, by the one who has already been justified in the pauline sense. Finally, the 'faith which justifies' means for Paul the commitment of the whole man to God wherein is contained also the acceptance of the moral requirements of the gospel; it is a faith which is effective through love in the one justified (Gal 5:6). That faith, which James opposes to works, on the other hand, is a purely theoretical faith, a speculative and doctrinal hypothesis which has no further influence on life and which is, in fact, a 'dead' faith (Jas 2:17, 26), similar to the sterile belief of the evil spirits (2:19). Objectively, therefore, James and Paul take their stand on the same ground from the doctrinal point of view. This means that the arguments of James cannot in any way be taken as a polemic directed against Paul; they were probably directed against a falsely conceived paulinism of some kind which, in the interests of a certain libertinism, rejected the necessity of moral conduct for christians, and for this purpose made use of certain ways of speaking found in Paul's preaching. Paul himself had more than once to issue warnings against attaching such false meanings to his teaching (Rom 3:8; 6:1, 15; cf also 2 Pet 3:16).

Bibliography: ↗ righteousness. See also B. Bartmann, *St. Paulus und St. Jacobus über die Rechtfertigung*, Freiburg 1897; E. Tobac, *Le Problème de la justification dans Saint Paul*, Louvain 1908 (new impression, Gembloux 1941); M.-J. Lagrange, *Saint Paul. Épître aux Romains—Études Bibliques*, Paris 1922[3], 119–41; H. D. Wendland, *Die Mitte der paulinischen Botschaft Die Rechtfertigungslehre des Paulus im Zusammenhang seiner Theologie*, Göttingen 1935; W. Mundle, *Der Glaubensbegriff des Paulus*, Leipzig 1932; Meinertz I, 237–42; C. Haufe, *Die sittliche Rechtfertigungslehre des Paulus*, Halle 1957; P. Bläser, *Rechtfertigungsglaube bei Luther*, Münster 1953; E. Lohse, 'Glaube und Werke',

ZNW 48 (1957), 1–22; E. Käsemann, 'Zum Verständnis von Röm 3:24–6', *ZNW* 43 (1950/51), 150–54; W. G. Kümmel, '*paresis und endeixis*', *ZTK* 49 (1952), 16off; S. Schulz, 'Zur Rechtfertigung aus Gnaden in Qumran und bei Paulus', *ZTK* 56 (1959), 155–85; F. Lau, *Paulus—Augustinus—Luther*, Berlin 1961; P. Bergauer, *Der Jakobusbrief bei Augustinus und die damit verbundenen Probleme der Rechtfertigungslehre*, Vienna 1962; V. Vajta, *Gelebte Rechtfertigung*, Göttingen 1963; O. Modalsli, *Das Gericht nach den Werken*, Göttingen 1963; E. Wilkens (ed.), *Helsinki 1963: Beiträge zum theologischen Gespräch des Lutherischen Weltbundes*, Berlin–Hamburg 1964; *Rechtfertigung heute*, Stuttgart 1965; K. Kertelge, *Rechtfertigung bei Paulus*; *T. F. Torrance, 'Justification: Its Radical Nature and Place in Reformed Doctrine and Life', *Christianity Divided*, ed. D. J. Callahan, H. O. Obermann, and D. J. O'Hanlon, New York 1961 and London 1962, 283–305; *H. Küng, 'Justification and Sanctification according to the New Testament', *Christianity Divided* (op. cit.), 309–35; *H. Küng, *Justification*, London and New York 1964.

Peter Bläser

Kingdom of God

We usually translate the central concept of the preaching of Jesus as the *kingdom of God* but it might be better to use the expression ↗ *kingship* or *the kingly rule of God* according to the Hebrew–Aramaic substratum of the expression, since *kingdom of God* corresponds more or less closely only to some metaphorical expressions (for example, 'to enter into the kingdom') referring to the final cosmic rule of God at the end of the world, whereas practically always the reference is to the kingly power of God and the exercise of this power. This concept has a long and rich history going far back into the Old Testament but reaches its climax in the message of Jesus and, later still, undergoes certain further developments.

The expression 'the kingdom of Heaven', which is used only by Matthew (thirty-three times), involves a paraphrase of the divine name and has the same meaning as 'the kingdom of God'. All too often in today's common usage is found a refined and false use of the term, a use which is in urgent need of reconsideration and revision on the basis of the statements found in the New Testament. It is therefore worth our while to try to grasp the thought of Jesus against the background of the Old Testament, comparing it with ideas then in common currency, basing our study on the traditions about Jesus as contained in the gospels. We shall also have to study the change which takes place in the preaching of the early church, the passage from the Jesus who preaches to the Jesus who is preached, and therefore the connection between kingdom of God and ↗ church.

A. *The Old Testament beginnings.* 1. *God's rule over Israel and the world.* Although it is disputed by competent scholars whether God was known and honoured under the title of king before the establishment of the political monarchy over undivided Israel, this *concept* at least must have been present right from the time of the wandering in the wilderness when God led his people as their leader and shepherd (see, for example, the 'Song of the Sea of Reeds': Ex 15:11–13, 18), overcame their enemies (see the Oracles of Balaam, Num 23:21f; 24:8), brought together the tribes (see Deut 33:5), remained in their midst and instructed them (see Ex 33:7–11). In the time of the judges, the fact of God being the only real ruler was so strongly experienced that Gideon the Judge refused the hereditary position of ruler on account of the unique sovereignty of God (Judg 8:23). Later on we find Samuel the seer indignant over the people's demand for an earthly king (1 Sam 8:6; 12:12). After the establishment of the political ↗ kingship, the king in Israel never appears as the incarnation of the god as in Egypt and Babylon where the king was divinised; he is always represented only as the vice-regent of God. Yahweh accepts the king anointed on Sion as his son (2 Sam 7:14; see Ps 2:7; 89:27f). According to the view of the Chronicler, the throne in Jerusalem is 'the royal throne of Yahweh over Israel' (1 Chron 28:5; 29:23; 2 Chron 9:8). In the temple of Solomon, the Ark of the Covenant was regarded as the throne upon which God sat (1 Kings 8:6f).

The *kingship of God* is not, however, limited to the people of the covenant. Since God is enthroned in the sanctuary in Jerusalem, the prophet Isaiah sees 'Yahweh of the hosts' on his heavenly throne, surrounded by the Seraphim who praise him as the Lord of heaven and earth (Is 6:3, 5). Yahweh as God of heaven and king of the world is not for Israel a figure taken from a mythological background but the result of her monotheism and her belief in creation. This mighty figure of the eternal, omnipotent lord of all confronts us in various poetical descriptions (Job 38; Ps 104), in prayer and in song (1 Chron 29:11; Ps 29; 74:12–17; 145). Jesus also speaks of him when admonishing his hearers to fear God: heaven is his throne, the earth is his footstool, Jerusalem is the city of the great king (Mt 5:34f).

In spite of this, the pious worshipper

in the temple was able to achieve an intimate personal relationship with this mighty ruler of the world who was, at the same time, the covenant God of his people (Ps 74:12; 103:17–22) and, full of trust, addressed him as 'my king and my God' (Ps 5:2; 44:4; 68:24; 84:4; 145:1).

A certain conviction was bound to grow up at length that Yahweh was king also of other peoples outside of Israel, no matter how strong and uncoercable they appeared to be. This would spring from both aspects of *the idea of kingship: the protective rule of God over his people and his universal rule.* Already in Amos Yahweh appears as the ruler of history, lord of the Philistines and Aramaeans (Amos 9:7). The great prophets, who reflect a refined monotheistic concept of God, witness to his absolute supremacy as ruler even when they do not use the title 'king' (possibly on account of their criticism against the political Israelite monarchy). 'Who would not fear thee, O King of the nations? For this is thy due; for among all the wise ones of the nations and in all their kingdoms there is none like thee!' (Jer 10:7; see also Is 40:12–25). Certainly this kingship of God over the nations is not yet so explicit; but this is also the object of a hope full of promise for the last age of salvation as can be seen in the small 'Isaian Apocalypse' (Is 24–7), in the second part of the Book of Isaiah (41:21; 44:6; 52:7–10; 6off) and in the more recent prophets (Obad 21; Zech 14:9, 16f; Mal 1:14). (See also under 3).

2. *The cultic kingdom of God.* Among the cultic hymns which praise the kingship of Yahweh there is a group of psalms which, on account of the acclamation: 'Yahweh is king!' (or, 'has been proclaimed king!'), are more often than not referred to as 'Psalms of accession to the throne' (Ps 47; 93; 96–9). Several scholars—in particular S. Mowinckel and the so-called 'Uppsala School'—postulate the existence of a special festival, that of the accession of Yahweh, to correspond with these psalms, one which would be related in some way to the Babylonian New Year festival. Others, however, dispute the existence of this festival, or prefer to speak of a 'royal festival of Sion' which was the occasion of a procession which represented the entry of Yahweh into Sion commemorating the transference of the Ark (see 2 Sam 6:15; 7; 1 Kings 8:1–13). This is the theory of H. J. Kraus. This question must remain uncertain, but at any rate the kingship of Yahweh must have been represented and publicly manifested in some special way in the liturgy and in the temple. Ps 24:7–10; 68:25–30 describe God's royal entry into the sanctuary and attach to this event the element of remembrance, hope and supplication. In liturgy the past is made present, the present moment of the divine sovereignty the future completion of which in the kingdom of God is seized on as an object of lively hope. The 'enthronement psalms' unite the themes of the divine sovereignty in the world over all creation and mankind, the kingly rule of God over Israel in the present and throughout its history, and the final completion of his rule in the latter days manifested in judgement and salvation. This represents the climax of the whole idea of *basileia* (kingship) in the Old Testament.

3. *The eschatological kingdom of God.*

The kingdom of God as an eschatological reality stands out more clearly in the announcement of salvation of the prophets than in the liturgy. The less they dared to hope for a political resurrection brought about by their own efforts after one or other of the national catastrophes that struck Israel, catastrophes which were seen as the judgement of God on his people unfaithful to the covenant, the stronger grew the expectation of a divine intervention. God himself would finally set up a kingdom of universal peace in which he would reunite the tribes of Israel, hand over the rule to them in accordance with his promises and subject the pagan nations to them. Thus Micah, speaking of the catastrophic end of the northern kingdom, also threatens Jerusalem with destruction (3:12) but prophesies that Yahweh would once again be king on the mountain of Sion (4:7). Very ancient representations of the messianic Shepherd–King keep on recurring (see 2:12f; 7:14f) and are used to describe with lively colours the last age. Isaiah describes the future pilgrimage of the nations to the Mountain of God (2:1–4) from which Yahweh rules the peoples and promulgates his doctrine—an eschatological figure this, which preserves its vitality right down to New Testament times (see Mt 8:11f).

The rest of creation also has a share in the blessings of the time of salvation. The peace of paradise will be brought back (Is 11:6–9), and, in general, this kingdom of God fulfilled in the last age takes on universal characteristics even though Israel has always the place of honour. It also has cosmic dimensions and a clearly religious and moral character—salvation and peace and the law of God established as the basis of the world order.

In a new and highly individual way Deutero–Isaiah describes the kingly manifestation of God (40:5) and takes on the role of a real proclaimer of his eschatological kingdom. God comes borne along on the royal way (40:3f) and reveals his kingly majesty (43:15; 44:6). The good news proclaimed by Jesus attaches itself directly to the joyful message of the herald who hurried on ahead to announce that God is assuming royal power (Is 52:7; cf Mk 1:15). In addition, the cosmic dimensions and the religious profundity of the presentation of this eschatological kingdom in Deutero–Isaiah prepare the way for the message of Jesus. In the jubilation caused by the redemption of Israel all creation will take part (42:10; 49:13); all flesh will see the salvation of God (40:5); the nations will do him homage (45:14–17); the temple will be a house of prayer for all the nations (56:7; see also Mk 11:17). There is only one element which is wholly absent here: that a descendant of David will be the instrument by which God will bring his kingdom into existence. This ancient expectation lived on in another line of the prophetic movement which is evidenced in Amos 9:11f; Hos 1:10f; Is 7:14–16; 9:6; 11:1; Mic 5:1–5; Jer 23:1–5; 30:9; Ezek 34:23f; 37:24f; Zech 9:9f. The decisive fact, however, is that Jesus attached his teaching firmly to the promises of an eschatological kingdom of God found in the prophets. This thought, and this alone, must be seen as the object of his proclamation of the *basileia*.

B. *The influence of views current in late judaism.* 1. *The expectation of a messianic kingdom of Israel.* The eschatological hopes of Israel at the time of Jesus were very much alive externally but there is no uniformity. There is, in the first place, less mention of the royal sovereignty of God than we might expect. The most common form these hopes take can be gathered from the Psalms of Solomon (first century BC) especially 17:23–51: the Messiah, son of David, will overthrow the foreign oppressors, purify Jerusalem from the heathen, gather Israel together and rule over it in such a way that it will live in justice and holiness. The pagan nations will come from afar to look upon the glory of God in Jerusalem. God rules on earth through his Anointed Ones but 'the Lord himself is our king for ever and ever'. This is a representation which is reflected in the gospels where it appears however as a popular belief of that time. But it is found also—with many variations—in the Apocryphal writings (Jub 1:17f, 28; 23:26–31 [here without mention of the Messiah]; Enoch [Eth] 89f; Test Jud 22:2f; 24:5; Bar [Syr] 72:2–6; 4 Ezra 12:32; 13:35–50; Sib III, 47ff, 808 etc), in ancient Jewish prayers (the Eighteen Petitions, the Qaddish, the ᶜ*Alenu*: see SB I, 178) and the rabbinical theology of the learned classes—although there is here a different view of the rule of God (see under 2). In many circles, especially among the Zealots, this national expectation had been elaborated into a political concept and a programme of action: that the messianic kingdom be imposed in open opposition to the Romans by means of an armed rising in which, it was hoped, God would take a decisive part (cf also the War Scroll from Qumran). Not only did Jesus dissociate himself completely from these active political groups but he came out against this religious–national expectation in general, at least insofar as it was understood in relation to a kingdom of this world which included and gave preference to all Israelites.

2. *The rabbinical teaching of a kingdom of God at present hidden but to be revealed in the future.* The rabbis developed a very broad concept of the kingdom of God which included also the idea of his world-rule. Although its supernatural nature was strongly emphasised, God's kingdom is nevertheless active in the world and in history and in particular among the people of the Covenant. As regards the manifestation of its earthly power, this kingdom of God has its periods of triumph and of failure. Thus the generation which lived at the time of the flood 'rejected' the commandments of God and threw off his yoke (Enoch [Slav] 34:1). At that time God was in effect considered as king only over the heavens, but 'Abraham made him king over the heaven and the earth' (Sifre on Deut 32:10 §313). In Egypt and on Sinai Israel accepted for itself the Kingdom of God, but when they sinned 'the Kingdom was taken from them and given to the nations of the world . . . but tomorrow when they will do penance, he will take it back from the nations of the world and give it to Israel again' (Midrash on Esther 1:2)—hence the necessity of penance, of keeping the law, observing the sabbath etc. 'To take the yoke of the Kingdom of Heaven upon oneself' signified to recognise God as the one true God and to accept the Torah; it

was then used as a formulaic expression for the recitation of the Shema ('Hear, O Israel!') which became the daily expression of the will of God in this respect. Jesus himself never speaks of such a hidden kingdom to which man subjects himself through observance of the *law*. His *concept of the basileia* overlaps rather with what the rabbis refer to as *the future age, the time of salvation, the fullness of salvation*. But Jesus threw new light upon and gave new weight to this eschatological reality.

3. *The apocalyptic expectation of a cosmic and universal kingdom of God which would suddenly appear.* There emerges in the apocalyptic literature a special element which can be detected elsewhere only in a very obscure and partial form: these writers look forward to a future world which will be quite different and in which the conditions obtaining in the previous, earthly existence will be either removed or profoundly modified; they see the future kingdom of heaven as coming about through a wonderful intervention of God which will take place after a period of most bitter tribulations. The prototype of this representation is found in the Book of Daniel with its different visions—especially the images of the world empires and the kingdom of God in chapters 2 and 7. It is well represented also in the parables of the Book of Enoch (Enoch [Eth] 37–71), in which we find also that the heavenly, pre-existent 'Son of Man' takes over the role of the ruler who brings salvation. There are several aspects which Jesus will take over and make use of in his eschatological message: the sudden 'appearance' of the kingdom of God established over the whole of creation depending solely upon the will and the power of God (AssMos 10:1, 7; see also Enoch [Eth] 1:3f); the final catastrophe of the earth which will take all by surprise together with the unheralded judgement (Enoch [Eth] 94:6–11; 97: 2–5; etc; 4 Ezra 11:44ff; Sib III, 670ff); the severe and exclusively moral criterion by which each one will be judged (4 Ezra 7:33ff; Sib IV, 40–46); the possibility of salvation extended also to the pagans (Enoch [Eth] 48:4); the exaltation and happiness of the just and the chosen ones (Enoch [Eth] 58:3f; 62:15f; Enoch [Slav] 65:8ff; Bar [Syr] 51; see also Wis 3:6–8). Side by side with these, however, there are other typical 'apocalyptic' desires and points of view which Jesus rejected: claims to secret knowledge, calculating in advance the time of the end on the basis of various signs, juggling with numbers, fantastic descriptions of the tribulations of the last age, visionary journeys to heaven, revelations about different heavens and hell, descriptions of paradise, etc. Jesus, therefore, took up a position of opposition to and clearly dissociated himself from certain ideas which were current among his contemporaries; he seized on the one point of the expectation of the eschatological kingdom of God but purified it of every trace of purely human thinking.

C. *The proclamation of Jesus.* 1. *The basic message.* What is peculiar to the message of Jesus about the *basileia* or kingdom is that he announces the eschatological kingdom of God as something close and even imminent, a reality the existence of which can already be detected and which is already active, something which brings salvation and which forces those who hear the message to come to a decision. All this is mysteriously bound up with his person and his mission. God has brought into existence a new reality through him (Mk 2:21f and parallels; Lk 16:16; see also Mt 11:12f), in him the Old Testament prophecies are fulfilled (Lk 7:22f = Mt 11:4ff; Lk 4:18ff) the eschatological era of salvation has broken in (Mk 1:15). The destruction of the sovereign rule of the devil and the other demons (Lk 11:20 = Mt 12:28; see also Mk 3:27 and parallels; Lk 10:18), the preaching of salvation, forgiveness of sins and healings—these all are signs that the rule of God is now present; not present certainly in power and glory, nor manifesting itself as cosmic event, but implicit in the activity of the hidden Messiah which reveals itself only to the eyes and the ears of those who believe (Lk 10:23f) but which remains a stumbling-block for those who do not believe (see Mt 11:6). This presence of the rule of God in the person, the word and activity of Jesus is the 'mystery' (Mk 4:11) which finds its explanation in the decree of God. The rule of God announced by Jesus is God's offer of salvation now that the last hour has come (cf Lk 12:56) containing a real possibility, but the *only* possibility, of sharing in God's eschatological kingdom which is imminent. It is a reality which is *purely religious and universal* since it offers to all men who have been converted and who believe (Mk 1:15) the mercy of God, at the same time promising them perfect salvation.

2. *The rule of God in the future and the present.* Jesus, then, announces the eschatological rule of God but with a peculiar twofold application: as a future event and at the same time as a present reality. The problem arising out of this has occasioned the most diversified answers the most important of which we can summarise more or less as follows: a. *consequent eschatology*: Jesus did not proclaim the kingdom of God as present but as coming in the near future, either during his earthly ministry or shortly after his death (J. Weiss, A. Schweitzer, M. Werner, E. Grässer, and others); b. *realised eschatology*: The kingdom of God has already come in its fullness in Jesus and his ministry; all that remains is for each one to make the decision for or against (C. H. Dodd, and various anglican exegetes); c. *anticipated eschatology*: The kingdom of God is already active in the present with the coming of Jesus but presents itself to man only under symbols and in an anticipatory manner; its real coming is still in the future; d. *understood in a progressive sense*: The kingdom of God is already really present and active in the words and the activity of Jesus, but has to undergo a progressive development until we come to the final stage. In this process of becoming it is generally identified with the church (this is a theory formerly popular among catholics); e. *the dialectical view*: According to this view, we can with equal justification speak of the kingdom of God as present *and* future. The dialectic of 'already' and 'not yet' is not the product of chance; it results in two ways of looking at the one and the same reality of the kingdom of God (this theory assumes various forms, and is defended by—

among others—catholic scholars such as R. Grosche and F. M. Braun).

The first two theories—(a) and (b)—are one-sided and do not do justice to the texts; the third, (c), runs the risk of underestimating the presence of salvation in Jesus; the fourth, (d), is right in seeing the beginning and the presence of the eschatological kingdom of God in the person and ministry of Jesus, but does not avoid the risk of inserting the kingdom into the innerworldly historical process thus understanding it falsely as a merely this-worldly institution; the last theory, (e), recognises correctly the element of tension, but fails to explain this tension within the thought-categories of the bible. This tension should rather be explained on the basis of the history of salvation directed to a final end. This way of viewing it sees the last (eschatological) age as having a beginning and an end, the beginning of its fulfilment and its final consummation. The interim or penultimate period (the *vorletzte Zeit* of O. Cullmann) is truly part of the time of salvation, and yet salvation has not yet been completely revealed. It is the time of the ingathering of the chosen ones, time of trial and of struggle for those who are saved, time of the church and its activity in furtherance of the coming perfected kingdom of God. *This dynamic manner of viewing the kingdom in the context of sacred history*, therefore considers the future event and the present reality as closely related together: *since the kingdom of God with all its salvific power is present in Jesus and his ministry its complete and perfect revelation in the future is already assured. But this fulfilment is as yet an object of hope and the working out of salvation in this present time is but a suggestion, a beginning or a sign and anticipation of what is to come.*

The justification of this fundamental interpretation with reference to the texts can only be briefly hinted at here. Most of the proof-texts have to do with the perfected kingdom of God, the future kingdom of glory as, for example, expressions such as 'to enter into the kingdom' (Mt 5:20; 7:21; 18:3 and parallels; 19:23f and parallels; 21:31; 22:12; 23:13; 25:10, 21, 23; Mk 9:47; Jn 3:5), 'the heirs of the kingdom' (Mt 25:34; see also 5:5), the prayer for the coming of the kingdom (Mt 6:10), the figure of the eschatological meal (Mk 14:25 and parallels; Lk 22:30), and in particular the representations of the marriage feast and the guests invited to the banquet (Mt 8:11f; 22:2–10, 11–13; 25:1–12; Lk 14:16–24). There are also the expressions about ruling with Christ in the kingdom (Lk 22:30; see also Mt 19:28; 20:23) and other ways of representing the eschatological redemption and ensuing happiness (Mt 5:3–10, 19; 13:43; Lk 12:32, 37).

The expressions which speak of the kingdom as a present reality are not nearly so numerous (the clearest example is Lk 11:20 = Mt 12:28) and are more often than not of uncertain interpretation (Lk 16:16; cf Mt 11:12f; Lk 7:28 = Mt 11:11; Lk 17:21). But if we take into consideration the texts in which Jesus speaks of his own person as identical with the inbreaking of the kingdom of God in the present together with others in which he speaks of salvation being present in his ministry as a reality which can be experienced (Lk 7:22f = Mt 11:4f; Lk 10:23f = Mt 13:16f; Lk 11:30f = Mt 12:41f; Lk

4:18ff; 10:18; 19:9), then the number greatly increases. Moreover, in the supposition that Jesus wished to maintain his 'messianic secret' it is understandable that he would not reveal 'the mystery of the Kingdom of God' (Mk 4:11) to everybody. It is in this context that we can best understand the important but very disputed parables inculcating watchfulness, that is, the parables of the sower (Mk 4:3–9 and parallels), the seed growing by itself (Mk 4:26–9), the mustard seed and the leaven (Lk 13:18–21 and parallels), and the wheat and the cockle (Mt 13:24–30). The parable of the fishnet (Mt 13:47–50) should not be considered in this connection. Harvest and full maturity were for Christ's hearers familiar figures of the eschatological kingdom; but Jesus spoke also of a preliminary sowing, an unobtrusive beginning, and this certainly referred to the fact that the kingdom of God was already present and operative in his person (indicated by the sower?). He addresses his teaching to those who will understand having already believed. In spite of all opposition and setbacks the harvest time comes, the time of glorious fulfilment, just as certainly as the reaping follows the sowing, the fruit the seed, the grown bush the one grain of seed. It is this evident contrast that Jesus emphasises rather than the organic development that lies between the two extremes. He does not wish to illustrate a process immanent in history but rather the wonderful action of God (the seed growing by itself, for example), not the extensive and intensive 'spreading of the kingdom of God on earth' but rather the certainty of fulfilment (the mustard seed and the leaven).

How will the future *basileia* appear? The primitive church understood Jesus in the sense that he himself would bring in the kingdom as the ↗ 'Son of Man' coming with power (see Mk 9:1 with Mt 16:28). Taking the words of Jesus which have come down to us on this subject we must admit that we are led to the same conclusion, despite the objections raised by some critics, and admitting that not every logion of Jesus is now accessible to us in its original form. This view is powerfully reinforced by the saying in Mk 8:38 = Lk 9:26 with its parallel form preserved in Lk 12:9 = Mt 10:33 and by the public statement of Jesus before the High Council in Mk 14:62 and parallels; but also by the eschatological aspect of the last supper in Mk 14:25 and parallels, taken in conjunction with the tradition preserved in Luke 22:16, 18 and 22:29f. Jesus saw the future kingdom as coming in only as a result of his atoning death, as the institution of the eucharist in particular clearly shows and saw himself not only as the ↗ servant of the Lord who obediently accepts his death but also as the future glorified ↗ Son of Man.

As to the question *when* the definitive kingdom of God would come, what Jesus really thought about this is a hotly disputed problem and one of great importance. It is certain that he proclaimed the *basileia* with prophetic insistence as an imminent reality; but does not perhaps this basic characteristic of his proclamation belong to the category of prophetic—eschatological preaching the purpose of which is to call men to a decision and arm them against the future? We have to consider over against the difficult *texts which refer to an expectation of an imminent kingdom* and which would appear to contain a reference to a limit within the lifetime of the generation then living (Mk 9:1 and parallels; 13:30 and parallels; Mt 10:23), some other texts which reject any attempt to calculate the time (Lk 17:20) and reserve the knowledge of the fixed time to the Father (Mk 13:32 and parallels). Is not the early church itself the best interpreter here which, in spite of the keen expectation of a proximate advent of the kingdom, yet remained clearly conscious of the fact that the hour was unknown? (See 1 Thess 5:1–11.) This problem can only be dealt with in a wider context, but at any rate the whole question should not blind us to the fact that the decisive moment of the coming of the kingdom has already taken place and that its final manifestation remains hidden, that it is already the time of salvation although we still have to wait for the approach of its complete fulfilment.

3. *The kingdom of God and the church.* In view of the 'interim period' between the first inbreaking of the kingdom of God with the preaching and salvific activity of Jesus and its appearance in power at the end of this aion, Jesus set up his redeemed community (↗ church) which takes the place of Israel, the old people of God, after they had rejected the Messiah (see Mt 16:18f and the 'new covenant' in Lk 22:20 and parallels). She is not yet the perfected community which shares in the future kingdom but the multitude of those who are called to membership, those who are prepared or are preparing themselves for this participation. The *ekklēsia* (=assembly, church) is the gathering place of the *eklektoi* (=chosen, elect).

What is the relationship between the rule of God as now in existence and this community? Following on what we have said, we cannot conclude that they are identical, for the kingdom of God is not an earthly institution and organisation. At the same time, even after Jesus had left this earth the power of the kingdom of God remained active and it was not removed with him. The disciples of Christ undertake the work of preaching and receive the same powers that Christ had (see already in Lk 10:9–11, 17–19; then Mt 28:18–20); in particular the power of binding and loosing (Mt 16:19; 18:18; see also Jn 20:23) stands in immediate relationship with the present and the coming kingdom of God. Peter receives the keys of the kingdom of God, that is, the authority to decide who will enter into the future kingdom (Mt 16:19a; for the figure of the keys, see Mt 23:13). The power of ↗ 'binding and loosing', which includes not only doctrinal decisions but also acts which lead directly to salvation, above all the forgiveness of sins (see Jn 20:23), is given with divine authorisation ('in heaven' = as from God). Therefore Peter and with him the other apostles (Mt 18:18) receive the task and the authority, in the words of O. Cullmann, 'to lead God's people into the kingdom of the resurrection'; but this bestowing of a special power is also an expression and the outcome of a kingdom of God in the present, which continues even after Jesus had left this earth. In the celebration of the eucharist the community experiences the presence of its Lord himself, the power of his atoning death and the cultic anticipation of the eschatological table-fellowship. The members of the redeemed community do not, however, obtain from this any certain guarantee of a share in the future kingdom of God but must rather preserve themselves by moral endeavour (Mt 7:22f) and by perseverance and constancy in believing (Mk 13:13, 20–23). The church, in the sense of the new community of God which takes over the inheritance of the old, is the anticipation and preparation for the blessed community of God in the future kingdom, the place where those who are waiting and preparing for the kingdom of God for the most part gather.

Considered as *existing in the interim period*, between the beginning of the salvific action of God and the definitive conclusion, the church has a dual character: it belongs in its whole nature to the future aion while at the same time remaining part of the present. It is 'eschatological' from the point of view of its destiny, the powers which have been given to it and the divine sovereignty which is exercised in it as in Jesus and his mission. It is not, however, eschatological in the entirety of its appearance and elements. It should therefore not be spoken of as a modality or a temporary configuration of the kingdom of God; even to refer to it as an organ of God's rule or kingdom would be open to misunderstanding. The church certainly undertakes the proclamation of the kingdom of God and the salvation of those who have gone astray; but she is not the visible aspect of an earthly form of divine rule. The kingdom of God must not be allowed to lose its strictly supernatural and eschatological character; it becomes a 'cosmic kingdom' only at the end at the 'restoration of all things'

(Acts 3:21) in a new manner of existence which is impossible for us to imagine. By then the task and also the age of the church will have been accomplished and it will become part, once the wicked have been separated from it by the judgement, of the perfected, eternal community of the saved which is the kingdom of God. If the community formed by Jesus upon earth is referred to in Mt 13:41 as the 'kingdom of the Son of Man' (distinguished from the 'kingdom of the Father', v 43), this would be another example of a usage connected with the terminology current in the early church but would not be the same as the 'kingdom of God' as found in the other texts we have considered.

4. *The kingdom of God considered in its moral demands.* As we have already clearly implied, the kingdom of God is from start to finish the result of God's activity ('Saat und Tat Gottes', in the phrase of Rudolph Otto). Expressions such as 'building the Kingdom of God on earth', which are never met with in the New Testament, are the outcome of false ideas about what the kingdom of God is. Since, however, the kingdom of God as proclaimed now in this present age is first and foremost the offer of salvation on the part of God, the message of Jesus demands a response from its hearers in the form of ↗ conversion, that is, a complete turning away from anything opposed to God and a ceaseless endeavour to submit oneself to his will and to believe the Good News (Mk 1:15). Those, however, who truly 'seek after the kingdom of God' (Lk 12:31 and parallels) and are willing to give up everything for this treasure, this pearl of great price (see

465

Mt 13:44–6), must also fulfil the difficult conditions which Jesus has in the name of God laid down for all who are waiting for the kingdom of God (see the Sermon on the Mount, Mt 5–7; Lk 6:20–49), namely moral conduct based on the purest of intentions and perfection in action going so far as even to love one's enemies. This ethic of the kingdom, so difficult to grasp, with its radical demands, its uncompromising character and unworldliness is, from another point of view, summarised in the great commandment of love (Mk 12:28–31 and parallels) and can be discerned in its true nature also in the warnings against the demonic attraction of riches (see Mk 10:17–31; Lk 16) and power (Mk 10:42–5 and parallels). The searching after the kingdom of God and the struggle required to enter it is, however, crowned with success when, according to the graphic figure used by Jesus, one succeeds in entering through the 'narrow door' (Lk 13:24 and parallels) and thus becoming part of Jesus' company of disciples. This group was at first limited to the community of his disciples during his lifetime, but after Jesus had left this earth all believers were bound by these moral requirements in accordance with the circumstances of each once they have received their personal call. This could imply doing without earthly belongings, separation from home and family (Lk 14:26f, 33), acceptance of suffering and persecution for the sake of the name of Jesus (Mk 13:12f and parallels), denying oneself even to the point of giving up one's life (Mk 8:34–8 and parallels). Corresponding, however, to these almost superhuman demands, Jesus promises a

reward exceeding great (Mk 10:29f and parallels) and gives his assurance that the help of God's grace will be available to make up for human weakness (see Mk 10:26f; see also the assurance that prayers will be heard, Mt 7:7–11 and parallels; Mk 11:24; Lk 11:5–8; 18:2–8).

D. *The proclamation of the early church as the continuation of the message of Jesus.* 1. *From Jesus who proclaims the kingdom to the Christ of early christian preaching.* Seen from the point of view of the *basileia* concept, the proclamation of the early church offers at first sight a rather strange picture, insofar as the central idea in the preaching of Jesus does not figure largely in that of the apostles. True, the Acts of the Apostles speaks when the occasion offers of the preaching of the kingdom of God, but in a noticeably general and unemphatic way (8:12; 14:22; 19:8; 20:25; 28:23, 31). The same applies to the epistles (for Paul, see under 2). Nevertheless, this change in the centre of gravity in the preaching of the early church is, from the point of view of the history of salvation and revelation, only too easy to understand and was practically inevitable; the reason is that with the resurrection and exaltation of Jesus a new phase in the history of salvation has begun which has repercussions also for the concept of the *basileia*. God has given the Messiah the royal throne at his right hand (Acts 2:32–6; Phil 2:9–11), exalted him to be leader and saviour (Acts 5:31), and given him power as the Son of God (Acts 13:33; Rom 1:4). God exercises his rule which brings salvation in a new way by delegating it to the exalted Messiah, Jesus the *Kurios*, who through his death on the cross has overthrown the forces opposed to God finally and definitively, even if not in a final trial of strength before the whole world, and created for himself in his church a definite scope for his activity. It is now the church's duty to proclaim him in whom, after the redemptive event on Golgotha, all salvation for mankind is to be found (cf Acts 4:12); and just as in the present order the communication of salvation is bound up with Jesus the Messiah and Lord, so when we look into the future his glorious parousia occupies the forefront only when we think of it as leading into the perfected kingdom of God. This shift of emphasis over to Christ which we find in the preaching of the apostolic church is therefore no accident nor is it a dilution or an obscuring of the message of Jesus. It is, on the other hand, fully intelligible as a stage in the history of salvation and represents a further development in the forward progress of revelation.

2. *Kingdom of God, kingdom of Christ, and the church.* This now leads us to a distinction as regards the content of christian preaching and the terms which are used in connection with it. Since from the point of view of Jesus the coming kingdom of God was also *his* kingdom (see Lk 22:30) insofar as he would bring it about and he and his disciples would be assembled together in it, the early church can already in the interim period speak of a kingdom which belongs to him who has been exalted to the right hand of God and even speak of itself as being 'the kingdom of the Son of Man' (see Mt 13:41). This is the kind of wider usage which we find in Paul, if not always uniformly. For the most part, this great theologian

keeps to the old idea of the future eschatological kingdom of God especially in the characteristic expression 'to inherit the kingdom of God' (1 Cor 6:9f; 15:50; Gal 5:21) which, however, is changed in Eph 5:5 to 'having an inheritance in the kingdom of Christ and of God'. This future eschatological sense is also retained in 1 Thess 2:12; 2 Thess 1:5 and Col 4:11 (see also the reference to the future kingdom of Christ in 2 Tim 4:1). Apart from this, however, Paul also speaks of the present *basileia* of Christ, most clearly in Col 1:13, but see also Rom 14:17 and 1 Cor 4:20 where the reference is clearly to God's kingdom which is already *realised* in Christ. Christ has obtained after his resurrection the position of exalted Lord in heaven in which also christians on earth have a share once they have been wakened from sleep and brought to life through baptism (Col 2:12f; Eph 2:5f). God has transferred them to the kingdom of his beloved Son (Col 1:13) and made them sit with him in the heavenly places (Eph 2:6). This comes about through their being members of the 'body of Christ' which is the church, and which is therefore already a 'heavenly' entity (see L. Cerfaux). But the lordship of the exalted Christ does not just extend to the church, but concerns the whole cosmos even, if in a way which is as yet hidden and not fully active. The basis of Paul's great cosmic conception of the church can already be discerned in 1 Cor 15:24–8: after his resurrection Christ must rule until God subjects all enemies under his feet. The last enemy to be annihilated, at the resurrection of the dead, will be the power of death itself, and then Christ will give back the lordship to God the Father upon which 'God will be all in all'—an expression which refers to the consummation, the future kingdom. The cosmic lordship of Christ is described with glowing colours in the Letters of the Captivity, as for example in the great description of Phil 2:9–11 and especially in the Letters to the Colossians and Ephesians. On the cross Christ triumphed over the rebellious cosmic powers and principalities and made them take part in his triumphal procession into heaven (Col 2:15; Eph 4:8–10). God subjected them placing them under the feet of Christ his co-regent (Eph 1:20–22). The reconciliation of everything with God through Christ (Col 1:20) and the recapitulation of everything in Christ (Eph 1:10) is the final goal. Christ, therefore, has a double position of eminence: over the church and over the whole of creation (cf Col 1:18 with 2:10; Eph 1:22b–23 with 21–22a), which is, however, exercised in a different if not unconnected way. The kingship of God in Christ is made present in the church (see H. Schlier), the area where it is immediately active and which it benefits; but it also takes in the whole cosmos insofar as it holds down the hostile forces which have not been so reconciled. The church's part, therefore, is to proclaim and mediate salvation to mankind (see Eph 3:6–8), but also at the same time to show up the forces opposed to God in the world, for what they are, even though their power is illusory (see Eph 3:10)—a profound theology this, which would require further treatment in depth (see F. Mussner, H. Schlier, V. Warnach). It provides us with the raw materials to enable us to distinguish more carefully between the kingdom of God, the kingdom of Christ, and the church; between God's present rule which is realised in Christ and his future cosmic kingdom; between Christ's rule over the church and over the world; and, finally, between the earthly and heavenly character of the church, how it shares in the lordship of Christ and serves to prepare for his kingdom.

3. *The transcendent (heavenly) and coming (eschatological) kingdom.* The uncertainty in the use of terms, which grows out of the various points of view from which one can regard the idea of the *basileia*, shows up especially in the later writings of the New Testament. Paul in 2 Tim 4:18 hopes that the Lord will save him 'in his heavenly kingdom', referring to the heavenly region as the *basileia* of Christ in which Christ already at this moment sits enthroned in manifest glory (see Col 3:3f) and in which the apostle hopes to achieve, but only after his death, the direct and full association with Christ (2 Cor 5:8; Phil 1:23). This is a way of speaking which, although familiar to us nowadays, occurs very seldom in the New Testament (see also Lk 23:42, according to a probably secondary reading, 'when you come into your kingdom'). Rather exceptional, too, is the hope expressed in 2 Pet 1:11 of finding entry into the 'eternal kingdom' of Jesus Christ, that is, into his future, eternal kingdom (whether eternal in the sense of quality or duration is not clear). The eschatological kingdom which emerges at the end already now exists in heaven and is certainly, like all transcendent realities, like all that pertains to God, an eternal and durable entity. This

must have been the persuasion of the author of the Letter to the Hebrews; some day, whether after death or at the parousia is unimportant for this consideration, we shall receive this 'kingdom that cannot be shaken' (12:28).

Elsewhere, and in a context of different theological suppositions, the Christ of John's gospel explains to Pilate that his 'kingdom' is not of this world (Jn 18:36). Christ certainly pronounced these words conscious of his imminent exaltation and glorification which would give him power 'over all flesh' (see 17:1f). But also here in John (3:3, 5), as in Paul (and in Jas 2:5), there occurs the expression of the Jesus of the synoptics about 'inheriting the kingdom of God', and this concept of the eschatological kingdom comes through once again strongly in the Book of Revelation. Here the whole frightful eschatological event—the plagues, trials, and judgement of punishment—hasten towards the final episode which the heavenly community already sings in anticipation in its glorious hymns of triumph: 'The kingdom of our Lord and of his Messiah has come over the whole world; and he will reign for ever as king' (11:15; cf 11:17; 12:10; 19:6). What exactly is meant by 'the thousand years kingdom of Christ' (Rev 20:1–6; ↗ millenarianism) is not easy to determine, but the definitive kingdom of God over the whole world and in a world renewed (21:1–5) is described clearly and magnificently by the visionary with every colour and image which he had at his disposal. He describes it above all as Jerusalem come down from heaven (21:10–27), as a reality which, in the last analysis, is beyond the power of

words to describe, the consummation of all things and of all history, perfect salvation and the blessedness of the redeemed who with God 'reign as kings for ever' (22:5). Our way of speaking of this subject must be deeply indebted to this biblical usage we have been describing; but for the understanding of the kingdom of God in the present we must bear in mind those distinctions which have been suggested by Paul.

Bibliography: On the question as a whole: B. Bartmann, *Das Reich Gottes in der heiligen Schrift*, Münster 1912; J. Schmid, *Das Evangelium nach Markus*, Regensburg 1954[3], 31–9; Meinertz I, 27–146; P. van Imschoot, Haag 1412–18; J. Bonsirven, *Le Règne de Dieu*, Paris 1957; R. Schnackenburg, *God's Rule and Kingdom*, London and New York 1963 (with further bibliography); T. Blatter, *Macht und Herrschaft Gottes*, Fribourg 1962; P. Hoffmann, *HTG* II, 414–28. See also: A. von Gall, *Basileia tou theou*, Heidelberg 1926; G. Dalman, *The Words of Jesus*, Edinburgh 1902; G. von Rad, K. G. Kuhn, and K. L. Schmidt, *TDNT* I, 563–94 (with bibliography; =*BKW* VII); G. Lündstrom, *The Kingdom of God in the Teaching of Jesus*, Edinburgh and London 1963; R. Otto, *The Kingdom of God and the Son of Man*, London 1943; H. Ridderbos, *De komst van het Koninkrijk*, Kampen 1950; J. Héring, *Le royaume de Dieu et sa venue*, Paris 1959[2]; E. Fascher, 'Gottes Königtum im Urchristentum', *Numen* 4 (1957), 85–113; N. Perrin, *The Kingdom of God in the Teaching of Jesus*, London 1963; G. E. Ladd, *Jesus and the Kingdom*, London 1964.

On A: Eichrodt I, 329f etc; M. Noth, 'Gott, König, Volk im AT', *ZTK* 47 (1950), 157–91; M. Buber, *Königtum Gottes*, Heidelberg 1956[3]; A. Alt, *Gedanken über das Königtum Jahwes*, Munich 1953, 345–57; H. J. Kraus, *Die Königsherrschaft Gottes im AT*, Tübingen 1951; J. Bright, *The Kingdom of God*, New York 1953; J. de Fraine, *L'aspect religieuse de la royauté israélite*, Rome 1954; S. Mowinckel, *Zum israelitischen Neujahrsfest und zur Deutung der Thronbesteigungs-Psalmen*, Oslo 1952; S. Mowinckel, *He that Cometh*, Oxford 1956; H. Widengren, *Sakrales Königtum im AT und Judentum*, Stuttgart 1955 (with bibliography); H. Gross, *Weltherrschaft als religiöse Idee im AT*, Bonn 1953; H. Gross, *Die Idee des ewigen und allgemeinen Weltfriedens im alten Orient und im AT*, Trier 1956; V. Maag, 'Malkut Jhwe', *Congress*

Kingship

Volume, Oxford 1959 (*VT* Suppl. VII), 129–53;
L. Rost, *TLZ* 85 (1960), 721–4; W. Schmidt,
Königtum Gottes in Ugarit und Israel, Berlin 1961;
M. Hopkins, *God's Kingdom in the Old Testament*,
Winona (Minn.) 1963; J. Gray, 'The Kingship
of God in the Prophets and Psalms', *VT* 11
(1961), 1–29.
On B: Dalman, *The Words of Jesus* (see
above); W. Bousset and H. Gressmann, *Die
Religion des Judentums im späthellenistischen
Zeitalter*, Tübingen 1926³, 213–22; P. Volz,
*Die Eschatologie der jüdischen Gemeinde im ntl.
Zeitalter*, Tübingen 1934²; G. F. Moore,
Judaism I Cambridge 1927, 431–7; G. E. Ladd,
'The Kingdom of God in the Jewish Apocry-
phal Literature', *Bibliotheca Sacra* 109 (1952),
55–62, 164–74, and 318–31; and *Bibliotheca
Sacra* 110 (1953), 32–49.
On C: R. Grosche, *Reich Gottes und Kirche:
Pilgernde Kirche*, Freiburg 1938, 41–76; E.
Walter, *Das Kommen des Herrn* II, Freiburg 1947;
F. M. Braun, *Neues Licht auf die Kirche*, Ein-
siedeln 1946; V. Schurr, 'Reich Gottes in der
Verkündigung', *Paulus* 23 (1951), 16–32; J.
Theissing, *Die Lehre Jesu von der ewigen
Seligkeit*, Breslau 1940; Schnackenburg 3–10
and 95–100; Y. de Montcheuil, *Das Reich
Gottes und seine Forderungen*, Mainz 1961;
H. Schürmann, 'Das hermeneutische Haupt-
problem der Verkündigung Jesu', *Gott in Welt*,
ed. K. Rahner, Freiburg 1964, 579–607.
See also: W. Michaelis, *Täufer, Jesus,
Urgemeinde*, Gütersloh 1928; W. Michaelis,
Reich Gottes und Geist Gottes nach dem NT, Basle
1931(?); H. Windisch, 'Die Sprüche vom
Eingehen ins RG', *ZNW* 27 (1928), 163–92;
G. Gloege, *Reich Gottes und Kirche im NT*,
Gütersloh 1929; H. D. Wendland, *Die Eschat-
ologie des Reich Gottes bei Jesus*, Gütersloh 1931;
E. Sommerlath, 'Reich Gottes und Kirche',
ZST 16 (1940), 562–75; C. H. Dodd, *The
Parables of the Kingdom*, London 1936²; N. A.
Dahl, 'The Parables of Growth', *ST* 5 (1952),
132–66; J. Jeremias, *The Parables of Jesus*,
London 1954 (with bibliography); H. B.
Sharman, *Son of Man and Kingdom of God*, New
York 1944²; O. Cullmann, *Königsherrschaft
Christi und Kirche im NT*, Zürich 1946²; R.
Morgenthaler, *Kommendes Reich*, Zürich 1952;
W. G. Kümmel, *Verheissung und Erfüllung*,
Zürich 1953² (with bibliography); T. F.
Glasson, *His Appearing and His Kingdom*,
London 1953; R. H. Fuller, *The Mission and
Achievement of Jesus*, London 1954; H. Roberts,
Jesus and the Kingdom of God, London 1955;
M. Burrows, 'Thy Kingdom Come', *JBL* 74
(1955), 1–8; P. Vielhauer, 'Gottesreich und
Menschensohn in der Verkündigung Jesu',
Festschrift G. Dehn, Neukirchen 1957, 51–79;

J. A. T. Robinson, *Jesus and His Coming*,
London 1957; S. Aalen, '"Reign" and
"House" in the Kingdom of God in the
Gospels', *NTS* 8 (1961/2), 215–40; G. E.
Ladd, 'The Kingdom of God—Reign or
Realm?', *JBL* 81 (1962), 230–38; T. van der
Walt, *Die Koninkrijk van God-Nabij!*, Kampen
1962; E. Jüngel, *Paulus und Jesus*, Tübingen
1962, 87–215; N. Perrin, *The Kingdom of God
in the Teaching of Jesus* (op. cit.); G. Lundström,
The Kingdom of God in the Teaching of Jesus (op.
cit.); G. E. Ladd, *Jesus and the Kingdom* (op. cit.).
On D: J. Gewiess, *Die urapostolische Heils-
verkündung nach der Apostelgeschichte*, Breslau 1939,
99–106; A. Wikenhauser, 'Die Belehrung der
Apostel durch den Auferstandenen nach Apg.
1:3', *Vom Wort des Lebens* (Festschrift M.
Meinertz) Münster 1951, 105–13; A. Wikenhauser, *Die Kirche als der mystische Leib Christi
nach dem Apostel Paulus*, Münster 1940², 41–7;
L. Cerfaux, 'L'Eglise et le Règne de Dieu
d'après S. Paul', *ETL* 2 (1925), 181–98;
L. Cerfaux, 'La Théologie de l'Eglise suivant
S. Paul', Paris 1948², 293–8; H. Schlier and
V. Warnach, *Die Kirche im Epheserbrief*,
Münster 1949; F. Mussner, *Christus, das All und
die Kirche*, Trier 1955 (with bibliography);
V. Warnach, 'Kirche und Kosmos', *Enkainia*,
Düsseldorf 1956, 170–205; H. Schlier, 'Über
die Herrschaft Christi', *GL* 30 (1957), 246–57.
See also N. A. Dahl, *Das Volk Gottes*, Oslo 1941
(with bibliography); H. J. Westerink, *Het
Koninkrijk Gods bij Paulus*, Hilversum 1937
(dissertation); *Ein Buch von der Kirche* (Sammel-
werk), Göttingen 1951; A. Oepke, *Das neue
Gottesvolk in Schrifttum, bildender kunst und
Weltgestaltung*, Gütersloh 1950; R. Frick, *Die
Geschichte des Reich Gottes-Gedankes in der alten
Kirche bis zu Origenes und Augustin*, Giessen 1928;
E. Staehelin, *Die Verkündigung des Reich Gottes
in der Kirche Jesu Christi*, Basle 1951.

Rudolf Schnackenburg

Kingship

In view of the extraordinary importance
which has been attributed in recent
years to the phenomenon of kingship—
especially by those attached to the
Scandinavian school—it would appear
useful to set out the theories now current
on this subject followed by a brief

application to the question of the Israelite monarchy.

A. Some English scholars (the 'Myth and Ritual School'), and even more so some Scandinavian scholars (I. Engnell and G. Widengren, of the University of Uppsala) have attempted to expound something like a *pattern* of king-ideology, that is, *a common scheme of the monarchical institution in the Ancient Near East* (Mesopotamia, Egypt, Canaan including Phoenicia, etc). According to this fundamental scheme, usually called the 'divine kingship pattern', the king in the region of the Fertile Crescent must be considered under three aspects:

1. Considered in himself, the ruler must be taken as a divine being, that is to say, as a being who moves in the divine sphere. Hard pressed by some recent criticisms, the 'patternists' are drawn more and more to concede that the epithet 'divine' must be toned down and that it would be better to speak of 'sacral' kingship. It is in fact only in Egypt that the Pharaoh is really equated with the gods in a thorough-going way (that is, from the *static* point of view), whereas in Mesopotamia the divine character of the monarch shows itself rather in certain *transitory* acts of cult, eg, the *hieros gamos* (=sacred marriage).

2. The ruler appears as the representative of the gods, in particular of the national gods, that is, as he who 'makes them present' among their subjects. The kingly attributes, including all their prerogatives as legislators, judges, and wielders of arbitrary power, are merely different ways of sharing in the divine majesty of the gods. The king is the 'chosen' of the gods; the historical origin of the institution of monarchy has to be considered from the religious point of view and this theological interpretation has to be transposed into the stuff of real history.

3. The king exercises the function of bringer of salvation with respect to his subjects. The monarch is 'the channel through which the divine blessing flows to the people' (S. Mowinckel). All divine gifts are destined for him in the first place since he represents a 'corporate personality' incorporating in himself, as it were, all his subjects. What concerns the king concerns also his people: all salvation and righteousness, any military victory, is given to the people always through the ruler as the mediator. He is in truth the 'king of righteousness', the means of increasing the divine blessing, 'the prince of peace' who lavishes perfect happiness upon those who belong to him.

B. The *institution of monarchy* as it appears in the two kingdoms of Israel and Judah (above all in Judah) betrays certain peculiar characteristics which alter in a radical way the *pattern* described above. This alteration must be explained on the basis of the idea of 'the holy'. In bible lands this element of the 'divine' was not conceived of as so often elsewhere as an impersonal mana, a personification of the anonymous forces of nature, but rather as a personal, living God.

1. It follows from this that in Israel an even superficial divinisation of the monarch was out of the question. The Israelites were always keenly aware of the difference between the personal and therefore one God and the human king. Even if the divinity of the king is

471

understood as 'concentrated supernatural sacrality' we still have to bear in mind that the whole bible gives the greatest emphasis to the fact that the Lord of the covenant is radically different from the human personality of the ruler.

2. Nevertheless there exists a close bond between the human ruler and Yahweh, the national God. As a result of the investiture—even more so of the anointing—the king, chosen under the influence of the Spirit of Yahweh, is 'changed into another man' (1 Sam 10:6) and clothed with holiness and divine inviolability. Basically the Israelite king has a share in the eternal kingship of Yahweh and 'sits on the throne of Yahweh's kingship over Israel' (1 Chron 28:5). If it is true of any king of Israel that he represents the God of Israel (he is 'an angel of Yahweh': see 2 Sam 14:17), this will be true above all of David, the great king of Judah, and, 'on account of David', of those who succeed him 'for ever' (Ps 18:50; 45:6; 132:11). Among these successors it is the Davidic king *par excellence*, the messianic king, who will realise here on earth the theocratic ideal. Of no king can it be said so certainly as of the Messiah, *the* anointed king, that he rules in the name of Yahweh, since no king is nearer to the personal God than he is whom Isaiah refers to as the 'strong God', 'eternal father' and 'prince of peace' (Is 9:6).

3. The Old Testament often mentions the 'redeemer-king'. The ruler of Israel was celebrated as 'king of righteousness' who defended the rights of the poor (Ps 45:7; 72:1–4, 12). He brings 'salvation' on the battlefield, that is, military victory (1 Sam 8:20;

9:16; 2 Sam 3:18); there are some texts which even ascribe a military function to the Messiah (Ps 2:9). In a certain sense the Israelite king takes over one or other of the functions of the priesthood without, however, being a 'priest' in the strict sense of the word— that is, literally, he who offers the sacrifice. He has, however, a prominent position, acting practically as representative of God in liturgical functions. All kings 'offer' sacrifices, that is, they at least provide the material for sacrifice and receive the divine blessing before their subjects though indeed they receive it also *for* their subjects. Since the king is 'shepherd' of his own (2 Sam 5:2) he represents an essential element in the material and spiritual well-being of the people—he is rightly referred to in Lam 4:20 as 'the breath of our nostrils', that is, our very life. From this point of view the Messiah appears above all as the ideal king (Ps 72:7, 16; Ezek 34:23f; 37:24; Jer 23:5) and as vicegerent of the divine Shepherd. (↗ kingdom of God).

Bibliography: J. de Fraine, 'L'aspect religieux de la royauté israélite', *Analecta Biblica* 3 (Rome 1954: with bibliography); A. R. Johnson, *Sacral Kingship in Ancient Israel*, Cardiff 1955; G. Widengren, 'King and Covenant', *JSS* (1957), 1–32; S. H. Hooke (ed.), *Myth, Ritual and Kingship*, Oxford 1958; K. H. Bernardt, *Das Problem der altorientalischen Königsideologie im AT* (*VT* Suppl. VIII), Leiden 1961.

Jean de Fraine

Knowledge of God

A. *Knowledge of God in the Old Testament*. 1. In the pre-exilic prophets, 'to know God' means above all *a practical and active recognition of God, confession or gratitude.* Jeremiah expresses what was understood by this in a severe warning addressed to Jehoiakim (Jer 22:15f): 'Did not your father eat and drink, and do justice and righteousness? Then it was well with him. He judged the cause of the poor and needy; then it was well. Is not this to know me? says the Lord'. In the messianic age the 'knowledge of God' is the characteristic basic attitude which Yahweh himself kindles in the heart of his people (Jer 24:7; see also 31:33f). It is Yahweh himself who makes it possible for the heart of man to acknowledge him and, full of faith, live in dependence on him since the land is full of the knowledge of the Lord (Is 11:9; Hab 2:14).

In the way that Hosea uses the term there is not contained principally the idea of a knowledge of the propositions of faith and the law of Yahweh, that is, a knowledge *about* God (as A. W. Wolff maintains), but the basis of theological thinking is knowledge of God conceived as the core of true religious feeling (Hos 5:8–6:6). A study of the terms used in parallelism and as synonyms of knowledge shows that 'knowledge of God' is not meant to refer to a mere *act* of knowing—an act of a discursive or intuitive kind—but rather the subjective attitude of Israel to Yahweh, a spontaneous preoccupation with the interests of Yahweh and the moral demands which he makes. All of these terms belong to the field of practical piety: only those 'know' God who 'seek' Yahweh (Hos 6:3; 10:12; Is 58:2; Ps 9:10), who are prepared to 'accept conversion' (Hos 6:1; Jer 24:7), to 'show steadfast love' (Hos 6:6; 10:12; 2:19; Jer 9:23; 22:16; Mic 6:8) and

practise 'righteousness' (Hos 2:19; 10:12; Jer 9:23; 22:15).

When the prophets lament the lack of the knowledge of God, this practically amounts to *apostasy and idolatry* which bring on future evils and punishment. 'Their deeds do not permit them to return to their God for the spirit of harlotry is within them, and they know not the Lord' (Hos 5:4; see also Jer 2:8; 4:22). Those who 'know not Yahweh', who are 'faithless' (Hos 5:7) and 'apostate' (Is 1:2; Jer 2:8), are said to 'abandon' him (Hos 4:10; Is 1:4), 'forget' (Hos 4:6), 'disdain' (Is 1:4), and 'despise' him (1 Sam 2:12, 30). Those who 'deal crookedly' do not know him (Jer 2:8; Hos 4:1f; 5:4); they 'worship Baal' (Hos 2:13), 'sacrifice' to him (Hos 11:2), and 'prophesy' through him (Jer 2:8). They do not 'repent' of their error (Jer 8:6) and are not prepared to 'be converted' (Jer 8:5; Hos 11:5; 5:4). Moral decline is intimately connected with this absence of the knowledge of God.

2. The expression so characteristic of Ezekiel, 'know that I am Yahweh' (seventy-one times), occurring mostly at the end of oracles announcing judgement but also in those which announce salvation, shows without a doubt that the initiative within history of the God who permits himself to be known, that is, reveals himself, is anterior to any human 'knowledge of God'. The formula 'I am Yahweh' which implies this self-revelation, underlines the character of what happens in history seen as epiphany or theophany. If Yahweh annihilates the worship of idols (Ezek 6:6, 13) or allows the land and people to become sterile on account of the godlessness of all its inhabitants

473

(12:20; 15:8), Israel comes to know by personal experience how mighty God is in history. In the same way, judgement passed on the enemies of Israel is for her a convincing manifestation of her God, he who constantly leaves signs of his presence within history (see Ex 10:2) in order to reveal himself to his people. Disastrous on the other hand is the fearful experience and knowledge of Yahweh which falls to the lot of the heathen nations which oppose Israel (Ezek 25:7, 11, 14; 26:6; 28:22, 23; etc). Even though these enemies praise the might of their gods and despise the God of Israel, yet will they not escape the justice of Yahweh but will know and will be forced to recognise in the punishment meeted out to them the sanction of Yahweh.

In the prophetic preaching salvation and condemnation are closely connected as the outcome of divine judgement. In the historical books, unlike the prophets, the experience and knowledge of condemnation take second place to the experience of salvation. Through experience Israel comes to know her God in a continual process of salvation, assistance and deeds of mercy (Ex 6:7; 16:12; 29:45; Deut 4:35; 7:9; 2 Kings 5:15; etc). Israel's experience of the self-revelation of Yahweh in power to the heathens is also accompanied by the same feeling of being redeemed (1 Kings 20:13, 28).

It is not, however, just Yahweh's judgement issuing in punishment and saving interventions which is the source of the knowledge of God; the tradition of the people of God, that is, the history of Israel itself, brings man to the knowledge of God, of his will and his plans (2 Chron 13:5; Jos 2:9). The

actual fulfilment of a prophetic oracle was for them the divine seal on the prophetic message and at the same time a sign by means of which the supernatural mission of the prophets could be known (Zech 2:9, 11; 4:9; 6:15; 11:11; Ezek 17:21; 20:38; 33:33; etc). Since the observance of the sabbath was also considered a divine sign which required of Israel a confession of faith, this also constituted for the gentiles a means of knowing that Yahweh had chosen and sanctified Israel as his own people (Ex 31:13; Ezek 20:12, 20).

It is possible to experience in and through events the divine action inherent in the power of God; man is able to encounter the power of Yahweh which issues in salvation and punishment, is involved in this for weal or woe and, so aroused in his sentiments and will, is called to make a decision for or against. This encounter has an irresistible force and cannot be set aside. In Deut, to a greater extent than in Ezek, this 'knowledge' is accompanied by movements of the will leading to an acknowledgement of God. In the Psalms it is at times the divine answer to prayer which meets us rather than the direct action of God and it is this which makes it possible for the religious man to have certainty and knowledge of the God who is ever ready to help, a certainty and knowledge which are full of faith.

Bibliography: G. J. Botterweck, '*Gott erkennen*' *im Sprachgebrauch des AT*, Bonn 1951 (with bibliography); G. J. Botterweck, *WW* 14 (1951), 48–55; W. Zimmerli, *Erkenntnis Gottes nach dem Buche Ezekiel*, Zürich 1954; W. Zimmerli, *Mélanges bibliques* (Festschrift A. Robert), 1957, 154–64; H. W. Wolff, *ET* 12 (1952/3), 533–52 and *ET* 15 (1955), 426–31;

E. Baumann, *ET* 15 (1955), 416–25 (against Wolff); J. L. McKenzie, *JBL* 74 (1955), 22–7.

G. *Johannes Botterweck*

B. *Knowledge of God in the New Testament*. 1. *New Testament usage in this respect continues that of the Old Testament*. a. As in the Old Testament, '*to know God*' is understood as *an expression of genuine religious feeling*. It stands, therefore, for the acknowledgement of God and of his will (see Lk 19:42, 44; Rom 2:18; 1 Cor 1:21; 2 Cor 8:9; Gal 4:8f; 1 Thess 4:5; Heb 3:10). 'L'idée de connaître Dieu enveloppe toute la vie religieuse et morale' (Dupont p. 530). In exact correspondence with this, its opposite 'not to know God' means not to accept his message, not to submit oneself to his will and therefore to reject faith completely (see 1 Cor 15:34; Eph 4:18; 2 Tim 3:7; 1 Pet 1:14). The process of conversion can therefore be equated with coming 'to the knowledge of the truth' (see 1 Tim 2:4; 2 Tim 2:25; Heb 10:26 cf Col 3:10) exactly in the same way as it is expressed in the Old Testament.

b. In the New Testament, we meet the phrase which occurs so frequently in the Old Testament, and there particularly in Ezekiel, 'Know that I am Yahweh'. It occurs, however, in some characteristic transpositions: applied to God in Rev 2:23; applied to Christ in Jn 8:28 (see H. Zimmermann, *Das absolute 'Ich bin' als biblische Offenbarungsformel*, Bonn 1952 [dissertation]; 'Das absolute *ego eimi* als die ntl. Offenbarungsformel', *BZNW* 4 [1960], 54–69 and 266–76; and 'Das absolute 'Ich bin' in der Redeweise Jesu', *TTZ* 69 [1960], 1–20).

2. *That which is peculiar to the New Testament usage*. a. *Jesus*. The peculiar element in New Testament usage can be seen in the saying of Jesus in Mt 11:27 (=Lk 10:22), the so-called johannine logion in the synoptics: 'All things have been delivered to me by my Father; and no one knows the Son except the Father, and no one knows the Father except the Son and any one to whom the Son chooses to reveal him'. The first part of the verse—'All things have been delivered to me by my Father'—is explained by the saying on reciprocal knowledge which follows. Jesus is, in a unique sense, the revealer of the Father since he alone 'knows' the Father as the Father 'knows' him. Here 'to know' is used in the johannine sense to express the inner relationship which exists between Father and Son which Jesus had come to reveal and at the same time communicate to others.

b. *Paul*. There can be no doubt that Paul gives to the knowledge of a christian a place of considerable importance. This in spite of the fact that in 1 Cor 13:13 it is said of faith, hope and love that they 'remain', while in the same 'Canticle in praise of Love' *gnosis* is only a kind of stopgap which will be made void, unlike love which 'builds up'. Faith presupposes *gnosis*, and must of necessity be bound up with it (cf Eph 3:17ff; 4:13), in fact penetrating into the concept of love (1 Cor 8:1ff; 13:2ff). It remains, however, something given by the Spirit to the christian so that he may be able to perceive the gift of the grace of God (cf 1 Cor 2:13). As such, knowledge is freely associated in Paul with the idea of 'wisdom' (see Rom 11:33; 1 Cor 12:8; Col 1:9; 2:3)—in fact, *sophia* can even be used as a synonym for *gnōsis* (1 Cor 2:5ff). Knowledge as a gift of the Spirit makes possible the penetration of the divine mysteries; by means of it the invisible world of God is opened up to the christian while remaining closed to the man who remains on the purely natural level (*anthrōpos psukhikos*). It is reserved for the 'perfect' and represents in fact a higher level of faith (see 1 Cor 2:6–16). In 2 Cor 4:6 the apostle mentions the 'heart' as the human organ of this knowledge which comes into existence through the Spirit. In speaking in the same text of *phōtismos tēs gnōseōs* (lit. = light of the knowledge) he is probably thinking of baptism through which this new knowledge is communicated (see also Eph 1:18).

What does such knowledge consist in? As we have already indicated, it is essentially a 'knowledge of God' (2 Cor 4:6; 10:5; Col 1:9, 10; 2:2). This will also be the case when we come across 'knowledge' standing by itself (Rom 15:14; 1 Cor 1:5; 12:8; 2 Cor 2:14; 6:6; 8:7; 11:6; Phil 1:9) or the phrase 'knowledge of the truth' (see 1 Tim 2:4; 2:25; 2 Tim 3:7). Nevertheless, we find that 'the knowledge of the glory of God' has been shown forth 'in the face of Christ' (2 Cor 4:6), meaning that the revelation of God is made visible through Christ and in this way communicated to others. Hence one can speak also in a similar way of the 'knowledge of Christ' (Phil 3:8; Eph 4:13) since 'all the treasures of wisdom and knowledge are hidden' in him (Col 2:3). The expression 'the knowledge of Christ' refers at the same time to that which is given to man through Christ (see 1 Cor 2:13; cf 2 Cor 8:9; Eph 1:18; 3:19; Col 1:5f;

Philem 6). The object of this knowledge is an intimate association with Christ which finds its expression in ↗ love (see 2 Cor 13:5; Eph 3:19; Phil 3:8) since we find that 'to love God' can be equated with 'to be known by him' (1 Cor 8:3).

If knowledge is to lead to such a deep association with Christ and God, it must perforce manifest itself in the conduct of one's life. Hence the apostle prays that his christians may have knowledge which can lead to conduct making them 'worthy of the Lord' (cf Phil 1:9, 10). It follows from this that *gnōsis* can take its place in lists of virtues together with others which are recommended to christians (see 2 Cor 6:6).

The whole point of the function of an apostle is to lead as many men as possible to such knowledge. Hence Paul can say, using an image which we find he employs in 2 Cor 2:14, 15, that God spreads abroad through him 'the odour of knowledge' and even that he himself is 'the odour of Christ'.

c. *John*. In Johannine usage, the verb *ginōskein* is met with very often (about eighty times) but the noun *gnōsis* not at all. This corresponds exactly to the way in which *pisteuein* (= to believe; ↗ faith) is used.

The text of Jn 10:14, 'I am the good shepherd; I know my own and my own know me' shows that it is presupposed in the fourth gospel—just as it is in Mt 11:27—that 'to know' applies in the first place to the relation between Father and Son. This relation is expressed elsewhere in John by such phrases as: 'I and the Father are one' (10:30; cf 17:11), 'I am in the Father and the Father is in me' (14:10; cf 10:38; 17:21), or it finds expression in the verb *agapan* (= to love; see 3:35; 10:17). Understood in this way, the verb 'to know' refers to the loving association which exists between the Father and the Son in which the subject, the one knowing, is identified through the nature of the object, the one known: 'For as the Father has life in himself, so he has granted the Son also to have life in himself' (5:26).

Christ has been sent into the world to reveal and communicate this ↗ life to man: 'I came that they might have life, and have it more abundantly' (10:10). One enters into this life through knowledge, hence the conclusion can be drawn: 'This is eternal life, that they know thee, the only true God, and Jesus Christ whom thou has sent' (17:3). At the same time, Christ reveals and communicates, together with life, also 'knowledge', since there exists the same relationship between him and his disciples as there is between him and his Father: 'I know my own and my own know me, as the Father knows me and I know the Father' (10:14–15). Here 'to know' expresses that loving association between Christ and his own which, in its close uniting bond, can be compared only to the association between the Father and the Son and which is in fact based on and mysteriously hidden within that association (see 17:21ff; cf 14:20).

The object of knowledge is, moreover, identical with that of faith since in johannine usage 'to know' and 'to believe' belong closely together (↗ faith).

Since knowledge is an expression of a loving union with God, it must have its practical effect on the moral life of the christian. This is emphasised above all in 1 John. Keeping his commandments is precisely the means whereby one is certain that one knows him (1 Jn 2:3), for Christ is for the christian the type of moral conduct (1 Jn 2:6): 'If anyone keeps his word the love of God is truly perfected in him. In this way we know that we are in him' (1 Jn 2:5).

This is true in particular of the command to love one's neighbour, as explained in 1 John (see 2:7ff) but also in the gospel of John (see 13:35).

d. The origins of this special use of the verb *ginōskein* in the New Testament are disputed. Among recent commentators we might name scholars like E. Norden, R. Bultmann, R. Schnackenburg, and H. Schlier who defend the gnostic origin of this concept. According to the last named, the use of *gnōsis* would be an example of fighting the enemy (the Gnostics) with their own weapons and at the same time giving the word a new meaning. Here it is worth while recalling that *gnōsis* is a very diversified concept and one which, for the time that the New Testament was coming into existence, is very difficult to grasp. On the other hand, scholars like A. Schlatter, L. Cerfaux, and J. Dupont emphasise the derivation of the word in its peculiarly New Testament usage, from the usage of the Old Testament. Here we should note that the way in which Paul uses the noun *gnōsis* or John the verb *ginōskein* betray often enough a clear distinction from the use of the Hebrew verb *yādaᶜ* and its derivatives in the Old Testament.

Very carefully pondered is the position of Dodd (*The Interpretation of the Fourth Gospel*, 151–69). Dodd holds that the word comes from the Old Testament as regards its essential content, but through being translated into Greek it has taken on a hellenistic meaning—a process which can be followed in LXX in the case of *gnōsis* and *ginōskein*. The fact that such a hellenisation of the Old Testament idea of knowledge can be discerned in the Wisdom literature, in the apocrypha and, recently, also in the Qumran scrolls, is in agreement with this view. It is not possible, nevertheless, to speak in this case of *gnōsis* (see H. Schlier, *Der Brief an die Epheser*, 19 *n* 1) since the real 'gnostic' usage is in fact in marked contrast to this (see A. S. van der Woude, 'Die messianischen Vorstellungen der Gemeinde von Qumran': *Studia Semitica Neerlandica* 3 [Assen Neukirchen 1957], 11; Nötscher 38ff; see also the bibliography).

Bibliography: E. Norden, *Agnostos Theos, Theosophische Untersuchungen zur Formengeschichte religiöser Rede*, Darmstadt, 1956; F. Büchsel, *Der Geist im NT*, Gütersloh 1926, 323–30; A. Fridricksen, 'Gnosis: Et Bidrag til Belysning ave den Paulinske Terminologi og Erkjennelsesteori', *Festschrift E. Lehmann*, Lund 1927, 85–109; E. Prucker, *Gnōsis theou: Untersuchungen zur Bedeutung eines religiösen Begriffes beim Apostel Paulus und bei seiner Umwelt*, Würzburg 1937; J. Dupont, *Gnosis: La Connaissance religieuse dans les Epitres de Saint Paul*, Louvain and Paris 1949; R. Schnackenburg, *Die Johannesbriefe*, Freiburg 1953, 82–7; R. P. Casey, 'Gnosis, Gnosticism and the New Testament', *Festschrift C. H. Dodd*, Cambridge 1955, 52–80; Bo Reicke, 'Traces of Gnosticism in the Dead Sea Scrolls?', *NTS* 1 (1954), 137–41; W. Davies, 'Knowledge in the Dead Sea Scrolls and Matthew 11:25–30', *HTR* 46 (1953), 113–39; Nötscher 15–79; H. Schlier, *Der Brief an die Epheser*, Düsseldorf 1958[2]; C. H. Dodd, *The Interpretation of the Fourth Gospel*, Cambridge 1958[4], 151–69; L. Cerfaux, *DB(S)* III, 659–701; R. Bultmann, *TDNT* I, 689–719; Haag 594–9; P. van Imschoot, Haag 605–07; R. Schnackenburg, *LTK* III[2], 996–1000.

Heinrich *Zimmermann*

Lamb of God

In Jn 1:29, 36 Christ is designated as Lamb of God. Tradition understands this title in terms of the death of Jesus which he underwent for the sin of the world, of the paschal lamb, or in the spirit of Is 53:7 (see also Acts 8:32). There are other similar explanations which have been proposed in recent years. As against all this, however, we cannot avoid asking the question: how could John the Baptist have spoken about the death of Jesus right at the beginning of Jesus' public life? We have to distinguish between: 1. the meaning which the term had for the Baptist; and 2. what it meant at the end of the first century in the gospel of John.

1. The Aramaic *talya* can mean either 'servant' or 'lamb'. According to one view, the Baptist spoke of Jesus as the Servant. The text of his sermon would therefore have been taken from the Book of Consolation (Is 40ff). It is from this collection that he quotes when he designates himself as 'the voice which cries in the wilderness' (Is 40:3) and it is to this that he refers in Jn 1:34 where he confesses: 'I have seen and have borne witness that this is the Son of God' (compare Is 42:1: 'Behold my Servant whom I uphold, my chosen in whom my soul delights! I have put my spirit upon him that he may bring truth to the nations'). What led the Baptist on to acknowledge the identity of Jesus was the coming down of the Spirit (Jn 1:32f) in the same way that in Is 42:1 the Spirit is characteristic of the mission of the servant of the Lord (see Mk 1:10f = Is 42:1). John is therefore thinking not of the servant in the fourth Song of the Servant, but of

the servant of the Lord at the outset of his career as found in the first song in the same way that the baptism of Jesus inaugurates *his* career (↗ servant of the Lord).

The continuation—'who takes away the sins of the world'—according to this interpretation would be johannine (see 1 Jn 3:5) and would form, together with 1:29, a reinterpretation of the words of the Baptist, who, following on Is 42:1–4, would probably have gone on to speak about the Servant bringing to the nations his doctrine which was the truth—the idea of the knowledge of the law and wisdom as having power to atone for sins was a common theme in post-exilic judaism (Sir 24:22; Prov 9:6; Ps 119:11; see also 4 Ezra 9:31; Baruch [Syr] 48:24; TestLevi 18:9; Enoch 6:8 and 1 QS 4:20–23).

2. The expression 'taking away sin' can be paraphrased exactly on the basis of a reading of 1 Jn 3:5f; there is, in fact, an exact parallelism between 1 Jn 3:4–8 and Jn 8:31–47. The phrase 'to take away sin' corresponds there to 'to set free (from the power of Satan)', and it can be said that by means of 'the truth' (see Jn 15:3) Christ is 'the lamb of God that takes away the sin of the world': he blots out sin in that his word brings to mankind the truth, and with it the means to withstand the attack of the Evil One.

3. At the time of his baptism the death of Jesus could not have been foreseen, but he himself calls his death a baptism (Mk 10:38f; Lk 12:50) and his passion will be compared with the suffering of the servant of the Lord (Is 53). According to 1 Jn 5:6 he is the one who came not with water alone

but also with blood (see Ignatius, *Ep. Eph* 18:2). After the resurrection, the early church could understand the servant of the Lord of the baptism episode (Is 42:1) to be identical with the Suffering Servant of Is 53. To express this conviction more clearly *talya* (in the second of the two meanings) was translated as 'lamb' bringing to mind at the same time the paschal lamb (Jn 19:36 = Ex 12:46; Num 9:12). The whole of the redemptive work of Jesus accomplished through teaching and through suffering was summed up in the unique amalgamation of the images of servant and lamb (see also 1 Cor 5:7; 1 Pet 1:19; Heb 9:28). The Book of Revelation presents in two series of expressions, the lamb as slain (5:6ff and 13:8) and as victor and judge of his enemies (6:16f; 14:10; 17:14). Here we have an expression on the one hand of the permanent identity of the exalted Christ with the crucified and on the other hand of the certainty of the final overthrow of the world forces opposed to God.

Bibliography: J. Jeremias, *TDNT* I, 338–41; *TDNT* v, 702; and *ZNW* 34 (1935), 115–23; P. Joüon, *NRT* 67 (1940), 318–21; E. E. May, *Ecce Agnus Dei: A Philological and Exegetical Approach to John 1:29–36*, Washington 1947; F. M. Braun, *RT* (1948), 347–93; J. Leal, *VD* 28 (1950), 98–109; C. H. Dodd, *The Interpretation of the Fourth Gospel*, Cambridge 1953, 230–38; A. George, *Bible et vie chrétienne* 9 (1955), 85–90; M. E. Boismard, *Du Baptême à Cana*, Paris 1956, 43–60; B. Prete, *Sacra Doctrina* 1/1 (1956), 13–31; I. de la Potterie, *Bibbia e Oriente* 1 (1959), 161–9; J. W. Doeve, *TT* 14 (1959/60), 57–65; W. Grossouw, Haag 984–6; H. W. Surkau, *BTHW* 329–31; S. Virgulin, 'Recent Discussion on the "Lamb of God"', *Scripture* 13 (1961), 74–80; T. Holz, *Die Christologie der Apokalypse des Johannes (TU* 85), Berlin 1962, passim.

Johannes B. Bauer

Law

A. *In the Old Testament.* Law was for the Israelites at the time of our Lord *the great religious reality.* The Torah really stood on a higher level than all the other books of scripture. Through the law 'we learn the divine things as is becoming and human things insofar as they are of use to us' says the author of the apocryphal Fourth Book of Maccabees (1:17), and Rabbi Ḥanina adds: 'When two sit together and pronounce the words of the Law the Shekinah (the divine presence) is among them' (Pirke Abot 3:2). Christ himself shows the greatest respect for the Law: 'Truly I say to you, till heaven and earth pass away, not an iota, not a dot, will pass from the law till all is accomplished' (Mt 5:18). The law was, then, an uncommonly rich religious reality, a gift of God, which constitutes the religious life of Israel. How was it given? What did it contain? What was to become of it in the context of the new revelation? These are the three points which we have to deal with.

1. *The formation of the Law.* The great lawgiver of Israel is *Moses* and the whole Torah, the Pentateuch, is called 'the book of the law of Moses' (Josh 8:31; 2 Kings 14:6) or 'the law of Moses' (Neh 13:1; 2 Chron 25:4), at least in the latter part of the Old Testament. But as every jurist will realise, the great lawgivers do not complete their work in a single day— on the contrary, the greater they are the more they influence those who come after them who solve new difficulties by allowing themselves to be guided by the principles which have already been laid down.

The work of forming legal corpora had begun in the Ancient Near East long before Moses' time. We know of law books of Lipit-Ishtar, of Eshnunna, and Hammurabi from the first half of the second millenium as well as Assyrian and Hittite collections from 1400–1300 BC. These are collections of legal obligations with specifications and modifications apropos particular points. The articles of these codices present the case in this way: 'If anyone should do this or that, cause this or that damage, commit this or that crime . . .', and go on to give the solution proposed in the judicial sentence with the purpose of restoring peace as well as the respective punishment or equivalent penal task imposed. These judgements intended to fit each specific case served as judicial pronouncements, in Hebrew *mišpāṭ* (from *šāphaṭ*—to pronounce a judicial sentence, to judge). In Ex 21:18–22:16 there is a whole series of *mišpāṭîm* in which critical analysis sees archaic characteristics, since they do not mention either kings or cities and presuppose an even more rudimentary stage of imparting justice, addressed as they are to a community which has its riches, its real estate, in its herds, even if it is already in possession of agrarian land. There are good grounds for ascribing this first collection to Moses himself.

In this connection, however, the bible speaks not of *mišpāṭîm* but of 'words' (*debārîm*) (see Ex 24:3). In fact the collection of *mišpāṭîm* is connected with a series of other texts (22:27–23:14) in which, unlike other legal books of the Ancient Near East, the legislator addresses himself *directly to the Israelites*: 'You shall not give out false rumours. . . . You shall not allow justice to be perverted. . . .' These are in the style of the Decalogue ('You shall not kill!'), that is, a series of imperatives. We have here another source of Israelite legislation of a much more individual type which links the law to God's word and to the moral demands of the God of Israel. Albrecht Alt has singled out this type of law and given it the name 'apodictic'. He has shown that it represents the oldest Israelitic tradition which should in all probability be dated even before the conquest of Canaan. This apodictic system of law is a unique feature that should be distinguished from 'declarative' pronouncements or moral counsels and prohibitions. It should be noted that the lawgiver intended to present the whole of the law-book contained in Ex 20:24–23:14 (15f is additional) under the kind of headings we have been referring to which introduce and round off the whole compilation.

The small law-book contained in Ex 34:17–27 is composed similarly of 'words'; but in this case the prescriptions are governed by an essential structural relationship to the three great liturgical festivals. We have to do here principally with the liturgy and the regular pilgrimage to the national sanctuary (v 24), namely, to the Temple (v 26). With its mention of the sacrifice of the paschal lamb this law-book presupposes the prescriptions for the celebration of the Passover as found in Ex 12:21–7. This was *the* great national festival. Since, on the other hand, there were texts in which this legislation was inserted, it is probable that these ancient prescriptions were codified at the time of the united

monarchy, under Solomon who built the temple.

Side by side with these ritual prescriptions there were also regulations which kings in antiquity promulgated with the object of governing life in the palace which was generally situated near the temple. We know of similar regulations among the Assyrians (published by Weidner in *AfO* xvii, 257ff) and Hittites (published by E. von Schuler). In Israel these regulations were called *ḥuqqîm*, that is, decisions of the *meḥōqēq* or prince (Judg 5:9; Gen 49:10). This would be yet another source for Israelite law.

There was, however, another source of an even more directly religious character. This consisted in the *ʿūdôth* or *ʿēdôth* (Deut 4:7; Is 8:16–20), that is, oracles given by the prophets (in Palestine and Syria they were called *ʿddm*; Zakir 1:12; Wenamon 1, 38). The sanctuary was called *ʾôhel môʿed*, the tent of the oracle. Once the priest had promulgated the oracle or communicated a decision of the deity, however, it was referred to rather as *tôrâh* (in Akkadian, *tirtu*; see Amos 2:4; Is 8:18). This word, which corresponded to a *divine decision*, and which perhaps originally derives from the verb *to throw* (*yrh*) with reference to the sacred lots, Urim and Thummim (1 Sam 14:41 in LXX), had come into use in Israel and was used to designate *the law of God* since it brought out to best advantage the fact of the divine intervention in the government of Israel. Deuteronomy, which refers to all its articles of law indifferently as *mišpāṭîm*, *debārîm*, *ḥuqqîm*, and even *mitswôth* ('commands') designates its law-book as a whole as 'this torah' (eg in 32:46). This new codification, which contains elements which are much older than the redactional stage, was probably edited on the basis of legal collections from the sanctuaries of the Northern Kingdom after the fall of Samaria. It fits in with a monarchical society rich in institutions (*see* chapter 18), and a society which is no longer merely agrarian but also artisan, and so the law refers not just to the offering of the harvest fruits but also to the remission of debts (chapter 15). Stamped with a deep religious and humanitarian spirit, this law is conceived as the expression of the will of the national God who desires to save his people and make them prosper in their own land.

Other collections of laws of this kind are similarly referred to as Torah as, for example, Chapters 1–7 of Leviticus which present the Torah of sacrifices (Lev 7:37). There are several laws for the various cases of leprosy and legal impurity (Lev 11:46; 13:59; 14:32), but other collections such as Lev 17–26, nowadays referred to as 'the Law of Holiness', appear to be more archaic and do not have this designation (Lev 26:46). Nevertheless, all these texts betray a similar spirit, that of Ezekiel who codified the prescriptions which made it possible for Israel to come into the presence of its God in the temple (Ezek 48:35) and which in fact constitute the 'Torah' of the temple (43:12).

It is for this reason that nowadays these texts are referred to as a whole as the Priestly legislation. This literary strand shows how God marks the various stages of sacred history by means of the great institutions which he establishes: the law of multiplying the species with Adam, that of reverence for blood with Noah, the law of circumcision with Abraham, that of the sanctuary with Moses and Aaron. It is precisely this literary corpus which has provided the framework for the whole Pentateuch and even in Joshua (Chapter 20) there is an expanded body of legislation. In this case, however, Joshua did nothing but make use of and adapt the law of Moses in the same way that he brought it to the knowledge of the people in Shechem (Josh 8:30–35). The Torah considered in this way, therefore, takes in the five books of Moses, that is, the Pentateuch.

2. *The theology of the law.* This simple presentation of the process of formation of the law shows the significance of the natural, economic, geographical, social and historical factors which contributed to the evolution of Israelite law. All these elements which went to make up the concrete life of the people of Israel, however, are always considered in the Scriptures as an expression of God's providence—as his word or his Torah. In order to understand these texts, one must always read them in their concrete social situation in which alone they can be grasped. It is not a moral or metaphysical law but rather a divine intervention by which God gives his people a statute for their guidance in this or that particular stage of their development.

These juridical texts and prescriptions governing special cases must be interpreted in a juridical and sociological context—*gratia non tollit naturam*! They reflect, nevertheless, a definite theology: thus the 'Book of the Covenant' which is intimately connected with the Decalogue, reminds us of the moral demands of the God of Israel who is not a deity in the manner of other oriental deities. The Book begins with the law of the Altar and ends with the prohibition to swear by false gods (Ex 23:13). It contains not only rules for the correct handling of disputed cases but also ordinances aimed at defending the weak (22:21–26; 23:6–12). It is stated that God knows even those things which are unknown to men (22:7f), he hears and gives force to the law (23:26). If we compare this text with the edict of reform of Pharaoh Horemheb we perceive that the God of Israel occupies the same position in regard to his people as the pharaoh with regard to his in Egypt. Thus faith in the God of the Fathers shows itself capable of assimilating the high political wisdom of the Egyptian scribes.

Ex 34 shows us how the same faith had assimilated the canaanite festivals and the understanding of the forces of nature which these incorporated. The three great seasonal feasts continue, but the feast of the unleavened bread is linked with the passover which becomes the predominant element. The presence of God can be experienced in his sanctuary and anything which smacks of magic such as the custom of seething a calf in its mother's milk is forbidden. Yahweh takes over the functions of the divinity of a population of sedentary cultivators of the soil but remains the national God, who set them free from the land of Egypt, who demands from his worshippers who depend upon him that they walk in his presence.

Deuteronomy contains a *thoroughly worked out theology* of the divine Torah. Even though the Decalogue has been given to men directly from God (Chapter 5) the bulk of the individual laws have been communicated through an intermediary, Moses. This law is not only a decree, an imperative, it is *wisdom* (Chapter 4), the *wisdom which leads to life*. The Torah is the expression of the divine act of will, and being God's will for man it is near to his heart: 'This commandment which I command you today is not too hard for you, neither is it far off. It is not in heaven that you should say, "Who will go up for us to heaven, and bring it to us, that we may hear it and do it?" ... But the word is very near you; it is in your mouth and in your heart, so that you can do it!' (30:11, 14). It is a gift of God, a revelation which promises happiness and life: 'The secret things belong to the Lord our God; but the things that are revealed belong to us and to our children forever, that we may do all the words of this law' (29:29).

The laws of the sacerdotal law-book are the regulations peculiar to the people of God by means of which God educates them, at least in the case of those members who keep themselves ritually pure, leading them on to the ideal of the holiness of God: 'Be holy for I, Yahweh your God, am holy' (Lev 19:2).

A very special holiness is attributed to the priesthood since only priests may consume the food offering made to God and remain permanently in the sanctuary over which the divine 'glory' descends. The Law was regarded as of absolute value (see M. Noth, *Die Gesetze in Israel*, p. 118ff). It was the eternal expression of the divine act of will revealed to Israel by a privilege of

God's grace. For this reason it was loved as being a divine reality as can be seen in Ps 119 (cf also Ps 1 and 18) which praises its beauty and benefits.

The post-exilic prophets emphasise the messianic expectation which aimed at extending also to others the privileges of the sadokite priesthood (Zech 14:21) and which nourished the hope of the proclamation of the Torah to all nations as is the case in Is 42:4. There is, finally, a whole stream of thought in late Judaism which contributes to keeping alive this concept of the Torah and the necessity of knowing it. Baruch (3:24, 34) equates the law with wisdom and Ben Sira sees this wisdom as originating from the Most High and identical with the 'book of the Covenant of the Most High' (Sir 24:18–32). It is fruitful, bringing forth precious fruits and growing in that Paradise which was seen by the prophets.

Bibliography: H. Kleinknecht and W. Gutbrod, *TDNT* IV, 1022–91 (=*BKW* XI); M. Noth, *Die Gesetze im Pentateuch*, Halle 1940; G. Oestborn, *Tora in the Old Testament*, Lund 1945; D. Daube, *Studies in Biblical Laws*, Cambridge 1947; H. Cazelles, *DB(S)* V, 497ff; H. Cazelles, *Études sur le Code de l'Alliance*, Paris 1946; von Rad (see index); Jacob 219–23; Nötscher (see index); Haag 563f; A. Deissler, *Ps 119 und seine Theologie*, Munich 1955; A. Alt, *Kleine Schriften zur Geschichte des Volkes Israel* I, Munich 1953, 278–332; W. Zimmerli, 'Das Gesetz im AT', *TLZ* (1960), 85, and 481–97.

Henri Cazelles

B. *Law in the New Testament*. I. *Vocabulary*. In dependence on and agreement with the terminology as used in late judaism the New Testament uses the term *law* throughout as a technical term for the Mosaic Law. This is a general rule to which there are but few exceptions. In Rom 7:21 the word *nomos* is made to refer to the fact of experience that man, in trying to do what is good, finds evil the easiest course. In Rom 7:23 Paul speaks of the 'law of sin' and in Rom 8:2 of the 'law of sin and death' by which he means the firmly-established, prevalent world-order, the organised power of sin and death. Opposed to this we find in Rom 8:2 the 'law of the Spirit of life in Christ Jesus' which must be understood as the organised power of the Spirit as a permanent order of existence over against the former. In speaking of the 'law of the mind' against which 'the law in my members' makes war (Rom 7:23), he is referring to an immanent, constant tendency of the will guiding the intellect which is opposed by another inner tendency which has its origin in a man's 'members'. Paul has also another idea of law in mind, different from that of the mosaic law, when he speaks in Gal 6:2 of the 'law of Christ' or in Rom 3:27 of the 'law of faith' which he sets over against the 'law of works' by which he doubtless means the mosaic law (see under IV: law of Christ).

When we hear of the Torah, the law, in the writings of later judaism, we have to remember that it can refer to one of four things: 1. The ensemble of all the commandments and stipulations which are to be found written in the Pentateuch and which God gave to his people on Sinai through Moses. 2. The Pentateuch itself, the five books of Moses as such as a part of scripture; everything which is written in the Pentateuch; it is not just the legal but also the historical parts which belong to the 'law'. In this sense the word 'law' is distinguished from 'tradition', that is, the collection of all the other books of scripture. In the same sense, the formula 'the law and the prophets' is used as a designation for the whole of scripture. 3. Since the Pentateuch is the most important part of Holy Scripture according to the view of later judaism, the whole of scripture as contained in the Old Testament can also be referred to simply as 'the Law'. 4. Quite apart from its application to scripture, there is found a use of the term *law* as referring to the oral tradition, that is, the explanations of the law passed on orally by the rabbinical schools.

While we have no indication that the word is found in the New Testament with this last meaning (in Gal 1:14 Paul uses the expression 'traditions of the fathers' to refer to stipulations of law imposed by word of mouth) the term *law* or *law of Moses* is used here to designate both the law of Sinai and also the Pentateuch as a part of scripture and also for the scriptures as a whole. In speaking of law in the New Testament we have to bear this diversification of meaning, referring to entirely different objects, well in mind. The reason is that what the New Testament says about law as scripture will not necessarily apply to law as the moral order coming from God, nor vice versa. While all christians down to the time of Marcion were unanimously convinced that the Old Testament as scripture (and therefore also the law) was divine revelation which still retained its validity and which could claim the highest possible authority even for a christian, in the same early christian period there raged a very keen battle as to whether the law as the moral order

coming from God still retained the same validity. And so there arose from the very earliest days the paradoxical state of affairs that Paul, in waging war against the law as a system still valid (the moral demands made by God), appealed more and more to the law considered as scripture. If, therefore, law is taken as the equivalent of scripture, there never was any dispute in the early church; but if it is taken as the moral demands of God then it is seen as the most difficult problem with which the early christians had to wrestle and which all but broke up the unity of the church.

How disastrous the failure to distinguish these two basic meanings of law in the New Testament is, can be studied in the expression 'letter' (*gramma*) which Paul uses as a synonym for law (Rom 2:29; 7:5; 2 Cor 3:6f). In 2 Cor 3:6 we read: 'The letter kills but the Spirit gives life'. If we interpret the first part of this sentence as referring to scripture the reference would be to the external and material written word as such in direct opposition to the Spirit (that is, the spiritual sense) which lies behind the material words, and it would thus be regarded as something which brings man everlasting death. Such an interpretation, however, is entirely foreign both to the Old and the New Testament. The letter is here rather the immediate expression of divine revelation and has a claim to the highest authority. Paul, therefore, evidently intended the phrase to refer to the law as the moral demands of God presented in the Old Testament. He uses the title 'letter' for this law meaning thereby a purely external demand made by God which is nothing more than a prescription and has no power of itself to give to man the possibility of fulfilling the moral demand made. It is in this sense that the 'letter', that is, the mosaic law, kills, since it brings man who is subjected to it and who cannot fulfil its demands under the curse of God and thus into eternal death. This affirmation fits in, therefore, with others made by the apostle; the mosaic law is seen to possess a similar power of destruction with regard to those who are subject to it (Rom 4:15; Gal 3:10; 1 Cor 15:56).

Since the question of the significance for the early church of the scriptures contained in the Old Testament does not fall under the real question of law in the moral sense as it is presented in the New Testament, we must restrict ourselves in what follows to the law considered as the moral demands of God as incorporated in certain writings. This is the basic meaning of the term in the context of late judaism, and is in the foreground in all the New Testament texts which speak of law.

II. *The content of the law.* As for the Old Testament, so also for the New Testament and for late judaism, the mosaic law consisted in an intrinsically indissoluble unity made up of moral, ritual, and juridical regulations. It is this ensemble which is referred to when there is mention of the law in the New Testament, though of course the weight of emphasis and the way of looking at it can be different in different texts. It is evident, for example, that the ritual element has great importance in the dispute of Jesus with the Pharisees apropos the validity of the mosaic law, for in this context it is a case of ritual and sabbath regulations more than

anything else. But the antitheses of the Sermon on the Mount (Mt 5:21–48), in which the subjects of discussion are murder, divorce, impurity, and the relation with one's neighbour, show clearly that the dispute is concerned with the content and validity of the Old Testament law in itself not just with ritual prescriptions.

The same is true of Paul's struggle for a gospel free of the law. Here also the ritual laws have a definite part to play, for example, when it is a question of circumcision (Rom 2:28; 3:1; Gal 2:3, 7; 5:6) or the observance of certain festivities (Gal 4:10). But in the last analysis the struggle is over the law as such and it is the moral requirements of the law which occupy the place of importance. That stands out clearly in the fact that Paul takes as the essential content of the law the injunction: 'You shall not covet' (Rom 7:7), that when he is speaking of transgressing the law he refers to transgressions of the moral law (Rom 2:13–29) and, finally, that he identifies the content of the law quite simply with the 'good' (Rom 7:12). It would therefore be a tragic misrepresentation of the pauline teaching on justification and would not correspond to the truth if we were to represent the thesis of the apostle— namely that no man can be justified on the basis of the law or the works of the law—in the sense that the observance of the ritual commandments of the Old Testament law were not enough for a man to be justified by God and that he, in order to achieve this end, must also observe the moral laws. This mistake is, unfortunately, often made in exegesis. The thesis of Paul goes much deeper: it states that the Old Testament law as such, including its moral requirements, cannot give fallen man righteousness which can come to him only as a gift from God. In the same way, one must conclude that when Paul is speaking of the abrogation of the law, he is referring to the Old Testament moral law.

Together with the Old Testament and writers of the later Jewish period, the New Testament evinces the firm conviction that the Old Testament law considered as a whole derives from God as its author. It is, to be sure, called the law of Moses, but Moses is only the mediator of the law (Gal 3:20). In the last analysis, it is the law of God (Rom 7:22); therefore it is holy and good (Rom 7:12, 16). It is an expression of the holy will of God (Rom 2:27). Even during the bitter polemic against the judaic element which considered the law as necessary for salvation for those christian communities converted from paganism, primitive christianity never succumbed to the temptation of solving the problem at issue in the manner of Marcion who denied the divine origin of the Old Testament law. This difficult problem of the law in the New Testament is based directly on the fact that, on the one hand, the divine authority of the law is fully accepted but that on the other hand this same law is no longer in force.

III. *The validity of the law.* 1. *The attitude of Jesus to the law.* Since the question of the law loomed so large in the early church it was natural that the evangelists, who had the intention at least in some cases of giving answers to questions of actuality in the communities of their day, which answers can be found in the gospels, should give much space to the position of Jesus with regard to the Law of the Old Testament. This position can be studied in the way Jesus acted but, above all, in the dispute-sayings with the scribes and Pharisees and in the basic affirmations of Jesus on the validity of the law. The material which the gospels offer is so varied that it has not been possible so far to reduce all the individual items, which to some extent are intelligible only within the context of a particular situation no longer known to us, to a common denominator and thus to draw them together into a single presentation. There is, at all events, this dual attitude of Jesus to the mosaic law: acceptance and criticism, faithful observance and transgression are found side by side.

This is true first of all in the case of the ritual prescriptions of the law. Thus Jesus carried out the pilgrimages to the temple on the great feasts which were prescribed by the law (Jn 2:13; 5:1; 7:10). He recognised the temple as the house of prayer and, full of zeal, made his protest against its desecration (Mt 21:12f; Jn 2:13–22). He celebrated the Passover with his disciples (Mt 26:17–19; Lk 22:7–15). We are certain at least in the case of the Passover offering that Jesus took part in the sacrificial system since the celebration of the Passover without the previous offering of the Passover victim was unthinkable and out of the question. Also the fact that the disciples, after the ascension of Jesus, continued taking part in the liturgy of the temple (Lk 24:53) allows us to draw the certain conclusion that they had already been in the habit of doing this when in the company of Jesus and believed that in so doing they were acting according to his desires. In his parables and discourses Christ takes it for granted that people go to the temple and there make their sacrifices (Mt 5:23f; 23:16f).

But even if the Old Testament ritual law seems to have been accepted by Jesus in theory and in practice, this affirmative approach has one important limitation, namely, that according to Christ's view, it is not the sacrificial system but moral conduct that takes the first place in religious life. This liturgical piety must not become a substitute for moral conduct and reconciliation has precedence over sacrifice (Mt 5:24). Above all, it can even become sinful if one should withhold from one's parents their rights and lawful sustenance on the grounds of a specious appeal to cult obligations (Mk 7:9ff). More important than any form of liturgical piety are the great moral commandments—justice, mercy, and fidelity (Mt 23:23f).

According to what we find in all the evangelists it was the sabbath ordinance which provided the greatest source of conflict in the polemic of Jesus against the scribes and Pharisees. We may suppose that in general Jesus observed the law of the sabbath rest. We even find in the eschatological discourse an affirmation of Jesus to the effect that this command would continue in force during the time of the threatened judgement of punishment on Jerusalem. In fact the admonition: 'Pray that your flight be not in the winter or on the sabbath' (Mt 24:20) would appear to be intelligible only in the light of the fact that flight would be impossible on the sabbath on account of the sabbath law which forbade a journey longer than about two-thirds of a mile—the so-called 'sabbath-journey'. Despite this, however, the accounts we have in the gospels show that Christ took up an attitude of interior freedom with regard to the sabbath law and rejected the kind of rigoristic observance demanded by the scribes and Pharisees. He not only allowed the disciples to pluck the ears of corn (Mt 12:1–8) but he himself often healed the sick on the sabbath day (Mt 12:9–14; Lk 13:10–17; Jn 5:9), thus breaking the law. He based this attitude not only on the precedence of the love of the neighbour over a cult law but especially on the affirmation: 'The Son of Man is also lord of the sabbath' (Mt 12:8), by which he claimed the right as messiah to determine *how* the sabbath law should be put into practice in individual cases, therefore placing himself basically *above* this commandment.

Jesus took up an attitude of even greater freedom in the case of the law of ritual purity. Here too he not only allowed his disciples to transgress the strict prescriptions of legal purity elaborated by the rabbis (Mk 7:1ff) but he defended their conduct. What is more, he too transgressed these stipulations by touching a leper (Mk 1:41) and a corpse (Mk 5:41; Lk 7:14). In the great discourse about the law of purity (Mk 7:14–23) Jesus explains how this idea of levitical purity is essentially irrelevant—'There is nothing outside a man which, by going into him, can defile him; but the things which come out of a man (that is, out of his heart) are what defile him' (Mk 7:15). He then substitutes for this the law of moral purity. In this way the law of ritual purity becomes entirely void of any further validity. This radical clarification of the question is given even greater force insofar as Jesus, as Mark expressly mentions in the introduction to the discourse, calls together the crowds and in their presence publicly repudiates this law of purity.

Jesus takes up a basically positive attitude to the moral specifications of the Old Testament law. He refers the rich young man, who asked him what was the way to find life, to the ten commandments (Mk 10:19). At the same time, the critical note is not absent even here. In the antitheses of the Sermon on the Mount (Mt 5:21–48) it is not just a question of correcting the rabbinical interpretation of the law but involves a criticism of the Old Testament law itself. This law is not just interiorised insofar as in the case of the first, second and fourth of the antitheses the inner disposition is shown to be necessary in addition to the external deeds demanded by the law, but this law itself is really and truly abrogated as is implied in the even more radical demands made in the remaining three antitheses. All this, it must be noted, falls under the word of power: '. . . but *I* say to you' by means of which Christ proclaims himself as the new lawgiver who promulgates the will of God in its absolute perfection since this will corresponds with the kingdom of God which had entered into history with his coming.

If one takes in the whole of the material that the evangelists offer on the subject of Jesus' position faced with the law of the Old Testament, one is led more or less to the following conclusion: the absolute will of God which finds its essential expression in the two commandments of loving God and loving the neighbour (Mt 7:12; 22:34–40; Mk 12:28–34; Lk 10:25–8) is the critical norm which Christ applies to discern the validity of this Old Testament law. To the extent that this law embodies an expression of God's will it is accepted; where, however, it is in opposition to it or lags behind it is either rejected or radicalised. Therefore the compromise arrived at on account of the hardening of men's hearts (Mk 10:5) is applied retroactively (Mt 5:31–42). Those stipulations of the Law which are concerned only with details of external conduct are either abrogated or interiorised in that it is the internal disposition which is enjoined as the decisive element in a true obedience (Mt 5:21–30). It is also in the same sense of an inner deepening and perfectioning that we are to understand the thematic proposition of Mt 5:17 which states what is characteristic of the attitude of Jesus to the Old Testament law: 'Think not that I have come to abolish the law and the prophets; I have come not to abolish them but to fulfil them.' It is this renewed, 'fulfilled' law of Christ that is mentioned also in the following proposition (Mt 5:18): 'Truly, I say to you, till heaven and earth pass away, not an iota, not a dot, will pass from the law till all is accomplished.'

2. *The attitude of the apostle Paul to the law.* The dispute about the meaning of the law of Moses within the context of sacred history which had already begun in early christianity—the discourse of Stephen (Acts 7) and the baptism of the pagan centurion Cornelius by Peter (Acts 10) are typical examples of this—reached its climax in the career of Paul

who was conscious of having been called to be the apostle of the nations (Gal 1:16). At the same time, however, it was solved on the theological level. Our sources for this struggle of Paul on behalf of a gospel free of the law are chiefly the account in Acts of the apostolic Council of Jerusalem together with the preparation for it (Acts 15) and the pauline epistles which reflect in different degrees the internal and external dispute and debate of the apostle with judaism. In this connection the letters to the Galatians and Romans and the two letters to the Corinthians take on a special importance.

We can pick out two lines of thought in the way the Apostle represents the meaning of the law which, although mutually interdependent and also at times fused in the way he expounds them, are nevertheless distinct: (a) whether the law is a valid means towards justification; and (b) whether the law is of binding character with regard to christians converted from paganism. While Paul fights for the freedom of these latter from the Law of the Old Testament he also at the same time contends against the view that this law is necessary for salvation. Conversely, on the basis of the demonstration that man is justified not by works of the law but by faith in Christ, he concludes to the fact that christians converted from paganism are free of the law. It is certain that what has the greatest weight here theologically is the idea of salvation as an absolutely free gift of God and, at the same time, the thesis that there is no way to justification through the law. In his own missionary work, however, a work which had such christians as its object, it was often the other theme that was uppermost, namely, that these converts from paganism were no longer bound by the law. The starting point of both lines of thought is the apostle's faith in Christ, his conviction that in Christ alone all salvation for mankind is bound up and that the redemptive death of Christ is the one and only cause of all justification. The arguments which Paul adduces in favour of a gospel free of the Law are of so many different kinds that we can offer here only a very brief summary.

a. *On law and justification.* For Paul any possibility of ascribing to the law a significance for salvation is excluded by the fact that God has now revealed his justice (Rom 3:21-6) in the vicarious, redemptive death of Christ which comes from God's grace as his own saving act and in which is included righteousness as a free gift to man. Seen in the light of the cross of Christ, all human righteousness appears as it really is, a free gift, and the only way to come by this righteousness is therefore faith. From this flows the thesis that Paul never tired of proclaiming, that righteousness cannot come from the law and that no man can be justified on the basis of works of the law but only on that of faith (Rom 3:20, 28; Gal 2:16, 21; 3:11). The reason is that since the law and the works of the law are concerned uniquely with the requirements which God makes and, flowing from this, human activity aimed at fulfilling these requirements—it is always a question of one's own activity when fulfilling the law (Gal 3:12)—a righteousness proceeding from the law would be a man's own doing and therefore something which, in the strictest sense of the word, he had earned. This would imply that a saving death of Christ could have no significance: 'Christ would have died to no purpose' (Gal 2:21). In Paul, law and Christ, and their correspondent works of the law and faith, stand over against one another as two mutually irreconcilable means of attaining to salvation. The recognition of the one necessarily leads to the rejection of the other. The great theological significance of the work of the apostle lies precisely here, that he clearly showed this irreconcilability and adduced the necessary arguments to prove that Christ and not the law was the one and only way to salvation for all men at all times.

The argument from scripture plays a great part in this demonstration. His basic thesis, that no man will be justified by God through works of the law, is already enunciated in a scripture text (Ps 143:2) the significance of which Paul broadens by adding 'by works of the law'. He goes on from this point to show, by means of the example of Abraham, that according to the testimony of scripture (Gen 15:6) the law was never intended to be (and in fact never was) a way to righteousness but that, on the contrary, righteousness such as Abraham's was given to man only as a result of faith and that means as an absolutely unmerited grace of God (Rom 3:31–4:25; Gal 3:6–9). This basic text was implemented by the quotation from Habakkuk: 'He who through faith is righteous shall live' (Hab 2:4), which Paul adduces in two important contexts (Rom 1:17; Gal 3:12) as a proof that scripture bases eschatological existence not on works

of the law but on faith. The text from the Psalms is also adduced to the same effect (Ps 32:1f): 'Blessed are those whose iniquities are forgiven and whose sins are covered' (Rom 4:7). In this quotation from the Psalms, as he states expressly in Rom 4:6, Paul sees the scriptural proof for the thesis that 'God reckons righteousness apart from works'. He finds another scriptural proof for the same thesis in the fact—related in Gen 12:7; 13:15; 18:18—that God gave Abraham the promise that all nations would be blessed in him or in his seed (see Gal 3:8, 15–19). Therefore the law, and that means one's own effort, cannot be the basis for the fulfilment of the promise since in this case the promise would lose its character *as* promise, that is, as an absolutely free gift (Gal 3:17; Rom 4:14). Therefore also works of the law cannot be the basis of salvation since God gave the promise of salvation in the form of a testament, four hundred and thirty years before the law was first proclaimed, and this testament cannot be altered (Gal 3:15–17).

In addition to scriptural proof Paul also argues from experience in his struggle for a gospel set free from the law and, in the first place, his own personal experience of the law. In Rom 2:1–3:20 he shows how the law had not in fact been a way leading to righteousness for the Jews themselves, for experience had proved that they who had appealed to the law as a way of salvation had not themselves observed it. On the contrary they had violated it and thus become sinners. Paul also bases this fact of observation upon a text quoted at length in which various individual texts have been put together to form a kind of mosaic of proof-texts and from which can be deduced that neither pagans nor Jews are righteous but rather all stand subject to sin (Rom 3:9–20). Paul goes on from this demonstration from history of the incapacity of the law to provide a way to salvation to the principal proof, in Rom 7:7–26, that the law is utterly incapable in itself of leading man to righteousness and that when unredeemed man and the law confront each other the result is necessarily transgression of the law and therefore the very opposite of righteousness. This is because the law does not confront man as such but man sold under sin (Rom 7:14) through Adam's disobedience (Rom 5:12–21). Between the law which is spiritual and man who is determined by the flesh (Rom 7:14) there opens up an unbridgeable chasm. Fallen man cannot lift himself up to the level of the law; he can assent to it with his reason but has not in himself the strength to do what is good but inevitably—even if not compelled physically to it—does what is evil. On the other hand, however, the law, the 'letter' (*gramma*) is just a precept and cannot give man the strength to do that good which it demands of him. It even forms with its commandment 'You shall not covet' (Rom 7:7) a continual incitement and starting-off point for sin to become effective in man (Rom 7:8–11). It is a 'power of sin' (1 Cor 15:56), brings on God's anger (Rom 4:15), and a curse on man (Gal 3:10, 13). Paul states incisively that this was in fact the purpose which God had in giving the Law; it is 'added because of transgressions' (Gal 3:19) and that can only mean, according to Rom

5:20 'to increase the trespass'. This was certainly not the final or the chief purpose pursued by God in giving the law. This chief purpose is referred to by Paul in Rom 5:21: 'Where sin increased, grace abounded all the more, so that, as sin reigned in death, grace also might reign through righteousness to eternal life through Jesus Christ our Lord'. This means that within the context of salvation-history the law had the task of making apparent the sinful tendency of man so that against this dark background the saving power of the grace of Christ might shine all the brighter. From this point of view Paul can go so far as to call the law a 'custodian' which holds men captive under the power of sin (Gal 3:22–4). Nevertheless it remains as a certain fact for Paul that the law is not sin (Rom 7:7), that, on the contrary, it is holy and just and good (Rom 7:12), that it is a law of righteousness, that is, a law which requires righteousness (Rom 9:31) and those who put the law into practice are declared to be just (Rom 2:13). Despite all this, however, it is not a means to righteousness. That would be so only if it were 'life-giving', if it gave to man the power to fulfil its demands; only in this case would righteousness really derive from the law (Gal 3:21). The Old Testament law, however, does not have this strength; essentially it makes demands upon man and nothing else as distinct from the law of Christ which is a law of the Spirit of life.

b. *On law as a standard of obligation.* Paul bases the freedom from the Old Testament law of christians converted from paganism upon the proof that this law, according to the intention of God, has a validity limited to a certain period of time. It is but a stage in the unfolding of the saving plan of God. It 'came in' (Rom 5:20) and was intended for the time up to the coming of Christ (Gal 3:19) and of faith in him (Gal 3:25). Above all, Paul illustrates the temporary validity of the mosaic law by means of the reference to the glory on the face of Moses, which came as a result of the giving of the law but which was transient in nature unlike that permanent glory connected with the proclamation of the gospel (2 Cor 3:7–18). In this figure freedom from the law is based on the presence of the Spirit which is given with and in the gospel, that Spirit which is identical with the risen and exalted Lord. This implied that with the coming of Christ the law had lost its validity; Christ is therefore in reality the end or goal of the law (Rom 10:4). By his death on the cross he had deprived this law of commandments of all its strength (Eph 2:15) and had taken upon himself at the same time the curse of the law 'for our sake', thus freeing us from this curse and from the law itself (Gal 3:13). This liberation in principle from the law through the cross of Christ is actualised, realised for each one in baptism, in dying with Christ (Rom 7:1–6). This idea of being set free from the law through baptism as a being crucified with Christ is also clearly stated in Gal 2:19f.

Since, therefore, according to Paul the law never had a salvific function, not even in Old Testament times, it follows that the emphatic statements of the apostle on the abrogation, nullifying, and 'cancelling' (Col 2:14) of the law cannot have the meaning of the law being abrogated as a system of salvation but must be understood in the sense of the abrogation of the law as a preceptive rule. For Paul, freedom from the law means that for christians the law is no longer binding even though it is God's law; and when he speaks of law he is thinking, as we have seen, of the law as a whole including and giving special emphasis to its moral prescriptions. It is only in the supposition that freedom from the law implies also freedom from the moral prescriptions of the law that the question contained in Rom 6:15 can be raised at all, following up the fact that the christian is no longer under the law. This question asks whether the christian so freed can now give himself up to a life of sin. This question clearly presupposes that for Paul the state of not being under the law is equivalent to being free from a rule which prohibits sin. It comes to the same thing when in Gal 5:13 he strongly emphasises the christian's liberty (and that means according to the context a liberty from the law) and then goes on at once to define this liberty more exactly by stating that it should not be abused by being interpreted as an opportunity for the flesh. These statements would lose their whole meaning if one were to think of the christian's freedom from the law as being just a freedom from the ritual elements of the law or from the law as a means to salvation. For Paul, the law of Christ takes the place of the law of Moses as the decisive norm in the life of christians.

3. *The position of the Letter of James with regard to the law.* Having considered the gospels, Acts, and the pauline letters, there remains only the

Letter of James to consider for the question of the situation of primitive christianity with regard to the law. The term itself occurs ten times in this letter, and at first sight it might appear that the writer was taking up a position contrary to that of Paul with regard to the Old Testament law. A closer investigation of what the author says about the law, however, shows that this latter term does not refer to the mosaic law, but is related to what Paul refers to as the law of Christ. The law of loving one's neighbour is mentioned as part of the content of this law (2:8–16) just as is found in Gal 6:2. It is identical with the saving word which 'can save your souls' (1:21) which implies that it is the same as the christian message of salvation or the gospel. Hence it is referred to as the 'royal law', the 'perfect law of freedom' (2:8; 1:25). ↗ Justification in the Letter of James.

IV. *The law of Christ.* It is clear from the way in which the synoptics describe the position of Jesus with regard to the Old Testament law that he proclaimed himself as the new lawgiver who promulgated the will of God with authority in his own person and in so doing fulfilled the law of Moses. In the dual commandment of love of God and of the neighbour this law of Christ has its real content. We find the correspondent to this in the Gospel of John, where the love of the neighbour is characterised as the 'new commandment' (Jn 13:34; 15:12; 1 Jn 3:23). It is not possible in this matter to make a clear distinction between the law and the person of Christ; on the contrary, the two form together an intrinsic unity. Since the kingdom of God itself has come with Jesus, there is revealed in

him the radical and absolute moral requirement of God as corresponding to this same kingdom. Whence the law of Christ is really identical with the call to become disciples of Jesus which we meet with constantly in the gospels (Mt 8:22; 9:9; 10:38; 16:24; 19:21; Jn 1:43; 12:26).

Paul uses the express term 'law of Christ' twice in his letters. In 1 Cor 9:21 he calls himself *ennomos Khristou,* that is, one who remains within the law of Christ, and in Gal 6:2 he refers to the moral standard which applies to christians as the law of Christ referring primarily, as the context of the passage shows, to the law of love for the neighbour. In this, however, there are included all the admonitions, commandments, and prohibitions which find expression in the numerous pauline imperatives found in the letters. The law of Christ has in common with the law of the Old Testament this essential moral content; it is the 'summing up' or 'fulfilment' of the mosaic law (Rom 13:8–10). For Paul also the law of Christ is bound up essentially with the person of Christ; one grows in familiarity with this law to the extent that one grows in familiarity with Christ (Eph 4:20). Above all, union with Christ is for Paul not just a reason for but also the standard of all moral conduct. The ethical imperatives that we find in his epistles appear only as the necessary consequence of this union with Christ. This gives to the law of Christ as conceived by Paul a strongly dynamic character. The new life which is given through union with Christ or, as Paul often puts it, through the Spirit (*pneuma*), is here not only the standard and the reason for moral conduct but also supplies the necessary strength for it. Unlike the Old Testament law, the *gramma*, which is merely preceptive, the law of Christ is a law of the Spirit (Rom 8:2), for there is an intrinsic correspondence between it and the divine power which is the *pneuma*. Whence it is that this law of the Spirit can bring about in us what the law of Moses was never able to accomplish, the freeing from the law of sin and death, so that we cannot ascribe the same death-dealing effects to the law of Christ as Paul ascribes to the mosaic law. Since it is the necessary result of the new, supernatural existence of man and in principle is identical with this existence it is not, like the Old Testament law, a law of slavery (Gal 4:24; 5:1) but of liberty (Gal 5:1, 13), the 'perfect law of liberty', as James puts it. In Rom 3:27 it is called the 'principle of faith' because just as the person and the mission of Christ, which is the redemption of mankind, are the object of faith, so also must be the moral requirements which follow from union with Christ. This is brought out clearly by Paul, but especially in Rom 12:3-6.

Bibliography: R. Schnackenburg, *God's Rule and Kingdom*, London and New York 1963; W. Trilling, *Das wahre Israel: Studien zur Theologie des Matthäus-Evangeliums*, Leipzig 1959; H. Ljungmann, *Das Gesetz erfüllen. Mt 5:17ff und 3:15 untersucht*, Lund 1954; G. Barth, 'Das Gesetzesverständnis des Evangelisten Matthäus', *Überlieferung und Auslegung im Matthäusevangelium*, ed. G. Bornkamm, G. Barth and H. J. Held, Neukirchen 1960, 54–154; H. Schürmann, 'Wer daehr eines dieser geringsten Gebote auflöst . . .', *BZ* 4 (1960), 238–50; J. Schmid, *Das Evangelium nach Matthäus*, Regensburg 1948, 67–71; P. Bläser, *Das Gesetz bei Paulus*, (*NA* 19 1–2), Münster 1941 (with bibliography); P. Bläser, 'Glaube und Sittlichkeit bei Paulus', *Vom Wort des Lebens* (Festschrift M. Meinertz), Münster 1951, 114–21; C. H. Dodd, *Gospel and Law*, Cambridge 1951; S. Lyonnet, *Liberté chrétienne et loi nouvelle*, Paris 1953; G. Bornkamm, *Das Ende des Gesetzes: Paulusstudien*, Munich 1952; G. Söhngen, *Gesetz und Evangelium*, 1957; P. G. Verweijs, *Evangelium und neues Gesetz in der ältesten Christenheit bis auf Marcion*, Utrecht 1960; P. Bläser, 'Gesetz und Evangelium', *Catholica* 14 (1960), 1–23; E. Neuhäusler, *Anspruch und Antwort Gottes*, Düsseldorf 1962; J. Bommer, *Gesetz und Freiheit im Katholizismus*, Lucerne and Munich 1963; W. Andersen, *Ihr seid und Freiheit berufen: Gesetz und Evangelium nach biblischem Zeugnis*, Neukirchen 1964.

Peter Bläser

Laying-on of hands

The expression *the laying-on of hands* implies more than a mere extending or stretching out of the hands (Lev 9:22; Sir 50:20), more than just raising them up (Lk 24:50). It also implies more than just touching (Mt 17:7), even when the hand (or, the right hand) is expressly named as the means of this contact (Rev 1:17). It represents rather an action by means of which a transference is either just symbolised (in which case the laying on of hands is a pure symbol) or really brought about (in which case it is a symbol which is also an efficient cause). This symbolism, which has a real effect given the necessary conditions, is based on the much used symbolism of the hand as a figure standing for power, strength or might (Deut 1:27; Judg 6:13; Mt 17:22 etc). Its frequent use in the New Testament is explained sufficiently by the prior use in the Old Testament as can be seen from numerous texts. A derivation from extra-biblical sources or usage either from ancient times or from the pagan Mysteries or the Mandaeans is therefore unnecessary.

The *Old Testament* is familiar with

495

the laying on of hands as a sign of a (private) giving of a blessing (Gen 48:9, 14, 20). There is also evidence in the Old Testament of the laying on of hands which took place on the occasion of offering a sacrifice as already was the case in Egypt. The layman who was offering the sacrifice laid his hands (rested them, more exactly) on the head of the animal that he had brought. He then killed it, whereupon the priest caught the blood and sprinkled it about the altar (Lev 1:3ff; 3:2, 8, 13; 4:4f etc). If the party offering was the nation as a whole or a group, the imposition of hands was carried out by a representative (Lev 4:15). This custom is found in connection with the burnt offering (Lev 1:4), the sacrifice of peace (Lev 3:2, 8, 13) as also the sacrifice for sin (Lev 4:4, 15, 24, 29, 33 etc). In all these texts the laying on of hands has the same meaning, that of an act of transference symbolising substitution. The sacrificial animal dies in place of the one who is offering the sacrifice. This symbolism of transferring to a substitute stands out with particular clarity in the case of the sacrifice for sin where the laying on of hands symbolises in particular the transference of sin and guilt; cf, apart from the texts already referred to, Lev 8:14 and especially Lev 16:21: on the great day of expiation, the high priest (Aaron) lays both hands on the head of the goat of expiation thereby confessing the sins and transgressions of the people which at the same time he transfers to the animal through the laying on of hands ('he puts them upon the head of the goat').

This idea of transference is also basic to the laying on of hands when used in connection with an act of judgement. The witnesses of a serious offence who, according to Lev 5:1; Deut 13:9, had the duty of testifying and therefore at the same time are the prosecutors, laid their hands on the head of the guilty party (Lev 24:14; Dan 13:34). The community as a whole had to assume responsibility for a capital offence committed in their midst especially when the perpetrator of the crime could not be identified (Deut 21:1–9; a rather similar stipulation in the Code of Hammurabi, 23f). In this regard the laying on of hands was the means of transferring the responsibility from the community, which was answerable as a whole, to the guilty individuals. Finally, the same custom is found in the Old Testament in connection with the transference of office or commissioning with some special task. Thus the first-born of Israel had the duty of taking part in the liturgical worship of the Lord as being the special property of Yahweh; but he chose the Levites to substitute for them in this task (Num 3:11f). The Israelites laid their hands upon them thus transferring to them the duty which was incumbent on the whole people or, more exactly, on the firstborn (Num 8:10ff). On the occasion when Joshua was appointed to take the place of Moses the latter transferred to him, by means of an act of laying on of hands ordered directly by God, not only the office of leader of the people (Num 27:18, 23; Deut 34:9) but also the grace of state necessary for the exercise of the authority connected with this office. In fact, as a result of the laying on of hands, Joshua was seen to be 'full of the spirit of wisdom' (Deut 34:9).

According to the *rabbinical writings* the Jewish scribes also made use of this custom as a means of conferring a blessing (see SB I, 807). Apart from this, they also made use of the same symbolic action to transfer to their disciples the authority to teach and to judge, the same authority which they themselves had received by means of an identical ceremony (SB II, 648–55). In the talmudic period beginning about AD 280, the laying on of hands was omitted at the ordination of a new rabbi; by AD 300 it was even expressly rejected (SB II, 655).

In the *New Testament* the laying on of hands is, in the first place, a means of conferring a blessing, as in the Old Testament. According to Mk 10:13 and parallels they brought children to Jesus 'that he might touch them' and the Lord 'blessed them, laying his hands upon them' (v 16). It is evident from the context that the 'touching' solicited by those who brought the children (Lk 18:15 is the only one to mention this) was in fact a laying on of hands and that by this means a blessing was conferred. This same action is found with particular frequency in connection with healing diseases, whether this is asked for of Jesus for this purpose (Mt 9:18 = Mk 5:23; 7:32) or whether the healing is really brought about by this means (Mk 6:5; 8:23, 25; Lk 4:40; 13:13). Unlike the case of conferring a blessing, there is no mention in the healings of Jesus pronouncing a prayer when laying on his hands.

The risen Lord promised his disciples that they too would be able to impart healing by laying on their hands (Mk 16:18). At least in the case of Paul it is stated expressly that he restored a sick person to health by means of prayer and the laying on of hands (Acts 28:8). He himself was given back his sight by the same means at the hands of Ananias after he had lost it on the road to Damascus (Acts 9:12, 17f). The significance of this action when used as the sign, and in some cases also as the means, of a transference of power or authority, stands out clearly in the cases in which in the early church the bestowal of an office was made by means of the laying on of hands. (It is never stated that Jesus endowed his disciples with their various offices by this means: see Mt 18:18; Mk 6:7; Lk 9:1; Jn 20:22f; 21:15ff. Matthias was not given his office of substitute for Judas through the laying on of hands but by election: Acts 1:15–26.) On the other hand, the apostles officially installed the Seven in their new office by means of the laying on of hands accompanied by prayer after they had been elected by the people at the suggestion of the apostles themselves (Acts 6:1–6). It is not so certain whether the laying on of hands conferred on Barnabas and Saul, as recorded in Acts 13:3, was an official action implying the delegation to office. In favour of this interpretation there is the strong argument that the action in this case is closely connected with prayer and, in particular, also with fasting. This ensemble of rites would appear to be of too solemn a nature to admit the interpretation that the two missionaries were being delegated to their task merely by the invocation of a divine blessing. There is no doubt, on the other hand, that in the three texts which mention this practice in the pastoral epistles—1 Tim 4:14; 5:22;

2 Tim 1:6—it is a question of the conferring of an office, more exactly, an act of consecration (the office of bishop). The 'gift' which was received 'when the elders laid their hands upon you' (1 Tim 4:14) does not refer to any of the gifts of the spirit (charismatic gifts) which were at that time of frequent occurrence—these are never conferred through the laying on of hands (cf 1 Cor 12–14)—but to the special grace of state pertaining to the office of church leader which in 2 Tim 1:6 is described as a 'gift of God', that is, as a something which God gives freely.

The laying on of hands is, finally, the sign of and also the means towards the giving of the Spirit. The apostles Peter and John prayed for the inhabitants of Samaria that they might receive the Holy Spirit (Acts 8:15). Then they laid their hands upon them 'and they received the Holy Spirit' (v 17). 'The Holy Spirit' in this context does not refer to a charismatic gift such as the gift of tongues no more than in the case we have just considered and for the same reason. In the New Testament the charismatic gifts are never called simply *the Holy Spirit*. The quite clear parallels which exist between the accounts in Acts 8:14–17 and 2:1–13 make it certain that the inhabitants of Samaria received, through the laying on of hands, the same Holy Spirit as the primitive community at Pentecost. They experienced *their* Pentecost when they received the Holy Spirit which was their confirmation. We have to assess in the same way the laying on of hands received from Paul by the twelve men in Ephesus after they had been previously baptised by another (Acts 19:5f). The laying on of hands which

is mentioned in Heb 6:2, together with baptism, the resurrection from the dead, and the eternal judgement, is also generally understood of the sacrament of confirmation.

The theory is occasionally proposed, especially by dogmatic theologians, that the mention of the laying on of hands in 1 Tim 5:22 (see above) has to be understood as part of a penitential ritual. This, however, is doubtful, to say the least. The very fact that the expression is never used in the New Testament in connection with any kind of penitential act should put us on our guard against it as also the fact that in 4:14 of the same letter, as indeed always in the pastoral epistles, the laying on of hands is mentioned only in connection with the appointment to the office of church leader. A similar conclusion is required by the immediate context of 1 Tim 5:22 in which vv 17 and 18 speak of genuinely good priests, v 19 speaks of others whose conduct is not above suspicion while in v 20 the author is concerned with priests who are morally reprehensible and how they are to be corrected. It is not just a question of sinners in general; this is proved by the use of the participle in attribution—'those *persisting* in sin . . .' instead of the noun 'sinners' as used previously in 1:9, 15. It fits in very well with this list of priests in descending order of moral excellence to interpret v 22 as warning against ordaining by a too rapid laying on of hands those priests who give grounds for fearing that in their future ministry they will be unworthy. The descending order starting with the really good through those who are suspect down to those who are clearly defective morally is rounded off well by the reference to those whom one fears will be unworthy in the future. Therefore both from the point of view of the remote as of the immediate context of 1 Tim 5:22, the meaning required points to the laying on of hands as in the sense of ordination and not of a penitential ritual. This interpretation is also suggested by the way in which the text is worded.

Bibliography: N. Adler, *Das erste christliche Pfingstfest*, Münster 1938; N. Adler, *Taufe und Handauflegung*, Münster 1951; J. Coppens, *L'imposition des Mains*, Paris 1925; E. Kalt, *BRL* I², 754f; *DB* III, 847–50; *DTC* VII, 1302–425; *LTK* IV², 1343–5; P. Galtier, 'La Réconciliation des Pécheurs dans la Première Épître à Timothée', *RSR* 39 (1951), 317–20; C. Spicq, 'L'Évêque selon les Épîtres pastorales', *Témoignages* 8 (1955), 113–21; N. Adler, 'Die Handauflegung im NT bereits ein Bussritus?', *Festschrift Josef Schmid*, Regensburg 1963, 1–6. See also: J. Behm, *Die Handauflegung im Urchristentum*, Leipzig 1911; E. Löhse, *Die Ordination in Spätjudentum und im NT*, Göttingen 1951; SB I, 807f and II, 647–61; P. Volz, 'Die Handauflegung beim Opfer', *ZAW* 21 (1901), 93–100; N. Adler, 'Imposicion de manos', *Enc. Bibl.* IV (1965), 131–5.

Nikolaus Adler

Life

A. *The concept of life (ḥayyîm)* goes to the very heart of Old Testament thinking, and for that matter the same can be said with regard to the New Testament (*zōē*). In both the word is used in the first place of the natural life of man. Right from the start, however, it is more than just mere physical existence. Existence is not sufficient for life. The biblical idea of life is more inclusive than the philosophical or biological concept, and fuller than the connotation which the word has in popular usage. It is a pregnant term,

rich with meaning, giving the idea of fullness both in the quantitative and qualitative sense. Life does not just imply duration but also health, good estate and happiness. Sickness implies ↗ death, and recovery from sickness, life (Num 21:8; Mk 5:23; Jn 4:50). This explains how life can be so close in meaning to light (Ps 27:1; 36:9; Job 3:20), peace (Prov 3:2), happiness (Prov 19:23; Deut 8:1), dwelling in the land (Deut 4:1; 5:33). Life not only presupposes all these things, but it is the sum total of them.

Undeniably there is a close relationship between the Old Testament idea and representations of life common in the East. For example, the original seat of life is taken to be the blood (Gen 9:4; Lev 17:11). This view, however, leaves room for another which sees life as residing in the breath or ↗ spirit as the *principle of life*. This does not solve the problem of the relation between body and soul since soul (*nepheš*) very often means quite simply life. Similarly in the New Testament life is dependent on the possession of *psukhē* or *pneuma*.

In the metaphorical sense we find the following used as symbolical images of living persons: spring water (Gen 26:19), the ↗ word of God (Acts 7:38; Heb 4:12; 1 Pet 1:23), hope (1 Pet 1:3), and also bread (Jn 6:51) and stones (1 Pet 2:4f).

It is of special significance that *the Old Testament treasures life* as the highest good (Prov 3:16). No higher good can be desired—hence the exclamation 'Long live the king!' (1 Sam 10:24), implying a wish that he live not just for a long time but in happiness and joy (1 Kings 3:11). A man will give everything in exchange for his life (Job 2:4).

Even a live dog is better than a dead lion (Eccles 9:4). The ideal is a long life, the crowning unhappiness an untimely death, which is generally understood as divine punishment (Job 8:13; Ps 37:34f). Job and Ecclesiastes (Qohelet) in particular lament the brevity of human existence (see also Ps 90:10; Sir 18:8f). It is only in the time of the Maccabees that we meet the idea, common among the Greeks, that a glorious death in battle is to be preferred to a shameful life (1 Macc 9:10).

An essential element in the biblical concept of life is its *close relationship to God*. Life in its fullness is possible only through union with God. He who seeks him finds life (Amos 5:4, 6, 14). He is the living God (Deut 5:26; Josh 3:10; Jer 23:36; Mt 16:16; 26:63; Acts 14:15), he who lives for ever (Deut 32:40; Dan 12:7; Sir 18:1; Rev 4:9; 10:6), the immortal One (1 Tim 6:16), he who has life in himself (Jn 5:26) in opposition to the false gods who are dead (Ps 135:15ff; Hab 2:19). The Israelite swears by the living God (the formula occurs forty-three times in the Old Testament); God himself swears by his own life (Is 49:18; Rom 14:11).

All life derives from God (Acts 17:25-8); his breath constitutes man as a living being related to God (Gen 2:7). His life is dependent on God (Deut 8:3) who also gives life to his people (Deut 32:6; Hos 1:10) and is himself this very life (Deut 30:20). God is the source of life (Ps 36:9; Jer 2:13; 17:13), he gives death and life (Deut 32:39), he conserves (Ps 66:9) and protects life. There is therefore at work in all life a divine element,

and life is seen as the most precious gift of God to man, who possesses this life only as on loan to him from God.

It follows from this that *God is the absolute lord of life and death* (Num 27:16; Job 12:10; 34:14f; Ps 104:29f; Mt 10:28f). Man's life depends on God's word (Mt 4:4) and he places before man the choice of life or death (Deut 30:15-20). The word of God is man's life (Deut 32:47). Fidelity to God's prescriptions and commandments assures man of a long and happy life (Lev 18:5; Deut 4:1; Amos 5:6, 9, 14; Jer 21:8).

In the Wisdom literature we find mentioned as *life-giving forces*, besides the word of God, ⁄ wisdom (Prov 3:16, 18; 8:35), *the words of the wise* (Prov 3:2; 4:4, 10, 22), *precepts and laws* (Prov 19:16), the *fear of God* (Prov 14:27; Sir 1:12), *instruction* (Prov 4:13; 6:23), for all of which life is promised as a reward and this reward is represented plastically as a source of living water (Sir 21:16), the tree of life (Prov 3:18; 11:30; 13:12; 15:4) and the way of life (Prov 15:24; Ps 16:11).

On the other hand, ⁄ sin stands for diminution of life. Man who was at first created immortal (Gen 2:17; Wis 2:23) lost this immortality through sin (Sir 25:24; Job 8:4; Rom 5:12; 1 Cor 15:22). Sin is therefore the reason why the lives of the patriarchs were shortened (Gen 6:3). Life (here and now) is promised to the just (Ezek 18:5-9, 21-5), death to the sinner (Is 1:28). Life and ⁄ death are correlative with good and evil. Life is dependent on the moral conduct of each one and his observance of the law.

The patent contrast between this belief and the experience of every day was a serious difficulty for the faith of the pious man of the Old Testament (Job 21:7–15; Ps 73:2–12), a difficulty which was resolved only with the gradual and progressive revelation of survival after death—a revelation which was rather obscure and uncertain in its earlier phase—the ↗ resurrection of the dead, ↗ retribution after death, and immortality. This revelation was completed only in the New Testament.

The *land of the living* mentioned in the Old Testament stands for a reality in this present world and life here below (Is 38:11; Jer 11:19; Ezek 32:23–6; Job 28:13; Ps 27:13) though blessed, of course, by God. There are also glimmers of a hope for a life for ever in association with God, even if these remain indefinite and mysterious (Ps 16:10f; 49:16; 73:24ff, 28) and it must be admitted that these texts are exceptional. It was only after the hard experience of captivity and the wars of the Maccabees that we find clear evidence of the belief in the ↗ resurrection and *eternal life* (Is 26:19; Dan 12:2; 2 Macc 7:9, 11, 14, 23, 29). The Book of Wisdom shows clearly the concentrated result of this new belief and consciousness (Wis 4:14; 5:15). At any rate, the Old Testament concept of life remains, right from the beginning, open to development and fulfilment, more so if we have to regard this idea of life as *the final object of the messianic expectation.*

B. *In the New Testament*, too, life is used first of all in the straightforward sense. It is transitory (Jas 4:14), limited (Rom 7:1–3), its end is death (Phil 1:20). This life, however, is only a prelude to another (1 Cor 15:19; 1 Tim 4:8): it is life in the flesh (Gal 2:20), whereas true life is not to be limited to this world (1 Tim 4:8) and is simply called life, *the* life (Mt 7:14; Mk 9:43; 1 Pet 3:7). It has burst out of the framework of this earthly life after the resurrection of Christ (2 Tim 1:8ff) and the sending down of the living Spirit of God (1 Cor 15:45; 2 Cor 3:6; Rom 8:6).

In the *synoptics*, life is not mentioned very often; they speak almost always of *eternal life* (Mt 19:16; 25:46; Mk 10:17). For the synoptic gospels, life is practically always seen as a purely eschatological entity, since the resurrection has already taken place. They speak, theocentrically, more of the Kingdom of God, for which the correspondent in John, whose gospel is christocentric, is eternal life.

Life is referred to more often in *Paul*, the present life and the future life both, however, being intimately connected with each other (see Rom 6; 8:2–11). Earthly life for him is a daily dying (2 Cor 4:11) in which, however, the life of Christ becomes manifest.

In *John* the life idea achieves its final form; it is, as it were, a passing over from the battlefield to the celebration of victory (see Guillet, *Leitgedanken der Bibel*, 215). In John life is even more firmly rooted in the present. The concept of life is here characterised by a radical christocentricity, an interiorisation; it is moreover personified and universalised. For John life is the all-inclusive concept of salvation. It takes in everything which the Saviour of the World sent by God brings to men (for this, see Mussner). All other good things pertaining to salvation are included in the gift of life and are not given apart from it: the passage from death to life which signifies a new birth (Jn 1:13; 1 Jn 2:29; cf Jn 3:3–8); being set free from the dominion of the ruler of this world; the taking away of sin (1 Jn 3:8f); the being saved from the judgement of death (Jn 5:24, 29); the divine sonship as a result of being born of God (1 Jn 3:1f); possession of the Spirit which gives life (Jn 6:63); fellowship with the exalted Christ and, through him, with the Father (1 Jn 3); enjoyment of the love of God, of joy and peace and a pledge of the resurrection (Jn 6:39f, 44, 55).

Life understood in this sense is revealed only in *Jesus Christ*. It is he who has brought imperishable life to light (2 Tim 1:10); he is the one who leads into life (Acts 3:15) for in him *is* life (Rom 8:2; 2 Tim 1:1; 1 Jn 5:11). This life is free from all those things which trouble our earthly life, from sickness, suffering and death and from the cause of all these, sin.

The Father has life in him and gives it to the Son (Jn 5:26; 6:57), and the Son, like the Father, gives life to whom he will (Jn 5:21). Christ is life in person, the life which was sent into the world. He it is who reveals God, for the task which he has been given is to bring eternal life (Jn 12:50); he has life in himself (Jn 1:4; 1 Jn 1:1; 5:11). He is the true God and eternal life (1 Jn 5:20). He can say of himself: 'I am the resurrection and the life' (Jn 11:25; 14:6). His words are spirit and life (Jn 6:63, 68). He gives living water (Jn 4:10; 7:38); he is the bread of life and gives this bread as food (Jn 6:35, 48). This bread is both living and able to communicate eternal life (Jn 6:58).

Christ himself is our life (Gal 2:20; Phil 1:21; Col 3:4). This is the whole point of his mission, the purpose of his coming, that we should have life and have it more abundantly (Jn 10:10; 1 Jn 4:9). It was for this purpose that John wrote his gospel, that we should have life in his name (Jn 20:31).

The content or nature of true life can be described in the same way as that of the Kingdom of God with which it is identical, that is, as ↗ righteousness, ↗ peace, and ↗ joy in the Holy Spirit (Rom 14:17). It is an object of hope as is the kingdom but already present by anticipation. Eternal life does not just imply duration without limit but the fulness of salvation which has yet to be revealed. In this sense it can also be referred to as the life to come (1 Tim 4:8). Life on this earth is, in comparison with this, more like death (Mt 8:22; Col 2:13). For christians, however, eternal life is already a present reality (Eph 2:5f) even if still hidden in Christ (Col 3:3). In this way, since it is the fruit of salvation which lasts for ever, it is eschatological and therefore the hoped-for fulfilment of the life of the christian. This final revelation comes in the last age (Eph 2:7). The resurrection of the body is the final integrating element of eternal life (Jn 5:21; 6:40, 54; 11:25; 1 Cor 15:35–55; 2 Cor 1–5).

Despite this we are already in a certain sense risen with Christ (Col 3:1) and therefore have passed over into life (1 Jn 3:14). This does not, however, leave the way open for any easy-going attitude but rather imposes moral obligations (Eph 4:1); by means of mortification, dying with Christ, life is renewed from day to day (2 Cor 4:10–18).

God reserves to himself the exclusive

right of disposing of life (Acts 13:48). We only inherit it (Mt 19:16; Mk 10:17; Lk 10:25), we receive it (Mk 10:30). It is our attitude to God and the revelation of God in Christ which decides whether we are worthy of life (Mk 10:29f; Rom 2:7). Similarly in the New Testament, the whole course of life has to be decided with respect to the word of God; it compels us to a new way of life. Man must live no longer to himself but to God (Rom 14:7f; 6:11, 13; Gal 2:19) and to Christ who died for him and rose again (2 Cor 5:15). Life in the Spirit demands that we walk in the Spirit (Gal 5:25).

Since life consists in the knowledge of God and of the One sent by God (Jn 17:3), ↗ faith must be *the basic condition* for life. He who believes in Christ will have life (Rom 6:8-13; 1 Tim 1:16). The just man lives by faith (Hab 2:4; Rom 1:17; Gal 3:11). He who believes has life already in the present (Jn 3:16, 36; 20:31) and has passed from death to life (Jn 5:24). The proclaimed word is a prerequisite for life as it is for faith (Rom 10:17). It communicates life (2 Cor 2:16; 3:6), it is the Word of Life (Phil 2:16; Jn 6:63, 68); the Easter message 'He is alive!' (Mk 16:11; Lk 24:5; Acts 1:3) is the centre of the christian proclamation (Rom 6:10; 14:9; 2 Cor 13:4).

Through faith and baptism the christian comes into newness of life (Jn 3:5; Rom 6:4, 11). After having died with Christ, Christ lives in him (Rom 14:7ff) and he has a share in Christ's eternal life (Rom 6:1-11, 23; Gal 2:19f) which will know no end (Jn 4:14; 6:27; 12:25). The flesh and blood of Christ is not only nourishment

but a pledge of this life (Jn 6:27, 30, 50f, 58).

Life is the overflow of the love of God (Jn 3:16) and we have passed from death to life because we love the brethren (1 Jn 3:14), even to the point of being ready to lay down our lives for them (Jn 15:13). In the last resort discipleship of Christ implies giving up this life in order to win eternal life (Mt 16:25; Jn 12:25).

Bibliography: G. von Rad and R. Bultmann, *TDNT* II, 832-75 (=*BKW* XIV, 1-8, 12-27, and 33-84); H. Schmidt, *BTHW* 336-40; J. Burnier, Allmen 234-7; B. J. Alfrink, Haag 993-7; P. Kleinert, 'Zur Idee des Lebens im AT', *TSK* 68 (1895), 693-732; L. Dürr, *Die Wertung des Lebens im AT und im antiken Orient*, Münster 1926; J. Lindblom, *Das ewige Leben*, Uppsala-Leipzig 1914; Guillet, *Leitgedanken der Bibel*, Lucerne 1954, 194-218; F. Mussner, '*Zöë*': *Die Anschauung vom Leben im 4. Evangelium*, Munich 1952; E. Schmitt, *Leben in den Weisheitsbüchern Job, Sprüche und Jesus Sirach*, Freiburg 1954; E. Schmitt, *HTG* II, 25-30; W. Zimmerli, '"Leben" und "Tod" im Buche des Propheten Ezechiel', *TZ* 13 (1957), 404-508.

Ernst Schmitt

Light

A. *Light and darkness in the Old Testament*. The contrast between light and darkness in the Old Testament is derived in the first place from the alternation of day and night, that is, from the natural rhythm of light and darkness in the ordinary sense. This temporal division, which is an element of world-order, is something given by God and contributes to the glorification of God the Creator. With the creation of light and the division between light and darkness God brought to an end the primordial condition of Chaos

(Gen 1:3f), and right from the beginning the work of creation moves forward according to this alternating rhythm of day and night (Gen 1:1-2, 3). The idea of a primitive mythological struggle between light and darkness is foreign to the bible or, at any rate, its traces have been covered up by monotheism and the belief in creation as a divine act. There is therefore no chance of any cosmological dualism developing. This is true also of the poetical descriptions in Ps 104 and Job 26 and 38 which look at light and darkness as regular occurrences in nature which derive from the will of God which creates order in the world. 'Thine is the day, thine also the night; thou hast established the luminaries and the sun' (Ps 74:16)—this is the basic motif of these religious contemplations of the world and nature (see Ps 104:19-23; Job 26:10; 38:12; Am 4:13; 5:8; Jer 31:35; 33:25). This order has been created with reference to man's salvation (Ps 104:23); and so when it is violated or destroyed it is a sign of divine punishment for the sins of men. Darkness by daytime will proclaim the great day of judgement, the 'day of Yahweh' (see Jer 4:23, 28; Am 8:9; Joel 2:2, 31; 3:14). Since the daytime and light are experienced as the time of life, of activity and happiness, the morning or, in other texts, the rising sun, are greeted as bringing blessing from God on their arrival (cf Ps 3:5f; 5:3; 19; 46:5; 57:8; 90:14; 130:6; 143:8; Is 33:2; Zeph 3:5). The practice of praying at sunrise with the face to the east and with raised arms, which is found among Essenes, Therapeutae, and the members of the Qumran community, should

be explained on this basis—and not with reference to Pythagoreanism (see Flavius Josephus, *Bell. Iud.* II, 128; Philo, *de Vita Contempl.* 89; 1 QS x). Night is the time of lamentation and sighing (see Ps 30:5; 77:2; 119:147). The Israelite, who loves life, can only represent the kingdom of the dead, the underworld, as the land of darkness and shadow (cf Ps 49:19; 88:11-12; Job 10:21f; 38:17; Eccles 6:4f).

With this last we have already passed over to a metaphorical and symbolical application of light and darkness. Living in the light signifies happiness; light and life belong together as do darkness and death, darkness and damnation (cf Ps 56:13; 97:11; Job 22:28; 30:26 etc). This ordinary human symbolism is seen as religious since God is the source of light and life—'for with thee is the fountain of life; in thy light do we see light' (Ps 36:9), meaning that we receive from God happiness and salvation (cf Ps 18:28; 118:27; Is 9:1; 58:8). More than this, God is himself our 'light' and salvation (Ps 27:1; Mic 7:8), an idea which ties up with the concept of the ↗ 'glory' (*kābôd*) of God as described eschatologically (Is 60:1-3, 19f; 62:1f; 66:18f; Zech 2:5, 8). To *walk in the light* refers to the direction in which one walks, *the right way*, for it is the 'light' of the Lord which leads the pious Israelite (Ps 43:3; Job 29:3; Is 2:5; Mic 7:8). In this way 'light' becomes a metaphor for *the law of God* (Ps 119:105; Prov 6:23; Wis 18:4; see also Ps 19:8; Is 51:4 which speaks of a 'light for the nations') and for *wisdom* (Eccles 2:13; see also Wisd 7:10, 26; Bar 4:1f). Faith in God was so strong that the obscure tragic forces and the power of darkness in the world never become overpowering; and the Old Testament knows nothing of any personified 'demonic' Powers of Darkness.

B. *In later judaism.* We notice a clear-cut *dualism* for the first time in later judaism (from about the second century BC). Corresponding to the division between light and darkness in Gen 1:4, it was presumed that there was also a division between the spirits which were in men (Enoch [Eth] 41:8; see also Testament of the Twelve Apostles), a twofold division of just and sinners. According to Enoch [Slav] 8–10 the patriarch who had been taken up by an ascension into heaven sees the good in paradise, situated in the third heaven, guarded by angels shining with light, and the wicked in a fearful place where there is 'darkness and fog and no light of any kind'. There they are tortured by merciless angels. The opposition between life and death, truth and falsehood, light and darkness dominates thinking in this period (we find it already in Sir [Gk] 36:14; Test. Asher 5). 'You cannot accomplish the works of light if you abide in darkness' (Test. of Nephthali 2:10); 'Choose for yourselves between light and darkness, between the Law of the Lord and the works of Beliar!' (Test. of Levi 19:1). By means of good works 'light comes into the mind and the darkness gives way' (Test. of Benjamin 5:3). Light and darkness are therefore seen as strongly *contrasted areas to one or other of which men belong in accordance with their moral condition.* The doctrine of the Two Ways (see Barn. 18–20; Did 1–5) is very closely tied up with this; according to Enoch (Slav) 30:15 God showed Adam the two ways, that of light and of darkness, in order to discover whether he really loved or hated God and in order to recognise those among his descendants who would love him. Thus mankind is divided into a 'progeny of light' and 'those born in darkness' (see Enoch [Eth] 108:11 with 14).

This dualism stands out even more clearly in the Dead Sea Scrolls. There we find arrayed against one another the 'sons of light' and the 'sons of darkness' (see 1 QM, that is, 'The War of the Sons of Light against the Sons of Darkness') and behind these two hostile groups are arrayed the good and the evil spirits: 'These are the spirits of truth and of depravity. On the side of light are the sources of truth and from the fountain of darkness come the generations of evildoers. In the hand of the Prince of Light is the rule over the children of righteousness who walk along the ways of light; but in the hand of the Angel of Darkness is all the rule over the children of evil who walk along the ways of darkness' (1 QS 3:18–21). It almost seems as if it were irrevocably determined to which group a man should belong (determinism), but nevertheless in other texts there is clearly implied the possibility of free decision (see Nötscher). The chosen members of the 'Covenant of God' (that is, the community of Qumran) assume the obligation 'to love all the Children of Light, each one according to his share in salvation in the Council of God, and to hate all the Children of Darkness, each one according to his guilt in the avenging design of God' (1 QS 1:9f). Of these latter 'the deeds take place in darkness and their desire is for such' (1 QS 15:9f). This dualism is not purely anthropological and ethical since it is traced back to forces which are operative in the world (the 'spirits' of light and darkness); there is always present the idea of God the creator and lord. All that exists and all that happens comes from the 'all-knowing' God and its purpose is determined by him (1 QS 3:15). It is he who has created all the spirits of light and darkness (1 QS 3:25). God or, in some texts, Michael the Prince of Light to whom the task is delegated, leads the Sons of Light to victory (1 QS 13:10) in order to 'humble the darkness and make strong the light' (1 QS 13:15).

In addition to this, light and darkness are also used in a symbolic sense already familiar to the Old Testament. The light of knowledge and wisdom comes from God, that is, in practice, the Law and its right interpretation which indicates the way to be followed (see the Hodayoth or Hymn Scroll). Above all, light and darkness stand for ↗ salvation and condemnation; the 'eternal light' is the future life already referred to in Enoch [Eth] 58:3: 'The just are then in the light of the sun and the chosen ones in the light of eternal life' (see Bar [Syr] 48:50; 51). The struggle of the 'Sons of Light' mentioned in Qumran lasts until 'all the ages of darkness are at an end; but in God's time his exalted majesty will shine forth for ever . . . for salvation and blessing, glory and length of days for all the Sons of Light' (1 QM 1, 8f). These will attain to 'eternal light' (1 QS 4:8) since 'the destiny prepared by God is [determined] as the light [of life]' (1 QM 13:5).

If we take into account this dualism clearly attested in later judaism it is hardly necessary any more to adduce rather far-fetched parallels from pagan syncretism and gnosticism, in particular from Mandaeism, to throw light on the New Testament, even granted that contacts with gnostic terminology and its whole thought-world have to be gone into in connection with the Gospel of John. We can say on the whole that the way in which the New Testament speaks of and represents light and darkness is nourished by roots in the thought-world of later Judaism.

C. *In the New Testament.* Here we find a wide variety in the metaphorical use of the terms light and darkness. The logion in Mt 6:22f = Lk 11:34 is based on a semitic way of thinking; the eye is understood not as the organ but the source of light for men, while the 'inner light' corresponding to this refers perhaps to association with God which makes the entire man whole and sound (this is the opinion of E. Sjöberg, *ST* 5 [1951], 89–105). It is a universal and generally recognisable trait that where God is and where he reveals himself—that is, in a theophany, cf also the appearances of Christ and angels—there is brilliant light which is either already there or which suddenly flashes forth (see Lk 2:9; Mt 17:2, 5 and parallels; 28:3; Acts 1:10; 9:3; 10:30; 12:7; etc). The great revelation of salvation, however, consists in this, that 'the people who sat in darkness have seen a great light' (Mt 4:16; quoted from Is 9:2). The light of God for those in sin and the shadow of death is Jesus Christ himself, the Messiah, the 'light for revelation to the Gentiles' (Lk 2:32), a title which had already been applied to the Servant of the Lord in the Songs of the Servant (Is 42:6; 49:6). The light of God can also refer to 'the gospel of the glory of Christ' or, finally, to God himself who through Christ and his good tidings of salvation has shone forth in our hearts like the light of the morning of creation (2 Cor 4:4–6; see also 2 Tim 1:10). God has called even pagans from the darkness into his marvellous light (1 Pet 2:9).

Light is a constant figure for the salvation which comes in as the eschatological reality with Christ and finds its completion in the future kingdom of God. 'To be thrown into the outer darkness' means to be excluded from the banquet hall of God (which is full of light), that is, from his eschatological kingdom (Mt 8: 12; 22:13; 25:30). In one case darkness is even represented as an evil power which is active and aggressive; in the text in which Jesus says on being arrested 'this is your hour, and the power of darkness' (Lk 22:53). Similarly in Eph 6:12 those angelic powers which have rebelled against God and which threaten the salvation of mankind are called 'the world rulers of this present darkness'.

He who answers the call of Christ becomes himself 'a Child of the Light'. After the discovery of the Qumran texts it is no longer a surprise to us to find Jesus contrasting the 'Sons of Light' with the 'Sons of this age' (Lk 16:8). According to Mt 5:14 he calls his disciples 'the light of the world', certainly in a comprehensive sense since the following verse draws the direct consequence of this for the moral conduct of the disciples. Early christian preaching gives great importance to the warning about living one's life in the light (see Rom 13:12; Eph 5:8; 1 Thess 5:4ff; 1 Jn 1:7; 2:9f). This

ethical trait comes from judaism, and there are also cases here and there where the choice of words betrays knowledge of or relation of some kind with the Qumran texts, as when Paul asks: 'What fellowship has light with darkness? What accord has Christ with Belial?' (2 Cor 6:14f—this is the only New Testament use of this appellation for the Devil!) or where he explains how Satan can 'disguise himself as an angel of light' (2 Cor 11:14). There are also striking parallels in the Qumran texts for the fine statement that God the Father has 'qualified us to share in the inheritance of the saints in light . . . [and] delivered us from the dominion of darkness' (Col 1:12–13), for in these texts the 'Sons of Light' hope 'to participate in the inheritance of the saints (= those in heaven, the angels) and to be united with the Sons of Heaven' (1 QS 11:8; see also 1 QH 3:21ff; 11:9–14). The exhortation to the 'Children of Light' (Eph 5:6–14) could also betray the same influence, but just here where towards the end we find quoted some verses from a baptismal hymn, we find revealed the true *Sitz im Leben* (original situation) in the early church, namely, the *baptismal sermon*. This enables us to identify unmistakably the early christian way of thinking: through baptism christians are delivered from darkness 'into light' and are made members of the heavenly Kingdom of Light. They must therefore avoid the works of darkness and act as Children of the Light. The ethical exhortation is based on the sacramental event which comes about through the grace of God and the decision of man to believe. Such baptismal preaching is contained particularly in Eph and 1 Pet but can be detected in very many other texts in the epistles. There is already present in the New Testament the later designation of baptism as 'enlightenment' (cf 2 Cor 4:6; Eph 1:18; 2 Tim 1:10; Heb 6:4) following on the metaphorical sense.

In the *johannine writings* the concept of light and the dualism as between light and darkness come through most clearly. Here Christ refers to himself as 'the light of the world' (Jn 8:12; 9:5). The man who follows him in faith does not walk in darkness (that is, in this present earthly cosmos estranged from God) but will have 'the light of life' (8:12); he will not stumble and fall (cf 11:9f) but will become a 'child of the light' (12:36). Being identical with the life of God himself, the pre-existent *Logos* was the 'light of men' whom the darkness could not overcome (1:4f) neither in the pre-existent stage nor when the incarnate *Logos* came into this darkened world for the salvation of mankind (12:46). The frightful and inconceivable guilt of mankind consisted in this, that 'they loved the darkness more than the light' (3:19) on account of their evil deeds which made them shun the light (3:20). The dualism of a superior world of light and an inferior world of darkness and between the ascent and descent of the Saviour is strongly reminiscent of the gnostic concept of the two worlds and the gnostic Saviour-myth; but the christian bringer of light and life is divested of all mythical traits and established firmly in human history through the incarnation and his death on the cross (see 1 Jn 5:6). His task is not to gather together the scattered sparks of light from the material world in order to bring them together in the higher realm of light; rather does he offer to all men the possibility of possessing once again the light and life of God and demands at the same time that they 'walk in the light'. This is referred concretely in 1 John to the love of the brethren (2:9-11); without this love the affirmation that one is 'in light', that is, in association with God, is devoid of significance and a lie. God himself is light in whom there is no darkness (1:5), that is, his nature consists above all in the most absolute holiness and he tolerates nothing unholy to be associated with him. This is true also of God in the Old Testament, which shows that the johannine concept of light used with reference to God is deeply rooted in the Old Testament, though it develops within the context of the christian message of redemption, leaving itself open at the same time to hellenistic thought (see the hermetical writings). Beginning with Christ and by means of Christ who is the 'true light' (Jn 1:9), but also by means of christians who have received his light and life within themselves and put it into practice through brotherly love, God's kingdom of light spreads outwards and forces the darkness to yield (see 1 Jn 2:8).

Bibliography: S. Aalen, *Die Begriffe 'Licht' und 'Finsternis' im AT, im Spätjudentum und im Rabbinismus*, Oslo 1951 (with full bibliography); F. Nötscher, *Zur theologischen Terminologie der Qumran-Texte*, Bonn 1956, 92-148; J. C. Bott, 'De notione lucis in scriptis s. Joannis Ap.', *VD* 19 (1939), 81-91; E. Percy, *Untersuchungen über den Ursprung der johanneischen Theologie*, Lund 1939, 23-79; J. Dupont, *Essais sur la Christologie de S. Jean*, Bruges 1951, 61-105; R. Schnackenburg, *Die Johannesbriefe*, Freiburg 1963²; H. Schlier, *Der Brief an die Epheser*, Düsseldorf 1958²; B. Bussmann, *Der Begriff des Lichtes beim heiligen Johannes*, Münster 1957; G. Stählin, 'Jesus Christus, das Licht der

Welt', *Universitas* (Festschrift A. Stohr) 1, Mainz 1960, 58–78; L. R. Stachowiak, 'Die Antithese Licht-Finsternis: ein Thema der paulisnischen Paränese', *TQ* 143 (1963), 385–421. See also: R. Bultmann, 'Zur Geschichte der Lichtsymbolik im Altertum', *Philologus* 97 (1948), 1–36; E. R. Goodenough, *By Light Light: The Mystic Gospel of Hellenistic Judaism*, New Haven 1935 (on Philo); *Alte Sonnenkulte und die Lichtsymbolik in der Gnosis und im frühen Christentum* (Eranos-Jahrbuch x), Zürich 1944 (several authors); S. Edlung, *Das Auge der Einfalt*, Uppsala 1952; H. Preisker, *TLZ* 77 (1952), 673–8; G. Molin, *Die Söhne des Lichts. Zeit und Stellung der Handschriften vom Toten Meer*, Vienna–Munich 1954; H. W. Huppenbauer, *Der Mensch zwischen zwei Welten*, Zürich 1959; F. N. Klein, *Die Lichtterminologie bei Philon von Alexandrien und in den hermetischen Schriften*, Leiden 1962.

Rudolf Schnackenburg

Likeness

A. *Old Testament.* 1. Of fundamental importance for the biblical doctrine of man's likeness to God is the following passage in the first creation narrative: 'Let us make man according to [or 'as'] our image, after our likeness' (Gen 1:26). This first chapter must be kept distinct from the second. Let us carefully examine what its author meant to convey by these words. In view of the ambiguity of the Hebrew prepositions it must remain an open question whether we should render 'according to' or '*as*' our image'. To express what likeness means the author makes use of two connected terms, image (*ṣelem*) and likeness (*demûth*). This special way of expressing it has no theological implications. Thus it cannot be deduced from the use of two terms that two likenesses are meant, one on the natural, the other on the supernatural plane (Irenaeus). No trace of any such idea is

to be found in the context. Moreover later on, when they are used in a more general sense in Gen 1:27; 5:1, 3; 9:6 the two terms are clearly interchangeable. On similar grounds, and especially in view of the statement that Adam generated Seth 'in his own likeness and after his image' (5:3), the translation of either one or both of these terms as 'faithfully reproducing the plan' (Caspari) is to be rejected. Neither in the case of Seth being in Adam's likeness, nor in that of man being in God's likeness, is any third point of common reference presupposed such as an idea, a plan, or a picture produced by the imagination. God in the first example, Adam in the second, are the only models from which the image is copied. Likeness then primarily implies that man is like God himself and that God recognises himself in man as in an image.

2. The passage immediately following on from the doctrine expressed in Gen 1:26 seems intended to convey that *the root meaning of likeness is dominion* (von Rad) over 'the fish of the sea, the birds of the air, the cattle, every wild beast of the plain, and over every creeping thing that creeps upon the earth'. Likeness then makes man like God precisely inasmuch as man represents God as Lord of creation and acts as God's vizier in the work of creation; it also makes man like God in that creation itself is, in a certain sense, ordered to man. In this respect the assertion in Ps 8:6–9 approximates very closely to Gen 1:26, although in the psalm the relevant terms for likeness do not occur. The psalmist may have avoided them deliberately, for the phrase 'a little lower than the *'elōhîm*' is equivalent to

a paraphrase of what is meant by likeness. Admittedly a certain dialectical tension is apparent in the idea of likeness as it is found in the psalm; on the one hand man *is lower* than the *ᵓelōhîm,* on the other he is *only a little* lower. Man is image; that is his limitation. He is an image of *ᵓElōhîm,* and that is his greatness. This is emphasised by the statement that God has imparted 'glory' (*kābôd*) and 'honour' (*hᵃdar*) to man. In immediate connection with this we are also told in Ps 8 that man is appointed as overlord over 'the work of thy hands'. Does the author mean to convey by this that the likeness in question consists in the possession of authority, in other words that it is merely a 'function'? We can by no means disregard the fact that man's overlordship is based on his superiority to the sub-human creatures and we may assume that the biblical author was aware of this as a pre-requisite for such overlordship. Thus likeness as found in Gen 1 can be defined as *that specific superiority over lesser creatures which is imparted to man by God* in such a way that these lesser creatures are subject to man and are, in a certain sense, ordered to him in virtue of his special status as person.

3. The question now arises what it is in man that reflects God's likeness; whether the likeness is predominantly physical (von Rad) or whether it is to be thought of as belonging to the 'spiritual sphere' (Heinisch, etc). At this point it must be observed that the author of Gen 1 does not consider man as made up of two basic constituents, 'dust' and 'breath of life'. Nor does he give a separate account of the creation of woman. He views man as a whole,

and so the body cannot be excluded from his conception of likeness. Further confirmation of this may be adduced from Ps 8, for the dominion (glory) with which God has crowned man must be taken in the widest sense of the term. To mention only one point, it includes 'the heavens' too (Ps 19:1) so that these bear witness to God and for God as an emanation of his own radiance. It is not the spirit alone but the whole of creation that bears witness to God. Here of course the body is regarded not as an anatomical form but as a phenomenon in its entirety. It is no objection to this point of view to point out that physically speaking there are many creatures to which man is not superior. The very fact that he stands upright gives him a far greater superiority than that which consists in mere muscular strength. Moreover, from the fact that the body is included in this idea of man's superiority it cannot be deduced that God is to be thought of in physical terms, so that man's likeness to him would be understood as something like that of a cast to its original. Let us take an example. On the one hand the words for likeness are used of the begetting of Seth. This rules out any exclusively spiritual interpretation of the concept of likeness. On the other hand it is a demonstrable and generally acknowledged fact that the author of Gen 1 works from a wholly spiritualised concept of God. For him it must have been clear that likeness was to be understood only as a figure of speech, and not as something that was achieved in the same dimension of existence as God. Thus likeness is manifested in man as *a physical-spiritual whole,* and it is this likeness to God that raises him above the rest of creation.

4. This likeness to God appears equally in woman as in man, for the statement 'male and female he created them' (Gen 1:27) is made in immediate connection with their creation as image. Thus on woman's equality with man Gen 1 agrees with Gen 2, however widely they differ in their manner of presenting it.

How does the differentiation between the sexes reflect as image some aspect of God? Are man and woman 'for' one another in a personal or a social sense? These are questions which the meagreness of the information does not permit us to answer. There is no mention of God being love; only his personhood and that of the two human beings are indicated.

The blessing of fruitfulness is more clearly connected with the idea of likeness to God. Fruitfulness results from God's life-giving and creative power, and is the image of this. Perhaps all that the author had in mind was the likeness that consists in this quite general relationship between man and woman. We cannot proceed any further in this line of argument without recourse to the New Testament mystery of the Trinity.

5. As presented in Gen 1 the 'likeness' idea has a very narrow application. Nevertheless this does not prevent us from recognising that with the development of Old Testament theology in general we have been able to achieve a fuller and more detailed knowledge of the breadth and richness of this idea in particular. Thus within the same strand of tradition (Priestly, or P) to which Gen 1 and 5 are equally ascribed

a primary shade of meaning can be established in that the begetting of Seth is seen as a handing on of likeness. In this tradition Seth is not just anyone but the one who is to bring the heritage of Adam into the line of the patriarchs and the elect, and so to hand it on through that line to Abraham. In this way Seth's likeness to Adam, himself created after the image of God, becomes the sign of a special election and grace. It is from this aspect that it is fundamental for the idea that the chosen race is superior to the rest of mankind, who have not been chosen.

But apart from this the actual idea of likeness to God has also been further developed and we have no grounds (against von Rad) for excluding the references in Wis and Sir as interpretations of the biblical concept of likeness. The opening verses of Sir 17 manifestly refer to the connection between man's likeness to God and his dominion over lesser creatures as presented in Gen 1:26. But they go beyond this to give details and draw consequences which have not previously been expressed. In Sir likeness is manifested in the 'powers' which God imparts to man, in the 'fear' emanating from man, which is an extension of the fear pertaining to God himself as Numen, but above all in the personal endowments of intellect and freedom, understanding and will. Here too, although the spiritual side receives special emphasis, the idea of likeness is applied to man as a whole, as is clear from the way in which the author refers to the fear that emanates from man. As image of God it is man's duty to 'order his way of life' (see 17:14), and this gives a quite unambiguous answer to a question which, so Caspari believed, should be left open, namely whether we are to infer that 'being in God's likeness imposed a series of obligations' (p. 208). Being in God's likeness does have ethical consequences in relation both to God and to one's fellow men.

In Wisdom a fresh view can be perceived. A concept which is central to this book is the immortality of man. This is represented as being in its original form (ie, before the fall) a consequence of being in God's image (2:23). This primordial immortality was lost, but the author does not make it clear at this point whether he believes that likeness too was lost as such and in its entirety or only immortality as one of its effects. The question must therefore remain open. At all events, as the teacher of wisdom understands it, likeness to God did not survive unscathed in man. In place of this human image he has knowledge of an 'unspotted mirror of God', namely wisdom itself, which he calls 'image (*eikōn*) of God's goodness' (7:26). This way of conceiving of likeness introduces a somewhat different element into the idea. Here wisdom is said to be not 'under God' but (due allowance being made for the influence of personification and hypostatisation) equal in essence to, indeed identical with God.

B. *New Testament.* 1. Fuller evidence could be adduced from extra-biblical sources for the idea which Wisdom introduces. But sufficient evidence has been given here to enable us to understand the similar development of the idea which can be discerned in the New Testament. Heb 10:1 sets 'image' in contrast to 'shadow'. In this way it establishes a connection between it and the original in identity, fullness and colour.

From this Paul could pass on quite naturally to presenting *Christ* as 'the first-born of all creation', as 'before all things', and as 'fullness'; he also described him as 'the image of the invisible God' (Col 1:15). The reality which John expresses as 'Word' (1:1) and elsewhere as 'Son', namely 'the glory of God in the face of Christ' (2 Cor 4:6), is here called the 'likeness of God' (2 Cor 4:4) or again 'the very stamp of his nature' (Heb 1:3). By emphasising likeness to God in Christ, Paul intends to assert not that Christ is 'under God' but that he is 'with God', that is of the same nature as, equal to, and metaphysically one with God.

With regard to *the likeness to God in man* as expressed in Gen 1, Paul gives a somewhat narrower idea of this in one passage, namely 1 Cor 11:7. Here he refers to it in the course of explaining how the husband comes to be the head of the wife because, according to Gen 2, he was created first. This would imply that only man was directly in God's likeness, while woman would be so only indirectly through man, in that she was formed from him. However we can see from Col 3:10 that this mode of reasoning is only a rhetorical device. In this passage he exhorts his hearers to put forth all their strength in the effort to make actual in their own lives and persons 'the image of the Creator'. Here there can be no difference whatever between man and woman. Beside the special shade of meaning in the idea which appears here, it may be inferred from this pericope that likeness is to be conceived at once as a gift and a task. It is capable of being developed and imposes a moral obligation on man to develop it within himself. But, as the apostle goes on to explain, this development would not be possible unless we had 'put on the new man' who is Christ. In this way the idea of likeness is changed in Paul's writings. It acquires new content and is given a place in the theology of redemptive grace. As a result of this 'the image of the earthly' and first Adam has had to be changed into 'the image of the heavenly' and second Adam (1 Cor 15:49). A two-fold likeness emerges from this. In fact, since Christ, likeness is only made present in us when we are 'conformed to the image of his Son' (Rom 8:29). In virtue of being 'changed into the same image' (2 Cor 3:18) we behold 'with unveiled face . . . the glory of the Lord'. In the New Testament then it is no longer a question of man having dominion over the lesser creatures. The idea of likeness is raised wholly into the supernatural order and consists finally in likeness to Christ and union with Christ. It is Christ now who is at once model, artist and pledge of true likeness to God in us. The relationship of being 'in Christ' leads on to that of being 'with Christ' and so to being 'of Christ'. In the same way a whole series of degrees of likeness to God is included in the idea of image, from the moment of grace when the christian community first began to take shape to the ultimate consummation of the deed of salvation, from the redeeming Christ to the glorified Christ, from the redeemed christian to the christian who participates in the glory of heaven.

Bibliography: J. Hehn, 'Zum Terminus "Bild Gottes"', *Festschrift E. Sachau*, Berlin 1915, 36–52; W. Caspari, 'Imago divina Gen I', *Reinhold-Seeberg Festschrift*, Leipzig 1929, 197–208; T. C. Vriezen, 'La création de l'homme d'après l'image de Dieu', *OTS* 2 (1943), 87–105; L. Koehler, 'Die Grundstelle der Imago-Dei-Lehre: Gen 1:26', *TZ* 4 (1948), 16–22; P. Althaus, 'Das Bild Gottes bei Paulus', *TB* 20 (1944), 81–92; *TDNT* II, 388–97 and IV, 742–55.

Othmar Schilling

Lord's day

How, when, where, and under what stimulus the community of Jesus transferred their holy day from the Jewish Sabbath to Sunday—these questions are lost in obscurity. There is no evidence that the risen Lord gave directions for the observance of this day to the apostles. On the other hand, however, in the life of the early church the institution of the Lord's day is so much taken for granted that clearly we must suppose that it was dedicated to the celebration of the resurrection and last supper by the apostles, and that too at a period before the missionary activity of Paul (see Dumaine, 895f). Of its very nature Sunday was quite different from the Sabbath. Sunday was not a day of rest and fasting, but a day of festal celebration, a commemoration of the resurrection (the Sabbath rest continued to be observed together with it chiefly by christians converted from judaism). Sunday, then, was far from being an institution opposed to the Sabbath and designed to replace it, though this has sometimes been maintained (see Dölger). Eusebius declares of the sect of christian Ebionites: 'This branch, like the other [Jewish Ebionites] observed the Sabbath and the rest of the Jewish customs, *but with it they* also celebrated the Lord's day like ourselves to commemorate the Resurrection of the Redeemer' (*Hist. Eccl.* III, 27:3–5). From this it can clearly be seen that there was nothing anti-Jewish in the observance of Sunday, and further that its celebration goes back to a Jerusalemite custom, namely the celebration of the resurrection.

In Acts 20:6 we are told that Paul comes to Troas and remains there for seven days, and then 'on the first day of the week' the faithful assemble in the evening (after work) in order to celebrate the last supper. Already before this, in 1 Cor 16:1f, Paul designates the 'first day of the week' as the day of assembly, when he gives directions for the collection to be made on this day. In Rev 1:10 it is on 'the Lord's day' that the 'risen' Christ appears to John the Seer, at a time when at home the community observes the celebration of the risen one. In Lk 24:30 the risen Christ celebrates the sacred meal in person with his astonished disciples on the day of his resurrection, in the evening 'on the first day of the week'.

In the life of the early church Sunday acquired a significance similar to that which the Sabbath bore in judaism. Ignatius of Antioch (†110) writes to the Magnesians 9:1: 'The Jews who have come to the new hope no longer celebrate the Sabbath but keep the Lord's day, on which life began through Christ'. The Epistle of Barnabas gives the same testimony (15:9). The pagan Pliny writes to Trajan at this time (*Letter* X, 96, 97) among other things that the christians assemble *stato die* (on a fixed day) before dawn, which is undoubtedly meant to call to mind the hour of the resurrection. The apocryphal gospel of Peter, which appeared in Syria before 150, already designates the day of the resurrection as *kuriakē*, 'the Lord's (day)'. Contemporaneously with this the Didache was written, of which chapter 14 treats expressly of the celebration of Sunday. Justin and Tertullian testify likewise to the celebration of Sunday. When they are addressing pagans they call it 'Sun-day' (*dies solis*), but when they are addressing christians they call it 'the Lord's day'. Further testimony may be adduced from Bardesanes of Edessa (†222) and Dionysius of Corinth (in Eusebius 4:23, 11) in a letter to Pope Soter written between 166 and 174. Again, soon after the middle of the second century, Melito, bishop of Sardis in Lydia, wrote a special treatise on Sunday. About the same time the question was raised among the rabbis how the '*day of the Nazarene*' should be regarded. Among the pagans no business can be conducted for three days before and after their feasts . . . the fourth and fifth days of the week (Wednesday and Thursday) remain for the christians (SB I, 1053).

Thus Sunday certainly did not originate in judaism, but it did not originate in the pagan world either. Of the pagans, the Romans did not specially celebrate the *dies solis*. Among them it was rather Saturn's day (Saturday) that was the equivalent of the Jewish Sabbath, for since Saturday was considered an unlucky day, people avoided beginning any business on it and so rested (Ovid, *Ars amat.* I, 415; *Rem. am.* 219f; Suet., *Aug.* 76:2; Seneca in Augustine, *Civ.* 6:11. Hence Flavius Josephus, *Contra Ap.* II, 39, thinks that all the pagans already celebrate the Sabbath too).

The 'Sunday' of the christians was not a day of rest, but one of liturgical celebrations, of joy, of the Lord's resurrection. The Syrian Didascalia contains a tradition of one of the Lord's sayings: 'It is not permitted for you to fast on the first day of the week, for that is the day of my resurrection' (21. S. 107, Flemming). On this day of joy there is no fasting at the ceremonies, nor any kneeling down (Tertullian, *De cor. mil.* 3; *De orat.* 23).

The pagans began the week on Saturn's day, as is shown by the calendars written on stone and clay which have been discovered. The system of reckoning and observance which the christians had long practised first became official under Constantine.

The decisive question is: 'How could the early church have arrived at this unanimous concept of the celebration of Sunday in opposition to the Jewish Sabbath? Paul gives us the answer: 'Let no one pass judgement on you in questions of food and drink or with regard to a festival or a new moon or a Sabbath. These are only a *shadow* of what is to come; but the *substance* belongs to Christ' (Col 2:16). Compare Gal 4:10f against the judaisers: 'You observe days and months and seasons and years! I am afraid I have laboured over you in vain'. Through the consummation in Christ the old festivals have found their fulfilment. They are the shadows, Christ is the substance, the reality, which *discards* these shadows! In him all is fulfilled; if someone decided to celebrate the old festivals still, he would set himself back in the old covenant, and forfeit the redemption.

Christ himself scrupulously observed all the Jewish festivals with his disciples up to his resurrection (Mt 26:18ff and parallels; Lk 2:41f; 4:16; 23:54f; etc). The fourth gospel is particularly concerned to emphasise that Jesus attended the Jewish festivals (2:13ff, Passover; see also 12:12ff; 11:56; Purim, 5:1; Tabernacles, 7:2ff; The consecration of the temple, 10:22). But the very fact of his doing so contains, in some sense, an implicit affirmation that he, Jesus, is the reality, the fulfilment of these festivals. This is the force of the saying of the Lord in Mt 5:17: 'Think not that I have come to abolish the law and the prophets; I have come not to abolish them but to fulfil them'. It is a question of fulfilment in him, a fulfilment which at the same time means their completion and their end, 'for Christ is the end of the law, that everyone who has faith may be justified' (Rom 10:4).

Jesus' sayings about the temple point in exactly the same direction: he who worships in spirit and in truth has no more need of a temple (Jn 4:21ff). Thus the imminent ruin of the temple and its replacement by a spiritual building is announced not as a catastrophe but as an advance: Jn 2:19ff: 'Destroy this temple and in three days I will build it up . . . but he spoke of the temple of his body' . . . Christ himself, his body, his mystical body, the church, the community of the faithful in him (1 Cor 12:27 etc), that is the new temple, the new reality.

'Something greater than the temple is here', says Jesus to the pharisees when they blamed his disciples for plucking ears on the Sabbath (Mt 12:1ff), and further: 'the Son of Man is Lord of the Sabbath'. It is precisely the Sabbath day that Jesus often chooses for the performance of his miracles. On this day he preaches in the synagogues. This day above all is the day on which he 'works' as the father works (Jn 5:17), that is, the day on which the future world actually breaks in upon the present one. Thus he fulfils the expectation of rest and the divine presence which was prepared for by the Sabbath. In this way the Sabbath becomes his day. He is Lord of the Sabbath. This is not, so to say, the expression of antiformalism as a principal, but the sign of his messiahship.

He is Lord of the Sabbath in order to redeem mankind (Lk 13:15; 14:5 etc). The Sabbath is there for man's sake, not the other way about (Mk 2:27f). Certainly he who transgresses the Sabbath law for any reason other than the coming of Christ is a lawbreaker and accursed, as an agraphon in the form of a saying of Jesus which is undoubtedly genuine reminds us: 'On the same day, seeing a man working on the Sabbath, he [Jesus] said to him: "Man, if you know what you are doing, you are blessed; but if you do not know, you are accursed and a transgressor of the law"' (Lk 6:5 [Codex D]; see J. Jeremias, *Unknown Sayings of Jesus*, London 1957). He who believes in Jesus the Messiah, therefore, is freed from the Sabbath commandment (Mt 12:1ff), as well as from circumcision and the temple—a new Israel!

What applies to the temple applies also to the Jewish Passover. It was only a type, a shadow: 'Christ is our paschal Lamb' (1 Cor 5:7).

In accordance with this replacement of shadows by reality the Sabbath also must go. It is the *church* which takes the

teaching about the new Israel unequivocally to heart, even though voices are raised here and there from among the Jewish christians who want the observance of the Sabbath to be acknowledged *as well* (Col 2:16; Gal 4:10). Certainly the apostles have to continue to observe the customs of the Jews in order to conduct their mission among them. Above all they must attend their assemblies on the Sabbath and hold their preaching then (see Acts 9:20; 13:5; 14:42ff; 14:1; 16:13; etc). Thus even now they still went into the temple (Acts 3:1; 5:20, 25). But they were fully conscious of the fact that they were no longer Jews.

The Sabbath was the sign of the covenant (Ex 31:17; see also Ezek 20:12): '. . . that they might know that I, the Lord, sanctify them'. Now the old covenant is abrogated, and its sign along with it. By instituting the new covenant God has declared the old one to be obsolete and annulled: *to de palaioumenon kai gēraskon engus aphanismou* (lit. = 'what is becoming obsolete and growing old is near disappearance', Heb 8:13). *Aphanizō* (lit. = to make unseen) is used of the deletion or abrogation of laws (Lysias, *Con. Nichomach.* 35; Dion. Hal., *Ant.* 3, 178). Compare 2 Cor 5:17; Lk 5:36ff; Lev 26:10; and the rabbinical axiom, 'one will renders another void' (Baba Bathra 8:5).

The new covenant is sealed in the blood of the Lord. The Messiah is delivered up for our sins and raised to life for our justification (Rom 4:25). Thus by his resurrection our redemption is once and for all achieved. If Jesus had not risen from the dead our faith would be vain. Once again this day, the day of the resurrection, the first day of the week, the day of 'the Lord', marked by special festal celebrations, is thought of as the sign of the new covenant. In Lk 2:34f Jesus himself is called a 'sign'; and the 'sign of Jonas', which will be given to the unbelieving generation, is clearly the resurrection of Jesus.

Sunday is designated as the ↗ 'Day of the Lord' after the prophets, who spoke of the judgement day of the Lord (Is 13:9; cp 2:12; Joel 2:31 etc). It is the day of the great banquet, from which he who is wearing no festal garment (=penance, Mt 22:11f) will be cast out. The Lord's day is also connected with the celebration of the eucharist (Acts 20:7. Perhaps already implicit in the meeting with the disciples on the way to Emmaus?). All this points on to the second coming of the Lord Jesus at the end of days. This too will be marked by judgement and a banquet. Both elements are anticipated every Sunday in the celebration of the liturgy, and in this anticipation the christians' hope that Christ will return in glory becomes true and real.

The Lord's Day—memorial of the resurrection, anticipation of Christ's return—is therefore the day, between these two events, on which supremely the work of salvation is accomplished; so that to experience a christian Sunday is to expose oneself to the grace of the redemptive mystery of God. We could have arrived at the same conclusion by considering, instead of the Lord's Supper, the preaching, that went with it (Acts 20:7ff); for preaching, quite as much as the Lord's Supper, is embedded in the eschatological work of God:

it, too, recalls the resurrection of Jesus (Acts 2:24ff, etc); it too, by gathering the elect (see Lk 5:10; Mt 9:37ff), anticipates the return of the Lord (cf Mt 24:31). It may be said, therefore, that the Lord's Day constitutes the church. It may also be said, that those who think it their duty to abandon Sunday to keep the sabbath instead are in effect denying the passage from the Old Covenant to the New, and therefore the Messiahship of Jesus. [Allmen, 125.]

Bibliography: On the sabbath: Haag 1443-77 (with further bibliography); more fully: J. Botterweck, *TQ* 134 (1954), 123-6 and 448-57; R. North, *Bbl* 36 (1955), 182-201. On Sunday: Haag 1538f, Allmen 123-6; Friedrich, *BTHW* 547-50; Lecher and Eisenhofer, *Liturgik*, Freiburg 1953, 131ff (with bibliography); H. Dumaine, 'Dimanche', *DACL* 458-886; C. Callewaert, 'La synaxe eucharistique à Jérusalem, berceau du dimanche', *ETL* 15 (1938), 34-73; F. J. Dölger, *Antike und Christentum* 6 (1941), 202-38; J. M. Nielen, *Das Zeichen des Herrn*, Freiburg 1940; P. Louis, *Der Christ und sein Sonntag*, Würzburg 1950; J. Wagner and D. Zähringer, *Eucharistiefeier am Sonntag*, Trier 1951; J. Froger, 'Origines et histoire du dimanche', *VS* 76 (1947), 502-22; J. Barbel, 'Der christliche Sonntag in der Verkündigung', *TTZ* 60 (1951), 17-30; F. Steinmetzer, 'Arbeitsruhe', *RAC* I, 592-5; F. Pettirsch, *ZKT* 1951; A. Deissmann, *Licht vom Osten*, 1923⁴, 304ff; W. Foerster, *TDNT* III, 1095f; E. Cattaneo, *Enciclopedia Cattolica* IV, 1817-19; E. Dekkers, *Tertullianus en de geschiedis der Liturgie*, Brussels 1947, 126-30; R. Hoomaert, 'Le dimanche chrétien', *Quest. Lit. par.* 16 (1947), 90-97; J. Hild, 'La mystique du dimanche', and L. Leloir, 'Le sabbat judaïque, préfiguration du dimanche', *MD* 9 (1947), 7-51; H. Rahner, *Griechische Mythen in christl. Deutung*, Zürich 1946, 141ff; W. Kornfeld and J. Kosnetter, *Der Tag des Herrn*, Vienna 1958, 11-31 and 33-57; E. Lohse, *TWNT* VII, 1-35 (with extensive bibliography); H. Riesenfeld, 'Sabbat et jour du Seigneur', *Festschrift T. W. Manson*, Manchester 1959, 210-17; Y. B. Trémel, 'Du sabbat au jour du Seigneur', *LV* 11/58 (1962), 29-49; W. Rordorf, *Der*

Sonntag (Abhandl. z. Theol. d. AT u. NT 43), Zürich 1962; P. Pas, 'De Zontag', *Colectanea Mechl.* 47 (1962), 5–29; E. Hilgert, 'The Jubilees Calendar and the Origin of Sunday Observance', *Andrews University Seminary Quarterly* 1 (1963), 44–61; W. Wiefel, 'Voraussetzungen und Anfänge des christl. Kirchenjahres', *TLZ* 89 (1964), 714f.

Johannes B. Bauer

Love

A. *The linguistic evidence.* The Hebrew term most closely corresponding to our word *love* is ᵓ*ahaḫâh*, or, in the verbal form, ᵓ*āhaḫ*. The less frequent *ḫāpēṣ*, meaning 'love' in the sense of 'take pleasure in' (eg, Ps 51:6) or *rāḫam* = 'love ardently' (with God as subject 'to take pity on' Ex 33:19; or of man's love for God, Ps 18:1) have a more restricted range of meaning. ᵓ*āhaḫ*, on the other hand, can signify the natural love of a father for his child (Gen 22:2), of spouses for each other (24:67); it can also mean friendship (1 Sam 18:1, 3) or the dependence of slaves upon the benevolence of their master (Ex 21:5), or even sexual passion (2 Sam 13:1, 4, 15). But it can also mean love of one's neighbour (Lev 19:18) or of strangers (19:34), and above all of God (not before Ex 20 [Elohist]), which is religiously motivated. ᵓ*āhaḫ* can even be used of the love which God offers to man, especially to the people of Israel (eg, Deut 4:37).

With regard to the Greek bible one cannot fail to be struck by the fact that in translating words of the ᵓ*āhaḫ* group LXX uses the terms *erōs* or *erasthai* only once or twice, though these are the words most frequently used in both classical and hellenistic Greek; the renderings *philia* and *philein* are also infrequent. The use of *agapēsis* or *agapan*, though, is almost universal: in this connection it should be noticed that these latter words are less emotionally charged than those previously mentioned. As used outside the bible they designate a sober kind of love—love in the sense of placing a high value upon some person or thing, or of receiving them with favour. In sacred scripture, however, they acquire a religious content which is, in many respects, new. A further sign of this is the introduction of the substantive *agapē*, which was hardly usual in earlier writings. This word appears already to have come to the fore in the *koinē* of Egypt (A. Ceresa-Gastaldo), but its presence in pre-LXX literature has so far not been able to be established with certainty (against W. Bauer, *Wörterbuch* 5, 9; cf Spicq, *Agapē*, 32–6 and 208ff). This can hardly have happened without reason, and must be taken into account in the theological interpretation of the word; for the implication of this fact of linguistic history, noteworthy as it is in two respects, is that the biblical doctrine of love differs essentially from pagan ideas on the subject.

In the writings of the New Testament the exclusion of *erōs* and *erasthai* is carried still further towards its logical conclusion, and at the same time the deeper meanings of *agapē* (*agapēsis* is completely absent in these writings) and *agapan* are fully explicitated. By contrast *philein* and its derivatives, although we encounter them more frequently here, are nevertheless less relevant theologically speaking. In the synoptics the substantive *agapē* occurs admittedly only twice (Mt 24:12; Lk 11:42); nor is the verb *agapan* particularly frequent.

Yet for all this the reality signified by these words is no less clearly thrown into relief. Apart from the instructions and parables of the Lord concerning the 'altogether different' love which embraces even the poor, sinners, and enemies, they have handed down to us the revelation of the unique manifestation of the love of God in the work and sacrifice of the Son. And it is precisely the fact that they have done this without any overlay of theological interpretation that makes their testimony especially valuable to us. In Paul and John, however, it is a 'theology' of *agapē* that confronts us. A comparison of the pauline vocabulary with the johannine reveals that the former has a remarkably strong preference for the substantive *agapē* as against the verb, *agapan* (78:36), whereas the converse is true of the latter, where it is the verbal form that predominates (30:71). Admittedly, it would be wrong to conclude from this that the pauline view is focused upon static substances, while the johannine, by contrast, is focused upon dynamic acts. On the contrary, as we shall see, there is essential agreement between the two conceptions of *agapē*.

For all this, however, these findings from the statistics of the language used do indicate differences in perspective, inasmuch as Paul is more concerned with the 'essence' of *agapē* as revealed in the salvific work of Christ, especially in the mystery of the cross, and in the transmission of its salvific effects to the faithful, while John concentrates rather on the movement of love outwards from, and inwards to, God, the basic unity of meaning and reality which underlines the particular concrete forms

in which love was for a time embodied, and by which it was characterised—in other words, the manifestation of the divine *Logos* become flesh in the person of Jesus Christ.

B. *Love in the Old Testament.* Biblical thought is, from the outset, orientated theocentrically—one might almost say 'theocratically'—and therefore has as its central point the idea of God as Creator and Lord of all, as well as deliverer and judge of mankind. For this reason it is of the love which is predicated of God himself that we must first speak.

1. *God's love for men.* This is attested even in the earliest sections of the bible. True it is seldom mentioned *expressis verbis*, but nonetheless it is expressed clearly, though indirectly, in the numerous *narratives* of how he acted towards men. First the creation is considered as a work of God's kindness (Gen 1:4, 10, 31; see also Ps 136:1–9; Sir 16:26–30; 39:33). But foremost in this work is the formation of man, whom God made to his own 'image' (Gen 1:26f; 9:6; Wis 2:23), richly endowed with gifts and set in the garden of bliss (Gen 2:7ff [J or E source]; see also Wis 9:2ff; Sir 17:1–14). Even when man has wantonly fallen away from him and become a sinner God does not altogether cast him off, but promises to redeem him in the future (Gen 3:14f). Thus in the midst of the general corruption Noah 'found grace (*ḥēn*) in the eyes of Yahweh' (6:8), and after the Flood he, together with his descendants, is deemed worthy of a covenant of blessing (9:1–17). In particular God took Abraham under his protection and sealed a covenant with him based on mutual faithfulness (*'emeth* 15:6 [J]),

renewing this with the other patriarchs (with Isaac, Gen 26:3–6, and with Jacob, 28:13ff; 35:11ff). The paternal love which Yahweh bore towards Israel his 'first-born son' (Ex 4:22 [L]) was manifested above all in his miraculous liberation of his people from the forced labour imposed upon them by the Egyptians (esp. Deut 1:30ff). This was constantly recalled, either as the subject of joyful thanksgiving (Ex 15:1–18) or as a basis for exhortations (Deut 4:32–8; 32:1–47; Jos 24:2–13). In the same way the Sinai covenant, by which Yahweh chose Israel for himself as 'his special possession', as 'a kingdom of priests' and 'a holy people', regardless of its juridical character, is a work of his mercy and kindness (Ex 19:4ff [L]; 34:9f; Deut 4:31; 7:7f).

However, direct evidence too of God's love is not lacking in the pentateuch. Admittedly the earliest occurrence of the verb *ʾāhaḇ* as used of the divine love in its free choice of Israel is in Deuteronomy (4:37; 7:7f; 10:15). But the loving attitude of God towards men is often expressed by related terms, thus by *ḥēn* (attraction, favour, ↗ grace Gen 6:8; 19:19; Ex 33:12f, 16f) or *ḥānan* (be gracious to, confer upon, Gen 33:5, 11; 43:29; Ex 33:19), by *ḥesed* (favour, ↗ goodness Gen 19:19; Ex 20:6; Deut 5:10; 7:9, 12; forgiveness Num 14:19f) and by *rāḥam* or *meraḥēm* (to have mercy on (Ex 33:19; Deut 17:18; 30:3) or *raḥamîm* (compassion Deut 13:17). Since Yahweh is at the same time the 'truthful' or 'faithful' covenant God (Deut 32:4) his dominion is characterised as one of '(loving) kindness and truth' (*ḥesed weʾemeth* Gen 24:27; see also 24:12), a usage which gradually came to have

the force of a declaratory formula (2 Sam 2:6; Pss 25:10; 40:11; 57:3; 89:14, 24, 33; Mic 7:20; Tob 3:2; etc; ↗ truth). Typical of the idea of God in ancient Israel is the saying: 'Yahweh [is] a merciful (*raḥûm*) and gracious (*ḥannûn*) [God], slow to anger and abounding in steadfast love and faithfulness, keeping steadfast love for thousands, forgiving iniquity and transgression and sin, but who will by no means clear the guilty' (Ex 34:6f [L]; see also Ps 86:15; 103:8; 111:4; etc). Thus the earlier parts of the Old Testament do seem to know of God's forgiving love (see also Num 14:17ff), and to see the effects of it even in the sufferings which are sent as chastisements, inasmuch as it is God's will to bring men by them truly to convert their ways (Lev 26:40–45; Num 14:20–25; Deut 4:25–31; 30:1–10). Of its nature the love of God is spontaneous and free (Ex 33:19); but in accordance with the nature of the covenant, the institution of which is its outcome, God expects and requires that man shall serve him, keep his commandments and love him in return. This already finds expression in the earliest passage in which God's love is declared: 'I, Yahweh your God, am a jealous God, visiting the iniquity of the fathers upon the children to the third and fourth generation of those who hate me, but showing mercy to thousands of those who love me and keep my commandments' (Ex 20:5f [J]; see also Deut 5:9f; 7:9–15 and *passim*). 'Zeal' or 'jealousy' here is used merely for the basic purpose of signifying the unconditional nature and the depths of God's love. But characteristic once more is the close connection between punitive justice and merciful kindness (*ḥeseḏ*), which nevertheless presupposes a reciprocal love on the part of man, realised in the observance of the commandments (see B.2 below).

In the course of history Yahweh constantly showed fresh instances of his love with its aspects of election, grace and forgiveness, to the Israelites in general, and especially to David and his house, always provided that they for their part remained loyal to the covenant and did not apostatise to strange gods (eg 1 Sam 2:1–10; 2 Sam 7:14ff; 1 Kings 3:6; 8:23–6; 9:3–9; 2 Kings 13:23; Neh 1:5–11; 9:17–33). But it is above all in the prophets that the love of God is thrown into relief, being preached by them with great force and conviction. In contrast to the 'dead idols' (Jer 11:12), which are 'insubstantial nothings' (Is 2:8), Yahweh alone can bestow help and salvation (Is 38:6; Jer 16:9; 42:11; Hos 1:7; Ezek 13:21). For his kindness (*ḥeseḏ*) 'endures for ever' (Jer 33:11), even though it is always complemented by ⁄ justice (*ṣᵉḏāqāh*) (9:24; see also 32:18). On the other hand, however, this love is often associated with the motif of compassion (*raḥᵃmîm*) (Hos 2:21 [19]; Is 54:8; 60:10; 63:7; Zech 1:16), which is abundant to pardon (Is 55:7; see also Mic 7:19), though of course only when the sinner has repented and been converted (Hos 1:6; Jer 18:8; 21:4–7; Ezek 18:27). Thus Habakkuk can actually unite the wrath of God with his compassion (3:2; see also Nahum 1:2f), especially since the ultimate motive for his forgiveness is the honouring or 'hallowing' of his name (Hos 11:9; Ezek 36:22f, 32). In this we can discern a veiled

pointer to the revelation of the divine nature as *agapē* in the New Testament (see below, C1). The love of God for men is not only the love of the Creator for his work (Is 43:1–7, 21), but is basically the love of a father (Hos 11:1–4; cf Is 1:4; 30:1, 9; Jer 3:19; 31:20); indeed it is greater than the love of a mother for her own child (Is 49:15; cf 66:13; Mal 1:6). Not infrequently the prophets use *'āhaḇ* to express this trait of warm affection (Hos 9:15; 11:1, 4; 14:4; Mal 1:2f), which is already connoted by the word *ḥāšaq* = 'be attached to' as used in Deut 7:7 and 10:15. The close connection between *'ahᵃḇāh* and *ḥeseḏ* as the expression of the essence of this quality is particularly clear in the words addressed by God to Israel in Jer 31:3: 'I have loved you with an everlasting love; therefore I have continued my favour to you so long'. The message of Is 63:9 is similar: 'In his love and in his forbearance (*ḥemlâh*) he redeemed them (the children of Israel), he lifted them up and carried them all the days of old'. In these passages soteriological motifs are adumbrated, which are also connected with the image of the 'shepherd of Israel' (Hos 4:16; Mic 2:12; 4:6; 7:14) and those of the 'doctor' (Is 30:26; Jer 3:22; Hos 6:1; 14:4) or ⁄ 'saviour' (Is 43:3, 11; 49:26; 54:5; Hos 11:3; 13:4; etc), but above all with the figure of the husband who strives to win back his unfaithful wife when she has become involved with other gods as her 'lovers' (*mᵉ'ahᵃḇîm*) (esp. Jer 2f; Hos 1:2; 2:4–15; 3:1–5; 4:12f; Ezek 16:23). If she acknowledges her fault and sincerely returns to her Lord, then he will receive her graciously again (Jer 3:12,

14, 22; 4:1; Ezek 16:53–63; Hos 2:16–25; Is 49:15; 54:5–8; 62:4f). This group of images, which is probably connected with ideas prevalent in the ancient Near East concerning the marriages of the gods, or 'sacral marriages' (see esp. Song of Solomon) serves to characterise the covenant between Yahweh and Israel as a living union of love. What is probably the most profound revelation of divine love in the Old Testament is presented in the figure of the suffering messiah, the ᵓ*ebed Yahweh* (↗ Servant of the Lord), who delivers himself up as a sacrifice of atonement for the faithless people (Is 42:1–9; 50; 53). Here the dynamism of salvation history, which is inherent in the Old Testament conception of love, comes fully to the surface. Yet the 'new' and 'eternal' covenant which the Servant of the Lord is to institute by his sacrificial offering of himself (Is 54:8–10; Jer 31:31–7; 33:19–26) is to unite all peoples (Is 2:2–5; Jer 3:17; Mic 4:1–7; Zeph 3:9; Zech 9:10; Mal 1:11).

The idea of God in the *Psalms* and *Wisdom Books* is also, in its essentials, inspired by an awareness of Yahweh's unwavering kindness and covenant faithfulness towards his people (eg, Ps 89:4ff; 103:17f; Wis 12:19–22; Sir 50:19–24). At the same time a fresh impetus is provided by the emphasis on Yahweh's love for individual men (thus Ps 4:1; 25:6f; 119:76f; 143:12; 146:8). These submit themselves trustfully to his care, and hence are called 'children' (Ps 29:1; Wis 5:5; 16:26) and 'friends' of God (Ps 60:7; 108:6; 127:2; Wis 7:27; see also 7:14; Sir 4:10). His 'ever enduring' mercy (Ps 100:5; 136) however, is extended not

only to mankind but to all creatures (86:5; 145:9, 16; Wis 11:24–6; 15:1). Certainly his unswerving justice never ceases to be accompanied by the kindness with which he gives help to men (*ḥesed* = *eleos*), the magnanimity with which he bestows gifts upon them, and, indeed, his forbearance also, and his readiness to forgive (eg Pss 36:7ff; 145:7–21; Wis 12:8–18; Sir 17:23f; 18:1–14). Hence it is that especially in the Wisdom literature the divine love is experienced not so much in the form in which it was initially bestowed, free, spontaneous, and unconditional (as it is in the prophets), but more as God's response to man's submission of himself in obedience, and his faithful observance of the laws (Prov 8:17, 21; 15:9; Wis 4:10; Sir 4:14 etc).

In the writings of *later judaism* this idea is emphasised by reason of the dialectic which is to be found between the divine kindness and the divine justice (eg, Hen 91:17; 92:4 etc), even though here too the awareness of the patience and compassion of Yahweh is in no way diminished (eg, 4 Ezra 7:132–9; see esp. 8:47). The conception of love in the sectarian writings lately discovered near the Dead Sea, specifically in the 'Rule of the Community' of Qumran, is characterised by a certain dualism. God, who is compassionate of himself (1 QS 1:22), does indeed love creatures 'throughout all ages' and showers graces above all upon the just (2:1); but yet he does 'abhor with an everlasting hatred' (4:1) the wicked, and especially the 'spirits of darkness'.

2. *The love of men for God.* In the Old Testament the love which God bestows upon men, above all on the chosen

people, is for the most part understood as faithfulness to the covenant. In view of this it is not surprising that the reciprocal love of men should likewise be conceived of as consisting essentially in the acceptance of covenant obligations. Hence it is that this reciprocal love is thought of in the first instance as a 'commandment', indeed as *the* commandment in an absolutely basic sense, one which is most intimately connected with the service of God (including the cult) and the keeping of the rest of the clauses of the covenant law (thus already in Ex 20:6; more fully in Deut 6:2–9; 7:9; 10:12f; 11:1, 13; 30:10, 16; Jos 22:5; 23:6–16 and *passim*). This explains why the love of God (*'āhaḇ*) should be intermingled almost inextricably with the fear of God (*yārē'*, eg, Deut 10:12; 13:4f), and why its exercise should consist chiefly in honouring Yahweh as the one true God to the utter exclusion of every sort of idolatry (Ex 20:2–6; 22:20; 23:32f; 34:11–17; Deut 4:19f). For all this, however, man's love for God is far from being expressed in sheer legalism or external observance of the cult; on the contrary, it engages the whole of man, with all his powers; it must come from 'his whole heart' (Deut 4:29; 6:5f; 10:12; 11:13; 13:3; 30:6) and must lead to a 'cleaving to' (*dāḇaq*) God (Deut 10:20; 11:22; 13:4; 30:20; Josh 22:5; 23:8; 2 Kings 18:6) that is living and dynamic. An attitude of thankfulness (Deut 8:1–10; Josh 22:4f; cf 24:1–18; 1 Sam 12:7–11; 1 Chron 16:7–36; 29:13f,↗ thanksgiving) and trust (Gen 15:6; Deut 10:12ff; 1 Sam 14:6; 2 Sam 24:14) is the essential characteristic of such interior love of God.

It is precisely upon these deeper impulses that the *prophets* have laid the greatest possible emphasis, throwing them into bold relief by their condemnation of externalism in the sacrificial forms of worship and of piety that is merely superficial (Is 1:10–15; 29:13f; 58:1–5; Jer 7:21–8; Ezek 33:10–20; Hos 6:6; Mic 6:6f), and by demanding genuine piety (*ḥesed*) in its place (Hos 4:1; 6:4–6; 10:12; 12:7). Hence they call again and again for true conversion of the heart (Is 1:16 to 20; 55:6f; Jer 3:12f; Ezek 18:30ff; Amos 5:14f; Joel 2:12f; Jonah 4:2). In all this the love of God continues to mean in essence faithfulness to Yahweh's covenant, which must be made real by keeping the commandments (*'ahaḇâh* only Jer 2:2; *'āhaḇ* Is 56:6; cf Jer 11:1–5; 26:3f; 31:31ff; Bar 2:6–10; 4:1–4).

This line of thought is pursued further in the *Psalms*, which, in accordance with their literary character as prayer-chants, are intended to express chiefly the love of thankfulness and trust (*'āhaḇ*) towards God (eg, 5:12; 31:24f; 97:10; 116:1; 138:2; 145:20). The interior depths of this love is emphasised by the use of *rāḥam* (18:1) and *ḥāšaq* (91:14), and in general the demand for God to be near and to be seen is particularly prominent in these chants (27:8; 42:2f; 63:1, 8; 73:23–8).

In the *Wisdom literature* we also encounter a 'mystical' attitude, eg, in Wis 3:9: 'Those who trust in him will understand truth (*alētheia*), and the faithful will abide with him in love (*en agapē[i] prosmenousin autō[i]*); because grace (*kharis*) and mercy (*eleos*) are upon his elect'. The love of wisdom, which is, in the last analysis, essentially love of the Creator (Sir 7:30; 47:8), leads to 'nearness to God' (Wis 6:19) and to 'friendship with God' (*philia pros theon*: 7:14), as also to 'living with' him (*sumbiōsis theou*: 8:3; see also Sir 2:3: *kollēthēnai autō[i]* = 'to be joined with him'); but at the same time it consists quite simply in observance of the commandments (Wis 6:18f); indeed, it is itself an observance of the law which blots out the guilt of sin (Prov 16:6) and promises reward (Sir 2:8; see also Prov 3:1ff; 19:16; etc). The cultic aspect of the love of God appears, for example, in Sir 4:14, where it is identified with the 'service of the Holy one' (*leitourgein tō[i] Hagiō[i]* according to LXX; note that *latreuontes* ['those who serve'] = *agapōntes* ['those who love']). Thus in the piety of post-exilic times fear of the Lord and trust in his unfailing paternal love are united (Prov 3:5–7; Sir 2:7–18; 7:30ff).

The Old Testament teaching on love survives in *late judaism*, only the legalistic aspect is still more strongly emphasised. Symptomatic of this is the appearance of the *šᵉmaᵓ* prayer, which had to be recited three times a day, and which, in accordance with Deut 6:5 and 11:13, constantly called to mind the commandment to love God. Together with this the philosophical element, which has already been brought to our attention in the Wisdom literature, makes itself felt to the extent that the love of God is made equivalent to love of ↗ wisdom or of ↗ truth (eg, TestRub 3:9), which Philo significantly calls *erōs sophias* (*Quis rer. div. her.* 14). But occasionally here we also come across the recognition that the love of God is properly only the free gift of his own grace (*Letter to Aristeas*, 229); just

as in the rabbinical literature we actually find references to a love of God that is pure and disinterested; this is exemplified in the tractate of the Mishna entitled Sota 31a (see *Pirqe Abot* 1:3) or in the tradition of Rabbi Akiba (b Ber 61b). Admittedly such statements are unusual, and belong to the second century after Christ, and are therefore hardly to be explained otherwise than as falling under christian influence.

3. *The love of men for each other* is likewise principally motivated by covenant ideas. But this love is represented as due first and foremost to fellow Israelites, who have all equally entered into covenant with Yahweh. The principle, therefore, of mutual 'steadfast love and faithfulness' (*ḥesed wᵉᵓemeth*, Gen 24:49; 47:29; Josh 2:14; etc) applies in these human relationships also. In the background is the strong sense of solidarity (↗ people of God) as developed chiefly in the patriarchal system of society. The fact of being descended from the same ancestor (genealogy!) makes a man regard those who belong to his people as 'brothers', and actually feel himself bound to them by natural and family ties (eg, Lev 10:6; Josh 2:12f; 1 Sam 30:23; Tob 1:3; 14:7; Mal 2:10; ↗ brother, ↗ neighbour). Hence even in the Old Testament love of neighbour does not stop short at a coldly legalistic kind of loving, but takes on the character of heartfelt fraternal feeling (Lev 19:17f; Ps 133:1; Sir 13:16; 25:1f; 1 Macc 10, 12:17). By contrast its essentially religious aspect is thrown into particularly strong relief by the fact that it is sanctioned by Yahweh's authority (Lev 19:10, 18, 34) and thereby raised

to the status of 'service of God'—
indeed united to the love of God (Deut
10:17ff; Is 58:6f; Mic 6:8; Zech 7:9f;
8:16f; Tob 14:11). For this reason
genuine love of neighbour can never
remain at the stage of a mere sentimental impulse, but must be made real
in act. Furthermore it is noteworthy
that it is not confined to fellow Israelites
in the narrower sense, but that, on the
contrary, under divine instruction it is
to be extended to aliens too (Ex 23:9;
Lev 19:33f; Deut 10:19). Even enemies
must not be excluded (Ex 23:4f; Prov
24:17, 29; 25:21f), as in general forbearance and readiness to forgive are
to be exercised instead of destructive
hatred (Lev 19:17f; Prov 16:7; 19:11;
Sir 27:30–28:7). Yet in spite of this the
lex talionis still remains in force as a
general principle (Lev 24:17–21), and
love is confined within nationalistic
limits. Not until the post-exilic period
does any change take place, and even
this takes a philosophical and cosmo-
politan direction (thus, eg, Wis 12:19;
Sir 13:19 [15]), probably under the
influence of hellenistic, and more
specifically of Stoic ethical teaching.

By comparison with this the motif of
brotherhood characteristic of early Israelite tradition becomes once more a
potent force, especially in Essene circles.
The Damascus Document or the Rule
of the Community from Khirbet Qumran are to some extent examples of this,
for here it was actually expressed in the
cult (1 QS 3:6–9; 5:13f; 6:16) by
means of an admission ceremony (connected with a two-year novitiate).
Admittedly when we are told of God
continuing to forbear 'because of the
purification of the many' (6:16) the
underlying thought is not so much of

the solidarity of the people as of the
esoteric character of the community,
which regards itself as the 'holy
remnant' of the final age of the
messiah. In these sectarian writings,
and especially in the Rule of the Community, the 'love of grace' or 'faithfulness' plays a peculiar part; on the
one hand it is connected with 'truth and
humility in the good', on the other
hand with the 'care and righteousness
that are to come first' (2:24f; see also
5:3f; 8:1f; 10:26). Here love for God
and love for one's brothers as 'the sons
of light' seem to be inextricably intermingled, while conversely the sons of
darkness are to be hated, in accordance
with the divine will to take vengeance
(1:9). Here too, therefore, we encounter the same peculiar form of
dualism! Elsewhere, admittedly, hatred
is rejected because of its diabolical
origin (eg, TestGad 5:2), and sometimes love of enemies was positively
recommended (Letter of Aristeas 227);
but there is no mention of love of
neighbour that is exercised towards
non-Israelites until we come to the
rabbinical writings of the second century AD.

4. *Summary.* It is always difficult to
render adequately in modern language
what is signified by the use of *ʾāhab* or
agapan and their derivatives in the Old
Testament unless *agapē* is adopted as a
'loan-word'. The English word *love* is
in many respects too vague, while in
others it is too much weighed down
with meaning to be regarded as
equivalent for all purposes, and without
being able to make additions and
explanatory glosses to it. Even the
translation recently proposed by Spicq
(*Agapè*, 210), namely *prédilection*, has

been found too narrow and one-sided, for the kind of love that is meant in the bible is no merely instinctive or purely emotional impulse; but then, as Spicq rightly insists, neither is it merely a 'détermination de la volonté, que l'on peut impérer' (*Agapè*, 210f). It is to be understood, rather, as constituting from the outset a movement of the whole being, one which stems 'from the whole heart', and in which all man's powers are engaged, including, precisely, the cognitive faculties. For *ʾāhaḇ* and *yāda*ʾ are closely connected not only in the sexual sphere (eg, Gen 4:1) but in the spiritual and religious one too (Deut 4:35–40; 7:9; 11:1ff; see also Ex 33:12f; Is 41:8; Jer 16:21; Hos 6:3, 6; Ps 98:2f; 106:7). Certainly love as presented in the Old Testament is primarily characterised by freedom of choice, less frequently however, by preference and selectivity, for in general it does not depend upon particular prior merits or considerations. On the contrary, it is spontaneously bestowed, is diffused to others with great generosity, is magnanimous in forgiving, shows itself active in helping others, even enemies and, if necessary, is ready to lay down its life in sacrifice. Grace and mercy are essential elements in it, especially when it is predicated of God. From the side of man it consists especially in worship and the dedicated submission of self, and is connected with the attitude of joyful thanksgiving. Even though it can also often appear to be all too severely cramped by legalistic and ritualistic norms, it still remains ultimately true that the parties to a ↗ covenant have obligations one towards another because this faithfulness has to be proved in the observance of the commandments and in the service of God.

It seems, then, that the Old Testament conception of love already contains many of the traits which are usually regarded as appearing for the first time in the New Testament conception of *agapē*. To that extent we are fully justified in speaking of the revealed teaching on love in the New Testament being prepared for in the Old. Yet if we were to confine ourselves to the Old Testament many questions would remain unsolved as, for instance, how law and grace are related, or election and ↗ freedom, and especially the key problem, how can man attain to salvation and thereby to a share in the divine love, when the law can offer no real deliverance?

At the same time it cannot be maintained, though many seek to maintain it today, that Old Testament religion stands in glaring opposition to the New Testament because unlike the latter it is inspired not by love, but ultimately by fear. Unquestionably love does not play so prominent a part in the writings of the Old Testament as, for instance, the motifs of ↗ life, power, and ↗ justice, which are, moreover, more consonant with the Semitic mentality. Yet even here the idea of love exercises a controlling influence which is not the less strong for being hidden. Thus the idea of God in early Israel was certainly characterised chiefly by the all-transcending immensity (*geḏúllâh, megalosunē*) and all-embracing power (*ḥayil, dunamis*) of Yahweh, which stood revealed in his majestic ↗ glory (*kāḇôd, doxa*) beside his justice (*seḏāqáh, dikaiosunē*), unshakeable because all-powerful, which, however, in its turn often took the form of kindness, even of pity (so, eg, Ps 71:2, 15–19, 24; 85:11f). But in addition to these it is precisely the paternal love of Yahweh, providing for all and determining their ultimate end, that constitutes a true manifestation of the nature of God, to which men must respond by thankfully and obediently loving him in return, as well as by showing the love of mutual help and forgiveness to each other. The basic conception of the Old Testament is reminiscent of a saying of Ben Sirach: 'As his (God's) majesty is, so also is his mercy' (Sir 2:18; see also, eg, Deut 10:17f; Pss 86:8–13; 107:5f; 145:4–9).

C. *Love in the New Testament.* Against the background of the complex, yet ultimately unified doctrine of the Old Testament, the uniqueness, newness and depths of the New Testament conception of love stand more clearly revealed. Yet the revelation of the love of God reached its highest point when the eternal *Logos* became flesh, and especially when he offered himself in sacrifice upon the cross; it is only in the light of these events that the numerous particular points which have come to light can be grasped in the full depths of their significance as well as in their underlying coherence.

1. *The basic forms of Agapē.* a. In the New Testament writings too the most important meaning of *agapē* or *agapan* is *God's love for men.* It cannot indeed be decided with certainty in every case whether *agapē tou theou* is intended as a subjective or an objective genitive, in other words whether the love that proceeds *from* God or that which is directed *to* God is meant. Probably it is not infrequent for both to be intended in a single phrase, thus in Lk 11:42;

Rom 5:5; Eph 3:19; Jn 5:42; 1 Jn 2:5; 3:17; 4:12; 5:3, though admittedly the emphasis varies from instance to instance. But Rom 8:39; 2 Cor 13:14; 1 Jn 4:9 are unambiguously to be referred to God as subject. The God of the New Testament is simply 'the God of love' (2 Cor 13:11).

As already adumbrated in the Old Testament the love of God is primarily *a father's love* (Mt 5:45; 6:9–12; 1 Jn 2:15; 3:1; cf 2 Cor 13:11, 14). Even though God has absolute freedom of choice, and bestows his love on whomsoever he will (Rom 9:11–18), he still shows his kindness in providing for his 'beloved children' (Eph 5:1) and for all creatures (Mt 6:8, 25–32; 7:11; Lk 12:22–32). But he does employ fatherly chastisement in order to educate his people (Heb 12:6 citing Prov 3:12). His *agapē*, which consists in a *saving* love (*theos sōtēr*, Lk 1:47; 1 Tim 1:1; 2:3; Tit 1:3; 2:10f; 3:4; Jude 25) is extended to all men (1 Tim 2:3f; 4:10; 2 Pet 3:9) or to mankind as a whole or to the 'cosmos' (Jn 3:16), but particularly to those that believe (Rom 8:37; Eph 2:5; 1 Thess 1:4; 2 Thess 2:13; Jn 17:23; 1 Jn 4:9f, 19). It is bestowed upon the cheerful giver (2 Cor 9:7) and those who faithfully observe the commandments of Christ (Jn 14:23; see also 14:21), but it is also extended to sinners who are, as such, his enemies (Rom 5:8; cf Mt 5:44f; Lk 6:35). Hence this love often takes the form of forgiveness (Mk 11:25f; Mt 6:12, 14f; cf 18:23–5), a fact which is also illustrated by parables such as that of the Good Shepherd who goes after the sheep that strays (Mt 18:12ff; Lk 15:4–7), or of the father who receives the son that was lost once more into his favour (Lk 15:11–32). The love of God, therefore, is not only kindness or ⁊ goodness (*khrēstotēs*: Rom 2:4; 11:22c; Eph 2:7; Tit 3:4 with *philanthrōpia*; also *kharis*: Acts 14:26; see also Mt 19:17b and parallels, God =*agathos*), but at the same time patience (*makrothumia*: Rom 2:4; 9:22; 1 Pet 3:20) and pity (*eleein*: Mk 5:19; Phil 2:27; see also Rom 9:15f, 18; 1 Pet 2:10; *eleos*: Rom 11:30; 15:9; Eph 2:4; Tit 3:5; Heb 4:16; 1 Pet 1:3; Jude 21; *oiktirmoi*: Rom 12:1; 2 Cor 1:3; see also Jas 5:11). Elements of the *ḥesed* motif are still to be found, and together with these the idea of God's covenant faithfulness to the fathers (Lk 1:50, 54, 72) especially in the infancy narrative preserved for us by Luke. Here it is actually the 'innermost depths' (*splankhna eleous*) of our God's mercy with which he has visited us (Lk 1:78) that is spoken of; in the same way, the substitution of *oiktirmōn* in Lk 6:36 for *teleios* in Mt 5:48 is not without significance.

The *agapē* of God physically confronts us in *Christ*, the 'beloved' (*agapētos*=*yāḥid*; Mk 1:11 and parallels; 9:7 and parallels; Mt 12:18; Col 1:13) Son of the Father, who likewise loves us (*agapan*: Gal 2:20; Eph 5:2; Rev 1:5; *agapē tou Khristou*: Rom 8:35; see also 1 Thess 2:13, 16), and indeed with a merciful love of sinners (*splankhnizesthai*: Mk 1:41; 8:2; Lk 7:13; or *eleein*: 1 Cor 7:25; 1 Tim 1:16; *eleos*: Jude 21; see also Mk 2:12–17 and parallels; Mt 11:28ff; Lk 4:17ff). The love of Christ is concentrated with special intensity upon his 'brethren', ie, the men who are to be redeemed (Heb 2:11f); according to John it is concentrated upon the disciples, 'his own' (Jn 13:1, 34; 15:9, 12), or 'the disciple whom he loved' (13:23; 19:26; 21:7, 20), and not least upon the church (Eph 5:25; see also Rev 3:9; 20:9).

b. *The love of men for God.* It is true that in the New Testament this is not directly connected with the idea of the covenant, but we do encounter it here as a 'commandment', indeed as the first and highest commandment, for even more clearly than in later judaism it is regarded as connected with love of neighbour (in connection with Deut 6:4f and Lev 10:27f; see also Mk 12:33f; further 1 Jn 4:19–21; 5:2f). Since this double commandment regulates the entire relationship of man with God and his fellow men alike, it follows that it brings the Old Law, with its numerous clauses and prescriptions, to its true fulfilment and therefore too to its end (Mt 22:40; Rom 13:8–10; Gal 5:14; cf 6:2; Jas 1:12; 2:5). The love of God is therefore unconditional. As in the Old Testament, it requires to be exercised by the whole man and demands of him an ultimate decision (Mt 6:24; Lk 16:13; see also Mt 12:30; Lk 11:23), one which proves itself in unreserved trust (Mt 6:25, 32), and then in the subject's concentrating all his attention exclusively upon 'the kingdom of God and his justice' (6:33), ie, in a total and absolute assent to, and performing of the divine will of the Father (6:10; 7:21; see also 26:42 and parallels; Mk 3:35). This attitude of loving obedience is also understood as 'following Christ' by self-denial and by carrying one's cross (Mk 8:34f and parallels; 10:28ff and parallels; see also 10:21 and parallels). For this reason it must manifest itself in patient acceptance of suffering and persecution for the sake of Christ or 'of justice' (Mt 5:10f; Mk 4:17 and parallels; 13:9, 13 and parallels). It can be seen, then, that this does not imply any falling back into legalism, even though in John, in accordance with Old Testament tradition, the love of God is combined with the keeping of the commandments (14:21–4; 15:10; 1 Jn 5:3; see also 2:4–8; 3:23f): so far from this, the keeping of the commandments is the obvious prerequisite for union with God and with Christ (Jn 14:23f; 1 Jn 2:5f). He who truly loves God must also observe his commandments, in which the protective love of God as Father is made known.

Paul too speaks unambiguously of man's love for God, not merely in passages in which he is following the tradition of the community (thus perhaps Rom 8:28) or in which he is referring to passages in the Old Testament (as in 1 Cor 2:9 citing Is 64:4), but in passages which are quite genuinely original too, such as 1 Cor 8:3: 'If one loves God, one is known by him'—a typically pauline idea (see 13:12; Gal 4:9). Moreover, by reason of the *eis* which precedes it, *agapē tou theou* in 2 Thess 3:5 must be considered as primarily referring to our love for God; in the same way this must be at least connoted as a secondary meaning in many other genitive constructions in which it is difficult to decide whether a subjective or an objective genitive is intended. Rom 5:5 and Eph 3:19 are cases in point. It does emerge from these passages, however, that our love for God is ultimately only a participation in the love that proceeds from God, and which is poured into our hearts by the Holy Spirit. Hence A. Nygrens assertion (80–83) that Paul does not recognise any *agapē* directed from men to God is to be rejected as erroneous, although it must firmly be maintained that this human love is always a response to the prior love of God, made possible by God's own grace, in other words a love of thankfulness expressed and exercised chiefly in the cult (*eukharistein*: Eph 5:19f; Col 3:15f; Rev 11:17; see also 4:9; 7:12; 2 Cor 4:15; 9:10–15; Phil 4:6; Col 2:7; 4:2; 1 Tim 2:1; 4:3f) and in service of one's neighbour (on this see C.1.c below). Our love is also and particularly directed—as far as the New Testament is concerned this is obvious—to Christ (*agapan*: Eph 6:24; Philem 5; 1 Pet 1:8; Jn 8:42; 14:15, 21, 23f, 28; 21:15f; *philein* 16:27; 21:15ff; 1 Cor 16:22); but we all give thanks for his deed of salvation.

c. *The love of men for one another* is most frequently described as 'love of neighbour'. This, as we have seen, is most closely connected with the love of God, and together with it constitutes *the* commandment *par excellence*. (Besides the passages cited under C.1.b see also Jas 2:8; 1 Jn 3:10f, 16f, 23; see also 2:8–11; Jn 13:34). In the New Testament, however, a neighbour is not merely a fellow-member of one's tribe or people; the alien too, and even the sinner (2 Cor 2:8) are also one's neighbour, as is one's enemy, whether in a personal or a national sense—in short everyone who by God's providential disposition of things is brought 'near' to me in order that I may serve him, or he me, in love. This is the teaching which Jesus himself expounds in the parable of the Good Samaritan

(Lk 10:30–37). For as the love of God is extended to all men, so also must ours be (Mt 5:44f; Lk 6:31–6; etc). In this respect alone the teaching of the New Testament surpasses the views which predominated throughout judaism in general; but it also surpasses the hitherto negative formulation of the 'golden rule', in that this is transformed into a positive one: 'Whatever you wish that men would do to you, do so to them' (Mt 7:12; Lk 6:31). That this is not to be understood in the sense of the old rule, 'do ut des' is clear from the sayings of the Lord in Lk 6:32ff. Here it is explicitly emphasised that in our love we are not to confine ourselves merely to reciprocating the love of those who love us. One profound effect of true *agapē* is that it causes us to love our enemies (6:35; see also 6:27–30; Mt 5:44f). True *agapē* neither defends itself nor takes revenge, but rather endures injustice patiently (Mt 5:39ff; Lk 6:28ff; 17:3f; Rom 12:14–20). As inspiring 'heartfelt pity' (*oiktirmōn*, Lk 6:36) it does not judge, is silent under condemnation, yet magnanimous in forgiveness, and even does good to those that hate it (6:37f; see also 6:27; Mt 6:14f; 18:21–35).

But as 'brothers' (eg, Acts 6:3; Rom 16:23; Eph 6:23; see also Mt 25:40) believers are in a special manner to bestow *agapē* upon each other (*allēlous*: Rom 13:8; 1 Thess 4:9; 1 Pet 1:22; Jn 13:34f; 15:12, 17; 1 Jn 3:11, 23; 4:7, 11f; 2 Jn 5; see also 2 Cor 8:7; 1 Thess 3:12; *philadelphia*: Rom 12:10; 1 Thess 4:9; Heb 13:1; 2 Pet 1:7), and that too though their 'brotherhood' (*adelphotēs*: 1 Pet 2:17; 5:9) is based upon the event of

salvation in Christ, the highest proof of divine *agapē* (Rom 8:29; Heb 2:10–18; see also 1 Thess 1:4). The result is that properly speaking, when they bestow *agapē* upon each other in this way christians are no more than giving back the unmerited love of God which they have experienced (Mt 10:8; Rom 15:7; see also 1 Pet 3:8f). When, therefore, we find precisely brotherly love so strongly inculcated in John (Jn 13:34; 15:12, 17; 1 Jn 3:10f, 14, 23; 4:20f; etc), this should not be interpreted in the sense of sectarian exclusiveness, but as pointing to the depths and intimate closeness of the community (A. Šuštar 70). It must be added, however, that we may here have before us a link with the Essenes, especially with the people of Qumran (see the Book of the Rule, 1 QS 2:24f). For the same reason the relationship between the apostle and the community whom he addresses is determined not merely by his authority but precisely by *agapē* (1 Cor 16:24; 2 Cor 2:4; 12:15; 2 Jn 1).

In this greater value is placed upon the inner dispositions, the genuineness (*anhupokritos*: Rom 12:9; 2 Cor 6:6; 1 Tim 1:5; 1 Pet 1:22; *en haplotēti*: Rom 12:8; 2 Cor 8:2; 9:11f; cf 1 Cor 13:4ff; Phil 2:1–4) and sincerity of the love (*ek kardias*: Mt 11:29; 18:35; 1 Tim 1:5; 1 Pet 1:22). But they must also prove themselves in action by helping and serving others (*diakonia*) no less than in a willing disposition, ready to follow the example of Christ in self-sacrifice (Mk 10:45 and parallels; Jn 13:15; 15:13; Rom 12:7–10; 16:4; 2 Cor 8:4; 9:11ff; Gal 5:6, 13; Jas 2:8, 13–26; 1 Jn 3:16–18). While Jesus sometimes puts acts of love before the observance of cultic prescriptions (Mt 5:23f; Mk 2:23–3:6 and parallels; Lk 13:10–17) this in no sense implies that he wishes to do away with cult as such (see C.1.b above); it is rather that he wishes to bring before our eyes the supreme importance of genuine love. Again, that love and true reverence for God are in no way opposed to each other is apparent from the fact that love of neighbour (Mk 12:31 and parallels), no less than love of enemies (Mt 5:44f; Lk 6:35) is motivated by love of God.

d. In the fourth gospel *the love that is interior to the Godhead*, that is between Father and Son, is frequently alluded to. The Father loves the Son because he has laid down his life (*agapan*: 10:17; see also 3:35; 17:23, 26; *philein*: 5:20; see also Mt 11:27; Lk 10:22), but he did love him already 'before the foundation of the world' (Jn 17:24). This fact is also implicit in the description of Christ as the 'beloved' Son (Mk 1:11 and parallels; 9:7 and parallels; 2 Pet 1:17; see also Mt 12:18; Eph 1:6; Col 1:13), a description which also recalls that of the Servant of the Lord in Is 42:1. God's paternal love of Christ, therefore, has a 'pre-salvation' aspect as well as one which applies to him in his salvific work. For his part the Son also loves the Father by carrying out the task he has given him (Jn 14:31; cf 15:10). It follows that the union between Father and Son must be characterised as *agapē*, and from this point it is only a short step further to the basic statement contained in 1 Jn 4:8–16: *ho theos agapē estin*. This derives from the very nature of God, or, more precisely, the unique manifestation of God's nature is characterised as *agapē*

(see also 2 Cor 13:11, 13). This is the way in which the johannine 'procession' finds its starting-point and return: from God, who is himself *agapē*, it goes out in Christ to the world and to those men who, united by fraternal love into a true *agapē*-community (the church) return to their origin in the love of God precisely in order to be made one with God in *agapē*, and through God with one another as Father and Son are one (Jn 17:21–6).

e. Of great significance, finally, is the *absolute* use of *agapō* and *agapan*, ie, the use of these words without the addition of an object to which they can refer. This usage is found everywhere in the New Testament. Instances of it already occur in the synoptics, but it is chiefly employed by Paul and John. In these it is evident first that *agapē* is presented as the purpose which determines all that takes place in the history of the world (predestination, Eph 1:4f), but more particularly in the history of salvation (2 Cor 5:14; Eph 2:4f; 1 Jn 3:1, 16; 4:9f), and in the actual achievement of salvation in the concrete (Rom 5:5; 8:35–9; 15:30; Eph 3:19; 1 Jn 2:5, 15; 3:17; 4:16). It has, indeed, an eschatological bearing (with *krisis*: Lk 11:42; see also Jn 5:42; 1 Jn 4:17). *Agapē* appears not infrequently as the 'new' being, the reality of salvation itself, to the extent that it in some sense forms or upholds the sphere (aeon) of salvation 'in' which we are, or in which we must 'abide' (*menein*) and walk (*en agapē[i]*: 1 Cor 16:14; Eph 3:17; 4:15f; 5:2; Col 2:2; Jn 15:9f; 1 Jn 4:16; 2 Jn 3; see also 1 Thess 5:13; 1 Tim 2:15; Jude 21). Hence it is that *agapē*, together with *eirēnē* (=peace), constitutes the subject of the apostle's invocation (Eph 6:23; Jude 2). *Agapē* in this absolute usage is found most frequently as a designation of the fundamental attitude of believers (eg, Lk 7:47; Rom 12:9; 1 Cor 8:1; 13:4ff; Gal 5:22; Eph 4:2; Phil 1:9, 16; 2:1f; 1 Thess 5:8, 13; 1 Tim 4:12; 2 Pet 1:7), often with the accent on its nature as existential decision (esp. 1 Cor 13:1–3; also Rom 13:8–10; 14:15; Col 3:14; 1 Tim 1:5; Philem 9; 1 Pet 4:8; 1 Jn 3:14; 4:7, 18f; 5:3; 2 Jn 6; Rev 2:4), occasionally with an explicitly eschatological reference (Mt 24:12; 1 Cor 13:8–13; 2 Thess 2:10). Often it is associated with *pistis* (= faith: 1 Cor 16:13f; Eph 6:23; 1 Thess 3:6; 1 Tim 1:14; 4:12; Titus 2:2; Rev 2:19; etc). Frequently, too, it is combined with *elpis* (= hope) as well (eg, 1 Thess 1:3; 5:8; Col 1:4f; Heb 10:22ff; 1 Pet 1:21f; Jude 21), but in such a way that *agapē* appears primary (1 Cor 13:13). Next to its effects (Gal 5:6, 13; Philem 7; Heb 6:10; 10:24; 1 Jn 3:18) its power to unite the community is chiefly emphasised (1 Cor 16:24; 2 Cor 8:7f), so that it can actually signify the unity of Christians in the church (Eph 3:17; 4:2ff, 15f; Col 2:2), or their fellowship with God (Rom 8:35–9; Jn 14:21ff; see also 1 Jn 1:3) or with Christ (Jn 15:9f; 17:26). It is precisely this absolute use of *agapē* that makes it clear that throughout all its transmutations of form it is a single reality. What the nature of this reality is must now be briefly described.

2. *The nature of agapē.* The fact that God loves is, of course, already known to us from the Old Testament, but the full depths and significance of this fact are not disclosed until the revelation of Christ. It must have seemed unheard of, indeed as 'folly' (1 Cor 1:23) above all to those formed by hellenistic culture. Aristotle, for example, regards it as senseless to believe that the gods love us mortal men, on the grounds that they have no need of us whatever (*Nic. Eth.* IX, 1158 b 35). This example throws light precisely upon the fact that the love spoken of in the New Testament is quite different from the *erōs* of the philosophers. Unlike *erōs*, it is not an avid longing, arising from a deep-felt want, for a higher good that has the power to make us happy, but rather a giving of one's life that does not stop short of total sacrifice of self. Whereas *erōs*, as a demand of the soul based on feeling, remains always orientated to the self, and seeks, in the first instance, only that which conduces to its own ultimate fulfilment and blessedness, *agapē* seeks to serve others and is ready, when required, even to offer itself in sacrifice on their behalf. For 'she seeks not that which is her own' (1 Cor 13:5), but that which is beneficial to others (10:24, 33; Phil 2:4). Certainly motives for *agapē* are sometimes adduced (eg, Lk 7:42), even when it is the love of God that is in question (2 Cor 9:7; Jn 10:17; 14:21, 23); nor does it exclude love of self or desire for one's own happiness (Mk 12:31 and parallels; Rom 13:9; Eph 5:28); but it is totally independent of these inducements and its act of giving is exercised precisely where neither claim nor reward are present, but only a need which it can help to answer (Mt 10:8; Lk 6:34f; 10:30–37; 14:13f).

Hence it is that, unlike *erōs*, which always proceeds upwards from below in its demand for ever greater enrichment and happiness, *agapē*, on the contrary, is directed downwards from above. Of its nature it stems 'from God' (1 Jn 4:7), and descends from God to the world, not, of course, to lose itself in the world, but by the graciously indwelling power of God to return once more to its origin. In this it also follows the pattern of history as seen by the New Testament, for this always teaches that beside the initial *katabasis* (descent) from God, there is always an *anabasis* (ascent) too, or better a return to him (eg, Eph 4:9f; Phil 2:5–11; Jn 16:28). Both *de*scent and *a*scent characterise the course of *agapē*. On these grounds *agapē* cannot be described as simply indifferent to value or 'unmotivated' (Nygren 45f), or as love purely in the sense of *katabasis* (Scholz 77; Nygren 142). Of course it does not represent any achievement or 'virtue' which man can attain to by his own efforts, but is always initially an unmerited gift of grace on God's part, or, as later theology puts it, a 'divine' or 'infused virtue'. In this it is connected with what Paul is speaking of when he says: 'God's love has been poured into our hearts through the Holy Spirit which has been given to us' (Rom 5:5). In these words the true nature of *agapē* is expressed. It is essentially spiritual ('pneumatic') love, that is a love which is generated in the 'heart' or *pneuma* of man (1 Cor 2:11; cf Rom 1:9; 8:10, 16 etc) by the *pneuma* of God (*agapē tou pneumatos*: Rom 15:30; *agapē en pneumati*: Col 1:8; see also Gal 5:22; Eph 3:16f; 2 Tim 1:7). The heart (*kardia*) as the bible sees it is not merely the seat of the feelings and emotions, but the innermost centre of man, different even from his soul (*psukhē*:

1 Thess 5:23; Heb 4:12). It is the focal point of his life, in which all the powers of knowing, willing, and feeling are brought together to produce a single unified effect (Mk 7:21f and parallels; Rom 10:1; 2 Thess 3:5). Hence as the true 'love of the heart' *agapē* is an act of the whole being, a fact which is already emphasised in the Old Testament (Deut 6:5 cited in Mk 12:30 and parallels; see also Col 2:2f). At the same time the heart represents the source of interior 'other-worldly' (transpsychic) existence in man, his true depths, in which he is open to God and receptive of his grace (Rom 8:27; 10:8–10; 1 Thess 2:4), and in which, above all, *agapē* is generated as the new 'form' of existence from God (1 Cor 13:2; Jn 17:26; 1 Jn 2:10; 3:1f, 14; 4:7, 16 etc). This *ontic* character of *agapē* appears particularly in the fact that it is considered as an 'aeon' or sphere of existence in the New Testament, one in which we find ourselves placed as a result of the salvific deed of Christ, and in which we must remain (*menein*: see above C 1 e). In terms of ontological reality *agapē* is a form of existence (*Da-Sein*) which consists in a 'being-for' others. This is made actual in the giving of help and in self-sacrifice.

Now since all that exists is called into being by God's creative word (eg, Gen 1:3, 6; Ps 33:6, 9; Rom 4:17; Heb 1:3), the being of man is, of its nature, likewise dependent upon a word, namely the word which God spoke once and for all when he lovingly 'called him (*klēsis*=determination as person: cf 1 Cor 7:20; see also C. 3 below) by his name' (eg, Is 43:1). To this word only the man concerned

Love

can give the appropriate response or
'counter-word' (*Ant-wort*), by lovingly
speaking his thanks. Thus he has
an inalienable 'responsibility' (*Ver-
antwortung*) for the word spoken to him
by God. The essentially *personal* character of *agapē* is therefore evident, and
this is underlined still more by the
fact that it is always based on a free
decision. In fact freedom (*eleutheria*)
belongs so essentially to *agapē* that if it is
withdrawn, or even substantially en-
croached upon, then *agapē* ceases to be
present (Gal 5:13f; cf Jas 1:25ff;
1 Pet 2:16f). In Paul free will or
spontaneity is a special characteristic of
agapē (*authairetos*: 2 Cor 8:3, 7; see also
8:3–20; 9:7; *kata hekousion*: Philem
14; cf 1 Cor 16:2; Rom 12:8; *hekousiōs*:
1 Pet 5:2). In another respect also
agapē is free, namely in that, unlike
erōs, it does not depend upon the value
of the object loved; instead of this,
agapē, by its basic affirmation, confers
upon that object or other person the
personal value which it is once and for
all to possess, that is as this particular
concrete 'thou'. It does this even
when, or precisely when the object in
question does not, of itself, inspire love
(love of the poor and the sick), or when
it has actually shown itself unworthy
of love (love of sinners and enemies).
It loves the other person, therefore, not
because he is good, pleasant or suitable
to be helped, but *in order that he may
become* good, and may attain to the
fulfilment in fact of that particular
significance as person which God
ascribed to him when he called him
by name (see, eg, 2 Cor 12:14;
also 1 Cor 8:3; 13:12). Finally,
the love of *agapē* is exercised in
co-operation with the summoning,

creative, and redeeming love of
God.

The community founded upon *agapē*
is also spiritual in character (*koinōnia
pneumatos*: Phil 2:1f), and is based upon
mutual intercourse and interchange
between persons who are free to take
their own decisions (*agapan allēlous*:
Rom 13:8; etc. See C 1 c above; see
also 2 Cor 8:7; Gal 5:13; Eph 1:15;
4:2; 2 Thess 1:3; 1 Pet 1:22; 4:8). As
already appears from the actual terms
employed (C 1 c above), this community is essentially a 'brotherhood',
in which, precisely in virtue of *agapē*,
even an enemy becomes a 'brother'.
It does not depend upon the constantly
relative and transient preferences of
those who love, or upon their inclinations and dispositions, but is unshakeably 'faithful' (*pistos*: 1 Cor
4:17; 2 Tim 2:2; *pistis* = *'emeth*, 2 Thess
1:4; Gal 5:22; Tit 2:10; 3:15), and
for this reason unceasing; for it consists in a spiritual union of being
(*henotēs pneumatos*: Eph 4:2ff; cf 1 Cor
6:17) which becomes effective above
all in the ↗ church as the body of Christ
(Rom 12:4–13; Eph 4:4; Col 3:14f;
etc). In spite of its being a real and
concrete entity the *agapē* community is
radically different from any kind of
essentially numerical group (multitude)
because it is brought together neither
by being directed towards an external
aim to be achieved, nor by the imposition of force, but rather represents
an end in itself and presupposes that its
members take personal responsibility
one for another ·(Rom 14:1–15:7;
1 Cor 10:23–33), as well as maintaining
sincere trust in one another (*peithesthai*:
2 Cor 2:3; 2 Thess 3:4). This love is, of
its nature, characterised by a two-fold

paradox: the more one acquires the command over one's self of true freedom (not egocentrically) the more open one is to others; and the more one unites one's self to others in true fellowship, the more one arrives at command of one's self (see Mk 8:35 and parallels; Jn 12:25).

In this personal-spiritual union of *agapē* the ancient biblical *principle of solidarity* of the community finds its true realisation inasmuch as the dynamic sense of sharing in a common destiny is here fused with the motif of the body of Christ. It is both demanded and made possible by *agapē* that those who love shall share most deeply in the lot of others. What is the experience of one is the lot of another (2 Cor 5:14: 'If one has died for all, then all have died'; cf Phil 1:29–2:11). And precisely as members of the single spiritual ('pneumatic') body of the Lord we are united with one another in a bond of common being and common destiny (Rom 12:4f, 15; 1 Cor 12:26). The background to this idea in salvation history will be treated of in C 3.

A further characteristic of *agapē* is that, unlike *erōs*, it is not 'binary'— that is, it is not confined to a relationship between two individuals. Such a relationship can easily be exclusive and provoke jealousy. But of its very nature *agapē* is necessarily 'trinary', and thereby open to others, indeed basically to all. He who loves God should also love his brother (1 Jn 4:19f), and he who loves his brother with the love of *agapē* loves God at the same time (4:11f). From this point onwards the 'trinary' aspect of *agapē* becomes evident; it is not only of divine origin but divine of its essence, for basically it always remains the love of God which has been poured into our hearts by the Holy Spirit, or the grace of participating in the eternal love which the Father and the Son bestow upon each other in the Holy Spirit (cf 2 Cor 13:13). In that we are permitted to share in the fullness of this love in the interior life of the Trinity we become 'one', in fact perfectly 'one' (Jn 17:21–6; cf 1 Jn 1:3). This sharing in the perfection of the threefold *agapē* of God is possible only on condition that we love '*even as*' Christ has loved us (Jn 13:34; 15:12; cf 15:9f; also Eph 5:1f), for as employed here the function of *kathōs* (='even as') is not merely to compare our love to Christ's but also to convey that his love is the cause of ours—is, indeed, in a certain sense identical with ours, inasmuch as it is the perfection of love in which we participate. At all events *agapē* always bears a *christological* stamp (*agapē tou Khristou*: Rom 8:35; 2 Cor 5:14; Eph 3:19; or *en Khristō[i]*: Rom 8:39; 1 Cor 16:24; 1 Tim 1:14; 2 Tim 1:13) because only by Christ and in Christ is it made available to and possible for us.

3. *The work of agapē*. When we view as a whole the numerous New Testament sayings about *agapē*, it is undoubtedly the aspect of salvation history that stands out as the determining factor. However, the significance of *agapē* for the whole of world history, and in particular for the *work of creation*, is far from being overlooked; in general, creation history and salvation history are not separated from each other in biblical thought. Thus the plan of the divine will, the 'archmystery' by which everything without exception is determined, is initially and

most deeply motivated by *agapē*. Yet the eternal 'design' (*prothesis*) or 'predetermination' (*proorizein*), as well as the actual 'calling' (*klēsis*) and 'election' (*eklogē*) represent no dark fate that sways men blindly, as does the *moira* of the Greeks or the *fatum* of the Romans; these are rather aspects of the process by which the love of God takes effect (eg, Rom 8:28ff; see also 9:11–26; 11:28–36; Gal 5:8, 13; esp. Eph 1:4–11; 3:9–12; 4:1–4; Phil 3:14; 2 Tim 1:9; Jas 2:5; 1 Pet 2:9f). Hence those who have been 'called' are referred to simply as the 'beloved of God' (Rom 1:7; Col 3:12; see also 1 Thess 1:4). That the creation is the work of God's paternal love—a fact already known to the Old Testament—is made clear to us not least from the end to which it is directed, for the *anakephalaiōsis* (=uniting) of all in Christ (Eph 1:10) can be understood only on the basis of *agapē* (cf 3:9ff with 3:18f; further 1 Cor 8:6; 15:28; Col 1:13, 22f; also Jn 17:21–6).

In all these assertions, however, the true interest is a *soteriological* one, and in fact it is in the *oikonomia*, the work of salvation accomplished by God through Christ, that the full depths of his *agapē* are revealed. The unanimous message of the New Testament writings is that it was God's compassionate love alone that, despite the fact that man had disdained and betrayed that creative love, took him once more under his protection when he had wantonly apostatised from him. What is indicated in a more veiled and indirect manner in the synoptics, namely that the Son of Man came to heal and to redeem (Mk 2:17 and parallels; Lk 4:17–19; see also Acts 10:38), and to lay down

his life 'as a ransom for many', that is for all (Mt 20:28; Mk 10:45), is expressed by Paul quite openly: 'God showed his love for us in that while we were yet sinners Christ died for us' (Rom 5:8; see also 8:32; Eph 2:4f; Tit 3:4f). John too says, almost in the same terms, 'In this the love of God was made manifest among us, that God sent his only Son into the world so that we might live through him. In this is love, not that we loved God but that he loved us and sent his Son to be the expiation for our sins' (1 Jn 4:9f; cf Jn 3:16; also 1 Pet 1:3).

God put this plan of salvation, the outcome of his *agapē*, into effect by sending his Son 'in the likeness (*en homoiōmati*) of sinful flesh' so that he might share our fate as sinners and by these means might conquer it (*peri hamartias*: Rom 8:3). By an inconceivable condescension Christ divested himself of his 'equality with God' and took 'the form of a servant . . . being born in the likeness of men and being found in human form', humbling himself even to the death of the cross (Phil 2:6ff). By becoming flesh the eternal Son of God entered into our mode of existence and shared it with us, his 'brothers', in order thereby to atone for our fault (esp. Heb 2:14–18). This unheard-of idea inspired Paul to some of his boldest expressions: 'Christ redeemed us from the curse of the law, having become a curse for us' (Gal 3:13), or even 'For our sake he (God) made him to be sin who knew no sin, so that in him we might become the righteousness of God' (2 Cor 5:21). The pregnant 'for (*huper*) us' here has the force of 'in our place' (thus, too, Rom 5:6, 8; see also 14:15; 1 Cor

8:11; 15:3; 2 Cor 5:14; Col 2:14). By his substitutional sacrifice of atonement, offered by Christ from pure *agapē* (Gal 2:20; Eph 5:2; Rev 1:5; see also Jn 10:17f) he bestowed upon us 'peace' with God (Rom 5:1, etc) and peace in general (Col 1:20f), by himself becoming 'our peace' (Eph 2:14).

Thus by concentrating on the motif of *agapē* the mystery of our redemption has been opened to us in its deeper significance. We have already established in C 2 above that the principle of solidarity is fully realised precisely in the *agapē* of the New Testament, and this is of decisive importance for the economy of salvation. For according to Heb 2:11 'He who sanctifies and those who are sanctified have all one origin' (see the 'Christ/Adam' parallel in Rom 5:12–19; 1 Cor 15:20ff). But union in guilt and salvation demands that fellowship in which we share the same mode of existence and the same destiny, and it is in this that the 'wonderful exchange' is achieved (Mt 8:17 citing Is 53:4; 2 Cor 8:9; Jn 1:29; 1 Pet 1:22ff). It was precisely for this that the Son of God became flesh, and he has endured the hardships brought upon us by our sins so that through him we may attain to the grace of being children of God (Jn 1:12ff; Gal 4:4f). Hence it is that Christ had to travel the hard way of the Cross in order to blot out the guilt of our sins by the bloody sacrifice of himself; but precisely in his body sacrificed upon the cross he has given us 'entry into the sanctuary' (Heb 10:19f) and 'access to the Father in the Spirit' (*pneuma*: Eph 2:14–18; 3:12).

These findings throw light upon the mystery of the ↗ church, which is at once the fruit and the continuation of Christ's work of salvation in history. The church, too, is essentially conditioned by the factor of solidarity of existence and the bond of a common destiny shared by all her members. In virtue of the fact that they belong to Christ as the 'last Adam', believers are already included in the destiny of their new 'forbear' (compare Rom 5:8–11 with 5:15–19 and 6:3–11; see also 1 Cor 15:20ff). But as members of his spiritual Body they participate even more in the destiny of the 'head' (Rom 7:4; Eph 5:25–30; Col 1:18–22; see also Rom 12:5; 1 Cor 12:26; see further Eph 1:22f with 2:14–18). In fact Christ is not merely the source (Heb 5:9) but also the pioneer of salvation (2:10), the 'first fruits' (1 Cor 15:20, 23), the 'first-born among many brethren' (Rom 8:29; cf Col 1:18). We are to 'follow' him (*akolouthein*: Mk 10:21, 28 and parallels; Lk 9:59–62; Jn 8:12; 12:26) as the 'forerunner' (Heb 6:20) above all by taking the cross [upon us] (Mk 8:34 and parallels; Mt 10:38; Lk 14:27) 'to continue with [him] in his trials' (Lk 22:28) and 'share the chalice of suffering' (Mt 20:22ff; Mk 10:38f; cf Jn 15:18–21; 16:1–4; 1 Jn 2:6; 4:17). This sharing in the fate or, more precisely, in the Passion of the Lord, which is also attested in Heb 13:13 (see 12:1–11) and 1 Pet 2:20f (see also 3:13–18; 4:12f) is the special concern of pauline theology, in which it is expressed chiefly by the characteristic *sun-* constructions. In Rom 8:17 the apostle gives the primary and basic principle which dominates the whole of his teaching on salvation, and his 'Christ mysticism' in particular: 'provided

537

(*eiper*) we suffer with him in order that we may be glorified with him'. We must respond to the 'Christ for us' with a 'we for Christ' (2 Cor 12:10; Phil 1:29; see also Col 1:24). We must remember, therefore that the soteriological task of the church consists chiefly in proclaiming and establishing union with the Redeemer in his death and resurrection.

The community of the church itself is also characterised by its members being bound together by a common destiny, for it pertains to its very essence that her members should all be united in a single body (Rom 12:5; 1 Cor 12:26). It must, therefore, always be formed and maintained by *agapē*. The *agapē* of God and of Christ is the sphere of life 'in' which believers are firmly 'rooted and grounded' (Eph 3:17; see also Col 2:2; Rom 8:35–9; 1 Tim 2:15; 2 Tim 1:13; Jn 15:1–10), and in which they must therefore 'walk' (Eph 5:1f; see also 1 Cor 16:14; Phil 2:1f). *Agapē* is that which above all holds firm the unity of the church (Eph 4:1–6), that too in which its growth is perfected (4:15; cf 4:11–13). Hence active fraternal love is the sign of a membership of the church that is living (Rom 13:8; 1 Thess 4:9; Heb 13:1; Jn 13:34f; 1 Jn 3:11–18; 4:19ff), and it must be shown especially to the leaders and helpers of the community (Gal 6:10; see also Heb 13:7, 17), as also by one community to another (Rom 15:25f; 2 Cor 8:1–8; 9:1ff).

4. *How agapē is to be made actual in men.* Just as salvation history is to be understood as of its essence the effect of *agapē*, so too the application of salvation to the individual is to be thought of in the same way. It originates in the acceptance of the preached word by ↗*faith* (esp. Rom 10:17; see also Jn 1:12; 5:24). This consists not merely of an affirmation on the part of the intellect or an assent on the part of the will, but in a positive seizing hold by the whole man with all his life-force; and this must lead to a true encounter with God in *agapē*. Hence faith is intimately connected with love (for passages see C 1 e above), chiefly because its ultimate motive force is the *agapē* which God bestows on us unmerited (1 Jn 4:16), and because faith itself, on its side, must work through *agapē* (Gal 5:6; see also Col 1:4f; Jas 2:14–26).

But faith as such embraces only the 'inner man', his 'heart'. In order, therefore that the whole man, body included, may be possessed by the grace of Christ, redeemed and sanctified, we have been given the *sacrament*. And here precisely we see *agapē* in action. For the salvation which Christ won for us by his sacrificial death upon the cross is not merely made over to us but, by the co-operation which the sacrament is designed to make possible for us, we are allowed actively to participate in the divine deed of salvation. Paul gives expression to this fact chiefly by his use of the *sun* construction; thus especially with reference to ↗ baptism, which is interpreted as a 'dying *with*' Christ, or a 'being buried *with*' him in death'. Again Paul speaks of 'our old man being crucified *with*' Christ, so that from this may ensue a 'being raised *with*' him and a 'being given life *with*' him (Rom 6:3–5; Col 2:12f). By this active co-operation in Christ's way of salvation believers acquire a new mode of existence, being engrafted as members into the spiritual ('pneumatic') body of the Lord that is the church so that they may achieve a saving participation in his life of *agapē*. But *agapē* as crucified confronts us most directly in the Lord's supper (↗ eucharist), in which we receive the actual sacrificed body of Christ, and are thereby received ever more deeply into the 'fellowship of the body of Christ' and in it are also united ever more closely to each other (1 Cor 10:16f). More than this, the eucharist is a sacrificial mystery (Mk 14:24: *ekkhunomenon* = 'being poured out' (present participle); compare Lk 22:19f; 1 Cor 10:14–21; 11:24f), for it consists of a commemorative act in which the Lord's death is declared (*kērussein* = proclaim) to be present (1 Cor 11:24–6). Because of this we are given in this sacrament a unique possibility of acting *with* Christ by offering *with* him the death which he offered in sacrifice once and for all. Thus in the sacrament that community of existence and of lot which the christians have with Christ becomes a completely concrete reality, which it is the church's salvific function to maintain.

This sacramentally based union with Christ in his death and resurrection naturally has effects in the *practical life* also, for this is to be not merely an 'imitation' of the Lord (1 Thess 1:6; Eph 5:1f), but above all a real 'participation' (*koinōnia*) in his suffering and a 'being conformed to his death' (Phil 3:10; cf 1 Pet 2:21; 4:13). Thus, for instance, our everyday sufferings become 'the sufferings of Christ' (2 Cor 1:5) provided that we bear them with 'Christ's patience' (2 Thess 3:5) in

order thereby to become worthy to bear 'witness' (*martus*) to them also (1 Pet 5:1). Again the profound 'Christ-mysticism' of Paul, which is, in the last analysis, always a cultic mysticism too (Rom 12:1f; Phil 3:3; 4:6; Col 3:16f; etc), is inspired by this 'existential' *agapē* and bears its stamp. This is all the more true because our love in Christ and in God is ultimately nothing else than a participation in the working out of God's love as Father, as made known in the salvific work of Christ (Rom 5:5; 2 Cor 5:14; Gal 2:20). *Agapē* likewise constitutes the most basic principle of New Testament *ethics*. For it is the first 'fruit of the Spirit' from which all other dispositions follow: 'love, joy, peace, patience, kindness, goodness, faithfulness, gentleness, self-control' (Gal 5:22f). Hence *agapē* is shown to be a force which generates life, and among the ways in which it manifests itself in act the works of mercy, corporal and spiritual alike, are not the least (Mt 5:7, 16, 42, 44f; Lk 14:13f; Rom 12:13; 1 Pet 4:9; 1 Jn 3:14–17; etc). Paul traces the roots of active fraternal love back to the unity of the spiritual ('pneumatic') body of the Lord, in which we are 'members one of another' (Rom 12:4ff; Eph 4:25). The closest fellowship of common life and destiny binds us to each other (1 Cor 12:25f), but also at the same time to Christ, so that we serve the Lord in our brother (Mt 10:40; 18:5 and parallels; 25:35–40, 42–5), but offend him also when we commit offences against our brother for whom Christ died (Rom 14:15; 1 Cor 8:11f). Hence fraternal love is the one debt that we have to pay to one another, and it continues to be a debt because we can never love enough to discharge it completely. When, however, we bend all our attention to practising this love without reserve, then this by itself is sufficient to 'fulfil the law' (Rom 13:8ff).

In this world the fulfilment of the christian ideal always remains imperfect, for the 'pledge of the Spirit' is all that we have received (2 Cor 1:22; 5:5). Hence our ex-istence presses on to the end as its ful-filment, and this end (*telos*) is nothing else than *agapē* (1 Tim 1:5), because it is at the same time the *teleion* and that which truly 'abides' (1 Cor 13:10–13). By reason of its divine or spiritual ('pneumatic') nature it is not 'of this world', but, in its true mode of being, transcendent or '*eschatological*' in the sense in which the New Testament speaks of the 'last things' which 'have already come upon us' (1 Cor 10:11; 1 Pet 4:7; 1 Jn 2:16). The eschatological character of *agapē* is also apparent from the fact that in virtue of the uncompromising decision which it demands it actually confronts us with the judgement already in the present life (Mt 23:23; Lk 11:42; Jn 5:42; see also 3:16–20; Jas 2:12f) as well as at the end of time (Mt 25:31–46; see also 24:12; 2 Cor 5:10; 1 Jn 2:28; 4:17f). On the other hand death, our 'last enemy', is deprived of his 'sting' (1 Cor 15:26, 56ff) by this *agapē* because it 'covers a multitude of sins' (1 Pet 4:8). As a 'dying with Christ' (see 1 Thess 4:14) through baptism, death now means, not a descent into corruption, but an ascent to a new and eternal life. This is achieved in co-operation with Christ's victorious 'passing over' from the world to the Father, and in it we recognise that the Lord has indeed 'loved us to the end' (Jn 13:1).

5. *Final summary*. In relation to the Old Testament the New Testament theology of *agapē* has the effect of illuminating, refining, and deepening what has gone before, although the continuity of revelation is preserved in all its essentials. Prior to this theology of *agapē* certain elements were unrelated to one another, and also unreconciled between themselves. Nor were the terms 'āhab and its Greek equivalent *agapan* sufficient to unite these elements in a true synthesis. But when *agapē* theology was introduced it had the effect of revealing the inner coherence and unity of the elements in question, because its exponents had found in the 'mystery of Christ' the key term that was related to all the rest, and of giving meaning to them all. Here *agapē* is supreme without qualification, and it owes this supremacy chiefly to its function in salvation history; indeed it is the true motive for God's intervention in the history of man in the person of Christ, and therefore for the form which the mystery of Christ assumed (Eph 3:2–11, 17–19). The doctrines of creation and salvation, christology and ecclesiology, moral and mystical teaching, the doctrine of the sacraments no less than that of the last things—all these are illuminated by the theology of *agapē* in their inner significance and in their consistency one with another. The other fundamental motifs, such as *doxa* (glory), *kharis* (grace), and *dikaiosunē* (righteousness, justice), together with the key ideas *phōs* (light), *zōē* (life), and *pneuma* (spirit) all congregate about *agapē* as the motif of motifs, the ultimate 'arch-motif' and 'arch-idea'. Even human

love (sex and *erōs*) finds its highest fulfilment in *agapē*, a fact which Paul brings out more or less explicitly in the section on marriage (Eph 5:23–33). Yet for all that the essentially unique character of *agapē* remains inviolate. It is always spiritual ('pneumatic') love, which becomes, by grace, our personal love, yet in doing so never ceases to be 'divine' love, because it is poured into our hearts by the Spirit of God and can only truly become effective when we participate in the threefold love of God. Hence it is essentially different from all other forms of love including the religious one, and even from the Indian *Bhakti*, which seems so closely related to it (see our survey in F. König, *Religionswissenschaftliches Wörterbuch*, 1956, 18ff). The *agapē* of the New Testament, therefore, is a reality which, while it embraces all other realities, cannot be mistaken for any of them; it is the factor which, first and last, exercises a decisive influence upon the whole of the world's course, for this course is fundamentally nothing else than the working out of the 'mysteries of *agapē*' (Clement of Alexandria, *Quis dives salvetur* 37:1 GCS Clem III, 183).

Bibliography: *General*: H. Riesenfeld, 'Etude bibliographique sur la notion biblique d'Agape', *Coniect. Neotest.* 5 (Uppsala 1941), 1–27; H. Riesenfeld, 'Note bibliographique sur 1 Cor XIII', *Nuntius* 6 (1952), 47f; V. Warnach, *Agape*, Düsseldorf 1951, 660–65; V. Warnach, *LTK* I² (1958), 217f; C. Spicq, *Agapè dans le Nouveau Testament. Analyse des textes* I–IV, Paris 1957–61. *On the Terminology*: B. B. Warfield, 'The Terminology of Love in the New Testament', *Princeton Theol. Rev.* 16 (1918), 1–45 and 153–203; E. Peterson, '*Agápē*', *BZ* 20 (1932), 378–82; E. Stauffer, *TDNT* I, 35–8 (=*BKW* I); A. Ceresa-Gastaldo, '*Agápē* nei documenti estranei all' influsso biblico', *Rivista di Filologia e di Istruzione classica* 31 (1953), 347–56; A. Ceresa-Gastaldo, 'Ancora sull' uso profano di *Agápē*', *Riv. di Fil. e di Istr. class.* 32 (1954), 1f; J. E. Steinmüller, '*Erān, philein, agapán*', *Extra-Biblical and Biblical Sources* (Miscellanea A. Miller), Rome 1951, 404–23; C. Spicq, 'Le verbe *agapaō* et ses dérivés dans le grec classique', *RB* 60 (1953), 372–97; M. Paeslack, 'Zur bedeutungsgeschichte der Wörter *philein, philia, philos* in der LXX und im NT unter Berücksichtigung ihrer Beziehungen zu *agapán, agapé, agapētos*', *Theol. Viatorum* 5 (1953/4), 51–142. *On the Old Testament*: G. Quell, 'Die Liebe im AT', *TDNT* I, 21–35; C. Spicq, *Agape. Prolégomènes à une étude de théologie néo-testamentaire* (Studia Hellenistica 10), Louvain–Leiden 1955; Guillot, *Leitgedanken der Bibel*, 29–111; J. Ziegler, *Die Liebe Gottes bei den Propheten* (*AA* XI/3), Münster 1930; F. Buck, *Die Liebe Gottes beim Propheten Osee*, Rome 1953; O. Schilling, 'Die atl. Auffassungen von Gerechtigkeit und Liebe', *Wort des Lebens* (Festschrift M. Meinertz), Münster 1951, 9–27; R. Sander, *Furcht und Liebe im palästinischen Judentum* (*BWANT* IV/16), Stuttgart 1935; G. Nagel, 'Crainte et amour de Dieu dans l'AT', *Rev. de Théol. et de Philos.* 23 (1945), 175–86; E. Sjöberg, *Gott und die Sünder im palästinischen Judentum* (*BWANT* IV/27), Stuttgart 1938; E. Stauffer, '"Lieben" im Judentum', *TDNT* I, 38–44 (=*BKW* I); O. Loretz, 'Zum Problem des Eros im Hohenlied', *BZ* 8 (1964), 191–216. *On the New Testament in general*: W. Lütgert, *Die Liebe im NT*, Leipzig 1905; W. Lütgert, *RGG* III², 1638–41; J. Moffatt, *Love in the NT*, London 1929; H. Preisker, *Die urchristliche Botschaft von der Liebe Gottes im Lichte der vergleichenden Religionsgeschichte*, Giessen 1930; E. Stauffer, *TDNT* I, 44–55 (=*BKW* I); W. Schlatter, *Die Liebe Gottes in der Mannigfalt ihres biblischen Selbstzeugnisses*, Berlin 1935; V. Warnach, *Agape*, Düsseldorf 1951, 88–179; W. Harrelson, 'The Idea of Agape in the New Testament', *Journal of Religion* 31 (1951), 169–82; J. Gaer, *Love in the New Testament*, Boston 1952; W. G. Cole, *Sex and Love in the Bible*, London 1960; C. Spicq, *Agapè dans le Nouveau Testament* I–IV, Paris 1957–61. *Synoptics*: C. E. Raven, *Jesus and the Gospel of Love*, London 1942²; F. X. Durwell, *La charité selon les synoptiques et les épîtres de S. Paul*, Brussels 1955; E. Mersch, 'Le plus grandes des commandements', *NRT* 69 (1947), 1009–26; G. Bornkamm, 'Das Doppelgebot der Liebe', *Ntl. Studien für R. Bultmann* (*BZNW* 21), Berlin 1954, 85–93; O. Michel, 'Das Gebot der

Nächstenliebe in der Verkündigung Jesu', *Die soziale Entscheidung*, Tübingen 1947, 53–101; P. Fiebig, 'Jesu Worte über die Feindesliebe', *TSK* 91 (1918), 30–64; A. Wikenhauser, 'Die Liebeswerke im Gerichtsgemälde Mt 25:31–46', *BZ* 20 (1932), 366–77; G. Braumann, 'Jesu Erbarmen nach Matthäus', *TZ* 19 (1963), 305–17; W. Pesch, 'Das Liebesgebot in der Verkündigung Jesu', *BK* 9 (1964), 85–9. *Paul*: P. Dupont, *Gnosis*, Lyons–Paris 1949, esp. 379–543; J. A. Ubieta Lopez, 'Caridad fraterna en las parenesis de Ef. 4:25–5:2 y Col. 3:8, 17', *Cuadernos Pont. Colegio Español* 2 (1955), 63–95; A. Fridrichson, 'Charité et perfection', *Symbolae Osloenses* 19 (1939), 41–5; K. Nomaniak, *L'amour du Père et du Fils dans la sotériologie de Saint Paul*, Rome 1961. *Specifically on 1 Cor 13*: A. Brieger, *Die urchristl. Trias Glaube, Liebe, Hoffnung*, Heidelberg 1925 (dissertation); A. Vitti, 'Excellentior via: caritas', *VD* 9 (1929), 43–52; G. Bornkamm, 'Der köstlichere Weg (1 Kor 13)', *Jahrb. der Theol. Schule Bethel* 8 (1937), 132–50; R. Guardini, *Die christliche Liebe. Eine Auslegung von 1 Kor 13*, Würzburg 1940; H. Riesenfeld, 'La voie de charité. Note sur 1 Cor 12:31', *ST* 1 (1947), 146–57; H. Schlier, 'Über die Liebe: 1 Kor 13', *Die Zeit der Kirche*, Freiburg 1956, 186–92; A. Barr, 'Love in the Church. A Study of 1 Cor 13', *SJT* 3 (1950), 416–26; G. Harbsmeier, *Das Hohelied der Liebe*, Neukirchen 1952; T. G. Bunch, *Love. A Comprehensive Exposition of 1 Cor 13*, Washington 1952; A. Descamps, 'L'hymne à la charité (1 Cor XIII)', *Rev. Dioc. Tournai* 8 (1953), 241–5; J. Brennan, 'The Exegesis of 1 Cor 13', *ITQ* 21 (1954), 270–78; C. Spicq, 'L'agapè de 1 Cor XIII', *ETL* 31 (1955), 357–70. *Johannine writings*: A. Sustar, *De caritate apud Joannem apostolum*, Rome 1951; C. Oggioni, 'La dottrina della carità nel IV Vangelo e nella I lettera di Giovanni', *Script. theol.* 1 (1953), 221–93; L. Moraldi, *Dio è amore. Saggio sul concetto di amore in S. Giovanni con introduzione al IV Vangelo*, Rome 1954; L. Cerfaux, 'La charité fraternelle et le retour du Christ (Jn 13:33–8)', *ETL* 24 (1948), 321–32; S. Gil Salafranca, 'Agape en S. Juan 17:26', *Cultura Bibl.* 12 (1955), 272–81; H. Schlier, 'Glauben, Erkennen, Lieben nach dem Johannesevangelium', *Besinnung auf das NT*, Freiburg 1964, 279–93. *Theology of Agape*: H. Scholz, *Eros und Caritas*, Halle 1929; A. Nygren, *Eros und Agape*, Güttersloh 1956²; L. Malevez, 'Amour païen, amour chrétien', *NRT* 69 (1937), 944–68; E. Walter, *Glaube, Hoffnung und Liebe im NT*, Freiburg 1940; E. Walter, *Wesen und Macht der Liebe*, Freiburg 1955; M. C. D'Arcy, *The Mind and Heart of Love*, London 1947⁴; E. L. Allen, *A Christology of Love* (in John), London 1950; V. Warnach, *Agape*, Düsseldorf 1951; V. Warnach, *LTK* I², 178–80; F. Prat, 'Charité', *Dict. de la Spirit* II (1953), 508–23; P. A. Sorkin, *The ways and the power of love*, Boston 1954; L. Colin, *Caritas*, Turin 1954; L. Colin, *Il commandamento nuovo*, Turin 1954; F. O. de Urtaran Diaz, 'Esperanza y Caridad en el Nuevo Testamento', *Script. Vict.* 1 (1954), 1–50; C. Charlier, 'L'amour en Esprit', *Bible et Vie chrétienne* 10 (1955), 57–72; G. Lefebvre, 'Le mystère de la divine Charité', *Vie spir.* 94 (1956), 563–86; R. Bultmann, 'Aimer son prochain, commandement de Dieu', *RHPR* 10 (1930), 222–41; E. Fuchs, 'Was heisst: "Du sollst deinen Nächsten lieben wie dich selbst?"', *TB* 11 (1932), 129–41; C. H. Ratschow, 'Agape. Nächstenliebe und Bruderliebe', *ZST* 21 (1950), 160–82; G. Salet, 'Amour de Dieu, Charité fraternelle', *NRT* 77 (1955), 3–26; R. Völkl, *Die Selbstliebe in der Hl. Schrift und bei Thomas von Aquin*, Munich 1956; R. Spiazzi, *Teologia della carità*, Rome 1957; G. Lefébvre, *Aimer Dieu*, Paris 1960; J. Coppens, 'La doctrine biblique sur l'amour de Dieu et du prochain', *ETL* 11 (1964), 252–99.

Agape and ethics: H. Preisker, *Das Ethos der Urchristentums*, Gütersloh 1949²; W. Lütgert, *Ethik der Liebe*, Gütersloh 1938; Schnackenburg, esp. 56–71, 151–6, and 224–9; C. Spicq, 'Die Liebe als Gestaltungsprinzip der Moral in den synoptischen Evangelien', *Freiburger Zs. f. Theol. u. Philos.* 1 (1954), 394–410; C. Spicq, 'La morale de l'agapè selon le NT', *LV* 21 (1955), 103–22 and 383–402; Bo Reicke, 'Neuzeitliche und ntl. Auffassung von Liebe und Ehe', *NT* 1 (1956), 21–34.

Viktor Warnach

Man

A. *In the Old Testament*. 1. The principal words for mankind are ʾādām and ʾenôš. Despite all obscurities with regard to etymology, it is certain that ʾādām and ʾadāmāh (= arable land, cultivated land) go together (see Gen 2:7). Man and tilled soil are thus connected with each other. ʾādām is almost exclusively a collective concept, yet in Gen 2:5ff it becomes from this simultaneously the name of the ancestor of the human race.

The derivation of *ʾenôš* is likewise uncertain, but to a Hebrew ear it clearly suggests the verb *ʾānaš* (= to be weak). Thus its use is especially favoured in contexts where men are spoken of as weak and mortal: 'I will make men more rare than fine gold, and mankind than the gold of Ophir' (Is 13:12); 'Who are you that you are afraid of man that dies, of the son of man who is made like grass?' (Is 51:12); 'Put them in fear, O Yahweh! Let the nations know that they are but men' (Ps 9:20); 'As for man, his days are like grass' (Ps 103:15); etc.

2. The Old Testament knows of no philosophical definition of the essence of man and of his constituent elements. Thus the question of whether man should be conceived of as made up of two or three basic parts is irrelevant. Here man is seen rather as a living whole, of which *bāśār*, *nepheš*, and *rûaḥ* are the principal aspects. As ↗ 'flesh' *bāśār* stands for the corporal side of man, which he shares with animals (see 'all flesh' as an expression for man and beast in Gen 6:17, 19 etc); but it can be simply a synonym for *ʾādām* (see Ps 56:4, 11 etc). In the use of *baśar* the connotation of frailty often comes well to the fore (cf Is 31:3; Jer 17:5; Deut 5:26 etc). *nepheš* (originally = throat, neck, 'windpipe') designates quite generally that life which is implicit in the very notion of breath, while blood stands for the element in which that life is properly located (see Gen 9:4; Lev 17:10, 11, 14; etc).

'Soul' is therefore to a large extent makeshift translation, in so far as the life of the soul is often included in the meaning of *nepheš* (see Gen 34:3; Is 1:14; Hos 4:8; Ps 11:5; 42:6; 86:4; etc), while spiritual perception (see Prov 19:2; Ps 139:14; Lam 3:20; etc) and even the religious activities of the soul (see Deut 4:29; 6:5; etc. Ps 42:2f; 62:6; etc) are implicit in it. In these cases *nepheš* becomes a synonym for 'heart' (*lēb*, *lēbāb*; see Deut 6:5), which is, for the Israelites, the seat of thinking, willing and feeling. *rûaḥ*, usually translated 'spirit', is, to a large extent, etymologically and semantically parallel to *nepheš*, and can therefore be used even of the animal realm (see Gen 6:17; Ps 104:29f; etc). As applied to men the word is often more sharply defined than *nepheš*, and serves as a precise indication of the seat of knowledge and sensory perception, often being parallel to heart (cf Ps 51:12, 17; etc; Ezek 11:19; 18:31; etc; Is 57:16; etc). Thus *nepheš* and *rûaḥ* designate, although with somewhat different emphases, a single life-force, to which the spiritual, animate, sensitive, and vegetative manifestations of life can be reduced.

These concepts are, however, very far from attaining to the fullness of the idea of a spiritual soul. They are so essentially bound up with the concept of *bāśār* that such meanings as to think, to hope, to wish, to be glad, to be frightened, to sin, etc can be expressed by this self-same root *bāśār* used as a predicate (see Ps 63:1; 84:2; 119:120; Prov 4:22; Job 14:22; 21:6; Eccles 5:5; etc).

Just how strong this sense is in the Old Testment of man as an essentially corporal being is also revealed by the fact that spiritual functions are ascribed not only to the heart, but also to the bowels (Is 16:11; Jer 4:19; 31:20; etc), the kidneys (Ps 7:10; Jer 11:20; etc), the liver (Lam 2:11; Prov 7:23; Ps 16:9; etc). It is not until the Greek period, and in the Book of Wisdom in particular, that we find an approximation to the Greek view of man as a compositum of spirit and body. The doctrine of the immortality of the soul is for the first time stated clearly and unequivocally in this last-named Book of Wisdom (see 2:22f; 3:4; etc). In Israel too, of course, the conviction was widely held that some kind of substratum of man (not to be equated with the spiritual soul) continues to exist in the underworld. But that this existence could be real life, or even life in communion with God, seems to have been guessed at or actually expected only by a few. So much can be gathered from Ps 16:9ff; 17:15; 49:15; 73:23ff. The resurrection of the individual man at the end of time comes nearer to the Old Testament view of man as an integral whole, and it is of this that Is 26:19 probably, and Dan 12:2f; 2 Macc 7:14 certainly speak.

3. It is a general principle that Old Testament authors convey the essence of a thing by describing how it came to be. And this is primarily true of their teaching about man. Like everything else man is brought into being by an act of creation on God's part, but he is God's creature in an eminent manner that sets him apart from the rest. The earlier of the two creation narratives testifies to this in Gen 2:7 (J). Certainly we find there that man is taken from the earth like the beasts (see 2:19), and

therefore he is, like them, of his very nature mortal (cf Ps 104:29; Job 34:14, 15); but in him the 'breath of life' (*nišmat ḥayyim*) is drawn from the 'exhalation' of God, something which is not stated of the creation of beasts (see 2:19). Thus the life-principle in man (*nišmāth ḥayyim* is a synonym for *rûaḥ*, see Job 27:3; Is 57:16; etc) stems directly from the divine breath of life, so that man, in spite of his mortality (his destiny to become dust), so often stressed in the Old Testament, has of his essence a special relationship with the Creator. Thus he can 'call the beasts by their names' (2:19f). This naming of the beasts expresses man's position of authority, but besides this it draws attention to his godlike faculty of speech. In this connection it is significant that the Hebrew chooses to call animals, especially large animals, *beḥēmâh* (see Gen 3:14; etc), ie, the dumb ones, although they have loud cries.

The later creation narrative shows (Gen 1:26ff [P]) how man is special and distinct among creatures by recording God's solemn word of decision by which he raises him into existence: 'Let us make man in our image, after our likeness!' 'Divine image' is the distinguishing characteristic of his nature. The significance of this relationship to God as image is illustrated by man's dominion over nature, and especially over the animal realm (cf 1:26 b; Ps 8; Sir 17:3f). Clearly, however, it is not the 'image relationship' in its entirety that is revealed here. This consists essentially in the personhood of man, just as the dominion of God is rooted in his absolute personhood—he is absolute 'self'. But this means that a two-fold relationship is intrinsic to man's essential nature. He is the representative of God in the material world and at the same time he is the 'thou' whom God addresses in that world. This I–Thou relationship between God and man is, of its essence, fundamentally mutual and interchangeable even though man is mere 'dust and ashes' (see especially Gen 18:27) before the holy and everlasting God.

This divine dignity which is inherent in human nature, applies in equal measure to man and woman. This is expressly stated in Gen 1:27, and in Gen 2:21ff (J) the vivid account of the creation of woman likewise includes, as a theologically deducible axiom, the essential unity of nature between man and woman.

What the Old Testament has to say concerning the creation of the first man, and thereby of mankind, is to be evaluated as a statement not of natural science but of theology. For this reason it cannot be adduced as a legitimate argument against the theory of evolution insofar as this theory remains strictly within the bounds of natural science. On the other hand what is expressly taught and maintained here is that man, regarded as a creature with a particular nature, assumes a privileged position in the visible world. This privileged relationship to the Creator is constitutive of man's existence and nature. This applies primarily to mankind as a whole. But besides this, God is, in a mysterious manner, active in the coming into existence of each individual man, as Job 10:8ff; 31:15; Ps 119:73; 139:13; etc testify, even though this does not imply any express 'creationism'.

4. Against this background of the order of creation the statements concerning man are re-applied in Old Testament revelation in the order of grace. Such are: the calling of the first man to special partnership with God (without humanity's present subjection to decay and death); the misuse of freedom involved in the first sin; the handing over of fallen humanity to suffering and death; the persistence of God's will to make covenant with man throughout all the judgements of the primaeval age; the new calling of humanity to covenant with God begun with Abraham, carried further with Israel as covenant partner and bearer of the covenant laws and promises, springing up afresh in the promised bringer of salvation (the Messiah) who is to inaugurate the age of salvation and the final age.

Bibliography: The relevant sections of the standard works on Old Testament Theology, above all Eichrodt II, 65–77 and Imschoot II, 1–38. In particular: P. Zapletal, 'Das Ebenbild Gottes im Menschen, Gen 1:26', *Schweiz. Kirchenzeitung* 71 (1903), 125–6, 136–8, and 143–4; E. Montmasson, 'L'homme créé à l'image de Dieu . . .', *Echos d'Orient* 14 (1911), 334–9, and 15 (1912), 154–62; J. Hehn, 'Zum Terminus "Bild Gottes"', *Festschrift E. Sachau*, Berlin 1915, 36–52; W. Caspari, 'Imago Divina Gen. 1', *Reinh.-Seeberg-Festschrift* I, 1929, 197–208; F. Dander, 'Gottes Bild und Gleichnis in der Schöpfung nach der Lehre des heiligen Thomas von Aquin', *ZKT* 53 (1929), 1–40, and 203–46; H. Junker, 'Der Mensch im AT', *Festschrift Tillmann*, 1934, 3–13; P. Humbert, *Etudes sur le récit du Paradis et de la chute dans la Genèse*, 1940, 153–75; '"L'imago Dei" dans l'AT' (see A. Bea, *Bibl* 25 (1944), 83–4); Th. C. Vriezen, 'La création de l'homme d'après l'image de Dieu,' *OTS* 2 (1943), 87–105; K. Barth, *The Doctrine of Creation* (*Church Dogmatics* III/1), Edinburgh 1958; K. Galling, *Das Bild vom Menschen in biblischer Sicht*, 1947, 11–12; W. Eichrodt, 'Das Menschenverständnis des AT', Zürich 1947; L. Köhler, 'Die Grundstelle der Imago-Dei-Lehre, Genesis 1:26', *TZ* 4 (1948), 16–22; W. Zimmerli, *Das Menschenbild des AT*,

1949; K. L. Schmidt, 'Homo Imago Dei im A und NT', *Eranos-Jahrbuch* 15 (1948), (149–95); A. R. Johnson, *The Vitality of the Individual in the Thought of Ancient Israel*, Cardiff 1949; B. Brinkmann, 'Geschaffen "nach dem Bilde Gottes"' (Gen 1:26f; 9:6)', *Wending* 2 (1951), 129ff; G. Söhngen, 'Die biblische Lehre von der Gottebenbildlichkeit des Menschen', *MTZ* 2 (1951), 52ff; M. Seligson, *The Meaning of 'ṭen lepeš' in the OT*, Helsinki 1951; C. R. Smith, *The Biblical Doctrine of Man*, London 1951; G. Pidoux, *L'homme dans l'AT*, Neuchâtel 1953; L. Köhler, *Der hebr. Mensch*, Tübingen 1953; A. Deissler, *Der Mensch als Gottesbild*, Oberrh. Pastbl. 1953, 204ff; W. Rudolph, 'Das Menschenbild des AT', *Festgabe Schreiner*, 1953, 238–51; J. J. Stamm, 'Die Imago-Lehre von Karl Barth und die alttestamentliche Wissenschaft', *Antwort K. Barth z. 70. Geburtstag*, Zollikon–Zürich 1956, 84–98; A.-M. Dubarle, 'La condition humaine dans l'AT', *RB* 63 (1956), 321ff; A.-M. Dubarle, *SP* 1 (1959), 522–6; B. de Geradon, 'L'homme à l'image de Dieu. Approche à la lumière de l'anthropologie du sens commun', *NRT* 80 (1958), 683–95; H. Sommers, 'L'homme image de Dieu. Origine du thème', Bijdragen 20 (1959), 126–45; G. Duncker, 'L'immagine di Dio nell'uomo (Gen 1:26–7)', *Bbl* 40 (1959), 384–92; D. Lys, *Nephesch: Histoire de l'âme dans la révélation d'Israel au sein des religions proche-orientales*, Paris 1959; J. Jervell, *Imago Dei (FRLANT* 58), 1960; R. Laurin, 'The concept of man as a soul (néphesch)', *Expository Times* 72 (1960), 181–4; A.-M. Dubarle, 'La bible a-t-elle une doctrine sur l'âme et le corps?', *L'Ame et le Corps*, 1961, 183–200; H. Gross, 'Die Gottebenbildlichkeit des Menschen', *Festschrift Junker*, 1961, 89–100; J. de Fraine, *Adam und seine Nachkommen: Der Begriff der korporativen Persönlichkeit*, Cologne 1962; E. Schlink, 'Die biblische Lehre vom Ebenbilde Gottes', *Pro Veritate* (Festgabe L. Jaeger and W. Staehlin), 1963, 1–23; G. Söhngen, 'Die biblische Lehre von der Gottebenbildlichkeit des Menschen', *Pro Veritate*, 23–57; Haag 2–4 and 1104–6; G. von Rad, 'Die Gottebenbildlichkeit im AT', *TDNT* II, 390–92; *RGG* IV³, 861–3.

Alfons Deissler

B. *In the New Testament.* The New Testament too, in contrast to the Greek picture of man, offers no philosophical description of the nature, components and characteristics of man. The New Testament writers understand man only as coming from God and directed towards him; that is to say, they are writing the history of God with men and of sinful man's answer to God's call. Biblical anthropology is inextricably entwined with soteriology. The New Testament picture of man comes above all from the epistles of St Paul, but also from the preaching of Jesus in the synoptic gospels, and from the johannine writings.

I. *The New Testament teaching on man.* In line with the Old Testament view, man is conceived of as a living totality, an indivisible unity made up of *sōma* (*sarx*), *psukhē* and *pneuma*.

1. *Sōma* means first of all, like *bāśār* the body as opposed to the 'soul' or 'spirit' (cf 1 Thess 5:23; 1 Cor 5:3; 7:34; also 1 Cor 6:13–20; 7:4; 9:27; 13:3), then its members (Mt 5:30; Rom 12:4f; 1 Cor 12:12–26).

As a result of the semitic total view, however, *sōma* in Paul often means (esp. Rom 12:1; Eph 5:28; Phil 1:20) not the shape of the body and even not only the body, but rather *the human person as such*, the real *I* of a man. 'Man does not have a *sōma*, he is *sōma*' (Rudolf Bultmann). In his use of *sōma* Paul did not, like the Greeks, have a dualistic understanding of the visible body, as the prison of the soul, from which it is freed at death. Quite the opposite! He longs for the resurrection of the body, the body which will then no longer be dominated by the transitory *sarx* (Col 2:11), by sin (Rom 6:6), or by death (Rom 7:24), but by the life-giving *pneuma* (Rom 8:23; 7:24; 1 Cor 15:35–49), by *doxa* (Phil 3:21).

2. *Psukhē*, the 'soul', in precisely the

same sense as the Hb *nepheš,* means the physical life (Mt 2:20; 6:25; Lk 12:22f; Jn 10:11; Rom 11:3; 16:4; Phil 1:27; 2:30; 1 Thess 2:8) or life as the precondition for all earthly or eternal goods (Mt 16:26; 20:28; Mk 8:36f; 10:45; Lk 9:25; 1 Thess 2:8; Rev 12:11), also the natural life-force or *life-principle* (Mt 10:28; Lk 12:19f; Acts 2:27; 1 Thess 5:23) as distinct from the body and thought of as immortal (Mt 10:28; 1 Thess 5:23; Rev 6:9; 20:4), and the whole man, the *personality* (Rom 2:9; 13:1; 2 Cor 12:15), the living man, the life-essence (2 Cor 15:45; = Gen 2:7), 'everyman' (Rom 2:9; 13:1), the emphatic 'I myself', etc (Acts 2:27; 2 Cor 1:23; 3 Jn 2).

In the trio 'spirit, soul and body' there is no threefold division. Paul is not thinking, on Greek lines, of the three elements, 'intellect, soul and body', but of the old Hebrew concepts *rûaḥ* and *nepheš,* both of which can describe the life-breath or the seat of the emotions and thoughts. Perhaps this is simply a case of a rhetorical formula from the liturgy.

3. Like *psukhē, pneuma* (↗ spirit) can mean, like the Hebrew *rûaḥ,* the life-spirit or life-principle which lives on after death (Mt 27:30; Lk 8:55; 23:46; 1 Cor 15:3; 2 Cor 7:1; Col 5:2; Heb 12:23), the *person* or a personal pro-*noun* (1 Cor 16:18; 2 Cor 2:13 [= 2 Cor 7:5]; 7:13; Gal 6:18; Phil 4:23; Philem 25; 2 Tim 4:22).

In Old Testament usage *psukhē* and *pneuma* describe inner impulses and affections, and within this general category the feelings of the *appetitus concupiscibilis,* such as joy, grief, pain, etc, are ascribed to *psukhē = nepheš* (Mt

11:29; 22:37; 26:38//; Mk 14:34; Lk 2:35; Jn 10:24; 12:27; Eph 6:6; Col 3:2), and the nobler feelings of the *appetitus irascibilis,* such as anger, excitement, mildness, patience, etc, to *pneuma* = *rûaḥ* (Mt 26:41//; Jn 11:33; 13:21; 1 Cor 4:21; 5:3; Gal 6:1; Eph 4:23).

4. *Kardia* (= ↗ heart—Hebrew; *lēb, lēbāb*), constitutes the one central organ through which God approaches men. It is in the heart that the whole inner (as opposed to outer) life of man is carried on (1 Thess 2:17; 2 Cor 5:12; 6:11).

a. In the heart are the roots of the *emotional life,* with the impulses of the *appetitus concupiscibilis* and *appetitus irascibilis,* such as joy (Jn 16:22; Acts 2:26), pain and grief (Jn 16:6; Rom 9:2), love (2 Cor 6:11; 7:3; 8:16; Phil 1:7), wish and desire (Rom 10:1), despair (Jn 14:1; 2 Cor 2:4), rage (Acts 7:54), etc.

b. From the heart as the seat of the *intellectual life* come thoughts and reflections (Mt 9:4; Mk 2:6, 8; Lk 3:15; 24:38; 1 Cor 2:9; 2 Cor 4:6), stupidity and laziness (Lk 24:25), etc.

c. From the heart come *expressions of the will,* such as 'purposes' (1 Cor 4:5) and decisions (1 Cor 7:37; 2 Cor 9:7; Lk 21:14; Eph 6:22; Col 4:8).

d. From the heart as the chief source flow the good and bad expressions of the religious and moral life, such as faith and doubt (Mt 15:8; Mk 11:23; Rom 10:6–10; 2 Cor 1:22; Gal 4:6; 1 Thess 3:13), good and bad deeds (Lk 6:45), love of God and our brother (Mt 22:37 and parallels; Lk 24:32); obduracy (Mk 6:52; Rom 2:5; 16:18; 2 Cor 3:14f), evil desires (Mt 5:28; 15:19; Mk 7:21; Rom 1:24) and moral decision (Rom 2:15).

e. Since the Holy Spirit dwells in the hearts of men (2 Cor 1:22; Rom 5:5; Gal 4:6), it is God himself 'who searches the heart' (Rom 8:27), 'tests' it (1 Thess 2:4) and therefore will eventually bring to light the 'purposes of the heart' (1 Cor 4:5).

Besides these main concepts the New Testament makes use of some other expressions, such as *nous* and *suneidēsis*. By nous is meant knowledge about something, willing and planning (Rom 1:25), the orientation of the will (Rom 12:2; 1 Cor 1:10) towards or away from God (Rom 7:23). Paul also expresses this idea by the term 'inner man' (Rom 7:22 *nous* = 7:23), which applies to non-christians (Rom 7:22) as well as christians (2 Cor 4:16; Eph 3:16), in contrast to the 'outer man' (2 Cor 4:16, RSV 'outer nature'), the transitory 'body of sin' (Rom 6:6) and 'body of death' (Rom 7:24), that is, the body under the power of sin and death.

Suneidēsis (= conscience) practically owes its place in the christian vocabulary to Paul. The idea is familiar to the Old Testament, but not the word, which however comes thirty-one times in the New Testament and nineteen times in Paul alone. It stands for that knowledge in man by which he judges his own position in the light of God's law (Rom 9:1; 13:5; 1 Cor 8:7–12; 10:25–30; 2 Cor 1:12; 4:2).

II. *The theology of man in the New Testament.* The New Testament picture of man, which has just been traced in its most important features, is overshadowed by a hostile force, ↗ sin. Sin directs its attacks in the first place against the vulnerable ↗ flesh, which in the New Testament, in a sense analogous to that of the Hebrew *bāśār*, means natural man as a weak, transitory and above all sinful creature (cf Rom 7:13–25; 6:19; 2 Cor 1:12) who cries out for salvation.

The New Testament is only interested in the question of the position of man before God. The question of man as sinful and in need of redemption occupies only a subordinate place.

1. According to the testimony of the synoptic gospels, Jesus sees man only in his relationship to God, as dependent on God. He values him, like the lilies of the field and the birds of the air, as God's *creation* (Mt 6:26–30; 10:31; Mk 10:2–9; cf Acts 17:25–8), on which God lavishes his care (Mt 5:45; 10:30; Acts 14:17), more than on the animals and the angels (Mt 6:26; 10:31; Heb 2:16).

But man refuses to acknowledge God's rule (Lk 17:7–10; 25:14–30) or do his will (Mt 21:28–32; Lk 12:47). He has turned his back on God the king (Lk 9:62; 13:1–5; 15:11–32; Rom 1:19–21) and lives 'according to the flesh' (Rom 8:5, 12), that is, in sin; he has given himself over to sin, which has laid the whole of humanity and every individual under its sentence (Mk 14:38; Jn 8:34; Rom 7:14–24); he is abandoned to weakness, helplessness, and mortality. Jesus sees man as a *sinner*.

In order to free man from the grip of sin and to protect him from the judgement which threatens, Jesus has proclaimed the demand for ↗ conversion, and added to this the gift of *God's sonship*: 'The time is fulfilled and the kingdom of God is at hand; repent, and believe in the gospel' (Mk 1:15), that is, the good news of God's *fatherhood* (Mt 6:9;

Lk 11:13; cf Mt 5:16, 48; 6:1; 7:11; Lk 6:36; Jn 8:41; 20:17) and man's status as *son of God* (Mt 5:9, 45; Lk 20:36).

2. While Jesus in his teaching about man as a son of God only hints at the likeness of God in man (cf Mt 5:48), and keeps the expression 'son of God' for the eschatological time of fulfilment, *Paul* speaks explicitly of the *eikōn* (not in the gospels, Acts, Rev) and of the baptised as sons of God (Rom 1:7; 1 Cor 1:3; 8:6; 2 Cor 1:2; Gal 1:3-4; Eph 1:2; Phil 1:2; Col 1:2; Philem 3; 2 Thess 1:1), appealing to Gen 1:26-7 as his basic text.

a. Developing this text from the priestly account of the creation, Paul hails the dawn of the new creation with the 'last Adam' (1 Cor 15:45), *Christ.* It is to the apostle of the gentiles that the task falls of preaching 'the gospel of the glory of Christ, who is the ↗ *likeness of God*' (2 Cor 4:4). In this context Paul means that the ↗ glory (*doxa* = *kābôd*) of God the creator became visible for us through faith in the face of the risen and exalted Lord (2 Cor 4:6). In the baptismal hymn Col 1:15-20 he praises Christ as 'the image of the invisible God', since he is the Son of God and as such his likeness (cf Gen 5:3), and since the Son of God made man shows forth the visible likeness of the 'invisible God' (cf Rom 8:29; Phil 2:6; Jn 1:14, 18; 1 Jn 1:1, Heb 1:3). The beginning of the new creation is simply Christ as the 'new man' (cf Eph 2:15; 4:13).

b. In the exhortatory passage Col 3:5-10 Paul insists that his christians 'have put off the old man (RSV 'natural') with its practices (see the catalogues of virtues and vices at Eph 4:17-5:2; 1

Pet 1:14-17) and have put on the new man (RSV 'nature'), who is being renewed in knowledge after the image of his creator (ie, God)' (Col 3:9-10; cf Rom 6:4-6; Eph 4:24). In the sacramental new creation (see Ps 51: 12; Ezek 36:25-9; 39:29) of baptism the original divine image in man is reproduced and has as its consequence the 'knowledge' of God's will (cf Is 11:9) which demands a change to a holy life, which here means in particular genuine love of one's brother.

c. In his inner life the believer has already, through baptism, died to sin and been raised with Christ to a new life (Rom 6:1-11), but it is only at the resurrection of the dead at the end of time that he will be conformed in his bodiliness to the image of the exalted Lord. Not in vain do we wait 'for the redemption of our bodies', for 'those whom he foreknew he also predestined *to be conformed to the image of his Son*' (Rom 8:23, 29; cf Phil 3:21). The image of Christ in the whole man is also the theme of 1 Cor 15:49: 'Just as we have borne the image of the man of dust, we shall also bear the image of the man of heaven.' Christ, 'the second man', 'is from heaven' (1 Cor 15:47) because he is *the Son of God made man.* Now we are still tied to the form of Adam (ibid 48), but after the resurrection of the dead we shall also bear the 'image' of the transfigured and glorified Lord on our bodies, that is, like the Lord, we shall put on a transfigured, glorified and immortal body.

In contrast to Rom 8:29, 1 Cor 15:49 and Phil 3:21, 2 Cor 3:18 says that something of the glory of the transfigured Lord already shines in us: 'We all, with unveiled face, reflecting

[RSV margin, text 'beholding'] the glory of the Lord, are being changed into·his likeness from one degree of glory to another; for this comes from the Lord, who is the Spirit.' In opposition to the 'dispensation of death' (2 Cor 3:7) or 'dispensation of condemnation' (v 9), ie, the mosaic preaching, the 'dispensation of the Spirit' (v 8) or 'dispensation of righteousness', ie, the apostolic preaching of the good news, already shines in secret with 'permanent' splendour. When believers open their hearts and minds to the gospel preached by the apostle, the Spirit of the Lord, which they have received in baptism, changes them secretly into the heavenly image which the transfigured Lord bears and which he reveals through his apostles in the gospel. On the *eikōn* image in 1 Cor 11:7 see↗ image.

3. The johannine writings see man even more sharply in his relationship to Christ. The fourth gospel unfolds within the framework of a cosmic process the dramatic confrontation between the redeemer and 'the world', between the power of 'darkness' (8:12; 12:35f, 46; 1 Jn 1:5; 2:8–11), the 'prince of this world' (12:31; 14:30; 16:11), and the 'light' (1:4, 5; 3:19; 8:12; 12:36, 46; 1 Jn 1:5), the 'saviour of the world' (4:42). Whoever freely chooses separation from Christ and enmity towards him is 'of the flesh' (3:6; 6:63), 'from below' (8:23), 'of the devil' (8:44; 12:38; 1 Jn 3:8), 'of the world' (*ek tou kosmou:* 8:23; 15:19; 17:14–16; 18:36; 1 Jn 2:16; 4:5) or of the earth' (*ek tēs gēs:* 3:31). Whoever on the other hand chooses closeness to Christ and friendship with him is born 'of the Spirit' (3:6), 'from above' or 'anew' (3:3, 7), 'of God' (1:13; 7:17;

8:47; 1 Jn 3:10), 'of truth' (18:37; 1 Jn 2:21; 3:19). Faith in Christ and rebirth are a gift of the Father: 'No one can come to me unless the Father draws him' (6:44).

John's individual teaching about the 'world' does not mean, however, that simply 'being *in* the world' (13:1; 17:11, 13) blocks the way to Christ or leads to falling away from him; what does this is 'being *of* the world', ie a personal sinful position. Thus Jesus prays to the Father for his disciples 'who are in the world', not that he should take them 'out of the world', but that he should keep them from the evil one (17:15). The believer, who can do nothing without Jesus (15:5), ought to, and can, make a free choice for Christ by listening to his voice (10:3–5, 16, 27; 18:37), letting Christ's words abide in him (15:7), keeping his commandments (14:15, 21; 15:10; 1 Jn 2:3), doing 'what is true' (3:21; 1 Jn 1:6). In this man finds 'eternal life' and his true greatness.

Bibliography: H. H. Wendt, *Die Begriffe Fleisch und Geist im bibl. Sprachgebrauch,* Gotha 1878; H. W. Robinson, *The Christian Doctrine of Man,* Edinburgh 1911; E. de Witt Burton, *Spirit, Soul and Flesh,* Chicago 1918; W. Schauf, *Sarx. Der Begriff Fleisch beim Apostel Paulus,* Münster 1924; F. Ruesche, 'Blut, Leben und Seele', *Studien zur Geschichte und Kultur des Altertums,* Paderborn 1930; J. Jeremias, *TDNT* I, 141–3; J. Jeremias, *TDNT* I, 364–7; E. Käsemann, *Leib und Leib Christi,* Tübingen 1933; W. Gutbrod, *Die paulinische Anthropologie (BWANT* IV/5), Stuttgart 1934; J. M. Nielen, 'Der Mensch in der Verkündigung des Evangeliums', *Festschrift F. Tillmann,* Bonn 1934, 14ff; K. T. Schaefer, 'Der Mensch in paulinischer Auffassung', *Festschrift F. Tillmann,* 25ff; H. Kleinknecht, *TDNT* II, 388–90; G. Kittel, *TDNT* II, 392–5; G. Kittel, *TDNT* II, 395–7; J. Behm, *TDNT* III, 447–54; J. Behm, *TDNT* III, 611–14; W. Foerster, *TDNT* III, 1028–35; K. L. Schmidt, 'Homo Imago Dei im A und NT', *Eranos-Jahrbuch* 15,

Zurich 1948, 149–95; K. Galling, *Das Bild vom Menschen in bibl. Sicht,* Mainz 1947; W. G. Kümmel, *Das Bild des Menschen im NT,* Zurich 1948; S. V. McCasland, '"The Image of God" according to St Paul', *JBL* 69 (1950), 85–100; H. Mehl-Koehnlein, *L'Homme selon l'Apôtre Paul,* Neuchâtel–Paris 1951; C. R. Smith, *The Biblical Doctrine of Man,* London 1951; J. A. T. Robinson, *The Body,* London 1952; C. H. Dodd, P. J. Bratsiotis, R. Bultmann, and H. Clavier, *Der Mensch in Gottes Heilsplan,* Newcastle 1952; J. N. Sevenster, *Die Anthropologie des NT* (*Numen* Suppl. II 1955), 166–77; W. D. Stacey, *The Pauline View of Man,* London 1958; F. W. Eltester, *Eikon im NT* (*BZNW* 23), Berlin 1958 (review by M.-E. Boismard, *RB* 66 [1959], 420–24); R. P. Shedd, *Man in Community,* London 1958; S. Läuchli, 'Monism and Dualism in the Pauline Anthropology', *Biblical Research* 3 (1958), 15–27; R. E. Murphy, 'Der Begriff "Fleisch" in den Qumran-Schriften und im Römerbrief', *SP* II, Paris–Gembloux 1959, 60–76; R. M. Wilson, 'Gen 1:26 and the New Testament', *Bijdragen* 20 (1959), 117–25; O. Kuss, *Der Römerbrief,* Regensburg 1959, 506–40; J. Jervell, *Imago dei* (*FRLANT* 76), Göttingen 1960; J. Schmid, 'Der Begriff der Seele im NT', *Einsicht und Glaube,* ed. J. Ratzinger and H. Fries, Freiburg–Basle–Vienna 1962, 112–31; Haag 2–3 and 1106–7; J. Schmid, *LTK* I², 604–15; F. Mussner, *LTK* IV², 1087–90; N. A. Dahl, *RGG* IV³, 863–7; H. Mehl-Koehnlein, Allmen 250–53; V. Warnach, *HTG* II, 145–60; P. van Imschoot, *Dictionnaire Encyclopédique de la Bible,* 832–5; E. Schweitzer, F. Baumgärtel, and R. Meyer, *TWNT* VII, 98–151; E. Schwiezer and F. Baumgärtel, *TWNT* VII, 1024–91.

Robert Koch

Marriage

In this article we will not be considering marriage in its juridical aspects, but will rather confine ourselves to the task of gathering the materials needed for the construction of a biblical theology of marriage. In other words we shall be assembling and evaluating the theologically significant statements in scripture in order finally to be in a position to discuss how the image of the marriage

bond comes to be used not only literally but also as a symbol of the relationship between God and his people.

A. The *Old Testament* seems to show in its earliest traditions an awareness of some still surviving vestiges of matriarchy and polyandry (Gen 24:28; 42:38; Lev 19:3; Judg 8:19, 31; 9:1–6). Later it is clear that patriarchy and polygamy predominate, and naturally it is the evil consequences of these that are spoken of (Gen 16:4f; 1 Sam 1:6; Deut 21:15–17). In the Yahwist (J) creation narrative monogamy is proclaimed as ordained and willed by God. Woman is fashioned out of man (Gen 2:23), therefore a man leaves his father and mother and cleaves to his wife, and they become one flesh (Gen 2:24). But before this God declares: 'It is not good that man should be alone; I will make him a helper fit for him' (Gen 2:18; see also 2:20). The wife is designated *primarily* as a helper, a support (*ʿēzer* is masculine!) for her spouse on a basis of natural equality. It is noteworthy that *ʿēzer* is chiefly predicated of God (Ex 18:4; Deut 33:7, 26, 29; Ps 20:2; 33:20; 115:9–11; 121:2; etc). The reason, namely that it is not good for man to be alone, is constantly adduced in later passages, in Sir (36:29f), referring to Gen 2:18, 20: 'Where there is no wife man is unstable and transient'; 'a man that has no wife is no man' (Yeb 63a), 'he is without joy, without blessing, without goodness' (Yeb 62b). While the J tradition simply records the fruitfulness of the first marriage as a fact in Gen 4:1, the later Priestly (P) creation narrative knows of a special blessing of God conferred upon the first couple, and of the command, 'Be fruitful!'

(Gen 1:28). This expresses the *further* end of marriage, namely increase through progeny. The blessing of children is a gift of God and a reason for joy (Ps 127:3ff; 128:3-6). Conversely, childlessness is a misfortune and a penalty from God (Lev 20:20f; Is 47:9; 1 Sam 1:15f etc).

Marriage, then, has a place in God's creative order. Hence it is under his care and protection. It is a↗ covenant, a divine covenant, a covenant of Yahweh (Prov 2:17; Mal 2:14). Just as, in Gen 2:22, God brings Adam his spouse, so the Lord 'appoints' a wife to a man (Gen 24:14, 44), 'prepares her for a man from all eternity' (Tobit 6:17). Just as these texts give expression to the idea that it is the providence of God that brings spouses together, so it is one of the incomprehensible mysteries how a man feels himself drawn to a young woman and so begets children (Prov 30:18f; see Knabenbauer *ad loc.* against D. Buzy, *RB* 42 [1933], 9f and V. Hamp *ad loc.*; see also Wis 5:10-12).

Death (and also being a prisoner or missing in time of war) and divorce dissolve a marriage. Only the husband can declare that a divorce takes effect, and he does so by some kind of formula as in Hos 2:4 or later, as Deut 24:1ff shows, by making out a bill of divorce. (In Elephantine, on the other hand, the wife too has the right to divorce her husband.) It is said to be a ground for divorce if the husband finds something repugnant in the wife or 'dislikes' her (an expression for relative impotence Deut 24:3; 2 Sam 13:14-18). The prohibition of the husband's retaining the purchase-price of the wife in a divorce is intended to prevent divorce being too easy. The admonishment in Mal 2:10-16 sharply condemns adultery and divorce (on this cf the detailed interpretation of G. J. Botterweck, *Bibel und Leben* 1 [1960], 179-85). The gravity of the sin of adultery can be seen from the fact that in the↗ decalogue its prohibition comes between that of murder and theft. In the early traditions it incurs the death-penalty (Lev 20:10; Deut 22:22).

B. The *New Testament.* Jesus emphasises once more the original meaning and the original law of marriage and puts an end to the possibility of divorce conceded to the Jews because of their hardness of heart (Mk 10:5-9; Mt 19:4-8). The exception 'for impurity (*porneia*)', added in Mt 5:32; 19:9 by the evangelist, should, according to the traditional explanation, be understood to mean that in such a case separation from bed and board is permitted, but not an absolute dissolution with freedom to marry again. The following interpretation is the best founded. First, on linguistic grounds, Mt 19:3 should be translated : 'May a man put away his wife for any reason?' There follows an apparent exception, which in fact is not an exception. *Porneia* means an unlawful marriage, in particular marriage between blood relations (Lev 18:6ff; Acts 15:20, 29), which was practised among the gentiles and regarded among them as lawful. Such marriage relationships, which could sometimes be found among applicants for baptism, had to be dissolved (cf 1 Cor 5:1), and this could give the impression of a divorce such as had been forbidden by Jesus. The matthean redaction is an attempt to meet this problem as it arose in gentile christian circles. In the world to come there will be no more marriages (Mk 12:25 and parallels); all will be 'as' the angels. For the sake of the future world, for the sake of the state of preparedness in which the ↗ parousia is the object of man's longing, it must be realised already in the here and now that 'to woo and to be wooed' does not exhaust the whole meaning of life (see Lk 17:26–9; Mt 24:37–9).

Paul answers a series of questions (the nature of which we know only by his replies) in 1 Cor 7, and in doing so recommends his own way of life, ↗ virginity, while explicitly emphasising that everyone has his own gift of grace, his ↗ charisma, one for one state, another for another (1 Cor 7:7). Here it is clearly expressed that the married state is no less charismatic than the unmarried. For Paul, marriage is a divinely willed and divinely instituted bond, by which men and women are freed from the fire of lust (1 Cor 7:1–5, 9) and so guarded from being led by Satan into temptation (v 5). Besides this, the marriage of a christian stems from a *power which sanctifies* the married partner (even when he or she remains an unbeliever; 1 Cor 7:14). Relying upon this power, Paul advises that in cases where spouses remain unconverted the marriage relationship should be preserved (unless these latter want a separation), for 'perhaps you, wife, [husband] can save your husband [wife]!' (1 Cor 7:16). Paul refers to an express commandment of the Lord that marriage must not be broken. But above all this commandment declares inadmissible the remarriage of partners who have been separated (1 Cor 7:10f). 1 Cor 7:15 is probably to be understood in the same sense: if the unbelieving partner wants to be separated the believer is not 'bound like a slave'. He should not attempt to continue at any price his married life with the unbeliever. The question of a second marriage does not arise. As is taught in 1 Cor 7:39 (and also in Rom 7:1–3) death alone makes such a thing possible. Certainly the earliest and also some of the most recent exegetes find in 1 Cor 7:15 an expression of the so-called pauline privilege (in a broader sense the *privilegium fidei*), namely that in a marriage between a christian and a non-christian the bond can be dissolved (*ou dedoulōtai* [= 'is not bound like a slave'] is in that case interpreted as applying to the marriage bond; but against this interpretation is the fact that in 1 Cor 7:39 and Rom 7:2 Paul uses *dedetai nomō(i)* [= 'for is bound by the law'], and furthermore refers the freedom of which he is there speaking *explicitly* to the admissibility of a second marriage, all of which is not stated in 1 Cor 7:15). The church's practice in admitting the *privilegium fidei*, although it oversteps the limits of the pauline text (even according to the traditional interpretation), is not affected by a strict exegesis of the passage in 1 Cor 7:15, for this practice is based on a 'divine' privilege, a fact which has constantly been maintained since Prosper Lambertini (Benedict XIV).

Husband and wife are exhorted to maintain mutual christian love (*agapē*) for each other in marriage (Col 3:18f; Eph 5:22–33). Such an exhortation is also found in 1 Pet 3:7: the husband must preside over the household with love and understanding; he must show reverence to the woman as the weaker part, for women are still heirs to the grace of life just as much as men. Eph 5:21–33 provides the deepest revelation of the sacramentality of marriage, which is deducible not merely from the sacramentum magnum (v 32), but from the whole context. Marriage is not only an image of the union of Christ with his bride, the church, but is, of its very nature, constituted by that union. In the dimension of salvific grace what is effected in the one union is closely parallel to what is effected in the other: 'Husbands, love your wives, as Christ loved the church and gave himself up for her, that he might sanctify her, having cleansed her by the washing of water with the word [ie, through the sacrament of baptism]' (v 25f). 'The husband is the head of the wife as Christ is the head of the church, his body, and is himself its Saviour' (v 23). Thus married love bestows sanctifying power on each of the partners (see above on 1 Cor 7:14). The spouses have a soteriological function to perform each for the other. It is in this that the 'pregnant mystery concerning Christ and the church' (v 32) consists. When, for instance, Jesus is explaining his relationship to his own, he compares the function which a vine performs for its branches with the soteriological function which he performs for his disciples. This is likewise a mystery of salvation. As the vine is to its branches so Jesus is to his disciples. But in Eph 5 the husband is for the wife what Christ is for the church: a saviour (v 23).

According to 1 Tim 2:15 'the wife finds her salvation (literally "will be redeemed") through motherhood, on condition of course that they (both spouses, or wives especially? or the children?) persevere in developing a high-principled way of life in faith, love and humble striving after holiness' (↗ humility). And in this the redemptive function of the husband is manifest once more, for if the wife *remains alone* she cannot *produce fruit* (see Jn 12:24f), a principle which is 'universally' valid, on the natural, as well as on the supernatural plane (↗ work). At this point too it is probably apposite to refer to Tobit 6:17, where it is foretold to Tobias that he will take Sara to wife and *rescue* her, for they will have children together ('rescue' not from the demon, for he does not threaten Sara at all, but rather her husbands, see 6:14f). 1 Tim 2:15 may also be directed against certain tendencies to despise marriage deriving from gnostic and ascetic movements, as is the case in Heb 13:4: 'Let marriage be held in honour among all, and let the marriage bed be undefiled; for God will judge the immoral and adulterous, even though their sins remain hidden from men'.

C. The *symbolic meaning* of marriage. Hosea experiences and claims the ↗ covenant of God with Israel as a marriage bond. Hosea loves the unfaithful Gomer in spite of all, in order to prophesy that Yahweh never ceases to love his people in spite of the fact that they have shown themselves to be adulterers, that is violators of the covenant, by turning away from him to strange gods. Jeremiah describes the two divided kingdoms as the unfaithful spouses of Yahweh (3:6–13) and equates the making of the covenant with a marriage between God and people (31:32). In Ezek 16 and 23 the picture of adultery consisting of apostasy from God and turning to idolatry is painted in drastic hues. God the husband punishes the unfaithful one in order to move her to return (Hos 6:4f; 11:8f; Jer 12:7); yet by the bill of divorce he does not repudiate her for ever, but only for a time (Is 49:15; 50:2; 54:4-8; 60:15), after which he shows himself once more to be gracious and loving towards her. The Song of Solomon enriches this wedding symbolism with a variety of images. This is the case whether it acquired this meaning in its incipient stages, as lyric poetry, perhaps as a collection of non-religious love-songs, or whether, as catholic exegetes have maintained recently, it is only the expressions of joy in love-play and the pleasure of love that have been borrowed, while the extremely positive value ascribed to marriage is due to the inclusion of this book in the canon (see A. M. Van den Oudenrijn, *Divus Thomas* 31 [1953], 257-80; A. Dubarle, *RB* 61 [1954], 67-86; J.-P. Audet, *RB* 62 [1955], 197-221; and K. Barth, *Church Dogmatics*, iii/1:365: 'To judge from the Song of Solomon, the Old Testament is aware of the weight of meaning contained in the relationship between the sexes precisely when viewed as such and in its ultimate literal sense. Hence it presumes to represent the union between Yahweh and Israel precisely as a man-and-wife relationship').

The New Testament applies marriage symbolism to Christ and the church. Certainly it is not already present in the gospels, for neither in the parables of the ten virgins and the wedding feast, nor in Mk 2:19f and parallels and Jn 3:29, is it the bride that is spoken of. In 2 Cor 11:2 the apostle appears as the spiritual father of the community at Corinth who conducts his daughter as a virgin bride to Christ the bridegroom. Here his ↗ parousia is regarded as the point in time at which she will be handed over. (For Eph 5:21-33 see above under B.) Revelation has a developed wedding symbolism at its command. In 19:7f the bride, the celestial community, has already bedecked herself for the marriage of the ↗ Lamb; in 22:17, 20 she, together with the Spirit (as groomsman), cries out for the coming of the bridegroom to lead her home to the everlasting nuptials. According to 21:2, 9 the pre-existing city of God (21:1 draws on Is 61:10), the Jerusalem which comes down out of heaven, is the community of the saved 'prepared as a bride adorned for her husband': 'the bride, the spouse of the Lamb'.

Bibliography: On A: W. Kornfeld, *DB(S)* v, 905-26 (with bibliography); A. Oepke, *RAC* iv, 650-66; G. Delling, *RAC* iv, 666-731 (with bibliography); H. Bardtke, *EKL* i, 996-8; F. Horst, *RGG* ii³, 316-18; A. Van den Born, Haag 355-64; J. Haspecker, *LTK* ii², 675-7. On B: H. Cazelles, *DB(S)* v, 926-35; H. Thimme, *EKL* i, 998-1000; Oepke, Delling, Van den Born as above; H. Greeven, *RGG* ii³, 318-20; H. Greeven, *ZEE* i (1957), 109-25; J. Michl, *LTK* iii², 677-80; B. Reicke, *NT* i (1956), 21-34; for the adultery clause cf most recently M. Zerwick, *VD* 38 (1960), 193-212 (with bibliography). On 1 Cor 7: J. Jeremias, *Festschrift Bultmann* (*BZNW* 21), 1957², 255-60; J. B. Bauer, *BL* 22 (1954/5), 142f; V. Neckebrouck, *Bijdragen* 24 (1963), 171-91; further ↗ Virginity bibliography. On the *Privilegium Paulinum*: P. Dulau, *CBQ* 13 (1951), 146-52; J. B. Bauer, *BL* 22 (1952/3), 82f. On 1 Pet 3:7: B. Reicke, *Festschrift Bultmann*, 1957², 296-304; J. B. Bauer, *BL* 22 (1954/5), 143f. On Eph 5, 21-33: H. Schlier *ad loc.*; P. Dacquino, *Scuola Cattolica* 86 (1958), 321-31; L. Johnston, *Scripture* 11 (1959), 1-6; E. Neuhäusler, *Bibel und Leben* (1963), 155-67. On C: J. Schmid, *RAC* ii, 528-64; Eichrodt i, 232-9; H. Gross and F. Mussner, *LTK* ii², 660-62; L. X. Léon-Dufour, 'Mariage et continence selon S. Paul', *Festschrift A. Gélin*, Lyons 1961, 319-29;

V. Dellagiacoma, *Israele Sposa di Dio: La metafora nuziale del VT*, Verona 1961; P. Grelot, *Mann und Frau nach der Hl. Schrift*, Mainz 1964; A. Alberti, *Matrimonio e divorzio nella Bibbia*, Milan 1962; W. Plautz, 'Monogamie und Polygymie im AT', *ZAW* 75 (1963), 3–27; W. K. Grossouw, 'Enkele bijbeltheologische opmerkingen over het huwelijk', *Jaarboek 1961: Werkgenootschap van kath. Theol. in Nederland*, Hilversum 1963, 63–77; T. de Kruijf, *De Bijbel over sexualiteit*, Roermond–Maaseik 1963; J. J. von Allmen, *Pauline Teaching on Marriage* (Studies in Christian Faith and Practice 6), London 1963; T. V. Fleming, 'Christ and Divorce', *TS* 24 (1963), 107–20; J. B. Bauer, 'Die matth. Ehescheidungsklausel', *BL* 38 (1964/5), 101—6; *E. Schillebeeckx, *Marriage: Secular Reality and Saving Mystery. I. Marriage in the Old and New Testaments*, London and New York 1965; *G. N. Vollebregt, *The Bible on Marriage*, London 1965.

Johannes B. Bauer

Mary

The name Mary, in the Greek of the New Testament generally *Maria* though sometimes in the later form *Mariam* as in LXX, corresponds to the Hebrew *Miriam*, a name borne by the sister of Moses and Aaron (Ex 15:20; Num 26:59; etc). Despite many attempts we are still uncertain as to the meaning of this name. As its relatively frequent occurrence shows, it must have been very popular in the inter-testamentary period. For example, a Hasmonaean princess, the second wife of Herod I, bears the name Mariamne which is a hellenistic expansion of the Semitic name. We also find many women of this name in the New Testament: Mary the mother of the Lord's brethren James and Joses (Mk 15:40; Mt 27:56; Lk 24:10; etc), Mary of Magdala (Mk 15:40; Mt 27:56; Lk 8:2; Jn 19:25; etc), Mary the sister of Martha (Lk 10:39; Jn 11:1; etc), Mary the mother

of John Mark (Acts 12:12), and another Mary, otherwise unknown, who performed great service in the Roman community (Rom 16:6). But the most important woman bearing this name was Mary, the mother of Jesus, and in what follows we shall be speaking of her alone.

A. *Introductory questions.* Mary mother of Jesus is not mentioned often in scriptures. Leaving aside texts which can only be applied to her by accommodation (eg, Prov 8:12–36; Sir 24:3–22) or by unsound exegesis (eg, Is 11:1; Jer 31:22), there are only three relevant texts in the Old Testament, of which one (Is 7:14) is referred to Mary in Mt 1:23, another (Mic 5:2), simply refers to the mother of the Messiah, and the third (Gen 3:15), is associated with her only in post-biblical tradition. Naturally there are more references to her in the New Testament, though only a few of the New Testament writings mention her, namely, the four gospels, though in different degrees, and Acts on one occasion. Paul refers on one occasion to Jesus born of a woman (Gal 4:4), but neither gives her name nor says anything about her. The vision of the Woman of the Apocalypse (Rev 12:1–6, 13–17), which in christian tradition has often been referred to Mary, must be left on one side, since this figure represents the people of God, the true Israel, as was correctly noted from the earliest period of the church's history (Hippolytus, Methodius, Victorinus). At the most, the vision could be referred to Mary only in the spiritual sense.

The information on Mary provided by the gospels comes, to a considerable extent, from the so-called 'infancy narratives' in Matthew and Luke. Recent gospel criticism takes the view that these are wholly or in great part unhistorical narratives, chiefly on account of the miracles and mysterious events which they record. Even if we regard this judgement as too extreme, there remains the problem of the literary genre of the narratives contained in the infancy narratives. Here we cannot disregard the possibility of a certain similarity with the Jewish genre of haggadic midrash according to which historical events are not simply reproduced but rather interpreted theologically. This genre allows for structural additions which cannot be called historical in the strict sense of the term. So, for example, the influence of Jug 13, the conception of Samson, and 1 Sam 1f, that of Samuel, on the Lukan history of the infancy is unmistakeable. Despite this, however, we find in these chapters of Matthew and Luke very early Palestinian traditions which have been elaborated, so that a reasonable criticism has to take account of a historical nucleus in these narratives. (For the virginal conception of Jesus, which constitutes the chief objection to the historical credibility of these chapters, see under C 1 b below.)

The historical value of the information on Mary found in the fourth gospel depends on the historical evaluation of the passages in which this information comes to us. It is certain that this evangelist wished to write history, not just allegory—at least, he himself considered his narratives as historical. With regard to the gospel writers in general this claim cannot indeed be proved by positive means; but neither have we any decisive grounds for considering their work as simply unhistorical.

B. *Historical information.* a. *the synoptic tradition.* Here Mary appears as the mother of Jesus (Mk 6:3 = Mt 13:55) married to an artisan (*tektōn*, Mt 13:55) named Joseph (Lk 4:22 taken with Mk 6:3). Jesus has brothers and sisters (Mk 3:31-5 and parallels), though it is not clear what their relationship to him was (↗ brethren of Jesus). For some of them at least a mother different from the mother of Jesus is mentioned (Mk 15:40 taken with 6:3).

b. *The infancy narratives.* In the infancy of Matthew, Mary conceived Jesus without having had intercourse with a man. This conception is attributed to the divine power, the Holy Spirit (1:18, 20). This had taken place before Joseph had 'known' her, that is, before the celebration of marriage and cohabitation (1:18). Alarmed by the pregnancy of his betrothed, Joseph wanted to send her away quietly, that is, leave her free to marry another man (1:19), but was informed by an angel of the real state of affairs and ordered to take Mary to himself (1:20), which he did at once (1:24). It is again emphasised that before the birth of the child they had not had marital relations (1:25). In due course Mary gave birth to the messianic child in Bethlehem in the time of King Herod I (37-4 BC), received the visit from the Magi from the east who wished to worship the child (2:11), fled with her husband and child to Egypt (2:13f), where they remained until the death of Herod (2:19), when the family settled in Nazareth (2:20-23). Allowing for the fact that these narratives, especially that of the visit of the Magi, are told with a certain latitude as regards historical detail, there is no need to doubt that they contain a historical nucleus. This is true of the miraculous conception of Jesus, the birth in Bethlehem, and the avoidance of danger to the child by exile in Egypt.

According to the Lukan infancy narrative Mary is a young maiden living in Nazareth betrothed (1:27: *emnēsteumenē*, which can also mean 'married' as in 2:5 but which, on account of the context, is here generally and rightly understood as 'promised in marriage') to Joseph of the house of David (1:27). The narrative does not tell us whether she too belonged to the Davidic line or to any other: Davidic descent is not excluded by 1:36, nor does it follow from Rom 1:3. She is then represented as receiving from the angel Gabriel the divine commission to become mother of the Messiah. This will be brought about by God, through the Holy Spirit and 'the power of the Most High' (1:35), without relation with any man. As the 'handmaid of the Lord' she declares herself ready to fulfil the task (1:38). Soon after she visits her relative Elizabeth, the mother of John the Baptist (1:39–45), who by the Holy Spirit recognises her as the mother of the Messiah (1:41–3). At this point Mary utters the 'Magnificat' (1:46–55), a hymn of thanksgiving to God which, in the form in which we have it, may have been attributed to her at a later date. She stays about three months with Elizabeth and later returns to Nazareth (1:56). On the occasion of a census ordered by the Emperor Augustus (2:1f; a reference which is not without its historical difficulties), Joseph went with Mary to Bethlehem where the expected child was born in the greatest poverty (2:1–7). Soon after, the shepherds of the neighbourhood came to see him, warned by an angel that the Messiah was about to be born (2:8–20). Eight days after birth the child was circumcised, on which occasion he received the name 'Jesus' (2:21; see also 1:31). After the period of purification was over (see Lev 12:2–4) Mary went with Joseph and the child to Jerusalem to offer the sacrifice of purification (see Lev 12:6–8) and present the child in the temple as her 'firstborn' (Lk 2:22–4, 27; see also Ex 13:13). There she met a pious Jew named Simeon who prophesied about her and the child (Lk 2:25–35): the child was to be a 'sign' of contradiction and a 'sword' would pass through the soul of Mary (2:34f). After the presentation in the temple the holy family returned to Nazareth (2:39).

On the occasion of the Passover, Joseph and Mary went up once again to Jerusalem on pilgrimage with the child, who by now was twelve years old (2:41–50). Without the knowledge of his parents Jesus stayed behind in the city among the teachers in the temple (2:43, 46) and astonished the hearers by his understanding and the answers he gave (2:47). When his parents eventually found him and Mary asked him why he had treated them so (2:48) he justified his conduct by replying that he must be in his Father's house, that is, in the temple (v 49)—an answer which they did not understand (v 50). On two occasions, at the birth of Jesus and the events surrounding it and on this occasion, Luke tells us that Mary noted and pondered over these experiences (2:19, 51).

These two infancy narratives of

Matthew and Luke show no sign of any mutual dependence one on the other; on the contrary, they are difficult to reconcile at some points, as for example, the return to Nazareth (Mt 2:23 and Lk 2:39). They do agree, however, on the most important points as, for example, the names of Jesus's parents, the conception of the child by a virgin with the co-operation of the Holy Spirit, Bethlehem as the birthplace, the fact that the family later on settled at Nazareth, and so on. It is therefore not too difficult to reconcile the two accounts. As far as Mary is concerned, we are told that when she received the promise that she would be mother of the Messiah she was betrothed but not yet married and that the marriage followed later, probably after her return from visiting the mother of the Baptist but in any case before the birth of Jesus.

c. *Information found only in Luke.* In Lk 11:27 a woman, impressed by the way Jesus spoke, declared his mother blessed. In Acts 1:14 Mary, together with the first apostles, the brethren of Jesus and several women, belongs to the community which after the ascension of the Lord engaged in common prayer in Jerusalem. This is the last mention of Mary in the New Testament.

d. *Information found in John.* According to one reading of Jn 1:13, supported especially by Vetus Latina versions (Codex Veronensis; Irenaeus, *Adv. Haer.* III, 16:2, etc; also Epistula Apostolorum 3[14]—which have 'natus est' instead of 'nati sunt'), we have a reference to the virginal birth of Jesus. Unfortunately, the reading is not original or authentic. The fourth gospel refers only to 'the mother of Jesus' without giving her name. It mentions her as present at the marriage-feast of Cana (2:1–11), on a journey of Jesus to Capharnaum together with his brothers and disciples (2:12), and finally at the crucifixion (19:25–7). At Cana she draws her son's attention to the lack of wine in the assurance that he will help and receives the answer: 'O woman, what is that to me and to you? My hour has not yet come' (or, 'has my hour not yet come?', 2:4). Evidently expecting him to perform a miracle she admonishes the waiters to do everything that Jesus will say to them (v 5). At Golgotha she stands at the foot of the cross together with other women including a 'sister' who may have been either Mary wife (daughter?) of Clophas or another woman otherwise unknown to us (19:25). Here too Jesus addresses his mother as 'woman' (v 26) and commits to her care the so-called 'Beloved Disciple' as a son in his own place, and her to this disciple who was, according to an old and well-founded tradition, none other than John himself (19:26f). From then on this disciple takes her to himself (v 27). The unsemitic form of address 'woman' was probably attributed to Jesus during the formation of the tradition. Since it implies respect rather than disregard, the evangelist probably chose this way of expressing the respect which Jesus had for his mother.

e. *Results.* The New Testament gives us no information on the time and place of Mary's birth or about her parents. She appears for the first time in Nazareth as engaged to Joseph. As the result of a miracle worked by God she became mother of the Messiah without losing her virginity. After her marriage to Joseph she brought Jesus into the world in Bethlehem in circumstances of the greatest poverty. After a period of exile in Egypt she lived with her husband and child in Nazareth. During the public ministry of Jesus she remained in the background but is found on a few occasions near him. Finally, she was staying in Jerusalem with other women from Galilee when her son was executed and was part of the community which stayed together in that city after the ascension. After the death of Jesus she remained closely associated with John the Beloved Disciple. No reliable information has survived bearing on her later life and her death.

C. *Biblical mariology.* Any theological reflection about Mary must begin from scripture. The bible provides us with some direct information about Mary while other conclusions can be deduced indirectly from them. Hence it is that the church, with the help of tradition, has deduced from scripture more than is warranted by historical and critical exegesis by using a kind of interpretation which it is not easy to define with any exactitude. There are some theologians who go even further and develop doctrine about Mary for which scripture offer no justification apart from the most general principles.

1. *Doctrine clearly witnessed to in scripture.* a. *Mary is the mother of Christ, the Son of God.* In giving birth to Jesus Mary became the mother of the Messiah, the Christ foretold by the prophets (Mt 1:16, 21; Lk 1:32f; 2:11). According to the faith of the early church this Christ Jesus enjoyed the unique relationship to God of Son to Father (Mt 11:27; Lk 10:22; Jn 5:19–23; 10:30; 17:1, 5; Gal 4:4) and

is himself God (Jn 1:1; Phil 2:6). Mary therefore is the mother of Christ and the mother of the Son of God—'mother of God' (*theotokos*), as she is called by theologians as early as the third century. Since the scriptures know of only one Christ Jesus who is at the same time man and God, they provide no justification for the view that Mary gave birth only to Christ as man not to Christ as God, a view held by early heretics such as Cerinthus and later Nestorius. Since Christ is at the same time truly God and truly man, and this from the first moment of his incarnation (Jn 1:1; Phil 2:7; 1 Jn 4:2), we must conclude that Mary conceived and gave birth to Christ as the God-man (Gal 4:4). Both the divine-human existence of Jesus and the divine motherhood of Mary are deep mysteries which go beyond the power of human reason, yet they follow necessarily from what we find in the New Testament.

b. *Mary is the virginal mother of Christ.* The scriptures also testify that Mary is the virginal mother of Christ. According to Mt 1:18–25 (see also 1:16) and Lk 1:34f (see also 3:23), Mary conceived Jesus without prior intercourse with a man, when she was yet a virgin betrothed to Joseph, but before she cohabited with him (Lk 1:27, 34; see also Mt 1:18, 25). Mt 1:22f sees in this marvellous conception the fulfilment of Is 7:14 according to which Emmanuel will be conceived and born of a 'virgin' (Hebrew: *'almâh*; LXX *parthenos*; other Jewish translators into Greek have *neanis*; Vulgate: *virgo*). Both the Hebrew text and the Greek translations leave it an open question whether a young woman already married is referred to or a girl who is still virgin; but the

Gospel of Matthew interprets the text as a prophecy of the miraculous conception of the Messiah from a virgin. The gospels ascribe this conception to the Holy Spirit (Mt 1:18, 20), or the Holy Spirit and the power of the Most High (Lk 1:35). This implies a conception brought about in Mary by divine power, but not of course in the literal sense of the theogonies found in Greek mythology (eg, Zeus and Danaë) —an idea which is completely alien to the biblical way of thinking—but by a miraculous causation understood in a totally spiritual sense.

While, strictly speaking, the scriptures refer only to a virginal conception, the apocryphal Gospel of James speaks of the virginity of Mary as preserved in the birth of Jesus, a teaching which, after some controversy in the patristic age, was to become an explicit part of church teaching (Lateran Synod, AD 649, under Pope Martin I, can. 3: DS 503 [= DB 256]). In keeping with this Is 7:14, which speaks of a virgin giving birth to Emmanuel, was understood not only of a virginal conception followed by a normal birth but of a perpetual virginity preserved also at the birth of the child. Though the literal sense of the passage does not lead necessarily to this interpretation it does not exclude it either. In more recent times the question has come up once again for discussion among catholic theologians as to how we are to understand this received teaching of Mary's virginity in the birth of her Son.

The New Testament says nothing explicitly about the virginity of Mary after the birth of Jesus. It would, of course, be excluded if only some of the brothers and sisters of Jesus mentioned were born of Mary. But as early as the apocryphal Gospel of James (9:2; 17:1) the so called brethren of the Lord are understood to be sons of Joseph by an earlier marriage. The view which is beginning to emerge here, that Mary remained a virgin after the birth of Jesus, is not based on any historical tradition, but is argued by Origen as congruent with Mary's position (*In Matthaeum* x 17, 463) and became the teaching of the church in the Lateran Synod of 649 (see above). No objection can be brought against this on the grounds of either Mt 1:25, Lk 2:7, or the references to the brothers and sisters of Jesus (⁊ brethren of Jesus).

If, as the tradition affirms, Mary remained a virgin after the birth of Jesus, we may ask whether this had been her purpose from the beginning. The answer to this question depends on the interpretation of her words to Gabriel (Lk 1:34): 'How can this be since I know not man?'. This means: how can Mary conceive the Messiah since she has had no intercourse with any man. Augustine (*De sancta virginitate* 4:4 [*PL* 40:398]; *Sermo* 291:5f [*PL* 38:1318f]) deduced from this text that Mary had already vowed her virginity to God. This view came to be widely accepted from the time of Augustine, especially in Latin christianity, though it was generally supposed that she had simply resolved to live virginally rather than make a vow of virginity (which was unknown at that time)—which, however, is much the same thing in practice. This interpretation is, however, untenable, especially since Mary is represented as betrothed to a man (Lk 1:27) and therefore contemplated marriage in the normal way. The words of Mary which are used to give support to this view are clearly susceptible of another explanation even though a completely satisfactory interpretation has not yet been found. They could, for example, simply refer to the fact that she and Joseph had not yet begun to live together. We may conclude then that her decision to live virginally in spite of her marriage with Joseph was first made under the influence of the unparalleled miracle of the conception of Jesus without male co-operation.

In general it may be said that modern criticism rejects the virginal conception of Jesus in Mary's womb. It sees this as a legendary embellishment of the tradition inspired perhaps by the desire to express a theological truth. Such legends could have arisen on the basis of Is 7:14, as supposed by Adolf Harnack and earlier scholars, or as parallels with pagan thinking according to which certain great men were conceived as the result of intercourse between a god and a human woman (Eduard Norden and others). According to this view, the story of the virgin birth would be an early essay in christology having the purpose of testifying that Christ was not like other men but was the gift of god to the the world (H. F. von Kampenhausen and many other critics). For a defence of this view we must refer to the commentaries on Matthew and Luke and the monographs on the ⁄ virgin birth.

Here we limit ourselves to saying briefly that the virginal conception of Jesus represented something absolutely new which cannot really be explained as a development of Is 7:14 or by reference to the parallels adduced by certain critics from the history of religions. It is a miracle without parallel which one must either accept or deny even when considered against the background of the entirely different world-view which the story presupposes. Many non-Catholic critics do not go so far as those named above. While accepting the virginal conception of Jesus they tend, however, to deny that she remained a virgin after the birth of Jesus. This is understandable if christian tradition, the main source for this belief, is left aside, as it commonly is by scholars who take their inspiration from the Reformation.

II. *Doctrines which the church takes from the scriptures only indirectly, by way of tradition.* a. *Mary is full of grace.* According to Lk 1:28 Mary is greeted by the angel as *kekharitōmenē*, highly favoured or 'graced', translated by the Vulgate *gratia plena*, full of grace (Vetus Latina has *gratificata*, a less elegant translation but one which is nearer to the original). As with Stephen, who is described by means of the same word in Acts 6:8, it refers to the possession of grace which is given by God, a close union with him which in the case of Mary consists in the fact that she is destined to be the mother of the Messiah (Lk 1:31-3). Christian tradition has concluded from the greeting of the angel and the unique destiny reserved for Mary that she was given grace in a special measure and united with God in such a way that she was 'full of grace'. As early as the patristic age the greeting of the angel was understood in this way to signify that Mary was filled with grace (eg, Ambrose, *Exposition Evangelii sec. Lucam* II 9 [*CCSL* 14]), and *Ineffabilis Deus* of 8 December 1854 refers to this and other elements of tradition in its teaching that Mary was conceived without original sin (Mansi 47, col. 122 C/D; see also DS 2800–4).

The bull *Ineffabilis* found another basis for its teaching in the interpretation of the so called Protoevangelium of Gen 3:15 (Mansi 47, 121 D/122A) which was already underway in the patristic age (Justin, *Dial.* 100:5f; Irenaeus, *Adv. Haer.* III 23:7; IV 40:3; V 21:1f). According to this text God had set enmity between the serpent and the woman, between its seed and hers, after the sin committed in paradise. The seed of the woman would tread on the serpent's head but the serpent would wound the heel that crushed it. In the context the woman is the spouse of the first man, who is given the name Eve (Gen 3:20). Her seed, that is, her descendence, is the human race. If with christian tradition we interpret this text not only of the natural opposition which exists between snakes and human beings but also and especially of a moral struggle between the human race and the Serpent understood as the Devil, it follows that God has taken away from the latter his power and domination over men but that men will always be troubled by his attacks though eventually they will overcome. The course of sacred history shows that men—more exactly the righteous—can only overcome Satan because God has become man and has overcome the adversary in his death and resurrection. If therefore we have here a prediction of a victory of mankind over the Devil this victory can only be won by Christ the head of redeemed humanity. Therefore we can say that Christ is referred

to indirectly and inclusively (making use of the *sensus plenior*) in this text.

The mariological significance of the text presupposes this christological significance. It means that we may find in this text also a prophecy about Mary who overcomes Satan in union with her son. In accordance with its reading: *ipsa* (ie, *mulier* rather than *ipsum*, ie, *semen*) *conteret caput tuum*, the Vulgate understands the woman herself, not in the first place her 'seed', as crushing the serpent's head. Since this is not true of Eve, we are obliged necessarily to think of another woman, namely Mary, either directly and exclusively (Mary only without Eve) or indirectly and inclusively (Eve through Mary). But since the text was seen to refer to Mary following on its christological content even before the Vulgate reading became prevalent (in the second half of the fourth century), and was considered to contain a reference to the Mother of God who would crush the head of the serpent (so in Irenaeus), catholic theology and, following it, the bull *Ineffabilis Deus*, sought to interpret Gen 3:15 in a mariological sense quite apart from the Vulgate reading which was not in conformity with the original text. This was no easy task, and it has so far led to no unanimous conclusion. Almost all catholic theologians now accept that the text refers to Mary and not just in an accommodated sense. Only a few (D. J. Unger, B. Rigaux) see Mary as referred to directly in this text, a view which is, however, excluded by the context. Most see the Mother of God as referred to in a spiritual or typological sense, Eve being the typological representation of Mary the new Eve (P.

Heinisch, *Probleme der biblischen Urgeschichte*, Lucerne 1947, 91 etc) or according to the *sensus plenior*. In this case 'the woman' refers not just to Eve but women in general and hence indirectly her who gave birth to the one who was to overcome the serpent (J. Coppens, M. Brunec). This is in keeping with the so called theory of corporate personality according to which an individual can recapitulate his or her descendants and symbolise them.

Another approach is to see Mary as intimately related to Christ as his mother in the victory which he has won over the Evil One (P. Morant, *Die Anfänge der Menschheit*, Lucerne 1960; M. Schmaus, *Mariologie*, Munich 1961[2]; see also *Ineffabilis Deus*). This insistence on the association of Mary with Christ has been widely represented from the Middle Ages down to the present. We should, however, make one methodological observation, namely, that the spiritual sense of a biblical passage cannot have probative force in the strict theological sense (Aquinas, *Summa* I qu. I, art. 10 ad 1), and that in appealing to a *sensus plenior* we have to avoid the danger of presupposing as proved what we hope to get from the text. We can, at any rate, conclude that Gen 3:15 refers to Mary not in itself but considered in the light of tradition.

b. *At the end of her life Mary was taken up body and soul into heaven.* 1 Cor 15:23 teaches that first Christ was raised by God and then at the return of the Lord those will be raised up who belong to him. This text appears to exclude the possibility that anyone other than Christ would be raised up in the body before the *parousia*. But since the New Testament testifies to a coming of the Lord before the end of the world (Jn 14:18f, 21, 23), what we might call an anticipated parousia, in much the same way that it allows for an anticipated judgement (1 Pet 4:17), the possibility may be left open that someone could be raised by God before the end of the world. This cannot be absolutely excluded by what Paul says, since he may well have been thinking of the parousia as subsumed in one moment of time. While it is true that no such exception is known to scripture, the church has in fact assumed that such an exception was made in the case of Mary. We find this view stated for the first time in apocryphal writings of the fifth century (especially in the *Transitus beatae Mariae virginis*). As from this time it was theologically elaborated and finally proclaimed as a dogma on November 1st 1950 (*Munificentissimus Deus*). In support of this doctrine the tradition appeals to the unique position of Mary as mother of Christ who is life itself (Jn 1:4; 11:25; 14:6), not subject to corruption (Acts 2:27, 31), and in whom all are made alive in God (1 Cor 15:22; cf Jn 5:21). Appeal is further made to Mary's own holiness, even with regard to her conception, so that death which is the wages of sin (Rom 6:23) can have no power over her. In particular, the kind of theological interpretation which lies behind the constitution *Munificentissimus Deus* refers to the 'protoevangelium' which implies a complete victory of Mary over the Evil One (see under a). But such a victory would have to include a victory over sin and its consequence death (Rom 5:12, 17-21; 8:10f; 1 Cor

15:25f, 54f; Heb 2:14). We can therefore conclude that though the doctrine
of the bodily assumption of Mary is not
explicitly present in the scriptures it is
founded on them and so understood
and developed in the tradition. We
therefore have good guarantee, in both
this case and that of the holiness of Mary
and her freedom from original sin, that
these doctrines have been accepted as
true by the church, which goes beyond
what can be found explicitly in the
scriptures.

III. *Other doctrines which are based on
the scriptures.* For a mariological doctrine
to be sound it must be in accordance
with the scriptures. This means that it
must at least be based on the scriptures,
even though not found expressly in
them, or be taken from the scriptures
by the church in reliance on tradition.
All the prerogatives of Mary elaborated
by catholic theologians are in one way
or another a development of the
scriptural teaching of her divine motherhood. These would include her representing mankind in its way towards
salvation, her participation in the
sufferings of Christ as she stood by the
cross, her spiritual maternity, her
powerful intercession before God, the
mediation of grace through her, however this is conceived, and her status as
queen. In addition many of the prerogatives attributed to her are not proper to
her but belong in some way to all
christians, though of course they belong
to her in a special way on account of her
position as mother of Christ the Son of
God. Together with those texts which
speak of her as mother of Christ we
should therefore note those many
others which speak of the justified as
brothers of Christ and members of his

body, though these too apply to Mary
in a way commensurate with her unique
dignity.

D. *Mary in the Apocrypha.* A section of
the Testament of the Twelve Patriarchs
which is certainly of christian origin
(XI Test. Joseph 19:8) speaks of a
virgin who gives birth to a lamb. The
Ascension of Isaiah (11:2–14) describes
the miraculous birth of Jesus from the
virgin Mary of the line of David. This
description is clearly based on the
infancy narratives in the gospels though
it contains many legendary embellish-
ments. The christian sibylline literature,
also in dependence on Luke's gospel,
refers to the virginal birth of the *Logos*
from Mary (VIII 456–79; see also
269f, 357f). The nineteenth Ode of
Solomon (6–11), which is of gnostic
origin, celebrates the conception and
painless birth of the Virgin. The third
epistle of Clement (5:12–14) and the
Epistula Apostolorum (3 [14]; 14 [25])
also refer to the conception of Jesus from
Mary, the former as the incarnation of
the Spirit, the latter (14 [25]) as that of
the Logos who appeared to the Virgin
in the shape of Gabriel. A writing
dedicated exlusively to Mary, the first
of its kind, is the Gospel of James from
the second century. It speaks of Joachim
and Anna as the parents of Mary who
brought her up a virgin in the temple.
At the age of sixteen she conceived
Jesus (12:3) and gave birth to him
while still remaining a virgin (19:2f;
20:1). Various elements taken from
this history contained in the Gospel of
James found their way into popular
christian piety and legend and even to
some extent into the liturgy (eg, the
names of her parents, the feast of the
Dedication of Mary on 21 November).

The *Transitus beatae Mariae Virginis*, composed not earlier than the fifth century, achieved a significance not dissimilar from that of the Gospel of James. It is in this writing that we find the account of how Mary ended her days and of her assumption body and soul into heaven.

Bibliography: On account of the great abundance of literature relevant to the subject references will be to a great extent limited to commentaries on the relevant biblical texts and works of a more general and inclusive nature: F. Ceuppens, *De Mariologia Biblica*, Rome 1948; R. Laurentin, *Queen of Heaven*, Dublin and London 1956; R. Laurentin, *Structure et Théologie de Luc I–II*, Paris 1957; K. H. Schelkle, *Maria im NT: Maria in Glaube und Frömmigkeit*, Rottenberg 1954, 5–38; K. H. Schelkle, *Maria, Mutter des Herrn*, Leipzig 1956; K. H. Schelkle, *Die Mutter des Erlösers*, Düsseldorf 1958; F.-M. Braun, *La Mère des fidèles: Essai de théologie johannique*, Tournai 1954²; P. Gaechter, *Maria im Erdenleben*, Innsbruck 1955³; G. M. Roschini, *Mariologia* I–IV, Rome 1957–8²; *Lexikon für Marienkunde*, Regensburg 1957ff; J. Galot, *Marie dans l'Evangile*, Paris 1958; S. Garofalo, *La Madonna nella Bibbia*, Milan 1958; L. Deiss, *Marie, Fille de Sion*, Paris 1959; M. Schmaus, *Katholische Dogmatik* v, Munich 1961²; A. Feuillet, 'La Vierge Marie dans le NT', *Maria, Etudes sur la sainte Vierge* VI, Paris 1961, 15–69; F. Spedalieri, *Maria nella Scrittura e nella tradizione della Chiesa primitiva*, Messina 1961; F. Spadafora, *Maria santissima nella S. Scrittura*, Rome 1963; M. Peinador, *Los temas de la mariologia bíblica*, Madrid 1963; *E. Schillebeeckx, *Mary, Mother of the Redemption*, London 1964.

On C I: E. Norden, *Die Geburt des Kindes*, Leipzig 1931; M. Dibelius, *Jungfrauensohn und Krippenkind*, Heidelberg 1932; D. Haugg, *Das erste biblische Marienwort*, Stuttgart 1938; A. Mitterer, *Dogma und Biologie der Heiligen Familie*, Vienna 1952; G. Delling, *TDNT* v, 824–35; O. Graber, *Die Frage Marias an den Verkündigungsengel*, Graz 1956; J.-P. Audet, 'L'annonce à Marie', *RB* 63 (1956), 346–74; R. H. Fuller, *The Virgin Birth: Historical Fact or Kerygmatic Truth?*, Chicago 1957; J. B. Bauer, 'Monstra te esse matrem, Virgo singularis!', *MTZ* 9 (1958), 124–35; K. Rahner, 'Virginitas in partu', *Theological Investigations* IV, London 1966, 134–62; J. Gewiess, 'Die Marienfrage, Lk 1:34', *BZ* 5 (1961), 221–54; H. F. von Campenhausen, *Die Jungfrauengeburt in der Theologie der Alten Kirche*, Heidelberg 1962; T. Boslooper, *The Virgin Birth*, London 1962; J. A. de Aldama, 'La virginidad "in partu" en la exégesis patrística', *Salmanticensis* 9 (1962), 113–53; J. A. de Aldama, 'Virgo in partu, virgo post partum', *Estudios ecclesiásticos* 38 (1963), 57–82; L. Legrand, 'L'arrière-plan néotest. de Lc 1:35', *RB* 70 (1963), 161–92; M. Rehm, 'Das wort ʿalmāh in Is 7:14', *BZ* 8 (1964), 89–101; *L. Hermans, *The Bible on the Childhood of Jesus*, London 1965.

On C II: F. Drewniak (P. Leander), *Die mariologische Deutung von Gen 3:15 in der Väterzeit*, Breslau 1934; M. Jugie, 'L'Assumption de la S. Vierge et L'Ecriture Sainte', in *L'Année théologique* 2 (1942), 1–46; L. G. da Fonseca, 'L'Assunzione di Maria nella S. Scrittura', *Bbl* 28 (1947), 321–62; T. Gallus, *Interpretatio mariologica Protoevangelii (Gen 3:15) tempore postpatristico usque ad Concilium Tridentinum*, Rome 1949; T. Gallus, *Interpretatio mariologica Protoevangelii posttridentina usque ad definitionem dogmaticam Immaculatae Conceptionis* I, Rome 1953; II, Rome 1954; A. Bea, 'La Sacra Scrittura "ultimo fundamento" del domma dell 'Assunzione', *Estratto de La Civiltà Cattolica*, Rome 1950; A. Bea, 'Maria Santissima nel Protovangelo', *Marianum* 15 (1953) 1–21; A. Bea, 'Bulla "Ineffabilis Deus" et hermeneutica biblica', *Virgo Immaculata III: De Immaculata Conceptione in Sacra Scriptura*, Rome 1955, 1–17; J. Coppens, 'Le Protévangile: Un nouvel Essai d'exégèse', *ETL* 26 (1950), 5–36; J. Michl, 'Der Weibessame (Gen 3:15) in spätjüdischer und frühchristlicher Auffassung', *Bbl* 33 (1952), 371–401 and 476–505; D. J. Unger, *The First Gospel: Genesis 3:15*, Louvain and Paderborn 1954; B. Rigaux, 'La Femme et son Lignage dans Genèse III, 14–15', *RB* 61 (1954), 321–48; R. Laurentin, 'L'Interprétation de Genèse 3:15 dans la Tradition', *Etudes Mariales* 12 (1954), 77–156; H. Cazelles, 'Gen III, 15: exégèse contemporaine', *La Nouvelle Eve* 3 (Paris 1957); M. Brunec, 'De Sensu Protoevangelii (Gen 3:15)', *VD* 36 (1958), 193–220 and 321–37.

On D: E. Cothenet, 'Marie dans les Apocryphes', *Maria. Etudes sur la Sainte Vierge* VI, Paris 1961, 71–156.

Johann Michl

Mediation

Neither Hebrew nor rabbinical language have any special term of their own for 'mediation' (see however *pillêl* = 'act as go-between', 'intervene', 1 Sam 2:25; Ps 106:30), but the Greek *mesitēs* and the Latin mediator, respectively derived from *mesos* and *medius* (middle) show that the *mediator* is one who stands in the middle (*between*). His function as intermediary means that he brings two or more parties into contact with each other or nearer to each other. He *unites*, he *reconciles* by bringing nearer. The histories of the relationships of the unique and transcendent God with the people of Israel and with the disciples of Christ are respectively summed up in the two institutions of covenants. They leave a permanent place for the intervention of mediators.

A. *The Old Testament.* Long before Moses God preserves part of mankind from the punishment which he has imposed through Noah (Gen 6:11f). Abraham acts as intercessor on behalf of Sodom (Gen 18:22f) and Abimelech (Gen 20:1–17). Unbelievers are brought back to the way of their fathers through the judges (Judg 2:18, 22). Above all it is the king who, at least in the beginning, is anointed by Yahweh (1 Sam 24:7–11; 26:9, 11, 16, 23; 2 Sam 1:14, 16) to represent the people before God. David and Solomon present offerings (2 Sam 6:13, 17f; 1 Kings 8:5). On the other hand Ezekiel does not ascribe any religious function to the prince, and Zechariah presupposes the separation of the royal from the cultic sphere of power (4:3, 11–14; 6:13). Only in the person of the Messiah will they be validly united (Ps 110).

The *constitutional organ* of mediation is the *priesthood*. By the help of its teaching and its prescribed rites it makes it possible for man to enter into union with God. On the one hand it guards and hands on the teaching and is responsible for seeing that it is applied to the life of the individual no less than to that of the nation: 'The priests teach Jacob thine ordinances and Israel thy law' (Deut 33:10; see also 17:18; 26:1–11; Jer 18:18; Ezek 7:26). On the other hand the 'ministers of the sanctuary' mediate the divine blessings (Lev 9:22; 1 Chron 23:13) and are consecrated for the performance of the liturgy. God had already entrusted the house of Eli with three functions: 'to go up to my altar, to burn incense, to wear an ephod before me'. In the Priestly Document, and above all in the Code of Holiness, this office is seen as including a wider range of functions. The priests present offerings, especially for atonement (Lev 10:17; Ex 28:38; Num 18:1) and for purifying from sins (Ex 29:36; Lev 9:15). After the Exile their service in praising the Lord was more developed (1 Chron 15:16–22; 16:4, 41; 23:5; 2 Chron 29:25–30; Ezra 3:10f). Because they draw near to Yahweh, who is holy, the priests must be separated from the people and even from the Levites, and they must keep themselves in a special state of ritual and moral purity (↗ clean and unclean). This applies above all to the high priest, who represents the chosen people and the priesthood. As a mark of distinction he wears: 1. a gold plate with the inscription 'Holy to Yahweh' (Ex 28:36f): as a result of this state of consecration his offerings are accepted by God (v 38); 2. The oracle pouch fastened to the ephod on the breast and embroidered with twelve stones each of which bears the name of one of the sons of Jacob. This last feature signifies that the high priest protects the interests of the whole nation. The climax of the high-priestly functions is the liturgy of the Day of Atonement (Lev 14). In this way the priests exercise a twofold mediatorship, one that is directed both upwards and downwards. They bring prayers before God and show him honour; they announce the will of God to men and guard the religious traditions.

The *function of prophet*, in so far as it is an institution and ordained to regulate the life of Israel, is *not hereditary*. It is a charismatic function to which men are called by the Spirit (Is 6; Jer 1; Ezek 1–3). It manifests itself first as the *office of interceding* (Jer 7:16; 14:11; 15:1; Ezek 14:13–20), as 'having access' to God on behalf of individuals (1 Kings 17:20; 2 Kings 4:33) or for the people (Amos 7:2, 5; Ezek 11:3; Dan 9:4–20). Chosen by the Lord and living in extremely close union with him, the prophet is 'a man of God'. He is assured of the divine favour, and, as a result, is totally dedicated to the work of praying for the people. But his most characteristic function is *to impart revelation* and to act as its authentic interpreter. Sent by God in order to impart his thoughts, he has nothing else to do but to repeat what he has heard (Jer 23:28; see also 1:9; 5:14, 15, 19). It is the prophets too who, in the course of centuries, add to the original revelation of Moses those expansions and more precise definitions in which their own teaching for the chosen people consists.

In the Israelite, and still more in the Jewish–hellenistic tradition, the highest and most perfect form of the prophetic function is found in *Moses*, considered as a military and political leader no less than as a prophet and priest. Thus he is *the* mediator of the old covenant. He is this as a prophet who intercedes not only for individuals or for a group, but for the people of Israel (Deut 9:18f, 25–9): during the plagues of Egypt (Ex 8:4, 8, 9, 24–7; 9:27–9, 33; 10:17–19), in order to arrest the fire that threatens the Israelites (Num 11:2), and to appease the wrath of Yahweh (Num 14:13–20; see also 21:7). Moses' prayer at Rephidim brings victory over the Amalekites (Ex 17:11–13). After the episode of the golden calf 'Moses propitiates the countenance of the Lord that (this time too) he may let himself repent' (Ex 32:7–14). In his innocence he is able to intercede on behalf of the guilty and to obtain pardon for them (vv 30–34). As mediator of revelation Moses proclaims Yahweh's law and his will as set forth in the torah (⟋ law). At Sinai the people, though they have taken their stand at a distance from the mountain, are so transported with terror at the theophany that they beseech their mediator to stand between them and it (Ex 20:18–21). Moses draws near to the cloud: 'I stood between the Lord and you . . . you were afraid because of the fire' (Deut 5:5, 22–30). The Rabbis go still further, explaining because of their sins the Israelites could not look upon the countenance of their mediator (*sarsôr*, see Pesiqt. 5:45a). In the 'tent of meeting' God converses with his servant, his 'middleman', face to face, 'like a man with his friend' (Ex 33:7–11; cf Num 12:1–8). Yahweh holds converse with Moses again (Lev 17:1; 18:1; 19:1; 20:1) in order to hand over to him the laws which his people had to observe (Ex 34:29–35).

In the post-exilic period, the ↗ word, ↗ wisdom, and ↗ Spirit of God are presented as mediators from the higher to the lower sphere, or rather they inspire and lead human mediators. The angels (*mal'akîm*, that is 'sent ones') regard it as their task to serve the elect and to fulfil the designs of providence. They live in heaven and there, in the presence of God, they act as intercessors (Job 5:1; Zech 1:12; Job 12:12). They also lead and protect men, and this is especially the function of the angel of Yahweh (2 Kings 19:35; see M. J. Lagrange, 'L'ange de Jahvé', *RB* [1903], 214f). Philo too applies the title 'mediator' to these spiritual messengers (*De somn.* 1:142) and presents them as the priests of the temple that is the world (*De spec. leg.* 1:66).

In a transcendent dimension and in a mysterious manner the ↗ servant of God appears as the mediator par excellence (Is 42f), for he is, of his essence, the embodiment of 'the covenant of God' (Is 42:6); as spiritual messiah and king he releases those who have been imprisoned; as teacher he will be a light for the Gentiles; as innocent victim in expiation he offers himself of his own will. As the Targum of Is 53:4–12 pertinently explains, 'He prays and receives an answer; before he opens his mouth he is heard'.

B. *The New Testament*. The term *mediator* does not appear in the gospels or in Acts. In fact it is created by the early church in order adequately to express the place of Jesus in the order of providence and his work of salvation (Gal 3:19f; 1 Tim 2:5; Heb 7:6; 9:15; 12:24). No doubt the term is partly connected with the themes of mediation and intercession in the Old Testament,

but it is enriched with the new meaning of mediatorship from the hellenistic period. Thus *mesiteuein* comes actually to mean 'to provide a guarantee', 'to give a security' (Heb 6:17; Philo, *De spec. leg.* 4:31; Pap. Rainer, 1:19); the *mesitès* himself is either a guarantor, a giver of security (Diod. Sic. 4:54:7; Epict. 33:5; Joseph., *Antiq.* 4:6:133) or an arbitrator in legal transactions (Pap. Lill. 28:11; P. Cattaoui 1:3; P. Goodsp. Cair. 29:3:5), and the rabbis, by their use of the commercial term *sarsôr* (=middleman, negotiator), make the mediator something more than an intermediary, namely an agent. Thus the mediator is no longer conceived of in the primary sense as a simple party to an agreement, a delegate or representative. He plays an active part in business matters, possesses authority and takes initiatives. He is not merely a salaried official (P. Magd. 30:3; see *PSI*, 6:551–10), but actually makes himself personally responsible for the security.

According to Gal 3:18f the promises given to Abraham were spoken by God directly, while the law was given to Moses through angels and through a mediator. This difference in the mode of promulgation permits us to conclude that the Mosaic law was subordinate to the promises in importance. According to the Palestinian and Hellenistic tradition 'the higher blessings were imparted to mankind by God himself, the lesser ones through his angels and logoi (Philo, *De leg. alleg.* 3:177; cf Sifr. Deut 11:14, 80a; Heb 2:2). The phrase 'through the hands of a mediator' is rabbinical and applies to Moses, not, however, as God's emissary or representative, but as 'agent'. In fact Moses used considerable initiative in negotiating, and it was not without difficulty that he achieved an agreement with an obstinate people. This implies on the one hand that the old covenant is imperfect (Heb 8:7f): through the intervention of human factors a transient and time-conditioned element had been introduced. On the other hand it implies that when God entrusted himself to his servant in all that concerned the copying of the law, he did not thereby intend to bind himself by the power of the curse which gave it authority (Gal 3:10–13). When he promulgated his promises, on the contrary, God gave a pure and undistorted gift to man, which was guaranteed by his own immutability (see D. Bornhäuser, 'Der Mittler', *NKZ* [1928], 21–4).

Unlike the foregoing instances, all the rest of the *mesitēs* passages in the New Testament are connected with the *hellenistic concept of mediator*. Primary in importance is 1 Tim 2:5: 'For there is one God, and there is one mediator between God and men, the man Christ Jesus, who gave himself as a ransom for all'. Here mediatorship is envisaged as operating in an upward direction. The redeemer represents men to God and must therefore be identified with them. Hence the strong emphasis on his humanity. United to his brethren by a common destiny, Jesus makes himself answerable for sin (2 Cor 5:21; Gal 3:13) and gives the 'ransom' which obtains pardon for them from God. He who is mediator is at the same time security. His blood is the purchase-price (1 Cor 6:20; 7:23; Tit 2:14). The atoning death of the righteous was already foretold in Is 53:11f. But the New Testament, when it describes this redemption as intercession or advocacy with God (1 Jn 2:1f), gives it a central place in the economy of salvation and confirms its reality.

These aspects are especially developed in the *Letter to the Hebrews*. If Christ, the high priest, is superior to the Levitical priests, that is because he is 'mediator of a better covenant, since it is enacted on better promises' (8:6). Both covenants have a priesthood as their basis, but the new covenant is unsurpassable, for its mediator obtains blessings that the priests of the old covenant could not attain to. Christ presents a heavenly sacrifice of unfailing efficacy (8:1–5). He acts for us in God's presence and is himself the guarantee that the promises will be fulfilled. The *enguos* (='surety', see 7:22) undertakes all the obligations of a contract supported by guarantee. He makes himself liable for a third part of his security, and this is no empty gesture, for he is bound to fulfil his obligations in his person or in his property even to the extent of laying down his life (see Sir 29:15). This is exactly what the redeemer has done. However worthless the unbeliever considers this security (10:29), believers still value this blood which was poured out at its true worth. They hold without doubt that the New Covenant is efficacious and eternal, for it has been sealed and guaranteed by the death of the Son of God (13:20). 'Therefore he is the mediator of a new covenant, so that those who are called may receive the promised eternal inheritance, since a death has occurred which redeems them from the transgressions under the first covenant' (9:15). Still more clearly than in this example mediatorship is connected with the idea of *ransom-redemption* (*apolutrōsis*). The mediator is priest and victim at the same time. He not only gives security, but is himself the security. That is why his intervention is of such value. Moreover it is more the *person* than the work of Christ that is in question. The redeemer does not confine his work of mediation to the offering of a victim of atonement. Rather he is in the position of a testator who makes a will disposing of his estate, and then dies of his own free will in order to enable his children to enter into their inheritance (vv 16f). In this fresh development an aspect of mediatorship is revealed which is verifiable only of the priest-king according to the order of Melchizedek, and which extends beyond the sphere of liturgy and cult. Jesus dominates and unites in himself the entire design of salvation, the entire economy of salvation in history, the entire kingdom of grace (Heb 2:10). Far more than as agent or guarantor he rules as king over the faithful, as 'pioneer and perfecter' (Heb 12:2; see 10:14) of the covenant, as the focal point of revealed religion (2 Cor 1:20). It is as high priest and leader of redeemed mankind that Jesus is mediator. And the point at which this mediatorship of his becomes effective with power and authority is unique (cf Jn 17:5–12). All that is needed in order to be taken with him into the blessed city and to join the choirs of angels in praise is to trust to this leader, to be subject to this king: 'You have come hither . . . to Jesus, the mediator of a new covenant, and to the sprinkled blood that speaks more graciously than the blood of Abel' (Heb 12:22, 24).

Concluding theological considerations. In the New Testament we find numerous instruments for mediating the knowledge and will of God: ↗ angels, ↗ apostles, ↗ prophets, etc. But there is only one single mediator in the true sense, Christ Jesus (1 Tim 2:5). In fact mediation is essentially a property of him alone, for in him alone is the position of 'standing between' realised in its most perfect form. On the one hand he is truly man and able to represent the whole of mankind (Heb 2:14, 17f). His life on earth has put him in a position to know from his own experience the cares and sorrows of his brethren so that he sympathises with them in their trials, and is zealous in bringing their needs before God: 'For every high priest chosen from among men is appointed to act on behalf of men in relation to God' (Heb 5:1). On the other hand Jesus did not claim this office of mediator for himself. He was called by God (Heb 5:4), and is therefore certain of being favourably received by God. More than this, he is God's own Son (Heb 1:2; 4:14; 5:5, 8; 7:3), of one nature with the Father (Heb 1:3). This gives him an authority without parallel, because he can speak with God on equal terms (Heb 1:8f; 7:26). Christ is an *ontological* mediator because the fullness of the godhead dwells corporeally in the Word made flesh (Col 2:9; see also Jn 1:14; Phil 2:7; Heb 2:16). In his own person he unites and reconciles godhead and manhood. As God he possesses the divine nature in its plenitude. But he possesses it to communicate it (Jn 1:16f), and he shares it with men (Col 2:10; see also Eph 3:19). Conversely he is the living way which leads to God (Heb 10:20); his Person is the entrance

571

and the sure access to the Father (Jn 14:6). In him man looks for and attains the goal.

If the proper *nature* of this mediator is altogether unique, his *work* is equally so. He exercises:

a. *a prophetic function,* by which he spreads the divine light (Mt 10:40f; 13:57; 23:37; Lk 10:16). He alone is the final and complete revealer of the mystery of God (Jn 1:18; 3:12; Lk 10:22). Therefore he transcends the order of prophets (Jn 7:48). Moreover whereas the other mediators only hand on the word of God or consecrate themselves to God's service, he *is* the Word of God (Heb 4:12). He also exercises:

b. *a priestly and atoning function.* Priest because God–Man, he is the consummation of the cult and offers himself as a victim of atonement, to purify the hearts of men (Heb 1:3; 2:17; 5:1; 10:8, 11) and reconciles sinners to God (2 Cor 5:18; Eph 2:16; Col 1:20, 22). In heaven he issues forth to act as mediator and to impart grace (Heb 8:2; 9:11), for his will to surrender himself abides and determines the form of the liturgy in the true temple of heaven (Heb 9:7). There is no need of further sacrifices or further victims. The sacrifice of Calvary, offered in a mode that is spiritual and eternal, is laid upon the living and speaking altar that is Christ's own person (Heb 13:10; Rev 16:7). The glorified redeemer does not cease to make effective the merits of his passion (Rev 5:7, 9, 12) and to be heard by his Father. In the exercise of his eternal priesthood Christ truly becomes the mediator of grace (Jn 1:16f), for he imparts to those who are his own all the privileges of the covenant, above all divine life (Jn 15:1f; Acts 3:15; Rom 6:23; 1 Pet 3:7; 2 Pet 1:4). He also exercises:

c. *a cosmic and kingly mediatorship.* As the new Adam Christ is the head of regenerate mankind, whom he vivifies with a life that is truly divine (1 Cor 15:22, 45; cf Jn 5:21; Rom 4:17; 5:17, 19). He 'recapitulates' the universe, that is he sums up all its elements in his own person and he is its head (Eph 1:10; cf Col 1:17). He has been anointed as king (Heb 1:8f; cf Jn 18:37) and has at his disposal a plenitude of power over all that the messianic kingdom contains (Lk 22:29f; Heb 9:15–17). God has made the world to come subject to him and designated him as heir to all things (Heb 1:2; 2:5; 3:5f). Thus he is head and origin of the new creation, founder and teacher of the new covenant, head and ruler of the church (Eph 4:15f). As Lord he presides over the faithful in his human nature. They are his 'servants', who look upon him as 'crowned with glory and honour' (Heb 2:2). The gospel is the proclamation of his kingdom. This mediator, who is at once king, priest and prophet, is endowed with the utmost plenitude of power, and he uses this to free the universe from the dominion of Satan and to perform his redemptive function, conjungendi et uniendi, mediating between creaturehood and God until the consummation of the world (Eph 2:13–16).

To be redeemed man needs only to cleave to his person, 'to be in Christ' (1 Cor 1:30; cf Col 1:27; 3:11). Christian ⁄ faith is epitomised in the mediatorship of the Son of God become man: 'Therefore, brethren, we have confidence to enter the sanctuary by the blood of Jesus, by the new and living way which he opened for us through the curtain, that is, through his flesh . . . we have a great priest over the house of God' (Heb 10:19–21).

Bibliography: W. F. Adeney, *A Dictionary of the Bible* III, ed. J. Hastings, Edinburgh 1906⁶, 311–21; M. Schulze, 'Der Mittler', *Festschrift R. Seeberg*, Leipzig 1929, 225–38; E. Brunner, *Der Mittler. Zur Besinnung über den christlichen Glauben*, Tübingen 1930²; A. Aeschimann, *Dictionnaire encyclopédique de la Bible*, Valence 1935, 135–41; F. von Bodelschwingh, *Jesus der Mittler des NT nach dem Zeugnis des Hebr.*, Bethel 1939²; A. Oepke, *TDNT* IV (1967), 598–629; H. M. Estève, *De coelesti mediatione sacerdotali Christi iuxta 8:3–4*, Madrid 1949; A. Cody, *Heavenly Sanctuary and Liturgy in the Epistle to the Hebrews*, St Meinrad (Ind.) 1960; A. Hegermann, *Die Vorstellung vom Schöpfungsmittler* (*TU* 82), Berlin 1961; M. P. Nilsson, 'The High God and the Mediator', *HTR* (1963), 101–20; H. Clavier, 'Mediation in the Fourth Gospel', *SNTSB* I (1963), 11–25; J. Scharbert, *Heilsmittler im AT und im alten Orient*, Freiburg 1961; A. Robert and C. Spicq, *DB(S)* v (1957), 997–1083; *J. Smith, *A Priest for Ever: A Study of Typology and Eschatology in Hebrews*, London 1969, esp. 103ff.

Ceslaus Spicq

Meditation

Among the terms for 'be mindful of, remember' one in particular is *hāgāh*. Originally it signified the cooing of doves, but subsequently it came to mean 'to read in a soft voice, to reflect upon with murmuring', the Hebrew equivalent of our 'to consider, meditate'. In a consecration formula in Ps 19:14 (similar formulae are to be found in Ps 104:34; 119:111) we find that what is consecrated is not only the words of the suppliant's mouth, but also the thoughts of his ⁊ heart. The suppliant hopes to find favour with God not only by means of the prayer which he utters with his lips but also by the thoughts which he enunciates. Basically these constitute his acceptance and active embracing of divine ⁊ revelation as formulated in precepts, an acceptance which is constantly renewed. These precepts must remain constantly in the individual's heart, and must be present in every situation in which he finds himself (Deut 6:6–9; Prov 6:22; Josh 1:8). Besides these, he must also keep alive the memory of God's deed of might and ⁊ miracles (Ps 77:12ff; see also 105:4ff), which give rise to fresh confidence in the fact that God has chosen his people and not cast them off for ever. By night the suppliant reflects upon their power and grace of God's redemption Ps 4; 5; 63:6–9; 77:6; 119:55, 148). It is by night too that the Lord gives him counsel (Ps 16:7). God's word and the enlightenment of his law are an ever-present subject of meditation (Ps 1:2f; 119:14f, 24, 97, 129f, 148; Sir 6:37).

Ps 1:2f describes the devout man who meditates upon God's law as a flourishing tree. The consideration of God's dispensations can only have the result that one observes his precepts and in this way reaps blessings; 'This book of the law shall not depart out of your mouth, but you shall meditate on it day and night that you may be careful to do according to all that is written in it for then you shall make your way prosperous, and then you shall have good success' (Jos 1:8). Meditating upon the works of God leads further to ⁊ knowledge of God, his power and his glory (see Ps 19:2ff; Job 12:7–9; Wis 13:1–9).

In Gen 37:11; Dan 7:28 and also

in Lk 2:19, 51 we find it said that a person keeps something in their ⌐ heart. Mary keeps the message of the shepherds and the words of her Son in her heart, realising their profound significance, and ponders upon them. Jesus himself exhorts his followers to meditate upon the events of sacred history and the examples which it provides (Lot's wife, Lk 17:32), and institutes the ⌐ eucharist 'in commemoration of him'. The apostles call to mind the memory of the risen Lord Jesus (2 Cor 4:14–18; 2 Tim 2:8) in order to encourage the persecuted believers in the midst of their sufferings, and to strengthen their ⌐ hope by meditating upon these sacred events (cp Rom 8:18–25). Paul shows how intense and concentrated this meditation must be by the comparison with one who runs a race. So long as he runs he has nothing else in mind except the goal. He is conscious of this alone and forgets everything else apart from it (Phil 3:12–21).

Meditation upon the law is referred to in Jas 1:25, but in a new sense. It is the perfect law of liberty, that is, according to 1:21: 'the implanted word which is able to save your souls'. He who meditates upon this and so, as it were, looks into a mirror and retains an impression of what he has seen there, will also be blessed in his actions.

Bibliography: E. Kalt, *BRL* I, Paderborn 1931, 253–5; A. Deissler, *Psalm 119 (118) und seine Theologie*, Munich 1955, 106f, 243f, and on the passages referred to above; O. Michel, *TDNT* IV, 675–83; J. Behm, *TDNT* IV, 948–51 and 971–3; P. A. H. De Boer, *Gedenken und Gedächtnis in der Welt des AT*, Stuttgart 1962; ⌐ Knowledge.

Johannes B. Bauer

Mercy

Mercy is closely connected with ⌐ grace, ⌐ goodness, ⌐ love. In Hebrew it is rendered by the roots *ḥnn* and *rḥm*, and in Greek by *eleos* and *oiktirmos* and their derivatives. *eleēmosunē* (= 'compassion'), is found in the New Testament only in the sense of beneficence, ⌐ almsgiving.

God's mercy is a special instance of his grace and love. One of Israel's earliest religious experiences is of Yahweh as 'a gracious and merciful God' (Ex 34:6). In Hos 11:8f mercy is said to belong to the divine nature: 'My heart recoils within me and my mercy grows warm and tender. I will not execute my fierce anger [⌐ wrath] . . . for I am God and not man'.

But '. . . I will show mercy on whom I will show mercy' (Ex 33:19). God's mercy stems from his absolute freedom, yet the sinner can still hope in it (cf Ps 51; 130 etc).

The New Testament too knows of God's mercy, which lies at the heart of his work of salvation. The canticles in the Lukan infancy narrative, the Magnificat and Benedictus, testify most eloquently to this fact (Lk 1:50, 54, 72, 78); similarly in Mk 5:19: those who had been possessed were told to go home and relate how the Lord had mercy on his own. The parable of the prodigal son (Lk 15:11–32) illustrates what is meant by Paul's phrase, 'Father of all mercies' (2 Cor 1:3), and the parable of the merciless servant (Mt 18:23–35) throws this quality of divine mercy into relief against a negative background.

Lk 6:36 'Be merciful even as your Father is merciful' presents the attitude of God towards men as the absolute ideal. In this connection it must be remembered that it is not the emotion of compassion that is in question here, but rather practical works of mercy, the deeds which emanate from and correspond to this attitude of mind. In connection with Hos 6:6 Jesus explains unequivocally how mercy, that is practical love of one's neighbour, comes before sacrifice (Mt 9:13; 12:7; 23:23; ⁊ neighbour B). God himself shows his mercy to him who is merciful, and does not show it to him who is himself unmerciful (Mt 18:32f; cf the '. . . as we forgive them . . .' in the Our Father Mt 6:12; 6:14f; Jas 2:13). For this reason the mercy of men is included in the list of virtues (Eph 4:32; 1 Pet 3:8), just as, conversely, mercilessness appears in the list of vices (Rom 1:31; see also Did 5:2; Barn 20:2).

Bibliography: R. Bultmann, *TDNT* II, 477–87; V, 159–61 (with bibliography); F. Asensio, *Misericordia et Veritas*, Rome 1949; Eichrodt I, 237f; Schnackenburg, 64f and 104–7; J. Schmid, *Matthäus* (*RNT* 1) 1956, 351–6; A. Deissler, *LTK* I, 125f; A. Vögtle, *LTK* I, 1253f.

Johannes B. Bauer

Messianism

A. *Old Testament*. Messianism in the broader sense is taken to mean the biblical *expectation of an aeon of salvation at the end of time which will culminate in the setting up of a kingdom of God*. In contradistinction to the cyclic concept of history of the ancients, the biblical concept is of a meaningful and irreversible process, with a beginning and an end, reaching out towards a goal predetermined by God. This applies in a special sense to the history of Israel, the definitive characteristic of which is the master idea of the covenant. In the bible this history is presented as *salvation* history. At its mid-point stands the Messiah, the bearer of salvation in the final age. It is he who will restore the relationship between God and man which was destroyed by sin, and who will set up a kingdom of peace and justice. This expectation of a personal dispenser of salvation constitutes that theme of biblical messianism in the stricter and more proper sense, which is the backbone of the Old Testament.

The name *Messiah* is a Greek transliteration of the Hebrew *māšiah* or its Aramaic equivalent, *mešiha*, which may be rendered as 'anointed one'. In the Old Testament this description was applied to the reigning king of Israel (1 Sam 24:6, 10), to the high priest (Lev 4:3), and later to all the priests (2 Macc 1:10). The Persian king Cyrus is also described as 'anointed one' (Is 45:1) in that he furthered Yahweh's design in history. As a name for the future Messiah it first appears in the extra-canonical books at the end of the Old Testament period, in dependence on Ps 2:2.

Messianic expectation in the bible cannot be explained as deriving from purely natural factors. It cannot take its origin from the vain expectation of a national kingdom of Israel, for messianic hope in the bible antedates the monarchy. Nor can the messianic idea be explained as a reaction against the preaching of judgement by the prophets, that is as a means of consoling the people when they had fallen into despair. For 'weal' prophecy antedates 'woe' prophecy. Nor can the bridge to belief in the Messiah be supplied by the so-called 'court-style', in which the actual reigning king was allegedly depicted in messianic hues and represented as a divine king. Divine kingship is irreconcilable with Israelite monotheism, and in any case the difficulty still remains of explaining how this path could have led to a hope for the Messiah at the end of time. Nor can messianic hope be explained in terms of the so-called New Year festival or Enthronement festival of Yahweh. At this festival, it is held, there would have been a ceremonial commemoration of the assumption of kingship over Israel by Yahweh himself, who would also bestow help on his people in the future. We have no evidence that such a festival existed in Israel. Even in Babylon, supremely the land of the new year festival, no hope for a messiah at the end of time developed. Israel's own unique presentation of her God, and her faith in Yahweh's readiness to help her, may have stimulated and developed messianic hope as we find it in the bible, but they cannot have provided its origin. In the last analysis it goes back to divine revelation.

We encounter *messianic hope* already in the opening pages of the bible. The so-called *protoevangelium* (Gen 3:14ff) contains the promise made to fallen man that in the struggle between the woman and the serpent, and between her seed and its, her seed would be victorious. The context shows that the woman is Eve, while her seed is the human race considered as participants in the struggle against the devil and his followers, to whom the wicked too belong. The gospel shows us how it is Christ, the seed of woman in a most

special sense, who appears as head of the entire human race and crushes the head of the serpent underfoot.

Noah's blessing of Shem (Gen 9:26) announces that the salvation of the world will come through Shem and through the ethnic group of peoples descended from him, namely the Semites. From among these Abraham is chosen as the bearer of the promise, in whose seed the peoples of the earth shall be blessed (Gen 12:1–3; 18:18; 22:18). For salvation comes out of Israel (Jn 4:22). The blessing of Jacob narrows the circle of transmitters of salvation down to Judah, the patriarch's fourth son; from his tribe will arise he to whom the sceptre will belong, and who will receive the obedience of the peoples (Gen 49:8–12). In this passage the Messiah confronts us as a firmly delineated figure of authority. His kingdom is described as a kingdom of peace (Gen 49:11, 12). The oracle of Balaam (Num 24:15–19), which is dependent on the foregoing passage, proclaims him as a star out of Jacob and as a warrior prince who will overthrow Moab, Edom and all the warriors of similarly warlike peoples. Both oracles have been worked over by a redactor of the time of David, but they do contain elements of an earlier tradition. Since they are only partially fulfilled in David—for he could not subdue these peoples permanently—they point on to the messianic king.

The so-called *gospel of Nathan* (2 Sam 7:3–16) applies the messianic hope to the house of David. It is not David who will build a house for the Lord (the temple) but, as Nathan expresses by means of a pun, the Lord who will build a house for David, for he will make the son who comes after him his successor and set David's throne firm for ever. Initially, no doubt, this promise applies to Solomon, without, however, excluding his descendants. For in Hebrew usage 'for ever' often means only 'for a very long time'. But in the light of the Last Words of David, in which the messianic king appears as a late descendant of the family of David (2 Sam 23:7), this promise is primarily directed towards the Messiah.

The portrayal of the Messiah in the *Royal Psalms* is influenced by the central conception of the oracle of Nathan, and it is probably to this that Ps 2:7 refers (cf Gelin 1178). It is true that this psalm also initially pre-supposes an actually reigning king, and is to be understood in terms of the context and historical circumstances in which it was composed, for example a coronation. Nevertheless he whom it honours is the messianic king of the last age. It was all the easier to pass from the actual to the eschatological king because the sense of Nathan's promise and of Old Testament modes of thought in general is such that each successive king of the Davidic dynasty was 'a link in the chain of succession leading to the Messiah' (Schilden-berger, Benediktinische Monatsschrift 29:129) and his place-holder, shining with the reflected splendour of the Messiah himself. In Ps 2 the *king* whom Yahweh sets over Zion appears as his son—more is implied here than in the mere formula of adoption in 2 Sam 7:14—and as ruler of the world to whom all kings must do homage. Ps 110:4, 6 acclaims the Messiah as *priest* and universal *judge*. The expres-

sions created to describe the Messiah in the two psalms go far beyond the natural order. They can hardly be explained as hyperboles typical of the so-called court-style. In Ps 16:10 the singer can only be speaking in the name of the Messiah when he declares him-self certain, in his union with God, that Yahweh will not abandon his soul to the underworld and will not suffer his holy one to see corruption. In Ps 22 the petitioner has been cruelly slain. His resurrection and the conversion of the Gentile world are envisaged as the reward of his sufferings. Only when this psalm is interpreted in a messianic sense does it yield an intelligible message.

Some connection with Nathan's pro-mise is also apparent in the earliest of the *writing prophets. Amos* (9:11-15) prophesies that Yahweh will raise up once more the hut of David which has collapsed under the storm of judge-ment, and that the old national king-dom will be replaced by a kingdom which embraces the entire world, so richly blessed as to suggest that Paradise has been restored. Hosea, his younger contemporary, predicts that at the end of days Israel will once more seek after David (3:5) and, in unison with Judah, will recognise him as king over all (2:2).

The *Isaian 'Emmanuel trilogy'* also has its roots in the ideology of the royal Messiah. The sign of Emmanuel, which is foretold as a sign both of weal and of woe (7:14ff), is the prophet's answer to the refusal of the Davidic dynasty in the crisis of the Syro–Ephraimite war. It is a sign of weal in that Emmanuel is the guarantee that the house of David will survive; it is a sign of woe in that he who is born of the virgin makes it known that the male line of the dynasty has been rejected. It was in 734 BC, at a time when the Northern kingdom was laid low and the greater part of its territory was made over to Assyria, that Isaiah foretold the birth of the child Messiah. He calls him Wonderful Counsel, Mighty God, Eternal Father, Prince of Peace (9:5–8). Even though Isaiah and the Old Testament in general may not have had any explicit understanding of the divine Sonship of the Messiah, nevertheless depths of messianic meaning are implied in these titles. Emmanuel is the ruler of Israel (8:8) who will raise up and set firm the throne of David anew. The prophet's third oracle is associated with the miraculous deliverance of Jerusalem in 701 BC (2 Kings 19:34ff). When the trunk of the Davidic house has been cut down to the roots, the messianic shoot sprouts and grows from it. The ruler is armed with the Spirit of God as a sevenfold gift of grace. Thus equipped he is to found a kingdom of justice and peace (11:1–9), to sit in David's tent (16:5) and to be set upon Zion by Yahweh as the living corner-stone of this kingdom (28:16). This kingdom will be open to all peoples (2:2–4; 11:11–16) and consist not only in spiritual benefits but in power to heal physical infirmities too (35:5f).

Micah, Isaiah's contemporary, follows the same path. His prophecy of the woman in travail whose son is to be he who saves men from their need (5:2) is reminiscent of Isaiah (7:14ff). Almost in Isaiah's own words he speaks of the Messiah's world-wide kingdom of peace (4:2–4) which will issue from Beth-lehem and from the ancient house of David (5:2).

In the Messiah as *Jeremiah* presents him the shining traits of the Isaian Messiah are admittedly no longer apparent. The kings of his period were totally ignorant of their theocratic function. But he confronts them with the shoot of righteousness (23:5) which Yahweh will raise up to David, and thereby he recalls once more the prophecy of Nathan. His messianic name, 'Yahweh is our righteousness', represents a deliberate protest against the corrupt kings of his period. The messianic ruler will spring up from the midst of Israel and will be endowed with the further gift of the dignity of the priesthood (31:21). But Jeremiah compensates for the meagreness of his portrayal of the Messiah by comparison with that of Isaiah. He does this by his interiorisation of the complex of ideas associated with the Messiah. An example of this is the magnificent promise of the new covenant, which is to usher in pure knowledge of God and the forgiveness of sins (Jer 31:31–4).

Psalms 45 and 72 belong to the period of the earlier writing prophets. They look beyond the actual to the messianic king. The first is a marriage song which celebrates the nuptials of the Messiah with his bride (the Church). Here, as in Is 8:5, he appears as divine hero (4, 7) whose throne stands firm for ever (6). The second psalm is in praise of the ideal king of social justice and peace, whose dominion is limitless in space and time and who is associated with the seed of Abraham (v 17 cf Gen 18:18).

According to the prophet *Obadiah* Israel's theocracy will one day become a world theocracy (Obad 1:21). Zephaniah's message of judgement upon a world in need of moral renewal contains an element of hope for world-wide salvation (Zeph 3:9–17).

Ezekiel's prophecy too contains anti-dynastic elements. He describes in a parable (chap 17) how the top of the Davidic cedar will be broken off and brought to Babylon. This signifies the deposition of the Jewish king Jeconiah and his deportation to Babylon by Nebuchadrezzar in 598 BC. His uncle Zedekiah was set up as king in his place or, as Ezekiel figuratively puts it, he was transplanted. But because he broke his word to the king of Babylon, Nebuchadrezzar's transplanting was shown to be in vain. Therefore Yahweh undertakes a fresh planting. From the top of the cedar he breaks off a slender shoot and sets it in Israel, where it grows up into a lordly cedar so that all the birds can live under its crest. It is the Messiah who is to issue from the descendants of Jeconiah. The withered tree will be brought into leaf once more. In punishment for his apostasy Zedekiah will lose crown and kingdom, but this will not be utterly the end for the forlorn throne of David. For the Lord will give the crown to him to whom it rightfully belongs (Ezek 21:30–32). Here Ezekiel is alluding to the prophecy of Gen 49:10. In place of the former kings, who were so oblivious of their duty, Yahweh will set up a single shepherd over the whole of Israel. It is his servant, David (Ezek 34:23f; 37:22–5). He will pasture her and be her prince, and will seal a covenant of peace with the people. This David is not David redivivus but the Messiah who is a shoot of David (Ezek 17:22).

Ezekiel, who had experience of the period when Israel had no king, prefers to call him prince. There is no evidence to support the view that by 'prince' he meant a series of kings rather than the Messiah. The prince in the temple vision (45:7) enjoys few prerogatives and is not described as a shoot of David. He can therefore hardly be regarded as the Messiah. In his vision of the spring of the temple (Ezek 47:1–12) the prophet speaks of the plenitude of grace which the messianic age will bring.

Deutero-Isaiah uses the image of a new exodus to prophesy the home-coming of the exiles and the setting up of a kingdom ruled by Yahweh (Is 52:7), and numbering the Gentiles too among its citizens (Is 49:19f; 54:3). An eternal covenant will be sealed, and it will be a covenant of peace (Is 54:10), through which the people will be granted a share in the graces bestowed on David (55:3). Here, then, the covenant of David is alluded to. In the Songs of the ⁄ servant of the Lord, which have been subsequently inserted into Deutero-Isaiah, the Servant himself confronts us as a mediator of salvation to the whole world. The third part of the book of Isaiah (chap 56–66) depicts in vivid hues the splendour of the new Jerusalem as the religious centre of the whole world, where Yahweh will receive the Gentiles' prayers too (Is 56:7; 66:23) and from which he will call priests from the midst of her (Is 66:21).

In the *Psalms of Yahweh's kingship*, 47 and 96–100, we find messianism without a Messiah. Connected with Deutero-Isaiah, these psalms proclaim the advent of a world-wide kingdom of God, and honour Yahweh as Lord and judge.

According to the most recent research the royal psalms would have undergone a process of re-editing after the fall of the Davidic dynasty. In this way they acquired an explicitly messianic and eschatological stamp (cf Gelin, 1189).

It is the main interests of the *post-exilic prophets* that determine the fresh lines on which the theocracy is to be re-established, and in their picture of the theocracy king, priesthood and temple operate as a three-pointed star to throw light upon its messianic character. When *Haggai*'s countrymen weep at the plainness of the design for the new temple he consoles them with the promise that the splendour of the new temple will be greater than that of the old. For in this place the Lord will dispense peace (Hag 2:9)—this is a prophecy of the age of salvation in which the mediator of salvation is not named—and the Gentiles shall bring their treasures to this shrine (Hag 2:7). The Vulgate renders the expression here translated 'treasures' as 'Desideratus' and takes it to mean the Messiah. In Haggai's eyes the messianic hope (2:5) is attached to Zerubbabel, 'the signet ring on the hand of the Lord'. It is the same hope which Jeconiah, his grandfather, had once disappointed (cf Jer 22:24).

In the prophet *Zechariah* we find a symbolic description of the purifying of the priesthood in the person of the high priest Joshua (3:4f). He is a type and a guarantee of the coming Messiah, whom Zechariah, influenced in this respect by Jer 23:5; 33:15, calls a Branch (Zech 3:8), and who will bring purgation of sin. The subsequent crowning of the high priest by the prophets is symbolic in character, for its refers not to him but to the Messiah who is to grow up from that which is beneath him. This latter phrase alludes to the obscure circumstances in which his life is to begin (Zech 3:8–10). Not Zerubbabel but the Messiah will build the temple of the future (cf 2 Sam 7:13). He will wear signs of exalted rank and will sit on the throne and rule (Zech 6:11–13). For the following stych translators often follow Jerome in rendering: 'And he (the messiah) shall be a priest upon his throne and the counsel of peace shall be between them (the powers) both'. On this rendering the passage is understood to refer to the union of royal and priestly dignity in the person of the Messiah. The effect of this union would be that the rivalry between the two powers which had prevailed in the past, and which perhaps still prevailed between Joshua and Zerubbabel, would be removed. But it is more justifiable grammatically to translate: 'And a priest shall sit upon his throne, and between priest and king harmony will reign'. This would express the idea that in the spirit of Jer 33:11 and Zech 4:14 it was promised that in the new theocracy the Davidic kingship and the Levitical priesthood would endure for ever.

The second part of the book of Zechariah is ascribed by critics to a different author, or authors. Here the prophet speaks of the processional entry of the messianic king of peace into Jerusalem. The Gentiles will be chastised and then Israel will be re-established within her ideal boundaries and the Messiah, riding an ass's foal, will enter his capital city and set up a world-wide kingdom of peace (9:9–10). The mysterious one 'whom they have pierced' is also a messianic figure for, although he will be put to death through the fault of his people, they will look upon him with sorrow and repentance (Zech 12:9–14). The massoretic reading, 'They will look upon *me*' is certainly corrupt. At the end of the passage (13:1) a spring is spoken of which will bring to the house of David cleansing from sin and defilement.

Malachi prophesies the judgement day of the Lord: 'the Lord whom you seek will come suddenly to his temple; the angel of the covenant in whom you delight' (Mal 3:1). As often in scripture, the angel of the covenant can be a form in which Yahweh appears (Deut 23:20) but it may also signify the Messiah. The prophet also speaks of a pure sacrifice which will be offered once and for all (Mal 1:11).

Joel's prophecy of the outpouring of the divine spirit upon all flesh (Joel 2:28) looks to the messianic age. It is concerned with the eschatological theme of the moral renewal of the world, of which Isaiah (32:15) and Ezekiel (36:26; 39:29) also speak.

In the theology of history of the book of *Daniel* world history is conceived of as the history of the kingdom of God. The kingdoms of this world must disappear so as to make way for the coming kingdom of God (Dan 2:44). As the ruler of this kingdom the ↗ Son of Man appears (7:13). The vision of the messianic age also includes the prophecy of the seventy weeks of years (9:24–7). Here the prophet speaks of the end of wickedness and sin, the expiation of unrighteousness and the establishment of eternal justice. Certainly this state of things will not begin after seventy years (cf Jer 25:1, 11) but after seventy weeks ('sevens') of years, ie, after a very long time. An editor living in the age of the Maccabees divided the seventy weeks of years into three periods: 587–538 (the advent of Anointed One, ie, Cyrus); 538–171 (the slaying of the high priest Onias III) and the seventieth week of years (the disruption of the temple services under Antiochus IV). The author did not expect the messianic salvation predicted in v 24 to arrive until this oppressor and oppression had come to an end. The weeks of years are to be interpreted symbolically, for from Cyrus to Onias not 434 but only 367 years elapsed.

Chronicles takes up once more the promise bestowed on the Davidic house, but introduces a clear element of messianism into it. It idealises the Davidic king, whose figure is fused with that of the king of the last age (1 Chron 17:11–14). His throne will be called God's throne (1 Chron 28:5), and his kingdom God's kingdom.

In many passages in the *Wisdom literature* the divine wisdom appears to be hypostatised in such a way that it can hardly be understood as mere poetic personification. This is found in the hymn (Prov 8:22–31) in which the gifts of the Spirit bestowed on the Messiah (cf Is 11:2f) are transferred to Wisdom; in the Book of Wisdom (7:22–8:1); and in Ecclesiasticus (24:3–6a, 9), so that a second flowering of messianic prophecy has been spoken of. However these passages in the Old Testament are not understood in a messianic sense and the divine wisdom is not assimilated to the Messiah.

Joshua ben Sira (45:25) and 1 Macc 2:57 mention the promise of Nathan clearly in its messianic aspect. Thus when Mathathias is dying he says that David, for his devotion, received the kingly throne for all time. Apart from this we find only isolated indications of the survival of the messianic hope in the later books of the Old Testament (Tob 23:10–18; 14:5–7; Sir 35:22–5; 36:7–18; and 2 Macc 2:18).

B. *New Testament.* ↗ Jesus Christ.

Bibliography: P. Heinisch, *Theology of the OT*, Collegeville 1955; P. Heinisch, *Christus der Erlöser im AT*, Graz–Wien–Köln 1957; J. Obersteiner, *Die Christusbotschaft des AT*, Wien 1947; J. Schildenberger, 'Messiaserwartung', Haag 1116–36; A. Gelin, 'Messianisme', *DB(S)* v (1955), 1165–212; Berlin 1925; L. Dürr, *Ursprung und Ausbau der israelitisch-jüdischen, Heilandserwartung*, F. Ceuppens, *De prophetiis messianicis in AT*, Rome 1935; J. Coppens, *L'Attente du Messie*, Bruges 1954; R. Mayer, 'Der Erlöserkönig des AT', *MTZ* 3 (1952), 221–43 and 367–84; H. Gross, 'Zum Problem Verheissung und Erfüllung', *BZ* 3 (1959), 3–18; E. König, *Die messianischen Weissagungen*, Stuttgart 1925²; H. Gressmann, *Der Messias*, Göttingen 1929; O. Procksch, *Theologie des AT*, Gütersloh 1950; W. Vischer, *Das Christuszeugnis des AT* i, Zurich 1948; ii, Zürich 1952.

Jakob Obersteiner

Millenarianism

The concept of the millennium (the kingdom which will last for a thousand years) is found in Rev 20:2–7. The term *millennium* (*khilia etē*) occurs six times. It designates one of the stages of the eschatological age. During this period, which is to come after the parousia, the just are to reign with Christ (Rev 20:4–6). Its inauguration will be marked by the resurrection of all those who have been found just, an event which John calls the 'first resurrection' (Rev 20:5ff). Throughout this period Satan will be chained in the abyss (Rev 20:3). What is *essential* here is the idea of a *resurrection of the just which is to precede the general resurrection*, an idea which is also found elsewhere in the New Testament (1 Cor 15:23; 1 Thess 4:16) and in judaeo-christianity (Asc Is 4:14–17). It is above all noteworthy that in 1 Cor 15:23, just as in Rev 20, the resurrection of the just precedes the final overthrow of Satan. The idea of the thousand-year kingdom, in which the just who have been raised from the dead will have a share, is already found in Ezekiel (36–40). But the pre-christian Jewish literature draws no distinction between a messianic and an eternal kingdom as periods following one upon the other in time. Rather it sets both concepts side by side without making clear how they are related.

But why is the rule of the just described by the word *millennium* (*khilia etē*)? It has been suggested that the concept is related to the seven millennia which go to make up the 'cosmic week'. But this connection is secondary. The 'thousand years' belong to *paradise symbolism* and represent that *paradisical length of life* which is presupposed in Gen 5:5, 8, 11, 27. Outside Paradise even the most just of men cannot attain to an age of a thousand years. This is clearly expressed in Jub 4:20: 'Adam died when he was seventy years old, before he reached a thousand years'. The 'thousand years' bring back paradisical length of life (Is 65:20–22). It is noteworthy that the LXX version of Is 65:22 brings in the 'tree of life': 'The days of my people will be as the days of the tree of life'. Thus the 'thousand years' are one aspect of paradise symbolism along with the ideas of harmony among the animals and the fruitfulness of the earth. In Rev 20:2 Satan is called 'the ancient serpent' (*ho ophis ho arkhaios*). Clearly this is a reference to Gen 3:1 so that it confirms our interpretation of the millennium as a restoration of the conditions of Paradise.

In the theme under consideration this *paradise symbolism* is combined with another kind of symbolism, namely *messianic*. During the thousand years the just will *reign with Christ* (Rev 20:4,6). This messianism is at once priestly and Royal (Rev 20:6). The same symbolism is found again in 1 Cor 15:24f. It includes two concepts. The first is of *the reign of Christ upon earth* after the resurrection of the just and before the final overthrow of Satan. Thus the reign is here conceived of as an intermediate stage (1 Cor 15:24f). The second concept is that *the just are to have a share in this royal dominion of Christ's* (Rev 20:4, 6). This royal dominion of the just consists above all in the fact that they preside with Christ in judgement; hence thrones are allotted to them (Rev 20:4). This last feature recalls Mt 19:28 though here the logion follows upon the 'hundredfold'. In its original form as preserved in Mk 10:30, this logion draws a contrast between the hundredfold that is to be given in this present world (*en tō[i] kairō[i] toutō[i]*), and the eternal life which will be bestowed in the world to come. A comparison of this with the ideas contained in Revelation strongly suggests that the hundredfold refers to

the messianic kingdom (Irenaeus, *Adv. Haer.*, v 33:2).

These then are the biblical data in the question. Naturally they are open to different interpretations, and we actually encounter such differences of interpretation from the outset. This primarily affects the state in which those risen from the dead are conceived to live. A whole group has taken it in a purely material sense in that they have related the biblical prophecies of the eschatological Paradise to the age of the millennium. Yet even here there is no lack of diversity in the various shades of meaning proposed. Papias, Irenaeus, and Justin speak only of the unwonted fruitfulness of the earth (*Adv. haer.* v, 33; *Dial.* 80f). Lactantius actually thinks of fruitfulness among men (*Div. inst* VII, 24:3), an idea which is irreconcilable with the symbolism of the millennium. Methodius, on the other hand, rejects both kinds of fruitfulness equally strongly (Conv., 9:1). Justin and Irenaeus take the messianic theme as applying to the restoration of the earthly Jerusalem (*Dial.* 81:3; *Adv. Haer.* v, 35:2). The same 'this-worldly' judaeo-christian messianism is especially stressed in the writings of the Ebionites and Cerinthus. Materialistic millenarianism is a non-biblical development deriving from certain judaeo-christian circles but unknown in the rest of the judaeo-christian texts such as Asc. Is.

Apart from this the duration of time symbolised by the millennium acquired a material sense when it became involved with speculations concerning the duration of the world. Such speculations make their appearance in Jewish apocalyptic, undoubtedly under

Iranian influence, and lead to the doctrine of the seven millenia in the Jewish apocalyptic writings of the second century AD (Test Abr 7). The judaeo-christians combine the theme of the messianic reign of a thousand years with this doctrine. By this route they arrive at the idea that the cosmic age is 6,000 years in extent, and is followed by the seventh millennium, namely the messianic reign. This in turn is followed by the eighth day, that is eternal life (2 Enoch 33:4; EpBarn 15:3-8; Iren v 28:3). This conception was general up to the time of Augustine. On this view the millennium loses the symbolic meaning which it bears in Revelation, and becomes a piece of chronological data on which calculations are based.

From the point of view of *biblical theology* the meaning of the thousand-year reign is that at the *parousia* the just will be raised from the dead and will participate in the glory of Christ before entering the world to come with him. This is expressed in paradisical and messianic images. By interpreting this image language in a material sense the judaeo-christians and the first christian writers arrived at a state of mind in which they ascribed a content and a duration to that event of which there is no mention in the New Testament. First Origen and then Augustine rightly repudiated this judaeo-christian millenarianism and then its official condemnation was finally pronounced by the church. On the other hand the interpretation of the thousand years as the age of the church, which is found in Tyconius and Augustine and finally in Allo, appears to be equally a distortion of the teaching of the New Testament.

Bibliography: L. Gry, *Le millénarisme*, Paris 1904; H. Bietenhard, *Das tausendjähriges Reich*, Zürich 1955; H. Bietenhard, 'The Millenary Hope', *SJT* 6 (1953), 12-31; W. Bauer, 'Chiliasmus', *RAC* II, 1073-8; O. Cullmann, *Königsherrschaft Christi und Kirche im NT*, Basle 1941; J. Daniélou, *Théologie du judéo-christianisme*, Paris 1958, 342-70; J. Daniélou, 'La typologie millénariste de la semaine', *VC* 2 (1948), 1-16; J. Sickenberger, 'Das tausendjährige Reich in der Apokalypse', *Festschrift S. Merkle*, 1922, 300-15; A. Wikenhauser, 'Das Problem des tausendjährigen Reiches in der Apokalypse', *Röm. Quartalschrift* 40 (1932), 13-27; A. Wikenhauser, 'Die Herkunft der Idee des tausendjährigen Reiches in der Apokalypse', *Röm. Quartalschrift* 45 (1937), 25-43; J. W. Bailey, 'The Temporary Messianic Reign in the Literature of Early Judaism', *JBL* 53 (1934), 170-87; R. Schmidt, 'Aetates Mundi', *ZKG* 67 (1956), 288-317; A. Luneau, *L'histoire du Salut chez les Pères de l'Eglise*, Paris 1964.

Jean Daniélou

Miracle

A. *A miracle is an event, apprehensible to the senses, through which the intervention of God in the world is accomplished.* It is not itself 'the holy', but a sign (Ex 4:8f; Is 7:11, 14) which points to it. Hence it is to be distinguished from the actual manifestation through which the holy itself may obscurely be discerned. Miracle derives its meaning from its character as sign, and Israel's experience of this 'sign' character on the occasion of the crossing of the Red Sea (Ex 13:17ff) was so profound that her entire thinking was shaped by it. Hence miracle is never unintelligible, but is always to be traced back to the activity of a personal God, who reveals his nature and his glory (1 Sam 6:19f; 2 Sam 6:7; Ex 15:11; Ps 77:14), but above all his power. For this reason his 'mighty acts' are spoken of (Deut 3:24; 2 Kings 8:4), his 'works' (Is

12:4), his 'marvellous' (Ex 15:11), 'terrible' (Ex 34:10) or 'mysterious' (Is 29:14) ways, or his 'signs and wonders' (Ex 7:3 etc). Such descriptions are never used for their own sakes but constantly with God in view. At the same time they reflect the reaction of man; his boundless astonishment at finding himself confronted by something which is beyond comprehension (Gen 18:14), something which he can approach only with trembling and from afar (Ex 14:31) though with praise too (Ex 15:1ff). In an earlier age God often employed special bearers of the Spirit (Moses, Elijah, Elisha). These, by their preparatory prayers (1 Kings 17:20; 2 Kings 4:33), by the use they make of sacred objects (Ex 4:2ff), or by their observance of specific directions given to them by God (Ex 7:9ff), emphasise their dependence upon him. In this way any element of magic is radically eliminated, for its incompatibility with the nature of God is recognised (Deut 13:2ff). Now it follows from this that miracles have no absolute value in themselves. They can be understood only in the relation they bear to the structure of revelation as a whole. As expressions of the holy, miracles have in common with it the quality of being strange and extraordinary. This may appear in the event itself (Jos 10:11ff; Is 38:8; Jer 19:3) or in the manner of its taking place. For a natural event (the miracle of the quails and manna Ex 16:3ff) may break out of the normal and expected course and acquire a decisive significance in the lives of the men involved in the miracle. Natural portents belong to this class, above all storms (Ps 135:7; Job 37:11ff); but so

too do confrontations with men who, by the very way in which they present themselves, are signs pointing to the authority of God (Is 8:18; 20:3; Zech 3:8). This leads on to a further and connected characteristic of miracles, namely their dynamism. When the holy breaks in upon the world, this intervention does not take place without design; rather it unleashes forces and directs them towards a goal. Mere exhibitions of miraculous power for their own sake are therefore impossible. What God seeks to achieve by his process of sanctification is to fill the entire earth with his glory, and in this process miracles prepare the way. This begins right from the creation itself (Gen 1:1ff). Here the word 'create' (*bārā᾿*), which is only used of God, expresses a union between him in his 'otherness' on the one hand, and the transient world of matter on the other. In history this same purposive energy is manifested above all in the journey into the promised land with its accompanying miracles, and in the process by which Israel gradually becomes a people. It reaches its conclusion at the end of days when as 'mighty God' and 'wonderful counsellor' (Is 9:6) the Messiah ushers in the age of salvation, which was foreshadowed in the sign of Immanuel (Is 7:14). The gulf which lies between God and man is bridged by leaders equipped with charismatic power. Among these Moses occupies a unique place. He it was who comprehended the meaning of the Red Sea episode (Ex 13:17ff) in all its fullness and depth, his insight piercing through and beyond the external fact of the miracle to the interior reality of the will of God, so that he became its proclaimer, showing its bearing on every aspect of life. For it is in this that the deeper meaning of the miracle consists. It is not the concrete fact that is important but the meaning hidden within it, which is understood as a summons from God. The converse is indeed true of the oracles of the prophets. Here the meaning lies in the word, while the sign attests its credibility (Is 7:11; 38:7). But this close connection between word and visible sign only serves to indicate the complexity of the process of revelation, in which the various elements are interdependent and interchangeable in their functions.

Apart from this the cult contributed to the religious education of the people. It was not merely that its sacred chants awakened memories of God's interventions in their history, in which his loving care for them was manifested. These chants also served as their response, their Credo, by which they acknowledged what he had done for them (Ex 15:21). In this way man is summoned to a decision. For him who closes himself to God, or who coldly refuses a sign (Is 7:12) the miracle becomes a judgement (2 Kings 21:12; Joel 3:3). But for others it effects that salvation which at the end of time, and in the light of the divine radiance, will be manifested in the form of peace and joy (Is 9:1ff). It is precisely in the miracle that it becomes clear that God thinks thoughts of peace and not of evil.

Since miracles could be conceived of (apart from a few minor exceptions in the Elisha cycle 2 Kings 4–6) only in relation to the living God, the earliest instances of the idea hardly penetrate below the surface. But according to the demands of the time the points of view were altered. Thus, to take the idea of creation, the Priestly code lays greater emphasis on its salvific implications (Gen 1:1ff), while the Wisdom literature stresses the element of mystery in it (Job 5:9ff; Ps 139:14). The problem which they were attempting to throw light upon was the problem of 'God and Israel'. It is not until later times, when faith has begun to waver, that a shift of interest is apparent. From now on it is the extraordinary nature of the event that is thrust into the foreground, and this is regarded as a condition for acknowledging God (the Apocrypha). The temptation of Christ is a good example of this (Mt 4:1ff).

B. *Miracles acquire a special significance in the New Testament.* Here several different terms are used to express the idea (*terata, sēmeia, dunameis,* 2 Cor 12:12; *thaumasia,* Mt 21:15). But though various shades of meaning are reflected in these, they all point to a single common factor, namely the character of miracle as sign. As signs, miracles should lead men to God, but they must be sharply distinguished from the apparent wonders worked by Satan (2 Thess 2:9). The element of dynamism is particularly prominent. From being distant the holy has thrust into the here and now. In the figure of Christ, whose miraculous birth ushers in the age of salvation (Lk 1:35), it is present, veiled in the midst of men. Miracles and signs bear witness to his mission and his Messianic status (Mk 8:17; Mt 11:4ff; Lk 4:23; Jn 3:2), reveal his ↗ glory (*doxa,* Jn 2:11; 9:3; 11:4) and are therefore inseparably connected with his words (Mt 9:35; cp the

586

ordering of the material in Mt 5:7; 8f and in Jn 6:8f). Thus they make access possible to the inward hidden reality of his person. Now that the distance between the holy and the profane has been diminished, the manifestations of the holy through portents in the elements of nature recede far into the background. They occur only at decisive points such as the crucifixion (Mt 27:51), the miracle performed for the apostle (Acts 16:26), and the *parousia* (Mt 24:15ff). From now on their place as the principle kind of miracle is taken by the healings, which go beyond human experience in any sphere. The 'otherness' of these miracles to the things of this world is thrown into relief by various factors: by the suddenness with which someone is cured of a chronic illness (Mk 1:40ff), by circumstances external to the miracle itself such as the faith of strangers (Mk 2:1ff), and above all by the fact that they are performed at a distance from the sufferer (Mt 8:5ff; Mk 7:24ff; Jn 4:46ff). Such factors as these exclude the possibility of autosuggestion or magic, and make it clear that the cures take place as a result of an act of will. If external media are sometimes used (Mk 7:31ff; 1:41; Jn 9:6) this is either so that the healing power can be imparted by contact, or as symbols of the Spirit (laying on of hands Mk 6:2), in whose power the miracle is performed (Mk 6:13; Mt 10:8); it is not therefore in pursuance of any psychological or medical end.

Apart from this miracles are milestones on the road to the kingdom of God and have a symbolic character. This is something which John in particular has recognised in all its depth, and which he uses the special term *semeion* to describe, among other instances in the multiplication of loaves (Jn 6:1ff), the healing of the blind (Jn 9:16), and the raising of Lazarus (Jn 11:47). The healings of the sick which Isaiah predicted would take place in the final age (Is 35:5ff) become present realities with the coming of Christ. The casting out of devils (Mk 1:23ff; 5:1ff; Lk 8:2f) show forth his victory over the dominion of Satan, for the unholy was regarded as such. This dominion will finally be overthrown, in spite of numerous counter-miracles, by the miracle of the epiphany at the *parousia* (2 Thess 2:8). This being the end in view, there can be no momentary miracle performed to overcome some material need (Jn 6:26; see Christ's withdrawal from the multitude: Mk 1:35f), or to create a sensation (Mt 4:5f; Lk 23:8ff; see also the command to be silent Mk 5:43, etc), or for his own glorification (Mt 26:53). The process, accompanied by miracles, by which the world is sanctified, is accomplished by working from the lowest to the highest, that is, from man to man. For this reason miracles are not general but particular and personal in their application. It is the lower levels of society (women: Mk 1:29f; 5:21ff; 7:24ff; Lk 8:2; 7:13; 13:10ff; a servant: Mt 8:10) who are favoured with them in the first instance. Yet because the individual is inseparably bound up with the community, the miracle has a central significance for all, summoning all to a *prise de position*. In this connection a distinction must be drawn between those who are actually favoured with the miracle and the onlookers.

The former, or their immediate en-
tourage (Mk 5:36; 7:29; Mt 8:10) are
representatives of the religious feeling
of the community. From these Christ
expects, often as a prior condition, an
attitude of faith and trust in his power,
even though this faith may sometimes
be rudimentary in character (Mk 5:34;
10:52; Lk 17:19), amounting to a
vague awareness that the holy is near.
Through the miraculous event this
awareness is then brought by the holy
himself to the point of explicit recognition and decision (Mk 2:5; Jn 9:35).
Thus the way leads from belief in the
miracle to belief in God, from the
visible exterior to the invisible centre
and source. The healing of the body
becomes a sign of the peace of the soul
(Mk 2:1ff). The dynamism of this
process is strikingly conveyed in the
words: 'I do believe, help thou my unbelief.' It lies in the nature of things
that in all these cases a breakthrough
to genuine faith must ensue. Otherwise
the miracle is refused (Mk 6:5; Lk
23:8ff).

The effect on the onlookers is different. The great majority stop short at
astonishment, which produces various
reactions ranging from excitement (Lk
23:8) to praise for the kindness and
benevolence of the miracle-worker (Acts
10:38), attitudes which often supplied
the immediate motive for the Lord's
works (Mk 8:1; Lk 7:13). Yet how
totally his actions could be misconstrued is seen in the attempt to make
him king by force (Jn 6:15). Often it is
enough for the bystanders, after a
critical examination of the facts confronting them, to recognise with their
minds that they are real (Jn 9:8ff),
while attempting to reconcile them with

the findings of human reason (Mt
12:9ff; Lk 6:6ff; Jn 9:16). Or else
recourse is had to other-worldly explanations which, however, do not
imply any kind of self-commitment (Mt
8:27; Jn 3:2; 7:31; 9:32f). The leaders
of the people on the other hand sense
that the miracles carry with them a
claim that is religious and demand a
decision from those who witness them.
Their repeated demand for signs (Mk
8:11f; Mt 12:38ff; 16:1ff; Lk 11:29;
Jn 2:18ff; 6:30; 1 Cor 1:22) reveals
their inner disquiet, but at the same
time too their lack of faith, for they
seek to make recognition of revealed
truth dependent upon a particular
work (Jn 6:30ff). What they cannot
understand is what was revealed in the
sign of the crib (Lk 2:12), namely that
God makes himself present in hidden
ways (Jn 7:3f), so that in the last
analysis blessed are they who do not see
and yet who believe (Jn 20:29).
Therefore they react with anger which
leads to calumny (Mk 3:22), hostility,
persecution (Jn 5:16; 9:34) and finally
to the taking prisoner of the object of
their wrath (Jn 11:47). The decision
for Christ cannot be forced, but must
be taken in free and willing response to
him. It leaves no part of the believer's
life unaffected, for it touches him in the
very depths of his being. Thus the response of faith reveals itself not in the
acknowledgement of the lips but in the
action which proceeds from repentance
(Mk 1:15; Mt 11:20). To him whose
heart is evil the miracle will bring that
downfall (Mt 11:20ff; 12:39; 23:37;
Acts 5:1ff; 2 Thess 2:9) to which the
sign of Jonah bears witness in its
function as foreshadowing the ↗ *parousia*
(Lk 11:29). But men of goodwill will

find salvation and joy coming to meet them (Lk 2:10; 11:34f).

The miracles worked by the apostles as emissaries of Christ (Mk 16:17ff), which were already becoming rare by the time Heb 2:4 was written, have a special significance, for they are signs of the activity which proceeds from the Holy Spirit to fashion and create the world anew (Acts 2:43; 3:6; 5:12ff; 9:34ff; 19:11). The idea of miracle is so inseparably connected with Christ that it has always been preserved from any diminution of its sacred character. In the episode of Acts 8:19f we find how strong the reaction was against any attempt at such diminution or vulgarisation. At the same time, in virtue of this connection with Christ's person, miracle is sharply opposed to the 'signs and wonders' of the false messiahs (Mk 13:21f; 2 Thess 2:9).

Bibliography: M. Buber, *Stationen des Glaubens*, Wiesbaden 1956, 20–26; Bultmann II, 44ff; Eichrodt I, 325ff; Haag 1723–8; Grundmann, *TDNT* II, 290–305; Procksch 454–8; von Rad I, 449f; J. Schmid, *Markus* (*RNT* 2) 1954², 52–5; Schnackenburg 14–18; G. Söhngen, *Wunderzeichen und Glaube, Die Einheit in der Theologie*, München 1952, 265–85; see also R. Bultmann, 'Zur Frage des Wunders', *Glauben und Verstehen* I, Tübingen 1954, 214–28.

Elpidius Pax

Mission

The whole of sacred scripture bears witness to the fact that when God has a message to impart, his normal way of conveying it to the men concerned is through intermediaries. In the Old Testament this task is entrusted on the one hand to the ↗ angels, on the other, and in a broader sense to the ↗ prophets

(see Jer 7:25) whom Yahweh sends or 'com-missions' (for a famous example, see Is 6:8). This principle applies to the whole history of revelation, but is realised most perfectly in the New Testament. This being the case, no detailed presentation of the relevant passages from the Old Testament will be attempted in this article since all the essential elements in the concept of revelation recur and are fully represented in the New Testament.

'Mission' also has its place in *the purely human sphere*. As the New Testament shows, men avail themselves of other men as their emissaries for the most diverse reasons. Evil intentions may lie behind their action (see Lk 20:20 and parallels). Or the explanation can be physical (Lk 7:20 John the Baptist in prison) or moral impossibility (Jn 11:3 Mary and Martha after Lazarus' death). Highly-placed officials send delegates (eg, the Jewish authorities send emissaries to John, Jn 1:19—according to v 24 it is the 'Pharisees'—as well as to Jesus, thus Jn 7:32), but so does the centurion when he wants to give a special mark of his humility (Lk 7:3). Apart from the first of the reasons adduced, each of the other motives for missions can contribute to our understanding of why God's work is accomplished again and again by means of missions.

As in the Old Testament, so in the New, God uses angels as his messengers: Gabriel is sent to Zechariah (Lk 1:19) and to Mary (Lk 1:26) to announce the good news first that the forerunner, and then that the Redeemer himself, have been conceived. In John the Baptist the Old Testament promise is fulfilled: 'Behold I send my "angel" before thee' (Mal 3:1; see also Ex 23:20 = Mt 11:10; and Mk 1:2; Lk 7:27). He is sent to give witness of the light (Jn 1:6f; see also Jn 1:33; 3:28). This gives him a place in the long series of messengers sent by God to his people. Moses himself was sent to the Israelites as leader and rescuer (Acts 7:35—and is, for this reason, a type of Christ). In the course of his parables Christ often refers to the fact that throughout the entire length of the Old Testament period God used human mediators of this sort (the householder sends workers into the vineyard Mt 20:2–7—without intending to allegorise here!; the king sends servants to the tenants, Mt 21:34, 36 and parallels; the bridegroom's father sends servants with invitations to the wedding Mt 22:3f; Lk 14:17). But it is John the Baptist who in a special way sums up this long series of divine messengers: he is the background which throws into relief him to whom being sent by, and coming from God applies in a unique and absolute sense, Christ the Lord (see Mt 11:18 and parallels: John hungers and thirsts, Christ eats and drinks). Every other mission from God takes place only with a view to the utterly unique mission of Christ!

Christ's sayings concerning his mission and his coming (for both concepts must be kept parallel here) represent his essential self-proclamation. In the *synoptics* Christ has the most pregnant expressions for his mission. He is sent to proclaim the good tidings of the kingdom of God (Lk 4:43). His task is a fulfilment of the promises of the prophets: 'to preach good news to the poor, release to the captives, and recovering of sight to the blind, to set at liberty those who are oppressed, to proclaim the year of grace of the Lord' (Lk 4:18 = Is 61:1f; see 58:6; Lev 25:10). His mission is confined to the lost sheep of the house of Israel (Mt 15:24). He has come to accomplish this mission, to fulfil the old order of salvation (= the 'law'), not to destroy it (Mt 5:17). As Jesus himself emphasises in his meeting with the Syro-Phoenician woman, his coming benefits sinners (see 1 Tim 1:15), not the just (Mt 9:13 and parallels). The Son of Man has come to seek out those that are lost and to rescue them (Lk 19:10); here belong the three parables in Lk 15, of which that of the prodigal son is particularly relevant. Without either denying or evaluating the 'righteousness' of the 'just', it is intended to invite them once more to rejoice with the Father, that is to be completely of one mind with him. The difficult logion in Mt 9:13 and parallels has a similar meaning (see W. Beilner, *Christus und die Pharisäer*, 1959, 106–09). In the fulfilment of his mission he is willing to spend himself utterly and unreservedly ('not to be served but to serve [as a slave], and to give his life in atonement for many' Mt 20:28 and parallels; Lk 12:50). But the fulfilment of his mission will not bring any utopian result: 'I am come to bring not peace but the sword' (Mt 10:34). This applies to himself as well as to those whom he will send. Lk 12:49 has a similar bearing: 'I have come to cast fire upon the earth, and what will I, but that it be kindled?' The ultimate fulfilment of his mission will be the Parousia (Acts 3:20).

An incomparably higher number of passages than in the synoptics (self-proclamatory as well as interpretative) concerning the mission and the coming of Christ are found in the *johannine writings*. Here as nowhere else does Christ insist upon the fact that he is *sent*. His mission from the Father is the basis of all his work. All the sayings converge upon the assertion that he who is sent is one with the Father who sent him (Jn 10:30). Christ knows the Father because he is with him and because he has been sent by him (Jn 7:29). Christ emphasises that it is not of himself that he has gone forth and that he has come, but that his coming is based upon his mission from the Father (Jn 8:42). Christ speaks the words of him who sent him, precisely because he has been *sent* (Jn 3:34). His teaching is not his own, but the teaching of him who sent him (Jn 7:16). The Father commands him what to say (Jn 12:49; see also 14:24). The Lord insists that man can attain to God only by the Way that lies through him whom the Father has sent: the work of God is to believe in him who he has sent (Jn 6:29). He who believes in Christ believes not in him but in him who sent him (Jn 12:44f). Eternal life consists in knowing the only true God and him whom he has sent (Jn 17:3). In order to avoid the judgement it will avail to believe in him who has sent Christ (Jn 5:24). It is not blind faith in his claims and in his mission that Christ demands. The Father who has sent Christ has borne him witness (Jn 5:37; see also 8:18). It is through his works that this testimony is manifested (Jn 5:36). Christ gives thanks to the Father for restoring Lazarus to life because this is a sign bearing witness that Christ has been sent by the Father (Jn 11:42). The Lord shows from scripture that his unheard-of claim is based precisely on the grace of his calling (just as the judges of the Israelite people may be called 'gods' in the psalm, so, and with far greater reason, may he be called God whom the Father has sent into the world, Jn 10:36). And through all this Christ is compelled to assert that the people of Israel ('the world') does not believe in him whom the Father has sent (Jn 5:38). Again and again the Lord cries out to the unbelievers: as the Father is true (Jn 7:28; 8:26), so too is he who comes in his name (Jn 7:18). But how can Christ expect them to believe in him when they do not know the Father who has sent him (Jn 7:28)? Since the Father who has sent Jesus does not draw them, they cannot come to him (Jn 6:44). But those whom God has given to Christ (Jn 17:6) have believed (Jn 17:8) and known (Jn 17:25) that the Father has sent the Son into the world (see also 1 Jn 4:9, 10f). Since his task is accomplished by this, Christ returns to him who sent him (Jn 7:33; 16:5). The task of the believers now is to be one among themselves as the Father is in Christ and Christ in the Father, that the world may believe that the Father has sent Christ (Jn 17:21) in proof of the fact that the Father loves the believers as he loves him whom he has sent (Jn 17:23).

When the apostle confesses: 'We have seen and bear witness that the Father has sent his Son as Redeemer of the world' (1 Jn 4:10; see also Rom 8:3: to condemn sin in the flesh), he is here repeating in summary form what the Lord said of himself. It is the will of the Father who has sent Jesus, that he shall lose nothing of all that God has given him, but raise it up at the last day (Jn 6:39). Christ has come as light into the world (Jn 12:46), that his own may have life (Jn 10:10). His task is accomplished in that 'hour' from which the Son of Man shrinks, but to endure which he has come (Jn 12:27). Through this endurance he becomes expiation for our sins (1 Jn 4:10). He has accomplished his task because his food is to do the will of him that sent him (Jn 4:34; see also 5:30; 6:38). He has worked the works of the Father who sent him so long as it was day (Jn 9:4). Therefore the Father too has not left him alone; for he has always done what was pleasing to him (Jn 8:29). This love of the Father (that he has sent his only-begotten Son into the world in order to give us life, 1 Jn 4:9; see also 1 Jn 4:10) does not produce its effects in men in any magical way. It is achieved by appropriating that redemption for the accomplishment of which the Son was sent. This in turn is effected by a man's relationship towards the one who was sent, and, as a consequence of this, towards the sender. This is best expressed in the paradoxical words which Christ spoke concerning the judgement which had been entrusted to him and which was exercised by him. It is equally true that the Son of Man was sent into the world not to judge it but to save it (Jn 12:47; see also 3:17; and Eph 2:17: he came and preached peace), and that he has come into the world for judgement (Jn 9:39). Man brings his own judgement upon himself by the way in which he relates himself to the One whom the Father has sent (Jn 3:18)!.Thus the judgement of Christ is a just judgement because he

is not alone: he who has sent him is with him (Jn 8:16).

It would not be true to say that the principle of mission came to an end with Christ or that it had no further developments. He now has emissaries of his own in his turn, whom he sends into the world (↗ apostle, ↗ disciple). His chosen missioners are 'the twelve' (Mt 10:5). When he sends them out in twos (Mk 6:7) without material means of support (Lk 22:35), as sheep in the midst of wolves (Mt 10:16 and parallels) to proclaim the good news (Mk 3:14 and parallels), all these details show that their mission is intended as a 're-presentation', a making present of the mission of Christ in all its aspects. Jesus tells them explicitly that they are to share in the fate of prophets, that is, to lose their lives (Mt 23:34, 37 and parallels). As Jesus sent out messengers before him in his journeys on earth (see again Lk 9:52) so together with the twelve, the other 'seventy (-two)' can prepare the way for his word in virtue of the mission which they have received from Christ (Lk 10:1). The special power of sending disciples derives from the Lord's self-giving (Jn 17:19: 'I consecrate myself for them, that they also may be consecrated in truth'). Thus they can reap where they have not sown (Jn 4:38 in accordance with John's whole mode of presentation. He seeks to understand things in the light of the post-Easter perspective). From their union with the Lord in spirit (cf Jn 6:63) they will obtain strength and a source of life on this mission: 'As the living Father has sent me . . . so he that eats me will live because of me' (Jn 6:57). In quite general terms he says: 'As the Father has sent me, so I send you' (Jn 20:21). Thus if they find that persecution is their lot, that can only be because the persecutors do not know him who sent Christ (Jn 15:21). Those sent by Christ send out yet others in their turn (Acts 8:14) and finally hand on their own mission to others still.

If one side of the significance of Christ is revealed in the mission (using the term in the broader sense) of apostles and disciples, the other, namely equality of nature with the Father who sends, is revealed in the sending or mission of the Paraclete (using the term 'mission' in its deepest and truest sense). The Father will send the Paraclete to the disciples in the name of Christ, so as to teach them and to recall to their minds all that Christ revealed to them (Jn 14:26). Equally Christ can say that he will send the Paraclete who proceeds from the Father in order that he (the Paraclete) may assist in bearing witness on the Son's behalf (Jn 15:26). The Seer of Revelation sees Christ's promise to send the Paraclete (Jn 16:7) abundantly fulfilled in the image of the seven horns and eyes of the slain Lamb, for these are the seven spirits of God (the sevenfold Spirit of God) sent out into all the earth (Rev 5:6).

Bibliography: K. H. Rengstorf, *TDNT* I, 398–406; M. Carrez, Allmen 396–8; Bultmann I, 42f and II, 105ff; J. Pierron and P. Grelot, *DBT*, 322–5; see also the bibliographies under 'Apostle' and 'Disciple'.

Wolfgang Beilner

Moses

A. *Old Testament*. 1. The bible interprets the name 'Moses' as meaning 'He who was drawn out of the water' (Ex 2:10). In contrast to the meanings ascribed to other names in the bible, this one has no connection with the part played by its bearer in the theology of salvation, for the active sense of 'drawer' or 'leader out' (Schedl) is not supported by the biblical evidence. Etymologically the name must be of Egyptian derivation, and this is in accordance with what we know of the early circumstances of Moses' life. On this showing the root-meaning would be 'son' (compare 'Ahmoses', 'Thutmoses').

2. Moses is a historical figure. It is very clear that 'the charisma, the special individual endowment of a [particular] person' stands at the source of Israelite religion and history, and that 'to such an extent is the whole structure based on it, that without it it would be inconceivable' (Eichrodt I, 292). Moreover the gradual elucidation of references to contemporary history has prevailed over the prejudices of an exaggeratedly critical approach and has led to the recognition that 'in many respects the extremely ancient narrative of Moses actually stands closer to the realities of history than Homer does to the prehistoric age of the Greeks' (Auerbach). 'The exodus from Egypt, and the incidents leading up to it, have authentic Egyptian elements' (Gordon).

It does not appear that Moses was already equipped for his work in the history of salvation with those qualities which would have made him suitable for the comprehensive organisation of a people and its religion. He was neither a member of a priestly caste nor an officer. He neither belonged to a circle of ecstatics nor had ancient lineage on which to rely. The authenticity of the traditional portrayal of Moses in the Old Testament is shown precisely by the fact that it makes him neither a priest—for this office belonged to Aaron (Ex 28:1f)—nor a general; Moses prayed instead of taking up the sword himself (Ex 17:10ff). The Old Testament is faithful in representing him as the person he actually developed into: prophet and man of God (Deut 34:10).

Three factors contributed to his formation and equipped him for his task: (1) Moses' religion was rooted in the traditions of his people—he had not lost contact with them (Ex 2:13); (2) he had received an Egyptian education (as a royal scribe?) and training (Acts 7:22); and (3) in Midian he had experience of a lively faith which, in respect of its origins (tribal traditions deriving from Abraham?) and emphasis (monolatry?), seems surprisingly to have been related to his own traditions. This called to life all the powers latent in him. Thus Moses was made ready for the experience of the thornbush (Ex 3).

3. With regard to temperament Moses was endowed with the one most suited to the position of authority which he was to hold. There can be no doubt that he had a powerful temper. His murder of the Egyptian (Ex 2:12) and his reaction in the episode of the golden calf (Ex 32:19) show as much. Yet the greatness of his personality, his attitude of responsibility in his work, and the periods of suffering which he underwent set such a curb upon his temperament that he appeared the meekest of men (Num 12:3). How far this meek-

ness was from being natural to him and how strongly he was tempted by rage is shown by his reaction at Meribah, a reaction which was held against him as a sin, and in punishment for which he forfeited the privilege of entering the promised land in person (Num 20:10ff). Whether this was caused solely by the behaviour of the people at the waters of Meribah or whether their refusal to break directly northwards into the promised land was a contributing factor, the fact is that Moses reacted against the designs of God. He was forced to make a detour and had to die on Mount Nebo before the gates of the promised land (Deut 34:5).

4. Moses' significance for the history of salvation lies in the fact that through him the stream of salvific grace is directed into the channel of specifically Israelite history. In a certain sense the taking of the land entailed an anticipatory eschatology in relation to the earlier promises, just as subsequently the land which had been won was to provide the scene and the starting-point for new epochs in the history of salvation.

The historical circumstances in which Moses was required to involve himself, the tasks which fell to his lot, the achievements which he accomplished are of the most diverse order. Primarily he is to be regarded as a charismatic. For without the fundamental religious experience of the thorn-bush, overwhelmingly powerful as it was (Ex 3), his superhuman work, so far transcending the limitations of his environment, is incomprehensible.

The task which was laid upon him by way of preparation would have taxed a master of psychological tactics. He had to apply his persuasive powers in two different directions: to his own people (Ex 4:27ff) and to Pharaoh (Ex 5). Force and compulsion were excluded here. Faith and personality alone could achieve success.

During the entire journey through the wilderness he had to undertake the leadership and the responsibility, and to stand firm against and master the adversities of fate and the churlish behaviour of the people. Tradition represents Moses as devoid of political ambition yet as a leader-figure.

There can be no doubt that the religious (Ex 24) and legislative (↗ decalogue) formation which Moses, acting as God's intermediary, gave to the people during the wilderness sojourning represents the peak of his achievement. We have no means of knowing whether he formed the people into a community after the pattern of an amphictyony or in some other way that upheld the theocratic principles. In any case the community which he had brought together was united around a *single* sanctuary and before Yahweh *alone* and was governed by a single moral code. However rudimentary we may have to imagine this to have been —the existing accounts of it are reflections from various periods—we must recognise that it pointed the way that had to be followed decisively and unambiguously (see Josh 24:16–24).

Moses is given numerous titles of honour in other parts of the Old Testament besides the Hexateuch, especially in the psalms (Ps 105:26; 106:23). It is noteworthy that in the prophets (apart from the later books Bar 2:28; Dan 9:11, 13 and Mal 4:4) Moses is not called lawgiver; the only references are to his position in the journey through the wilderness (Is 63:11f). The explanation is that as spokesmen of God and proclaimers of an ethic which was to some extent hostile to the concept of the law entertained by the people and perhaps by certain priestly circles too, the prophets had perforce to appeal to Yahweh directly. It is only in the later period of stagnation that reflections upon the law, now crystallised in written form, come to the fore. This also explains why in late judaism Moses came to be absolutely apotheosised (*TDNT* IV, 849ff).

As on so many points, so here too Qumran differs from the apocrypha and pseudepigrapha in its sobriety and its firmer hold on scripture. But the point at which it shows itself to belong precisely to the old covenant is its unmistakable reliance upon Moses and his law (*CD* 15:7–9).

B. *New Testament.* In his attitude towards Moses and his law Jesus Christ would have been as badly received at Qumran as he was among the Jews at Jerusalem, for it is beyond question that Christ let himself be known as a new source of divine revelation and a new interpretation of the divine will. Christ intended to present himself and did present himself as greater than the Old Testament and Moses alike. In spite of this the New Testament portrayal of Moses is more vivid and positive than a consideration of the basic 'Christ/Moses' tension might lead one to suppose (cf also Jn 6:31ff).

1. For all the sharpness of the antithesis 'You have heard that it was said to the men of old . . . but I say to you' (Mt 5:21) Christ did not conduct a

polemic against Moses in person, although he did sharply oppose the interpretation of Moses upheld by the Jews of his period (Mt 12:10ff). It would be quite wrong to think of Christ's 'evaluation of Moses' as though he regarded him as the 'evil tree' which could only bear the fruit of 'hypocrites', 'offspring of vipers' and the whole 'adulterous generation'. Rather it was so much that was false in judaism that aroused the animosity of Jesus Christ precisely because the law of Moses had not been observed (Mt 23:23). Accordingly Moses will be the accuser of the Jews in the coming judgement (Jn 5:45). The limitations of Moses were seen and stated, but with a certain understanding, as is shown by the discussion about divorce (Mk 10:5). Certainly Moses was covered with the 'veil' (2 Cor 3:13f), but the light that shone from God was not thereby distorted (2 Cor 3:7). Thus Moses still has his place with Christ (Jn 1:17) in virtue of his divinely willed vocation as covenant founder. The position he occupies is indeed antithetic to that of Christ, but it has its value.

2. Hence it should not surprise us that Moses is also significant as a type that points on to the mediator of the new covenant (Heb 12:24). According to Deut 18:5 Moses is *the* prophet without further qualification and therefore points on to the Messiah as prophet (Jn 1:21). The inclusion of Moses in the early stages of the transfiguration (Mk 9:4) is probably to be explained in the same way.

It has been suggested that the periods spent in the desert by the Baptist and by Christ respectively have a typological meaning in that they refer back to Moses (*TDNT* iv, 865). In the light of Qumran, however, this opinion can probably no longer be upheld. The typological sense is clearer in connection with the discussion of baptism in 1 Cor 10:2 and also with regard to Moses' function as deliverer (Rev 15:3).

3. No attempt should be made to interpret the description of Moses as a man of God tried by sorrows (Acts 7:25ff) in a typological sense. Moses' sufferings are spoken of in order that he can be praised as a man of faith (Heb 11:24–9) and virtue (Acts 7:25ff).

4. The reference to Jannes and Jambres (2 Tim 3:8) must derive from the apocryphal literature, as also must the mention of Michael's struggle over the body of Moses (Jub 9; see perhaps ApocMos 8:43).

Bibliography: J. Jeremias, *TDNT* iv, 848–73; H. Cazelles and A. van de Bom, Haag 1160–69; M. Noth, *The History of Israel*, London 1963; C. Schedl, *Geschichte des Alten Testaments*, i and ii, Innsbruck 1956; C. H. Gordon, *Introduction to Old Testament Times*, Ventnor (N.J.) 1953; E. Auerbach, *Moses*, Amsterdam 1953; J. Bright, *The Authority of the Old Testament*, London 1967; R. Smend, *Das Mosesbild von H. Ewald bis M. Noth*, Tübingen 1959.

Othmar Schilling

Mountain

Among the most widespread and primitive phenomena known to the history of religions are the various manifestations and objectivisations of the numinous which take place on hills and mountains. These are attested wherever there are mountains or wherever a particular people recalls some particular mountain or mountains in the country from which it originally came, and lead to the setting up of sanctuaries on mountains or the building of temples which are artistic representations of a mountain. We know of countless religious traditions which are familiar with a sacred mountain in the centre of the world whose summit touches heaven and whose roots reach down into the underworld. This mountain constitutes the *axis mundi* which binds together the three cosmic regions of heaven, earth and underworld. Such a representation comes through with particular clarity in the cosmologies of the ancient Near East, India (see B. Meru) and China. The cosmic mountain is seen as the central point of the world where the gods dwell and around which the constellations turn. According to Babylonian mythology the great gods are born on the cosmic mountain to the east of which there was thought to be the 'mountain of the east' on which the gods decided the destiny of the world on the feast of the New Year. The Gilgamesh epic speaks of a cedar-mountain as the dwelling of the gods in much the same way as the Ras Shamra texts refer to the holy mountain Zaphon as the dwelling-place of Baal. It was for this reason that Baal is known as 'Baal Zaphon' and the cult of this deity was brought to Corfu by Phoenician sailors.

We find traces of this mythological thinking in the Bible as, for example, when it is said of an overthrown tyrant that he wished to make himself like God and set up his throne on the top of Zaphon (Is 14:13–15). In much the same way the king of Tyre is represented as being established, along with Melqart the divine ruler of the city, on the mountain of God (Ezek 28:14–16).

The exigencies of a particular cult tended to transfer the cosmic mountain into particular neighbourhoods. Not only the ziggurats, which were stepped towers belonging to Babylonian temples, but also natural mountains (eg, Mount Olympus in Greece) could serve as types or models of the original mythical archetype and be associated with the representation of the mid-point of the earth or the 'navel of the world'. Jerusalem, for example, is the mid-point of the earth in Ezek 5:5 and Gerizim is the navel of the earth in Judg 9:37. There may also be an etymological connection between *ṭabûr*, Hebrew for 'navel' (Ezek 38:12) and Mount Tabor in Galilee (Josh 19:22; Judg 4:6, 12, 14). Many of the more impressive mountains of Palestine were associated with cult in the pre-Israelite period. For example, Zaphon the dwelling-place of Baal was identified with *jebel el-aqra*ʾ north of Ras Shamra, and was known at a later time as Mount Casios where Zeus-Casios was worshipped in the hellenistic period as the successor of Baal. There were other holy mountains in Canaan, conspicuously Lebanon and Syrion, referred to as Hermon in Deut 3:9. Both of these mountains are mentioned in Hittite treaties of the second millennium BC. On Hermon there were to be found the ruins of religious sanctuaries which were being visited as late as the fourth century AD. Tabor was likewise identified with the mountain of the transfiguration well-known in Christian tradition (Mt 17:1), and it too was an ancient sanctuary probably referred to in the Blessing of Zabulon (Deut 33:19). Hos 5:1 refers to Tabor as the centre of an apostate cult which contributed to the downfall of the people of Israel; LXX has at this point *Itabyrion*, the *Atabyrion* found in Greek writers, and it is probable that the sanctuary of Zeus Atabyrios on the island of Rhodes can be traced back to the worship of Baal of Tabor.

There was a sanctuary of Baal Peor (Num 23–5) at Peor, a city over which Israelites and Moabites fought one another. We have so far no record of a pre-Israelite deity of Gerizim but this mountain, together with Ebal which stood opposite it, was thought to be sacred by the Israelites (Deut 27:4–8; Josh 8:30ff), and it was for this reason that the Samaritans built their temple there in the fourth century BC. A long cultic tradition also attached to Carmel. It is referred to as the 'holy promontory' in Egyptian topographical lists going back to Thutmoses III, is characterized as holy to Zeus by Pericles of Skylax in the fourth century BC, and Vespasian offered sacrifices on its summit. Since Phoenicians and Israelites disputed the ownership of this mountain, Baal and Yahweh also fought over it (1 Kings 18). Yahweh laid claim to all mountains consecrated to the worship of other gods. It was he who created Lebanon and Syrion (Ps 29:6); Zaphon, Tabor and Hermon praise his name with joy (Ps 89:12).

However, the mountains which were uniquely sacred to Yahweh were Sinai, where he revealed himself, and Sion, where he dwelt. Sinai-Horeb is described as the mountain of God (Ex 3:1; 4:27; 18:5; 24:13; 1 Kings 19:8), and the mountain-sanctuary of Jerusalem is Yahweh's dwelling-place (1 Kings 8:10–13; see↗ temple). Zion is the holy mountain *par excellence*

(Ps 2:6; 3:4; 15:1; 43:3; 99:9; Is 27:13; 56:7; 57:13; 65:11; 66:20; Jer 31:23 etc), which will be raised even higher in the messianic age (Is 2:2f = Mic 4:1f). Ezekiel is probably thinking in these terms when he describes the ideal Jerusalem of the future as built on a very high mountain (40:2 cf Zech 14:10).

Bibliography: J. Jeremias, *Der Gottesberg*, Gütersloh 1919; O. Eissfeldt, *Baal Zaphon, Zeus Casios und der Durchzug der Israeliten durchs Meer*, Halle 1932; B. Alfrink, 'Der Versammlungsberg im aussersten Norden', *Bbl* 14 (1933), 41–67; W. F. Albright, 'Baal-Zephon', *Festschrift Bertholet*, Tübingen 1950, 1–14; J. Lewy, 'Tabor, Tibar, Atabyros', *HUCA* 23 (1950/51), 357–86; R. Mouterde, 'Antiquités de l'Hermon et de la Beqa^c', *Mélanges de l'Université S. Joseph* (Beirut) 29 (1951/2), 22–37; M. Avi-Yonah, 'Mount Carmel and the God of Baalbek', *IEJ* 2 (1952), 118–24; K. Galling, 'Der Gott Karmel und die Achtung der fremden Götter', *Geschichte und Altes Testament* (Festschrift Alt), Tübingen 1953, 105–25; O. Eissfeldt, *Der Gott Karmel*, Berlin 1953; H. V. Herrmann, *Omphalos*, 1959; de Vaux 279–81.

Walter Kornfeld

Mystery

Although the great era of the so-called 'history of religions' explanation of Christianity already lies behind us, we find ourselves confronted even today with a host of theories, each diverging from the others, concerning an alleged connection in origin between christianity and the mysteries of antiquity. To anticipate here: even certain catholic exegetes are not disinclined to believe that the *forms* in which the basic facts of christianity were *presented*, even in the earliest stages, would have been influenced to a certain extent by the mysteries. Manifestly error is possible here, because there is a danger on the one hand of underestimating the capacity of christian preaching to produce a definite mode of expression from its own resources as the need arose, and on the other of simultaneously overestimating the power of the mysteries to exercise a psychological influence on christian preaching.

These, however, are harmless questions compared with other hypotheses which are concerned not merely with linguistic peculiarities or certain ancillary ceremonies, but with the very fundamentals of Christian teaching and Christian ritual. In explaining how these would normally have originated, they allege that both the teaching and that essential Christian practice, *the sacraments*, would have been modelled after patterns found in the pagan mysteries. What is in question here is that combination of teaching and practice which belongs to the basic sacraments, ↗ baptism and ↗ eucharist, as well as the soteriology on which it is based, the salvific work of the Lord with its two culminating points, the ↗ cross and ↗ resurrection. With regard to christianity's ritual heritage, attempts are made to attribute to the influence of the mysteries not so much the mere external form of the rites, but rather the connection between the rites and the effects of grace attached to them. It is believed that the meaning which was ascribed to the rites originally, that is among Palestinian Christians, was radically transformed when the Church passed over to pagan soil. For it is only at this point, so the theory goes, that the uncompromising realism of the *opus operatum* was introduced. Now the early Christian sources have handed down

the narratives of institution for both these sacraments (for baptism cf Mt 28:19; Mk 16:16; Jn 3:5, and for the eucharist the commentary on the eucharistic discourse in Jn 6 may be adduced). The hypothesis is, then, that as a result of the encounter at an early stage between christianity and paganism the entire meaning of this symbol underwent the most shattering and radical transformation. Now the only way to make this hypothesis credible is to do violence to the sources and to call their reliability in question. Again the evangelists provide clear evidence of the fact that the Lord himself announced that his own death would be a death offered willingly in expiation. Here too the view is widely held that this fundamental dogma is to be explained in terms of the history of religions. And here too, of course, this view can be maintained only by the same procedure of calling in question the historical value of the relevant supporting texts.

The inadmissibility of this procedure from a methodological point of view will be apparent. It is all the more striking because this attitude of scepticism towards the New Testament sources is in glaring contrast to the boundless trust which is placed in a certain group of ancient non-Christian sources. These are the so-called 'Hermetic writings'. Since R. Reitzenstein, sayings drawn chiefly from them have been used to support the theory with which we are here concerned, namely that the parallels to and prototypes of the Christian views in question which are found in the pagan mysteries are of early origin. Here it may be said that not one of these writings derives from the cultic mysteries. They belong to a quite different type, namely the so-called 'literary mysteries' (*Lesemysterien*). In these the devotee strove to achieve by reading alone effects similar to those sought after in the ancient cultic mysteries: above all assurance of happiness in the next world and the attainment of special relationships with the deity. (In Hermetic circles, however, this had been divested of its mythological elements and had its place within that ancient group of ideas in which God was conceived of as interior to the world.) Perhaps the devotee had to combine this reading with some sort of exercises. These, however, he would have performed in private (in late antiquity, at a time when 'theurgy' flourished, they were often magical in character). Again it is uncertain whether a single one of the sixteen Hermetic tractates (most of them very short) was already in existence at the time when the writings of the New Testament first saw the light. The late origin of most of these tractates is a firmly established fact. These are factors to be borne in mind in considering the research which has gone into our present question. They should prove to us that in this work of research the emphasis has been laid not on interpreting the New Testament sources but on determining their historical origins and estimating their reliability.

Clearly in a mere survey article belonging to a manual word-book of the bible the exposition of the subject matter must be extremely circumscribed. Even with regard to questions which are important for biblical theology only the main principles can be stated which are essential

to elucidate the conclusion arrived at.

1. Etymologically no certain explanation has been given of the resources of the Greek language which lie behind the word *mustērion*. At the same time the derivation from *muō* (= 'I shut my eyes') has a certain probability. In the earliest instances the word is found as a designation of secret rites. In this usage it is found in the plural always in earlier times and nearly always in the later too.

In the context of Greek religion mysteries are a collection of cultic practices in which the ceremonies were carried out in concealment and in which all publicity was excluded. Many Greek cultic movements have in addition to their public ceremonies supplementary practices which are performed in secret, but since we do not always know what form these practices took it is difficult to establish in all cases the real reason for their being kept concealed. Often the requirement of secrecy is to be explained by the fact that it is fertility rites that are in question and these extend into the sexual sphere and are reserved to women (thus in the secret rites of the Athenian Thesmophoria).

Secrecy was also a means of raising the estimation in which the rites were held and to ensure their popularity. In the case of one or two of the cultic movements it is also possible that they were practised by a section of that amalgam of peoples called the Greeks which was of Indo–Germanic origin. This too would be a partial explanation of the attitude of secrecy. These autochthenes or indigenous inhabitants could have had reasons for concealing their cult for as long as possible from the waves of invaders who were breaking in. Thus what was originally a quite understandable measure of self-protection would later have been transformed into a binding law so that the mysteries derived their name from it. The fact that they are always spoken of in the plural is probably to be explained by the fact that the emphasis was placed on the ceremonies and these always involved a number of actions.

It is a fact of linguistic history that the word *mustērion* very soon appeared in the singular too as a designation of things outside the cult which were secret. This can be explained as a secondary extension of meaning. But the alternative explanation is at least equally probable, namely that the general meaning 'secret' without further qualification was the original one. At all events this neutral application of the Greek word is supported by the usage of LXX, for here it is taken as equivalent to the Aramaic *rats*, which has no necessary connection with the cult whatever.

The plural *mustēria* is occasionally used in the very late books of LXX to designate pagan mystery cults. This of course represents sheer borrowing from the religious language of paganism for the sake of reference. Apart from this, *mustērion* in LXX, together with the semitic words which it stands for, shows no connection whatever with any cultic background. When it is applied to things pertaining to God it belongs to the general context of revelation and appears together with terms which have this connotation.

The recent discoveries at the Dead Sea have shown in a surprising way

that as a designation of an occult saying of God the word *mustērion* was extremely popular at least among the sect of Jewish pietists who lived in the monastery of Qumran. (And besides these many similar groups living elsewhere should be taken into account.) In view of this we can no longer be surprised to find the word in the synoptics on the lips of Jesus used to describe the kingdom of God (the parable of the sower). Again with regard to the literary contacts which lie in the background of Paul's plentiful use of the term, it has been established long ago that these were confined wholly to the bible (and later Judaism). The proof adduced for this lay in his adherence to the linguistic usages of the canonical literature of the Old Testament. Now, with the Dead Sea discoveries, this position is still more strongly confirmed.

The New Testament contains some twenty-five occurrences of *mustērion*. They are very unevenly distributed. Three passages are in the gospels, but they all belong to a single complex, that of the mystery of the kingdom of God (Mt 13:11 and parallels). The great majority of the occurrences are found in the Pauline writings. These can be divided into two groups. The first consists of the major texts which we are about to enumerate; they can be reduced to five (or six according to how the material in Ephesians is divided). The second group consists of the less important passages, among which we can include that in Eph 5 on marriage, which Paul himself calls 'the great mystery'. For here, after all, the theological content which the word *mustērion* carries does not attain to the depth and pregnancy of the five or six mystery passages of the first group, so full of import as they are for christology and the theology of salvation. In any case it is contestable how exactly *mustērion* should be rendered in this passage of Eph 5. How one decides this depends upon what precisely one takes *mustērion* as referring to. One can regard the actual text cited from Gen 2:24 as such as the object which Paul here calls mystery (in which case *mustērion* would be roughly equivalent to 'type'). Or it may be marriage itself, the natural bond spoken of in this text from Genesis that Paul has in mind as the object of his description. Or rather it may even be marriage in its New Testament status (in that case the sense of *mustērion* here would almost approximate to that of an institution conferring salvation, and the way from there to the further idea of a sign effective of salvific grace is no longer so terribly far). To sum up, three possible lines of interpretation have their champions even today. But none of them leads us outside the circle of ideas which are basically biblical.

The use of the word *mustērion* in Revelation is not influenced by the cult. It is connected rather with the basic meaning of the word (mystery or mysterious sign).

In view of these passages the question must now be put: Has not Paul, merely by choosing the word *mustērion* to stand for christian teaching as a whole, straightway turned the minds of his Greek catechumens, without any further suggestion on his part, to the thought of some similarity between this sum total of christian teaching and the ideas of the mystery cults?

The question thus put must be solved

according to the rules of the psychology of language. When a broad area of association and application is attached to a word, so that it is normally used in one particular context, then no one should lightly suppose that the user of that word intended his use of it to suggest a quite different context and a quite different sphere of associations. In what follows we shall be examining more closely, and with a view to their theological content, those passages in which Paul especially chooses to employ the word *mustērion*. Beside these we have his secondary applications of the word, such as that in Eph 5 which we have just been considering, and these are more or less closely connected with the first. From this we shall conclude that this word was precisely not associated with the cultic sphere. It was the pagan usage of the plural of *mustērion* familiar to Paul's gentile catechumens, which first focused attention on this association. What was uppermost in the mind of Paul himself was rather the unfathomable depths of meaning to be found in God, and his love as revealed in the counsel that brings salvation, ideas which are conditioned by the concept of the divine wisdom planning all things. In the five or six major passages in which Paul treats of mystery he enlarges upon its content with satisfying clarity and depth, so that even if the reader came from a gentile background he could not fall into the temptation of sliding into the quite different area of application which was attached to the word *mustērion* among the pagans. Now supposing that by chance one day the question were put to Paul (as in the long run it was inevitable that it should be): 'What is your own personal opinion of the pagan mystery cults?' If the question were thus openly raised, the underlying thought would make it a question about the *thing*, the real object designated as *mustērion* by the gentiles, as opposed to the import or meaning of the *word* as used either by christians or by pagans.

Paul's way of speaking about *mustērion* could at most afford a superficial pretext for a question of this sort concerning a concrete entity. Even if he had found it possible to answer (and in view of his general attitude to paganism even that is far from certain) he would have treated it as a problem which was totally distinct from his message concerning the mystery of Christ. The fact that he had spent his youth in the midst of a pagan environment already gave Paul a certain familiarity with pagan cults (it was in fact a form of vegetation cult that prevailed at Tarsus, the Sandan-Heracles cult with a funeral festival at its mid-point, the ceremonies of which had not, however, been developed into mystery rites in the proper sense). It may be supposed that a question of this sort, concerning the religious value of the pagan mysteries, would have awakened in Paul's mind an image of celebrations held at religious or pseudo-religious assemblies, for it was these that were chiefly referred to as mystery communities or associations of mystics in the sphere known to him through his missionary journeys.

In Asia Minor and Ionia, where Paul worked for the longest period, what were chiefly called mystic brotherhoods were probably less influenced by the barbaric cult-forms of Attis and the Magna Mater. Neither was the secret form of Egyptian idol worship overpredominant, although the Austrian excavations in Ephesus may have laid bare a magnificent temple of the Egyptian deities. Certainly there were also the mysteries of Ephesian Artemis, but by comparison with the public cult of this goddess they had even less influence. What most frequently appeared in a city like Ephesus, manifesting itself in the form of organised brotherhoods or *thiasoi*, as they were called, was the veneration of Dionysus. This was the form of cult with which brotherhoods masked their true nature. For among them there was very little religion, and probably not much more of the special rites of the Dionysian mysteries left alive. These would have included omophagia, the consumption of raw meat. It was rather the Dionysian delight in life that the members of these confraternities gave themselves up to. Most of their observances were conducted openly and took the form of those *kōmoi* (= revellings) against which Paul issues warnings in Rom 13:13 and Gal 5:21. At the same time we find here an indication of the answer which, we may suppose, Paul would have given to our question about the mysteries.

2. No thorough understanding can be achieved of the relationship between the ancient mysteries and the christian mystery of salvation without *a historical outline of the mysteries themselves*. For this purpose we may select the cult of Eleusis as typical. This procedure seems justified not least because although the origins of this cult are shrouded in obscurity the most recent excavations have shown that it belongs to the pre-Greek level of the population of Hellas.

This means that it probably reaches back into the religious world of Crete and Mycenae with its strong emphasis upon earth-mother-fertility worship, a world which scholars have long since found it possible to reconstruct from the profusion of ancient Cretan monuments.

The rites are divided into three stages of consecration, Myesis, Telete, and Epopteia. It was prescribed that a year's interval had to elapse between the two last stages. The precept of silence was less strictly applied in the case of Myesis. It could be performed in Athens itself. The formula which tells us what took place in the middle stage, the Telete, has been preserved for us by Clement of Alexandria. (It had to be recited as proof that this stage had been completed according to rule so that the candidate could be admitted to the third). It speaks of a fast (clearly a ritual re-enactment of the fast which the goddess Demeter observed as an act of mourning when she was searching for her daughter), of the taking and transferring of certain unknown objects from a sacred coffer into a basket (*kalathos*), and of some 'work' which was simultaneously performed with these objects. No firm conclusion has been arrived at from the discussion of the obscure formulas, a state of affairs which will probably continue unless some archaeological discovery makes available fresh source material (and this is hardly to be expected). However certain discoveries pertaining to an offshoot of the Demeter cult in Priene have shown that this possibility is not altogether excluded. For although Eleusis was the place specially dedicated to the worship of Demeter and Kore, offshoots of this kind had been estab-

lished here and there in the course of the Hellenistic age. (Apart from Priene, one such existed at Alexandria, and there were others too.) The discoveries at Priene are sexual in character. Even if they may be regarded as the objects referred to by Clement (an inference that is not far-fetched) it still remains an open question how they were used. They could have served to symbolise that the user stood in the relation of a child to the cult deity, Demeter.

It seems too that the principal episodes in the myth of Kore would have been shown in exciting representations. Thus the following would have been called to mind: the rape of Kore by Hades, the mother's search for her daughter, then too, probably, her visit to Eleusis where, in return for her kind reception at the house of King Celeus, she instituted the mysteries and revealed the art of cultivating corn (to disseminate this knowledge the hero Triptolemus was sent out into the world), her enquiries after the place where her daughter was sojourning, the protestations to Zeus by Demeter made sick by her frustrated mother-love, and finally the compromise solution arrived at at the instigation of the father of the gods, namely that for at least part of the year (the sources vary as to the exact period stipulated) Kore should leave her husband Hades and should be restored to her mother to live in the upper world.

It is in this outcome that the real point of the myth and the cultic symbolism becomes clear: Demeter herself represents the power of all-fruitful nature, while her daughter symbolises the actual life of nature, the fruit of this elemental vitality. The course of this life is governed by rhythmic laws, the two main stages being decline and fresh upsurge, death and life. Unlike human life, geared as it is to the advance of history, this course of nature is not a 'once and for all' process. Instead it unfolds in an apparently endless series of cyclic repetitions, for this precisely is the distinctive characteristic of the organic and non-historical life of nature. Human destiny, then, in the existentialist sense, has a 'once and for all' quality, whereas the life of nature consists of cyclic periods, each of which returns to its point of origin. So sharply does the first differ from the mythical ideology which represents the second that the only connection between them lies in the fact that the idea of organic vegetable life is embodied in a divine figure in human form, Kore, the daughter of Demeter. In addition to this Kore occupies a position at the side of Hades, the lord of the dead proper, and from this aspect she has acquired the title of mistress of the dead.

Thus the devotee attempted to achieve a special union with the mistress of the underworld by means of solemn rituals of consecration. Thereby he hoped to have found a way of ensuring that a better life awaited him in the world to come. That it is precisely this kind of benefit that the mysteries were expected to confer is attested by the earliest record of the Eleusinian myth, the Homeric hymn to Demeter (sixth century BC). They did not give rise to hopes which altogether transcended the limitations of the popular conceptions of the after-life, but within those limitations they did claim something special for the consecrated ones, an improvement of their position in Hades.

On his way from Athens to Corinth Paul passed through Eleusis. At that time various philosophical movements were responsible for undermining by their criticisms belief in the gods of Eleusis (or for that matter any other gods), at least in the sense represented by the ancient myth, in the minds of all educated Greeks. Thus the special benefits for the after-life which devotees hoped to gain by participating in the cultic ceremonies were deprived of their particular basis. Now Corinth lay very close to Eleusis. Yet although Paul spent a longer period of his missionary activity in Corinth than in any other Hellenistic city (except Ephesus), no allusions to the cult of the mysteries practised at Eleusis can be discerned in his epistles. Even though a single passage in 1 Cor 12:2 has been supposed to refer in general to the mysteries, it is not certain that it does so. It is possible to take this 'being led astray to dumb idols' as intended to characterise the pagan attitude to idols in general. In Eph 4:19 Paul may perhaps be referring to the second main cult of Greece, which also gave rise to mysteries, namely the cult of Dionysus. Possibly we should see an allusion to the same cult in the warnings against unruly drinking sessions in general, which the participants so often attempted to justify by sheltering under the aegis of the Dionysian cultic prescriptions.

The pattern of a Dionysian consecration was derived from the four elements to which purifying power was ascribed. According to the evidence of archaeological monuments the ancient

Greek winnowing-fan was also used. Orphism is found as an independent offshoot of the Dionysian worship, but one which is of so little significance precisely for the New Testament period that it must remain outside the scope of the present discussion.

A glance at the Eastern mysteries. In their basic essentials the ideology of the Eastern forms of the cult are in harmony with that of Eleusis, considered as the cult of the decay and renewal of nature. The Phrygian (Attis–Cybele), Syrian (Adonis and Astarte, the latter adopted into Greek mythology as Aphrodite), and Egyptian (Isis–Osiris) forms are representative of this Eastern ideology. By comparison with the mistresses of nature who are their consorts in each case, the three male figures are inferior. They suffer violent deaths. Not a single ancient writer before Firmicus Maternus has spoken of one of these heroes being resurrected. The description 'dying and rising gods' is a product of the modern imagination. In one passage Tertullian may be saying that in the Mithras cult an *imago resurrectionis* was enacted (or perhaps more simply introduced 'inducit'). In the myth Mithras is represented neither as dying nor as rising from the dead (on this point in general, see K. Prümm, 'Dei morti e risorti', *Gregorianum* 2 [1958]).

Apart from this, let us consider the actual content of the tradition-complexes which centre upon the three archetypal figures referred to—Attis, Adonis, and Osiris. A closer examination of these brings certain features to light which rule out any closer approximation to the message of the atoning death and resurrection of the Lord.

1. Not one of the three archetypal figures dies voluntarily. Even allowing for the fact that death was forced upon them, not one of them imparts to this death, even retrospectively, the significance of being designed to benefit mankind. It is the *venerators* of these deities who first introduce this meaning in that they hope, by uniting themselves in spirit to the cult god's fate, to obtain some sort of advantage for themselves. These are the ones who introduce a salvific meaning into a religious experience originally shared openly in communal celebrations, but subsequently made private and individual.

2. But when they participate in a way that is pleasant in the fate of the cult deity the benefit they expect to gain thereby is not sought in the sphere of moral values, at least not to the extent of making them wish to compete with the aspirations of christianity, a wish that might otherwise have exercised a christianising influence. The *deliverance* which an Attis is expected to bring to his devotees is *not freedom from the burden of sin and guilt*. In all these cults the atmosphere which we encounter is far from being laden with any sense of the oppressive burden of sin. What preoccupies the participants in the cult is at best the tragedy latent in man's life in general, namely the inescapability of death. But not even this symbolism, basic as it in some sense was to the various forms of cult, entered the thoughts of many. When Heraclitus of Ephesus (fifth century BC) says of the Dionysian revels that the true object of their celebrations was Hades, he wishes to express a significance of which even these devotees of the god were hardly conscious, drowning it rather in the wildness of their clamour.

We have just been calling attention to the weaknesses of the mystery cults. The underlying reasons for these will appear more clearly in the light of the comparison which we are about to make with the fundamental aspects of the mystery of Christ.

But lest we be accused of injustice let us mention straight away what is of positive good in these mysteries. It lies in the fact that at a time when religion had openly become a political and 'this-worldly' matter, they made the other world the object of their earnest attention and desire and sought to establish a means of solving the problem of the dark future. The mysteries represent a view of the world which, unlike the official religion of the state, did not soften the harsh reality of man's fate. Yet to such an extent did this remain a pagan view of the reality in question that they could not, of their own convictions, draw any real distinction between human death and the blind unconscious decay of plants and animals as a purely organic occurrence. Thus thick darkness continues to hang over the true meaning of death. This consists in the fact that it brings to a close a life which is personal and which carries with it duties for the discharge of which men must answer.

3. *The content of the pauline mystery of Christ and the pagan cultic mysteries.* *Mustērion* has a special pre-eminence for Paul. It is found in the five passages which treat of the mystery of Christ, namely 1 Cor 2:6–3:2; Rom 16:25–7; Eph 1:10ff; 3:3ff; Col 1:26f; 2:2ff; 1 Tim 3:16. The word designates the divine plan of salvation which centres upon the person of the Lord. Although it was announced by the prophets it was

hidden for long ages until Christ appeared. Now it is revealed (in the revelation of deeds and the revelation of words), and it will be made known in the apostolic preaching. In the fuller *mustērion* passages of the apostle the distinction between these three phases in the mystery of salvation is apparent throughout. As the subject of revelation the mystery must be deeply pondered, and so, on the part of those receiving it, it finds its counterpart in a series of receptive acts. The most fundamental of these is always ⁊ faith, but this must attain to gnosis, and in this in turn several stages are apparent.

Only in one single passage, namely, 1 Cor 4:1, does *mustērion* appear in the plural in Paul. Here it is evidently intended to express the fact that the divine work of salvation, God's hidden plan right from the beginning but now brought to light, includes a number of elements which have been together entrusted to the apostles to administer (in view of his basic conception of the apostolate, what Paul has primarily in mind here is certainly the function of preaching). Now it is to be observed that on the one hand the mystery of salvation also includes as one of its elements the fact that it is to be given to men, something which is ordinarily accomplished by means of the sacramental rites. On the other hand Paul himself is of course acutely aware that the apostolate includes not only the right and duty of evangelising, but the specifically priestly functions too. In view of these considerations it seems highly probable that in this passage of 1 Cor 4:1 the apostle intends the sacraments too to be included among the elements of the mystery of salvation entrusted to him in virtue of his apostolic ministry.

Most often Paul refers briefly to 'his mystery' without further qualification. In the background of his thought here is the immediate connection between the mystery and God, the culmination of all reality. In a special study (K. Prümm, *Bbl.* 37 [1956], 135–61) we have interpreted this mode of reference as follows: '*The mystery is properly located in God.* It is the mystery of his gracious and powerful will. But just because God's will is not irrational in its exercise, so, naturally, the mystery of the divine wisdom making its plan is not irrational either. Viewed objectively it carries the stamp of order and design, and it is by this that the mystery is informed. Now the primary connotation of order is the idea of things being directed towards and determined by a single end in view. Of course this end in view or goal has in turn several different aspects from which it may be regarded. Seen from the point of view of God the end in view or goal consists in the manifestation of his glory, *doxa*, and the realisation of this implies simultaneously the plenitude of honour for the Lord and the plenitude of grace for the redeemed, grace which raises them to the status of children of God and members of the Body of Christ. But because it implies a renewal of creation this plan also includes the world of angels.'

The very fact that this ultimate end in view is the explicit manifestation of God's *doxa* implies that there must be faith, that there must be believers there to recognise this glory. This in turn implies that the mystery is of its very nature intended to be preached. Both its

content and its progressive realisation in the world must be made known to the believers. For this reason God reveals himself not only in the deeds by which he puts his plan into action but also in words which make him known in his gracious activity, words which throw light upon the meaning latent in the objective reality of his creative acts. This revelation is given first to those who are called to be the mouthpieces of God, that is to the apostles and prophets who are to impart the mystery to others. Their task is to do their utmost to preach the mystery without any reserve, having regard both to the capacity of their hearers to receive it and to the extent to which the actual content of the mystery can be made intelligible to human minds. That the mystery is meant to be imparted universally to all without exception is apparent from the very fact that the sphere in which the plan of salvation is to be put into practice is extended so as to include the whole of mankind. Thus of its very nature the mystery demands to be made known openly to all. The christian message is immediately intelligible to all, and is in this respect diametrically opposed to the esoteric knowledge claimed by the adherents of the ancient mysteries.

Besides the passages in which he speaks of the *mustērion* of God or of the divine will, Paul several times calls it the *mustērion* of Christ (Eph 3:4; Col 1:27; 2:2). Knowledge of the person of the Lord that is clear and based on revelation is therefore included as a primary element in the mystery.

In many passages (besides Gal 4 cf Phil 2:5ff or Rom 1:3ff and 8:3) Paul recognises the divinity of the Lord, at the same time asserting that he has a human nature in common with ourselves. So plainly and unequivocally is this expressed that it amounts to a clear distinction between the two natures in Christ. This conclusion with regard to the two distinct natures in the Lord is irreconcilably opposed to the way in which the chief figures of the mysteries, Osiris, Attis, and Dionysus were regarded, that is as anthropomorphic deities or demi-gods. Such a conception would never be fully reconcilable either with the idea of God or with that of a man as these terms are understood in scripture. From a phenomenological point of view these figments of mythological tradition are therefore 'mixed forms', and since they are not fully human they cannot identify themselves fully with the human race.

Christ came into the world of his own free will, a truth that can perfectly be reconciled with the fact that his coming was decreed by the Father. For this applies to the work of redemption as a whole. It is this idea of the complete unison and accord which exists between the totally free decision on the Father's part and the no less totally free carrying out of what has been decided on the part of the Son which is absolutely primary in Paul's mind when he speaks of *mustērion*. The 'planning' of salvation by the Father and the 'carrying out' of salvation by the Son together make up the miracle of God's wisdom and love and for that reason they awaken reactions of astonishment and of love in return. What the christian cherished and honoured before all else in Christ, the focal point of the mystery of salvation was not

death as such, for this, as far as it went, was ascribed to the heroes of the oriental mysteries too. Rather it was a 'dying on behalf of'. Everything, even the entry of the Lord upon his earthly life, was conditioned by the goal he had set himself of bringing salvation to others. It was with this in view that the Lord took human nature in the state in which it actually existed, namely as liable to suffering and as leading to an early death. Paul expressly states this in Rom 8:3. We must put this forward as our principal justification for asserting that the so-called *hieroi logoi* (lit = 'sacred words') of the mysteries could not possibly have appeared to the apostle to have anything whatever in common with his gospel of Christ. It should be explained that according to one theory these *hieroi logoi* were legendary accounts which served as a sort of running commentary upon the rites performed in honour of the fertility gods. The fate of these gods symbolised human destiny as such, that is as conditioned by the historical event of the fall and the penalty of death which it entailed. In no sense did it imply a redemptive victory over death. And if Paul did turn his attention to historical figures who could provide a pattern for christian behaviour either because they foreshadowed Jesus or because they imitated him, he would take the great heroes of faith in the Old Testament who offered all they had in the hope of salvation (Heb 11), or else he put himself and the other apostles forward as models to be imitated (Phil 3:17).

If we were asked where to look in Paul's writings for the briefest statement of what the true purpose of the mystery of Christ was, we should point to Eph

3:6. Here we find it asserted that the ultimate end towards which the mystery is directed, and at the same time the chief point which it contains, is that the gentiles are to become 'fellow heirs, members of the same Body, and partakers of the promise in Christ Jesus'. In this passage Paul finds that the essence of the mystery lies in the fact that christianity is to be universal. Now this universality is bound up with the plan for the work of salvation in history. It is precisely in its universality that *the continuity of christianity with the religion of the Old Testament* is most clearly manifest. More than this, indeed, it is in the light of this universality that we can best understand Augustine's statement that the true religion was in existence *ab origine mundi.* In the psalms and many of the prophets the universality of salvation has received loud and solemn expression. The calling of *mankind* to a single religion (which is nothing else than leading them to their salvation) can be rightly valued only against the background of the singleness of God. Thus a geographical and a temporal universality can be spoken of, which is essential to the mystery of Christ as Paul sees it. Now since the mystery cults are devoid of any awareness of such a unity of mankind based upon a divine plan, it follows that they also lack any sense of an interior calling to a universal mission to the world.

4. *Concluding judgement.* It cannot be sufficiently emphasised how irreconcilable the difference is between christianity on the one hand, considered as the full revelation of salvation by God, and the mystery religions on the other. *They exist on two different planes.*

When they are placed side by side a certain similarity is apparent between the goals at which they are respectively aimed; that is their ultimate religious aspirations. But the question always comes back to the means which are available to either movement for the attainment of its goal. This in turn depends on the resources available to each of the religious movements being compared. Let us take christianity first. First it has an assurance, imparted to it in the course of the Old Testament history of revelation, that the goal will one day be attained. Secondly, it is also assured that all preparations have been made, all the foundations have been laid (ie, the objective deed of salvation has been performed by Christ; atonement has been made by him on behalf of all mankind, and the possibility of achieving justification in God's eyes has been extended to all). Thirdly, the way has been exactly laid down by which the individual can attain to these graces, imparted to the whole of mankind. The entire edifice of the christian religion rests upon a foundation of historical facts, and the nature of these facts is such as to guarantee that the truth they contain is one and continuous with the truth of God— consider in this connection the role of *alētheia* (↗ truth) in Paul and John, and the *monoi met'apodeixeōs* (= 'they alone with proof') of the Alexandrine. These who, more than any others, found themselves in open confrontation with the spiritual world of paganism, and who sometimes made concessions which were not approved by the church as a whole, have nevertheless been the first to formulate this difference between christianity and all pagan cults in clear and scientific terms. Even in their writings, therefore, the struggle between christianity and paganism does not primarily take the form of a competition in which each strives to show that its doctrines deserve the place of honour. It is rather a question of the authentication of those doctrines. In other words christianity, *in concreto* the church, was able to authenticate its message as historically revealed.

Bibliography: The relevant ancient sources have been published in easily accessible form in the collection of texts by N. Turchi, *Fontes historiae mysteriorum aevi hellenistici*, Rome 1925. For a more detailed justification of the position adopted here, the author would refer to the article which he wrote in collaboration with R. Follet, 'Mystères', *DB(S)* VI (1958), 1–225; see also H. Krämer, 'Zur Wortbedeutung "Mysteria"', *Wort u. Dienst* (Bethel-Jb), 1959, 121–5; R. E. Brown, 'The Semitic Background of the New Testament Mysterion (I)', *Bbl* 39 (1958), 426–48 and 40 (1959), 70–87.

Karl Prümm

Name

Among the Semites a name (*šēm*) is far from being a mere empty word. Rather it means something powerful, something which, the moment it is used, makes the person named present (1 Sam 25:25): to know a person's name means to be able to exercise power over him. Hence the pagan gods keep their names secret (Gen 32:29; Judg 13:6). To pronounce someone's name over something means to put that thing in his power (2 Sam 12:28). The women in Is 4:1 who want to have a name of a man 'called upon' them, want to have him as their lord and master. He who writes Yahweh's name on his hand becomes his servant (Is 44:5). To alter the name means to change the personality (see 2 Kings 23:34; 24:17). The priest lays Yahweh's name upon the people, and Yahweh protects and blesses them (Num 6:27). Yahweh's name is a shelter and a refuge (Prov 18:10), exorcisms are performed in his name (see Acts 19:13; Lk 9:49). Certainly the invocation of Yahweh's name in Israel has no magical import as though a man could force Yahweh to do what he wanted (Job 23:13 is a clear assertion of the contrary, and throughout the Old Testament an awareness of being utterly dependent on Yahweh is apparent—see Gen 18:27). Such a 'sacrilegious' use of the name of God was severely punished (Ex 20:7; Deut 5:11). In the name of Yahweh the Israelite prays, swears, blesses, takes refuge, conquers (Gen 4:26; 13:4; 1 Sam 20:42; 2 Sam 6:18; 2 Kings 2:24 etc). Finally name can express the greatness, fame and ↗ glory of its bearer: for the sake of the name something is expected to happen or must happen etc (Josh 7:9; Ezek 36:22; cf the use of name and glory in parallelism Is 42:8; 59:19; Ps 102:15). More than this, the name can be used as a substitute for Yahweh himself (cp 1 Sam 20:42 with Josh 2:12; 1 Kings 1:17 or 2 Kings 2:24 with 1 Sam 17:43). To profane Yahweh's name (Amos 2:7), hallow it (Is 29:23), love it (Ps 5:11), praise it (Ps 7:18), exalt it (Ps 34:4) means nothing else than to profane, hallow, love, praise, and exalt Yahweh himself. In some passages the name is used as though it were, in some sense, a representative of Yahweh. It manifests Yahweh to men (Is 30:27; Ex 23:20f; Ps 20:1, etc). When Yahweh causes his name to dwell in the temple, etc (Deut

12:5; 26:2 etc), this is to be explained in terms of a particular literary tradition which wants to make it clear that Yahweh is not enclosed in or confined to the temple (1 Kings 8:27); it is merely that he prefers to manifest his presence and his protection in this place.

The *New Testament* is continuous with the Old in the way that it uses 'name'. God's name must be hallowed, that is the holiness of God must be declared everywhere (cf Mt 6:9). This is the first petition that Jesus gives us to repeat after him. Here as in John the 'name of God' designates his essence inasmuch as it is turned towards man with loving attention, the 'revelation aspect' of God (Bietenhard). Jesus proclaims this name, this essence of God to all as that of a loving Father (Jn 17:3, 6, 26). In this name of his the Father will keep the disciples, just as up to that point Jesus has kept them in this name (Jn 17:11ff), ie in that true knowledge of God which Jesus had received from the Father and which he had revealed to those who were his own. In this name they will be one as Jesus and the Father are one (Jn 17:21). The disciples are to be drawn into that sphere of power which consists in union with God. Thus in the commandment to baptise (Mt 28:19), the name of the Father, the Son and the Holy Ghost expresses the divine essence as one. For the baptised person it means that 'by entering into communion with the Son, who is united to God, he receives forgiveness and comes under the influence of the Holy Ghost' (Bietenhard).

The name of Jesus (Mt 1:21 and parallels: Jesus = saviour from sin) expresses his mission and his omnipotence. Salvation in all its aspects is accomplished in his name (1 Cor 6:11; Acts 10:43; 1 Jn 2:12), in no other name is there salvation (Acts 4:12; see also Mt 12:21 = Is 42:4), the whole christian life is subject to it (Col 3:17). To pray in this name (Jn 14:13ff; 15:16; 16:23, 26) means to utter it while praying, or to invoke it in the course of one's prayer. Such prayer is assured of a hearing because he who prays knows that he is united to Jesus the Son of God, whether the prayer is directed to him and relies upon him, or whether it is addressed to the Father with an invocation of the Son. He who calls upon this name will be saved (Rom 10:13; Acts 2:21). He belongs to the community of christians (1 Cor 1:2) upon whom the name of Christ is pronounced because they are Christ's own (Jas 2:7), and are therefore called christians (Acts 11:26; 26:28).

Because salvation is bound up with this name of Jesus, it is proclaimed in preaching (Acts 8:12; 9:15, 27f; Rom 1:5; see 15:20; 3 Jn 7). To believe in his name is equivalent to believing in him (Jn 2:23, cf 1 Jn 5:10). The power of this name to effect salvation in the invisible sphere (of faith) is made manifest simultaneously in the visible sphere (in immediate conjunction with the preaching of salvation) (Lk 10:17; Acts 3:6; 16:18). 'By what power or by what name did you do this?' (Acts 4:7; note that here power and name are parallel concepts). The Jewish authorities would have liked to suppress preaching of this kind, accompanied by evidence of the power of Jesus' name (Acts 4:17f; cf 5:28, 40).

The line between believers and unbelievers is drawn by the attitude they adopt towards this name (1 Cor 12:3). Unbelievers blaspheme his name (Rom 2:24; 1 Tim 6:1; Jas 2:7; Rev 13:6; 16:9), while the faithful proclaim it, praise it, pray in it, believe in it, and suffer for its sake.

Bibliography: H. Bietenhard, *TDNT* v, 242–83; Imschoot I, 207–12; P. van Imschoot, Haag 1194–7; Eichrodt I, 219f; von Rad I, 179–87; E. Lohmeyer, *Das Vaterunser*, Göttingen 1946, chapter 3; Bultmann (Index); J. Schmid, *Matthäus* (*RNT* 1), 1956³, 128f; A. Wikenhauser, *Johannes* (*RNT* 4), 1957²; C. Biber, Allmen 191–3; A. M. Besnard, *Le mystère du nom*, Paris 1962; M. A. Brongers, 'Die Wendung *beschēm jhwh* im AT', *ZAW* 77 (1965), 1–19.

Johannes B. Bauer

Neighbour

A. *In the Old Testament*, *rēʿâh* comes from the root *raʿâh*, 'to associate with' (in LXX it is usually rendered *ho plēsion*). It is used indiscriminately to designate various degrees of association between men, ranging from friendship (Deut 13:6; 2 Sam 13:3; Ps 35:14; etc), love (Jer 3:1, 2; Hos 3:1; etc), comradeship, companionship (Job 30:29; Prov 17:17; see also Ps 45:14; Judg 11:38), and neighbourliness (Prov 3:29; 25:8), to any other kind of association at all. Often it means no more than another person (Prov 6:1, 3; 18:17; 25:8; 26:19; 1 Sam 28:17; etc).

In the law codes (⚹ law) *rēʿâh* occurs in the Book of the Covenant and in the Decalogue with the same range of meaning as has been indicated above. In Deuteronomy and the Holiness Code, on the other hand (see especially the formulation of the commandment

of love in Lev 19:16–18), the terms *rēʿâh* and *ʾāḥ* (⚹ brother) are used to designate those who are bound to each other by the covenant, the members of the community. Hence the commandment to love one's neighbour actually applies only to those who are bound to each other in virtue of the covenant with Yahweh. It is not until Deut 10:19 that this commandment is extended to the aliens (*gēr*) living in the land as well (an idea which is endorsed by the narrower interpretation of Lev 19:16–18 mentioned above), while aliens who are merely passing through the land (*nokrî*) are not included in this.

The interpretation of the law in later judaism narrows down the application of the command once more to Israelites and full proselytes (*gēr hatsedeq*). It is no accident that the Greek tradition of translation chooses *plēsion* as the appropriate rendering. This is a broader, more general expression, reflecting the other tendency in judaism, to advocate the broadest possible application of the commandment of love. It is in this sense that the Greek translation of Sir 13:15 runs: 'Every man loves his neighbour' (instead of 'him who is of like mind', which is what the Hebrew text actually says).

B. *In the New Testament* the word is found firmly established in the command to love one's neighbour (⚹ love). Who is the neighbour here? The use of *plēsion* and *heteros* in parallelism in Rom 13:8–10 indicates how broad a concept *plēsion* was in the New Testament; but above all this is seen in the vivid and concrete definition of neighbour in the parable of the Good Samaritan (Lk 10:29–37): do not ask in an academic sense, 'Who is my neighbour?' In reality he is your neighbour who comes to your help in your hour of need, without asking if you are his neighbour. He is not in the least concerned that you are a stranger to him and do not belong to his circle. In other words the 'neighbour' is not to be thought of as belonging to a definite category of men. Rather he is 'he whom one meets': *plēsion* implies 'near' both in a temporal and in a local sense. Our word *stand-by* strikingly includes both elements in a single expression to 'be there' and to help. What puts the Jewish questioner to shame in the reply he receives in parallel form is the fact that he is not told whom he is to regard as his neighbour, but who will treat him as a neighbour!

It is true that a certain narrowing down of the idea of neighbour so as to mean 'brother in the faith' (↗ brother) is clearly implied in the New Testament (as in Rom 15:2), but this is not explicitly stated either in the New Testament itself or in the apostolic fathers, although in practice the neighbour is often one's fellow christian.

Bibliography: J. Fichtner, *Wort und Dienst* (Bethel Jahrbuch 4, 1955), 23–52; J. Fichtner and H. Greeven, *TDNT* VI, 311–18; H. W. Beyer, *TDNT* II, 702–4; G. J. M. Bartelink, *Lexicologisch-semantische Studie over de taal van de apostolische Vaders*, Utrecht 1952, 144; J. Schmid, *Lukas* (*RNT* 3), 1955, 193–5; W. Michaelis, *Die Gleichnisse Jesu*, Göttingen 1954, 143ff; F. Mussner, *TTZ* 65 (1955), 91–9; S. De Diétrich, Allmen 305–6; H. Braun, *Spätjüd.-häret. und frühchristl. Radikalismus* (2 vols.), Tübingen 1957 (Index); C. Spicq, *Agapè, Analyse des textes* I, Paris 1958 (Appendix); C. Spicq, *Die Nächstenliebe in der Bibel*, Einsiedeln 1961.

Johannes B. Bauer

Oath

As used in the bible an oath is usually a *sworn affirmation* or an *invocation of God* in confirmation of a promise. Thus Rahab the harlot exacts an oath from the spies that when the city is conquered her family will be treated with clemency (Josh 2:12–14). Joseph had to bind himself with an oath to bury his father in the land of Canaan in his own grave (Gen 50:5–7). We find examples of the misuse of promissory oaths in Esther 5:3, 6 and Mk 6:23–6. For the most part oaths in the bible are strikingly similar to vows, so that it is almost possible to speak of a 'vow-oath'. The transition from the sphere of private life to that of official law-court procedure and the administration of justice is fairly easy. Here the purificatory oath is far the most familiar (Gen 14:22–4; Ex 22:7–10; Lev 6:2–5; Num 5:12–31; Josh 22:9–34; Job 31:1–34). It is this that brings the oath into the religious sphere proper. To call upon God or the gods in the cult and to swear an oath are actions which are closely interconnected (Josh 23:7; Is 48:1). God himself swears an oath to the patriarchs (Gen 22:16; Deut 1:8), to David (Ps 132:11–12), to the king referred to in the psalms (Ps 110:4), to Zion personified as a woman (Is 54:9), to the prophets (Is 14:24; 45:23; Amos 4:2). Oaths by his 'great name' (Jer 44:26) and by 'the pride of Jacob' (Amos 8:7) raise a special problem. Again Yahweh swears an oath in his wrath (Ps 95:11). Moreover it is incontestable that the oath is connected with the ↗ curse. There are numerous formulae, gestures and rituals which men use in order to bind either themselves or others by 'conditional curses' (Deut 28; 29; Josh 22:22–9: Neh 5:12–13). The person taking the oath calls down a power which must take effect immediately if the oath is broken. This applies particularly to cases in which a pact is to be concluded (Gen 31:44–53; Josh 21:1–7). God intervenes as arbitrator between the two parties. Gestures which accompany oaths are the raising of the right hand or of both hands Ps 106:26; Dan 12:7), the touching of the genital organs, euphemistically called the thigh (Gen 24:2; 47:29), passing between the severed pieces of a sacrificed animal which has been cut in two (Gen 15:17 ↗ covenant). In this case the animal is representing the fate of him who breaks the pact. Reference to the abuse of oaths are found in the moralising references in Ps 15:4; 24:4. In these and other passages all double-dealing in legal disputes and matters involving justice is severely castigated. According to Jesus ben Sira the practice of taking oaths for trivial reasons must actually have become the order of the day (Sir 23:9–11). It is possible that at that time different oath formulae were considered to have varying degrees of binding force. Thus for instance an oath might be more or less solemnly binding according as it had been sworn by heaven, earth, the temple or some part of the body. In the Old Testament we meet simply the oath by Yahweh. In Song 2:7 and 3:5 the intention is to invoke the gazelles and hinds of the field merely as witnesses; thus an oath is taken in their presence but not 'by' them. A similar idea underlies the etymological meaning of the Hebrew word to 'swear', namely to 'seven'

oneself: from this it is to be understood that the oath was taken in the presence of seven persons or seven animals. The Essenes regarded any form of swearing as such as an act of perjury, and considered the word as of itself more powerful and more effective than the oath. However, according to the Qumran texts and the Damascus document, their actual practice seems to have been somewhat different (*TLZ* [1956], 495–8). At least it is known that an oath had to be taken on entering the sect, and that an oath could only be taken before the judges. In the same way it is valuable to see how far the statements in the New Testament and the practice reflected there agree with each other. Jas 5:12 is clearly intended as an absolute prohibition of all oaths, while Mt 5:33; 14:7; 26:70–74; Lk 1:73; Acts 2:30; Gal 1:20; Heb 6:16; etc corroborate the statements of the Old Testament and *a fortiori* their practical application. Again the saying of Jesus in Mt 5:37 in the form in which it has been handed down raises no objection to the lawfulness of oath-taking. For a double affirmation or a double denial already counted as an oath. It is however possible that the simple affirmation or denial prescribed in Jas 5:12 represents a genuine community tradition of the saying of Jesus.

Bibliography: J. Schneider, *TDNT* v, 458–6´; *Encyclopaedia Judaica* v, 316–32; *Universal Jewish Encyclopaedia* viii, 261–3; F. Horst, 'Der Eid im AT', *ET* 17 (1957), 366–84; Theophilus ab Orbiso, *VD* 29 (1951), 65–76; J. Pedersen, *Der Eid bei den Semiten*, Strasbourg 1914.

Meinrad Stenzel

Obedience

Like the English word *obedience*, derived from the Latin *ob-audire*, both the Hebrew and the Greek words meaning 'to obey' are connected with the words for 'to hear'. To obey means to hearken to the expression of another's will, to respond to it and to comply with it. To obey is to hear and to do (Gen 22:18; Ex 15:26; Deut 5:31–3; Mt 7:21; Mk 3:35; Jn 12:47; Rom 2:13; Jas 1:22–5).

Old Testament religion is essentially a religion of the word that has been and that must be heard, the word to which man must respond by his actions. It is a religion of obedience to the revelation of God in the word of the law and the prophets. Its essential demand is expressed in the sentence: 'Hear, O heavens, and give ear, O earth, for the Lord speaks' (Is 1:2; cf 1:10; Jer 2:4; 7:21–8). God's greatest reproach against his people is expressed in these terms: 'When I spoke to you persistently you did not listen, and when I called you, you did not answer' (Jer 7:13; Hos 9:17). The promulgation of the law in Deuteronomy begins with the words: 'And now O Israel, hear the statutes and the ordinances which I teach you. Observe and follow them' (4:1–6). The father and founder of the chosen people proves himself by 'hearkening' (Gen 12:4; 17:1; 22:2).

The worship of God consists essentially in obedience. 'Does the Lord take delight in burnt offerings and sacrifices? He requires obedience. Behold, to obey is better than sacrifice, and to hearken than the fat of rams' (1 Sam 15:22; cf the account of Saul's rejection 1 Sam 15:10–35; Ps 40:7–9; 50).

The ⇗ covenant which God has made with Israel demands obedience to the covenant statutes (for the covenant with Abraham, Gen 17:9; for the Sinai covenant, Ex 19:5f: 24:7f). Obedience is the condition necessary for the fulfilment of the covenant promises (Ex 15:26; 20:6; 23:22, 25; Lev 20:22ff; Deut 6:1; 5:32f; 8:1; 28:1–14). The obedience required by the covenant is no longer in danger of being withheld once God establishes the new covenant, once God writes his law in men's hearts, giving them the will to obey as a gift (Jer 31:31–4; Ezek 36:25–8; Is 55:3; 59:21; 61:8; Ps 51:12).

The narrative of the fall provides a most impressive example of what the Old Testament conceives of as the essence of ⇗ sin: the disobedience of man to the will (commands) of God, his Lord. The basic reason why even injustice against one's fellow man is a sin is that it involves a deviation from the divine will (Ps 51:6). Man must pass through life by a determined path, which is pointed out to him by the will of God (Ps 1:1). If he deviates from this path by a free decision of his own will he commits sin (1 Sam 15:22ff, 26; Jer 6:16–18: 7:24; Deut 11:26ff).

In the period after the exile the ⇗ law becomes the power that governs all things. Obedience to God becomes obedience to the law. Ethical thinking is dominated by the ideal of legal obedience (2 Macc 7:1–42; Ps 119).

In the *New Testament* Jesus rules his entire life by obedience to his Father. In the temptation he is confronted with the decision of how he is to fulfil his messianic mission. It is from obedience that he decides not upon the way offered to him by Satan but on his

Father's way; he repeatedly refers to some precept of the law in order to express what obedience means to him (Mt 4:1–11; Lk 4:1–13). When Peter wants to prevent him taking the way of suffering, he repulses him as a tempter, and points out that it is not the words of men but the words of God that he has to fulfil (Mk 8:33 parallels). The prayer at Gethsemane shows what depths of suffering his obedience to the will of his Father leads him into (Mt 26:39, 42; Mk 14:36; Lk 22:42).

Conformity with the will of God is his whole life. He praises (*exhomologoumai*, lit. = 'give thanks') the Father for revealing to little ones the news that the rule of God has broken in upon the world, and he pronounces the 'yes' of his assent to the good pleasure of God (Mt 11:25f; Lk 10:21). He finds the will of God expressed in the law and he fulfils it. He takes part in the religious life of the people, richly laden as it is with tradition, and regulated by the law (synagogue service, Mk 1:21 and parallels; 6:2; Lk 4:16; 13:10; pilgrimage festivals, Lk 2:41; Jn 2:13; 5:1; 7:14; 10:22; 12:12; Mk 11:1f; payment of the temple tax, Mt 17:24ff). He recognises the will of God laid down in the law (Mt 5:17). Certainly he is conscious of being sent to disclose the will of God in its original meaning, to explain it with divine authority in cases of doubt, and when necessary to proclaim new requirements of it, as well as how the old ones are to be conclusively fulfilled (the antitheses Mt 5:27–45).

Jesus' life, especially as presented by Luke (Grundmann, *TDNT* II, 22f), is determined by the 'must' of the will of God. It is this that underlies Jesus' actions (Lk 4:43; 13:33; 19:5), and

that leads him on to his passion and his glorification (Lk 9:22 and parallels; 17:25; 24:7, 26); it is based on the will of God as laid down in holy scripture, which Jesus uncompromisingly fulfils (Lk 22:37; 24:44).

In his preaching of the obedience due to God Jesus requires the obedience of a servant (Lk 17:7–10). The message of the kingdom of God implies at once an offer of salvation and a moral demand. For this reason it is not enough merely to hear the message. Deeds are also required. The first condition for entering the kingdom of God is to take the demands of the decalogue fully to heart (Mk 10:17ff), so that the will of God expressed in them may be fulfilled in its deepest and most radical sense as preached by Jesus (cf the antitheses of the sermon on the mount according to Mt 5:21–48; Lk 6:20–49: fulfilment which amounts to total refusal of all concessions to human weakness). The prayer taught by Jesus (the Our Father) shows the direction in which his message leads: that the dominion of God may break in upon the world, that his holy will may be imposed throughout the earth and that all obstacles to his dominion may be overcome (Mt 6:9–13). They are true disciples of Christ who do the will of his Father (Mt 7:21; Mk 3:31–5 and parallels).

The demand that the law shall be obeyed is freed from the formalism with which contemporary judaism has surrounded it. Jesus requires obedience as an attitude of mind and conscience (Mt 15:1–20). What he wants is awareness of how the spirit of the law is to be fulfilled (eg, in the question of the Sabbath Mk 2:27f; 3:4; Lk 14:1). He sums up the manifold precepts of the law in the chief commandment to love God and one's neighbour (Mt 22:34–40; Mk 12:28–34).

In the preaching of the kingdom of God obedience to God becomes obedience to Jesus in whom that kingdom comes. Nature (Mk 4:41), the devils (Mk 1:27), sickness and death itself (↗ miracles) 'hearken' to him. Men too must hearken to him: 'He calls [men] to a personal discipleship. This personal attachment is a new and unprecedented element in the claims of Jesus' (R. Schnackenburg, *God's Rule and Kingdom*, London 1963, 110). Jesus demands complete surrender of one's own will (Mk 8:34–8).

The *pauline* corpus makes a more frequent use of the words meaning to 'hearken' or obey than do the rest of the New Testament writings. However it cannot be deduced from this statistical finding that obedience is 'one of Paul's favourite concepts', deriving from the 'obedience theology' of the rabbis, in which he revelled, and that it has led to a distortion of the teaching of Jesus (the view of E. Stauffer, *Die Botschaft Jesu*, 1959, 18).

For Paul obedience is the key concept for the soteriological work of Jesus. By the incarnation Jesus becomes subject to the law of Moses so that he can free those others who are subject to it (Gal 4:4). Obedience is the meaning of Jesus' life and death (Phil 2:8). The disobedience of Adam brought all that is contrary to salvation into the world. Salvation is founded upon Jesus' act of obedience (Rom 5:19). It is through the obedience of faith that salvation is appropriated (Rom 1:5; 16:26). Faith is obedience to the preach-

ing of the message of salvation (Rom 10:16; 2 Cor 7:15; 2 Thess 1:8). The purpose of the apostolic kerygma is that the gentiles may obey (Rom 15:18), that every thought may be taken captive for the obedience of Christ (2 Cor 10:5). A christian is a man who is obedient to the gospel of our Lord Jesus (2 Thess 1:8), one who hearkens to the truth (Rom 2:8; Gal 5:7), one who glorifies God by his obedience in acknowledging the gospel of Christ (2 Cor 9:13). Obedience to the message of salvation takes the place of obedience to the law of Moses. The life of christians is informed by obedience (Phil 2:12). By the grace of God they are led from obedience to sin, which leads to condemnation, to the obedience which consists in acknowledging the teaching; this obedience arises from the free decision of the will led by the divine spirit (Rom 6:16–17). The christian's life of obedience counts as righteousness and achieves his sanctification (Rom 6:19). Finally it is God who makes good his claim through the Lord Jesus Christ (Rom 6:22; 10:9).

Paul regards the attitude of submission to authority as the true foundation of the house of christianity just as it is the foundation of political life. In the lists of virtues and vices obedience is required from wives to husbands (Eph 5:22; Col 3:18; see also 1 Pet 3:6), from children to their parents (Eph 6:1; Col 3:20ff), from slaves to their masters (Eph 6:5; Col 3:22; Tit 2:9; 1 Pet 2:18). In submitting to authority one should have the Lord in view 'in the fear of Christ' (Eph 5:21f). Such submission is prompted by a reverent awareness that Christ is judge. One should obey the civil authorities

618

on grounds of conscience (Rom 13:1–7; see also Tit 3:1; 1 Pet 2:13–16). Obedience to God takes precedence over obedience to the state (Acts 5:29; 4:19; Tobit 2:8; 1 Macc 2:22).

In expounding the high-priesthood of Christ the *Letter to the Hebrews* relies especially on the obedience of Jesus in his earthly life. The incarnation in its significance for the high-priesthood is regarded as an act of obedience. Since God took no pleasure in the sacrifices and burnt offerings of the Old Testament cult, Christ brings as an offering his readiness to do God's will (10:5–10; Ps 40:8). Obedience in the acceptance of suffering is the way to ↗priesthood according to the order of Melchizedek (a perfect and eternal priesthood) (5:7–10). Chist's offering of himself in sacrifice takes place 'in the eternal spirit', in the Holy Ghost who sets alight the obedience of Jesus (9:14). By this priestly act he brings salvation to those who hearken to him (5:9). If the people are to find a home in the Sabbath rest of God it must be a people that is obedient to the word of God (4:9). The gospel which requires obedience (the word of obedience) will remain with those who hear it and hearken to it by faith. Disobedience will cause them to fail in the attainment of their goal (4:6, 11). Disobedience brings ruin in its train (2:2). Obedience and submission must be shown to the leaders of the church not with sighs but with joy (13:17; see also 1 Thess 5:12; 1 Pet 5:5).

The Lukan infancy narrative of Jesus is to be understood in the light of the spiritual teaching of Gal 4:4 ('born of a woman, born under the law'). The incarnation takes place through the obedience of Mary (1:38).

He is born in Bethlehem in obedience to the command of Augustus (2:1f). All the requirements of the law which affect the firstborn child who is a male are scrupulously fulfilled (circumcision, presentation, redemption offering, 2:21ff). From his youth upwards Jesus is obedient to the pious custom of making pilgrimage to the temple (2:41–50); he is obedient to his parents (2:51), and still more to his Father in heaven (2:49).

John has presented Jesus as a source of revelation. He has done this in two ways. First he expresses it in terms which amount to an assertion that Jesus has dignity and authority equal to that of God. God has given all things into his hand, so that he has the same power as God himself to dispose of them (3:35; 10:28; 13:3; 17:2ff); he has given it to the Son to have life in himself, as the Father has life in himself (5:26). As the Father raises the dead to life, so too the Son brings to life whoever he will (5:21). The Father has handed over to him all judgement (5:22). Jesus can claim honour equal to that of the Father. The second way in which John presents Jesus as a source of revelation appears in such passages as that in which Jesus explains that he has not come down from heaven to do his own will but the will of him who sent him (6:38). He works in obedience to the Father's command (10:18; 12:49; 14:31; 15:10). His meat is to do the will of him who sent him, and to perfect his work (4:34). His work is to accomplish the task laid upon him by the Father (5:36; 9:4; 10:32, 37; 17:4). His last word is 'It is accomplished' (19:30). The same obedience is expressed in negative formulae: Jesus has come not by his own authority but as one sent by the Father (7:28f; 8:42). He acts (5:19f; 8:28) and speaks (7:17; 12:49; 14:10, 24; 17:8) only as the Father directs him, not of himself. The greatness of Christ lies in this obedience of his; for, because he does not speak of himself, God speaks in him (3:34). He who sees him thereby sees the Father (14:9). His disciples attain to salvation when they fulfil the Father's commands in obedience (14:15, 23).

Obedience is the basic attitude inculcated by the *First Letter of Peter*. Christians are 'children of obedience' (1:14; cf 1:2, 22). Slaves must be subject to their masters (2:18), wives to their husbands (3:1ff), the younger members of the community to the elders (5:5), all christians to those in authority (2:13f). Clearly a false concept of freedom had sprung up, a certain libertinism. True to the word of Christ, he who is in command must serve (Mk 10:42, 45). Those who have authority must not rely upon obedience, but must strive to win respect by their attitude of considerate love. Husbands are forcibly admonished to live with their wives in understanding and reverence (3:7). Priests must be an example to the community (5:3).

Obedience occupies a key position in the history of God's salvation. Obedience to revealed truth is not compulsory, but is an expression of the freedom of the children of God, devotion to God, the life of one who has been made subject to God's dominion and permeated with divine life.

Bibliography: F. Kittel, *TDNT* I, 216f; E. Kalt, *BRL*, 618–24; F. K. Schumann, *RGG* II³, 1265; L. Nieder, *LTK* IV², 601f; K. H. Schelkle, *Die Passion Jesu in der Verkündigung des NT*, 1949,

passim; S. Gross, 'Der Gehorsam Christi', *GL* 29 (1956), 2–11.

Alois Stöger

Original sin

A. *Old Testament*. All that the account of the fall in Gen 2:8–3:24 explicitly asserts is that the first sin brought upon *the first parents themselves* the loss of familiar intercourse with God (3:23), toil and suffering (3:16–19), and also death (2:17; 3:3, 19, 22). Since, however, the narrative is undeniably aetiological in character, it does say, at least indirectly, that if since the fall men have found themselves in the same unhappy situation as their first parents, the reason for this is to be traced back to the first sin. Admittedly in the Hebrew literature of the Old Testament the account in Genesis has never been explained in this sense in so many words. The first clear evidence for the doctrine of *death as the outcome of original sin*, ie, the idea that the physical death to which all men are subject is a consequence of the sin of paradise, is to be found in Sir 25:24: 'From the woman came the beginning of sin, and because of her we must all die'. The idea is taken up again in Wis 2:23f: 'For God created man incorruptible, and to the image of his own likeness he made him. But by the envy of the devil death came into the world, and they who belong to him will experience it'. Since v 24 undoubtedly refers back to Gen 3 (vv 1–13), death is traced back to the sin of the first human couple. But 'death' here is probably not physical death alone, but also the spiritual and eternal death, repudiation by God (see 1:12,

13, 16). However a specific statement that the sin of the first parents is transmitted to each of their descendants—that is, the idea of original sin—is nowhere to be found. The Old Testament does indeed emphasise in numerous passages the universality of sinfulness or guilt (see Gen 6:5; 8:21; Job 4:17; 14:4; 15:14; 25:4; 1 Kings 8:46; Is 64:5; Eccles 7:20; Sir 8:5; Prov 20:9; Ps 130:3; 143:2). But in such passages it is obvious that what the writers have in the forefront of their minds is simply the fact of experience that all men commit personal sins. This must be recognised even though the statements in question are so frequent and so emphatic that they might give the impression of an underlying awareness of a state of sin permeating the whole of humanity down to each individual member of it, from which the actual sins spring up as from a hot-bed. Certain passages even appear to speak of a sinfulness that is innate: thus, Gen 8:21: 'The imagination of man's heart is evil from his youth'; Job 14:4: 'Who can bring a clean thing out of an unclean? There is not one'; Ps 51:5: 'Behold I was brought forth in iniquity, and in sin did my mother conceive me'. But this innate sinfulness is to be understood rather as an innate proneness to sin than as an inherited state of sinfulness; and, most important of all, it is not connected with the fall of the first parents as its *fons et origo*.

B. *The extra-canonical Jewish literature* contains a whole series of instances of the idea of death as an inherited penalty. In Enoch (Slav) 30:17 we find only a remote echo of it: Yahweh made Adam a wife 'in order that through his wife death might come upon him'. In the *Vita Adae et Evae* the death of Eve (§ 18) and of Adam (§ 26) is represented as a consequence of the fall. But in the Greek recension which goes by the name of the *Apocalypse of Moses* it is the death of the entire human race that is regarded as a result of this, § 14: 'Then Adam said to Eve: What have you done to us? For you have brought great anger upon us, namely death which (now) rules our entire race' The example in 4 Ezra 3:7 is no less clear: After Adam had broken the commandment of God, 'Thou didst straightway ordain death for him and his descendants alike'. The doctrine of death as an inherited penalty occurs several times in the Syrian *Apocalypse of Baruch*. Thus in 17:3: Adam 'brought in death and shortened the years of those who were begotten by him'; 23:4: With the sin of Adam 'death was decreed upon all who were born'; 54:15: 'Adam sinned first and brought a premature death upon all'; 56:6: 'As soon as he had sinned, sudden death ensued'. The instances of this idea in the rabbinical literature are numerous. Thus a saying of Rabbi Jehuda (circa AD 150) runs: 'You are children of the first man, who has brought death as a punishment upon you and upon all his descendants who come after him until the end of all generations' (Siphre Deut. 32, § 323), further instances in SB III, 227f, and F. Heimes, *Der jüdische Erbsündenbegriff im Zeitalter der Tannaiten und Amoräer*, Münster 1920, 13–59. Admittedly side by side with these examples we also find sayings of the rabbis which, in order to avoid exposing the doctrine of man's personal responsibility to danger, explain men's personal sins as the cause of their death (instances in SB III, 228f).

Apart from death, evil in general, in all the manifold forms in which it occurs, is also traced back to the first parents. Their fall from grace brought physical pain upon Eve and her descendants (*Vita Adae et Evae* 34), 'Transgression and sin upon our whole race', 'Every evil' (*ibid* 44); 'the whole great multitude came down upon him who had been corrupted' (Syr ApocBar 48:43); 'The sublimity of humanity was debased, and virtue withered up' (*ibid* 56:6). Probably too it is evil in general—and not sin specifically—that the author of 4 Ezr 7:118 has in mind: 'O Adam what hast thou done? When thou didst sin thy fall came not only upon thee but also upon us, thy descendants'. An unambiguous witness to the doctrine of original sin, that is to the idea that sin was in some way inherited from the first parents by their descendants, is lacking in this literature also. Even Eve's lamentation in ApocMos 32: 'All sin has entered creation through me' (*pasa hamartia di'emou gegonen en tē[i] ktisei*) is not a sure example, for it may simply have in mind the relationship between the origin and the further development of sin, and in any case the passage has possibly already been subjected to christian editing. Flavius Josephus explains that selfishness is a natural disposition of mankind (*Antiq.* III, 190: *phusei pantas einai philautous*; see also v, 215), Philo interprets sinfulness in general in the same way (*De Vita Mosis* II, 147: *panti genētō[i] ... sumphues to hamartanein*; similarly, *De sacrif. Abelis et Caini* 15; *De spec. leg.* I, 252). Again, in one of the Qumran documents we find

the assertion: 'Man lives in sin from the womb of his mother', and the rabbis speak of an evil impulse which is innate in man (SB IV, 466–83). In all these examples what the writers have in mind is not a state of sin or of guilt in which man finds himself prior to any personal sin on his part, but rather his propensity to sin; above all, this natural disposition is not regarded as deriving from the sin of the first parents.

C. *New Testament.* In the gospels we find only a few remote allusions to the fall. The description of the devil as 'a murderer from the beginning' (Jn 8:44) clearly refers to the tradition that the devil brought *death* upon mankind by leading Eve astray. It seems to follow from Mk 10:5–8 parallels that man as he left the hand of God was still free from 'hardness of heart', and that it was only subsequently—and that surely can only imply through the fall—that he incurred this defect. This should be compared with Jn 3:5f, which could be taken as asserting that man when not renewed by the Spirit finds himself in a state of uncleanness that is innate. Neither here nor elsewhere in the gospels, however, is any innate stain of this kind unambiguously traced back to the fall of the first parents. But on the other hand neither is the idea of an innate state of sinfulness excluded, as might be thought from Mk 10:14f and parallels. For this saying of the Lord's is not based upon any idea of freedom from sin in infancy. The most significant statements are to be found in Paul. He teaches in unambiguous terms the doctrine of *death as an inherited penalty.* Thus in I Cor 15:21f: 'For as by a man (*di' anthrōpou*) came death, by a man has come also the resurrection of the dead. For as in Adam (*en tō[i] Adam*) all die, so also in Christ shall all be made alive'. In other words, the reason for the fact that all men die is to be found in Adam. It is apparent from Rom 5:12 that this amounts to a reference to Adam's fall. In this latter passage Paul likewise bases his argument on the Adam/Christ parallel: 'Therefore as sin came into the world through one man and death through sin, and so death spread to all men because all men sinned—'. The consequence of Adam's sin was that death entered the world and henceforward laid hold of all men. It is not merely death as an inherited penalty that Paul teaches, however, but also the doctrine of *original sin* (Trent: DS 1510-15 [=DB 787-92]). This idea appears already to be presupposed in 1 Cor 15:22, although there the connection of all men with Adam by reason of whom all must die is not explained in greater detail, still what Paul has in mind is doubtless that all men share in the punishment of Adam, and, since punishment presupposes guilt, evidently they all also share in Adam's guilt. He expresses himself more clearly in Rom 5. Admittedly the passage in 5:12d, earlier regarded as the classical passage for the church's doctrine of original sin, is disputed. The idea that the words *in quo* in the Vulgate refer to *homo* (or also to *peccatum*) was upheld by the Latin interpreters up to Erasmus exclusively. This view is certainly untenable. But even if the words *eph' hō(i)* are understood not as a relative clause ('on which') but as a conjunction ('on the basis of the fact that', 'because'), an approach which modern exegesis is

almost unanimous in upholding (on this, see also J. Gross, *Byz. Zschr.* 52 [1959], 316f), several interpretations are still possible. Most catholic interpreters take *hēmarton* ('they sinned') as referring not to the personal and actual sins of men but to the sin of Adam in which, in a mysterious manner, all Adam's children share. For this so-called collective interpretation the following arguments are adduced: 1. As Adam by his sin brought death upon the whole of mankind, so Christ, by his work of redemption, brings justification and life to all. Now if the vital point in this statement is taken to be that the sin of *one man*, Adam, incurred death for all, then *hēmarton* must be taken as referring to the *one* sin, and must mean: 'All have become sinful through the sin of Adam'. 2. In 5:13f it is stated that the sins of men before Moses are not reckoned as crimes worthy of death in the same sense as Adam's sin, because in this period before the law there is no penal code imposing the death penalty for specific crimes. In spite of this, so the argument goes, those men also died. Thus the physical death of the men before Moses—Paul does not explicitly draw this conclusion but comes very close to it—cannot be ascribed to their individual sins, but must have its origin in the guilt inherited from Adam. 3. It was possible for Paul to assert with perfect justice that all men died, but on the other hand it was not open to him to assert that all men committed personal sins. The statement in 5:12d can be applied to children who have died in infancy only if *hēmarton* is taken in a collective sense.

Certain more recent catholic exegetes,

however, basing themselves especially upon Rom 3:23 (*pantes gar hēmarton* = 'for all have sinned') and the exegesis of the Greek fathers, have championed the view that what Paul has in mind when he uses the word *hēmarton* in 5:12 is actual sins, and that he is not thinking of infants here any more than in 3:23. They regard Rom 5:12d as a digression, and explain it as arising from the apostle's endeavour to maintain the responsibility of the individual, or else they argue that Paul wishes here to emphasise that men by their personal sins ratify, as it were, the situation of guilt deriving from Adam. In this case the verse in question does not represent an unambiguous instance of the idea of Adam's sin being transmitted to all men, even if 'death' is taken in the broadest possible sense (Lyonnet: *abalienatio a Deo*). Yet there is a clear expression of this idea to be found in v 19: 'For as by one man's disobedience many were made sinners (*katestathēsan*), so by one man's obedience many will be made righteous'. The parallelism here between type and antitype is underlined by the use of the verb *kathistasthai*. (On the meaning of this, see Freundorfer, 260–63 and Oepke, *TDNT* III, 445) in both the first and second clauses. From this parallelism it follows that when it is said that the many (ie, all men) have become sinful through Adam's disobedience, this is to be understood as having taken place, in the last analysis, just as independently of the individual acts of men as the justification of men by the obedience of Christ. Just as the justification of men through Christ has no basis in their personal achievements, so too the sinfulness envisaged here as having been incurred by men through Adam has no basis in their personal sins. We may conclude, therefore, that in this passage Paul really is speaking of a state of sinfulness to which all men are subject, and which has been caused by the sin of Adam. All the children of Adam are, in a mysterious manner, which Paul makes no attempt to examine more closely either here or elsewhere, sharers in the sin of their first parent. It is evident that Paul is also thinking of this sinfulness which, prior to any personal sin on their part, is present in all men since Adam's fall and through that fall in Eph 2:3: 'We were by nature (*phusei*) children of wrath like the rest of mankind' (see H. Schlier, *Der Brief an die Epheser*, Düsseldorf 1957, 107).

Bibliography: J. Freundorfer, *Erbsünde u. Erbtod beim Apostel Paulus*, Münster 1927; N. P. Williams, *The Ideas of the Fall and of Original Sin*, London 1927; J.-M. Vosté, *Studia Paulina*, Rome 1928, 69–86; J. H. Oemmelen, *Zur dogmatischen Auswertung vom Röm 5:12–14*, Münster 1930; M. Jugie, *Dict. de la Théol. cath.* XII, Paris 1933, 275–317; W. G. Kümmel, *Das Bild des Menschen im NT*, Zürich 1948, 36–9; T. Barrosse, 'Death and Sin in St Paul's Epistle to the Romans', *CBQ* 15 (1953), 438–58; P. Seidensticker, 'Taufe und Tod. Das Problem des leiblichen Todes im Römerbrief', *Studii Biblici Franciscani (Liber Annuus* IV), 1953/4, 117–83; M. Delcor, 'L'homme et le péché dans les documents de Qumran' (probably not yet published. See *Bbl* 36 [1955], 467 *n.* 3); S. Lyonnet, *Quaestiones in Epistolam ad Romanos. Prima series*, Rome 1955, 182–243; S. Lyonnet, 'Le sens de *eph' hō*(*i*) en Rom 5:12 et l'exégèse des Pères grecs', *Bbl* 36 (1955), 436–56; S. Lyonnet, 'Le péché originel et l'exégèse de Rom 5:12–14', *RSR* 44 (1956), 63–84; S. Lyonnet, 'Le sens de *peirazein* en Sap 2:24 et la doctrine du péché originel', *Bbl* 39 (1958), 27–33; P. de Haes, 'Doctrina S. Scripturae de peccato originali', *Collect. Mechlinensia* 41 (1956), 474–85; O. Kuss, *Der Römerbrief*, Regensburg 1957, 224–75; F. Lafont, 'Sur l'interprétation de Romains 5:15–21', *RSR* 45 (1957), 481–513; J. Mehlmann, *Natura Filii irae. Historia interpretationis Eph 2:3 eiusque cum doctrina de Peccato Originali nexus*, Rome 1957; I. Romanides, *To Propatorikon Hamartēma*, Athens 1957; A.-M. Dubarle, *Le péché originel dans l'Ecriture*, Paris 1958; J. M. Gonzáles-Ruiz, 'El pecado original según San Pablo', *Estudios Biblicos* 17 (1958), 147–58; J. Scharbert, *Solidarität in Segen u. Fluch im AT u. in seiner Umwelt* I, Bonn 1958, 264–6; W. Barclay, 'Rom 5:12–21', *Expository Times* 70 (1958/9), 132–5 and 172–5; K. Barth, *Christ et Adam d'après Rom 5*, Geneva 1959; R. Bultmann, 'Christus nach Rom 5', *ZNW* 50 (1959), 145–65; L. Ligier, *Péché d'Adam et Péché du monde*, Paris 1960; S. Lyonnet, 'Le péché originel en Rom 5:12', *Bbl* 41 (1960), 325–55; F. Spadafora, 'Rom 5:12', *Divinitas* 3 (1960), 289–98; B. Willaert, 'Aantekeningen bij de erfzondeleer', *Coll. Brug. et Gandavenses* 6 (1960), 498–519; W. B. Neenan, 'The Doctrine of Original Sin in Scripture', *ITQ* 28 (1961), 54–64; J. Gross, *Entstehungsgeschichte des Erbsündendogmas*, Munich-Basle 1961; F. J. Thonnard, 'Sur le péché en S. Augustin', *Revue des Etudes Augustiniennes* 7 (1961), 250f; A. Vanneste, 'S. Paul et la doctrine augustinienne du péché originel', *Stud. Paulin. Congressus* II, Rome 1963, 513–22; P. Schoonenberg, *Man and Sin: A Theological View*, London and South Bend (Ind.) 1965, 98–191; S. Lyonnet, *DB(S)* VII/38, 486–567; U. Vanni, 'Rom 5:12–14', *Rivist. bibl. ital.* 11 (1963), 337–66; A. Stenzel, 'Zur Geschichte des Erbsündedogmas', *Scholastik* 39 (1964), 407–12; H. Haag, *Is Original Sin in Scripture?* New York 1968; *A. Hulsbosch, *God's Creation: Creation, Sin, and Redemption in an Evolving World*, London 1965, 15–57; *A. Cunningham, *Adam*, London 1968.

Joseph Blinzler

Parable

In all languages we encounter comparative figures of speech involving the use of images. Images provide the most agreeable form of expression in popular wisdom, and elevated language without comparisons is unthinkable.

As far back as the rhetoric of Greece and Rome, scholars were preoccupied with the problem of how to comprehend and to classify the various possible forms of linguistic comparison. Since then it has been customary to draw an initial distinction between the image or simple simile (in which image and object compared are set side by side: Achilles fights like a lion) and the metaphor (the image takes the place of the object compared: the lion [=Achilles] fights). In the same way the similitude or the parable (a comparison extended to a whole sentence or a whole narrative) is distinguished from allegory (a series of metaphors).

A. *In the Old Testament*. The word *parabolē* is used very frequently in LXX. Apart from certain isolated exceptions it serves as a rendering of the Hebrew *māšāl*, and thus deviates from Greek linguistic usage elsewhere in acquiring the broad range of meaning attached to *māšāl*. *Māšāl* stands first and foremost for the proverb, the popular proverb or household word (cf 1 Sam 10:12; 24:13), and particularly the mocking saying (to become a *māšāl* = to become an object of mockery; see 1 Kings 9:7), and also the wisdom proverb (see 1 Kings 4:32), which can develop into a whole wisdom speech (Job 27:1; 29:1). Again the oracle of blessing imparted by Yahweh to Balaam is called *māšāl/parabolē* (Num 23 and 24). The same is true of the tasks laid by God upon Ezekiel, for these have obscure allegorical meanings which are hard to interpret (Ezek 17:2; 21:5; 24:3). In the same way *māšāl/parabolē* is an extremely favoured term among the apocalyptic writers who use it to designate a type of prophecy which takes the form of mysterious word-pictures (especially Enoch). Similitudes properly so called are never referred to as *māšāl/parabolē* in the Old Testament. It must be added, however, that very few are found anywhere in the Old Testament.

B. *In the New Testament*. Apart from Heb 9:9; 11:19 the word *parabolē* occurs only in the synoptics. Here it has a wide range of meaning similar to that of *māšāl/parabolē* in the Old Testament, and it can mean a proverb (Lk 4:23) or an occult saying (Mt 15:15; Mk 7:17). But contrary to Old Testament usage it is employed above all to designate the numerous similitudes which occur in the teaching of Jesus. John does not use the word *parabolē* at all. But the literary form elsewhere so designated is found in his writing, though admittedly to a significantly smaller extent. In addition to isolated images and similes he has three genuine similitudes: the two shepherd similitudes, 10:1–5 and 11–13, and the similitude of the woman in travail, 16:21. Above all he has the 'I am' passages. Admittedly these are not word-pictures in the true sense, but they do show how for John the entire earthly sphere is made up of images and figures and is in this respect the antithesis of the reality of the divine sphere.

The synoptics, on the other hand, quite apart from the numerous similes and metaphors which they contain, have handed down to us a whole range of similitudes taught by Jesus. Since A. Jülicher it has been customary to divide these into three groups:

1. *Similitudes proper:* the mustard-seed (Mk 4:30–32), the seed growing by itself (Mk 4:26–9), the budding fig-tree (Mk 13:28f), the door-keeper (Mk 13:34–7), going before the judge (Mt 5:25f), the children at play (Mt 11:16–19), the leaven (Mt 13:33) the

treasure in the field (Mt 13:44), the pearl (Mt 13:45f), the seine-net (Mt 13:47–50), the lost sheep (Mt 18:12–14), the burglar (Mt 24:43f), the faithful and unfaithful servants (Mt 24:45–51), the choice of places at the feast (Lk 14:7–11), the tower-builder and the king contemplating a campaign (Lk 14:28–32), the drachma (Lk 15:8–10), the servant's reward (Lk 17:7–10). The imagery in these similitudes is drawn from customs the meaning of which would be obvious to everyone. These are usually related in the present. The compelling clarity of the image illumines the truth which is to be explained.

2. *Parables in the true sense:* the seed that falls upon different kinds of ground (Mk 4:3–8), the wicked vine-growers (Mk 12:1–12), the tares among the wheat (Mt 13:24–30), the unmerciful servant (Mt 18:23–35), the equal reward for unequal amounts of work (Mt 20:1–16), the sons who were unlike each other (Mt 21:28–32), the supper (Mt 22:1–10), the guest without a wedding-garment (Mt 22:11–14), the ten virgins (Mt 25:1–13), the talents entrusted to the servants (Mt 25:14–30), the two debtors (Lk 7:41–3), the friend asking for help (Lk 11:5–8), the barren fig-tree (Lk 13:6–9), the prodigal son (Lk 15:11–32), the unjust steward (Lk 16:1–8), the unjust judge (Lk 18:1–8). The subject of the comparison here is not some obvious and generally accepted custom but something that was done by someone once (in the past). In this case improbable features may occur at any point. In most cases these even have a special meaning.

3. *Examples in narrative form:* the good Samaritan (Lk 10:30–37), the rich fool

(Lk 12:16–21), the rich man (Dives) and the poor Lazarus (Lk 16:19–31), the pharisee and the publican (Lk 18:9–14). The example in narrative form is essentially different from the similitude and the parable. It is meant to hold up a mirror to the hearers, and so to stir them into an examination of their religious and moral behaviour.

With regard to *the meaning of the synoptic similitudes* it is especially noteworthy that not one of the similitudes of Jesus which have been handed down is a pure allegory. Certainly we do find similitudes with allegorical features. This raises the question, especially in those cases in which an interpretation has been appended to the similitude, of whether these allegorical elements do not represent a subsequent expansion of the similitudes as told by Jesus. This problem can best be illustrated by taking as an example the parable of the seed which falls on different kinds of ground (Mk 4:1–9). The numerous semitisms, as well as the method of sowing seed described, which is typical of Palestine, tell us that here, as also in the other synoptic similitudes, what we have to deal with is 'a fragment of the original rock of tradition' (J. Jeremias, 11). A farmer sows his field. This has lain uncultivated since the last harvest and has only been softened by rain. The path which has been trodden hard has not yet been ploughed up. The thorny scrub grows rampant. The innumerable stones have only a very light covering of earth. In spite of these unfavourable conditions some of the seed does take root and brings a rich yield. When we compare this similitude with the rest of the similitudes about sowing (the seed growing by itself, Mk

4:26–9; the mustard seed, Mk 4:30–32; the tares among the wheat, Mt 13:24–30) and with the similitude of the leaven (Mt 13:33), the point of the comparison in the similitude with which we are concerned is not difficult to see. It lies at the end. However small its beginnings may be (mustard-seed, leaven), however many obstacles and preliminary failures it may have to overcome (tares, barren soil), still the kingdom of God is in the end achieved. The interpretation appended to the parable (Mk 4:13–20 parallels) does not attempt to answer the question 'What is the *tertium comparationis?*' It draws no judgement from the imagery which it can then apply so as to illumine the truth which that imagery represents, although this is what is required for the true understanding of a similitude. In this method of interpretation the parable is regarded rather as an allegory, and an attempt is made as it were to translate it trait by trait from mysterious figurative speech into intelligible language. 'The sower sows the word. And these are the ones along the path . . .' (Mk 4:14f). The unevennesses in this interpretation show in the clearest possible way that it cannot be a wholly accurate representation of the intention of the original speaker. The interpretation placed upon the parable by the early christians arrives at a quite new conclusion, one which corresponds to the altered situation of the primitive church in which the gospel was preached ('a second *Sitz-im-Leben*'). What was originally an eschatological parable is turned into an allegory in which the main concerns are psychological and parenetic: 'It applies to you!' The similitude of the tares among the wheat

(Mt 13:36–43) acquires a similar interpretation. Thus the attempt to interpret similitudes allegorically can be traced to the period of the early christian church. At a later period this method of interpreting similitudes completely blocked the way back to the original meaning of the similitudes and parables. If we want to realise and to explain the original teaching contained in the similitudes of Jesus we must make a conscious effort to guard ourselves against allegorisation. This is not, of course, to deny that isolated allegorical traits did occur in the similitudes even as they were spoken by Jesus. But it must be upheld as a principle that 'To treat something as allegory merely because it could perhaps be so is arbitrary. Only that which cannot possibly be taken in its literal sense is to be treated as allegorical. However full of imagery a passage may appear, so long as it is capable of another interpretation than the allegorical one, so long does the advantage lie with that other interpretation' (A. Jülicher, 68).

The purpose of a similitude is to make comprehensible by the use of images drawn from familiar surroundings abstract truths that are difficult to grasp. This applies to the numerous similitudes and parables of Jesus. They are intended to convey revealed truth in comprehensible form. That this is the reason why Jesus taught in parables is expressly stated in Mk 4:33: 'With many such parables he spoke the word to them, as they were able to hear it'. However this is not to deny that those who lacked the necessary predisposition of good will would naturally find it easier to shut their ears to truth presented in parable form. Nevertheless

the awe-inspiring saying in Mk 4:11f cannot be in its original historical context and cannot be a statement of the reason why Jesus spoke in similitudes either. It must rather be intended to underline the fact that 'The revelation of this mystery (= the mystery of Jesus's messiahship) is to be understood as an act of grace proceeding from the free sovereignty of God' (J. Schmid, *Markus*, 94). Admittedly many of the synoptic parables are obscure to us of today. The reason for this, however, is not the form in which they were originally preached by Jesus but rather the fact that today we know these images only in a form in which they have been uprooted from their original context.

Bibliography: A. Jülicher, *Die Gleichnisreden Jesu* (2 vols), 1899, reprinted 1910; P. Fiebig, *Altjüd. Gleichnisse und die Gleichnisse Jesu*, 1904; P. Fiebig, *Die Gleichnisse Jesu im Lichte der rabb. Gleichnisse des ntl. Zeitalters*, 1912; O. Eissfeldt, *Der Maschal im AT*, 1913; A. Feldmann, *The Parables and Similes of the Rabbis*, 1927[2]; D. B. M. Smith, *The Parables of the Synoptic Gospels*, 1937; E. Schweitzer, *Ego eimi*, 1939; G. C. Morgan, *The Parables and Metaphors of Our Lord*, 1943; C. H. Dodd, *The Parables of the Kingdom*, 1946[9]; M. Hermaniuk, *Les paraboles évangéliques*, 1947; D. Buzy, *Les paraboles*, 1948[10]; M. Meinertz, *Die Gleichnisse Jesu*, 1948[4]; A. Wikenhauser, *Das Evangelium nach Johannes*, 1948, 111f; J. Pirot, *Paraboles et allégories évangéliques*, 1949; F. Hauck, *TDNT* v, 744–61; F. Mussner, 'Gleichnisauslegung und Heilsgeschichte. Dargetan am Gleichnis von der selbstwachsenden Saat (Mk 4:26–9)', *TTZ* 64 (1955), 257–66; J. A. T. Robinson, 'The Parable of Jn 10:1–5', *ZNW* 46 (1955), 233–40; J. Jeremias, *The Parables of Jesus*, London 1963[2]; W. Michaelis, *Die Gleichnisse Jesu*, 1956; R. Bultmann, *History of the Synoptic Tradition*, London 1963, 166–205; G. Fohrer and N. A. Dahl, *RGG* II[2] (1958), 1615–19; J. Schmid, *Das Evangelium nach Markus*, 1958[4], 87–100; M. Dibelius, *Die Formgeschichte des Evangeliums*, 1959[3], 149–258; J. Schmid, *LTK* IV[2] (1960), 958–60; F. Mussner, *Die Botschaft der Gleichnisse Jesu*, 1960; J. Herz, 'Die Gleichnisse der Ev Mt, Mk u.

Lk', *Bekenntnis zur Kirche*, 1960, 52–94;
E. Linnemann, *Gleichnisse Jesu*, 1961; H.
Schürmann, 'Die Botschaft der Gleichnisse
Jesu', *Bibel und Leben* 2 (1961), 92–105, 171–4,
and 254–61; H. Kahlefeld, *Gleichnisse und
Lehrstücke im Evangelium*, 1963.

Elmar M. Kredel

Paradise

A. *Old Testament.* 1. *Terminology.* Both
the Greek word *paradeisos* of LXX, from
which the Latin *paradisus* and the
English *paradise* derive, and the Hebrew
pardēs are loan-words from the Persian
pairi-daeza, meaning an enclosed garden. The Hebrew *pardēs* occurs only
three times in the Old Testament, and
then with the purely profane meaning
of 'garden' or 'park' (Song 4:13;
Eccles 2:5; Neh 2:8). In LXX, on the
other hand, *paradeisos* is used far more
often and in other passages besides
these three. In most instances it is a
translation of the Hebrew *gan* (Num
24:6; 2 Chron 33:20; Jer 39:4) or
gannâh (Is 1:30), meaning 'garden'.
We also find it with this meaning
in Sir 24:30 and in the story of
Susannah (twelve times). Gen 2 and
3 treat of a particular garden. Here
paradeisos, like the Hebrew *gan*, designates what we understand by 'paradise'
in English, namely, the garden which
God designed for the first men (Gen
2:8ff, 16; 3:1ff, 8, 10). In 2:8 the
position of this garden is described in
greater detail: it lies 'in *ʾeden* (LXX:
en Edem)', somewhere 'in the east'.
Eden, then, is a geographical proper
name for a particular district. The
Hebrew text then speaks several times
more of *gan ʾeden*, that is, of the 'garden
of Eden' (2:15; 3:23f), whereas LXX

takes *ʾeden* no longer as a proper name,
but as a noun derived from the root
ʾādan (= to be pleasant, delightful), and
translates it by *truphē* (= bliss). In this
way the Hebrew *gan ʾeden* ('garden of
Eden') becomes in Greek *paradeisos tēs
truphēs* ('garden of bliss'), and both
modes of expression have influenced a
series of other passages in the bible.
Because paradise was a garden planned
by God it could be spoken of as *gan
elohim* or *gan Jhwi* (= *paradeisos tou
theou* or *paradeisos tou kuriou*), that is, as
'garden of God' or 'garden of Yahweh
(the Lord)' (Gen 13:10; Is 51:3; Ezek
28:13; 31:8). We again meet the
phrase *gan ʾeden* and its Greek equivalent
paradeisos tēs truphēs in Joel 2:3. But
instead of 'garden of Eden' it was
possible to say, more briefly, 'Eden'
(or, in Greek, *truphē*): thus we have
'trees of Eden' = *xula tēs truphēs* (Ezek
31:16, 18), and in Ezek 31:9 this is
even expressed pleonastically as 'the
trees of Eden . . . that were in the
garden of God'. LXX extends this
pleonastic phrase still further: *ta xula
tou paradeisou tēs truphēs tou theou* (lit. =
'the trees of the garden of the bliss of
God'). Since paradise was endowed by
God's blessing with an especially rich
abundance of fruits, any fruitful garden
could be called by analogy 'a blessed
Eden' (*ʾeden berākâh* = *paradeisos eulogias*,
Sir 40:17, 27). Only in this passage has
the Septuagint made Eden equivalent
to *paradeisos*. Elsewhere it translates it
by *truphē*. The idea of paradise is not,
of course, covered in its full extent by
these terms.

2. *The paradise story in Gen 2:4–3:24.*
Individual motifs of the paradise story
in the bible are occasionally found in
the myths of ancient Near-Eastern

peoples (the myth of Adapa, the Epic of Gilgamesh). Such are: the tree of life, the loss of eternal life (but not through a sinful fall), men conversing confidently with the Deity, inconceivable fruitfulness, and unbroken peace in the primaeval age. But while recognising this fact it must still be said that considered as a literary unity the paradise story in the bible is wholly without counterpart in the literature of the Ancient Near East. In this story we may select the following motifs as essential: a. God first creates all that is necessary for the life of man by fashioning and ordering the rest of the world to that end. Then, at the climax of his creative work, he forms man himself and breathes into him the breath of life (2:4–7). b. God prepares a fruitful garden for man in Eden, a land unknown to us. In the midst of it, beside fruit-trees of all kinds, he puts the tree of life and the tree of knowledge. Its fertility is guaranteed by a copious stream of water (2:8–14). c. In this garden man is set. He must develop his physical and spiritual powers by cultivating the garden, but he can also enjoy the abundant fruits growing everywhere by God's blessing. Man must, however, recognise the dominion and authority of God by observing his command not to eat of the fruit of the tree of knowledge. If he does transgress this prohibition death will be imposed as a limit to his life and happiness (2:15ff). d. Man lives in this paradise at peace with the animals, but he does exercise a small degree of control over them. Yet since he is by nature inclined to communal life he remains lonely and dissatisfied because he has no-one of his own kind with whom to converse (2:18ff). e. Then God creates woman. She is 'one flesh and one bone' with man, ie of the same nature as he. Love, marriage, family, communal life is now possible for the first time, and thereby human nature is fulfilled (2:21–4). f. The first men live in circumstances of pure happiness, moral purity and perfect harmony in their sensible and spiritual dispositions (2:25). g. This peace with the surrounding world and with God is broken into from without by a power hostile to God which takes the form of a serpent. The narrator gives this serpent the characteristics of malice, cunning, envy and hostility towards man. It stirs up mistrust of God in man, makes light of the danger incurred by transgressing the divine command, awakens cupidity and induces man to attempt to gain divine powers by tasting of the fruit of the forbidden tree so as to withdraw himself from the claims of God's dominion. In this way the first sin is committed (3:1–6). h. Sin results in the loss of unconstrained spontaneity and of harmony in the instincts. It also brings in its train anxiety in God's presence and a bad conscience (3:6–13). i. God punishes sin by imposing upon men a lot of suffering, toil and final death. He banishes them from paradise and withdraws himself from the open, confident friendship which had previously prevailed between himself and man. Since then the whole of mankind is subject to the burden of suffering, the fate of death, guilt and separation from God. The way to paradise is blocked (3:16–24). j. Yet mankind does not remain altogether without hope. The serpent is accursed. God pronounces sentence of eternal enmity between it and its brood on the one side, and the woman and her descendants on the other. And he holds out the prospect that even if the serpent and its brood bring harm to the 'seed' of the woman, in the end that seed will crush the serpent's head (3:14ff).

This narrative contains all the points that are essential for a theological anthropology, although they are admittedly wrapped up in figurative language belonging to a type of literature which can be defined neither as myth nor as history-writing in the modern sense (DS 3864). Neither the classical nor the ancient Near Eastern categories of literature can be applied to this narrative. Even if it has certain traits in common with myth or fairy-tale (the speaking serpent, the tree of life, the tree of knowledge, a garden of inconceivable fruitfulness etc), it is meant to express something true about the real situation of the first man and his relationship with God. In view of this, the encyclical *Humani Generis* regards the paradise story as historical 'in certain sense which is true even though it has still to be more closely examined and defined by the exegetes', for it 'presents both the most important truth on which our striving for eternal salvation is based, and the origin of the human race in the simple figurative style accommodated to the understanding of a people of little culture' (DS 3898 [=DB 2329]). The following elements are considered historical in the decision of the Papal Biblical Commission of 30 June 1909: the creation of the world by God; the special creation of man, the forming of the first woman from the first man, the unity of the human race; the happiness of the first

man in the state of grace in which he possessed a nature that was unblemished and immortal; a command given by God to man to test his obedience; the transgression of this command as a result of temptation by the devil; the exclusion of man from that primordial state of innocence; the promise that a Redeemer would come (DS 3514 [=DB 2123]).

3. *The subsequent persistence of the idea of paradise in the Old Testament.* Not only the expressions 'Eden', 'garden of God', 'trees of Eden' which were mentioned under 1, but also other elements in the paradise story are echoed in subsequent passages in the Old Testament. We may note above all that the ideas of indescribable fruitfulness, of unbroken peace among men and animals, and of eternal life have entered into the Old Testament expectation of salvation. The epoch of messianic salvation is described by means of images which are taken, at least in part, from Gen 2 and 3. In the expected epoch of salvation Zion or the land of Israel will be turned into a new Eden, a garden of God (Is 51:3). A stream of water flows ceaselessly to ensure its inconceivable fruitfulness (Is 33:21; Ezek 47:1-12; Joel 3:18; Zech 14:8). The toil and also the disappointments of work on the land will be removed (Is 27:6; 30:23f; 35; Hos 2:14f; Amos 9:13). Peace will reign among the animals (Is 11:6f; 65:25) and among men (Is 2:2ff; 9:6; Mic 4:1-4), but also between animals and men (Is 11:8; Hos 2:18). Men will live to a very great age (Is 65:20f; Zech 8:4). Indeed, death will be generally abolished (Is 25:8; 26:19), and intimate friendship with God will once more be established (Is 25:6-12;

Jer 31:31–4; Hos 2:21f). Thus paradise will return; in fact the happiness of the age of salvation will actually exceed that of the first man in paradise.

The passages in the Old Testament which recall the loss of paradise by the sin of the first man are only very few and late. Sir 25:24 connects death as the lot of mankind with the sin of the first woman. According to Wis 2:23f God intended man to be immortal, but death came into the world through the envy of the devil.

Bibliography: On Gen 2 and 3: J. Jeremias, *TDNT* v, 765–73; Haag 1260f and 1566–9; C. Hauret, *DB(S)* 3 (1960), 908–26; E. Cothenet, *DB(S)* 34 (1960), 1177–220; J. Begrich, 'Die Paradieseserzählung', *ZAW* 50 (1932), 33–116; A. Weiser, 'Die biblische Geschichte von Paradies und Sündenfall', *Deutsche Theologie*, 1937, 9–37; G. Lambert, 'Le drame du jardin d'Eden', *NRT* 76 (1954), 917–48; I. Lewy, 'The Two Strata in the Eden Story', *HUCA* 27 (1956), 93–9; C. Schedl, *Geschichte des AT* I, Innsbruck 1956, 64–114; A. M. Dubarle, *Le péché originel dans l'Ecriture*, Paris 1958; L. F. Hartmann, 'Sin in Paradise', *CBQ* 20 (1958), 26–40; J. Dus, 'Zwei Schichten der biblischen Paradiesgeschichte', *ZAW* 71 (1959), 97–113; M. Metzger, *Die Paradieseserzählung*, Bonn 1959; H. Renckens, *Urgeschichte und Heilsgeschichte*, Mainz 1959; F. Hvidberg, 'The Canaanite Background of Gen 1–3', *VT* 10 (1960), 285–94; P. Morant, *Die Anfänge der Menschheit*, Lucerne 1960, 101–216; T. Schwegler, *Die bibl. Urgeschichte im Lichte der Forschung*, Regensburg 1960; L. Ligier, *Péché d'Adam et péché du monde*, Paris 1960, 152–231; H. Haag, 'Die Themata der Sündenfallgeschichte', *Festschrift H. Junker*, Trier 1961, 101–11; J. B. Bauer, *Die bibl. Urgeschichte*, Paderborn 1964², 33–47; *SB* IV, 1118–65. On the hope for the return of paradise: J. Alonso, 'Descrición de los tiempos mesiánicos en la literatura profética como una vuelta al Paraíso', *Estudios Eclesiásticos* 24 (1950), 457–77; B. J. van Merwe, *Pentateuchtradisies in de Prediking van Deuterojesaja*, Groningen 1955; H. Gross, *Die Idee des ewigen und allgemeinen Weltfriedens im Alten Orient und im AT*, Trier 1956, 66–8; J. Ringborn, *Paradisus Terrestris*, Helsinki 1958; J. J. Stamm and H. Bietenhard, *Der Weltfriede im Lichte der Bibel*, Zürich 1959; G. Fohrer, 'Die Struktur der atl. Eschatologie', *TLZ* 85 (1960), 401–20 (esp. 415f).

Josef Scharbert

B. *New Testament*. The primordial paradise of Genesis is not mentioned in the New Testament. Yet the story of paradise is occasionally referred to (Mk 10:6–8; Mt 19:4–6: indissolubility of marriage; 1 Cor 11:7–9: the formation of woman from man; Rom 5:12: advent of sin and death; see also Rom 3:23; 8:20). As in the late Jewish pseudepigrapha (ApocMos 37; Bar[Syr] 4:6; 51:11; Enoch [Slav] 8:1; 42:3) so in the New Testament, where the concept of paradise does occur it means a place of bliss above the world. Jesus promises the thief crucified with him that together with him he will enter paradise (Lk 23:43), that is, the place where the just live in bliss and which is probably to be found in the heavenly sphere rather than in some hidden paradise on earth.

About the year 43 Paul underwent a mystical experience in which he was caught up into 'the third heaven', 'into paradise'. Here he heard 'things that cannot be told' (2 Cor 12:2–4). Although it is not quite clear it is probable that what Paul is saying here is simply that something happened to him; he was taken up into the world beyond. In that case the 'third heaven' is a synonym for 'paradise' (many interpreters, however, consider the two places as distinct and consequently take Paul as referring to two distinct experiences). In this passage Paul is using the Jewish ideas of his period to describe his closeness to God, and according to these ideas 'paradise' was a place where God was surrounded by the assembly of the just. Not invariably but in some passages this place is to be found in 'the third heaven' (ApocMos 37; Enoch[Slav] 8:1; cf 9:1; 42:3 in the longer recension).

Revelation too speaks of paradise in the sense of the place of the blessed in heaven (Rev 2:7): Christ promises to him who conquers that he will give him fruit to eat from the tree of life which stands 'in the Paradise of God'. Allowing for the idiom of the time, what this promise means is the eternal life which Christ is to bestow on his disciple when he triumphs over the suffering and persecution of the world. Now in the same book the tree of life is said to stand in the heavenly Jerusalem (22:2, 14), which comes down from heaven to earth at the consummation of the world. It follows that this city is really identical with paradise, and both concepts point to that salvation which the blessed will receive at the end of time, their eternal life, their joy and the security they find in being taken up into the glory of God.

Bibliography: SB IV/2, 1118–65; J. B. Frey, 'La vie de l'au-delà dans les conceptions juives au temps de Jésus-Christ', *Bbl* 13 (1932), 129–68; P. Volz, *Die Eschatologie der jüdischen Gemeinde im ntl. Zeitalter*, Tübingen 1934², 395f and 412–19; H. Bietenhard, *Die himmlische Welt im Urchristentum und Spätjudentum*, Tübingen 1951, 161–91; J. Jeremias, *TDNT* V, 765–73; H.-G. Leder, *Die Auslegung der zentralen theologischen Aussagen der Paradieseserzählung (Gen 2:4b–3:24)*: *I. Im AT, im Judentum u. im NT*, Greifswald 1960 (dissertation).

Johann Michl

Parousia

In spite of the Greek idiom in which it is expressed, the *parousia*, or coming of the Lord in messianic glory, can be understood in its depths only against the background of Old Testament thought. In the early stages of Israel's existence her wanderings had been marked by powerful and purposive interventions of God. Right from the outset this had directed her attention to the history in which God revealed himself in one theophany after another. In this history man sees the meaning of his life. It is not focused upon the individual, for concerning the fate of the individual after death one can only speculate anxiously and timorously (Is 26:19). What is central here is rather the community belonging to God, which must be established 'politically' as a power in history. At first confined to the one particular people of Israel (Jer 23:6), this community is later extended so as to include the entire world (Zech 11:10). Moreover it follows from this that present and future often overlap imperceptibly with each other (Ex 3), and it is hard to define the point at which the future hope becomes eschatological in character (Is 30:27ff; 40:3ff; 59:19ff). The expectations of the community are based primarily on the promises, which are partially fulfilled when the land is taken (Ex 3:8). Thereby they seem to give a guarantee that the kingdom of peace will in fact be achieved (Gen 49:8; Num 23:21).

In contrast to this often too self-confident attitude, the prophets present God's activity as the ⤢ holy breaking in upon the world with a power that no one can evade. On the ⤢ 'day of Yahweh' this will appear in the sight of all. Either a historical event of supreme significance or an eschatological event may be being thought of here.

633

In hellenistic circles it is calculated that it will arrive after the present aeon has run its course (Dan 12:7; Enoch[Eth] 85ff). This intervention is of its nature designed to have a twofold effect: it brings both destruction and salvation. In pre-exilic times it is the first of these that is chiefly stressed, but from the exile onwards the emphasis falls on the second. The initial impact of the holy upon the profane leads on immediately to a judgement which is directed not only against the gentiles (Is 14:24ff), but against Israel too (Is 10:1ff). It is manifested in afflictions (Is 30:25; 34:2), catastrophes in nature (Is 13:10; 24:18ff), and miracles, among which the epiphany in fire is the chief (Amos 2:5; Jer 17:27; Zeph 1:18; the idea of a world conflagration however does not appear before the Sibylline Oracles). In the apocalyptic literature these manifestations are depicted more fully and more vividly (Dan 7:2ff; Hen [Eth] 37–71). In this way space will be made for the advent of an order of salvation which, according to Isaiah, is to extend to the entire cosmos (Is 30:26) and to result in a new heaven and a new earth (Is 65:17). It is thought of under the image of the new Jerusalem (Is 60:1ff). What is primary and central in the prophets' thought is the light in which the glory of God (*kabod*) is manifested, and to which all the peoples stream (Is 9:2). This is interpreted as a return to paradise (Hos 2:21ff; Is 2:2ff; 11:6ff).

The gulf between God and man is bridged by the 'anointed one' who has, through his obedience as representative of the people, become God's own. He shares the responsibility of accomplishing the sanctification of the world. Hence

the salvific age is connected with ⁄ kingship (2 Sam 7:17). And when this fails, the hope of salvation is transferred to the Messiah. This figure is indeed promised by God; but at the same time he must emerge, in response to God's summons, from among his fellow men and, indeed, from the house of David. He evinces either warlike (PsSol 17:21ff) or peaceful (Zech 9:9) traits. Sometimes too a distinction is drawn between a priestly and a subordinate political messiah (TestRub 6:7ff; Rule of the Community 1 Q 9:11). Alternatively the Messiah may introduce only an 'intermediary age' which will be followed by the age of salvation brought about by God (4 Ezr 7:26ff). In circles associated with the Book of Enoch these ideas were displaced because attention was centred upon the figure of a redeemer called the ⁄ Son of Man, who was conceived to have a prior existence in heaven before appearing on earth, and who was to arise out of the sea and to come upon the clouds (4 Ezr 13; Enoch [Eth] 37–71; see also Dan 7:23 where the interpretation of the Son of Man as an individual figure (as opposed to a symbolic representation of a collective entity such as the people of Israel—translator's note) may represent a secondary theological reflection. Whereas the Messiah appears only once, we must also take into account the related view that the prophet (Elijah: Mal 4:5; Enoch: Enoch[Eth] 90:31) will return at the end of time. This figure is regarded as a forerunner of God, and sometimes too of the Messiah. Apart from the prophets all this hope was expressed in and sustained by the cult, and the royal psalms which belong to this are undoubtedly messianic in character (Ps 2; 21; 45; 72; 110; 1 Sam 26:9).

In the New Testament the situation has been fundamentally altered. In the person of Christ the kingship of God (↗ kingdom of God) has already become a reality. The promised Messiah has actually appeared, not however as man, but as Son of God (Mk 14:61f). Certainly his power and glory are still veiled. Believers however can recognise them in the miracles which he performed considered as signs (Jn 2:11), or these attributes shine out at decisive moments such as the transfiguration (Mk 9:2ff), but chiefly in his Easter apparitions, his ascension, and in the sending of the Holy Spirit. At the *parousia* this power and glory will be finally and fully revealed in all its brilliance (Mt 24:27), and in Heb 9:28 the parousia is expressly referred to as a return.

Thus the *parousia* is to be classed among the manifestations of the divine. It has in common with them the suddenness of its advent (Mk 13:35; Mt 24:43; Lk 17:30f; 1 Thess 5:4), but it deviates from them precisely in the fact that it is not transient but lasting: it represents the inauguration of the age of salvation which from now on is to be made manifest to all. Yet this difference is only a formal one. In reality *parousia* is the final completion of *epiphany*, the purpose of which is precisely unveiling. Hence Paul actually uses the word *epiphany* in the sense of the second coming of the Lord (2 Thess 2:8; 1 Tim 6:14; Tit 2:13). It is necessary for ↗ epiphany and *parousia* to be separated from each other by the so-called 'intermediary age' because it is not until they are at some distance from the actual events that the community can recognise the true nature of its Lord. The connection with Christ implies that the final revelation of the kingdom of God comes not as the conclusion of a prior development, but as an event, unexpected, determined by God (Mk 13:32) and accompanied by miracles. Because of the manifest difference between holy and profane, these eschatological miracles, in contrast to the deeds of power performed by Jesus during his earthly life, are of irresistible force. Hence they are depicted in apocalyptic hues which are often suited to the ancient view of the world (Mk 13:24ff). Moreover present and future are often telescoped into each other in a foreshortened perspective (Mt 24:29), and from this fact literary conclusions can be drawn with regard to the authorship of particular passages (Lk 21:20f).

The *parousia* itself is a complex event consisting of several different stages. First comes the afflictions of the lawless one (2 Thess 2:2ff) or ↗ Antichrist (see Rev), who by his miracles attempts to imitate the *parousia* (2 Thess 2:9). The *parousia* proper is ushered in by a cosmic catastrophe (Mk 13:24ff; Rev 8:7ff; 9:1ff; late Jewish and Iranian influences are reflected in the reference to the world conflagration in 2 Pet 3:6ff). Then follows the mysterious sign first interpreted as a ↗ cross in ApocPet 1, which represents the advent of the 'Son of Man' (Mt 24:30f) appearing upon the clouds and shining with radiant light. Alternatively the sign may perhaps be identical with the Son of Man (see the sign of Jonah, Mt 12:40) As an expression at once of lowliness and of sublimity Christ's

635

description of himself as Son of Man unites in one harmonious whole both the veiled and unveiled aspects of his nature. Merely by appearing, without any further action on his part, he annihilates Satan (2 Thess 2:8; Rev 20:9ff). At the trumpet-call sounded by the angels who surround him the dead are roused from sleep (1 Thess 4:16; 1 Cor 15:52). At the same time the cosmic judgement which extends to all men is inaugurated. In it Christ acts as judge by separating the good from the wicked, taking as his ultimate criterion for this task that ideal of love which is the culminating point of all the requirements of religion (Mt 25:31ff).

The salvific age follows as the outcome of this, freed from sin and death and brought to its fullness by the exercise of his office as mediator and high priest (Heb 9:28). Participation in it represents what is essential in the parousia, a fact which John has evidently seen, for while he hardly speaks of *parousia* at all (Jn 21:22; 1 Jn 2:28) he does speak instead of eternal life (Jn 4:10; 6:68 etc) which we already have on earth; for as he sees it, epiphany and *parousia* are interwoven. Not is this contradicted by the terminology. The word *parousia* was used in the Jewish diaspora in a cultic sense (Jos. Ant. 3:80, 202) and is not found in an eschatological sense before the christian era. The choice of this word arises not so much from theological as from psychological considerations. These often lead men to call an event after some striking feature which occurs at its commencement. The 'day of the Lord' (1 Cor 1:8; Lk 17:24; 1 Thess 5:2) is taken from the Old Testament.

Since the salvific age is connected with the person of Christ, paradisal descriptions of it are dispensed with. It is described rather as attended by glory (Mk 10:37), light (Lk 16:8), refreshment (Acts 3:19), rest (Heb 4:1), and joy (Mt 25:21). Now this can only take place in that sphere in which the veiled epiphany has also taken place, that is not in some remote heaven but on the earth transformed and made new. This is shown in John's references to water (Jn 4:14), bread (Jn 4:35), and places to live (Jn 14:2), etc.

It follows further that the question of date cannot be of central importance, and the announcement of the *parousia* cannot contain any contradictions whatsoever on this point. Christ can say that the kingdom of God is in our midst (Lk 17:21) or, alternatively, contrary to what we find in the apocalyptic literature, that only the Father knows the day and the hour (Mk 13:32). When the nearness of the *parousia* is emphasised (Mk 13:32) this refers not so much to a definite point in time laid down for it to arrive as to the inexorability with which history, through all its vicissitudes, grows ripe for its fulfilment. Already we are living in the final phase (see the so-called '*parousia* parables', Mt 25:1ff etc). There is no doubt that a great number of early christians (Mk 9:1; 13:30; 1 Pet 4:7; Rev 1:3), including for a time even Paul (Rom 13:11; 1 Thess 4:15ff; 1 Cor 7:26), hoped for an early *parousia*. But the fact that its evident delay did not lead to any crisis of faith—the scoffers of 2 Pet 3:1ff are heretical teachers—is proof enough that there can be no question of a so-called postponement of the *parousia*. Rather, the attention of the early christians was left free for the enormous significance of the 'intermediary age'. This appears especially in Luke, who presents Christ as the centre of time: his life is preceded by the age of the Old Testament and followed by the time of the ↗ church (Lk 9:2ff; Acts 1:6ff), characterised by the missionary precept. This is to be brought to a close by the *parousia*.

Thus the *parousia* is the fulfilment of God's promise right at the outset that he would sanctify the world (Mt 6:9f). The unbreakable connection between present and future is characteristic of this. It appears above all in the cult in which ↗ baptism makes one share in the death and resurrection of the Lord (Rom 6:3ff) and the eucharistic meal proclaims the death of the Lord until he comes again (1 Cor 11:26). The eucharistic meal also points on to the marriage supper of the Lamb (Rev 19:9), while in the cry *maranatha* (1 Cor 16:22) prayer is made for the coming of the Lord. But sanctification implies at the same time a summons to men. For this reason the *parousia* occupies a central place in the teaching of Jesus, and all that is said about it is said with the purpose of summoning the individual to a decision which means punishment or ↗ reward, salvation or perdition. In this way the *parousia* becomes a motive for moral behaviour. The summons to ↗ conversion and repentance is to be explained by this (Mt 3:2; 12:41; Rev 3:19), as are the exhortations to watchfulness (Mt 24:42; Lk 12:37; etc), and the counsel to withhold oneself from the things of this world (1 Cor 7:31). But in addition to these the *parousia* doctrine also lies in the background of the ex-

hortation not to let eschatological pre-occupations make one neglect one's daily duties (2 Thess 3:11). In the light of the *parousia* even ↗ sufferings can appear meaningful and power to resist evil is also strengthened (Mt 26:64; 2 Pet 3:13; 1 Jn 2:18ff; 1 Cor 1:7). If these demands gradually lose their intensity (see for example, the *parousia* parables and the pastoral epistles), this is not to be explained by the theory that under the influence of the alleged post-ponement of the *parousia* an 'interim ethic' was developed. It is rather that when the early christians fixed their gaze upon the ascension (Acts 1:11) they were concentrating on that which was essential, that upon which the *vita christiana* was based, that which was realised and lived out in the familiar circumstances of every day (1 Thess 3:13; Phil 1:10; 1 Pet 1:13). But as they did so these early christians were conscious of being supported by the Holy Spirit bestowed upon them as a pledge of the glory to come (2 Cor 1:22). Hence this attitude of theirs is characterised by ↗ faith (2 Cor 5:7), ↗ hope (Rom 8:23), and ↗ love (2 Tim 4:8), and in all this the elders of the community bore the responsibility (1 Pet 5:1ff). The interval between epiphany and *parousia* is thus occupied with the formation of the christian (*paideia*: Tit 2:11ff; ↗ discipline).

The immense power of the *parousia* doctrine in Old and New Testament alike has made any unified or systematic presentation of it impossible. It may be regarded as surrounded on all sides simultaneously by the scriptural writers so that a different aspect of it is available to each according to his particular standpoint. Hence it is only when these fragmentary aspects are blended together into a composite whole that we can gain any picture of the significance of the *parousia*.

Bibliography: B. J. Alfrink, Haag 1711–15; M. Buber, *Stationen des Glaubens*, Wiesbaden 1956, 44–51; Eichrodt I, 472ff; Feine 129–32, 299–302, and 282–4; Jepsen, Meyer, and Conzelmann, *RGG* II, 655–72; W. G. Kümmel, *Verheissung und Erfüllung*, Zürich 1953; A. Oepke, *TDNT* v, 858–71; A. Oepke, 'Die Parusie-Erwartung in den älteren Paulus-Briefen', *Das NT Deutsch* 8, Göttingen 1953, 144–6; E. Pax, *Epiphaneia*, Munich 1955, 208–44; F. J. Schierse, 'Himmelssehnsucht und Reich-Gottes-Erwartung', *GL* 26 (1953), 189–201; M. Schmaus, *Katholische Dogmatik* 4/2, Munich 1953, 18–70; J. Schmid, *Markus* (*RNT* 2), 1954³, 244–6; Schnackenburg 127–34; Cullmann 12–29 and 109–94; Procksch, 582–600; E. Grässer, *Das Problem der Parusie-verzögerung in den synopt. EV.*, Berlin 1957; A. Strobel, *Untersuchungen zum eschatologischen Verzögerungsproblem*, Leiden 1961.

Elpidius Pax

Passion of Christ

It is the memory of a historical fact that is preserved in Acts (2:23f; 3:13–15; 4:10, 27f; 13:27–31) when it records that the subject of the earliest apostolic preaching was the passion of Christ (here taken to include his death and his exaltation both together). So too, right from the outset it was the passion which the early christians firmly upheld in their creeds and celebrated in their cultic chants (Phil 2:6–11; 1 Pet 2:21–4; 3:18–22). This must have been the case: 1. because the crucifixion of the Messiah had been carried out with full publicity and needed to be explained and interpreted in instruction and preaching; and 2. because the passion had to be preached as the focal and climactic event in the salvation

which had been achieved. From the outset those who recounted it gave it a messianic interpretation (chiefly by means of references to scriptures, as in Acts 4:10f, 25–8; 1 Cor 15:3f). From the outset, too, if the cross was to appear anything but a meaningless catastrophe, the preachers had to link it with the resurrection and to interpret it from the perspective of the resurrection in their preaching (Mk 8:31; Acts 2:24 Rom 8:34).

From a form-critical point of view it must have been the same: the passion narrative established itself permanently and necessarily as the primary constituent of the gospel. Again, this narrative at once gives information and bears witness; and it is expressed in a form which not only interprets the facts but summons the hearer to respond to them. Whereas the rest of the gospel accounts of the deeds and words of Jesus are only loosely connected with each other, and are sometimes arranged merely according to subject-matter, the passion narrative relates the events in their temporal (Mk 14:17, 28; 15:1, 33, 34, 42) and geographical (Mk 14:17f, 26, 43, 54; 15:1, 16, 22) sequence. This was the only way of making comprehensible their terrible culmination on the cross, brought about by the collaboration of the Jews and the Romans. At the same time, however, this narrative too was interwoven with numerous isolated details of apologetic, dogmatic, or paranetic value. It was on account of these values that the memory of such details was preserved and that they were mentioned in the gospel. The theological motivation underlying them appears ever clearer in the narrative as we turn from the earlier to the later gospels. In part they may be compared with the motives which embellish the ancient acts of martyrs written by secular authors, Jewish and subsequently christian too. But there are also parts of the passion narrative of Jesus which are beyond comparison (such are the Gethsemane episode, or words such as those found in Mk 15:34), and it is precisely this that reveals the uniqueness of him who suffers here.

On apologetic and dogmatic grounds the evangelists wanted to show that it was not for a crime and not as a victim of brute force that Jesus suffered and died, but in his innocence and as Lord of the passion. That is why they assert again and again that he had prior knowledge of his own death (Mk 14:8, 18–21, 27–31; Lk 22:15; Jn 13:1, 3; 18:4; 19:28) and took it willingly upon himself (Mk 8:31; 14:42; Mt 26:52–4; Jn 19:17). His conflict in Gethsemane over the necessity of his imminent suffering is, by comparison with Mk 14:33–6, toned down in Mt 26:37–9 and Lk 22:29–36; and Luke adds the more consoling detail (22:43f) of the apparition of the angel. The evangelists show ever more clearly that it was of his own free will that Jesus underwent his passion. They show this in their accounts of how he was taken prisoner (Mt 26:52–4; Lk 22:51; Jn 18:4–9). Even the opponents of Jesus are forced to recognise his innocence and his righteousness (Mk 14:55; Mt 27:19, 24; Lk 23:4, 14, 15, 47). In the fourth gospel Jesus appears as the accuser of his own judge (Jn 18:19–23), and it is before Pilate that he reveals his transcendent kingship (Jn 18:36), just as it is here that he has

to bear witness to the fact that he is the Son of God (Jn 19:7). Finally even his opponents recognise it (Mt 27:54). The account of the crucifixion, too, is progressively toned down. Whereas Mk 15:34, 37 and Mt 27:46, 50 tell us only of his exclamation of dereliction and his death cry, Luke (23:34, 43, 46) knows of words which, in accordance with the basic theme of the third gospel, reveal him as he dies as the saviour of sinners and as one who is perfect in patience. In his last words as given in the fourth gospel, Jesus fulfils the commandment of love to the very last (Jn 19:26); he is obedient to scripture (Jn 19:28) and testifies to the consummation (Jn 19:30). In accordance with the rich symbolism of this gospel Jn 19:26ff can bear a still deeper meaning. It is Origen who already finds (explanation of Jn 1:6) implicit in Jn 19:28 an extension of Mary's motherhood. Medieval and later theologians have found a basis for their doctrine of the universal motherhood of Mary in this passage. The narrative is able to show abundant proof that in the passion of Jesus the Old Testament is fulfilled (Mk 14:13, 21, 24, 27, 49; 15:23, 24, 29, 34; see also Mt 26:15, 54; 27:9f; Lk 22:37; Jn 13:18; 15:25; 17:12; 19:28, 31–7). Thus the motif becomes increasingly prominent and further instances of it are found outside the gospels in the preaching of the apostles (Acts 4:25–8; 1 Thess 2:14ff; Heb 11:26; Rev 11:7ff). If the Old Testament is fulfilled in the passion of Jesus it follows that, so far from affording an argument against his messiahship, it actually provides proof in its favour. The abundance of the proofs, as well as the fact that they are often closely connected with the text of the narrative, makes it possible to recognise that these proofs from prophecy are not the work of a single mind, but rather that of the community as a whole. They read such texts as Pss 22 and 69 as prophecies of the passion, and were convinced that in doing so they were continuing the interpretation of the Old Testament initiated by Christ (Lk 24:25–7, 44–6).

Again, those details and motifs in the passion narrative which consisted in moral exhortation were understood and their meaning was brought out and strengthened: the command to watch in the hour of darkness (Mk 14:38); the command to love one's enemies (Lk 23:34) and self-surrender to God's will (Lk 23:46; Acts 7:59f). The saying about taking up one's cross and following Jesus was originally intended as an exhortation to the effect that the disciple should be ready for all things, even to lay down his life. But it is taken up and developed so as to mean following the crucified Lord in an ascetical and mystical sense (Mk 8:34; Mt 10:38; Lk 14:27; see also Heb 13:13). This interpretation was also introduced into the historical account of Simon of Cyrene carrying the cross (Lk 23:26).

Luke is especially concerned to present those elements in the passion of Jesus which are appealing and moving. Christ for him is the man of patience, the martyr. Jesus is sorrowful as he celebrates the last Supper with his disciples (22:15). In the Garden of Olives his sweat falls to the ground as heavy as drops of blood (22:44). He stands revealed as a saviour when he heals the ear which has been cut off (22:51). His gaze moves Peter to repentance when he has denied him (22:61). He comforts and exhorts the weeping women (23:27–31). On the cross he prays for his enemies (23:34), forgives the penitent thief (23:43), and dies as a man of patience and devotion to God (23:46). Finally beneath the cross all are deeply moved. They beat their breasts and so return home (23:48). These details are exclusive to Luke. It is this evangelist then who provides a basis for that feeling, that experience of *compassion* with the Lord in his passion which is to move christendom in the future.

In the gospel narratives of the passion alone its salvific value is clearly attested (Mk 14:24 = Mt 26:28; cf Mk 10:45), for in them sayings of the Lord such as those we have been considering could be understood by the disciples in the light of the late Jewish theology of suffering (as in 4 Macc 6:28f; 17:22; see also 1 QS 8:2f; 9:3). Behind and beyond the narrative which lies in the foreground one can sense that the whole of creation is affected, that it is being shaken in sympathy (Mt 27:45, 51–3), while the powers of heaven and hell struggle with one another (Mk 8:33; Lk 22:3, 31, 53; Jn 14:30; 1 Cor 2:8).

In the passion narratives of the gospels history and theological interpretation are closely and indissolubly interwoven. This connection cannot be attributed to an evangelist. It was arrived at either consciously or unconsciously in the faith and preaching of the church, and it was the gospel materially contained in this faith and preaching that subsequently acquired written form at the hands of the evangelists. Mark must have been the first to commit to writing in the Greek tongue a complete passion narrative. Matthew and Luke followed his version, making additions here and there by way of interpretation and expansion. Luke in particular had a comprehensive source at his disposal, which he could perhaps have taken from an account given in a different context from that of the gospels.

The motifs implicitly contained in the gospel narratives of the passion are made explicit in the form of dogmatic statements in the epistles and writings of the apostles. They describe the willingness and the obedience of the Son, who took the cross upon himself (Rom 5:19; Phil 2:6–11; Heb 10:5–10; 12:2ff). In the preaching of the apostle the salvific value of the passion and the graces deriving from it are unfolded in the form of a constantly developing dialectic. The salvific death of Christ is ransom (Mk 10:45; 1 Tim 2:6; Heb 9:12), atonement (Rom 3:25; Heb 2:17), and sacrifice (1 Cor 5:7; Eph 5:2; Heb 7:27). Its effects are deliverance from sin (Mt 26:28; 2 Cor 5:21; 1 Jn 1:7; 1 Pet 3:18), from law (Rom 7:4; Gal 3:13), from death (1 Cor 15:55; Heb 2:15) and from powers (Jn 16:11; Col 2:15; Rev 12:11). It effects salvation (Acts 4:12; 1 Thess 5:9f), sanctification (Eph 5:25–7; Heb 10:10), purification (Heb 10:2; 1 Jn 1:7), reconciliation (Rom 5:10ff), peace (Col 1:20), righteousness (Rom 3:24f), life (Jn 3:14f; Rom 6:4; 1 Pet 1:3). The salvific death of Christ is endured vicariously on behalf of the entire world (2 Cor 5:19) and on behalf of the people of all ages (Heb 9:12).

The cross represents the entire content of the preaching (1 Cor 2:2). The passion of the Lord is made in the church and its power is made effective in the sacraments of baptism (Rom 6:1–7) and the eucharist (1 Cor 10:16; 11:26). Christians must share in bringing the passion to its final fruition in their daily lives. The apostles lay special emphasis in their epistles on the duty of following the example of Christ who sacrificed himself utterly in the passion, becoming the servant of all (Rom 15:3; 2 Cor 4:10; Phil 2:5–8; Heb 12:2; 1 Pet 2:21–4; 3:18–4:1; 1 Jn 3:16). But sin and apostasy are a denial of the cross (Heb 6:6; 10:29).

In its entire life, in its word, its sacraments as in its ethos, the church is a representation and an actualisation of the death and exaltation of its Master.

Bibliography: H. W. Surkau, *Martyrien in jüdischer und frühchristlicher Zeit*, Göttingen 1938; W. Hillmann, *Aufbau und Deutung der synoptischen Leidensberichte*, Freiburg 1941; T. Innitzer, *Kommentar zur Leidens- und Verklärungsgeschichte Jesu Christi*, Wien 1948[4]; K. H. Schelkle, *Die Passion Jesu in der Verkündigung des NT*, Heidelberg 1949; E. Benz, *Der gekreuzigte Gerechte bei Plato, im NT und in der alten Kirche*, Mainz 1950; J. Blinzler, *Der Prozess Jesu*, Regensburg 1960[3]; E. Lohse, *Märtyrer und Gottesknecht*, Göttingen 1955; L. Morris, *The Apostolic Preaching of the Cross*, London 1955; V. Taylor, *Jesus and his Sacrifice*, London 1955; V. Taylor, *The Cross of Christ*, London 1956; W. Rehkopf, *Die lukanische Sonderquelle*, Tübingen 1959; J. Schmid, 'Die Darstellung der Passion Jesu in den Evangelien', *GL* 27 (1954), 6–15; G. Schille, 'Das Leiden des Herrn', *ZTK* 52 (1955), 161–205; N. A. Dahl, *Die Passionsgeschichte bei Matthäus*, *NTS* 2 (1955/6), 17–32; T. A. Burkill, 'St Mark's Philosophy of Passion', *Novum Testamentum* 2 (1958), 245–71; *DB(S)* VI, 1419–72; E. Lohse, *Die Geschichte des Leidens und Sterbens Jesu Christi*, Gütersloh 1964.

Karl Hermann Schelkle

Passover (Easter)

Easter is the equivalent of the Greek and Latin word *pascha* which corresponds to the Hebrew name for the Jewish and Christian festival, namely *pesaḥ* (in Aramaic, *pishā'*) derived from an earlier form *phashā'* (see *TDNT* v, 896f). For the Jews the feast celebrates their national deliverance, for christians the victory of the Lord Jesus over death (Rom 1:4). The resurrection of Christ the Lamb of God (Jn 1:29, 36), corresponding to the Passover lamb which was sacrificed on the 14th of Nisan (Jn 18:28; 19:31, and especially v 36 referring to Ex 12:46), forms the link between the Jewish and christian feasts.

A. *Passover in the Old Testament.* The etymology of the word *pesaḥ* is uncertain and the relevant Hebrew roots throw little light on it. Is 21:5 seems to depend on texts which refer to this festival. No decisive conclusion can be reached by referring to the cognate languages including Egyptian. Two attempts at a solution which ought to be mentioned are: (a) allusion to a sacred dance (compare the verb *pāsaḥ* in 1 Kings 18:21); and (b) a borrowing from the Akkadian *pashahu* which in ritual texts refers to placation of a deity.

1. *The Passover ritual.* In Ex 12–13 the Passover ritual is described in two forms. 12:21–3 appear to contain an abbreviated form of a more elaborated text which is found in vv 1–14. It is presumed that the shorter text (coming from J) is the more ancient, and its essential elements occur again in Ex 34:25. It evidently refers to a sacrifice which takes place at night. After the slaughter of the animal, either a lamb or a kid, the elders of Israel dip a bunch of hyssop in the blood and smear the doorposts with it. In this way the house is protected from the deity when he proceeds to smite the firstborn of Egypt. The text really tells a story. It is explained that the asymes mean bread which has not been allowed to ferment. The ritual is apotropaic in character, designed as a protection against the God depicted in such a fearful light as Moses encounters him in Ex 4:24.

The ritual of Ex 12:1–14 is more complete and combines very archaic characteristics with more detailed prescriptions of the priestly type (it comes from the P source). We evidently have here a family ritual with few participants, at the most a few neighbours. The meal is incorporated into the blood-ritual. The animal must be roasted whole, it must not be cooked, and none of its bones must be broken, as is stipulated in an additional note in v 46. It must be eaten by those at table with unleavened bread and bitter herbs and the participants must be dressed for a journey. While it is, as we have seen, meant as a protection against the last of the plagues (vv 12f), it is even more clearly a memorial day in recollection of the exodus (v 14; see also v 11). One of the most recent elements in the ritual is the fixing of the date which is the month of Abib (13:4), the first month of the year (v 2). Only four days must separate the choice of the animal (on the tenth) and its slaughter (on the fourteenth, 'towards evening', vv 3, 6). Other stipulations have to do with the participation of foreigners (12:43ff), but throughout Passover is clearly distinguished from the feast of Azymes which follows it.

2. *Origins of the festival.* Scholars are inclined to trace the sacrifice of the Passover animal back to the time when the Hebrews were semi-nomads. Abib is the spring month and this is the time of year when the Arabian bedouins carry out their sacrifices (the month of Radshab). This is supported by the fact that it takes place at night, by the roasted flesh, the bitter herbs (desert plants used for seasoning) and the unleavened bread similar to the flat cakes which the nomads bake on hot stones. The ritual is certainly apotropaic—the desert nomads attribute protective power against evil demons to blood. As regards the sacrifice there is no consensus of opinion. For some (eg, de Vaux), it is simply a question of a gift made to the deity at the time when the nomad sets out for new pastures; for others (eg, J. B. Segal) it is a New Year sacrifice made in the spring unlike the autumn New Year festival of the Canaanites. Others again consider the animal sacrificed to be a substitute for the firstborn of men which belong to God (Ex 22:29) and whose existence is threatened (Henniger); and it is precisely in the spring that the flocks have their young. The connection between the ritual and the striking of the firstborn (Ex 13:15), and the fact that during the patriarchal period an animal was offered instead of the firstborn (Gen 22), make this last hypothesis the most probable. On account of the liberation of Israel from the power of Egypt, the sacrifice which the Israelites wished to celebrate before their departure (Ex 5:1) became a memorial service of the protection and salvation of Israel by its God.

3. *History of the feast.* After the settlement in Canaan this ancient spring festival was linked up with another feast, namely Azymes, during which bread without yeast and roast barley were eaten after the offering of the first sheaf (Lev 23:10, 14). In Jos 5:10f we can see the problem clearly: Passover comes before the eating of the firstfruits of the land. The Canaanite ritual, which is part of an agrarian calendar of feasts, and which was celebrated on the occasion of the sowing of the fields and the harvest (see a Phoenician inscription from Karatepe IV, and also Ex 34:22), was more of the nature of an annual New Year's festival. Though this was celebrated in the autumn under the monarchy it was changed to the spring from the time of the Babylonian captivity and is attested in Jewish tradition (*Rosh hashanah*). The J account testifies that the feast of Azymes was already in existence at the time of the exodus but can trace the eating of unleavened bread only to the time of the revelation on Sinai (Ex 34:18). At this time Passover was not yet part of the liturgical calendar. It was a kind of independent festival, though one of considerable significance (v 25), but did not have to be celebrated 'before Yahweh' and at the national sanctuary (compare v 23 with v 24). In fact, until the time of Hezekiah and Josiah, Passover was displaced in favour of the autumn festival which was attached more to the monarchy than to the nation as a whole. Solomon holds a solemn dedication of the temple (1 Kings 8:2) and Jeroboam introduces a rival festival after his accession (12:32). With the decline of the monarchy and the return in the prophetic writings to the origins (1 Kings

19; Hos 12:14), the old festival of Passover came back into its own. Yet the so-called Elohist (E) strand of the Pentateuch has very little indeed to say about this festival (at first sight Ex 24:8 seems to refer rather to the Feast of Weeks; see also Ex 19:1).

The restoration of Passover began after the fall of Samaria. While *Kings* informs us that the feast which had not been celebrated since 'the days of the Judges' was first taken up again under Josiah (2 Kings 23:22), *Chronicles* mentions a Passover celebration under Hezekiah, in the second month of his reign (2 Chr 30:12ff), though this information is of doubtful historicity. If Deuteronomy really goes back to northern circles at the time of Hezekiah, it would seem to be attempting to contribute to the restoration of this feast. In Deuteronomy, Passover is really the national festival (16:1ff), the more so that it ceases to be celebrated locally (v 5) and takes place exclusively at the national sanctuary. It absorbs the feast of Unleavened Bread which ceases to be regarded as the firstfruits of the harvest and begins to be thought of as 'the bread of affliction' eaten in Egypt. The sacrificial animal need no longer be one of the smaller kind and it can from now on be cooked as well as roasted. Passover also takes over the seven days of Unleavened Bread. The character of the former as a festival celebrated at night is artistically combined with this period of seven days and despite the centralisation of worship can still remain a family feast, retaining the memory of the tents on the morning after its celebration.

The more recent law in Lev 23 disregards these innovations and holds on to the distinction between the Passover on the fourteenth day of the month and Azymes on the fifteenth and following days (see the ritual in Ex 12:1–14 followed by 15–20 referred to earlier). It appears that the change in the calendar favoured Passover which, as a result of the change, was celebrated in the first month, while the autumn festival was divided into three separate feasts. Although the autumn festival retained its significance (see Neh 8), the torah of Ezekiel gives pride of place to Passover (Ezek 45:21–4), preceded by the feast of the purification of the temple and the altar. After the return from exile the autumn festival of worship was taken up again, but Ezra 6:19ff goes on at once to state that Passover was celebrated in accordance with the mandatory laws of ritual purity associated with it. From this time on it became the great feast when the entire diaspora was invited to assembly at the temple, so much so that provision had to be made for a second Passover for those who had been unable to comply with the purity laws.

The evening preceding the Passover was the so-called 'day of preparation'. This is referred to as early as the Jewish papyri from Elephantine. In 419 BC the members of this Jewish colony received a rescript from the Persian court giving them the date of Passover and the ritual of purification for the feast of Azymes.

Bibliography: J. B. Segal, *The Hebrew Passover*, Oxford 1963; H. Haag, 'Pâques', *DB(S)* 6, 1120–49; J. Jeremias, *TDNT* v, 896–904; R. de Vaux, *Les Sacrifices de l'Ancien Testament*, Paris 1964, 7–27; E. Kutsch, 'Erwägungen zur

Geschichte der Passafeier und des Massotfestes', *ZTK* 55 (1958), 1–35; *de Vaux 484–93.

Henri Cazelles

B. *Easter (Passover) in the New Testament*. 1. *The Feast of Passover in the New Testament*. The Old Testament distinguishes between Passover, which is celebrated on the evening of the fourteenth day to the dawn of the fifteenth day of Nisan (Ex 12:3–14; Lev 23:5; Num 28:16; Ezra 6:19–21; 2 Chr 35:1, 17), and the feast of Unleavened Bread, closely associated with it, which was celebrated from the fifteenth to the twenty-first of Nisan (Lev 23:6–8; Num 28:17; Ezra 6:22; 2 Chr 35:17). Following the usage of contemporary judaism (Josephus: *Ant.* XIV 2:1, §21; XVII 9:3 §213; XVIII 2:2 §29; xx 5:3 §106; *Bell. Ind.* II 1:3 §10; Mishna: Pes 9:5; Hag 1:3) the New Testament, on the contrary, takes Passover to refer to both feasts (quite clearly in Lk 22:1; also 2:41; Jn 2:13, 23; 6:4; 11:55; 12:1; 13:1; 18:39; 19:14; Acts 12:4 point in the same direction).

Several events in the life of either Jesus or his disciples are associated with Passover. When twelve years old Jesus goes with his parents on a Passover-pilgrimage to Jerusalem and during the feast he stays in the temple (Lk 2:41–50). According to John, Jesus went to Jerusalem for Passover some time after the miracle of Cana (2:1–11), on which occasion he ejected the traders from the temple and performed miracles (2:14–23). Again according to Jn (6:4), the multiplication of bread also took place a short time before the celebration of Passover (cf Mk 6:35–44 and parallels; Jn 6:5–13). Most important of all, Jesus died during this festival (Mk 14:1f and parallels; Jn 12:1, 12; 13:1). The synoptics describe the last supper of Jesus with his disciples as the ritual Passover meal (Mk 14:12–16 and parallels; Lk 22:15) so that, according to them, Jesus died on the 15th of Nisan. According to John, however, who also reports this meal (13:1–30), it took place on the evening between the 13th and 14th of this month, so that Jesus was crucified on the 14th (see 18:28; 19:14). So far these two representations have not been successfully reconciled. Finally, Agrippa I had Peter arrested during a Passover a short time after he had had James son of Zebedee executed (Acts 12:2–4).

We have no direct evidence to show that the early christians celebrated the Passover and, if so, in what way. We can, however, suppose that later christian usage with regard to the celebration of Easter goes back to a primitive christian celebration of Passover which would certainly have had a different content and meaning from the Jewish feast. We find some indications pointing in this direction in the New Testament. For example, the fact that the days of Unleavened Bread are given prominence allows us to suppose that they were also of significance to christians (Acts 12:3; 20:6).

It would have followed naturally from the fact that Jesus died during Passover that from quite early on he would have been regarded as the Passover lamb (1 Cor 5:7). This comparison is the nucleus of a rich typology which we come across repeatedly in the New Testament and the church's liturgy. In the coming time of salvation the hopes inherent in Passover would be fulfilled (Lk 22:16). The christian community is compared with unleavened bread, and moral attitudes appropriate to the celebration of the christian Passover are demanded of it (1 Cor 5:7f). Finally, the moral task of the christian is inculcated with reference to motifs taken from the Jewish Passover (1 Pet 1:13–21): they are to gird up their loins in a spiritual sense (v 13) since they are in a time of exile, (v 17) though redeemed by the blood of Christ the lamb (v 19). As for the use of Passover typology in the liturgy, we may refer to the practice still in use of reading the Passover ritual (Ex 12:1-11) on Good Friday—earlier on Holy Saturday—and of singing the Exultet during the Easter vigil. In the preface for Easter Sunday there occurs the reference, taken from 1 Cor 5:7, to Christ as our Passover lamb which has been sacrificed.

2. *The resurrection of Jesus.* The christian feast of Easter, which historically is the continuation of the Jewish feast of Passover, even though its content is quite different, is for the christian determined by the thought of *the resurrection of Jesus.* It is true, of course, that in the early period of the church's history the resurrection was intimately associated with the passion and death of the Lord until, in the fourth century, death and resurrection were celebrated on two different days, Good Friday and Easter Sunday. For the resurrection of Jesus as an historical event, see ⁊ Jesus Christ. Here we limit ourselves to some remarks on the significance of the resurrection.

According to the New Testament the resurrection has a double significance. On the one hand, God has vindicated Jesus with regard to both his mission and his claim by raising him from the dead (Mt 12:40; Rom 1:4). Further, the significance of the resurrection has to be seen in the context of the history of salvation: negatively, as the overcoming of sin and its outcome which is death; positively, as the beginning of a new life (Rom 4:25; 1 Cor 15:14, 17, 22).

Since the resurrection is a vindication of Jesus it is natural that we should find expressed in the early Christian preaching of the resurrection certain christological motifs. Jesus is now 'exalted' (Acts 2:33; 5:31) 'to the right hand of God' (Acts 2:33; 5:31; Rom 8:34; Col 3:1; Heb 12:2), taken up into the glory of God (Phil 2:11). As such, despite his condemnation on earth, he appears as 'the holy and righteous one' (Acts 3:14), a new prophet and a second Moses (Acts 3:22f), 'the servant of God' (Acts 3:13, 26), 'lord' and 'messiah' (Acts 2:36), as 'Son of God' (Rom 1:4) whom God has exalted above all creation in return for his humiliation even to the death of the cross (Phil 2:9–11), and to whom all authority in heaven and earth is given (Mt 28:18).

As a result of his resurrection Jesus has a unique place in the whole history of the redemptive design of God. As the risen and exalted one he is active in power through all time and is near to his church (Mt 28:18, 20). He is the fulfilment of the promise made to the patriarchs (Acts 13:32f). He has passed into the glory of God after his resurrection as the firstborn of the multitude of those who sleep (1 Cor 15:20, 23). As he himself lives in a new kind of existence he can be called 'the author of life' (Acts 3:15), 'leader and saviour' (5:31 cf Heb 2:10; 12:2), the heavenly and last Adam (1 Cor 15:45, 47), and mediator of the divine Spirit (Acts 2:33; see also Rom 1:4; 1 Cor 15:45).

The outcome of the resurrection for christians is that they recognise him as lord and believe that God has truly raised him from the dead (Rom 10:9). In baptism they have already risen with him from the death of sin to a new life (Rom 6:4, 11; 7:4; Col 2:12f; 3:1, 3) in order to live in fellowship with him (Rom 7:4; 8:2, 10; 12:5; Gal 2:20; Eph 3:17) and in the possession of his Spirit (Rom 8:9; Eph 4:30; 5:18), which is the Spirit of life (Rom 8:2), as a 'new creation' (2 Cor 5:17; Gal 6:15). Since Christ has risen from the dead the christian may reasonably look forward in hope to a coming salvation (1 Pet 1:3). The expectation of the resurrection from the dead and of a life of happiness with God is possible only because Christ himself has risen to this new life (1 Cor 15:20–22). If this were not so there would be no resurrection for the christian; his faith would be in vain and the preaching of the apostles a delusion (1 Cor 15:12–19). But just as God has first raised Christ from the dead, so also will he raise the christian to a life of glory (1 Cor 15:23; 2 Cor 4:14).

On the basis of this resurrection faith the paranetic instruction found in the New Testament warns the christian to keep in mind his heavenly goal (Col 3:1f), to avoid what is evil (Rom 6:12f; Col 3:5–9), put off 'the old man' and put on 'the new man' (Col 3:9f; Eph 4:22–4), undertake a new way of life (Rom 6:4), bear fruit for God (Rom 7:4), live a virtuous life characterised by mercy, goodness, humility, meekness, and patience, living by love and mutual forgiveness (Col 3:12–14). Side by side with the joy and sense of exaltation at the new life which has already been given through the resurrection, there is the sober warning to avoid both unrealistic retirement from the world and undue excitement (2 Thess 2:1–3; 3:6–12). Conscious of living in the last age, one must be aware of the seriousness of the situation (1 Pet 4:7–11; 1 Jn 2:18–28) and be ready for the return of the Lord (1 Jn 2:28; 3:2).

Bibliography: J. Schmitt, *Jésus resuscité dans la prédication apostolique*, Paris 1949; F.-X. Durrwell, *The Resurrection: A Biblical Study*, London 1969³; E. Kretz, *Die Auferstehung Jesu als Heilsmysterium*, Salzburg 1958; W. Künneth, *Theologie der Auferstehung*, Munich 1951⁴; H. Schürmann, 'Die Anfänge christlicher Osterfeier', *TR* 130 (1951), 414–25; Haag 123–31; B. Lohse, *Das Paschafest der Quartadezimaner*, Gütersloh 1953; J. Jeremias, *TDNT* v, 896–904; R. Morgenthaler, *Christ ist erstanden*, Zürich 1955; P. Grelot and J. Pierron, *La Nuit et les Fêtes de Pâques*, Paris 1956; J. Schmitt, W. Bulst, and K. Rahner, 'Auferstehung Christi', *LTK* I, 1028–41; S. Lyonnet, 'La valeur sotériologique de la résurrection du Christ selon Saint Paul', *Gregorianum* 39 (1958), 295–318; G. Koch, *Die Auferstehung Jesu Christi*, Tübingen 1959; K. H. Rengstorf, *Die Auferstehung Christi*, Witten 1960⁴; J. Schildenberger, 'Der Gedächtnischarakter des alt- und neutestamentlichen Paschas', *Opfer Christi und Opfer der Kirche*, ed. B. Neunheuser, Düsseldorf 1960, 75–97; D. M. Stanley, *Christ's Resurrection in Pauline Soteriology*, Rome 1961; J. Sint, 'Die Auferstehung Jesu in der Verkündigung der Urgemeinde', *ZKT* 84 (1962), 129–51; R. Marlé and A. Kolping, 'Auferstehung Jesu', *HTG* I, 130–45; N. Füglister, *Die Heilsbedeutung des Pascha*, Munich 1963; J. B. Segal, *The Hebrew Passover*, London 1963; R. Le Déaut, *La Nuit Pascale*, Rome 1963; H. Grass, *Ostergeschen und Osterberichte*, Göttingen 1964³.

Johann Michl

Peace

A. *Old Testament.* 1. The Hebrew word *šālôm* has a wider range of meaning than either the English *peace*, the Latin *pax*, or the Greek *eirēnē*. Etymologically it is derived from the Sumerian root *silim* and the Akkadian root *šalâmu* = 'to be whole, uninjured'. Hence *šālôm* as applied to inorganic objects acquires the meaning of 'undivided'; as applied to artefacts it comes to mean 'undamaged', and as applied to living creatures 'sound', 'healthy'. As applied to the community *šālôm* is equivalent to 'well ordered as a society living in prosperity so far as outward circumstances are concerned'.

The idea of peace is a dominant factor in the life and thought of the ancient Near East. From time to time a certain hope wells up in the hearts of men and peoples and breaks out in the unpeaceful present in which they find themselves situated. It is hope for lasting and universal peace, and it springs from two different sources:

a. From *the memory*, more or less vividly preserved, *of a vanished golden age* at the beginning of time. All sorts of different situations may prepare the way for this to be recalled to mind.

b. From the *natural dispositions* of the human soul, which *longs for* that tranquillity of order in which peace consists. It can be perceived that these two basic impulses are complementary and interdependent. It is their memory that rouses and stimulates men's longing to represent to themselves the hoped-for future in the hues of the vanished primordial age as they imagine it once to have been.

2. Turning now to Israel herself we can paraphrase the range of meaning expressed by *šālôm* as follows: 'Peace means total harmony within the community. It is founded upon order and permeated by God's blessing, and hence makes it possible for man to develop and increase free and unhindered on every side'. This, then, explains why *šālôm* is used so often and with so wide a range of meaning, being found both in the context of everyday life and as the object of the most profound religious expectations. Bodily health is expressed by it (Is 57:18f; Jer 6:14). It serves as a form of greeting (Gen 29:6; 43:27; 1 Sam 16:4f). Men 'go in peace' (Gen 26:29; Ex 18:23), 'strive for peace' (Deut 23:6; Jer 29:7), 'sleep in peace' (Ps 4:8), 'are buried in peace' (Gen 15:15; 2 Kings 22:20).

It will be apparent from the foregoing that in the earlier period *šālôm* did not stand for the opposite of war. It consisted rather in complete harmony among those who had united to fight, both in battle and in victory. In 2 Sam 11:7 David paradoxically informs himself of the *šālôm* of the war. Victory over an enemy or the taking over of his territory is regarded as peace (Judg 8:7ff; 2 Sam 19:25, 31; 1 Kings 22:28). In fact from the outlook of the earlier generations of Israel a man was always in a state of peace when he could point to success in his undertakings. But in all these earlier expressions a further idea is implied, namely that peace is at root a *religious benefit*. In the last analysis it is dependent on God and is his gift.

3. *Later*, above all in the preaching of the prophets, a new development estab-

lishes itself, by which *war* is conceived of as *the opposite of peace*. For the full enjoyment of peace a fresh factor is now necessary, namely the absence of war (Is 2:4; 9:4). As this insight developed a parallel idea went with it, namely that as a sign of God's blessing true peace could only be established on the basis of righteousness and could only flourish in that condition which can quite generally be described as a life ethically ordered in all its aspects. Hence from time to time we now find peace linked with righteousness (Is 32:16f; Ps 72:3, 7; 85:10). In order to understand the connection between these two we must remind ourselves that all the promises of God's blessing, especially the chief one, that of enjoying peace, are conditional upon the observance of the law (see Lev 26:6; Deut 28:1–14).

A further and more negative aspect of the concept of peace is to be seen in the fact that in their conflict with the so-called 'prophets of well-being' the prophets had to distinguish true peace from a false idea of *šālôm*. Traces of their struggle are apparent in the episode of Micaiah the son of Imlah (1 Kings 22:5–18), but above all in Jer 6:14; 14:13; 28; Ezek 13:16. In place of this false concept of *šālôm* they threaten that because of the beguilement of the people and because of the externalisation of their cult judgement and punishment, *the opposite of 'well-being'* (Is 48:22; 57:21; Jer 6:14; 12:12; 30:5; Ezek 13:10) will come upon them. For in the last analysis God bestows *šālôm* only when the people are loyal to the covenant obligations into which they have entered (Is 26:12; 45:7). In the time of blessedness which

is to come God will actually enter into a new covenant, a 'covenant of peace' with the converted and purified people (Is 54:10; Ezek 34:25; 37:26). Thus united to God the people will receive from this covenant a plenitude of grace and favour.

4. This brings us to those aspects of the meaning of *šālôm* which most of all come to the fore in the eschatological expectation of the Old Testament. As used in this context, the word *šālôm* stands for *the essence of well-being and happiness*, that towards which Old Testament revelation directs all men, seeking with urgency and vigour to bring them to it. As particular definitive characteristics included in this universal and all-embracing eschatological peace, the following may be distinguished:

a. Paradisal fruitfulness in a degree never known before (Gen 49:11; Is 32:15–20; Joel 3:18; Amos 9:13–15);

b. Peace in the animal realm both among the animals themselves and between animals and man (Is 11:6–8; 35:9; Ezek 34:25; Hos 2:18);

c. Peace among men as individuals (cf Is 11:9; 65:25; Jer 31:31–4; Zech 9:9f);

d. Peace among nations (Is 2:2–4; 19:23–5; 54:13f; Mic 4:1–4; Zech 8:23).

These elements in the peace of the final age are not to be understood as having a merely 'symbolical' or spiritual meaning and so as open to any interpretation which we may choose. They are, on the contrary, full of real meaning as expressing the transformation of the world into that ideal state which it will achieve in the final age.

Thus they have as their content the *ideal reality of the eschaton free from all those earthly limitations and disadvantages* by which the men of the present age are oppressed. But even more than bringing earthly peace, the happiness of this eschatological peace will be a completely free *gift* and dependent on Yahweh (Is 2:2–4; 32:17; Zech 2:4f; 14:11; Ps 46:9f; 85:11). Yet a series of passages tell us that God will not bring about this peace by his own direct act but will give the Messiah, 'the prince of peace' (Is 9:6) the task of achieving this final happiness (Gen 49:10; Is 7:14; 9:6f; 11:1–5; 53:5; Dan 7:13, 18, 22; Mic 5:1–3; Zech 9:9f). This peace and happiness is not, however, bestowed unconditionally but depends on whether and how the faithful, in the course of their earthly lives, have shown themselves to be working for its realisation by their just and blameless conduct, and by their loyalty to God's revelation and law (Is 11:3–5; 32:15–18; Ps 72:1f; 85:9–14). Finally this will be made possible for man by the fact that God changes his inconstant heart (Jer 31:33f; Ezek 36:24–7). In this way he is put in a position freely and spontaneously to keep himself loyal to God. Naturally it is not in this aeon that everlasting peace is achieved. For the present it remains only a hope. In the age to come, on the contrary, it will be attended by an inconceivable harmony extending throughout the entire cosmos, and man will make that state of bliss completely his own, for the disease of sin will be fully healed in him. This peace will appear in the form of a new covenant of friendship with God and of complete happiness. It will bring with it the consummation of the All. From the history of salvation now coming to an end will issue the age of salvation which will be everlasting.

B. *New Testament.* 1. How far the range of meaning of *šālôm* extends may be seen by the fact that the LXX uses more then twenty terms in the attempt to give a precise rendering of the various shades of meaning in it which come to the fore from time to time. Finally, however the word *eirēnē* established itself as the appropriate translation, for the manifold uses to which this word is put have had the effect of broadening its conceptual field in many respects. Of itself *eirēnē* manifestly expresses the opposite of *polemos* (= war), the blessing of the *polis* (= city, state) which is dependent upon the favourable attitude and acts of the gods. In the subject matter which it represents *eirēnē* serves, in accordance with the increased understanding of the New Testament, to deepen the Old Testament idea of peace and to extend it further along the lines there laid down. Thus in the proems to many of the pauline letters (1 Cor 1:3; 2 Cor 1:2; Gal 1:3; Eph 1:2; Phil 1:2; Col 1:2, 1 Tim 1:2; 2 Tim 1:2; Tit 1:4; Philem 3) *eirēnē* is used with *kharis* (= grace) as a form of greeting. In Mt 10:13; Lk 10:5f when the disciples are sent on their mission the first thing they are commanded to do is to greet people by invoking peace upon them. The well-being of the young Church is also described as peace (Acts 9:31). The *eirēnē* referred to in these formulae of greeting is the immediate effect of that salvation which the Messiah freely bestows in the time of fulfilment from the hands of God. It is a characteristic of his self-manifestations (Lk 1:79;

2:14; Mk 5:34). It is this salvation which is proclaimed in the 'gospel of peace' (Eph 6:15). Jesus gives it to his own in his own way (Jn 14:27; 16:33). For God is the 'God of peace' (Rom 15:33; 16:20; 1 Cor 14:33). He establishes this peace through his Son (Acts 10:36; Phil 1:2; Col 1:20).

2. With regard to its content, the *eirēnē* which Christ bestows is characterised by the fact that it is parallel to ↗ *life* (Rom 8:6; see also 2 Pet 3:14). This idea is developed in 1 Thess 5:23 and a similar usage is found in Heb 13:20f. It implies that in the state of *eirēnē* the whole man is sound and whole in body and soul alike. Its chief effect is that through Christ, who is 'our peace' personified (Eph 2:14), man is in a state of peace with God. For according to Eph 2:14–18 Christ has established peace in two ways (cf Col 1:27; 3:14f):

a. between mankind and God (Rom 5:1);

b. of men among themselves, in that he has torn down the barrier between Jew and gentile and opened a way to God by which both may enter in one and the same Spirit through Christ (Eph 2:18; see also Lk 19:38; Acts 10:36). This peace then is already a present fact in the here and now of the church. It follows that peace is *an essential concomitant of the kingdom of God* (Rom 14:17; 1 Cor 7:15; Eph 4:3; 2 Tim 2:22; Jas 3:18). It is not only a gift, however, for it lays upon Christians the task of constantly seeking peace (1 Pet 3:11). Thus the New Testament idea of peace agrees with that of the Old in that it awaits the consummation of eschatological peace in the final age.

Bibliography: A. Bea, 'L'idea della pace nel Vecchio Testamento', *XXXV Congreso Eucaristico International*, Barcelona 1952, 49–59; J. Comblin, 'La paix dans la Théologie de S. Luc', *ETL* 32 (1956), 439–60; J. Comblin, *Theologie des Friedens*, Graz 1963; H. Gross, *Die Idee des ewigen und allgemeinen Friedens im Alten Orient und im AT*, Trier 1956; Haag 495–7; N. Peters, *Weltfriede und Propheten*, Paderborn 1917; G. von Rad and W. Foerster, *TDNT* II, 400–20; F. Sauer, *Die Friedensbotschaft der Bibel*, Graz 1954; E. Vogt, 'Pax hominibus bonae voluntatis', *Bbl* 34 (1953), 427ff; J. Zingerle, 'Die Weissagungen des Propheten Isaias (11:6–8) vom messianischen Friedensreich', *ZKT* 4 (1880), 651–61. See also: W. Caspari, *Vorstellung und Wort 'Friede' im AT*, Gütersloh 1910; W. Eichrodt, *Die Hoffnung des ewigen Friedens im alten Israel*, Gütersloh 1920; W. S. van Leeuwen, *Eirene in het NT*, Wageningen 1940; J. J. Stamm and H. Bietenhard, *Der Weltfriede im A und NT*, Zürich 1959.

Heinrich Gross

People (of God)

A. *Terminology*: The Old Testament uses several terms to designate the people of Israel as a religious entity but these are not synonyms. The noun *gôy* (pl. *gôyîm*) stands for a collection of individuals (hence in Joel 1:4 it is even applied to a swarm of locusts) who represent the whole population of an area without taking into account its inner unity. This is the word which the Old Testament normally uses for the foreign peoples with whom Israel comes into contact or whose existence she has heard of. Hence we can often translate by the term 'pagan'. It is true, however, that on occasion Israel herself is also described as *gôy* (Is 60:22; Ezek 35:10; Ps 106:5). The individual belonging to a *gôy* had no inward spiritual relationship with it, so that in referring to his own people a man would never say 'my/your/his *gôy*'. Only in the course of a prophetic address to the land (Ezek 36:13ff), and once in addressing Yahweh (Ps 106:5), is reference made to 'your *gôy*'. The phrase '*gôy* of Yahweh' is never used. LXX usually translates *gôy* as *ethnos*. It is only when the translator has understood *gôy* as referring to Israel that he writes *laos* (Josh 3:17; Is 9:2; Jer 9:8; etc).

The word *lᵉ'ôm* (pl. *lᵉ'ummîm*) only occurs in poetry, and is used as a general description of peoples and races. Here too 'my/your/his *lᵉ'ôm*' is never spoken of (*lᵉ'ummî* in Is 51:4 should probably read *lᵉ'ummîm*). The usage '*lᵉ'ôm* of Yahweh' is likewise unknown to the Old Testament. LXX uses *ethnos* in most cases to translate this term, but it does use *laos* too, eleven times.

The people considered as a unity consisting of men bound together by ties of common blood, speech, and moral and social standards, as well as by a common history and mutual solidarity, is *'am* (pl. *'ammîm*). Originally this term means 'clan ties', 'tribal relationships' (Gen 25:8, 17; 35:29; Ex 30:33, 38; Lev 19:16; Deut 32:50; 2 Kings 4:13; Jer 37:12; Ezek 18:18). But the expression can also mean 'people' in the broadest sense, 'population' (Judg 3:18; 1 Kings 19:21; 2 Kings 4:41; Ruth 4:9; Jer 39:10), and even stranger nations or peoples (Num 21:29; Deut 14:2; Ezra 3:3; Neh 10:28). Indeed it can even be used of a group of animals of the same species (Prov 30:25f). But *'am* is the favourite term used to designate Israel. In this case the expressions 'my/your/his *'am*' or ''*am* of Yahweh' are used, and the corresponding term in LXX is normally *laos*.

The noun *qālāl* can mean a crowd or

a loose assembly of men (1 Sam 19:20; Ps 26:5), but in most cases it stands for the conscription of the free menfolk of Israel for war (Num 22:4; Judg 20:2; 21:5, 8; 1 Sam 17:47) to deliver judgement (Ezek 16:40; Prov 26:26), to take decisions in matters of importance affecting the whole people (1 Kings 12:3), but above all for worship (Ex 12:6; Lev 4:13f; Num 16:33; 17:12; Deut 23:2ff, 9; 31:30; 1 Kings 8:14, 22, 55; Ps 22:22, 25; etc). It stands therefore for the people as it appears in relation to other peoples or to Yahweh when it exercises its functions as a whole through its duly appointed members. LXX almost always translates this expression as *ekklēsia*.

'ēdâh is closely similar in that it is used of groups of people of good (Ps 1:5) or evil intent (see the 'rabble of the company of Korah' Num 16:5f; see also Ps 22:16; Sir 16:6) assembled together for common consultation and action. Hence too it is used of the people who come to make up the assembly (Judg 20:1; Prov 5:14). In the majority of passages, above all in the Priestly (P) tradition of the Pentateuch, it is used to designate Israel as a religious (Ex 12:3; 16:1; Lev 8:3f; etc) or juridical community (Josh 9:21; 20:9 etc). The corresponding term in LXX is, with few exceptions, *sunagōgē*.

Yisrā'ēl (=Israel) is attested as the name of the people of God in the Old Testament from the earliest times (Song of Deborah, Judg 5:2, 7ff; Stele of Merneptah, line 27: *AOT* 20–25). As far as is known from the Old Testament the name stood from the very outset for something conceived to be sacred. Those who bore it comprised all the tribes together assembled round the ark of the covenant and united in the worship of Yahweh, that is, the people of God whom Yahweh had chosen. When the kingdom was divided after the death of Solomon the name Israel was confined to the Northern tribes and to the 'Northern kingdom' which they had established. Yet the prophets still refer occasionally to the people as a whole as 'Israel'. Thus Isaiah (8:14) speaks of 'both the houses of Israel'. After the downfall of the Northern kingdom (722) that section of the people in the Southern kingdom which had remained loyal to the Davidic dynasty, and which chiefly consisted of the tribe of Judah, became the embodiment of the people of God and once more bore the name *Israel*, which had once been applied to all the twelve tribes (Is 5:7; 8:18; Mic 2:12; 3:1, 8f; etc). After the exile it was the Jewish people living in Palestine and in the diaspora, now an ethnic and a religious community rather than a political one, that regarded itself as the heir to the ancient people of the twelve-tribe confederation and therefore took over the name Israel.

The name *Israel* is associated in the Old Testament with the ancestor of the people, Jacob. After his experience at the Jabbok Yahweh had changed the name Jacob to that of Israel (Gen 32:28ff). Hence the people are not infrequently referred to as 'Jacob' (eg, Num 23:7). In the period of the monarchy this name, like Israel, is at first used as a designation of Israel only (Amos 7:2, 5), but after the fall of Samaria it is applied to Judah too (Is 2:5f; 14:1; 29:22; Mic 2:7; 3:1; etc). On the other hand the names *Ephraim*, originally the name of one of the Northern tribes (Is 7 passim; 9:9;

Hos 4:17–14, 8, thirty-seven times; Ezek 37:19; etc), and *Joseph* (Ezek 37:16, 19; Amos 5:6; 6:6; Ps 80:1; etc) are applied as names of peoples either to the Northern tribes or to the Northern kingdom, while the name *Judah* is confined to the Southern tribes or to the Southern kingdom (1 Kings 12:23; 15:1; Is 22:21; Jer 7:30; Lam 1:3 etc). The name *'ibrî* (=Hebrew) as a designation of the Israelites is chiefly found on the lips of non-Israelites (Gen 39:14, 17; 41:12; Ex 1:16; 2:6; 1 Sam 4:6; etc) or as a way of describing themselves when addressing foreigners (Gen 40:15; Ex 1:19; 2:7; 9:13; Jon 1:9; etc). Although the name *Habiru* is found repeatedly in the records of the ancient Near East from the second millennium onwards, the connection between this and *'ibrî* has not so far been explained. In the Persian and hellenistic period *Israel*, *Jews*, and *Hebrews* are found side by side to stand for the Jewish people as an ethnic and religious unity, while the chief form of self-designation found on the lips of the Jews is, of course *Israel*, meaning their own people as the chosen people of God.

B. *The theology of the people of God in the Old Testament.* As the Old Testament conceives of it the individual man can gain access to God and so salvation only in union with the people of Israel whom God has chosen. The people of Israel and its members constitute an organic unity which is quickened and held together by a life-principle; for as such we may regard their solidarity in blood, in thought and desire, in moral and social standards, in worship and in acknowledgement of Yahweh. Israel has been made one people by descent from the patriarchs, the bearers of the promise, by the gracious choice of Yahweh, and by the covenant which Yahweh keeps.

Yahweh blessed the patriarchs and so made them a people (Gen 12:1ff; 17:4–8; 35:11). When the descendants of the patriarchs had become a people consisting of twelve tribes Yahweh freed them from the bondage of Egypt and chose them to be his own people and his special possession (Ex 19:3–8; Deut 7:6; 14:2; etc). At Sinai–Horeb Yahweh sealed a covenant of grace with this people (Ex 19–24; 34; Deut 5). It was in this way that Israel became the people of Yahweh (Ex 6:7; 19:5f; Lev 26:9–12; Deut 7:6ff).

Certainly it was only those who were descended from Abraham or from Jacob/Israel who normally belonged to the people of Yahweh. Yet on the one hand not everyone who was so descended from Abraham or Jacob *ipso facto* participated in the promises and blessings of the covenant, and on the other it was possible for those who were not descended from the patriarchs to become heirs to the promise. To specify this, other signs of belonging to Israel were required beside that of physical descent. One such sign was *circumcision*. It is a sign of the covenant and a sign of belonging to the people of God (Gen 17:10–14; Josh 5:2–9). Only males were circumcised. The women acquired their membership of Israel in virtue of the fact that they belonged to the head of a family. A further sign of belonging to the covenant people is *communal worship*, ie, the observance of the cultic ordinances laid down by Yahweh, especially that of the sabbath (Ex 31:13–17), the prescriptions for eating meals

(Lev 11; 17:10–14), the regulations for purity (Lev 12–15) and the observance of Passover (Ex 12:2–28, 43–49; Num 9:1–14; Deut 16:1–8). Anyone who transgresses these ordinances is 'cut off from his clan', ie, to be expelled from the community (Gen 17:14; Ex 12:15, 19; 30:33, 38; 31:14; Lev 7:20; 17:4, 9, 14; 22:3; 23:29; Num 9:13; etc).

In addition to these exterior signs of belonging to Israel interior ones too were required, namely loyalty to Yahweh and his commandments (Ex 20:1–17; Deut 5–7; 28). All these marks make the people as a whole a 'holy people' (Ex 19:6; Num 16:3; Deut 7:6; 14:2; 26:19; 28:9) and its individual members holy (Lev 19:2; Deut 33:3; Dan 7:18, 22, 27; etc). He who breaks God's covenant and does evil is, in spite of his physical descent, not a son of Abraham but of Canaan, the prototype of all immorality (see the story of Susanna).

Since the people of God is a community not only in blood but in life, moral standards and faith, it follows that it is possible to become a member of it even for one who is not descended from Abraham, namely one who accepts circumcision, the laws of the covenant, and faith in Yahweh (Ex 12:48; Num 10:29–32; Deut 23:8f; 1 Kings 8:41ff; Ezra 6:21; Judith 14:10; Is 2:2ff; 19:22–5; Mic 4:1ff; Zech 8:23). In general everyone who acknowledges that he is blessed in Abraham and in his 'seed' can become an heir to the promise (Gen 12:3; 22:18; 26:4; 28:14; Jer 4:2).

Implicit in the Old Testament concept of the people of God are the following *relationships of solidarity*:

1. *Earlier and later generations:* Just as

654

in a family a father can become a mediator of blessing and happiness (Gen 6:18; 7:1; 19:12; Ex 23:25f; Num 14:24; Ps 25:13; 37:25; 112:2; 128; Prov 14:26; 20:7) or of cursing and ruin (Gen 20:17f; Ex 20:5; 34:7; Num 16:32f; Deut 5:9; 11:6; Jos 7:24f; 1 Sam 2:31; Jer 11:22f; 18:21ff; Amos 7:17; Ps 17:14; 109:6–14) for his entire house and generation, according to his moral and religious attitude, so too earlier generations in Israel play a large part in deciding whether later generations are to be blessed or cursed. The influence of the progenitors is above all decisive in determining the relationship between God and the tribes and peoples descended from them. It is from them that the entire community inherits either the blessing and the promise (Gen 9:26f; 12:1–7; 13:15f; 15:5; 16:10; 17:1–9, 19f; 22:16; 26:3; 28:13f; 35:11f; 48:15f, 19f; 49:8–27; Num 14:24; Jos 14:9; Jer 35:18f) or else the curse (Gen 9:25; 49:3–7). In fact humanity itself in its entirety is subject to the curse pronounced upon its progenitor for his sin (Gen 3:16f). Not only does the progenitor give life to the community descended from him, but he determines too the character, the habits of life, the morals and the religion of the entire clan—the people is conceived of as a macrocosm of the clan. Hence in the last analysis it is conformity with 'the fathers' in religious and moral thinking and acting that is decisive, rather than belonging to the line of inheritance of the blessing (Gen 17:13f; 18:19; Lev 26:40ff, 45; Is 51:2) or of the curse (Jos 24:14f; Is 43:27; Jer 11:3f, Dan 13:56; Hos 12:2, 14). For it is precisely he who does not conform to the fathers

in morals and religion who will be 'cut off from his people', ie, expelled from the community.

But the blessing and curse which are extended to the people as a whole derive not only from the patriarchs but from earlier generations in general. God's promises to the earlier generations, to the 'fathers', are applicable only to the extent that the later generations walk in the way of the fathers. If they deviate from it then the promises will fail to take effect and the blessing will be changed into a curse (Deut 11:28; 30:17; Judg 2:19–22; Is 63:10ff; Jer 2:30, 32; 7:25f; 9:12f; Ezek 2:3ff; Hos 9:10; 10:9; 12:14; Amos 2:4; Zech 7:7–13). The prophets reproach their contemporaries for having imitated the sins of the fathers, indeed for having gone even further in the same evil direction than the fathers; in this way they have forfeited the promised blessings (Jer 7:26; 11:10; 44:9–17; Ezek 2:3ff; Hos 9:10; 12:15; Amos 2:4, 7). Their descendants therefore are not inevitably predestined to the curse, but make the curse actual for themselves by their own fault. Hence the proverb which arose about 590 BC: 'The fathers have eaten sour grapes and the teeth of the children are set on edge', is false (Jer 31:29f; Ezek 18:2). It was intended to shift the blame to the fathers in the judgement, and to represent perdition as an inevitable fate. The opposite of this is demanded in Lev 26:40 and Jeremiah (3:22ff; 14:7, 19f), namely, repentant acknowledgement of the people's own and their fathers' sins. One must separate oneself then not only from one's own sins but also from the guilty fathers, and return to the moral and religious behaviour of those who once bore the promise. After the exile the acknowledgement of 'the sins of our fathers and our sins' becomes a characteristic of Jewish prayer (Ezra 9:6–15; Neh 1:6; 9:6–37; Judith 7:28; Tobit 3:2–5; Ps 106:6; Lam 5:7, 16; Bar 1:15–3, 8; Dan 9:15–19). The pious feel themselves ensnared in the sins of the fathers and wish to remove the guilt both of the fathers and of the present generation, that is the general guilt which oppresses the people of God. They try to do this by penance, confession of their sins, patient endurance of suffering, and intercession.

2. *Mediator and people.* This solidarity in blessing and curse also applies to all the members of the people who are alive at the same time. But God has called specific individuals to act in a special way as mediators of blessing and wellbeing. Such mediators are:

a. The great men of God, especially Moses, who by their sorrowful intercession before God rescue Israel from the judgement (Ex 32:31f; 34:9f; Num 14:5; 21:4–9; Deut 9:18, 25–9). Conversely even Moses incurs God's wrath because of the people's sins (Deut 1:37; 3:23–6; 4:21f).

b. The priests and prophets: the acts of expiation performed by the priests rescue Israel from perdition (Num 14:5f; 17:9–13; 25:6–15) and mediate blessing to her (Lev 9:22; Num 6:23–6; Deut 10:8; 21:5). The prophets not only announce God's will to the people, but also make intercession for Israel (Jer 14:7ff, 19–22; 21:2; 37:3; 42:1–4; Ezek 9:8; 11:13; Amos 7:1–6; Mic 7:18f). Indeed Yahweh actually delays his judgement in the hope that priests and prophets may yet be found to 'stand in the breach' on behalf of the sinful people and to 'build a wall' so that his wrath might be stayed (Ezek 13:5; 22:30; Ps 106:23; Sir 45:23). Of course a change of disposition must also take place in the sinners; those whom the mediating activity of the men of God is intended to benefit must somehow acknowledge, at least retrospectively, that they have taken him as their mediator and thereby declare their solidarity with him (see Ex 33:4ff; Num 12:11–14; 21:7; Jer 7:16; 11:14; 14:11; 15:1; Ezek 9:8ff; Is 53:1–6; Zech 12:10–14). The judgement upon Israel is inevitable when even the priests and the prophets fail and do not fulfil their functions as mediators (Ezek 13:5; 22:30; cf Is 28:7–13; Jer 2:8ff; 6:13; Hos 4:4ff; 5:1).

c. The king: the king plays a certain part in the Israelite cult. He is a dispenser of blessing (2 Sam 6:18; 1 Kings 8:14, 55f; 1 Chron 16:2; 2 Chron 6:3) and an intercessor (1 Kings 8:22–53; 2 Kings 19:15–19; 2 Chron 6:12–33; 30:18f). But the sins of the king bring evil on his people too. As it was conceived of in the earlier period it took the form of a great national misfortune brought upon the people by some transgression of the king's, yet as a punishment not of the people but of the king. It is he, not the people, who will be hit (D. Daube: 'Herrscherstrafe' [=punishment of the overlord]; Gen 20:9; 2 Sam 21:1f, 14; 24:11–17; 1 Kings 9:6f; 18:18; 20:42). The attitude of the king towards religion determines that of the people too. Godless kings become a snare for their people because they lead them into idolatry. For this reason the history writers and prophets regard the people themselves as guilty in the judgement because they have allowed themselves to be led astray by their kings (1 Kings 14:15f; 15:30; 2 Kings 17:20–23, 35–40; 23:26f; 2 Chron 12:1; 21:11; 33:9f; Jer 32:32; 36:31; Sir 47:23ff; 49:4f). In the cult the community prays for the king, knowing that prosperity and blessing depend upon him (1 Kings 8:66; Ps 20:9; 21; 61:7ff; 72; 84:9).

d. The martyrs: Old Testament revelation is also concerned with the solidarity which exists between the individual and the people. This reaches its highest point in the references to vicarious expiatory suffering. The 'Servant of Yahweh' (Is 52:13–53:12) and the 'pierced one' (Zech 12:9–14) vicariously atone by their suffering and death for the guilt of the 'many' and thereby avert the judgement of God (↗ Servant of God). The three youths in the furnace (Dan 3:23[16f]) consider the laying down of their lives upon which they have decided as an expiatory sacrifice on behalf of their people. The Maccabaean martyrs hope that God's anger over Israel will 'be arrested' by their sufferings (2 Macc 7:38). The idea of vicarious substitution in these passages has nothing to do with magic, as is shown by the acknowledgement implicit in the 'we' in Is 53:1–9 and the mourning of the people in Zech 12:10–14. Those who are benefited by the vicarious suffering of the martyrs must declare themselves, at least retrospectively, one with the mediator in solidarity, and must separate themselves from sin.

3. *The pious man or the sinner and the people.* But the simpler members of the people too exercise an influence on the happiness or unhappiness of the whole community according to whether they are pious or sinners, just as, conversely, they have a share in the merit and the guilt of the fathers and of the people as a whole. As a community Israel set itself under the law of the covenant and bound itself to observe the commandments. It must therefore ensure that the order prescribed by the covenant is observed by individual members too. If a limb of the communal body is diseased, ie, if it has incurred guilt, then the whole suffers the consequences with it (Josh 7; 1 Sam 14:27, 37). Conversely, the individual cannot withdraw himself from the judgement incurred by the majority of the people for their sins. But in this case the pious man patiently accepts his share of the suffering in order to remove the guilt of the people (see above under 1). On the other hand the pious individual feels himself protected among his people which is heir to the promises, because he knows that by this he too will have a share in the promised happiness (Ps 105:5–9; 106:45; Sir 44:19–23; Wis 12:21; 18:22). Even when only a small ↗ remnant is delivered from the judgement this remains the people of God and the heir to the promises (Is 4:3; 10:20; 11:11–15; 24:13–16; 65:8ff; Jer 30:10ff; Mic 2:12; Zeph 3:12).

In the Old Testament therefore the people is not a collective entity in which the individual completely loses his identity; but neither is each single member an 'individual' who is only interested in his own happiness. Thus the Old Testament conception of the relationship between people and individual can be appropriately described

657

neither by the term 'collectivism' nor by that of 'individualism': at most it can be described as 'solidarity'. As the people of God Israel is a visible community made up of sinners and just, of 'fathers' and 'sons', a 'hierarchy' and 'layfolk'. In it each individual receives through the whole life, grace and happiness; but as a member of the whole he also mediates life or death to the people. The people of God is not a static organisation, but an organism that is continually developing, renewing itself, at times too, it must be admitted, becoming sick and transforming itself, but in the last analysis immortal by reason of the promises made to it. For even when the visible Israel of the Old Covenant has vanished the ideal spiritual Israel still remains, the holy 'remnant' of those who will come through judgement and penance to receive life from God and to experience the fulfilment of the promises brought by the Messiah, the mediator and servant of God *par excellence*. By this faith the Old Testament prepares the way for the New Testament concepts of the church and the mystical body of Christ.

C. People of God in the New Testament,⁊ church.

Bibliography: A. On the people of God: G. Bertram, K. L. Schmidt, and H. Strahtmann, *TDNT* II, 364–9; III, 530–31; and IV, 29–39; A. Cody, 'When is the Chosen People Called a Goy?', *VT* 14 (1964), 1–6; H. Wildberger, *Jahwes Eigentumsvolk*, Zürich 1960; E. A. Speiser, '"People" and "Nation" of Israel', *JBL* 79 (1960), 157–63; R. Martin-Achard, *Israël et les nations*, Neuchâtel 1959; J. Pedersen, *Israel, its Life and Culture*, I–IV, Copenhagen–Oxford 1959; J. Maier, *Zum Gottesvolk- und Gemeinschaftsbegriff in den Schriften vom Toten Meer*, Vienna 1958 (dissertation); H.-J. Kraus, *Le peuple de Dieu dans l'AT*, Neuchâtel 1960; J. D. W. Kritzinger, *Qehal Yahwe. Wat dit is en wie daaraan mag behoort*, Kampen 1957; D. W. Watts, 'The People of God', *Expository Times* 67 (1955/6), 232–7; J. R. Wiskerke, *Volk van Gods Keuze*, Goes 1955; F. Asensio, *Yahweh y su pueblo*, Rome 1953; N. A. Dahl, *Das Volk Gottes*, Oslo 1941; L. Rost, *Die Vorstufen von Kirche und Synagogue im AT* (*BWANT* IV/24), Stuttgart 1938; N. A. Dahl, *Die Bezeichnungen für Land und Volk im AT* (Festschrift O. Procksch), 1934, 125–48; N. W. Porteous, *Volk und Gottesvolk im AT* (K. Barth zum 50. Geburtstag), 1936, 146–63; G. von Rad, *Das Gottesvolk im Deuteronomium* (*BWANT* 47), Stuttgart 1929; *G. von Rad, *Studies in Deuteronomy*, London 1953, esp. 45–59.
B. On the names *Israel*, *Judah*, etc; G. von Rad, K. G. Kuhn, and W. Gutbrod, *TDNT* III, 356–91; W. Zimmerli, 'Israel im Buche Ezechiel', *VT* 8 (1958), 75–90; H. W. Hertzberg, 'Jeremia und das Nordreich Israel', *TLZ* 77 (1952), 595–602; A. R. Hulst, 'Der Name "Israel" im Deuteronomium', *OTS* 9 (1951), 65–106; G. A. Danell, *Studies in the Name of Israel in the OT*, Uppsala 1946; L. Rost, *Israel bei den Propheten*, Stuttgart 1937.
C. On solidarity between people and individual: J. Scharbert, *Heilsmittler im AT und im Alten Orient*, Freiburg 1964; N. Lohfink, 'Wie stellt sich das Problem Individuum-Gemenischaft in Deuteronomium 1:6–3:29?', *Scholastik* 35 (1960), 403–7; J. de Fraine, *Adam et son lignage. Etudes sur la notion de "personnalité corporative"* dans la Bible*, Bruges 1959; J. Scharbert, *Solidarität in Segen und Fluch im AT und in seiner Umwelt* I, Bonn 1958; G. E. Wright, *The Biblical Doctrine of Man*, London 1954; F. Spadafora, *Colletivismo e Individualismo nel VT*, Rovigo 1953; J. de Fraine, 'Individu et société dans la religion de l'AT', *Bbl* 33 (1952), 324–55 and 445–75; D. Daube, *Studies in Biblical Law*, Cambridge 1947, 154–89; A. V. Ström, *Vetekornet. Studier över individ och kollektiv i NT*, Stockholm 1944; W. Eichrodt II, 157–83; J. Hempel, 'Das Ethos des AT', *BZAW* 67 (Berlin 1938), 32–93; H. W. Robinson, 'The Hebrew Conception of Corporate Personality', *BZAW* 66 (Berlin 1936), 49–62.

Josef Scharbert

Perfection

A. *The Old Testament*. I. The Hebrew root *t-m-m* with its derivatives is chiefly used to express the idea of human perfection. Admittedly the verb is found in this ethical sense only once, in Ps 19:13. But this may be taken as symptomatic of something that applies to all the words formed from the root *t-m-m*: their chief connotation is sinlessness and freedom from punishment. The adjective *tām* belongs to typical Wisdom language. In Job 1:1, 8; 2:3 it is a synonym for 'upright' (*yāšar*, often in this sense), God-fearing, an enemy of evil. The negative aspect of its meaning (=free from punishment) is especially prominent in Job 9:20–22; Prov 1:11 (corrected). The adjective *tāmîm* has a wider range. In the language of sacrifice (Priestly [P] tradition, forty-one times; Ezek, eleven times) it is predicated of the animal victim with the sense of 'free from defect', 'unblemished'. In the religious and moral sphere it is striking how often it is combined with 'way' and 'walking': thus in Gen 6:9; 17:1 (both P); Ps 15:2; 18:33; 101:2, 6; 119:1; Prov 11:20; 28:18. This is still more true of the substantive *tōm*: see 2 Sam 15:11; Job 4:6; Prov 2:7; 10:9; 19:1; 20:7; 28:6; Ps 26:1, 11. According to this usage man is 'perfect' when he walks with God or in God's way, and avoids any way which is sinful and so leads him away from God. Often too *tōm* is used of the state of the heart in the sense of a pure and sinless conscience (see Gen 20:5, 6 [*Elohist!*]; Ps 78:72; 1 Kings 9:4).

II. No Old Testament doctrine of perfection can be constructed on the basis of the terminology alone. What Yahweh requires of his human covenant partner and what he regards as the ideal of covenant partnership is stated in manifold ways in the revelation of Yahweh's will. The decalogue, as the heart and centre of the covenant charter, undoubtedly contains the principal statement of this. Its basic ideas exercise a decisive influence not only upon the legal traditions but also upon the prophetic and sapiential ones. It is true that the formulae in which the decalogue is expressed are almost exclusively negative—hence it is not surprising that the chief aspect of the meaning of the root *t-m-m* is sinlessness—but this negative formulation is no more than the outward garb of an eminently positive demand, namely the 'yes' of assent to God and to one's neighbour (cf the two tables of Moses). This is not revealed for the first time in the New Testament (see Mt 22:37f and parallels). It is attested again and again in the Old Testament too. If we enquire more closely into the essential claims which Yahweh makes on his covenant partner the following must be mentioned:

1. *Faith as a basic attitude.* The ⁊ decalogue has nothing explicit to say concerning faith, but it does presuppose it as axiomatic, especially in the first table (also on this compare Ex 19:8 with 19:3ff). As far back as the sealing of the covenant with Abraham it is clearly apparent that a role of fundamental importance in the covenant partnership is assigned to faith (see Gen 15:6). Num 14:11; 20:12; Is 7:9; 43:10; Ps 106:24 point in the same direction. In all this it is apparent that faith follows the same basic pattern throughout: believe in Yahweh because of his covenant. Faith is therefore an act which proceeds from person to person: the believer receives the word of revelation from God, especially the

word of his promise, and makes it the foundation of his life (the Hebrew equivalent for 'believe', *heʾĕmîn*, literally means 'to take one's stand upon . . .').

2. *The living 'yes' of assent to God as Lord of, and as partner in, the covenant.* a. *The turning of the heart to him.* Ex 20:6; Deut 6:5ff; Josh 22:5 are the chief texts which speak of this. This thought is, from the very outset, implicit in the use of the word *love* to express man's relationship with God. It is the Deuteronomist (D) school which is particularly preoccupied with it, and this is, in turn, influenced by the prophets and especially by Hosea precisely in this respect. Love is expressed and maintained in the keeping of God's commands—hence in Deuteronomy and elsewhere 'love' and 'fear' are used as parallel terms—and this truth is explicitly asserted in various different ways (Ex 20:6; Deut 5:10; 7:9; etc). It is true that the tone of moving warmth is absent from the P version of the law, which points austerely to the absolute duty of obedience; but by this it means nothing else than the surrender of the will to God.

b. *The turning of the word to God.* It does not need to be specially emphasised that alike in Israel and in the ancient Near East the just man stands before God as one who speaks to him. For the believers of the Old Testament the dialogue with their covenant God has, as it were, an 'existential' significance. This speech with God and in God's presence reaches its highest point in prayer. The duty of praying is included by implication in the first commandment of the decalogue. The prophets constantly show themselves to be men of great prayer. A passage in Hos 14:2 contains the cry: 'Take with you words and return to Yahweh!' and goes on to set prayer above other offerings as 'the fruit of our lips'. It is the psalter especially, with its rich store of prayer forms (hymns, thanksgiving, laments, psalms of trust etc) which provides evidence of the central place which prayer took in the covenant partnership. According to Ps 50:15 to entreat is of itself to honour Yahweh. According to Ps 50:14; 51:17f prayer is better than animal sacrifice.

c. *The making over of the good things of life to him in sacrifice and cult.* The religion of Israel maintains the sacrificial form of worship in common with other religions of the general area to which she belongs. Particularly clear evidence of this is provided by the discoveries at Ras-Shamra-Ugarit. But the meaning which is ascribed to such sacrifices in the Old Testament is different from that entertained by other peoples. At a very early stage Moses had established the 'worship of the word' (ie, the word of God and the response of men) as central to the liturgy of the covenant (Ex 24:7). The prophets, especially Hosea, preached that the pith and essence of sacrifice was the making over of oneself to the covenant God by paying heed to his instruction and by personal morality. Even the priestly version of the law, for all its preoccupation with cultic forms, is stamped with this idea. For though the manner in which sacrifices were offered was governed by strict rules and rubrics, they were still regarded in this tradition purely as evidence of their offerers' obedience to God in his holiness. The basic exhortation of the priestly tradition is 'Be holy, for I, Yahweh your God, am holy!' (Lev 11:44f; 19:2; 20:26 etc. And even if this has strong cultic connotations, still no one could fail to hear in it the universal summons to surrender the will to Yahweh. Unlike the foregoing the Deuteronomic law emphasises also the joy which the Israelite experiences in taking an active part in the celebrations at the sanctuary, especially in the sacrificial meal over which the covenant God presides as host. It calls the bringing of the sacrifice to the temple 'rejoicing before Yahweh' (see Deut 14:26; 16:13ff). Similarly the sabbath, which occupies a central place in the cult laws, is regarded by Deuteronomy not only as a day on which time as the chief blessing of life is offered, but also as a refreshing day of rest for man and beast (see Deut 5:14; Ex 23:12).

3. *The 'yes' of assent to the covenant God as a 'yes' of assent to one's fellow man.* However closely the sacrificial cult was bound up with the religion of Israel it did not constitute its heart and centre. This fact shines out from the message of the prophets with unmistakable clarity, especially in the case of Mic 6:6ff. Here, in a spirit of penitence, the people pose the question of what Yahweh requires of them, and in doing so it is natural that they should think in terms of unbloody or bloody sacrifices. 'You have been told, O man, what is good, and what Yahweh requires of you: to act justly to love the spirit of brotherhood and to walk in a spirit of humble service with your God!' The fact that in the decalogue religious and moral obligations are indivisibly connected made one point clear from the outset: every violator of

justice and love between men flouted by his offence the will of the covenant God for all men and so constituted a breach of the covenant. The solemnity of the condemnations in Is 1:10ff; Jer 7:21ff; Amos 5:21ff; Hos 6:6 confirm such an interpretation. Micah summarises this central tradition of revelation and gives it its most impressive formulation, and he even presents the 'yes' of assent to one's neighbour as the principle which it is most important to teach. What Yahweh demands of man is that in his life no less than in his act of faith he shall give his assent to the will of his covenant God and so, in union with him, shall live in harmony with everyone to whom the favour of the covenant God is extended. Certainly in ancient Israel this applied primarily to one's fellow Israelites, but at least the basic ethical demands had a universal application (see Gen 9:6; Ex 22:20; 23:9; Deut 14:29; Lev 19:34; Amos 2:1 etc). Thus in the demand 'to walk with God in a spirit of humble service' we have before us a summary not only of the first table of the decalogue but of the covenant instruction in its entirety. It is the most eloquent expression of the covenant ethos of the Old Testament as a whole. It contains echoes of the memory of the exodus when Israel set out on the way not only into the promised land but also into her own history with Yahweh as her *leader*. Our minds must be open to this association when we meet such expressions in the Old Testament as 'walking with God' (see also Gen 5:22, 24; 6:9; Mal 2:6), 'walking after God' (1 Kings 14:8), 'walking in Yahweh's ways' (Deut 19:9; 28:9; 1 Kings 2:3; 2 Kings 21:22; Ps 81:13),

661

or 'walking in God's sight' (see Gen 7:1; 17:1; 24:40; 48:15; 1 Kings 3:6; 9:4; etc). Hence it is not unnatural to find the idea of perfection so often associated with 'way' and 'walking'. Certainly 'walking' in such passages is close to the idea which we express in English by 'travelling' or 'wandering', but the Hebrew word in question never has quite this force. From this aspect too, and not only from that of faith directed towards the future, human existence before God acquires in the Old Testament a uniquely dynamic quality and an openness to the future which could almost be called eschatological.

The Old Testament doctrine of perfection contains no idea of the *status perfectionis* properly so called. It is true that in the early history of Israel we do find sporadic references to the Nazirite state as a life-long consecration to God (Judg 13:5; 1 Sam 1:11), the external sign of which was that the Nazirite allowed his hair to grow uncut. But later men became Nazirites only for a time (cf Num 6), incurring the obligations of not cutting their hair, refraining from wine, and avoiding all contact with corpses. Even the so-called Rechabites (cf 2 Kings 10:15ff), who strove to imitate the life of the wilderness period in the midst of the fertile land, cannot truly be claimed as belonging to a special category of the perfect, even though they earned high praise for their loyalty to Yahweh (Jer 35:6ff). The Old Testament knows nothing of voluntary poverty, although the 'poor of Israel' acquire a special place in revealed tradition as devoted and loyal believers in Yahweh. The ideal here is to bear social oppression

and religious persecution with patience and fortitude. The celibate state is imposed only on Jeremiah (16:1ff), and that by way of exception and for reasons of symbolism. Vows of obedience such as those taken at a later period at Qumran are still unknown to the Old Testament. The ideal of perfection of the Old Testament thus envisages the covenant people as a whole, and remains within the limits of what every member of the people of God can aspire to and attain.

Slowly but ever more clearly in the course of Old Testament revelation it became apparent that God had decided to call from the midst of the Old Israel, ever stubborn in resisting his will, the head and representative of a new covenant people. From the moment when this figure is first conceived of, the ideal of the perfect covenant partner of God shines out from him. He is distinguished by his specially close relationship with God (Is 9:6; 11:2). His chief mission is to be just himself and to establish justice between men throughout the covenant people (cf Is 9:6; 11:3–5). He will rule his people as a good shepherd (see Mic 5:4; Ezek 34:23). Not only will his heart be with the poor and the oppressed, but he will identify himself completely with them (Zech 9:9). Although deputed to bring salvation, not only to Israel but to the gentiles too (Is 42:6; 49:6), he will be despised and insulted (see Is 49:7), yet he will surrender himself to the hard destiny marked out for him by God (cf Is 50:4ff). His sense of brotherhood will be so intense that he will be ready to endure death as a victim on behalf of men to atone for their breaches of the covenant and to intercede for them before the covenant God (Is 53:12). These are all features which, according to Mic 6:8 characterise the perfect human covenant partner of Yahweh. In the messianic bringer of salvation they are made present in a pre-eminent degree and, as it were, in concrete tangible form. It is in the new covenant that that concrete tangible form comes into actual existence, drawing men to follow it.

Bibliography: The relevant sections of the various theologies of the Old Testament (eg, Heinisch, 140–89; Eichrodt III; E. Jacob, 122–219; Imschoot II, 83–338; Proksch, 677–99; von Rad I, 382f). Especially: J. Hempel, *Das Ethos des AT*, 1964²; J. I. Dickson, *The Idea of Perfection in the Old Testament*, Vanderbilt University 1954 (dissertation); P. Delhaye, 'Le recours à l'AT dans l'étude de la théologie morale', *ETL* 31 (1955), 637–57; A. Deissler, 'Das Vollkommenheitsideal nach dem AT', *GL* 1959, 328–39; A. Vanhoye, *DBT* 375f.

Alfons Deissler

B. *Later judaism*. The Old Testament demands perfection in the sense of 'completeness', 'wholeness', and this is chiefly expressed in the terms tom, tam, tamim. This determines the ideal of piety for later judaism too, especially in the esoteric circles influenced by apocalyptic writings and in Qumran. The idea of 'wholeness of heart' (*tom = haplotēs*) has a major part to play (see Edlund), above all in 'The Testament of the Twelve Patriarchs'. The *Essenes of Qumran* are notable in regarding themselves as 'the perfect of the way' (I QS IV, 22; I QSa I, 28; I QM XIV, 7; I QH I, 36), 'those who walk perfectly' (I QS I, 8; II, 2; III, 9; IX, 19; I QSb I, 2; V 22), 'a house of perfection and truth in Israel' (I QS VIII, 9), 'men

perfect in holiness' (CD XX, 2, 5, 7). Especially noteworthy here is the connection of 'perfect' ('perfection') with 'way' and 'walk'. This points both backwards to the Old Testament and forwards to the New. Yet the ideal of perfection upheld by the community of Qumran goes far beyond that of the Old Testament, for this community regards itself as the 'holy remnant' of the final age, which has gained a deeper knowledge of the way of God in the Torah than the rest of the Israelites, and which knows of the 'mysteries' of God. The perfect, then, are the saints of the final age! Yet this esoteric awareness of perfection is strangely complemented by the simultaneous conviction that 'perfection' only 'comes from the hand of God' (see I QS XI, 2:10f; I QH IV, 30). Hence the birth of the new man who is perfect already in the here and now (see Kosmala) takes place at Qumran in the power of God's spirit. Thus the tension between indicative and imperative is already apparent here.

For *Philo of Alexandria*, 'perfection' (*teleiotēs*) means 'nothing else than the summit of life, where the vision of God is associated with the most virtuous mode of life, where the whole of existence is conceived of as service of God and service of the brothers, where everything is received in experience as a gift of God and produced in act as a *mimēsis theou*' (Völker, 262f): this represents a synthesis of the Old Testament and Jewish ideal of perfection with that of the Greek Stoics.

In *rabbinical tradition* the idea of perfection is chiefly associated with the concept of the '*Tsaddiq*' ('the just man': on this, see R. Mach, *Der Zaddik*).

C. *The New Testament*. 1. *Jesus*. So far as the concept goes there are only two passages in the gospels in which Jesus makes explicit statements about 'perfection'. Once in the Sermon on the Mount we find the exhortation: 'Be ye also perfect as your heavenly Father is perfect' (Mt 5:48). Behind this lies the late Jewish conception of the *imitatio Dei*, which is based on God's exhortation in the Old Testament: 'Be holy, for I the Lord your God am holy!' (Lev 19:2). The text which we have already cited from the Sermon on the Mount is connected with the preceding logion by the conjunction *oun* (= therefore), and it is possible to recognise from this preceding logion that the 'perfection' for which the disciples of Jesus must strive consists above all in boundless *love*, which takes its measure from God. The extent to which this love exceeds the normal measure (*perisson*) is shown precisely in the fact that it is extended even to enemies. In this respect the righteousness of the scribes and pharisees is 'far' exceeded (see 5:20).

The 'christian' element in Jesus' teaching on perfection appears in the pericope of the rich young man according to Matthew's version (see Mt 19:21). The element that is 'wanting' for the perfection which the rich young man seeks is total renunciation of possessions and, as a concomitant of this, discipleship of Jesus. Perfection, then, as understood here means something more than devotion to the torah, however earnestly intended, though this too can lead to life (cf 19:17). This does not imply that Jesus teaches a 'two-category' ethic. Rather it re-emphasises once more the *perisson*

which belongs to the *teleion* as he sees it. It is the life of the disciple, taking into account the radical demands it makes upon those who embrace it, that now constitutes the 'perfect' and the new. Here of course the Jewish doctrine of the 'perfect *way*' has been absorbed into the idea of *following after* (discipleship of) Jesus. Thus the imitation of God has become discipleship of Jesus. What is more, Jesus' call to 'perfection' is not left to a final state, but permeates his whole moral teaching.

2. *Paul*. For the apostle too the will of God is directed primarily towards the *teleion* (Rom 12:2). Thus according to Col 4:12 the prayers of Epaphras are likewise offered in order that the Colossians may 'stand as perfect'. In the context this may be interpreted as 'being filled with the will of God in its fullness'. It is because the christians receive with faith the ultimate message of God, the 'foolish' gospel of the cross, and because they are not intoxicated by the false wisdom of the world, that they are already 'the perfect' (1 Cor 2:6). And yet for all that perfection remains constantly a goal that lies before them, towards which they are directed by the apostles' exhortations (1 Cor 14:20; Phil 3:14; Col 1:28; 4:12). 'All who would be perfect' must be of one mind in this with the apostle (cf Phil 3:15). Yet we learn from 3:12 that he himself is not yet 'perfect' and that for him too the *teleion* still lies before him as *ta emprosthen*, as 'a goal', as 'the prize of victory' which he pursues. The standard of christian perfection may be considered from two aspects. On the one hand it is for Paul (as for Jesus) love, which binds all the other virtues together into one (Col 3:14). This, in

contrast to that 'scaffolding' which passes away, survives even in the 'life beyond' because it is the 'perfect' (1 Cor 13:9f). From another point of view the standard of christian perfection is to be found in the glorified Christ himself; for in him is that goal which is to be set before the eyes of every man as 'perfect', that goal towards which all the strivings and exhortations of the apostles are directed (Col 1:28). This is the New Testament's interpretation of the ideal 'perfect man' referred to in terms drawn from judaism in Eph 4:13. It signifies that eschatological *state of maturity* which corresponds to the 'coming of age' of Christ, the state of *perfect* glory to which he has finally come in heaven. This 'perfect manhood', then, brings the christian to maturity and makes him steadfast against all preachers of falsehood and false philosophies (4:14), setting him on the way of truth and love and making him 'grow' wholly into Christ, who is the heavenly head (4:15). Thus the glorified Christ himself becomes the pattern and the goal of all christian perfection. Here the idea of discipleship in the gospels is interpreted in a mystical and eschatological sense and elevated above the earthly sphere. In the epistle to the Hebrews a further and unique aspect of it is revealed.

3. *The Letter to the Hebrews.* In this epistle of the New Testament the idea of perfection is wholly subordinated to its main purpose as stated in 13:22: it is intended as a *logos parakleseos*, a 'word of encouragement' for a community which has grown dispirited. Jesus is held up before the eyes of these faint-hearted ones as the sublime pattern and goal of that perfection which all

christians strive to attain. 'Therefore ... let us set aside every obstacle and sin which so easily ensnares us, and let us run with perseverance the race that is set before us, *looking to Jesus, the pioneer* and perfecter of our faith, who for the joy that was set before him endured the Cross, despising shame, and is seated at the right hand of the throne of God' (12:1f). In the view of Hebrews, therefore, the christian life is regarded as *the life of a wanderer* with Jesus and to Jesus in heaven. It is this conception that gives the doctrine of perfection as expounded in this epistle its unique quality, although its roots can be traced back to the Jewish conception of the exodus (way) and the New Testament idea of discipleship. As a result of this interpretation of the 'way' of perfection the course of Jesus' life is presented in this epistle as 'parallel' to that of his 'brethren' (see eg, 2:10–18; 3:14–16; 4:14–5:10; 13:13). At the same time the *earthly* dispensation of the Old Testament is evaluated 'dualistically' in that the eschatological goal to which the christian way of perfection leads lies in the *heavenly* sphere. Here Christ is to be attained both as he who consummates (or perfects) salvation and as its actual consummation (or perfection) (see especially 9:11; 12:22–4; 13:13f). As the author of Hebrews sees it, there is no consummation or perfection either of the christian man or of christianity in this world.

While the law and the cult of the Old Testament could never 'perfect the things to come' (see 7:1, 19; 9:9; 10:1), Christ as the eschatological high priest has himself 'attained to perfection' (5:9) by the obedient sacrifice of his suffering, and has also 'by (this) single offering . . . perfected for all time those who are sanctified' (10:14; see also 5:10; 7:17). However as fellow travellers on the way of Jesus the 'forerunner' and 'perfecter', these must also engage their own personal efforts in the struggle for perfection, and strive to attain the heavenly goal by means of penance, ascetical practices and moral effort. In all this the verb *teleioun* has a peculiarly cultic connotation: it means to sanctify, to 'consecrate' as a willing sacrifice. Yet the cultic language is completely subordinate to the parenesis, the demands of 'conscience' (see 9:9), the moral imperative. Such teaching is 'solid food for the full-grown' who are no longer 'immature' (5:14). It speaks no longer of 'the elementary foundations of Christ's teaching' but of its 'full and perfect' truths (see 6:1). In other words the teaching on perfection in this epistle, hard and austere as it is, and devoid of illusion and compromise, is taken to be *the substance of Christian preaching and practice*. Thus Hebrews represents the climax of New Testament teaching on perfection. The way traced out by the earthly Jesus through Golgotha to the heavenly sphere of God is presented as the norm of christian life. Here, no less than in the pauline epistles, the author does not have to rely on the gnostic myth to see and express this truth. The way has been prepared in judaism both for the idea and for the language in which it is expressed. They are integrally connected with the New Testament kerygma of Christ.

4. *The Letter of James*. The expressions 'perfect work' (= 'full effect' in RSV) (1:4), 'perfect gift' (1:17), 'perfect

law' (= teaching of Jesus: 1:25), 'perfect man' (3:2) are taken from the biblical idea of wholeness. They serve to designate that which is fully achieved, the final version (in which no further revisions are possible), the undivided and indivisible. As used here the term *teleios* has no special eschatological connotation.

5. *John*. According to Jn 17:23 the eschatological end of the union of the disciples with God and Christ is to be their 'perfection' in the indivisible 'union' of love. 'Perfection' in love of God is shown by keeping his commandments (1 Jn 2:5) and by love of one another (4:12). Here, in contrast to the emphasis placed by gnostic heretics on 'knowledge', *the primacy of love* is stressed. Love that has been perfected gives the christian 'confidence' for the day of judgement and casts out the fear of appearing before the divine judge (4:17f). Thus the johannine teaching on perfection is wholly in line with Jesus' demand for perfection in the Sermon on the Mount.

Bibliography: J. Dupont, '"Soyez parfaits" (Mt 5:48), "Soyez miséricordieux" (Lk 6:36)', *SP*, Paris–Gembloux 1959, 150–62; C. Edlund, *Das Auge der Einfalt*, Copenhagen–Lund 1952; N. R. Flew, *The Idea of Perfection in Christian Theology*, Oxford 1934; W. Hillmann, 'Perfectio Evangelica', *WW* 19 (1956), 161–262; E. Käsemann, *Das wandernde Gottesvolk. Eine Untersuchung zum Hebräerbrief* (FRLANT 37), Göttingen 1939; J. Kögel, 'Der Begriff *teleioun* im Hebräerbrief', *Theol. Studien f. M. Kähler*, Leipzig 1905, 35–68; H. Kosmala, *Hebräer-Essener-Christen*, Leiden 1959, esp. 208–39; R. Mach, *Der Zaddik in Talmud und Midrasch*, Leiden 1957; O. Michel, 'Die Lehre von der christlichen Vollkommenheit nach der Anschauung des Hebräerbriefes', *TSK* 106 (1934/5), 333–55; F. Nötscher, *Gotteswege und Menschenwege in der Bibel und in Qumran* (BBB 15), Bonn 1958; F. Nötscher, 'Heiligkeit in den Qumranschiften', *RQ* 2 (1959/60), 163–81 and 315–44; P. J. de Plessis, '*Teleios*': The Idea of

Perfection in the New Testament, Kampen 1959 (with bibliography); B. Rigaux, 'Révélation des mystères et perfection à Qumran et dans le NT', *NTS* 4 (1957/8), 237–62; F. J. Schierse, *Verheissung und Heilsvollendung, Zur theol. Grundfrage des Hebräerbriefes*, Munich 1955; R. Schnackenburg, 'Die Vollkommenheit des Christen nach den Evangelien', *Geist und Leben* 32 (1959), 420–33; C. Spicq, 'La perfection chrétienne d'après l'Epître aux Hébreux', *Mémorial J. Chaine*, Lyon 1950, 337–52; G. Stählin, 'Fortschritt und Wachstum, Zur Herkunft und Wandlung ntl. Ausdrucksformen', *Festgabe J. Lortz* II, Baden-Baden 1958, 13–25; Suitbertus a S. Joanne a Cruce, 'Die Vollkommenheitslehre des l. Joh-Briefes', *Bbl* 39 (1958), 319–33 and 449–70; F. Torm, 'Om *teleioun* i Hebraeerbrevet', *SEA* 5 (1940), 116–25; W. Trilling, *Das wahre Israel*, Leipzig 1959, 165–9; W. Völker, *Fortschritt und Vollendung bei Philo von Alexandrien* (*TU* 49/1), Leipzig 1938; A. Wikgren, 'Patterns of Perfection in the Epistle to the Hebrews', *NTS* 6 (1959/60), 159–67; E. Neuhäusler, *Anspruch und Antwort Gottes*, Düsseldorf 1962; J. Gnilka, *BZ* 7 (1963), 57–62; R. Schnackenburg, 'Christian Adulthood according to the Apostle Paul', *CBQ* 25 (1963), 254–370; F. Mussner, *Der Jakobusbrief*, Freiburg 1964; J. Blinzler, *LTK* x, 863f.

Franz Mussner

Persecution

A. *The Old Testament*: The word derives initially from the language of war. Whenever Israel takes the field to wage God's ↗ war(s) she will have the power to persecute (ie, 'hunt down') her enemies (eg, Lev 26:7f: five will be able to hunt down one hundred, and one hundred will be able to hunt down ten thousand; see also Deut 32:30; Jos 23:10). But if Israel breaks faith with God, her protector and Lord himself warns her that she herself will undergo exactly the same terrible experience of being hunted down by her enemies (Lev 26:17 actually states that they 'shall flee when no-one hunts you

down'!). The Book of Judges shows how this twofold promise of God is fulfilled again and again (Judg 2:11–23 is the key passage here). Again in the account of the Maccabaean period the same basic message is conveyed (see 1 Macc 2:47; 3:5).

As attention is increasingly focused on the individual as distinct from the community, more and more narratives are found of the persecution of individuals on various religious grounds. David, the elect of God, is exposed to persecution at the hands of Saul (1 Sam 19:9ff). In the psalms the suppliant complains of the persecutions which he has to endure (see Pss 7:1f; 35:1, 7, 15, 21; etc). Without regard to God the wicked seek to deprive the good of life and property. Persecution, in a sense which corresponds most nearly to our contemporary situation, and which is at the same time closest to the New Testament usage of the word, is in a special degree the destiny of the ↗ prophets. Jezebel represents the prototype of all religious persecutors (1 Kings 18:4; 19:2). Amos is persecuted for his prophecies of woe (Amos 7:10ff [–?]: again and again we find that the underlying motive of religious persecution is some 'political' transgression!). Right from the outset of his prophetic mission God predicts the persecution that threatens Jeremiah (Jer 1:19). Again and again (Jer 37–8) the prophet actually experiences this as a fate which he laments (Jer 15:15). But in all persecutions, whether they affect the people as a whole or the individual, the persecuted one is aware that God can bring succour. The Old Testament has preserved numerous prayers for us for the prevention of such oppression at the hands of the godless (see Ps 7; 35; 79; Jer 15:15–21. In this last example we encounter a state of despair which is quite absent from the psalms).

B. *The New Testament*: For the authors of the synoptic gospels the time of the church is the time of persecution (Mt 13:21 'persecution on account of the word'; Mk 10:30 reward multiplied many times over, here in this time, 'with persecutions'). They recognise these persecutions, to which many will succumb and so forfeit their salvation (Mt 13:21) as the fulfilment of Christ's own prophecies of persecution. To the apostles (Mt 10:23) as well as to their future persecutors, the Jews (Mt 23:34), the Lord predicted that the messengers of Christ would be persecuted from city to city. At the same time the Lord directed those who remained true to him to flee from persecution wherever it might break out (Mt 10:23; hence the saying in Jn 10:12 cannot be pressed too far!). Persecutions are a sign of the approaching eschaton (Lk 21:12). While the words of Christ himself imply that persecutions are to be accounted the hardest of tests (flight from them is allowed), they still remain—and here we plumb the depths of the paradox of christianity—a reason for profound joy (Mt 5:12) and blessedness (Mt 5:10, 11). Hence even on these grounds one should not be surprised at the command to pray for one's persecutors (Mt 5:44).

It is precisely in the fact of persecutions that the basic harmony between the Old and New Testament dispensations appears in their bearing upon salvation and life (Mt 5:12; see also Acts 7:52). In the New Testament too the community of the saved *in general* (not merely individual members of it) is subject to persecution, only in place of the people of Israel we have precisely the new community of the church or some particular community representative of it (Acts 8:1).

Paul epitomises in his own person the types of persecutor and persecuted. Beyond measure (Gal 1:13) and with burning zeal (Phil 3:6) he has persecuted the church of Jesus Christ (1 Cor 15:9; Gal 1:13, 23; Acts 22:4; 26:11) and thereby Christ himself (Acts 9:4f). But now that he himself has been seized by the grace of Christ and so has become Christ, he himself *must* suffer persecution. The Jews cannot forgive him for his 'apostasy' (Acts 13:50), and even Jewish christians, his own brethren, apparently prepare persecution for him (Gal 5:11: he suffers persecution for no longer preaching circumcision). His life has become a life of oppression and persecution (in 2 Tim 3:11 Timothy is called upon to bear witness to this). Yet he rejoices in the midst of, and on account of his weaknesses, the insults offered him, his needs, persecutions and oppressions (elsewhere too in the New Testament it is noticeable that persecution is only one of the tests to which christians are subject, and that it is far from coming first in the list) because the power of Christ dwells in him, and in part because of these sufferings (2 Cor 12:10). Paul knows that everyone who wishes to live devoutly in Christ Jesus (2 Tim 3:12) must reckon with persecution. Finally the behaviour of Ishmael to his brother Isaac is a type of this (Gal 4:29). So Paul gladly endures persecution (1 Cor 4:12) so long as he knows that he is not forsaken (by Christ) (2 Cor 4:9). Indeed he has the blessed certainty that no power and no deprivation of rights (and persecution is expressly mentioned amongst others) can separate him from the love of Christ (Rom 8:35). And when he finds christians who, like him, are ready to endure persecution, he boasts of their patience and their faith in the midst of these persecutions (2 Thess 1:4).

In the three passages in which John explicitly mentions persecution (ultimately the entire Book of Revelation is *the* book about persecution) he provides a most penetrating summary of virtually all that can be known of this concept. Christ himself had to suffer persecution at the hands of the Jews on account of his claim to be equal to God (Jn 5:16). His disciples too will be persecuted likewise (Jn 15:20). But in the last analysis every persecution derives from Satan: the dragon constantly persecutes the woman (Rev 12:13) for he wishes to destroy her son (Rev 12:4). And this is to continue until the seducer is thrown into the lake of fire and brimstone (Rev 20:10).

Bibliography: A. Oepke, *TDNT* II, 229f; C. Biber, Allmen 324–5; W. Nauck, 'Freude im Leiden, Zum Problem einer urchristlichen Verfolgungstradition', *ZNW* 46 (1955), 68–80; E. Lohse, *Märtyrer und Gottesknecht* (*FRLANT* 64), Göttingen 1955; N. Brox, *Zeuge und Märtyrer*, Munich 1961; R. Deville, *DBT* 376–8.

Wolfgang Beilner

Possession by evil spirits

The first clear and unequivocal reference to the phenomenon of possession is found in the New Testament. The phrase 'an evil spirit from God came upon Saul' (1 Sam 16:14–16; 23; 18:10; 19:9) should be compared with the statement in Jn 13:27 that 'Satan entered into Judas'. Neither of these instances can be regarded as referring to possession in the full sense. In both cases the conviction which is being expressed is merely that men who of their own free choice obstinately continue in sin may as a punishment be allowed to fall from time to time under particularly strong demonic influence.

As against this, possession as *a lasting and abnormal state* is first spoken of by the *synoptics*. Here we encounter the possessed (*daimonizomenoi*) as a class which, both in the general summaries (Mk 1:32 and parallels; Lk 6:18 and parallels) and in the more detailed descriptions (Mk 1:23–6 and parallels; 5:2–13 and parallels; 9:17–29 and parallels), is clearly distinguished from that of the sick. All the possessed in these accounts exhibit symptoms of organic and psychological disturbance of the gravest character: the evil spirit makes its victim dumb (Mt 9:32; Lk 11:14), deaf and dumb (Mk 9:25), dumb and blind (Mt 12:22), moonstruck (Mt 17:15), subject to outbreaks of frenzy and convulsions (Mk 1:26; 9:18–20; Lk 4:35). Popular belief does in fact ascribe all kinds of illness, but above all nervous and psychological disorders, to the influence of demons. But that it is not such a popular belief that is in question here is evident from the fact that not only do the synoptics tell us of possessed persons and their exorcism at the Lord's hands, but Jesus himself claims to have this fullness of power and expressly distinguishes it from the power to heal the sick (Lk 13:32). He adduces it as proof of his messianic mission (Lk 7:21–2; 11:20), imparts it to the twelve apostles (Mt 10:8), and then to the seventy-two disciples (Lk 10:17–20), and finally bequeathes it to his church as a lasting possession, as a sign of his victory over the 'prince of this world' (Mk 16:17; Acts 8:7; 16:16–18; 19:12–27). Whereas in his dealings with his disciples Jesus takes every opportunity to correct superstitious or otherwise erroneous views (for instance this is more or less what he is doing in the question concerning the 'fault' of the man born blind Jn 9:3), he never does this where cases of possession are concerned. Indeed in his controversies with the Pharisees (Lk 11:14–26) he makes use of the same expressions as they use in order to prove that he is the awaited messiah precisely by his exorcisms.

That possession does in fact constitute a phenomenon *sui generis* also becomes clear when healing of the sick and exorcism are compared. Indeed the distinction between them is particularly clear in cases in which the sick persons and the possessed show similar symptoms. Thus the healing of a deaf mute (Mk 7:33–5) may be compared with the exorcism of one who is deaf and dumb by reason of possession (Mk 9:25). To the sick the Lord acts as a kind and sympathetic doctor. The word of authority, the healing gesture are always directed to themselves. But with the possessed it is quite otherwise. Here Jesus addresses himself to a hidden and malignant being, who is designated unequivocally as the cause of the victim's pathological behaviour, and whom he intends to subdue (Mk

9:25; Lk 13:16). He puts questions to him (Mk 5:9) or commands him to be silent (Mk 1:25), threatens him (Mk 1:25), casts him out (Mk 1:34: compare the frequent use of the term *exebale* with Jn 12:31), banishes the demons, whole companies of whom sometimes inhabit a single possessed person, into a herd of swine (Mk 5:13). Conversely the possessed person is said to have an evil or an unclean spirit (Mt 9:25), that this spirit dwells in him (Lk 11:26), and that it decisively controls both his speech and his behaviour. At the approach of the Lord he is seized with fear which rises to a paroxysm (Mk 1:26). He throws himself to the ground (Mk 5:6), weeps and pleads for grace, for a little more time, for forbearance (Mt 8:29–31). He claims to recognise that the Lord is a supernatural being (Mk 1:24, 34; 3:12; 5:7). He resists, unleashes all his impotent fury once more upon his victim (Mk 1:26; 9:26), but has to yield to the all-powerful command of the Lord (which sometimes achieves its effect at a distance [Mk 7:29]), however great the number of his confederates may be. Taken together these statements make it impossible for the exegete, or indeed the scientific historian, to call in question in any degree whatever the reality of the phenomenon of possession.

In order to describe in closer detail the essential factors in possession it is necessary to take account not only of the factual records of the synoptics but in addition of all those passages which treat of the dominion of Satan as the prince—indeed as the god of this world, and of his tyranny over mankind (Jn 12:31; 14:30; 2 Cor 4:4; Eph 2:2; Heb 2:14; ⁊ Satan). The original cause of this dominion, and the point at which it started, is the sin committed in Paradise, by which man of his own free will separated himself from God and, by the ensuing loss of *integritas*, withdrew his body and in fact the entire order of earthly creation from the sole dominion of God, and subjected it to the influence of Satan. In the order of irrational creaturehood this influence takes effect in the form of catastrophes in nature and of harmful disturbances of the cosmic forces (Eph 2:2; Rev 8:10; 9:2). In its impact upon men it manifests itself in the whole range of evil effects familiar to us, extending from mere transitory temptation (Gen 3:1–5; Mt 4:1–11), to physical and spiritual afflictions (Job 1–2; Rev 9:4–7) and finally to possession in the full sense as depicted in the synoptics. It must therefore be regarded as a state in which the subject is deprived of all freedom, a state of utter and complete slavery (Lk 13:16), 'in which the centre of personality, the volitional and active ego, is impaired by alien powers which seek to ruin the man and sometimes drive him to self-destruction'. (W. Foerster, *TDNT* II, 19.) It is the work of Satan, the 'murderer from the beginning' (Jn 8:44), *par excellence*, for in it the personal dignity and freedom of man is brought down to the very depths. It is an expression of that hatred with which Satan persecutes 'the children of the woman' (Rev 12:12, 17). But for this very reason it also follows that the exorcism of the possessed, the freeing of man from enslavement to the devil, is the work precisely of him who '. . . appeared to destroy the works of the devil' (1 Jn 3:8) and to set men 'free for freedom'

(Gal 5:1). From these considerations it will be clear what a deep significance the exorcism of the possessed has in the gospels and Acts of the Apostles—and what a deep significance it must still have today in the preaching of the word. The christian of today must be brought back afresh to an awareness of the reality of diabolical influence, an influence which in the final age will in fact grow to gigantic proportions (2 Thess 2:3; Rev 13:7). But at the same time he must also be brought to a new awareness of the far mightier reality of the victory of Christ and his church. He must learn to see for himself the hand of the Father in the terrible mystery of possession, for Satan himself, albeit unwilling, is forced to play his part in the design of the divine love formulated by the Father. Even possession, the worst of all evils, is rooted, whether it is meant as punishment or as purification, in God's eternal plan of salvation.

Bibliography: J. Smit, *De daemoniacis in historia evangelica*, Rome 1913; F. M. Catherinet, 'Les démoniaques dans l'Evangile', *Satan*, Paris and Bruges 1948, 315–28; F. X. Maquart, 'L'exorciste devant les manifestations diaboliques', *Satan*, 328–52. See also: Alois Mager, *Mystik als seelische Wirklichkeit*, Salzburg 1945, 355–63; Giovanna della Croce, 'Mystische Theologie', *Jahrbuch* 1957, Klosterneuburg 1956; W. Grossouw, Haag 186f.

Myriam Prager

Poverty

At the time when Israel was still a child, that is during the transition from semi-nomadic to sedentary existence, poverty as a sociological problem, or even as a theological problem, was wholly unknown. The leading men of the tribes could not be otherwise than rich; riches were a natural concomitant of charismatic endowment, of leadership. The closely knit unity of tribe and family ensured that at least nobody starved while another had more than he needed. With the advent of the monarchy it was quite otherwise. As a result of commerce and trade, money made its appearance in the land, and with it social differences too (1 Sam 2:5, 7–8; Is 3:16–23; Amos 6:1–6; etc). Hebrew contains several words to describe the poor, of which *raš, dal, 'ebyôn, 'ānî,* and *ānāw* may be mentioned here. The 'poor' man is the oppressed, the humiliated, the one reduced to servitude. Hence in almost all cases the mighty, the rich and the powerful are the guilty and have brought about this moral evil. Only in the rational speculations of the proverbial literature do we find instances here and there of a man becoming poor through his own fault (Prov 6:6–11). It is the duty of those who are well off to come to the help of their poor brethren, to whom they are bound by ties of blood (Deut 15:7–11). If the pre-exilic prophets passionately espoused the cause of all the downtrodden classes, this is not to be ascribed to egoism—the prophets themselves might belong to the wealthier classes—but to the fact that Yahweh was in a special sense the friend of the poor. To intervene on their behalf meant simply to intervene on behalf of the people of God (Amos 2:7; Is 3:13–15; Mic 2:8–11; 3:1–4). In Prov 30:8 when the modest Agur prays, 'give me neither poverty nor riches', this is far from representing a solution to the theological problem of poverty as seen by the Old Testament. For in the course of the exilic and post-exilic period the concept of poverty underwent a significant transformation. Thenceforward poverty (*'anāwâh*) came to be the equivalent of humility and submissiveness to God (cp the similar shades of meaning in *islam* and *muslim*). When we read in Zephaniah: 'Seek Yahweh, all you humble of the land, who do his commands; seek righteousness, seek humility . . .' (2:3) or: 'I will leave in the midst of you a people humble and lowly, they shall seek refuge in the name of the Lord' (3:12), these seem to be instances in which post-exilic supplements have been added on to the pre-exilic text of Zephaniah. The poor are now equated with the pious, who are contrasted with the wicked holders of power and wealth. During this exilic and post-exilic period Israel herself came to be regarded as the poor one whose fate had been foretold in the prophetic descriptions of Jeremiah, and who was actually present to view in the figures of the Servant of the Lord and Job. The Servant of God, the just one who fears Yahweh, the perfect, is the poor man, whose rights are championed by the Most High, and whom he protects. Ideas of this and similar kinds are to be found again and again in the psalms and other writings composed during the post-exilic period. The poor man is presented as the opposite of the rich and powerful (Wis 2:10–14) and at the last judgement, once he himself has survived the test, he is to sit in judgement upon his enemies (Wis 3:6–9) and to exercise kingly power (Dan 7:22). Whether these poor ones originally derived from one particular section of the people and then subsequently came to form a united party is a disputed question. Do we not perhaps feel that even in post-exilic times it is by no means in every case that the context permits us simply to equate the poor with the righteous? In the same way it may be doubted whether riches and piety are in every case mutually exclusive.

Right at the beginning of the New Testament, continuity with this ancient theological theme of the poor is assured by the mention of the *ānāwîm* in the Magnificat. What Is 61:1 regarded as the prime task of the messiah, Jesus deemed to be fulfilled in the synagogue at Nazareth (Lk 4:18). Again when Jesus begins the Sermon on the Mount with the words: 'Blessed are the poor in spirit!', he is speaking in the spirit of the Old Testament. By poverty he understands here an attitude which is totally orientated to God. Certainly lack of possessions is included in this, for these always represent an obstacle between God and those who are religiously disposed. Because the poor are thus committed to God they will be persecuted, tortured and oppressed. The phrase 'in spirit' here, which is missing in Lk 6:20, is an addition taken from passages of the bible such as Is 57:15. The *ānwe rûaḥ* mentioned in 1 QM XIV, 7 is likewise a description of the true Israel, the community of the new covenant. Here too we should bear in mind Old Testament modes of expression and the *ānāwîm* theology of the Old Testament. Again the messiah depicted in Zech 9:9 (cf Mt 21:5–11) is called an *ānî* because he rides meekly upon an ass and not upon a horse after the manner of a great world conqueror. Jesus regarded riches as an

obstacle to the way of life required for the kingdom of God (Mt 6:24; 10:9f; 19:21–6; Mk 10:23–31; Lk 12:15–21; 14:33; 18:22–30). At no time, however, did he demand a revolution in social and economic relationships. In Acts 4:32 we are presented with an ideal of christian living which was certainly never imposed as of obligation. The disciple of Jesus had to commit himself to it freely and voluntarily. It is significant, however, that Luke, who probably had a profound familiarity with early christianity, should show such an inclination to speak of the deprived, the downtrodden and the poor, and to introduce images and parables of these (15:11–32; 16:19–31; 21:1–4). Care for the poor is one of the principal themes in the preaching and apostolic activity of the apostle Paul. But it is the epistle of James which appears expressly to favour the poor, and that not without a certain hostility towards the rich (see 1:9–11; 2:1–13; 5:1–6). It may be that in this epistle, representative as it is of Jewish christianity, we are encountering the after-effects of the late Old Testament idea that only those who are bereft of possessions can truly be devoted to God.

Bibliography: *TDNT* VI, 37–40; *LTK* I², 878–81; *RGG* I³, 622ff; Haag 101–2 and the literature recorded there; A. Gelin, *Die Armen—Sein Volk*, Mainz 1957; M. Vansteenkiste, 'L'ani et l'anaw dans l'AT', *Divus Thomas* 59 (1956), 3–19; P. Gauthier, *Die Armen, Jesus und die Kirche*, Graz 1965.

Meinrad Stenzel

Power

As used in its broadest sense the word 'power' covers a whole group of concepts, chief among which may be summarised as follows: physical strength; military power (resources for war, armed forces); the capacity or ability to act (in business, etc—means of power, possessions, wealth); and influence with or power over others (dominion, majesty, lordship).

From the Greek conceptual field we should notice above all the two expressions *dunamis* and *energeia*, which Greek philosophy was at pains to explore in depth, especially in its efforts to explain the forces at work in the cosmos. Whereas in Plato *dunamis* is the dominant term, for Aristotle the two concepts together are important, namely, *dunamis* (= ability, capacity) and *energeia* (= active power).

While the bible knows nothing of the philosophical concerns of the Greeks (characteristic here is the total omission in LXX of the word *energeia* as a translation for any Hebrew idea of power), almost fifty expressions are found in the Hebrew part of the bible to convey the various forms of power as something possessed and as something exercised. Generally speaking it is not possible to define the individual words in such a way as to distinguish them precisely from each other and so establish a semasiological order between them. Often the same word is used in the same way to designate utterly different kinds of power: thus, divine power or majesty, the power of the ruler, the armed forces—for these the word *ḥayil*, which occurs frequently in all parts of the Hebrew bible, being used 245 times in all, is a specially favoured term, as also is *tsābā'*, with 479 occurrences. To translate these terms LXX generally employs *dunamis*—

163 times for *ḥayil*, and 125 times for *tsābā'*.

In this connection *dunamis* is also occasionally used as a translation in such expression as *'anāšîm* (= men), *gedûd* (= force one's way in/incursion, raid—used chiefly of smaller groups of soldiers), *ḥāmôn* (= tumult, throng), *maḥaneh* (= camp, levy of troops), *ḥalûts* (= equipped for war, armed), *'ebed* (singular used collectively = servants, men), *'am* (= people—in the sense of a nation capable of waging war). The word *tsābā'* (= force, host) mentioned above has also a special usage which must be brought in at this point: the plural form of the word is found 279 times in the stereotyped epithet attached to God—Yahweh (God) 'of hosts'. LXX, in addition to the translation *tōn dunameōn* (= of the powers), also employs the Greek transliteration *sabaōth* (= of hosts), and, as a freer translation, the word *pantokratōr* (= omnipotent—used 100 times), which is good Greek. It must be admitted that this last expression also occurs sometimes as a translation of *'elōhîm* or *Yahweh* (= God), and still oftener (sixteen times) for *šaddai* (= almighty).

This wide range of meaning of the individual terms is well illustrated by such words as *'ôn*. This is used alike of the power of God (Is 40:26) and of that of the hippopotamus (Job 40:16), of procreative power (Gen 49:3; Deut 21:17 etc) as well as of resources (in the sense of riches, Hos 12:8; Job 20:10). In the rabbinic literature it can also designate a legally valid bill of sale (or deed of gift).

The meaning of the expression *gebûrâh* (= power: LXX *dunamis* and *iskhus* [= strength] thirteen times apiece) is frequently extended so as to apply to the power of God. It is used to designate both the power residing in the godhead and God's 'deeds of power' (*aretai*) (eg Deut 3:24; more often in the psalms). In addition to this it can also signify the power (especially for war) of men, strength of resolution (2 Kings 18:20; Is 11:2; 36:5), victory and success (many times in the Books of Kings), self-mastery (Jn 10:18) the 'mighty rising' of the sun (Judg 5:31). The precise sense of this word in Ps 90:10 is disputed: it may be 'life-force', 'miracle', or, if used adverbially, 'at the most'.

Two further terms which are frequently used are *kōaḥ* (LXX *iskhus* ninety-eight times, *dunamis* six times) and derivatives of the root *ḥzq* (=be strong); other expressions signify 'high' or 'sublimity' (*gōḇah*, *rûm*). Images are also used to depict strength: chief among these are the mighty hand and '(outstretched) arm' as expressions of the divine power in history (*passim*, see Ex 15:6; Deut 3:24; Is 9:12; 51:5, 9 etc). The word *'oz* is found in the same connection, especially in contexts in which the mighty deeds of God are being praised (LXX *iskhus* twenty-eight times, *dunamis* twenty-two times).

The term *me'ōḏ*, which is found as an adverb throughout the bible (300 times), but very rarely as a substantive, is found in its substantival form in the important passage of Deut 6:5, which contains the command to love God 'with your whole strength'.

As the biblical writers see it, every manifestation of power has at its source, not some universal power of nature, but the personal might of the one God. This is revealed in the act of creation (see, in addition to the narratives in Gen, Is 40:26; Jer 27:5; etc) and in the personal interventions of God in the course of human history, above all in that chain of events which led from the exodus from Egypt through the institution of the covenant at Sinai to the taking of the promised land (eg Ex 15:1–18, the Canticle of the Reed Sea; 32:11; Deut 9:26, 29; 26:8).

Since therefore Yahweh unfolds the plenitude of his power in nature and history (see the poetic description in Job 12:7–25), the people and the individual members of it can and should have recourse to God's power to help them when they find themselves in need or danger (thus in the sermon in Deut 8, esp. vv 17–18, in the Book of Consolation of Is 40–55, and in numerous psalms). A special manifestation of God's power is the power that is laid upon the prophets (Mic 3:8; *kōaḥ* and *geḇûrâh*) and the power of the messiah (Is 9:6; 11:2).

This line of development is taken up in the New Testament (Lk 1:35; 4:14, 36; 24:19). The messianic power is in Jesus. It 'goes forth from him' (Mk 5:30 and parallels; 6:14; Lk 8:46); his power to perform miracles is *dunamis* (sing.), his miraculous works are *dunameis* (pl.) (Mt 7:22; 11:20; 13:54; 14:2; Mk 9:39); this power of his proves the plenitude of his authority (*exousia*: Mt 7:29; 9:6 and parallels; 10:1 and parallels; 28:18). It is manifested especially in the resurrection ('in power' Acts 4:33), but will appear as it really is for the first time at his second coming (Mt 24:30 and parallels). This power works in the apostles (who act 'not from their own power', Acts 3:12); it works in the gospel which is 'power for salvation' (Rom 1:16; similarly 1 Cor 1:18).

But the wicked, the forces of darkness (Lk 22:53; Rev 13:2), have a kind of power too, which, however, is ultimately dependent upon God's permitting them to have it (Jn 19:11), for God is simply he who 'has power' (Rev 16:9), to whom 'nothing is impossible' (Lk 1:37; Mt 19:26 and parallels). Hence 'power' can be used as a paraphrase for the divine name, and Jesus uses it in this sense before the Sanhedrin (Mt 26·64 and Mk 14:62—Luke adds an explanatory 'of God' in 22:69).

In summary it can be said: the unique holder of power is God. The power that is at work in nature and in history, in angels and devils, in men and in beasts, is ultimately his. Moreover the order of God's creation reflects in its manifold forms the absolute power gathered up in him. The image of this power is, so to say, refracted as light is by a prism, into the host of the various limited powers, abilities, sources of strength and resources which are distributed throughout the created order. But God's power is at work in a special manner in the deed of salvation, which was prepared for by the prophets, and which achieves its consummation in the messiah, he who bears the divine power in his own person.

Bibliography: A. Berthold, *Das Dynamische im AT*, 1926; W. Bultmann, 15; W. Grundmann, *Der Begriff der Kraft in der ntl. Gedankenwelt*, 1932; F. Preisigke, *Die Gotteskraft in frühchristlicher Zeit*, 1922; G. Quispel, 'Mensch und Energie im antiken Christentum', *Eranos Jahrbuch* 21 (1952), 109–68. On *'on*: E. Mowinckel, *Psalmenstudien* I, 1921, 1–58. On evil powers and arts: J. Pedersen, *Israel* 1/2, 1926, 431. On magic power: Hjelt, *Stud. Orient.* 1 (1925), 61ff. On magic: H. Schlier, 'Mächte und Gewalten im NT', *TG* 9 (1930), 289–97; P. Biard, *La puissance de Dieu*, Paris 1960; E. Fascher, *RAC* IV, 415–58 (with bibliography) and V, 4–51 (with bibliography).

Suitbert H. Siedl

Praise

In his *Polyhymnia catuceatrix*, published in 1619, Michael Praetorius wrote: 'in heaven all are engaged in music; what will the man who has no interest in music here on earth find to occupy him there?' In Luther we find the view expressed that music stands very close to theology. Two conclusions may be drawn from these views: first, that these men understand music to be a part of the worship and praise of God to which every page of the bible summons us, and second, that they were conscious of the fact that to praise God is the essential mode of existence of the christian community. In the Book of Revelation the church triumphant in the heavenly world is represented as continually living and praising God; but the church militant here on earth also shares in this praise. In praising God she performs already that service which she is destined to perform in heaven thereby repelling the attacks of the Evil One and showing herself to be the chosen and protected by God. This explains why the liturgy of all denominations is full of divine praise and seeks to honour God starting out with song, music and art.

The beginning of this process lies in the Old Testament. In the Old Testament the demand is continually made to praise and honour God. Throughout we hear the voice of the covenant community or of the individual member intoning hymns of praise. Particularly well known examples of such hymns of praise can be found in the hallelujatic psalms prescribed for the Passover *seder* (Ex 15; Judg 5; 1 Sam 2:1–10) and the hymn sung by the three men in the fiery furnace. Such hymns are found throughout, from the earliest strata of Old Testament tradition (parts of Ex 15 and Judg 5) to more recent times (Dan 3:24ff). The main Hebrew verbs for this activity of praise are: *giddel, šîr, hillel, bārek.* The object of praise is the divine ↗ glory, ↗ light, ↗ holiness. Sometimes the song of praise states the reasons for praising God explicitly, as Ex 15:1f; Ps 21:4; 8:3; 116:1; Sometimes too they speak of quite material things; but if we take in the context of the Old Testament as a whole, not forgetting passages such as Is 6 (the vision in the temple) and Dan 7:10 (the heavenly court around the Ancient of Days), we shall have to conclude that it is not just a question of asking for external goods and help in present distress but is, basically, in virtue of the covenant. When God gives his assistance he manifests his fidelity to the covenant and his mercy, and proves to the one who receives the benefit what it means to belong to the covenant people. The threefold acclamation of the holiness of God in Is 6 shows that the praise of the earthly community is but an echo of the heavenly chorus of praise and a response to the glory, majesty and loving kindness of God. Every form of praise on earth is a proclamation of the glory (*kābôd*) of God, and is verified even if one does no more than pronounce the name of God aloud (Gen 12:8).

We find much the same thing in the deutero-canonical books. Tobit 12:7 speaks of the glory of revealing the works of the Lord (*endoxōs anakaluptein erga theou*); Sir 39:10; 44:8, 15 of the praise (*epainos*) of God by the assembly (*ekklēsia*). We hear this strain of praise most clearly where God on his side has given to man *epainos* and *eulogia* (Wis 15:19). Among the writings of the Qumran community we also find a collection of hymns of praise, the *Hodayoth.*

In the New Testament the praise of God reaches its highest peak and at the same time the function of praise is seen in a clearer light. The canticles contained in the New Testament (Lk 1:46–55, 68–79; 2:29–32) continue along the lines of the Old Testament hymns of praise; the *megalunein* of Lk 1:46 reflects the Hebrew *giddel* (magnify). The praise which greeted Jesus on his entry into Jerusalem (Mt 21:9) takes us back directly into the Old Testament, with *eulogein* reflecting the Hebrew *hillel.* The wonderful deeds of Jesus inspire the people to praise God for his wonderful deeds (Lk 18:43; 19:37). As is clear from Lk 2:13 and Revelation, the origin of this activity of praise is to be found in the heavenly world. The angels and the court of heaven are engaged incessantly in the praise of God (Rev 4:8f; 5:11f; 7:12; 14:3; 15:3; 19:5). Here too we find echoes from the Old Testament (eg 15:3ff). The court of heaven renders to God glory, honour, and thanksgiving (*doxa, timē, eukharistia*), The angels bear the prayers of the saints before God as sweet-smelling incense so that they too may be taken up into the chorus of heavenly praise (Rev 5:9). These prayers are certainly the psalms, hymns and spiritual canticles of the earthly community (Eph 5:19; Col 3:16). Eph 1:3 speaks of a 'spiritual blessing' (*eulogia pneumatikē*) and 5:19 of 'spiritual hymns' (*ō[i]dai pneumatikai*). This implies the important consideration that not anyone can sing hymns or psalms to the glory of God. Praise is only possible through the Holy Spirit who dwells in the community. The Spirit comes from the Kyrios, and it is he who sustains and gives meaning to the praise even though it is in his honour. It is Christ himself who is the great gift of God enabling the church to sing and praise, and in comparison with this gift all others pale into insignificance. It is in him that the new covenant is made to which anyone, whether Jew or gentile, can belong. Hence the whole *ekklēsia* joins in unison in the hymn of praise of the angels in Lk 2:13 which greets Christ as he appears on earth.

The New Testament is full of hymns and doxological formulae which certainly come from divine service as practised in the early church (the word *a[i]dō* = 'sing' is used in the Book of Revelation where the author describes the heavenly liturgy). This is true both of the community as a whole and of individual christians to whom forms of praise are attributed.

The verb *aineō* and the nouns *ainos* and *epainos* are often used in the New Testament (Mt 21:16; Lk 19:37; Acts 2:47; Rom 2:29; 13:3; 15:11; 1 Cor 4:5; 2 Cor 8:18; Eph 1:6, 12; 1 Pet 1:7). The verb stands for the joyful praise of God and the corresponding noun is used in secular Greek literature for 'praise'. It is often found later on in the writings of the church fathers. The second noun is met with in LXX where it stands for the recognition by the community or even by God of the piety of an individual (Sir 39:10; 44:8, 15), as also for the attitude of worship adopted by the community in its relation to God (Ps 35:28; 22:4; 1 Chron 16:27). Both of these connotations can be found also in the New Testament (Rom 2:29; 1 Cor 4:5; 1 Pet 1:7; 2 Cor 8:18; Rom 13:3f; 1 Pet 2:13f). As used of the hymn, the word signifies the stammering, uncertain expression of the community's worship and confession of faith (Eph 1:6, 12; Phil 1:11). In these two texts and in 1 Pet 1:7 *epainos* is combined with *doxa*. With this last (and the corresponding verb *doxazein*) we come upon the word that expresses the christian attitude more clearly than others such as *a[i]dein*, *ainein*, *eulogein*, *eukharistein*, *anthomologein* (Mt 5:16; 6:2; Lk 2:14, 20; 18:43; Acts 4:21; Eph 1:6, 12; Phil 1:11; 1 Tim 3:16; 1 Pet 1:7). *Doxazein* implies participation in *doxa*, and *doxa* (*kābôd*) signifies the very being and existence of God. Whoever is near to God reflects this proximity in some way (Ex 34:29f, 35). Whoever acknowledges and expresses the divine *doxa* in praise comes himself to share in it. Here we have the basis of all exultation and praise in the New Testament, namely, that God's *doxa* has come to us in Christ. The goodwill of God shines upon us (Lk 2:14— *eudokia*). We live already in this life in the light of his *doxa*. In the life to come we will see it (1 Cor 13:12) and in the heavenly *ekklēsia* glorify, praise and give thanks to him who was and is and is to come (Rev 4:8).

Bibliography: H. Schlier, *TDNT* I, 163–5 and 176f; Kittel, *TDNT* II, 253f; Preisker II, 583–5.

Georg Molin

Prayer

A. *In the Old Testament. Prayer and ↗sacrifice together constitute the cult.* Not only are they frequently conjoined in the relevant passages (see Ps 50:8, 14; 66:13f), but they actually belong together from the outset. This can often be deduced from the basic meanings of verbs: the expression *heˤetîr* belongs to the language of sacrifice (Arabic *ʾatara* ='to sacrifice'; see Ex 8:25; 9:28; etc). To seek Yahweh means not only to supplicate him in prayer (Ex 33:7; Deut 4:29; 2 Sam 12:16; Is 45:19; 51:1; Jer 29:13; Hos 3:5) but also precisely to sacrifice (Hos 5:6). Correspondingly *tôdâh* signifies not only the prayer of praise and thanksgiving (Ps 100:1; Is 51:3; Jer 30:19; etc) but also the thank-offering (Jer 17:26; 31:12; 2 Chron 29:31; Amos 4:5; Ps 56:12). It is difficult to decide whether the 'sacrifice of thanks' (Ps 107:22; 116:17) should be understood literally as a thank-offering (so most exegetes) or, with an epexegetical genitive force (so Zorrell, Lex. Hebr. 890), as meaning that the sacrifice is constituted by the thanks (see Ps 50:14, 23; 141:1f).

The actual words meaning to pray (*heˤetîr* and *hithpallēl*, lit. 'to make cuts in oneself', cf 1 Kings 18:28) are seldom used. Usually other designations of prayer are substituted for them, chiefly to cry, to call out (*qārāʾ*) either *to* Yahweh (Deut 15:9; 1 Kings 8:43; Jer 11:14; etc), or *in the name of* Yahweh (Gen 4:26; 12:8; etc), originally referring to the calling out of the divine name in the course of the cult. In addition to these we find *hithhanēn* (='to propitiate', 'to entreat': Hos 12:4; Job 9:15; 19:16; Sir 13:3) and also *ḥillâh* or *panîm* (literally ='to caress', originating from the practice of touching and kissing the images of gods, 'to mollify the countenance of Yahweh': Ex 32:11; 1 Sam 13:12; Zech 7:2; 8:21f; Ps 119:58; Dan 9:13). To glorify and to praise constitute a major element in prayer. Hence *hillēl* (=to rejoice, praise) and similar terms, among them those expressive of↗joy, jubilation and exultation constantly recur (thus *gîl*, *ˤālats*, *ˤālas*). The expression of thanks (↗thanksgiving) constitutes a distinct form of prayer in addition to the obvious one of supplication. This latter form is divided into collective supplication (Ps 44; 60; 79; 80; Ezra 9:5-15; Neh 9:5-37; Dan 9:4-19; etc), which seeks to bring to God's notice the needs of his people and the afflictions which they suffer and to implore him to deliver them, and individual supplication, which is chiefly concerned with material requirements: prosperity, riches, length of life, blessing of offspring, deliverance from enemies or illness. Occasionally however more spiritual benefits are also sought, thus wisdom (1 Kings 3:7ff; Ps 25:4f; Sir 51:13; Wis 7:7; etc), forgiveness of sins (Ps 25:7; 51; 130), preservation from error (Ps 141:3-17; Sir 22:27; 23:1-6), the happiness of union with God (Ps 16:11; 17:15; 73:25; etc). Besides these,↗blessing and↗cursing are also the subject of supplication.

The following gestures of prayer are noteworthy: to cast oneself down (*hištaḥªwâh*: Gen 18:2; 19:1; etc), to fall on one's knees or to bend the knee (2 Chron 7:3; 29:29; Ps 22:30; 72:9), and—once only—to bow the head upon the knees (1 Kings 18:42, an act of homage similar to the two gestures mentioned above; this is found also in Egyptian and Ugaritic texts; see A. Jirku, *WZKM* 103 [1953], 372; a parallel which has not been noticed is found in Berakot 34 b, where Ḥanina ben Dosa uses this posture when entreating for a cure from illness). Other gestures are standing upright (1 Sam 1:26), stretching out (Is 1:15) or raising the hands (Ps 28:2). It is a characteristic of Old Testament prayer that it is directed exclusively and directly to Yahweh. Not until after the exile are angels found as mediators (Zech 1:12; Job 5:1; Dan 12:1. According to Tobit 12:15 in LXX Raphael brings the prayers of the saints before the divine majesty. Similar doctrines were current in the literature of late judaism). This attitude of prayer in which everything is focused upon Yahweh is based upon his absolute faithfulness to the covenant (↗ covenant, truth). Hence the petitioner's unshakeable trust in 'his God', 'his rock' (2 Sam 23:3; Deut 32:30; Is 17:9f; 30:29), who is his 'refuge' (Ps 14:6; 46:1; 61:3; etc), his 'stronghold' (Ps 62:2, 6; 94:22; etc), his 'shield' (Gen 15:1; Deut 33:29; etc).

Besides this it is also noteworthy that the omnipotence of God is emphasised as a strong motive for trust. 'Our help is in the name of the Lord, who made heaven and earth' (Ps 124:8; 102:26–9; cf Ps 8; 19; 29; 104; 147; 148).

A further characteristic is that the worshipper is discouraged from prolonging his prayer with many words (Eccles 5:1), and from repeating the same formulae of prayer again and again (Sir 7:14; see also Mt 6:7). In this respect 'heathen' prayer is manifestly devoid of the necessary trust in God, as also of the reverence which is due to him. Again, prayer as conceived of in the bible is utterly different from 'incantation', the three essential characteristics of which are the magical invocation of the divine name, the murmuring of prayers with the lips, and above all the sustained repetition of the prayer in the same words. There is no trace of any irreligious attempt at bringing force to bear by one's prayer on the will of God. This can be learnt not least from the gestures of prayer employed. These bear witness to the total submission of the petitioner to a higher will.

A feature which may justly be remarked is the total absence from Israel's prayer of any element of the portentous or the pompous. It is also noteworthy that the distinction between liturgical or cultic prayer and private prayer is very slight. These factors indicate the strength and sincerity of Israel's prayer life. That mystical prayer which consists in dying to the self and entering into the infinity of God has significantly found no place among the attitudes of prayer represented in the Old Testament. With Heiler and Eichrodt it must be maintained: The God of the Old Testament reveals himself not in the guise of static being which is blessed in itself, but as the eternal king whose will is all-commanding. Correspondingly the pious Israelite is not a mystic who, having renounced this world, drinks deep of other-worldly delights. Rather he is a fighter who, even in his prayers, has to struggle to attain the object of his longing, that life filled with dynamic power which union with the divine Lord brings. His goal is the Ultimate considered not statically as the *summum bonum*, but dynamically as the universal dominion of God.

Bibliography: Heinisch, 204–12; Imschoot II, 166–73; Eichrodt I, 172–6; J. Herrmann, *TDNT* II (1935), 785–800; W. Grossouw, Haag 509–13; A. Maillot, Allmen 329–32; J. Döller, *Das Gebet im AT*, Vienna 1914; A. Greiff, *Das Gebet im AT*, Münster 1915; J. Hempel, *Gebet und Frömmigkeit im AT*, Göttingen 1922; F. Heiler, *Das Gebet* (numerous editions); R. Storr, *Die Frömmigkeit im AT*, München-Gladbach 1927, 175–91; A. Wendel, *Das freie Laiengebet im vorexilischen Israel*, Leipzig 1932; F. L. Lefevers, *The Place of Prayer in Hebrew Worship as Reflected in the OT*, South-Western Baptist Seminary 1952 (dissertation); Claus Westermann, *Das Loben Gottes in den Pss*, Göttingen 1954; G. Bernini, 'Le preghire penitenziali del Salterio', *Anal. Greg.* 62, Rome 1953; D. R. Ap-Thomas, *VT* 6 (1956), 225–41; A. Bea, *LTK* IV² (1960), 538–40.

Johannes B. Bauer

B. In the New Testament. I. The prayer of Jesus. As with the life of the God–Man in general, so too with the prayer of Jesus two factors are definitive: Jesus prays as a scion of his people, and simultaneously as the only Son of his heavenly Father. As a scion of his people he recites those prayers which at his period were customarily recited at prescribed hours during the day (morning, afternoon and evening). When he reproaches the Pharisees, who make an exhibition of their piety before men, it is, no doubt, the abuse of these prayers that he is condemning rather than the prayers themselves (cf Mt 6:5ff).

The 'Our Father' attests the fact that he was familiar with the prayer of the eighteen petitions as customarily recited during his period. Similarly he knows the *shema*, which every pious Israelite recited daily. In fact he answers the

question of the scribes as to which is the greatest commandment with the opening words of this prayer: 'Hear, O Israel, . . .' (Mk 12:28ff). Again he follows the practice of all pious Israelites in refusing to take so much as a piece of bread, a cup of wine, or *a fortiori* a meal, without first saying a prayer. So far from omitting this, just as he himself teaches his disciples to pray for their daily bread (Mt 6:11; Lk 11:3), so he recites the thanksgiving over the bread before breaking it and distributing it according to custom (Mk 6:41; Mt 14:19; Lk 9:16; Mk 8:6; Mt 15:36; Jn 6:11; Mk 14:22; Mt 26:26; Lk 22:19; 24:30, 35). In connection with the last supper he prays the 'great hallel' together with his disciples (Mk 14:26; Mt 26:30).

As the only Son of his heavenly Father he feels so great an inner compulsion to pray that, as the testimony of all the evangelists agree, all important crises in his life on earth are accompanied by prayer. Indeed his entire life is supported by his interior communion with the Father, which finds its visible expression in prayer. He prays at his baptism (Lk 3:21), at his initial entry into Capernaum (Mk 1:35; Lk 5:16); he prays after the miracles which he performs (Mk 6:46; Mt 14:23); he prays before the choosing of the Twelve (Lk 6:12), as well as before the moment of decision at Caesarea Philippi (Lk 9:18); before his passion he prays as an intercessor on his disciples' behalf (Lk 22:32), and himself strives in prayer with his Father (Mt 26:36–46 and parallels). It is above all the evangelist Luke who portrays Jesus as the great man of prayer. For whole nights at a time the Lord remains in prayerful intercourse with the Father (Lk 3:21; 5:16; 6:12; 9:29; 10:21ff; 11:1; 22:32; 23:34, 46). By portraying him thus Luke surely intends to give expression to the fact that Jesus is united to the Father in a communion of prayer that is unceasing. Moreover, according to this evangelist he requires the same attitude from his disciples: they must pray always (Lk 18:1). Admittedly his unique position prevents him from ever joining his disciples in a common prayer to the Father.

Specific prayers of Jesus have been recorded by the evangelists word for word. A factor common to them all—with the exception of the prayer cried out on the Cross, which is taken from Ps 22—is that God is addressed as 'Father'. In this 'Abba' (Mk 14:36) is latent all the childlike submission of the Son to the Father. Christ addresses his heavenly Father as a child speaks to his human Father. In the cry of joy contained in Mt 11:25f he *thanks* the Father for having hidden the mystery of the kingdom of God from the wise and prudent, yet revealed it to little ones. Before the miracle of the raising of Lazarus he gives thanks to the Father for having heard him (Jn 11:41f). His filial trust in his Father appears especially in his *entreaties*: in the priestly prayer (Jn 17) he prays for his own. He prays to the Father before entering upon his passion (Mt 26:36–46; Mk 14:32–42; Lk 22:40–46; cf Jn 12:27, 28; Heb 5:7). He prays for those who put him to death (Lk 23:34). But the depths of his prayer can be glimpsed in the prayers he utters on the cross, above all in the cry which bursts from him in the extremity of his need: 'My God, my God why hast thou

forsaken me?' (Mt 27:46; Mk 15:34 = Ps 22:2). To this is appended, in the very moment of death, a saying from Ps 31: 'Into thy hands I commend my spirit' (Lk 23:46 = Ps 31:5). The only variation is that Jesus uses it with the invocation 'Father'. 'In this *single* word "Father" lies the all-holy mystery of his life—and of his prayer' (J. Jeremias, 'Das Gebetsleben Jesu', 140).

II. *The prayer of christians.* 1. For those whom he has made his own Jesus does not only represent the great example of prayer; *he himself actually teaches his disciples to pray*, and gives to his church that prayer which is called 'the Lord's prayer', and which, until the end of time, the church must make most deeply and intimately its own. The evangelist Luke is probably the most historically correct in his account of the situation in which it was first uttered. Jesus himself has been praying; then one of the disciples, speaking in the name of the rest, asks him: 'Master, teach us to pray just as John taught his disciples to pray'; and then the Lord teaches them *his* prayer (Lk 11:1–4). Matthew on the other hand, in accordance with his usual method of arranging his material, inserts the 'Our Father' into the Sermon on the Mount, connecting with what has gone before by means of the theme-word 'prayer' (Mt 6:5–13). Just as these two evangelists, Matthew and Luke, differ in the motives which prompted them to record the Lord's prayer, so too they differ in the actual forms in which they have handed it down to us. It is right to recognise, however, that both versions derive from the same basic form (Schmid, *Matthäus* ad loc; see also Lohmeyer, *Das Vaterunser*, 174ff).

According to Matthew's version it consists of seven petitions of which the first three are concerned with God himself. They can be summarised in *one* of these petitions, that namely which asks for the coming of God's kingdom. The last four petitions are concerned with man. They consist of entreaties for the needs of daily life. What appears to be a wide gulf between the petition for the coming of the kingdom and that for daily bread is bridged by the invocation 'Father'. Both are bestowed by the Father in heaven. Even as he is seeing to the attainment of the great object of man's petition, the advent of the kingdom, he makes the small everyday needs of man no less his concern. The attitude of trustful self-surrender, in which man speaks to God as a child to his father, and lays all things in his hands, is a distinctively christian characteristic which marks off the 'Our Father' as the christian prayer *par excellence*.

Corresponding to the prayer which the Lord teaches to his disciples are the instructions which he gives for praying rightly (Mt 6:5-8). Prayer must be made before God and not before men. This is what is meant by 'praying in your private room', but this image should not be taken as excluding public or communal prayer (see Mt 18:20). Prayer should not be full of words as is that of the heathen, who think to 'weary' the gods with the multiplicity of their words. Christians should rather pray with childlike simplicity, for all is known to the Father even before man prays to him (Mt 6:8). This should not, of course, be taken as meaning that all petition should be set aside as meaningless. Jesus himself shows how wrong this would be by insistently exhorting his disciples to entreat their heavenly Father earnestly and persistently for all things (Lk 11:5-8; Mt 7:7-11; Lk 11:9-13; 18:1-8).

The parable of the Pharisee and the publican (Lk 18:9-14) cannot be improved upon as an illustration of how prayer should be made, according to the teaching of Jesus, if it is to be an expression of true devotion. Precisely because in his prayers the christian approaches God as the Father, he is, like the publican, aware of his guilt, and knows that in all things he needs God's grace.

In conclusion, by his own prayer and by his teaching on prayer Christ gave to his disciples an unqualified certainty of being heard: 'Whatever you ask in prayer believe that you receive it and you will' (Mk 11:24; see also Lk 17:5f and parallels).

2. *Prayer and sonship of God.* Jesus' teaching that God was to be addressed as 'Abba' represented an unheard-of innovation in his time. Concomitantly with this he introduces a new relationship of sonship to the heavenly Father, and it is this effect of Christ's work that is presupposed by christian prayer properly so-called. Not only can the christian *call* God his Father, but he has actually become his son (see 1 Jn 3:1). As the child of his heavenly Father he can pray for *all* things (Mk 11:24).

In the gospel of John this mode of praying is called praying 'in the name' of Jesus (Jn 14:13f; 15:16; 16:23, 26). To pray 'in his name' signifies: to pray by his authority, according to his will, but also by actually invoking his name or—to sum up both factors in a single idea—to pray in that kind of union

U

with him that is described in c. 15 of the gospel of John. It is to the same kind of prayer that the Lord refers when, in the course of his dialogue with the Samaritan woman, he speaks of worshipping 'in spirit and in truth' (Jn 4: 23, 24). For this expression should not be taken as in any sense implying that the worship which must be offered must be purely spiritual in character, that is, freed from all material conditions and from that true knowledge of God that goes with them. The intention is rather to describe that kind of worship which is possible only for the children of God, that is for those to whom Christ has given access to the reality of God, those who are born of the Spirit (see Jn 3:5). 'Worshipping in spirit and in truth' might be paraphrased as 'worshipping in union with the Spirit of God as this has been bestowed by Christ'. The apostle Paul in particular connects the prayer of a son of God with the Spirit through whom that sonship has been imparted to man. It appears certain that Paul is thinking of prayer when he says: 'It is the Spirit himself bearing witness with our spirit that we are children of God' (Rom 8:16). And when he says, just before this, 'You have received the Spirit of sonship by which we crỳ "Abba, Father"' (Rom 8:15), this should be taken as an actual quotation from the beginning of the 'Our Father'. According to Gal 4:6 it is the Spirit of God himself who cries 'Father' within us. Of himself man is wholly ignorant of how to make his prayer effective before God. But then the Spirit comes to the help of his infirmity and pleads for him with 'sighs too deep for words' (Rom 8:26). Thus Paul sees christian

prayer as made effective by the Holy Spirit, and it is for this reason that it is assured of a hearing (Rom 8:27).

3. *The prayer of the early church.* From all this a picture of christian prayer is formed as it was in fact put into practice in the early church. This can be gathered from the testimony of the Acts of the Apostles, the epistles, and the Book of Revelation.

So far as the externals of prayer are concerned the early christian community adheres to the hours of prayer customarily observed among the Jews: at the ninth hour Peter and John go to the temple to pray (Acts 3:1); at the sixth hour Peter rises up to pray on the roof of his host's house (Acts 10:9); the early christians continue to go to the temple and the synagogue to pray, but also assemble for prayer and the liturgy in the houses of their fellow christians (Acts 2:42ff; see also 4:23ff; 12:5). Prayer is offered standing upright (Mk 11:25; see also Lk 18:9–14) or kneeling as Jesus knelt in Gethsemane (Mk 14:35; Acts 7:60; see also Acts 21:5). Obviously communal prayers are recited in the liturgical assembly (1 Cor 14:13ff; see also Mt 18:19, 20).

With regard to content the attitudes of thanksgiving and praise exercise a largely decisive influence upon the form of early christian prayer. Paul and Silas praise God in the prayers they offer in prison (Acts 16:25). Again it will no doubt be remarked how often Paul gives thanks to God and praises him in his epistles (Rom 7:25; 9:5; 11:33–6; 16:25–7; 1 Cor 15:57; 2 Cor 1:3; 9:15; Eph 1:3ff; 3:20, 21; Phil 4:20; 1 Tim 1:17).

According to the instruction of the Lord (Mt 7:7ff) however, petition too plays a major role in prayer. All that the christian needs and all that conduces to the coming of the kingdom of God is the subject of petition. In the prayer recorded in Acts 4:24-30 the early christian community prays for strength to preach the word of God with boldness and for the 'signs' which are to accompany this preaching. The christians at Jerusalem pray unceasingly for Peter to be freed from prison (Acts 12:5). Following the teaching and example of Christ, the dying Stephen prays for his enemies (Acts 7:60; cf Mt 5:44; Lk 23:34). Paul constantly makes mention of those whom he has made his own in his prayers of intercession (Rom 1:9; 1 Thess 1:2; 2:19; 2 Tim 1:3), that God will grant them unity of mind (Rom 15:5), that he may fill them with joy and peace (Rom 15:33; cf 2 Thess 3:16), that he may bestow upon them love and knowledge, in short, all that is needful for the 'new man' (2 Thess 3:5; Eph 1:17-19; 3:14-21). It is not surprising therefore that the apostle himself transforms the conventional formula of greeting with which a letter customarily opened to a wish that his readers might be blessed (Rom 1:7; 1 Cor 1:3; 2 Cor 1:2; Gal 1:3; Eph 1:2; Phil 1:2; Col 1:2; 1 Thess 1:1; 2 Thess 1:2; Philem 3; 1 Tim 1:2; 2 Tim 1:2; Titus 1:4; see also: E. Lohmeyer, *Briefliche Grussüberschriften: Probleme paulinischer Theologie*, Stuttgart n.d., 9-29; O. Roller, *Das Formular der paulinischen Briefe* [*BWANT* 58], Stuttgart 1933). This invocation of blessing is probably modelled upon the blessing used in the liturgy (Nielen, 151). But conversely Paul himself asks in turn for the prayers of the brethren so that by this means he and they may be united in the common struggle, exercise mutual charity towards each other and fulfil the task of their apostolate (Rom 15:30-32; 2 Cor 1:11; Eph 6:19).

Prayer is normally directed to God the Father 'in the name of our Lord Jesus Christ' (Eph 5:20; cf Col 3:17). But prayers are also addressed to Jesus himself. In fact both personal prayer can be directed to him, as in the case of the dying Stephen (Acts 7:59, 60) or of Paul in his time of need (2 Cor 12:8), and also liturgical doxologies (Rom 9:5; 2 Pet 3:18; Rev 1:6; cf Rev 5:9, 10, 12, 13). Among the earliest of christian prayers is the cry 'Marana tha' (1 Cor 16:22; see also Rev 22:20). On the evidence of this prayer we must rule out one theory as to how the practice arose of calling upon Christ as Lord. It is the theory that this was first made possible when the hellenistic communities transferred the title *kurios*, which derives from LXX, to Jesus (Greeven, *TDNT* II, 805f).

In addition to the petitions of the 'Our Father' (see above), the above mentioned cry 'Marana tha' (1 Cor 16:22; Did 10:6), (which has been preserved in the original Aramaic), at least in the sense which it bears in Rev 22:20, enables us to conclude that prayer in the New Testament is eschatologically orientated (see Greeven).

'Marana tha' probably derives from the liturgical prayer of the early community. Paul mentions liturgical prayer in the course of his exhortation in Eph 5:19, 20 (see H. Schlier, *Die Zeit der Kirche*, Freiburg i. Br. 1956, 252ff), likewise in 1 Cor 14:6ff; 1 Thess 5:16ff; cf Heb 13:15. Echoes of liturgical prayers or hymns seem to have survived in Phil 2:6–11; Col 1:15–20; 1 Tim 3:16 and also perhaps in the prologue of the johannine gospel (see R. Schnackenburg, 'Logos–Hymnus und johanneischer Prolog', *BZ* 1 [1957], 69–109). In the same way the heavenly liturgy depicted in Revelation (see especially chapters 4 and 5) may have had its counterpart in the earthly liturgy of the church.

Bibliography: A. Klawek, *Das Gebet zu Jesus* (*NA* 6/5), Münster 1921; J. M. Nielen, *Gebet und Gottesdienst im NT*, Münster 1937; J. Jeremias, 'Das Gebetsleben Jesu', *ZNW* 25 (1926), 123–40; F. Cabrol, *La prière des premiers chrétiens*, Paris 1929; H. Greeven, *Gebet und Eschatologie im NT*, 1931; E. Orphal, *Das Paulusgebet*, Gotha 1933; G. Harder, *Paulus und das Gebet*, Gütersloh 1936; J. Jeremias, *Das Vaterunser im Lichte der neueren Forschung*, Stuttgart 1963; W. Ott, *Die Mahnung zu unablässigen Beten bei Lukas*, Würzburg 1964 (dissertation); P. Ketter, 'Vom Gebetsleben des Apostels Paulus', *TPQ* 91 (1938), 23–40; H. Greeven, *TDNT* II, 775–84 and 800–08; Haag 509–16; H. Schürmann, *Das Gebet des Herrn*, Freiburg 1958.

Heinrich Zimmermann

Preaching

Usually 'proclamation' or 'preaching' are used to translate the Greek word *kērugma*. This word occurs eight times in the New Testament if we omit the brief Markan conclusion, ie, in Mt 12:41 = Lk 11:32; Rom 16:25; 1 Cor 1:21; 2:4; 15:14; 2 Tim 4:17; Tit 1:3. It is absent in the johannine writings, and is found only four times in LXX: 2 Chron 30:5; Prov 9:3; Jn 3:2. *Kērugma* is distinct from *katekkēsis* and *didakhē*, which expound at length christian doctrinal and moral teaching, from *parainēsis*, which points up especially the basic demands of morality, and from *didaskalia*, which is a higher form of religious instruction aiming at providing a basis for the christian faith and going into it more deeply. A careful examination of the texts referred to above shows that *kērugma* may be used to designate the earliest form of the proclamation of the christian mystery. It denotes a preaching of the necessity of conversion and decision, a missionary preaching, a preaching of renewal in the context of the church.

The word *kērux* (=herald) occurs only three times in the New Testament: 1 Tim 2:7 and 2 Tim 1:11 with reference to Paul, 2 Pet 2:5 with reference to Noah. It is used only four times in LXX: Gen 41:43; Sir 20:15; Dan 3:4; 4 Macc 6:4. Why, we may ask, does the New Testament hardly ever speak of the human 'herald', an expression which would fit the christian preacher so well? It is never used of the person of the preacher who proclaims the message since the only bearer of the proclaimed word is either God himself or Christ. The human preacher must remain in the background behind Christ who alone is the true 'proclaimer'.

The frequent use of the verb *kērussein* (=proclaim) supports this conclusion. It occurs sixty-one times in the New Testament: nine times in Matthew, fourteen times in Mark, nine times in Luke, eight in Acts, nineteen in Paul (Romans four, 1 Corinthians four, 2 Corinthians four, Galatians two, Philippians two, Colossians one, 1 Thessalonians one, 1 Timothy one, 2 Timothy one), once in 1 Peter, and once in Revelation. This verb does not occur at all in the johannine writings, but is substituted by *marturein* (=bear witness). By using this verb so often while neglecting the corresponding noun, the New Testament writers may well be indicating the enormous importance of the *kērugma* since it is, in the last analysis, God or Christ who speaks by means of the herald. LXX uses the verb thirty times, generally as a translation-word for the Hebrew *qara*.

In addition to this verb the New Testament also makes use of *euangelizesthai* which has much the same meaning, as also other synonyms.

A. *'Kērugma' in the Old Testament*. In the Greek milieu the verb brings to mind the herald who, in the name of and fully authorised by the king or lord, proclaims some decisive event of the reign with a loud voice in the public square.

In the Greek Old Testament *kērussō* occurs thirty-three times corresponding to a whole series of Hebrew verbs and expressions: eighteen times to *qārā* (Gen 41:43; Ex 32:5; 2 Kings 10:20; 2 Chron 20:3; Esther 6:9, 11; Prov 1:21; 8:1; Mic 3:5; Joel 1:14; 2:15; 3:9; Jn 1:2; 3:2, 4, 5; Is 61:1; Dan 3:4—in Jer 7:2 and Ps 105:1 only Symmachus translates *qārā* [to cry or call out] with this verb); four times to *rûaᶜ* (=‘to make a noise’, ‘raise the alarm’: Hos 5:8; Joel 2:1; ‘to break out into a cry of joy’: Zeph 3:14; Zech 9:9); twice to *heᶜebîr qôl* (Ex 36:6; 2 Chron 36:22=‘to let out a cry’, ‘fecit ire seu resonare per regionem vocem=proclamavit’: F. Zorell, *Lexicon* 568); once for *zāᶜaq* (=‘give forth a cry of lamentation’, Jn 3:7); once for *karaz* (=‘cry out publicly’, Jer 5:29

Theod), once for *nāthan qôl* (=‘lift up the voice’, 2 Chron 25:9), and once for *dābar* (=‘cry out’, Jer 20:8 Symm). It also occurs in 1 Macc 5:49; 10:63, 64. It follows from the multiplicity of Hebrew correspondents that this verb is not a fixed expression for one particular kind of proclamation, but that for the most part it has the sense of crying or calling out.

In the political life of the city and the state it refers to the activity of the herald who proclaims festively and publicly some decisive event which is imminent, eg the proximate arrival of some one high up in the kingdom (Gen 41:43; Esther 6:9, 11; 1 Macc 10:63, 64; Dan 3:29) or of any enemy (Joel 3:9; Hos 5:8). This profane 'proclamation' has three characteristics: its official character, reference to an important occurrence, and the proximity of this occurrence.

The *prophetic* proclamation is usually in the form of an arresting and disturbing appeal (Joel 1:14; 2:15; Jn 1:2; 3:2, 4, 5, 7; Jer 7:2; cf 2 Chron 20:3) which rings out in the name and by the power of God and announces a coming festival, (Joel 2:1 cf Ex 32:5; 2 Kings 10:20) or the day of the Lord and/or the day of judgement (Joel 2:1; Is 61:1 cf Jer 20:8; Mic 3:5; Hos 5:8). 'Blow the trumpet in Zion; sound the alarm on my holy mountain! Let all the inhabitants of the land tremble, for the day of the Lord is coming, it is near' (Joel 2:1). Hence the demand which is made: 'return to me with all your heart, with fasting, with weeping and with mourning; rend your hearts and not your garments. Return to the Lord your God' (2:12–13). When the voice of the herald is heard speaking out in the name of Yahweh (see Prov 1:21; 8:1 referring to Wisdom) it is always a proclamation of the day of judgement which is imminent. Hence the sinful people is thereby recalled to penance and conversion.

B. *'Kērugma' in the New Testament.* The prophetic preaching is the seedbed from which the New Testament kerygma emerges and develops. Our rather eviscerated term 'preaching' does not by any means exhaust the full meaning of the verb *kērussein.* It is not a case of an artistically arranged and impressively delivered sermon which aims at instruction, admonition or edification. What this verb implies is rather the solemn and official announcement of an event made in the name of God or Christ, an idea which is best conveyed in the word 'proclamation'. A study of the relevant vocabulary in the New Testament reveals that the emphasis is not on the *kērux* (herald; three times), not even on the *kērugma* (proclamation; eight times) but on the act of proclaiming (*kērussein*; sixty-one times). In other words, what turns the scales is not the messenger, and basically not even his message, but the act of proclaiming, which is effected by the Spirit. It is brought about by the Spirit of God in the same way that the word is in the Old Testament. It is therefore a charismatic operation. Since the prophets were filled with the divine Spirit (see Hos 9:7; Mic 3:8; Is 8:11; 30:1–2; 61:1; Ezek 2:2; 3:24; etc) they received not only the instructions of God but also the task and the ability to proclaim them without fear. Much the same can be said of the bearers of the *kērugma* in the New Testament. Having received the gift of the divine

Spirit (Jn 7:37–9; Acts 2:4, 33; 5:39; 11:21; 1 Cor 12:8; 1 Tim 4:14; 2 Tim 1:14; 3:16; 1 Pet 1:1–2), the apostles announce the 'gospel of God', God's message of salvation brought about in Christ.

This raises a whole series of questions: *who* preaches or proclaims? *what* is to be proclaimed and *how*? *to whom* is the proclamation addressed? *where* is the proclamation to take place?

I. *Who preaches or proclaims?* The New Testament refers to a considerable number to whom the *kērugma* is entrusted whose situation is different with regard either to the whole economy of salvation or to the church's mission. In the last analysis, however, the real bearer of the message is the exalted Christ himself; it is he who speaks through the human instruments.

1. In the first place, Christ is himself mysteriously present in christian preaching since it is a task commissioned by God (or by Christ) and since the object of preaching is the glorified Lord himself.

a. In much the same way as the prophets Joel and Jonah, *John the Baptist* was commissioned by God (Mk 11:30–33) to raise the sound of alarm in order to rouse his contemporaries from sleep and tell them of *the kingdom of God* (Mt 3:1–2) which was breaking in on them and the imminent coming of the king-messiah (Mk 1:7–8). For this reason he announced with a clear voice a 'baptism of repentance for the forgiveness of sins' (Mk 1:4 = Lk 3:3; Acts 10:37 cf 13:24). In this way John associates himself with the *kērugma* of the prophets who announced the advent of the kingdom of God, the coming of the Messiah and the forgiveness of sins.

b. With *Jesus* the time of the *kērugma* was fully present (Acts 13:24 speaks of the pre-kerygmatic stage of the Baptist's ministry). As with John, Jesus proclaimed the message in virtue of a divine mission (Lk 4:18, 43): 'the time is fulfilled, and the kingdom of God is at hand; repent, and believe in the gospel' (Mk 1:14–15; see also Mt 4:17–23; 9:35). At the same time, the *kērugma* of Jesus is basically different from that of the Baptist. Jesus does not speak just as a prophet who announces the kingdom of God. By the very act of proclaiming or preaching (Mk 1:38, 45; 1:39 = Mt 4:23; Lk 4:44; Mt 11:1) he realises the good news (Mk 1:14) of the kingdom of God (Mt 4:17; see also 4:23 = 9:35; 24:14) and calls men to repentance (Mk 1:14 = Mt 4:17). The kerygma of Jesus brings about what it proclaims. It comes about by the Spirit of God and therefore is charged with power. This conviction is expressed by Jesus himself: 'today this scripture has been fulfilled in your hearing' (Lk 4:21). 'Today'—that means here and now—the salvation promised in Is 61:1 is *proclaimed*, that is, fulfilled and realised in the release of captives and the acceptable year of the Lord. '[Jesus] does not announce that something will happen. His proclamation is itself event. What he declares takes place in the moment of its proclamation' (G. Friedrich, *TDNT* III, 706). Following on this, Paul is sent 'to preach in its fullness' 'the gospel of Christ' (Rom 15:19) or 'the word of God' (Col 1:25). In both cases the verb *plēroō* is used. The Lord stood by him and gave him strength (*endunamoō*) so that through him the

kērugma might be 'fully proclaimed' (*plērophoreō*, 2 Tim 4:17). These expressions do not mean that Paul has preached the gospel or the word of God or the *kērugma* completely, without leaving anything out, or that he has preached it in every place. According to the context it signifies that he has brought it to its full development, that, in other words, he has actualised or realised it; for in all three texts Paul attributes the success of his preaching to 'the power' which he has received (Col 1:29; 2 Tim 4:17) or to 'the Holy Spirit' (Rom 15:19).

c. In the time before the resurrection Jesus sent out his *disciples* to 'proclaim' publicly on the streets and from the rooftops (Mt 10:27 = Lk 12:3) the proximate coming of the kingdom of God (Mk 3:14 = Mt 10:7 = Lk 9:2) and to call the hearers to conversion (Mk 6:12). Unlike the *kērugma* of the Baptist, that of the apostles is accompanied by the healing of the sick. After the resurrection the disciples are to carry on until the end the *kērugma* of Jesus in virtue of their divine mission (Mt 24:14; 26:13 = Mk 14:9; 13:10; 16:15, 20; Lk 24:47–8; Acts 10:42).

d. The apostle *Paul* is conscious of preaching the same *kērugma* as that of the first apostles, as can be seen from the frequency with which he speaks in the plural: we preach, our preaching (Rom 10:8, 1 Cor 1:23; 15:11; 2 Cor 1:19; 4:5; 11:4; 1 Thess 2:9). This also emerges from the fact that he attributes his *mission* to God or to Christ rather than to the Twelve, but not to Christ of the earthly ministry but to the exalted Lord (see Gal 1:16; 1 Cor 1:17; 2 Cor 5:18; Eph 3:7). But he distinguishes his *kērugma* from that of the first apostles by appealing not just to an immediate revelation but also to the apostolic tradition (compare 1 Cor 15:11–12, 14 with 15:1, 3; see also Col. 1:23; Gal 2:2).

e. In the post-apostolic age the *kērugma* becomes *the preaching of the church*. The preaching of the word takes on more and more the form of *didakhē* and *didaskalia*, that is, the exposition of faith and moral conduct together with a more elaborated kind of religious instruction. Phrases such as 'sound teaching' (*didaskalia*; 1 Tim 1:10; 2 Tim 4:3; Tit 1:9; 2:1), 'sound words' (*hugiainontes logoi*; 1 Tim 6:3; 2 Tim 1:13), 'sound speech' (*logos hugiēs*: Tit 2:8), 'sound in the faith': Tit 1:13; 2:2) occur only in the Pastorals and refer to solid exposition and interpretation based on the fixed tradition of the gospel, 'in accordance with the glorious gospel of the blessed God' (1 Tim 1:11). This sound doctrine in keeping with the tradition must be distinguished from the preaching of the basic events of salvation. This is 'a distinction which the modern kerygmatic theology—and not only the modern kerygmatic theology—ignores and thereby loses the saving events, abandoning the saving history to the here and now of a proclamation aimed at arousing faith' (H. Schürmann, *LTK* VI², 123).

2. Christian preaching is carried out by a divine commission and has Christ as its centre. But the exalted Lord also speaks *directly* by the mouth of the apostle. Paul sees himself as 'sent on behalf of Christ' (2 Cor 5:20) to do 'the work of the Lord' (1 Cor 16:10) in preaching 'the gospel of Christ' (1 Cor 9:12; 2 Cor 2:12; 9:13;

2 Thess 1:8; etc). In Rom 10:14 it is probably the exalted Lord himself to whom one must belong in order to attain to faith. In Rom 16:25: 'according to my gospel and the *kērugma* of Jesus Christ', 'Jesus Christ' should not be taken as objective genitive, namely, as the object or content of the preaching (as H. Ott), but rather as subjective genitive in keeping with the parallel 'according to my gospel'. In other words, it is here a question of the message which Jesus Christ himself proclaims, but not Christ in his life on earth (as G. Friedrich) but rather the exalted Lord. As Augustine put it, Jesus Christ preaches from his heavenly throne.

As the glorified Christ justifies men through the Holy Spirit (compare Gal 2:16 with 1 Cor 6:11), sanctifies them (compare 1 Cor 1:2 with 6:11) and seals them (compare Eph 1:13 with 4:30), so does he himself speak by the Spirit of God bestowed on the one who preaches. Paul says expressly that Christ with power watches over the word of the one sent by him (2 Tim 4:17; see also Lk 24:47–9; Mk 16:20) so that the apostolic preaching may sound forth 'in the manifestation of spirit and power' (1 Cor 2:4; see also 1 Cor 15:10–11), 'full of life and power' (Heb 4:12). Christian preaching is therefore integrally part of the charismatic gifts.

If, however, Christ speaks through the Holy Spirit (2 Cor 3:17) in the one commissioned by him it must follow that he has not just spoken 'then' but continues to speak here and now to those who listen today. 'In preaching, Christ himself continues to appear before men, offering himself to them as lord and redeemer and calling them to decision. It is by means of the word that the church comes into existence and is established' (V. Schurr, 236).

II. *What is to be preached and how?*—these two questions are intimately related to each other.

1. In the first place, what is preached is not a truth or a precept but a *person*: the exalted and glorified lord, Jesus Christ. The person of Jesus Christ constitutes the heart and soul of the *kērugma*. Without him the *kērugma* would be like a watercourse without water, a body without soul, a husk without grain, a sky without sun.

By proclaiming the imminent coming of the kingdom of God and an urgent call to conversion Jesus not only presented himself as the bearer of the *kērugma* but became its very centre, as is clear from his interpretation of Is 61:1–2 in the synagogue of Capharnaum: '*today* this scripture has been fulfilled in your hearing' (Lk 4:18–19, 21). Jesus therefore did not become the centre of the *kērugma* only after his resurrection. What happened after the resurrection was a shift of emphasis: the primitive christian *kērugma* was permanently centred on the figure of the dying Saviour, even more so on the risen and exalted Lord. It was grounded in the resurrection of Christ. From that point until his glorious return the exalted Lord was to be the heart and soul of the christian proclamation (see Acts 8:5; 9:20; 19:13; 1 Cor 1:23; 15:12; 2 Cor 1:19; 4:5; 11:4; Phil 1:15; 1 Tim 3:16). The *kērugma* takes in the whole mystery of Christ: the cross (1 Cor 1:23), the resurrection (Rom 10:8–9) and the return of Christ in glory as universal judge (Acts 10:42).

Since God and his decisive act in Christ form the centre of the *kērugma*, it can be described as the proclamation of the kingdom of God (Mt 13:19; Lk 9:2; Acts 28:31) and the preaching of Christ (Acts 8:5; 9:20; 1 Cor 1:23; 2 Cor 4:5). Seen in its effects it may be paraphrased as 'the word of salvation' (Acts 13:26), 'the word of grace' (Acts 14:3; 20:32), 'the word of faith' (Rom 10:8), 'the word of truth' (Col 1:5; Eph 1:13; 2 Tim 2:15), 'the atoning word' (*logos tēs katallagēs*, 2 Cor. 5:19), 'the word of life' (Phil 2:16), 'the word of the glory of Christ' (2 Cor 4:4) or simply as 'the word' (2 Tim 4:2; Acts 17:15D). Since this word is effected by the Spirit of God it brings about and realizes what it expresses: salvation, grace, faith, truth, atonement, and life.

2. Since the exalted Lord speaks and acts through the proclamation of his messengers who are filled with the Spirit, it follows that the personality of the preacher must fall into the background, leaving room for the Lord who is mysteriously present through the word. The decisive factor is the presence of Christ and his Spirit. The personality of the preacher who proclaims the word is of no consequence since the true preacher is God, or God speaking through Christ. Hence in the New Testament little attention is paid to the *kērux*, the herald, seen in the fact that this word occurs there only three times. This explains the peculiar and unique function of the christian preacher such as we find it described in Paul's letters. More than any of the other apostles he set himself to fathom the mystery latent in the christian proclamation.

691

It follows from all this that the power of Christ comes through most clearly in the *weakness* of the one who proclaims the message (2 Cor 12:9). Paul admits to the Corinthians that he came to them 'in weakness, in fear and with much trembling' and preached to them 'not in lofty words of wisdom' but in 'the demonstration of the Spirit and power' so that their faith should not be grounded on 'human wisdom' but on 'the power of God' (1 Cor 2:2–5). Since the apostle of the Gentiles was deeply conscious of the fact that when he preached his own role was a secondary one, he did not put much store by 'earthly wisdom' (2 Cor 1:12) or by skill in speaking (11:6). The treasure of the word of God is borne for the apostle 'in earthly vessels' so that 'the transcendent power may belong to God and not to us' (4:7).

The mystery of the christian proclamation and preaching is founded in belief in the power of God's Spirit and in knowledge of the weakness of the human instrument. Here we have the key to its irresistible progress and power. Despite all his setbacks the apostle continued to boast of his weakness (2 Cor 11:30) and enjoy the consoling presence of God (1:3–4).

Whether free or in chains, the bearer of the message continues his mission—'the word of God is not fettered' (2 Tim 2:9). His voice is silenced by death but the word of the Lord continues to resound throughout the centuries (see 2 Thess 3:1).

III. *To whom is the proclamation addressed?* If we study the texts we shall see that the apostolic *kērugma* was not addressed exclusively to the gentiles or ↗ heathen. The New Testament *kērugma* does not refer exclusively to the first proclamation of the mystery of Christ in terms of a call to conversion and decision, but takes in also, even primarily, the preaching of the renewal of life within the christian community.

In preaching to the Jews, who were always on the lookout for signs, Jesus compares his mission to that of the prophet Jonah (Mt 12:40 = Lk 11:32). According to Rom 16:25 Paul addressed the *kērugma* of Jesus Christ to the christian community of Rome by means of which the exalted Lord himself strengthened by his word the christians of that city. The *kērugma*, therefore, was not just addressed to pagans. Paul reminded his christians in Corinth that by means of the *kērugma* God had saved all of them *who had believed in it* (1 Cor 1:21). This implies that in what was already a believing community the word of God continued to be present as a power of salvation 'for those who believe' (cf 2 Tim 4:17). According to 1 Cor 15:14 the apostle's *kērugma* is also a preaching of the resurrection which is addressed to *christians*. Without the risen and exalted Lord his preaching would be 'void' and the faith of the community vain. This too, therefore, must be considered as a preaching not of conversion but renewal (see also Tit 1:3; 1 Tim 3:16).

In writing to the Corinthians, 'My speech and my message were not in plausible words of wisdom but in demonstration of the Spirit and power' (1 Cor 2:4), Paul was certainly referring to his first preaching among them. But the whole context shows that he was not concerned with who had first preached the gospel but *how* it had been preached. Since they are filled with spirit and power the words of his preaching are superior to discourses inspired by gnostic wisdom. Since he is referring in 1 Cor 2:4 to a generally valid characteristic of his preaching, it can be concluded, especially in view of what he says in 1:18–31 and 2:6–16, that the reference throughout is in the present tense. Right from the beginning and throughout, the preached word of the apostle is full of the power of God's Spirit.

The texts we have adduced should not lead us to suppose that the *kērugma* refers exclusively to the first preaching of the gospel. It must continue to resound in the church even after the apostolic age. The faithful take their place at 'the table of the word of God' in order to be continually renewed in the Holy Spirit and strengthened in their resolve to live a christian life in accordance with the will of God.

IV. *Where does the proclamation take place?* The apostolic preaching always takes place in public: 1. in an assembly of non-christian listeners whom the preacher wishes to win over to faith in the risen and exalted Lord as, for example, on the first Pentecost (Acts 2:14–36), in the household of the Roman centurion Cornelius (Acts 10: 34–8), or on the Areopagus at Athens (17:19–31); 2. Within the assembly of a believing community (Acts 14:27; 15); 3. Above all, during the divine service, where the divine host himself proclaims anew in a mysterious way the message of salvation through the mouth of his herald who is filled with the Holy Spirit. This proclamation has the purpose of recalling the christian hearer to conversion and to a renewal of life. Throughout the centuries the

christian church continues to preach the *kērugma* to bring into the hearts and lives of both christian and non-christian alike 'the word of Christ' (Col 3:16).

Bibliography: C. H. Dodd, *The Apostolic Preaching and its Developments*, London 1956; J. Gewiess, *Die Urapostolische Heilsverkündigung nach der Apostelgeschichte*, Breslau 1939; R. Asting, *Die Verkündigung des Wortes im Urchristentum*, Stuttgart 1939; A. M. Hunter, *The Unity of the New Testament*, London 1944; H. Schürmann, *Aufbau und Struktur der ntl. Verkündigung*, Paderborn 1949; A. Rétif, 'Qu'est-ce que le kérygme?', *NRT* 81 (1949), 910–22; A. Rétif, 'Témoignage et prédication missionnaire dans les Actes des Apôtres', *NRT* 83 (1951), 152–65; A. Rétif, *Foi au Christ et mission d'après les Actes des Apôtres*, Paris 1952; J. R. Geiselmann, *Jesus der Christus*, Stuttgart 1951; K. Stendhal, 'Kerygma und kerygmatisch', *TLZ* 77 (1952), 715–20; P. Hitz, *L'Annonce missionnaire de l'Evangile*, Paris 1954; L. Cerfaux, 'Témoins du Christ d'après le livre des Actes', *Recueil L. Cerfaux* II, Paris–Gembloux 1954, 157–74; H. Schlier, *Kerygma und Sophia*, Freiburg 1956, 206–32; C. F. Evans, 'The Kerygma', *JTS* 7 (1956), 25–41; J. D. Vincent, 'Didactic Kerygma in the Synoptic Gospels', *SJT* 10 (1957), 272–3; W. Baird, 'What is the Kerygma?', *JBL* 76 (1957), 181–91; E. L. Allen, 'The Lost Kerygma', *NTS* 3 (1957), 349–53; K. Goldammer, 'Der Kerygma-Begriff in der ältesten christlichen Literatur', *ZNW* 48 (1957), 77–101; U. Wilken, 'Kerygma und Evangelium bei Lukas', *ZNW* 49 (1958), 223–37; H. Ott, 'Kerygma', *RGG* III, 1250–54; K. E. Logsturp, 'Verkündigung', *RGG* VI, 1358–60; G. Friedrich, *TDNT* III, 683–718 (with bibliography); G. Friedrich, *TDNT* II, 707–37; D. Grasso, 'Il kerygma e la predicazione', *Gregorianum* 41 (1960), 424–50; H. Schürmann, 'Kerygma', *LTK* VI, 122–5; Bultmann 63–92 and 306–14; H. Schlier, *Wort Gottes*, Würzburg 1962²; J. Audrisseau, *DBT* 838–43; A. Regan, 'The Word of God and the Ministry of preaching', *Studia Moralia* I (1963), 389–449; I. Hermann, 'Kerygma und Kirche', *Neutestamentliche Aufsätze* (Festschrift J. Schmid), Regensburg 1963, 110–14; K. Rahner, 'Die missionarische Predigt', *Handbuch der Pastoraltheologie* I, Freiburg–Basle–Vienna 1964, 220–29; V. Schurr, 'Die Gemeinde predigt', *Handbuch der Pastoraltheologie* I, 230–65; D. Grasso, *L'annuncio della Salvezza*, Naples 1965 (with bibliography).

Robert Koch

Predestination

The world is perfectly ordered. All is designed for a purpose (Prov 16:4) and nothing takes place, not even evil, without the will of God (Gen 45:8; 50:20; Amos 3:6; Sir 11:14; Acts 4:28). To this ordering of the universe to a predetermined end in the order of nature corresponds, on the supernatural plane, the reality known as predestination: all that is connected with Christ, the chosen people, the Christians, has been foreseen, willed and prepared from all eternity by God. Still more precisely, the divine plan which was conceived of for the ↗ redemption of believers, accomplished by Christ and revealed in the preaching of the apostles, will unfailingly be fulfilled down to its final effects in the glorification of the elect.

This doctrine, while not developed systematically, nevertheless does bring out one aspect of the biblical authors' faith in the absolute supremacy of ↗ God (Ps 29; 89:6f). He is omnipotent (1 Tim 6:15; Rev 19:6), Lord (Lk 2:29; Acts 4:24), the first and also the sole cause of the cosmos and of everything that takes place within it, both in the sphere of nature (Job 27:15; Ps 104; Mt 6:30a; 10:29) and in the human sphere (Is 41:25; 45:1f; Jn 6:44; Phil 2:13). 'He has done whatever he pleased' (Ps 115:3; Is 55:11). What he planned from of old he now brings to pass (2 Kings 19:25; Is 22:11); he also plans what is to happen in the course of history (Is 14:24; 37:26; Ps 139:16), and in fact brings it to pass at a point in time determined by himself (Acts 17:26, 31). Nothing, not even events which appear to be accidental, falls outside his control (Gen 24:52, 56; Prov 16:33).

I. *The divine plan.* Such knowledge as we can acquire concerning the purposes of God can be conceived of only by analogy with the processes of human psychology. In terms of these the intended end is first conceived of, desired and decided upon, and only then, by the use of the selected means, finally attained. In a similar way it could be said that God has a plan for creation, an overall economy determining the religious history of mankind (1 QS 3:15; 11:11). This is what Paul, the teacher of the doctrine of predestination, calls the 'counsel of his will' (Eph 1:11), his plan or his purpose (*prothesis*), which he characterises as 'gracious decision' (*eudokia*, Eph 1:9; cf 2 Tim 1:9), taken from sheer kindness (Rom 8:28), and determined upon from all eternity (Eph 3:11; cp 1:4; 2 Thess 2:13; Col 1:26), 'fixed upon before all ages' (1 Cor 2:7). In contrast to all the instability and mutability of human decisions this mysterious decision of his will, which he has taken freely (Eph 1:9), is not merely unalterable and final (Rom 11:29), but also unfailing in its accomplishment. Prior to all history and exercising an influence upon it, this plan has been worked out in sovereign independence without regard to the qualities or the reactions of the men involved (Rom 9:11f), but solely for the honour of God, ie in order to make manifest his graciousness; all is done 'for him' (Col 1:16).

As it is the task of ↗ wisdom in general to prepare the means for a given end, and to adapt them to that end, so in the case of God this undertaking or purpose of which we have been speaking is identical with his wisdom (1 Cor 2:7). It has as its object our glorification (1 Cor 2:7; Rom 9:23), an inconceivable happiness 'that he has prepared for those that love him' (1 Cor 2:9) as a heritage (Gal 4:7; Eph 1:14; Heb 9:15), as salvation (2 Tim 1:9; 2 Thess 2:13). The object of God's design may be stated still more precisely. It is our assimilation to Christ—including physical resurrection as the final stage in the process by which we are conformed to his glorified Body (Rom 8:28f), and, even more than this, 'our being adopted children of God in Jesus Christ' (Eph 1:5). This in turn presupposes the gift of grace (v 6), by which we are changed into the likeness of Christ (2 Cor 3:18), and also all kinds of spiritual blessings (Eph 1:3), above all the remission of sins (v 7), the gift of faith and sanctification (2 Thess 2:13), in short the entire ordering of the cosmos in so far as this decides the destiny of the elect in a favourable sense.

II. *Knowledge and choice.* This deciding of destiny and these actual gifts are not directed to all men, but only to those who love God, the faithful who respond to God's summons, the members of the church. Most properly it applies to the elect and to those of whom God has had foreknowledge (*prognōsis*, Rom 8:29; 11:2; 1 Pet 1:20). As the bible understands it this knowledge is not only an act of the speculative intellect, but an act of God's benevolent will also, by which he sets certain creatures apart to himself. These are separated from the rest precisely in order that he may be a benevolent God to them (1 Cor 8:3; Gal 4:9). By this knowledge, then, is designated not merely an act of the intellect but, as a concomitant of this, an act of the will proceeding from love (Hos 3:5; Amos 3:2; Ps 1:6). The plan of salvation is based not only upon prior knowledge (Judith 9:6) but on a prior selective recognition of specific individuals who are to be preferred before the rest as the object of divine favour. Hence this plan is also called the 'plan of God's free choice' (Rom 9:11).

Divine choice (*eklogē*) and divine knowledge or recognition are equivalent in meaning. For the concept of election (*bahar*, selectively to examine) includes as its inseparable concomitant the movement of the intellect in drawing the initial distinction upon which the preference and special favour determining the choice are based. The 'elect of providence' (1 Pet 1:1f) can equally well be described as 'those whom God foreknew' (Rom 8:29), and also as 'those whom God chose from the beginning to be saved' (2 Thess 2:13). In this last instance, however, greater emphasis is laid upon the affective aspect, for 'to choose' is often equivalent to 'prefer' (Is 1:29; 1 Chron 16:13; Ps 89:3; Mt 12:18; Lk 9:35). The reason is that what is involved in such cases is the act by which a man claims for himself that which he loves. Thus Israel was elected because God loved her (Deut 4:37; 7:8; 10:15; Rom 11:28). Christians for their part are elected because they are the object of the love of God and Christ (1 Thess 1:4; 2 Thess 2:13). Assurance is given that the objects of the divine choice, the chosen race (1 Pet 2:9), will share in the new distribution of all treasures of grace (1 Cor

1:27–30; Eph 1:4). It is reiterated that this election is a favour (Rom 11:5), the outcome of benevolent care (Eph 1:9), love that is not due to any merit of theirs: 'So it depends not upon man's will, nor upon exertion, but upon God's mercy' (Rom 9:16).

III. *Predestination.* The eternal design of God (*prothesis*), the outcome of loving knowledge and enlightened choice, is essentially dynamic. In order to become effective too, and to attain to its full realization in time and eternity, it needed a determination of the will (Acts 2:23), a decision (11:29) which finds its expression in a decree (*imperium*). It is in this decree (*to hōrismenon*, Lk 22:22) that predestination formally consists. The New Testament does in fact mention divine resolves and decrees (Acts 17:26; Heb 4:7). Some of these refer to Christ, who is declared to be judge over the whole of creation (Acts 10:42; 17:31), and to be 'Son of God with power' (Rom 1:4), ie endowed with all the qualities needful for his mission. Other such decrees refer to the elect whose names are written for ever in the Book of Life. When however it is the final and predestined decision of the eternal plan of God that is in question, the New Testament uses a verb (*proörizō*, lit = 'to predestine') and not the corresponding noun, whereas elsewhere noun and verb are used without distinction to express the fore-knowledge or prior choice of God. From this it can be deduced that no logical distinction is drawn between the three acts. By its etymology alone the third word implies a definitive ruling and determination which admits of no exceptions or modifications. On this point the commentary of Aquinas is wholly to be upheld: 'Differt [praedestinatio] a praescientia secundum rationem, quoniam praescientia importat solam notitiam futurorum, sed praedestinatio importat causalitatem quandam respectu eorum' (*In Rom* VIII, lect 6: 'the essential difference between foreknowledge and [predestination] is that foreknowledge denotes a simple awareness of future things, but predestination denotes a certain causality in respect of them'). It should be noticed, moreover, that foreknowledge and choice have as their proper object the actual persons concerned, and only secondarily the maintenance of favour (2 Thess 2:13f), whereas predestination applies rather to the economy of salvation and its realization in progressive stages, and only secondarily to the persons involved. From this one is led to conclude that the knowledge and choice of God bear chiefly upon the end, whereas predestination bears chiefly upon the means: the course which the elect must follow considered as a whole.

There is no need to insist too much on these fine distinctions. What is certain is that election connotes chiefly the preference and love of God, whereas predestination is specifically Christian in that it decides that the lot of the elect is to be in fellowship with Christ. Once God has separated off his elect to himself, he destines them to become like his Son (Rom 8:29; Eph 1:5). This is a great destiny which goes back to the plan of the divine wisdom (1 Cor 2:7; Eph 1:11; 2 Tim 1:9). Henceforward man knows the way and manner and basis of the 'preparation for glory' (Rom 9:23; see also Mt 25:34). It is not so much a question of the happiness of the elect as of the formation of a new race, the head and firstborn of which is Christ, as Adam was in the beginning for mankind, so that a family of children of God (⁊ sonship) can be formed, among whom Christ is the chief. Predestination is directed to this as its concrete end, and to the means whereby it is to be attained; the gift of faith, of grace and of the Holy Spirit, of the remission of sins, of sanctification, of bearing one's Cross and entering heaven are nothing else than particular means, following one upon another, of becoming united and conformed to Christ (Rom 3:25f; Gal 4:4–6; Col. 1:19f; 1 Pet 1:19–21). While special callings do exist also (Mt 20:23; Acts 22:14), there is, nevertheless, only one predestination for all the elect: to become 'Christ'.

IV. ⁊ *Vocation*, ⁊ *justification*, and ⁊ *glory*. If God has 'predestined us to be his sons (⁊ sonship) through Jesus Christ' (Eph 1:5), he has also actually put this decision into effect (Jn 1:12). Indeed he has chosen the right point in time for doing this, for in his decisions he takes the smallest factors into account and determines the exact point in time at which they are to be accomplished (Acts 17:26; Heb 4:7; cf Jn 7:30; 12:27; 13:1; 17:1). To the three stages in the divine intention: foreknowledge, election, predestination, correspond three stages in the accomplishment: vocation, justification, glorification as the three links in a chain which brings the elect to heaven. 'Those whom God predestined he also called, and those whom he called he also justified; those whom he justified he also glorified' (Rom 8:29f). The apostle wishes to arouse in all christians an absolute

trust in the present grace, which is the seed of, and at the same time the pledge of, their supernatural beatitude: 'For it is through hope that we are saved' (Rom 8:24). 'Hope will not be put to shame' (Rom 5:5). Each one can entertain a firm hope of future glory because through justification in faith he has been set right and made ready to enter the kingdom of God. He has received forgiveness for his sins because he has actually received a call from God to believe. He has received this call because he is predestined by God. He is predestined because God, from all eternity, has set him apart and has loved him.

V. *Predestination and* ⁊ *freedom*. Predestination is infallible in attaining its object and cannot be lost. Hope does not deceive (Rom 5:5); love does not cease (1 Cor 13:8; Eph 6:24); graces will henceforward never be revoked (Rom 11:29). The elect are redeemed once and for all (Mt 24:24). The bible speaks as though there were no such thing as human freedom. On the other hand everything happens as though there were no such thing as predestination. For the New Testament ceaselessly exhorts christians to live worthily of their calling (Eph 4:1; 2 Pet 1:10). Since good will is precisely the sign of election, effort is necessary in order to enter into the promised rest (Heb 4:11). This may be compared to the situation of a prize-fighter who wins the crown of victory only when he has fought for it (1 Cor 9:24; Phil 3:12–14; 2 Tim 4:7): the keeping of the commandments is therefore presupposed (Mt 19:17; Lk 13:23f). Each one is responsible for his own actions and will be judged according to his works (Mt 25:34f, 41f; 2 Cor 5:10). Thus in the last analysis he forges his own happiness or unhappiness (Mt 22:12f; 25:3-12, 21-30). In other words grace brings no coercive force to bear, and the integrity of human freedom remains unimpaired.

The problem of how free will can be reconciled with predestination, a problem which does not present itself in the New Testament, is for the theologians to solve. From an exegetical point of view all that can be said on this point is that the merits and good works of men, which God foresees, do indeed have no influence whatever upon his decision. This is arrived at quite without reference to human presuppositions, a fact which may be gathered from the figure of the choosing of one of two twins (Rom 9:11f; see also Mal 1:1f). On the other hand, however, this doctrine is the opposite of quietism, for man has the power to render God's grace ineffective (2 Cor 6:1). He can reject the gifts God offers him (Heb 4:2) in the same way that a bad field can prevent good seed from bearing fruit (Heb 6:7; Lk 8:5-15). Everything depends upon the attitude of the ↗ heart, which is hardened (Heb 3:8, 12f, 15), rebels, and refuses obedience to God (Rom 10:6), and finally prefers darkness to ↗ light (Jn 3:19). There is therefore human co-operation in the work of salvation (Col 1:24; 2 Tim 2:10).

VI. *Reprobation.* The mystery of how the elect are chosen and other men are reprobated is a terrible one. Can it really be that only those who believe will be in heaven (Heb 11:6), those preferred by God who have been redeemed by the ↗ blood of Christ, and

whose names are written in the ↗ Book of Life (Rev 13:8; cf 3:5; 17:8; 21:12, 27; Phil 4:3)? Election implies selection from a greater number, namely the number of those who remain left to their own resources and untouched by the mediatorship of Christ (Jn 17:9), those too who on account of their sins are subject to the dominion of ↗ wrath (Eph 2:3), that is, liable to chastisement. This state of alienation from God prepares for and entails the state of final separation from him in eternal death. 'God has mercy upon whomsoever he wills, and he hardens the heart of whomever he wills' (Rom 9:18).

We are here confronted with the mystery of the fact that God's gifts are bestowed without merit, and that his ↗ love is free, with depths, then, that are unfathomable, and with a mystery which no man can comprehend (Rom 11:33; cf Rom 9:20f; Sir 33:10-13; 1 QS 11:22).

It still remains true that God's will to save is universal. God wishes all men to be saved (1 Tim 2:4), that none of them should perish (2 Pet 3:9), and again and again he sends out his call and his help to them so that they can convert their ways: 'All day long I have held out my hands to a disobedient and contrary people' (Rom 10:21). It is not God, then, who rejects 'the vessels of wrath' (Rom 11:1f; cf 9:22), but rather they who reject what is offered to them. 'How often would I have . . . and you would not' (Mt 23:37). Nowhere do we find reprobation presented as the result of God's decision (as at Qumran, 1 QH 15:12-20), preparing the wicked for condemnation as his predestination prepares the elect for glory (cf the significant change of verbs Rom 9:22–33 and 1 Thess 5:9). Some are infallibly preserved by God (Jn 6:37; 10:28), others not (17:11f), and God gives them up, or leaves them to effect their own perdition (Rom 1:24, 26, 28). Reprobation, then, is purely negative in character; it is an effect and not a cause.

It is in this sense that God is said to 'harden' sinners (Rom 9:18; 11:17), as he did in the case of Pharaoh. The blindness ensuing upon sin is the inexorable punishment of this initial disobedience. It renders them incapable of returning to their senses (↗hardness of heart).

The sinner who is thus hardened is quite simply disqualified, literally 'not admitted' (*adokimon*, 1 Cor 9:27; 2 Cor 13:5–7). God has no reason to intervene in his favour; he treats him as though he were not there. Forgiveness and glory, which he bestows upon the elect, are gifts of his love, whereas eternal↗death is the just requital of ↗sin.

God, then, is not responsible for the misery of the sinner. On the contrary he treats him with patience in order to give him time for repentance (Rom 2:4; 3:25; 2 Pet 3:9, 15). Admittedly these observations cannot, without further qualification, be applied to heathens and unbelievers who have never heard the gospel. For chapters 9–11 of the Letter to the Romans refer more to communities than to individual men, more to the temporal role of these in the course of history than to their moral behaviour, their fate in eternity and the acts of election based upon the divine foreknowledge (Gen 25:23; Mal 1:1f). In fact the hardening of Israel (Rom 11:7f) was only partial and restricted in time, and was ordered to the conversion of the heathen. God will attain this goal through his mercy (Rom 11:25–32).

VII. *Conclusion.* When God's will to save or his plan for salvation or election and predestination are in question, Paul continually refers to the benevolence of God (Eph 1:11), his unmerited↗goodness (Rom 11:5; Eph 1:6–9; 2:5–8), his↗mercy (Rom 9:11, 16, 23; Tit 3:5), and above all his↗love (1 Thess 1:4; 2 Thess 2:13; Rom 8:28; 11:28; Eph 1:3f). The predestined man is the beloved of God (Rom 9:13, 25). The biblical mystery is not terrible, but rather a mystery of love. God destines those men for whom he entertains a prior love to eternal glory, and this destiny is accomplished thanks to the dispositions which he has made, based upon his prior knowledge. These dispositions *per fas et nefas* work in their favour. Turning to the opposite case of those others whom God is no less desirous of delivering, his salvific will is no less generous to these, for he does indeed offer his grace to them too (Tit 2:11). But this does not take effect because the men concerned resist it. God is unjust to no man, even if to those whom he wills he is something more than just—loving (Mt 20:13f). Thus Florus the Deacon, as cited by the third Council of Valence, can assert: 'Nec ipsos malos ideo perire quia boni esse non potuerunt, sed quia boni esse noluerunt' (DS 627 [DB 321]: 'not even the wicked perish because they have been unable to be good, but because they have been unwilling to be good').

It is no less important to remember that election and predestination are only means to an end which goes far beyond themselves: the glory of God, that is the manifestation of his kindness in its most extreme form, that namely of ⁊ mercy (Eph 2:4f). Certainly God detests evil, but Jesus has revealed that he loves sinners, and the Holy ⁊ Spirit characterises his own essence as love (1 Jn 4:8, 16). On the historical plane it is already established that where 'sin increased grace abounded all the more' (Rom 5:20). Yet the scope of the divine plan of the created order is vast enough to include a time during which evil is allowed to continue: 'For God has shut up all in disobedience, that he may have mercy upon all' (Rom 11:32; see also Gal 3:22; 2 Pet 3:9).

Towards this mystery the apostle recommends a threefold attitude of spirit; first strong and ardent trust (Rom 8:28f; cf on this Thomas Aquinas: 'Promotis a Deo nullus potest nocere'), next 'work out your salvation with fear and trembling', ie with great earnestness (Phil 2:12–16), for the obligation of responding to the gifts of grace is all the greater for the fact that they are quite unmerited (Lk 11:21–6, 31f); finally the apostle recommends that no pains shall be spared in the performance of good works, so that we can put into effect the plan laid down by God (Eph 2:10; Tit 3:8). A twofold criterion of predestination has been clearly provided, which enables assurance of salvation to be given to every heart (1 Jn 3:19f; 4:18f). This is the love of God (Rom 8:28), which is inspired by the Holy Ghost (Rom 5:5), and the love of one's brother, which shows that one has taken the step from death to life and that one has been born of God (1 Jn 3:10, 14, 19; 4:7).

Bibliography: E. B. Allo, 'Versets 28–30 du c vⅢ ad Romanos', *RSPT* (1913), 263–73; E. B. Allo, 'Encore Rom 8:28–30', *RSPT* (1924), 503–5; M. J. Lagrange, *L'Epître aux Romains*, Paris 1916, 244–8; R. Liechtenhan, *Die göttliche Vorherbestimmung bei Paulus und in der Posidonianischen Philosophie*, Göttingen 1922; E. von Dobschütz, 'Prädestination', *TSK* 106 (1934/5), 9–19; F. Davidson, *Pauline Predestination*, London 1946; J. Dupont, *Gnosis*, Louvain–Paris 1949, 88–104; F. Ceuppens, *Theologia Biblica* I, Rome 1949, 237–79; Ⅲ, Rome 1950, 199–201; A. Feuillet, 'Le plan salvifique de l'Epître aux Romains', *RB* (1950), 336–87 and 489–529; J. M. Bover, 'La reprobación de Israel en Rom 9–11', *Estudios Eccl.* (1951), 63–82; F. Heese, *Das Verstockungsproblem im AT*, Berlin 1955; S. Lyonnet, *Quaestiones in Epistulam ad Romanos*, Rome 1956; J. Munck, *Christus und Israel. Eine Auslegung von Rom 9–11*, Copenhagen 1956; H. G. Wood, 'God's Providential Care and Continual Help—Rom 8:28', *Expository Times* 69 (1958), 292–5; C. Spicq, *Agapè* I, Paris 1958, 246–59; J. B. Bauer, 'Röm 8:28', *ZNW* (1959), 106–12; E. Schweizer, 'Zur Herkunft der Präexistenzvorstellung bei Paulus', *ET* (1959), 66; A. Lemonnyer, 'Prédestination', *DTC* xⅡ/2, 2809–15; P. Maury, *La Prédestination*, Geneva 1957; F. Nötscher, 'Schicksalsglaubein Qumran und Umwelt', *BZ* 3 (1959), 205–34 and 4 (1960), 98–121; H. M. Dion, 'La Prédestination chez S. Paul', *RSR* (1965), 5–43.

Ceslaus Spicq

Priest(hood)

1. *Nature*. According to Deut 33:8–10 Levi has charge over the Tummim and Urim (the sacred lots by means of which oracles were taken). He also teaches justice and the law of God (Jer 18:18; Ezek 7:26). All cases of dispute and all acts of violence are submitted to the decision of the priest. He also blesses in the name of the Lord (Deut 21:5) and offers sacrifices on the altar of God (Deut 26:1–11). The priest

is a messenger of the Lord (Mal 2:7). The designations *kōhēn* (soothsayer) and *lēwî* (oracle-giver) are probably derived from the function of presiding over the sacred lots. *hierens* too is almost synonymous with *mantis*: Homer, *Iliad* I, 62). In the New Testament I Pet 2:1–9 defines the nature of the priesthood by means of its twofold function and ministry: witness and sacrifice or, more generally, word and worship (v 9 and v 5). What both aspects of the priestly ministry have in common is the function of mediatorship (⟋ mediation). In the case of the word the mediator exercises his ministry by conveying the word *from* God *to* the world; in the case of sacrifice he brings offerings *from* the world *to* God. Priests are mediators between God and men. Since the word as presented in holy scripture is never powerless, but always accomplishes what it signifies (⟋ word), the blessings of God are also included in the words which are brought by the priests (Lev 9:22f; I Chron 23:13). Similarly in sacrifice all aspects of the cult (the praise of God, the forms of which were elaborated after the exile) are entailed.

2. *Priesthood in the Old Testament.* In the pre-Mosaic period there were no special cultic officials in Israel, set apart from the rest and legislated for by positive laws. Instead the priesthood was exercised by those who in greater or lesser degree represented the interests of the community (family, tribe, nation). Cain and Abel (Gen 4:3f), Noah (Gen 8:20), and the patriarchs (Gen 12:8; 15:8–17; 22:1–13; 26:25; 33:20; see also Job 1:5) offered sacrifices. 'The fact that religious priesthood and profane leadership were united corre-

sponded, therefore, to the patriarchal way of life' (Schedl, *Geschichte des AT* II, 178). In the period of judges laymen too carried out ritual acts (Judg 6:18–24; 13:19). Kings claimed the right to exercise priestly functions (David: 2 Sam 6:17; see also 8:18; Solomon: I Kings 3:4; 8:22, 62). But there is no lack of cases in which the king's sacrifice is condemned as an act of usurpation (I Sam 13:13, 14; 2 Chron 26:16–21). The prophet Elijah too offers sacrifices (I Kings 18:32–8). Whether a priestly office in the true sense was evolved during the period of the sojourn in Egypt, in the course of which the families of the patriarchs developed into a people, is not certain (cf Schedl II, 178 against *BRL* II, 410). Moses exercises priestly functions, even though he survives in tradition as a lawgiver and not as a priest. He is the great mediator of the people. He celebrates the sacrifice of the covenant (Ex 24:4ff), consecrates the sacred tabernacle and its equipment, presents the first offerings on the altar of incense within the sanctuary and on the altar of burnt offerings in the court of the tabernacle (Ex 40:16–33), consecrates Aaron and his sons as priests (Lev 8), and is chosen and consecrated by God (Lev 21:10–15).

By the terms of the *Mosaic law* the priesthood was transferred exclusively (Num 17:5; 18:7; cf 3:10; 16:1ff) to Aaron of the tribe of Levi and his male descendants (Ex 28f; Lev 6; cf also Ezra 2:62; Num 16:17). The function of the remaining members of the tribe was to be God's 'own possession' (Num 3:6–13) and as such to minister to the priests in the cult. Aaron himself, and in succession to him one of his descendants, was to be set up as head of this 'hierarchy' and to be high priest with special powers and rights and with special robes of office. 'The great antiquity of this institution cannot be doubted, even though it was only in the course of time that its further accretions and later developments were added to it' (F. Nötscher, *Biblische Altertumskunde*, 306; on the history of the Levites, see Schedl II, 181; *RGG* IV², 1488–92; *TDNT* III, 257–65). Prerequisites for receiving or exercising the priesthood were: legitimate membership of the priestly tribe (Ezra 2; Neh 7; 11f; 1 Chron 6:1–53; Josephus Flavius, *C. Ap* 1,7), and the fulfilment of the laws regarding the touching of corpses (Lev 21:11f) and regarding marriage with prostitutes, defiled or divorced women, and non-Israelite women (Lev 21:7–9; Ezra 10:18–44; Neh 13:28f). The law also records physical 'impediments to ordination': blindness, lameness, deformity, etc (Lev 21:17–24). Even though the priesthood was hereditary the priest had to receive consecration and investiture (see the ritual prescribed for Aaron and his sons Ex 29; Lev 8). The high priest was bound by strict laws of purity (Lev 21:10–15). The priests had the task of ministering in sacrifices (Lev 1–7). Only the more remote procedures could be carried out by those who were not of priestly stock. The service of the altar was also their responsibility (Ex 30:7; 2 Chron 26:18; Lev 1:9), and with this went service within the sanctuary: the renewal of the shewbread (Lev 24:5–9), tending the lights of the seven-branched candlestick (Ex 30:8; Lev 24:3f), the blessing after the morning offering (Num 6:22–7; Lev 9:22; see also Lk

1:22). In addition to their liturgical duties the priests were responsible for seeing that the laws of purity were carried out (Lev 13f; Mt 8:4). It was their duty also to instruct the people in religious doctrine and law (Lev 10:11; Deut 33:10; Ezek 22:26; 44:23; 2 Chron 15:3; Jer 2:8; 18:18; Hos 4:5ff; Mal 2:7—(the priest is 'a messenger of the Lord'), and even to give judgement in the more difficult cases of dispute (Deut 17:8f; Ezek 44:24; 2 Chron 19:8, 11; see also Deut 19:17; 21:5). After the exile the task of interpreting the law and of instructing the people in it became more and more the province of the scribes; only the cult was left to the priests. The ministry of the high priest was characterised by three elements: his calling and election by Yahweh, his privilege of entering the Holy of Holies, and his atoning function (Lev 16:1–28; Num 17:11–15; Sir 45:6–22; 50:1–21). The high claims were never realised, and pagan syncretism (Jer 2:26; Ezek 8), disrespect for the law (Zeph 3:4; Ezek 22:26), resistance to the prophets (Amos 7:10–17; Is 28:7–13; Jer 20:1–6), selfishness (Mic 3:11; see also 1 Sam 2:12–17; 2 Kings 12:5–9), and lukewarmness in worship (Mal 2:1–9) were all known to the prophets and condemned by them as unworthy of the priesthood.

Priesthood also became a part of the *messianic* hope. In Ps 110:4 the author greets the king (probably on his coronation day) as 'priest for ever according to the order of Melchizedek'. In pre-exilic Jerusalem the king of the city must have exercised priestly functions (Gen 14:18). The dignity of this office of priest-king is then transferred to the Israelite overlord (H. J. Kraus,

Psalmen 2, Neukirchen 1960, 760). Just as the mysterious king of Canaanite antiquity was at once king and priest so the new king must be priest as well. His priesthood, however, is to transcend the existing one, for it is eternal. Ps 110 is messianic (for judaism, see SB v, 452–65; in the New Testament it is frequently cited and applied to Christ: Mt 22:44; Mk 12:36; Lk 20:42; Acts 2:34f; Rom 8:34; etc). Melchizedek (*TDNT* iv, 568–71), was the 'king of justice', king of Salem (Jerusalem) 'who brought forth bread and wine' (primarily as a meal but at the same time as a sacrificial offering too, for the meal was considered to be bound up with a sacrificial act), 'the priest of the most high God', who blessed Abraham. In judaism this figure, while not actually identified with the Messiah, is so with other eschatological figures (*Elijah redivivus*, the high priest who is to accompany the messiah in the final age, he is also interpreted as the Logos and priest of God in Philo, *Leg. alleg.* iii, 79; *De congr. erud.* 99; on the historicity of Melchizedek, see Haag, 1101f). The union of kingship and priesthood in a single person belongs to a very early age. It is also expected in the future. According to Ex 19:6 Israel is 'a kingdom of priests and a holy nation' (J. B. Bauer, *BZ* [1958]). The prophet Zechariah is directed to crown the high priest Joshua (Zech 6:9–14). The crowning of the high priest signifies that he is entrusted with the civil power. In the Maccabaean period this uniting of the two spheres of authority becomes an actual fact (Jonathan, 1 Macc 9:30f; 10:20f; Simon, 1 Macc 14:41: 'Now the Jews and priests had agreed that Simon should be their perpetual leader

and priest, until a trustworthy prophet should arise'). The Maccabaean influence upon this mode of combining the two offices appears chiefly in the Test xii (cf Test Lev 5:1–7; 8:1–19; 17:1–11; 18:1–14; Test Jud 24:1–6). In later judaism a distinction is drawn between a priestly and a royal messiah, a messiah from the tribe of Levi as well as one from the tribe of Judah, the royal messiah being subordinated to the priestly (Test Jud 21:2–5). Examples of this are found in the Qumran texts (Rule of the Community I QS 9:11 and I QSa 2:12ff), the Damascus Document (12:23; 14:19; 19:10; 20:1), and the Testaments of the Twelve Patriarchs (Test Rub 6:7; Sim 7:2: 'The Lord will make to arise a high priest from Levi and a king from Judah . . . Thus he will deliver all the gentiles and the house of Israel'). According to this conception priest, king, and messiah are connected. Priest and king are 'anointed ones' ('messiah'). See J. Maier, *Die Texte vom Toten Meer* ii, Munich 1960, 32f.

3. *Priesthood in the New Testament.* a. *Christ the High Priest.* Jesus was convinced that at his coming the temple and its cult would be brought to an end (Mt 26:61 and parallels; Jn 2:19ff). The survival of the offices of high priest and priest was thereby called in question. Jesus himself describes himself as 'more than the temple' (Mt 12:6). He gives a messianic interpretation of Ps 110 (Mt 22:43ff) and applies it to himself. According to his statement before the sanhedrin the privilege of sitting at the right hand of God, which is to be bestowed upon the Son of Man, is bound up with the idea of the priest-king according to the order

of Melchizedek (Mt 26:64 and parallels). He interprets his death as a sacrifice (Mk 10:45; 14:24; see also Ex 24:8), and preaches the law of God in a more perfect way (Mt 5:17f). In the messiah as realised in Jesus' own person the hope for the ideal priestly figure finds its fulfilment. Jesus is conscious of being the hoped-for high priest *and* messiah. In the references in the New Testament the prophetic role of Christ appears more clearly than the priestly one (Lk 4:18; Mt 7:29; Mk 1:22; Mt 21:10f; Jn 4:19; see also Mt 23:37; Lk 4:24; 16:31).

The theology of Christ the high priest is presented in the Epistle to the Hebrews. The author of this epistle has been deeply impressed by the obedience, compassion, and faithfulness to his God-given vocation which Christ manifested throughout his life and in his death, and has viewed these in the light of his subsequent exaltation. These factors, together with the Old Testament revelation concerning Melchizedek (Gen 14:17–20; Ps 110:4), have had a decisive influence upon the conception of the high-priesthood of Christ in Hebrews. The Levitical high-priesthood of the Old Testament had certain essential functions attached to it. These, viewed in the context of the liturgy of the Day of Atonement, have served as a background to the presentation. In the field of vision of Hebrews stands the exalted Christ, 'the great high priest who has passed through the heavens, Jesus, the Son of God' (4:14; 5:10). Already during his earthly life Christ has lived his high-priesthood; he carries it a stage further when he makes himself present after his resurrection;

finally he will perfect it when he comes 'for the second time' (9:28). Moreover the three fundamental aspects of Jesus' work are included in the high-priesthood of Christ: the work on earth which he accomplished once and for all, that which he continues to perform when he makes himself present to us in his exaltation, and that which he will accomplish at the second coming.

The high-priesthood of Christ is based upon the following factors: the eternal decree of God for him, his union with the rest of men by reason of having the same nature as they, his calling by God and his proclamation as high priest. The eternal decree of God is revealed through the image of Melchizedek as delineated in Gen 14 and Ps 110. Christ the high priest is taken from among men (5:1), made like in every respect to mankind, his brethren (2:17; see also 2:10–18), one in nature with them (2:11), 'in the flesh' as they are (5:7), weak and tempted (2:18; 4:15) in order that he may mitigate the impact of his wrath against sin (5:1), yet himself without sin (4:15; 7:28; see also 2 Cor 5:21; 1 Jn 3:5; 1 Pet 2:22). The divine calling coincides with the declaration that he is the Son of God (cf Ps 2:7; Heb 1:5). In as much as Christ is both God and man he can be the perfect mediator (↗ mediation) and priest. The precise point in time at which the priesthood is entrusted to him is not brought into consideration (incarnation, baptism, transfiguration). After Christ has proved himself by the selfless offering of his passion, by the holy fear which he shows before God, and by his obedience to the will of God (5:7f), he is proclaimed high priest according to the order of Melchizedek. The way to the high-priesthood in the heights leads through the priesthood lived in lowliness. As representative of mankind before God he is compassionate (2:17), and as mediator from God to man he is faithful (2:17; 3:2).

The greatness of the high-priesthood of Christ appears in its transcendence over the Levitical, and over every earthly priesthood. With the priesthood of Christ God initiates a new order of worship (4:8; 7:11, 28). This priesthood stands forth in the light of the final consummation and of eschatology. Christ is royal high priest. The type which foreshadows him is the priest-king Melchizedek (7:1). He brings 'justice and peace' (see Is 9:7; Jer 23:5; Mic 5:4; Dan 9:24; Zech 9:10; Mal 4:2) and 'consummation': remission of sins (9:14), redemption (9:12), purification of conscience (9:12), fulfilment of the divine will (10:9). Christ is high priest for all eternity (7:3f). His priesthood has eternal validity (7:20–25) and cannot be bestowed upon another. He is the sole high priest of the New Testament (7:23f).

Christ the high priest is perfect in every respect (7:26ff). He possesses all the personal and moral perfections which he needs to equip him for the perfect form of worship. For he is holy in every sense of the term, 'separated from sinners', without blemish, transcendent over every creature and near to God, wholly steeped in the divine. He lives in a constant and active relationship with God, stretching out to him in a never-ending act of worship ('with God': see Jn 1:2; Ex 18:19). The priestly activity which Hebrews chiefly holds in view is sacrifice. The sacrifice of atonement occupies the forefront of its thought, but it shows familiarity with sacrifice in general ('to serve the altar with care' 7:13). A further part of the high-priest's work is intercession (7:25). Heb 7:1 also mentions the blessing of Melchizedek, but no analogous act is ascribed to the new high priest. Nor does he occupy himself with instruction or giving judgement. He devotes himself to the cult alone, and hence his countenance is turned more to God than to men. The sacrifice which Christ offers is a perfect sacrifice. He offers it once and for all, so that there is no need of any further sacrifice. He offers himself as a sacrifice. Thus the innermost depths of his significance (*sacerdos et hostia*) find expression in the cult. The complaint found in the prophets and psalms concerning the gulf between interior dispositions and exterior cult (sacrifice) is silenced. He offers himself wholly on behalf of others, for as the sinless one he has no need of atonement. Perfect too is his ordination as priest (7:28). For this high priest is set up not in virtue of a transient law, but by the unbreakable word of God and by an oath. Hence he is also called to be priest for ever. Christ is a priest not incidentally but of his essence. His consecration as divine and the proving of his faithfulness establish for ever his moral perfection, his being lastingly accepted by God, and his nearness to him which is to endure for ever.

It is true that in the New Testament writings Christ is never called 'priest' or 'high priest', but what is material to the idea of the priesthood of Christ is often implied or expressed. Jesus is the sole mediator (1 Tim 2:5). The apostles have emphasised that in the passion the initiative lay with Jesus (Gal 2:20; Eph 5:2). The Redeemer is not only the sacrificial lamb without blemish (1 Pet 1:19). He himself has carried his body to the altar of the cross and sacrificed it there (1 Pet 2:24; cf Heb 7:27; 9:28; 13:12). We have access to God through Christ alone (Rom 5:2; Eph 2:18; 3:12; 1 Pet 3:18). Christ acts as mediator by his intercession (Rom 8:34: cf Heb 7:25). John in particular explores the image of Christ as priest. In Rev 1:13, where the Son of Man appears in the midst of the seven lamps, the girdle which reaches to his breast signifies that he is a priest. In the gospel of John, more strongly than in those of the other evangelists, it is emphasised that Jesus surrendered his life to death of his own free will (10:18). The form he has given to the passion narrative is wholly derived from this idea. Jesus' prayer at parting from his disciples has rightly been called the 'high-priestly prayer' (by D. Chytraeus, the protestant theologian, 1531–1600). It is the canon of the sacrificial offering of the cross. If anyone has sinned, Christ is his 'paraclete' before the Father (1 Jn 2:1). This 'paraclete' function of Christ is also seen being exercised in the works of the paraclete whom he sends down to earth.

b. *The priestly office.* Protestant exegesis and theology of the New Testament recognises only the general priesthood of the church as a whole, and not, therefore, the priesthood officially conferred upon individual members (the priestly office). According to Bultmann it is clear 'that everywhere—and especially in Hebrews—the idea is given

up that God's grace must or can be won by humanly offered sacrifices; and that led by implication to the insight that the church does not need persons of special quality (ie, priests) to mediate between it and God' (Bultmann I, 115; see also I, 147f and II, 110). It has been noticed that although Christ never described himself by the appellation 'priest' or 'high priest', his work was still priestly in character. In the same way, although he did not describe his apostles as 'priests', still he did give them the task of continuing his mission (Mt 10:40; Lk 10:16; Jn 13:20; 17:18; 20:22), and did present their apostolic ministry (↗apostle) as one of mediation and hence as a priestly ministry. The apostles are called to a ministry of mediation between God and men, and for this purpose they are created anew (Mk 1:16–20; 3:14). Their mission consists not merely in preaching the word but in mediating salvation as well. They not merely preach the forgiveness of sins, but actually make it come to pass (Mt 18:18; Jn 20:23). They not merely speak of the sacrificial death of Christ, but actually make it present (the task of consecrating the eucharist, Lk 22:19; 1 Cor 11:24, 25). It is through the ↗laying on of hands by Peter and John that the newly baptised in Samaria receive the ↗Spirit (Acts 8:15–18). It is the Holy Spirit who institutes—certainly through human mediation—the bishops and elders (Acts 20:28). The rank of presbyter carried with it the power of healing the sick and forgiving their sins by means of prayer and anointing with oil (Jas 5:14). Paul conceived of and presented his ministry as a priestly activity. He is aware that in his preaching of the word he is a mediator between God and man bringing atonement or judgement (2 Cor 5:18ff; 1 Cor 5:3ff), life or death (2 Cor 2:14ff). He plainly declares that he has the function of a mediator and priest to fulfil in the world. He is 'minister (*leitourgos*) of Christ Jesus to the gentiles, in the priestly service of the gospel of God, so that the offering of the gentiles may be acceptable' (Rom 5:15f: 'intensely cultic terminology'). He conceives of the work of his mission as cultic (Rom 1:9), his apostolate to the Philippians, through which they came to the faith, as the exercise of a cultic and priestly ministry. If he has to endure a martyr's death he will regard this as supplementary to, and the consummation of the sacrifice which he has offered to God in the community of believers, and he will rejoice that he has been able to offer himself as the consummation of this act of worship (Phil 2:17f). He regards his sufferings in the light of his awareness of ministering as priest on behalf of the church (2 Cor 1:6; 4:12; 12:15; Col 1:24). The apostles are mediators of God's salvific work in the world. They are 'fellow workers of God' (1 Cor 3:9; 1 Thess 3:2; cf Mt 9:37). In them salvation (2 Cor 1:15) and the glory of Christ enter the world (2 Cor 8:23; see also Jn 17:22).

The original bearers of the apostolic office, as also those who later succeeded them, fulfil in word and deed the ministry of mediators and priests. The fact that they are never called priests in the New Testament is due to the necessity of avoiding a certain misconception, namely that in the church an individual could of his own power, and independently of Christ, be a priest, like gentile or Israelite priests who practised their ministry independently, taking oracles and soothsaying, and offering sacrifices (K. H. Schelkle, *Discipleship and Priesthood*, 116ff). Preaching and the priestly ministry have another meaning in the New Testament from that which they bear in nonchristian circles. In relation to the human community on behalf of which he appears before God the priest is no longer in the position of their direct representative. He stands rather for the one who alone is capable of representing mankind before the Father, namely Christ. In the unified ministry of preaching and cult the emphasis lies upon preaching. Only in the word is it revealed in what the sacramental priestly act consists.

The apostles appointed fellow workers in their ministry and installed leaders in the communities when they were compelled to leave these. In the earliest period 'presbyters' (Acts 11:30; 15:2-6, 22f; 16:4; 21:18) worked with the apostles after the pattern of the Jewish Sanhedrin. In his first missionary journey Paul appointed 'presbyters' with prayer and fasting in every community that he founded (Acts 14:23; see also 20:17). About 58 AD the community of Ephesus is led by presbyters (or bishops: Acts 20:17–38). Again, though the earlier pauline epistles do not use the word *presbuteros*, they clearly refer to leaders (see 1 Thess 5:12; Rom 12:8). Among the gifts of grace enumerated by Paul are those of leading and administering (1 Cor 12:28; cf Col 4:17; Heb 13:7). In the absence of the apostle these leaders directed the community. He himself retained the ultimate authority. In Phil 1:1 the holders of official positions are called 'bishops and deacons', while in the pastoral epistles the term presbyter is added to these two designations. 1 Peter speaks of presbyters, but seems also to know of *episkopoi* (= bishops: see 1 Pet 2:25). James mentions presbyter as a single office. 'Bishop' and 'priest' are used to designate the same office (compare Acts 20:17 with 20:28; 1 Tim 2 with 5:17–22; Tit 1:5 with 1:7). To the leaders thus designated the ministry and authority of the apostle are transferred. They too, therefore, exercise a priestly ministry, have to administer the heritage of the apostle, to follow his example, to preside over the community, to watch over it, to preach sound doctrine and to defend its infallible message against teachers of error (Acts 20:17–35; 1 Tim 1:3; 3:5; 4:11; 2 Tim 2:1f; 1 Pet 5:1–5), and to bring salvation to men by the power of the sacraments (Jas 5:14f). Ministers are ordained by the ⁊ laying on of hands accompanied by prayer (Acts 14:23; 1 Tim 4:14; 5:22; 2 Tim 1:6) and in this the Spirit of God is active (Acts 20:28). Whether candidates for the office of bishop or presbyter are suitable depends above all on their moral qualities (1 Tim 3:1–7; Tit 1:6–9).

c. *The general priesthood of believers.* In the Old Testament the chosen people of God is called a 'royal priesthood' (Ex 19:6), a priesthood which belongs to God as king, and which shares in his dignity. The prophets announce that in the time of salvation Israel will be a priestly people (Is 61:6), that all will exercise priestly functions (Is 56:7; 60:7; see also 56:6; 59:21) and will enjoy priestly privileges (60:11). 1 Pet 2:9 transfers the title 'royal priesthood'

to the people of God of the New Testament. As a royal priesthood this people is to preach the mighty deeds of him who has called her out of darkness into his wonderful light. Built together as living stones into a temple in the Holy Spirit, into a holy priesthood chosen by God and belonging to him, under the guidance and by the power of the Holy Spirit dwelling within them, they are to offer sacrifices which through Jesus Christ are made well-pleasing to God. Christians exercise the two essential functions of the priestly ministry: word and worship. The sacrifices which are here being thought of are both corporal and spiritual in character: selflessness and good deeds (Heb 13:16), supporting the poor and the forlorn (Jas 1:27), the giving of gifts (Phil 12:1), thanksgiving and prayer (Heb 13:15): the offering of the eucharistic sacrifice by the faithful is not mentioned. The priestly ministry of the faithful is exercised 'through Jesus Christ'. He is the unique mediator and priest of the church. The priestly office is exercised only in union with him and in dependence upon him. Under the influence of Ex 19:6; Rev (1:6; 5:10; 20:6) calls the faithful 'priests before God' (the phrase 'royal priesthood' in Ex 19:6 is repeated in 2 Macc 2:17; Jub 33:20. Philo refers to 'kings and priests').

The ⁊ church is a cultic community. It is a holy temple of God (1 Cor 3:16f; Eph 2:21). Christians are 'holy', separated from the world and established in the service of God (⁊ holy). According to Paul the church has the task and the honour of offering a living and pleasing sacrifice to God in a form of worship that is spiritual (Rom 12:1).

Primacy

The gift of the church at Philippi is 'a fragrant offering, a sacrifice acceptable and pleasing to God' (Phil 4:18). By its gift the community exercises a priestly function. The faith (living by the faith) of the Philippians is a sacrificial offering (Phil 2:17). The church offers to God a sacrifice of praise and of acts of love (Heb 13:15), an assertion which is probably connected with the celebration of the ⟋ eucharist. Women are exhorted to make their lives worthy of the holiness of their (priestly) calling (Tit 2:3). The cultic service which, according to Rom 1:9 the apostle himself performs is also the duty of the faithful (Lk 1:74f; Phil 3:3; Tit 2:3; Heb 12:28). To help widows and orphans in their need counts as 'religion that is pure and undefiled before God and the Father' (Jas 1:27). In these passages concerning the general priesthood of the faithful there is no intention of asserting that all baptised persons participate in the priesthood of Christ in the same way; in no sense do they exclude the official priesthood, any more than the general priesthood of the people of the Old Testament excluded the official priesthood of the Levites.

Bibliography: *DB* III, 295–308; V, 640–62; *RGG* IV², 1188–92; Eichrodt I, 392–436; *TDNT* III, 257–65 and 265–83; *TDNT* VI, 651–80; F. Stummer, 'Gedanken über die Stellung des Hohenpriesters in der atl. Gemeinde', *Episcopus* (Festschrift Faulhaber), Regensburg 1949, 19–48; J. Blinzler, 'Hierateuma', *Episcopus*, 49–65; R. Schnackenburg, 'Episkopos und Hirtenamt in Apg 20:28', *Episcopus*, 66–88; E. Lohse, *Die Ordination im Spätjudentum und im NT*, 1951; A. Stöger, 'Der Hohepriester Jesus Christus', *TPQ* 100 (1952), 309–19; C. Spicq, *L'Epttre aux Hébreux* II, Paris 1953, 119–31; E. Walter, *Quellen des lebendigen Wassers*, 1953, 223–70; H. von Campenhausen, *Kirliches Amt und geistliche Vollmacht*, 1953;

K. Weiss, 'Paulus, Priester der Kult gemeinde', *TLZ* 79 (1954), 355–64; C. Spicq, *La spiritualité sacerdotale d'après Saint Paul*, Paris 1954; A. Vitti, 'La dottrina di San Paolo sul Sacerdozio', *Rivist. Bibl. Ital.* 4 (1956), 1–16; C. Schedl, *Geschichte des AT* II, Innsbruck 1956, 176–89; Cullmann 82–107; K. H. Schelkle, *Discipleship and Priesthood*, New York 1965 and London 1966; F. Wulf, 'Die Spiritualität und Frömmigkeit des Weltpriesters', *GL* 32 (1959), 39–43; *HTG* II, 340–44; O. Kuss, *Der Brief an die Hebräer* (*RNT* 8), Regensburg 1966², 126–38; *J. Smith, *A Priest for Ever: A Study of Typology and Eschatology in Hebrews*, London 1969, 66–136.

Alois Stöger

Primacy

1. *The position of Peter in the early church.* The earliest written witnesses to the fact that a position of supreme authority was accorded to Peter are to be found in the pauline epistles. In the Letter to the Galatians Paul informs us that he has gone to Jerusalem 'to visit Cephas' (1:18). At this period (37), then, the 'rock' was certainly the man in authority at Jerusalem, and thereby in the church as a whole. In 1 Cor 15:3–7 Paul tells us of an important tradition in which the official witnesses of the resurrection (the women being excluded from this!) are named. Here the 'rock' (*kēphas*) is given the first place, and is set apart from the twelve. This again indicates that a primacy of rank was accorded to Peter. Admittedly little evidence can be deduced from this for a primacy of leadership. But it does show that Peter was placed before the twelve (⟋ disciples) as the foremost witness of the resurrection, and as such as the foundation in a special sense, supporting the faith of the entire church.

In Gal 2:9 the 'rock' (*kēphas*) no longer occupies the first position. It

709

may be that Paul named James first because he was the man of importance precisely in the matter under discussion. This cannot of itself be taken as an unqualified statement concerning Peter's position in the council of the apostles. But the Acts of the Apostles too bears witness to the fact that after his departure from Jerusalem (circa 42 AD) Peter played a less prominent part. James had taken over the leadership of the primitive community and Peter—unlike James and Paul too precisely in this respect—was not the man to assume the leadership whatever the circumstances and whatever difficulties he had to surmount in attaining it. There are no grounds for concluding that because Peter withdrew from the leadership, a general withdrawal from the position of having a leader at all must have taken place. Above all we must guard against the fallacy of measuring the relationships in the early church by modern standards. In the council of the apostles too Peter was the 'rock' (*kēphas*), and remained so even during the period when he had retired from the leadership of the primitive community. Conversely Jerusalem, the original capital of christendom, became less and less significant.

It is certain however—and this is very important for the question of the authenticity of Mt 16:18f—that the Jerusalem presided over by James was not a place where the formation or even the development of a tradition such as that found in Mt 16:18f could have taken place.

2. *The name 'Rock'*. Jesus gave sobriquets to three of the twelve: he called the two sons of Zebedee *boanērges*, 'sons of thunder' (Mk 3:17), and to

Simon, as all four evangelists attest, he gave the name *Petros*/Kephas. This fact, namely that Jesus himself was the originator of the name Peter, is today undisputed. It is however interesting to compare the two sobriquets. That bestowed upon the two sons of Zebedee needed no explanation. Anyone who knew the two knew the reason for it. Simon, on the contrary, was far from having a rock-like nature. So far from being self-explanatory, therefore, this name demanded an explanation. The name *boanērges* did not become established precisely because it was not felt to be important. But the sobriquet which Simon received actually succeeded in completely suppressing his original name (indeed Paul seems to have been quite ignorant of it!) and became a real proper name, whether it was preserved in its original Aramaic form (*kēphas*, thus Paul) or translated into Greek (*Petros*). It is precisely the fact that it was so translated that has, once again, a special significance. Normally a name was not translated into another language but only transcribed. At the time that this name was translated, therefore, it was the objective properties of 'rock' that were being thought of. Both factors, that the sobriquet actually blotted out the proper name and that it was translated into Greek, prove what significance was attached to the name 'Rock' in the early church.

3. *Mt 16:18f*. The *authenticity* of the logion addressed by the Lord to Peter has been called in question again and again since the last century. At the present day this logion is above all difficult to reconcile with a 'consequent (thoroughgoing) eschatology',

according to which Jesus never envisaged a church, and therefore did not conceive of founding a church upon Peter either (↗ church). However it is incumbent upon all those who contest the authenticity of this logion to find where the source of this 'Peter' tradition lies. It is generally recognised that the text of Matthew is based upon an Aramaic tradition. This fact rules out Greek-speaking communities as a possible place of origin. But the primitive Aramaic-speaking community cannot be considered as the originator of the tradition either (see section 1 above). Hence no other course is left open to us than precisely to recognise the authenticity of the 'Rock' logion. Furthermore the name 'Rock' leads us back to Jesus himself and demands (see section 2) an explanation ultimately not from the early church but from Jesus himself. If we did not have the actual text of Matthew we would have to postulate a logion of Jesus which was similar in tenor to it. No objection to the authenticity of the logion can be raised on the grounds that in Matthew this saying of Jesus to Peter is out of its historical context, and that it has been inserted by Matthew in the Markan tradition (the acknowledgement by Peter in Mk 8:29 and the prophecy of the passion in Mk 8:31 belong together). In our quest for the historical context of our logion perhaps Luke sets us on the right path (see Lk 22:32).

Our best way of attaining to a deeper knowledge of the meaning of this saying of Jesus to Peter is to examine more closely the symbolic meaning of the word 'rock'. Rock is used as a symbol currently throughout the ancient Near East. In the Old Testament it is very frequently employed as a figure for Yahweh. Hence the saying that Yahweh is the rescuer, the unshakeable refuge from the 'waves of death' (Ps 18:2ff). Isaiah calls the rock of Zion (=Yahweh) 'He-who-believes-will-not-waver' (28:16). Here again death-dealing floods are presented as the antithesis of the Rock of rescue. It is not arbitrary to recall another tradition proper to Matthew, namely the episode of Jesus walking upon the waters of the Sea of Galilee (Mt 14:28–31). Just as here Jesus rescues Peter with his little faith from sinking in the deep, so Peter himself is to become a Rock of rescue for his brethren. Admittedly this will be not through the strength of his own faith but through the grace of God: 'I have prayed for you that your faith may not fail, and do you . . . strengthen your brethren' (Lk 22:32). Thus a living man, whose weakness has been exposed when put to the test, becomes a shield for the faith of his brethren. The Lukan text, therefore, yields the same basic meaning as the Matthaean, only without the image. This function of Peter's, namely of being a Rock of rescue, is especially significant because it applies to Peter alone (in direct contrast to his brethren). This leads us immediately to the question: 'How long does the church need this rescuing function to be discharged by a living Peter?' To this there can only be one answer: 'As long as the powers of hell continue to threaten it'. (In the same way the church needs the Shepherd [Jn 21:15–18] as long as it exists in the world.)

Besides this function of rescuing, however, the 'Rock' has a further basic function to fulfil. Jesus will build his Church on this foundation. This task Peter shares with the Twelve (⤳ disciples; 1 Cor 15:5; Eph 2:20; Rev 21:14), but he is the foremost witness of the resurrection, and the *most basic* foundation of the faith of the church. As the function of the Twelve as constituting a foundation is unique and unrepeatable, so also is that of Peter (in contrast to his other function as being a rock of rescue). Just as Peter shares the function of being a rock of foundation with the Twelve, so too he shares the power of binding and loosing (the power of the keys and the power of binding and loosing are merely two images of a single reality) with the rest of the disciples (Mt 18:18). Even here, however, the fact that Peter was singled out to receive this promise of power indicates that he has a special position as the apostle who is a Rock.

Bibliography: F. Kattenbusch, 'Die Vorzugsstellung des Petrus und der Charakter der Urgemeinde zu Jerusalem', *Festgabe Karl Müller*, 1922, 322–51; R. Bultmann, 'Die Frage nach der Echtheit von Mt 16:17–19', *TB* 20 (1941), 265–79; H. Strahtmann, 'Die Stellung des Petrus in der Urkirche', *ZST* 20 (1943), 223–82; A. Oepke, 'Der Herrnspruch über die Kirche Mt 16:17–19, in der neuesten Forschung', *ST* 2 (1949), 110–65; J. Ludwig, *Die Primatworte Mt 16:18, 19 in der altkirchlichen Exegese* (*NA*) 1952; A. Vögtle, 'Messiasbekenntnis und Petrusverheissung', *BZ* 1 (1957), 252–72 and 2 (1958), 85–103; P. Gaechter, *Petrus und seine Zeit*, Innsbruck 1958; J. Schmid, 'Petrus "der Fels" und die Petrusgestalt der Urgemeinde', *Begegnung der Christen* (1959), 347–59; M. Roesle and O. Cullmann, *Begegnung der Christen*, Frankfurt 1960², 347–59; O. Cullmann, *Peter: Disciple, Apostle, Martyr*, London 1960²; O. Cullmann, *Das Evangelium nach Matthäus*, 1959⁴, 251–60; O. Cullmann, *TDNT* VI, 95–112; F. Obrist, *Echtheitsfragen und Deutung der Primatstelle Mt 16:18f.* (*NA*) 1960; J. Schmid, *HTG* II, 306–12.

Elmar M. Kredel

Principalities and powers

A. *Jewish.* 1. *Old Testament.* The expressions ᵓelōhê hatstsᵉbāᵓ ôth ('God of armies') or *Yhwh tsᵉbāᵓ ôth* ('Yahweh of the armies') are familiar from the Old Testament (⤳ Angel B a). LXX translates these designations as *ho theos ho pantokratōr* ('God the almighty': Hos 12:6; Amos 3:13; 4:13; etc), *kurios pantokratōr* ('the Lord almighty': 2 Sam 5:10; 7:8; 1 Chron 11:9; 17:7, 24; etc), and frequently too as *kurios tōn dunameōn* ('the Lord of the powers': 2 Sam 6:2, 18; 1 Kings 18:15; 2 Kings 3:14; Ps 24:10; 46:8, 12; 59:6; 69:7; 80:5, 8, 20; 84:1, 3; Jer 40 (Hebrew 33):12; etc). Besides these the stars are called the 'army' (*tsābāᵓ*) of heaven, which the Greek translates by the collective noun *dunamis* (=power) of heaven (Ps 33:6; Dan 8:10 Theodotian; see also Is 34:4 cod B). The expression 'army' or 'power' of heaven therefore also stands for the astral gods of the pagans, which were sometimes worshipped by the Jews (2 Kings 17:16; 21:3, 5; 23:4f). The 'powers', therefore, are not the 'army' of God, the instruments of his omnipotence: they are, at least in the later occurrences, the angelic hosts. But the stars, too, are a 'power', and—inasmuch as they were venerated in a pagan manner—represent a 'power' that is hostile to God.

2. *The pseudepigraphal literature of later judaism.* Here still more preternatural beings of this kind interposed between God and men are referred to, not frequently perhaps, but still occasionally. In addition to the angels and the spirits the Book of Jubilees also mentions the 'powers' of God (15:32: trans.

E. Littmann in E. Kautzsch, *Die Apokryphen u. Pseudepigraphen des AT* II, Tübingen 1900). In Enoch (Eth) 'angel' and 'power' are occasionally juxtaposed (41:9: trans. A. Dillmann, *Das Buch Henoch*, Leipzig 1853; for this 'angel' and 'power': trans. G. Beer in Kautsch). 'Angels of the powers' (*angeloi tōn dunameōn*) is also found (Enoch [Eth] 20:1), as also 'angels over the powers' (*angeloi epi tōn dunameōn*: Bar [Gr] 12:3). An early list in Enoch (Eth) 61:10 enumerates in all ten categories of angelic beings, and among them 'the whole army of heaven', 'the army of God', 'all the angels of the power', 'all the angels of the domains' and, in conclusion, 'the other powers' which are on dry land and water (trans. A. Dillmann and G. Beer in Kautsch). Test Lev 3 informs us that in the third of the seven heavens are to be found *hai dunameis tōn parembolōn* ('the powers of the camps') which take vengeance upon the spirits of error and of Belial (the devil) on the day of judgement (v 3). It also tells us of the *thronoi* (thrones) and *exousiai* (powers) in the seventh heaven, which praise God continually (v 8). A further list, likewise of ten groups of angelic beings, in Enoch (Slav) 20:1 (the longer recension) names 'powers' (*dunameis*) and 'dominions' (*kuriotētes*), 'principalities' (*arkhai*), 'forces' (*exousiai*), and 'thrones' (*thronoi*): all these according to their rank stand in worship before God or sing hymns to him (vv 3f).

None of these passages makes it clear what the different terms are intended to designate. They could be abbreviated descriptions of angels of God's dominion, throne, etc (see Enoch[Gr] 20:1; Bar[Gr] 12:3; 2 Thess 1:7: 'angels of his power').

In that case they would express the connection of the angels concerned with the power, might, dominion or throne of God. Alternatively, could this be a portrayal of the world similar to that of the later gnostic movement, in which these names designate cosmic rulers? Nor is it possible to recognise the difference between the individual orders, and not much can be concluded on this point from the names used. Certainly it is intermediate beings which are in question here, higher than man and lower than God in the hierarchy of being, and evidently angelic in character. Even though occasionally fears are expressed concerning a particular 'power' that it could act in a manner contrary to the will of God (Jub 15:32; Enoch[Eth] 41:9), still as a rule these intermediate beings serve and glorify God, and therefore have no element of hostility to God or of the demonic in them. They appear rather as good beings.

The rabbis are probably familiar with the idea of 'forces of heaven' (*ḥēlê šᵉmayyaʾ*: eg, Targum on 1 Kings 22:19; Ps 96:11), which are equivalent to the 'armies of heaven'; that is they designate angels or stars. But those further categories mentioned above as being found in certain of the apocrypha, have no place, so it appears, in the rabbinical writings. Clearly it was only one particular movement (the Essenes?) in so-called later judaism that was familiar with them.

B. *Christian*. 1. *New Testament*. Here such beings are mentioned in the so-called principal epistles and the captivity epistles of Paul, and also in 1 Pet, a letter which stands close to the spiritual world of Paul. There are powers' (*dunameis*, Latin *virtutes*: Rom 8:38; 1 Cor 15:24; Eph 1:21; 1 Pet 3:22; see also 2 Thess 1:7), 'forces' (*exousiai, potestates*: 1 Cor 15:24; Eph 1:21; 3:10; 6:12; Col. 1:16, 2:10, 15; 1 Pet 3:22), 'principalities' (*arkhai, principatus*: Rom 8:38; 1 Cor 15:24; Eph 1:21; 3:10; 6:12; Col 1:16; 2:10, 15), 'dominions' (*kuriotētes, dominationes*: Eph 1:21; Col 1:16), and 'thrones' (*thronoi, throni*: Col 1:16). It cannot be discerned in what the difference between these categories consists or why they are thus designated. These beings have been created through Christ and for him (Col 1:16). But for reasons which are nowhere mentioned, a 'disturbance' of this relationship took place, which has only been repaired through 'atonement' in the blood of Christ (Col 1:20). Certainly this relationship was disturbed in the order of being. But whether it was also disturbed in the order of obedience, and if so to what extent, is not stated. Now, however, Christ is the head of every 'principality' and every 'power' (Col 2:15). By exalting him to his right hand God has made him Lord over all these groups (Eph 1:20f; see also Col 1:17). The 'forces' and 'powers', like the angels, are subjected to the exalted Lord (1 Pet 3:22). In the church established by Christ on earth the 'principalities' and 'forces' in heaven recognise the wise purpose of God to save men (Eph 3:10).

These passages seem to indicate that as in late judaism it is good beings that are meant, even though a passage may be found here and there which could be taken as referring to evil ones. Other statements, however, do clearly ascribe demonic traits to these powers. Thus

through the death of Christ God has taken away the strength of the 'principalities' and 'powers' and has treated them as conquered enemies (Col 2:15). In spite of this, their noxious power has not yet been fully overthrown. It is true that neither angels, nor principalities, nor powers can avail to separate christians from the love of God (Rom 8:38f). But the christian must struggle against principalities and powers, those overlords of the world which lies in the power of darkness (Eph 6:12). They are 'spirits of wickedness' and are allied to the devil (Eph 6:12; see also v 11 and 2:2). The 'principalities', 'forces', and 'powers' assume in the present age of the world a dominant position in the world as a whole. But they will lose this power when the eternal kingdom of God is inaugurated (1 Cor 15:24).

The difficulty of reconciling these two kinds of reference to preternatural beings is hardly to be overcome by assuming that all the groups involved consist of demonic powers. On the contrary, as with the related concept of 'angel', a distinction must be drawn between the good and the bad among these beings. Concerning the functions of these creatures, which are at once more than human and less than divine, little is said. Even the question of whether it could ever be possible for man to obtain help from them as from the angels goes unanswered. All that we hear on such points is a few warnings concerning the danger which threatens mankind at least from those of them which are demonic in character.

2. *Post-biblical and early christian writings*. 'The powers of Satan', which are to be overcome by the frequent

celebration of the christian liturgy (Ignatius, Eph 13:1), are familiar to us. We know also of the 'dominions' and 'thrones' which, together with the angels and archangels, have fallen away from God (Irenaeus, *Demonstr. apost. praedicationis*, 85). The devil has 'dominions' and 'powers' about him (Asc Is 1:3; 2:2; see also 4:4). There are 'evil and corrupting powers' (Clement Alex, *Stromata* II, 68:1), 'hostile powers' (Origen, *De Orat.* 12:1; see also 13:3), 'principalities and powers of darkness' (Clemens Alex, *Stromata* IV, 96:1; Clement also considers the 'principalities' referred to in Rom 8:38 as Satanic), 'powers and spirits of forces' (Clement Alex, *Stromata* IV, 47:1), which are 'principalities of darkness' (47:2). 'Every principality, every force and power' must be overthrown by the christians (Origen, *De Orat.* 25:3; see also 1 Cor 15:24).

Side by side with these, however, other passages are to be found, in which these beings are regarded as good and as belonging to the celestial order (Irenaeus, *Adv. Haereses* II, 30:6 [see also II, 30:3, 9]; Origen, *De Orat.* 17:2; *Contra Celsum* IV, 29 [see also VI, 71]; in Greek, the Legends of Isaiah 2:40). 'Powers' is also used in a quite general sense to designate the spiritual beings who serve God (Athenagoras, *Legatio* 24:2; Irenaeus, *Demonstr. apost. praedic.* 9; Clemens Alex, *Stromata* V, 36:4; Origen, *De Orat.* 6:5; 27:11; *Contra Celsum* VIII 64; etc), and in fact as the cherubim and seraphim who praise God (Irenaeus, *Demonstr. apost. praedic.* 10). In a similar manner, though less frequently, 'forces' is employed as a collective designation for angelic beings (Tertullian, *Apolog.* 46:1;

Augustine, *De diversis quaest.* 83, q. 67:7: the angels are simply called 'virtues' and 'potestates').

Now, therefore, that the five groups mentioned in the pauline letters were thought of as good spirits belonging to heaven, they were associated with the angels, archangels, cherubim, and seraphim. From this arose the idea which finally held the field that the choirs of angels were nine in number. From the fourth century onwards this idea prevailed in the East (Cyril of Jerusalem, *Catech. mystag.* v, 6; John Chrysostom, *In Gen. Hom.* IV, 5; Test Adae 4:5–22) and also in the West (Ambrose, *De Apologia David* 5:20). It led to the speculations of Pseudo-Dionysius, who arranged the groups in a pattern, dividing them hierarchically into three triads (*De Cael. Hierarchia* 6:2; 7–9; *De Ecclesiast. Hier.* 1:2). In the west the teaching thus developed concerning the nine choirs of angels became familiar from the time of Gregory the Great (*In Evang. Hom.* XXXIV, 7; *Moralia* XXXII, 48; *Epist.* v, 54). Even though as early as the third century it was already recognised that in Paul's references to the various groups at least some of them are regarded as hostile beings (eg, Clement of Alexandria and Origen: see above), as speculation on this subject developed this view faded into the background, and the beings in question were considered to be good, celestial, angelic spirits.

C. *The theological importance of the teaching concerning principalities, powers, etc.* The church adheres very firmly to the doctrine that supernatural or preternatural beings do exist, either angelic or demonic in character, and regards this as a matter of faith. At the same time the church has never made any declaration on the question of whether these beings are divided into specific orders, or, if so, what the character of these orders is. Even though the powers, forces, and other similar beings were originally figures belonging to an antiquated picture of the world which we have since abandoned, we may nevertheless conclude from the references to these beings in the New Testament that there are indeed spiritual beings higher than men but lower than God, both good and evil, which have various ways of existing and acting. It is this that we can gather to a certain extent from the New Testament. But there is no support in scripture for the idea that these beings are hierarchically ordered in the manner suggested by Pseudo-Dionysius.

Bibliography: M. Dibelius, *Die Geisterwelt im Glauben des Paulus*, Göttingen 1909; G. Kurze, *Der Engels- und Teufelsglaube des Apostels Paulus*, Freiburg 1915; E. de los Rios, 'S. Paulus de angelicis hierarchiciis', *VD* 9 (1929), 289–97; K. L. Schmidt, 'Die Natur- und Geistkräfte im paulinischen Erkennen und Glauben, *Eranos-Jahrbuch* 14 (1947), 87–143; G. H. C. Macgregor, 'Principalities and Powers: the Cosmic Background of St Paul's Thought', *NTS* 1 (1954/5), 17–28; G. B. Caird, *Principalities and Powers: a Study of Pauline Theology*, Oxford 1956; H. Schlier, *Principalities and Powers in the New Testament*, London and New York 1961; J. Michl, *RAC* v, 79f, 98f, 112–14, 171–6, 180–2, and 194–8. See also the relevant articles in *TDNT* and the bibliographies under ↗ demon and ↗ angel.

Johann Michl

Prophet

The word *prophet* is a translation of the Hebrew *nābī'*. This could be connected with the Akkadian *nabû* = to call, and, in accordance with the passive force for the most part expressed by katil forms, its meaning could originally have been 'the one called (by God)' (W. F. Albright, *From the Stone Age to Christianity*, 303). However the nature of the prophets' calling, which was to be sent by Yahweh in order to announce his words to the people (see Jer 7:25; 25:4; 2 Kings 17:13), was such that it caused the word *nābī'* to be thought of as having the sense of 'proclaimer' or 'spokesman' (of God), even though this was not the original meaning (compare Arab. *naba'a* = 'to announce', 'to execute a commission'; Ethiop. *nabāba* = 'to speak'). Thus in the case of Ex 7:1, where Moses is metaphorically called Elohim (god) and Aaron is called his *nābī'*, an explanation of this is given in v 2, namely that Aaron is to convey to Pharaoh the words which Moses speaks to him—is therefore to be the spokesman, the interpreter of Moses (see Ex 4:15f: 'He shall be a mouth for you, and you shall be to him as God'). The Greek *prophētēs* too means not 'predictor of the future' but 'spokesman for someone' or, still better perhaps, 'crier', 'proclaimer' (Fascher). Terms less frequently used are *rō'eh* (=seer: see 1 Sam 9:11) and *ḥōzeh* (discerner: Amos 7:12; Is 30:10). What is expressed by these terms is that the individuals concerned have been given insight into the world of the divine, which is hidden from the rest of men. The interior bond between such individuals and God is also expressed by the term 'man of God', a phrase which is confined almost exclusively to the narratives of Samuel, Elijah and Elisha (see 1 Sam 2:27; 9:6; 1 Kings

17:18; 2 Kings 4:9). 1 Sam 9:9 tells of a change in linguistic usage: 'He who is now called a prophet was formerly called a seer'. Yet immediately afterwards we find 'prophets' mentioned as belonging precisely to this earlier period in which Samuel lived (1 Sam 10:5, 10). The passages in question speak of a band coming down from the high place of sacrifice, who to the accompaniment of harps, tambourines, flutes, and lyres 'prophesied' (the root from which *nābī'* is derived), that is, they were so possessed by religious ecstasy that they danced and sang. The scenes described in Ex 15:20ff (significantly Miriam is called a prophetess) and Num 11:25–9 refer to similar ecstatic manifestations. Prophets of this kind always appear in bands. The fact that they appear at places of worship implies that they have a connection with the cult: see, in addition to 1 Sam 10, 2 Kings 2:3 (Bethel); 1 Sam 19:18 (Rama; see also 7:17), 2 Kings 4:38 (Gilgal); 2 Kings 23:2; Jer 26:7f, 11, 16 (the temple at Jerusalem—priests and prophets are also mentioned together in Hos 4:4f). The prophets of Baal in 1 Kings 18:19ff likewise take an active part in the cult and 'prophesy', ie, dance and cry out in ecstasy. Similar external manifestations are found in the world surrounding Israel; for example the narrative of the journey of Wen Amon tells of an ecstatic of this kind at Byblos (Gressmann, *Altorientalische Texte*, 71–7). We may compare in our own day the frenzies of the dervishes. What is characteristic of the companies of prophets in Israel is not their external behaviour but their being filled with the spirit of Yahweh. Hence men such as Samuel (1 Sam

19:18ff), Elijah and Elisha (1 Kings 18:4, 13, 22; 19:10; 2 Kings 2:3, 5, 15f; 4:1; 5:22; 6:1) maintain friendly relations with them. That God gave actual revelations to men thus wholly given over to religion appears, for example, from 1 Kings 20:35–42 (see also 1 Sam 28:6). The Levite Jahaziel too (2 Chron 20:14) is clearly a cult prophet. Working in communities, these cult prophets gave answers from God to questions put to them; they could, however, become corrupt as is shown in 1 Kings 22:6ff. Thus they became false prophets, not sent by Yahweh, and prophesying from their own hearts. This brought them into bitter conflict with the true prophets (Jer 23:9ff; 26:7ff; 27:9f; 28; Ezek 13; Mic 3:5ff; Zech 13:2ff). As criteria for true and false prophecies respectively Deut 13:2–6 lays down that it should be seen whether they agree to disagree with the tenets of Yahwistic faith, while Deut 18:21f states that they are true or false according to whether or not they are fulfilled. But the second criterion is not sufficient without the first (Deut 13:3). As a further criterion Jer 28:8 gives the agreement or otherwise of the prophecy concerned with the earlier (true) prophets who have announced God's punishments. A prediction of good fortune can be proved to be genuinely from God only when it has been fulfilled (Jer 28:9). Jeremiah himself is convinced that threatening oracles such as those in 28:16 and 26:6 do come from God. In the first of these instances the people are to receive proof of the authenticity of the oracle when it is fulfilled (28:17). In the second the fact that the prophet has

717

indeed been sent by God is to be recognised in the attitude of quiet and unshakeable firmness which he shows in adhering to his word (26:16). In the case of another divine revelation Jeremiah himself does not recognise that it was from God until it has come true (32:8). However, on most of the prophets called by Yahweh to be his messengers to the people an interior enlightenment is bestowed, which gives them an immediate certainty of the fact that they have indeed encountered God (Amos 3:8; 7:15; Jer 15:16; 20:9).

There were men of God of this kind in Israel from the outset. In this sense Abraham is already a prophet (Gen 20:7), for Yahweh lets him know what his designs are so that he may show the way of Yahweh to his house (Gen 18:17, 19). Moses, the covenant mediator (see Ex 19f; 24), is called the greatest of the prophets (Deut 34:10ff; see also Hos 12:13), and, as is attested by the immediate and literal sense of Deut 18:15, an unbroken succession of holders of the prophetic office is to come after him. In the period of the judges, it is true, 'the word of Yahweh was rare; there was no frequent vision' (1 Sam 3:1), but it was during this period that the influential prophetess Deborah appeared (Judg 4f), and also two other prophets, both of them representatives of the religious and moral order (Judg 6:8f; 1 Sam 2:27ff). From Samuel onwards we have an unbroken succession of prophets until after the exile (see Acts 3:24). The earlier prophets have not bequeathed to us any collections of their sayings under their names. They often intervened decisively in the destiny of the people of God; thus Samuel (1 Sam 7–16), Nathan (2 Sam 7:2; 1 Kings 1), Ahijah (1 Kings 11:29), the powerful Elijah (1 Kings 17ff; 21; 2 Kings 1ff), and Elisha (2 Kings 2ff). The period of the so-called 'writing prophets' begins with Amos (circa 750 BC): collections of the writings of these have come down to us, some of them assembled by the prophets themselves but most by their disciples. These collections have been further enriched with secondary products of the prophetic charism by men writing in the spirit of the original authors. These works contain sayings, and narrative sections in the first person ('Ichberichte': eg Hos 3) and in the third ('Erberichte': eg Hos 1). It is probable that the latter do not, for the most part, come from the hands of the prophets concerned, but from those of their disciples. Such 'Erberichte' are to be found, for example in the book of Jeremiah, written by his secretary Baruch (eg, Jer 36–45). The basic forms of the prophetic saying are the *reproach* (eg, Is 3:14f), the *exhortation* (Amos 5:4ff, 14f), the *announcement of punishment* (Is 1:24f; 5:13f), often following the reproach and introduced by the conjunction 'therefore', and the '*weal oracle*' (Jer 32:15). However in addition to these the prophets do use other forms, for instance the 'song of the vineyard' in Is 5:1ff is lyrical in form, while Amos 5:2 is a funeral lament.

The significance of the prophets consists chiefly in the following four factors: first, their superb exposition of the object of Israel's faith (Yahweh is the God of the whole world, the controller of world history); secondly, their demand that their hearers shall prove themselves true servants of God by maintaining righteousness, love of neighbour, humility, and trust in God (see Is 1:16f; 7:9; 30:15; Mic 6:8); thirdly, their deepening of the personal relationship between God and man (Jer 31:31ff; Ezek 36:25ff; Hos 2:16, 21f; 14:2ff), a relationship the full force of which is to be made effective in the future; fourthly and finally, their portrayal of the messianic age to come (↗ messianism, ↗ Servant of Yahweh).

The *prophetic predictions of the future* (see Is 2:2ff; 11:11ff; Jer 30ff) are to be distinguished from *the portrayal of the final age as presented in the apocalyptic writings*. The distinguishing features of these are their vividly evocative images of earthly realities, and their intensified used of symbols and also of symbolic numbers. Apocalyptic is also characterised by its frequent presentation of mysteries which can be understood only when interpreted by an angel. This form is adumbrated, eg, in Ezek 38f; 40–48; Zech 1:7–6:8; 14; Joel; Is 24–7; 34. It appears as fully developed in Dan 7–12 and Rev, as well as in the apocalypses of the apocrypha. In these the visions and prophecies are ascribed to some figure of the past distinguished for his piety, eg, Adam, Enoch, Baruch, Ezra. To some extent at least this is also the case in the visions of the Book of Daniel, where a basic document from earlier times is adapted so as to apply to the Maccabaean period (see the expansions in Dan 2:43; 7:7 [conclusion], 8, 11, 20ff, 24f; Junker). The whole of Dan 8–12 may derive from an inspired author of the Maccabaean age, in which case chapters 8–11 would be a theology of history in the guise of predictions of the future (see Menasce

and Lusseau. It had already been accepted earlier that the precise historical data in chapters 10f are interpolations from the hand of a redactor of the Maccabaean period). Especially in Dan 2 and 7 a wonderful vision of history is revealed in which the world empires, while the threat which they represent even to the dominion of God is allowed to assume ever greater proportions, are, by the counsel and plan of God, permitted to develop their power only for a limited period, and are destined finally to be annihilated and banished from the eternal kingdom of God.

The references to the Old Testament prophets in the *New Testament* are chiefly concerned with their messianic prophecies (Mt 26:56; Lk 1:70; 24:25, 27, 44; Acts 3:24; 10:43; 13:27; Rom 1:2; 1 Pet 1:10ff). As the last and greatest of the prophets of the old covenant John the Baptist is the immediate forerunner of the messiah himself and prepares the way for him (Lk 1:17, 76; 7:26ff; Mt 11:9ff). By reason of his knowledge of hidden things (Jn 4:19) and of his miracles (Lk 7:16; Jn 9:17) Christ himself is regarded as a prophet (see also Mt 21:11; Mk 6:15; 8:28). Even though the disciples on the way to Emmaus were too dispirited by his death on the cross to think of him any longer as the messiah, they did nevertheless regard him as 'a prophet mighty in deed and word' (Lk 24:19). Those who referred to him as 'the prophet' were probably thinking for the most part of the figure which Deut 18:15, 18 had led them to expect (see Acts 3:22; 7:37), whether they actually identified this figure with the messiah (Jn 6:14) or regarded him as the immediate forerunner of the messiah, and therefore as a separate figure (Jn 7:40; see also 1:21. The rabbis do not interpret Deut 18:15, 18 as referring to the messiah, SB II, 626f). The chanting of Zechariah under the inspiration of the Holy Spirit is called 'prophesying' (Lk 1:67). The widow Anna who, like Simeon (Lk 2:26f), receives an illumination from the Holy Spirit concerning the advent of the messiah, is called a 'prophetess' (Lk 2:36).

Prophets were also to be found in *the early church*. Together with other charismatics they had the task of 'building up' the church, the body of Christ (Eph 4:11f). Paul expressly assigns them to the second rank: the first is taken by the apostles (1 Cor 12:28; see also Eph 4:11), this designation being applied to a wider group than merely 'the Twelve'. According to Eph 2:20 the faithful are 'built upon the foundation of the apostles and prophets, Christ Jesus himself being the chief corner-stone'. The 'prophets' are to be understood as including those of the early church, for the mystery of Christ is revealed by the Holy Spirit to the apostles and to them; namely, that the gentiles are to have an equal right to share in the promise in Christ (Eph 3:5). The prophets of the New Testament, therefore, like those of the Old, receive from the Holy Spirit revelations of divine mysteries. Apart from the great mystery of salvation through Christ, these may also concern the hidden thoughts of men (1 Cor 14:24f), or future things. Thus the prophet Agabus predicted the famine which occurred during the reign of the emperor Claudius (Acts 11:27f), and

later the imprisonment of Paul. In this latter case he performed a symbolic action (Acts 21:10f) after the manner of the ancient prophets (see Jer 19:1, 10f; Ezek 4f). In this connection too the four 'prophesying' daughters of Philip the deacon appear (Acts 21:9), and in general in the course of this journey of Paul from city to city the Holy Ghost bears witness to him, clearly through the medium of prophets, that imprisonment and afflictions await him (Acts 20:23). It was through prophets that he, together with Barnabas, was first 'separated off' for his apostolate (Acts 13:1f; cf also 1 Tim 4:14). The prophet is different from those who 'speak in tongues' in that he pronounces 'upbuilding and encouragement and consolation' (1 Cor 14:3ff) in speech that all can understand. This could have happened even in cases in which the prophet did not receive and impart a revelation of events and truths otherwise unknown to him. However, under the power of the Spirit he did speak with such force and conviction that the faithful sensed the breath of the Spirit and were deeply stirred in a manner conducive to their salvation (Acts 15:32). In imparting to others the illuminations which he has received the prophet is free; he is not an ecstatic, therefore, who has no command over his faculties (1 Cor 14:32). Thus for the celebration of the liturgy at Corinth Paul directs that two or three prophets are to speak one after another, and that the first is to cease when a revelation is imparted to another; but women endowed with the gift of prophecy are to keep silence during the liturgy (1 Cor 14:29–34). Whereas the Corinthians set too much store by charismatic gifts, Paul had to write to the Thessalonians warning them not to despise the gift of prophetic speech and not to suppress the Spirit (1 Thess 5:19f). Certainly the community—and clearly this applies particularly to its leaders (see Acts 14:23; 20:17, 28ff; Phil 1:1), to those endowed with the charism of distinguishing between spirits (1 Cor 12:10) and to the prophets who are in a position to hear—must put all that purports to be prophetic speech to the test (1 Cor 14:29; 1 Thess 5:21), and must only retain what is good. For just as there are 'false apostles' (2 Cor 11:13) and false teachers (see Gal 1:7; Phil 3:2), so too 'many false prophets have gone out into the world', hence the exhortation: 'Do not believe every spirit, but test the spirits to see whether they are of God' (1 Jn 4:1). The decisive characteristic is whether they agree or not with the preaching of the apostles (1 Jn 4:2f; Gal 1:8f; see also Deut 13:2ff). The Didache (11:8ff) points with special insistence to the way of life of the prophets, and asks whether they conform to that of Christ. Similarly Hermas (11th Mandate) inquires whether the prophet is unassuming, gentle, humble, and free from all bad qualities, and whether he does not speak superficially to men as he pleases. According to Didache 15:1 'the prophets and teachers' held a leading position in the communities, and clearly too in the liturgy, especially when the eucharist was celebrated (cf also 10:7; 13:3). The theory that they received priestly powers simply in virtue of their charism (O. Casel, 'Prophetie und Eucharistie', *Jahrbuch für Liturgiewissenschaff* 9 [1929], 1–19), or in virtue of the recognition of their

charism on the part of the church (J. Colson, *Les fonctions ecclésiales*, 360, *n*. 1), cannot be verified with any certainty even though this idea may have been to some extent influential (see Hippolyt, *Apostolic Tradition* 10: a witness to the faith who by his sufferings in prison has been proved to be manifestly a bearer of the spirit has no need of consecration by the laying on of hands for the office of priest and deacon). Even though the author of the Didache has accepted this, the fact that this document (which is probably post-apostolic, belonging to the first half of the second century) has not found general acceptance shows that it does not necessarily represent in all respects the generally binding doctrine of the early church (against the early dating suggested by J.-P. Audet, *La Didachè*, Paris 1958, see L. Cerfaux, *RHE* 54 (1959), 515–22; F. M. Braun, 'Le quatrième Evangile dans l'Eglise du second siècle', *SP* II, Paris–Gembloux 1959, 270–73; E. Peterson, 'Didachè', *Enc. Catt.* IV, 1563f). Peterson (*RSR* 36 [1949], 577–9) understands the 'liturgy' in Acts 13:2 as referring to a ceremony mentioned in Hermas, *Similitudes* 5:1, 1; 5:3, 3, 8 and corresponding to the fasts later observed on station days. This interpretation is favoured by the context in which the ceremony in Acts occurs: 'while they were worshipping the Lord and fasting', whereas in v 3, which does treat of an actual liturgy we find: 'Then after fasting and praying they laid their hands on them'. In Did 15:1ff 'prophets and teachers' are juxtaposed in a manner not found elsewhere. Probably the passage was written with Acts 13:1 in mind, with the result that the liturgy mentioned in Acts 13:2 is understood as referring to a celebration of divine service. According to the interpretation given above this cannot be correct. In any case Acts 6:3–6 makes it improbable that the charismatics were able to celebrate the eucharist without the laying on of hands or sacramental ordination: here the seven men 'full of the Spirit and of wisdom' and also Stephen 'full of faith and of the Holy Spirit' were ordained for their office in the church by the laying on of hands. Again, the proselytes who gathered round Cornelius the centurion still underwent baptism even though the Holy Spirit had already come upon them and they had spoken with tongues (Acts 10:44–8).

Bibliography: M. van den Oudenrijn, *Nebuah.* Rome 1926; L. Dürr, *Wollen und Wirken der atl. Propheten*, Düsseldorf 1926; E. Fascher, *Prophētēs*, Giessen 1927; H. Junker, *Prophet und Seher in Israel*, Trier 1928; E. Tobac and J. Coppens, *Les prophètes d'Israel*, Malines 1932; J. Schildenberger, *Vom Geheimnis des Gotteswortes*, Heidelberg 1950, 174–204; M. Buber, *The Prophetic Faith*, New York 1960; M. Buber, *Sehertum, Anfang und Ende*, Cologne–Olten 1955; P. van Imschoot, Haag 1367–83; G. Rinaldi, *I Profeti minori*, Turin 1953, 1–120; G. Quell, *Wahre und falsche Propheten*, Gütersloh 1952; Beguerie, Leclercq, and Steinmann, *Etudes sur les Prophètes d'Israel*, Paris 1954; C. Kuhl, *Israels Propheten*, Munich 1956; E. Balla, *Die Botschaft der Propheten*, Tübingen 1958; A. Néher, *L'Essence du prophétisme*, Paris 1955 (see H. Duesburg, *Bible et vie chrét.* 11 [Paris 1955], 100–12); A. Robert and A. Feuillet, *Introduction à la Bible* I, Tournai 1959², 468–582 ('Prophets' by A. Gelin), 695–707 ('Daniel' by H. Lusseau); H. Bacht, 'Wahres und Falsches Prophetentum. Ein kritischer Beitrag zur religionsgeschichtlichen Behandlung des frühen Christentums', *Bbl* 32 (1951), 237–62; J. Brosch, *Charismen und Ämter in der Urkirche*, Bonn 1951; J. Colson, *Les fonctions ecclésiales aux deux premiers siècles*, Paris 1956; Krämer, Rendtorff, Meyer, and Friedrich, *TDNT* VI, 781–861; R. Schnackenburg, *Die Erwartung des Propheten nach dem NT und den Qumran-Texten (TU 73)*, 1959, 622–39; O. Procksch, *Theologie des AT*, Gütersloh 1950; G. Fohrer, 'Neuere Literatur zur atl. Prophetie', *TR* 19 (1951), 277–346 and 20 (1952), 193–271 and 295–361; O. Plöger, 'Priester und Prophet', *ZAW* 63 (1951), 157–92; H. W. Wolff, 'Hauptprobleme atl. Prophetie', *ET* 15 (1955), 446–8; J. Lindblom, 'Zur Frage des kanaanäischen Ursprungs des altisrael. Prophetismus', *BZAW* 77 (1958), 89–104; *RGG* v³, 608–38; H. von Reventlow, 'Prophetenamt und Mittlerprophetie', *ZTK* 58 (1961), 269–84; R. Rendtorff, 'Erwägungen zur Frühgeschichte des Prophetentums in Israel', *ZTK* 59 (1962), 145–67; J. Lindblom, 'Prophecy in Ancient Israel', Oxford 1962; N. Füglister, *HTG* II, 350–72; *LTK* VIII², 794–802 (see also 803ff); J. Scharbert, *Die Propheten Israels bis 700 v. Christus*, Cologne 1965; *E. W. Heaton, *The Old Testament Prophets*, Harmondsworth 1958; *J. Rhymer, *The Prophets and the Law*, London 1964.

Johannes Schildenberger

Providence

A. The English word *providence* comes from the Latin *providentia*, which is a translation of the Greek *pronoia*. The word itself and the particular connotation of what it represents comes to us from the world of Greek thought. Faith in the divine *pronoia* was understood by the Greeks cosmocentrically. It was orientated to the world, explained in rational terms, and related consciously and expressly to mankind and its place in the world. By reflecting on the totality of nature and the world and on the knowledge of a world-reason which governed the world in a meaningful and purposeful way and which was considered to be divine, the Greeks arrived at the idea of a divine *pronoia*, a divine government of the world which is provident, by which everything is ordered according to an absolute purpose, which is good, and which acts with reference to a definite goal. This teaching on providence spread from the

Stoics, in whose harmonious body of doctrine *pronoia* played a central role, to hellenistic judaism and early christianity, and thus became a part of the spiritual history of Europe. This was no doubt due to the intrinsic religious strength of this doctrine which inserted the individual into the ordered and predetermined harmony of the cosmic whole.

B. The fact that the *Old Testament* is familiar with the idea of divine providence, often strongly emphasised, and yet does not contain an elaborated *concept* which defines it, takes us at once to the essential characteristics of what the Old Testament has to say on this subject. Hebrew thinking was backward in the formation of abstract concepts precisely because it was orientated to a concrete way of representing reality. Thus the concepts of 'nature' and 'cosmos' are not found at all in the Old Testament. The 'world' was not conceived of as a self-sufficient, stable, harmonious and all-embracing order of reality, but as a context of existence which was imponderable, incalculable and beyond the free disposal of men. It was, in the last analysis, 'a sustaining activity of Yahweh' (G. von Rad 1, 427).

Hence we find the idea of providence expressed more often than not where Hebrew man testifies in faith to the historical experience of what Yahweh has done (exodus, the wandering in the wilderness, conquest of the land) and where he reflects aloud on the deeds of Yahweh by which in wisdom and grace he brings about the salvation of the people and, within this social context, that of the individual Israelite. In this sense, the 'world' is open to the future

of God. Human existence cannot be assured and rationally ordered by means of intelligible and manageable concepts; it has to be lived out in faith and trust in 'the ground of being', in Yahweh God of the covenant. It is no coincidence that the first attempt to express the idea of divine providence in the Old Testament does not speak of the 'providence' of God (in the etymological sense of seeing in advance, *pro-videre*) but of his care for men (Job 10:12, *pᵉkuddā*), the thought which he gives him and the protection he offers him (only in Wis 14:3 and 17:2 do we find the Greek term *pronoia* understood as a paraphrase for 'God'). In the Old Testament, therefore, providence is not a dimension of the cosmos thought of as a closed system but as the ground of the being of both the world and man understood and experienced in personal terms, that is, as Yahweh who in grace, freedom and goodness guides everything wisely and purposefully to its appointed end. The tension between the freedom of human action and the all-powerful activity of Yahweh can be preserved not by identifying or juxtaposing the two but by seeing them as mutually inclusive.

C. *The experience of the providence of Yahweh* is confirmed in the first place by his government of his people throughout their history, especially in the lives of the patriarchs (Gen 12; 20; 22; 37; 39), but also in the exercise of his lordship over nature and in the experience of the individual Israelite. Under the influence of prophetic thinking (especially of Isaiah) this was also seen to be true of the nation as a whole. According to the priestly point of view it could be seen also in the provident wisdom of God in giving his people a law. In these and many other different ways the idea of divine providence finds expression in the Old Testament.

I. In the first place divine providence is at work in guiding *the history* of his chosen people (Amos 3:2) which he has created (Is 43:1, 15; Ps 95:6) in accordance with his antecedent decree (Deut 32:39; Josh 24; Neh 9; Judith 5; Is 43:18–21; Ps 78; 105; 106). Yet he also guides the historical destiny of other peoples (Amos 9:7) which serve his purposes (Gen 11:1ff; 49:1; 1 Kings 19:15ff; Is 10:5–14; Jer 27:3ff; Job 12:23). Yahweh sees the whole course of history in advance (Is 22:11; 44:7) and choses instruments for the accomplishment of his designs (Is 49; 54:16; Jer 1:5). The Deuteronomistic view of history discerns in what happens to the people of Israel the reward and punishment of Yahweh (Deut 4; Judg 2:11–15; 3:7–12; 1 Sam 4–6:7; 1 Kings 13:33f; 14:22–4). Daniel and the authors of apocalyptic in the later Jewish period divide history into periods and see in the succession of different ages the activity of Yahweh who leads history towards its conclusion in the establishment of the kingdom of God.

2. As *creator* of heaven and earth (Gen 1) Yahweh is continually and directly operative in the world, governing it as a wise father (Wis 7:22ff; 14:1–5; Hos 2:10; Ps 65:7–14; 104; 145:15f; 147: 8f; Job 9:5f). He maintains an appropriate order in nature (2 Macc 7:28; Jer 5:22; 8:7; Ps 19:4ff) which is subject to his laws (Gen 8:22; Jer 31:35f; Ps 148:6; Job 38:33), cares for all created things (Gen 27:28; Ps 65:7–14; 104; Job 38:19–41), bestows life (Is

42:5; Ps 104:29f; Job 10:12; 12:10; 33:4; 34:14) and fertility (Gen 1:22, 28).

3. *The individual* who experiences God's providential guidance in the first place as a member of the people of God knows from the prophets and wise men that his life is in God's hands (Is 41:4; Ps 16:5; 22:10f; 90:3; Prov 16:9; 20:24; Job 5:18ff; 10:8ff; 1 Macc 3:60). Even the things which seem to happen by pure chance or by accident come from God (1 Sam 6:9; 10:19ff; 14:41; Prov 16:33; Ruth 2:3). Even what is evil (Ex 4:21; Is 45:7; Amos 3:5f) is caused by Yahweh. It is by his sovereign decree and action that men are punished for the sins they commit (Ps 1:4f; 112:10; Wis 11:14–17; Sir 5:1–15; 10:12–17), a conviction which is expressed most clearly in the speeches made by Job's friends. But in punishing them he also leads them to greater maturity (Job 34:31f; 36:5–21) and purifies them (Job 33:15–30; Wis 3:5; 11:9; 12:13–27; 2 Macc 6:16; 7:18). There is nothing which cannot serve the purpose of Yahweh's salvific design, which is beyond the understanding of men (Gen 50:20; Is 47; 55:8f; Hab 1:12ff; Job 42:1ff).

D. The *New Testament* never speaks explicitly in so many words of the divine *pronoia*, but presupposes the Old Testament view of providence.

1. Jesus' eschatological proclamation of the salvific and holy will of God now at last definitely revealed in him stresses even further and deepens the idea of a divine providence since it culminates in the revelation of the unlimited goodness of God as Father (Lk 6:36; 15:1–31; Mt 5:43–8; 20:1ff). In this goodness one can now find com-

plete security and protection (Mt 6:25–34). The loving care of the heavenly Father for all creatures (Mt 6:25–31; Lk 12:22–9; Mt 10:29f; Lk 12:6f) reflects his fatherly care and preoccupation for the salvation of men (Mt 6:32; Lk 12:30; Mt 7:7–11; Lk 11:9–13), which has found incomparable and unsurpassed expression in his merciful turning towards sinners in the person of Jesus (Mt 5:45; Lk 6:35; 7:36ff; Mk 2:17; Mt 18:11; Lk 19:10). Jesus reveals the will of God not only for salvation but also sanctification; for him God remains always the holy, righteous, and sovereign lord and judge (Mt 5:34f; 20:1–16; 10:28; Lk 12:5, 20, 25; 17:7–10; Mk 10:40). In Jesus' mission, in what he proclaimed by word and deed, God's salvific goodness and love (and therefore also his providence) are made visible and manifest once and for all as an eschatological reality (Mt 13:16; Lk 10:23).

2. In the providential Christ-event brought about by God, in the origin and destiny of Jesus (Mt 1–2), in his suffering (Mt 8:31 and parallels; 9:31; 10:33), crucifixion and resurrection (Acts 2:23f; 2:30–32; 3:18ff) the universal activity of God aiming at the salvation of the world has reached its goal (1 Cor 2:7–9; Rom 10:9ff; 5:1ff; etc), his gracious providence has already in principle decided the outcome of man's destiny which is to be salvation. In the victory of the Lamb who reveals the eternal design of God (Rev 5:1ff), God has overcome this transitory world (Rev 11:17f; 12:10f), which has now only one goal of fulfilment, namely Christ, who has already appeared (Eph 1:3–14; 4:10, 13). The christian who believes in God and in the resurrection of the Lord Jesus may be unshakeably certain that he is guarded and protected by God (Rom 8:28ff). The love of Christ has permeated the very ground of our existence (Rom 8:35). The belief in providence found in the New Testament rests on the certainty that 'neither death, nor life, nor angels, nor principalities, nor things present, nor things to come, nor powers, nor heights, nor depth, nor anything else in all creation, will be able to separate us from the love of God in Christ Jesus our Lord' (Rom 8:38f).

Bibliography: Haag 1691–4; *TDNT* IV, 1009–17; *RGG* VI³, 1496–9; J. Dheilly, *DB* 975f; Eichrodt, *Theology of the OT*, I and II; von Rad I, 157f and 427f; Bultmann I, 71; R. Bultmann, *Urchristentum im Rahmen der antiken Religionen*, Hamburg 1963, 20–30, 92, and 128ff; R. Völkl, *Christ und Welt nach dem NT*, Würzburg 1961, 29f; W. Eichrodt, 'Vorsehungsglaube und Theodizee im AT', *Procksch Festschrift* 1934, 45ff; J. Schmid, *Das Evangelium nach Matthäus* (*RNT* I), 124–8; F. Nötscher, *Gotteswege und Menschenwege in der Bibel und in Qumran* (*BBB* 15), 1958; J. Schreiner, 'Führung—Thema der Heilsgeschichte im AT'. *BZ* 5 (1961), 2–18; A. Vögtle, 'Jesus', *LTK* v², 922–32; H. Schlier, 'Jesus Christus und die Geschichte nach der Offenbarung des Johannes', *Aufsätze* II, 1964, 358–73; T. Blatter, *Macht und Herrschaft Gottes*, Freiburg 1962, 86–92.

Rudolf Pesch

Rebirth

The actual expression 'rebirth' (*palingenesia*) is used to designate the basic salvific event of the christian's life only in one passage of the New Testament, namely, Titus 3:5. The same idea is expressed in verbal form in 1 Pet 1:3, 23 (*anagennaō* = 'to be born anew') and Jn 3:3 (*anōthen gennēthēnai* = 'to be born again'; *anōthen* can also signify 'from on high' (see Jn 3:31; 19:11), that is, 'from God' (see Jn 1:13; 1 Jn 2:29; 3:9; 4:7; 5:18), but this birth which comes from God, in contrast to the physical one, is also a new birth, a rebirth). On designations which are related in meaning in the New Testament, see A. Harnack, *Die Terminologie der Wiedergeburt und verwandter Erlebnisse in der ältesten Kirche* (*TU* III, 12, 3), 1918, 97–143; J. Dey, 4ff.

The concept of *palingenesia* is probably derived from philosophy. In the physics of the Stoic school it is used to designate the re-emergence of the world after its periodic destructions by cosmic conflagration (↗ restoration). In an earlier representative of the Stoic school only the verbal phrase *palin gignesthai* (= 'to become, be born, again') is attested. In the doctrine of the transmigration of souls, rebirth is expressed by *palingenesia* together with *metempsukhōsis* and *metensōmatōsis*, but the examples are rather late. Among neo-Platonists the maintenance of life by reproduction is regarded as a rebirth. In everyday speech every sort of renewal—return to earlier conditions, restoration or resumption of former relationships, termination of imprisonment or exile, recovery of health or adoption (for actions corresponding to these, see Dey, 128–31)—can be described as a rebirth. In the Hermetic writings rebirth is considered from a spiritual point of view as the restoration of the spiritual soul to its sphere by releasing it from its bondage in the body.

To *explain* the New Testament idea of rebirth we must turn to the *history of religions*, and in particular to that branch of it which deals with the mystery religions. Most of the evidence for these belongs to the centuries after Christ. Because of the fact that their tenets were kept secret, and also because the accounts of them by Christian writers are often presented from polemical or apologetic points of view (K. Rahner, *Greek Myths and Christian Mystery*, London 1962) it is difficult to understand what is essential in the beliefs and ceremonies of the mysteries. A prudent judgement may arrive at the following conclusion: in the Eleusinian mysteries, the mysteries of Isis, the so-called 'liturgy of Mithras', etc. the idea of rebirth is either not discernible or else expresses something quite different from the christian concept. Any influence upon the development of the New Testament and early christian idea of rebirth is excluded either on chronological grounds (the lateness of the evidence for these mysteries—for instance the *Taurobolion* inscription [*CIL* VI, 510] from the year 376), or by reason of the fundamentally different basis from which the relevant doctrine was evolved (gnostic dualism in the case of the Hermetic writings). (For a more detailed exposition of this, see Dey, 36–128; Prümm, *Religionsgeschichtliches Handbuch für den Raum der altchristlichen Umwelt*, Freiburg 1943; Nilsson, *Geschichte der griechischen Religion*, Munich 1950). ↗ Mystery.

The idea of rebirth may have been *prepared for by the thought of the restoration and renewal predicted by the prophets for the messianic age of salvation* (↗ restoration). But the idea of a rebirth which applies to individual men in the present age, such as we find in the New Testament understanding of the term, is not yet foreshadowed in writings pertaining to the old covenant, just as the idea of a twofold coming of the messiah is not yet expressed in the prophets of the Old Testament. Again the statements in the later writings of the Old Testament concerning life as a blessing of the age of salvation (Dan 12:2: *ḥayyê ᶜôlām zōē aiōnios*; 2 Macc 7:9; *eis aiōnion anabiōsin zōēs*) apply only to the state of the righteous after the resurrection and the last judgement (for bibliography, see Nötscher 141, *n.* 97). The Qumran community also believed in eternal life in the final age, but nothing is said of how it is to begin or of other details (texts, Nötscher, 150f). It is 'the sons of righteousness' who are to participate in this blessing, though now they are suffering and oppressed.

For judaism we have a rabbinical rule which describes the proselyte's state of righteousness in relation to God and the law in the following terms: 'The proselyte is like a new-born child' (SB II, 423). But this expression is not meant to refer to a 'moral renewal' (SB II, 421). The baptism of the proselyte was originally a washing intended to remove the uncleanness incurred during his time as a gentile. By about the end of the first century AD it, together with circumcision, had acquired a greater significance (for examples, reasons and the opinions of various schools on this point, see SB I, 102–8). But even in this sense the baptism of proselytes has no salvific effect; it is a sign, rather, of the subject's conversion to judaism, with the juridical and legal consequences which this entailed under the Levitical law. In contrast to this we find that rebirth as conceived of in the New Testament has the effect of conferring new life on the individual in the present.

1 Pet 1:3–5: God accomplishes rebirth, or better new generation (*anagennēsas*), already here in the present world. The purpose of this is the redemption, the salvation (*eis sōterian*) which will be revealed openly in the last time (*en kairō[i] eskhatō[i]*); then the entry into the 'inheritance which is imperishable, undefiled and unfading, kept in heaven for you' will ensue (see Col 1:5, where the actual hope for this is said to be 'laid up in heaven'). Salvation, then, is the object of hope, and, indeed, of a living hope, that is, one which is actually developed in the course of life. 'Salvation of the soul' is also the 'final goal of faith' (1:9), a faith which can, precisely, be set alongside hope (1:21). 'For a little while' (1:6f; see also v. 5) it must be proved and tested by suffering. Rebirth is an effect of the divine compassion (see Eph 2:4f, where our being made alive together with Christ [*sunezōopoiēsen*] is based upon the richness of the divine mercy and our redemption is based upon grace); indeed this compassion is extended to us not only in the initial act by which God regenerates us into a state of grace, but also in the lasting state of being protected by God's power (1:5). It depends upon the resurrection (*di᾿ anastaseōs*) of Christ. But this is not only the basis of salvation. From the fact that it points back to the sufferings and on to the glory of Christ (1:11), it follows that these experiences which he underwent are ordered to our present life with its sufferings (1:6), and to the joy and glory to come (1:8). The exhortation to constancy and to uprightness of life (1:13ff) makes it clear that this rebirth is to be understood not only in an eschatological sense but as

having a vital significance for the present too.

1 Pet 1:23 takes up the idea of a new generation (*anagegennēmenoi*) again and emphasises that its effects are eternal, just as the source whence it derives is 'the imperishable seed, through the living and abiding word of God' (as opposed to the perishable seed of earthly generation). By undergoing this 'in the living and abiding word of God', man is allowed to participate in 'the fullness of life and the eternity which belong to God' (Michl, *RNT* ad loc.) In Jas 1:18, too, it is said that God brought us forth (*apekuēsen*) by 'the word of truth'. In 1 Pet 2:2 (*artigennēta*) it is only a simile that is being presented, but a simile which is probably inspired by the idea of rebirth. No other means of achieving rebirth is considered except baptism, which, while it is not explicitly mentioned in 1 Pet 1:3, 23, is not excluded either.

Jn 3:3–8: The idea of a rebirth is brought strongly to the fore in response to the uncomprehending question put by Nicodemus. It is characterised as an effect of the Spirit, not within the power of man to accomplish, and opening his eyes to the kingdom of God. Baptism is the means by which rebirth is achieved, and, unlike the baptism of repentance or the baptism of John, it is not presented as something extra and external to the reception of the Spirit, undertaken to obtain pardon for one's sins. Jn 1:13 emphasises once more the contrast between this rebirth and natural birth, and serves to add weight to the thought of Jn 3:5 (see 1 Jn 2:29; 3:9; 4:7 and R. Schnackenburg, *Die Johannesbriefe*, on these passages). The process of being baptised appears as a salvific act on the part of God, and is accomplished upon man, not by him. That the baptised person is not merely being given the appellation 'child of God' but is really being admitted to a new form of being is shown in 1 Jn 3:1 (see Schnackenburg ad loc.).

From a linguistic point of view Titus 3:4–7 admits of several different explanations (Dey, 133ff). It must, however, be firmly maintained that *anakainōseōs* does not signify a further procedure in addition to the washing, such as confirmation. (Paul too emphasises in 1 Cor 12:13a that in baptism the power of the Holy Spirit is really operative). The washing is the baptism and, according to Paul, it is always this that is the means of our salvation (see Rom 6:3f; 1 Cor 12:13; Gal 3:27; Eph 4:5; Col 2:12). Eph 5:26 also speaks of baptism as a washing which has the effects of cleansing and consecrating, but there is no mention here of rebirth. In 1 Cor 6:11 washing is presented as an image of purification. It is to be observed, however, that over and above the moral effects, namely purification from sin, consecration and justification are conferred as a new state, a truly new dimension of life, by which men receive and possess the Spirit of God (see Kuss, *RNT* ad loc.). This in turn requires that the gift which has been received shall be made fruitful in the moral sphere, in that the baptised person must relinquish the sinful way of life of his gentile past. It is to baptism that Heb 10:22 refers.

The idea of a renewal of men by God is found in the Old Testament. When the prophets speak of the new and eternal covenant (Jer 31:31–4; Ezek 37:26; see also Is 54:10) they are

728

thereby indicating the interior effects of right moral and religious attitudes brought about by God in the souls of men (Ezek 11:19; 36:26). But the moral acts of man are also included (Ezek 18:31; see also Dey, 146f). The sprinkling with 'the spirit of truth' in the Qumran community (1 QS iv, 21; Molin, *Die Söhne des Lichtes*, 23: 'the spirit of right conscience') is a purification from sin and achieves success in judgement (in the Thanksgiving Psalm XI = 1 QH vii, 6 the outpouring of the Spirit upon the worshipper signifies the help and support of God in alien surroundings).

In contrast to this, Titus 3:4–7 declares: It is in the washing of rebirth that God accomplishes upon us the decisive act of redemption. He does this not because of our (natural or legal) righteousness but because of his grace. Through the medium of the washing, the baptism, the Holy Spirit sent by Christ effects our rebirth and renewal. The goal of this salvific process is our justification and preparation in expectation of eternal life. Eschatological considerations may have influenced or inspired the choice of the words *palingenesia* and *anakainōsis*; but from the fact that a contrast is drawn between the way of life connoted by them and that led by the Godless and sinful (3:3) it may be concluded that the salvific event involved is ordered to this present epoch, with its moral strivings, and therefore that the renewal is to be made fruitful in the subject's altered attitude towards the commandments of God, in *metanoia*. A magical effect, such as 1 Cor 15:29 might be taken to suggest, is ruled out by the fact that the necessity of faith is pointed to (see amongst other passages Gal 3:26f, where faith and baptism are mentioned together; Col 2:12), and also by the constant references to God's gracious activity in the bestowal of salvation. But apart from this it is also explicitly denied by Paul (1 Cor 10:1–13).

In none of the New Testament passages does the image of rebirth receive any further explanation (such as that of Justin, *Apol.* 1, 61:10); it is intended, rather, simply to throw light upon the way in which salvation is effected (Schnackenburg, *Das Heilsgeschehen*, 128). Hence it becomes evident that it is not the idea of rebirth that was primary, but rather the event of salvation. The ideas and modes of expression which were current at the relevant period provided in the term 'rebirth' the appropriate concept to throw light upon this. If one and the same act of receiving salvation can be described as rebirth, putting on Christ and circumcision in Christ, it follows that it is not the terminology of the mystery religions that we are encountering, but the language of images (Schnackenburg, *Heilsgeschehen* 56; Harnack, *Terminologie*, 141). Braun ('Das "Stirb und Werde" in der Antike und im Christentum', *Libertas Christiana* [Festschrift F. Delekat], 1957, 25) rightly notes that the actual ceremonies by which baptism was conferred, in contrast to those of the mystery religions, appear not to be emphasised. Certainly the effects of baptism cannot be confined to the moral sphere; it must also be regarded as causing salvation as a state, as is indicated by such turns of phrase as 'in Christ', pointing to the fact that the baptised become children of God.

The doctrine of rebirth finds its classic formulation in the dogmatic exposition of the Council of Carthage, AD 418 (DS 223 [=DB 102]: 'Etiam parvuli ... baptizantur, ut in eis regeneratione mundetur, quod generatione traxerunt'). The idea of rebirth at baptism finds expression several times in the liturgy. It appears particularly clearly in the words used at the blessing of baptismal water on the night preceding Easter Sunday: 'Qui hanc aquam, regenerandis hominibus praeparatam, arcana sui numinis admixtione fecundet: ut, sanctificatione concepta, ab immaculato divini fontis utero, in novam renata creaturam, progenies caelestis emergat' and in the preceding prayer, 'ad recreandos novos populos, quos tibi fons baptismatis parturit, spiritum adoptionis emitte'. A poetic conception of the theology of baptism, in which it is interpreted in the sense of a rebirth, has survived from the time of Sixtus III (432–40) on the distichs of the baptismal church near the Lateran basilica at Rome. (Text etc. in Kaufmann, *Christliche Epigraphik*, Freiburg 1917, 187. In the translation it must of course read: 'all of whom one fount, one Spirit, one faith unites'; see Eph 4:4f; on the origin and authorship of the inscription, see F. J. Dölger, 'Die Inschrift im Baptisterium S. Giovanni in Fonte', *Antike und Christentum* II [1930], 252–7.)

↗ Baptism, Circumcision, Creation, Justification, Life, Resurrection.

Bibliography: J. Dey, *Palingenesia* (*NA* 13, 5) 1937; R. Schnackenburg, *Das Heilsgeschehen bei der Taufe nach dem Apostel Paulus*, *NT*, Munich 1950; R. Schnackenburg, 'Le Baptême dans le NT', *LV* 26, 27 (1956); R. Schnackenburg, *Die Johannesbriefe*, Freiburg 1953, 155–62;

J. Michl, Exkurs 'Die Wiederzeugung des Menschen aus Gott', *RNT* 8 (1953), 204–6; F. Büchsel, *TDNT* I, 673–5 and 686–9.

Josef Dey

Reconciliation

A. *Old Testament*. I. *Terminology*: Reconciliation with God presupposes in addition to a definite understanding of the deity a *relationship* with God (↗ covenant) conceived of as taking place within certain specific limits. This kind of relationship also implies that man has acted injuriously towards God; it can be impaired and even completely broken but, given certain preconditions, can also be re-established, though this can take place only on God's initiative. By reconciliation or atonement we understand, therefore, in the first place, the final and conclusive act by which the original relationship between God and man is re-established. This act is manifest in the assurances given by means of the word of God that Yahweh will once again be Israel's God and Israel once again his people. Reconciliation is therefore the end-result of this process of re-establishing a broken relationship. In order to understand and accept this we have to presuppose on the part of God a basic disposition towards reconciliation since without such a disposition the whole process would be impossible. The account we have given of this process can also be expressed in a logical and systematic way, and signs of this are present even to some extent in the Old Testament. This could hardly have been otherwise, since a great deal is said on this subject in the Old Testament.

We should, however, add that there is nothing approaching a doctrine of or treatise on reconciliation there, and not even a specific term which can be satisfactorily distinguished from the complex of ideas and statements centred on the word *kipper* (= atone). In speaking therefore of reconciliation in the Old Testament context we have to do with a number of different connotations which touch on this subject and which find expression in the words ↗ atonement, ↗ covenant, election, ↗ grace, ↗ justification, ↗ righteousness, the forgiveness of sins (intimately associated with ↗ sin, guilt, and punishment). This appears to be the only way of representing the necessary connection between reconciliation as present in the Old Testament though terminologically not distinct, and the way in which it is conceptualised and differentiated as a theological doctrine today.

2. *The subject of the reconciling act.* We are indebted to K. Koch, J. B. Bauer, L. Moraldi, and other scholars for the deeper realisation which we now have of the fact that in the whole complex of expressions about expiation, the forgiveness of sins, and atonement it is always Yahweh who appears as the one who acts and brings about what is implied in these expressions. He desires reconciliation and therefore makes it possible for men to undertake expiatory actions. In all this Yahweh is the subject of the action of reconciliation not the object. Of himself man cannot either initiate or bring about reconciliation. The only guarantee that the expiatory actions undertaken may succeed lies in Yahweh alone; in fact, it is precisely the recognition of the fact that Yahweh has

opened up this possibility which makes the expiatory act what it is. Taken by itself, merely as an act undertaken by man, it would be worth nothing. Therefore the whole idea of finding means of placating the deity, as was the case with pagans in relation to their gods, was unthinkable in Israel. At the same time, we have reason to believe that in Israel as elsewhere acts of expiation did not escape being misunderstood in a mechanistic and magical sense and therefore being put to bad use; the more so that as regards their origin and formation these acts are reminiscent of others practised in the pagan world before the time of Israel and also by Israel's neighbours (pre-Israelite cultures in Palestine, Babylonian influence, etc). It is understandable, therefore, that there was a constant need to correct misunderstandings and one-sided explanations—and this precisely *because* of the prevalence of acts which correspond in such a concrete way to the religious needs of man in his human existence.

3. *How the act is mediated.* There are texts in the Old Testament in which certain persons play an important mediating role in re-establishing a broken relationship between God and man. One example is the intercession of Abraham on behalf of Abimelech and his house (Gen 20:17f), though this act of mediation was arranged by Yahweh himself (v 7). The intercession of Moses happened at the request of Pharaoh after the plagues of Egypt and proved efficacious (Ex 9:27ff, 33ff; 10:16ff), though within limits specified by Yahweh, as the context makes apparent. Moses also acted as intercessor after Miriam had been struck by

leprosy (Num 12:13ff) and when the Israelites were threatened by serpents (21:6–9). But if a significant role is given to intercession and to mediation, it is made clear that this is only one of several ways open to Yahweh. He is and remains the master and lord and brings about reconciliation when and how he wishes. This is clearly seen in the fact that he can refuse reconciliation in spite of intercession as, for example, when he forbids an act of intercession in advance (Jer 11:14; 14:11) or states that it will be without effect (Jer 15:1; 'though Moses and Samuel stood before me...').

The most impressive figure in the Old Testament of those who mediate the reconciling act of God is the Servant of Is 53 who takes upon himself the guilt of all. But precisely here we see that the mediator is no independent figure in his own right; his function is only made possible by Yahweh's disposition to reconciliation and will to save men. He is the Servant of Yahweh.

4. *Conditions necessary for reconciliation.* Though reconciliation is a gift of Yahweh freely given, it still remains necessary for man to submit to the process by which he shares in the gift. Man must seek Yahweh (2 Sam 12:16; Is 55:6; Hos 10:12; Amos 5:4, 6), seek his face (2 Sam 21:1; Hos 5:15), return with all his heart to him (1 Sam 7:3), humble himself before him (2 Kings 22:19) and experience a change of heart (Ezek 18:31). The attitude demanded of man is subsumed in one of the most central concepts of the prophetic preaching (especially in Hosea, Jeremiah, and Deutero–Isaiah): he must be converted, return to Yahweh. This new attitude must find expression in acts (Jer 7:3–7; 26:13). Though the conversion is the work of Yahweh (clearly expressed in Jer 31:31–4), the necessity of an attentive readiness and openness on the part of man is continually emphasised (Is 1:19f).

Prophetic preaching (eg, Is 1) gives great emphasis to the fact that, though expiatory acts may be accorded a greater or lesser value, without the right predispositions in the heart of man they are all worth nothing (this is true of all other external acts by which man seeks to give honour to God). The confession of sin and guilt is an absolutely necessary precondition for reconciliation with God whether on the part of the individual (eg, David: 2 Sam 12:13) or the community (1 Sam 7:6). This is sometimes induced by serious illness (Ps 6; 32; 38), the infliction of punishment (2 Sam 24:17), the warning words of a prophet (1 Sam 15:24) or the prospect of liberation (1 Sam 7:6). A public and ceremonial confession of sins was held every year on the great Day of Expiation (Lev 16:21).

5. *Extent.* Reconciliation as the re-establishment of a relationship with God was mandatory to the extent that that relationship had been impaired by human guilt and sin. This illustrates the close association between expiation, the forgiveness of sins, and atonement on the one hand, and sin and guilt on the other. Taken together, these entities make up a reality which appears differently at different periods of history but is always closely related to the changing understanding of God, man and the world. In order to answer the question of what the concept of reconciliation includes (with regard to its presuppositions, effects, etc) and how

far it extends (its content in the strict sense) we have to try to grasp the way in which this total relationship was thought of in the particular context in question. So, for example, if we wish to understand something about modern man and how he thinks about these things we would have to go beyond our own ideas about sin and reconciliation and ask such questions as which actions would today be regarded sinful and which not, what specifically makes actions evil and what does not, to what extent is sin a social and to what extent a purely personal phenomenon, and so on.

The idea that the relationship between God and man is broken automatically when certain circumstances enter into play, quite irrespective of the question of responsibility, is a very ancient one, though the texts in which it finds expression often come from a much more recent time. Examples would be the infliction of a mortal wound or murder when the perpetrator remains undetected (Deut 21:1–9), Achan's violation of the ban which constituted a threat to the entire people (Josh 7:11f), unwitting adultery which is judged in the same way as premeditated adultery (Gen 20; 26:7–10), unconscious or unintentional infractions of ritual prescriptions which are regarded as sins worthy of punishment (Lev 4:3). Corresponding to such sins are the various means of expiation when such are applied. On some occasions it is deemed necessary to 'cut off' the offending party from the people (Lev 17:4, 9, 10, 14; Num 9:13). In this respect there is a great difference between the pre- and post-exilic periods, though of course we must be careful not to generalise too much. Interpreted in the light of the preaching of judgement in the pre-exilic prophets the setbacks and defeat of the people on the political, economic and military level give rise to a new and critical assessment of the question of sin. We find that this term acquires a much wider connotation and there develops a much stronger and more personal sense of sin. Correspondingly, acts of expiation, including ritual acts, acquire greater importance (see Ezekiel and P). All are subject to the need for atonement, priests and people alike (even the temple and the altar, see Ezek 43:20). Rites of expiation are given a fixed place in the calendar: the feast of the new moon (Num 28; 29) and especially the great Day of Expiation (Lev 16). Sacrifice has a predominantly expiatory character, though it is difficult now to discover how this process began. Even Passover became subject to the same process (2 Chron 30).

6. *Effects.* Since it consists in a re-establishment of the broken relationship between God and man, reconciliation also includes the removal of guilt and punishment consequent on sin. This, however, cannot simply be described as an annulment, quite apart from the question how such an annulment could take place. So, for example, we find a deferment of punishment (Ex 32:34), but the punishment is still inflicted on those who have sinned, as 32:33 makes clear (see Ezek 18). The case in Ex 34:7 is different again, since here the punishment will be visited on later generations. We also find both deferment and diminution of punishment, as in Num 14 and 2 Sam 12. This way of thinking is not very

733

accessible to us today. In order to understand it we have to take into account the fact that for the early Israelite it was impossible to break the chain made up of sin, guilt, and punishment. It would have been quite foreign to the Israelite way of thinking to break up the continuity in these factors which seemed so powerfully operative in human life by the application of abstract and logical categories of thought. According to Old Testament understanding, sin, guilt, and punishment did not make up some kind of a spiritual (much less other-worldly) reality in the context of a personal and private relationship of man to God. By means of sin 'something evil is set in motion' (von Rad) which is brought to a halt only when punishment has been exacted. Punishment redresses the balance. The individual, according to this view, does not just live for himself. His existence is caught up in that of society, and the present society lives on in the generations which follow it. In addition, the different areas of life formed a unity. There was just *one life*; any kind of clear-cut distinctions were out of the question. The indissoluble unity of the various interrelated aspects of life which was experienced much more strongly then now provides a context of understanding which must be taken into account in the discussion of the present theme. This enables us to understand how reconciliation was thought of as experienced in the enjoyment of the ordinary good things of life: restoration of health, a long life, defeat of enemies, protection from all kinds of danger (eg, from wild beasts, the failure of the crops, and so forth).

The preaching of the prophets did not basically change this understanding of how reconciliation was experienced. What it did was to strengthen and deepen the idea (which they were not the first to state) that reconciliation with Yahweh and material well-being were not necessarily to be identified or put on the same level. The prophets further indicated that those affected by the fearful visitation of Yahweh could, by accepting and living out the judgement imposed on them, find themselves already on the path towards reconciliation which Yahweh had indicated (Jer 29:10–14). While these distinctions drawn by the prophets should not be underestimated, their writings also convey the conviction that he who passes through the fire of divine judgement in order to be reconciled with Yahweh will also in time have his due of earthly goods in full. In addition, we find here traces of eschatological thinking which open up the hope for a definitive reward for the just and a final reconciliation with God. There is also a tendency to restate the complex: sin, guilt, punishment with direct reference to the individual. Where we find the effects of reconciliation (with respect to the individual) transferred to a life after death we may be sure that this comes from a later period (2 Macc 7:9, 14, 23, 36).

7. *Good and bad dispositions with regard to reconciliation.* Though the many different experiences and points of view found in the Old Testament are too complex to allow of any easy classification, it is at least possible to state in general terms what is required for reconciliation with God to come about. This will be easier to accomplish if we place in the centre of the picture the

gracious action of Yahweh on behalf of Israel (election, covenant), rather than starting out from a simple enumeration of texts giving to each of them an absolute and independent value which it does not possess. In this way the basic demand on man to prepare himself and be well disposed for the reconciling action of God stands out in sharper relief (see Ex 34:6; Num 14:18; Ps 86:5; Ps 103:8–10; Jer 5:1; etc). In Num 15:30ff we have an equally clear statement on the kind of disposition which excludes reconciliation and the consequences which necessarily follow on obduracy, sin committed 'with a high hand'. We find the same refusal depicted in other texts, eg, 1 Sam 3:14; 2 Kings 24:4; Is 22:14; Jer 5:7; 7:16. The prophetic passages in which Yahweh himself makes the refusal show clearly that 'the leitmotiv of judgement is the love of God who wishes to win back his people' (H. W. Wolff). This is true even when Yahweh forbids intercession to be made for the guilty people (Jer 7:16; 11:11, 14) or allows no further appeal for repentance to be made (Hos 5–7), since Israel does not yet seem to be ready to receive such appeals. The punishment is inflicted without any vindictive passion since its aim is the bringing back of Israel to the knowledge of Yahweh as the lord of its history and into fellowship with him (5:15; 6:6). (See H. W. Wolff, *Dodekapropheton I: Hosea*, Neukirchen 1961, 166.) In the last resort the love of Yahweh for his people is seen even when, for a time, they refuse his offer of reconciliation.

Bibliography: See the various Theologies of the Old Testament; J. J. Stamm, *Erlösen und Vergebung im AT*, 1940; S. Herner, *Sühne und Vergebung in Israel*, 1942; L. Moraldi, *Espiazione sacrificiale e riti espiatori nell'ambiente biblico e nell'AT*, Rome 1956; K. Koch, *RGG* vi[3], 1368–70; E. Speiser, 'Ritual Expiation in Mari and Israel', *BASOR* 149 (1958), 17–25; S. Lyonnet, 'De Notione Expiationis', *VD* 36 (1958), 129–48, 37 (1959), 336–52, and 38 (1960), 65–75 and 241–61; S. Perubčan, *Sin in the Old Testament*, 1963; W. Mann, *HTG* i, 468–79.

Odilo Kaiser

B. *New Testament*. 1. We only find anything approaching a theology of reconciliation or atonement in the pauline corpus (Rom 5:10f; 11:15; 2 Cor 5:18–20; Eph 2:16; Col 1:20f). If we leave out of account the terms associated with atonement (principally *hilaskesthai*), we are left with the following terms which are relevant for the theme of reconciliation: the noun *katallagē* (=reconciliation: Rom 5:11; 11:15; 2 Cor 5:18f), the verb *katallassō* (=to reconcile: Rom 5:10; 2 Cor 5:18–20), and the augmented verbal form *apokatallassō* (=to reconcile: Eph 2:16; Col 1:20, 22). In addition we have *diallassō* (=to reconcile) in 1 Cor 7:11 (and in Mt 5:24, though this lies outside the context of reconciliation theology, as also *sunallassō* in Acts 7:26).

2. We must not identify the characteristically pauline theology of reconciliation with pauline soteriology in general, as if any soteriological expressions and motifs found in his epistles could be put under the heading of a theology of reconciliation. Despite its uniquely pauline characteristics and its fairly thematic development in 2 Cor 5:18–20 and Col 1:20, 22, the theme of reconciliation occurs so sporadically in Paul (as, for example, in

Rom 5:10f, where it serves to give point to what he says about justification, and in Rom 11:15 and Eph 2:16) that it cannot assume this role. It must therefore be regarded as one of several fundamental soteriological motifs together with the forgiveness of sins, ↗ redemption, sanctification (↗ holy), and ↗ justification. It stands in particularly close association with this last (Rom 5) as it does with the idea of vicariousness, but all of these different motifs play their part in the full development of pauline soteriology.

3. It is a well-founded view that, from the point of view of the history of the tradition, the theme of reconciliation has its origin in 'the doxology of the hellenistic community' (Käsemann 49), that is, in a hymnic and liturgical tradition. In view of their immediate context Col 1:20, 22 and Eph 2:16 presuppose such a hymnic tradition, though in their present form they have been worked over by Paul. Paul himself could have arrived at the theme of reconciliation and made it the basis of what he has to say on this subject starting from such a tradition, as would seem at least plausible on the basis of an analysis of Rom 11:15 and especially 2 Cor 5:19–21. As is suggested by its *Sitz im Leben* in the hellenistic community, this tradition could have originated in the cosmological aspect of the concept of reconciliation which took in the cosmic totality, the world as a whole (2 Cor 5:19; Col 1:20). Under the influence of eschatologically coloured thinking orientated towards the church and emanating from judaeo–christian circles, it could then have been given a new meaning emphasising the anthropological aspect with reference to the

reconciliation of the faithful. This is suggested by the juxtaposition of both aspects in 2 Cor 5:19f and Col 1:20, 22. Among the texts which refer to the cosmological aspect of reconciliation there are those which emphasise the reconciliation of the world with God (2 Cor 5:19) and others which speak of reconciliation within the cosmos, that is, within a divided humanity (Rom 11:15; Col 1:20; Eph 2:16).

4. The whole idea of reconciliation or atonement was developed against the dark background of the knowledge of a lost condition of wholeness, of division and rebellion (Eph 2:2), of mutual hostility, alienation under the law and the power of sin (Rom), disobedience (Rom 8:7), estrangement of man from God (Eph 2:12), and the revelation of the anger of God (Rom 1:18–32; see also Eph 2:16b; Col 1:21; etc). In his great love (Rom 5:5, 8; Eph 2:4) God has opened a way for many out of this hopeless situation, and this is the way of atonement, the result of his gracious will (Col 1:19). In the Christ-event, in the death and resurrection of Jesus, God has reconciled the world and mankind to himself and established peace (Rom 5:1; Eph 2:15; Col 1:20), removed hostility (Rom 5:10; Eph 2:14), saved sinners from his anger (Rom 5:9), not reckoning to them their sins (2 Cor 5:19; cf Rom 5:8). The death of Jesus on the cross (Col 1:20, 22; Rom 5:6–11) brought about the reconciliation of man with God and opened up to them the way to the Father (Eph 2:16) and access to grace (Rom 5:2). Mankind, previously divided into the Jew and gentile, is reconciled 'in one body' (Eph 2:16). The establishment of the lordship of Christ in the cosmic totality

which followed on the resurrection brought about a universal reconciliation (Col 1:20).

5. Reconciliation is the result of God's act deriving from his sovereign and absolutely free initiative. It is not sinful men who carry out the reconciliation nor does it have anything to do with cult and sacrifice. All that men do is receive the reconciling act of God (Rom 5:10). God reconciles the world and especially mankind to himself (2 Cor 5:18; see also Col 1:20, 22; Eph 2:16). It comes about independently of any disposition on the part of men, from the pure grace of God to sinners (Rom 5:8) and those who were his enemies (5:10). As brought about by God, reconciliation is a reality, a condition which is already in existence (Rom 5:11; 2 Cor 5:18–19) even before it is accepted and appropriated by men (2 Cor 5:19). Reconciliation occurs, this antecedent reality becomes event, when the message concerning this reality is delivered to the community through 'the ministry of reconciliation' (2 Cor 5:18), in the preaching of 'the word of reconciliation' 5:19), when it is announced and offered by its ministers who take the place of Christ and when those addressed, those to whom the invitation is made, answer and accept the offer. This antecedent reality reaches its goal in this process of offering and acceptance but man also participates in it. His indispensable contribution is to allow this abiding reconciling activity of God to become an event for him; he must himself be reconciled to God (2 Cor 5:20). His action in the whole process is to 'allow' it to happen. He has to listen to the message of reconciliation and take hold of the new

existence in peace and friendship with God which reconciliation opens up to him. In this way reconciliation considered as antecedent event and as a process stands within the unique tension in pauline theology between the indicative and the imperative of salvation, between the gift of salvation and the need to accept the gift.

6. The newly created possibility of association with God opened up by reconciliation or atonement takes the form of a new life lived for God 'in Christ'. Sinners are justified by the blood of Christ (Rom 5:9) and reconciled to God by his death (v 10). Reconciliation takes place through Christ, God has reconciled the world to himself through Christ (2 Cor 5:19), through the blood of his cross he has established peace (Col 1:20). In the blood of Christ Jew and gentile have come close together (Eph 2:14), reconciled to God through the cross (2:16). Christ can therefore be regarded, in Eph 2:16, as the subject of the reconciling action, the 'architect' of reconciliation, since it comes about by virtue of his death 'in his body of flesh' (Col 1:22). If we start out from the christological aspect of reconciliation we shall find many points of contact with other basic New Testament statements about the salvation which comes from the death of Jesus (especially Heb 2:17; 1 Pet 1:18f). Though in itself not a primary category of pauline theology, reconciliation is permeated with some of the most fundamental themes found in his writings.

7. The seemingly untheological expression in 1 Cor 7:11 can also find its place in the pauline theology of reconciliation by virtue of the context (vv

12–16). The peace to which the spouses are called by God and in which they are to live (v 15) is that brought about by God which enables them to be reconciled to each other irrespective of human views on their problems. Finally, the warning of Jesus in Mt 5:24 takes on a new urgency against the background of the theology of reconciliation, since the duty encumbent on men to be reconciled to each other is founded on the reconciling act of God.

Bibliography: Apart from the commentaries on the texts referred to, see F. Büchsel, *TDNT* I, 255–9; R. Gyllenberg, *RGG* VI[3], 1371–3; Léon Roy, *DBT*, 423f; A. Nygren, *Die Versöhnung als Gottestat*, Gütersloh 1932; E. Percy, *Die Probleme der Kolosser- und Epheserbriefe*, Lund 1946; V. Taylor, *Forgiveness and Reconciliation*, London 1946; J. Michl, *TQ* 128 (1948), 442–62; J. Dupont, *La Réconciliation dans la Théologie de Saint Paul*, Paris 1953; E. Lohse, *Märtyrer und Gottesknecht*, Göttingen 1955, 158–62; H. Schlier, *Littérature et théologie pauliniennes*, 1960, 127–41; G. W. H. Lampe, *Reconciliation in Christ*, London 1956; K. Prümm, *Diakonia Pneumatos* II/1, Rome 1960, 127–41; E. Schweizer, *TLZ* 86 (1961), 241–56; L. Cerfaux, *Christ in the Theology of Saint Paul*, London and New York 1959; E. Käsemann, *Bultmann Festschrift*, Tübingen 1964, 47–59; A. Vögtle, *LTK* X[2], 734–6.

Rudolf Pesch

Redemption

A. The most general term for to redeem is *hôšiya'* (Gk: *sōzein*), 'to help', 'to deliver'. Yahweh is the redeemer, ↗ saviour *par excellence*. The way in which the meaning develops is significant: first, deliverance from temporal needs and dangers (see Judg 15:18; 1 Sam 10:19; 2 Sam 22:3); then the term comes to be applied to the chosen people in their deliverance in the episode of the Reed Sea at the time of their exodus from Egypt (Ex 14:13; 15:2) or else in their being delivered from exile (Is 45:17; 46:13; 52:10); finally it is deliverance from sin that comes to be emphasised (Is 33:22f; Ezek 26:28f). Thus the word comes to express messianic salvation, and this is its primary meaning in the New Testament. Here it designates not only rescue from needs and from sin, but has a positive meaning too, namely the possession of all the blessings of the eschatological age. Even in the case of the healing of the sick the meaning of *sōzein* extends beyond that which it bears in profane usage (Lk 7:50; 17:19; Mk 5:36; 10:52; cf Acts 4:9–12): sickness and death were regarded as consequences of sin.

The salvation which Jesus brings begins in the temporal order. The first group of New Testament passages which speak of messianic salvation are those which refer to the foreshadowings of it in the Old Testament (Acts 7:25; Judg 5; Heb 11:7; 1 Pet 3:20); next are chiefly Mt 1:21; 10:22; 18:11; 19:25, and many other passages: Jn 3:17; 5:34; 10:9; 12:47; Acts 2:21; 4:12; etc. Paul speaks solely of messianic salvation. This includes the resurrection (Phil 3:20). Hence the question may be raised whether it is conceived of purely in an eschatological sense or as already present, being, at least incipiently, already in the possession of the faithful. (On Rom 8:24. ↗ hope.) The problem is wholly similar in the case of the ↗ kingdom of God, which in the writings of Paul bears a more eschatological aspect (see 1 Cor 6:9; Gal 5:21). But salvation is also represented as already commencing

(2 Cor 6:2) or even as having commenced (Tit 3:5; 2 Tim 1:9; see also Eph 2:5, 6, 8; Col 2:12). This tension between present and future appears not only in the concept under consideration here but also in the other messianic concepts such as ⁄ kingdom of God, ⁄ epiphany, ⁄ *parousia*, and ⁄ justification (see Gal 5:5). It is upon this tension that the ethical prescriptions for the christian life are based. Salvation has been achieved by Christ on earth, and will be completed. As a community the believers already possess it; but as individuals each one must persevere to the end; no one possesses salvation in such a manner that he cannot lose it.

B. We come now to the more specific terms. The first of these are *gāʾal* and *pādāh* (both are rendered by *lutroun* and its derivatives).

1. *gāʾal* (originally 'to protect', 'shelter'). It is used of persons who are responsible for upholding the rights and interests of those related to them, the persons and possessions of their family (in the broader sense). This responsibility extends even to marriage rights, for by the law of the levirate marriage a childless widow is to be freed from the reproach which this state implies by her nearest kinsman (Lev 25:25f, 48f, 54; Ruth 3:9, 12; 4:1, 6). Yahweh acts in this manner towards his people, for whose salvation he has made himself responsible (by reason of election and ⁄ covenant). He is also the protector, in this sense, of the individual members of the people, the religiously zealous, widows and orphans (see Is 40–55; 62:12; Ps 107:2; 119:54; etc; Prov 23:11). Admittedly when this word is predicated of Yahweh it loses its basic meaning; *gāʾal* then means simply the

act by which God redeems men from alien powers (there is no question here of paying 'ransom' or any kind of compensation for them). Like *hôšiyaʾ gāʾal* comprises three degrees: redemption from temporal evils, which is conferred upon zealous individuals (Prov 23:11), that bestowed upon the chosen people at the exodus (Ex 6:6), and finally that to be bestowed in the salvific age (Is 41:14).

2. *pādāh* means to ransom quite in general, that is to acquire something from the possession of another by payment of something of corresponding value. It is also used of the ransom of the firstborn according to sacred law (Ex 13:13, 15; 34:20; Lev 27:27; Num 18:15ff; Ps 49:8). Yahweh ransoms Israel from Egypt (Deut 9:26; 15:15; 21:8; etc; Mic 6:4); in this the idea is introduced that what has been thus acquired is his 'possession', although no purchase price is mentioned (Is 43:3f represents an exception to this, but it is rhetorically expressed). God always ransoms men of his own grace, and since he is the absolute Lord of the world, he gives no recompense when he ransoms (Köhler, 225). Again here we find a threefold redemption: as the people were led out of Egypt, so too individual men who are zealous for Yahweh's cause are redeemed: David (2 Sam 4:9; 1 Kings 1:29), Jeremiah (Jer 15:21) and others (Jer 31:11; Hos 7:13; 13:14; Zech 10:8; Ps 25:22; 34:22; Job 5:20; 6:23; 33:28; etc). Finally ransom comes in the salvific age: Israel is made free of her sins (Ps 130:8); the redeemed return home rejoicing to Zion (Is 35:10; 51:11).

C. *An exact correspondence is to be found between the chosen terms for redemption in the New Testament and the adumbrations of it in the Old.* What is said of Yahweh in the Old Testament is said of Christ in the New. (See Lk 1:68; 2:38; 24:21. In the Qumran texts an anointed one (messiah) is never substituted for God as the subject of *hôšiya²*, *gā²al*, and *pādāh*. This sect held extreme views on the subject of predestination, regarding themselves as the already chosen remnant of Israel, and the others as destined to perdition; it is consistent with these views that they should have regarded a redeeming messiah as unnecessary. See de Lorenzi, 220–23.) In most contexts a purchase price to be paid to someone is excluded. The dominant feature is the granting of freedom, which makes man God's own possession. He redeemed Israel 'for himself' (Esther 13:9 [16]). Eph 1:14 is to be understood in the same sense: it treats of a ransom which at the same time gives rights of possession over the object ransomed. This does not exclude the idea that for the accomplishment of this redemption Christ has paid a price (Rom 3:24; 1 Pet 1:18ff;⁊ blood of Christ), namely his own death, his blood! From this point of view *lutron* (ransom) is to be understood in the sense in which Philo uses it (eg, *De sacr. Abelis et Caini,* 121; *Quis rer. div. heres,* 124; etc), as the means whereby the redemption is effected (thus Tit 2:14; see also Mk 10:45; 1 Tim 2:6). In place, therefore, of ransom money being literally paid to the overlord of the imprisoned and the slaves, we have the labours and the life of him who takes up the cause of those in bondage as their loving and generous benefactor. *agorazein* (= to buy) does however occur in the New Testament (1 Cor 6:20; 7:23; Gal 3:13; 4:5; 2 Pet 2:1; Rev 5:9; 14:3f), and the converse of the same idea is expressed when it is said that sinners are 'sold under sin' (Rom 7:14). Hence the question presents itself whether the purchase price which Christ has paid is his own blood (Rev 5:9) or the curse which he has taken upon himself (Gal 3:13). Is it paid to the devil as lord of this world? To avoid this conclusion it has been assumed that what Paul had in mind was not the sort of bargaining that is carried out in the market-place, but the price paid for the release of slaves. The slave saves money and purchases his freedom by bringing this money to a temple and observing a prescribed ritual whereby the master of the slaves sells him to the particular god of the temple (and thereby obtains the money). In this manner the slave is bought by the god and presented with his freedom. Admittedly this explanation is uncertain. The slaves in question must themselves put forward the money, which finally accrues to their master. The *libertus Caesaris* was previously a *servus Caesaris* and is now free from this slavery; the *libertus Domini* (1 Cor 7:22), on the other hand, was formerly the slave of the devil and is now the slave of God; not only is the christian not free from the service of God, he is actually transferred to Christ as his own 'property' (1 Cor 6:20; 7:23; 2 Pet 2:1). In view of these differences it is advisable to seek a solution in the Old Testament realm of ideas. By the covenant Israel becomes the purchased property of Yahweh (Ex 19:5ff; see Deut 7:6; 14:2; 26:18; see also esp. Mal 3:17 and Ps 135:4). This idea recurs again and again in the

New Testament, especially in 1 Pet 2:9; Tit 2:14; and above all Acts 20:28: 'The Church of God which he obtained with his own blood' that is (referring back to Ex 19:5ff), with 'the blood of the covenant' 'he', that is, the Father (as in the Old Testament) obtained her by the blood of his Son, or else the Son obtained her with his own blood. Hence the manner in which christians are bought by Christ (or by God) is not the fictitious manner in which pagan slaves were 'purchased', but the manner in which Israel was bought from Yahweh by the covenant which was sealed (by blood) so as to make her Yahweh's possession. Further on this ↗ blood, ↗ atonement, ↗ messianism, ↗ passion of Christ, ↗ sin.

D. Not only do the blood, passion and death of Jesus enter as active elements into the redemption which he accomplishes, but also his *resurrection*, Rom 4:25: 'who was put to death for our trespasses and raised for our justification'. The glorified and exalted Lord is author of life (Acts 3:13, 15). 'If Christ had not been raised, then your faith would be 'illusory' and you would still be in your sins' (1 Cor 15:17). The pauline conception is that as in Adam, so too in Christ, mankind is one (one body). His resurrection is not only an example; nor, again, is it only the evidence on the basis of which we believe. Rather he is the firstborn (v 20) of mankind which is to be led back from death and sin to the Father and to life. In Christ, in his death and resurrection, man returns to God. Admittedly by a personal act of his own ↗ freedom exercised in ↗ faith and ↗ baptism (see Rom 6:3ff), every individual Christian must enter into this union with Christ and must 'grow together' with him (Rom 6:5). Thus the death and resurrection of Christ is really the cause of our redemption, which bestows upon us release from guilt and at the same time newness of life.

Bibliography: J. J. Stamm, *Erlösen und Vergeben im AT*, Bern 1940; Köhler, 225–7; von Rad I, 177f; A. R. Johnson, *VT* Suppl 1 (1953), 67–77; A. Médebielle, *DB(S)* III, 1–262; F. Büchsel, *TDNT* I, 124–8 and IV, 328–56; A. van den Born, Haag, 414–21. See also: S. Lyonnet, *De peccato et redemptione*, Rome 1958; S. Lyonnet, *Gregorianum* 39 (1958), 295–318; S. Lyonnet, *VD* 36 (1958), 3–15; 37 (1959), 136–52; and 38 (1960), 65–75 and 241–61; A. Kirchgässner, *Erlösung und Sünde im NT*, Freiburg 1950; Daniel a Conchas, *VD* 30 (1952), 14–29, 81–91, and 154–69; L. De Lorenzi, 'Alcuni temi di Salvezza nella letteratura di Qumran', *Riv. bibl. it.* 5 (1957), 197–253; F. X. Durrwell, *The Resurrection: A Biblical Study*, London 1969³; J. Gewiess, *LTK* III², 1016–20.

Johannes B. Bauer

Remnant

The idea of the remnant plays a prominent part in the divine economy of salvation right from the outset. Noah together with his family appear as a remnant of the kind in question in their deliverance from the flood (see Gen 7:23). Under the aegis of Joseph, himself granted particular guidance by God, the family of Jacob develops into 'a great band of survivors' (Gen 45:7) whose lives have been preserved. At the time of Elijah, when the chosen people fell into grave apostasy, the following promise from God is pronounced: 'I will leave seven thousand in Israel, all the knees that have not bowed to Baal' (1 Kings 19:18). In the light of this we can understand how the writing prophets, in whose oracles the remnant idea acquires a growing significance, found this concept already to hand in a developed form and were able to incorporate it in their messages, eg, Amos 5:15: 'remnant of Joseph'. In the concept of the remnant in general a twofold aspect can be discerned: 1. when the people as a whole are subject to a threat only *a remnant* of it will escape; 2. but the fact that a remnant *does survive and does remain* is full of promise and extends beyond the particular downfall which is threatened into the future. On this showing the remnant as viewed by the prophets is a small chosen part of the people which survives the threatened condemnation and punishment by the mercy of God in order to become the new bearers of the promises. For the judgement of God never brings absolute and unmitigated punishment upon the sinners. The possibility of repentance and conversion always remains, the remnant that is to be delivered is never lacking. In the light of this it also becomes intelligible that right from its origins the idea of the remnant is connected with that of Israel's eschatological hope.

In the history of revelation, at least in its broad outline, three stages of development in the concept of the remnant may be distinguished:

1. In the *pre-exilic period* Amos, Micah, and Isaiah are the chief predicters of a remnant which is to survive God's condemnation and punishment, which he allows to be accomplished by means of the Assyrian army, and to remain in the promised land (Is 1:9; 17:5ff; 24:6, 13; Amos 3:12; 4:11). As against this it must be admitted that Is 11:11–16 does give the impression that the delivered remnant is to consist of homecoming captives. In the vision in which Isaiah receives his vocation he undergoes a ritual purification (Is 6:7) which has the force of an example for this remnant. It stands solidly in union with the prophet and as a result its basic nature receives the stamp as does his, being admitted to a share in the divine holiness; for it is this that transforms and moulds afresh not only Isaiah's nature but that of the remnant too (see Is 6:13; 4:3). According to Is 7 (see the name of Isaiah's son 'a remnant shall return' 7:3) faith is the *criterium distinctionis* between the remnant that remains faithful to God and the broad mass of the people, who are destined to ruin together with Ahaz. In the last analysis the remnant owes its conversion and survival to the compassion of God (Is 10:20f; 17:7f; 28:5; Mic 5:6f). Is 14:32 is to be understood as presenting a new factor in determining who is to belong to the remnant. According to this passage it is to consist of the 'poor', this term being understood not in the sociological but in the religious sense which it came increasingly to bear in the course of the progressive unfolding of revelation. Thus in the preaching of the prophets, and above all in that of Isaiah, the 'quantitative' Israel was replaced by a people chosen on a qualitative basis from the holy, the faithful, and the 'poor'—*in fact, the holy remnant.*

2. At the time of *the Babylonian exile* the titles of honour belonging to the remnant were transferred to the returning exiles (Jer, Ezek, Zeph), see Jer 23:3; 24:5–8; 31:2–7. The journey home to Palestine, the new exodus made possible for the remnant by God's

mercy (Ezek 48), will again inwardly transform the rescued captives, will prepare them for a new covenant with God, will make of them a new Israel (Ezek 11:13–20). Once the remnant has returned home it will enter into the closest possible union with God in a new temple (Ezek 40–42) in a new holy city that is to be called after God and to bear no other name (Ezek 48:35).

3. In *the period after the exile*, then, the identification of the holy remnant with the newly constituted community of Israel is fully achieved. It is within this general period that we encounter the special interests apparent in the chroniclers' version of history, which were supported by the post-exilic prophets. It was sought to prove that the great, but hitherto unfulfilled promises to Israel, including the messianic ones, were in fact realised in the theocratic community of post-exilic times (see Zech 8:11–15; Ezra 9:8, 13–15).

The remnant, then, represents a link between the community threatened with condemnation and punishment on the one hand, and that awaiting the fulfilment of the promises on the other. In the development of revelation we can trace its course from a stage at which it is applied to groups of the present (Gen 7:23; 45:7; 1 Kings 19:18; Is 1:8f—the ↗ prophet, together with his disciples and children also count as a remnant, Is 8:16–18) to a stage at which it signifies a future entity (Is 7:10ff; Ezek 11:13ff). The constitution of this remnant is determined not quantitatively according to its numerical size but qualitatively by the faith and holiness of its members. To it, as the nucleus which remains loyal, *all the privileges of the chosen people* are trans-ferred. Above all it becomes *the bearer of the promises of salvation*; God's plan of salvation is accomplished for it and through it. Hence too its close connections with the hope for a messiah (Is 7:10ff; 9:6; 11:1ff) and for the Zion of the final age (Is 4:2–6; 28:16f; 37:32).

Is 10:22f and 1:9 are cited in Rom 9:27ff. The New Testament concept of the 'little flock' (Lk 12:32) is close in meaning to the Old Testament idea of the remnant. But there is a great difference between Jesus' message and the radical interpretation of the remnant idea in, eg, pharisaism or Qumran.

Bibliography: R. de Vaux, 'Le "Reste d'Israel" d'après les prophètes', *RB* 42 (1933), 526–39; W. E. Müller, *Die Vorstellung vom Rest im AT*, Leipzig 1939 (dissertation); Herntrich and Schrenk, *TDNT* IV, 194–214; J. Jeremias, 'Der Gedanke des "Heiligen Restes" im Spätjudentum und in der Verkündigung Jesu', *ZNW* 42 (1949), 184–94; E. W. Heaton, 'The root *š'r* and the Doctrine of the Remnant', *JTS* 3 (1952), 27–39; F. Dreyfus, 'La Doctrine du Reste d'Israel chez le Prophète Isaie', *RSPT* 39 (1955), 361–86; B. J. Alfrink, Haag 1427f; J. Morgenstern, 'The Rest of Nations', *JSS* 2 (1957), 225–31.

Heinrich Gross

Renewal (newness)

Everything earthly is subject to transitoriness and must be renewed from time to time. According to Aeschylus (*Prometheus*, 955 and 960) even Zeus and the gods of Olympus are called 'new gods' (*hoi neoi theoi* or *neōteroi theoi*), since the ancient race of Titans whom they overthrew ruled before them. As is well known, Socrates was condemned

because, so it was alleged, he worshipped new gods (*Apol.* XIII: *hetera de
daimonia kaina*). In the worship of the
ruler during the hellenistic and Roman
periods the word *neos* was often used in
connection with the name of a particular god (Dionysos, Asklepios, etc) to
emphasise that the monarch in question
represented the deity in question in a
new form (see *TDNT* IV, 896). The
Greek Stoics spoke of a renewal of the
earth through fire (see H. Diels,
Doxographi Graeci, 1929, 609, line 18:
tōn ontōn ananeoumenōn ek puros . . .).

As regards the use of terms: though
the two Greek words which correspond
to the English *new* (*kainos* and *neos*) have
slightly different nuances—in modern
Greek *kainos* is more literary, while *neos*
belongs to everyday speech—both occur
as synonyms in LXX and in the New
Testament (see *TDNT* III, 447f). In the
Hebrew Old Testament *ḥādāš* generally corresponds to both.

In the *Old Testament* renewal can be
referred to profane realities such as the
treaty between the Jews and the
Romans (1 Macc 12:1, 3, 10, 16), or
friendly relations of old standing with
the Spartans which were renewed by
the Maccabees after their victory (1
Macc 14:22; 15:17). Any mention of
new gods was naturally taboo (see
Deut 32:17).

The striking prophetic lament for the
destruction of Jerusalem issues in the
trustful prayer that God may renew the
good fortune of times gone by (Lam
5:21). This prayer was heard, as was
that of a later time found in Ben Sirach
over the persecution of Israel by the
Syrians in the second century BC: 'show
signs anew, and work further wonders . . . destroy the adversary and wipe

out the enemy' (Sir 36:6–7). Naturally
the sacred vessels of the temple which
had been removed must also be
replaced (1 Macc 4:36) and a new
altar set up (4:47). The music available
for temple worship also had to be
continually increased and expanded
(Ps 33:3; 40:3; 96:1).

The texts which speak of the renewal
of man are obviously much more
important. God renews the youth of the
psalmist like the eagle's (Ps 103:5).
This is based on the ancient belief that
after a certain number of years the
eagle acquired a new plumage. After
his serious lapse into sin David prayed
the Lord to renew a right spirit within
him (Ps 51:10). Of course, man's body
was also renewed throughout his whole
lifetime (Ps 38:3). The patient Job
thinks sadly of the good days of the past
before his misfortunes came upon him,
days in which his glory and reputation
were renewed from day to day (Job
29:20), while now he lies sick and
despised by all.

In the messianic age Zion will be
given a new name (Is 62:12) and
Yahweh will give to those who fear him
a new heart and a new spirit (Ezek
11:19; 18:31; 36:26). He will enter
into a new covenant with all the house
of Israel (Jer 31:31) despite the fact
that they had broken the old covenant
(v 32). His intention is to renew Israel
in love (Zeph 3:17). Divine wisdom
remains unchanged and unchangeable
but it constantly renews the whole
cosmos (Wis 7:27). As early as Is 65:17
we hear of an eschatological re-creation
of the entire cosmos: 'for behold, I
create new heavens and a new earth,
and the former things shall not be
remembered or come to mind'. Much

744

the same is expressed in Is 66:22: 'for as the new heavens and the new earth which I will make shall remain before me ... so shall your descendants and your name remain'.

The prophets await a new cosmos since they hope for a humanity renewed in its innermost being and more faithful to God, a humanity which will have a heart no longer insensitive as stone but a heart of flesh (Ezek 36:26). This was an ideal representation which was only to be fulfilled in Christ, who was meek and humble of heart (Mt 11:29) and showed compassion for the ignorant and erring (Heb 5:2; 4:15).

In the *Old Testament Apocrypha* we find reference to both individual and cosmic renewal. In the small book entitled *Joseph and Asenath*, Joseph in Egypt prays for his Egyptian bride Asenath, the daughter of a priest from Heliopolis (see Gen 41:45): 'Lord God of the fathers of Israel ... bless this young girl, give her life and renew her through thy Holy Spirit' (8:9). Just before her conversion to judaism Joseph said to her: 'from now on you are created and given life anew' (15:5). The *Testament of Levi* mentions a consoling event in the history of the Jews: 'they returned home to their desolate land and renewed there the house of the Lord' (17:10).

In the *Ethiopian Book of Enoch* (72:1) the angel Uriel reveals to the author the course of world history divided into epochs, a history which unfolds until 'the new creation which lasts for ever will be created'. As 91:16 makes clear, this refers to 'the new heavens' which will give seven times more light than now. In much the same way the *Book of Jubilees* (1:29) speaks of 'the day of

the new creation when heaven and earth and all that they contain will be renewed' (see also 4:26).

This idea of a renewal, a transformation of man into a 'new creation', occurs also in the rabbinical literature (see SB II, 421), though the reference here is not to a moral renewal brought about by grace, in the sense in which the New Testament speaks of man being born again, since this would only be possible in the messianic age. He who turns to judaism becomes a 'new man' or a 'newly born child' in a juridical sense by accepting proselyte baptism (see further SB II, 422f).

In the *Qumran texts* the concept of renewal or newness plays a certain role in so far as the community refers to itself simply as the new covenant in the land of Damascus (CD VI, 19; VIII, 21). The 'men of scorn' have spread false reports about this new covenant and its prescriptions and have fallen into apostasy (CD XX, 11; see also CD XIX, 34 and 1 Qp Hab II, 3). This idea of renewal also has a liturgical aspect not unconnected with the heavenly bodies: 'on the occurrence of the festivals according to the days of the month ... when they are 'renewed' (i.e, come round again), the great day for the All-holy One ...' (1 QS x, 3-4). The duty of putting off the old man of sin and renewing oneself is expressed within the Qumran community most clearly in the community hymn book (the *Hodayot*): 'for the sake of thy glory thou hast purified man from sin that he may be holy ... and that he may be united with the sons of thy truth ... in order to renew himself with everything that is ...' (1 Q x, 10-14). There is also occasionally a reference to a new creation (as in 1 Q IV, 25), but without further specification. (See on this whole question Kosmala 226ff who thinks in terms of a renewal in two stages at Qumran: the first, which is imperfect, takes place during this life, the second at the end of life.)

Philo records the view of some Stoics that after the great cosmic conflagration when the new earth will be created (*De Aeternitate Mundi*, cap. 18), the fire will not be entirely extinguished but a part of it will remain in the form of phantom shapes or chimerae (*plasmata*). We learn from the same author that not every renewal is for the good. He gives the case of the emperor Caligula, a young man very keen on renewal but devoid of any human feeling since he intended to set up a statue of Jupiter in the temple of Jerusalem (*Leg. ad Caium*, cap. 29). It was understandable that in this case the Jews should expect at least one thing from the army of occupation, that they should not attempt any innovation with regard to the temple and its worship (see cap. 32).

As is well known, the harmony and health of the human body only obtains for a short time, but the beauty of the spirit adorned with virtues can be renewed and rejuvenated as long as life lasts (*Vita Mosis*, cap. 15). Other references to renewal in Philo can be studied by referring to the index of H. Leisegang (Berlin 1930), I, 417 and II, 544ff.

The *New Testament* speaks of newness, as the very title of the collection suggests. We are told that those who listened to Jesus wondered at his 'new teaching' (Mk 1:27). This may refer in the first place to the external form in which his teaching was presented, since

he taught 'as one having authority and not like the scribes' (Mt 7:29). The arresting formula 'but I say unto you . . .' with which he introduced his sayings on the Old Testament laws, enlarging, correcting, or even superseding them (e.g, the law about divorce, Mk 10:6; Mt 19:10 and parallels), as well as many rabbinical rules (Mt 12:2ff; 15:2ff), shows clearly that he could with justice speak of his teaching as new wine which could no longer go into old wineskins (Mt 9:17), in other words, into old forms and rites. Whereas the old covenant on Mount Sinai was sealed with the blood of young oxen (Ex 24:5–8), Christ sealed the new covenant between God and man with his own sacrificial blood (Lk 22:20). He is therefore the mediator of this covenant (Heb 9:15; 12:24). We read of a new covenant as early as Jeremiah (31:31). Paul rejoiced to be a minister of this covenant (2 Cor 3:6). But Christ has brought us not only new teaching and a new covenant but also a 'new commandment' (Jn 13:34), new at least in its motivation and comprehensiveness since by it we are even commanded to love our enemies (Mt 5:44). At the end of his sacrificial life Jesus speaks of the new wine of the eschatological banquet (Mk 14:25), and is buried in a new grave, that is, one not previously used (Mt 27:60; Jn 19:41). Soon afterwards we find his followers speaking in new languages (Mk 16:17; Acts 2:4). God can now be approached by the new way which has been opened up (Heb 10:20).

This new religious ideal—which was, initially at least, quite incomprehensible to the Athenians (Acts 17:19ff)—required for its fulfilment a new humanity, a new creation (Gal 6:15). Here the institutions of the old order, circumcision in particular, had no further role to play. Christ himself created this new humanity when he broke down the old wall of division between Jew and gentile (Eph 2:14) by his death on the cross. What is important now is a new mind (Rom 12:2), a new spirit (Rom 7:6) and a new life (Rom 6:4)—in a word, to put off the old man and put on the new (Eph 4:22ff). This new way of life is mediated through baptism, in which our 'old man' is mystically buried with Christ and rises to a new life with him (Rom 6:3–6). When anyone through baptism is 'in Christ' he is a new creation (2 Cor 5:17): 'the old has passed away; behold, the new has come'. In Tit 3:5 baptism is described as a rebirth and renewal by means of the Holy Spirit. Christ is not just the basic cause but also the prototype and model of this new way of life (Eph 4:24). Paul never tires of bringing home constantly to the Christians he addresses the serious duty of a continual personal renewal. This emerges clearly in Eph 4:23 and especially in 2 Cor 4:16 if we assume with J. Dupont (*Sun Khristō[i]* 1, Paris 1952, 129) that Paul, in speaking of the 'inner man' who must be renewed from day to day, understands this term in much the same way as the 'new man' of Eph 4:24 and elsewhere. This continual renewal of the baptised Christian takes place by means of 'the knowledge after the image of his creator', as Col 3:10 states in the illuminating prospective of the future contained in this letter. In the light of this there is no longer gentile or Jew, barbarian, Scythian, slave, or free; only Christ who is all and

in all. (In the light of the movement for racial equality today we can see how 'modern' the thought of Paul is.)

According to Heb 6:4 it is clearly impossible for those who have been once enlightened (baptised) and have tasted the heavenly food to be 'renewed in repentance' (*anakainizein*) if they fall away from their faith by a conscious act of will. It may be possible however to accept the interpretation of O. Michel that, though it may be impossible for man to do so, it is not beyond the reach of God (see Mk 10:27). We can at least say that this objective impossibility (of finding the true way once again) is due to the subjective incapacity of the one who, through religious obtuseness, throws away the precious gift of faith (see H. Strahtmann, *Der Brief an die Hebräer*, 1963, 105).

G. Schneider holds the view that since Jesus never speaks explicitly in the gospels of a new creation Paul must have taken this *theologoumenon* from the Old Testament or the Apocrypha. This latter hypothesis is entirely possible and there is not a great difference in time between some of the Apocrypha and Paul; but we should recall that Jesus spoke to Nicodemus of the absolute necessity of being born anew of water and the Spirit (Jn 3:5). This could well have been a decisive influence on Paul at the time when he was composing what we may call a theology of baptism in Rom 6. We may suppose that he was acquainted with the ruler of the Jews to whom Jesus addressed his words. Hence it is neither necessary nor even likely that Paul borrowed from Zoroastrianism, the Stoics, or the gnostics. We could in any case have concluded this from texts such as 2 Cor

6:14. (See the remarks on this subject in Schneider, 262f and 269f: he rightly points out that Christ does not merely restore what was lost in Adam as the gnostics supposed. Through him man obtains much more than what he had previously and therefore we can speak of a new creation in the real sense of the term.)

The point of departure for the renewal of humanity and the cosmos as the saving event of Christ and its fulfilment is described in *Revelation*. Here we find a description of the glory of the new (heavenly) Jerusalem (3:12; 21:2) and the announcement of a new heaven and a new earth (21:1; see also 2 Pet 3:13) in much the same terms as is Is 65:17; 66:22. New names will be given (2:17; 3:12), new hymns will be heard (5:9; 14:3). The mighty apocalyptic vision ends with the permanent renewal of the cosmic whole (21:5). This shows that the 'total otherness of the christian situation' (Bultmann II, 206) applies not just to men. Inanimate creation will also be freed from the bondage of decay in order to share in the glory of the children of God (cf Rom 8:21).

Bibliography: H. D. Wendland, *Vom Menschenbild des NT* (Festgabe H. Schreiner), Gütersloh 1953, 306–27; R. A. Harrisville, 'The Concept of Newness in the New Testament', *JBL* 74 (1955), 69–79; E. Sjöberg, 'Neuschöpfung in den Toten-Meer-Rollen', *ST* 9 (1955), 131–6; F. Baudraz, Allmen 210ff; G. Schneider, 'Die Idee der Neuschöpfung beim Apostel Paulus und ihr religionsgeschichtlicher Hintergrund', *TTZ* 68 (1959), 257–70; H. Kosmala, *Hebräer-Essener-Christen*, Leiden 1959, 209–39; E. Larsson, *Christus als Vorbild*, Copenhagen 1962, 197–210; *DBT* 694–8; Bultmann II, 203ff; H. W. Bartsch, *BHHW* 1302f; G. Ladner, *RAC* VI, 240–75; SB II, 421f; *TDNT* III, 447–54 and IV, 896–901.

Johannes Kosnetter

Rest

The *rest of God* after his work of creation is not to be understood anthropomorphically (as though in some way God rested after work as man rests after the ↗ work which he has done), but expresses a theological idea: the ↗ creation is the first act of salvation history, and after its completion God rests. It is now that he can make a ↗ covenant with his creation, just as it is the rest after the flood that makes it possible for him to enter into covenant with Noah (Gen 9:8–17). The sign of the covenant in the latter case is the rainbow, in the former the sabbath (de Vaux, 480f). Thus the rest of God has significance as an element in salvation history.

For *mankind* rest (*menûḥâh*, etc; *anapausis, katapausis*, etc) is primarily an interval amid the toils and sufferings of everyday, of human life in general. There is above all the rest which man longs for after his work in the heat of the day (Eccles 4:6; 6:5; Sir 11:19 etc). But the recovery of health after the torment of fever is also rest (Sir 38:14), as also is sleep (Sir 40:5f) and even death (Sir 30:17; 38:23; Job 21:13). For a young woman marriage means rest in the house of her husband (Ruth 1:9; 3:1), while the wife is 'a pillar of rest' for the husband (Sir 36:25). This rest is a gift of God (Ruth 1:9), as also is the deeper form of rest which God bestows on his people, namely, rest from hostile incursions by alien peoples. When the land which Yahweh had given his people as an ↗ inheritance was finally taken possession of by them, this marked the point at which he finally 'brought Israel to rest' (Deut 12:9f; 25:19; Josh 1:13; 11:23; 21:43–5).

Yet the promises are not yet finally fulfilled; as promises they point on to a time of fulfilment in the future far beyond the time of Joshua (see Heb 4:8 and von Rad II, 383). Meanwhile the struggles continue. What was initiated in David's reign had to be continued under Solomon (1 Chron 22:9): 'He shall be a man of rest. I will give him rest from all his enemies round about'. Already during the wilderness wanderings this gift of rest bestowed by God was closely connected with the cult. The ark of the covenant marked out where the place of 'rest' is to be (Num 10:33), and David had the intention of building a 'house of rest' for the ark even while devoting himself wholly to the quite unrestful activity of conquering the promised land (1 Chron 28:2). Again, Jerusalem is to become the place of rest for the messiah (Is 11:10). Solomon can build the temple (1 Kings 5:18) and pray to God: 'Come to your resting-place!' (2 Chron 6:41). For the writers of Chronicles, covenant and cult are made actual in the temple of Solomon, and it is there precisely that rest is achieved (1 Chron 22:9, 18; 28:2). Again, Yahweh dwells in Jerusalem for ever (1 Chron 23:25). Rest and a reign of peace (1 Chron 17:9) are characteristic privileges of the theocracy, which is associated with the covenant made with the patriarchs (see A. Noordtzij, *RB* [1940], 161–8). Again the rest of God appears in connection with the covenant and salvation.

In the wisdom books wisdom, seeking a place of rest among the peoples, settles upon Zion (Sir 24:7). It is in a certain sense identified with the sanctuary at Jerusalem (see Ps 132:8–14). Yet we may recognise a spiritualisation in the manner in which this presence is conceived. The emphasis is placed upon the attitude of God towards men, the benefits which he confers upon them and the happiness which he bestows: the disciple of wisdom finds rest with her after labour and toil (Sir 6:28; 51:27; Wis 8:16).

The *New Testament* is familiar with rest (*anapauein, anapausis*) from physical strain (Mk 6:31; 14:41; Lk 12:19), but also, and primarily, with refreshment of the inner man (1 Cor 16:18; 2 Cor 7:13; Philem 7, 20), and then the eschatological 'rest' of the redeemed mentioned in Rev (14:13). The messianic age of salvation, which is to usher in the ↗ restoration of all things (↗ *parousia*) is to be a time of reinvigoration (*kairoi anapsuxeōs*) (Acts 3:19f). When the Lord comes with power he will give rest (*anesis*) to the oppressed (2 Thess 1:7), which means union of life with Christ (1 Thess 4:17), participation in the ↗ kingdom of God (2 Thess 1:5), and in his ↗ glory (2 Thess 1:12). With this is to be connected the saying in Mt 11:28f, where (as Bauernfeind, *TDNT* I, 353 penetratingly remarks) 'the word comprehends the whole saving work of Jesus'. Certainly it is not the rest of Sir 51:27 that is in question here—that, namely, which the teacher of wisdom has gathered as the fruit of his study. The rest and reinvigoration spoken of by Jesus is the reward of discipleship, and it is he who takes the yoke of Jesus upon himself who enters upon it. No doubt the word *yoke* here also serves to emphasise how different this yoke is from the yoke of the law prescribed by the rabbis; by their rigid and formalistic interpretation of the law they have imposed a crushing burden on the devout. But this is not the essential aspect of the promise. It is not as though the arduous demands which Jesus sets before his disciples did not call for at least as much heroism as the burdensome fulfilment of the minutiae of the law demanded by these fanatics. The difference is that in the latter case it is blind heroism that is demanded, whereas in the former (the requirements of Jesus) it is a heroism that has its eyes open; the blindness imposed by the rabbis leads to an all too literal sabbath rest, whereas the demands of the Lord lead to life, for rest is in fact 'the future kingdom, eternal life' (2 Clem 5:5). An early illustration of the connection between 'yoke' and 'rest' is to be found in the vividly imaginative language of a neo-Babylonian incantation addressed to Ishtar: 'I have taken up thy yoke: give me rest (in return)' (E. Ebeling, *Die akkadische Gebetsserie 'Handerhebung'*, 1953, 60–63: line 26).

A special development of the idea of rest appears in the Letter to the Hebrews (3:7–4:11). The way of the believer leads *from* God *to* God, from the Creator who rests after his work to the final accomplisher, who is the ultimate goal and the final source of rest of the believer. The ethical teaching of the bible points the way which must be followed in order to attain to the goal. In the typological exegesis of Ps 95 Israel is the type of the new people of God, the exodus is the type of the christian's life on earth, Moses is the type of Christ, who leads the way to life, the promised land is the type of messianic ⁄ peace. Many Israelites did not succeed in reaching Canaan (4:8), and God's promise that they are to enter into rest remains in force (4:1), 'so then there remains a sabbath rest for the people of God' (4:9). With regard to those who share in the heavenly calling (3:1), those who believe (4:3), those who have accompanied Christ (3:14), it is no longer the promised land that they will attain, but ⁄ heaven. Thus the doctrine of a mystic rest contained in Hebrews is based upon a christological interpretation of one of the principal themes in Israelite religion. Rest designates alike the rest of God after the work of creation, the temporal ideal of the Israelites, namely entry into Canaan, and now the religious ideal of christians. The rest of the soul is to be in harmony with the will of God (Jer 6:16 = Mt 11:29) and still more eschatological union with God.

Bibliography: H. Lesétre, *DB* v, 1049f; von Rad ɪ, 45, 147f, 225, 231, 288, 304, and 353; and ɪɪ, 269 and 383; de Vaux, 480ff; R. Bultmann, *TDNT* ɪ, 367; O. Bauernfeind, *TDNT* ɪ, 350f and ɪɪɪ, 627f; C. Schneider, *RAC* ɪ, 414–18; C. Spicq, *L'Epître aux Hébreux* ɪɪ, Paris 1953, 95–104; J. B. Bauer, 'Requiem Aeternam', *Heiliger Dienst* 8 (1954), 91–6; J. B. Bauer, 'Das milde Joch und die Ruhe (Mt 11:28f)', *TZ* 17 (1961), 99–106; T. Ohm, *Ruhe und Frömmigkeit*, Cologne 1955; H. Fine, *GL* 33 (1960), 335–48.

Johannes B. Bauer

Restoration

The word *apokatastasis* is chiefly associated with one concept in the teaching of Origen, according to whom human souls and the demons will in the next world be cleansed by a gradual purification and thus come to a resurrection, a reconstitution or *apokatastasis* which excludes the eternity of hell and thereby seems to realise, in the only way possible, the condition in which God can be 'all in all' (1 Cor 15:28).

Apokatastasis, attested since the fourth century BC, means bringing a thing back to its original state. It refers therefore in medicine to healing (compare the use of *apokathistanai* in Mt 12:13 and parallels; Mk 8:25 in connection with miraculous cures; Ex 4:7), in law to restitution, in astronomical language to the return of the stars to their original conjunction. In this sense the conservation of cosmic order, according to *Corpus Hermeticum* VIII, 4, is also founded on the *apokatastasis* (Oepke, *TDNT* I, 390). On the basis of these astronomical suppositions the Stoics taught that after a certain time the world would be destroyed by a conflagration and then return to its former state. In this *apokatastasis* every thing and every person would reappear, although some Stoics spoke only of a similarity, not an identity. It is apparent from the use of the word that it may be identified with *palingenesia* (= ↗ Rebirth). Méhat maintains that the idea of an *apokatastasis* originates in gnosticism (see '"Apocatastase" Origène, Clément d'Alexandrie, Acts 3:21', *VC* 10 [1956], 196–214). It is the main theme of the Valentinians (see Irenaeus, *Adv. Haereses* I 2; 4–5; 8:4), and the term is used by them in the same sense as in Origen: 'the return of things and souls to an original and perfect state' (Méhat, 199).

Although the word *apokatastasis* does not occur in LXX (though the verb

apokathistanai does), the Old Testament is familiar with the idea of a messianic restoration (Proksch, 'Wiederkehr und Wiedergeburt', *Festschrift L. Ihmels*, Leipzig 1928, 1–18; Dietrich, '*šûb šebûth*, Die endzeitliche Wiederherstellung bei den Propheten', *ZAW* suppl. 40, Giessen 1925). In the preaching of the apostles, messianic salvation (*tas hēmeras tautas* = 'these days', Acts 3:24; *peri tēs eis humas kharitos* = 'concerning [God's] grace for you', Eph 3:2f) is represented as the fulfilment of the testimony of the prophets. The idea of return and restoration was often expressed by the phrase *šûb šebûth* (for examples see Proksch). It has been demonstrated since Ewald's article in *Jahrbücher der biblischen Wissenschaft* (Göttingen 1855)—and Proksch and Dietrich are in agreement with him—that *sebuth* does not come from sabah (= to take captive), as supposed in LXX, but from *šûb* (= to return, be restored). Aquila, which disagrees with LXX, has *epi(apo)strephein tēn aikhmalōsian* (= to turn back captivity), and the Vulgate has *convertere captivitatem* and similar expressions. It is therefore here a question of an etymological figure: *šebûth* is the construct state of *šābûth*, and since the noun is always accompanied by another word—eg 'Israel', 'my people', 'the tents of Jacob', 'Judah'—the absolute infinitive, otherwise the usual form, would not be appropriate here. That this expression can also be used outside a messianic context can be seen in Job 42:10—a text, moreover, which, like Ezek 16:53, admits a derivation only from *šûb*, not from *šābāh*. The idea expressed in this term is to be understood as that of *apokatastasis*, and is verbally expressed by *apokathistanai*

751

or *apokathistanein,* which in fact are frequently used in this sense.

The return to an original state is mentioned in Amos 9:11–15; Hos 14:2f; Joel 3:1; Jer 30:18–21; 31:2–9, and is thought of as the period of happiness after days of defeat and disaster, as the time when Israel will return to Yahweh and the Lord will turn in favour towards his people.

It is, however, quite another question whether the restoration announced by the prophets always and exclusively denotes a return to an original state, as it is called in Ezek 16:55 (*leqadnāthān*—the reference is to the conversion of Sodom), or whether a new element, something which was not there before, is contained in the new state. This idea is expressed in the proclamation of the new covenant which God will make with his people in the last days (Jer 31:31–4), the everlasting covenant of peace (Ezek 37:26; Is 54:10). This is not simply the renewal of a previous covenant, but a completely new one, founded on the new disposition of man resulting from both the fruitful operation of divine grace (Ezek 11:19; 36:26) and free human endeavour Ezek 18:31). This renovation includes not only the people of Israel and all mankind, but the whole of the universe as well, and is therefore a re-creation (Is 65:17; 66:22; see also Rev 21; 2 Pet 3:11–13). The bringing about of a new state may also be expressed by *apokatastasis* and *apokathistanai.* Méhat (200) very rightly observes that in combination with a verb the prefix *apo-* not only denotes separation but also completion (cf 'off' as in 'to finish off').

The idea of a restoration and a new world persistently occupied the minds of the apocryphal writers (see SB IV/2. 799–815). The Sibylline Oracles also show familiarity with the idea of a restoration of the world after the world-fire, and of a renovation of man (eg, IV, 45, 173, 179ff; VII, 139–50); this new world, where misery and pain do not exist, is, of course, reserved for the just only.

The expectation of the end (to come about even in the present generation: Elliger, *Studien zum Habakuk-Kommentar vom Toten Meer,* Tübingen 1953, 278) is very conspicuous in the texts of Qumran (Elliger, 276). It is 'the completion of the kingdom of God' (see Molin, *Die Söhne des Lichtes,* Vienna and Munich 1954, 153), the unqualified observance of his law, everlasting life for the just after the present life with its struggle and hardship, the divine presence, salvation (for texts, see Nötscher, 151).

In the New Testament the word *apokatastasis* occurs only once (Acts 3:21). It corresponds in meaning to *palingenesia* in Mt 19:28 where it explains Christ's second coming for the last judgement. Here (3:21), however, his coming is apparently connected with the 'times of refreshment'. The function of the relative clause introduced by *hōn* . . . (=of which) cannot be clearly defined (see the commentaries). It is evident from the passage that the idea of *apokatastasis* in the New Testament has not been influenced by the Stoics; the destructions and restorations embraced in their philosophy are periodical, whereas Christ's Coming is a unique event in history.

Morphologically, this instance is related to Acts 1:6: *ei en tō(i) khronō(i) toutō(i) apokathistaneis tēn basileian tō(i) Israēl* (=will you at this time restore the kingdom to Israel?), and to Mt 17:11; Mk 9:12 (compare Mal 3:23; Sir 48:1–11), and proves that the idea is natural to the Jewish mind of the time. It appears from the context (Peter speaking to the Jews in an attempt to convert them) that *apokatastasis* here includes all that people expected from the messianic time of salvation (for the benefits of this salvation see SB IV, 2, 887–92). The Syrian translation *mūlôjô dezabne* (fulfilment or fullness of time) shows that the object of this expectation was not a mere return to a former state.

It is used in a much richer sense in the passages which describe Christ's work, re-establishment and completion (1 Cor 15:24–8; Eph 1:10; Col 1:20), even though the actual word *apokatastasis* or the corresponding verb has not been used. According to 1 Cor 15:25–8, this completion consists in the subjection of all things to God, even of the devils, to whose dangerous power mankind is still exposed (Eph 6:12), and in the victory over death, so that God's vital power will be effective in those who are saved (cf context).

According to Eph 1:10, Christ's work of perfection or completion consists in this, that 'all things should be united in Christ as the head' (see H. Cazelles, *Bbl* 40 [1959], 342–54). The use of the rare word *anakephalaiousthai* (= to be summed up: Schlier, *TDNT* III, 681f) can be explained on the basis of the apostle's teaching that Christ is the head of the church (Eph 1:22; 4:15; 5:23; Col 1:18), but also of the principalities and powers (Col 2:10). He is Lord and Head 'from the outset' (*pro pantōn*, Col 1:17); he takes the world into the church, into the 'fullness

of the godhead' (Schlier, *TDNT* III, 680; Staab, *RNT* on Eph 1:23). Col 1:20 characterises the achievement of Christ as (re)conciliation (*apokatallaxai*).

The texts referred to have been taken as an *apokatastasis* in Origen's acceptance of the term—that is, as a universal reconciliation. This attempt is understandable, since the doctrine of the universal saving will of God and his all-encompassing grace seem to exclude the doctrine of the eternity of damnation, or to reduce it at least to an impenetrable mystery (it is noteworthy that salvation from eternal fire through the intercession of the just is contemplated in the Sibylline Oracles II, 332f, and that the possibility of an end to the punishments of the underworld is taken into consideration by Seneca, *Apocol.* 14:3). Finally, Michaelis (Gumligen–Bern 1950) understands the general reconstitution as a universal reconciliation (for a brief review of the history of the question and bibliography see 7–12, 16ff). Quite apart, however, from the texts on the eternity of hell which go against this (Mt 25:46; Mk 9:43, 48; Jn 3:36; 2 Thess 1:9), and the reference to the second death (Rev 2:11), it is difficult to accept his view. *Telos* (– end) cannot be understood as 'remnant'—'those who are left'. Eternal damnation is not inconsistent with the universal dominion of God; the context of the other passages does not necessarily imply that 'all' means the whole of mankind, righteous and sinners, faithful and unbelievers. Stauffer (225–31) does not entirely disregard the doctrine of eternal reprobation which is so obvious and explicit in Jn 3:36 and Revelation; yet he accepts a final, universal reconciliation in Paul on the

753

grounds of 1 Cor 15:22–8; Col 2:15 and especially Phil 2:10ff). But universal recognition and praise of Christ does not necessarily imply universal salvation (Jas 2:19). Moreover, the serious warning (Phil 2:12 *hōste ... meta phobou kai tromou*=wherefore ... with fear and trembling) concerning the 'Day of Christ' which follows immediately proves that Paul is concerned not to exclude an irrevocable reprobation.

Bibliography: A. Loosen, *LTK* 1², 708–12; A. Lenz, *RAC* 1, 510–16; A. Oepke, *TDNT* 1, 387–93; G. Müller, *TZ* 14 (1958), 174–90.

Josef Dey

Resurrection

A. *Old Testament*. No actual term for resurrection is to be found in Old Testament Hebrew. Moreover it is only at a late date that we find the resurrection explicitly mentioned as an object of effective and general hope. Nonetheless, in view of the affirmative attitude which the Old Testament does adopt with regard to the question of life after death, it can be said that this hope for resurrection is in harmony with its overall message.

Admittedly a point which Cullmann has recently emphasised with regard to the New Testament does apply also to the Old. It is that we must be careful not to restrict our field of vision within the confines of a 'doctrine of the soul' in the Platonist sense. This could only have the effect of distorting our interpretation by representing the hoped-for resurrection as 'dematerialised', and therefore as a deviation from Old Testament ideas in general. Certainly at all periods of Old Testament writing an awareness of the problem of 'the flesh' is apparent. But this problem is not solved by eliminating the 'body' or by the idea that the soul is 'released' from it, as though the human entity were divided into two. Prior to the hellenistic period the Old Testament has nothing to say of what happens to a man's *nepeš* (=soul) and *rûaḥ* (=spirit) after he dies. For all that death is not conceived of as the end. On the contrary the whole 'I', with its distinctive characteristics as an individual, enters the realm of the dead. It is true that this 'concept of the after-life' (*Fortsetzungsvorstellung*, Köberle) is far from leading to the hope for resurrection as its logical consequence. But it does have the effect that when the idea of resurrection does finally emerge it is conceived of simply as the return of this whole being, which was already believed to live on after death; the idea of the resurrection is not weighed down by reactions against the body. Only in this sense is it valid to assert that 'it is a fundamental idea of the Israelite community that where graves are, there too are resurrections' (*ATAO* 775).

A further point is that, in seeking to understand the essential content and the development of the concept of the resurrection, our minds can only do justice to it if we take cognizance of the fact that the ideas contained in the bible have not been developed *in abstracto* or from a desire for knowledge as an end in itself. Rather these other ideas have constantly been orientated towards and influenced by the idea of God, have been developed in the light of it and permeated by it.

Moreover the basis on which they have been developed has been the progressive achievement of salvation, and hence they have also been related to the idea of retribution. It must be understood, therefore, that in spite of the presence of external influences the Old Testament in its early stages contained no developed idea of the world to come, and that its vision was restricted, rather, to a *preliminary eschatology*, namely the entry into 'the land that I will show you' (Gen 12:1), or the 'land flowing with milk and honey' (Ex 3:8).

The idea of God, which first set a limit to the conception of the world beyond the grave, also provided the roots for this idea. Attempts have been made to trace the idea of the resurrection back to myths of dying and rising gods (thus Baudissin, Sellin; see also Nötscher), or alternatively to the religion of Zarathustra (thus Langton, Pilcher; against this view, see recently F. König). But none of these theories as to the idea having been derived from non-Israelite influences has led to unequivocal and convincing conclusions.

B. Through the whole of the Old Testament we can trace an awareness that God 'makes the dead to live', or alternatively that he can 'bring down to Sheol and raise up' (1 Sam 2:6; Wis 16:13). This statement, with the real conception which it contains of *the absolute power of Yahweh over life and death*, also remains valid in cases in which, following the tendency of Hebrew linguistic usage, 'the consequences of an act are identified with the act itself' (Ehrlich). An instance of this would be a situation in which similar terms were used to describe an escape

from dire need and the actual state of need itself, as for example: 'Thou hast put me in the depths of the Pit' (Ps 88:6), or again: 'Thou hast brought up my soul from Sheol [and] restored me to life' (Ps 30:3). Thus the 'restoration to life' expressed in such terms as these is not resurrection. Allowing for the device of linguistic hyperbole which is used in such cases, we may regard it as equivalent to 'continuing to live', 'not dying'.

This conviction that Yahweh has power over life and death has been embodied in the stories of the lives of the prophets Elijah and Elisha, which contain accounts of the *reawakening* of dead children and also of people who have been buried (1 Kings 17:22; 2 Kings 4:35; 13:21). These awakenings from the dead still do not amount to resurrections, for what is envisaged is only a *return to the earthly mode of existence*, which has no connection with the idea of a transformation of the condition and state of the persons thus restored, to take place at the end of time. Nevertheless we should appreciate their importance as links in the chain of development of the idea, above all because of their clarification of the idea that Yahweh has power over life and death.

C. It is noteworthy that at first no conclusions of universal application were drawn from the concept of Yahweh's power over life and death or from the accounts of awakenings from the dead. In the Old Testament way of regarding such matters the decisive factor in all cases was still the will of God and the effacement of the individual. In the vision of the valley of dry bones when God asks Ezekiel

755

whether these bones, now scattered and dried up, can live, even he gives the circumspect reply; 'Lord, thou knowest' (37:3). From this it is clear that he does indeed ascribe to God the necessary knowledge and power, but that the hope for a general resurrection had not yet become an element in the content of faith. In consequence his vision of the revivification of the bones is merely *parabolic in character*: the bones signify the people in the 'death' of the exile, and the restoration to life is to be understood as a promise of their return to Judah.

The expressions and the realities referred to in Amos 5:2 and Hos 6:1f are of a similar kind. Thus the 'rising on the third day' is not evidence for the presence of the idea of resurrection in the Old Testament, nor, in consequence, can it be taken as evidence for the resurrection of Christ on the third day (↗ three).

D. The cry in Is 26:19 can be understood in a similarly figurative sense (Schwally, Sutcliffe): 'Thy dead shall live, their bodies shall rise, O dwellers in the dust, awake and sing for joy. For thy dew is a dew of light, and on the land of the shades thou wilt let it fall'. The so-called apocalypse of Isaiah belongs to a special literary *genre*, and in consequence the interpretation of this verse concerning the resurrection has usually been made to depend upon the assignment of the chapter to its existing position at a particular time. It cannot be overlooked, however, that the announcement: 'He will swallow up death for ever' (Is 25:8) as well as the context as a whole become clearer if they are taken to point to a real resurrection. Thus this passage is to be regarded as genuinely expressing the expectation of an *eschatological resurrection* (thus also Martin-Achard, Gelin). In terms of content it is connected with the expectation of deliverance and applies to Israel alone (see 26:13f), before whose eyes the prophet sets the increase of the people through the future resurrection as God's compensation for having decimated them in judgement.

In the last of the Servant poems resurrection is not directly spoken of, but in interpreting the promise made to the Servant of God of length of life (53:10), it cannot be overlooked that the image of the lamb which is applied to him, and the sacrificial character of his submission of himself, could not have failed to signify slaughter and death in the minds of Israelites. Correspondingly the new life with its 'vision of light' (1 QIs^a) and the 'satisfaction' which it is to bring, is to be interpreted as a resurrection. To that extent it is to be understood as an individual resurrection involving a transformation of condition and state. Moreover it is related to the ideas of retribution and salvation.

The prophecy of resurrection in Daniel is uncontested and incontestable. The influence of Parsism has been assumed (Bentzen, etc)—not least upon Dan 12:2. It is true that a clear advance in the idea of resurrection is apparent: as used here resurrection is no longer a term confined to those who are to receive salvation; for only some, that is the faithful covenant people, are to 'awaken to eternal life', while the others, on the contrary, are to awaken to 'eternal shame'. But it is precisely these points, the sharp division between the two groups and the eternity of perdition envisaged, which are, of themselves, quite foreign to the eschatology of Parsism. For the latter envisages happiness for all as the final end after purification has been undergone (see Martin-Achard). In Daniel too the idea of resurrection is developed in connection with, and within the limits of the Old Testament's understanding of God and of election. A special feature of the resurrection here is the idea referred to in 12:3 to the effect that 'those who are wise shall shine like the brightness of the firmament; and those who turn many to righteousness, like the stars for ever and ever'. By this image a transformation of state and an illumination is indicated, although it admittedly remains an open question whether these are to be understood as taking place in this world or the next. The section closes with an oracle of consolation addressed to the prophet himself: after his 'rest' he too is to 'stand in your allotted place' (12:13). In spite of the omission of the usual term for resurrection, *qûm*, the context shows that it is this that is meant to be expressed (Bentzen, Nötscher).

The references to resurrection in 2 Macc are also undisputed. Here resurrection is spoken of seven times in the most varied ways. The mother and her sons, that is the so-called Maccabaean martyrs, are convinced that God will give them back 'breath and life' (7:23) and even their tortured 'limbs' (7:11). They hope to be 'raised up . . . to live again for ever' (7:9) and to obtain 'resurrection' (7:14). Admittedly the application of these references is too individual, and the whole episode is too strongly coloured by the hope for recompense, for us to deduce a doctrine

of general resurrection from them. It is expressly denied that the tyrant will be 'raised to life' (7:14). In interpreting this last reference the decisive question is whether the final words 'to life' are added merely to strengthen the idea of resurrection, or whether they are intended to specify that particular risen state which was spoken of in Dan 12:2. If the latter is the case then what is being denied to the tyrant is not resurrection as such but that which it is expected to lead to for the just, namely salvific bliss. Now in 2 Macc 12:43 this term 'resurrection' is used without the additional words 'to life', and in a context in which it is the resurrection of those who will first need to be absolved from their sins that is envisaged. In view of this it does seem more reasonable to assume that it is a general resurrection that the author has in mind, though one which will, admittedly lead to salvific bliss only for those who are already just or else absolved from their sins.

E. The *didactic literature* has not much to contribute to the idea of resurrection. So far as the Psalms are concerned neither the term 'awaken' in Ps 17:15, nor the phrase 'thou dost not give me up to Sheol', in Ps 16:10 are sufficiently clear and unambiguous. It cannot be established that the term 'awaken' in the former instance is used in the sense which it bears in Dan 12:2. These examples do not permit of assured conclusions with regard to the idea of the resurrection. One feature, however, which is undeniably present in the psalms is a growing hope in the possibility of achieving a union with God that will overcome death (Ps 49 and 73 in contrast to 37). This hope

757

goes beyond any of the basic attitudes to life belonging to earlier centuries (Söderblom, Martin–Achard). Hitherto the 'concept of the after-life' had been neutral in character, promising neither happiness nor sorrow to those who were to experience it. But now, under the impulse of faith, a new hope develops of salvation beyond the grave; the 'I' is conscious of being protected by God in spite of death and in death in such a way that this protection is extended to the body too. The earlier Wisdom books do not contain any belief in the resurrection (Hamp). The Wisdom of Solomon could not give prominence to the body because it was written in reaction against hellenism and materialism. To that extent it has adhered to theories which it found ready to hand among the Greeks with regard to the 'immortality of the soul' (Wis 3:1). Yet from the manner in which the final age is depicted the author appears to have presupposed that the dead, just and wicked alike, were to enter upon a form of existence that embraced the whole man, including the body (4:20–5:25 [Bückers]). The text of Job 19:25ff is unfortunately corrupt, with the result that although the Vulgate takes it as referring to the resurrection, this interpretation has not so far been confirmed.

F. The *Apocrypha* display a variation of attitude towards the resurrection similar to that which we have found in the books of the Old Testament. Some are silent on the subject (AscIs; Enoch [Slav] 65:9f); others cling stubbornly to the ideas of the after-life and of Sheol which belong to ancient times (AssMos; 3 Macc). A further idea which is found is that the whole of Israel will be carried off to heaven (AssMos 10:9f), or again in some passages the body is expressly excluded from the state of bliss to which the soul is destined (Jub 23:31). 4 Macc 18:17 quotes Ezek 37 but it remains obscure what sense it attaches to this passage.

Other aprocrypha speak of the resurrection of the just, sometimes of specific individuals of Old Testament history (TestJud 25), sometimes of the just in general (Enoch 90:10; PsSol 3:16).

Still others, however, do recognise a general resurrection of both just and sinners (Bar [Syr] 50). The denizens of heaven and hell will confront one another (4 Ezr 7:35ff). The resurrection is also found with the formula 'to glory and to shame' attached to it (TestBenj 10:8).

The Qumran texts do not enlarge upon the resurrection. But it is probably justifiable to interpret 'the awakening of the sons of truth' who 'sleep in the dust' (1 QH 6:29f, 34) or the 'raising of the dead from the dust of worms' (1 QH 11:12) as referring to the resurrection of the just. Of sinners it is stated that they 'shall be no more' (1 QH 6:30 [Del Medico, Nötscher]).

G. *New Testament. The synoptics.* In *the judaism of New Testament times* a similar attitude of indecision towards the idea of the resurrection can be established. The Pharisees—and this probably implies the official circles of judaism—believe in the resurrection (Acts 24:15); the Sadducees, who admit only the Torah as scripture that is binding upon faith, reject the resurrection (Mt 22:23). The position adopted by Christ to both of these factions is remarkable, for he does not identify himself with either of the two theories. Against the Sadducees he is completely decisive in defending belief in the resurrection (Mt 22:31), but he also corrects the ideas of the Pharisees, who conceive of the resurrection as a return to a comfortable and secure way of life. Christ points out that after the resurrection 'they neither marry nor are given in marriage, but are like angels in heaven' (Mt 22:30)—that, in other words, the resurrection will entail a transformation of condition and state and an illumination which transcends earthly modes of life. In this way Christ extended the doctrine of the resurrection by adding an element of decisive importance to it, he clarified it, and he also confirmed it. By adducing the argument that God is a God not 'of the dead but of the living' (Mt 22:32), he adds a further idea to those already contained in the Old Testament, namely that the 'I' of the patriarchs Abraham, Isaac and Jacob are to survive as integral beings and that the body too is to be included in the future salvific bliss which is awaited.

Apart from this the resurrection also plays a predominant part in the message of the synoptics as *the inauguration of salvation which is expected for the just.* Nevertheless it would surely be a misunderstanding of the phrase 'resurrection of the just' if it were sought to deduce from this formula that sinners were to be excluded from the resurrection. There is a special reason for adding the qualification 'of the just' to the word 'resurrection' here. It is to bring out the idea of resurrection as a reward for that love of neighbour without regard to person which is required of us by the Lord (Lk 14:13).

Again the references in the synoptics to the general judgement at which good and evil are to appear in the same manner imply that there will also be *a general resurrection* (Mt 11:22; 12:41 and parallels). Acts 24:15 speaks more explicitly of 'the resurrection of both the just and the unjust'.

H. *John.* The statements in John concerning the resurrection are more plentiful, more clear, and more comprehensive than those of the synoptics. It is taught that 'all who are in the tombs will hear his voice' and that some 'will come forth . . . to the resurrection of life', others 'to the resurrection of judgement' (5:28f). The majority of passages, however, are concerned with the resurrection of the just and faithful, for whom Christ promises that he will be 'the resurrection and the life and he who raises them up at the last day' (6:39, 44, 54). The statement that when the Lord returns upon the clouds 'every eye will see him, [including] every one who pierced him' (Rev 1:7) must surely also be understood as referring to a general resurrection. The 'second resurrection' (Rev 20:12f) should be taken in a similar sense; it is a judgement upon all 'according to their works' that is announced.

I. *Paul.* 'For to me to live is Christ, and to die is gain . . . My desire is to depart and be with Christ, for that is far better' (Phil 1:21, 23). This exclamation of Paul, in which death is directly connected with entering into 'being-in-Christ', appears wholly to ignore the factors of resurrection and final fulfilment, and instead of taking these into account to relate all expectation of salvation to the immortality of the soul. Death appears to be regarded as a natural event to be desired, as a friend and liberator, while concerning the body Paul's opinion might seem to be similar to that enunciated in the Phaedo 'that we must make ourselves free of it and regard things with the vision of the soul alone'. But to understand Paul would be to misunderstand him. Cullmann has rightly drawn attention once more to the possibility that the biblical understanding of death and the after-life may have come under the influence of Greek thought and so have been transformed. The exclamation of Paul must be viewed in the context of his eschatological teaching as a whole. The apostle's yearning for death has quite different origins and aims than the corresponding feeling in Plato. Death for Paul is not the liberator who allows the higher element in man to unfold, but the 'last enemy' whom the Redeemer, the true liberator, has been brought precisely to destroy (1 Cor 15:26). With Paul the desire for death springs not from the opposition between body and soul but from that between flesh and spirit—which is far from identical with it, and which, so far from excluding the idea of the resurrection, precisely includes it. But is Paul's desire 'to be with Christ' connected with the expectation of a resurrection to follow immediately after death has taken place? This question must be answered in the negative, for Paul awaits the resurrection as a general event and, indeed, one which is not to take place before the 'return of the Lord' (1 Thess 4:15). This negative answer is still valid even if it is held that Paul must have imagined the return of the Lord as something that would take place in the not too distant future. Thus

Paul speaks of 'being with Christ' as an intermediate state between death and resurrection. Cullmann feels himself compelled to recall that the bible describes the state after death as 'sleep' (Mk 5:39). Paul too speaks of 'those who have fallen asleep' (1 Thess 4:13). Cullmann's point is justified if this expression is intended to describe the 'caractère provisoire' (p 15) of the state before the resurrection. But any over-emphasis, such as the theory that the dead are plunged into complete unconsciousness, is inconsistent with Paul's thought, for this would in fact bring Paul forthwith into a state of total paralysis, still more pitiful, therefore, than the earthly life. This earthly life would at least have signified a state of 'being in Christ' with a heart alert and watchful, with a love that was ardent, and with zealous exercise of his apostolate. In that case Paul's yearning for death would have been 'absolutely senseless' (Meinertz II, 222). Paul must have promised himself more than this in the intermediate state. At this point, therefore, Wis 3:1 may surely be adduced: 'The souls of the virtuous are in the hands of God, no torment shall ever touch them'; here we have before our eyes a genuine harmonisation of anthropological and theological understanding of man. This passage too, on an unprejudiced interpretation, ascribes consciousness to the dead and thereby the existence of a spiritual substratum which ensures the dead man's identity with himself. Thus it is precisely the book of Wisdom that shows how the errors of Greek thought can be avoided, how what is good in it can be retained and can be used to express a concept of eschatology that is in accordance with revelation; for the 'blessedness' of the just consists not in lack of consciousness but in 'peace in God', and is therefore not identical with immortality in the philosophical sense, but is 'grace and mercy' (Wis 3:9). Only one whose view of creation and redemption is all too contradictory can assert that the assumption of an immortal soul makes the resurrection an affair 'of man and his manipulation of himself' (Leeuw 22). Biblical anthropology and doctrine of the after-life are not logically thought out and harmoniously systematised. On the contrary the statements in which they are embodied are expressed in the language appropriate to the period in which they were formulated and in accordance with the conditions and circumstances then prevailing. This however does not give us any right to see more in the image of 'sleep' than an image which emerged at a period when earthly life was regarded as life in its full form. This was then taken up by the authors of the revealed documents as an indication of the fact that death is not the end. If Paul expected to be with Christ already in the interval between death and resurrection, his statements on this point are surely to be supplemented and filled out from his eschatological teaching as a whole. On this basis it can only be that in this expectation of his the resurrection was to be experienced as a further perfection and fulfilment of himself, one which up to that point he would not enjoy. But according to Heb 6:2 the resurrection belongs to the 'elementary doctrines' of the christian faith, and false views upon this point would be liable to destroy faith in general (2 Tim 2:18).

For the rest Paul—differing in this from the *catholic epistles*, which contain no mention of the resurrection—defended and confirmed various aspects of the doctrine of the resurrection in his epistles and addresses. He showed where the basis of this doctrine lay, and explained the circumstances and conditions which would attend upon it. He defended it against the Sadducees and all those before whom he appeared in his speech at the trial which took place after he had been arrested (Acts 23:6ff; 24:15; 26:23); he also defended it against the hostility of the Greeks in his speech on the Areopagus (Acts 17:31f) and against those among the Thessalonians who mourned unduly for their dead and those who were of little faith. These last he assured that those still living at the parousia would by no means enter into union with Christ before their fellows who had died, for 'The dead in Christ will rise first. Then we who are alive, who are left, shall be caught up together with them . . . to meet the Lord' (1 Thess 4:16f). In the same context he had already presented *the resurrection of Christ as the grounds and the guarantee of the hope of christians* for their own resurrection (1 Thess 4:14); he expounds this more fully in the passage in which he takes to task certain movements in the christian community at Corinth: 'Now if Christ is preached as raised from the dead, how can some of you say that there is no resurrection of the dead? . . . But in fact Christ has been raised from the dead, the first fruits of those who have fallen asleep. For as by a man came death, by a man has come also the resurrection of the dead' (1 Cor 15:12,

2of). Thus Christ 'makes the beginning' by himself rising from the dead (1 Cor 15:23). It follows that anyone who denies the resurrection in general thereby also denies the resurrection of Christ and the fundamentals of the christian faith (1 Cor 15:13–19). Now this *'beginning by Christ'*, so far from being understood in an exclusively temporal sense, is also to be taken *causally* and *soteriologically*: 'one man's act of righteousness leads to acquittal and life for all men . . . For if we have been united with him in a death like his, we shall certainly be united with him in a resurrection like his' (Rom 5:18; 6:5). The Spirit works in union with the Redeemer to effect the salvation of men. Hence the Spirit is given to any who possess it as a 'guarantee' that 'what is mortal may be swallowed up by life' and that all may 'be further clothed' (2 Cor 5:4f): 'If the Spirit of him who raised Jesus from the dead dwells in you, he who raised Christ Jesus from the dead will give life to your mortal bodies also through his Spirit which dwells in you' (Rom 8:11). Now since 'flesh and blood cannot inherit the kingdom of God' (1 Cor 15:50), what is being treated of in all these statements is that aspect of the resurrection which pertains to the theology of salvation. The resurrection of the godless is no longer explicitly mentioned by Paul in his epistles.

Although flesh and blood cannot inherit the kingdom of God a revivifying of the 'mortal body' is spoken of. Hence the question arises of *what state and condition of life* we may expect to be achieved by, and to ensue upon the resurrection. In view of the impossibility of adequately conceiving of and expressing the conditions of the supernatural state it would be asking too much of the apostle and of the message of the bible in general to expect him to provide some sort of 'television documentary' of eschatology. The matter can be effectively presented only 'per modum percipientis'. Paul speaks with special emphasis of the *'transformation'* which will take place at the resurrection (1 Cor 15:51). This he illustrates by means of the expression *'being further clothed'* (2 Cor 5:4) and also by pointing to the change that takes place in the growth of corn between the seed and the developed plant (1 Cor 15:38). He also avails himself of the manifold possibilities of illustration provided by the physical forms of the animal realm and those of the terrestrial bodies (1 Cor 15:39ff). In order to convey the superiority of the body as transformed by the resurrection he also uses a series of contrasts: corruptibility—incorruptibility, dishonour—glory, weakness—power, physical body—spiritual body (1 Cor 15:42ff). A further contrast is contained in the statements concerning the transformed conditions of the risen body. It is that of 'continuity—difference', and serves to indicate *the identity of the body* in question. Neither the theory of a pre-existing heavenly body (which is based on a misunderstanding of 2 Cor 5:1), nor that of a total loss of individuality on the part of risen man, can be reconciled with these words. Certainly these statements of Paul were made without any precise knowledge of the nature of matter and they do not give us any information on which the idea of the identity of the body before and after resurrection can be based. But whatever view we take of the question, an unprejudiced interpretation will prevent us from taking these statements concerning the resurrection in the sense proposed by Leeuw, even in order to maintain its status as an object of faith. It is not true, then, that in the resurrection we first perish 'irrevocably and totally, so that nothing of us remains unless God performs a miracle of creation and lets us rise again. From this it would follow that the term 'survival' is misleading. It presupposes a continuity between the life of God and our life . . . but the bond does not reside in us or in anything in us, but in the justifying grace of God alone' (Leeuw 23). For it is not the view of Paul that the resurrection and redemption are founded upon a 'nothing'. On the contrary they are based upon the creation of man, one element of the *continuity* of which is achieved precisely by its connection with the physical, even though it is 'groaning in travail' (Rom 8:20ff). Although it is not 'of its own will' that the creation was subjected to transience, still its 'hope to be set free from its bondage to transience' is surely to become true through the almighty power of God alone. Paul has left no doubt upon this point either when he says: 'God raised the Lord and will also raise us up by his power' (1 Cor 6:14).

To the question 'resurrection of the flesh or of the body?' (Bieder, *TZ* 1, [1945]) we should reply, therefore, on the basis of what has been said above, that these two concepts do not constitute true alternatives, for both of them are intended to assert and to emphasise that the resurrection implies a fresh beginning of a physical mode of existence at the final age. Only if 'flesh' were to be understood as the return of man as unredeemed, untransformed and sinful would these two concepts be mutually exclusive. But from the point of view of the bible the question 'what is the risen body to consist of?' must remain open. Is the material element to play no part in the process by which the continuity of the individual before and after the resurrection is maintained? Is this continuity to be achieved by the fact that 'I' or my soul remains the same? Or is something of the individual body too to survive and to return? Our knowledge of the transmutation of matter etc, even in this earthly life tells against this last idea. If this is ruled out then the formulation 'resurrection of the flesh' could be taken to imply 'resurrection of the man' involving a new formation of the body in the sense of a new creation of the material element in the human substance.

Paul likewise expresses the physical reality, as well as the spiritualised mode of being of the risen body in a saying that may well be taken to represent the culmination of the christian belief in the resurrection: 'who will change our lowly body to be like his glorious body, by the power which enables him to subject all things to himself' (Phil 3:21).

Bibliography: W. Baudissin, *Adonis und Esmun, Eine Untersuchung zur Geschichte des Glaubens an Auferstehungsgötter und Heilgötter*, Leipzig 1911; E. Sellin, *Die atl. Hoffnung auf Auferstehung und ewiges Leben*, Zürich 1919; J. Scheftelowitz, *Die altpersische Religion und das Judentum*, Leipzig 1920; F. Nötscher, *Altorientalischer und atl. Auferstehungsglaube*, Würzburg 1926; P. Volz, *Die Eschatologie der jüdischen Gemeinde im ntl. Zeitalter*, Tübingen 1934²; H. Bückers, *Die Unsterblichkeitslehre des Weisheitsbuches*, Münster

1938; C. V. Pilcher, *The Hereafter in Jewish and Christian Thought*, London 1940; T. Nikolainen, *Der Auferstehungsglaube in der Bibel und ihrer Umwelt*, Helsinki 1944/6; E. F. Sutcliffe, *The Old Testament and the Future Life*, London 1946; O. Schilling, *Der Jenseitsgedanke im AT*, Mainz 1951; R. Martin-Achard, *De la mort à la résurrection d'après l'AT*, Neuchâtel 1956; G. van der Leeuw, *Unsterblichkeit oder Auferstehung*, Munich 1956; O. Cullmann, *Immortalité de l'âme ou Résurrection des morts?*, Neuchâtel 1956; Thomas Aquinas, *Summa Theologica*, III, 253, aa. 1–4; W. Marchel, *VD* 34; (1956), 327–41; G. J. Botterweck, *WZKM* 54 (1957), 1–8; A. Ahlbrecht, *Tod und Unsterblichkeit in der evangelischen Theologie der Gegenwart*, Paderborn 1946; F. König, *Zarathustras Jenseitsvorstellung und das AT*, Vienna 1964; B. Alfrink, 'L'Idée Résurrection d'après Daniel 12:1–2', *Bbl* 40 (1959), 355–79.

Othmar Schilling

Retribution

A. *In the Old Testament and judaism:* 1. *The earliest doctrine of retribution in the bible* is closely connected with the two concepts of election and ↗ covenant; it is not conceived of in juridical terms, but envisages the divine initiative as always primary, and the human deed to which God reacts as secondary. It is in these terms that the unhappy situation of the world and of mankind is explained in numerous passages which are aetiological in character (Gen 3:16–19; 6:3; 11:6–9; 19:24ff; etc). At first retribution was often understood as collective punishment imposed upon the enemies of Israel (Ex 23:27; Josh 24:12); later it was also understood to include the anger of God against the covenant people when it was found guilty (Num 25:3; Josh 22:20), either collectively (Ex 32; Num 11:1; 13:25–14:38; 17:6–15) or in its individual members (Josh 7), of violating the sanctity of election and covenant. Later the prophets developed these ideas still further: 'You only have I known of all the families of the earth, therefore I will punish you for all your iniquities' (Amos 3:2). Since retribution as conceived of here was envisaged as taking place only in this world, all the events of history considered as Yahweh's deeds, all the powers of nature and of human activity were considered to be the instruments of retribution. This doctrine of retribution constituted the earliest theology of history. At the same time it served to provide a basis for religious and moral demands. This was the case especially in the prophets (↗judgement) and in Deuteronomy. In particular it was soon developed further into the doctrine of a retribution consisting of punishments and rewards (see Ex 20:12). In Deuteronomy and in the so-called Deuteronomist writing we find the theses representative of this doctrine in the form of the major sections of blessings and cursings (Deut 28; see also 4:40; 5:33; 6:3; 7:12–26; 15:4–10; 30:15–20), proofs in support of these theses in the work of editing earlier sources according to the pattern 'sin-chastisement-conversion-restoration to God's favour' (Judg 2:11–23; 3:7–9; etc), a work which was carried out at the same time; the consequences of this doctrine as applied to past and present, the careful laying down of measures designed to guard against any misunderstandings (Deut 29:18ff), and the descriptions of the brighter future which was to come in the promised land, when God payed the people the full reward for their deeds (Deut 11:10–25). All this is far more than a mere doctrine 'of the fateful deed', according to which man himself is the author of his own retribution, while God merely applies it and, so to say, plays the part of a midwife in bringing it into effect. This would be to deny that the initiative lay with God, who was a God of revenge and punishment, and who, apart from any question of merit or lack of merit on man's part, could chastise (Amos 4:6–11), instruct and put to the test (Job 5:17–26), defer punishment (Amos 7:1–3), alter it (Amos 5:15), or remit it altogether (Hos 11:8f; Jer 3:12; Ezra 18:23f). He was a God who, of his free will doubled the reward or increased it a thousandfold, extending it generation after generation (Deut 5:10). It does of course remain true that it would be inadmissible to speak of an 'Israelite dogma of retribution'. It also remains true that because retribution was envisaged as taking place only on the earthly plane, the idea of how a deed and its retribution were connected appears in the nature of things rather limited. This fact is attested by the very images of retribution which were sometimes employed, such as seed and harvest, growth and fruit, conception and child.

2. *Collective and individual retribution.* The earliest teaching was of a collective retribution. It laid down that punishments and rewards (Ex 20:5f; Deut 5:9f) had to be bestowed on just and sinners together (Judg 3:7f; 13:1; 2 Kings 17:7–23; Amos 7:17), on the people as a whole together with its individual members (Num 16:20–22; 2 Sam 24:16f), on the offspring together with their forebears (Num 14:18). A reaction against the strict doctrine of collective retribution soon manifested

itself (Ex 34:7ff; Num 12:10f; 2 Sam 6:6f; etc), especially in proverbs belonging to the age of enlightenment before the exile (Jer 31:29). Jeremiah still thinks in the categories of collective responsibility (11:22; 22:6; 29:32), but he also taught that individual retribution would prevail (Jer 31:29f) in the age of the new covenant which was to come (31:31ff). From Ezekiel onwards, and in connection with the political events which broke up the unity of the people, this doctrine acquired a special significance in the preaching of the prophets concerning the present (Ezek 18; 33:10–20). Divine retribution as applied to individuals (Sir 16:11–23) is especially well attested in the liturgical writings (Ps 1; 32:10; 62:12; 94; etc) and the wisdom literature (see also 2 Chron 21:15–18; 24:24; 25:27; 26:16–20). God rewards (Tobit 14:9–11) and punishes every deed (Prov 24:12; Eccles 3:17; 11:9; 12:14), every word and every thought (Wis 1:7–11; ⁊ harvest). The extra-biblical writings and the developing proselytising propaganda attest the growth of this individualism in judaism. The doctrine of judgement is enriched at this period by the doctrine of an individual retribution after death or at the cosmic judgement, and all spirituality is orientated to retribution for individuals, whose individual acts God will weigh in the balance or find recorded in books. The names of such individuals are written in the book of life (see L. Koep, *Das himmlische Buch in Antike und Christentum*, Bonn 1952, 18–39). The interest on their heavenly capital is paid to them already here and now in the form of prosperity and well-being. Such ideas still find only slight support in passages from the Old

Testament. They 'represent the culmination of the doctrine of retribution in its atomised form' (Volz, 290). How varied the views held on retribution were is reflected in the fact that side by side with the doctrine of individual retribution in the Old Testament (Dan 9:16; see J. Scharbert, 'Unsere Sünden und die Sünden unserer Väter', *BZ* 2 [1958], 14–26) and in extra-biblical judaism, the idea of collective retribution remained alive, especially in the context of nationalist expectations (Volz, 368–81; etc).

3. *The process of spiritualisation.* The primitive teaching of a retribution which is to take place in this life is never altogether left behind in the Old Testament. It is because of this that victories and defeats, prosperity and trials, sickness and want, fruitfulness and abundance of offspring, happiness, health and wealth, friendship, love and honour were all counted as retribution coming from God (eg Prov 3:2f; 10:16, 24, 27, 31; 4:10, 22; 8:18f; 9:11; 10:22, 29; 11:8; 12:2, 21; 13:21; 15:8, 29; 16:17, 31; 22:4; etc). Human experience taken as a whole was regarded as made up of 'good' and 'evil', 'life' and 'death'. The difficulties involved in these explanations of retribution in terms of this present life led to scepticism (Eccles 7:15; 8:14) and helplessness (Job) or else to an obstinate reiteration of the doctrine (Ps 37). Ps 49 and 73 contain references to the realm of the dead and to the state of friendship with God as retribution (Ps 49:15; 73:25–8), although these ideas are still vague in the extreme. Later statements are made concerning the 'names' of the righteous (Sir 41:11–13), their descendants (Sir 44:12;

47:12), and the fates they are to meet at the hour of death (Sir 11:21, 26ff). Others recommend blind trust in God (many of the psalms; Job 42 and 19:25ff) or, from the exile onwards, turn their eyes to the world to come as the object of eschatological expectations and to the hoped-for resurrection of the just, which would give them a share in this future world (Dan 12:2f; 2 Macc 7:9–23; 12:44f; 14:46). Finally, under hellenistic influence, the idea of retribution as absolutely spiritual and transcendent was put forward in the doctrine of immortality of the Book of Wisdom (H. Bükkers, *Die Unsterblichkeitslehre des Weisheitsbuches* [*AA* 13:4], Münster 1938, 181): it was held to bring either everlasting union with God and a share in his eternal kingship and dominion, or alternatively the loss of this (Wis 1–6; especially 3:7ff; 3:14; 4:2; 5:16; 6:19). Death and life, originally conceived of as epitomising all the ideas of earthly retribution, here become, after many intermediary stages (Prov 11:19; 12:28; Ps 16:11), the favourite expressions for a wholly transcendent retribution (Wis 5:15; see also Lk 16:19–31; Rev 20:14f; 21:8), which at this time played a major part in the extra-biblical teachings too. Whereas even as late as the second century rabbinism still retained only materialistic ideas of the future, the reward depicted in the Similitudes of Enoch (Eth) is spiritual in character: righteousness (38:2; 48:1), eternal life (58:6), similarity to the angels (51:4), union with the Son of Man and God (45:4f; 62:14). With the sections of 4 Ezra (eg, 5:121–5; 6:52ff) there is a similar situation. In several instances the reward is said to take place actually in heaven (Bar [Syr] 51; AssMos 10:9). In these descriptions the eschatology of Jesus attains the transcendental plane. The Qumran literature is also familiar with the idea of eternal life as the retribution (1 QS 4:7f) of those who are to stand for ever before God (1 QH 7:31), and eternal condemnation (1 QS 2:15; 5:13) for all those who are destined to an existence in eternal fire (1 QS 2:8). However, in all the instances of this doctrine of a spiritual retribution as formulated in the writings of later judaism, it is found only in conjunction with many other ideas which are either materialist in character or on the border-line between the material and the spiritual or wholly confined to the sphere of this world.

4. *The dogma of retribution in late judaism.* The spirituality of later judaism concerned itself first and foremost with the law, which it regarded as the final and definitive revelation. The differences of opinion are reflected in the fact that many regarded fulfilment of the law as a duty of gratitude, for which no reward should be expected. Others conceded that the reward might be a motive for acting in conformity with the law but dismissed all attempts at equating achievement with reward as meaningless in view of the freedom of God. In Qumran too thoughts and actions were often influenced by the idea of a retribution which was to be put into effect within time or at the end of time, in this world or the next. But here all the minutely itemising casuistry and the 'huxter' attitude of pharisaic orthodoxy is quite absent (1 QS 10:18; 1 QH 3:19-23). The authoritative circles, however, incul-

cated both in theory and in practice a doctrine of retribution according to which every human act incurred a retribution exactly proportionate to it, which was determined by God, and the human lot considered as a whole, both on earth and in heaven, constituted such a retribution, corresponding to men's deeds. In upholding this theory God was made dependent upon the law, which even he himself had to study, and dependent too upon men's deeds. In consequence it was believed that God counted all these deeds, recorded them, weighed them in the balance, and laid them up in a storehouse of merit, so that on this basis it would be decided once and for all at the last judgement what their retribution was to be. Sometimes it was taught that God reckoned up the sum of good and evil deeds at the end of each day and each year. What fortune the next day and the next year would bring depended on the result of this test. This was the prevailing teaching, and it was rationalist through and through. It had the unintentional effects of on the one hand externalism, reward-seeking and pride in personal achievement, on the other despair and fatalism. (For examples, see Pesch, 90–104; J. Bonsirven, *DB*[*S*] IV, 1200–2; etc.)

B. *In the New Testament.* 1. *In the teaching of Jesus on retribution* (Mk 8:35; 9:41; 10:28-30; 12:1-9; Mt 5:12 and parallels; 6:1-6, 16-18, 19-21; 7:24-27; 10:32f; 11:28ff; 19:28 and parallels; 20:1-15; 25:31-45; Lk 14:7-14; 15:11-32; 16:19-31; 17:7-10; 18:9-14; 19:12-27 and parallels; etc) all the lines of development in the Jewish doctrine of retribution which are in conformity with revelation converge, but his teaching differs characteristically from all Old Testament and Jewish doctrines.

a. *Retribution within time and at the end of time* are here united in a synthesis. This applies to eternal bliss and eternal woe (Lk 6:20–26 and parallels; etc), to the promises of reward for the disciples (eg, Mk 10:29f and parallels), to the assurance of interior peace, and to the announcement of the punishment which was to befall Jerusalem (Mt 23:37ff and parallels; see also Lk 19:41–4). Jesus designates eternal life and eternal punishment as retribution (Mt 25:46; see also Mk 8:35; 9:43, 45). He foresees an eschatological judgement and presents us with the image of treasure in heaven (Mk 10:21; Mt 6:19ff and parallels). The sayings concerning entry into the kingdom of God are eschatological (see H. Windisch, *ZNW* 27 [1928], 163–92), as are the images of the meal (Lk 13:29) and of the unquenchable and eternal fire (Mk 9:43, 47f) which was prepared for the devil and his angels (Mt 25:41).

b. *Retribution as immanent and transcendent.* On occasion Jesus also finds retribution in an earthly event (Mk 2:5; Lk 13:1–5; 19:41–4), yet this retribution always transcends all powers of conception (Lk 13:1–5; 17:20f), and comes wholly from the love of God (Mt 20:1–15; Lk 12:32; 22:29). According to the teaching of Jesus transcendental retribution exceeds all our ideas of earthly place (Mk 13:31; Mt 5:18 and parallels) and quality (Mk 8:36; 12:25; Lk 12:20f), is not confined in any way to the heavenly sphere, and also transcends all earthly time (Mk 8:36; Lk 13:25; 16:26; Mt 25:13). In these expressions the epithet 'eternal' has been made into a distinguishing characteristic of transcendence (Mk 9:43–8 and parallels).

c. *Collective and individual retribution.* Jesus also announces punishment which is to fall upon an entire people, a city, or a generation (Mk 9:19; Mt 11:20–24; 12:38–42; 23:37ff), but he denies that any individual incurs punishment for the fault of another, and also any laying claim to the privileges of the fathers (Jn 8:33–40; Lk 16:26; see also Mt 8:12). The sole exception, his own death 'for the many' (Mk 10:45), is in reality that which finally puts an end to all ideas of collective retribution, for here he means mankind without exception, each individual who must opt for him by being converted and believing (Mt 10:32f) or by love of neighbour (Mt 25:31–45).

d. *The distinctive element in Jesus' teaching on retribution.* Jesus never follows the teaching of late judaism at the price of the purity of his own teaching. He does not accept what is handed down uncritically. This appears primarily in what he omits. Even in cases in which his teaching is couched in contemporary turns of speech the preaching of Jesus avoids all minute calculations, all totting up of misdemeanours and good works. It also avoids any extended description of punishment and reward, or the assertion of any equivalence between achievement and reward. The independence of Jesus appears above all in the radical character of his teaching. He recognises only an 'either/or'. The reward, however, according to him, is a 'reward of grace', which the Father bestows from pure love. Jesus defends this conception against all misinterpretations of a mercenary kind (Mt 20:1-15; Lk 15:11-32). All the characteristics which have been mentioned are united in the kingdom of God as proclaimed by Jesus. This is the reward (Mt 5:3, 10; 25:34); to be excluded from this is the punishment. Now stated in non-figurative terms this means that Jesus recognises no reward apart from God himself. God himself is the reward of the just, who remain unprofitable in his sight (Lk 17:7-10) and sinners (Lk 18:10-14). When man makes this 'reward' the motive of his deeds, and fears to be punished by being separated from God, he is acting very religiously. But Jesus presents himself in his own person as the suffering (Mk 10:45) and glorified (Mt 28:18ff) Messiah in place of the Jewish law (Mt 11:27, 28ff). The retribution of God is determined according to the attitude which man adopts to this Lord (↗ judgement).

2. *The doctrine of retribution in the rest of the New Testament.* This consists of a development of this teaching of Jesus. According to it each one will be rewarded according to his works (Rom 2:6; 2 Cor 5:10; Rev 20:12; cf also 1 Cor 1:8; 2 Cor 11:15; 2 Tim 2:12). In Paul we find a reference to divine retribution in an earthly event (1 Cor 11:30). Yet apart from this, retribution is always expected to come on the day of the *parousia* and the judgement (2 Cor 5:10; Jas 5:9; 1 Pet 4:13; 5:4; Rev 22:12), on the last day (Jn 12:48; 1 Pet 1:4f). As well as by works (Jn 5:29) retribution is determined according to man's faith in the Lord (Jn 12:47-50; 2 Thess 1:7). In spite of all metaphorical expressions detailed calculations are to be found nowhere in the New Testament. Instead of these we are presented only with the great alternative: eternal life or eternal death. The reward appears as glory, honour and immortality (Rom 2:6f), as peace (Rom 2:10), joy (1 Pet 4:13), and entry into the eternal kingdom of our Lord (2 Pet 1:11), while punishment is presented as death (Jn 5:24; 8:51; Rom 1:32; 6:21ff; Jas 1:15), which is to last for ever (Rev 2:11; 20:6, 14; 21:8) as ruin and destruction (Phil 1:28; 1 Thess 5:3; 1 Tim 6:9; Heb 10:39; 2 Pet 2:1; etc). In this connection the reward and punishment which are to come at the end of time can be regarded as a reality already present (↗ judgement). In Paul's presentation the motifs of punishment (1 Thess 4:6; Gal 5:21; 1 Cor 6:9f; Eph 5:5f; Col 3:6; see also Rom 14:10ff) and reward (Gal 6:7-10; Eph 6:2f) evince a special quality which is also important. Divine retribution for him is that which leads up to, and is organically connected with the supernatural life in which man participates (Gal 6:7-10). Man, however, is only able to sow according to 'the flesh'; God must first bestow the 'Spirit' upon him. If he reaps destruction from the flesh, then the ensuing punishment is wholly due to himself, but if he reaps life from the Spirit this reward is doubly a free gift (Rom 6:23), that is the retribution involved proceeds wholly from the redemptive work of Jesus (see L. Nieder, *Die Motive der religiös-sittlichen Paränese* in *den Paulinischen Gemeindebriefen,* Munich 1956, 109-12). For the apostle it is this that silences all boasting over one's own achievements (Rom 3:27); all is the working of the Spirit (Rom 8:14-17; see also 2 Cor 1:22;

5:5), the gift of God's grace freely bestowed upon sinful man (Gal 5:22; Phil 2:13; 1 Cor 15:10). The reward is a 'reward' of pure grace, and the gift of the kingdom of God (1 Cor 15:50; Col 1:13). It is also the incomparable (1 Cor 15:42f) glory of Christ (Col 3:4; Rom 8:18).

Bibliography: Alfrink, Haag 1671-7; Leuba, Allmen 369-71; Würthwein and Preisker, *TDNT* IV, 707-14; W. Pesch, *Der Lohngedanke in der Lehre Jesu*, Munich 1955 (with bibliography 147f); G. Didier, *Désintéressement du Chrétien. La Rétribution dans la Morale de St. Paul*, Paris 1955. See also: K. Koch, 'Gibt es ein Vergeltungsdogma im AT?', *ZTK* 52 (1955), 1-42; F. Horst, 'Recht und Religion im Bereich des AT', *ET* 16 (1956), 49-75; E. Pax, 'Studien zum Vergeltungsproblem der Psalmen', *Studii Biblici Franciscani* XI (1960/61), 56-112; H. Braun, *Spätjüdisch-häretischer und frühchristlicher Radikalismus* (2 vols), Tübingen 1957; H. Graf Reventlow, '"Sein Blut komme über sein Haupt"', *VT* 10 (1960), 311ff.

Wilhelm Pesch

Revelation

No precise concept of revelation is developed in the bible, and nowhere do we find any explicit account of the bible's own conception of revelation. On the other hand it does bear witness, with every word contained in it, to the event in which revelation has taken place, and it is from the statements in the bible itself that a correct understanding of this is to be obtained. God's revelation to men is proclaimed in manifold ways and in a language that is rich in symbolism, and this revelation can be described in general terms as the effective proximity of God in the history of this world, in which he intervenes for the salvation of men. In this description the specifically biblical element has already found expression. For whereas in the thought of the non-biblical religions practised among Israel's neighbours revelation is chiefly understood as a sign given by God, an oracular or prophetic saying, or as the imparting of knowledge of God or special and saving knowledge, or else as instruction concerning the other world and concerning realities which are mysterious and hidden, what the bible is primarily concerned with is revelation considered as a specific *event*. The biblical experience of revelation is characterised not by the fact that in it man's awareness is extended to depths which have hitherto been unattainable, and to a knowledge of other-worldly spheres, but by his special and unique encounter with God in this world. In this the emphasis is laid exclusively upon the divine initiative. God has shown himself and reveals himself whenever he wills to do so. For men the decision between life and death depends upon their encounter with him. For his revelation lays claims upon man with the absolute authority proper to God himself, and man can either refuse this claim or prove himself in his response to it. For man the revelation of God brings astonishment and blessing at the same time. When man opens himself to the epiphany of God then he finds salvation. The special concept of God which is proper to the bible becomes apparent *ipso facto* in the very manner in which he reveals himself.

A. For the *Old Testament* the revelation of Yahweh is *par excellence* the act of instituting and creating, because it is the act of choosing Israel. God chooses her as his people by intervening in her life to direct her, to care for her and to lead her, and by revealing himself to her in his 'glory' (Ex 40:34f) he shows that he is Israel's God in accordance with his promise (Gen 17:7). God's presence to Israel was not simply an obvious fact to be taken immediately for granted. It was manifested in history and was experienced as relevation. Yahweh 'became' the God of Israel. It is difficult to point to any one outstanding factor in the complexity of the Old Testament revelations and make that the focal one. Of central importance are the revelation of the name of Yahweh (Ex 3), the exodus from Egypt (Ex 5–15), the making of the covenant at Sinai (Ex 19–24), the conquest of the land (Jos 2–11). In these decisive encounters with God Israel is summoned into an enduring relationship with God, and has the duties of this state laid upon her. For God reveals himself as the 'Thou' who acts and speaks, bestows favours and delivers, a 'Thou' who demands a response from the people. God's address to Israel is heard in all that takes place, in the prosperous events of history no less than in its catastrophes, in the destiny of the people no less than in the fate of the individual, in the present no less than in the past, which is the subject of praise. All, whether it be an event in history or an utterance of Yahweh, constitutes the ↗'word' of God. In all his requirements are proclaimed, in all he reveals himself, his nature and his will. The encounter with him takes place in the way in which he leads the people by his 'arm'. The books of the Old Testament present the evidence for, and the interpretations of this

unfailing revelation of Yahweh to his people, and the fickle and changeable loyalties shown by that people. But in the sanctuary too, in prescribed places blessed by his presence his ↗'glory' makes itself manifest, and he is accessible to his people in their ↗sacrifices as the object of their thanksgiving and prayers for forgiveness.

From the very outset Yahweh's revelation to his people points beyond Israel to the pagan world. The pagans too must become sharers in this revelation on the ↗'Day of Yahweh', when he reveals his dominion. The fullness of God's self-revelation is still to come (Amos 5:18; Is 2:17; Jer 30:7; Ezek 7:10; 30:3; Zeph 1:14). The particular revelations, for all their complexity, have an underlying unity and cohesion in virtue of this final act of God, constantly awaited in the future, in which he will reveal himself, and also in the present, in which his people experience his power.

According to the Old Testament God reveals himself in the most varied ways. He speaks through visions, auditions or ↗dreams, in ecstasy or in interior promptings. Man comes to know him through his messengers (↗angel eg Gen 16:7; 18:2; 48:16), or he makes his presence felt in portents in nature (Ex 19:16; 2 Sam 5:24; 1 Kings 19:12f). He is close to the people in the pillar of cloud and fire (Ex 14:24; Num 9:17ff). In this sense the ↗creation too is one of his revelatory acts (eg Ps 19:1ff; Is 40:12ff, 22ff; Job 38; 39). Finally his 'hand' is felt in the troubled course of history. He manifests himself as the holy one and the gracious one, in his power as also in his ↗wrath (Ex 9:15f; Is 66:14; 30:30; Jer 16:21;

Ps 78:15f; 107:8), as he who 'is' (Ex 3:14) *there* for his people. In this the concept of ↗ 'glory' (*kāḇôḏ*) constitutes a more general category for the modes in which he appears. In the New Testament this concept is taken up and expressed by the word *doxa*. It is intended to indicate the 'weight' of the divine presence in all its overwhelming fullness (eg Num 14:21; Is 6:3; 42:8; Ps 19:2; 29:9; 57:5, 11; 72; 97; 108:5ff). In addition to the revelatory events Yahweh's enlightening word of ↗ consolation and of ↗ judgement is found upon the lips of those whom he has commissioned as their 'portion', and it comes to them through his ↗ Spirit, with which he fills them.

Amid the complexity of the figures which are used to describe the revelation of God expression is given to Israel's single and abiding conviction that God has shown his 'countenance', and that in this he wills to become 'Thou' to his people, speaking to them and able to be spoken to by them, and that he imparts his name to them: 'I am Yahweh' (Gen 28:13; Ex 20:2; see also 3:6; 6:2, 29; Hos 12:10; 13:4; Is 45:5f, 7, 18, 21f; 46:9; 48:12). The mighty 'deeds' of God in history, however, are added to this in order that his power and divinity may be made visible not merely to Israel, but to the ↗ heathen also (Ex 7:5, 17; 11:7; 14:4, 18; Ezek 12:16; 21:4, 10; 25:7, 11, 17; 36:23; Is 43:10; 45:3, 6; 49:26). The God who reveals himself makes himself known as refuge, salvation, and deliverer by him who recognises his power, submits to his election, and allows himself to be guided by his instructions. For he speaks to the people.

B. The *New Testament* is dominated by the awareness that the God of Israel, as a continuation of his self-revelations in the history of this people, has revealed himself in a manner which is totally new, unsurpassable, and therefore final, ie, eschatological, at the 'end of the ages' (1 Cor 10:11) in his Servant Jesus, who is his Son and is now Christ the glorified Kyrios. With Jesus a new beginning, or alternatively the end of the long history of the revelation of God to men, has arrived. From this perspective what has gone before seems like an accumulation of revelations which has been followed by one unique word in Jesus: 'In many and various ways God spoke of old to our fathers by the prophets, but in these last days he has spoken to us by a Son' (Heb 1:1f). The way of God with men has arrived at its end. The Old Testament is recognised as a preliminary history. Viewed as a whole it was a revelation which promised what has now come to pass. All that has been revealed hitherto by God finds its ↗ fulfilment in Jesus Christ, 'for all the promises of God find their "yes" in him' (2 Cor 1:20). Thus it is not a linear conception of revelation that we meet with here. The events pressed on to that very end which God has now brought about. An aspect of the Old Testament which constantly comes to the fore is its 'openness to the future'. Now, in the New Testament understanding of time and history, this finds its full flowering. God's revelation, his self-bestowal, becomes here at the end clearer and more 'complete'. The time is 'fulfilled' (see Gal 4:4). God not merely speaks now—he himself *is* Word and as the Word 'has become flesh' (Jn 1:14).

He could not have come closer to men than he has done in the *kairos* of his coming. The 'end' which is already present is fuller than the earlier age, for 'the new has come' (2 Cor 5:17) through God's present revelation.

But in that God has become flesh, has appeared as man, has willed to be 'a curse' and 'sin' (Gal 3:13; 2 Cor 5:21), he has revealed himself in a manner that is unexpected and even scandalous (1 Cor 1:23). He has become 'like in all things' to men (Heb 2:10–18). As appears finally and for all time in the crucifixion, he has chosen the guise of poverty and 'weakness' (eg, 1 Cor 1:27f) as the manner and 'vehicle' of his eschatological revelation. This implies a scandal for men: to be forced to recognise God in lowliness and obscurity (Phil 2:6–8; Rom 8:3; Gal 4:4). The disciples' protest against the prediction of the Passion (eg, Mk 8:32f) may be taken as a paradigm of the necessity on man's part of rethinking his ideas. Now it is the Cross that designates the form and manner of God's ↗ epiphany in this world, and it cannot have been felt to be in conformity with men's expectations. The form of faith is determined by the form of this new revelation of God. Man is summoned to respond to God's 'foolish' election of him (1 Cor 1:27), and to accept the revelation of salvation in this self-manifestation on God's part in the lowliness and 'failure' of a human life.

Faith in 'Christ crucified' (1 Cor 1:23) recognises the wisdom of God in foolishness, the exalted Christ in Christ crucified, *doxa* (glory) in his abasement. For as the way of revelation the Cross is, symbolically speaking, the ↗ 'exal-

tation' (Jn 3:14; 8:28; 12:32–4). In their reactions to 'habitual contact' with the person of Jesus men fall into the two groups of those who have no respect for him (Mk 6:3) and those who are eager to hear him (Mk 1:22, 27; 2:12). The manner in which God reveals himself in the humanity of Jesus brings the decision of faith to its crisis-point. Since God reveals himself on the Cross this revelation can only be accepted by a believer who lets himself 'be crucified with him' (see Rom 6:6; Gal 2:19), and recognises the 'weakness' in which '(God's) power is made perfect' (2 Cor 12:9) as the focal point of revelation and as the manner in which it is brought to men in Jesus Christ.

For all this God's self-disclosure in his Son Jesus Christ is also experienced as 'glory' (*doxa*). In spite of all their lowliness the events of revelation are transparent to the eye of faith, which sees in them the 'radiance' of God breaking through to this world. The birth of Jesus is attended by this radiance (Lk 2:9; cp 2:14, 32). As with the ↗ transfiguration of Jesus (Lk 9:29f), the 'glory' is the 'state' of unveiled revelation into which Jesus will finally enter after his abasement (Lk 24:26). But God permits the faithful to 'see' this glory even in the lowly form of the Incarnation of the Son (Jn 1:14; 1 Jn 1:1ff). As the fullness of power and grace it appears in the miracles of Jesus and the signs performed by him as a portent, a 'flash' (see Mt 11:4–6; Jn 2:11). In Jesus the reflection of the glory of the Father radiates out (Heb 1:3).

A further consideration, however, is that Jesus 'was raised from the dead

773

by the doxa of the Father' (Rom 6:4). His presence was experienced in a manner which was wholly new. He showed himself in the unveiling of his epiphany, at which men, in their 'otherness', were terrified (eg, Lk 24:37); but then as they partake of the meal with the risen Lord (Lk 24:30f; Jn 21:12f; Acts 10:41) this new revelation assures them of his consoling presence. He lets the church see his 'glory' (2 Cor 3:18), while the unbelievers remain excluded from this vision (2 Cor 4:4).

Although in the coming of Jesus his cross and resurrection were eschatological events—that is, they constituted the ultimate in revelation—the decisive event of the unveiled self-revelation of God has still to come. We await with hope the 'appearing of the glory of our great God and Saviour Jesus Christ' (Tit 2:13), for he will reveal his power unreservedly and unveiledly at his Second Coming (Mk 13:24–7 and parallels; Rev), and since 'God will be all in all' (1 Cor 15:24–8), this revealing of himself introduces radically new circumstances, those namely of the 'world to come'. These are also referred to as the 'new heaven and new earth' (Rev 21:1), and the 'holy city Jerusalem' (Rev 21:10). The life-bestowing light of this city will be the 'glory of God', which is even now experienced in his revelation, and the ↗ Lamb (Rev 21:23), the 'Lord of glory' (Jas 2:1). The revelation in the lowliness of the Passion and Cross is directly connected with the disclosure of the glory of God at the end, and with sharing in that glory (eg, 1 Pet 4:13).

For those men whom God's revelation to Israel and in his Son, Jesus Christ, has failed to reach, or who have not been touched by it, his power and presence are manifested in (provisional) ways even in the works of creation (Acts 14:15–17; 17:24ff; Rom 1:19f).

In the New Testament too, therefore, revelation is not merely the imparting of teaching, but primarily an *event* and God's enlightening *word* made manifest in the unveiling of the decree of his will (Eph 1:11; Col 1:19f). With the coming of Jesus the ↗ kingdom of God, the age of salvation, is inaugurated (Mk 1:15). He is the first-born of the dead (Rom 8:29; Col 1:18; Rev 1:5). His resurrection is the beginning of salvation. In him the kindness and benevolence of God our redeemer have appeared (Tit 3:4), 'the grace of God as salvation for all men' (Tit 2:11). The Cross is the form in which revelation is conveyed for the time of this world, and Jesus explicitly rejects the role of overlord, a revelation in power to overcome opposition by force (Mt 4:1–11). It is through that element which at first appears scandalous in the form which this revelation takes, namely in the unprepossessing character of the historical events, that man is made to realise the nature of this world and set upon the one way of salvation in it for him, because he is referred to the salvation of God revealed and made accessible to him in history. He is summoned by God to utter his 'yes' to this which has been offered to him, which does not compel his assent by means of miracles, but confronts him in the freedom of his heart. Now is the time of the 'mystery which was kept secret for long ages but is now disclosed, and through the prophetic writings is made known to all nations according to the command of the eternal God, to bring about obedience to the faith' (Rom 16:25; see also 1 Cor 2:6–16).

Bibliography: R. Bultmann, *Der Begriff der Offenbarung im NT*, Tübingen 1929; H. H. Hubert, *Der Begriff der Offenbarung im Johannesevangelium*, Göttingen 1934; E. F. Scott, *The New Testament Idea of Revelation*, New York 1935; A. Oepke, *TDNT* III, 563–92; H. Schulte, *Der Begriff der Offenbarung im NT*, Munich 1949; W. Schmauch, *Orte der Offenbarung und der Offenbarungsort im NT*, Göttingen 1956; von Rad I and II *passim*; W. Eichrodt, *RGG* IV³, 1599–1601; O. A. Piper, *RGG* IV³, 1603–5; R. Schnackenburg, *LTK* VII², 1106–9 (with bibliography); J. R. Geiselmann, *HTG* II, 245–9; F. G. Downing, 'Revelation in the New Testament and among its Expounders', *Studia Evangelica* II (*TU* 87), Berlin, 183–6; D. Lührmann, *Das Offenbarungsverständnis bei Paulus und in paulinischen Gemeinden*, Neukirchen-Vluyn 1965.

Norbert Brox

Reward

1. *Reward* as used in the bible means the recompense due for specific things (Ex 22:14; Is 23:18; see also Gen 30:16), the soldier's pay (Ezek 29:18f; see also Jer 46:21; 1 Macc 6:29), the portion of the Levites (Num 18:30) and priests (Mic 3:11; see also Judg 18:4), but especially the wages of hired workers (Ex 2:9; Deut 15:18; Mt 20:1–15; see also Lk 15:15–19; Jn 10:12f), who were for the most part day-labourers (but see also Lev 25:53). The basic principle, 'Every labourer is worthy of his hire' (Lk 10:7; 1 Tim 5:18), corresponds to the commandment of God (Deut 24:14f; Mk 10:19), and the fact that all men have been made by God (Job 31:15) and must love one another (Sir 7:20f). Hence

short payment (Deut 24:14; Mal 3:5) or deferment of wages (Lev 19:13; Deut 24:15), evading the payment of wages (Sir 34:22), and imposing forced labour without payment (Jer 22:13); all these are counted as grievous sins. In such cases the recompense due cries to heaven like the blood of Abel (Sir 34:22), and brings down God's just judgement upon the exploiter (Jer 22:13–19; Jas 5:1–6).

2. 'The wages of unrighteousness' (Jude 11 and dependent upon this 2 Pet 2:13–15) is to be understood not in the metaphorical sense, but rather, as the comparison with the hire of Judas shows (Acts 1:18) as 'profit made by sin' (see Lk 16:9). In connection with the Jewish traditions concerning Balaam (see Deut 23:5; Neh 13:2) the expression alludes to material advantages gained by false teachers (see 2 Pet 2:3; Tit 1:11), which will bring condemnation upon these in the judgement of God.

3. For reward in the figurative sense ⁄ retribution.

Bibliography: F. Nötscher, *Altertumskunde*, 104f (see the more extensive bibliography there provided); Preisker, *TDNT* IV, 703–6; de Vaux 76f; W. Bienert, *Die Arbeit nach der Lehre der Bibel*, Stuttgart 1956², 88–96; K. H. Rengstorf, 'Die Frage des gerechten Lohnes in der Verkündigung Jesu', *Festschrift Karl Arnold*, 1955, 141–55.

Wilhelm Pesch

Riches

A. In the *Greek Old Testament* various Hebrew words are translated by *ploutos*. The word-group connected with this is found thirty-two times in the historical books (six times in the Pentateuch), thirty-four times in the prophets (seventeen times in Isaiah alone!), sixteen times in the Psalms, and ninety-three times in the Wisdom literature. It follows compellingly from this summary that it was chiefly the teachers of wisdom of the post-exilic period who were preoccupied with the question of wealth or riches.

1. In the earlier period the fullness of earthly blessings, the possession of herds of cattle, of menservants and maidservants, gold and silver was consistently regarded as the mark of God's special favour (see Gen 13:2; 24:35; 26:12-14; 30:29f; 41ff; Deut 6:11; 28:1-14; 33:18f).

2. Subsequently, in the period of the monarchy, in which the structure of social relationships was changed, a rich upper class emerged. As a result grave abuses gained ground, which the prophets most bitterly combated. Such abuses were the harsh forced labour imposed upon the poorer classes of the people (Amos 5:7-12), the inhuman drudgery exacted from slaves (Jer 34:8-11), the brazen exploitation of widows and orphans (see Amos 4:1; 6:1-14; 8:4-14; Mic 3:2; Is 5:8-24; 10:1-2; Jer 5:28) by falsehood and deceit. 'Like a basket full of birds their houses are full of treachery; therefore they have become great and rich' (Jer 5:27). The prophet Isaiah is still more severe in his judgement upon the rich, who will be blown away like dust (Is 29:5), whose mistresses will be thrown into poverty (Is 32:9-14), and, together with the high and exalted in rank of Jerusalem, will be thrown down into the underworld (Is 5:14).

3. The teachers of wisdom speak from a rich experience of life of the gain, the advantages, and also the dangers of riches. Riches can be gained honestly by diligence (Sir 31:3), by ability (Prov 10:4; 11:16), by prudent administration (Prov 24:4), by a life that is free from hindrances (Sir 19:1ff). Goods unjustly gained do not prosper (Sir 13:24).

Riches also carry great advantages with them, such as friends (Prov 14:20; 19:4), honour (Sir 10:30), peace (Sir 44:6), a life that is happy and secure (Prov 10:5; 18:11, 16; Sir 44:1-8), the possibility of distributing alms (Sir 31:9; Tobit 12:8).

While the teachers of wisdom certainly do take a positive attitude towards riches, nevertheless they do not for a moment deny the dangers which they incur. Riches lead all too easily to perverse ways (Prov 28:6; Sir 31:3, 5, 8f), to the pride that goes before a fall (Prov 18:10ff; 11:28; 28:11). They lead to false security (Sir 11:19; Ps 48:7; 52:7), bring about unrest (Prov 17:1; Eccles 2:4-11; 5:9-11), and are conducive to sin (Sir 27:1; 31:5-11).

The earlier concept, according to which riches were considered as a blessing from God, is still to a large extent retained (Prov 10:22; 15:16; Sir 11:14ff). On this showing riches and piety, poverty and godlessness belong together (see Prov 10:15; 22:4; Sir 13:24; 44:6). For this reason the apparent good fortune and riches of the godless, and also the real unhappiness and the deep poverty of the devout, cause the teachers of wisdom the greatest difficulty (see Job 21:7; Ps 37; 49; 73; Eccles 7:15; 8:11-14; Jer 12:1f; Mal 3:15).

The sages of the Old Testament

strove to find *solutions* which were more or less satisfying. They point to the restoration of the just ordering of things by God (see Ps 37; Job 20; etc). It may be some consolation to the poor that the rich cannot take their riches with them to the grave (see Ps 48:7; Eccles 5:12–19; Sir 11:17ff).

Of greater value is the conception of the teacher of wisdom according to which riches do not represent the highest good. Above earthly treasures stand the benefits of health, freedom, and happiness (see Sir 29:22 [LXX]; 30:14–16), of a good name (Prov 22:1), of wisdom (Wis 7:8). Moreover earthly possessions entail disadvantages which the poor man does not know, such as sleeplessness and care (see Eccles 5:12; Sir 31:1f).

Gradually the ideas of poor and devout on the one hand, rich and godless on the other become increasingly closely connected in the mind of the teacher of wisdom to the extent that they often become actually interchangeable (see Ps 86:1f; 37; 73; Sir 13:23; 14:3–16; Wis 7:7–10). For all his patience Job had to undergo a long interior conflict before he achieved the conviction that his poverty was not necessarily a manifestation of God's displeasure (Job 42:1–6), and the psalmist acknowledges: 'Better is the little that the righteous has than the abundant possessions of the wicked' (Ps 37:16). The idea that the fear of God is more precious than all riches raises us to a plane as elevated as that of the New Testament (see Ps 34:9; 37:16; Prov 13:7; 11:28; 15:16; 17:16; Eccles 7:11f; Tobit 4:21).

B. The *New Testament* has a radically different attitude towards riches, which it views in the light of the gospel of the kingdom of God.

1. Among the *synoptics* (John does not allude to this question) it is Luke in particular who condemns riches most sharply, although he could not be accused of any radical hostility to riches or of being an Ebionite. The Christ of the synoptic gospels does not reject riches as such, but only the *evil use* to which they are put, because of the immense dangers which they carry with them.

a. Riches represent a danger first to God's inalienable claim to supreme authority over the blessings of creation. All the treasures of the world belong by right to the Lord (see Lev 25:23; Ps 16:5f; 105:44; Acts 2:8). They are only 'loaned' to man (see Sir 5:1, 3, 8), and therefore remain 'the property of another' as long as they are in his hands (Lk 16:12; cf Job 1:21). To strive avariciously to increase one's earthly possessions is manifest folly, because the rich man can lose all his treasures, together with his life in a single night, as Jesus illustrates so startlingly by the example of the rich corn-grower (see Lk 12:15 with 12:16–20; see also Eccles 6:1–6; Sir 11:18–20). Two passages from the Letter of James carry an echo of this (Jas 1:10f; 4:13–16).

Further, the avaricious man is in constant danger throughout his life of falling away from God. The rich man throws himself on his knees before the demonic power of 'Mammon' instead of rendering to God the tribute of his prayers and homage (Lk 16:13; Mt 6:24).

b. The rich man also imperils his own entry into the kingdom of God. The cares of riches and the pleasures of the world choke the seed of the word of God, ie, the gospel of Jesus Christ, as the Lord so vividly illustrates in the parable of the sower (Mt 13:22; Mk 4:19; Lk 8:14). Therefore Jesus proclaims in the Lukan *woes* that the 'rich', the 'full' and 'those that laugh' will be shut out from the kingdom of God (Lk 6:24–5). In the *beatitudes*, on the other hand, he promises the kingdom of heaven to the 'poor', the 'hungry', and 'them that weep' (Lk 6:20–21; Mt 5:3–6). Later Jesus embodies the 'curse against the rich' and the beatitudes pronounced over the poor in the incomparably vivid and deeply moving image of the rich reveller and the poor Lazarus (Lk 16:19–31).

If riches almost invariably entail eternal perdition, the solution to the problem can only be 'Away with riches, together with the extreme dangers which they carry with them'. It is to these that the rich but pusillanimous young man succumbs (Mt 19:16–22; Mk 10:17–22; Lk 18:18–23). 'Away with riches' which block the way to the kingdom of heaven, so that Jesus declares with deep emotion, 'How hard it will be for those with possessions to enter the kingdom of God. For it is easier for a camel to go through the eye of a needle than for a rich man to enter the kingdom of God' (Mt 19:24; Mk 10:25; Lk 18:24f; see also Mt 16:26).

Poverty, on the other hand, actually leads towards the kingdom of God: 'Blessed are you poor, for yours is the kingdom of God' (Lk 6:20). Matthew interprets this Lukan formulation correctly when he says that basically the poor in question here are those who are emancipated from all earthly possessions, and depend on God alone, who do not rely on their own strength and their own achievements but solely on God: 'Blessed are the poor in spirit' (Mt 5:3). The widow's mite and the pharisee's gold pieces throw the clearest light upon what is demanded for the kingdom of God. Admittedly it is an undertaking that exceeds the powers of man, but any man, be he rich or poor, who, with the help of God, with whom all things are possible (Mt 19:26; Mk 10:27; Lk 18:27) has emancipated himself interiorly from riches for the sake of Christ will obtain a recompense many times over already in this life, and eternal life in the world to come (see Mt 19:27–9; Mk 10:28–30; Lk 18:28–30). Christ leaves no room for doubt. That disciple of his who seeks first the kingdom of God and its justice will obtain over and above this all that he needs for his life (Mt 6:33f; see also 16:24–6), while care for earthly things is the mark of a heathen way of life (see Mt 6:25–32).

c. Riches entail the danger of failing to fulfil the duty of kindness to one's brother. Avarice closes up the heart of man to the needs of another. In rejecting his brother in his need the rich and hard-hearted man ultimately rejects Jesus Christ. *Fratrem vidisti, Christum vidisti!* (see Mt 25:31–45). Thus there can be no mistaking the tenor of Jesus' demand: 'Sell your possessions, and give alms; provide yourselves with purses that do not grow old, with a treasure in the heavens that does not fail, where no thief approaches and no moth destroys' (Lk 12:33f; Mt 6:19–21). In the saying which Luke attaches to the parable of the unjust steward Jesus says: 'Make friends for yourselves by means of un-righteous mammon, so that when it fails they may receive you into the eternal habitations' (Lk 16:9), ie, 'Use it to make the *poor* your friends, so that they may intercede for you in heaven'. In the parable of the great supper (Lk 14:15–24; see also vv 12–14) it is in fact 'the poor and maimed and blind and lame' (14:21; see also v 13) who are to sit down at table with the king of heaven and earth.

The kingdom will be freely bestowed upon him who *prays* for it, and guards himself against demanding back pos-sessions which have been stolen from him (Lk 6:30 = Mt 5:42a). Ridding oneself of one's own possessions for Christ's sake also becomes in the statements concerning *borrowing*: 'If you do good only to those who do good to you what credit is that to you? For even sinners do the same. And if you lend to those from whom you hope to receive what credit is that to you? Even sinners lend to sinners to receive as much again. But love your enemies and do good, and lend expecting nothing in return, and your reward will be great (Lk 6:33–45; see also 14:12–14). He who acts in this manner *de facto* gives his possessions away (Lk 6:33ff = present, Mt 5:42b = aorist!). He who gives and lends to anyone without hope of restoration is on the right road. The spirit of the heroic commandment of love breathes in the early church at Jerusalem, and its voluntary decision to hold all goods in common stands out as the visible sign of Christ for all times (Acts 2:44–5; 4:32; 5:1–11).

In connection with the parable of the foolish corn-grower Jesus has concisely formulated the worthlessness and danger of riches when he says 'So is it with him who lays up treasure for himself and is not rich towards God' (Lk 12:21).

2. Wholly in the spirit of the synoptic gospels, *Paul* warns us of the dangers incurred in foolish and harmful greed for riches (1 Tim 6:9). He exhorts the rich not to trust to their unreliable riches, but in God, and to become rich in good works! (1 Tim 6:17–19). The apostle of the gentiles follows through to the end the way which the synoptics have trodden. It is incontestably the achievement of the great theologian to have pressed on to the only true riches, the kingdom of God in Jesus Christ, with which the christian communities must be filled.

God reveals his riches in Jesus Christ in compassion (Eph 2:4), in kindness, patience and longsuffering (Rom 2:4), in grace for the forgiveness of sins (Eph 1:7), in wisdom and knowledge (Rom 11:33), in glory (Rom 9:23). Paul is called 'to preach the unsearchable riches of Jesus Christ' (Eph 3:8).

The christian obtains a share in these riches of Christ through prayer: 'The same Lord is Lord of all, rich unto all who call upon him' (Rom 10:12). Christ's unheard-of joy in giving is ultimately rooted in his work of love: 'You know the grace of our Lord Jesus Christ, that though he was rich, yet for your sake he became poor, so that by his poverty you might become rich' (2 Cor 8:9; cf 1 Cor 1:5).

It is immediately obvious that these riches in Christ are accounted in the eyes of the world as poverty and foolish-ness (cf 1 Cor 1:23; 3:18), but that so far as the pastor and the christian are concerned they represent a stimulus and a warning: to make others rich by one's own poverty (2 Cor 6:10). The true riches of the teaching and the learning church find their fullness in total self-giving in love, which does not seek its own (see 1 Cor 13:4–13), which maintains an open hand and a kind heart for the neighbour's need (cf 2 Cor 8:1–10; 9:6–14). For every possession and all earthly goods are such that they represent not riches or security of life but are merely means for the exercise of love, and have no value of themselves, as Paul warns the community at Corinth (1 Cor 7:31) (Hauck/Kasch).

Bibliography: H. Rahlfs, *ᵓanî und ᵓānāw in den Psalmen*, Göttingen 1892; O. Schilling, *Reichtum und Eigentum in der altkirchlichen Literatur*, Freiburg 1908; J. Leipoldt, *NKZ* 28 (1917), 784–810; F. Hauck, *Die Stellung des Urchristentums zu Arbeit und Geld*, Gütersloh 1921; E. Lohmeier, 'Soziale Fragen im Urchristentum', *Wissenschaft und Bildung* 172 (1921); H. Birkeland, *ᵓanî und ᵓānāw in den Psalmen*, Oslo 1933; K. Bornhäuser, *Der Christ und seine Habe nach dem NT*, Gütersloh 1936; A. Kuschke, *ZAW* 16 (1939), 31–57; P. Régamey, *La pauvreté*, Paris 1941; J. Schmid, *Das Evangelium nach Markus*, Regensburg 1950², 155–7; J. van der Ploeg, *OTS* 7 (1950), 236–70; A. Gelin, *Les pauvres de Yahvé*, Paris 1963; P. Humbert, *RHPR* 32 (1952), 1–6; A. George, 'Le Dieu des Pauvres', *Evangile* 9 (1953); C. van Leeuwen, 'Le développement du sens social en Israel avant l'ère chrétienne', *Studia Semitica* 1 (1955); R. Koch, 'Die Wertung des Besitzes im Lukasevangelium', *Bbl* 38 (1957), 151–69; J. Dupont, *Les Béatitudes*, Bruges–Louvain 1954, 184–244; E. Kalt, *BRL* II, 504–11; Haag 101–10 and 1408–20; Allmen 270–5; Osterloh 473f; *TDNT* III, 136–8; *TDNT* IV, 388–90; *TWNT* VI, 37–40, 58–63, 266–74, 318–32, and 885–915 (with bibliography); *TWNT* VIII, 1–27; *RGG* II³, 363–5; Schnackenburg 79–86.

Robert Koch

Righteousness (justice)

A. The *Old Testament*. Righteousness, or justice, is generally taken to be one of the centrally important biblical and theological concepts, but being rather protean and many-sided it is difficult to define. It would be too much to say, as Heinisch does, that the entire history of Israel is a revelation of the righteousness of God—the same could be said also of grace and, less appositely, of holiness, though it is decidedly difficult to distinguish justice from this latter. Our word *righteousness* is a not sufficiently comprehensive and not very apt rendering of the Hebrew *tsedeq* and *tsᵉdāqâh* (there is no essential difference between the two forms) with at times *mišpāṭ*. We have no expression in English which corresponds exactly to these terms and takes in the same area of meaning. The basic significance of *ts d q* is disputed: *conformity to a certain standard, mutual keeping of faith, established order or conformity to such an order, straightforwardness* or even *victory, being blessed with victory*—none of these quite hits the mark. What is clear, at any rate, is that it is a term which implies *relationship*. Righteousness comes to the fore in the relationship between God and either the people or an individual person, as well as between man and man. It can therefore be used either of God or of man, but there are certain other cases where it applies to things—laws, for example (Ps 19:9; 119:172), or a way of life, a sacrifice (Ps 4:5; 51:19), even of weights and measures (Lev 19:36). The word is not, however, used in a material, spatial sense as a field of energy which can benefit man (see von Rad I, 373f). Justice operates on the *juridical, social, moral, and religious* level, but since the implementation of law is, in the last resort, reserved to Yahweh and has to be carried out in the way laid down by him, and since social injustice is also religious injustice, the two aspects, juridical and social on the one hand and moral and religious on the other, are difficult to distinguish. This means that the question whether the word's original field of meaning was purely juridical or religious is really otiose. It is, at any rate, *a dynamic concept*, belonging more to action than existence.

It is often said both of God and of men that they 'do' or 'exercise' righteousness, though not of course in the same way. The people are righteous when they do not omit their duty to their God (Is 58:2), and the individual is so insofar as he leads a perfect life from this point of view (Ps 15:2; Is 56:1; etc). Yahweh is righteous and is guilty of no unrighteousness as men are insofar as he honours what he has undertaken to do in the covenant (that is, his promises) and shows forth his deeds of justice every day (Zeph 3:5). He does not destroy the just with the sinner (Gen 18:25), but shows grace, redress, and justice (Jer 9:24), especially to those who are oppressed (Ps 103:6).

1. In the pre-exilic period, up to the time of Zeph and Jer, it does not appear to be stated explicitly that Yahweh is righteous or possesses righteousness as something proper to himself, though there appears in Amos a strict sense of divine justice in the way we understand it today, a justice which will brook no contrary act. This emerges here as a basic characteristic of the divine being. In Hosea, on the other hand, it is rather God's grace which stands out. In addition, there are some personal names such as Josadaq and Sidqia, as well as the messianic title

Yahweh-sidqenu (= 'Yahweh is our righteousness': Jer 23:6), which imply the fact of God's justice.

This righteousness is manifested as judgement and retribution, in the form of punishment justly inflicted, bringing salvation to the just man and annihilating the evildoer with fire and sulphur (Ps 11:6). In ↗ judgement Yahweh manifests himself as holy by means of his righteousness (Is 5:16; see also 10:22; 1:27). It sweeps away all sinners leaving only the purified remnant which accepts conversion (cf Is 28:17). One of the results expected from the exercise of his righteousness is that the principle of retribution be put into operation. This works to the good of the just man who will enjoy the fruit of his good works, but it bodes ill for the wicked man whose works will be his own ruin (Is 3:10f; see ↗ retribution). It cannot be maintained that righteous punishment is a contradiction in terms (von Rad I, 376) or that the divine righteousness will come upon the sinner only in the way that we find in the account of the Last Supper in the New Testament (1 Cor 11:29 [Procksch, 573]). Either consciously or unconsciously there is always somewhere in the background when this view is stated—namely, that divine righteousness can issue only in a 'high beneficence' or 'saving power'—in the manner of the reformation idea of justification by faith alone.

It is clear that in the Old Testament *justice* and *the grace of God* (↗ grace) are not used as opposites in the way we do today. They are *two facets or aspects of the same divine activity* which corresponds to the Hebrew *ts^{e}dāqâh*. The further we go on in the Old Testament, it is true, the more grace comes to the fore, but not to the extent that the aspect of punishment disappears entirely. Yahweh shows grace and favour to thousands, but he does not leave sinners and the guilty unpunished (Ex 20:5; 34:6f). The 'righteousness of God' which is manifested in retribution and judgement brings to the one salvation, to the other eclipse and ruin; which means that we can ascribe to God under the same heading both justice *and* grace. These two appear, especially in the Psalms, *as parallel ideas, even as identical expressions*, at least in the mind of the pious Israelite who is waiting for salvation and help from God (Ps 36:10; etc). He sees in his 'righteous God' the God who is ready and willing to help him (Ps 44:2), and in the manifestations of his righteousness, *ts^{e}dāqôth*, certain proofs of his grace (Ps 103:6; Mic 6:5). It is these *ts^{e}dāqôth* which Israel has experienced in the course of her past history and which she awaits as a future↗ salvation.

The righteousness of God can also be the object of thanksgiving (Ps 51:14; 71:15, 24) when it takes the form of help in the time of need (Ps 31:1; 35:24). It is practically identical with *grace*, especially in the Psalms (5:8; 33:4f; 40:10f; 70:5; 143:1) and, above all, with *salvation* in Deutero–Isaiah (Is 51:8; 56:1; etc; see also Dan 9:24; Esther 9), and this salvation is brought about by God himself through the servant of the Lord. The righteousness and fidelity (*'emeth*) of God, his grace and salvation (*šālôm*) are within the same order and, far from being mutually exclusive, interpenetrate one another (Ps 85:11f, 13; 89:14). They are occasionally personified in poetic

writings and appear as the supports of the divine throne (Ps 89:14; 97:2).

The righteousness of God works naturally and in the first place in favour of Israel in general and of the religious man in particular. It is, however, at the same time all-inclusive (Ps 9:4, 8), extends even to the animal creation (Ps 36:6; 71:19), and lasts for ever (Is 51:8; Ps 119:142; Dan 9:24). It is at work on all sides and at all times. Yahweh is judge not just over Israel but over all peoples and is the lord of the whole world (Ps 99:2; 98:2) and can therefore make the beneficial influence of his righteousness felt in every region (Ps 98:9).

God's righteousness is also for the religious man the object of an unshakeable faith; it is something absolutely incontestable (Jer 12:1; Ps 51:6; 99:4). It was left to experience, however, especially in the form of the great difficulties which life offers, to bring this belief to perfection. Jeremiah and Job in particular find that things can at times go very badly indeed with the religious man and that evildoers can flourish in undisturbed happiness and prosperity (Jer 12:1ff; Job 9:20; 23:13–17; see also Ps 73:2ff; Hab 2:4). If we restrict our view merely to earthly retribution, as in fact was the case at that time, we do however find some form of retribution, since we see Yahweh as the judge who tests the heart and the mind (Jer 11:20). The great majority of people do not understand the apparent contradiction involved and protest against it, as they do against the thought of the transmission of the effects of their ancestors' sins: 'The fathers have eaten sour grapes, and the children's teeth are set on edge' (Jer

31:29; Ezek 18:2; see also Ezek 33:17, 20). Jeremiah awaits the solution of the difficulty in the future (31:30) whereas Ezekiel (chapter 18) develops the idea of personal retribution, in a hypothetical form, in an almost casuistic way. Job has to be content with the insight that human knowledge cannot take in the divine designs and plans. Any doubt about the reality of divine righteousness is groundless, but suffering, trial, and even the martyrdom of the righteous are not thereby excluded.

It is not expressly stated that God is just in his capacity as *lawgiver*, but this is certainly implied. In accordance with this, his laws (see above) are designated explicitly as just (Ps 19:9; 119:172; cf also 119:7, 62, 75, 138, 160).

2. God can communicate his righteousness also *to men—either to Israel or to the individual—as a gift* (see Is 45:8; 61:11). It can also be communicated to them in the form of teaching (Hos 10:12). They receive it as *salvation* or as a *means of enabling them to conduct themselves in an upright manner*. It is above all the Anointed of Yahweh, either the reigning king in the present or the messianic ruler of the future, who receives the divine righteousness as the means of enabling him to rule justly and who has to enforce it in a special way as defender and advocate of the poor (Ps 72:1ff, 12–14; Jer 22:3; 23:5). The king's daily task is to pronounce judicial sentence (Jer 21:12; see also 2 Sam 15:2f; Ps 101:8) and in this way, as a God-fearing man, to maintain the social order as willed by God (see 2 Sam 23:3). Righteousness belongs to the essential characteristics of the messianic ruler (Is 9:7; 11:3–5; see also Jer 23:5f; Zech 9:9). Law and

righteousness are in force in his kingdom (Is 32:1–20; cf 11:9; Jer 31:23).

In this latter sense, righteousness is certainly *not exclusively considered as a gift of God*; it is also *a human achievement*, and is the result of man's own endeavour. In the form of an ordered, conscious, and impartial exercise of righteousness it is in fact a very considerable achievement which as a rule is credited in the scriptures to those responsible for it (Amos 5:24; cf Is 1:17; Jer 22:3). When it is lacking, it evokes the lament of the prophets, a lament which is constant and often couched in moving tones in the prophetic literature (Is 1:21, 23). They lament that in public life, above all in the places of judgement, it is *tseʿāqâh* not *tsedāqâh* (violation of law, not just sentence) which holds sway (Is 5:7). So it can happen that the upright man can be taken for an evil-doer and vice versa (Prov 17:15; also Is 5:23), that is to say, as a result of the perversion of right order the guilty party is set free and the innocent condemned, whereas in the technical juridical sense 'righteous' should be identical with 'absolved' and 'unrighteous' with 'sentenced'.

As a rule, however, the term *righteous*, *righteousness*, is not merely juridical but is used as *a moral and religious concept*, something like *yāšār* and *tāmîm* (honest, perfect) including, however, at the same time the social connotation. Hence, a just person is one who takes up the right attitude with regard to God and man and lives and acts in accordance with this. Noah is taken as an example of the righteous man understood in this sense (Gen 6:9; 7:1) since he was 'perfect' and 'walked with God'. The

783

same for Daniel and Job who were saved by their righteousness (Ezek 14:14, 20). Abraham's active faith was reckoned to him as righteousness (Gen 15:6) insofar as he achieved in this way the right relationship with God. This was a proposition which came to have great importance for the reformation view on the New Testament doctrine of justification (Rom 4:3; Gal 3:5).

At times the contrast between *righteous* and *unrighteous* corresponds objectively to that between *Israelite* and *non-Israelite* (cf Hab 1:13). This equation, however, is not really fundamental in the scriptures; the non-Israelite is as far from being identical with the unrighteous as all Israelites are from being themselves righteous. In fact they, or a great part of them, are often described as evil-doers. The ideal of the just Israelite or simply the just man comes through especially in Psalms, Job and Proverbs. We find it well developed above all in Job 31; 32:1; Ps 1; 15; 24; also Is 33:14–16; Ezek 18:5–9.

Side by side with religious and social probity or loyalty in a general sense (Is 1:21; 56:1; Ezek 3:20), there belongs here in particular fidelity to law for religious motives (Deut 6:25; Tobit 1:3), a right attitude in the application of law (Lev 19:15; Deut 16:19f; Prov 17:15), and activity inspired by genuinely upright social principles (Ex 23:6; Lev 19:32–7; Jer 22:3, 15f; Prov 22:22; Tobit 4:14). To this extent, justice is also the application of practical wisdom (Prov 2:1f, 9). It can become meritorious (Deut 24:13) and give one a claim to public recognition by God (ie, justification: Job 33:26;

Jer 51:10; see also Gen 15:6). When one prays, one's own 'perfection', which means the same here as righteousness, can even be the reason why the prayers will be heard (Ps 26:1, 11; 41:12) insofar as one's moral position can be adduced—a strange consideration, this, for us today—as the whole reason for the prayer for help and salvation. This attitude is not, however, one of self-righteousness—in fact, we find an explicit warning against this (Deut 9:4–6)—but rather a means of qualifying oneself, if in a very relative way, for receiving God's help. There exists certainly the consciousness of a universal sinfulness—in comparison with God no living person is just (Ps 143:2; cf 130:3)—and there are among human beings in addition various degrees of righteousness as of sinfulness. One can be more righteous and less charged with guilt than another (Jer 3:11; cf 5:4; Hos 4:14). The religious man feels that he is just in contrast with the public sinner who lives in happiness and rejoices at the expense of the conscience-ridden 'unhappy man' (that is, the just man: Jer 12:1–5; Ps 73:2–9; see also texts referred to above).

In the later Old Testament period the emphasis is placed on the practical application of piety to such an extent that righteousness (*ts^{e}dāqāh*) is placed in the same class as almsgiving and similar altruistic good works and is in fact practically identified with them. To these practices is ascribed the power to atone for sin and to bring salvation (Dan 4:27; Sir 3:30; Tobit 1:3; 12:8f; see also Sir 7:10; 29:12; Tobit 1:17; 4:7, 10, 16; 14:10f).

The relation between God and the people of Israel in the ↗ covenant rests on grace and promise, but gives rise in its turn to certain *rights* and *duties*. The *right which Yahweh has* corresponds to the *duty which the people has*. The same for the relation between God and the individual. In both cases this is expressed by *mišpat* (law), practically identical with our word *religion* (Jer 5:4f; Is 58:2), something which must be known and put into practice. This terminology, corresponding as it does to current semitic usage, passed into the New Testament. Thus the expression 'to fulfil all righteousness' (Mt 3:15) refers to all duties imposed on man by the divine law and which must be put into practice. In Mt 6:33, instead of 'seek the Kingdom of God and his (God's) justice', we should translate more exactly: 'Be solicitous for the Kingdom of God and for what his law, and therefore your duty with regard to God, is!'

Bibliography: Heinisch 57–64; Imschoot 1, 71–80 (see also Eichrodt 1, 239–49); Procksch 568–77; Jacob 75–82; Vriezen 132–4; von Rad 1, 370–83); Diestel, 'Die Idee der Gerechtigkeit, vorzüglich im AT, bibel-theologisch dargestellt', *Jahrbuch für deutschen Theologie* 5 (1860), 176ff; E. Kautzsch, *Die Derivate des Stammes ṣ d q im atl. Sprachgebrauch*, 1881; J. Martin, *Le Notion de la Justice de Dieu dans l'AT*, Berlin 1897; G. Dalman, *Die Bichterliche Gerechtigkeit im AT*, Berlin 1897; G. Wildeboer, 'Die alteste Bedeutung des Stammes ṣ d q', *ZAW* 26 (1906), 167ff; K. Cramer, 'Der Begriff der ṣedâqâ bei Tritojesaja und bei Amos', *ZAW* 27 (1907), 77ff and 146ff; F. Nötscher, *Die Gerechtigkeit Gottes bei den vorexilischen Propheten*, 1915; W. W. von Baudissin, *Der Gerechte Gott in altsemitischer Religion* (Harnack-Festschrift), 1921; K. H. J. Fahlgren, 'ṣedâqâ', *nahestehende und entgegengesetzte Begriffe im AT*, 1932; R. Leivestad, *Guds straffende rettfertighed* (Beihefte zu Norsk Teol. Tidsskrift), 1946; W. Kokemüller, *Die Gerechtigkeit Gottes in den Psalmen*, Jena 1936/7 (dissertation); A. H. van der Weijden, *Die Gerechtigkeit in den Psalmen*, Rome 1952 (dissertation); P. Rosenthal, 'ṣedâqâ

charité', *HUCA* 23 (1950/51), 411–30; H. Cazelles, 'A propos de quelques textes difficiles relatifs à la justice de Dieu dans l'AT', *RB* 58 (1951), 169–88; H. Ljungmann, *Gods Barmhartigket och Dom*, Lund 1950 (on the post-biblical period); R. Mach, *Der zaddik in Talmud und Midrasch*, 1957; H. H. Walz and H. H. Schrey, *Gerechtigkeit in biblischer Sicht: Studie zur Rechtstheologie*, 1955; H. J. Kraus, *Die prophetische Verkündigung des Rechts in Israel*, 1957; R. Nielsen, *Über den Begriff 'tsedeq'* (*Stud. Theol.* VI/1, 1952/3); N. M. Watson, 'dikaioō in LXX', *JBL* 79 (1960), 255–66; N. Jaeger, *Il diritto nella Bibbia*, 1960; K. Koch, 'Wesen und Ursprung der Gemeinschaftstreue in der Königszeit', *ZEE* 1961, 72–90; E. Beaucamp, 'La justice de Jahwé et l'économie de l'alliance', *Stud. Bibl. Francisc. Liber annuus* 11 (1960/61), 1–55; E. Pax, 'Studien zum Vergeltungsproblem der Psalmen', *Stud. Bibl. Francisc. Liber annuus* 11 (1960/61), 56–112; F. H. Breukelman, 'Gerechtigkeit', *Vox Theol.* 32 (1961f), 42–57; A. Dünner, *Die Gerechtigkeit nach dem AT 'tsedeq'*, Bonn 1963 (dissertation); J. P. Justesen, 'On the meaning of tsedeq', *Andrews University Seminary Studies* 2 (1964), 53–61; J. Becker, *Das Heil Gottes*, 1961. On the development of the concept *mišpat*: H. W. Hertzberg, *ZAW* 40, 256–87 and *ZAW* 41, 16–75; J. van der Ploeg, *OTS* 2, 144–55.

Friedrich Nötscher

B. Righteousness in the New Testament.
1. Outside Paul and James. In dependence on and agreement with Old Testament terminology, righteousness in the New Testament refers to the moral-religious uprightness of a man. The norm by which this is measured is the will of God. In Lk 1:6 the term *righteous* is explained as 'walking in all the commandments and ordinances of the Lord, blameless'. As in the Old Testament, the expression 'the way of justice' (Mt 21:32; 2 Pet 2:21) means life lived according to the commandments of God. In this sense, the just man is he who fulfils the commandments of God. Thus the epithet *righteous* is used of various persons in the Old and New

Righteousness (justice)

Testaments and also of Christ (Mt 13:17; 23:28, 29; Lk 1:6; 2:25; 2 Pet 2:7). The moral and religious content of this designation stands out clearly in those cases where the adjective *righteous* is used in conjunction with other adjectives within the moral-religious sphere to form one composite meaning: thus, 'holy and righteous' (Acts 3:14), 'righteous and devout' (Lk 2:25; Acts 10:22), 'good and righteous' (Lk 23:50). The same goes for the noun *righteousness*. The expression 'to serve God in holiness and righteousness' (Lk 1:74f) can be paralleled by numerous cases in the Old Testament, and has the same meaning in both. Since righteousness is said of the attitude of a person who is in conformity with the will of God, one can speak of 'working righteousness' (Acts 10:35) or 'fulfilling all righteousness' (Mt 3:15). This justice or righteousness of life is also referred to in the disputed saying of the Sermon on the Mount: 'Blessed are those who hunger and thirst after righteousness' (Mt 5:6). There is no ground for the supposition that the word *righteousness* has here a meaning which is unique in the whole of the New Testament with the exception of Paul, with reference, that is, to the divine action of judging and saving understood in an eschatological sense.

There are some features which characterise the New Testament idea of righteousness:

1. The righteousness demanded by Christ is greater and more perfect than that of the scribes and pharisees (Mt 5:20). Over against the legalism of the pharisaic concept of the ⁊ law, it emphasises above all the intention as the essential and decisive element in any moral action (Mt 6:1). But even with regard to its content, this righteousness goes beyond the demands of judaism and, in particular, also of the Old Testament, as the so called 'antitheses' of the Sermon on the Mount clearly show (see Mt 5:21–48).

2. Righteousness is essentially something given by God. It is therefore he who brings it about, which is true also of the kingdom in connection with which justice is mentioned (Mt 6:33). Justice also appears in the Beatitudes (Mt 5:6) as the inner substance and the fruit of salvation in God's kingdom. Here, too, it is clearly expressed that justice derives from the grace of God, on condition that the Beatitudes are understood as a *promise of the kingdom of God*—which is what in reality they are.

2. *Righteousness in Paul*. a. *The righteousness of God*. The expression 'the righteousness of God' occurs only in Paul with the exception of three texts (Mt 6:33; Jas 1:20; 2 Pet 1:1). Restricting our view to Paul, the word occurs, with the sole exception of 2 Cor 5:21, only in Romans (1:17; 3:5, 21, 22, 25, 26; 10:3 [twice!]). Here it has a decisively important meaning, which can be seen already in the fact that the essential theme of Romans is formulated in the expression 'the righteousness of God', for 'the righteousness of God is revealed through faith for faith' (Rom 1:17). In confirmation of this is the fact that this expression is strategically placed in the text which contains without any doubt the theological climax of the letter and in which Paul's teaching on salvation is presented *ex professo*, namely, in Rom 3:21–8. Opinions are, of course, many and various on the meaning of this passage

786

and what it is really saying. The discussion turns first of all on the question whether the reference here is to righteousness as *a property of God himself* or *a property of man*. The conviction is steadily increasing among exegetes that the question cannot be decided in the form of a radical Either/Or, but rather by examining both aspects of the answer and bringing them together into a unity, that is, a Both/And type of answer.

The righteousness of God is thought of first and foremost as a property of God, but understood in a dynamic rather than static sense, that is, as a divine activity which includes also immediately and necessarily the relationship to the human subject together with the effect of this activity, namely, the new being which is thereby given to man by God. In this way, the emphasis can be laid on the aspect of the divine activity in one text, while in another the result of that activity, namely the righteousness of man which comes to him from God, will occupy almost exclusively the field of vision. This dual aspect of the concept 'the righteousness of God' can be clearly discerned in Rom 3:26, a text which can be at once taken as an authentic definition of this concept. When we read here that God proves his justice in 'that he himself is righteous and that he justifies him who has faith in Jesus', both aspects of the concept are referred to: the righteousness which is proper to God alone, and the righteousness which he gives freely to man. It is significant for the dynamic character of this idea that it is said of it that it comes into existence through a revelation (1:17). According to normal New Testament terminology, this does not refer to a theoretical doctrine but to the emergence of a new reality. The justice of God is revealed in this, that it is put into practice and thus is *seen* to be a reality. It is actualised by being given to man and so, viewed in this way, the righteousness of man is really the righteousness of God himself.

As regards the individual texts in which the term 'the righteousness of God' occurs, we find at times different shades of meaning. Thus, in Rom 1:17 the author is thinking of an action which goes out from God for the salvation of man, as the contrast between the righteousness and the anger of God shows. We can, however, form an idea of how strongly the thought of the result of this action, namely, the righteousness of man himself, has influenced the idea of the righteousness of God, in that in 1:17b the thesis that the righteousness of God is revealed from faith to faith is based on the quotation from Habakkuk: 'the righteous [man] shall live by his faith' (2:4). What the quotation is meant to prove, namely, that man becomes righteous on the basis of faith, serves to demonstrate the thesis that the righteousness of God becomes operative on the basis of faith. There are, therefore, two things contained in the concept of the righteousness of God as presented in this text: the action of God and the result of this action, which is the righteousness of man.

In Rom 3:5 we find an opposition between the righteousness of God and the unrighteousness of man. There can be no doubt that it is a question here of righteousness as a property of God in the same way that unrighteousness is seen as a property of man.

In Rom 3:21–6 the theme already sketched out in 1:17 is taken up again and presented exhaustively. There is a close relation between the two texts, which thus help to explain one another. One result of this is that in Rom 3:21–6 the expression 'the righteousness of God' must be understood, as regards its essential nature, along the same lines as in 1:17. In 3:21–2 it is in the first place a question of God's saving action in the person and history of Jesus Christ; at the same time, however, the result of this action, that is, the righteousness of man, is mentioned. The righteousness of God is shared out to all those who accept Christ on the basis of faith.

In 3:25–6 there is mention twice of the 'proof' of the righteousness of God, and what is proved is 'that God himself is righteous and that he justifies him who has faith in Jesus'. Already the formula 'a proof of the justice of God' is a clear sign that the author is thinking in the first place of that righteousness which unites man to God. This is confirmed by the fact that this proof of the righteousness of God is more closely defined through the added note that he justifies him who has faith in Jesus. Since, however, it is evidently a question in this clause of the action of God which justifies, this also, in addition to the righteousness of the one who has faith, must be part of the overall concept.

In Rom 10:3 the righteousness of God is opposed to man's righteousness as the real end of all human endeavour. This opposition certainly makes it clear that the author is thinking of the righteousness of God as something to which man has a claim. This interpre-tation receives a quite authoritative confirmation from the fact that in Phil 3:9 there is, opposed to one's own righteousness which is based on the law, a righteousness of another kind. It is not here referred to, however, as the righteousness of God but more precisely as a 'righteousness *from* God that depends on faith'. In Rom 10:3 also the expression seems to have this meaning and refer to righteousness as something given to man by God. Despite this, however, the idea of a divine activity is not completely absent, since the expression 'they [the Jews] did not submit to God's righteousness' can be explained most naturally if we take the expression 'the righteousness of God' as referring not just to the substance of salvation but to the action of God which produces it. Here too, therefore, both aspects of the idea are present—the divine activity and the result of this activity which leads to salvation, the righteousness which is given by God and which justifies man, and so Rom 10:3 is a clear example of how closely these two aspects are connected.

In 2 Cor 5:21—'For our sake he made him [Jesus] to be sin who knew no sin, so that in him we might become the righteousness of God'—the human aspect is stressed directly and almost exclusively. The abstract noun-phrase 'the righteousness of God' doubtless stands in this text for the concrete 'justified by God'. The thought is at once clear: the vicarious expiation of Christ has, in the divine intention, the purpose that we who believe should receive that righteousness which pro-ceeds from God and which is brought about by him; or, in other words, that we should be justified by him. The case is similar in 1 Cor 1:30. If we read there that 'he is the source of your life in Christ Jesus, whom God made our wisdom, our righteousness and sanctification and redemption', this can be understood only in the sense that through or in Christ, wisdom, righteousness, sanctification, and redemption are given to man by God. Here too, therefore, righteousness appears as a gift of God even if the expression 'righteousness of God' does not occur in so many words.

A second question which is bound up with the expression 'the righteousness of God' has to do with the problem how this righteousness should be understood with regard to its content when considered as a property of God. Luther expressed the conviction that it had always been explained in catholic exegesis in the sense of a vindictive justice leading to punishment. H. Denifle (*Die Abendländischen Schriftausleger bis Luther über Iustitia Dei und Iustificatio*, Mainz 1905), however, has proved on the contrary that not a single exegete before Luther had understood the righteousness of God in this rigorist sense. The contrast between the righteousness and the anger of God in Rom 1:17f and the line of thinking in Rom 3:21–6 show very clearly that, in using this expression, Paul is referring to *God's saving goodness, the grace, mercy, and love of God*. When he says that the righteousness of God has been revealed we have to take it in the pauline sense that the grace and saving goodness of God have taken on reality in Christ. All that Paul is doing here is to take over usage already present in the Old Testament, especially in the prophetic

literature and the Psalms. Grace and righteousness, salvation and righteousness, goodness and righteousness—in the Old Testament these are linked up quite naturally in order to express that divine activity which brings help, redemption, and salvation to man. This usage can be traced back eventually to the idea of the covenant which already dominated all Old Testament piety. God had entered into a covenant with Israel, and so whenever he comes to the assistance of his people in moments of sore need, this is seen to spring from the covenant-relationship. It is precisely in this way that his righteousness is shown, namely, that he keeps his covenanted promise by intervening in the course of events to save Israel. The fact that in the course of time the saving action of God is no longer seen so much in external interventions but rather in his mercy and grace manifested in judgement (Ps 143:1ff; 69:28) is due to the progressive spiritualisation of the covenant idea. Paul also understands this concept of the justice of God in this spiritualised sense, and it is above all in Rom 3:5 that we can see what a decisive part the thought of covenant-fidelity plays in the concept of the righteousness of God. This statement is certainly couched in this way with the intention of replying to the rhetorical question of Rom 3:3; only in this verse it is a question in express terms of the fidelity of God and the infidelity of man. It would be possible, therefore, to translate Rom 3:5, without any change in the sense, as follows: 'If therefore our *infidelity* serves to show the *fidelity* of God . . .'—only it would not then be apparent that, according to Paul's view, the judgement of God consists precisely in this fidelity to his promises. What Paul understands by the righteousness of God is expressed tersely in 1 John 1:9: 'God is faithful and just, and will forgive our sins and cleanse us from all unrighteousness'.

b. *The justice of man*. Righteousness and justification are, in Paul's theology, two terms intimately linked together, since righteousness is the condition of man which follows from the act of justification. To *achieve righteousness* and *to be justified* are one and the same thing for Paul. (cf Rom 5:1 with 9:30; cf Gal 2:16 with 2:21.) This implies that the exact determination of what he means by righteousness will depend basically on what he understands by justification. (↗ justification.) Apart from this, however, we can extract from the letters of the apostle some important considerations on certain aspects of the concept of righteousness.

Since in the one term there is contained the idea of righteousness as a property both divine and human, it will be impossible for us to take the second of the two in a purely forensic sense, that is, as a purely external judgement of God on man. The reason is that the term does not have the connotation of a divine judgement passed on man, and so here can refer only to an inner property of God—it stands for the way that God exists and acts. If this is true of the divine aspect it must be for the human, unless we are going to admit that the term contains two entirely different ideas of righteousness in the two cases. And so here too righteousness must stand for the way that man exists and acts. This can be seen also in the fact that righteousness and sin are for Paul correlative though contrary ideas. The direct opposition between them stands out very clearly in the rhetorical question: 'What partnership have righteousness and iniquity? Or what fellowship has light with darkness?' (2 Cor 6:14). In the passage Rom 6:12–23, sin and righteousness appear as the two basic powers and possibilities of human existence between which the christian has to decide. But since the term *sin* belongs quite certainly to the moral category (in 6:19 it is paraphrased by the two terms impurity and lawlessness), the term righteousness must do so too.

A purely forensic idea of righteousness or justice is therefore totally absent here. Being set free from sin and subjected to righteousness (Rom 6:18) are really two aspects of one and the same reality. Righteousness means inner freedom from sin. The moral connotation of the term is clear above all in Gal 3:21: 'If a law had been given which could make alive, then righteousness would indeed be by the law' Basic to this thesis is the view that the Old Testament law was indeed a 'law of righteousness' (Rom 9:31), that is, it required of man that he be righteous. Being however only *gramma*, the letter, it was unable to give him the means of being righteous. The Old Testament law lacked the power to give man life, that is, to enable him to live up to moral standards. This power belongs only to the supernatural *pneuma* (2 Cor 3:6; see also Rom 8:4–6). In order to prove that the Old Testament law, though given on account of transgressions (Gal 3:19), does not in its essence oppose the divine promises the object of which is precisely righteousness, Paul adduces this hypothetical case: if the law *could* give life, then righteousness would really have come from the law. In saying this, we are admitting indirectly but nonetheless clearly that righteousness for Paul consists in the basic possibility of moral conduct and integrity. At the same time, we note that in Paul righteousness and holiness are named together and are in fact intimately related—'He has been made our wisdom, our righteousness and sanctification and redemption' (1 Cor 1:30). Christians must yield [their] members to righteousness for sanctification' (Rom 6:19). We read also that the New Man is created 'in true righteousness and holiness' (Eph 4:24).

Since righteousness is related to *moral conduct* in its very essence, this latter can also be referred to by Paul as *righteousness*. So he can speak of 'obedience leading to righteousness' (Rom 6:16), 'the fruits of righteousness' (Phil 1:11), 'the instruments of righteousness' (Rom 6:13; 2 Cor 6:7) and 'the breastplate of righteousness' (Eph 6:14). In treating each case in particular it might be somewhat difficult to fix on a definite meaning with regard to some turns of phrase used by the apostle, and especially to determine whether the term *righteousness* refers to the basic content of salvation or to moral life in the active sense. But this very difficulty makes it particularly clear what a decisively moral character the idea of righteousness possesses in Paul. It is only because of this that the two aspects referred to can be united and expressed in the one word.

The fact that righteousness comes entirely *from the grace of God* can be seen clearly in the designation 'righteousness of God', which, when used in the sense of something belonging to man, must be taken as a righteousness coming *from* God. In the same sense Paul speaks of 'the free gift of righteousness' (Rom 5:17) and says that grace reigns through righteousness (Rom 5:21). God 'reckons righteousness to man' (Rom 4:6), and this process of 'reckoning' is understood in the Old Testament sense of *hashab*, that is, a real putting to one's credit account, a genuine handing over and allocation.

Considered as *a gift or a grace of God*, the righteousness of God is opposed to one's own righteousness, that is, a righteousness which derives from the law, which can be achieved on one's own account through the fulfilment of the commandments of the law (Rom 9:31; Phil 3:9). Such a righteousness is possible only in a very relative sense, in the sense in which Paul can say that he had been blameless 'as to righteousness' during the period of his life that he lived under the law (Phil 3:6). In reality, however, this kind of righteousness is non-existent. This follows from the historical (Rom 2:1–3, 19) and ontological (Rom 7:6–26) proofs adduced by the apostle in support of the thesis that man who is under the law *only* has never and indeed can never fulfil its demands, but remains always the opposite of righteous, namely, a sinner. According to Paul's teaching on the law, the Old Testament law did not have, in the intention of God, the object of communicating righteousness to man. On the contrary, insofar as it was the occasion of his sinning, it aimed at making plain man's need and the

791

absolutely gratuitous nature of the righteousness which was communicated through Christ (Rom 5:20f; Gal 3:19, 22). What made this absolutely clear was the fact that Israel, while following the law of righteousness, never in fact achieved righteousness, while the heathens who had no such law received it as a gift (Rom 9:30).

The one and only basis of all righteousness is Christ, so that he can be called directly 'our righteousness' (1 Cor 1:30). It comes to the same thing when Paul affirms that we have become 'the righteousness of God' (2 Cor 5:21). The only means whereby man can share in righteousness is faith in Christ, which implies the acceptance by man in his total being of the saving revelation of God in Christ (↗ faith). Hence Paul can speak of the 'righteousness of faith' (Rom 1:17; 3:22; 4:11, 13; 9:30; 10:6; Phil 3:9). Viewed in this way, faith stands as diametrically opposed to all self-glory (Rom 3:27), that is, to the typical Jewish outlook of that time which understood righteousness as the result of one's own endeavour and therefore as merited. Faith and grace for Paul belong intimately and inseparably together, and either can be referred to indifferently as the basis of righteousness (Rom 3:22ff; 4:14, 16; Gal 5:4). Since righteousness comes from the grace of God it must therefore come from faith. He expresses this in another way: the promise, and righteousness that goes with it, are based on faith so that in this way it may be given as a free gift (Rom 4:16). To leave the way of salvation that has been opened up by faith would then imply rejecting the grace of God (Gal 2:21) or a falling from grace (Gal 5:4). Inasmuch, therefore, as faith, which is the necessary condition and the means of achieving the righteousness of God, is not conceived by Paul merely as trust in God but includes in its essence an affirmation of the moral demands of the gospel, it is evident that righteousness cannot just refer to a purely external relation to God but must be essentially a moral reality.

For righteousness in James ↗ justification.

Bibliography: On Part 1: A. Descamps, *Les Justes et la Justice dans les évangiles et le christianisme primitif hormis la doctrine proprement paulinienne*, Louvain 1950; J. A. Baird, *The Justice of God in the Teaching of Jesus* (New Testament Library 4), London 1963.

On Part 2: O. Kuss, *Der Römerbrief*, 1 (esp. from 1:1 to 6:11), Regensburg 1957, 115-31; Meinertz II, 115-34; Bultmann I, 271, 281, and 285-8; *TDNT* II, 182-225 (=*BKW* IV); S. Lyonnet, 'De "Iustitia Dei" in Epistula ad Romanos', *VD* 25 (1947), 23-34, 118-21, 129-44, 193-203, and 257-63; S. Lyonnet, 'Notes sur l'exégèse de l'Épître aux Romains', *Bbl* 38 (1957), 40-61; A. Kirchgässner, *Erlösung und Sünde im NT*, Freiburg 1949; W. Grundmann, 'Der Lehrer der Gerechtigkeit von Qumran und die Frage der Glaubensgerechtigkeit in der Theologie des Apostels Paulus', *RQ* 2 (1960), 237-59; E. Käsemann, 'Gottes Gerechtigkeit bei Paulus', *ZTK* 58 (1961), 367-78; C. Müller, *Gottes Gerechtigkeit und Gottes Volk* (*FRLANT* 86), Göttingen 1964.

Peter Bläser

Volume 3

Sabbath – Wrath

Sabbath

The word *sabbath* (Hebrew *šabbāth*) is found as a substantive only in the language of religion, and it signifies the seventh day of the week. The longer form *šabbāthôn* is used to designate several feast-days and days of rest, which, however, need not in every instance coincide with a sabbath (Lev 25:4). On grammatical grounds we must exclude the idea that the word is derived from *šebaᶜ* (=seven). As used in the bible the word *sabbath* represents, rather, a noun derived from the Hebrew verb *šābath*. The basic meaning of this verb is independent of the idea of sabbath, for it signifies quite in general 'to cease, keep still' (Gen 8:22; Josh 5:12; Is 24:8), an etymology which is supported by the text of the bible itself (Gen 2:2f).

With regard to the origin of the sabbath, attempts have been made to find this chiefly in Mesopotamia, where the Akkadian word *šapattu* designated a day of the full moon in the middle of the month, or alternatively the seventh, fourteenth, nineteenth (=forty-nine days, ie, 7 × 7 days, since the beginning of the previous month), twenty-first, and twenty-eighth days were considered to be *ûmu limnû*, ie, 'evil days', on which a series of tabus were in force (eg, the prohibition of eating meat, changing clothes, touching the sick, offering sacrifices, enquiring of oracles, etc.). Since many of the Old Testament passages associate the sabbath with the new moon as a feast day (2 Kings 4:23; Is 1:13; Hos 2:11; Amos 8:5; Ezek 45:18; Neh 10:33), and since, furthermore, the festivals of Passover and Tabernacles were celebrated on days of the full moon, it has been concluded that originally Israel would only have known of this sabbath which falls in the middle of the month as a day of rejoicing. In the exile Ezekiel (see 46:1) would have been the first to introduce the idea of the sabbath as a day of rest after six days of work, and at the same time as a sign of the covenant. Following the pattern of the *ûmu limnû* the sabbath would have had a series of prohibitions attached to it, and in order to avoid any contamination of star worship would have lost its connection with the phases of the moon, and would have been fitted into a calendar of weeks independent of the lunar month. A series of considerations, however, militate against this hypothesis. In contrast to the sabbath the *ûmu limnû* were 'unlucky' days. *šapattu* was used only as a designation of the day of the full moon, and never to signify an *ûmu limnû*. More than this, we have no evidence to justify the supposition that on the *šapattu* work came to a halt. It is true that sabbath and new moon occur in parallelism one to another. But the reason for this is to be found in the festal character which both these days have in common. The obvious relationship between the expressions *šabbāth* and *šapattu* can be explained from the fact that both are derived from the common root *šb/pt* (=cease), for on the *šapattu* the moon ceases to grow larger, and on the sabbath labouring activities come to an end, as also does the week.

Since the sabbath in Israel has come to be recognised more and more as an ancient institution, and since any direct Babylonian influence is improbable, many have supposed that Israel would

797

have taken over the sabbath from the Canaanites after they had appropriated their land, and that these Canaanites would have imported the sabbath at a still earlier date from Babylon. A fact which tells against this view, however, is that this assumption does not explain the difference between sabbath and *šapattu* or *ûmu limnû*, and furthermore neither the sabbath nor the division of time based on weeks were known to the Canaanites.

A theory which is no less ingenious, and also no less unprovable, upholds the view that Israel would have taken over the sabbath from the Kenites. These were related to the Midianites (Num 10:29), and even at a later stage the Israelites continued to have ties with them (Judg 1:16; 4:11, 17; 1 Sam 15:6). The name 'Kenites' would have meant 'smiths', and the working of the mines at Sinai could have accounted for the temporary settlement of a tribe of smiths in the Sinai region. Since one of the earliest sabbath laws prohibits the making of fire (Ex 35:3), this would have implied an interruption in the working of metal. Finally, among certain non-Israelite peoples the seventh day of the week was dedicated to the dark planet, Saturn, which corresponded to the Assyrian Kewân, a god whom Israel may have honoured in her cult during the sojourn in the wilderness (see Amos 5:26). Unfortunately, however, we know almost nothing of the Kenites—neither that they were smiths, nor that they had a time-division based on weeks, nor that they worshipped Saturn. The only fact that remains assured is that the sabbath goes back to the origins of Yahwism, and that the bible presupposes it as already in force before the promulgation of the law at Sinai (Ex 16:22–30). Indeed one tradition actually assigns it to the beginning of the world (Gen 2:2f).

In the various strata of the Pentateuch the sabbath is recognised as a day of rest after six days of work (Ex 34:21 J; Ex 23:12 [E]; Exod 31:12–17 P). Since the stipulations in Exodus were in force at latest at the beginning of the conquest of the land, and since the sabbath commandment is found in both of the passages of the decalogue (Ex 20:8–10; Deut 5:12–14), there is no room for doubt that the sabbath goes back to the time of Moses, that is to the origins of Yahwism. Whether it is modelled upon a pre-Mosaic institution cannot be established. In any case the seven-day week is irreconcilable with the lunar calendar, and for this reason the sabbath cannot be derived from the phases of the moon. For the rest the seven-day period is often found in Israel and her world (Marriage: Gen 29:27; Judg 14:12; Tob 11:19; Mourning: Gen 50:10; 1 Sam 31:13; Job 2:13; Judith 16:24; Sir 22:12; Sympathetic mourning: Job 2:13; Banquet: Est 1:5; Long period spent in wandering: 2 Kings 3:9; etc). Seven, therefore, was a small round unit used in divisions of time also. But whatever the origin of the sabbath may have been, it does remain a fact that in Israel the sabbath was a specific institution. But it had this significance not by reason of its periodic recurrence, the prescription of resting from work, or the various prohibitions, for all this is found in one form or another elsewhere as well. The distinctive element in the Israelite sabbath consists in the fact that it is held sacred by reason of its connection with the covenant God, and is, therefore, an intrinsic factor in this covenant. Just as the ↗ firstborn of the flock and the fruits of the field constituted a tithe representative of man's work, so the sabbath represented, as it were, a tithe of man's days, the rest of which were spent in toil. Hence the sabbath has its place within the framework of the Sinai covenant (Decalogue) and in the Book of the Covenant, considered as the document of the tribal confederation (Ex 23:12). Since the Deuteronomist writings mention only those festivals at which the Israelites had to come to the central sanctuary, the sabbath is not mentioned in Deut 12–26, but there is certainly a special emphasis on its importance in the Code of Holiness (Lev 19:3, 30; 23:3; 26:2), and the Priestly (P) document (Ex 31:12–17; Num 28:9f). Probably the sabbath commandment as originally formulated in the decalogue exhibited the same short and apodictic form as is apparent in the rest of the decalogue commandments. But when we consider the surviving versions in which it has come down to us, in Deut 5:14f it is associated with the mighty deed of God in freeing Israel from the bondage of Egypt, after which Israel was to find a 'place of ↗ rest' (Deut 12:9) in the land of the promise. During the sabbath rest it was this that she had to recall. Ex 20:11, on the other hand, associates the sabbath commandment with the work of creation, and sees it as following an example provided by God himself (Gen 2:2f). Just as the creation is the first act of salvific history, at the conclusion of which God pauses in

order to conclude a covenant with his creation, and just as it is only at the cessation of the Flood that the covenant with Noah is made possible, its sign being the rainbow (Gen 9:8–17), so in turn the sabbath is a sign of the Sinai covenant (see Ex 20:10, 11). In both of these motivations the sabbath is connected with the covenant. But in this Deuteronomy lays greater emphasis on the covenant people, while the Priestly document lays it on the covenant God. P, therefore, brings out the religious character of the sabbath above all. It is *for* Yahweh (Lev 23:3). It is the day which Yahweh has made holy (Ex 20:11). Therefore the observance of the sabbath carries with it an assurance of salvation (Is 58:13f), and its violation, for which the law requires the death penalty (Ex 31:14f; see also Num 15:32–6), brings down on the individual exclusion from the community of salvation, and on the people as a whole divine punishment (Ezek 20:13; Neh 13:17f).

This theological understanding of the sabbath only developed slowly. In the earlier passages the sabbath is a day of rest and joy (Is 1:13; Hos 2:13), on which no heavy work was done (Ex 20:9f; Deut 5:13f), no trading was engaged in, but probably small journeys were undertaken (2 Kings 4:23) and the relieving of the guard was carried out (2 Kings 11:5, 11). After 586, when the remaining feast days could no longer be celebrated, the importance of the sabbath increased and it came to be the essential sign of the ↗ covenant. Under post-exilic judaism it was laid down that on the sabbath the shewbread should be renewed (Lev 24:5–9) and supplementary sacrifices should be offered (Num 28:9f). The number of sabbath prohibitions were also increased (Is 58:13; Jer 17:21f), though the Jews made little effort to observe these, so that Nehemiah directed that the gates of Jerusalem should be closed on the sabbath (Neh 13:19-22) in order to compel the citizens to observe the sabbath rest. Gradually the sabbath prescriptions were imposed more and more strictly. In the period of the Maccabees the Jews preferred to submit to slaughter rather than to violate the sabbath rest by taking measures to defend themselves (1 Macc 2:32-8). Again, a successful pursuit of the enemy was broken off at the beginning of the sabbath, and only resumed when the sabbath had passed (2 Macc 8:25-8). According to Jub 1:8-12 marital intercourse and the preparation of meals were prohibited on the sabbath. The Essenes refused to move any object on the sabbath (Flavius Josephus, *Bell.* II, 8:9). At the time of Christ the pharisees said that on the sabbath it was unlawful for a man to carry his bed (Jn 5:10), to care for the sick (Lk 13:14), to pluck ears of corn (Mt 12:2) and to walk more than two thousand paces (see Acts 1:12). Jesus respected the sabbath (Mt 24:20; Lk 4:16), but rejected an unduly narrow interpretation of the sabbath commandment, and put man before the sabbath (Mk 2:27; 3:4; see also 2:23-6; 3:1-6; Lk 13: 10-17; 14:1-6). In the Mishna the upholders of judaism compiled a list of 39 works which were considered prohibited on the sabbath. In contrast to this Jesus as Lord of the sabbath (Mk 2:28) abrogated these, just as he also brought an end to the Old Covenant by introducing the New. Thus there is no connection either between the Jewish sabbath and the christian Sunday. The former represented the conclusion of the week, the latter its beginning, which, moreover, is for christian minds associated with the resurrection of the Lord (Acts 20:7; 1 Cor 16:2; Rev 1:10). Just as Jesus fulfils the whole of the Old Testament in his own person, so too Sunday, as the ↗ day of the Lord, constitutes a fulfilment of the sabbath which was a type of it.

Bibliography: N. H. Tur-Sinai, 'Sabat und Woche', *Bibliotheca Orientalis* 8 (1951), 14-24; G. K. Botterweck, 'Der Sabbat im AT', *TQ* 134 (1954), 134-47 and 448-57; R. North, 'The Derivation of Sabbath', *Bbl* 36 (1955), 182-201; E. Jenni, *Die theologische Begründung des Sabbatgebotes im AT*, Zurich 1956; W. Kornfeld, *Der Sabbath im AT: Der Tag des Herrn. Die Heiligung des Sonntags im Wandel der Zeit*, Vienna 1958, 11-31; E. Vogt, 'Hat Šabbat im AT den Sinn von Woche?', *Bbl* 40 (1959), 1008-11; E. Kutsch, *RGG* v³, 1258-60; de Vaux 475-83.

Walter Kornfeld

Sacrifice

Although sacrifices were offered in ancient times they were left undefined. Various primitive rites were current, the exact meaning of which was for the most part no longer exactly known, and which furthermore the offerer was able to vary. Thus in a papyrus from Ramesseum we can discern a new interpretation of the coronation rituals pertaining to the myth of Horus and Osiris: the Egyptian priests wished to explain the sacrifice as the victory of Horus over Seth. The popular explanation of sacrificial gifts in Assyria and Babylon is of a similar kind. It is that the gods devour the sacrificial gifts which are brought to them (see Dan 14). It is for the duty of providing these offerings that men are created, as the sixth table of the epic of creation declares (lines 32–9). But both in these regions and among the Hittites of Asia Minor it is even more clear that it was a duty laid upon men to offer sacrifices even though they were ignorant alike of their meaning and of the value of the rites employed in them. One of the pieces of advice which the hero of the Babylonian epic of the Flood gives to his children (see Meissner, *Assyrien und Babylonien* II, 421f) runs as follows: 'You shall honour your god every day with sacrifices, prayers, and the prescribed incense offering'.

The ancients seem to have regarded sacrifice chiefly as a *gift*, the *performance of a duty*, an *act of homage to the protecting deity*, the ruler of mankind. But the texts are not always so clear, and precisely in the case of the Semites and Israelites various theories have been proposed in recent times. The leading theorists interpreted sacrifice as a gift made to the godhead until W. R. Smith published his *Lectures on the Religion of the Semites* in 1889. Here he connected sacrifice not, as formerly, with the idea of a gift, but with that of *communion with the deity*. The believer strove to unite himself physically to the deity so that it would impart its power to him by partaking of a banquet with it consisting of the flesh of the sacrifice. Smith based his theory upon the primitive totemism of the Semites, but he did exaggerate. Lagrange produced a criticism of this work in his *Etudes sur les Religions sémitiques* (1905), and finally arrived at the following conclusion:

'The sacrifice of the Semites is neither a simple compact of participation nor the holding out of a (hungry) mouth to the gods, nor yet the renewal of a blood-bond with the deity by means of a sacrifice divine in character. Rather it is the expression of a ceremonial act with the concomitant idea that everything belongs to God. It is an acknowledgement of this right of his. At the same time, however, it is also an expression of the desire to draw near to God' (p 274). G. B. Gray (*Sacrifice in the Old Testament*, 1925) returns once more to the basic idea of a gift. But according to Gray there would have been a constant deepening of this idea of a gift, and the synthesis of Leviticus provides evidence of what man sought to achieve by it: *a spiritual union with the godhead*.

Great attention has also been paid to the development of sacrifice in Israel's own history. O. Eissfeldt ('Opfer im Alten Testament', *RGG* IV, 711–17) connects the idea of a gift with the entry into Canaan. A. Lods regards Leviticus as an attempt, not altogether successful, at achieving a synthesis of various ideas. Oesterly concentrates particularly on the sacrifices of the nomadic period (*Sacrifices in Ancient Israel*, 1937). He finds that already at this period three ideas of sacrifice had emerged: *gift*, *communion*, and *redemption*. After a syncretistic period during the agricultural stage and the more advanced stage of civilisation in Israel, sacrifices appear in the exilic period as *reconciliation with God*. R. Dussaud (*Origines cananéennes du Sacrifice israélite*, 1941[2]) emphasises that sacrificial rituals in Canaan and Israel were originally identical. Moses chooses Yahweh as his God and in his spirit codifies the Levitical ritual legislation. According to H. H. Rowley ('The Meaning of Sacrifice in the Old Testament', *BJRL* [1950]) Israel already possessed rites of its own when it came into contact with Canaan, but adapted many others to its own purposes. Sacrifice expresses various ideas such as those of gift, of communion, of propitiation, but the single factor which all these have in common is the idea of sacrifice as constituting an effective means in the hand of the offerer of presenting himself before God. L. Moraldi (*Espiazione sacrificale e riti espiatori*, Rome 1956) does not attempt to provide any comprehensive treatment of the problem of sacrifice, but insists on one aspect of it, namely the independent value of sacrifice as a victim substituted for the offerer to undergo his punishment. In an extremely penetrating study of the relevant texts he shows the connections between the Israelite ideas of sacrifice and those current in the world about her, but emphasizes the peculiarly spiritual aspects of the legislation in Leviticus: the clearer idea of sin, of the presence of God in his temple and his holy land, which gives life to his people provided that they do not profane this place by their conduct: the blood sacrifice has a cleansing value inasmuch as blood is life (Lev 17:11, 14).

This presentation enables us to realise how rich in ideas Israelite sacrifice can be shown to be. It would be perilous to attempt to opt for any one of these ideas at the expense of another. As the central idea of all we should probably hold fast to that of *sacrum facere*. The effectiveness of the act of sacrifice consists chiefly in the fact that by means of it the individual or the community transforms a living act into a consecrated act. The community sacrifice is certainly extremely ancient and makes manifest the union of the god with his people above all on festival days. Leviticus, however, does not give first place to these ritual meals, which were very widely practised among the Canaanites, but makes the whole burnt offering, in which everything is destroyed in honour of, or for the sake of the godhead, the chief form of sacrifice. This form of sacrifice, which is likewise extremely ancient, seems at first to have been conceived of as a kind of thanksgiving for an encounter with God (Judg 9, 13), but Leviticus ascribes an atoning value to it, as also to the two other kinds of sacrifice, *ḥaṭāʾâh* and *ʾāšām*, which presuppose transgression and liability to punishment. These sacrifices were well-known in the Semitic world, and had an expiatory value, whether this was achieved through punishment (penance) or through a *kuppuru* rite (in Assyria and Babylon), by which it was sought to heal one smitten with sickness by a deity whose indignation had been aroused by some transgression or fault or uncleanness in him. We believe, although this is still a disputed point, that Leviticus has merely 'canonised' these atonement rituals by attaching them to the Mosaic law, above all the *lex talionis*, but that in the case of the whole burnt offering, the *ḥaṭāʾâh* or the *ʾāšām* the blood of the slaughtered beast was regarded as a substitute for the life of the sinner, who would otherwise have had to die in accordance with the strict letter of this law. Passages exhibiting the same spirit, such as Ezek 30:12–16, connect atonement (*kipper*) with ransom (*kōper*). Thus the lawgiver ruled out all magic practices and all kinds of naturalism. This, however, was not the deepest sense of atonement, which above all represented the healing of an individual sick in body and soul. Christ restores the full value of the communion sacrifice to it. *Kipper* (Greek: *hilaskomai*) becomes in the New Testament the outpouring of the blood of Christ. *hilastērion* (Rom 3:25), which heals man, justifies him in faith by his sharing in the eucharistic meal: 'This Blood will be shed for many' (Mk 14:24). ↗ Eucharist, redemption.

Bibliography: Haag, 1229–35; N. H. Snaith, *VT* 7 (1957), 308–17; R. de Vaux 415–56; L. A. Rutschmann, *Altar and Sacrifice in the OT Nomadic Period, with Relation to Sacred Space and Sacred Time*, 1962 (dissertation, S. California School of Theology); D. Gill, 'Questions to Thysia and šᵉlāmīm', *Bbl* 47 (1966), 255–62; R. Rendtorff, *Studien zur Geschichte des Opfers im Alten Israel*, (*WissMonANT* 24), Neukirchen-Vluyn 1967; N. M. Loss, 'Oblazione quotidiana oppure oblazione stabile', *Rivista Biblica Italiana* 16 (1968), 409–29; H. Muszynski, 'Sacrificium fundationis in Jos 6, 26 et I Reg 16, 34?', *VD* 46 (1968), 259–74.

Henri Cazelles

B. *New Testament*. The many and varied ideas of sacrifice found in the Old Testament do not die out in the New Testament, but are transposed on to a higher plane. In the thinking of the primitive christian community they are concentrated on the death of Christ and given a new interpretation from this standpoint.

Full clarity and maturity are only achieved through separation from the religious community of judaism, theological reflection on Jesus' death on the cross, and the primitive church's deepening understanding of itself as the community of God whose life and duties flow from the sacrificial death of Christ.

1. Relation to the sacrificial ritual of judaism. Jesus' own attitude can no longer be completely reconstructed from the brief and selective accounts of the gospels, which give it a slant reminiscent of that of the great prophets: no total rejection of contemporary sacrificial rites (cf Mk 1:44 and parallels; Mt 5:23f; Lk 13:1), but sharp criticism of external religion (Mk 7:6 and parallels following Is 29:13) and dishonouring the sanctuary (the cleansing of the temple), the placing of the commandment to love above all sacrifices (Mk 12:33f). Jesus probably kept the passover (though hardly in the manner of the Essenes) until he 'reinstituted' it at the last supper (cf Mk 14:12–16 and parallels; Lk 22:15). The 'temple saying' (Mt 26:61; Mk 14:58; Jn 2:19; cf Rev 6:14) is not conclusive evidence of a rejection of the temple and its sacrificial ritual.

The attitude of the primitive church in this respect was at first neither clear nor unified; in spite of their connection with the temple (cf Acts 2:46; 3:1, 11; 5:12), the first christians must from the start have celebrated their own 'Easter' in place of the Jewish passover. In the circle of James the links with the Jewish sacrificial system were presumably maintained (cf Acts 21:23–6), but on the other hand Stephen (and with him the 'hellenisers') completely rejected the temple, Paul distanced himself from the Jewish sacrificial ritual (cf 1 Cor 10:18), and there grew up generally in the primitive (hellenistic) church the consciousness of a new christian system of worship without the Jewish (and pagan) practice of sacrifice.

2. *Theological distancing from the old sacrificial system.* The realisation of the 'new thing' which had taken place in and with Jesus through God's action, together with the destruction of the temple and the end of the sacrificial ritual in AD 70, led to a theologically conscious turning away from the old Jewish sacrificial system, which is surpassed and 'abolished' in the new eschatological order of salvation which came into being with Christ. This is the context in which Matthew uses Hos 6:6 (9:13; 12:7) and inserts in 12:6 the sentence 'Something greater than the temple is here [i.e. in Jesus]. John refers the 'temple saying' to the body of Jesus, the risen one (2:21f), and regards as brought to pass in Jesus the time when true worshippers will no longer pray to God in the temple but 'in spirit and in truth' (4:21–4). For Paul the eucharist surpasses the communion with God which was the aim of the Jewish 'peace offering' (1 Cor 10:14–18), and 'Christ, our paschal lamb, has been sacrificed' (1 Cor 5:7), that is to say, the new ('our'), genuine, eschatological paschal lamb; this idea is echoed in 1 Pet 1:19 and lies behind Jn 19:33f, 36 as a type.

The author of the Letter to the Hebrews, who has no need to take account of any still existing Jewish system of worship, regards the Jewish priesthood and sacrificial ritual as fulfilled and surpassed by Christ, the true high priest 'after the order of Melchizedek', and his once-for-all, complete and permanently valid sacrifice. The old covenant is not merely subordinated to the new covenant sealed in the blood of Jesus, but it is also abolished by it, because perfected (cf 8:13; 10:9b). Since Christ by his sacrifice 'has perfected for all time those who are sanctified' (10:14), and as high priest leads the people of God into the heavenly sanctuary (10:19ff), the meaning of every sacrificial system and the demands of the worshippers are now fulfilled, and the shadow must give way before the reality (10:1).

3. *The atoning death of Christ and ideas of sacrifice.* The earliest community understood the death of Jesus as representative atoning suffering (cf 1 Cor 15:3 'died for our sins in accordance with the scriptures', presumably referring to Is 53), and this idea is also expressed in the saying over the cup at the eucharist (Mk 14:24 'for many'; Mt 26:28 'poured out for many for the forgiveness of sins'; Lk 22:20, applied to the participants in the meal, 'poured out for you') and in Mk 10:45 = Mt 20:28 ('his life as a ransom for many'). This idea of representative atonement, which appears first in Is 53 and then has a continued existence in judaism (esp. 2 Macc 7:38; 4 Macc 1:11; 6:28f; 17:21f; 18:4) should be distinguished from views of sacrifice (cf Lohse), though it can be linked with such views, as perhaps already in the servant song of Is 53 itself (cf v 7, the image of the lamb; v 10 ʾašam). Mk 14:24, with its 'blood of the covenant', recalls the sacrifice which ratified the covenant on Sinai (Ex 24:8), during which the blood was also sprinkled on the people (v 8), and after which a sacrificial meal took place (v 11), and in this way it connects the two ideas. Jesus' death falls under the ideas of

sacrifice in another way when it is treated as the New Testament passover (see above).

In the Gospel of John the 'lamb of God' (Jn 1:29, 36) may be a fusion of the ideas of 'servant of God' (the Aramaic *talja'* can mean both 'servant' and 'lamb') and paschal lamb to describe Jesus. The 'lamb' (Gk *arnion*, strictly 'ram') of Revelation combines royal features with a reminder that it was 'slain' (5:8, 12; 13:8) and washes the garments of the redeemed with its blood (7:14). Wherever the blood of Christ is mentioned, the idea of the covenant founding (Ex 24) and atoning (cf Heb 9:22) effect of the blood of the sacrificial victim should be felt as well.

At the back of Rom 8:32 there certainly lies the typology of the sacrifice of Isaac, and according to Eph 5:2 Jesus gave himself as 'a fragrant offering and sacrifice to God'. The language of sacrifice is also used when, according to Jn 17:19, Jesus 'consecrates' himself for his own. Finally, the view of Christ's death as the once for all and definitive sacrifice which ends and surpasses all the sacrifices of the Old Testament, and of his blood as the totally efficacious, atoning, purifying and sanctifying ransom, is set out in full in Heb 9:11–10:18.

4. Eucharist and sacrifice. The sacrificial character of the eucharist, which many exegetes are unwilling to recognise in the texts of the New Testament, can be seen not only in its close relation to the sacrifice of the cross (the bestowal of the saving power of Christ's blood on the participants in the meal), but is also in the eucharist itself, inasmuch as it is treated as a representation of the sacrifice of the cross and as a sacrificial meal.

But Jesus' institution of the supper means more than a symbolic event which depicts and interprets the death on the cross; it is an action which makes present the sacrifice of the cross, applies and makes effective its atoning power for the time before the parousia (cf 1 Cor 11:26), and thereby shares in the sacrificial character of Christ's death. In 1 Cor 10:14–22 this sacrificial character is made clear by the analogy with Jewish (v 18) and pagan (v 20) sacrificial meals. If Paul is putting the christian celebration of the eucharist— though with a more exalted status—in the place of the previous Jewish sacrifices or sacrificial meals, then 1 Cor 9:13; 10:7; 11:28ff also support this view (S. Aalen).

The idea of the christian eucharist as a sacrificial meal is also present in Heb 13:10–14; its uniqueness, by which it surpasses the Jewish sacrifices, lies in the fact that those who celebrate the atoning sacrifice participate in the atoning event at the altar by sharing the sacrificial gifts. This linking of atonement (the sprinkling with the blood of the sacrificial victim) and sacrificial meal, found in the Old Testament in the sacrifice which ratified the covenant at Sinai, is completely fulfilled in the institution of Jesus (cf Mk 14:24), and gives the eucharistic celebration the character of a new sacrificial meal which makes present and effective the new covenant sealed in the blood of Christ (cf 1 Cor 11:25).

5. Effect of the New Testament idea of sacrifice on christian existence. When Heb 13:15f, after recalling the sacrificial death of Jesus, and the eucharistic community, immediately demands of christians a 'sacrifice' of praise of God and brotherly love, this is a transfer of meaning which can already be observed in judaism but which has developed out of the particular christian understanding of sacrifice and can be seen in other places in the New Testament.

Within hellenistic judaism the cultic ideas of temple, priest and sacrifice came to be 'spiritualised' (Wenschkewitz); in Qumran, where the priestly and sacrificial system of the Jerusalem temple was rejected as illegitimate, great value was placed, in a way formally similar to that of the New Testament, on the 'sacrifice of the praise of the lips' and moral living, as an 'acceptable and voluntary sacrifice' (1 QS 9:5; 10:14; CD 11:21). This did not, however, go with a depreciation in principle of cultic and ritual sacrifices, and there was on the contrary an expectation that these would be legitimately renewed in the last days (cf 1 QM 2:5f).

The renunciation on the part of christians of the old cultic sacrifices and the call to christians to 'offer' spiritual or moral 'sacrifices' arise from the evaluation of Christ's death on the cross as the unique atoning sacrifice, and from the consequences which were derived from this for those who followed him. This can be seen in the primitive christian use and interpretation of the Lord's sayings about taking up one's cross (esp. Lk 9:23 'daily'); there is no mention of 'sacrifice' here, but the idea of sacrifice is contained in those of self-denial and readiness to die. A sacrifice image lies behind the saying about 'being salted

with fire' (Mk 9:49; cf the alternative reading of some MSS), and also goes with similar sayings which demand a spirit of sacrifice from the disciples. Paul uses the image of a libation to express his readiness for martyrdom (Phil 2:17; cf 2 Tim 4:6). He requires all christians to present themselves 'as a living sacrifice, holy and acceptable to God' (Rom 12:1), and explains this as being not 'conformed to this world', i.e., renunciation of the world which is hostile to God and leads men astray from him, and inner renewal (v 2). Similarly, in 1 Pet 2:5, christians, as a 'holy priesthood', in the 'spiritual house', are to offer God 'spiritual sacrifices' through Jesus Christ. This refers to actions inspired and made possible by the Holy Spirit, the worship of God, brotherly love, the building up of the church through service, which belong to the 'priestly' vocation of christians. Christ has revealed the way to them through his sacrificial death (cf 1:18f); he himself is the cornerstone of God's holy building, and is to be their model, especially in suffering (2:21-5; 3:17f 4:1f). This is no 'spiritualising' of old cultic ideas, but an application of the central christian idea of sacrifice to the existence of christians in this world.

Bibliography: O. Schmitz, *Die Opferanschauungen des späteren Judentums*, Tübingen 1910; H. Wenschkewitz, 'Die Spiritualisierung der Kultbegriffe Tempel Priester u. Opfer im NT', *Angelos* 4 (1932), 71-230; J. Behm, *TDNT* III, 180-90; J. Blinzler, '*Hierateuma*: Exegese von 1 Pet 2:5 and 9', *Episcopus*, Munich 1949, 49-65; P. Seidensticker, *Lebendiges Opfer*, Münster 1954; E. Ruckstuhl, 'Wesen und Kraft der Eucharistie in der Sicht des Johannesevangeliums', *Das Opfer der Kirche*, Lucerne 1954, 47-90; E. Lohse, *Märtyrer und Gottesknecht*, Göttingen 1955; F. J. Schierse, *Verheissung und Heilsvollendung*, Munich 1955; H. Schürmann, *Der Einsetzungsbericht Lk 22:19-20*, Münster

1955; H. Schürmann, 'Abendmahl', *LTK* I², 26–31; O. Kuss, 'Der theologische Grundgedanke des Hebräerbriefes', *MTZ* 7 (1956), 233–71; J. Sint, 'Schlachten und opfern', *ZKT* 78 (1956), 194–205; J. Carmignac, 'L'utilité ou l'inutilité des sacrifices sanglants dans la *Règle de la Communauté* de Qumran', *RB* 63 (1956), 524–32; R. Schnackenburg, 'Die "Anbetung in Geist und Wahrheit" (Jn 4:23) im Lichte von Qumran-Texten', *BZ* 3 (1959), 88–94; A. Vögtle, 'Blut', *LTK* II², 539–41; H. Zimmermann, 'Mit Feuer gesalzen werden', *TQ* 139 (1959), 28–39; P. Neuenzeit, *Das Herrenmahl*, Munich 1960; J. Betz, *Die Eucharistie in der Zeit der griechischen Väter* I/1: *Aktualpräsenz*, Freiburg 1955; and II/1: *Realpräsenz*, Freiburg 1964²; B. Cooke, 'Synoptic Presentation of the Eucharist as Covenant Sacrifice', *TS* 21 (1960), 1–44; R. Hummel, *Die Auseinandersetzung zwischen Kirche und Judentum im Matthäusevangelium*, Munich 1963, 94–108; J. Bihler, *Die Stephanusgeschichte*, Munich 1963, 134–78; S. Aalen, 'Das Abendmahl als Opfermahl im NT', *NvT* 6 (1963), 128–52; L. Sabourin, 'Sacrificium ut Liturgia in Epistula ad Hebraeos' *VD* 46 (1968), 235–58.

Rudolf Schnackenburg

Salvation

For the extremely wide range of meaning attached to the concept of salvation the Greek bible uses the word-group constituted by *sōzein* (= to save) and its derivatives. In the Old Testament sections this is most frequently used as a rendering of the Hebrew root *yš* (266 times in all, of which the verb is used 131 times, the noun *sōtēria* eighty-three times, and *sōtērion* fifty-two times). But roots such as *mlt* (forty-eight times: 'to allow to escape', 'to deliver'), *nṣl* (twenty-three times: 'to pull out', 'to rescue'), *plṭ* (verb, twelve times; substantive, seven times: 'to escape', 'to be rescued'), *śrd* (six times: 'to escape', 'to survive'), *ḥyh* (five times: 'to live', 'to let live'), *ʿzr* (five times: 'to help') are also sometimes translated

by one or other of the forms of the *sōzein* word-group.

First the concept can be used in a completely general sense to signify the setting free from situations of all kinds of need the individual (danger, injustice, sickness) or the community (war, political upheaval, famine). The deliverance thus signified can be effected by the actual person threatened (who 'helps himself', 1 Sam 25:26, 31, 33), or by other men in a purely natural manner (eg, 1 Sam 11:3; 2 Sam 10:11, 19; 2 Kings 16:7), or alternatively by men who are clearly instruments in the hand of God. It can also be effected by interventions in the course of history by means of which God 'works salvation' (on this, see the theology of history of the Book of Judges, eg, Judg 2:16). God is in no way dependent upon the use of these creatures as his instruments, but often in the course of history he so arranges things that no connection whatever exists between the salvation which is effected and the means used by God, men or circumstances which are often quite inadequate to the end achieved. In fact in a certain sense it is precisely the powerless, the poor, who have special grounds for hoping for salvation from God (see many psalms). Thus it becomes ever clearer that in the last analysis it is God alone who 'works salvation' (Ex 14:13), indeed who 'is salvation' (Ex 15:2). In the Old Testament this idea of salvation can be traced from a primitive eudaemonistic optimism (both on the personal and national plane) to the idealised concept (which was regarded as more or less made actual in the age of David) of a salvation achieved on the political and national plane. This was

807

connected with the further idea of a glorified 'remnant' saved in the midst of catastrophes, to which a 'new heart' and a 'new spirit' would be imparted (Jer 24:7; 31:33; Ezek 36:26ff). The idea of salvation was developed further to a point where it was expected to usher in a new creation, and probably also to take a form that was primarily, though not exclusively spiritual in character in the *ʿōlām habbaʾ*, the new world which was to come at the end of this present age. It is only after the period of the prophets that the expected salvation becomes clearly connected with the expectation of a messiah (⁊ Jesus Christ, ⁊ redeemer, ⁊ saviour), who is to be the absolute bringer of salvation.

The New Testament takes over in all essentials this wide range of meaning connected with the concept of salvation as this has been developed in the Old Testament, and attaches it to the person of Jesus Christ, the Saviour, who has come to bring salvation to sinners and indeed to all men (1 Tim 1:15; 2:4). The condition for obtaining salvation, whether this signifies the healing of a sick man, the forgiveness of specific sins or the ultimate salvation in the broadest and most spiritual sense of the term, is first and foremost a turning back (⁊ conversion) to Jesus Christ in faith, hope and trust. Prayer and the fulfilment of one's duty (Paul instances child-bearing for women 1 Tim 2:15) also belong to the prior conditions necessary for becoming subjectively a sharer in salvation, which objectively Christ has achieved once and for all by his sacrificial death for all mankind.

Bibliography: M. Joseph, *Jüdisches Lexikon* II, 1514–15; E. G. Hirsch, *The Jewish Encyclopaedia*

x, 663–4; Löwe, *BTHW* 245; A. Gelin, *Die Botschaft des Heiles im AT*; ⁊ hope (bibliography); ⁊ redemption (bibliography); W. Wagner, *ZNW* 6 (1905), 205–35; J.-B. Colon, *RSR* 10 (1930), 1–39, 189–217, and 370–415; and 11 (1931), 27–70, 193–223, and 382–412; J. N. Sevenster, *Het verlossingsbegrip bij Philo, vergeleken met de verlossinggedachten van de syn. evangeliën*, 1936; M. Goguel, *RHPR* 17 (1938), 105–44; André Rétif and Paul Lamarche, *Das Heil der Völker*, Düsseldorf 1960; J. Scharbert, *Heilsmittler im AT und im Alten Orient*, Freiburg 1964.

Suitbert H. Siedl

Satan

A. It is consistent with the provisional character of the *Old Testament* that it provides only scanty indications of the nature of Satan and his place in the plan of salvation. The name *Satan* (from the verb *stn* = 'obstruct', 'oppose', 'show hostility to') is used first as the designation of an earthly enemy (1 Kings 11:14, 25). But even here we already find some adumbration of the idea that these 'adversaries' are sent by God to execute his punishment upon Solomon 'because his heart had turned away from the Lord' (1 Kings 11:9). The first mention of Satan as a demonic spirit occurs in 1 Chron 21:1: 'Satan stood up against Israel . . .', while the parallel account in 2 Sam 24:1 runs: 'The anger of the Lord was kindled against Israel . . .'. This correction does indeed attest a certain progress in theological thought, but leaves the actual problem of the part played by Satan still obscure. As *adversary* in the juridical sense, that is, as *accuser*, we encounter Satan in Zechariah (3:1–5), but above all in the Book of Job. Here he plays the part of the 'public prosecutor' of heaven. He is therefore the adversary not of God but of men, and is counted as one of the sons of Elohim. It is his task to go through the earth and to keep watch over men (Job 1:7; 2:2). He is not merely accuser, however, but calumniator and above all *tempter*, who has a double end to pursue: to make men rebel against God and to destroy them. Already here certain essential traits of the biblical portrayal of Satan are to be found, at least implicitly: he is not a partner on an equal footing with God, not an 'anti-God' as in the dualistic religions, but a *creature*, a *servant of God* who constantly needs special permission from God in order to carry out his destructive designs (catastrophes in nature, brigand raids, sickness, etc). The relationship of Satan to the rest of the demonic beings mentioned in the Old Testament, and also the exact reason for his role as adversary remain, however, wholly obscure.

B. It is only in the *New Testament* that we are provided with the definitive answer to this question. Here it is shown how it was possible for a rebellion to be made, an original sin committed in the cosmos created by God, how by Satan's influence this sin was extended from the sphere of the spiritual beings to the world of men, and how it extended its influence still further in this field until Christ 'appeared to destroy the work of Satan' (1 Jn 3:8). It describes the redemption in the form of a mighty struggle between the 'strong man and the stronger' (Mk 3:27 and parallels), which, in spite of the decisive victory of the Cross, will be brought to its conclusion only in the last days of the history of salvation.

As our point of departure we may take the passage in Jn 8:44 which puts the whole 'diabolism' of the bible in a nutshell: 'He [the *diabolos* = 'stirrer-up of tumult', 'calumniator'] was a murderer from the beginning, and has nothing to do with the ↗ truth, because there is no truth in him. When he lies, he speaks according to his own nature, for he is a liar and the father of lies'. *From the beginning*—John does not use any expression such as 'from the first moment of creation onwards', for it is a fundamental doctrine of the bible that 'God created all things as his own' and said that they were 'very good' (Wis 14; Gen 1, 3)—but more probably at the beginning of the *history of salvation*, at the dawn of creation, before man had been made. From that time, therefore, Satan had nothing to do with *the truth*, that is he rejected the truth, the 'word of revelation with which he was confronted' (Kittel), closed his mind to it, rejected the grace that was offered to him and thereby found that he could no longer stand even in *his own truth*, in his creaturely *reality*: 'I will not be that which thou thinkest or as thou hast seen me from eternity . . . I am the creature which escapes thee, which evades thy arm, which turns thy creative word into a lie' (*Satan*, 241).

Corresponding to the johannine expression 'having nothing to do with truth' (lit: 'not standing in the truth') is a passage to which too little attention has been paid in Jude 6–8: 'The [fallen] angels . . . did not keep their own position but left their proper dwelling'. The manner in which they did this can be gathered from the verses which follow, in which the comparison between the gnostics (v 8), the inhabitants of Sodom (v 7), and the fallen angels (v 6) permits an analogy to be drawn between the lower and the higher, the sin of man and the sin of angels. The inhabitants of Sodom rebelled against the order established by God on the sexual plane, and the gnostics on the intellectual and personal plane in that by indulging in unnatural sexual practices or by proudly disdaining the body they denied the need of a creature to be completed, and by this act of autonomous self-glorification they sinned at the same time against their own natures. In just the same way Satan, and with him the rest of the fallen angels, perpetrated on the broadest possible basis what was essentially the same sin: he *willed* to be sufficient to himself, persisted in his blind complacency in his own nature, and thereby lost his true value, his office, his rank (*arkhē*), perverted his nature to lying, and so became the *father of lies* who 'exchanged the truth about God for a lie' (Rom 1:25). So completely did he become the champion and protagonist of lying that between it and him complete identity was achieved: 'Everywhere where lying has become a principle of life, a principle of understanding, of willing, of acting, there Satan is directly at work' (A. Mager, *Satan*, 641).

That this rebellion against God proceeded from a ring-leader who had gathered companions of like disposition about him can be gathered from Rev 12:7–8. Other statements in the New Testament also, among which the 'Beelzebub' pericope (Mk 3:22–7) is particularly clear, permit us to recognize that Satan is the chief of all demons and that his kingdom is single and united. In the light of these statements

in the New Testament those of the Old Testament too acquire their full significance. These tell of how a mighty potentate and enemy of God rebelled against him, and how he was punished for this (Is 14:4–20; Ezek 28:12–17; Pharaoh, Nebuchadnezzar, etc).

Thrown down from heaven—the state of proximity to and friendship with God— *to earth* (Rev 12:9), the father of lies becomes a *murderer*, whose first victims are our own forebears. His tactics remain always the same. They consist of deception, of 'laying a smoke-screen', of uttering lies which are well-nigh impossible to observe. But here for the first time when the first human couple consented to him (↗ possession by evil spirits) these tactics succeeded, and gained for him a far-reaching influence over the cosmos. He became the *prince, the god of this world* (Jn 12:31; 14:30; 1 Cor 2:8; 2 Cor 4:4; Eph 2:2), the *lord of death* (Heb 2:14), because death is nothing else than the expression in the body of sin in the soul: 'By the envy of the devil sin came into the world, and through sin death' (Wis 2:24; Rom 5:12). The close connection between Satan, ↗ sin, and ↗ death is particularly clearly brought out in the pauline letters. Sin, which entered the world through the disobedience of one man (Rom 5:12)— true to the pauline manner of expressing things, which sums up in a single phrase a whole conceptual range from the original effective cause right down to the ultimate effect which it produces— is nothing else than the sinner *par excellence*, the constant adversary of God who avails himself of the instinctive life of man, the ↗ flesh, and even the law given by God himself in order to bring men under his deathly sway (Rom 7:11, 13–20; 1 Cor 15:26, 54–6). He holds humanity prisoner in the bondage of the fear of death (Heb 2:15) until Christ appears as the bringer of God's dominion (Mk 1:15), binds the strong man and robs him of his booty (Mk 3:27).

The stages in this spiritual combat can be followed exactly in the gospel: it commences in the wilderness and continues in the innumerable accounts of how devils are driven out. In these stories the behaviour of the possessed person clearly reflects the terror, torment and fury of the defeated devil before the irresistible advance of his conqueror. The struggle ends at Calvary, where the prince of this world is *cast out* from the whole sphere of humanity (Jn 12:31) just as formerly he was cast out of the individual whom he had enslaved (see the frequent use of *exebale* = 'he cast out' in the exorcisms of Jesus, eg, Mk 1:34). This victory of Christ over Satan is fully revealed in his resurrection, for in this he 'brought life and immortality to light' (2 Tim 1:10) for all who believe in him, becoming for them a 'life-giving spirit' (1 Cor 15:45), a new principle of life, the author of a rebirth by which they become children of God (Jn 1:12) from being 'children of wrath' (Eph 2:3).

But how can these statements concerning the decisive victory of the cross of Christ (Col 1:13; 2:15; 1 Jn 3:8; etc) be reconciled with those which refer to the work of Satan within the young christian community and in the life of individual christians, generating evil, raising obstacles to christian living and destructive in its effects? This is the real problem with which we have to deal. The devil steals the good seed from the hearts of the hearers (Mt 13:19), sows weeds among the wheat (Mt 13:25), seduces Ananias and Sapphira into an act of deceit (Acts 5:3), leads the chaste into temptation (1 Cor 7:5), stirs up dissensions in the community (2 Cor 2:11; Rev 2:24), and seeks in every way to inhibit the work of the apostle to the gentiles by crippling infirmity and other adverse conditions (1 Thess 2:18; 3:5; 2 Cor 12:7). But it is in the *secret revelation* above all that the part played by Satan within the church and within the whole course of world history finds its clearest expression. He has his 'synagogue' at Smyrna (Rev 2:9) and his 'throne' (Rev 2:13) at Pergamum, the centre of emperor-worship. The expulsion of the angels is mentioned for the first time here under the figure of the falling star (8:10), and after this in the following section the evil effects of this are described (8:11) and the satellites of Satan are introduced: locusts (9:3–11), hostile cavalry (9:13–19), the image of all that is terrifying, awe-inspiring, destructive, which has taken place or will take place from time to time in the world through the influence of Satan. After the defeat of Satan in heaven (12:8) the extensive description of his activity within human history begins (12:13–20:10). Under the disguise of the 'beast from the sea' (13:1–10) and the 'beast from the dry land' (13:11–17) as the power behind imperialism and pseudo-religion he rules over 'those who dwell on earth' (13:14; Mt 24:11–12; 2 Thess 2:10). But however mighty and terrible this coalition between brute force and glittering lies may be, at basis it is no more than the death-struggle of the 'beast which goes to perdition' (17:8), and is destined to everlasting bondage (Jude 6) and to eternal torment in the lake of fire and brimstone (Rev 20:10).

In the penultimate stage of this struggle, at the time when Satan's power is at its height, we find the saying which leads to the solution of our problem, at least to the extent that it is capable of being solved at all. As in the Book of Job, 'power to make war on the saints and to *conquer them*' (13:7) is *allowed by God* to Satan, only to an immeasurably greater extent. And it is allowed to him—so the seven letters to the churches tell us—in order that the christian may become the victor with Christ (2:26; 3:5, 12, 21; 21:7), his fellow combatant in the struggle against Satan. Those who seem to have been conquered by Satan are in reality those who follow Christ in his victory on 'white horses' (19:11–14). In order to give them an opportunity to prove themselves in battle Satan is allowed this power. In order to enable men to become 'fellow workers with God' (1 Cor 3:9) in full reality the strongholds of the beleaguered enemy remain standing in the territory which Christ has conquered. In the struggle against Satan there is neither neutrality (Lk 11:23) nor secret treaty-making (Mt 6:24; 1 Cor 10:21). Constant watchfulness (1 Pet 5:8), constant preparedness (Eph 6:10) is required, and above all uncompromising sureness of victory! Satan has in fact power only over those who 'give him opportunity' (Eph 4:27), who allow themselves to be led astray by the threefold lust (1 Jn 2:16), and thereby open the doors of their thinking, willing and acting to him.

But he who belongs to the body of Christ is withdrawn from the power of Satan: the Lord, the God of peace, will soon crush Satan under his feet (Rom 16:20) and guard that man from 'the evil one' (2 Thess 3:3; Mt 6:13).

Bibliography: (A): J. B. Bauer, 'Libera nos a malo', *VD* 34 (1956), 12–15; J. Guillet, *Leitgedanken der Bibel*, Lucerne 1954, 156–68; B. Langton, *Essentials of Demonology, a Study of the Jewish and Christian Doctrine, its Origin and Development*, London 1949; E. Lewis, *The Creator and the Adversary*, New York–Nashville 1948; H. B. Kuhn, 'Angelologia VT', *JBL* 67 (1948), 217–32. See also: M. Zerwick, *VD* 27 (1949), 179; B. Noack, *Satanas und Soteria*, Copenhagen 1949; M. Prager, 'Vater der Lüge, Aufriss einer biblischen Diabologie', *Gloria Dei* 7 (1952), 105–18; A. Romeo, 'Satana-Satanismus', *Enciclopedia Cattolica* x, 1948–61; *Satan* (*Etudes Carmélitaines* 27), Paris 1948 (with numerous articles and a copious bibliography); R. Schärf, 'Die Gestalt des Satans im AT', *Symbolik des Geistes*, ed. Jung, Zurich 1948, 153–319 (see Hempel, *ZAW* 63 [1951], 114f); K. L. Schmidt, 'Luzifer als gefallene Engelmacht', *TZ* 7 (1951), 261–79; F. Zeman, 'De daemoniis in scriptis prophetarum VT in luce daemonologiae Orientis antiqui', *VD* 27 (1949), 270–77 and 321–35; and 28 (1950), 18–28 and 89–97. (B): D. de Rougemont, *Der Anteil des Teufels*, Vienna 1949; C. S. Lewis, *The Screwtape Letters*, London 1942.

Myriam Prager

Saviour

In the Old Testament Yahweh is described, especially in the Psalms and Isaiah, as *Saviour* (Hebrew *yēša͏ᶜ*, *yᵉšûᶜâh*, *môšᵗᶜa*). The corresponding word in LXX is *sōtēr*. In Is 19:20 the Messiah is designated as the 'saviour' who is to come. In judaism this title is generally reserved to God. (When Moses is said to 'save' the people or other leaders of the people are given the title 'saviour', as in Judg 3:9, 15, these cases are exceptions which are to be explained precisely by the fact that it is God who works through these, his helpers.)

In hellenistic circles gods, heroes, and rulers are regarded as saviours in cases in which they have supplied some kind of need. The 'saviour' Asklepios brings healing from sickness. The divinised ruler acts as 'saviour' when he creates peace and order. The deity who breaks the power of death and matter in the mystery cults is likewise saluted as 'saviour'. Jesus was probably never called 'saviour' (*sōtēr*) during his lifetime. Nevertheless this honorific title seems to have been employed at a very early stage, as we can gather from Acts 5:31 and 13:23, and also Phil 3:20. In Lk 1:47 this title is used to designate God. But in Lk 2:11 it is Jesus Christ who is the 'saviour'. In the same way, too, in the Pastoral Epistles both God and Christ are designated by the title of *sōtēr*. When this *sōtēr* title is applied to Jesus it is chiefly as the deliverer of the people from sin and death; in other words on the basis of his work of redemption. In addition to this there is an *eschatological element* (absent from the hellenistic concept of *sōtēr*) in the 'epiphany in glory' which is still awaited, and in which the work of redemption will finally be completed (Tit 2:13; Phil 3:20). It may be that John deliberately chooses a mode of designation which closely resembles the formulae employed in the cult of the emperor as *sōtēr* (formulae of this description are applied to Hadrian), or alternatively he may even be reacting against the idea of Asklepios

as 'saviour' (his sanctuary at Pergamum is referred to as the 'throne of Satan' in Rev 2:13). But these points cannot be determined with any degree of certainty.

Bibliography: O. Cullmann, *The Christology of the New Testament*, London 1959, 246–52 (with extensive bibliography); K. H. Rengstorff, *Die Anfänger der Auseinandersetzung zwischen Christusglaube und Asklepiosfrömmigkeit*, Münster 1953; K. Prümm, *Religionsgeschichtliches Handbuch*, Freiburg 1943 (Index); S. Lyonnet, *VD* 36 (1958), 3–15; E. Pax, *LTK* v², 80–82; W. Foerster and G. Fohrer, *TWNT* vii, 866–1024; J. Zandee, *Numen* 11 (1964), 52–6 and 62–4.

Johannes B. Bauer

Scandal

The biblical word which we translate 'scandal', and which has entered our language in this form, originally designated the stumbling-block causing a fall, then the fall itself, and finally everything which provides the occasion for stumbling and falling, in other words a 'hostile influence'. The realisation of the image which lies behind this word makes it easier to understand many passages in the bible, and also explains the wider usage and field of significance attached to it.

In the New Testament the word *scandal* is not used primarily of moral danger, but of *influences hostile to faith*, and since faith provides the basis for obtaining salvation, all the words for scandal which bear upon this carry special weight. When it is a question of the agent by whom, or the occasion through which scandals are caused a significant difference is to be discerned: one line of thought leads back to God who in his inscrutable wisdom laid down ways to salvation which are hard for men to understand, and so put their faith to the test, and, indeed, represent a burden upon and a challenge to it. They can take scandal at this. Other statements refer to men who wickedly and culpably set pitfalls for the faithful and lead them to destruction, to falling away from the faith. At the very outset we find the aged Simeon prophesying that the child Messiah is 'set for the fall and the rising of many in Israel' (Lk 2:34), and this prophecy is fulfilled in Jesus' answer to the emissaries of the baptist: 'Blessed is he who takes no offence at me' (Mt 11:6). The significance of this is that the person and actions of Jesus run counter to almost all the contemporary messianic expectations of the Jews: his earthly origin (Mk 6:3; see also Jn 7:27, 41f), his renunciation of external power, and the aim of political liberation (see Jn 6:14f), the works of grace which he performs for sinners and the irreligious without any accompanying condemnation (see the questions addressed to him by the Baptist, Mt 11:2ff), and finally his passion and cross, which are incomprehensible even to his closest disciples (Mk 8:31–3 and parallels). In fact, as Jesus has predicted, the passion shakes their faith for a time, and scatters the little flock of the faithful until the risen Christ assembles them once more (Mk 14:27f). The taking of scandal on the part of the disciples here constitutes a fulfilment of scripture, and, like the betrayal of Judas (Mk 14:21), pertains to the divine plan. For, without absolving the individuals concerned from responsibility (see the presumptuous attitude of Peter (Mk 14:29f), it

was part of this divine plan that the Son of Man should undergo the deepest humiliation and the most total abandonment (see Mk 14:41; Jn 16:32). In the johannine gospel this becomes still clearer, for here Christ simultaneously veils and unveils his divine glory, and so compels men to an inescapable decision between belief and unbelief. The scandal which men take in the person and revealed message of Jesus (6:61) can be endured in faith (6:68f), but unbelief is a sin, indeed is *the* sin (15:22–4; 16:9). Of its nature, then, the divine activity has the effect of challenging faith and putting it to the test, and this effect continues in the subsequent course of salvific history. The hatred and mortal enmity incurred by Jesus are transferred to his disciples, whose faith can be severely shocked by it (Jn 16:1). But only those men whose faith is not deeply rooted enough fall away (cp Mk 4:17). The temptation and scandal to faith to which men will be exposed in the time of eschatological affliction will be especially terrible (Mt 24:10; see also Mk 13:5f, 22f). The faith and constancy of the elect will then indeed be put to the proof (see Mk 13:13, 23).

Scandals are among the inevitable phenomena of this present age. Nevertheless Jesus invokes a terrible woe upon him by whom they come. It would have been better for him that a mill-stone should have been hung about his neck and that he should have been submerged in the sea (Lk 17:1f). This is the other view of the culpable giver of scandal: here too it is certainly the temptation to fall away from faith that is envisaged. For the 'little ones' who must be preserved from scandal arc the innocent believers (cf Mk 9:42), the simple members of the community (cf Mt 10:42), whom, nevertheless, no-one may despise (Mt 18:10), since it has pleased God to reveal Jesus' message to those who are childlike in their lack of wisdom (Mt 11:25). A particularly vicious tempter in the last age will be the ↗ antichrist who in the power of Satan will actually perform deceitful signs and wonders (2 Thess 2:9f).

The early church remains conscious of the fact that scandal can be taken at the idea of Jesus as Messiah. It makes an appropriate use of the image of the 'stone of stumbling and rock of scandal' (Is 8:14), which causes unbelievers to fall, but combines with this image that other one which Jesus himself has already employed (Mk 12:10 and parallels), that namely of the stone which the builders rejected and which has become the 'corner-stone', that is, for all those who believe in him (see Rom 9:32f; 1 Pet 2:6–8). Paul regards the event of the cross as the climax of the paradoxical action of God in salvific history, at which men can take scandal. From this he develops his profound ideas on the 'scandal of the cross'. All human wisdom will be confounded at the 'word of the Cross'. It can be received and accepted only by faith. God has deliberately laid down this way of 'folly' because the world with its wisdom has failed to recognise God (1 Cor 1:21). To the Jews, who expect a mighty Messiah and demand signs of his coming, the shamefulness of the cross is a scandal; to the Greeks, proud of their wisdom, it is folly (1:23). But God has chosen those who are weak and foolish in the eyes of the world in order to confound the exalted and the wise so that no man can boast in his presence (1:29). The scandal of the cross, however, has a profound effect upon christian life, for it demands of christians that they shall take up the cross of their master and with him endure contempt and persecution. In contrast to the judaising teachers of error, who confuse the Galatian communities and in Paul's opinion are merely striving to obtain fame in the eyes of their Jewish compatriots and want to escape persecution (Gal 6:12), Paul himself demands that the scandal of the cross shall not be made void (Gal 5:11). For his part, through the cross of Christ the world has been crucified to him and he to the world (6:14). Thus the scandal of the Cross designates the path that the christian must follow through this world, and it can be overcome only by faith in the resurrection of Christ and its power, which can already be felt in the present (2 Cor 4:16ff; 13:4), and by hope in the christian's own resurrection (Phil 3:10f).

But the New Testament also recognises *moral scandal*. The logion concerning the members of the body which give scandal (Mk 9:43–7 and parallels) has a unique power to unveil all the urgency and radicalism of Jesus in moral matters. When a man's hand, foot, or eye gives him scandal—that is, becomes an occasion of grave sin—he must be ready to pluck it from him and to enter eternal life (or the kingdom of God) without it rather than be thrown into hell with two hands, feet or eyes. In the interpretation of the parable of the tares among the wheat it is said that the angels of God will one day remove 'all causes of sin and all evil-doers' from the kingdom of the Son of Man (Mt 13:41). The similarity of the expressions employed makes it probable that this refers to those men who, being corrupt themselves, give rise to scandal so as to corrupt others. More often we are confronted with exhortations not to give any occasion of sin to our Christian brother by our own behaviour. In the question of whether it is permissible to eat flesh and wine Paul concedes that those who see nothing unlawful in it are right; but at the same time he requires of them that they shall voluntarily go without if by their eating and drinking they lead the 'weak' astray as to act against their conscience and fall into sin. Love prescribes that we should avoid even those actions which, while not in themselves bad, nevertheless by force of circumstances become a cause of sin to others, and can bring about the downfall of a brother 'for whom Christ died' (Rom 14:13–15, 20f; see also 1 Cor 8:13). 1 Jn 2:10 also contains an exhortation to brotherly love. But here, by reason of the figurative language, it is not clear whether he who loves his brother and 'walks in the light' has nothing scandalous in him, or offers no scandal to others, or whether it means that in his walking in the light he does not encounter anything scandalous. To give scandal is always something terrible (see also Rom 16:17; Rev 2:14), because thereby the salvation and redemption of another is threatened, but in the community it is particularly so because 'a little leaven leavens [ie, a little sin corrupts] the whole lump' (1 Cor 5:6), and because 'a "root of bitterness" [can] spring up and cause

trouble, and by it the many become defiled' (Heb 12:15).

Bibliography: G. Stählin, *Skandalon*, Gütersloh 1930; G. Stählin, *TWNT* vii, 338–52; A. Humbert, 'Essai d'une théologie du scandale dans les Synoptiques, *Bbl* 35 (1954), 1–28; R. Schnackenburg, 'Vom Ärgernis des Kreuzes', *GL* 30 (1957), 90–95; K. H. Müller, *Der paulinische Skandalon-Begriff*, Würzburg 1965 (dissertation). See also: O. Schmitz, *Vom Wesen des Ärgernisses*, 1925[2]; W. A. Berruex, *La notion de scandale dans le NT*, Lausanne 1953 (dissertation).

Rudolf Schnackenburg

Scripture

1. *The concept.* Jews and christians have a collection of books which are accounted normative for faith and morals. The collection bears the designation 'scripture', 'holy scripture', or 'bible'. From the aspect of salvific history the compilation is divided into the *Old* and the *New Testaments*, but of these the Jews recognise only the former, while christians recognise both Testaments as normative.

These collective designations have a history which goes back right into the period of pre-christian judaism, or at least into that of early christianity. The New Testament speaks repeatedly of the 'scriptures' (*graphai*) in the sense of books that are normative, and which are already in existence among the Jews (Mt 21:42; 22:29; 26:54, 56 ['scriptures of the prophets']; Mk 12:24; 14:49; Lk 24:27, 32, 45; Jn 5:39; Acts 17:2, 11; 18:24, 28; Rom 15:4; 16:26 ['prophetic writings']; 1 Cor 15:3f; 2 Pet 3:16), but only once of the 'holy scriptures' (Rom 1:2; a similar expression is found in 2 Tim 3:15). Often, too, the New Testament speaks in the singular, but in a collective sense, of 'scripture' (Jn 2:22; 7:38, 42; 10:35; 17:12; 19:28; Acts 8:32; Rom 4:3; 9:17; 10:11; 11:2; Gal 3:8, 22; 4:30; 1 Tim 5:18; 1 Pet 2:6; 2 Pet 1:20; in a non-collective sense 2 Tim 3:16). The word *scripture* here can also be used to designate a particular passage in scripture (Mk 12:10; 15:28; Lk 4:21; Jn 13:18; 19:24, 36f; Acts 1:16; 8:35; Jas 2:8, 23). In a few exceptional cases the term is even applied to a work not elsewhere regarded as authoritative (thus Jas 4:5). In the Old Testament such terms do not yet occur, but the expression 'the holy scriptures' probably is familiar to Philo and the adherents of hellenistic judaism, and that too in a sense corresponding to that in which it is used among the rabbis (instances in *TDNT* 1, 750f). Besides this we should mention the Talmudic designation 'writings' for a group of Old Testament books which is additional to the Torah and the Prophets in the narrower sense (Babylonian Talmud, Baraitha, Baba Bathra 14b).

Already in post-exilic judaism we find mention of the 'books' in the sense of normative writings (Dan 9:2), of the 'holy books' (1 Macc 12:9); frequently in Philo and Josephus [*TDNT* 1, 615f]). Instances also occur of the singular usage 'the holy book' (2 Macc 8:23). Apart from this the Torah in particular is referred to as the 'Book of Moses' (Ezra 6:18; 7:6, 9), a turn of phrase which is also found in the New Testament (Mk 12:26; see also Gal 3:10: 'The Book of the Law'). Similarly reference is made to the

'book of the psalms' (Lk 20:42; Acts 1:20), the 'book of the words of Isaiah' (Lk 3:4; cp 4:17), and the 'book of the prophets' (Acts 7:42). But the New Testament never speaks of the 'books', the 'holy books', or even of the 'book' without further qualification in the sense of the biblical writings. It is not until the end of the first century AD that the Epistle of Clement (43:1) re-introduces the old Jewish expression 'the holy books'. Such turns of phrase as these were rendered in Greek by the words *biblos* and *biblion*, both terms for 'book', and in Latin this word was retained as a loanword, *Biblia*. In accordance with its Greek origin this word was first treated of as a neuter plural, but later (certainly from the twelfth, and probably from the ninth, century onwards) as a feminine singular. It is this that lies behind the English term *bible* and the corresponding terms in other European languages.

The terms *Old Testament* and *New Testament* represent anglicisations of the Latin designations *Vetus Testamentum* and *Novum Testamentum*, terms which belong initially to salvation history and are primarily intended to refer to the Old Covenant of Moses at Sinai and the New Covenant of Jesus at Golgotha. As early as the prophecies of Jeremiah we find a proclamation of a 'new covenant' (31:31), which Jeremiah contrasts with the earlier covenant made at the time of the exodus from Egypt (31:32). Subsequently the New Testament speaks of a 'new covenant' instituted by Jesus (Lk 22:20; 1 Cor 11:25; Heb 9:15; 12:24), so that Paul can refer to the earlier one as the 'Old Covenant' (2 Cor 3:14). But all these references to covenants do not yet constitute a name for a collection of books. At the same time, however, Paul does speak (2 Cor 3:14) of the 'reading of the old covenant (testament)', and thereby paves the way for the subsequent development in which the expression came to be used as a name for a collection of books. Later, at the turn of the second and third centuries AD, the designation 'New Testament', which had originally been used in the sense of 'New Covenant', likewise comes to stand for a series of writings. It has become general practice in English to speak of the old and new covenants when referring to the institutions in salvation history, but of the Old and New Testaments when it is the collections of books that is in question.

2. *Range and extent.* The books which the Jews or christians hold to be normative for their faith and their lives constitute the 'canon' (a concept which has become native to christian theology at least since the fourth century) of the holy scriptures. 'Canon' here signifies not a list of such writings, but the norm which these books provide for the church. The canon of both the Old and the New Testaments has undergone a prolonged development until it was finally defined as a dogma for the Catholic Church by the Council of Trent (Fourth Session, 8 April 1546: DS 1501–4 [=DB 783ff]). According to this decree, the canon of the Old Testament includes five books of Moses, or the Torah, ie, Genesis, Exodus, Leviticus, Numbers, and Deuteronomy; and further, the books of Joshua, Judges, Ruth, the four Books of Kings, (ie, 1 and 2 Samuel and 1(3) and 2(4) Kings); 1 and 2 Chron-

icles, Ezra and Nehemiah (also called 2 Ezra), Tobit, Judith, Esther, Job, Psalms; the five Books of Wisdom (ie, Proverbs, Qohelet [Ecclesiastes], Song of Solomon, Wisdom, Sirach [Ecclesiasticus]); the so-called four 'major prophets' (ie, Isaiah, Jeremiah [together with Lamentations and Baruch], Ezekiel and Daniel); the so-called twelve 'minor prophets' (ie, Hosea, Joel, Amos, Obadiah, Jonah, Micah, Nahum, Habakkuk, Zephaniah, Haggai, Zechariah, and Malachi); and, finally, 1 and 2 Maccabees— forty-six writings in all, of greater or lesser extent.

The following books are considered to belong to the canon of the New Testament writings: the four gospels (ie, Matthew, Mark, Luke, and John); the Acts of the Apostles; the thirteen letters of Paul (ie, Romans, 1 and 2 Corinthians, Galatians, Ephesians, Philippians, Colossians, 1 and 2 Thessalonians, 1 and 2 Timothy, Titus, Philemon, and also Hebrews); the seven so-called 'catholic epistles' (ie, James, 1 and 2 Peter, 1, 2, and 3 John, and Jude); and finally, Revelation.

References to the normative status of individual books of the Old Testament also occur in the later writings of the Old Testament itself (Sir 46–9, especially 49:10; 2 Macc 2:13), and also in the New Testament (Mt 23:35; Lk 24:44; Jn 5:46, etc). In Flavius Josephus (*Contr. Ap.* 1, 8 §§ 38–42) we also find a reference from about the end of the first century AD to the total number of the books, namely twenty-two. It is evident that various writings which are nowadays enumerated individually have here been taken together. A list of the sacred books dating from the second century AD is also to be found in the Babylonian Talmud (Baraitha Baba Bathra 14b). This Jewish 'canon' includes only books which have been preserved in Hebrew or Aramaic. Those writings which are in Greek or which have been handed down as complete books only in Greek are omitted from it. Such are Tobit, Judith, 1 and 2 Maccabees, Wisdom, Sirach (Ecclesiasticus), Baruch, and the Greek additions to Esther and Daniel, which, since the sixteenth century, have been described as 'deutero-canonical' writings, in contrast to the universally acknowledged 'proto-canonical' writings (the designation *deutero-canonical* was first used by Sixtus of Sienna [1520–1569]). The christian church took over the canon of the Jews, but the 'Deutero-canonical' books, which were prized especially in the circles of hellenistic judaism, only came gradually to have equal value with the proto-canonical writings. As early as the fourth century there is evidence that they had this value here and there in the Western church (Synod of Rome, AD 382; Augustine, *De Doctrina Christiana* II, 8, 13). But against this they were not so valued by Jerome, who on this question allowed himself to be guided by the views of the synagogue, whereas in the East it is only from the seventh century onwards that they can be shown to have been accorded canonical status (Trullanum 692).

The canon of the New Testament has been developed within the christian church. Apart from the heretical list of the scriptures composed by Marcion, it is first attested in the so-called Canon of Muratori (called after the Italian historian Ludovico Antonia Muratori [1672–1750], who discovered it in the Ambrosiana at Milan), which belongs to the second half of the second century. Admittedly it is not yet as extensive as subsequent versions, which appear in the West at the end of the fourth century (Synod of Rome, AD 382), and in the East perhaps already in the third century in Origen (*In Jos. Hom.* VII 1), and certainly in the fourth century in Athanasius (*Festal Epistle* 39 from the year 367; *Ench. bib.* n 15). The canonicity of certain of the writings of the New Testament was disputed in the first centuries: that of Hebrews in the West, and that of Revelation in the East. Furthermore the canonicity of the catholic epistles was everywhere disputed, even though 1 Peter and 1 John were recognised as canonical in most cases.

In the Middle Ages the limits of the canon were not seriously called in question either in the case of the Old Testament or in that of the New, and the Council of Florence confirmed the canon as it had come down to it in its Bull *Cantate Domino* of 4 February 1441 (*Decretum pro Jacobitis*: DS 1334 [=DB 706]). In the sixteenth century, however, questions arose in catholic and reformation circles alike concerning the full authority of several books for questions of the faith, and doubts were raised as to whether entire writings or particular parts which had not been included in all the earlier manuscripts did in fact belong to the canon. Against such ideas the Council of Trent issued its decree mentioned above, and in the nineteenth century this was invoked by the First Vatican Council (c.4, *De Revelatione*: DS 3029 [=DB

1809]). In Luther's time, although the canon had been established by tradition, it had not yet been formally defined. He and the protestants who followed him admitted only those Old Testament books which were recognised by the Jews as canonical. The rest, the Deutero-canonical writings, were called 'apocrypha'. Luther also excluded from the New Testament Hebrews, James, Jude, and Revelation. Since the seventeenth century, however, the lutherans have reverted to the traditional canon of the New Testament, to which the calvinists have consistently adhered.

3. *The nature of scripture.* The declaration that a document belongs to the canon *ipso facto* implies that it is inspired by God. Logically speaking, the difference between being inspired and being canonical corresponds to the difference between being something and being recognised as such.

Inspiration (as a technical term for the biblical authors and books the word is current from the seventeenth century onwards) in the passive sense implies that sacred scripture is of divine origin, while in the active sense it signifies the charisma of the biblical author, which enables him to compose an inspired work.

The New Testament does indeed notice in passing that every scripture (by this it means the normative books of the Old Covenant) is inspired by God (2 Tim 3:16: *theopneustos*; Vulgate: *divinitus inspirata*), and further that God, the Holy Spirit, or even Christ himself has spoken in the books of the Old Testament (God: Rom 1:2; 3:2; Heb 1:7–13; 2:6, 11:11–13; 5:5f; the Holy Spirit: Acts 1:16; Heb 3:7;

Christ: Heb 10:5–9); but the compelling proof for the inspiration of the biblical writings as a whole is found in the tradition which already manifested itself in the Epistle of Clement (45:2; 63:2). The church has defined her views on this conviction that the holy scriptures are inspired in the Bull of the Council of Florence already mentioned (*Decretum pro Jacobitis*: DS 1334 [=DB 706]), and has proclaimed it as a dogma at the Council of Trent (Fourth Session: DS 1501 [=DB 783]). The Tridentine decision was renewed by the First Vatican Council (Third Session, 24 April 1870, *Constitutio dogmatica de fide catholica*, c. 2: DS 3006 [=DB 1787]; also c. 4: DS 3029 [=DB 1809]). According to the doctrine of the church, inspiration is a grace exercising a supernatural influence by which God moves the intellectual faculties of the author in such a way that he conceives of within his own spirit, intends to write down, and faithfully does write down that which according to the will of God must be written and must be imparted to the Church (see Leo XIII, *Providentissimus Deus*, 18 November 1893; DS 3293 [=DB 1952]).

This inspiration of holy scripture must be distinguished from prophetic inspiration, which does admittedly also represent a supernatural and divine influence upon an individual man. The purpose of prophetic inspiration, however, is not the composition of a book but rather that the man endowed with the grace of it may impart some message to others in accordance with God's will. Moreover as a rule the message is an oral one. Certainly prophetic inspiration and scriptural inspiration can be bestowed upon the same man if he is both prophet and biblical author at the same time, but there is no necessity in such a combination. Either kind of inspiration can be bestowed without the other. This important distinction is numbered among the achievements of the more recent theology. In taking over Jewish views on prophetic and scriptural inspiration, all earlier christian authorities combined the two (hence, too, they spoke of 'prophecy' and 'prophetic' where we today speak of 'inspiration'). The effects of this conception have survived to the present day, and have raised unnecessary difficulties in the solving of many questions relating to the bible. The consequence of this earlier opinion was that scholars were compelled to seek among prophets or apostles (to whom a similar endowment of the Spirit was ascribed) for the authors of the biblical books, for on this view there was no other way of explaining the inspiration of a given document than through the prophetic or apostolic charisms with which its author was endowed. It is not until recent times, and as a result of the progress in historical and critical knowledge of the New Testament now summed up in modern works of introduction to it, that a change has gradually come about, and that the fresh knowledge which scholars have acquired concerning the manner in which the biblical writings were composed has compelled them to draw the necessary distinction between prophetic or apostolic inspiration on the one hand, and scriptural inspiration on the other.

The fact that a biblical writing is divinely inspired does not diminish the human freedom of its author. In the writing of it God is at work in a mysterious and, for us, an inscrutable manner, and simultaneously the human author works with complete freedom. Thus a biblical document is wholly a product of God and no less wholly a product of its human author. This explains why the books of the bible should differ one from another in presentation and style. Such differences, and many shortcomings as well, derive from the work of the human author whose personal qualities are no less actively present for the fact that he is inspired. Thus a certain tension prevails between the divine and the human elements in the bible, a duality of effect which is remarkable.

Certainly inspiration extends to the actual truths which are taught in sacred scripture, and even to the individual words to the extent that these are necessary for rightly expressing such truths. We must at least, therefore, recognize the presence of a so-called 'real' inspiration. But as soon as one reflects more deeply upon the nature of inspiration one feels inclined to postulate an influence which extends still further, one namely which bears even upon the individual choice of words. This is the so-called verbal inspiration, admittedly not in the antiquated sense of a mechanical influence exercised upon the human author by God, but in the sense of an inspiration that is verbal in the psychological sense. On this hypothesis not only the content of the bible, but the actual biblical text itself would be wholly the work of God and wholly the work of man. This view has the advantage of consistency, but various observations with regard to the biblical books themselves seem to exclude it and to indicate simply a 'real' inspiration (thus the possibility that an uninspired collaborator imposed his own style on the ideas of the inspired author, and committed them to writing (see DS 3395 [=DB 1998]; and DS 3593 [=DB 2178]), or errors of memory such as are found in Mk 2:26; 6:17; Mt 23:35; 27:9; 1 Cor 1:14, 16. Again the loss of the original text of several of the writings of the bible, and the high estimation in which a translation, namely the Vulgate, has been held rather than the original text throughout many centuries of the church's life might be adduced in favour of this view).

The principal effect of inspiration is the so-called inerrancy of sacred scripture. This fact follows necessarily from the concept of inspiration, but it is important to obtain a correct understanding of what this inerrancy really means. It is not an absolute inerrancy, though the not altogether happy expression 'inerrancy' might be taken to suggest this. On the contrary the term 'inerrancy' requires to be qualified in certain particular respects. It is not possible to enter more deeply into these extremely difficult questions at this point. Here we must confine ourselves to a brief mention of certain aspects which are important for a correct understanding of what inerrancy means.

Inerrancy applies only to the assertions, the judgements of the inspired author, not simply to everything which is included in the bible. Admittedly it is not always easy to say what the author intends to assert or to teach. In every case a distinction must be drawn between the actual content of the saying and the form in which it is presented. The literary genre of a passage, or indeed of whole books, must be taken into account before one is able to recognize the true significance of a saying or the presentation of an idea. If it is apparent that earlier traditions have been edited, as is very frequently the case, the biblical author must not be held responsible for them, at least not in all details, without further qualification. The question arises, therefore, of what he himself intends to assert or to teach. Because inspiration is not revelation, not the unveiling of things otherwise unknown, it follows that the biblical recorder of history, just like any other, had first to look for sources on which to base his work, and had to edit them. In this there was much that he was no longer in a position to verify in all its details, a fact which subsequently appears in his own presentation. Finally the inspired author writes history as a child of his age in the manner appropriate to his age, with a freedom which was common in antiquity, but which may seem strange to us, accustomed as we are to modern methods of historical research.

Divine truth is made present in the bible through men who, even though inspired, did not cease to be men, and it is only through the medium of their human modes of expression, conditioned as they are by circumstances of epoch and environment, that we are allowed to have access to the truth of God.

4. *Interpretation.* The interpretation of holy scripture, or 'hermeneutics' (*hermeneutikē* [*tekhnē*] = [the art of] interpretation) was concerned with the

question of the multiplicity of senses in the bible. After a prolonged development originating far back in antiquity the following presentation of the matter was arrived at by Aquinas (*Summa Theologiae* I, q. 1, a. 10): he drew an initial distinction between the literal and the spiritual sense. Then he subdivided this spiritual sense first into the *allegorical* sense, as he called it— the sense which today we call the typical, or typological, sense—in which episodes which took place under the old covenant foreshadow those of the new. Aquinas' second subdivision of the spiritual sense was the *moral* sense, in which that which befell Christ or those who went before him and foreshadowed him is presented as an example for us to imitate in our conduct. Aquinas' third subdivision of the spiritual sense was the *anagogical* sense. In this the events in the life of Christ or those who foreshadowed him are once more taken as types and patterns, but now patterns of what is to come in the future age of eternal glory.

All sound interpretations of scripture invariably take as their starting-point the literal sense, the sense which arises directly from the actual words and the context in which they appear, except in cases in which the words are intended to signify something different from what is immediately expressed (as, for instance, in an allegory). But this is to be determined from the context. Again, according to Aquinas (*Summa Theologiae* I q. 1, a. 10, ad 1), who adduces Augustine in his support (*Epistola* 93 [*Contra Vincentium Donatistam*] 24), theological truths can only be adduced by means of the literal sense. Nevertheless the question of the existence of a

spiritual sense over and above the literal one, which in recent times has been thrust into the background with the development of an exegesis based on historical criticism, still has its importance in certain spheres even to this day. Thus it enables us to understand the use of the Old Testament in the New or the importance of the bible in the liturgy and in other departments of the church's life.

But in contemporary thought hermeneutics has acquired a new meaning, now that the question has arisen: How is scripture to be understood as a whole? This problem initially arose from the modern conception of the world, which in recent times has ousted the ancient and mediaeval ideas on the subject. As a work deriving from antiquity the bible shares these latter views concerning the cosmic order, which are today so outmoded. In addition to this the history of religion and culture has contributed further new insights and also not infrequently ideological prejudices, so that all this, whether justifiably or not, has contributed to a transformation in our understanding of scripture. The case of Galileo in the seventeenth century constitutes an outstanding landmark in this development, and in our own times the call for a demythologising of the New Testament raised by Rudolph Bultmann has drawn attention to the problem of understanding scripture in a manner which cannot be ignored.

Under the influence of the modern natural sciences it has long been customary to take the work of the six days in Gen 1 no longer in a literal sense. A different interpretation of it is necessary than that which earlier generations made. But should we not come to a similar conclusion with regard to ↗ angels and ↗ demons, and with regard to concepts such as those of the Holy Spirit and ↗ grace, and doctrines such as the virginal conception of Jesus (↗ virgin birth) and his ↗ resurrection? It is indeed possible to decide in general terms how the biblical authors would have understood their own statements. But in particular cases are not we of the present day, with our new knowledge and new insights, justified and perhaps indeed compelled either to interpret the data afresh or simply to disregard it altogether? Often enough, it is true, we cannot arrive at any short conclusion on the basis of scripture alone. Illustrations of this are, for instance, the discussions carried on in protestant circles concerning the significance of the virginal conception of Jesus or the message of his resurrection.

In the sphere of catholicism the case is different. Here, in addition to scripture itself, we have tradition as a further aid for the interpretation of scripture, and finally we have the teaching of the church in her official function as interpreter of the bible. Certainly even with this assistance many questions do still remain open as to how such and such a passage in scripture should be understood. But in those points which are basic to Christian faith sureness is the predominant note. Not only doctrines such as that of the virginal conception of Jesus and his resurrection, but also those of his messianism and his sonship of God, and many other points, which have long since been proclaimed and estab-

lished by the church as dogmas, can never be revoked or reinterpreted in a different sense. In this way biblical research, while remaining constantly aware of the problems entailed by bringing contemporary knowledge and thought to bear on sacred scripture, does have a firm guiding line by which its course can be directed.

Bibliography: Apart from works of introduction to the Old and New Testaments and the appropriate sections in general treatises of dogmatic theology, *In general and on 1*: G. Schrenk, *TDNT* I, 615–20 and 742–69; B. Hessler, *LTK* II², 335f. *On 2*: SB IV, 1, 413–34; P. Katz, 'The Old Testament Canon in Palestine and Alexandria', *ZNW* 47 (1956), 191–217; F. V. Filson, *Which Books Belong in the Bible? A Study of Canon*, Philadelphia 1957; H. Bacht, 'Die Rolle der Tradition in der Kanonbildung', *Catholica* (*Jahrbuch für Kontroverstheologie* 12), Münster, 1958, 16–37; A. Jepsen, 'Zur Kanongeschichte des AT', *ZAW* 71 (1959), 114–36; J. Schildenberger, J. Michl, and K. Rahner, *LTK* v², 1277–84; F. Hesse, 'Das AT als Kanon', *ZST* 3 (1961), 315–27; P. Neuenzeit, *HTG* I, 777–90; K. Aland, 'Das Problem des Ntl. Kanons', *ZST* 4 (1962), 220–42. *On 3*: SB IV 1, 435–51; A. Bea, *De inspiratione et inerrantia Sacrae Scripturae*, Rome 1947; A. Bea, *LTK* v², 703–11; E. Florit, *Ispirazione biblica*, Rome 1951²; N. H. Snaith, *The Inspiration and Authority of the Bible*, London 1956; J. Schildenberger, 'Inspiration und Irrtumslosigkeit der Heiligen Schrift', *Fragen der Theologie Heute*, ed. J. Feine and others, Einsiedeln 1957, 109–21; L. Vagaggini, 'Ispirazione biblica e questioni connesse', *Problemi e orientamenti di teologia dommatica*, Milan 1957, 171–229; B. Brinkmann, 'Inspiration und Kanonizität der Heiligen Schrift in ihrem Verhältnis zur Kirche', *Scholastik* 33 (1958), 208–33; K. Rahner, *Inspiration in the Bible*, London and New York 1961; K. Rahner, 'On the Inspiration of the Bible', *The Bible in a New Age*, London 1965, 1–15; S. Tromp, *De S. Scripturae inspiratione*, Rome 1962⁶; D. M. Beegle, *The Inspiration of Scripture*, Philadelphia 1962; W. Harrington, 'The Inspiration of Scripture', *ITQ* 29 (1962), 3–24; A. V. Bauer, 'Inspiration als sakramentales Ereignis, zum Verhältnis von Wort, Sakrament und Menschheit Christi nach der Theologie Karl Barths', *TTZ* 72 (1963), 84–104; P. Grelot, 'L'inspiration scripturaire', *RSR* 51 (1963), 337–82;

P. Benoit, *Inspiration and the Bible*, London 1965. On 4: J. Coppens, *Les Harmonies des deux Testaments, Essai sur les divers sens des Écritures et sur l'Unité de la Révélation*, Paris 1949; J. Coppens, *Vom christlichen Verständnis des AT*, Louvain 1952; J. Schildenberger, *Vom Geheimnis des Gotteswortes, Einführung in das Verständnis der Heiligen Schrift*, Heidelberg 1950; W. Schweitzer, 'Das Problem der biblischen Hermeneutik in der gegenwärtigen Theologie', *TLZ* 75 (1950), 467–78; R. Bultmann, 'Das Problem der Hermeneutik', *ZTK* 47 (1950), 47–69; J. Daniélou, *Sacramentum Futuri, Études sur les origines de la typologie biblique*, Paris 1950; O. Schilling, 'Der geistige Sinn der Heiligen Schrift', *TG* 44 (1954), 241–54; A. Bea, 'Biblische Hermeneutik', *LTK* II², 435–9; A. Bea, '"Religionswissenschaftliche" oder "theologische" Exegese? Zur Geschichte der neueren biblischen Hermeneutik', *Bbl* 40 (1959), 322–41; E. Fuchs, *Hermeneutik*, Bad Cannstatt 1954; E. Fuchs, *Zum hermeneutischen Problem in der Theologie: Die existentiale Interpretation*, Tübingen 1959; E. Fuchs, 'Das NT und das hermeneutische Problem', *ZTK* 58 (1961), 198–226; R. Hermann, *Gotteswort und Menschenwort in der Bibel, Eine Untersuchung zu theologischen Grundfragen der Hermeneutik*, Berlin 1956; R. Hermann, 'Zur Theologie der Schriftauslegung: Bild und Verkündigung', *Festschrift H. Jursch*, Berlin 1962, 71–83; K. H. Schelkle, 'Heilige Schrift und Wort Gottes, Erwägungen zur biblischen Hermeneutik', *TQ* 138 (1958), 257–74; K. H. Schelkle, 'Hermeneutische Zeugnisse im NT', *BZ* 6 (1962), 161–77; K. H. Miskotte, *Zur biblischen Hermeneutik*, Zollikon 1959; H. Wildberger, 'Auf dem Wege zu einer biblischen Theologie, Erwägungen zur Hermeneutik des AT', *ET* 19 (1959), 70–90; H. de Lubac, *Exégèse médiévale, Les quatre sens de L'écriture* (2 vols), Paris 1959/61; C. Westermann (ed.), *Probleme atl. Hermeneutik: Aufsätze zum Verstehen des AT*, Munich 1960; R. Rendtorff, 'Hermeneutik des AT als Frage nach der Geschichte', *ZTK* 57 (1960), 27–40; S. Amsler, *L'Ancien Testament dans l'Église, Essai d'herméneutique chrétienne*, Neuchâtel 1960; L. Steiger, *Die Hermeneutik als dogmatisches Problem, Eine Auseinandersetzung mit dem transzendentalen Ansatz des theologischen Verstehens*, Gütersloh 1961; J. D. Smart, *The Interpretation of Scripture*, New York 1961; E. Käsemann, 'Zum gegenwärtigen Streit um die Schriftauslegung', *Das Wort Gottes und die Kirchen*, Göttingen 1962, 7–32; P. Grelot, *Sens chrétien de l'Ancien Testament*, Tournai 1962; A. N. Wilder, 'New Testament Hermeneutics Today: Current Issues in New Testament Interpretation', *Festschrift Otto A.*

Piper, New York 1962, 38–52; O. Rodenberg, *Um die Wahrheit der Heiligen Schrift, Aufsätze und Briefwechsel zur existentialen Interpretation*, Wuppertal 1963²; R. Marlé, *Le problème théologique de l'herméneutique, Les grands axes de la recherche contemporaine*, Paris 1963; L. A. Schökel, 'Hermeneutics in the Light of Language and Literature', *CBQ* 25 (1963), 371–86; W. Vischer, 'Zum Problem der Hermeneutik', *ET* 24 (1964), 98–112; S. Neill, *The Interpretation of the New Testament 1861–1961*, London 1964; *A. Deissler, R. Schnackenburg, A. Vögtle, H. Schlier, and K. H. Schelkle, *The Bible in a New Age*, London 1965, 16–152.

Johann Michl

Sea

In ancient cultures we usually encounter the idea of a deity of the sea, as a rule conceived of as masculine, who rules over all the waters. We also meet with a belief in various spirits and demons which inhabit streams, springs, etc. Certain Old Testament passages contain geographical references (eg, 'spring of the goats', Josh 15:62; 'spring of the serpents', Neh 2:13; 'mistress of the well', Josh 19:8; 'god of the river', Num 21:19) which perhaps represent an echo of ancient local traditions and remnants of what were once popular beliefs. At all events Yahwistic monotheism recognises Yahweh alone as creator and ruler (see Ps 93:4; 135:6) of the three divisions of the cosmos, heaven, earth, and sea (Gen 1; Ex 20:4; 1 Chron 16:31f; Hos 4:3). In accordance with the idea of the cosmos which was general throughout the ancient Near East, the Israelites distinguished between the 'upper sea' above the firmament, in which Yahweh dwells (Ps 104:3; see also Amos 9:6; Ezek 28:2) and the 'lower sea' (see Gen 1:2–9), which is

referred to either as *tehôm* (= 'primordial waters', Gen 1:2; 'cosmic sea on
which the earth rests', Ezek 26:19;
'flood', Ps 42:7; 'depths of the sea',
Ps 107:26) or as *yām* (= 'open sea',
Ps 104:25, a term for the various oceans
of the earth).

In the cosmogonies of the peoples of
the ancient Near East it is emphasized
that the character of the divinised sea
is a hostile one, and that it must be
conquered in a struggle between the
gods. In Chapter 175 of the Egyptian
Book of the Dead the sea is considered
as a remnant of primeval chaos which
constantly threatens the world. In
Ugaritic mythology Yam, the god of
the wide and dangerous sea, tries to
subjugate the earth and the gods, and
is ultimately conquered by Baal, the
god of the wind. In the Mesopotamian
epic *Enuma eliš* two primeval oceans are
mentioned: Apsu, the soft sweet water
on which the earth is constructed, and
Tiamat, the salt water, peopled by
monsters. Tiamat is killed by Marduk,
the city god of Babylon, by means of
the hot wind, and then dismembered.
Many of the turns of phrase in Gen 1 (P)
are reminiscent of the extra-biblical
cosmogonies, but there are essential
differences in the way in which the
content of the creation narrative is
arranged, for it contains above all a
revelation of the power, person and
absolute authority of Yahweh. *Tehôm*
(parallel to the Babylonian Tiamat)
is here wholly demythologised and is
presided over by the *rûaḥ* of Yahweh
(= ↗ 'spirit of God', not wind as in
the *Enuma eliš*). The work of dividing
light from darkness (= the chief allies
of Tiamat in the Babylonian epic), and
the division of the upper and lower

waters (death and dismemberment of
Tiamat) may to some degree be
reminiscent of the Mesopotamian cosmogony (see *ANET* pp 60–61). At any
rate in its theological and psychological
presentation the Old Testament commits itself to the idea of *creatio ex nihilo*
(↗ creation) even though it does not
refer to the making of the *tehôm*
expressis verbis (according to Prov 8:24
wisdom existed before the *tehômôth*),
and even though it only mentions
God's 'power over the *yām*' (Ps 95:5;
Jon 1:9).

Again, in the narrative of the flood
Yahweh appears as absolute Lord
(Gen 7:4; 8:1f), whereas in the
Babylonian epic of Gilgamesh the gods
flee from the floods to the highest
heaven of Anu. The poetic and prophetic passages of the Old Testament
employ images of a contest (Ps 104:6ff;
Hab 3:15), victory (Ps 65:7; 89:10;
Job 38:8ff) and destruction (Job 9:8),
to express Yahweh's position of sovereignty over the sea. In particular
mention is often made of Yahweh's
contest with the sea monsters Tannin
and Rahab (Job 7:12; 26:12;
Ps 74:13), as well as with Leviathan
(Job 3:8; 41:1; Ps 74:14; 104:26;
Is 27:1), which are stabbed and dismembered or caught like a great fish
(Ezek 29:4f; 32:3ff). Whether these
presentations are influenced to any
extent by the divine struggle as set
forth in the *Enuma eliš* or in the
Ugaritic myth of the contest of Baal
with Yam cannot be established with
any certainty. But in no case is it a
cosmogonic theme that is being treated
of in the passages in question. However
it is plausible to regard the sea monsters
as images of political sea powers which

were hostile to Israel, for Tannin and Rahab are used as symbols of Egypt (see Ps 87:4; 89:10f; Is 30:7; Ezek 29:1–16). At any rate the monsters are not on an equal plane with Yahweh but are his creatures (eg, Leviathan in Job 41:25), for which he alone is a match.

In spite of Yahweh's sovereignty over it the sea constitutes a continual danger for sailors (Ps 107:23ff), and is associated with the abode of the dead. The dead fall into the sea, into its currents (Ex 15:5; Ps 69:2, 15), into its streams (2 Sam 22:5), into its innumerable waters (2 Sam 22:17), into its depths (Ps 88:7). It is in the sea that the gates to the world of the dead are to be found (Job 38:16f), ie the sea is connected with the underworld, although how it is connected is nowhere systematically set forth. The *tehôm* instills fear into men. It is the 'land without return' (Jon 2) where man is no longer united to God (Ps 88:11f). God alone can draw his faithful ones out of these depths (Ps 32).

This brings us to the part played by the sea in apocalyptic and eschatological literature. The sea contains the enemies of God (Ps 68:23; Amos 9:3), as also darkness and unclean spirits (Mk 5:13). The waters of the *tehôm* foster and nourish the tree which is a symbol of Egypt in her hostility to God (Ezek 31:4ff). From the sea the monstrous enemies of God arise (Dan 7:2f; Rev 13:1–8). The roaring of the sea is a sign of the return of Christ (Lk 21:25), and it is only at the end of the aeons that the sea will disappear together with the danger of destruction and death which it represents (Rev 21:1).

But for all its diverse aspects, the sea remains a creature of God and manifests the glory of Yahweh (Ps 69:34; 96:11), and by reason of the springs that issue from the lower ocean and the rains coming down from the upper it can be referred to as a medium of blessing (Gen 49:25).

Bibliography: O. Kaiser, *Die mythische Bedeutung des Meeres in Ägypten, Ugarit und Israel* (*BZAW* 78), Berlin 1959; bibliography ↗ water.

Walter Kornfeld

Seal

Seal (Hebrew: *ḥôthām*, many times; LXX [usually] and New Testament: *sphragis*): means first the instrument with which one seals, that is the stamp or signet, and then the actual imprint made by the seal.

A. *In the history of culture*. Nowadays when we want to give legal validity to a document we sign it. But not infrequently we also affix a seal, or at least a stamp as well. This usage represents the survival of an ancient custom. The use of a seal impress instead of a signature was familiar throughout the entire ancient Near East (1 Kings 21:8; Is 29:11; Jer 32:10). Lengthier documents were closed by being rolled up into a scroll and then sealed (Is 8:16; Dan 12:4–9; Rev 5:1f; 22:10). Stones used for closing the mouths of tombs, vaults, pits, etc were also sealed in order to guard against unauthorised opening of the place concerned (Dan 6:17; Mt 27:66; Rev 20:3). Every free citizen could carry his seal. Many seals still survive, and provide some detailed information of the various forms which were used. From the aspect of the particular techniques employed we must distinguish between two kinds of seal, the roller or cylinder seal and the seal stamp. The special technique employed for the first of these consisted of rolling it on clay tablets so that the device affixed to the cylinder was impressed upon the tablet. The imprint of the seal stamp, on the other hand, was obtained merely by pressing it down on the tablet. Seals bore the names of their owners and often, a picture (symbol, distinguishing mark) in addition. They were made of stone (semi-precious stones, chiefly quartz: see Ex 28:9–11; Sir 32:6), and were carried on a neck band (Song 8:6; see also Gen 38:18, 25) or a ring on the finger (Gen 41:42; Esther 3:10; 8:2; Jer 22:24; Hag 2:23).

B. *As used in figurative language.* Even in the Old Testament seals are referred to in a symbolic sense, although there are only a few instances of this. Thus the earth is said to be changed under the light of morning 'as clay under the seal' (Job 38:14), ie, as a lump of clay receives the picture affixed to the seal when this is pressed down upon it, so the light of morning makes the forms and outlines of the earth appear under it, all of them having previously been unrecognisable in the darkness of night. Another passage, of which the precise interpretation is uncertain, is Ezek 28:12. Here the king of Tyre is called a 'fairly fashioned seal full of wisdom and perfect in beauty'. 'Seal' here may be an expression of the underlying meaning of the qualities which are being praised.

The New Testament speaks especially frequently of 'seals' and 'sealing' in a figurative sense. God has 'sealed' Jesus (Jn 6:27), ie, authorised him as the bringer of his salvation, made manifest in the works of divine power which Jesus performs. When a man by receiving Jesus' words with faith 'sets his seal to the fact that God is true', (Jn 3:33) this means that he confesses, recognises by his faith, the revelation of God which has taken place in Jesus as truth, and thereby confesses also that God himself is true. When Revelation tells us that the book of God is closed with seven seals (5:1f etc) this idea is based upon an ancient usage. What it means is that the decrees of God for the world are hidden, and are disclosed and executed only by Christ. Thus Abraham receives circumcision 'as a seal of the righteousness which he had by faith' (Rom 4:11), so that in his case circumcision was equivalent to the confession mentioned above in bringing about his justification from faith alone. When we read that the community at Corinth is 'the seal of his apostleship' for Paul (1 Cor 9:2), it means that the existence of this community is the guarantee of the fact that Paul really has an apostolic task, the 'seal' which Christ has, so to say, imprinted upon this apostolate. In another passage (2 Tim 2:19) the church is said to bear as a 'seal' the words: 'The Lord knows those who are his own' and 'Let everyone who names the name of the Lord depart from iniquity'. This means that the sayings quoted are, so to speak, affixed to the edifice of the church as seal inscriptions, signifying that they apply to the church. Paul wishes to 'seal' his collection conveyed to the christians in Jerusalem from the communities in the hellenistic sphere (Rom 15:28). One meaning of this is certainly that the undertaking is now definitively discharged. Whether the phrase is intended to express still more than this we cannot discern—at any rate not with any degree of certainty.

In particular the seal which is metaphorically said to be imprinted on a man is a sign that he belongs to the possessor of the seal, whether God or Christ, and can rejoice in the protection of his owner (Rev 7:2–8; 9:4; see also Ezek 9:4, 6; Rev 14:1; 22:4). Thus God has 'sealed' the christians (2 Cor 1:22) in that he has made them his own in the act of ↗ baptism, and has, indeed, sealed them with the Holy ↗ Spirit (Eph 1:13; 4:30). It is in line with this manner of speaking that from the second century onwards (Hermas, *Sim.* VIII 6:3; IX 16:3–5, 7; 17:4; 31:1, 4; 2 Clem 7:6; 8:6; Acta Pauli et Theclae 25; etc) 'seal', *sphragis*, becomes a name for baptism.

Bibliography: F. J. Dölger, *Sphragis, Eine altchristliche Taufbezeichnung in ihren Beziehungen zur profanen und religiösen Kultur des Altertums*, Paderborn 1911; F. Nötscher, *Biblische Altertumskunde*, Bonn 1940, 67 and 233–5; K. Galling, 'Beschriftete Bildsiegel des ersten Jahrtausends v. Chr. vornehmlich aus Syrien und Palästina', *ZDPV* 64 (1941), 121–202; S. Moscati, 'I Sigilli nell' Antico Testamento', *Bibl* 30 (1949), 314–38; A. Reifenberg, *Ancient Hebrew Seals*, London 1950 (with illustrations); Haag 1512–14; W. Michaelis, 'Zeichen, Siegel, Kreuz, Ein Ausschnitt aus der Bedeutungsgeschichte biblischer Begriffe', *TZ* 12 (1956), 505–25; N. Avigad, '*ḥotām*', *Encyclopaedia Biblica* III, Jerusalem 1958, 68–86 (with illustrations); J. G. Février, 'Les sceaux et cachets', *DB(S)* XXXIII, 955–64; G. Fitzer, *TWNT* VII, 939–54.

Johann Michl

Seeking God

A. *In the Old Testament.* The expression 'to seek God' (*darāš* or *biqqēš 'et YHWH*; from *daraš* the word *midrāš* is derived: it stands for a literary category characterized chiefly by the activity of *seeking* for that meaning in an Old Testament passage which is relevant and appropriate to a given age) signifies a basic religious attitude of the man of the old covenant which is closely related to ↗ fear of God and ↗ faith. The occurrence of this term, so pregnant in meaning as it is, in relatively early passages enables us to recognise that even in the earliest times the relationship between God and Israel, far from being maintained on a mere collective basis, was in the highest degree personal and individual.

In the J and E passages of the *Pentateuch*, as also in the books of Samuel and Kings, the primary meaning of the phrase 'seeking God' is to ask the Lord for counsel in some specific matter, to request an oracle from God. Thus Rebekah sought the Lord when she felt twins moving in her womb—that is, she went on pilgrimage to a sanctuary in order to ask the Lord the meaning of this preliminary sign, perhaps through the mediation of a non-Israelite 'man of God' (Gen 25:22 J). Later Israel was able to seek judgement from Yahweh through Moses, the accredited spokesman of God (Ex 18:15[E]) or to seek the Lord directly in the Tent of Meeting (Ex 33:7[EJ]). The fact that even after the death of Moses there was no lack of God-given mediators for the people is attested in 1 Sam 9:9: 'Formerly in Israel when a man went to enquire of

God he said "Come let us go to the seer"'. Again it is related of Jehoshaphat (1 Kings 22:5; 2 Kings 3:11) and Josiah (2 Kings 22:13, 18), as also of the wife of Jeroboam 1 (1 Kings 14:5), that in difficult situations they sought Yahweh or alternatively Yahweh's decision, in other words, that they obtained through the prophets a revelation of his will. But it is especially often stated of David that he made no decision on his own, and undertook no military operation without having first sought Yahweh (1 Sam 23:2, 4; 30:8; 2 Sam 2:1; 5:19, 23; 21:1; etc). The fact that this enquiry of God took place through the high priest and by means of the sacred lots which were kept in the ephod is illustrated in 1 Sam 23:9–12 etc.

The all-pervasive change in Israel's religion to personal and interior piety, which was achieved under the influence of the *prophets*, also left discernible effects upon the use of the expression 'to seek God', which henceforward exhibits fresh shades of meaning: voluntarily to turn to God, to turn away from evil, to fulfil the will of God, to turn to him with entreaty. Thus Amos contrasts the worthless externalism of the cult at Bethel, Gilgal and Beersheba, the homes of idolatrous cults, with that genuine seeking for God which alone can avail to ward off the catastrophe: 'Seek me that you may live . . . Seek the good and not the evil' (Amos 5:4, 14; see also Hos 5:6). Zephaniah, too, establishes the closest connection between seeking for God and morally good behaviour. Moreover in the message of this prophet of the ↗ 'poor of Yahweh', this attitude appears simultaneously as the 'virtue appropriate to the class' of the poor and humble (Zeph 2:3). But those who do not seek God and do not concern themselves with him (Zeph 1:6; Is 9:13), or else do this only with a penitence that is superficial and ungenuine (Hos 6:6; Ps 78:34, 36) prefer to rely upon earthly covenants and alliances as their defensive equipment instead of 'looking to the Holy One of Israel and seeking the Lord of Hosts' (Is 31:1). Such as these shall not escape the condemnation and punishment which is threatened.

Since the inevitable national downfall is ultimately intended simply to bring back the people to a true seeking for God, the pre-exilic prophets already proclaimed: 'I will return again to my place, until they acknowledge their guilt and seek my face, and in their distress they seek me' (Hos 5:15). It is not until the exile and the post-exilic period, however, that we are brought to recognise that it was indeed their apostasy from the true God that brought about the downfall of the two kingdoms (2 Kings 17:7–23; 24:1–4), but that a radical conversion, a true seeking of God, will discover a God who is forgiving and compassionate. 'From there [the exile] you will seek the Lord your God and you will find him if you search after him with all your heart and with all your soul . . .' (Deut 4:29; see also Jer 29:12–14; etc). This sure hope is taken up by Deutero–Isaiah and combined with an urgent exhortation to prayer and penance: 'Seek Yahweh *for* he can be found, call him *for* he is near. Let the wicked forsake his way . . . Let him return to the Lord' (Is 55:6; see also 45:19. P. Troadec has established convincingly, in his article cited below, that the particle *bᵉ* here, which is generally translated 'so long as', 'while', has here, as elsewhere in Deutero–Isaiah,—eg Is 60:1; 53:5; 57:17—a causal sense). God is near, and, for those who genuinely seek him, easy to find, for in a short time he will reveal himself by a mighty intervention in Israel's fate as her rescuer and redeemer. The point at which he leads her home from the exile is close at hand. The same promise, now on a universal scale, which prepares the way for the New Testament message of God's will to save all mankind, occurs in the final section of the Book of Isaiah: 'I was ready to be found by those who *did not seek* me (Is 65:1; see also Rom 10:20; a similar universalist expansion in Zech 8:22; Bar 4:28–9).

The expression 'to seek God' has a privileged position in the Books of Chronicles, in which it virtually constitutes a principal motif and recurs again and again with new applications. A comparison with the parallel passages in the Books of Kings reveals that by inserting the term 'to seek God' the author of the Books of Chronicles intended to give expression to his conception of the ideal king and of true devotion to Yahweh (compare eg, 2 Chron 14:3, 6 with 1 Kings 15:11–12; 2 Chron 16:12 with 1 Kings 15:23; 2 Chron 19:3 with 1 Kings 22:46; 2 Chron 22:9 with 2 Kings 9:28; 2 Chron 26:5 with 2 Kings 15:3). In all these passages, each according to the particular context, seeking for God would have to be rendered as 'pure faith, covenant loyalty, whole-hearted acknowledgement of Yahweh, conversion from idolatry, abolition of false cults', etc. When, for instance, it is said of Josiah that 'while he was yet a boy he began to seek the God of David, his father' (2 Chron 34:3), what is hinted at in this laconic statement is the religious reform just then commencing, and the final flowering of the Davidic kingdom (see 2 Chron 15:13, 15; Ezra 6:21; etc).

According to this, then, seeking for God is the attitude of one who turns wholly to God, an attitude which, in conformity with the stage reached by ↗ 'reward' theology at that time, brings ↗ peace and ↗ life, the very essence of all blessings. Correspondingly the opposite attitude, 'to pay no heed to God, to abandon him, to forget him, to turn aside from him', condemns those guilty of these sins to misfortune and ↗ death as already foretold by the prophets: 'Saul did not seek guidance from Yahweh [but rather from the spirits of the dead]. Therefore Yahweh slew him' (1 Chron 10:14; see also 2 Chron 12:14; 16:12).

A concept so rich in religious overtones was naturally used copiously in the *Psalms*. Here the chief applications of it are 'seeking the face of God', and 'rejoicing in being near to him in the temple' (Ps 24:6; 27:8; 34:10; 40:16; 69:32; 70:4). The exhortation 'always to seek' God's face (Ps 105:4 = 1 Chron 16:11) found an echo in the liturgy and in the christian life of prayer. In fact according to Augustine, 'the soul is never satisfied with what it has found, but continues seeking all the more eagerly the more it loves' (*PL* 37, 1392; see the postcommunion prayer of Septuagesima Sunday: 'Et percipiendo requirant, et requirendo sine fine percipiant').

In the *Wisdom books* we find echoes of the motifs in the Psalms (Prov 11:27; 15:14; Sir 14:22; 32:14; Wis 1:1). Special mention should be made of those passages in which Wisdom appears as a person in its own right, one emanating from God and one whom the wise man seeks to bring home 'as a bride' (Wis 8:2). She lets herself be found by those who love her easily and willingly (Wis 8:21). The same theme of 'seeking and finding' occupies a central place in the Song of Solomon. However much the question of the literary category to which this book should be assigned may be disputed, there can be no doubt that the bride who tirelessly seeks her beloved among the shepherds (1:7), upon her bed (3:1), in the streets and squares of Jerusalem (3:2; 5:6), is a figure of the covenant people of the post-exilic age which has finally taken to heart the prophetic exhortation to seek God in truth by interior conversion and renunciation of idols. The difference between the biblical and the Greek ideas of seeking appears very clearly precisely in the Song of Solomon. When the biblical man seeks God he does so like the bride in the Song of Solomon by engaging his whole person in the search, seeking genuinely with his whole heart (2 Chron 11:16), with the true resolve of his will (2 Chron 15:19), with his whole soul (2 Chron 15:13), with contrition of heart and abasement of soul (Dan 3:39[LXX]). By contrast for the Greeks seeking is first and foremost an intellectual activity. This is shown by the use of the expression *zēteō* (=examine), *zētēsis* (=investigation), and *to zētoumenon* (=subject under examina-

tion) as *termini technici* of philosophical speculation.

B. *In the New Testament*. The idea that God will allow himself to be found even by those who *do not seek him* (Is 65:1) represented the highest point to which the Old Testament could attain in the knowledge of God. But that God himself was to come in Christ in order to '*seek* and to save the lost' (Lk 19:10), and that having found them he would rejoice over them as a shepherd over a lost sheep that he has found, and as a woman over the recovery of a lost drachma (Lk 15:2–8), was reserved to the christian revelation. The christian himself must now respond to this experience of having been sought by himself seeking—and at this point the New Testament takes over all the depths of meaning inherent in the idea of seeking God in the Old Testament and brings it to its consummation. Whatever the Christian is directed to seek, whether it be 'the kingdom of God and his justice' (Mt 6:33; see also Gal 2:17) or 'that which is above' (Col 3:1) or the 'true fatherland' (Heb 11:14; 13:14), or 'glory, honour and immortality' (Rom 2:7)—at basis he is always seeking God in Christ Jesus, in the person of whom the kingdom of God has entered into the world, and who, as the bringer of salvation, is present and future both at once (*TDNT* I, 589). Therefore, when he engages in this seeking he must commit himself to it far more unreservedly, and be far more constant in his practice of it, than his forebears were under the Old Covenant. Like the pearl-trader who, in order to obtain the precious pearl which he seeks, joyfully surrenders everything else (Mt 13:45), so too the christian's *first* preoccupation, prior to all earthly cares or concern about food and clothing (Mt 6:31–2), must be to be a follower of Christ and to devote himself to his cause.

The promise which Jeremiah gave to those who truly seek God (29:12–14) is taken up by Jesus and confirmed: 'He who seeks finds' (Mt 7:7–11 and parallels). The context of this passage enables us to recognise clearly that seeking here is equated with praying: 'For prayer is seeking God if it is to be successful prayer, to open the door and to give access to God.' (Greeven, *TDNT* II, 893.)

Since the redemptive death of Christ all men are called and equipped for this task of seeking God. James gives expression to this truth at the first Council of the Apostles when (quoting freely from Amos 9:11–12 and Jer 12:15–16) he proclaims that the 're-building of the fallen hut of David' by Christ, the Son of David, is intended to make it possible for 'all the gentiles who are called by name to seek the Lord' (Acts 15:17). The expression has the same world-wide sense as it occurs on the lips of the apostle to the gentiles, when in his Areopagus speech to those who were groping to seek God he promises that fulfilment and the attainment of that goal will be found in Christ for *all* men who inhabit the face of the earth' (Acts 17:26–7).

Finally the Letter to the Hebrews records the conviction that God 'rewards those who genuinely seek him' (11:6), and who show that 'minimum of faith' which, as it is promised, will be rewarded by eternal salvation.

Bibliography: Eichrodt II, 157–207; M. Prager, 'Gottsuchen in der Heiligen Schrift', *Erbe und Auftrag* 6 (1959), 444–52; P. Troadec, 'La Parole vivante et efficace', *Bible et Vie chrétienne*, XI, 57–67.

Myriam Prager

Self-denial

When we speak of 'self-denial' we are, for the most part, thinking of that *agere contra*, that *abstine et sustine* by which we distinguish between the conquest of our evil inclinations and our endurance of suffering and trials. The first of these is conceived of as self-mastery and mortification, the second as sacrifice or love of the cross. While these requirements actually belong to the basic stock of christian 'asceticism' and religious training, they do not cover what is essential to the biblical concept of self-denial. This concept of self-denial in the traditional sense provides a graphic example of how, in the process by which theology, moral teaching and ⁊ asceticism are progressively emancipated from holy scripture, a saying of Jesus that is genuine has become obscured and changed from its original meaning so as to have a purely moralising application. The good tidings of the biblical message have been replaced by a gloomy 'ascetic' imperative, and this represents an impoverishment of one of Jesus' demands which is genuine and important.

A. Self-denial is a New Testament concept, and in the strict sense appears only in the synoptic gospels (Mk 8:34 and parallels) and in one passage in Paul (2 Tim 2:13). The New Testament knows only of the *verb* 'to deny one'self': *arneomai* or *aparneomai*.

In order to gain a deeper understanding of the concept all those passages must be adduced in which this verb appears either in its simple or its composite form. *arneomai* is used thirty-three times (Mt 10:33 ab = Lk 12:9a—Mt 26:70, 72 = Mk 14:68, 70; Lk 22:57; Jn 13:38; 18:25, 27—Lk 8:45—Lk 9:23—Jn 1:20—Acts 3:13, 14; 4:16; 7:35—1 Tim 5:8; 2 Tim 2:12ab, 13; 3:5—Tit 1:16; 2:12— Heb 11:24—2 Pet 2:1—1 Jn 2:22ab, 23—Jude 4—Rev 2:13; 3:8). *aparneomai* is used eleven times and, moreover, only in the synoptic gospels (Mt 16:24 = Mk 8:34—Mt 26:34, 35, 75 = Mk 14:30, 31, 72; Lk 22:34, 61— Lk 12:9b). The composite form of the verb, however, does not express any intensification of the concept, for both verbs are used interchangeably, both in the parallel passages (eg, Lk 9:23 = Mk 8:34—Mk 14:30, 31, 72; Lk 22: 34, 61 = Jn 13:38—Mt 10:33ab; Lk 12:9a = Lk 12:9b) and within one and the same sentence as well (eg, Lk 12:9).

B. As in classical Greek so also in the New Testament, *arneomai* is used in its original meaning of 'to say no': 'to refuse, renounce' either an admonition or acclaim, eg, 'to renounce irreligion and worldly passions' (Tit 2:12; see Acts 3:13, 14; Heb 11:24), or 'to give a negative answer' to a question, 'contest' it, eg, to Jesus' question, 'Who has touched me?' all *reply in the negative* (Lk 8:45). Peter gives a *negative answer* to the question of the maid-servant as to whether he belongs to the group of Jesus' disciples (Mk 14:68, 70 and parallels; Jn 18:25, 27; see also Acts 4:16; Jn 1:20; 1 Jn 2:22).

Since the gospel lays the principal emphasis not on the truth of salvation but on the bringer of salvation, the Saviour, the New Testament authors have perforce had to give a fresh meaning to the verb under consideration, that namely of 'to *deny a person*'. One can 'give a negative answer' to a truth, but one 'denies' the *proclaimer* of that truth. In contexts concerned with the person of Christ there may already be some underlying connotation of this latter meaning in the use of the word as signifying 'to give a negative answer to' (compare Mk 14:68, 70 with 5:30; Mt 26:70, 72; Acts 3:13, 14; Jn 1:20).

This fresh meaning appears in all those passages which primarily refer to the *person of Christ*, and it is palpably evident that it is only the *disciples* who can be said to deny Christ, and not Jews or gentiles. For only he who has once professed loyalty to Christ can deny him.

The disciple denies Christ when he fails voluntarily and solemnly to confess the *person of Jesus Christ* in his whole conduct. In this sense Peter *denies* his Lord and Master (see Mk 14:30, 31, 72; Mt 26:34, 35, 75; Lk 22:34, 61; Jn 13:38). About disciples who are disloyal Christ says: 'Whoever denies me before men, I also will deny before my Father who is in heaven' (Mt 10:33; Lk 12:9; see also 2 Tim 2:12; Jude 4). It comes to the same thing when the New Testament authors speak of 'denying faith in Christ', or 'denying the word and the name of Christ', rather than of 'denying Christ himself' (Rev 2:13; 3:8; see also Tit 1:16); this means failing to acknowledge the truth of his teaching (1 Jn 2:22, 23; 2 Pet 2:1), or refusing the just claims of one's brother (1 Tim 5:8; 2 Tim 3:5).

'To deny' Christ, therefore, means nothing else than 'to say no' to Christ, to refuse Christ, to fail to acknowledge him before men, 'to be ashamed of him and of his word' (Mk 8:35; Lk 9:26). The opposite of this is 'to say yes' to Christ, 'to acknowledge, bear witness to' Christ before all the world, to remain constant to Christ in life and death, to give up all things for Christ, to be prepared to lose one's possessions and shed one's blood, and even to lay down one's life itself. This requirement arises from Christ's claim to absolute dominion.

C. Self-denial must be regarded from this christological aspect. The classic passage is found in the following major section of Mark: 'And he called to him the multitude with his disciples, and said to them: (1) "If any man would come after me let him deny himself (*aparnēsasthō*) and take up his cross and follow me. (2) For whoever would save his life will lose it; and whoever loses his life for my sake and the gospel's will save it. (3) For what does it profit a man to gain the whole world and forfeit his [future] life? (4) For what can a man give in return for [to obtain once more] his life? (5) For whoever is ashamed of me and of my words in this adulterous and sinful generation, of him will the Son of Man also be ashamed when he comes in the glory of his Father with the holy angels". (6) And he said to them "Truly I say to you, there are some standing here who will not taste death before they see the kingdom of God come with power"' (Mk 8:34–9:1; see also Mt 16:24–8; Lk 9:23–7).

I. Taken as a whole the six sayings contained in this section were spoken by Jesus himself, even if not all on the same occasion (see V. Taylor, 380). The first, second, and fifth are found in different contexts in Matthew and Luke. From this it can be concluded that the word *for* (*gar*) which joins the individual sayings one to another is merely a particle of transition. The evangelist probably derived these sayings from an original collection of sayings, and all of them, or at least the first four (vv 34–7), teach us in what true 'following of Christ' consists. Mark has skilfully inserted them between on the one hand Peter's acknowledgement of the Messiah and the first passion prediction, and on the other the account of the transfiguration. Christ requires an acknowledgement not merely of his message, but of his person also as Son of Man, as suffering and glorified Lord, whose fate in life and death the disciple is called upon to share in obedience.

In the first saying it is striking that *twice* in the first sentence (Mk 8:34; Mt 16:24; Lk 9:23) Christ demands discipleship together with self-denial and bearing one's cross, even though in other contexts in Matthew and Luke (Mt 10:38 = Lk 14:27) he requires only the bearing of the cross and discipleship. This provides a basis for suggesting that in Mk 8:34 and parallels two originally independent sayings have been blended together: 1. 'He who will *follow me*, let him *deny himself*'; and 2. 'He who *does not take up his cross* and *follow* me is not worthy of me' (Mt 10:38), or: 'He who *does not bear his cross* and *follow* me cannot be my disciple' (Lk 14:27).

II. However this may be, self-denial and bearing one's cross (↗ cross) are

835

constitutive elements in the discipleship of Christ. The section as a whole (Mk 8:34–9:1) is preceded by the account of the confession of Peter at Caesarea Philippi, and of Christ's prediction of his passion (8:27–33); and followed by the narrative of the transfiguration of the Lord (9:2–8), which is led up to by the reference to the coming of the kingdom of God with power (9:1). Everything focuses upon the following of Christ, and on bearing witness to the suffering and glorified Lord by self-denial and carrying one's cross.

1. Viewed in this christological perspective the expression 'to deny oneself' is equivalent to 'to say no' to oneself as person, 'to yield oneself up', 'surrender oneself', that is to give up the individual 'I' with all its ideas, aims and desires, or as it is expressed in Luke: 'To hate one's life' (Lk 14:26).

The same demand that one should ruthlessly divest oneself of one's own selfish interests also finds expression in the verse which follows: 'Whoever *loses his life* for my sake and the gospel's will save it' (Mk 8:35; see also Mt 16:25; Lk 9:24; Mt 10:39; Lk 17:33; Jn 12:25). He who boldly exposes himself and his earthly life to a martyr's death will gain possession of his true self, and together with this, the true and the eternal life, and will enter into the kingdom of God. *psukhē* (lit. = soul) here means not the immortal soul as contrasted with the mortal body—this is a Greek idea—but that form of life which corresponds to the Hebrew *nepeš*, which embraces both body and soul, the man as a whole. If the disciple courageously surrenders himself in life and death he will win possession of himself and

eternal life at the resurrection. The anthropology of the Old Testament recognises no blessing which applies to the soul exclusively, only blessings which apply to man as a whole. The well-known missionary apostrophe, 'Save your souls!' is derived from Aristotelian thought. The question arises of whether the hypothesis which has recently been forwarded, to the effect that the 'resurrection of the flesh' begins to take place immediately after death, does not come closest to representing the true view of the bible, even though holy scripture itself does not pronounce explicitly upon this point.

Christ requires us to say 'no' to ourselves in a manner that is truly radical: 'He who will be my disciple, *let him take up his cross*' (Mk 8:34 and parallels). Was this demand in any sense comprehensible *before* Jesus' crucifixion? Would it not have been laid retrospectively upon Jesus' lips by the apostles or evangelists? Or may we even suppose that the saying of Jesus originally ran, 'Let him take up his yoke' (Mt 11:29), and that this would subsequently have been changed by the early church into 'Let him take up his cross'. Certainly the rabbinical literature knows nothing of any proverbial saying of this kind (see SB 1, 587), yet death by crucifixion was not unknown in Palestine under Roman domination (see Josephus, *BJ* II, 12:6; II, 14:9; *Ant* XVII, 10:4–10). Probably, therefore, what we have here is a genuinely dominical saying. In it Jesus is thinking of the moment at which one condemned to death by crucifixion takes the crosspiece (*patibulum*) on his shoulders and, amid mockery and insults, crawls as a defenceless and ignominious criminal to the place of execution. 'Everyone who decides to follow me must be ready to endure the pillory like a criminal on the way to execution'. Another question is whether Jesus was thinking of his own death on the cross, for he does not say, '. . . take up *my* cross', but '. . . take up *his* cross'. Jesus does not speak *expressis verbis* of his own death on the cross. The solitary mention of the crucifixion in the passion predictions (Mt 20:19) cannot be adduced against this. In the parallel passages in Mark and Luke (Mk 10:34; Lk 18:33) it is absent, which shows that it represents a subsequent insertion on Matthew's part. But the whole tenor of these sayings suggests that in view of the murderous hatred of his enemies our Lord did indeed have in mind a violent death, precisely the ignominious death of crucifixion.

The witness which the disciple must bear to Christ is pressed to its utmost possible limits, that is to martyrdom in the true sense of the word, the witness in blood which Stephen, the initiator of the endless procession of 'martyrs', was the first to bear. Certainly God requires martyrdom neither every day nor from all of his children. But this should not be taken as showing that martyrdom is a mistaken way of bearing witness, only that it represents an 'extreme situation'.

In view of the altered circumstances of the early christian communities, Luke (or the early church) speaks of a 'daily' bearing of one's cross. This does not represent any weakening of the sense; the accent is simply laid more upon one's interior readiness for mar-

tyrdom. The disciple must always be ready, if God wills it, to follow his Master on the way of the passion to the place of execution, and to undergo violent death in order to bear the witness of blood to his Lord. Everything bears upon the necessity of readiness. The underlying intention of Luke's retrospective interpolation is precisely to bring out the meaning of this readiness. It entails a radical renunciation of self as an essential and abiding attitude of spirit. In this sense those christians who are forced to renounce much in order to live chaste married lives, and perhaps to endure mockery on that account, are true witnesses to Christ. Again the Carmelite nun who in her quiet and hidden life follows the hard way of total self-renunciation practices self-denial in the truest sense. 'Martyrdom was the dream of my youth, and this dream returned in an intensified form in my convent cell' (Thérèse of Lisieux).

In Mk 8:36–7 Jesus goes on to speak of a concrete instance of self-denial. He sets side by side for comparison the two possibilities of gaining the world and losing one's life. This verse is connected with v 35 not merely in terms of externals, by the recurrence of the stich-word 'life', but also in terms of its actual interior meaning. He who decides to follow Jesus must be ready to surrender all worldly riches not merely because he will have to lose them all at his death, but primarily because he stands to lose eternal life. With the greatest possible emphasis Jesus warns us of the great dangers to the attainment of eternal life which earthly possessions entail. The *Sitz-im-Leben* of the saying here under

837

consideration is to be sought in the circumstances of the land-owning classes in Palestine. According to Jesus' teaching in the synoptic gospels, what represents the greatest danger to eternal life for these is not the temptations of sex but the thirst for money. In the gospel of John the question of money does not enter in. For Paul the immorality and idolatry of the hellenistic cities conjure up dangers which are at least as great as those entailed by avarice, even if he does also stigmatise this latter vice with extreme severity: 'The love of money is the root of all evils' (1 Tim 6:10; see also Col 3:5). In this the teaching of the apostle to the gentiles is in harmony with that of Jesus, who incessantly renews his warnings of the immense danger of riches. Almost infallibly they lead to eternal perdition: 'How hard it will be for those who have riches to enter the kingdom of God . . . It is easier for a camel to go through the eye of a needle than for a rich man to enter the kingdom of God' (Mk 10:23, 25; Mk 10:24, which interrupts the sequence of thought, is omitted in Mt 19:23 and Lk 18:24). The disciples rightly understood the words of Jesus as signifying that the difficulty spoken of here amounts to almost total impossibility. Hence the fear with which they ask, 'Then who can be saved?' (Mk 10:26 and parallels). Christ reminds them of the omnipotence of God: 'With men it is impossible, but not with God. For all things are possible with God' (Mk 10:27 and parallels). It is precisely when man is reduced to utter impotence that the power of God really comes into its own (see Gen 18:14; Job 10:13; Mk 14:36). God alone can

show himself supreme over the idol Mammon, which, like some sinister demonic power (see Gen 4:7), threatens to draw down the avaricious man into the eternal abyss (see Lk 16:13). And this means eternally and for ever; for at the last judgement man will have no redeeming price to offer in order to buy back or redeem the life he has lost (Mk 8:37).

2. Christ himself points out the supremely salient factor in the biblical idea of self-denial: 'For my sake and the gospel's' (Mk 8:35). This dominical saying tells us what is the definitive mark of self-denial, for it embodies the fundamental motivation which underlies all true self-denial.

The words 'and the gospel's' do not belong to the dominical saying in its original form. They bear the impress of the early church. For according to the evidence of the synoptics Christ himself constitutes the heart and centre of the 'euangelion'. For this reason the expression has actually been omitted in the parallel passages in Matthew and Luke, and rightly so (Mt 16:25; Lk 9:24; see also Mt 10:39). According to Mk 10:29 the disciple of Jesus leaves relations and possessions alike 'for my sake and the gospel's', whereas according to Mt 19:29 it is only 'for my name's sake', and according to Lk 18:29 'for the sake of the kingdom of God'.

One can only speak of self-denial in the biblical sense if it is exercised for Christ's sake. The person of Christ lies at the very roots of self-denial. Thus it is not primarily self-control or character-building or the purifying and perfecting of one's own personality that is in question, though certainly all this is not excluded. It will 'be added to you' (Mt 6:33).

The decisive factors, however, are bearing witness to Christ, giving up what is one's own, and unreserved consent to the divine will. Without Christ self-denial would be distorted into a rigid self-discipline. By the practice of self-denial in the biblical sense man grows beyond himself and shares in the glorious destiny of the life and death of his Lord. His individual personality, with the special talents belonging to it, is not thereby suppressed. It simply becomes free from the perverse inclinations of fallen humanity, free for the love of God, and free for the loving service of his neighbour (see Mk 12:28-34 and parallels; Lk 10:25-8 and parallels). In this way, therefore, the human personality can be developed and perfected. This imparts to self-denial as understood by the bible a dynamic quality, a true moral greatness, and an immense power to affect others.

Bibliography: Apart from the commentaries on the gospel of Mark by M. J. Lagrange (1947), J. Schmidt (1958), V. Taylor (1959), W. Grundmann (1962), and *D. Nineham (1963), see above all A. Friedrichsen, '"Sich selbst verleugnen"', *Coniectanea Neotest* 2 (Uppsala 1936), 1-8; R. Raitz von Frentz, *Selbstverleugnung*, Einsiedeln 1936; R. Raitz von Frentz, 'Selbstverleugnung oder Selbstveredelung', *Zeitschrift für Askese und Mystik* 15 (1940), 45-55; J. Lebreton, 'La doctrine du renoncement dans le Nouveau Testament', *NRT* 65 (1938), 385-412; J. Lebreton, '"Le Renoncement"', *Lumen Christi* (Paris 1947), 171-96; H. Riesenfeld, 'The Meaning of the Verb *arneisthai*', *Coniectanea Neotest.* 11 (Lund-Copenhagen 1947), 207-9; K. H. Schelkle, *Die Passion Christi in der Verkündigung des NT*, Heidelberg 1949, 217-38; A. Decourtray, 'Renoncement et amour de soi selon saint Paul', *NRT* 74 (1952), 21-9; F. Wulf, 'Selbstverleugnung und Abtötung als Übung der Nachfolge Christi und als Kennzeichen des neuen Lebens in Christus', *GL* 25 (1952), 4-42; R. Koolmeister, 'Selbstverleugnung, Kreuzaufnahme und Nachfolge. Eine historische Studie über Mt 16:24', *Charisteria Johanni Kopp octogenario oblata*, Stockholm 1954, 64-94; E. Dinkler, 'Jesu Wort vom Kreuztragen', *Neutestamentliche Studien für Rudolph Bultmann*, Berlin 1954, 110-29; W. K. Grossouw, *Bijbelse Vroomheid*, Utrecht-Antwerp 1964⁶; K. Rahner, 'Passion und Aszese. Zur philosophisch-theologischen Grundlegung der christlichen Aszese', *Schriften zur Theologie* III, Zurich 1955, 73-104; H. Schlier, *TDNT* I, 469-71; J. Jeremias, *Die Gleichnisse Jesu*, Göttingen 1958³, 183-4; H. van Oyen, *RGG* v, 1961³, 1679-82; J. Kahmann, 'Het volgen van Christus door zelfverloochening en kruisdragen', *TT* 1-2 (1961/2), 205-26; A. Schulz, 'Nachfolge und Nachahmen', Munich 1962, 79-92; W. Pesch, *LTK* IX², 629-30; *BTHW* 537.

Robert Koch

Servant of the Lord

A. *In the Old Testament*. 1. In the bible we find repeated references to men of virtue who are called the 'servants' (*ʿebd*) of God. This is the designation which Jacob applies to himself in his prayer to be rescued from the threat of Esau's anger (Gen 32:10). Solomon does the same in his prayer at Gabaon (1 Kings 3:7f). In various passages of the bible the expression is applied to Abraham (Ps 105:6, 42), Joshua (Josh 24:29), David (Ps 18:1), and Job (Job 1:8). Its original meaning, prior to subsequent modifications, is known to us both from the bible and from other texts of the ancient Near East. When the kings of Assyria, such as Assurbanipal, are addressing their gods they describe themselves as their servants. We find the Phoenician king Azitawadda calling himself the servant (*ʿbd*) of Baal in only the second line of his inscription. This role of servant includes the service of the cult, a fact which is reflected in the Babylonian epic of creation. According to this man was created after the rebellion of Tiamat so that he could be made responsible for the service of the gods. But this service has a much wider ambience than this. It comprises obedience in all areas of life. The kings are the servants of the nation's god, whose interests they uphold, and we even find King Sargon after his eighth campaign addressing a letter to the god Assur in which he submits a reckoning to him of the campaign he has conducted. For similar reasons the Canaanite princelings in the Tell-el-Amarna letters are called Abdi-Addi, ie, 'servant of the god Adad', Abdi-Aširta ('servant of Asherah), Abdi Ninurta etc. They also refer to themselves in quite general terms in their letters as 'servants' of Pharaoh, who, according to Egyptian ideology, is god and lord. But in the Letters of Lakish and on Israelite seal cylinders this expression is used in so general a manner that it cannot of itself be taken as implying the divinisation of the king.

2. The community of Israel was organised as a direct theocracy, and it is not primarily the prophets who are the 'servants of Yahweh' the true god, but even in the earlier passages (Ex 4:23; 7:16, 26; etc) it is said that Israel must 'serve' Yahweh. However it is only in later passages that we find mention of Israel as the 'servant of God'. Even the plural form 'servants of Yahweh' (2 Kings 9:7; 10:23) designates not the Israelites as a whole but the faithful who share the beliefs of the prophets.

3. It is not until we come to Is 40–55,

chapters which are now generally assigned to the final years of the exile, that the people of Israel in bondage appears as 'the servant of Yahweh'. As Babylon has the status of servant in relation to her gods Bel and Nebo (Is 46:1), so too Israel serves Yahweh, or, more accurately, should serve him; for God reproaches Israel for having neglected to bring him either sheep or sacrifices (43:22–4). Israel is a blind and deaf servant (42:19)—indeed a sinful servant (42:24; see also 43:24), yet God insists that he has chosen her from all the ends of the earth: 'You are my servant, I have chosen you and not cast you off' (41:9 see also v 8: 'Israel my servant, Jacob whom I have chosen, the offspring of Abraham, my friend'). This servant whom he has chosen is his witness (43:10); through him God will reveal himself. His descendants will receive the spirit and blessing of Yahweh, and will have nothing more to fear (44:2); he has a prophetic mission like that of Jeremiah, who was chosen and prepared for his mission from his mother's womb (44:2). This servant will never be forgotten by God, and his sins will be blotted out (44:22f). For his sake, and in order to keep his word, God raises up Cyrus (44:28; 45:4). Yahweh leads this servant, whom he has delivered, through the wilderness (48:21). In order that all may hear the voice, the word of this servant (50:10; see also 44:26), the command of God will become a light to the peoples (51:4), and the new Jerusalem will be far greater and more glorious than the former one, and all who hearken to God, seek Yahweh and abandon their sinful ideas will be able to be healed there (54f).

4. Understandably many authors, seeing the theme of Israel and its prophetic mission to the Gentile peoples, are inclined to regard the four songs inserted into these chapters, which treat in a quite special manner of the mission of the servant of Yahweh, as instances of the same theme. In language, in imagery, and in their general tendency these verses approximate very closely to the remainder of the chapters, but have noticeably abrupt beginnings (42:1; 49:1; 50:4; 52:13). Moreover, if this point too is contested, it can be shown that they interrupt the development of ideas in Is 40–55. The limits of the individual songs can best be determined by the following considerations: (a) the disquisition on idols, which is broken off in 41:29, is resumed in 42:8; (b) the description of the new exodus, which is interrupted by the gloss in 48:22 (from 57:21) and by the second 'Servant' song, is continued in 49:9b; (c) the divine judgement and condemnation outlined in 50:3 is completed in 50:9b—the images find their explanation in 51:6f; (d) finally, the return of the exiles to Jerusalem in 52:9f is completed by a renewed appeal to the repopulated Jerusalem in 54:1ff.

The four songs, the limits of which have been determined in this way (42:1–7; 49:1–9a; 50:4–9a; 52:13–53:12) 'individualise' the servant of Yahweh much more strongly, and distinguish him from sinful Israel. Each of these songs takes up, at least in its opening section, the theme of the mission to the Gentiles, which has already been adumbrated in 41:4f. The servant has the mission of imparting the law entrusted to him to the Gentiles (42:4). He is therefore a light to the gentiles, the glory of the peoples. He ensures that the gentile peoples and their kings shall receive not only knowledge of the Torah, but ↗ salvation and ↗ peace (*šālôm*: 53:5) as well. But he has also a further mission, that namely of setting free the blind and imprisoned Israel (42:7), of restoring the tribes of Israel and leading the remnant of Israel home (49:6), of justifying many and interceding for sinners (52:11f ↗ justification, mediator).

Whereas in chapters 40–55 the mission to the gentiles is only mentioned in passing, in these songs it constitutes the main theme. They even ascribe to the servant that mission of liberation which in the rest of these chapters appears to be ascribed to Cyrus. For this reason many have wished to regard Cyrus as the servant of God. Others again have seen in this figure a king or prophet of the past, present or future. The interpretation which is preferred at the moment would seem to be the collective one, according to which the servant of God is interpreted if not as Israel in general, then at least as the Israel that has been converted—all the more so since most of the manuscript traditions contain the reading in 49:3, 'Israel my servant'. Many speak of a *corporate personality*, and in terms of this suggest that the servant would have been *individual and collective simultaneously*. But traditional exegesis, which is derived from the New Testament, regards the servant as the Messiah, the heir of David, and this view still retains its force: in terms of the first view it is difficult to see how the converted Israel could conduct its liberating mission towards Israel as a whole, especially in view of the fact that this mission is directed precisely to the remnant, the 'redeemed' or 'preserved' of Israel (49:6). The servant does still retain in his own person certain traits which in the rest of Is 40–55 are ascribed to Israel. These are the sufferings which she underwent during the exile, her debasement, her humiliations, her condemnation and punishment, in other words her death, although it is surely far more difficult to assert this of Israel in spite of Ezekiel's vision of the dry bones (Ezek 37). The servant can be called 'Israel', for he takes upon himself all the sufferings of an Israel that has been contaminated with the sins of the Gentiles, and has incurred the same punishment on their account (53:4). Essentially he is the priest-redeemer who 'intercedes for sinners' (Is 53:12).

Against this view it does not appear difficult to see the victorious Emmanuel of Is 9 in this figure who liberates Israel—the more so since the same figures of light and victory recur in this final chapter. The David of Is 55:3–5 is prince and ruler of peoples whom he has never known hitherto. The author of the servant songs seems to have combined the liberating mission of First Isaiah with the universalist vision of Second Isaiah, and to have systematically inserted his oracles in such a way that the conclusion of the songs is connected with those passages in Is 40–55 which follow it. In this way he has imparted the depths of meaning in his songs to the earlier oracles also, and has given them the definitive traits of that universalist messianism which the New Testament constantly regards as fulfilled in the person of Jesus of Nazareth (Mt 27:29–31; Jn 12:38; 19:5; Acts 8:32f; etc).

Bibliography: *DB(S)* III, 90–100; A. Feuillet, *DB(S)* IV, 709–14; J. Jeremias, *TDNT* V, 654–700; J. Fischer, Haag 609–19 (all with copious bibliographical references); J. Scharbert, *BZ* 2 (1958), 190–213; H. Haag, 'Ebed Jahwe Forschung', *BZ* 3 (1959), 174–204; V. de Leeuw, *De Ebed Jahweh Profetieën*, Assen 1956.

Henri Cazelles

B. In the *New Testament* Israel (Lk 1:54), *David* (Lk 1:69; Acts 4:25), and five times Jesus (Mt 12:18; Acts 3:13, 26; 4:27, 30) are described as the *pais* (servant) of God. In the connected literature the title *pais theou* is found four times applied to Jesus in ancient prayers in the Didache (9:2f; 10:2f; 10:7: copt. fragm.), three times in 1 Clem (59:2ff), three times in MartPol (14:1–3; 20:2); always in liturgical and doxological formulae in which ancient phraseology has been preserved. Since in the New Testament Israel, too, and especially David are described as the servant of God, it is in no sense certain that in the 'christological' use of the title 'Servant of God' Jesus is always being interpreted as the *Isaian* servant of God—the more so as, in the passages quoted in Acts with the exception of 3:13, the idea of the (substitutional) suffering of the servant of God does not appear. It is probable, rather, that Jesus is thought of as the servant of God first and foremost simply in the sense of being the just one who obeys, who fulfils the will of God without reserve (see Mt 3:15). In particular in Acts 3:26 ('God raised up his *servant* for you first') it is not the Isaian servant of God that is being thought of but rather Jesus as *Moses redivivus* (see also 3:22; 7:37; and, on this, Deut 18:15, 18), especially as Moses is described as 'the Servant of God' in the Old Testament (Josh 14:7 [LXX]: *Mōusēs ho pais tou theou*; see also Josephus, *Ant.* v, 39). Jesus himself, as also the apostolic preachers, have viewed his messianic service in the light of the Isaian prediction of the servant of God, as a whole series of passages containing direct or indirect references attest. More important examples: 1. *In the preaching of Jesus*: the logion on ransom, Mk 10:45 and parallels (see also Is 53:12; but probably the formulation of this logion is secondary; see Lk 22:27); the words of Jesus expressing the significance of the distribution of the chalice in the eucharist: *ekkhunomenon huper pollōn* (see Is 53:12; this *huper* [*anti, peri*], which precisely gives expression to the 'substitution' idea, plays an important part in the apostolic preaching of salvation; Schelkle, *Die Passion*, 131–5); Lk 22:37 (see Is 53:12); the silence of Jesus at his trial (see Is 53:7); Jn 10:11, 15, 17 (see Is 53:10); behind the 'must' (*dei*) of his passion (see Mk 8:31 and parallels; Jn 3:14) Jesus certainly saw the will of God as revealed in the *scriptures* (see especially the psalms of lamentation and Is 53). 2. *In the apostolic preaching of the gospel*: (a) *direct*: Mt 8:17 (Is 53:4); 12:18–21 (Is 42:1–4); Lk 22:37 (Is 53:12); Jn 12:38 (Is 53:1); Acts 8:32f (Is 53:7f); Rom 15:21 (Is 52:15); (b) *indirect*: 1 Cor 15:3–5 (a very ancient tradition containing a reference to the fact that the atoning death of Jesus on behalf of others was *in accordance with scripture*); Rom 4:25 (Is 53:4, 5, 12

[LXX]); 8:32; Phil 2:6–12 (*doulos* = slave); humiliation—exaltation); Acts 2:23 (see Is 53:10); 1 Pet 2:21–5; Mk 1:11 and parallels (see Is 42:1); Jn 1:29, 36 ('Lamb of God'); 1 Jn 2:2; 4:10 (*hilasmos* = expiation); Heb 9:28 (see Is 53:12). Jesus also seems to have imparted a new dimension to the idea of the Son of Man by introducing aspects of the Isaian servant of God (see especially the predictions of the passion): the Son of Man must pass through his earthly life as the (anonymous) servant of God. Probably, too, the so-called messianic secret of the synoptic gospels is connected with this: precisely because Jesus is the unknown and unrecognised Servant of God his messianic secret must at first remain unspoken and hidden in public. This tension between the glorious and the suffering Messiah also determines the structure and way of life of the church and its members, and it is for this reason that Is 53 has a part to play in early christian parenesis (eg, Mk 10:45 and parallel; Phil 2:5–11; 1 Pet 2:21–5; Schelkle, 217–38). The description of Jesus as the servant of God belongs to the earliest tradition. Yet it soon died out because it was open to the danger of being misinterpreted in a subordinationist sense, and with the christological kerygma of exaltation greater and greater emphasis came to be laid upon the glory of Jesus *as God in heaven*. Since *pais* has also the meaning of 'child', the transition from the *pais* (=servant, child) to the *huios* (son) christology could be made without any difficulty.

Bibliography (a selection): A. von Harnack, *Die Bezeichnung Jesu als Knecht Gottes und ihre Geschichte*, 1926; K. F. Euler, *Die Verkündigung vom leidenden Gottesknecht*, 1934; J. Gewiess, *Die urapost. Heilsverkündigung nach der Apg.*, 1939, 38–56; K. H. Schelkle, *Die Passion Jesu in der Verkündigung des NT*, 1949; H. W. Wolff, *Jesaja 53 im Urchristentum*, 1949³; T. W. Manson, *The Servant-Messiah*, London 1953; C. Maurer, 'Knecht Gottes und Sohn Gottes im Passionsbericht des Mk-Ev', *ZTK* 50 (1953), 1–38; E. Lohmeyer, *Gottesknecht und Davidssohn*, 1953²; H. Hegermann, *Jesaja 53 in Hexapla, Targum u. Peschitta*, 1954; J. Jeremias, *TDNT* v, 700–717 (with bibliography); E. Schweizer, *Erniedrigung u. Erhöhung bei Jesus und seinen Nachfolgern*, 1955, 81–6; E. Sjöberg, *Der verborgene Menschensohn in den Evv.*, Lund 1955; E. Lohse, *Märtyrer und Gottesknecht*, 1955; G. Bertram, 'Praeparatio evangelica in der LXX', *VT* 7 (1957), 235–9; J. E. Menard, *Pais Theou*, a Messianic Title in Acts', *CBQ* 19 '(1957), 83–92; O. Cullmann, *The Christology of the New Testament*, London 1959; J. N. Sevenster, 'Jezus in de EJ', *TT* 13 (1958), 27–46; E. Fascher, *Jesaja 53 in christl. und jüdischer Sicht*, Berlin 1958; J. L. Price, 'The Servant Motive in the Synoptic Gospels', *Interpretation* (1958), 28–38; L. Krinetzki, 'Die Gottesknechtstheologie des hl. Paulus (Phil 2:6–11)', *BM* 34 (1958), 180–91; L. Krinetzki, *Der Einfluss von Is 52:13–53:12 Par auf Phil 2:6–11*, Rome 1959; M. Hooker, *Jesus and the Servant*, 1959; U. Wilckens, *Die Missionsreden der Apg*, Neukirchen 1961, 163–7; F. Hahn, *Christolog. Hoheitstitel (FRLANT 83)*, Göttingen 1963, 54–66; M. Rese, 'Überprüfung einiger Thesen von J. Jeremias zum Thema des Gottesknechtes im Judentum', *ZTK* 60 (1963), 21–41; W. M. W. Roth, 'The Anonymity of the Suffering Servant', *JBL* 83 (1964), 171–9; J. Jeremias, *Abba*, 1966, 191–216.

Franz Mussner

Shepherd

The work of a shepherd was familiar to the ancients as a matter of living experience. It is this that provides the basis for the figurative use of the term. In Sumer, Babylon, and Assyria 'shepherd' is already found as a soubriquet of the ruler who 'pastures' his subjects, gathers them when they are scattered, carries and cares for the weak. In Egypt it is the God of the other world who is the shepherd and tends his flock. The term is applied to the gods generally. Men are the 'flock of God, which he has made'. The idea of 'shepherd of the peoples' is familiar to Homer, and the image is current throughout antiquity.

The *Old Testament* is unfamiliar with the formalised use of the term (*rō'eh*) for gods and rulers, a usage which is customary elsewhere in the ancient Near East. Instead the manner in which individual traits of the shepherd function are applied to Yahweh shows that here the image is wholly subordinate to the context of a living faith. Yahweh leads his people, his flock (Ps 68:7; 23:3; etc), searches out pastures for them (Ps 23:2; Jer 50:19), calls them together when they are scattered (Zech 10:8), collects them (Is 56:8), bears them (Is 40:11; Ps 28:9). In the accounts of the exodus in Exodus and Deuteronomy terms drawn from the work of shepherds are used. Perhaps too Ps 23 has been influenced by these if we may take 'waters of rest' as referring to the promised land, and the 'restoration of my soul' (v 3) as referring to the miracle of the manna (Guillet, *Leitgedanken der Bibel*, 22f). The psalms and prophecies of consolation composed during the exile make manifold use of the 'shepherd' image, but Yahweh can also assume the other aspect of a shepherd. He can hand his people over as a flock to the slaughter and (instead of gathering them) can scatter them among the peoples (Ps 44:11; see also the image in Ps 44:22; Jer 12:3; Zech 11:4, 7).

The term *shepherd* does not occur in the Old Testament as a title for the king. The Messiah who is to come from the house of David is the first to whom it is applied. He will exercise the function of a shepherd, and he alone as the only shepherd will pasture his people (Ezek 34:23f; Israel and Judah will become one people under one shepherd: Ezek 37:22, 24). In this way the more ethical and social aspect of the task of the messianic ruler who is to come is set in contrast to a purely political understanding of the Messiah (significantly the 'shepherd' does not appear in the Qumran literature!).

In the *New Testament* the figurative use of the 'shepherd' (*poimēn*) idea continues. The image is applied to God only in Lk 15:4-7 in the parable of the lost sheep—if, indeed, it is not intended even there to apply to Christ 'who, by God's commission, brings back the sheep that has strayed' (W. Michaelis, *Die Gleichnisse Jesu*, Hamburg 1955², 133). It may be this latter interpretation that finds expression in the Gospel of Thomas (logion 107) when it declares: 'He left the ninety-nine and sought the one until he found it. After he had toiled [a reference to the Passion?] he said to the sheep, "I love you more than the ninety-nine"'.

Jesus does indeed apply to himself the saying in Zech 13:7 when he says that he goes to his death as a shepherd on behalf of his own (Mk 14:27 and parallel; see also Jn 10:11). He repeatedly insists that he has been sent to the lost sheep (Mt 15:24, etc), in order to seek out the lost, to gather them, to rescue them (Lk 19:10). Jesus is the true shepherd of those who believe in him, hearken to him, those whom he knows and who know him

(Jn 10:4, 14f). But he insists that it has been laid upon him as a shepherd to care for the 'other sheep who are not of this fold' (Jn 10:16). The early church describes Jesus with special emphasis as the 'great shepherd' (Heb 13:20), the 'shepherd and guardian' of our 'souls' (1 Pet 2:25), he who is the 'chief shepherd' (1 Pet 5:4) over the bishops and priests (Jn 21:15ff; Acts 20:28) who pasture the flock of God. In Rev 7:17 the image of the ⁄ lamb is combined with that of the shepherd: he will be the shepherd and will lead the perfect to the springs of life (see Jn 10:28). Again in Rev 12:5; 19:15 (see also 2:27) the power of the victorious Christ as judge is expressed as a power 'to lead to the pastures' (*poimainein*: see Ps 2:9 [LXX]) 'with a rod of brass'. In the same way in Mt 25:32ff Jesus himself had already described the carrying out of the last judgement by means of the image of the shepherd who gathers the whole flock in the evening and divides the (white) sheep from the (black) goats.

Bibliography: L. Dürr, *Ursprung und Ausbau der israel.-jüd. Heilandserwartung*, Berlin 1925, 116-24 F. Hintze, 'Noch einmal die Menschen als "Kleinvieh Gottes"', *Zeitschrift für ägypt. Sprache* 78 (1943), 55ff; J. M. A. Janssen, 'De Farao als goede Herder, Mens en Dier', *Festschrift F. L. R. Sassen*, 1954, 71-9; V. Hamp, 'Das Hirtenmotiv im AT', *Episcopus (Festschrift Faulhaber)*, Munich 1949, 7-20; E. Vogt, 'The "Place in Life" of Psalm 23', *Bbl* 34 (1953), 195-211; R. Criado, 'Los símbolos del amor divino en el AT', *Cor Jesu*, Rome 1959, 411-60 (esp. 427ff); M. Rehm, 'Die Hirtenallegorie Zach 11:4-14', *BZ* 4 (1960), 186-208; J. Jeremias, *TWNT* VI, 485-502; W. Jost, *Poimen, Das Bild vom Hirten in der bibl. Überlieferung und seine christologische Bedeutung*, Giessen 1939; T. K. Kempf, *Christus der Hirt*, Rome 1942; R. Schnackenburg, 'Episkopos und Hirtenamt', *Episcopus (Festschrift Faulhaber)*, 1949, 66-88; P. Samain, 'Le pasteur dans le

Bible', *Rev. Dioc. de Tournai* 5 (1950), 15–25; J. G. S. S. Thompson, 'The Shepherd-Ruler Concept in the Old Testament and its Application to the New Testament', *SJT* 8 (1955), 406–18; N. Catavassi, 'De munere "pastoris" in NT', *VD* 29 (1951), 215–27 and 275–85; J. B. Bauer, '"Oves meae" quaenam sunt?', *VD* 32 (1954), 321–4; V. Hamp and J. Gewiess, *LTK* v², 384–6; J. Botterweck, 'Hirt und Herde im AT und im Alten Orient', *Festschrift J. Frings*, Cologne 1960, 339–52. On the representation of the bearer of the sheep, see: T. Klauser, *Jahrbuch für Antike und Christentum* 1, 1958, 20–51; D. Müller, 'Der gute Hirte', *Zeitschrift für ägypt. Sprache* 86 (1961), 127–44; H. Thomann, *Jahwe, Hirte der Seinen;* Rome 1963 (dissertation); W. Tooley, 'The Shepherd and Sheep Image in the Teaching of Jesus', *NT* 7 (1964), 15–25; A. Stöger, 'Jesus der Hirte', *Oberrhein. Pastoralbl.* 66 (1965), 97–106.

Johannes B. Bauer

Sickness

A. *The Old Testament.* 1. *Sickness as a harsh Experience.* Old Testament man is conscious of the bitterness of being sick, and complains of it to God (see eg, Ps 31:11; etc). He knows how to prize the great benefit of good health (Sir 30:14–20: 'It is better to be poor and healthy of body than rich but physically sick').

2. *Sickness as a punishment for sin and a sign of sinfulness.* See, eg, Ps 32:3–5; 38:3 ('There is no soundness in my flesh because of thy indignation'); 41:4 ('Heal me for I have sinned against thee'), 8f; Job 8:13; 22:5–14; Sir 38:15 ('He that sinneth in the sight of his Maker shall fall into the hands of the physician'); 1 Sam 16:14; 2 Kings 5:27; 2 Chron 21:12–15, 18f; 1 Macc 9:54–6; 2 Macc 9:11f.

3. *The image of the 'sick' people as an expression of its sinful state.* See Is 1:5f;

Jer 8:21–3; 30:12–15; 51:8f. (There is no healing for Babylon).

4. *Sickness as the threatened penalty for falling away from Yahweh and his commandments, health as a reward for faithfulness.* See Ex 15:26; 23:25; Lev 26:15f; Deut 7:12, 15; 28:20–22, 27, 59–61.

5. *Prayer in sickness.* See, eg, Ps 6:2–8; 13:4; 30; 88; 102:24f; 118:17f; 119:149; Sir 38:9 ('Pray to the Lord and he shall heal thee').

6. *Help from Yahweh.* Ex 15:26 ('I am Yahweh your healer'); Ps 34:3f; 41:2–4; 103:3; 107:20; Jer 30:17; 33:6–8. But the human physician too is highly prized by reason of his skill in healing (Sir 38:1–15).

7. *The healing of sickness in the messianic age.* See especially Is 35:5f.

8. *The servant of God as the bearer of our infirmities.* See Is 53:3–5 (v 4: 'Surely he has borne our griefs and carried our sorrows'), and compare this with the promise in v 10 that Yahweh will heal him when he has been wounded. 'Infirmities' are already being used as an image of sins.

B. *The New Testament.* 1. *Jesus and sickness.* According to the witness of the gospels Jesus healed numerous sicknesses of the most diverse kinds. (Apart from the numerous individual narratives concerning healings of the sick, see the summaries in Mk 1:32–4 and parallels; 3:10 and parallels; 6:55 and parallels; Lk 5:15; 8:2. The apostles too receive the commission to heal the sick and the power to execute it from Jesus: Mt 10:8; Lk 10:9). In this the inauguration of the promised messianic age of salvation manifests itself irrefutably (see Mt 11:5 and parallels; 12:28 and parallels), and according to Mt 8:17 it represents a fulfilment of the prophetic saying concerning the servant of God: 'He has taken away our infirmities and borne our sicknesses' (Is 53:4). 'In his name' the apostles too heal the sick (see Lk 10:17; Acts 3:6, 16; 4:10; 9:34: 'Aeneas, Jesus Christ heals you'; Jas 5:14). In the saying which Jesus applies to himself, 'Those who are well have no need of a physician, but those who are sick' (Mk 2:17 and parallels). The passage which follows ('I came not to call the righteous but sinners'), and the context as a whole, together show that Jesus also considers his salvific work for the 'publicans and sinners' as a work of his office as messianic 'physician', who sees in sin a sickness from which man suffers and from which he must be healed.

2. *Sickness and sin*. In the New Testament it is recognised throughout that there is a connection between sin (the dominion of Satan) and sickness (see Mt 12:28f; Lk 13:16; Jn 5:14; Acts 12:22f; Rom 8:20, 22; 1 Cor 11:30; Rev). But Jesus breaks through 'the mechanical dogma of retribution' (Oepke), which was widespread in the Old Testament (see A 2) and later judaism (see Test XII Gad 5:11: 'That in which a man sins, in that will he be punished also'; Jn 9:2, 24). As illustrations of this, see Jn 9:3: 'Neither he nor his parents have sinned'; 11:4: 'This sickness . . . is for the glory of God, so that the Son of God may be glorified by means of it'; Lk 13:1–5). Admittedly God can also permit a sickness to fall on a man as a means of healing chastisement (see 1 Cor 11:32; 2 Cor 4:17; 12:7ff).

3. *Sickness as vicarious suffering entailed in the vocation of the apostle*. Paul speaks of this in 2 Cor 12:7f; see 2 Tim 2:10f. He boasts of his infirmity, which is manifested in his illness 'that the power of Christ may rest upon me' and 'that the life of Jesus may be revealed in our mortal flesh'. In this he sees a sharing in the 'sufferings of Christ' (2 Cor 1:5; Col 1:24), which vicariously benefit his 'body', the church (see the adumbration of this in Ezek 3:22–7; 4:4–8). This must apply to every christian who accepts his sickness as coming from the hand of God.

Bibliography: A. Lods, 'Les Idées des Israelite. sur la maladie, ses causes et ses remèdes', *BZAW* 41 (1925), 181–3; F. Fenner, *Die Krankheit im NT*, Leipzig 1930 (with bibliography); C. J. Brim, *Medicine in the Bible*, New York 1936; H. Greeven, *Krankheit und Heilung nach dem NT*, Stuttgart 1948; J. Scharbert, *Der Schmerz im AT*, Bonn 1955; J. Hempel, '"Ich bin der Herr dein Arzt" (Exod 15:26)', *TLZ* 82 (1957), 809–826; J. Hempel, *Heilung als Symbol und Wirklichkeit im biblischen Schrifttum*, 237–314; F. J. Schierse, 'Hat Krankheit einen Sinn?', *SZ* 84 (1959), 241–55; *DB(S)* v, 957–68; Haag 963f; G. Stählin, *TDNT* i, 490–93; A. Oepke, *TDNT* iii, 200–15; iv, 1091–8; L. M. Weber, *LTK* vi², 591–5.

Franz Mussner

Simplicity

The concept of simplicity is closely related to that of ↗ perfection.

It connotes not simplicity in the derogatory sense of silliness, but rather the virtue of a straightforward, upright and wholehearted disposition, which is immune to any kind of duplicity or deceit. This attitude, which bears the stamp of the union of God with men, is called *haplotēs* by the Greek translators of the bible and by the New Testament, and for this the most favoured translation in Latin is *simplicitas*.

For Plato and Aristotle this concept coincides with those of truthfulness and uprightness. For adherents of the Stoa it is the idea of being faithful to what is natural and unfalsified that is most emphasised. The simplicity of the cynics and the naturalness of their way of life are recommended. A philosopher who comes closer to the biblical concept of simplicity is Marcus Aurelius: in the virtuous man all must be honest and simple and full of good will (3, 4, 3). He decides for the good from a disposition that is simple and free (3, 6, 6). But Marcus Aurelius' 'simplicity' is strongly and decisively conditioned by the Stoic concept of impassivity as an ideal. One must be simple in the sense of refusing to allow oneself to be perturbed by anything (4, 26, 2). 'Simple' is related to 'immune to suffering', 'free from illusion' (4, 37). In 1 Macc 2:37 the doomed Jews encourage themselves by saying: 'Let us all die in the innocence of our hearts!' The ancient translations of 1 Kings 9:4 and Josh 24:14 may be compared with this. 'Simple' comes to express the inner meaning of all virtues, as is seen in the case of the *vir simplex et rectus*, Job (Job 1:1). Such is the simplicity of heart with which one must seek the Lord (Wis 1:1).

The derogatory sense of 'simple', which appears in non-biblical Greek, is unknown in the Old Testament. It is precisely the Proverbs of Solomon which praise the virtue of walking with an upright heart before God (↗ way). In the Testaments of the Patriarchs 'simplicity' is particularly emphasised, and here the concept seems to have been developed still further, for it embraces all virtues and is equivalent to integrity (TestIss v 4) and innocence.

In the New Testament the word does not occur so often (see Rom 12:8; 2 Cor 8:2; 9:11, 13; 11:3; Eph 6:5; Col 3:22 for the noun; and, for the adjective, Mt 6:22; Lk 11:34), but the reality signified by the word simplicity is to be found in children and those of tender age (Mt 18:3), who are the example used to illustrate this attitude. Christians must be 'as simple (ie, as immune to falsehood) as doves' (Mt 10:16). In the logion concerning simplicity (soundness) of the eye (Mt 6:22; Lk 11:34) Jesus requires entire and undivided self-giving to God's will as opposed to the divided and ambiguous piety of the pharisees. To be 'simple' means to be free from ulterior motives of self-interest, and carries the further implication of honesty and ↗ humility. Thus after the breaking of bread the community partake of food with joy and simplicity of heart, praising God (Acts 2:46f), and he who has anything to give gives it with simplicity (Rom 12:8).

Bibliography: C. Spicq, 'La vertu de simplicité dans l'Ancien et le Nouveau Testament', *RSPT* 22 (1933), 5–26; O. Bauernfeind, *TDNT* i, 386f; G. Bertram, *TDNT* iv, 912–23; C. Edlund, 'Das Auge der Einfalt', *Acta Sem. neotest. Upsaliensis* 19 (1952); H. Bacht, 'Einfalt des Herzens', *GL* 29 (1956), 416–26; H. Bacht, *RAC* 4, 821–40; O. Hiltbrunner, *Latina Graeca: Semasiologische Studien über lateinische Wörter im Hinblick auf ihr Verhältnis zu griechischen Vorbildern*, Bern 1958, 15–105; J. Kürzinger, *LTK* iii², 746; G. W. H. Lampe, *A Patristic Greek Lexikon* i, 1961, 186f.

Johannes B. Bauer

Sin

A. *Sin in the Old Testament.* It is difficult to define what sin is, but by means of the particular expressions which are employed for it we can deduce from the history of revelation in what it essentially consists.

1. 'Your iniquities have made a separation between you and your God!' (Is 59:2). This is, perhaps, the clearest saying concerning the essence of sin in the Old Testament (Köhler, 164). Something sundering comes between man and God. The first sin that is committed is recorded in the narrative of the fall in paradise. It is a sin of disobedience both interior and exterior. The ancestors of the race wish to be sicut dii, like gods, knowing good and evil! This is not equivalent to saying that they 'wish to know everything', or 'to distinguish between good and evil', but that they wish 'to decide for themselves what was good and what was evil, and to live according to this decision' (thus Coppens, de Vaux, etc). It is a question, therefore, of nothing less than outright moral autonomy which finds expression in pride and rebellion against the dominion which God claims for himself!

At the suggestion of the serpent, Eve believes that the word of God may not be absolute; she doubts the word of God and thinks that the command that comes from God has been given not for man's benefit but for the benefit of God himself (1. 'You will by no means die', 2. 'For God knows that you will be as gods'). Thereby man becomes a rival to God. The whole conception of the relationship between God and man is radically inverted. The evil of sin consists, therefore, not so much in the external act of disobedience as in the interior inversion of the right order.

The indirect effect of sin is an alteration in man by reason of which he flees from God (Gen 3:8: 'And they hid themselves', whereas formerly, on the contrary, 2:25: 'They were not ashamed'). At the same time punishment ensues also: ↗ death and expulsion from paradise. Man no longer had access to the tree of life (3:22–4). ↗ Life has the value of a supreme gift, one which God alone can give. Death, on the other hand, is nothing else than the deprivation of life. So long as no revelation has yet been given of survival after death, death means the absolute deprivation of all benefits without exception, and so the loss of salvation too. Wis 2:23 has also interpreted our passage in the same sense: 'God created man for immortality, and made him to the image of his own eternity. But by the envy of the devil death came into the world, and they experience death who are on the side of the devil'. In Rom 5:12 Paul adduces the revelation of Genesis in the literary form which it has acquired in Wisdom. With the transgression of Adam sin has entered the world of men, sin, here formally personified as a power which sets itself against God, and which so long as it remains in mankind separates it from God. This is the condition of separation which is of itself final and irremediable, and which Paul—in agreement here with the whole of tradition—calls 'death'—death, which is in consequence of the spirit and everlasting, the sign of which is physical death, which will not be followed by any glorious resurrection.

The chapters which follow in the primitive history of the bible relate how sin makes ever deeper incursions into the world of men, and how at the same time it takes away 'life' (see the genealogies in chapter 5, and 6:3). Indeed life would have been completely wiped out by the flood had not God relented and 'saved' Noah together with his family in the ark. (Hence it is that the ark becomes a type of salvation in the New Testament: I Pet 3:20ff). They are saved by God who makes his ↗ covenant with them. Men would not have been able to achieve salvation of themselves.

In the minds of the Hebrews the land of Egypt (see Ezek 20:5–9) was the land in which man lived *far* from God, the land of *sin*. And it is precisely there that it is revealed with unsurpassable clarity (the miracles of Moses!) that without the miraculous intervention of God all thought of deliverance would have been senseless from the very outset. Hence the constantly recurring motivation: 'For I am the God who brought you out of the house of bondage, out of Egypt'—thus especially in the prelude to the decalogue, Ex 20:2 and Deut 5:6 (see also Lev 22:33 and Ps 81:10), for the commandments of God are meant precisely to be a help to salvation and to life. They are given for man's well-being, so that he shall not fall into sin and finding himself far from God, encounter death.

What does sin mean for God? Does the Old Testament teach only that sin is committed against God, or does it go still further and say that it constitutes an actual injury to God? In itself the word *offence* does express this. In our terms it means 'damage' (as for

instance it might be said that the malignant talk of someone else has 'damaged' me), 'scandal', 'injury'. Admittedly the actual term is not exemplified in the Old Testament. Nevertheless the idea is there.

2. *The words for sin* in the Old Testament seem at first not very enlightening: *ḥāṭāʾ*, properly 'to miss a goal, blunder, commit a moral error', applies to the sin which is committed externally and which is apprehensible and visible to others; *pešaᶜ* as a designation for sin usually emphasises the aspect of rebellion, opposition to God; the word *ᶜāwôn* lays the chief emphasis on bad conscience, the evil intention involved in sin, and then (as can readily be understood) the fault.

3. Rather more can be deduced from the consequences arising from sin according to the teaching of the Old Testament. It provokes God's ↗ wrath (Deut 32:21); see especially Jer 7:18f; 'The children gather wood, the fathers kindle fire, and the women knead dough, to make cakes for the queen of heaven. And they pour out drink offerings to other gods to injure (insult) me. Is it I whom they injure? says Yahweh'. Is it not themselves, to their own confusion?' From these two verses one receives not merely their own particular message but also a striking insight into the theology of Jeremiah. Properly speaking it is not God who is injured but man! Again the word *nāʾats* means to 'treat irreverently'. The Greek bible (and, following it, RSV) translates 'to provoke to anger'. In any case it is precisely by this word that the idea of injury and offence is expressed, although in practice it is confined to the rejection of the counsel, law, or com-

850

mandment of God. The Old Testament strives as far as possible to uphold the transcendence of God. However certain it may be that sins are directed against God, it is no less certain that man cannot really affect him by them (Job 35:6: 'If you have sinned, what do you accomplish against him? And if your transgressions are multiplied, what do you do to him?').

Nevertheless the Old Testament does contain many contexts and many individual narratives from which it can clearly be shown that there is a true sense in which the sin of man does affect God also, without impugning his transcendence. In pagan sources we already have abundant evidence for the idea that by sin God is robbed of something, that he does not obtain something that is his by right. Traces of some such idea may well be found from time to time in the earlier passages of the bible, as for instance in the narrative of the sacrifice of the sons of Eli (1 Sam 2:12ff, especially v 17), and similarly in the story of the ark of the covenant among the Philistines (1 Sam 5:7ff). As a whole, however, the Old Testament adopts a hostile attitude to ideas of this kind. The prophets, for example, struggle to eradicate that attitude of mind among the Israelites in which they strive to appease God and offer him compensation in the manner of pagans: see Is 1:11; Ps 50:9ff, similarly in the section on the right kind of fasting, Is 58:5ff.

Sin is an 'injury', an 'insult' to God to the extent that it injures or damages a man whom God has under his protection. In 2 Sam 12 Nathan reproaches David with his sins against Uriah and his wife (vv 7f)—what ingratitude to God who has made David so great and rich, and has bestowed wives in plenty upon him! v 9: David has despised the commandment of God, therefore punishment will fall upon him; v 10: 'because you have despised *me*, and have taken the wife of Uriah the Hittite to be your wife'. But when the sinner acknowledges his sin and repents God removes his guilt from him (v 13). Only part of the punishment still stands in order that others may not be scandalised and imagine that David's guilt might go unpunished. In one way, therefore, sin does indeed affect God, namely by doing injury to men whom God protects and loves. The same idea is expressed in Ps 83 when it is said that the fury of the ↗ enemy is directed against God, and yet it is made clear in the same breath that it is only the Israelites who will experience it. They are, after all, *his* people! Whoever sins against them sins against God.

It is even more true that sin constitutes 'injury' and 'insult' against God in that it is a breach of the ↗ covenant between God and men, the covenant which came increasingly to be deemed as close as the marriage bond. Adam and Eve forfeit not only life as such, but life in friendship with God. God who, of his own free will, had bestowed every kind of love and every possible benefit upon them, is regarded by them as a tyrant and a rival. Then we have to take into consideration all the covenants (see Rom 9:4) which he made with Noah, Abraham and Moses. For this reason it is precisely idolatry (see Rom 1:21ff) which can be described as the sin of sins from which all other sins derive.

For in Israel's choice of other gods besides Yahweh, Yahweh himself is precisely supplanted as inadequate for the role of protector and friend. From early times onwards we find sin regarded as *adultery*. The marriage between people and God is broken. The marriage of Hosea perforce bears moving witness to this, the actual circumstances of it taking on this prophetic meaning (see also Ps 45, the Song of Solomon, Ezek 16, Is 5, and 54:5ff; etc). God loves his people as a wife, with a perfect and boundless love. Every time she is unfaithful and separates herself from him he follows her to induce her to ⤴ convert her ways and return home. He does this with all the urgency of a husband who cannot go on living without her. It is against this background that the expressions of divine jealousy are to be understood (the classic passages: Ex 20:5 = Deut 5:9; Ex 34:14; Deut 4:24; 6:15; Josh 24:19). This jealousy is turned into anger when confronted with the enemies of his people, but can also be turned against the Israelites themselves when they are unfaithful, in order to bring about their conversion (see Ezek 23:25 and 14:11). Thus the very punishment inflicted upon sinners by God can be regarded as an expression of his love for them. For if he did not love them, then he would not chastise them in order to induce them to convert their ways. Nowhere in pagan tradition is there any mention of such a love of God for his creatures, his men.

To summarise the doctrine of the Old Testament on sin: Sin is directed against, and in a true sense affects, God in that it 'strikes his love in the face'. For this reason it can be forgiven only by him. Equally sin is an *evil*, the evil that falls upon man himself because it deprives him of true life, and subjects him to the rule of Satan. The effect of sin upon the interior man is to produce in him a profound change for the worse, a change which the man himself cannot be the sole, or even the primary agent in removing and repairing. For this God himself must intervene—must 'wash him clean', 'renew his life', 'create him anew', to invoke the words of the unknown suppliant in Ps 51. It is precisely this sublime psalm of repentance which can be pointed to as the compendium of the Old Testament teaching on sin.

B. *Sin in the New Testament.* 1. *The synoptics.* The vocabulary does not throw much light on the nature of sin. On the contrary, one could be led astray by it if one decided to take as one's starting-point the word most frequently used in the synoptics and Acts, namely *aphienai* (lit. = 'to let go'), and assumed from this that sin in the New Testament is conceived of in purely juridical terms. Instead of such an examination of individual words it will be far more suitable to our purpose to take the New Testament as a whole, the sequence and context of the accounts it contains as the basis for our investigation of the nature of sin.

'Forgive us our debts as we also have forgiven our debtors' (Mt 6:12). Here Jesus is using an expression which was familiar to the Jews: *debt.* See Sir 11:15, where it appears as equivalent to *ḥaṭā᾿.* Thus also, in Ps 25:18, in place of the Hebrew word *ḥaṭāt* (=sin), the Targum (Aramaic paraphrase) puts *ḥôbā᾿* (= debt). In exactly the same way Lk 11:4, the parallel text to Mt 6:12, reads 'sin' in place of 'debt'. Naturally the use of this word does not open the way to a purely legalistic view of sin. It is rather that all must lay to heart the commandment of mutual forgiveness (see Sir 28:2ff; Mk 11:25; Mt 18:23–34). More can be learnt of the New Testament idea of sin from the concept of ⁊ 'conversion', which is extremely closely connected with it. Like John the Baptist, Jesus commences his preaching with a summons to repentance (see Mk 1:4, 15; Mt 3:7–10 and parallels; Lk 3:7ff). This presupposes that the men to whom it is addressed have already *turned away* from God. It is precisely in this turning away that sin consists. It is disobedience to God (Lk 15:21) and lawlessness (Mt 7:23; 13:41). In the ethics of christianity, God is the Lord and man is bound to obey him, whereas in the Stoa sin is regarded simply as a deviation from the ideal, from that which is in conformity with nature. Hence every sin carries with it the awareness of guilt, the awareness of having deserved punishment from God.

A still more perfect and more exact idea of sin is to be obtained from the parables concerning God's kindness, above all that of the prodigal son (Lk 15). In his case sin begins in the moment when he demands his share of the estate with the intention of spending it all on his own pleasure, to which end he takes himself abroad in order to withdraw himself from the surveillance of his father. These two elements, departure from the father's house and living for pleasure, together constitute a sin.

The three parables in Lk 15 carry us further, for they all exhibit one trait in common, namely that the Father, God,

of his kindness brings his lost children (sinners) home from afar. It makes no difference here whether the evangelist was in fact the first to put these parables together. The point is precisely that man, left solely to his own resources, cannot live for long without grave sin. Not only the psalmists but also the devotees of the Qumran sect were utterly convinced of this, and gave expression to their conviction again and again: it is God who guides man's steps into the right way (that is, the moral life). Without his help man cannot live a good life. When ⁊ temptation comes he is powerless before it without the divine help, like the prodigal son in the far country when a famine broke out. His position is brought home to him even more by this, and he is forced to notice how isolated and desolate man is far from his home. No-one is willing to help. This motif appears in all three parables, if indeed the leading figure is taken to be the Father in his kindness. It is manifest that sin is represented by the element of total deprivation, deprivation of the very meaning of existence by separation from God. The lost sheep is perishing in isolation, and, more than this, has thwarted the very meaning of its own life, namely to be of service to man. The same applies to the lost drachma. The sole purpose of its being there, the very meaning of its existence is that men shall avail themselves of it. When it is lost people can no longer avail themselves of it, and it is like a coin which has been withdrawn from currency, common metal, or— still worse—like forgotten matter. In a word, its 'drachma-being' is meaningless precisely because it has been cut off from its proper sphere of life. So it is with man. The meaning and goal of his life is God, the luminous will of God, his overflowing love. He who wilfully separates himself from this is not only lost but makes his very 'being a man' meaningless in itself. The necessary condition for the sinner receiving grace always remains his conversion (see Lk 15:7, 10). Admittedly this conversion does not of itself bring about the forgiveness of the Father, but rather the Father has been waiting for it from the first. As August-ine trenchantly puts it: 'Iam diligenti nos reconciliati sumus', 'He loves us already before we have been reconciled to him'. If Christ appears as ⟋ mediator between God and ourselves, then this is not to alter God's attitude towards us, but to demonstrate to us the love of God, who offers his only begotten Son on our behalf, who only waits for our conversion. This conversion, therefore, is necessary because man is free and a person, possessing free will and taking his own decisions (⟋ freedom). Jesus therefore has to alter our attitude, our state of lostness far from God, by his preaching of penance and conversion. By these means he prepares men to receive the forgiveness of their sins, for as the suffering ⟋ servant of God he lays down his life in expiation for many who come before and after him. It is only thus that the promise of the angel is fulfilled in its deepest sense. The name 'Jesus' means salvation, that is, that he will save men 'from their sins' (Mt 1:21; ⟋ redeemer, ⟋ Saviour). This significant feature in the messian-ism of Jesus was unknown to judaism (in spite of Is 53, etc: see H. Heger-mann, *Jesaja 53*, Gütersloh 1954, 131f), and *a fortiori* has no counterpart in any

of the saviour-figures in hellenistic religions.

A further point of fundamental importance (see Schmid) is the 'polari-ty' of the christian idea of God. God is at once absolute ⟋ holiness, and there-fore the strict and immovable Lord and judge, and at the same time absolute ⟋ love, the kind Father who recognises even the most abandoned of sinners as his child and takes him into his grace when he turns back to him. Both aspects of the christian idea of God are accorded their full force in the teaching of Jesus on sin. Hence the radicalism of Jesus' moral demands, his sayings on judgement and 'woes'. On the other hand Jesus teaches no less decisively that the Father's love knows no limits, that he does not will the death of the sinner, but rather his life, and that he only waits for the conversion of that sinner with open arms—indeed that he actually comes to meet him when he repents. This polarity in the idea of God is again underlined by the cir-cumstances of Jesus' own life. Certainly, the Father loves him in an infinitely higher manner than in his love for his human creatures, but on the other hand in a certain sense he owes it as an act of atonement to his affronted holiness (at least in the order of atonement once he has chosen this) that he both wills and accepts the sacrifice of the life of his beloved Son in expiation for the guilt of humanity.

⟋ *Satan.* In the preaching of Jesus and the apostles a further element of decisive importance can be discerned. Jesus comes to establish the kingdom of God in place of the kingdom of Satan (Jn 12:31; Col 1:13; Acts 26:18). This appears quite clearly from the narrative of the ↗ temptations of Jesus. In any case the Lord intended to lay it before his apostles as a fact of special importance for the understanding of his mission. As soon as he had received his solemn messianic investiture at baptism—anointing as messianic king by the Holy Spirit (see Acts 10:38)—he was impelled by the Spirit to go into the wilderness 'in order to be tempted by Satan'. However we choose to explain the individual elements in the temptation, one point is clear. We have here the prologue to the entire life of Jesus. His whole mission consists in the victory over Satan, and a victory won not with any kind of weapons but with those provided by the Father, which alone were effective. Satan suggests various apparently good means, and above all opportune means. Certainly in order to assuage his hunger he could legitimately make use of his power of working miracles. In order to convince the Jewish people he could hardly have thought of a more appropriate miracle than to cast himself down from the pinnacle of the temple, for then they would truly have been able to recognise him as the Son of Man in the guise foretold in Daniel's promise as 'he who comes upon the clouds of heaven'. The Jews themselves demanded a miracle of this kind from Jesus (Mt 12:38; 16:1; Jn 6:30). Josephus has a similar story to tell about the Jews of his time (see *Antiq.* 20:5, 1; 8:6). Jesus would indeed perform miracles, but of a different kind: the sign of Jonah, death as a proof of his love, and resurrection as a proof of his power, but all without eye-witnesses! And when (Jn 6:30) the Jews wanted a

miracle like the miracle of manna Jesus promised them a still greater, more sublime and more effective sign: the true bread from heaven. But they said 'this saying is hard' (v 60).

Christ rejects Satan's suggestions in the clearest possible manner. For him there can be no question of using any other means to establish the kingdom of God except those willed by God himself. Then Satan sees that he has been defeated by the steadfastness of Jesus and reveals his real intentions: I will give you all the kingdoms of the earth if you will adore me . . . the Son of God could no longer be in doubt. Satan, the conqueror of the old Adam, is now himself conquered by the new. But this conquest is only preliminary, only on the occasion of these temptations. Luke adds the significant statement: 'Satan departed from him until an opportune time' (4:13). This victory is only a preliminary one, an anticipated one (as in the transfiguration)—only now will the struggle with Satan run its full course through the entire life of Jesus.

Jesus and Satan during Jesus' public mission. The Jews held the conviction that sickness was a sign of bondage to sin and Satan. The 'woman who was bent over' (Lk 13:11ff) had a 'spirit of infirmity' (v 11). She was 'bound by Satan' (v 16), although it is not stated in so many words that there was a devil to be cast out of her. Certainly Christ does correct the opinion of the Jews and of his own disciples, but he also confirms what is true in this opinion: see Lk 13:1ff: Jesus receives news of the massacre of certain Galilaeans as they were in the act of offering sacrifice at the temple: 'And he answered them, "Do you think that these Galilaeans were worse sinners than all the other Galilaeans because they suffered thus? I tell you, No; but unless you repent you will all likewise perish". There is, therefore, a real connection between men's unhappy fate and sin. In a not dissimilar manner in the case of the man born blind (Jn 9:2f) Jesus explicitly denies that this man or his parents have sinned, but he sharply admonishes the man who has been healed at the pool of Bethzatha (Jn 5:14): 'See, you are well. Sin no more, that nothing worse befall you'. The healing miracles, therefore, are meant to prove more than that Jesus is the awaited Messiah (Mt 11:4), more too than that Jesus has power to forgive sins (Mk 2:10ff), or that he is the sole redeemer (Acts 4:12). These miracles prove more than this in that they constitute in themselves the beginning of redemption to the extent that they free men from the tyranny of the devil. It is no accident that the exorcism stories above all are told at great length. The casting out of devils bears witness to the fact that the kingdom of God has come (Mt 12:28; Lk 11:20). For the same reason the disciples too receive power to heal the sick and to cast out devils (Mk 3:15; 6:7; Lk 10:19). This downfall of Satan is to be understood figuratively as a spiritual demonstration by Jesus (see Is 14:12), and it signifies that the devil has lost the position of power which he has hitherto enjoyed (see Jn 12:31; 16:11). The struggle is at its keenest during the passion of Jesus. Luke has clearly brought↗ temptation and↗ passion into connection with one another (4:13): 'Then Satan departed from

him until an opportune time'; and (22:53): 'This is your hour and the power of darkness'; compare Acts 26:18, in which the phrase 'out of darkness' is used as a synonym for 'from the power of Satan'. Satan is quite exceptionally active at this time. He enters into Judas (Lk 22:3; see also Jn 13:2, 27). He wants to sift the apostles like wheat (Lk 22:31). Paul asserts the same thing in 1 Cor 2:8 when he holds the devils responsible for the death of Christ (the *arkhontes* have crucified the Lord). But as at the temptation Jesus triumphs over Satan in that he subjects his own will to that of the Father: 'Having become obedient to the death of the cross'. And while the others believe that he has succumbed to Satan and to the power of evil, in reality he conquers the devil by his most perfect act of love and obedience. Thus that dominion over all the kingdoms of the earth which Satan had promised to give to him (Lk 4:6) is indeed transferred to Christ: 'All power is given to me . . .' (Mt 28:18; see also Phil 2:9: 'He bestowed upon him the name which is above every name [ie, *Kurios*], that at the name of Jesus every knee should bow in heaven and on earth and under the earth').

Now every christian must obtain a share in this victory of Christ. As the whole life of Jesus was a struggle with Satan, so too the whole life of Christ's disciple must be the same (Eph 6:11). Compare the synoptics: the enemy sows weeds in the field of the farmer (God). This enemy is the devil (Mt 13:39), who avails himself of the night hours because he shrinks from the light of day. The 'evil one' snatches away what has been sown in the hearts of men (Mt 13:19), and Luke, who calls him by his name ('the devil') adds: 'Then the devil comes and takes away the word from their hearts that they may not come to ⁄ faith and be saved' (8:12).

As long as the christian remains united to Christ his struggle with Satan can only have a successful issue. In the light of this the duty of ⁄ prayer becomes manifest (⁄ temptation).

To summarise then: the message of the synoptics goes even further than that of the Old Testament. Here sin is regarded as something even stronger than 'bondage under the devil', not in external terms, as simply a 'debt', but as a state of being sundered from God and enslaved to Satan.

2. In the case of *John* it is striking that, unlike the synoptics, who constantly speak of 'sins' in the plural, he employs the singular form: Christ has come to take away the *sin* of the world (Jn 1:29; see also 1 Jn 3:5). Jesus takes all the sins—that is, the debt of sin— upon himself in order to lead the world home from its state of separation from God. In John the nature of sin as a state of being sundered from God finds its clearest expression. Jesus, who is one with God, is *without* sin (Jn 8:46). He is the light and the sinners are darkness (3:19). He is always heard by God, whereas God does not hearken to the sinners (9:31). For this reason John refers to sin simply as *anomia* (=lawlessness, godlessness) (1 Jn 3:4), that which places men in constant opposition to the will of God.

By sin, then, the sinner becomes precisely a child of Satan (1 Jn 3:8): 'He who commits sin is of the devil; for the devil has sinned from the beginning. The reason the Son of God appeared was to destroy the works of the devil'. In 1 Jn 3:9, on the other hand, we are told; 'No-one born of God commits sin'. The opposition between righteousness (=virtuous life 1 Jn 3:7) and sin is every bit as real and as insuperably great as the opposition between God and Satan.

The gospel has the same message to convey (8:34): The sinner is a son of Satan: 'You are of your father, the devil' (8:44); and this is intended in the full sense, as the context shows. The Jews practise lying and murder inasmuch as they set themselves against Jesus, who is truth itself, and inasmuch as they intend to kill him. This applies to every sin. In every sin the sinner does the works of the devil (1 Jn 3:8–11), that is he sets himself against the truth and becomes a murderer like Cain who, inspired by Satan, slew his brother because the works of that brother were good, whereas his own were evil. Why is the sinner a murderer? Because he who hates his brother is a murderer (v 15). The sign that men possess this ⁄ 'life' (the germ of eternal life which is what John means by 'life') is their love for their fellow men (1 Jn 3:10; Jn 13:35). Hatred of one's brother destroys this (eternal) life. Sin now means not merely a state of being sundered from God but hatred against God. The sinners are indeed impelled by the devil (as, according to John, Judas and Cain were), and do the works of the devil (Jn 3:19ff: 'This is the judgement, that the light has come into the world and men loved darkness rather than light, because their deeds were evil. For everyone who does evil hates the light'. This hatred against Christ, and thereby against God also, has led men to a point at which they will kill him. 'Now they have no excuse for their sin. He who hates me hates my Father also' (15:22f).

This is the drama of human existence: either love of God or hatred of God. Thus Christ becomes a sign of contradiction in that he reveals what sin really is, how penetratingly it takes possession of us, piercing into our innermost depths. In this situation only love could avail to help. There was no other way in which sin could be blotted out except by love. Only in this way could man attain a share in the divine love, in the love of him who is love itself and whose love is the ultimate and absolute love. As Ralph Luther says (*Ntl. Wörterbuch*, Hamburg 1951, 32f), Christ has in our name given to the Father that love which humanity should have given to God but did not give. A debt which we owed he has paid.

Satan is referred to by John no less than by the synoptics. It is the devil that impels the Jews, so that the passion of Jesus is described as the work of the devil and of the ⁊ 'world', which for its part is the instrument of Satan. Thereby the death and resurrection of Christ (both referred to by John by the single term 'glorification'), his victory over Satan, is the 'hour in which the prince of this world shall be cast out' (or better, 'cast away': Jn 12:31; see also Lk 10:18; the same image in Rev 12:9: 'And the great dragon was thrown down, that ancient serpent who is called the devil and Satan, the deceiver of the whole world . . . conquered by the Blood of the

Lamb . . .'). These last words signify that the fall of Satan is brought about by Christ's death on the cross. This brings us to the Book of Revelation. Here this idea is developed further, especially in chapter 12. Before the seer depicts the hard struggle of the church in chapters 13ff he places at the beginning that vision which can actually be regarded as a synthesis of this struggle as a whole and of its successful outcome, namely the victory of Christ. In a similar manner in the gospel John records the words expressing the triumph, the final victory, spoken by Jesus before his passion: 'Fear not, I have conquered the world' (16:33).

3. In *Paul* the Jewish mode of expressing sin and forgiveness, namely, 'debt' and 'remission of debt', only occurs incidentally, and where it does occur the word *remission* (Col 1:14: *aphesis tōn hamartiōn* = 'remission of sins'; Eph 1:7: *aphesis tōn paraptōmatōn* = 'remission of trespasses') is sometimes explained by other words such as *apolutrōsis* (= redemption) or *hilastērion* (= propitiation). The nearest Paul comes to this idea of sin is to be found in his reference to the cancellation of the bond (Col 2:14); see on this the Jewish prayer for the New Year, Abînu Malkênu: 'Of thy great mercy cancel all our bonds'. But in both these passages it is to be noticed that it is not a question of a debt being paid by a debtor, but of the total cancellation of the bond of debt. Moreover in the passage in Col 2:14 God the Father is the subject.

What therefore can be deduced from the actual words which Paul uses for sin? We have already referred to the fàct that the synoptics always use *hamartia* in the plural, whereas John employs the singular form far more frequently. He speaks of the Lamb who takes away *the* sin of the world. Paul goes still further. He reserves this word for cases in which he has a special meaning to express, elsewhere employing other terms. For him *hamartia* is a power, an active force in men which entered the world with the fall of the first parents and brings its lethal effects to bear through the law. In Rom 5:1–11 Paul refers to the christian's experience of peace with God and harmony of soul, which is based upon the unshakeable firmness of christian ↗ hope. And this in turn is based upon the ↗ love which God has for us as the ↗ Spirit attests to us. Christ actually underwent death for us while we were still sinners. Now a prior condition for this experience is that Christ has redeemed Christians from sin, ↗ death, ↗ law and ↗ flesh. In other words the entire redemptive work of Christ is aimed at removing this 'sin', *hamartia*.

From Rom 6 it can be deduced that man can be freed from this sin only by the death and resurrection of another, that is inasmuch as he becomes like the dead and risen Christ. This gives expression to the fact that man before and man after ↗ baptism differ basically from one another alike in their state of being and their mode of action. 6:4: we must walk in newness of life. To the extent that the sacrament of baptism makes the christian one with the being of Christ, it has reformed and fashioned anew our entire being. If we are one with him in death then we are one with him also in resurrection. In v 6 the old man is called the man with *hamartia*

(man before baptism). Our body was a body of sin, but when this was deprived of its effectiveness by baptism it ceased to be an instrument of sin. He who (according to v 7) has died has abandoned this body of sin, this instrument of sin, and is justified. The fact that man can fall back into sin once more appears from the whole tenor of the exhortation of the apostle of the Gentiles (vv 12ff). Sin, therefore, as we have already seen in Gen 3, is something which alters the whole man to his very depths. In Rom 7 Paul develops his doctrine of sin still further. Christ has redeemed man from sin, death, and flesh, but also from the law—in spite of the good effects which the law has had as leading up to Christ. As a wife is no longer bound to her husband by the law after he has died, and no longer becomes an adulteress if she takes another husband, so christians are free from the external law, the Mosaic law, for they are no longer in the flesh but in the Spirit. This death to sin and the flesh takes effect in them through the Body of Christ. In other words they have already begun to share in the life of Christ who, by his death and resurrection, has rid himself of his fleshly body in order to assume a spiritual body.

How is law now related to sin? Is it a cause of it? Is it identical with it? Law is indeed a cause of sin (Gal 3:19), but only as providing the occasion (*causa occasionalis*) for it, that is not a cause of sin in the strict sense, but of transgression of the law itself. This was in fact the case with the first sin. Two elements are present in it, the factor of evil cupidity, concupiscence, and the factor of the commandment. In fact the devil, as always, avails himself of this divine commandment, a commandment which, holy and God-given as it was in itself, was bestowed for the benefit of the first human pair and not for them to transgress. Without this law the devil would have remained powerless for ever. It was not without reason that God permitted this state of affairs. Man's first experience of the power of sin is of its death-dealing effects. By sin man is brought to an awareness that it sets him in opposition to God, sunders him from God, deprives him of his life. For life is a privilege granted by God. Thus the true sense of what Paul says can be recognized: 'It is only through the law that I have knowledge of sin'. Law is the *epignōsis hamartias*.

In vv 14ff Paul describes the consequences of sin for sinful man (not, as Augustine assumed after his Pelagian conversion, for the just). It is not man's nature that is totally corrupt; this remains sound, 7:22: 'I delight in the law of God, in my inmost self'.

The question therefore arises whether what Paul understands as *hamartia* is what we call original sin, the effects and the power of which are blotted out by baptism. Paul at least intends *hamartia* as *including* personal sin, for he speaks of sin having grown (see Rom 5:12).

A further question is whether he understands *hamartia* as meaning concupiscence, as the Council of Trent presumes. This can be maintained provided that the term *concupiscence* is taken to mean something more than merely fleshly concupiscence—in other words, if it is taken in a broader sense, in which its meaning might be paraphrased somewhat as follows: we are all led by a certain egoism with regard to ourselves, our neighbour, and God— ie, concupiscence here would mean what Augustine calls *amor sui ipsius*, self-love.

For our understanding of Paul's idea of the nature of sin it is also particularly illuminating to compare Rom 7 and 8. Here the state of grace is expressed in other terms, namely as the presence of the Spirit, while the state of sin is made equivalent to the absence of the Spirit (see the adumbration of this in Ezek 36). The restoration of man now consists in the fact that he passes from the state of being in the flesh to the state of being in the Spirit, from egoism to love (in the sense of *caritas*). Rom 8 shows us further that in the man whom Christ has redeemed there is no longer anything worthy of condemnation (8:1). He can now live the life that is divine, the life of the Spirit, and therefore too fulfil that which the law prescribes, or rather, what the law prescribes is fulfilled in him (v 4 in the passive); for it is rather that an effect is produced in the redeemed man than that he himself brings it about. Paul adds a further point of special importance: 'Insofar as he walks not according to the flesh but according to the Spirit'. For even when christians have been redeemed from sin and no longer live in the flesh (vv 8, 9), still they can once more hearken to that which is fleshly, and so fall victim once more to the dominion of sin. Thus right through their lives they remain under the law, but only as a matter of duty, not as a matter of compulsion.

The redeemed christians are not subject to the compulsion of the law because he who loves acts not because of the law but out of his love. They are indeed, however, under the obligation of the law because when they are lacking in love they see in it what they have to do.

From all this the position of law and sin in relation to each other is again made clear. If man lived wholly in the Spirit, and could no longer fall victim to the impulse of the flesh, then law would indeed be superfluous. Hence the assertion of the apostle of the gentiles in 1 Tim 1:9: 'The law is not laid down for the just but . . . for sinners' (see Gal 5:23).

Still further light is thrown upon the opposition between Spirit and flesh in the christian in Rom 8:5ff and Gal 5:16ff: 'The mind that is set on the flesh is hostile to God'. Actual transgression of the law is only the expression of this hatred against God. The essence of sin consists in the fact that he who hates God does not and cannot hearken to him. Paul's idea of sin as set forth here also appears in passages in which he is not speaking of sin in general, as in Rom 5–8, but in which he has specific transgressions in mind, as in Rom 1:21ff and 1 Cor 6:12ff. In Rom 1:21ff the sins of the pagans are described in the selfsame terms that are used of Israel (see Ps 106:20), who, even as God was speaking with Moses concerning the covenant, made idols for herself. Israel did not wish to have a distant transcendent God, but one to whom she could constantly have recourse, whom she could influence according to her own wishes, a God who would be 'at hand' for man. Like Adam and Eve the Israelites wanted to decide for themselves what was good and what was evil, what they

should do and what they should omit. This is precisely the reproach that is levelled against the pagans. They have not given due honour to God as God, and have not shown gratitude to him; both expressions have the same essential meaning.

Sin, therefore, is to be regarded as consisting essentially in the fact that man is no longer content to be dependent upon God but decides to be the principle of his own life, no longer acknowledging that it is God and not himself who has made him what he is. In sin man turns away from God and towards himself (see the statements in Col 1:21 and Eph 4:14f).

In 1 Cor 6:18 Paul says that the unchaste man likewise sins against his own body. But the gravity of the transgression consists in the fact that the body exists for the Lord, is the property of the Lord. Thus unrighteousness is directed against Christ. It has the effect of tearing his members from him (the christian is still a member of the body of Christ). Unrighteousness is directed against the Spirit and against the Father in heaven, whose temple the christian is. Even one who sins only against his own body is acting against God, and commits a crime of robbery against God, a sacrilege. When man offends against God it is not as though he could deprive him of something, but rather that he withdraws from him the man whom he loves. Thus Christ's entire work of ↗ redemption and ↗ atonement is aimed at giving back to the Father the man who has once more become Christ and is in Christ.

In the *Letter to the Hebrews* sin is conceived of in a manner wholly in conformity with the underlying meaning of the Hebrew *ḥāṭāʾ* ('to miss the goal'). It is the sin of one who is *en route*. As the leader of the caravan God requires obedience (3:7, 12:25). But the people murmur and doubt (3:8). Sin, therefore, is disobedience (2:2) and mistrust (4:6, 11). The result is that the sinner loses his orientation (3:13). He is a wanderer who has lost the caravan. He advances without any plan (2:1; 5:2; 13:9). His knees become weak (12:12). He becomes ever more feeble (4:15; 5:2; 7:28) and gives up (10:39; 4:1). He falls (3:17; 4:11; 6:6) and has no further hope of being rescued. Because he has given in to the temptations of fatigue he is condemned (6:8) and draws down upon himself the ↗Wrath of God (3:11, 17; 10:31). Sin is directly opposed to perseverance (10:36; 12:1f, 7; ↗hope): man must hold out 'to the point of shedding your blood' (12:4). The gravity of sin consists in the fact that it constitutes mistrust and unbelief in God (3:12, 19; 12:25). This giving up along the way (to God in obedience and trust) is the worst evil of all (6:4) because it sets us at a distance from God for ever (12:14). The meaning, goal and purpose of all human existence is thereby frustrated (see Prov 8:35f: *ḥāṭāʾ* = 'to miss the goal' on the one hand, and *mātsāʾ* = 'to find' on the other). For this meaning, goal and purpose of life is draw near to God and finally to find him.

Bibliography: Above all, see S. Lyonnet, *De Peccato et Redemptione* i, Rome 1958; S. Lyonnet, series of articles in *VD* 35 (1957)f. See also: G. Quell, G. Bertram, G. Stählin, W. Grundmann, and K. H. Rengstorf, *TDNT* i, 267–335 (=*BKW* iii); F. Hauck, *TDNT* v, 559–66; Eichrodt iii, 81–141; Proksch 632–53; Köhler 155–71; Jacob 226–39; Imschoot ii, 278–314;

J. Guillet, *Leitgedanken der Bibel*, Lucerne 1954, 112–55; A. George, *RB* 53 (1946), 161–84; J. Scharbert, *BZ* 2 (1958), 14–26; A. Kirchgässner, *Erlösung und Sünde im NT*, Freiburg 1950; J. Haas, *Die Stellung Jesu zu Sünde und Sünder nach den vier Ev.*, Fribourg 1953; J. Schmid, *Das Ev. nach Lukas (RNT* 3), 1955³, 150–55; E. Lohmeyer, *Probleme paulinischer Theologie*, Stuttgart n.d., 77–156; C. Spicq, *L'Epître aux Hébreux* i, Paris 1952, 284–7; K. G. Kuhn, *ZTK* 49 (1952), 200–22; O. Kuss, *Der Römerbrief*, Regensburg 1957, 241–75; P. Palazzini (ed.), *Il peccato*, Rome 1959; H. Vogel, 'Die Sünde im bibl. Verständnis', *ET* 19 (1959), 439–52; D. Daube, *Sin, Ignorance and Forgiveness in the Bible*, London 1961; E. Beaucamp, E. des Places, and S. Lyonnet, *DB(S)* 7 (1962), 407–568; E. Beaucamp, *Données bibliques pour une réflexion théologique sur le péché*, Paris 1963; S. Porúbčan, *Sin in the Old Testament*, Rome 1963; J. Becker, *Das Heil Gottes. Heils- und Sündenbegriff in Qumrantexten und im NT*, Göttingen 1964.

Johannes B. Bauer

Sonship

1. *Pagan sources.* The fact that in his prayers man thinks of and describes his relationship to God as the relationship of a son to his ↗father is one of the earliest of religious phenomena (see N. Söderblom, *Das Werden des Gottesglaubens*, Leipzig 1916, 176f). Among primitive peoples, who are close to nature, the earliest and most frequent name applied to the deity is that which designates him as father. The highest being recognised by the early Indo–Germanic peoples is called 'Father Heaven' (Dyāuš pitā, hence *Zeus patēr*, Jupiter). For Homer, Zeus is 'the father of men and gods' (Odyssey 1:28, etc). In general when he appeals to his relationship with God as son, all that man intends to express thereby is that he owes to the deity his life and existence, that he recognises his absolute

dependence upon that deity, and yet that in spite of this he can have confident recourse to him as of right. The 'father/son' relationship, however, was in various ways also understood in a natural sense in ancient pagan belief, and specifically among the Greeks. It was assumed not only of heroes but of whole tribes and families as well that they were descended from a divine ancestor. Like the kings of ancient Egypt, so later the hellenistic rulers and outstanding heroes such as Apollonius of Tyana liked to have themselves described as sons of god. The idea that every man is a son of god by nature found strong expression among the Stoics. We are all sons of god 'because we have all come to being through god' (Epictetus 1, 3, 1), 'have all sprung from him' (Cleanthes, *Hymn to Zeus*), and hence are 'of his race' (Aratos, Prologue to the *Phainomena*; see Acts 17:28). In the mysteries and the hermetic writings we encounter the idea that it is only by a personal act, namely by a↗ rebirth, that man becomes the child of god, ie, endowed with the divine nature.

2. *Old Testament and judaism.* The idea that man is the son of God by nature is alien to the religion of the Old Testament and judaism. The description 'sons of God' for the↗ angels (Ps 29:1; Job 1:6; 2:1; 38:7; 1 Enoch 6:2; 13:8; 14:3; 101:1) has no physical or genealogical background, but is simply intended to express how closely these heavenly beings are attached to God, whose courtiers, servants, and messengers they are. Whether the phrase 'sons of God' in Gen 6:2–4 is likewise intended to refer to angels, or whether it designates men with special power

(see Ps 58:1; 82:6), is a disputed point. In other passages in which the appellation 'son of God' is applied to men it is not simply the generality of mankind that is in question. Again it is not usually applied to individual Israelites but to Israel as a people (Ex 4:22f; Deut 1:31; 8:5; 32:5f, 18; Is 63:16; 64:8; Jer 3:19; 31:9, 20; Hos 11:1; 13:13; Mal 1:6; 2:10; Wis 12:19, 21; 16:10, 26; 18:4, 13; 1 Enoch 62:11; AssMos 10:3), or to the king as representative of Israel (Ps 2:7; 2 Sam 7:14; Ps 89:27; TestLev 17; TestJud 24). This sonship is based upon the election of Israel as the covenant people (Deut 14:1; Is 1:2, 4; 43:6; Mal 1:2f; 2:10). Even in those instances in which it is connected with the idea of creation, the underlying idea is not so much that God is the creator of men, but that he is the creator of Israel (Deut 32:6; Is 43:1; 64:8; see also 43:15; Mal 2:10). In view of this it should not be deduced from the fact that the designation 'firstborn son' is applied to Israel (Ex 4:22; Jer 31:9; 4 Ezra 6:58) that non-Israelites too were conceived to be sons of God. The Old Testament description of Israel as the son of God, as also its correlative, which is only found later and is used less frequently, namely the description of God as Father (Deut 32:6; Jer 3:4, 19; Is 63:16; 64:8; Mal 1:6; 2:10), are intended on the one hand to express the fact that Yahweh has chosen Israel before all the peoples as the object of his↗ love, protection, and help, on the other hand the fact that Israel will and must respond to this election by showing reverence, faithfulness and trust in Yahweh (see Deut 14:1f), and by mutual brotherly love (Mal 2:10;

↗ brother). The idea of sonship, however, does not play a predominant part in the religion of the Old Testament. The relationship between Yahweh and Israel is for the most part conceived of as the relationship of a lord to his slave (both ideas are found together in Mal 1:6), often also as that of a king to his people, a married man to his wife, or a bridegroom to his bride (↗ marriage). In later times, and probably under hellenistic influence, an individualisation of the symbol of sonship gradually established itself. The devout individual is accounted a son of God (Wis 2:13, 18; Sir 4:10; PsSol 13:9; Jub 19:29; Philo, *De Vita Mosis* II 39 § 288; *De Spec. Leg.* I 11 § 318; *De Confus. Ling.* 28 § 145) and uses in his prayers the form of address 'my Father' (Wis 2:16; 14:3; Sir 23:1, 4; 51:10; Ps 73:15; see also Tob 13:4). Moreover the first signs appear of an eschatological use of the appellation 'son'. The following passage in Jub 1:24f treats of the age of salvation: 'I will be a Father to them and they shall be my children, and they shall all be called children of the living God, and all angels and all spirits shall know it, and shall recognise that they are my children, and that I am their Father in firmness and righteousness, and that I love them'. According to PsSol 17:27, the Messiah will 'recognise them, that they are all sons of their God'. It is possible that the use of the term in this sense is already to be found in Wis 5:5. Josephus does not apply the expression 'son of God' to anyone, nor does the term 'Father' used as a form of address in prayer occur in his writings, but he does use the title 'Father' of God, and, indeed, in a universalistic sense: God is 'Father of the whole human race' (*Antiq.* 4:262; see also 1:20; 2:152; 7:380). In the Qumran literature Ps 2:7 is several times applied to the people of God (as well as to the Messiah), not, however, to the whole of Israel, but only to the elect of Israel. At the same time the sectarians avoid any presentation of themselves as 'sons of God', and apparently do not use the title 'Father' of God either. The idea that the Israelites are sons of God and that God is their heavenly Father frequently recurs in the writings of rabbinical judaism (*Abot* 3:14; *Yoma* 8:9; *Sota* 9:15; b. *Taanit* 25f; also in the *Šemone Esre* and *Abinu Malkenu* prayers). In this, however, the eschatological use of the 'Father/son' image is virtually absent. Sonship is regarded as entailing the duty of following the pattern laid down by God in one's life, occupying oneself with the Torah and with the fulfilment of the commandments. On the other hand it was also a guarantee of God's unfailing ↗ mercy and compassion. For Rabbi Meir, the attribute of sonship was a gift bestowed upon the Israelites unconditionally and remaining valid even for the sinners among them. Admittedly Rabbi Yehuda ben Elai opposed this view. The title 'son of God' was not usually applied to the Messiah even in circles which interpreted Ps 2 as referring to him (PsSol 17:21-5; Qumran documents, late rabbinical tradition).

3. *The synoptics.* When Jesus describes God as the Father of mankind ('your Father': Mt 5:48; 6:32; 7:11 [all passages from Q!]; Mk 11:25; 'thy Father'; Mt 6:4, 6, 18), and when he trains the disciples to address God as

'(our) Father' in their prayers (Mt 6:9; Lk 11:2), he proclaims the universal Fatherhood of God in the sense that God's fatherly love, kindness, and protection is extended to every man, even to the sinner (Lk 15:1–32). This does not mean, however, that Jesus was now promising divine sonship to all men as well. The designation 'children of God' is altogether absent from the synoptics. That of 'sons of God' only occurs in three instances (Mt 5:9; 5:45 [=Lk 6:35]; Lk 20:36 [however, a comparison with Mk 12:25 shows that this is a secondary Lucan formulation]), and in fact with an eschatological force. According to these passages sonship of God is a gift which is neither bestowed upon all men as God's creatures, nor upon the disciples already here below, but one which will be imparted to the elect only in the future age of salvation, and one which goes together with eternal bliss, the sharing in the kingdom of God. A further fact which may be connected with the idea that the Father/son relationship will be revealed and will take effect only at the final consummation, is that Jesus's sayings concerning the final consummation lay special emphasis upon the Fatherhood of God (Lk 12:32; 22:29; Mk 8:38 and parallels; Mt 20:23 [otherwise in Mk 10:40]; 25:34), and speak of the kingdom of the Father for the most part in a strictly eschatological sense (Mt 13:43; 26:29 [otherwise in Mk 14:25]; 6:9f=Lk 11:2). Jesus claims divine sonship for himself in a unique and exclusive sense (Mt 17:24–7; 11:27=Lk 10:22; Mk 13:22). This claim to be a son of God by nature can also be recognised in the

fact that Jesus never uses the designation 'our Father' in referring to himself together with others, but invariably confines himself to the designations 'my Father' or 'your (thy) Father'. In certain passages the terms 'son of God' appears as a messianic title (Lk 4:41; 22:70; see also Acts 9:20, 22). And it also appears to be used in this sense in Mk 14:62f and parallels, since there 'son of the Blessed One' is in apposition to 'Messiah'. In many cases we cannot arrive at a more certain conclusion on the question of whether 'son of God' is used as a description of Christ's nature or as designating his office as Messiah. For it is difficult to establish how far the terminology of the early Christian mission is present or absent.

4. *Paul.* In about forty passages God is called 'Father', mostly 'our Father' (Rom 1:7; 1 Cor 1:3; 2 Cor 1:2; Gal 1:3f etc), a few times 'Father of (our Lord) Jesus Christ' (Rom 15:6; 2 Cor 1:3; 11:31; Eph 1:3; Col 1:3), often too simply 'the Father' (Rom 6:4; 1 Cor 8:6; 15:24; Gal 1:1; etc). In this latter case it can be deduced, at any rate from the context, who is being thought of as the corresponding party to the relationship. The sayings which treat of divine sonship afford a clearer insight into the actual kind of 'father/son' relationship that is envisaged. In the nature of things Jesus Christ is the unique and only Son of God (Rom 8:3, 32; Gal 4:4; Col 1:13; see also 1 Cor 8:6; 2 Cor 8:9; Phil 2:6–8; Col 1:15f), but Paul also calls Christians 'sons of God', employing sometimes the expression 'sons of God' (Rom 8:14, 19; 9:26; Gal 3:26; 4:6f; 2 Cor 6:18; cf Heb 2:10; 12:5–8),

sometimes 'children of God' (Rom 8:16, 17, 21; 9:7f; Phil 2:15) without distinction. As applied to Christians sonship is based upon the fact that they have been accepted by God as his sons. The term *huiothesia*, which Paul uses to describe the Christian's status in Rom 8:15, 23; Gal 4:5; Eph 1:5, is used in Rom 9:4 of the Old Testament idea of Israel as son of God, a sign that Paul has transferred the concept in its eschatological fulfilment to the New Testament people of God. The word is a technical term for legal adoption, a practice which, while it was not general in judaism, was common throughout the hellenistic sphere, and was for this reason familiar to the apostle and his readers. 'The concept was entirely suitable to characterise the new and unique bond between men and God which had been effected by God's salvific work, while at the same time making due allowance for the special character of the "physical" sonship of God which was proper to Jesus Christ' (O. Kuss). The purpose of sending the Son of God into the world was to bring sonship to mankind as a whole, not merely to Israel (Gal 4:4f). To be a son or child of God in this developed sense is one of the benefits of salvation enjoyed in the present (Rom 8:16: 'We are children of God'; Gal 3:26: 'You are all sons of God'; 4:6: 'You are sons'), which man attains by ⚹ faith and by undergoing ⚹ baptism (Gal 3:26f). More specifically it is the pneuma (⚹ spirit) received in baptism by believers in Christ that brings about sonship (Rom 8:14f). Since this pneuma is 'the pneuma of his Son' (Gal 4:6), it imparts to the baptised person a quality which is

analogous to that of true sonship of God (Gal 3:27; see also Rom 8:29), hence it can also be called 'the pneuma of acceptation into the status of son' (Rom 8:15). This condition, by which baptised persons become children of God, is a fact which can be experienced and recognised to the extent that the pneuma of the Son causes the believers in their prayers to break out into the spontaneous cry of enthusiasm 'Abba, Father!' (Rom 8:15f; Gal 4:6, where *hoti* should hardly be taken in a causal sense, but rather in an elliptic and declaratory one). The status of sonship implies a right to inherit. The ⚹ inheritance which God has bestowed upon those whom he has accepted as his sons consists in ⚹ 'life' (Rom 8:13) or in ⚹ 'glory' (8:17). Since Christ has already entered upon this heritage christians are 'co-heirs with Christ' (Rom 8:17). Basically Paul understands the sonship of God to signify the same reality which he elsewhere calls 'righteousness'. This is clearly expressed in Rom 8:13-17. The reason underlying the clause in v 13b, 'If by the Spirit you put to death the deeds of the body you shall live', is given in vv 14-17. Whereas elsewhere the connecting link between Spirit and life is righteousness (righteousness as an effect of the Spirit: Rom 8:10; 1 Cor 6:11; as a prior condition of life: Rom 5:17, 18, 21; 1:17; Gal 3:11, 21), here Paul introduces in its place the idea of divine sonship, because this is manifested as a fact of experience in the cries of 'Abba!'; and so, with the assistance of the idea of inheritance, it can serve as a proof of the fact that the Christian has received life. In Gal 4:1-7, on the other hand, the motif of sonship is presented in its own right. For in this passage Paul's aim is to establish the thesis enunciated in 3:29: 'You are heirs'. His point is that a prior condition of being an heir is being a son. Divine sonship and ↗justification, or righteousness, complement one another in yet another respect. In both cases it is not a magical transformation of man that is in question, but rather a gift of grace which lays upon its recipient the duty of a moral life (at the same time equipping him to fulfil this duty). Thus the baptised man can be exhorted to 'walk in righteousness' (Rom 6:12–23 etc), as also to guard his state as a child of God (Phil 2:15; Eph 5:1; Rom 8:17). Both gifts appear sometimes as blessings of man's present state (righteousness or justification: Rom 3:21f, 24, 26, 28; 4:5; 5:5, 9, 16f; 6:18; etc; sonship: Rom 8:16; Gal 3:26; 4:6), sometimes as blessings to be hoped for in the future: according to Gal 5:5 'For through the Spirit by faith we wait for the hope of righteousness'; according to Rom 8:23 'We groan inwardly as we wait for adoption as sons, the redemption of our↗ bodies', ie the moment when we shall be fully and definitively established as sons and heirs of God at the↗ parousia.

John. In the fourth gospel and in the first two johannine epistles the title 'Father' as applied to God occurs more than 120 times. In this it is always God's relationship as Father to Jesus Christ that is being thought of, whether the word is being used absolutely ('the Father'), the most usual phrase, or otherwise ('my Father' [thirty-five times]). Jesus explicitly rejects the claim of the Jews that God is their Father (8:41–4). God is never referred to as Father of men. The only exception to this is Jn 20:17: 'I am ascending to my Father and your Father, to my God and your God'. What is expressed here by the fact that the risen Christ calls the disciples his brothers and God his Father and their Father is that by the resurrection the relationship between God and Jesus, on the one hand and the disciples on the other, has acquired an essentially more intimate character. But it is clear from the deliberate avoidance of the expression 'to *our* Father' that God is nevertheless Father of Jesus in another and a higher sense than that in which he is Father of the believing disciples. The uniqueness of God's relationship as Father with Jesus is made clear in numerous sayings of Jesus himself, and according to 5:18 is also recognised by the Jews, who wish to kill Jesus 'because he called God his Father, making himself equal to God'. This unique quality emerges no less clearly from those sayings of Jesus in John's gospel in which he refers to himself as the Son of God (3:18; 5:25; 10:36; 11:4), or as 'the Son' without further qualification (3:16f, 35f; 5:19–23, 26; 6:40; 8:36; 14:13; see too, 'thy Son': 17:1). There can be no doubt that the title of Son as used by John is not a paraphrase for Messiah, although both titles are closely connected with one another (11:27; 20:31). Rather this title of Son signifies the eternal (cf 1 Jn 4:14) Sonship of God by nature (see 20:28), in which the messianic function of Jesus is ultimately rooted. In some cases John underlines the uniqueness of the Sonship of Christ by affixing the adjective

867

ho monogenēs (1:14, 18; 3:16, 18; 1 Jn 4:9), which signifies 'the only begotten, sole descendant, only one'. Whether this is intended to lend additional force to the idea that it is God who has caused this begetting (birth), and to characterise Jesus as the only one who has been begotten from the nature of God is disputed, and in point of fact makes little difference, inasmuch as in John the title 'son' is applied to Jesus unambiguously as a designation of his origin, and for this reason implicitly contains the idea of his eternal begetting by God. Finally, the uniqueness of the sonship of Jesus Christ appears in the johannine writings in the fact that he has a special terminology for it, the title 'Son of God' being reserved for Christ alone. Insofar as John speaks of men being sons of God at all he never employs the term 'sons', but invariably confines himself to the phrase 'children of God' to express this. This derivative childhood of God is for him, just as for Paul, a blessing of salvation which has already been imparted in the present life to those who believe 'in his name', that is, in Jesus as the Messiah and Son of God (Jn 1:12; 1 Jn 3:1f; 5:1). The Pauline idea that the relationship of child has been brought about by an act of adoption on God's part does not, however, appear in the johannine writings. According to them, being a child of God is brought about rather by a new birth (Jn 3:3, 7), or by being begotten (born) of God (1:13; 1 Jn 2:29; 3:9; 4:7; 5:1, 4, 18). The new birth is characterised in Jn 3:5 as a birth 'of water and the spirit', which can only mean that it is accomplished by↗ baptism, and takes effect through

the↗ Spirit of God, who suffuses the subject in baptism, and re-creates him as a new being. The idea of↗ rebirth does admittedly occur elsewhere in the New Testament without any connection with the concept of being God's child (Tit 3:5; 1 Pet 1:3, 23; Jas 1:18). Again, when John speaks of 'being begotten (born) of God', in spite of the naturalistic overtones in this turn of phrase he means that the believer undergoes a purely spiritual process, by which the imparting of the Spirit to him gives him a new mode of existence which sets him in a wholly new and intimately personal relationship to God; and as with Paul the gift carries a task with it, and must bear fruit in the moral conduct of one's life (1 Jn 2:29; 3:9f; 4:7; 5:1–4, 18). Although the baptised believer enjoys the state of a child of God already here below, he still awaits its completion. This will only be revealed in the age of fulfilment ushered in by the↗ parousia, and will consist in being like God and seeing God (↗ vision). 'We know that when he appears we shall be like him, for we shall see him as he is' (1 Jn 3:2).

Bibliography: P. Baur, 'Gott als Vater im AT', *TSK* 72 (1899), 483–507; A. Dieterich, *Eine Mithrasliturgie*, Leipzig–Berlin 1903, 134–56; M.-J. Lagrange, 'La paternité de Dieu dans l'AT', *RB* 17 (1908), 481–99; S. Many, 'Adoption', *DB* I, 227–33; H. Lesêtre, 'Fils de Dieu', *DB* II, 2253–7; G. P. Wetter, *Der Sohn Gottes*, Göttingen 1916; A. von Harnack, *Die Terminologie der Wiedergeburt und verwandter Erlebnisse in der ältesten Kirche* (*TU* 42/3), Leipzig 1918; SB I, 219, 371–4, and 392–6; C. A. Bernoulli, 'Le Dieu-Père de Jésus d'après les Synoptiques', *Actes du Congrès international d'histoire des religions 1923* II, Paris 1925, 211–24; R. Gyllenberg, 'Gott der Vater im AT und in der Predigt Jesu', *Studia Orientalia* I (Helsingfors 1925), 51–60; M.-J. Lagrange, 'L'hermétisme', *RB* 35 (1926),

352–62; W. Bousset and H. Gressmann, *Die Religion des Judentums im späthellenistischen Zeitalter*, Tübingen 1926³, 377f; E. Wissmann, 'Gotteskindschaft', *RGG* II², 1394–6; M.-J. Lagrange, 'La régéneration et la filiation divine dans les mystères d'Eleusis', *RB* 38 (1929), 68–81 and 201–14; A. L. Williams, '"My Father" in Jewish Thought of the First Century', *JTS* 31 (1930), 42–7; A. Bertholet and H. Seeger, 'Vatername Gottes', *RGG* v², 1442–5; W. F. Lofthouse, 'Vater und Sohn im Joh.-Ev.', *TB* 11 (1932), 290–300; G. Kittel, *TDNT* I, 5f; J. Hempel, *Gott und Mensch im AT*, Stuttgart 1936², 170–78; J. Dey, *Palingenesia*, Münster 1937; W. Grundmann, *Die Gotteskindschaft in der Geschichte Jesu und ihre Religionsgeschichtlichen Voraussetzungen*, Weimar 1938; W. Twisselmann, *Die Gotteskindschaft der Christen nach dem NT*, Gütersloh 1939; A. Oepke, *RAC* I, 105–9; J. Leipoldt, *Jesu Verhältnis zu Griechen und Juden*, Leipzig 1941, 124–44; F. Büchsel, *TDNT* IV, 737–41; Haag 914f; J. Bieneck, *Sohn Gottes als Christusbezeichn. d. Syn.*, Zurich 1951; A. Oepke, *TDNT* v, 650–54; S. Zedda, *L'adozione a figli di Dio e lo Spirito Santo*, Rome 1952; S. V. McCasland, 'Abba Father', *JBL* 72 (1953), 79–91; P. Winter, 'Monogenês para patros', *ZRG* 5 (1953), 335–65; R. Schnackenburg, *Die Joh.-Briefe*, Freiburg 1953, 155–62; G. Schrenck and G. Quell, *TDNT* v, 946–1015; J. Schmid, *Das Ev. nach Mk (RNT 2)* 1954³, 17–20; J. Schmid, *Das Ev. nach Mt (RNT 1)*, 1956³, 124–8; W. Grundmann, *ZNW* 47 (1956), 113–33; A. Wikenhauser, *Das Ev. nach Joh. (RNT 4)*, 1957, 91–4; O. Bauernfeind, *RGG* II³, 1798–1800; J. Giblet, 'Jésus et "le Père" dans la ive Evangile', *Recherches Bibliques* 3 (1958), 111–30; O. Kuss, *Der Römerbrief*, Regensburg 1959, 596–608; P. Schruers, 'La paternité divine dans Mt 5:45 et 6:26–32', *ETL* 36 (1960), 593–624; O. Michel and O. Betz, 'Von Gott gezeugt', *Judentum, Urchristentum, Kirche* (Festschrift J. Jeremias), Berlin 1960, 3–23; E. Pax, *LTK* IV², 1114–16; I. Hermann, *Kyrios und Pneuma*, Munich 1961, 94–7; W. Grundmann, 'Zur Rede Jesu vom Vater im Joh.-Ev.', *ZNW* 52 (1961), 213–30; B. M. F. van Iersel, 'Der Sohn' in den syn. Jesusworten, Leiden 1961; E. Lövestam, *Son and Saviour*, Lund–Copenhagen 1961; G. Cooke, 'The Israelite King as Son of God', *ZAW* 73 (1961), 202–25; F. W. Danker, 'The huios phrases in the New Testament', *NTS* 7 (1961), 94; T. de Kruiff, *Der Sohn des lebendigen Gottes*, Rome 1962; F. Hahn, *Christologische Hoheitstitel*, Göttingen 1963; W. Kramer, *Christus, Kyrios, Gottessohn*, Zurich 1963; M. W. Schoenberg, 'St Paul's Notion on the Adoptive Sonship of Christ', *Thomist* 28 (1964), 51–75.

Josef Blinzler

Spirit

A. *The Spirit of God in the Old Testament.* The concept of spirit occupies a prominent place in the theology of the Old Testament. As a rule the word *rûaḥ* in the Hebrew text should be translated 'spirit', and there are about 380 occurrences to which this would apply. LXX, with only 355 instances, falls somewhat short of the Masoretic text. It usually renders *rûaḥ* as *pneuma* (264 times).

I. *Spirit in the Old Testament.* The Arabic words corresponding to the Hebrew *rûaḥ* (the verb, occurring only in the hifil, = 'to smell', hence the noun *rēaḥ* = 'odour') are *rîḥ* = 'wind' and *ruḥ* = 'spirit', both being derived from *raha* = to blow.

1. *rûaḥ* = wind. (a) *Concept.* In the earliest passages *rûaḥ* probably means the 'stream of air' which manifests itself in the movement of the wind, the soft 'current of air' (Gen 3:8[J]; 1 Kings 19:11; Job 4:15; 41:16; Is 57:13); the wind (Gen 8:1[P]; Num 11:31; 2 Sam 22:11; 2 Kings 3:17; Is 27:8; 57:13; Jer 2:24; 10:13; Ezek 17:10; 19:12; Hos 8:7; Amos 4:13; Hab 1:11; Zech 5:9; Job 28:25; 41:13; Pss 1:4; 83:13; 103:16; 104:3f); the tempest (Ex 10:13; 14:21; 1 Kings 18:45; 19:11; Is 32:2; 41:16; Jer 4:11; 13:24; 18:17; 22:22; 49:36; Ezek 1:4; 13:11; Hos 4:19; Jon 1:4; Job 1:19; 21:18; Ps 11:6; 18:11; 35:5; 55:8; 107:25; 135:7).

This sense is encountered in all areas of Hebrew literature, most frequently in Jeremiah and the Psalms. As the places whence the wind comes, the quarters of the heavens are called *rûḥôth* (1 Chron 9:24; Ezek 37:9; 42:20; Zech 2:6; 6:6; Dan 7:2; 8:8; 11:4). Since the wind, which man can neither see nor grasp (see Jn 3:8), is a suitable image for all that is vain and empty, *rûaḥ* comes to acquire the metaphorical sense of a vain, empty, and futile matter. 'All is vanity and a striving after wind' (Eccles 1:14; 2:11, 17; 4:6, 16; 5:16; 6:9; Is 26:18; Jer 5:13; Hos 12:1; Mic 2:11). Hence the idioms 'to speak words of wind' (Job 16:3), 'to sow the wind', and 'to reap the whirlwind' (Hos 8:7; Prov 11:29).

(b) *The effects of 'rûaḥ'*. Man in the ancient Near East experienced a reverent awe for the mystery of the wind. (i) For him the wind is equivalent to an overwhelming and mysterious power, which the gentile peoples honour as a divinity of nature, but which the Israelites, thanks to their superior monotheism, value only as an instrument for putting into effect God's purposes in salvation history. The *rûaḥ* represents a force of nature, of which God avails himself at all critical turning-points in the tempestuous history of salvation for carrying out his plans. The tempest is able to rend the mountains and shatter the rocks (1 Kings 19:11). At God's behest it brings an end to the flood (Gen 8:1[P]). At the time of the Egyptian plagues the east wind carried the assembled swarms of locusts into the land of Pharaoh, and the west wind threw them into the sea (Ex 10:13, 19). At the Exodus from bondage a strong east wind provided

the people of God, hard-pressed as they were, with a way to safety through the Red Sea (Ex 14:21f; see also 15:10f; Is 11:15). David describes, with a high degree of poetic imagination, how the Lord 'bowed the heavens and came down. . . . He flew hither, hovering upon the wings of the wind. The channels of the sea were seen' (2 Sam 22:10-16 = Ps 18:10-16). In the wilderness wanderings a strong wind drove a host of quails in from the sea, and a rain of manna down from heaven for the hungry people (Num 11:31f; Ex 10:19; 16:13-16; Ps 78:24ff). At the covenant institution at Sinai a strong wind, together with the loud blast of a trumpet ushered in the thunder and lightning which were the precursors of the divine Lawgiver (Ex 19:16; see also Acts 2:2f). At the Lord's command a strong wind will execute the divine sentence upon the unfaithful people which he pursue into the exile: 'The wind shall shepherd all your shepherds, and your lovers shall go into captivity' (Jer 22:22; see also 4:11ff). A terrible desert wind will come against Ephraim, a wind of the Lord which arises out of the wilderness and brings in ruin (Hos 13:15; Ezek 13:13). Again in the name of God the tempest carries out its destructive work upon the peoples (Is 57:13; Jer 51:1). At the return from Babylon the purified 'remnant' will be able to cross the Euphrates in sandals by the power of the wind sent by God (Is 11:15).

(ii) In certain passages, relatively few in number and late in date, a creative force is also ascribed to the wind sent by God. The oriental, with his close ties with the processes of nature, observed how the wind brings in clouds with the rain which fertilises the desert parched for water (see 1 Kings 18:45; 2 Kings 3:17; Hos 13:15; Job 1:19). According to the Priestly author (P) 'the earth was without form and void, and darkness was upon the face of the deep, and the wind (Spirit) of God was moving over the waters' (Gen 1:2), and then, by his word, God created heaven and earth and all that they contain (Gen 1:3–30). In the messianic era 'a *rûaḥ* from on high' will be poured out, and will transform the land into a garden of paradise (Is 32:15). The Hebrew, who judges by appearances, thinks of the wind, which is located in space (Ezek 37:9), as intimately connected with the word of God. The wind becomes, so to say, the bearer of the creative word. It is striking how in poetic passages the 'wind' is represented anthropomorphically as the 'breath of God', which instils life into creation and nature (Ex 15:8, 10 with Ex 14:21; 2 Sam 22:16 = Ps 18:15; Is 11:15; 27:8; 30:28; 33:11; 34:16; 40:7; 59:19; Hos 13:15; Job 4:9; 26:13; 37:10; 147:18). Even if this idea, based as it was on the sensible appearance of material things, was mitigated in the course of time, still it was never altogether discarded. 'By the word of Yahweh the heavens were made, and all their host by the breath of his mouth' (Ps 33:6; see also Gen 1:2; Judith 16:14). Even in the most recent book of the bible it is stated that 'the spirit of the Lord has filled the whole world' (Wis 1:7).

(iii) The wind is not an independent force, but a power controlled and directed by God for the furtherance of salvation history and creation. God 'has created the wind' (Amos 4:13). He 'brings forth the wind from his storehouses' (Jer 10:13; 51:16; 135:7). On account of this dependence of the wind upon God the wind is often depicted in poetic passages as 'the breath of Yahweh' or as 'the breath of Yahweh's nose' (Ex 15:8; Is 40:7; Ps 18:15; etc).

(iv) Just as man is unable either to see or grasp God, so too he is unable to see or grasp his messenger. He does not know whence it comes or whither it goes. The wind is shrouded in mystery (see Jn 3:8). Thus the properties of the wind are power and mystery. Because the God of the Old Testament is a God of power and mystery, the authors of sacred scripture appropriately describe the nature and attributes of God by the image of the wind, mysterious in its origin and powerful in its effects.

2. '*rûaḥ*' = *breath*. Just as in the context of nature *rûaḥ* is 'wind', so in man and beast it becomes 'breath' or 'respiration'. This sense is already attested in very early passages (Gen 45:27: Judg 15:19). (i) In the grandiose vision of the dry bones the *rûaḥ* is commanded to blow from the four quarters of the wind and to blow upon the bones so that they come to life (Ezek 37:9). The *rûaḥ* is a life-giving entity. Man lives precisely so long as he breathes in and breathes out. 'Dum spiro spero!' Hence the 'breath' becomes the seat and supporter, the source of life for man and beast (Gen 7:22[J]; Num 16:22; 27:16; Is 42:5; Job 34:14f; Ps 104:29f; Eccles 3:19). God blew into the nostrils of the first man the 'breath of life' (*nišmat ḥayyîm* = the *rûaḥ ḥayyîm* of Gen 6:17[P], 7:15, 22[P], both paralleled in Is 42:5;

57:16; Job 4:9; 27:3; 34:14; etc), so that he became a living being (Gen 2:7[J]; cf Gen 6:3[J]). The whole *span of man's life* depends upon the *rûaḥ*. All life must dissolve in death when God withdraws his breath of life (Job 27:3f; 34:14f; Ps 104:29f; 146:4; Eccles 3:18–21; 12:7). The 'breath of life', however, is only 'lent' for the short period of his earthly days. He cannot dispose of it as he wills (see Wis 15:8, 16; Lk 12:20). Yahweh alone is 'the Lord of the breath of life' (Num 16:22; 27:16; see also 2 Macc 14:46), which he imparts to man from motives of divine love and solicitude (Job 10:12).

(ii) It is entirely in harmony with the idea of the *rûaḥ* in men, both according to the senses and the intellect, that physical exhaustion or recuperation are represented as the withdrawal or the return of the breath of life (eg, Judg 15:19; 1 Sam 30:12; Ps 143:7; Job 17:1). At joyful tidings the breath of life is thrown into agitation. Intense astonishment renders one 'out of breath' (1 Kings 10:5; 2 Chron 9:4).

(iii) On the occurrence of some misfortune or under the impact of some strong emotion the 'breath' comes more quickly or more slowly, more strongly or more weakly. Because of this *rûaḥ* is used to describe the different emotions of the irascible appetite, such as anger (Judg 8:3; Job 4:9; 15:13; Prov 1:23; Eccles 7:9; Is 25:4; Zech 6:8); disquiet (Gen 41:8; 2 Kings 19:7); trouble (Gen 26:35; 1 Sam 1:15; 1 Kings 21:5; Job 7:11; Ps 34:19; Prov 15:4; Is 54:6; 66:2); despair (Ps 77:4; Is 61:3; Ezek 3:14); courage (Josh 2:11; 5:1; Sir 48:12; patience (Prov

17:27; Eccles 7:8; Sir 5:11); impatience (Ex 6:9; Job 21:4; Prov 14:29; Mic 2:7); jealousy (Num 5:14, 30; 1 Sam 16:14f, 23; 18:10; 19:9); and discord (Judg 9:23). Animal functions and the movements of the lower senses are invariably ascribed to the *nepeš* (normally = 'soul'), not to the *rûaḥ*, which in fact comes from above and has an element of nobility in it.

(iv) *rûaḥ* can also be used to describe those ways of conducting one's life which give expression to an interior attitude of mind. Here any sensible basis which we can apprehend vanishes more and more. Instances of this are humility (Prov 16:19; Is 57:15; Dan 3:39); pride (Ps 76:12; Prov 16:18; Eccles 7:8; Dan 5:20); faithfulness (Num 14:24; Ps 51:10, 12; 78:8; Prov 11:13); or quite in general, a 'disposition' (Ezek 11:19; 36:26; see also Prov 16:32; 25:28).

(v) Finally *rûaḥ* is considered the source of the higher, spiritual life from which stem aims and ideas (Ps 77:6; Job 32:8; Prov 1:23; Is 19:3; Jer 51:1; Ezek 11:5), as well as plans and decisions (Ex 35:21; 1 Chron 5:26; Hag 1:14).

The primary meaning of *rûaḥ* may be taken to be *wind*, the mysterious and irresistible power of which Yahweh avails himself in the execution of his designs in salvation history and creation. On the human plane it designates the *breath* with all its concomitant manifestations which permeates the lives of men (and beasts) from the first moment of their existence to the last. This breath of air and of life comes from on high, from God, and it permeates, brings to life and maintains all the inhabitants of the world together (see Wis 1:7; Acts 17:28). In this sense it is omnipresent (Ps 139:7).

II. *The Spirit of the Lord in the Old Testament.* Just as extraordinary events in nature are attributed to the power of the wind, so too astonishing feats performed by men in order to save the chosen people are attributed to the 'spirit of the Lord'. It is that mysterious force which proceeds from God and takes powerful effect in the history of the covenant people. It constitutes an historical phenomenon, which brings about the *magnalia Dei* through figures who are empowered by the spirit.

1. In the earliest passages what is attributed to the spirit of the Lord is transitory phenomena in the physical or psychological order, all of which have an element of the tempestuous and the violent in them. The spirit of the Lord 'impels' (Judg 13:25) or 'falls upon' someone (Ezek 11:5), 'carries him away' (1 Kings 18:12; 2 Kings 2:16), 'comes mightily upon him' (Judg 14:6). It arouses in a subject chosen by it for the benefit of the people of God gigantic physical strength (Judg 13:25; 14:6, 19; 15:14); heroic feats of arms (Judg 6:34; 11:29; 1 Sam 11:6f); prophetic raptures and ecstasies (Num 11:24–30; 1 Sam 10:5–13; 19:20–24), which seize upon Saul himself and even the messengers of Saul (1 Sam 10:10; 19:19–24; see also 1 Kings 22:10ff); physical as well as spiritual transports (1 Kings 18:12; 2 Kings 2:16; see also Acts 8:39; Ezek 3:12; 8:3; 11:1; 37:1; 43:5); the power to perform stupendous wonders (1 Kings 17:14, 17ff; 2 Kings 2:15; 4:1ff); an amazing gift of prophecy (Num 24:2; 1 Chron

12:18; 2 Chron 20:14; 24:20); and interpretation of dreams (Gen 40:8; 41:16, 38; Dan 4:5; 5:12; 6:3). In the passages referred to, the bestowal of the spirit is a free gift of God's grace. The Lord 'gives' the spirit (Num 11:25; 2 Kings 19:7). It is of divine origin. The spirit comes 'upon' the man concerned (Judg 3:10; 1 Sam 16:16). The *rûaḥ* of Yahweh manifests itself as a mysterious, supernatural, and miraculous force (Is 31:3).

2. In later passages particularly, charismatic leaders and prophets are endowed with the spirit of the Lord no longer in a tempestuous and intermittent manner, but continuously. It 'rests' upon Moses, the prototype of the leader of the people and of prophets (Num 11:17, 25; see also Is 63:11); upon the seventy elders (Num 11:25, 29); upon Joshua (Num 27:18; Deut 34:9); upon Saul (1 Sam 16:14); upon David (1 Sam 16:13; 2 Sam 23:2), whose hereditary form of kingship superseded the dominion that was charismatic and theocratic in character (1 Sam 16:13); upon Elijah (2 Kings 2:9); and upon Elisha (2 Kings 2:15).

But it is the prophets who are considered bearers of the spirit of God *par excellence*. It is correct to say that those belonging to the pre-exilic period never explicitly claim the spirit of the Lord as the source of their inspiration. What they appeal to is rather the word of God. This is probably because the frenzied ecstatic bands of prophets and the false prophets call upon the spirit of the Lord although these false prophets are only 'wind' (Jer 5:13). Yet there are sufficient passages to show that these true prophets were conscious of being endowed with the spirit of the

Lord. According to Hos 9:7 the ↗ prophet is in popular parlance simply called 'the man of the spirit'. Those who merely seem to be prophets are indeed equipped with a *rûaḥ*, but this is only 'wind', and so falsehood and deceit (Mic 2:11). In contrast to these Micah acknowledges: 'I am filled with power, with the spirit of the Lord and with justice and might to declare to Jacob his transgression and to Israel his sin' (Mic 3:8). For Isaiah the act of making a covenant which is not according to Yahweh's spirit is equivalent to acting against Yahweh's spirit or will, which is revealed in the prophet as the 'mouth' of the Lord (Is 30:1f; see also 48:16). After the exile all possible emphasis was laid upon the idea that it was through his spirit that Yahweh sent his instructions through the medium of the earlier prophets (Zech 7:12; Neh 9:30). Often in place of the 'spirit of the Lord' we find the parallel expression 'the hand of Yahweh', to which the same effects upon the spirit and will of the prophet are ascribed (1 Kings 18:46; 2 Kings 3:15; Is 8:11; Ezek 1:3; 3:14; 8:3; 37:1; 40:1; and compare Lk 11:20 with Mt 12:28). From the exile onwards the spirit of the Lord is clearly considered as the soul of prophetic inspiration (Ezek 2:2; 3:24; 11:5).

Through the spirit of the Lord the prophets receive first and foremost Yahweh's 'instructions' (Is 30:1; Zech 7:12), divine directives for the religious and political guidance of the people (2 Sam 23:2; 2 Chron 15:1; 20:14; 24:20; Is 11:2; 42:1; 61:1), as well as 'prophecies' in the strict sense (Num 24:2; 1 Chron 12:18). It is the spirit of the Lord too which imparts to the prophets the 'power' to preach boldly and to suffer heroically (Mic 3:8; 2 Chron 24:20f). The spirit of God transforms the prophet into 'a fortified city, an iron pillar' (Jer 1:18; see also 1:8; 20:11), makes his brow like 'adamant, harder than flint' (Ezek 3:9; see also Is 6:6-9).

3. It is noteworthy that in the earlier period only physical and psychological effects were attributed to the spirit of the Lord. It is only from the exile onwards that the *rûaḥ* Yahweh is also conceived of as a moral force in human life, though only for the just. The author of Ps 51 prays for the 'holy spirit', which is able to dwell lastingly in the soul of the just man, and to bestow upon him power to live a holy life (Ps 51:12). In a moving psalm of repentance (Is 63:7-19) from the time of the return from the exile the prophet extols the 'spirit of holiness' (vv 10, 11) which God has set in the inmost heart of Moses. Since the spirit is made parallel to the 'arm of Yahweh', which divided the water of the Reed Sea before them (v 12), he is probably referring primarily to a divine power which was bestowed on Moses to enable him to lead the people (see Num 11:17). This is all the more probable if the Jews have perhaps replaced the phrase 'spirit of Yahweh' by that of 'spirit of holiness' from motives of reverence for the tetragrammaton. A teacher of wisdom prays for the 'holy spirit of discipline' (Wis 1:5), or for the 'holy spirit' (Wis 9:17), which is identical with Wisdom (Wis 1:4ff; 7:14, 22-5) and which, in the last analysis, does not so much initiate the religious and moral life as maintain it and guard it from the dangers of sin

(Wis 1:5; 9:17; see also 1:3f, 6; 7:14, 23, 25). From this it becomes clear that only the just are endowed with this power to lead a virtuous life (Wis 1:4; 7:25; TestSim 4:4; TestBen 8:2; Jub 1:21), exactly as in Ps 51:12.

In other passages the phrase 'the good spirit' of God means not, strictly speaking, the power to live a moral life, but rather a teacher who guides and strengthens the just (Ps 143:10), or the chosen people (Neh 9:20; Zech 7:12) so as to bring them to a life that is pleasing to God.

Up to the exile the spirit of the Lord is not conceived of as a source of religious and moral living. But since this period it undoubtedly is so, although only for the just. The transformation of the sinner into a 'new creature' in the messianic period is promised by Ezekiel, and fulfilled in the New Testament.

For the doctrine of the 'evil spirit' in the sense of a personal being, a demon, the Old Testament affords only adumbrations. The 'spirit of jealousy' (Num 5:14, 30), of 'harlotry' (Hos 4:12; 5:4), of 'uncleanness' (Zech 13), of 'confusion' (Is 19:14), of 'stupefaction' (Is 29:10)—these are nothing but vivid personifications of an evil power or passion. It is probable, however, that when the men of those ancient times speak of the 'evil spirit' which Yahweh sent between Abimelech and the men of Shechem (Judg 9:23), or which at God's command came upon Saul (1 Sam 16:14ff, 23; 18:10f; 19:8f), they have in mind some obscure idea of a personal being which sowed 'dissension' or stirred up Saul's diseased jealousy. This conception is still more clearly expressed in 1 Kings 22:19-23, where Yahweh sets a 'lying spirit' (*rûaḥ* in the masculine) in the mouth of the prophets, that is a spiritual being distinct from and subordinate to God, a demon.

4. *The spirit of the Lord in the messianic age.* The finest of the writings of the great prophets have been devoted to the spirit of the Lord which will produce the most marvellous effects both in the psychic and the religious and moral orders in the Messiah, in the messianic community of the saved, and in its members.

(a) In an age which rejoiced in its kings first Isaiah presents a masterly portrayal of the future ideal ruler, who is to be endowed *lastingly* with the spirit of the Lord. On the messianic king 'rests' all the fullness (the single spirit of the Lord with its three spirit-pairs = the sevenfold gift in which this fullness consists) of the most precious and most variegated gifts of a ruler: the proverbial wisdom and understanding of Solomon, the counsel and strength of David, the knowledge and fear of the Lord of the patriarchs Abraham, Isaac, and Jacob (Is 11:1f). The Lord will equip the closest collaborators of the messianic king with the 'spirit of righteousness', so that 'the Lord of hosts will be a crown of glory and a diadem of beauty to the remnant of his people' (Is 28:5f). After the downfall of the royal house, Deutero–Isaiah portrays the coming redeemer with the traits of the compassionate 'servant of God' who, in the fullness of the prophetic spirit, will proclaim the true religion to the heathens, and will lead the Israelites home from the exile (Is 42:1–7). From the historical background of the post-exilic community arises the moving figure of the unknown prophet who in the power of the spirit of God will proclaim the good tidings of salvation to the ʿanāwîm (= the poor), and will restore justice (Is 61:1–3).

(b) According to the earlier passages the spirit of the Lord will renew the face of the messianic community of the saved. The great prophets now present us—and this is the element that is new—with a universal outpouring of the spirit of God, a divine power which will transform and make glorious nature and people alike. The 'spirit of judgement and of purification' will purify the daughter of Zion from all sin (Is 4:4–6). The 'spirit from on high', like a warm rain, will bring forth paradisal fruitfulness in nature, and perfect righteousness in the hearts of the people so that overflowing peace will issue forth (Is 32:15–20). In his Book of Consolation, Deutero–Isaiah promises that Yahweh will 'pour out' his spirit, the breath of life upon the seed of Israel, and thereby rouse the people who are dying out to a new life (Is 44:3ff; see also Ezek 37:1–14).

(c) After the return from the exile the small 'remnant' awaits the most glorious of all the gifts of the spirit, which will actually bring about a new creation in the members of the community. Then Yahweh will pour out his spirit 'upon all flesh', upon young and old, high and low, so that all will be thrown into prophetic ecstasy and will have both dreams and visions (Joel 2:28). The 'spirit of grace and of weeping' will wipe out every sin in the inhabitants of the Jerusalem of the final age, and will remove every cause of sin from them, for the Lord 'pours it out', or lets the 'fountain' stream forth (Zech 12:10–14; 13:1–6). Ezekiel, the priestly prophet, leads us to a plane as exalted as that of the New Testament. According to him the Lord will no longer 'pour out' his spirit as rain, but will 'sprinkle' it as the water of a cultic purification upon all the members of the community (Ezek 36:25), so as to purify them from all moral pollution. Then Yahweh will replace the 'heart of stone' in them with a 'heart of flesh', that is, he will give them a 'new heart' and will put a 'new spirit' (another disposition) within them; he will make them into a 'new creature' (Ezek 11:19; 18:31; 36:26; see also 2 Cor 5:17; Gal 6:15). Finally the Lord will fill the hearts thus transformed for ever with his spirit, with a superhuman power to lead a holy life according to God's 'commandments and precepts' (Ezek 36:27; 39:29; 37:14; see also Is 61:1–4; Jer 31:31–4; 32:38ff). From this point onwards it is only one step further to the mystery of the indwelling of the holy spirit in the souls of the just, which is rightly considered as the climax of the process of grace.

It is evident that neither the New Testament nor the present Church have completely exhausted the depths of these divine prophecies in all their richness. Their complete fulfilment will be achieved only with the true consummation of all, with the resurrection of the dead (Ezek 37:1–14) and with the 'new heaven and the new earth' (Is 65:17; 66:22).

5. *The nature of the Spirit of God.* From what has been said it will be seen that throughout the entire Old Testament the spirit of the Lord is conceived of not

yet as a person but merely as a force, as a physical reality, as a kind of extremely fine matter. The original interpretation is echoed more or less strongly in this. In the classic formula, 'The Egyptians are men and not God, and their horses are flesh and not spirit' (Is 31:3), it is not the 'spirit' that is in some sense contrasted with matter, the immaterial with the material, but rather the weak, mortal human nature with the powerful, immortal breath of God. When we are told of the spirit of the Lord that it is sent, that it envelops, breaks in upon, falls upon, guides and leads, sanctifies . . ., this means merely that an impersonal divine power receives a living human form, a form which can be recognised as the person of the Holy Spirit only in the light of New Testament revelation.

B. *The Spirit of God in the New Testament.* The New Testament terms corresponding to *ruaḥ* in the Old Testament is *pneuma*. It is found some 375 times, and exhibits the same range of meaning, though with a notable shift of emphasis. The synoptics mention *pneuma* seventy-nine times (Matthew nineteen times, Mark twenty-three, and Luke thirty-seven). The Acts of the Apostles has sixty-eight passages referring to the Spirit, far more than any of the other books. *Pneuma* also constitutes a major element in the earlier pauline letters: Romans thirty-two times, 1 Corinthians forty, 2 Corinthians seventeen, and Galatians sixteen (1 Thessalonians five times and 2 Thessalonians twice). Among the captivity epistles, the Letter to the Ephesians, with fourteen references, stands out from the others (Philippians five, Colossians two, and Philemon one), whereas there is hardly any mention at all of *pneuma* in the pastoral epistles (1 Timothy three times, 2 Timothy three times, and Titus once). Among the catholic epistles 1 John comes first with twelve references, and is followed by 1 Peter (ten), 2 Peter (one), James (two), and Jude (two). The Letter to the Hebrews contains twelve passages on the Spirit. John's gospel (with twenty-three references) and the Book of Revelation (with twenty-four) are evenly balanced. The development of the idea of the Spirit from the Old Testament to the New proceeds in a directly ascending line: the meaning 'wind' disappears almost completely. While, in the synoptics and Acts, the psychic effects of the Spirit predominate, the major epistles and John's gospel, with their teaching on the mystery of the new creation or rebirth, attain to a high point in the New Testament theology of the Spirit. The anthropological sense of *pneuma* receives peripheral mention, especially in the pauline writings.

I. *The Spirit in the New Testament.* 1. *Pneuma* in the original sense of 'wind' is only found in Jn 3:8 and Heb 1:7 (=Ps 104:4). While the basis in sense experience also disappears almost completely, so that the only surviving trace of it occurs in the episode of the mighty wind of Pentecost, still the characteristic quality of the tempest, namely mysterious and irresistible power, is permanently ascribed to the working of the Spirit of God.

2. *'Pneuma' in man.* Far more numerous are the passages in which *pneuma* is used to designate the spirit of man: the breath (2 Thess 2:8; see also Is 11:4; Jn 20:22; Acts 17:25): the

breath of life or the principle of life which comes from God and returns to him (Mt 27:50; Lk 8:55; 23:46; Jn 6:63; 19:30; Acts 7:59; Heb 4:12; Jas 2:26; Rev 11:11; 13:15); the spirit as the seat of perceptions and feelings (Lk 1:47; Jn 11:33; 13:21; 1 Cor 4:21; Gal 6:1; Eph 4:23; 1 Pet 3:4); of thought (Mk 2:8; 8:12; Lk 1:80; Acts 18:25; Rom 1:9; 2:29; 7:6; 1 Cor 2:11; 5:3, 4, 5; 6:17; 14:2, 12, 14, 15, 16, 32; 16:18; 2 Cor 2:13; 7:13; 12:18; 2 Tim 4:22; Phil 4:23; Philem 25), and of decisions of the will (Mt 26:41; Acts 20:22); a state of mind, an attitude of the spirit (Lk 1:17; Mt 5:3; Jn 4:23f; Rom 12:11; 1 Cor 2:12; 4:21; 2 Cor 4:13; 6:6; 7:1; 2 Tim 1:7; Phil 1:27; 2:1; 1 Jn 4:1f; 1 Pet 3:4); the 'spirit of truth and spirit of error' (1 Jn 4:6); the human personality (Gal 6:18).

3. *Evil spirits.* The New Testament very seldom speaks of spirits in general (Acts 23:8f), of good spirits or of angels (Heb 1:14; Rev 4:5), but far more frequently, especially in the synoptics and Acts, of the 'evil spirits', for which it has various designations: 'spirit' (Mk 9:20; Acts 16:18; Eph 2:2); 'spirits' (Mt 8:16; 12:45; Lk 10:20; 11:26; 1 Cor 12:10); 'evil spirits' (Lk 7:21; 8:2; Acts 19:12f, 15f); and 'dumb spirits' (Mk 9:17, 25). The term 'unclean spirits' is encountered particularly often. Of twenty-three passages referring to *pneuma* in Mark, fourteen are concerned with the 'unclean spirits' (or similar expressions Mk 1:23, 26f; 3:11, 30; 5:2; etc; Mt 10:1; Lk 8:29; 11:24; Acts 5:16; 8:7; Rev 16:13; 18:2). The 'spirits in prison' are also .called *pneumata* (1 Pet 3:19), as are the souls of the de-

parted (Heb 12:23). The expressions 'deceitful spirits' (1 Tim 4:1) and 'spirit of stupor' (Rom 11:8; ↗ Spirit of God in the Old Testament, ↗ Demon) have a wholly Old Testament ring.

II. *The Spirit of God in the New Testament.* With the new covenant the 'marriage' of the Spirit of God is inaugurated. The choice of the Greek and Latin adjectives—*pneuma hagion* (not *pneuma hieron*), *Spiritus sanctus* (not *Spiritus sacer*)—is enough by itself to show this. The full and lasting possession of the Spirit constitutes the great and blessed experience of newness for Jesus Christ. His glorified body constitutes the unquenchable source of the Spirit for the apostles, the church, the faithful—in fact, for the whole of creation.

1. *The Spirit of God and Jesus Christ.* In the person of Jesus Christ the most glorious bearer of the Spirit appeared, he who had been promised by the prophets (Is 11:2; 42:1; 61:1), and who was awaited by contemporary judaism (PsSol 17:42; Enoch 49:3f; TestLev 18:7; TestJud 24:2).

From his miraculous conception onwards, Christ is under the influence of the Spirit of God. The angel dispels the hesitation of Mary with the words: 'The Holy Spirit will come upon you, and the power of the Most High will overshadow you' (Lk 1:35; Mt 1:18, 20; see, too, the equivalent ideas in Acts 1:8). The angel attributes the miracle of the conception to the creative power of the Spirit of God (see Gen 1:2; Ps 104:30; Wis 1:7), who will descend upon Mary like a cloud, the sign of the divine presence (see Ex 13:21; 19:16; 24:16; 40:34). In the Old Testament every child born under

878

miraculous circumstances was dedicated in a special manner to God. Thus for example Isaac (Gen 18:14; 21:1), who was born according to the Spirit (Gal 4:29), Joseph (Gen 30:22f), Samson the Nazirite (Judg 13:2f, 7), Samuel (1 Sam 1:19f). In the same way the miraculous conception of Jesus represents the matchless masterpiece of the Spirit of God, who cannot increase his presence in Christ as he does in the Baptist (cf Lk 2:40 with 1:80), and who consecrates him as holy and as Son of God.

The Holy Spirit had already 'rested' (Jn 1:32; see also Is 11:2; Zech 3:8) upon the Son of God 'without measure' (Jn 3:34; Lk 4:1) from the moment of his birth. But at his baptism God 'anointed him with the Holy Spirit and with power' (Acts 10:38), ie, God revealed him and attested him in the eyes of all the world (see Lk 1:41, 44, 67; 2:25ff, and 37f) as the longed-for Messiah. The new creation begins with Christ filled with the Spirit, and yet the Baptist beheld the Spirit descending as a dove from heaven and hovering upon Jesus (Mt 3:16; Mk 1:10; Lk 3:21f; Jn 1:32f), just as on the morning of the first creation the *rûaḥ ᵉlōhîm* flew to and fro like a bird above the primordial waters as a power of fruitfulness and life (Gen 1:2), or as after the Flood the dove bore a fresh olive-branch in its beak as a sign of peace for the new humanity embodied in the Messiah (Gen 8:11).

At the beginning of his public ministry the Spirit of God drove Jesus, the 'new man', into the wilderness, where, like Moses (Ex 34:28) and Elijah (1 Kings 19), he fasted and prayed for forty days. And just as the first man was tempted by the devil, so too the second Adam was tempted by Satan. Triumphantly he overcame by power from above the subtle suggestions of the devil that he should build the messianic kingdom on the foundations of money, honour and power (Lk 4:1; Mk 1:12; Mt 4:1). Jesus ushered in once more the peace between man and beast which prevailed in Paradise (Gen 2:19; ApocMos 16). For according to Mk 1:13, when he had conquered temptation he sojourned 'among the wild beasts', and the evangelist may probably have intended to indicate by this that the paradisal conditions of the final age had been inaugurated (see Is 11:6–8; 65:25). And just as, according to the Midrash, in paradise food was prepared for Adam by the angels, so here angels provided heavenly food for the new man.

After this the Holy Spirit led him back to Galilee (Lk 4:14), where he prepared himself for his prophetic mission. (a) As he proclaimed for the first time the good tidings of the kingdom of God, as also throughout all his later preaching activity (Mt 12:18–21 = Is 42:1–4), he knew that he was endowed with the Spirit of the Lord (Lk 4:18f = Is 61:1f). (b) All the miracles which he performed were a sign of the Spirit of God, in whose power he drove out devils (Lk 4:36; Mt 12:28 = Lk 11:20: 'with the finger of God'; see also Ex 8:19; Deut 9:10), heals the sick and infirm, and raises the dead to life (Lk 5:17; 6:19; 8:54f; 13:32; Mt 12:18, 20). He prays in the Holy Ghost (Lk 3:4; 5:16; 6:12; 9:18; 9:29; 11:1; 22:32; 23:34–46), and is overflowing with joy in him (Lk 10:21). (c) In a further episode, while a radiant cloud upon the mountain, the 'majestic glory of God' (2 Pet 1:17), the symbol of the Spirit of God, over-shadowed Jesus, Moses, and Elijah, a voice proclaimed: 'This is my beloved Son' (Mk 9:2-13; Mt 17:1-13; Lk 9:28-36). Baptism and transfiguration reveal the divine sonship of Jesus. In his redemptive sacrifice upon the cross, through the 'eternal Spirit', Christ overcame (Heb 9:14) the weakness of his *sarx*, the mortality and limitations of his human nature (Mt 26:41). Then the 'Spirit that gives life' (Jn 6:63), ie, the creative power of God, raised Jesus to glory: 'If the Spirit of him who raised Jesus from the dead dwells in you, he who raised Christ Jesus from the dead will give life to your mortal bodies also through his Spirit which dwells in you' (Rom 8:11; see also 1 Pet 3:18).

The act of raising from the dead which the Father has accomplished through the mediation of the Holy Spirit as the executive organ is also attributed by Paul to the *dunamis* (lit. = power) which is equivalent to the Holy Spirit: 'Having the eyes of your hearts enlightened, that you may know . . . what is the immeasurable greatness of his power, which he accomplished in Christ when he raised him from the dead and made him sit at his right hand in the heavenly places' (Eph 1:18-20; cp 1 Cor 6:14; 2 Cor 13:14).

When Paul writes, 'Christ was raised from the dead by the *doxa* (*kābod*, ↗ glory) of the Father' (Rom 6:4), he is thinking of the cloud of light and fire, the shekina, which reveals the glory, presence and power of God (see Ex 24:17; 40:34; Num 10:34; Ezek 10:4), and in this respect the role of the cloud

has, with the passage of time, been transferred to the Spirit of God (see Is 63:10-14).

In his resurrection Christ also be-came transfigured by the Spirit. Above all he became, according to the law of the Spirit, designated Son of God (Rom 1:4). Thus he who on earth lived according to the psyche became in the Resurrection, in accordance with the nature of the Spirit, a spiritual being (1 Cor 15:45), so that from that time onwards he is pulsating with the over-flowing and life-giving power of the divine Pneuma: 'The Lord is himself the Spirit' (2 Cor 3:17; see also v. 6). So totally is the glorified Christ filled with the all-embracing and life-giving reality of the Holy Spirit that according to Paul it is justifiable to say that a man is in Christ (Gal 2:17) or in the Spirit (1 Cor 6:11), sanctified in Christ (1 Cor 1:2) or in the Spirit (1 Cor 6:11), sealed in Christ (Eph 1:13) or in the Spirit (Eph 4:30). And yet Paul does not regard the glorified Christ and the Holy Ghost as interchangeable. For while the believer is still sojourning in alien surroundings 'far from the Lord' (2 Cor 5:6), the Spirit of Christ is already dwelling within him (Rom 8:9).

In the power of the Holy Spirit Christ descended after his death to the 'spirits in prison', ie, in limbo, where he proclaimed the good tidings of sal-vation to those men who had perished in the flood, or announced to the devils the fact that they were finally bound and subjected to his power as *Kurios* (1 Pet 3:18-20).

It is the spiritualised and exalted body of the Lord, which is no longer subject to the laws of gravity, that the believer consumes in the ↗ eucharist. In other words, he eats the flesh of Christ, not in its earthly mode of existence, but as it is when transfigured by the Spirit. 'It is the Spirit that gives life, the flesh is of no avail' (Jn 6:63). This is Jesus' rejoinder to the Jews when they murmur against him and take scandal at the realism of his demands (Jn 6:52–63). The glorified body is a 'spiritual' food (1 Cor 10:3).

2. *The Spirit of God and the apostles.* During his earthly life Christ was the unique bearer of the Spirit, if we abstract from the charismatic figures who appear in the infancy narrative of Jesus (Lk 1:15, 41, 67; 2:25ff) and do not regard the power of working miracles extended to Jesus' disciples as an effect of the Spirit (Mt 17:19; Mk 16:17; Lk 21:15). It is with the Resurrection that the great mission of the glorified Lord begins, in which he pours out the Holy Ghost on all believers, the ↗ apostles first of all (see Is 28:6). According to the synoptics and the Acts of the Apostles it was not until Pentecost that Christ bestowed on the apostles (Acts 2:4, 33; see also 2:17) that 'baptismal fire', the Spirit of God which the Baptist had promised (Mt 3:11; Mk 1:8; Lk 3:16; see also Jn 1:22, 23), of which he himself had held out the prospect (Lk 24:49; Acts 1:2, 4, 5, 8; 11:16) and which he had ardently desired (Lk 12:49). For John, on the contrary, the sending of the Spirit is connected with the resurrection: 'If anyone thirst', says Jesus at the feast of Tabernacles, 'Let him come to me and drink, he who believes in me. As the scripture has said, "Out of him (Christ) shall flow rivers of living water"' (Zech 14:8; Ezek 47:1f; see

also Jn 4:1). The evangelist interprets this saying of the Lord: 'Now this he said about the Spirit which those who believed in him were to receive. For as yet the Spirit had not been given because Jesus was not yet glorified' (Jn 7:37–9; see also 16:7; 3:14f; 10:10). From the wound in his side when he was crucified (Jn 19:34; see also 1 Jn 5:6ff), from the glorified body of Christ as the messianic temple (see Jn 2:19; Ezek 47), the Spirit was indeed to be poured out over the whole earth and to the end of time. On the evening of the day of his resurrection he breathed (breath, exhalation!) upon the disciples with the words: 'Receive the Holy Spirit!', and by this gift he imparted to them the power to forgive sins (Jn 20:22f). The two authors do not contradict, but rather supplement, one another. Luke is concerned with the charismatic effects which he sees as deriving from the gift at Pentecost. John, on the other hand, has primarily in mind the sacramental graces which he sees as proceeding from the gift at the first Easter.

On the festival of Pentecost the apostles were assigned the charismatic function of prophets and leaders. They were equipped by the gift of the Spirit of God for preaching the word of God and for leading the church. Just as the Spirit of God had spoken through the mouth of the prophets (see Mt 22:43; Mk 12:36; Acts 1:16; 4:25; 28:25; Heb 3:7; 9:8; 10:15; 2 Tim 3:16; 2 Pet 1:21), so too he speaks through the mouth of their successors the apostles (Acts 5:39; 11:12; 1 Cor 12:28; 1 Pet 1:11f). The tongues of fire (Acts 2:3) point on to the preaching of the *magnalia Dei* (Acts 2:11) and also of the divine instructions (Rev 2:7, 11, 17, 28; 3:6, 13, 22). The Holy Spirit imparts divine authority and dignity to their inspired words (see 2 Tim 3:16; 2 Pet 1:21; Rev 14:13). Once the Holy Spirit has descended upon them they realise the immense significance of the message of the risen and exalted Lord (Acts 1:8; 2:33; 4:8; 6:5, 10; see also Rev 19:10) for obtaining a deeper insight into the mystery of Christ (1 Cor 2:10–14; 12:3; 2 Cor 4:13f; Eph 3:5, 16ff). The Holy Spirit does not reveal any new truths to the disciples, but reminds them of the teaching of Christ (Jn 14:25f; 15:18, 25f), which hitherto they have not understood (Jn 16:12). The reverential title 'Spirit of truth', which is accorded to him, is appropriate (Jn 14:17; 15:26; 16:13). Under the promptings of the Holy Spirit the christological meaning of the messianic prophecies of the Old Testament is disclosed (Acts 2:17–21 = Joel 2:28–32; 2:25–8 = Ps 16:8–11; 2:34f = Ps 110:1; 3:22f = Deut 18:15, 19; 4:25f = Ps 2:1f; etc).

At the same time the Holy Spirit equips them with superhuman power in order that in spite of opposition and persecution they may preach the 'word of God', ie, the message of Jesus Christ, with unflagging courage and burning zeal (Acts 2:29; 4:20, 29–31; 5:29; 9:27f; 19:8; 26:26; 28:31; 1 Cor 2:3f; 2 Cor 3:4–6; 4:1; 1 Thess 1:5), in 'the power of Christ' (2 Cor 12:9).

The success of their preaching is powerfully promoted by a whole series of impressive gifts of the Spirit such as inspired speech (Acts 2:4, 11, 15; ↗ charisma); the performance of major miracles (Acts 9:39–42; 12:5–17; 13:9–11; Rom 15:19); physical (Acts

8:39) and spiritual transports (Rev 1:10; 4:2; 17:3; 21:10); and prophecy in the strict sense (Acts 9:17; 20:23; Rev 2:1 = 8, 7 = 11; 2 Thess 2:2; 1 Tim 4:1; Jud 18; see also Lk 1:41, 67).

Like the leading figures of the chosen people, such as Moses (Num 11:17) or David (1 Sam 16:13), so too the apostles are equipped with charismatic gifts to exercise the functions of leader or pastor. By means of the ↗ laying on of hands they impart these to their disciples also (Acts 6:3; 20:28; 2 Tim 1:6; see also Num 8:10f).

The Spirit of God directs the young church through them (Acts 1:8; 13:2; 15:28; 20:28–31). In the Acts of the Apostles the chief protagonist is neither Peter nor Paul, but the Holy Spirit, by whose assistance the church grows (Acts 9:31). By the choice of Matthias (Acts 1:15–26) he brings the apostolic college to its full complement, making it the counterpart of the group of the twelve patriarchs of Israel. He determines who are to be the seven deacons (Acts 6:3, 5, 6; compare the seventy elders in Ex 24:1; Num 11:16), and who are to be the servants of the church (Acts 13:2). He institutes bishops (Acts 20:28; 1 Tim 4:12; 2 Tim 1:6); breaks down the inveterate prejudice against receiving gentiles into the church (Acts 10:19; 11:12; 15:28); guides and strengthens the 'apostles' (Acts 1:8; 5:3; 8:14–17) and the 'evangelists' (Acts 2:18; Eph 4:11; 2 Tim 4:5) on their hard missionary journeys (Acts 4:8; 6:10; 8:29; 10:19; 13:2–4; 16:6f; 20:24).

3. *The Spirit and the church.* According to the evidence of the Acts of the

Apostles, both the young church at Jerusalem, the 'Israel of God' (Gal 6:16), and also the gentile world (Acts 10:44f, 47; 11:15; 15:8f) celebrated a miniature Pentecost (Acts 4:31; see also 5:32; 8:17; 9:31; 19:2, 6) which was after the pattern of the prophecy of Joel (Acts 2:17=Joel 2:28).

With the exaltation of Christ and the sending of the Spirit (see Mt 16:18; Jn 7:39) the kingdom of God has begun (Acts 2:33; see also 1:3, 6; 2:20–36; 4:10f). The time of the church is essentially the time of the Spirit of God. Church and Spirit belong to each other inseparably as body and soul. According to Paul, the church is the glorified body of Christ, which is permeated by the living power of the Holy Spirit (1 Cor 12:13; Eph 4:2f). By him the believer's surrender of himself to Christ and his incorporation in the mystical body is sealed as a pact is sealed by the stamping of the seal upon it (Eph 1:13; 4:30). When Paul compares the church to a temple in which the Spirit of God dwells (1 Cor 3:16; Eph 2:22; cf 1 Pet 2:4f), this is another way of expressing the same truth.

The Holy Spirit was imparted to the individual members of the church by the imposition of hands (Acts 6:6; 8:17ff; 19:6; 1 Tim 4:14; 2 Tim 1:6; cp Deut 34:9). Since the charismatic gift of the Spirit of God was customarily bestowed only in view of a specific task, one who is already 'full of the Holy Spirit' by baptism is still open to further strengthening by the charismatic gifts of the Spirit (Acts 6:3, 10). The Samaritans had already received the baptism in water and the Holy Ghost, but it was only through the ⟋ laying-on of hands by the apostles

that the charismatic manifestation of their possession by the Spirit was granted to them (Acts 8:14–19; cf 19:5–7).

The Spirit of God breathed most powerfully through the young church, in which the primary result of his presence was the accomplishment of certain effects which were quite out of the normal course, and were most closely connected with the mission of the church. The church itself had abundant experience of being strengthened by the Holy Spirit (Acts 9:31), and it was due to him that the time of flowering in the christian life was so full of promise. Wholly characteristic of the Spirit of God was the aim of conquering the world for Christ. One expression of this aim was the courageous preaching of the word of God (Acts 4:31; 5:32; 6:5, 10; 11:24); others were the charismatic inspiration of the spoken and chanted liturgy (Acts 2:47; Eph 5:18–20); the gift of prophecy (Acts 8:19; see also Lk 1:15, 41, 67; 2:25ff); illuminations and inward promptings of the will (Acts 11:12); visions (Acts 7:55); prophecies in the strict sense (Acts 11:28; 21:4–11); miracles (Acts 3:1–8; Heb 2:4; 6:1f); ecstatic speech (Acts 10:44ff; 19:6; 1 Cor 12:10; 14:2–28; 1 Thess 5:19f) and its interpretation (1 Cor 12:10; 14:13, 27f); the ability to distinguish between spirits (1 Cor 12:10; 14:29; 1 Thess 5:21; 1 Jn 4:1); and the amazing wisdom and boldness of speech of the persecuted christians when they they were brought to judgement (Mt 10:20; Lk 12:12; Jn 14:26; Acts 6:5, 10).

4. *The Spirit of God and the faithful.* It is above all the pauline letters and the

883

fourth gospel which bring us into what is properly the domain of the Holy Spirit. According to these, with the resurrection of Christ the miracle of religious and moral transformation promised by the prophets (Ezek 36: 25ff; Jer 31:31, 34) has been accomplished. One day this work will be crowned by an act of glorification of mankind and of nature which will be absolutely comprehensive in its effects. In the pauline letters extraordinary feats have only a subordinate part to piay, while in the 'spiritual' gospel of the beloved disciple they go unmentioned altogether.

(a) The Holy Spirit dwells in the souls of the faithful as in a temple (1 Cor 3:16f; 6:19; Eph 2:22), but this is achieved no longer by the laying-on of hands, but rather by↗ baptism (Mt 28:19; Mk 16:16; Acts 8:12f, 16, 38; 9:18; 16:14f; 18:8f; Eph 4:5; Col 2:12), or by baptism in the name of Jesus (see Acts 2:38; 10:48; 19:5; 22:16; Rom 6:3ff; 1 Cor 1:13).

(b) The transformation accomplished by baptism is depicted by Paul as a new creation. Recalling the water of purification used in the cult (see Ezek 36:25; see also Is 4:4; 31:9; 66:15; Amos 7:4), he tells us how the soul is washed, sanctified and declared justified in the 'washing of the water' (Eph 5:26; Heb 10:22) of baptism from all guilt. This means that in fulfilment of the prophetic promise (see Ezek 36:27; 37:14) it is changed by the Holy Ghost into a new creature (cp 1 Cor 6:11; 2 Cor 5:17; Gal 3:27; 6:15; Eph 4:24; Rom 15:16; 1 Thess 1:5ff; 4:7f; 2 Thess 2:13; 1 Pet 1:2).

For this reason once they have been baptised the Jewish christians no longer

observe the↗ law 'of the letter', which was written on stone, but the law 'of the Spirit', which is inscribed in the hearts of christians (2 Cor 3:2–11). He who is free from the 'old written code' of the law 'serves in the new life of the Spirit' (Rom 7:6); but he who conducts himself according to the law fulfils the requirement of the law (Rom 8:4). The letter of the law now grown obsolete kills; only the 'new Spirit' brings about new life, the life that is in Christ Jesus, a new creation (see Rom 7:6; 8:1ff; Gal 6:8). Paul then goes on to draw this conclusion: '. . . walk not according to the flesh but according to the Spirit . . . To set the mind on the flesh is death, but to set the mind on the Spirit is life and peace' (Rom 8:4, 6; see also vv 7ff, 13). 'Walk by the Spirit and do not gratify the desires of the flesh' (Gal 5:16), ie, 'you shall not do the works of the flesh' (see Gal 5:19ff, 24), 'but will bring forth "the fruit of the Spirit"' (see Gal 5:22f, 25f). In this struggle against corrupted nature the christians are not alone. In the power of the Spirit they put to death the deeds of the flesh (cp Rom 8:13; Gal 5:13).

John conceives of the interior transformation of man achieved in baptism as a↗ rebirth, which is, in the last analysis, another way of expressing the same truth. According to the proclamation of the Baptist (Jn 1:33; see also Ezek 36:25f), in baptism the believer is born 'of God' (Jn 1:13), 'of the Spirit' (3:5, 6, 8), 'from above' and 'anew' (3:3: in John *anō* has both these senses). This is a divine new birth which is set in contrast to the birth 'from below' (8:23) 'of the flesh' (3:6), 'of the devil and the world'

(8:42–7; 15:19; 17:14, 16). In the 'bath of rebirth' we have been renewed by the Holy Spirit whom the Father, of his compassion, has poured out upon us in rich measure through Jesus Christ our Saviour in order that we, justified by his grace, may become heirs according to the hope of eternal life (see Tit 3:5ff).

(c) What effects do the pauline new creation or the johannine rebirth entail? Above all, sonship of God, the victorious act of faith, burning love for the brethren and the bearing of inspired witness.

In baptism the believer is in a mysterious manner 'baptised into' (see Rom 6:3ff) the dying and rising Lord, so that together with this newness of life his Spirit too is bestowed upon him, the Spirit of the Son, the Spirit of ⁊ sonship: 'And because you are sons God has sent the Spirit of his Son into our hearts crying "Abba, Father", so through God you are no longer a slave but a son, and if a son then an heir also' (Gal 4:6f). In baptism 'the flesh', that is the bondage of the earthly sinful man (Rom 8:1–8), is overcome by the 'Spirit' through whom God, together with his Son, has raised up us also to the new life of sonship (Rom 8:9–14). Henceforward the 'Spirit of God' (Rom 8:9), the 'Spirit of Christ' (Rom 8:9), the 'Holy Spirit' (Rom 5:5), or simply the 'Spirit' (Rom 8:11), dwells for ever in us and bears witness to the fact that we are sons of God (Rom 8:14–17). This Spirit of divine sonship obliges the christian as a son of God to persevere, 'to let himself be led by the Spirit of God' (Rom 8:14), 'to walk according to the Spirit' (8:4), 'to set his mind on the

things of the Spirit' (8:5), 'on life and peace' (8:6), 'on ⁊ righteousness' (8:10), that is true holiness.

The Spirit bestows upon us in ⁊ prayer a sureness of the fact that we are sons of God (Gal 4:6). He also teaches the christian the right manner in which he should pray to the Father in heaven (see Phil 1:19). Indeed he himself intercedes for him with sighs too deep for words (Rom 8:16, 26f; Jude 20; Phil 3:3). During the time 'when our Redeemer is absent', the Spirit of Christ arouses in us a prayerful longing for the return of our Lord (Rev 22:17, 20).

The Holy Spirit instils in us that ⁊ faith in Christ which does not derive from the works of the flesh (Gal 3:14; 5:5). It arouses in us an unshakeable faith in the person of the exalted *Kurios* (1 Cor 12:3).

In the power of the Spirit the christian maintains a superabundant ⁊ hope (Rom 15:13), and in this power he emerges victorious (Rom 8:1–7; Gal 5:16ff) over the desires 'of the ⁊ flesh', the 'old nature' (Gal 6:8).

The Spirit strengthens the interior man in faith and love (Eph 3:14f). The Spirit of the Father, 'a Spirit of power' (2 Tim 1:7), is efficacious in a quite special degree when he speaks through the mouth of his persecuted children (Mt 10:20; Mk 13:11; Lk 12:12; Jn 14:26), imparts strength to the martyrs to suffer and to lay down their lives for the sake of Jesus' name (1 Pet 4:14), the greatest possible proof of a love of Christ that is genuine (cp Jn 15:13).

According to Paul the spirit of brotherly love (⁊ brother) flows from the risen Christ into the soul of the baptised: 'God's love has been poured (perfect tense = lasting effect) into our hearts through the Holy Spirit which has been given to us' (aorist = initial occurrence: Rom 5:5; see also 15:30; Gal 5:22; Col 1:8; 2 Cor 6:6; Eph 3:16f) ↗ Love coincides so closely with the new life of the Spirit that 'to walk in the Spirit' is virtually synonymous with 'to love one another' (Gal 5:16, 18; see also Rom 8:4; Eph 5:2); to fulfil 'the law (of Christ)' (Gal 5:14; 6:2; 1 Cor 9:21) is virtually equivalent to 'to bear one another's burdens' (Gal 6:2).

The Holy Spirit watches with special care over the development of the beloved church. He instils daily brotherly love, ↗ joy, patience, friendliness, ↗ goodness, faithfulness, and gentleness (Gal 5:22; cp 1 Cor 13:4-7; Eph 4:2; Col 3:12), and ↗ humility (Eph 4:2). When the Spirit of love and the holiness of God is present in someone, through that love the law is fulfilled in the most perfect possible manner (Rom 13:10; Gal 5:14; Col 3:14).

Love is enthroned in the church as a queen. In the body of Christ it occupies the first place, for it has the same part to play as the Spirit (see Eph 4:16; Col 2:2). It immeasurably exceeds all other gifts of the Spirit (1 Cor 13:1-3, 8-10, 13; 14:1; see also 1 Jn 5:7), and includes them (Rom 15:30; Col 1:8; Gal 5:22). All charismatic feats performed in the service of the church are, in the last analysis, services of love for the brethren (see Acts 6:3). Without the Spirit of love the church would no longer be the church of Christ, but only a dead structure, a caricature of a church.

For John, too, the Spirit is so closely connected with love that he uses the words *Spirit* or *love* without distinction (1 Jn 4:13-17). When one compares 1 Jn 4:13-17 with Jn 17 one is tempted to discern in the love of the 'priestly prayer' the Spirit of the Lord himself who makes actual the unity of the faithful in the single Body of Christ (Jn 17; see also 1 Cor 12:4-12). The Holy Spirit draws the faithful into that relationship of love which unites the Father with the Son. Thus through the Holy Spirit man's encounter with God is made personal and living.

The Holy Spirit imparts a superhuman strength to the disciples of Christ in order that the ↗ witness which they bear to the exalted Lord shall be an inspired one.

5. *The Spirit of God and the glorification of creation.* In the 'new creation' or in the 'new birth' the entire man, and so the body too, takes part in the transformed life of glory. Paul explicitly enlightens us upon this: 'God has made *us* alive together with Christ . . . and raised us up with him and made us sit with him in the heavenly places' (Eph 2:5f [verbs in the perfect]; see also Col 2:12f).

The approaching ↗ resurrection, as foretold in the great vision of the dead bones (Ezek 37:1-14), is essentially and in principle already entered upon in holy baptism. There the Spirit is given to us as a 'pledge' of the physical resurrection (Rom 5:5; 8:11; Gal 3:2; 4:1; 1 Thess 4:8; Eph 1:13). More than this, indeed, the reception of the Spirit is the gift of first fruits (Rom 8:23), a 'down payment' or deposit on the part of God which guarantees the full outpouring of glory which will transfigure all without exception (2 Cor 1:22; 5:5; Eph 1:14).

In one passage, however, the raising of the body is regarded as the achievement of the Father, who will restore it through the power of the Spirit with its creative effect: 'If the Spirit of him who raised Jesus from the dead dwells in you, he who raised Christ Jesus from the dead will give life to your mortal bodies also through his Spirit which dwells in you' (Rom 8:11; see also 1 Cor 6:14). The Spirit is the miraculously life-giving force which will bring about the resurrection of the flesh (2 Cor 3:6; Gal 6:8; see also Jn 6:63).

Paul does something to throw light upon the question of 'how' the resurrection is to be effected (see 1 Cor 15:35-53). The earthly body, which is subject to the conditions of sense-experience, will then be raised into a 'spiritual body' which will be wholly permeated with and dominated by the life-force of the divine Spirit (1 Cor 15:44). Just as up to that point we shall have been conformed to the image of the 'first Adam', the earthly man, so then we shall be conformed to the image of the 'new Adam', the heavenly man, Christ (1 Cor 15:44-9; see also Rev 21:5). This is the image of 'incorruptibility' (1 Cor 15:42, 52f), of 'immortality' (1 Cor 15:53), of 'glory' (1 Cor 15:43; see also Rom 8:18; 2 Cor 4:17; Phil 3:21; Col 3:4).

The Spirit of God was at work in the first creation (Gen 1:2; cp 2:7). Through the ⁄ sin of man, to whom creation was handed over for better or for worse (cp Gen 3:17), it was thrown into 'the bondage of decay' (Rom 8:21), 'has been groaning in travail together until now' (v 22). But once the bodies are glorified, then the smitten world of creatures will also take part in the 'glory of the children of God' (v 21) through the creative power of the Spirit of God. Then it will find its redemption in the glorified Body of Christ and in that of man (Rom 8:18-23; see also Col 1:20; Eph 1:10; 2 Pet 3:13; Rev 21:5), 'in the new heaven and on the new earth' (Rev 21:1; Is 65:17; 2 Pet 3:13). Thanks to the living power of the divine Spirit, the paradise belonging to the beginning of time will break out once more in the glory of the eschatological new creation.

6. *The Spirit of God as person.* It may be concluded from the passages adduced that in most cases the Spirit of God is conceived of wholly in the sense of the Old Testament *rûah*, as a divine power. Only in this sense can we understand what is meant by such expressions as the outpouring of the Holy Spirit, baptising, anointing, sealing, filling, etc with the Holy Spirit. Often Spirit and power are found as parallel terms (Lk 1:17, 35; Acts 1:8).

Just as in the Old Testament, the Spirit of God is personified. He speaks through the mouths of the apostles (Acts 8:20; 13:2; etc) as he spoke through those of the prophets (Acts 4:25); he sends the disciples out (Acts 13:4); he leads the church (Acts 20:28). The Spirit can be found in place of ⁄ wisdom or power (1 Cor 2:4f, 13), and Paul means for the most part the supernatural presence and activity of God. For this reason 'God', 'Lord', and 'Spirit' can be used in parallelism to one another (1 Cor 12:4ff).

In the synoptics explicit reference to the three divine persons is found only in a single passage: the baptismal formula of Mt 28:19, which probably bears the stamp of later liturgical usage. In the Acts of the Apostles the passage: 'It has seemed good to the Holy Spirit and to us' (Acts 15:28), should probably be interpreted in the same sense. In the pauline letters certain passages point to the activity and presence of a distinct person of God. Among these passages are the trinitarian formulae in 1 Cor 12:4-6 and especially in 2 Cor 13:14. The fourth gospel and the Book of Revelation leave nothing to be desired in point of clarity. The Father sends the 'Supporter' (Jn 14:26) who proceeds from him (15:26) so that he can take the place of Christ in instructing the disciples (14:26) in order to bear witness to Jesus (15:26), in order to convince the world of sin (16:8-11; etc). The Holy Spirit occupies the place of Jesus Christ among the disciples and represents him (7:39; 16:7) during the long interval which must elapse before the return of the Lord (14:16). Again in Revelation, John the theologian envisages a person who is distinct from the Father and the Son. The Spirit speaks as a person to the community (Rev 2:7, 11, 17, 29; 3:6, 13, 22; 14:13). With John the theology of the Spirit of God as person achieves its definitive form.

Bibliography: On A: apart from the Old Testament theologies, see in particular: A. Westphal, *Chair et Esprit*, Toulouse 1885; J. Köberle, *Natur und Geist nach der Auffassung des AT*, Munich 1901; H. Gunkel, *Die Wirkungen des Heiligen Geistes nach der populären Anschauung der apostolischen Zeit und der Lehre des Apostels Paulus*, Göttingen 1909[3]; P. Volz, *Der Geist Gottes und die verwandten Erscheinungen im AT und im anschliessenden Judentum*, Tübingen 1910; J. Hehn, 'Zum Problem des Geistes im alten Orient und im AT', *ZAW* 43 (1925), 210-25; P. van Imschoot, 'L'action de l'esprit de Yahvé dans l'AT', *RSPT* 23 (1934), 553-87; P. van Imschoot, 'L'esprit de Yahvé, source de vie dans l'AT', *RB* 44 (1945), 481-501; P. van Imschoot, 'L'esprit de Yahvé et l'alliance nouvelle dans l'AT', *ETL* 22 (1936), 201-26; P. van Imschoot, 'Sagesse et esprit dans l'AT', *RB* 47 (1938), 23-49; P. van Imschoot, 'L'esprit de Yahvé, principe de vie morale dans l'AT', *ETL* 16 (1939), 457-67; P. van Imschoot, 'L'esprit selon l'AT', *Bible et Vie Chrétienne*, 2 (1953), 7-24; P. van Imschoot, 'L'esprit de Yahvé, source de piété dans l'AT', *Bible et Vie chrétienne* 6 (1954), 17-30; A. R. Johnson, *The Cultic Prophet in Ancient Israel*, Cardiff 1944; H. W. Robinson, *Inspiration and Revelation in the Old Testament*, Oxford 1946; B. W. Miller, *The Holy Spirit, What the Bible Teaches about Him*, 1950; R. Koch, *Geist und Messias. Beitrag zur bibl. Theologie des AT*, Vienna 1950; R. Koch, 'La théologie de l'Esprit de Yahvé dans le Livre d'Isaïe', *SP* 1 (Paris-Gembloux 1959), 419-33; R. Koch, 'Der Gottesgeist und der Messias', *Bbl* 27 (1946), 241-68; K. Galling, 'Der Charakter der Chaosschilderung in Gen 1:2', *ZTK* 47 (1950), 145-57; K. Prümm, 'Israels Kehr zum Geist', *ZKT* 72 (1950), 385-442; T. Maertens, 'Le souffle et l'esprit de Dieu', *Evangile* 14 (1954), 9-49; D. Lys, 'Ruach', *Le Souffle dans l'AT*, Paris 1962; D. Lys, 'Nephesh', *Histoire de l'âme dans la Révélation d'Israël*, Paris 1959; E. Haulotte, 'L'Esprit de Yahvé dans l'AT', *L'homme devant Dieu* (Mélanges H. Lubac 1), Paris 1964, 25-36; I. Herrmann, *HTG* 1, 642f; P. van Imschoot, Haag 527-35; M. J. Le Guillou, *Catholicisme* IV, 474-7; *TDNT* VI, 332-89 (=*BKW* IX); *RGG* II[3], 974-6 and 1270-72.

On B: see the well-nigh exhaustive details supplied in *TDNT* VI, 332-4. See also: H. Wendt, *Die Begriffe Fleisch und Geist im bibl. Sprachgebrauch*, Gotha 1878; J. Gloël, *Der Heilige Geist in der Heilsverkündigung des Paulus*, Halle 1888; G. Weinel, *Die Wirkungen des Geistes und der Geister im nachapostolischen Zeitalter bis auf Irenäus*, Freiburg 1899; M. Goguel, *La notion johannique de l'Esprit et ses antécédents historiques*, Paris 1902; E. Sokolowski, *Die Begriffe Geist und Leben bei Paulus*, Göttingen 1903; K. Deissner, *Auferstehungshoffnung und Pneumagedanke bei Paulus*, Leipzig 1912; H. B. Swete, *The Holy Spirit in the New Testament*, London 1912; H. Bertrams, *Das Wesen des Geistes nach der Anschauung des Apostels Paulus*, Munster 1913; W. Reinhard, *Das Wirken des Heiligen Geistes im Menschen*, Freiburg 1918; H. Leisegang, *Der Heilige Geist*, Leipzig-Berlin 1919; E. Scott, *The Spirit in the New Testament*,

London 1923; H. von Baer, *Der Heilige Geist in den Lukasschriften*, Stuttgart 1926; F. Büchsel, *Der Geist Gottes im NT*, Gütersloh 1926; R. B. Hoyle, *The Holy Spirit in St Paul*, London 1926; P. Gächter, 'Zum Pneumabegriff des heiligen Paulus', *ZKT* 53 (1929), 345–408; W. Michaelis, *Reich Gottes und Geist Gottes nach dem NT*, Basle 1931; E. Fuchs, *Christus und der Geist bei Paulus*, Leipzig 1932; W. Grundmann, *Der Begriff der Kraft in der ntl. Gedankenwelt*, Stuttgart 1932, 92–106; E. B. Allo, 'Sagesse et Pneuma dans la première Epître aux Corinthiens', *RB* 43 (1934), 321–46; N. A. Waaning, *Onderzoek naar het gebruik van 'pneuma' bij Paulus*, Amsterdam 1939 (dissertation); H. E. Dana, *The Holy Spirit in Acts*, Kansas City 1943; K. L. Schmidt, 'Das Pneuma Hagion als Person und Charisma', *Eranos-Jahrbuch* 13 (1946), 187–235; J. Loncke, 'Liber Actuum apte vocatur Spiritus Sancti Evangelium', *Collationes Brugenses* 46 (1946), 46–52; C. K. Barrett, *The Holy Spirit and the Gospel Tradition*, London 1947 (see also *Expository Times* 67 [1956], 142–5); F.-M. Braun, 'L'eau et l'Esprit', *RT* 49 (1949), 5–30; K. Prümm, 'Die katholische Auslegung von 2 Kor 3:17 in den Letzten vier Jahrzehnten', *Bbl* 31 (1950), 316–45 and 459–82; and 32 (1951), 1–24; J. Schmid, 'Geist und Leben bei Paulus', *GL* 24 (1951), 419–29; J. Michl, 'Der Geist als Garant des rechten Glaubens', *Vom Wort des Lebens* (Festschrift M. Meinertz), Münster 1951, 142–55; E. Schweizer, 'Geist und Gemeinde im NT und heute', *Theologische Existenz heute*, Munich 1952; E. Schweizer, 'The Spirit of Power: The Uniformity and Diversity of the Concept of the Holy Spirit in the New Testament', *Interpretation* 6 (1952), 259–78; H. D. Wendland, 'Das Wirken des Heiligen Geistes in den Gläubigen nach Paulus', *TLZ* 77 (1952), 457–70; S. Zedda, *L'adozione a figli di Dio e lo Spirito Santo*, Rome 1952; B. Schneider, 'The Meaning of St Paul's Antithesis of the Letter and the Spirit', *CBQ* 15 (1953), 163–207; *LV* 10 (June 1953); *LV* 1 (January 1953); T. Maertens, 'Le souffle et l'esprit de Dieu', *Evangile* 14 (1954), 9–49; T. Maertens, 'L'Esprit qui donne la vie', *Evangile* 17 (1955), 7–64; O. Cullmann, *Life After Death or Resurrection of the Body*, London 1958; E. Schweizer, 'Röm 1:3f und der Gegensatz von Fleisch und Geist vor und bei Paulus', *ET* 15 (1955), 563–71; E. Schweizer, 'Die sieben Geister in der Apokalypse', *ET* 15 (1955), 502–11; E. Schweizer, 'Gegenwart des Geistes und eschatologische Hoffnung bei Zarathustra, spätjüdischen Gruppen, Gnostikern und den Zeugen des NT', *The Background of the New Testament and its Eschatology* (Studies in honour of C. H. Dodd), Cambridge 1956,

482–508; M.-E. Boismard, 'La révélation de l'Esprit Saint', *RT* 55 (1955), 5–21; *Bible et vie chrétienne* 14 (May–July 1956); M. Dibelius, *Der Herr und der Geist bei Paulus*, Tübingen 1956; J. Goitia, *La noción dinámica 'pneuma' en los libros sagrados*, Madrid 1956/7; Neil Q. Hamilton, *The Holy Spirit and Eschatology in Paul* (*SJT* occasional papers no. 6), Edinburgh–London 1957; A. Dietzel, 'Beten im Geist', *TZ* 13 (1957), 12–32; P. Bonnard, 'L'Esprit Saint selon le NT', *RHPR* 37 (1957), 81–90; M. A. Chevallier, *L'esprit et le Messie dans le Bas-Judaisme et le NT*, Paris 1958; F. X. Durrwell, *The Resurrection: A Biblical Study*, London 1969³; D. E. Holwerda, *The Holy Spirit and Eschatology in the Gospel of John. A Critique of Rudolph Bultmann's Present Eschatology*, Kampen 1959; R. Padberg, 'Pneuma und christliche Wirklichkeit', *Kaufet die Zeit aus. Beiträge zur christlichen Eschatologie*, (Festschrift T. Kampmann), Paderborn 1959, 73–91; O. Kuss, *Der Römerbrief*, Regensburg 1959², 540–95; R. T. Fortna, 'Romans 8:10 and Paul's Doctrine of the Spirit', *ATR* 151 (1959), 77–84; P. Bläser, 'Lebendigmachender Geist', *SP* II (Paris–Gembloux 1959), 404–13; J. Hermann, *Kyrios und Pneuma*, Munich 1960; P. Biard, *La Puissance de Dieu*, Paris 1960; T. Blatter, *Macht und Herrschaft Gottes*, Fribourg 1962; K. Stalder, *Das Werk des Geistes in der Heiligung bei Paulus*, Zurich 1962; O. Betz, *Der Paraklet*, Leiden–Cologne 1963; R. Koch, 'L'aspect eschatologique de l'Esprit du Seigneur d'après Saint Paul', *Stud. Paulin. Congressus Internat. Cath.* 1, Rome 1963, 131–41; H. Schlier, 'Zum Begriff des Geistes nach dem Johannesevangelium', *Festschrift J. Schmid*, Regensburg 1963, 233–9; C. Huyghe, *Conduits par l'Esprit. Une école de la foi*, Paris 1964; K. Niederwimmer, 'Das Gebet des Geistes, Röm 8:20f', *TZ* 20 (1964), 252–65; E. Stauffer, *Theologie des NT*, Gütersloh 1948⁴, 144–7; Bultmann I, 153–64, 203–10, and 336–40; and II, 88–91; P. van Imschoot, Haag 535–40; M.-J. Le Guillou, *Catholicisme* IV, 477–82; R. Haubst, *LTK* v², 108–13; V. Hamp, *LTK* VIII², 568–70; J. Guillet, *DBT*, 499–505; I. Hermann, *HTG* I, 643–7; *TDNT* VI, 332–455 (=*BKW* IX); *RGG* II³, 976f, 1272–9, and 1283–6; P. H. Menoud, Allmen 168–72; W. D. Davies, 'Paul and the Dead Sea Scrolls', *Flesh and Spirit: The Scrolls and the New Testament*, 1957, 157–80; F. Nötscher, 'Geist und Geister in den Texten vom Qumran', *Mélanges A. Robert*, Paris 1957, 305–15; D. Flusser, 'The Dualism of "Flesh and Spirit" in the Dead Sea Scrolls and the New Testament', *Tarbiz* 27 (1958), 158–65 (in Hebrew).

Robert Koch

Suffering

A. *Old Testament.* 1. *Terminology:*
The Hebrew word for suffering in the
objective sense, ie, as an evil, is *ra*ᶜ
(= 'that which is evil'), but this can
mean both moral evil, that which is
vicious, and that which is harmful.
Besides this, the Old Testament expresses evil by means of paraphrases
based on the roots ᶜ*tsb* (= 'injure') *ḥly*
(= 'be sick'), *k*ᵓ*b* (= 'find oneself in a
terrible, desperate situation'), etc. The
Hebrew language has no term for
'pain' as a physical sensation, but can
only give a description of the external
appearance and behaviour of one
suffering pain, and so permit one to
deduce indirectly what the sensation of
pain is like, as well as the effect which it
has upon the spirit: ᵓ*ēḥel* and *tsyrîm* are
the symptoms of birth-pangs, but are
also used of pain and anguish in
general. *ḥîl* denotes the shuddering and
quaking of a body tormented with pain
and anguish; *ka*ᶜ*as* is the vexed, sullen
disposition of one suffering; ᵓ*ēḥel* is the
attitude of mourning; *mispēd* the lamentation and sorrowful behaviour of one
in mourning. Various expressions for
injuries, wounds, sickness, hard toil
(ᶜ*āmāl*), unpleasant sensation (*mar* =
'bitter'), etc, serve to indicate pain and
suffering, with the result that in a given
case it can only be decided with difficulty whether the pain referred to in the
passage concerned is physical or mental,
whether the expression is to be understood literally or metaphorically. This
must be borne in mind in interpreting
Lamentations, and passages such as
Is 53.

2. *Physiological and psychological concepts.* The following kinds of physical

suffering are mentioned in the Old
Testament: injuries, sicknesses, physical
chastisement, and birth-pains. Chastisement and birth-pains are considered as
so painful that they are the chief
images used to describe the extreme
anguish of mental suffering. The following causes of mental suffering are
mentioned in the Old Testament:
danger of death (2 Kings 20:1ff; Is
38:1ff); the death of children, whether
this is presumed, impending or has
already taken place (Gen 21:15f;
37:31–5; Judg 11:35; 2 Sam 19:1–5;
Tob 10:1–8), especially the death of a
first-born child or an only son (Jer
6:26; Amos 8:10; Zech 12:10).
Further causes of mental suffering are:
childlessness (Gen 15:2; 1 Sam 1:9ff);
homesickness (Ps 43; 61; 84; 137);
persecution and hostility (Num 16:15;
Jer 20:14–18; Ps 22; 38:13; 39:2f);
mockery and malicious gloating at one's
misfortunes on the part of enemies (Jer
20:7; Ps 22:7f, 13f; 31:11, 13; 42:10f;
55:3f; Job 19:18; 30:1–10); loneliness
and the sense of having been abandoned
(Ps 22:2; 31:12f; 38:10f; 88:9, 18; Is
53:3; Jer 15:17); ingratitude and
faithlessness on the part of one's own
friends and relations (2 Sam 13:19;
Jer 18:20; 20:10; Ps 41:9; 55:13ff;
Job 16:20; 19:17, 21f; Prov 10:1;
17:25; Sir 3:16; 30:9, 12); and also
the misfortune of friends and acquaint-
ances (Ps 35:13f; Job 2:11; 30:25;
42:11; Sir 7:34f)—the devout man
suffers especially when his own people
are in need (Ex 5:22; 32:11f; 2 Sam
1:11–27; Is 22:1–4; Jer 4:8, 19–31;
6:24f; 8:18–23; 13:17; 14:17f; Ezek
9:8; 21:12; Mic 1:8–16; Bar 4:9–20; Ps
44:10–23; 60:3–7; 74; 77:2–11; 79;
80:5–15; 89; 137; Lam; Neh 1:4;

Esther 4:1ff; 6:12; 2 Macc 3:16–22).

The oriental's capacity for suffering is such that any deeply felt suffering affects the entire body/soul compositum. Pain is connected with specific parts of the body: with the bones (Is 38:13; Jer 23:9; Ps 31:10; 42:10; Job 30:17); the kidneys (Ps 73:21; Job 16:13; Lam 3:12f); the liver and gall (Job 16:13; Lam 2:11; Prov 7:23); the bowels (Is 16:11; Jer 4:19; Job 30:27; Lam 1:20; 2:11); and the heart (1 Sam 1:8; Jer 4:19; 8:18; 23:9; Lam 1:20, 22; Ps 38:10; 55:4). Suffering impels the subject to outbursts of anger and cursing (Jer 11:20; 15:15; 17:18; 18:18–23; Ps 35:4–8, 26; 69:23–29; 109:6–15; 137:7ff; Job 3). It can make one physically sick (Neh 2:2; 1 Macc 6:8; 2 Macc 3:16f) and lead to despair and disgust with life (Gen 37:35; Jer 15:10; 20:14–18; Job 3; 6:8ff; 7; Lam 3:1–20; Tob 3:6). Old Testament man does not conceal his pain, but expresses it in weeping and pitiful lamentations. Such behaviour is not considered unworthy of a man. Suffering is avoided as far as possible. Any attitude of asceticism such as might in some sense lead one voluntarily to embrace suffering in order to bridle the lower instincts or to strengthen the body or the will is alien to the Old Testament. At the same time, however, the devout member of the Old Testament people does understand how to bear unavoidable suffering, especially when the service of God requires it, with exemplary fortitude.

3. *How suffering is judged of from a religious point of view.* The Old Testament considers the deeper cause of suffering to be any disturbance of the relationship between God and man

through sin, and the anger of God thereby incurred. Pain in bearing children, various kinds of troubles, hardships and suffering, sickness and death, came into the world as a result of the first sin (Gen 3:16–19; Wis 2:24). In spite of this 'aetiology of the origins' of suffering not all the actual sufferings recorded in the Old Testament are interpreted as the direct effects of sin or of the divine anger, as is the case in the Babylonian Laments. At the same time suffering is in many cases considered to be punishment for sin (Gen 42:21f; 44:16; Lev 26:14–40; Num 12:9–12; 21:6; Deut 28:15–68; Judg 2:1–4, 11–18; 3:7ff; 4:1ff; 6:1–7; 10:6–16; 2 Sam 12:11–18; 24:11–17; Is 57:17; Jer 4:18; Ezek 23:33; Ps 32:3ff; 38:4f, 19; 39:12; Lam 1:18–22; 3:40–7). Other factors which were regarded as painful experiences were remorse (Zech 12:10–14; Ps 51; Is 53:1–4), the incomprehensibility of the disposition of good and bad order in the world, ie, the prosperity of the wicked and the misfortune of the devout (Ps 35; 73), disappointments encountered in the service of God (Ex 5:20f; Num 11:11–15; Is 49:4; 50:6; 52:13–53:12; Jer 1:8, 17ff; 12:5f; 20:7–13; Ezek 2:6; 24:15–18), and above all the misfortunes of the people of God (see under 2 above).

Suffering always implies temptation, and even the devout man turns against God for a time and rebels under it (Ex 5:22; Num 11:11; Jos 7:7; Is 38:17; Jer 12:1; 15:18; 20:7; Ps 79:5; 85:6; Job 7:12; 9:22; 19:6–12; 30:17–22; Lam 3:10f), so that bitter reproaches against God are wrung from the sufferer, leading to the pressing questions: 'Why?', 'How long?'. But suffering also breaks down resistance against God, so that the sinner and rebel is brought to reflect and repent (Ps 32:3ff; 34:19; 51:19), and to acknowledge his fault (Ps 32:3ff; 38:4, 18; 39:2–12). It is precisely in the hour of bitterest suffering that the longing for union with God makes itself felt (Ps 17:15; 22; 42; 84:2f; 120; 123:2; Job 19:27ff; 29:2ff).

Even when it is the ⁄ wrath of God that brings suffering upon man, still God is moved to compassion by man's suffering so that he forgives and comes to his aid (Gen 21:17f; Ex 2:24; 3:7; 2 Kings 19:6f; 20:5; 22:19; Tob 3:16f; Ps 3:4; 17:6; 22:24f; 86:12–17). God richly rewards his devotees when they are faithful in enduring suffering (Gen 22:16; 1 Sam 2; 2 Macc 7:11, 36; Is 49:5; 52:13; 53:10ff; Wis 3–5; Job 42:10–17).

Thus the Old Testament achieves a rational explanation of suffering which goes far beyond all the futile attempts of other and earlier peoples and religions to find some meaning in suffering. According to the Old Testament conception suffering is intended to compel a man to decide which position he will take up, for or against God, and so to prove the faithfulness and devotion of the man concerned (Gen 22; Ps 30; Job 1:11; 2:5). It is intended to draw him out of his self-confidence, to remind him of his fault against God, and so to introduce the process of healing needful after sin (Ex 15:26; Deut 32:39; Is 19:22; 30:26; Jer 30:17; 33:6; Hos 6:1; 14:4). Suffering is indeed often a means of chastisement, but it is a chastisement that comes not from the hand of a heartless tyrant, but from God as loving Father (Jer 10:24;

30:11; 31:18; 46:28; Lam 3:33; Ps 30; 31; Wis 3:5). Suffering purifies devotion and deepens man's union with God (Sir 2:5; Wis 3:5). The Old Testament revelation on the meaning of suffering reaches its climax in Is 53; Zech 12:10–14; Dan 3:23(6)f; 2 Macc 7:37f): the suffering of the devout is a means of atonement which, by a process of substitution, takes away the guilt of the sinners and of the whole people, and so mediates salvation to others.

Already, then, in the Old Testament we find a realisation that suffering is a prior condition for the attainment of salvation on the part of sinful humanity. It is through suffering that man must enter into the joy of the kingdom of God. Between suffering and salvation there is a connection similar to that between a mother's birth-pangs and her joy (see Is 66:9f; Jer 30:6f; Mic 4:10). The most effective motive prompting the devout adherent of Old Testament religion to transcend his suffering inwardly is the thought that in suffering man draws closer to God, and contributes to the salvation of God's people. By contrast the hope of resurrection or belief in the after-life as a motive of consolation in suffering becomes a significant factor only at a very late stage (Dan 12:1f; Wis 3–5; 2 Macc 7; ⁄ resurrection).

It is only for the obdurate and finally reprobate (Dan 12:2; Judith 16:17; cf Is 66:24) that suffering has the function of punishment without the further significance of salvation. So long as man is not altogether cast off from God, suffering always continues to be a grace for him, because it can still bring about his 'contrition', and thereby his forgiveness also.

The Old Testament manner of speaking, which ascribes human feelings to God, also recognises a suffering on God's part. This is the suffering of disappointed love (Gen 6:6; 1 Sam 15:11, 35; Is 1:2–5, 21; 5:1–7; 39; 65:1–4; Jer 3:6–10, 19f; Ezek 16; Hos 10:1ff; 11:1–5; 12:14f; Mic 6:1–8), or of merciful sympathy with men (Is 49:15; 66:12f; Jer 31:20; Hos 2:16f), but it never ascribes to God the kind of suffering that comes from weakness.

Bibliography: E. Balla, 'Das Problem des Leidens in der Geschichte der israelitisch-jüdischen Religion', *Festschrift H. Gunkel*, Göttingen 1923, 214–60; N. Peters, *Die Leidensfrage im AT*, Münster 1923; L. B. Paton, 'The Problem of Suffering in the Pre-exilic Prophets', *JBL* 46 (1927), 111–31; J. J. Stamm, *Das Leiden des Unschuldigen in Babylon und Israel*, Zürich 1946; J. Scharbert, *Der Schmerz im AT*, Bonn 1955; J. Scharbert, *HTG* II, 37–44; J. L. McKenzie, 'Divine Passion in Osee', *CBQ* 17 (1955), 287–99; J. A. Sanders, *Suffering as Divine Discipline in the Old Testament and in Post-biblical Judaism*, Rochester 1955; E. F. Sutcliffe, *Providence and Suffering in the Old and New Testament*, Edinburgh 1955; H. Frey, 'Zur Sinndeutung des Leidens im AT', *Wort und Dienst* 6 (1959), 45–61; O. Garcia de la Fuente, 'El Problema del dolor en la religion babilonica', *La Ciudad de Dios* 174 (1961), 43–90; J. S. Croatto, 'El problema del dolor', *RB* 24 (1962), 129–35; C. T. Francisco, 'Evil and Suffering in the Book of Hosea', *Southwest Journal of Theology* 5 (1962/3), 33–41; A. R. C. Leany, 'The Eschatological Significance of Human Suffering in the Old Testament and the Dead Sea Scrolls', *SJT* 16 (1963), 286–301; J. Salguero, 'Finalidad del dolor segun el AT', *Ciencia Tomista* 90 (1963), 369–97; R. Bultmann, *TDNT* IV, 313–24; W. Michaelis, *TDNT* V, 904–39.

Josef Scharbert

B. *Later judaism*. The attitude of later judaism to suffering is determined by the concept of ↗ retribution. At the same time it is involved in a quest for a rational solution to the problem confronting theodicy, and it hopes to achieve this by recourse to this same idea of retribution. It takes as its starting-point the idea that all men are sinners, and goes on to assert that all sufferings are connected with sin. For the devout, who are likewise not free from sin, suffering is a means of divine discipline. Sufferings are intended to compel man once and for all to examine his course, and thereby to bring him to repentance. Thereafter suffering becomes a means of atonement which obliterates sin in the sight of God. In this way God gives the devout man the opportunity of atoning for his sins in this world so that in the world to come he may be preserved from punishment (Bar [Syr] 78:6), whereas he lets the wicked go unpunished and thus withholds from him this possibility of atoning for his sins. Moreover God rewards such minor acts of virtue as he performs by prosperity in order to allow him to feel the full weight of his punishment in the world to come. This principle applies to peoples and individuals alike (2 Macc 6:12–17). The sufferings of the devout, therefore, are the chastisements of love, and their purpose is to increase merit and reward. Finally, judaism also recognises suffering endured in atonement on behalf of others (↗ mediation), which serves the purpose of atoning for the sins of the entire people. The patriarchs, Moses, David, the prophets, and Job are counted as men who have suffered on behalf of the entire people in this way. But above all it is the death of the just and of martyrs which has this power of atonement, and so benefits the entire people. On the other hand no evidence is to be found in the literature of later judaism for the idea of the Messiah undergoing atoning suffering on behalf of others (as a development of the idea contained in Is 53). This is to be explained by the fact that the concept of the Messiah which prevailed in later judaism did not admit of the idea of a suffering Messiah.

C. *The New Testament.* For the New Testament suffering has a still greater significance than for judaism. Almost all the books of the New Testament speak of suffering in numerous passages. On one occasion Jesus designates the power of Satan as the origin of suffering (Lk 13:10–17; similarly Paul in 2 Cor 12:7; see also Acts 10:38). Nor is it disputed that suffering can be punishment for sins decreed by God. According to Lk 13:1–6 when Jesus encounters special cases of misfortune he sees in them on the one hand punishment that is deserved, on the other a warning to others. According to Jn 9:1, however, we should not enquire after the cause of the suffering of the man born blind, but rather its purpose. It is an opportunity for the works of God to be made manifest. The Jewish idea that sickness can be the result of sin and so punishment also finds expression in one passage of Paul (1 Cor 11:30–32). On the other hand, both Jesus (Lk 16:19–31) and the New Testament in general altogether deny the prevailing doctrine of the Pharisees that all suffering is retribution.

In order to understand the attitude of Jesus and of the New Testament towards suffering we must take as our starting-point the fact of his own suffering and what he has to say about it. His entire messianic work consisted of suffering in manifold forms. Jesus has neither home (Mt 8:20 = Lk 9:57), nor family (Mk 3:31–5), and as he journeys through the towns and villages of Galilee the works he performs there are exhausting. Yet he encounters a complete absence of understanding on the part of the people and bitter hostility from their leaders. The result is almost total failure and his death on the Cross. He has not only predicted this, but actually emphasised that it is willed by God (Mk 8:31; 9:31; 10:33; 14:21; Lk 13:32f). He is the suffering servant of God, who must lay down his life vicariously on behalf of the many (Mk 10:45; Lk 22:17). It is through suffering that he must enter on his glory (Lk 24:26). And just as suffering belongs to Jesus' own fate, so too it belongs to the life of his disciples. To be a disciple is to follow him in his suffering. It is to carry the cross after Jesus (Mk 8:34ff; Mt 10:38f = Lk 14:27). It is to tear oneself away from the most cherished human ties (Mt 8:19–22 = Lk 9:57–62). It implies a renunciation of life's enjoyments, of worldly esteem and repute (Mt 10:43f). It entails slander, hatred, persecution and even death as its consequences (Mk 13:1–13), and for this reason demands self-abnegation to the point of laying down one's life (Mk 8:34; Mt 10:39 = Lk 17:33; Jn 12:24f). Blessed is the disciple whom the Lord finds worthy to follow him even to a martyr's death! (Jn 11:28f). Only he who loses his life for Jesus' sake will save it (Mk 8:35). Jesus has come to bring division upon the earth, to introduce discord even into families (Lk 12:49ff = Mt 10:34–6), and this because he compels men to decide whether they are for him or against him. The reason for this manifold suffering consists primarily in the condition of this world, for which the gospel is a scandal and a folly, and which therefore hates and persecutes Jesus' disciples even as it hated and persecuted Jesus himself. But the ultimate reason for all this suffering is to be found in the will of God. It is precisely for this reason that the cross which the disciples must carry after Jesus is also the mark of election, and therefore reason for joy. Jesus pronounces those blessed who suffer slanders, calumnies, and persecutions for his sake (Mt 5:11f=Lk 6:22f).

The ↗ passion of Jesus represents a special problem, which is not confined merely to early christian apologetics. For in it the element of the divine is wholly hidden under weakness and deepest degradation. Here suffering becomes a problem of christology. What took place on Good Friday was not only a stumbling block to Jew and a folly to gentiles (1 Cor 1:23), but has appeared to christians also as incomprehensible and shocking (see Mk 8:31–3). There is one passage in which, in order to overcome this shock to faith, Paul views the passion in connection with the resurrection (1 Cor 15:3f), and then, connecting it further with Jesus' own words concerning the fact that his suffering was willed by God, goes on to explain it in the light of Old Testament prophecies, especially the Messianic interpretation of Ps 22. For the Jews, who demand signs (proofs of divine power), and for the Greeks, who seek wisdom, the preaching of Jesus crucified is indeed folly, but for those who are called it is precisely in him that the power and wisdom of God

stand revealed (1 Cor 1:22–4). It only seems that it is by his human adversaries that Christ has been laid low. In reality it was God who 'delivered him up' (Acts 2:23; 3:13–18; 4:10; 5:30f; 13:27–30; Rom 4:25; 8:32), and thereby made atonement for the world through him (2 Cor 5:19).

The words of Jesus concerning the necessity of suffering are also echoed throughout the entire New Testament in the life of the faithful. Probably the Jewish idea is also present, namely that suffering is a means of divine chastisement or ↗ discipline (Heb 12:4–11; Rev 3:19), that it is a test by which the believer must prove himself (Rom 5:3f; 1 Pet 1:7), and for this reason the christians should rejoice over their sufferings (Jas 1:2–4; 1 Pet 1:6). But this is not the specifically christian understanding of suffering, the theology of which has been developed above all by Paul. The many sufferings which the christians encounter they endure 'for the sake of the name of Jesus' (Acts 5:41), and in imitation of his example (Heb 12:1f; 1 Pet 2:20f). Suffering falls especially upon the preachers of the gospel (Acts 9:16). God has 'set them in the world as the last of all, like gladiators sentenced to death' so that they have become a spectacle for the world, for men and for angels (1 Cor 4:9ff). But Paul does not only suffer *like* Christ, in accordance with his example (1 Pet 2:20f), and '*for* him', that is for the sake of Christ (2 Cor 4:11): he also suffers *with* him (Rom 6:3ff). His sufferings proceed from the fact that he 'exists in Christ'. In what he has to endure day by day he continually bears the death of Jesus in his own body (2 Cor 4:10). Because in baptism, as Rom 6:2ff lays down, he has died with Christ and risen to a new life, he can and must also 'become like Christ in his death' (Phil 3:10). In suffering he takes the Cross of Christ upon himself (Gal 6:14), experiences what it is to have a share in the sufferings of Christ (Phil 3:10). Therefore he can call his sufferings 'the sufferings of Christ' (2 Cor 1:5; Phil 3:10; Col 1:24) and the marks of the wounds which have been inflicted upon him in the exercise of his apostolic ministry, the marks of the wounds (*stigmata*) of Jesus (Gal 6:17). Suffering brings the christian to an awareness of his own weakness and nothingness, and guards him against the self-presumption of relying on his own strength instead of the strength of God (2 Cor 1:9; 12:7). But Paul also knows that he does not suffer as an isolated individual for himself alone. The sufferings which come so copiously upon him are for the benefit of the church, and that too not only in the sense that they cannot be thought of apart from his work as an apostle (2 Cor 11:23-9), or that he, having been consoled by God in his sufferings, can also console others (2 Cor 1:4-7), but they contribute directly to the salvation of the church, the formation of the body of Christ (Col 1:24). If death is at work in him, this is in order that life may be at work in others (2 Cor 4:12-16). And because it has this significance for him he has overcome suffering inwardly. So far as he is concerned it no longer represents any problem of theodicy, nor is there any element of harsh compulsion in it. Rather it is a grace (Phil 1:20; see also 1 Pet 2:20), so that he can say: 'I rejoice in my sufferings'

(Col 1:24). This does not mean that he is in any sense a Stoic who meets the afflictions that come upon him from without with the strength of some immovable *ataraxia* or calmness. On the contrary he is acutely aware of the reality of suffering and experiences it for what it really is. But the strength which preserves him from breaking under the burden of his sufferings is the strength of Christ who lives in him. But for Paul, as for the New Testament in general (Acts 14:22; 1 Pet 4:13; Heb 2:10; 2 Tim 2:11ff), suffering is transcended by eschatology, and that too in a sense quite different from that which it bears in later judaism. The law, 'Through suffering and death to life and glory' does not apply to Christ alone. 'Provided we suffer with him in order that we may also be glorified with him' (Rom 8:17). Viewed in the light of the glory that is to come, Paul's present sufferings seem to him 'not worthy of mention' (Rom 8:18). 'For this slight momentary affliction is preparing for us an eternal weight of glory beyond all comparison. Because we look not to the things that are seen, but to the things that are unseen. For the things that are seen are transient, but the things that are unseen are eternal' (2 Cor 4:17).

The theology of suffering of the fourth gospel appears from the teaching concerning the 'world' which is peculiar to this gospel. Because the disciples called by Jesus out of the world have been chosen from the rest (15:19), they no longer belong to the world, even though they still exist in it. And for this reason they incur the hatred of the world, and participate in Jesus' own fate (15:18-21). The suffering which they must bear is a necessary corollary of their belonging to Jesus; therefore it is the beginning of that joy which, since it does not derive from the world, lasts for ever (16:21f).

Bibliography: On B: S. Büchler, *Studies in Sin and Atonement*, London 1922; SB II, 274–82; *TDNT* v, 617f; W. Wichmann, *Die Leidenstheologie*, Stuttgart 1930.
   On C: A. Juncker, *Jesus und das Leid*, Berlin 1925; R. Liechtenhan, 'Die Überwindung des Leidens bei Paulus und in der zeitgenössischen Stoa', *ZTK* 3 (1922), 368–99; J. Schneider, *Die Passionsmystik des Paulus*, Leipzig 1929; A. Wikenhauser, *Die Christusmystik des Apostels Paulus*, Freiburg 1956²; K. H. Schelkle, *Die Passion Jesu in der Verkündigung des NT*, Heidelberg 1949; Bultmann (see Index); *TDNT* IV, 313–27; *RGG* III², 1563–5; J. Coste, 'Notion grecque et notion biblique de la souffrance éducatrice', *RSR* 43 (1955), 481–523; E. F. Sutcliffe, *Providence and Suffering in the Old and New Testament*, Edinburgh 1955; J. Carmignac, 'La théologie de la souffrance dans les hymnes de Qumran', *RQ* 3 (1961/2), 365–86; *RGG* IV³, 297–300.

Josef Schmid

Taking up

References to bodily 'taking up' or ascension into heaven are to be found in the Old Testament where they are expressed by means of the technical term *lāqaḥ*.

1. According to the early passage of Gen 5:23 (P), after 365 years (one for each day of the solar year) Enoch, the seventh (the number of perfection, fullness) of the antediluvian patriarchs, was taken away (*lāqaḥ*) by God by reason of the holiness of his life. What is this 'taking away' or 'up' intended to convey? Probably the primary intention of the priestly writer is to emphasise that the prophet of cosmic religion (Jude 14) could not fall

victim to the penalty of the flood. This is why God took him to himself. Does this mean, then, that it was by a death that was in some sense premature? When he died he would not yet have attained the great age of the rest of the patriarchs. Nevertheless the fact that the years of his life were so immense in number was regarded in ancient times as a special sign of divine favour. It is only in the last century BC that death at an early age is ascribed to God's special favour (see Wis 4:7–20). Others envisage a physical taking up to heaven, so that Enoch would have provided a type of the resurrection and ascension of Jesus Christ. But until the resurrection of Christ heaven remained closed to unredeemed mankind (see Mt 27:52f). Medieval theologians, therefore, thought that it was a 'taking up' into paradise that was meant (this idea is already to be found in Jub 4:23; see also Gen 2:15). Others contend that the phrase signifies an 'ecstasy'.

Surely, however, the literary form in which the description is couched points in another direction. According to the Epic of Gilgamesh the hero Utnapishtim is taken up (*leqû*) by the gods together with his wife, and is admitted to their fellowship (Gressmann, *AOT* I, 1908, 55). The biblical author must have adapted this mythological idea to his monotheistic beliefs. After a life of great holiness Enoch would have been admitted into blessed fellowship with God without descending into Sheol, where man had to endure a diminished and shadowy form of existence far from God. But the sacred author does not go into any closer detail as to the manner in which this would have taken place.

897

However this may be, the mysterious fate of Enoch gave rise to an immense wealth of speculation in the literature of later judaism, eg, Sir 44:16; Wis 4:10f. In addition to the references here, which are relatively sober in character, the figure of Enoch became the centre of a whole group of legends in the apocrypha, and traces of these legends have survived in the New Testament as well. In Enoch (Eth)—from the first half of the first century BC—the 'taking up' of the patriarch does seem to approximate to an 'ecstasy' similar to that in which Paul was 'caught up' into the third heaven (2 Cor 12:2). In the course of his ecstasy Enoch is inaugurated in the mysteries of the heavenly cosmology and the plans of God (Enoch (Eth) 14:8–11, 70–71). Enoch (Slav), from the first century AD, describes the taking up of Enoch and his journey through the seven heavens, the purpose of which is that he may live there for ever (1–21; 22:4–10; 23:6; 33:8f; 47:2; 48:6; 50:4; 68:2; Jub 10:13. See *TDNT* II, 554f).

In the New Testament Heb 11:5 repeats ideas which have often been expressed in Enoch (Eth) and in Jub 10:17. Jude 14 appears to be taken word for word from Enoch (Eth) (60:8).

2. *Elijah* is separated from his disciple by a fiery chariot, and taken up (*lāqaḥ*) to heaven in a tempest (2 Kings 2:3, 5, 11). This too has been taken as referring to an 'ecstasy'. According to the context, however, this was the occasion on which Elijah bade farewell to Elisha for ever. Henceforward he no longer appears on the scene. The ancient tradition is that this great zealot for Yahweh's cause, like Enoch, escaped the fate of descending into Sheol and instead went straight to God. The fiery horses and the fiery chariot, like the pillar of fire at the Exodus and other examples, served merely to symbolise the fact that God was present in a special sense. According to the ancient popular conception the place for a man of such outstanding quality could only be close to God.

This background of mystery and the prophecy of the return of the prophet after he had been taken up (Mal 3:23f = LXX 4:4f) were still arousing lively interest in later times (see Sir 48:9, 12; 1 Macc 2:58; Enoch (Eth) 89:52; 93:8; Josephus, *Antiq.* 9:28) among the Jews of the New Testament period (Mt 16:14 and parallels; Mt 17:10–13 = Mk 9:11–13; Mt 27:47–9 = Mk 15:35–6; Lk 9:8 = Mk 6:15; Jn 1:25). According to Mt 17:12 the return of Elijah before the day of judgement as foretold in Mal 3:23 is probably to be understood, not in the sense that Elijah was to return in person, but rather of the advent of a man in the spirit and power of Elijah. Late judaism added further details to the miracle story. From the fact that Elijah was 'taken up' it was deduced that he was without sin. He was elevated to angelic status, and regarded as an intercessor for Israel, the friend of the poor and the deliverer of the oppressed. No less than three late apocalypses of Elijah were in circulation (see Haag 380f).

3. In the fourth of the 'Servant of Yahweh' poems we are told that after his atoning suffering on behalf of others this mysterious figure was 'taken up' (*lāqaḥ*) (Is 53:8), probably in glory to

God like Enoch and Elijah: 'By reason of his sufferings he shall look upon the light' (Is 53:11), ie, experience resurrection and glorification in his own body.

Thus the biblical concept of 'taking up' contained within itself, however obscurely, the germ of belief in the resurrection and ascension. A similar idea is to be found in two of the psalms. The pious suppliant hopes to be 'taken up' from his state of dire need into glory by means of an extraordinary intervention on the part of God: 'But God will ransom my soul from the power of Sheol. For he will take me up (*lāqaḥ*)' (Ps 49:15). 'Thou dost guide me with thy counsel and afterwards thou wilt take me up (*lāqaḥ*) into thy glory' (Ps 73:24). This hope, faint echoes of which are to be discerned in the ancient texts and the two psalm passages (see von Rad 1, 406f), is developed further in the post-exilic period (see Ezek 37:1–14; Is 26:19; Dan 12:2–3; 2 Macc 7:9, 11, 14, 23).

In this sense the ancient idea of 'taking up' remotely foreshadows and prepares for the ascension of Christ into heaven, the climactic event of salvation history.

Bibliography: Apart from the commentaries on Genesis and 2 Kings, see esp.: W. Bousset, 'Himmelsreise der Seele', *ARW* 4 (1901), 136–69 and 229–73; P. Billerbeck, 'Der Prophet Elias nach seiner Entrückung aus dem Diesseits', *Nathanael* 30 (1914), 43ff, 93ff, and 112ff; H. Bietenhard, *Die himmlische Welt in Urchristentum und Spätjudentum*, 1951; W. Reiser, 'Eschatologische Gottessprüche in den Elisa-Legenden', *TZ* 9 (1953), 327–38; J. Daniélou, *Holy Pagans in the OT*, London 1956, 45–59; *Elie le Prophète* I–II (*Etudes Carmélitaines*), Bruges 1956; K. Galling, 'Der Ehrenname Elisas und die Entrückung Elias', *ZTK* 53 (1956), 129–48; J. Steinmann, *Le prophétisme biblique des origines à Osée*, Paris 1959, 112–15; *TDNT* II, 556–60 and 928–41; Haag 380f, 399, and 688f; *RGG* II³, 424–7; *RGG* III³, 934f; *LTK* III², 905 and 806–10; *EKL* II, 159f; SB IV, 764–98.

Robert Koch

Temple

As with all religions, so too in the Old Testament the cult, the external worship paid to God, and the place of cult are located where this worship is manifested to the divinity, and where it hearkens to the believers and, at least during the actual cultic ceremonies, is thought to be present in a special way. The choice of the sanctuary does not depend upon human caprice, but is determined by God, who manifests himself to man for the purpose (Ex 20:24; Judg 6:24–6; 2 Sam 24:16–25). This place is sacred, and must be respected as such by man (Ex 3:5). The Old Testament traditions have preserved the memory of various shrines from the time of the patriarchs: Shechem (Gen 12:6f; 33:18–20), Bethel (Gen 12:8; 28:10–22), Mamre (Gen 13:18), and Beer-sheba (Gen 21:33; 26:23–5; 46:1–4). The sacred tabernacle employed during the sojourn in the wilderness is represented as conforming to the pattern of the Jerusalem temple (Ex 25:16; 40:20). It was used for Moses to speak with God (Ex 32:11), and for the encounter of God with Moses and the people (Ex 29:42f; 30:36). Before the temple was built at Jerusalem there were shrines at Gilgal (Josh 4:19), Shiloh (Josh 18:1; 21:2), Mizpah (1 Sam 7:5–12), Gibeon (2 Sam 21:1–14), Ophrah (Judges 6:11–32), and Dan (Judg 17–18).

The building of the temple of Solomon at Jerusalem was completed in the tenth century (1 Kings 6f). David had paved the way for this by transferring the ark to Jerusalem (2 Sam 6) and by the building of an altar there (2 Sam 24:16–25). The temple was built on the rocky outcrop at the north of the Ophel (2 Chron 3:1), where at a later date the temples of Zerubbabel and Herod were also built. It consisted of a vestibule (*'ûlām, 'êlām*: 1 Kings 6:3; 7:19), the Holy Place (*Hêkāl* = the principal division of the temple: 1 Kings 6:3), and the Holy of Holies (*Debîr*: 1 Kings 6:5, 19–23, also called *qōḏeš qadašîm*). In front of the entrance to the temple were placed two bronze pillars (1 Kings 7:15–22, 41f), which are reminiscent of the steles which stood before the ancient Canaanite sanctuaries. The names by which they were called, *Jākîn* (= 'he erects') and *Bō'az* (= 'with power') suggests that they were built after the model of the Egyptian Jed pillar, a symbol of permanence (of temple and dynasty) familiar throughout the ancient Near East at that time. In the forecourt were placed the altar of whole burnt offerings (2 Kings 16:14), the 'bronze sea' (1 Kings 7:23–6), and the ten lavers (1 Kings 7:27–39). In the Holy Place stood the altar of incense (1 Kings 6:20f), the table of shewbread and the ten lamps (1 Kings 7:48f). The Holy of Holies where the ark was enshrined (1 Kings 6:23–8) was separated from the Holy Place by a dividing wall of wood with a door to which five steps led up, and which corresponded to the 'thin walls' of Ezek 41:3, and the veil of the tabernacle (Ex 26:33) or in the temple of Herod (Josephus, *Bell.* v,

5, 5). In comparison with non-biblical temples this temple does exhibit certain similarities in detail, but there are differences also. The similarities are to be explained by the sacral architecture which was general at that time, and by the fact that non-Israelite builders were engaged for the work (1 Kings 5:6, 18). In the Assyrian temple there was no dividing wall separating the Holy Place from the Holy of Holies, so that the cultic image which stood upon the podium (Holy of Holies) was constantly visible. Unlike the immense temple tower at Babylon, which was likewise divided into three parts, the Holy of Holies did not constitute a temple situated at the summit.

Since the temple was built and maintained by the kings (1 Kings 15:15; 2 Kings 12:19; 15:35; 16:10–18), it was a royal sanctuary (Amos 7:13), but it was also essentially more than that, because David had intended a house for Yahweh (2 Sam 7:1f), and Solomon actually did build this and, together with all Israel, consecrated it (1 Kings 8:1–5, 13, 62–6).

The temple of Solomon was destroyed in 587 BC, and its equipment was carried off to Babylon (2 Kings 25:13–17; Jer 52:17–23). In the exile Ezekiel had his vision of a new temple (Ezek 40:1–44:9). This was not in fact ever realised in practice, but the prophet had known the temple of Solomon, and he ascribed the same proportions to his visionary temple, so that his description of it could have influenced both Zerubbabel and Herod. After the exile, under Sheshbazzar (Ezra 5:16), the rebuilding of the temple began, and it was completed under Zerubbabel in 515 (Ezra 4:24–5:2; Hag 1:1–2, 9;

Zech 4:7–10). The temple of Herod was begun in 20 BC and completed in all essentials ten years later. The building may not have been wholly completed, however, right up to the time of the destruction of Jerusalem in AD 70.

The temple of Solomon was the religious centre of Israel and continued to be so even after the division into two kingdoms, in spite of the schismatic sanctuaries of the northern kingdom at Dan and Bethel (see 1 Kings 11:32). After the ark of the covenant had been brought into the temple God took possession of it as his house, and the cloud filled the temple (1 King 8:10). It is recognised that a cloud is repeatedly mentioned as a type and symbol of the presence of God (see Ex 33:9; 40:34f; Num 12:4–10; Is 6:1–4; Dan 7:13; Mt 24:30; 17:5; Acts 1:9; 1 Thess 4:17), and the darkness in the Holy of Holies was also intended to recall this (1 Kings 8:12). The temple as the dwelling place of God for all eternity (1 Kings 8:13), combined with faith in the special presence of God in the temple, constitutes the basis for the temple cult and the honouring of the temple on the part of the believers (see Ps 27:4; 42:4; 76:2; 84; 122:1–4; etc). In spite of their alleged hostility to the cult the prophets shared this conception (see Amos 1:2). From the time of Isaiah onwards the name 'Zion' has a religious significance, for by reason of the temple it is the 'mountain of Yahweh' (Is 2:2; etc; ↗ mountain), the 'glorious throne' of Yahweh (Jer 14:21). Admittedly the prophets preached that the presence of Yahweh in the midst of his people is a free gift of grace which can be forfeited by the people's own unfaithfulness (Jer 7:1–

15; 26:1–15). Ezekiel saw the withdrawal of God's glory from the temple, which was profaned by sin (Ezek 8–10), but the Lord will return to a new temple in order to have his throne in the midst of the children of Israel for ever (Ezek 43:1–12). The idea that the temple is Yahweh's dwelling-place was also the principal motive which hastened the rebuilding of the temple after the Exile (Zech 2:13; 8:3).

This conception of the presence of God in the temple led, however, to theological difficulties. If Yahweh utters his voice from Zion (Amos 1:2; Is 2:3 = Mic 4:2) his presence still appears to be in some way connected with the material temple. How can the transcendence of the cosmic Lord be reconciled with his historical presence in Israel? The Deuteronomist editor of the Books of Kings puts this question on the lips of Solomon (1 Kings 8:27), and as the solution to it he lays down that the believer prays in the temple and Yahweh hears him in heaven (1 Kings 8:30–40). In other words, if we follow the meaning of the Deuteronomist way of putting the matter, the idea of the presence of God is mitigated to the extent that it is the 'name of Yahweh' which dwells here (1 Kings 8:17, 29; see also Deut 12:11; 14:23; 16:2, 6, 11; 26:2; Jer 7:12). Since the name represents the personality of its bearer, the presence of the 'name of Yahweh' means that God is present in a special sense. This theological speculation arrives at its logical conclusion in the conception of the *shekinah* in judaism, the idea that God is graciously present in the midst of Israel without his character as transcendent being thereby impugned.

The temple is above all a sign of the free and gracious election of God, who has himself designated the site for the temple by means of a theophany (2 Sam 24:16; 2 Chron 3:1), and thereby has chosen his dwelling-place (Ps 68:17; 76:2; 78:68; 132:13; Deut 12:5). In this connection the election of David and the endurance of his dynasty are often set in parallelism (see 1 Kings 8:16; 11:13, 32; 2 Chron 6:5f). The unexpected raising of the siege of Jerusalem by Sennacherib in the year 701 BC was greeted as an historical ratification of the promises of God (2 Kings 19:34; Is 37:35), and an unshakeable trust emerged in the inviolability of the temple (Jer 7:4). After the people's faith had been put severely to the test in the year 587, faith still arose once more during the post-exilic period in a new election of Jerusalem as the dwelling-place of the 'name of Yahweh' (Neh 1:9; Zech 1:17; 2:12; 3:2).

Under the influence of hellenism Jewish thinkers, in a manner similar to many of the fathers of the church and theologians of the Middle Ages, sought to discover a cosmic symbolism in the temple. Now it is true that the temple was built after the pattern of temples not mentioned in the bible which belonged to non-Israelite peoples. These, therefore, could have had symbolic meanings in mind when they built it, but this cannot be proved, and still less can it be shown that Israel would have known of these symbolic meanings and would have taken them over. Nowhere in the biblical text do we find mention of the temple having a cosmic significance, or of any intention to make the three divisions of the temple correspond to the three cosmic spheres (heaven, earth, underworld), or of the bronze pillars being connected with the sun and the moon, or the lamps with the five planets, or the lavers with rain-clouds, or the 'bronze sea' with the primordial ocean and more alleged correspondences of the same kind. Only the darkness in the Holy of Holies has a symbolism, but this is stated in the text, and is not cosmic in character, for the darkness symbolises the cloud with which God veiled his presence (1 Kings 8:12). Obviously the temple did have a symbolic significance, but one which can be deduced not from myths, but only from the history of the Old Testament. Just as the great cultic festivals recalled the liberation from the Egyptian bondage, and as the ark of the covenant recalled the covenant of God with his people, so too the temple constituted a token of the election of Jerusalem and of the Davidic dynasty by Yahweh.

The prophets had a positive attitude towards the temple, but resisted any over-emphasis on the cult of the temple at the expense of religious morality. When Nathan explains that in earlier times Yahweh neither possessed a house nor required one (2 Sam 7:5-7), this did not mean that the building was to be postponed until the time of Solomon —as the gloss to 2 Sam 7:13 and the redactor of 1 Kings 5:5 suggest—but that he absolutely refused to have a temple. In fact the building of a temple seemed to many Israelites tantamount to a breaking of faith with the bridal time of Israel in the wilderness, and a concession to pagan forms of cult. Moreover this negative attitude to the temple continued to survive even later, even if it was not always apparent on the surface. After the exile there were protests against the rebuilding of the temple on the grounds that Yahweh had no need of any temple (Is 66:1). Stephen too refers explicitly to this (Acts 7:48). When Jesus utters the prediction of the destruction of the temple and the rebuilding of another temple not built with human hands, (Mk 14:58) the material temple is transformed into a spiritual one; the living stones of this spiritual temple are the members of the New Testament people of God (1 Pet 2:4f), who are firmly knit together through Christ as their cornerstone (Eph 2:20–22). As *verbum incarnatum* he *is* the presence of God for ever, and it is through him that salvation is mediated. ⁊ Cult.

Bibliography: K. Galling, 'Das Allerheiligste in Salomons Tempel', *JPOS* 12 (1932), 43–6; W. F. Albright, *Archeology and the Religion of Israel*, Baltimore 1942, 142–55; J. Daniélou, *Le Signe du Temple ou de la Présence de Dieu*, Paris 1942; J. Daniélou, 'Le symbolisme cosmique du Temple de Jérusalem', *Symbolisme cosmique et Monuments religieux*, Paris 1953, 61–4; M. Schmidt, *Prophet und Tempel. Eine Studie zum Problem der Gottesnähe im AT*, Zollikon–Zürich 1948; A. Parrot, *Le Temple de Jérusalem*, Neuchâtel–Paris 1954; L. H. Vincent and A. M. Steve, *Jérusalem de l'AT* II–III, Paris 1956, 373–610; L. H. Vincent, 'Le caractère du Temple de Salomon', *Mélanges A. Robert*, Paris 1957, 137–48; S. Yeivin, 'Jachin and Boaz', *Eretz-Israel* 5 (1958), 97–104; E. L. Ehrlich, *Die Kultsymbolik im AT und im nachbiblischen Judentum*, Stuttgart 1959, 24–33; W. Kornfeld, 'Der Symbolismus der Tempelsäulen', *ZAW* 74 (1962), 50–57; de Vaux, 312–440.

Walter Kornfeld

Temptation

A. *The Old Testament*. The verbs *nāsâh*, *peiran*, and *peirazein*, 'to make an attempt, have experience of' etc (see 1 Sam 17:39; Eccles 7:23; Wis 2:24; etc), 'to prove, test' (1 Kings 10:1; Dan 1:12, 14; etc), are used in the profane sense, but they can also have a religious meaning, and it is this that is primary in the biblical usage. As used in this sense they can have either God or Satan or man himself as their subject.

1. The classic example is the temptation of Abraham (Gen 22:1–19). The result of this is expressed in v 12: 'Now I (God) know that you fear God'. By the use of his free will in taking a decision (⁊ freedom) the man proves himself to be godfearing, obedient to God. In exactly the same way God also puts the entire people to the test (Ex 15:25f; 16:4; 20:20; Deut 8:2; Judg 2:22) as to whether they keep his commandments, do not fall into pagan practices etc. This testing is part of his work of salvation, for his commandments are designed to show the way by which salvation can be attained.

2. This continues to be the basic purpose of testing even in cases in which (in later passages) ⁊ Satan appears as the tester or tempter, as in Gen 3:1–19; 4:1–16(?) or in the narrative framework of the Book of Job. This precise point is illustrated in Gen 4:7 in the words which God addresses to Cain: 'If you do well, you will be accepted, and if you do not do well, sin is couching at the door. . . .' Cain's testing consists in the fact that God, by a free decision of his will (see Ex 33:19), accepts Abel's offering, but refuses Cain's—no reason is assigned in the text for God acting thus—whatever the circumstances may be in which this has been made known

(perhaps in the success or lack of attained by the two brothers respectively).

In the Wisdom books Abraham is held up as an example of how to behave in temptation (Sir 44:20; see also Judith 8:25f; 1 Macc 2:52), although here (see especially Sir 2:1; 4:17; 33:1; Wis 3:5f) the idea of educating also has a part to play. God disciplines (↗ discipline) and educates man through ↗ suffering. This idea, characteristic of the Wisdom literature, also occurs in Philo, although in his case, as also in that of Josephus, the word *peirasmos* is not used. *nāsâh* is also absent from the Qumran texts, even though the reality being treated of there is testing or tempting. The 'sons of darkness' seek to lead the 'sons of light' into apostasy (1 QM), the angel of darkness and his wicked spirits strive to seduce the just (1 QS 3:21–5; 4:15–18; cp CD 14:5).

3. Man 'tempts' God when he doubts his will to save or his power to deliver. Wis 1:2: 'He is to be found by those who do not put him to the test, and shows himself to those who do not distrust him' (see Ex 17:1–7; Num 14; Ps 78:17f, 40f; 95:8f; 106:14; Is 7:12). The requirement not to tempt God (Deut 6:16f; Sir 18:23) is a requirement to exercise ↗ faith. The New Testament too recognises this kind of culpable want of faith and disobedience (compare 1 Cor 10:9 with Ps 78:18, and Heb 3:8f with Ps 95:8f), which constitute rebellion against God and incur severe punishment (Acts 5:9; 15:10).

B. *The New Testament.* 1. *peirasmos* is that alien factor in man's life by which he is brought into a state of wavering and instability so that he has already almost fallen into the power of the evil one. We do not often find it stated who brings this about. In Jas 1:13 objections are raised against describing God as tempter (in order to make him responsible for one's own sins). In Paul the 'tempter' is Satan (1 Thess 3:5; cp 1 Cor 7:5), as also in the saying of Jesus about Peter being 'sifted as wheat' (Lk 22:31). In 1 Cor 10:13 we find a reference to 'human temptation', that is, to one which human nature is able to endure. Clearly there is also one in which fall and sin are already implicitly present. As used in this sense it must be said that 'God himself tempts no man' (Jas 1:13), ie, he does not *seduce* anyone (into sin). The admonition to 'take heed to yourself lest you are led astray' in Gal 6:1 has the same basic meaning, and there is a parallel passage to this in 1 Cor 10:12: 'Let anyone who thinks that he stands take heed lest he fall'. Again, Mt 6:13 (Lk 11:4) is not a prayer for total immunity from temptation, but a cry for help in case of attack. It represents a negative formulation of the same idea which is expressed positively in the second half of the verse (parallelism): 'Deliver us from evil', ie, from the power of Satan. (The phrase *apo tou ponērou* is masculine and should be taken as referring to the evil one, see J. B. Bauer, *VD* 34 [1956], 12–15). The English words *tempt* and *temptation* are still too neutral in import. Like our term *seduce*, the New Testament word sometimes, as in the passages referred to above, of itself carries the implication of the evil outcome (precisely as opposed to any possible good outcome) of the temptation.

2. The ⁊ sufferings which christians must take upon themselves for Christ's sake are also called *peirasmoi*. Since these are, basically, tests of faith and constancy one should actually rejoice at them (Jas 1:2f, 12; 1 Pet 1:6; 4:12f, 17). Rev 3:10 and 2:10 contain references to the eschatological affliction, in which the devil makes special efforts to lead the faithful into apostasy. In this connection also we may mention the references to Jesus being tempted in Heb 2:18; 4:15. These are to be related not to the temptation stories in the synoptics, but (as can be seen from Heb 5:7–9) to the terrible sufferings of Gethsemane. He became 'in every respect tempted as we are' (Heb 4:15; cf Lk 22:28), ie, he endured all the sufferings which men have to endure (cf Lk 22:28), but without sin.

Sufferings do indeed constitute 'temptation' in that they can become the occasion of unbelief and lack of trust (as in the case of Cain); but they can also, as in the case of Job, become the occasion of boundless trust in God; see Heb 5:8, of Jesus.

At this point too it may be appropriate to recall a non-biblical saying attributed to Jesus: 'No-one can attain to the kingdom of heaven without being tempted' (Tertullian, *De baptismate* 20). See, too, Lk 24:26, in which *edei* (lit. = 'it was necessary') as used of Christ's sufferings is to be understood as implying, not that these constituted his unavoidable lot, but rather that they represented the task which God had laid upon him (see E. Fascher, *BZNW* 21 [1954], 228–54). See also Lk 22:28f (and on this again NmRabbah 15 [179a], SB 1, 136, and Ex Rabbah 31 [91c], SB 1, 822).

3. The temptation of Jesus (Mk 1:12f; Mt 4:1–11; Lk 4:1–13) is a repetition of the temptation of the chosen people in the wilderness. The Messiah must, as it were, undergo once more the great experiences of the history of Israel, must undertake these once more, and so bring that history to its consummation. Jesus emerges victorious from those temptations to which Israel succumbed in the wilderness, applying to himself certain readings from Deuteronomy (Mt 4:4; cf Deut 8:3; Mt 4:10; see also Deut 6:13). The essential significance of the temptation stories of Jesus is that they show: (a) that Jesus is the Son of God in that sense in which the title had been applied to him just before at his baptism; and therefore (b) not in the sense expected by his contemporaries. He remains true to the mission laid upon him by God in spite of the seductive ideas of a temporal and worldly messianism suggested to him by Satan (⁊ scandal, ⁊ sin B 1).

Bibliography: H. Seesemann, *TDNT* VI, 23–36; E. Lohmeyer, *Das Vaterunser*, Göttingen 1946, chapters 8f; K. G. Kühn, *ZTK* 49 (1952), 200–22; S. Lyonnet, *Bbl* 39 (1958), 27–36. On A2: M. Buber, *TZ* 7 (1951); J. B. Bauer, *Die Biblische Urgeschichte*, Paderborn 1956, 37–54; J. B. Bauer, *TPQ* 103 (1955), 126–33; J. B. Bauer, *Der Seelsorger* 24 (Vienna 1954), 226–9 and 328–30. On Qumran: K. Schubert, *TLZ* 78 (1953), 495–506; Nötscher, esp. 82f and 171–4. On B2: W. Nauck, *ZNW* 46 (1955), 68–80. On B3: R. Schnackenburg, *TQ* 132 (1952), 297–326; J. Dupont, *NTS* 3 (1957), 287–304; J. Guillet, *Leitgedanken der Bibel*, Lucerne 1954, 26–8; M. J. Sykes, *Expository Times* (1961/2), 189f.

Johannes B. Bauer

Thanksgiving

In the bible far more references are to be found to thankfulness towards God than to thankfulness towards men. Indeed, in the New Testament, the only instances of the latter are in Acts 24:3 —the words of one who is not a christian—and Rom 16:4. The thought of the bible is theocentric, and thanksgiving is the response to the freely offered gifts of God. In the Old Testament, thanksgiving towards God is expressed in the praises offered to him. Hebrew has no special word for thankfulness and thanksgiving, but expresses these periphrastically by the verbs 'to praise' and 'to glorify' (*yādâh, tôḏâh*: see P. Joüon, 'Reconnaissance et action des grâces dans le NT', *ETL* 29 [1939], 112–14). Israel expresses its thanks in the form of thank-offerings (Amos 4:5; Jer 17:26; 33:11; Ps 56:12; 100:4), and in psalms of thanksgiving (Ex 15:21; Ps 48; 66; 118; 124; 135). Some of these psalms were sung as accompaniments to thank-offerings (100:1; 50:14, 23; 107:22), others betray their cultic origin by the fact that they are designed to be sung by cantor and choir or by two choirs (Ps 107; 135).

In the later books of LXX the word-group *eukharistein, eukharistia* was introduced (Judith 8:25; then Esther 8:12; 2 Macc 1:11; 2:27; 10:7; Wis 18:2). Philo ascribes the greatest significance to *eukharistein*. For him thanksgiving is the highest form of honour paid to God, the highest virtue, an effect produced by God in the soul (see P. Schubert, 122–31). In the New Testament the word-group occurs only in authors affected by hellenistic influence (in Luke twice, Acts twice, Paul thirty-four times, John once, Revelation three times—never in the synoptics or the catholic epistles). Paul is not the creator of the word-group in the New Testament field. It was already established among the Greek-speaking Jews. Apart from brief interjections (Rom 1:25; 9:5; 2 Cor 11:31), only two of his prayers begin with the Jewish expression of praise 'Blessed be God' (2 Cor 1:3; Eph 1:3).

Jesus expresses his thanksgiving by praising his Father (Mt 11:25; Lk 10:21: *exhomologoumai*). Zechariah, too, begins his canticle in the manner of the Old Testament (Lk 1:68; see Lk 1:46–55; 2:29–32). Luke records that one of the ten lepers whom Jesus had healed returned and 'thanked' Jesus. Jesus expected this thanksgiving, and expressed his sorrow that only this single one had 'given honour to God' (Lk 17:18). The one who did so return was a foreigner (Samaritan). Acknowledgement, praise, and thanksgiving to God for benefits received is the most elemental and basic of religious acts. Lk 6:35 replaces 'the just and the unjust' (Mt 5:45) by 'the ungrateful and the selfish'. The prayer of thanksgiving becomes merely external and formal unless the attitude of thankfulness directs one's vision away from oneself to God. The self-righteous prayer of thanksgiving of the Pharisee in the temple becomes an obstacle to repentance and true righteousness (Lk 18:11). John says that Jesus 'thanked his Father for having heard him when he was preparing to raise Lazarus to life' (11:41).

'Thanksgiving' is a characteristic feature of the accounts of the institution of the eucharist: Mt 26:27; Mk 14:23

(Lk 22:17); Lk 22:19; 1 Cor 11:24, whereas the expression used in Mt 26:26; Mk 14:22 (see also 1 Cor 10:16) is 'to pronounce a blessing' (*eulogein*). According to the custom of his people, Jesus said the grace before and after the meal (*eulogēsen*: Mt 14:19; Mk 6:41; Lk 9:16; Mk 8:7 [the multiplication of loaves]; Lk 24:30; *eukharistēsas*: Mt 15:36; Mk 8:6; Jn 6:11, 23 [the multiplication of loaves]; Acts 27:35). The fact that the original *eulogein* ('to pronounce a blessing') has been replaced by *eukharistein* ('to give thanks') in the institution passages would have been due, not to the hellenising of the earlier word *eulogein*, but to the fact that it represents ancient 'eucharistic' terminology. Probably in his prayer over the third cup Jesus had already departed from Jewish custom in respect of form and content alike (see Mt 14:19 and parallels: 'to lift up the eyes', which was not a Jewish custom; Lk 24:30). Jesus would have been thinking with thankfulness of God's deeds of salvation of the New Testament era (see the interpretative elements). Following Jesus' example the apostolic communities were able to use at the celebration of the Eucharist a form of thanksgiving which was free and christologically motivated in place of the Jewish thanksgiving formula. Thus by reason of the special character of the eucharistic prayer of christians the eucharistic act comes to be designated as *eukharistia* at a very early stage. The episodes in the New Testament in which meals are described (such as the multiplication of loaves) became heavily coloured with this eucharistic terminology (see Meinertz 1, 132; H. Schürmann, *Der Paschamahlbericht Lk 22:[7–14], 15–18*

[*NA* 19/5], Münster 1953, 53–60). In Did 9:1–5; 10:1–4; Justin Dial 41:1; 70:4; Apol 1 65:5; 66:1f; Ignatius, *Eph* 13:1; *Smyr* 8:1, in which the prayer recited, the action performed, and the sacramental elements employed at the Lord's Supper are together called ↗ 'eucharist', the subject of thanksgiving is the mighty deeds of God, and it renders these present, so that at a very early stage it may have come to be thought of as a suitable form of *anamnēsis* (J. Betz, 158f). In the pauline communities the 'thanksgiving' in the liturgy is directed to be acclaimed by the members responding 'Amen' to it (1 Cor 14:16f; Just, *Apol* 1 65:3; see *TDNT* 1, 337). Such thanksgiving (also found in 1 Thess 5:18; Eph 5:20; Col 4:2; 3:16; 1 Tim 2:1–4) found expression in 'psalms, hymns, and spiritual canticles' (Eph 5:19f; see H. Schlier, *Der Brief an die Epheser*, Düsseldorf 1957, 246–50). Col 1:12–22 must represent a fragment of a liturgical eucharistia (G. Harder, 38ff). The celestial hymns recorded in Revelation are an echo of the eucharistic prayers of thanksgiving (Rev 4:9–11; 11:17; see also 5:9f, 12f; 7:12).

The apostle and theologian of thanksgiving is Paul. He adopts the epistolary form customary in the hellenistic world (see 2 Macc 1:11; A. Deissmann, *Licht vom Osten*, 145–50), but almost always—with the exception of Galatians, 1 Timothy, and Titus—inserts an expression of thanksgiving to God after the prescript (Rom 1:8f; 1 Cor 1:4–6 (2 Cor 1:3–4); Eph 1:15f; Phil 1:3–5; Col 1:3; 1 Thess 1:2–4; 2 Thess 1:3; Philem 4f; 2 Tim 1:3). The prescript has a special structure of its own: (a) an allusion to Paul's prayer on behalf of the recipient; (b) commendation of the community (2 Cor 1:2); (c) the thanksgiving formula; and (d) a transition to the eschatological perspective (1 Cor 1:4–9; Phil 1:3–11; Col 1:3–23; 1 Thess 1:2–4; 2 Thess 1:2–10). For Paul these introductions to his letters are not mere formal expressions of courtesy: rather, they are genuine prayers of thanksgiving. (This element emerges in a particularly cordial form in Philippians.) At the same time they represent a *captatio benevolentiae* in which Paul expresses his praise and appreciation of the communities, and so of God for having made them worthy of praise.

Thanksgiving is a duty. It is God's will in Christ Jesus that we should be thankful in all circumstances (1 Thess 5:18). To give 'honour and thanks' to God is among the basic acts by which we acknowledge God and show our devotion to him (Rom 1:21). Ingratitude is the vice characteristic of men in the last days (2 Tim 3:2). Just as *eulogein* (to praise or bless) is man's response to God's *eulogia* (blessing), so too *kharis, eukharistia* (thanksgiving) is his response to the *kharis* (grace or gracious gift) of God. *kharis* (in the sense of the grace of vocation to the apostolate) must bear fruit in the *eukharistia* (thanksgiving) of those who have been converted by the apostle (2 Cor 4:15). In thanksgiving God is given back what he himself has bestowed (1 Thess 3:9). Paul does not wish to be alone in giving thanks for the charisma of his redemption. Rather, many individuals must join in expressing this prayer of thanks; a choir of thanksgiving must proclaim God's praise (2 Cor 1:11).

Thankfulness is a motive for ethical conduct. The underlying motive of Paul's apostolic work is that the thanksgiving of men may overflow more and more to the glory of God (2 Cor 4:15). Apostolic grace (here personified) seeks constantly to extend its sphere of influence. The ultimate goal of this activity is that God shall be glorified. The medium of expression in which the first of these, apostolic grace, becomes fruitful in the second, the glorification of God, is that chorus of thanksgiving which is sent up to God from the growing number of believers in the liturgical assemblies. Charity is to be practised in order that by the prayers of thanksgiving resulting from it God may be glorified (2 Cor 9:11). Through the apostle who has brought about the assembly the gift which the Corinthians give, and which itself is a gift of God, causes God to be glorified by thanksgiving. The collect has two effects: the relieving of need at Jerusalem, and the copious thanksgiving by which the recipients of it praise God. The second of these effects quite overshadows the first. The work of external and material succour ('liturgy') leads on to the further work of liturgical worship ('liturgy' also). There is no mention of thanks being given to men. Even where thankfulness to the human givers does appear, it is inseparably united to an awareness that behind all stands the surpassing ↗ grace of God (9:14). Through thanksgiving, activities which are indifferent in themselves become consecrated for the most exalted aim of life. This applies both to words and deeds (Col 3:17), and also to eating and drinking. Paul presupposes that the Christians say their grace in the manner strictly prescribed among the Jews. Once it has been pronounced the entire meal becomes an expression of divine praise (*TDNT* II, 760f). Paul treats of this grace as a prayer of thanksgiving (thus Rom 14:6; 1 Cor 10:30; 1 Tim 4:3f). He himself recites it also (Acts 27:35). It is through his prayer of thanksgiving that food and drink are consecrated. 'For everything created by God is good, and nothing is to be rejected if it is received with thanksgiving. For then it is consecrated by the word of God and prayer' (1 Tim 4:4f). It is by this attitude of thankfulness that the christian acquires his decisive orientation towards the glorifying of God (1 Cor 10:31). All that the christian says or does he shall do in the name of the Lord, in that through him he gives thanks to God the Father (Col 3:17). It is the prayer of thanksgiving that provides the criterion for deciding the questions of diet: the question which arose at Rome about the strong not giving scandal to the weak in this matter (Rom 14:6), the question of the Corinthians as to whether flesh offered to idols should be eaten (1 Cor 10:30), and the question of the dietary rules laid down by heretical teachers, against which 1 Timothy is directed (1 Tim 4:3f). Thanksgiving certainly does not exempt one from paying due heed to the conscience of the weak (1 Cor 10:29f; Rom 14:20).

Paul constantly exhorts his hearers to express their thanksgiving in act. They must do this in communal worship (1 Cor 14:6f; Eph 5:20; Col 1:12; 3:17; 1 Tim 2:1) as well as in private (2 Cor 4:15; 9:11f; 1:11; Phil 4:6; Col 2:7; 4:2; 1 Thess 5:18). Christians must not pray for themselves alone, but must offer thanksgiving and prayers on behalf of all men (1 Tim 2:1). At all times (Eph 5:20; 1 Thess 2:13) and in all things (1 Thess 5:18) thanksgiving must rise up to God. The christians are 'givers of thanks' (Col 3:17). Thanksgiving is of the very essence of the christian life. The christian must show himself 'abounding in thanksgiving' (Col 2:7) because the graces which he has received are likewise superabundant (2 Cor 9:14; 1 Tim 1:14; Eph 2:7; Phil 4:7; 2 Cor 7:4; Eph 3:19; 2 Cor 12:7; see also 2 Cor 1:5; 11:23). Prayers of petition must be constantly intermingled with thanksgiving (Phil 4:6; Col 4:2). The christian's conversation is to be characterised not by stupid chatter and unseemly levity, but by thanksgiving (Eph 5:4). Joy and thanksgiving go together (Col 1:12). Both have their basis in the gift of salvation. Paul himself is a man of thankfulness. He utters prayers of thanksgiving for himself (1 Tim 1:12) and for his communities (Rom 1:8; 1 Cor 1:4; Phil 1:3 [Philem 4]; Eph 1:16; Col 1:3; 1 Thess 1:2; 2:13; 3:9; 2 Thess 1:3; 2:13; 2 Tim 1:3). He does not know how to find an adequate expression of his thankfulness (1 Thess 3:9). Exclamations of thankfulness are interspersed through the text of his epistles (in these cases the word used for thanks is always *kharis*: Rom 7:25; 1 Cor 15:57; 2 Cor 2:14; 8:16; 9:15; see also 2 Ezra 7:17).

God's deeds of salvation constantly occupy the centre of Paul's thought. He gives thanks for ↗ faith, ↗ hope and ↗ love (Rom 1:8: faith; Eph 1:15; 2 Thess 1:3; Philem 4f: faith and love; 1 Thess 1:3: the works of faith, the self-sacrifice of love, the steadfastness of hope; 2:13: acceptance of the word of God in faith). Paul also gives thanks for the grace of God and the charisms (1 Cor 1:4–6), for joy over the believers (1 Thess 3:9), for redemption and the fruits of redemption (Col 1:12–23), for redemption from the body of death through Christ (Rom 7:25), for his fellow-workers (2 Tim 1:3), for the guidance of God in apostolic work (1 Cor 1:14), for the conquest of death (1 Cor 15:57), for the vocation to apostolic work (1 Tim 1:12), for rescue from danger of death, because thereby the apostle can go on to convert many more individuals (2 Cor 1:11), for triumph in his apostolic work (2 Cor 2:14), for the zeal of Titus (2 Cor 8:16), for the inexpressible gift which God gives to the Corinthians, and which urges them to the work of charity (2 Cor 9:15). The gifts for which Paul gives thanks pertain to eschatological salvation. The final age has no further need of the prayer of petition, but only recognises the jubilation of thanksgiving (Rev 4:9; 7:12; 11:17). The prayer of the new aeon is a prayer of thanksgiving (see G. Harder, 128f and 184).

Prayers of thanksgiving are as a rule directed to God: to God (1 Cor 1:4; 1 Thess 1:2; 2:13), to 'my God' (Rom 1:8; Phil 1:3; Philem 4), to God the Father (Col 1:12; 1 Thess 1:3), to God the Father of our Lord Jesus Christ (2 Cor 1:3; Eph 1:3; Col 1:3). The ultimate source of all gifts is God the Father. Only in one single passage is thanksgiving directed to Jesus Christ (1 Tim 1:12). Paul gives thanks for having been called to be an apostle, for this too he habitually ascribes to the Father. In this connection he takes occasion to emphasise that he, like the rest of the apostles, has been called by Christ. Prayers of thanksgiving are uttered 'through Christ' (Rom 1:8; Col 3:17). The 'pneumatic' Christ is the mediator of thanksgiving (Rom 1:8; Eph 5:20; see G. Harder, 173–84). Thanksgiving returns to God by the same way by which his grace to men went forth from him. Through Christ the christian must hope that he can give thanks to God fittingly. Christ represents the 'solution to the crisis in prayer of antiquity' (G. Harder, 187). The Ephesians are to thank God the Father 'in the name of our Lord Jesus Christ' (Eph 5:20). This formula (and this is the only passage in the New Testament in which it is connected with 'thanksgiving') often points to the context of cultic worship as the situation in which it arose (1 Cor 5:4; 6:11; Phil 2:10; Col 3:17; 2 Thess 3:6). Thanksgiving is to be offered by the community which has assembled in the name of Jesus, and which is his mouthpiece (H. Schlier, *Der Brief an die Epheser*, 249). In the name of Jesus the fullness of those divine gifts of grace for which christians must give thanks is summed up (*TDNT* v, 272f).

Bibliography: J. Wobbe, *Der Charisgedanke bei Paulus* (*NA* 13/3), Münster 1932; G. Harder, *Paulus und das Gebet*, Gütersloh 1936; J. M. Nielen, *Gebet und Gottesdienst im NT*, Freiburg 1937; P. Schubert 'Form and Function of the Pauline Thanksgivings', *BZNW* 20 (1939); E. Kalt, *BRL* 1, 354f; E. Mócsy, 'De gratiarum actione in epistolis paulinis', *VD* 21 (1941), 193–201 and 225–32; Osterloh 81f; J. Betz, *Die Eucharistie in der Zeit der griechischen Väter* 1/1, Freiburg 1955, 156–62; H. Schürmann, *LTK* III², 158f; C. Westermann, *BHHW* 1, 320–22; B. Rigaux, *Paulus und seine Briefe*, Munich 1964, 171f.

Alois Stöger

Three

A. A ceremonial declaration or legal formula is repeated *three times* before witnesses in order to bring a legal enactment formally into force. This is what took place at the purchase of the cave of Machpelah by Abraham (Gen 23). This is still the custom in Palestine for the drawing up of a marriage contract or at the declaration of a divorce in accordance with Islamic law. In a cultural milieu where memory and the oral pronouncements of men have to be relied upon instead of written contracts, the part played by this legal form becomes immediately comprehensible.

When Jesus tells Peter that he is to be the pastor of his people (Jn 21:15–17) he employs the same form of *threefold repetition* because his words have the force of just such a legal enactment. From this it is clear that Jesus did in fact found a church with legal norms, in that by a solemn act of handing over legal authority he gave it a visible representative of himself.

Likewise in the vision of Peter (Acts 10:10ff [see also 11:10]) the *threefold* repetition of the declaration that the unclean food was clean probably has a similar purpose, being a formal legal guarantee that this declaration of God had full force.

In this connection *thrice*-repeated prayer should perhaps be mentioned. In Mt 26:39–44 Jesus solemnly submits himself to the will of the Father *three times*. In 2 Cor 12:8 Paul declares that *three times* he besought God with tears to take the sting from his flesh, but that he received the answer (*three times*?): 'My grace is sufficient for you'.

B. Like the English phrase 'a couple of', *three* can stand for a small number, 'some', 'several'. 'Three days' or 'on the third day' (both terms are materially identical) is equivalent to 'a few days', and this is a relative expression for what may be felt to be an extremely short period or, on the other hand, a long period, according to the point of view of the speaker or hearer. 'Three days' is a long time for looting to last (2 Chron 20:25), for a slaughter (2 Macc 5:14), for passing through a city (Jon 3:3), for a man to remain in the belly of a fish (Jon 1:17), for the disciples expecting some kind of sign (Lk 24:21), for parents seeking their lost child (Lk 2:46). On the other hand it represents a very brief interval for mobilisation of an army (Josh 1:11; 2 Sam 20:4), for a sickness to last until it is healed (2 Kings 20:8; Hos 6:2), for a temple to be built anew (Mk 14:58; 15:29; etc), for remaining in the realm of the dead ('resurrection in three days').

Bibliography: P. Gächter, *Petrus und seine Zeit*, Innsbruck 1957, 11–30 (on A); J. B. Bauer, *Bbl* 39 (1958), 354–8 (on B). For a more detailed treatment, see R. Mehrlein, *RAC* IV, 269–310.

Johannes B. Bauer

Time

The bible has hardly any speculations to offer on the nature of time such as are found in philosophy, at least from the time of Plato and Aristotle onwards. Hence there is no one unified concept of time in the bible and no single term for time. Instead we find various conceptions of time which find expression in the Hebrew words (or their Greek equivalents) for 'day', 'hour', 'eternity', 'aeon', 'end', 'moment', 'decisive point in time', 'now', 'today', 'festal time', etc. The biblical conceptions of time which lie behind these terms are different, in the first place, from mythological ideas of time in the ancient Near East, for these are determined by the cycles of the stars and the yearly seasons. In other words, in these mythological conceptions time is thought of in terms of cycles of time and cycles of history returning endlessly to their starting-points. But no less alien to the bible is the present-day conception of 'linear' time. In this, time is thought of as a straight line of limitless extent which, viewed from the present, extends backwards through past events and forwards through future ones. The bible, on the other hand, knows nothing of the idea of time as 'empty' space, as a prior entity which is subsequently filled out with the ordered succession of temporally distinct events. Yet it is precisely the history writing of Israel which orders the various traditions and occurrences of its own past as a people into an historical sequence so as to show their extent in time, and at the same time attaches them to cultic celebrations which are constantly and recurrently entered upon anew. On a simplified view of the matter, therefore, the biblical idea of time seems to lie between the mythical and cyclic on the one hand, and the 'linear' and accumulative on the other.

A. *Old Testament ideas of time.* The most important characteristic of the biblical idea of time is that of time which is 'filled', time 'for' something. It is based on the underlying psychology of the two Semitic or Hebrew tenses, which appears to recognise only two kinds of past, namely that of the completed event (perfect, *factum*) and that of the still uncompleted event (imperfect, *fiens*), in addition to the present and the future. Time, therefore, is conceived of subjectively from the standpoint of the beholder of history, who divides it according to the events which he himself regards as significant. These important times, referred to in Hebrew as *ʾēth* and *yôm*, were brought into connection with the periodic acts of revelation and salvation performed by God, and it is only from these that they derive their specification. They are never thought of as having any significance in themselves apart from these events, or purely as chronological points in the flow of time. Instances of this basic idea of time as specified by its content are, for example, the time for driving the flock (Gen 29:7), the time of Harvest (Joel 3:13; Mk 4:29), the time for giving birth (Mic 5:3; Lk 1:57; 2:6), the proper season for the tree to bear fruit (Ps 104:27; Acts 14:17). Thus there is a time for every matter under the sun (Eccles 3:1), which man has to use, and which imparts a rhythm to his life. The individual history of a man's life is made up, therefore, of the total sum of these rhythms in time (in the plural), and it is this history of his own life as an individual that the psalmist is referring to when he says in his prayer, 'My times are in thy hand' (Ps 31:15; see also Ezek 12:27; 24:1). The sum total of the salvific deeds of God in the life of the chosen people constitutes the time of salvific history in its total extent (see the summaries in Deut 26:5–10; Josh 24:2–13), considering these events in their relevance to the present life and worship of the individual Israelite. The word ʿōlām, which is translated 'eternity', means the time of God as extending away into invisible distances consisting of a vaguely imagined pre-history on the one hand, and an endless future on the other. As applied to mankind, however (1 Kings 1:31; Ps 73:12), it can also stand for a period which, though subjectively long, is objectively speaking of short duration, provided that the content of the period in question is of corresponding importance. As applied to God this is, of course, undoubtedly the case. Thus ʿōlām itself too is, in the last analysis, not a temporal but a qualitative concept. The Israelite experiences the impact of God's intervention upon him with special intensity at festal times, in which the salvific event which has taken place in Israel's history is rendered present in such a way that it is as though the times of the patriarchs are in some sense synchronised with those of the participators in the celebrations, who think of themselves as identical with their own forefathers (compare the later synchronisation in the Gospel of John). The events which took place at the time of the exodus from Egypt have in some sense so strongly specified that period that the individual who is engaged in commemorating them cultically believes himself to be carried back to that time, and in this way renders present the earlier salvific event (cf Mish Pesa 5:5, 10 and Ex 13:8; Deut 6:23). The idea of the 'corporate' or 'collective person' (Adam: see Rom 5; or Abraham: see Gal 4),

in whom the fate of all subsequent generations is determined, is the corresponding factor in the spatial dimension to this fusing of present and past in the temporal one. Thus from its temporal aspect salvific history is not to be equated with a process whereby the individual salvific deeds of God are assigned a place in an extent of time previously given. On the contrary the temporal sequence results, to some extent, as a byproduct, from the arrangement in a series of the events embodying God's gracious leadership of the people, which constitute times filled with salvific power.

In the prophets and in apocalyptic circles of later judaism the idea of time that is constituted by its own content, as upheld by earlier generations and in the traditions of the patriarchs, is transformed into a future hope of the judgement and fulfilment that is awaited. This now becomes as important as history for life in the present—indeed it takes the place of history. The future crisis is already making itself felt. And finally apocalyptic introduces the idea of periods by combining the mythological idea of cycles with the ancient and indigenously Israelite image of 'this-worldly' history in such a way that world history in its total extent is divided into two aeons (see 4 Ezra 7:26ff), and the approaching post-messianic aeon is presented as transcending the entire past (Enoch [Eth] 65:7f). The end to which time is directed begins to outdo its origins.

B. *The New Testament ideas of time* are based upon those of the Old Testament and judaism. With the event of Christ the new aeon, the aeon which is 'to come' has commenced (Eph 1:21;

2:7), though this does not mean that the present evil aeon has already been deprived of its power (Gal 1:4; Heb 6:5). Of special importance in the message of the New Testament is the idea of the *kairos*, the time which has as its content the work of Jesus (Mt 26:18; Jn 7:8) and the decision of man to accept or to reject this salvific event (2 Cor 6:2). In the *kairos* the gift of God and the demand that man shall lay hold of this offering of salvation on God's part is brought home to men in a definitive and unrepeatable manner (Lk 19:44; Jn 7:6), and this *kairos* of God gives certainty. In this it is unlike cosmic or human *kairos*, which has to remain in a constant state of readiness for all possible opportunities even when these are only remote. In the preaching of the kingdom of God by Jesus in the present the hour of decision has been ushered in (Lk 12:54ff), for now the turning-point of the ages has arrived. This hour of decision will remain as an enduring 'now' and 'today' until the approaching consummation, and scarcely admits of the further survival of salvific history after the Old Testament pattern, or in the sense of profane, chronological history. But in spite of its abiding expectation that Jesus' message of the kingdom of God is about to be realised, the primitive church does maintain a genuine openness to the possibility of a further stage in the revelation of God's salvific will, and for fresh acts mediating salvation to men to be performed, for a fresh beginning in the preaching of salvation, for a new 'now' of salvation history (A. Vögtle). New Testament eschatology, therefore, makes it possible for statements about the future and the present to stand side

by side. Thus the present salvation is 'redemption in hope' (Rom 8:24), hope that is entertained in a dynamic present which is imbued with the approaching end (1 Cor 7:29ff). The problem of the delay of the ↗ *parousia*, which arose from the fact that at first the return of Christ was expected in the imminent future, hardly arose as a problem at all in New Testament times, but nevertheless the post-Easter expectation of the end was based particularly upon the facts, events and truths of the revelation of Christ, though not on the knowledge of any definite appointed time at which the end was to come. In spite of this the eschatological ideas on time in Paul (R. Bultmann), the lukan conception of time in terms of salvation history (Old Testament: time of the promise; gospel: Jesus as the centre of time; Acts: the time of the church; see O. Cullmann), and the johannine historicisation of eschatology cannot be reduced to a single common denominator. What is common to them all, as also to the Book of Revelation, is the revelation of the 'time of grace', the 'day of salvation' (2 Cor 6:1f) and the 'today' of God (Heb 3:7ff), which, as the time of the Holy Spirit, is to be used by those to whom the message of the bible is addressed. But the power to transcend time for all those who are in the world can only come from Jesus Christ, 'Yesterday, today and for ever', and therefore in the last analysis only from God.

In that God himself fixes the time and brings it once more to an end, he shows that he is the Lord who transcends time, and who, in spite of the fact that his work is fitted into the time process, never undergoes a temporal dissolution, or remains imprisoned by it, but maintains his being independently of the human form of existence which is of its nature temporal, in a perfection that is eternal. [W. Eichrodt, p 123.]

Bibliography: O. Cullmann, *Christ and Time*, London 1962; O. Cullmann, *Heil als Geschichte*, Tübingen 1965; R. Bultmann, *History and Eschatology*, London 1957; R. Bultmann, *Glauben und Verstehen* III, Tübingen 1960; T. Boman, *Hebrew Thought Compared with Greek*, 1960; W. Eichrodt, 'Heilserfahrung und Zeitverständnis im AT', *TZ* 12 (1956), 103–25; G. Delling, *Das Zeitverständnis des NT*, Gütersloh 1940; E. Dinkler (ed.), *Zeit und Geschichte*, Tübingen 1964; E. Fuchs, 'Das Zeitverständnis Jesu', *Zur Frage nach dem hist. Jesus*, Tübingen 1960; W. G. Kümmel, *Promise and Fulfilment*, 1957; P. Neuenzeit, 'Biblische Zeitvorstellungen', *Geschichtlichkeit und Offenbarungswahrheit*, ed. V. Berning, P. Neuenzeit, and H. R. Schlette, Munich 1964, 37–65; E. Vögtle, 'Zeit und Zeitüberlegenheit in biblischer Sicht', *Weltverständnis im Glauben*, ed. J. B. Metz, Mainz 1965, 224–53.

Paul Neuenzeit

Tradition

Tradition derives its importance from the very nature of our religion, which is wholly the outcome of a revelation. This is not constantly recurring anew, but was imparted once and for all at a specific point in human history. All men remain bound by this privileged *kairos*.

1. The fact that the concept of tradition has so many aspects often makes theological discussion of it difficult. It is therefore essential to gain a clear idea of the complexity of the concept. First, then, the word can be used in an active, an objective, or even in a documentary sense. Tradition in the active sense is the human activity of 'handing on', or even—for activities can exist only as the accidents of substances—the author of such activity, the 'tradent'. But the word can also signify the object of the 'handing on', that which is 'handed on'. The handing on of a piece of tradition is made possible chiefly by means of certain material aids drawn from the past of the individual man. These are the *monumenta traditionis*, the witnesses, whether written or otherwise, to the past.

A further division is also important, that namely which is based on the distinction between the broader and more comprehensive use of the word tradition and a narrower sense which it can also bear. In the more comprehensive sense tradition stands for all methods of handing on, including therefore the 'handing on' (in an extended sense of the term) which is the function of sacred books. In this sense holy scripture is one form, one aspect, one part of tradition. In the narrower sense, on the other hand, tradition is confined precisely to those kinds of 'handing on' which do *not* constitute the 'handing on,' in this extended sense, of the sacred scriptures or, regarded objectively, to those matters alone which have *not* been passed down from one generation to the others by means of sacred writings.

The two divisions already mentioned must now be viewed in their bearing upon a third and still more important distinction, that namely between apostolic and ecclesiastical tradition. By apostolic tradition we mean that which derives from the apostles as its active bearers or 'tradents'. This may apply either to traditions which are of divine origin or to traditions which actually originated with the apostles. The church is obviously the bearer and source of traditions, and these too can be of various kinds. The church can hand down apostolic traditions. It can also itself be the author and originator of fresh traditions.

Obviously the theology of the church, as essentially bound by revelation, is primarily interested in apostolic tradition. The distinctions drawn above give rise to the following division at this point: I. Tradition as the act of handing down or as the subject who hands down. II. Tradition as material content and as document: (a) in the broader sense, (b) in the narrower sense: the *sine scripto traditiones, scripta* here being understood to apply solely to the inspired scriptures.

2. In the connection between scripture and tradition three main aspects are to be distinguished. The most important, and for many christians today the most perplexing, aspect arises from the fact that scripture, regarded from the human aspect, is itself a product of tradition. But what kind of tradition? One which is principally preservative or one which is creative and gives birth to new stories? It is the second aspect which emerges from the bible's own statements about tradition, which constitute a theme. This aspect is not, of itself, identical with the first. It is not always that one can experience the mystery of a personality from the statements which the individual concerned makes about himself. It is no less difficult to deduce the nature of the tradition of the New Testament merely from a survey of the

thematic statements upon this subject contained in the bible. Finally, there is a third aspect, which has a direct relevance to the current teaching of theology on our knowledge of God. The post-apostolic christian is indeed guided by the Spirit of God, but he no longer has any direct access to the act in which God reveals himself. Instead he is told to rely upon holy scripture and on non-biblical tradition to mediate this knowledge to him. Both can be called sources in the sense in which this term is employed in scientific history, and with reference to the knowledge of faith. But how are these sources of our knowledge in faith related one to the other? In considering the problems indicated here let us confine ourselves to the difficulties which arise in connection with the New Testament.

3. The problems which arise from the nature of scripture as tradition are admittedly not apparent in the thematic statements which scripture makes about tradition. In their presentation of these statements contemporary exegetes show hardly any perceptible divergence of view.

To express the phenomenon of tradition the New Testament employs the verb *paradidonai* and the substantive *Paradosis*. For the manifold use of these terms, which occur frequently in the New Testament as also throughout the Greek language, we may refer to the article of F. Büchsel, *TDNT* ii, 169–73.

'The religion of the Old Testament and judaism is a religion of tradition, and indeed of the revelation imparted to the fathers by Yahweh, which was set down in writing in the Torah. Side by side with this in later judaism oral tradition ("the tradition of the fathers")

916

acquires an ever increasing importance. By it the "law" is interpreted, supplemented and applied to fresh situations' (F. Mussner, 'Tradition', *LTK* x, 291). In his controversies (Mk 7; Mt 15) Jesus takes issue with the *paradosis tōn presbuterōn* (= 'the tradition of the elders': Mk 7:3, 5; Mt 15:2), with the *paradosis tōn anthrōpōn* (= 'the tradition of men': Mk 7:8), or with the *paradosis humōn* (= 'your tradition': Mk 7:9, 13; Mt 15:3, 6).

In Mt 11:27 and Lk 10:22 *paradidonai* is used in connection with the supreme power of Jesus as Messiah or Son of God: *panta moi paredothē* (= 'all things have been delivered to me'). Considerable use of *paradidonai* is also made in the passion narrative, where the frequency of its occurrence is equalled only by the frequency 'which is usual elsewhere too in accounts of trials or martyrdoms' (F. Büchsel, *TDNT* II, 172).

According to Jude 3, christian teaching is the *hapax paradotheisē tois hagiois pistis* (= 'the faith which was once for all delivered to the saints'); according to 2 Pet 2:21 it is the *paradotheisē hagia entolē* (= 'the holy commandment delivered [to them]'). 'In reality the church is aware right from the outset that the event of Christ and its abiding impact on the life of its community exercise a decisive influence on its very nature'. *paradidonai*, *paradosis* and *paralambanein* (= 'to receive [tradition]') are from the very outset terms which designate the manner in which tradition is developed (1 Thess 2:13; 4:1; Gal 1:9; 1 Cor 11:2, 23; 15:1, 3; Phil 4:9; see also Col 2:6; 2 Thess 2:15; 3:6; Jude 3; 2 Pet 2:21; 1 Clem 7:2; Did 4:13; Barn 19:11), and *parathēkē*

as used in the pastoral epistles is the term used for the deposit of teaching provided by tradition (1 Tim 6:20; 2 Tim 1:12, 14; see also 2:2), having been chosen, perhaps, as a juridical term in order to avoid using *paradosis*, which had been rendered suspect by the gnostics (von Campenhausen). The content of *paradosis*, *parathēkē* is normally right teaching as opposed to erroneous teaching. It can, however, also mean that which is ethically required (Did 4:13; Barn 19:11; 1 Clem 7:12; and in 2 Pet 2:21 probably moral requirement and teaching both together). 'The apostles' proclamation founded the tradition, and in the apostle concept the idea of tradition becomes the dominant factor' (R. Bultmann, *Theology of the New Testament* II, 119).

Already in the New Testament itself the dispute as to the authentic form and the rightful bearers of tradition is apparent (*successio apostolica*). In the post-apostolic church this goes further, and leads, among other things, to the establishing of the canon of scripture.

4. In the controversy between catholics and reformed christians concerning the theory of *sola scriptura*, the principal point of difference consists not in the acceptance or rejection of *sine scripto traditiones* (ie, traditions not contained in scripture), but in the basic religious orientation of the individual; in how he conceives of tradition in the active sense, what he thinks of the role of the church and of private judgement. This has been brought out very clearly by Newman in his *Lectures on the Prophetical Office of the Church*. In practice, for the reformed christian of the continental type, the individual conscience as enlightened by the Holy Spirit, and in

917

solitary engagement with the bible, probably always remains the ultimate court of appeal. He rejects every *sacrificium intellectus* of his historical or speculative understanding which 'the church' could possibly demand. The Anglican constantly commits himself to a *via media* position, which Newman unsuccessfully attempted to translate into terms of practical living. The distinctive element in the catholic's position derives from his doctrine of the church. This must never, indeed, suppress the historical or speculative understanding of the individual. In other words it must never demand an acknowledgement of the truth of propositions which are contrary to reason. But it certainly can go beyond the historical and speculative reason. Guided by the Spirit of God and of Christ, the church claims authority to interpret the will of God in applying revelation to the particular concrete situations as they arise, and it claims that its power to do this exceeds the clear reflexive understanding of the original recipient of the revelation concerned, and likewise the powers of our individual historical and speculative reason.

All this has, of itself, nothing to do with the question of the sufficiency or insufficiency of scripture in terms of its content. When and how did this question come to occupy the central point in the teaching of theologians on our knowledge of God?

The question of the *sine scripto traditiones* scarcely played any significant part before the late Middle Ages. *Sacra pagina* and *sacra doctrina* were almost synonymous terms. The concept of oral tradition is almost totally absent from the writings of Aquinas.

Admittedly, Aquinas does recognise that the apostles of the church have handed on certain prescriptions which were not set down in their writings. In practice, however, according to Aquinas, these directives are confined to the sacraments and other questions of the liturgy. He teaches, on the one hand, the sufficiency of sacred scripture with regard to subject-matter, and on the other hand that this subject-matter does include a definition of what is necessary for salvation, and that the truths necessary for salvation are not *ipso facto* identical with revelation in its entirety.

The view according to which sacred scripture contains all the truths necessary for salvation was still to be upheld by the catholic theologians of the sixteenth century. Thus, for example, Driedo and Robert Bellarmine. Again, many of the reformation theologians gave their allegiance to this idea in order to restrict the sphere of authority of the magisterium of the church. Soon the truths necessary for salvation came to be known as a fundamental article of faith, and in order to substantiate them the theologians took up the criterion formulated by Vincent of Lerins: *Quod semper, quod ubique, quod ab omnibus.* In the concrete these truths necessary for salvation were identified with the articles of the credal confession of faith interpreted in a comprehensive sense in the light of christian antiquity. In anglicanism the concept of the *fundamentals* is found in the works of G. Cassander, Hooker—the classic theologian of the *via media*—and after him many other anglican theologians, especially Bishop Laud (in his controversy with the Jesuit Fisher), G.

Calixt, and Jurieu. Not the least of those who upheld this doctrine was the anglican Newman. The doctrine of the *fundamentals* and the sufficiency of scripture and infallibility of the church as confined to this occupied the central point in his teaching on the *via media*.

In the late Middle Ages a shift of emphasis took place in the teaching of theologians on the knowledge of God. Aquinas was chiefly preoccupied with the·material object of faith, and more particularly with its salvific content. By contrast the theologians of the later Middle Ages preoccupied themselves increasingly with the external formal object of theology, and it was at this point that the ambiguous nature of the concept of truths necessary for salvation was borne in upon them, and led to a gradual abandonment of the theory of the sufficiency of sacred scripture, for the formal object of theology is not the eternal salvation of man but the authority of God who reveals. As a result of this the necessity of doctrines for salvation had to be measured not so much by their direct bearing upon eternal salvation as by their common character as revelation. The development of theology brought with it a multiplication of the doctrines which were regarded as revealed, and also an increase in the number of those doctrines which it was not believed possible to discover in sacred scripture. And when they reverted to the teaching of the past the theologians established that the idea that sacred scripture was insufficient in terms of content was traditional in the church. For instance, in their teaching on the nature of baptism, the fathers of the church too had derived this from tradition alone.

Yet to deny their teaching on this point was condemned as heretical and punished by excommunication from the church.

The polemics of the counter-reformation introduced an emphasis not merely on the formal insufficiency of sacred scripture but also on its insufficiency in terms of content. According to the definition of the Council of Trent concerning revelation (*DS* 1501 [=DB 783]), the gospel message is accessible to us *in libris scriptis et sine scripto traditionibus*, and the believer must adopt an attitude towards the apostolic traditions which are still in force in the church today defined as *pari pietatis affectu*, that is, he must treat them with the same reverence as sacred scripture itself. 'In consequence of this, the conception of tradition as a second material source side by side with sacred scripture came increasingly to the fore in post-tridentine theology' (J. Ratzinger, 'Tradition', *LTK* x, 297). In recent times the true significance of the tridentine decree, and the value of the post-tridentine development, have become the subject of numerous and impassioned discussions which we cannot pass over without drawing attention to certain facts.

According to the teaching of the Council of Trent the catholic must obviously accept *in principle* that the fact that a doctrine is not contained in sacred scripture is not a sufficient ground for refusing to recognise it as a revealed truth. But the council does not solve the question of whether *in fact* there are any important doctrines not contained in any way at all in scripture. For, however we interpret the statement of the council, it does not contain any information at all with regard to the number and the nature of the *sine scripto traditiones*, apart from the fact that they constitute elements in the gospel message. Let us take the extreme case of a theologian who, on concrete historical grounds, maintains that no document known to him justifies him in asserting that the apostles were explicitly aware of some particular point in our *fides divina et catholica* which was not contained in sacred scripture. Let us further suppose that this same theologian goes on to say, again on concrete historical grounds, that he would be unjustified in asserting that the point in question does in fact fulfil the necessary conditions for inclusion in this *fides divina et catholica*. In making this twofold assertion he would in no way be controverting the teaching of the Council of Trent.

It is possible to regret the 'two-source theory' of revelation of post-tridentine theology. At all events, one must be on one's guard against a mythical presentation of this theory. Its adherents have never presented the sources as separate and partial sources with differing contents, somewhat in the manner in which the power to govern may be divided between two parties, each having his own proper sphere of authority. The upholders of the theory have never maintained that what we today call 'tradition' in the church, that is, the handing down of the gospel message in word and deed from generation to generation, would not always have contained the whole of this gospel message. They have never denied that tradition *in sensu activo* has always been formed in the first instance as a commentary on and an explica-

tion of the content of sacred scripture. And it is surely difficult to perceive why the assertion—whether true or false—that scripture does not contain all the teaching and all the supplementary material which together make up the gospel must lead to the assumption of two bodies of tradition with two quite different contents, each incomplete in itself and parallel to the other.

Moreover the adherents of the so-called 'two-source theory' have scarcely left the catholic doctrine of the *analogia fidei* out of their considerations. They have for the most part emphasised the indirect evidence, the arguments *ex convenientia* that scripture offers in support of the theory of *sine scripto traditiones* which they maintain, and they have done this in fact better than many theologians of today, for whom everything is contained in scripture 'somehow'. The question may be asked whether the protestants of today do not often require a still greater *sacrificium intellectus* than was demanded in the centuries of the two-source theory.

Actually, the position of contemporary catholic and reformed christians with regard to the dogmas proclaimed in the previous century differs only in one important respect from the position of the post-tridentine christians with regard to the dogmas defined at the Council of Trent. The earlier generations had greater trust in the possibilities of finding theological solutions with the speculative reason, as well as in the possibility of direct historical proof, than most theologians of today. Progress in the methods of historical research since the middle of last century has probably been one of the most important factors in the development of the new theology. It has led to a prudent evaluation of direct historical arguments in theology, as well as of the premisses on which the arguments in speculative theology are based. Not least, it has also provided a better insight into the traditio-historical character of sacred scripture. It has shown that arguments from sacred scripture are often just as difficult to adduce as the so-called arguments from tradition. The effect of this has been to emphasise to an increasing extent the role of indirect proof, through the medium of the life of the church and its magisterium. So strongly, indeed, has this been emphasised that the magisterium itself has been forced to react against an exaggerated emphasis on its role and a corresponding neglect of directly historical and speculative methods of argument.

Apart from the progress in historical and other sciences, a further factor which led to a change of attitude towards the problem of tradition was the oecumenical atmosphere, borne of an altered situation of the world, in the relations between christian confessions. This has recently borne fruit in the *Dogmatic Constitution on Divine Revelation* of the Second Vatican Council.

5. 'The debates of the Second Vatican Council were characterised by a dialogue of a type which is classical in post-tridentine scholastic theology, and by efforts to achieve a deeper understanding of tradition on the basis of the heritage of the early Church. In this the legitimate concerns of reformation thinking were duly taken into consideration'. This is J. Ratzinger's accurate estimate (*LTK* x, 298). The efforts mentioned above were crowned with success.

Of the twenty-six paragraphs of the *Constitution on Divine Revelation*, no less than nineteen are concerned with sacred scripture. Sixteen are devoted to it exclusively. The apostolic preaching, it is stated, is 'expressed in a special way in the inspired books' (§ 8). The Council numbers sacred scripture, together with the Holy Eucharist, as among the most precious treasures of the church: 'The church has always venerated the divine scriptures, just as it venerates the body of the Lord, since from the table of both the word of God and of the body of Christ it unceasingly receives and offers to the faithful the bread of life' (§ 21). The sacred scriptures 'contain the word of God, and since they are inspired, really are the word of God; and so the study of the sacred page is, as it were, the soul of sacred theology' (§ 24).

The constitution devotes hardly more than three paragraphs to tradition. It presents sacred scripture as a privileged form of tradition. The council fathers again reiterate the tridentine teaching on the formal insufficiency of sacred scripture. Thus, 'it is not from sacred scripture alone that the church can draw its certainty about everything which has been revealed' (§ 9). The council takes up once more the *pari pietatis affectu* of the tridentine decree: 'Therefore both sacred tradition and sacred scripture are to be accepted and reverenced with the same sense of devotion and reverence' (§ 9).

In yet another respect emphasis is laid upon the formal insufficiency of sacred scripture: 'Sacred tradition and sacred scripture form one sacred deposit of the word of God which is committed to the church. Holding fast to this deposit the entire holy people, united with their shepherds, remain constantly steadfast in the teaching of the apostles. . . . The task of authentically interpreting the word of God, whether written or handed on, however, has been entrusted exclusively to the living teaching office of the church, whose authority is exercised in the name of Jesus Christ. This teaching office is not above the word of God, but serves it, teaching only what has been handed on' (§ 10).

In the *Constitution on Divine Revelation* the fathers of the council do not show an excessive concern to arrive at a precise analysis of the concept of tradition. In those passages in which they provide a statement of what the true function of tradition and of the teaching office of the church is they take this function to be, on the one hand, in the active sense, what J. Geiselmann calls 'living tradition', and on the other hand, in terms of content, or objectively regarded, what Y. Congar calls 'tradition in the comprehensive sense'. The question of the sufficiency or insufficiency of sacred scripture in terms of content, on the other hand, which has been at the centre of the controversies between confessions ever since the Council of Trent, is simply set aside. It is not treated of *ex professo* at all. All the statements on the relationship in content between the two basic types of the 'handing on' of divine revelation are kept neutral. There is no mention whatsoever of 'sources' of revelation.

The council leaves the question open.

It teaches neither the sufficiency of what is contained in sacred scripture nor its insufficiency. It is probably clear from the text that the doctrine of the insufficiency of what is contained in sacred scripture with reference to the content of revelation should not be regarded as the binding doctrine of the church. The question as stated pertains to the area of free theological and historical research. It can only be decided *a posteriori* in terms of particular cases, and on the basis of concrete evidence. It should no longer provide reasons for division between the confessions as such. The crucial point of difference in fundamental theology is to be sought elsewhere.

Bibliography: N. Appel, *Kanon und Kirche. Die Kanonkrise im heutigen Protestantismus als kontrovers-theologisches Problem*, Paderborn 1963; P. Asveld, 'Ecriture et Tradition', *ETL* 41 (1965), 491–529; J. Beumer, 'Die mündliche Überlieferung als Glaubensquelle', *Handbuch der Dogmengeschichte* 1/4, ed. M. Schmaus and A. Grillmeier, Freiburg 1964; H. Beintker, *Die evangelische Lehre von der Heiligen Schrift und von der Tradition*, Lüneburg 1961; G. Biemer, *Überlieferung und Offenbarung. Die Lehre von der Tradition nach J. H. Newman*, Freiburg 1961; Y. M. J. Congar, '"Traditio" und "Sacra Doctrina" bei Thomas von Aquin', *Kirche und Überlieferung*, ed. J. Betz and H. Fries, Freiburg 1960, 170–210; Y. M. J. Congar, *La Tradition et les Traditions* I, Paris 1960; and II, Paris 1963; G. Ebeling, *Wort Gottes und Tradition*, Göttingen 1964; J. R. Geiselmann, 'Das Konzil von Trient über des Verhältnis der Heiligen Schrift und der nichtgeschriebenen Traditionen', *Die mündliche Überlieferung*, ed. M. Schmaus, Munich 1957, 123–206; J. R. Geiselmann, *Die Heilige Schrift und die Tradition*, Freiburg 1962; J. R. Geiselmann, *HTG* II, 686–96; H. Holstein, *La Tradition dans l'Eglise*, Paris 1960; W. Kasper, *Die Lehre von der Tradition in der Römischen Schule*, Freiburg 1962; P. Lengsfeld, *Überlieferung. Tradition und Schrift in der evangelischen und katholischen Theologie der Gegenwart*, Paderborn 1960; P. Lengsfeld, 'Tradition innerhalb der konstitutiven Zeit der Offenbarung', *Mysterium Salutis. Grundriss heilsgeschichtlicher Dogmatik*, I, Cologne 1965, 239–

88; and 'Tradition und Heilige Schrift. Ihr Verhältnis', *Mysterium Salutis*, 463–96; J. L. Murphy, *The Notion of Tradition in John Driedo*, Milwaukee 1960; F. Mussner, *LTK* x², 291–3; K. Rahner, *Inspiration in the Bible*, London 1961; K. Rahner, 'Schrift und Tradition', *Das Zweite Vatikanische Konzil*, ed. K. Forster, Würzburg 1963, 69–91; K. Rahner and J. Ratzinger, *Offenbarung und Überlieferung*, Freiburg 1965; J. Ratzinger, *LTK* x², 293–9; P. Rusch, 'De non definienda illimitata insufficientia materiali Scripturae', *ZKT* 85 (1963), 1–15; H. Schauf, *Die Lehre der Kirche über Schrift und Tradition in den Katechismen*, Essen 1963; *Schrift und Tradition. Mariologische Studien*, ed. Der deutschen Arbeitsgemeinschaft für Mariologie, Essen 1962 (this work includes certain articles previously published elsewhere, which are important for our understanding of the most recent discussions); B. Decker, 'Sola scriptura bei Thomas von Aquin', *Universitas* (Festschrift A. Stöhr) i, Mainz 1960, 117–29; *Schrift und Tradition. Untersuchungen einer theologischen Kommission*, ed. K. E. Skydsgaard and L. Vischer, Zurich 1963; G. H. Tavard, *Holy Writ and Holy Church. The Crisis of the Protestant Reformation*, London 1959; M. Thurian, *L'unité visible des chrétiens et la Tradition*, Neuchâtel 1961.

Paul Asveld

Transfiguration

The motif of being changed into another form recurs frequently in the conceptual and imaginative milieux of the ancient religions. Sometimes it occurs in the form of stories about gods appearing to men in earthly guise (the metamorphoses of Greek mythology); sometimes the change is in the opposite direction, of man into a divine being by acquiring heavenly form (hellenistic mystery religions). The account of the transfiguration of Jesus on the mountain as recorded in the bible represents a metamorphosis which is totally different in character from these. Of the four accounts of this episode, that found in Mk 9:2–9, which is manifestly based upon the tradition handed down by Peter, must be considered the earliest. This in turn provides a basis for the parallel account in Mt 17:1–9, which differs from it only in inessentials, while Lk 9:28–36 has drawn not only upon the markan account, but upon another one as well, one which derives, perhaps, from John the son of Zebedee. Independent of the gospels a further version, admittedly only fragmentary, is to be found in 2 Pet 1:16–18.

In the interpretation of this event opinions have been, and continue to be, widely different. First, it is clear that what is in question here cannot be a revelation directed to Jesus himself. Baltensweiler's theory to the effect that the transfiguration would have been a subjective experience on Jesus' part, arising from his temptation to conceive of his messianic calling in political terms and in terms of the Zealot movement, cannot be reconciled with the accounts. These leave no possibility of doubting that, in the first instance at least, it was for the sake of the three apostles who were present as witnesses that the event took place. To them the true dignity of their Lord, hitherto concealed, was revealed by means of a vision which they saw and words which they heard. The only questions that arise are in what precisely this dignity is to be regarded as consisting, and why it was momentarily unveiled to the three witnesses. The answers which have been suggested to both these questions are extremely divergent (see Höller, 206–28). Recently attempts have been made to interpret the transfiguration as an anticipatory vision of the ↗ parousia (Boobyer) or as the inauguration of Jesus as messianic king presented after the pattern of the

Old Testament enthronement sequence (Riesenfeld). Notable arguments can be advanced in favour of both these theories. At the same time a theory in which every individual element in the story falls into place convincingly and without strain has yet to be discovered. The recognition of this fact has led some to doubt the unity of the narrative. Lohmeyer believed that Mk 9:3 was a fragment from a hellenistic myth which had been applied to Jesus. It could be separated from the rest of the narrative, in which transcendence of Jesus over the heroes of the Old Testament was depicted in the hues of Jewish eschatology. H. P. Müller finds two distinct sequences of ideas, an earlier one in which Jesus is proclaimed eschatological king after the pattern of Ps 2 as interpreted messianically (9:2ab, 7, [9]), and a later one in which Jesus appears as the heavenly Son of Man and as a divine being (9:2c–6, 8). But these hypothetical reconstructions give the impression of being far too artificial to be convincing. Moreover Lohmeyer later abandoned his hypothesis.

In any attempt at determining the theological import which the narrative would have borne for the community which handed it down, we must take the *vox interpretativa* of Mk 9:7 as our starting-point. Unlike the voice at the baptism, the voice here resounding from the clouds, the symbol of the divine presence (Ex 16:10; 19:9; 24:15f; 33:9; Num 11:25; 2 Macc 2:8), is clearly addressed to the disciples. Echoing Ps 2:7, it declares Jesus to be the beloved (=only) Son of God, ie, the Messiah, and thus provides *divine* confirmation of Peter's confession (8:29), to which, therefore, the interval

mentioned as having elapsed in 9:2 must, at least originally, have referred. Admittedly, for Mark and the primitive community the title 'Son of God' would not merely have designated Jesus' status as Messiah, but would have carried the further implication of his sonship of God in the metaphysical sense as well. In the second part of the utterance from heaven Jesus is indirectly declared to be the eschatological prophet promised in Deut 18:15, whose words are to be hearkened to and obeyed. With regard to the appearance of Moses and Elijah, some have regarded these as representatives of the law and the prophets; in spite of the paucity of the evidence, however, it is more probable that they were intended as forerunners of the Messiah (see Jeremias, *TDNT* II, 938f; IV 859f and 871). The presence of these figures, then, appears to have had the same significance of bearing witness to the messiahship of Jesus. By the transformation of his appearance and the unearthly whiteness with which his garments shone Jesus appeared for a moment in the state appropriate to the heavenly mode of existence (see Dan 7:9; 10:5; Acts 1:10; Rev 3:4f; 4:4; 7:9; Bar [Syr] 51:3, 5, 10, 12). Thereby he unveiled himself to the witnesses as the heavenly Son of Man (Dan 7:13f; 1 Enoch 46:1–3; [62:5; 69:29]; Mk 8:38; 13:26; 14:62; Rev 1:13f). In the mind of Mark the reason for this epiphany being imparted to the apostles precisely at this point is probably to be found in the passion prediction which precedes it in 8:31f. In that case the significance of the revelation which they received can be stated as follows: the fact that Jesus takes the path of a servant in lowliness and suffering, and not the path of a king in the acquisition of earthly power, as was generally expected, in no way alters the fact that he is the messianic Son of God of Ps 2:7, the eschatological prophet and teacher promised in Deut 18:15, the Son of Man endowed with heavenly glory as depicted in Dan 7:13. The fact that only the three closest of his disciples were privileged to receive this revelation, like the enjoinder to silence recorded in 9:9, is connected with the 'messianic secret'. In the parallel accounts in the other synoptics, and specifically in Matthew, the transfiguration has in all essentials the same meaning. The reference back to the passion prediction, which is only to be inferred in Mark, is in Luke stated plainly and explicitly. For according to him the conversation of the two Old Testament figures with Jesus was concerned with his 'departure' at Jerusalem (9:31). Furthermore, by introducing the term *doxa* (=glory) and applying it both to Jesus (9:32), and also to Moses and Elijah (9:31), Luke, even more than Mark, imparts to the vision of the three figures features which are characteristic and definitive of the heavenly mode of existence (see also 2 Pet 1:17).

Bibliography: J. Höller, *Die Verklärung Jesu*, Freiburg 1937 (with bibliography of the earlier literature); J. Blinzler, *Die ntl. Berichte über die Verklärung Jesu*, Munster 1937; E. Dabrowski, *La Transfiguration de Jésus*, Rome 1939; P. Dabek, '"Siehe, es erschienen Moses und Elias"', *Bbl* 23 (1942), 175–89; G. H. Boobyer, *St. Mark and the Transfiguration Story*, Edinburgh 1942; T. F. Torrance, 'The Transfiguration of Jesus', *Evangelical Quarterly* 14 (1942), 214–29; H. Riesenfeld, *Jésus transfiguré*, Lund 1947; B. Zielinski, 'De Doxa transfigurati', *VD* 26 (1948), 291–303; B. Zielinski, 'De Trans-figurationis sensu', *VD* 26 (1948), 335–43; J. Schildenberger, 'Die Verklärung des Herrn', *BM* 24 (1948), 23–9; A. M. Ramsay, *The Glory of God and the Transfiguration of Christ*, London 1949; F. X. Durrwell, 'La Transfiguration de Jésus', *VS* 35 (1951), 115–26; P. Bonnard, Allmen 429–30; G. B. Caird, 'The Transfiguration', *Expository Times* 67 (1955/6), 291–4; J. R. Macphail, *The Bright Cloud. The Bible in the Light of the Transfiguration*, London 1956; A. Kenny, 'The Transfiguration and the Agony in the Garden', *CBQ* 19 (1957), 444–52; M. Sabbe, 'De Transfiguratie van Jesus', *Collat. Brugenses et Gandavenses* 4 (1958), 467–503; A. Feuillet, 'Les perspectives propres à chaque évangeliste dans les récits de la Transfiguration', *Bbl* 39 (1958), 281–301; H. Baltensweiler, *Die Verklärung Jesu*, Zurich 1959; A. M. Denis, 'Une théologie de la Rédemption. La Transfiguration chez S. Marc', *VS* 41 (1959), 136–49; A. George, 'La Transfiguration (Luc 9:28–36)', *Bible et Vie chrétienne* 33 (1960), 21–5; H. P. Müller, 'Die Verklärung Jesu', *ZNW* 51 (1960), 56–64; J. Larisis, *Hē metamorphōsis tou Sōtēros hēmōn Iēsou Khristou*, Athens 1960; C. E. Carlston, 'Transfiguration and Resurrection', *JBL* 80 (1961), 233–40; P. Miquel, 'Le mystère de la Transfiguration', *Questions Litug. et Paroissiales* 42 (1961), 194–223; M. Sabbe, *La rédaction du récit de la Transfiguration. La venue du Messie*, Paris-Louvain 1963, 65–100.

Josef Blinzler

Transitoriness

The transitoriness of all earthly existence is a theme which is not confined to the bible alone. It pervades a major part of the literature of the ancient Near East.

The Old Testament has no abstract term for it. It depicts transitoriness by means of comparisons. All earthly existence seems like a dream (Job 20:8), like a garment devoured by moths (Is 51:6; Job 13:28), like smoke (Ps 102:3; Is 51:6), like grass and flowers (Ps 90:5–7; Job 14:1f; Is 40:6). The generations of mankind pass away and are succeeded by others (Eccles 1:4). Even memory vanishes (Job 18:17). All is vanity (Eccles 1:2). In all this evanescence there is only one who remains and whose years have no end, namely God (Ps 102:27; Dan 12:7). But this is not a fact in which man can *ipso facto* place his reliance, for his sins have drawn down the anger of God upon him, and with it death and liability to corruption (Gen 3; Is 6:5; Ps 90:7). Only in fear and trembling does the devout man attempt to trust in the eternity of God. He reminds God of the fact that in Sheol no-one can serve him (Ps 6:5; 30:9). He steeps himself in the Torah as a wellspring of life (Ps 119:92), he relies on the compassion of God. Only very seldom does he envisage an association with God which enables him to transcend the power of death (Ps 73:26). Only in the latest books do we find the consoling light of the idea of ⁊ resurrection (Dan 12:2; Is 27 [later interpolation]).

In the period of the deutero-canonical and pseudepigraphal literature faith in the resurrection was universal. In the New Testament it appears to be taken for granted. But it does not yet signify the overcoming of death and transitoriness. There is the second death (Rev 20:6, 14; 21:8). One can perish (*apollumi*: Mt 5:29; 8:32; 10:39; etc). ⁊ Death is the wages of sin (Rom 6:23). It is Paul who sees the importance of the fact that death, hell, and the devil belong together. It is not merely a man's individual sins but his whole being, which is in a state of alienation from God, that sets him in a condition of lostness, makes the 'flesh' transitory, threatens that he will pass away beyond all hope of return.

Because of sin the 'flesh' (ie, the natural, human existence, both spiritual and physical) is *phthartos* (= 'mortal', 'perishable': Rom 1:23; 8:21; Gal 6:8; 1 Cor 15:42; see also 2 Pet 2:12, and we are the slaves of corruption (2 Pet 2:10). But the New Testament is no longer devoid of hope as it confronts this transitoriness and liability to death on the part of creaturehood, which is the outcome of sin and the anger of God. The ⁊ hope which is tentatively hinted at in the Old Testament, that God can give ⁊ life which is no longer subject to death, has become a certainty. The Gospel of John is full of this message (5:21, 24; 6:58, 63; 11:25; 14:6). The Book of Revelation in its very first chapter shows us Christ as possessing the keys of hell and of death (1:18). It knows that death will be no more (21:4), and knows also of the tree of life, the fruits of which give life to those who were formerly alienated from God (22:2). Again Paul rejoices over the victory of Christ (1 Cor 15:55; 2 Tim 1:10). The cosmos which continues to exist apart from Christ does indeed remain *phthartos*. It is moving towards its end (1 Thess 4:17; Rom 13:11ff), but only in order to give place to a new world at the ⁊ parousia. Christ is the *arkhēgos* of this new world. He who is baptised in his death and resurrection, and who has his Spirit—he also has life, and no longer stands under the curse of transitoriness (Col 3:3; Rom 6:3, 8, 23; 5:12, 17; 10:9; Heb 2:14; Rom 8:10; Gal 6:8). Hence for christians there is no longer any mourning (1 Thess 4:13). What was transient has become intransient (1 Cor 15:53).

Bibliography: T. C. Vriezen and H. Conzelmann, *RGG* II³, 799ff (with bibliographical references); E. Lohse, *BHHW* 623; B. Reicke, *RGG* VI³, 912–21; *TDNT* I, 394–6.

Georg Molin

Truth

The biblical concept of truth is something quite different from that conveyed by the term 'truth' in popular parlance. This appears primarily from the Hebrew word ʾĕmeth which lies at its root. Originally and basically concrete in conception, this term has come to have a wide range of meaning attached to it, a range of meaning which has subsequently been taken over by the corresponding word in Greek, *alētheia*. ʾĕmeth (appearing in the Old Testament 132 times) is derived from ʾāmint, a part of the verb ʾāman, meaning 'to be firm, stand firm, be reliable, unchangeable'. The opposite of ʾĕmeth is šeqer, 'instability, nothingness, lie' (see Prov 11:18). Instances of this basic meaning of stability and sureness are to be found in 2 Kings 20:19 = Is 39:8 and Jer 14:13 ('peace and security', 'assured peace'). Again the phrase beʾĕmeth, 'in truth', 'truly', 'really', clearly implies the element of lastingness. Only that which has firmness, that which will not vanish in the next moment is real and true. In Is 16:5 beʾĕmeth should actually be translated 'for ever' (see Sir 37:15; 51:15).

Frequently—in more than half the passages, in fact—ʾĕmeth has a religious meaning. Either alone or in conjunction with ḥesed (↗ grace) it is often referred to as an attribute of God or of the divine law.

1. *As an attribute of God*: in this sense ʾĕmeth is connected with ↗ covenant and promise. (Sir 41:19 LXX [Vulg 24] is hardly the result of an accident, even if the verse seems out of place in the context; see 1 QH 10:30f). In Ex 34:5–7 Yahweh is said to be 'rich in ḥesed (grace, loving-kindness) and ʾĕmeth', and this is explained by the statement that he 'keeps this same ḥesed for a thousand generations'. ʾĕmeth, therefore, is the attitude of God by which he makes his kindness last and be stable. ʾĕmeth, therefore, must be translated literally as 'faithfulness'. In this sense the promises to David in Ps 89 constantly invite comparison with the declarations of Yahweh's ʾĕmeth (see Mic 7:18–20; Zech 8:8; etc). In this sense too Ps 132:11 is particularly enlightening: 'Yahweh swore ʾĕmeth to David, an oath from which he will not turn back . . .'. The object of the oath that is sworn is not some abstract entity such as faithfulness; rather it is connected with objects in the concrete. The *Liber Psalmorum* gives the appropriate rendering *promissum firmum*, 'a sure promise'. The basic connotation of stability contained in ʾĕmeth is applied in the context of the oath and the promise. The fact that ʾĕmeth is found side by side with the justice of God (Zech 8:8; Hos 2:21f [Vulg 19f]; Neh 9:33; ↗ righteousness) or with his holiness (Ps 71:22) shows that the word does not merely mean faithfulness as such, but carries the further connotation of permanence. In the passages referred to this permanence consists precisely in the favourable attitude and behaviour of God towards his own.

2. Another side of the concept ʾĕmeth appears in contexts in which it is used

927

to express the faithfulness of God inasmuch as this constitutes the refuge and sure protection of the just, and hence is often presented under the images of shield, rock and fortress (Ps 91:4; see also Ps 54:7). It is not the covenant faithfulness of Yahweh that is referred to in such passages, but his reliability and unwavering readiness to help quite in general (Ps 40:11; 42; 43; 54:7; 60:4; etc).

3. In four passages in the Old Testament the faithfulness of God is explicitly referred to: in the address of Moses (Deut 7:9) concerning his covenant faithfulness; Deut 32:4 and Is 49:7 in a general sense: God is faithful towards his people; in its most sublime form in Ps 31:6: God's faithfulness is the hiding-place, the refuge of the just; all his trust is based upon him (see also Sir 41:19 LXX; Vulg 24).

4. What does the combination *ḥesed weʾĕmeth* signify? Are the two words used (a) synonymously, (b) as a hendiadys, that is, as signifying lasting kindness, unfailing benevolence, or (c) simply as signifying 'kindness and faithfulness'? Ps 138:2-4 shows that both terms express the two aspects of the realities referred to (covenant and promise) inasmuch as these promises are expressions of the kindness and love of God (*ḥesed*), and inasmuch as God remains faithful to these promises (*ʾĕmeth*) (see Gen 24:27; 32:10; 2 Sam 2:6; 15:20; etc).

5. *ʾĕmeth* is also used of men, whether in respect of the relations of men to each other or in their religious life. 'Men such as fear God, men who are trustworthy', *ʾanšê ʾĕmeth* (Ex 18:21; Neh 7:2). While in both these passages the aspect of faithfulness which the author

primarily has in mind is loyal obedience, nevertheless the connection with the virtue of fearing God shows that the religious aspect is also included. This is also apparent in Hos 4:1f, where the synonyms show us that *ʾĕmeth* here is a social virtue, which applies to the whole range of duties towards one's neighbour. Far more frequently *ʾĕmeth* is used of duties towards God. This can also be deduced from the various similar expressions with which it is set in parallelism: 'Serve the Lord in total self-surrender and faithfulness (*ʾĕmeth*)' (Jos 24:14; see also Judg 9:16, 19). 'I have walked before thee in faithfulness and with a whole heart' (2 Kings 20:3; Is 38:3). 'Hezekiah did what was good and right and faithful (*haʾĕmeth*) before Yahweh' (2 Chron 31:20). 'Jerusalem shall be called the faithful city and the mountain of the Lord of hosts, the holy mountain' (Zech 8:3). Two particularly noteworthy usages are 'to walk in truth' (1 Kings 2:4; 3:6; 2 Kings 20:3; Is 38:3; Pss 26:3; 86:11; Tob 3:5), and 'to do *ʾĕmeth*' (2 Chron 31:20; Sir 27:9; Tob 4:6; 13:6; Is 26:10 [LXX]). In both usages it is faithfulness to God's law that is meant (see especially Tob 3:5) in attitude and in act. Again the phrase 'to practise *ḥesed weʾĕmeth*' is in some instances used of men (Gen 24:49; 47:29; Josh 2:14; Prov 3:3; 14:22; 16:6; 20:28). Here it is precisely steadfastness and faithfulness that *ʾĕmeth* adds to the idea of the exercise of kindness and favour. In some few passages we can even establish a juridical aspect of *ʾĕmeth*, as in Prov 29:14; Ezek 18:8; Zech 7:9: 'to judge in *ʾĕmeth*' is to judge truly because the judgement is immutable.

It can neither be influenced beforehand by corruption, nor retrospectively revised on the grounds that it was unjust. It is only a short step from the idea of *'ēmeth* as faithfulness and reliability to the further significance of integrity. This comes out very clearly in Prov 12:19: 'Truthful lips endure for ever, but a lying tongue is but for a moment'.

6. Truth in the narrower sense is neither a human nor a divine attribute, but simply a quality of speech: 'Truth (*'ēmeth*) is something spoken' which proves to be genuine and reliable even after it has been put to the test, an assertion which does not evaporate into nothingness upon closer examination (see the passage just quoted above from Prov 12:19). Thus the queen of Sheba, when she has seen everything with her own eyes, can confirm what she has heard of Solomon: 'The report was true which I heard . . .', or in a freer translation (Stenzel): 'What I have been told in my own land about your condition of life and your wisdom is in conformity with the facts' (1 Kings 10:6). When Micaiah, against the probabilities, predicts that Achab will be victorious, the king asks him: 'How many times shall I adjure you that you speak to me nothing but the truth in the name of the Lord' (1 Kings 22:16), in other words 'that which really will come to pass'. From these texts alone it can be seen that in Hebrew truth and reality are one and the same—*'ēmeth*. Not to speak the truth is the same as not to express the real state of affairs (see Jer 9:5; 23:28; Zech 8:16). What applies to statements and words also applies to realities. *'ēmeth* in the sense of reality, of a certain genuineness, can be used of these too: eg, Jer 2:21: 'I planted you (Israel) a choice vine, wholly of pure seed (*zerʿa 'ēmeth*). How then have you turned degenerate . . .?' (see also Is 5:2). *'ēmeth* is also used in the sense of the way (Gen 24:48), of a sign (Josh 2:12), of God (2 Chron 15:3; Jer 10:10), always in order to emphasise the genuineness and rightness of the object thus qualified, and to distinguish it from the false or deceitful way, sign or god.

7. Truth as a religious expression: 'The sum of thy words is *'ēmeth*, every one of thy righteous ordinances endures for ever' (Ps 119:160, cf 43), 'thy words are *'ēmeth*' (2 Sam 7:28). The usage 'to walk in *'ēmeth*' adduced above (§ 5) is also found in the form 'to walk in thy *'ēmeth*'. No basic difference is to be inferred from this. The second of these two usages adds only the element that the *'ēmeth* in question comes from God, is taught by him and commanded by him (thus as we find: 'Show me your way, teach me your law', etc). At this point, however, a development is introduced which leads to an identification of *'ēmeth* with the law of God, his revelation or his will: 'Teach me thy way, O Yahweh, that I may walk in thy *'ēmeth*' (Ps 86:11). This manner of speaking attains its full development in the Wisdom books and Daniel: 'For my mouth will utter truth; wickedness is an abomination to my lips' (Prov 8:7; see the verses following and Prov 22:21; Eccles 12:10). A striking combination of synonyms is apparent in Prov 23:23: 'Buy truth and do not sell it; buy wisdom, instruction, and understanding'. 'Truth' (*'ēmeth*) in this context is the teaching of the book as a whole (see 4:5, 7; 16:16; Sir 4:25). In Daniel *'ēmeth* comes to have a purely religious

meaning, for it is used in the sense of the revelation of God: 'In the place of the daily burnt offering transgression was laid down, and truth was thrown down to the ground' (8:12). The transgression here is the form of cult introduced by Antiochus, while the truth is the monotheistic religion of Israel (see also 8:26; 9:13; 10:1, 21; 11:2).

B. *Later Judaism.* In rabbinic judaism and in the Qumran texts *ʾĕmeth* is a term frequently used, and it reappears here with all the nuances and shades of meaning familiar to us from the Old Testament. Let us concentrate primarily on the specifically religious meaning (see A7 above): 1. God himself is the truth; 2. his *tôrâh* is truth; and 3. those who practise it are men of truth, are his faithful ones, the observers of his law, who are in covenant, in union with him.

1. 'As thou, God, art *ʾĕmeth*, so too thy word is *ʾĕmeth*' (Ex Midrash 29:1). God 'is the truth itself' (CD 2:10 [2:11f]), is a God of truth (1 QH 15:25).

2. The *tôrâh* likewise, therefore, as the utterance of the divine word, is *ʾĕmeth* (Midrash Ps 25 § 11). One can speak of a 'law of thy truth' (1 QS 1:15), as also of the 'truth of the law of God' (1 QS 1:12; CD 9:51 [20, 29]). In this case truth and law appear so interchangeable that it amounts almost to an actual identity between the two. Finally *ʾĕmeth* embraces the whole sphere of the divine in general; it designates true religion and the practice of religion, and contrasts these with the attitude of aversion from God and irreligion as expressed by the terms 'wickedness' (*ršᶜ*, *ᶜwl*) or lies (*kzb*, *šqr*).

3. Men are repeatedly said to 'do the truth' (see Tob 4:6; 13:6; Is 26:10 [LXX]; Sir 27:9b—In TestRub 6:9 and TestBen 10:3 it is required that man shall 'practise the truth' towards his neighbour). An equivalent usage (*ᶜabad kûštâ*) is found in Targ. Hos 4:1, and here the moral conduct which is so designated is clearly thought of as connected with the attitude of true religion. The people of Qumran are called 'men of truth who fulfil the law, whose hands do not slumber in the service of truth' (1 Qp Hab VII 10–12). This is synonymous with the service of God (1 QH 2:36). The opposite of it is 'the service of deceit' (*ᶜbwdt šww*), or the works of lies, to which the preacher of lies seduces many (1 Qp Hab X 9–12). Thus on the one side stand the 'men of truth who fulfil the law' (1 Qp Hab VII 10f; 1 QH 9:35), on the other all evil-doers and 'men of deceit' (1 QH 14:14) or 'violent men who rebel against God' (1 Qp Hab VIII 11).

In the Qumran texts, furthermore, much is said of the struggle between truth and perversity, truth and lies, between the 'sons of truth' and the 'sons of perversity'. The spirits are divided into spirits of truth and spirits of perversity (1 QS III 18f), that is into the groups of spirits of life and spirits of darkness. Two hierarchies of spirits, those of truth and light and those of perversity and darkness, are engaged in a struggle with each other, and carry this struggle actually into the hearts of men by the influence which they exercise over them. The whole world is subject to this dualistic influence until the end, the final victory of truth (1 QS IV 19). The 'judgement that is decreed' brings this struggle to an end, and with his 'truth' God purifies the deeds of men. He sprinkles 'the spirit of truth' like lustral water upon all the abomination of lies (*šqr*), (1 QS IV 20).

C. *The New Testament.* Recently doubts have once more been cast, not unjustifiably (von Friedländer), upon the etymology of *alētheia* as meaning a state of affairs which is unconcealed, unveiled, open to view. Here, however, we can leave this question aside, together with the further question of how the concept of *alētheia* was represented in Greek culture—the more so since, in terms of meaning, *alētheia* in the New Testament follows on from the corresponding term in the Old Testament and later judaism, *ʾemeth*.

1. In this connection it is not always easy to discern the precise aspect on which the emphasis is laid in any given instance. In Eph 4:21; Gal 2:5, 14; Rom 2:8 *alētheia* can be taken in the sense of 'validity', a 'valid norm'. But the fact that the opposite of it is mentioned (see Gal 1:6 and above A6) implies that there is an emphasis on genuineness here as well.

2. In Rom 3:7 *alētheia* means the 'faithfulness and reliability' of God (see the preceding phrases *pistis theou* = 'faithfulness of God' [Rom 3:3] and *theou dikaiosunē* = 'God's justice, righteousness' [Rom 3:5]). Exactly as in the Old Testament, it means his faithfulness to his promise (Rom 15:8).

3. In 2 Cor 7:14; 11:10; Phil 1:18; 1 Tim 2:7; 2 Jn 1; 3 Jn 1 *alētheia* means human integrity and honour.

4. In Rom 1:18 it is that which is manifest, well-known that is expressed by *alētheia* (similar to the usage in Wis 6:22). The subject here is the revelation of God which is made known even among the heathens. A little

further, in v 25, the *alētheia* of God is opposed to *pseudos* (= lie, falsehood). Thereby the aspect of *alētheia* which is brought to the fore is that of reality as opposed to deceitfulness, and of genuineness as opposed to falsehood (idols), a contrast which is wholly dependent upon the opposition between *ʾemeth* and *šeqer*.

Thus usages such as *en alētheia(i)*, etc signify *truly* (Col 1:6; see also Acts 4:27; 10:34; Rom 2:2; and especially 1 Jn 3:18).

5. In Acts 26:25; Mk 12:14, 32; Lk 4:25 it is the truth of a statement that is meant.

6. True doctrine (see above A7; see also Philo, *Spec. Leg.* IV, 178, where the proselyte is described as 'changing over to the truth'). Perhaps Gal 2:5, 14 (to which 2 Cor 13:8 is related), passages which have already been mentioned above under 1, should more appropriately be placed under this heading. In 2 Cor 4:2 ('the open statement of the truth') truth stands for the 'word of God' which has just been mentioned. In Rom 10:16 'to hearken to the gospel' has exactly the same significance as the expression 'to follow the truth' in Gal 5:7. Christian faith is 'obedience to the truth' (1 Pet 1:22). The preaching of the gospel is 'the word of truth' (Eph 1:13; Col 1:5; 2 Cor 6:7; etc). 'To arrive at a knowledge of the truth' (2 Tim 3:7 and frequently elsewhere) means nothing else than to become like Christ. In this phrase the words *epignōsis alētheias* (lit. = 'knowledge of the truth') mean 'christian knowledge' deriving from the true teaching, and bearing fruit in the subject's life. Hence in Titus 1:1 the term can appear side by side with

pistis (faith). Here, too, the word *sōthēnai* (lit. = 'to be saved')—as used specifically in the context of conversion to christianity, as it is, more or less, in Rom 8:24—can be made parallel to *eis epignōsin alētheias elthein* (= 'to come to the knowledge of the truth': 1 Tim 2:4). For the same reason, in 1 Tim 4:3, a passage intended to point to the true christians, these can be referred to as *tois pistois kai epegnōkosi tēn alētheian* (= 'those who believe and know the truth'; see Dibelius, 177). In this, too, the connotation of the genuine and unfalsified state of the christian teaching is repeatedly present (see 1 Tim 6:5; 2 Tim 2:18; 3:8; 4:4; Tit 1:14). Bultmann is justified in his apposite statement: 'As the concept of *pistis* [↗ faith] is determined by the thought of obedience, so *alētheia* is 'authoritative teaching'. The way is thus prepared for the historical development which fashions the concept of dogma, in which truth and law are conjoined.' (*TDNT* i, 244.)

7. It is only at this point that we are in a position to combine the two usages *peripatein en alētheia(i)* (= 'to follow the truth': 2 Jn 4; 3 Jn 3f) and *poiein tēn alētheian* (lit. = 'to do the truth': Jn 3:21; 1 Jn 1:6), although we have already pointed out the precise correspondence between the two above in A 5 and B 3. What the phrase expresses is that true integrity which loyalty to the law involves. And it is precisely the Qumran texts which show that this had been perceived. In this sense the corresponding elements in the New Testament cannot be understood otherwise than as referring to the way of life inspired by christian teaching: to do the truth no longer means loyally to observe the law of the Old Testament (and the tradition of the fathers), but to fulfil the law of Christ.

8. John shows a special predilection for the word *alētheia*, though he uses it in a wide variety of senses, and, in fact, frequently combines all the various shades of meaning which it has come to acquire. In addition to these a fresh shade of meaning comes to be expressed by *alētheia* and *alēthinos*, namely, 'that which alone really exists, the transcendent and eternal'. This fresh shade of meaning is acquired under the influence of the hellenistic and dualistic mentality as exemplified in Heb 8:2 (see Philo *Leg. All.* I, 32f; *Vit Mos* I, 289; etc). As it appears in the New Testament, however, it is not altogether unmodified, but is radically conditioned by revelation (as, for instance, in Jn 4:23, where 'the true worshippers' are those who worship in spirit and in truth, that is in the divine reality revealed through Jesus, and not merely through an understanding of God that is purged of anthropomorphisms and spiritualised). Likewise the 'true light' (1 Jn 2:8; Jn 1:9) is 'the light of life' (Jn 8:12). Thus in the johannine *alētheia* three elements are present simultaneously: the truth of the actual statement (in which the underlying reality is expressed), this reality itself, and the revelation of it through and in Christ (Jn 8:40–47; cp v 33 and 18:37). From this we can understand the functions ascribed to the 'truth': it sets free (Jn 8:32), and that not merely as the truth of the spoken word (in the formal sense) but as the reality of divine salvation, as saving knowledge and redemption from sins (Jn 8:33f).

It sanctifies (Jn 17:17-19; see also Jn 15:2f and 1 QS IV 19f; see above B 3). Christ is 'the way, the truth and the life' (Jn 14:6), that is, he has essentially made possible and inaugurated that which the Spirit will carry on, namely, 'he will guide you into all the truth' (Jn 16:13). This means further that in the revelation which Christ brought, word and deed constitute a single entity (one might say a sacramental entity): the word is not the means to an end, but a sign of the divine deed which is inseparable from it. What this 'truth' means for men is nothing less than entry into the sphere of the divine in terms of knowledge and in terms of existence (cf the striking exposition in 1 Pet 1:3-11). It means that they belong to God. 'To be of the truth' (Jn 18:37; 1 Jn 3:19) is the same as 'to be of God' (Jn 8:47). Here we may notice the emphasis which John lays upon the fact that those who are of God hear his word, while those who do not hear it are not of God. What he means by this is to specify the two spheres of influence in which the two groups which he mentions respectively stand. For it is the Christian form of existence, abiding in this truth (considered as the divine deed of salvation), which begins with the preaching and acceptance of the message of this truth; and this must go on to find expression in the conduct which corresponds to this new existence (1 Jn 3:11-20). In fact it must take the form of co-operating with the divine truth (considered as message and as work of salvation) in bringing it to unbelievers (3 Jn 8). Thus the truth 'abides in us and will be with us for ever' (2 Jn 2) because this existence in the truth is itself precisely the true and eternal life (Jn 14:6).

Bibliography: M. Dibelius, *Festschrift G. Heinrici*, Leipzig 1914, 176-89; R. Bultmann, *ZNW* 27 (1928), 113-63; R. Bultmann, *TDNT* I, 238-51; G. Quell, *TDNT* I, 232-7; G. Kittel, *TDNT* I, 237f; M. Zerwick, *VD* 18 (1938), 338-42 and 373-7; F. Asensio, *Misericordia et Veritas*, Rome 1949; I. de la Potterie, *VD* 27 (1949), 336-54; 28 (1950), 29-42; J. C. C. van Drossen, *De derivata van den stam ᵓmn in het Hebreeuwsch van het OT*, Amsterdam 1951; E. T. Ramsdell, *Journal of Religion* 31 (1951), 264-73; F. Nötscher, '"Wahrheit" als theologischer Terminus in den Qumran Texten', *Festschrift V. Christian*, Vienna 1956, 83-90; A. Wikenhauser, *Das Evangelium nach Johannes* (*RNT* 4), 'Exkurs zu Joh 8:39ff'; R. Schnackenburg, *Die Johannesbriefe*, Freiburg 1953 (*ad loc.*); W. Luther, 'Der frühgriechische Wahrheitsgedanke im Lichte der Sprache', *Gymnasium* 65 (1958), 75-107 (against Friedländer); J. H. Vrielink, *Het waarhedsbegrip*, Nijkerk 1956; I. de la Potterie, 'L'arrière-fond du thème johannique de vérité', *Studia Evang.*, Berlin 1959, 277-94; F. Moritz, *Die Wahrheit tun*, Rome 1960 (dissertation); H. Boeder, 'Der frühgriechische Wortgebrauch von Logos und Aletheia', *Arch. f. Begriffsgesch.* 4 (1959), 82-211; E. Heitsch, 'Die nicht-philosophische Aletheia', *Hermes* 90 (1962), 24-33; D. J. Theron, *Aletheia in the Pauline Corpus*, Princeton Theol. Sem. 1950 (dissertation); A. Vögtle, '"Die Wahrheit" als geoffenbarte Wirklichkeit und wirkende Gotteskraft', *Oberrhein. Pastoralblatt* 62 (1961), 1-8; J. Blank, 'Der johanneische Wahrheitsbegriff', *BZ* 7 (1963), 163-73.

Johannes B. Bauer

Vengeance

A law which is to be numbered among the earliest principles of justice known to the ancient Near East is the *lex talionis*. This lays down that when somebody has been wronged or deprived of his rights in any way the recompense which has to be made must be equal in value to the rights of which the injured party has been deprived ('ox for ox', Ex 21:36; 'Eye for eye, tooth for tooth', Ex 21:24); this principle finds its ultimate application in the law of blood vengeance ('life for life', Ex 21:23). The practice of exacting blood vengeance is rooted in the sense of corporate unity which manifests itself in various forms among the peoples of the ancient Near East according to the various ways of life prevailing among them. Some led a nomadic existence, while others had become sedentarised and had developed a peasant culture. These factors had a decisive influence upon the form in which this sense of corporate unity manifested itself. In nomad cultures the tribes living together constitute a unity based on a common 'mind' and 'soul' in which each individual is the representative of the whole, and conversely depends for his basic attitude and outlook upon the whole. This sense of belonging together is based upon a social structure which is patriarchal in character. The consciousness of common descent, whether real or imagined, constitutes a blood bond, and unites the individuals concerned into a community. And it is this community alone which makes it possible to lead a life which is in any sense fruitful. For outside this fellowship the individual has no rights to safeguard his well-being. Hence as a basic principle of justice blood vengeance implies that the tribe takes collective responsibility for the transgressions of any one of its members, and conversely that the community champions the cause of any member who suffers injury at the hands of those outside the tribe. In sedentarised cul-

tures, on the other hand, the exclusive unity of the tribe is dissolved, and local communities take the place of the tribe. These are based upon particular families, and it is to these that the sense of corporate unity is now transferred. In the sphere of justice and law, in place of blood vengeance we now have the *lex talionis*, in which the transgressor against justice is answerable to a greater extent for his own personal crimes, and individual responsibility progressively takes the place of tribal responsibility even though remnants of the nomadic conception of justice still exercise an influence here and there. In ancient Israel the nomadic heritage continued to survive long after the stage of sedentarisation, and for this reason the custom of blood vengeance was still recognised right into the period of the monarchy (Gen 4:23f; 9:6; 34; 1 Sam 25:33). The community was responsible for the acts of the individuals belonging to it (Judg 20:13f; see also Judg 15:9–13), just as, conversely, an entire family could obtain exemption from punishment because of the merits of one of its members (Josh 6:22–5; Judg 1:24f). Hence it was felt to be an obvious expression of divine justice that children were punished for the sins of their fathers (Ex 20:5). Nonetheless, after the sedentarisation of Israel, the village community became increasingly prominent, and urban culture more and more loosened the earlier communal ties. The protection of the individual became the responsibility of the local court, and the awareness of corporate unity was transferred from the tribe to the family. As a result of this the individuality of the particular member of the family was strengthened. Collective responsibility disappeared, the transgressor was held personally responsible for his own misdeeds, and those related to him remained unaffected by his punishment. True, in the grave cases of violation of the sacral law and high treason the family was included in the punishment of the offending member (Josh 7:24ff; 1 Sam 22:12ff; 2 Kings 9:26), but even here the aim of confining punishment to the offender alone is already apparent (2 Kings 14:6). Blood vengeance was already restricted by the prescriptions of the Book of the Covenant, which attached a different degree of guilt to deliberate assassination and manslaughter (Ex 21:13, 14), and, furthermore, made provision for the individual who had done manslaughter to take asylum in a sanctuary (Ex 21:13f). This right of sanctuary certainly also survived till a later stage, for many expressions in the psalms undoubtedly recall this (Pss 5:7–8; 27:2–5; 61:4f). In the nature of things the cities of refuge represented a more permanent institution (Josh 20:1–9; Deut 19:1–14; Num 35:9–34). It was here that the transgressor had to submit himself to the judgement of the elders of the community. In the case of premeditated murder he was delivered up into the hands of the *go'el*, the closest responsible relative of the victim, who incurred the duty of exacting blood vengeance. In the case of unpremeditated killing the perpetrator had to remain in the city of refuge until the death of the high priest. This was probably because the official accession of a new high priest was accompanied by a general amnesty. Since the disappearance of the earlier tribal solidarity entailed fresh dangers for the individual, from now on special emphasis was laid upon the protection of his rights by the reminder that God was his covenant Lord. The oppression of the poor and weak, which is attested in the prescriptions of Deuteronomy and in passages in the prophets and Proverbs (Deut 24:17; 27:19; Is 10:2; Jer 7:6; 22:3; Zech 7:10; Prov 23:10 etc), calls down the vengeance of Yahweh upon the oppressors (Deut 32:35; Is 34:8; 61:2); ie, in place of the earlier solidarity of the tribe, that of religion came to the fore as a determining factor in the people's lives, together with the sense of corporate unity entailed by the covenant with God. Already in the story of David we can discern a certain tendency to aim at meekness in the face of injury and to renounce vengeance for Yahweh's sake (1 Sam 24:7, 11, 19f; 25:31ff). Again, the message proclaimed by the prophets to the effect that the relationship with God was of its nature with the individual as distinct from the community had the effect of finally driving out the idea of collective sharing in guilt (Ezek 18). Finally it was possible for the New Testament to require a complete renunciation of private vengeance (Mt 5:38–42) because of the progressive perfecting of the official concept of justice and the growing sense of an interior moral code. ↗ Enemy, ↗ love, ↗ hate.

Bibliography: E. Merz, *Die Blutrache bei den Israeliten*, Leipzig 1916; H. Cazelles, *Etudes sur le Code de l'Alliance*, Paris 1946, 117–20; J. Scharbert, *Solidarität in Segen und Fluch im AT und seiner Umwelt* (BBB 14), 1958; Eichrodt II–III, 1964⁵, 157ff.

Walter Kornfeld

Victory

Victory and defeat exist as the outcome of ↗ contest, strife, and ↗ war in this world; and defeat exists as the consequence of finite limitations, ↗ sin and ↗ death. Victory is the expression of power (see Hebrew *gᵉbûrâh*), strength, and might. The strong and mighty triumphs in the victory. The weak or he who has been deprived of his power succumbs in the defeat. God's compassionate emptying of himself has overthrown the rulers of this world in the paradox of the Cross; eschatological victory appears in the guise of defeat in this world.

A. The *Old Testament* contains accounts both of the victories of Israel and of the victories of her enemies, defeats suffered by the people. In the interpretation of Israel's history, which is focused upon Yahweh's powerful and gracious leadership, the victories and military successes (Ex 15:1–18; 17:8–16; Josh 6:16; 10:10; Judg 7:15; 1 Sam 14:6; 2 Chron 14:10f) are ascribed to HIM who fights on his people's behalf (Ex 14:14; 2 Chron 20:15). 'To conquer' (=*yšᶜ* in the Hiphil) in Hebrew means 'to obtain help from God'. Yahweh himself fights for his people and makes them rich in victories (Deut 33:29; see also Hab 3:8). Yahweh, who alone is truly powerful (Ps 44:4; 48; Is 49:24–7), gives the victory (Deut 20:4; Josh 22:4; 1 Sam 14:45; 2 Sam 8:6). In their battles the people entreat Yahweh for victory (Ex 17:11). Victory depends upon him (Prov 21:31), and they receive it from him as a gift (Ps 18:32ff; 20:7–10; see also Ps 118:15f). It is not ascribed to their own power in battle

(Ps 33:16f; 1 Macc 3:19; 2 Macc 10:37f; 13:15; 15:8ff; Eccles 9:11; Judg 7:2ff; see also 1 QM III 5:8f; IV 13; XI 4f). But even though Yahweh is the unconquerable covenant partner of the people (Deut 32:22–43; Is 30:27–33; Nah 1:2–8; Hab 3; Judg 6:13ff), he can also give the victory to the enemies of the people and assign defeat to themselves (2 Chron 21:14; 24:20; 25:8–20; Jer 15:1–9; 27:6; Ezek 22). Moreover the people are aware as a matter of experience that in their victories, or in the victory of individuals among them, the power of evil is not finally broken. These factors keep alive their awareness, especially in the message of all the prophets, that every victory in this present age is subject to the ambiguity of that which is provisional and which merely foreshadows the final eschatological victory of God. This will take place in the final age, when God, either in person or through his Messiah, will enter into conflict, battle, war, as in the primordial age he waged war against the chaos dragon (Ps 74:13; 89:10; see also Is 51:9f; Job 26:11f), will overcome all the 'victories' of this world, of sin, death and Satan, and will finally set up his kingdom (Gen 3:15; Ps 51:62 [LXX]; see also Zech 14; Ezek 38f; Is 63:1–6) and usher in everlasting peace (Is 9:1–7; 11:1–9; Jer 23:5f; Ezek 34:23ff; etc).

B. According to the *New Testament*, in ↗ Jesus the one who is stronger has come, the one who conquers Satan and his accomplices (Lk 11:22; Col 2:15), the servant who brings justice to victory (Mt 12:20), the conqueror of the 'world' (Jn 16:33). In his preaching by word and deed, the victory of

God over the 'world', over the devils, sin, sickness, and death (see the miracle stories in the gospels), is accomplished. The victory gained in the death of Jesus (1 Cor 15:55)—in the world's eyes an ignominious defeat—has been confirmed by God through the resurrection. Jesus is the lion from the tribe of Judah who has conquered (Rev 5:5), the victor who has set out to conquer (Rev 6:2), the Lamb who was slain (Rev 5:12), who conquers the kings of the earth because he is the Lord of lords and the King of kings (Rev 17:14). The victory of Christ, won in death and resurrection, is only temporary, hidden (in defeat), and it is not until his ↗ *parousia* that it will finally be revealed for what it is. The victory of Satan and his forces (Rev 11:7; 13:7), which is now to be seen in the forefront of affairs, will have no enduring future because this 'victory' is only a 'constantly being on the point of' victory (Schlier), which is in despair of being able to hide the real defeat, and seeks to postpone the unveiling of the final victory of Christ.

Taken with Jesus in his failure, the christian has already in the present a share in the victory of Christ in faith, hope, and love (Rom 8:37; 1 Jn 2:13f; 5:4f; Rev 12:10f; 15:2), but he still remains engaged in the struggle (1 Cor 9:24; Phil 3:14), must show patience, steadfastness, and faithfulness (Rev 2–3), must fight against the 'world', against the forces of infidelity and immorality (1 Jn 2:13f; 5:4), in order that he may, as victor, be given a share of the kingdom with Christ (Rev 2:26; 3:21) and eternal life (Rev 2:7) in the blessed state of union with God (Rev 21:7). In faith and in love (especially as proved in the ordeal of martyrdom) the christian extends the victory of Christ in history already here below, the victory of Christ which consists in the fact 'that it is no longer the self-will which dominates history from within that prepares the immediate and the final future for itself, but the love of God, which has come to reign in Jesus Christ' (H. Schlier, *Besinnung auf das NT* II, 361). The christian can celebrate the victory of Christ already in the here and now in the words of the hymn: 'Thanks be to God who gives us the victory through our Lord Jesus Christ' (1 Cor 15:57).

Bibliography: *TDNT* IV, 942–5; F. Rienecker (ed.), *Lexikon zur Bibel*, Wuppertal 1960[2], 1295–6; *DBT* 553–5; R. Völkl, *Christ und Welt nach dem NT*, Würzburg, 1961, 430 and 454–63; H. Schlier, 'Jesus Christus und die Geschichte nach der Offenbarung des Johannes', *Besinnung auf das NT* II, Freiburg 1954, 358–73; H. Schlier, *Principalities and Powers in the New Testament*, London and New York 1961; R. Schnackenburg, *Die Johannesbriefe*, Freiburg 1963[2], 253–5.

Rudolf Pesch

Vigilance

The English concept of 'being awake' is used to cover several ideas which in biblical theology are distinct. What is common to them all is the emphasis on paying special heed. The most important of the aspects covered is that of preparedness or vigilance, which is particularly emphasised in the New Testament. At the same time, however, the other aspects must not on this account go altogether disregarded. Above all it is necessary to recognise which groups of ideas are mutually overlapping or even, in certain cases, synonymous.

A. *Old Testament*. The demand of God that his commandments, words and ways must be exactly observed is found in numerous passages in the Old Testament, together with warnings of punishment for non-observance. (Among the great number of these passages, see especially Ex 12:17, 24f; 13:10; 23:13, 15; Lev 8:35; 18:4f, 26, 30; 19:37; 20:8, 22; 22:9, 31; 25:18; 26:3; Deut 4:2, 6; 6:2, 17; 10:13; 12:28; 28:13; etc). Next among the prophets we find the Israelites reproached with having failed to maintain this observance, on which so much stress had been laid (see Mal 2:9; 3:7; Jer 16:11). Together with the more general exhortations we also find exhortations to maintain the same exact observance of individual commandments, especially the sabbath commandment (see Ex 31:13f; Lev 19:30; 26:2; Deut 5:12, 15; Is 56:2), but also the commandment prescribing unleavened bread for the Passover (see Ex 12:17; 23:15). The necessity of keeping guard over that which proceeds from the mouth is the subject of a special exhortation (Deut 23:23). In return for paying due heed to his will in the manner thus commanded God promises a reward (Ex 15:26; 19:5; 23:22; 1 Kings 6:12; etc). The greatest reward of God for loyal adherence to his commandments is the assurance that he in his turn watches over the devout (Ex 23:20: his angel goes before Israel; Ps 121:4, 7; 12; 17:8; 34:20; 89:28). The devout entreat God for this benevolent watchfulness over them (see Ps 16:1; 86:2; Jer 5:24; Ps

141:9). The idea of watchfulness (for the *parousia*) hardly occurs in the Old Testament.

B. In the *New Testament* also exact observance is referred to and required, and those who do not obey will be punished. The rich young man boasts of his observance of the law (Mt 19:20 and parallels). Stephen reproaches his adversaries with deficiency in this loyalty to the law (Acts 7:53; see also Gal 6:13). Blessed are they who keep the word of God exactly (Lk 11:28). He who keeps the word of Christ will not be judged by him (Jn 12:47). The clauses of the apostolic decree must be observed exactly (Acts 21:25). Timothy must hold firm to the teaching which has been handed down to him (1 Tim 6:20; 2 Tim 1:14).

Christians must guard themselves from devils (1 Jn 5:21) and in general pay great heed to themselves lest they lose the stability which they have acquired (2 Pet 3:17). Again, according to the teaching of the New Testament, God watches over the men who remain loyal to him (2 Thess 3:3; Jude 24). Christ has kept those who have been entrusted to him; the only exception is the son of perdition (Jn 17:12). The elders of Ephesus are exhorted to watchfulness over the flocks of God which have been entrusted to them (Acts 20:31). The same applies to the 'angel' of Sardis (Rev 3:2). The leaders of the churches watch over those who are under their authority and must render an account for them (Heb 13:17). By far the most significant statement concerning vigilance in the New Testament is the exhortation, which is so much stressed, to be ready for the *parousia*. Since we know neither the day nor the hour we must be ready and watch (Mt 24:42; 25:13). Just as a householder would watch if he knew at what hour the thief was to come, so we would watch if we knew the hour of the *parousia* (Mt 24:43). But the Father has hidden the day and the hour from us in this way (Mk 13:32 and parallels) in order that he might lay vigilance upon us as a task (Mk 13:34). This command to watch applies to the apostles, but likewise to 'all' (Mk 13:35, 37). Blessed are those servants whom when the Lord comes he shall find watching; the Lord himself will be their servant (Lk 12:37f).

The episode of the Garden of Olives shows how closely the prayer and the vigilance required of Christ are connected (Mt 26:38–41 and parallels). It is necessary (physically) to watch in order to pray; through prayer we keep watch in expectation of the coming of Christ. Clearly this impressive exhortation of the Lord has been taken up by the apostles (1 Cor 16:13; Col 4:2: 'Be watchful in prayer'; see also Eph 6:18; 1 Thess 5:6; 1 Pet 5:8).

In this case, as in so many others, the mysterious Book of Revelation takes up this exhortation of the Lord and unites many of his different sayings in a single one, that namely in which he is represented as saying: 'Blessed is he who is awake, keeping his garments that he may not go naked and be seen exposed' (Rev 16:15).

Bibliography: Meinertz I, 64f; A. Oepke, *TDNT* II, 338f; Bultmann 79; G. Friedrich, Osterloh 660f; M. Didier, *DBT* 563–5.

Wolfgang Beilner

Virgin birth

There can be no mistaking the special interest with which Matthew and Luke record, at different points in their respective infancy narratives, the mysterious manner in which Jesus was conceived by his virgin mother Mary (Mt 1:18–25; Lk 1:26–38). This was achieved by the Spirit of God without the intervention of a human father. Even if we accept the generally admitted position that both narratives are independent of each other from the literary point of view, still they do both derive from an earlier tradition which is common to them both. A further indication of this from the form-critical point of view is that the two accounts agree in all essentials in the basic structure and plan of the revelation episode: the imparting of the mystery—difficulties and ponderings on the part of the recipient—explanation by the angel—willingness and acceptance on the part of her to whom it is addressed. Thus the tradition reaches back beyond the stage at which the gospels were written to the first age of the Jewish–christian community, a fact which is confirmed in Matthew and Luke alike by the religious and linguistic colouring of the narrative.

In Matthew the uniqueness of Jesus' conception is already indicated at the conclusion of the genealogy of Joseph (1:16), and that too by means of a formula which he has probably employed of set purpose: 'the child and his mother' (2:11, 13f, 20f). Likewise in Lk 3:23 the immediate significance of the parenthesis *hōs enomizeto* (='as was supposed') is that it is an indication of the fact that it was only in the judgement of those among whom he lived that Joseph was counted as the father of Jesus, whereas the real mystery of Jesus' birth is imparted in Lk 1:26–38. Here a further point is indicated, namely that whereas the incarnation of Jesus was brought about miraculously by the Holy Spirit, at first this remained unknown to the generality of men, and the true facts were preserved only in the narrow circle of the initiated. In view of this, those who regard the silence of the rest of the New Testament as an argument against the historical truth of the virgin birth find that their objections are deprived of their force. The virgin birth was not included as an urgent and vital element in the early christian preaching because, according to Acts 1:22; 10:37 and according to the general outline and the content of Mark (see 1:1), this consisted essentially in the 'words and deeds' of Jesus (Acts 1:1) in the course of his public work. It began, therefore, with his baptism and continued up to the witness to the resurrection. So far as judaism was concerned, it was more important that the messianic characteristics of Jesus should be pointed out than the fact of his virgin birth, and first and foremost among these messianic characteristics was the proof of his Davidic descent as demonstrated by both the family trees of Joseph (Mt 1:1–17; Lk 3:23–38). This was all the more true in view of the fact that any idea of a virgin birth was quite unfamiliar to the Jews. Thus Paul too has no reason to speak of the virgin birth in connection with his message of redemption. Indeed his primary concern throughout was the preaching of salvation, and his interest in the history of Jesus was

secondary and subordinate to this. The phrase *genomenon ek gunaikos* (= 'born of woman') in Gal 4:4 is an expression for the birth of a man which also occurs in the Old Testament (see Job 14:1; compare Mt 11:11 with Lk 7:20). Again, 'without father, without mother' in Heb 7:3 is not meant to refer to the virgin birth, and the variant readings for Jn 1:13f (b, Iren., Tertul. have *natus est* in the singular), which might be adduced in support of the virgin birth (in the apocryphal Letter of the Apostles 3 the phrase is taken in this sense), cannot be maintained from the point of view of textual criticism. From the fact that the virgin birth is not included among the themes and statements regarded as essential from the outset in the early christian preaching, it can be deduced that it was not a 'creation' of the community belief, and that the idea of the virgin birth could not have been an assumption deriving from this.

While, therefore, the attestation of the virgin birth in the New Testament is relatively scanty, still no statement can be found in it which is opposed to the possibility or the actuality of the virgin birth. It is true that Jesus is described by his countrymen as 'the carpenter's son' (Mt 13:55; in the parallel passage of Mk 6:3 he is called simply 'the carpenter, the son of Mary' without any mention of Joseph), or as 'the son of Joseph' (Lk 3:23; 4:22; Jn 1:45; 6:42). Again in Lk 2:27, 41ff there is mention of his 'parents'. In Lk 2:33 we find a reference to 'his father and his mother', and in Lk 2:48 'your father and I'. But these references apply to the legal fatherhood of Joseph in the sense attested in Mt

1:1–17, and from this it is to be concluded that in the popular estimation Jesus was also regarded as the son of Joseph by physical descent (see Lk 3:23). It must be observed that neither Matthew nor Luke has felt that these statements represent any contradiction of what they have recorded in their infancy narratives concerning the conception of Jesus by the miraculous intervention of the Spirit, and without any human father. In fact this is expressed particularly clearly in the manner in which the generations follow strictly one upon another in the human genealogy recorded in Mt 1:1–17, and also in the revelation concerning the part played by the Holy Spirit in the conception of Jesus (Mt 1:18–25). From Mk 3:21 inferences have sometimes been drawn to the effect that when the 'friends' of Jesus took measures to restrain him Mary did not behave like a mother who was conscious of the miraculous and mysterious circumstances of his birth. But no argument can really be adduced from this passage, for it has nothing whatever to tell us either about whether his mother was present at all, or about her behaviour on this occasion. On the other hand we should maintain an equal reserve with regard to the exact meaning of the saying of Mary in the episode recorded in Jn 2:1–11. For apart from the unique style of the johannine presentation we cannot conclude with any certainty that the reference to his mother implies that it was her awareness of the mystery of the birth of her son that made her expect him to give miraculous assistance on this occasion.

It is equally impossible to establish that the infancy narrative, together with the tradition of the virgin birth, must represent a secondary embellishment subsequently prefixed to the earlier account of Jesus' public ministry. As has been mentioned above, from the aspects of religion and language alike various elements in the narrative evince a judaeo–christian character present in them from the outset, and this tells against any such assumption. This is true not only of Luke but equally of Matthew. On examining his work we can discern exactly the same methods of presentation and composition in the infancy narrative as in the main part of the gospel, so that the first two chapters must have grown up together with the gospel as a whole.

A. von Harnack attempted by means of arguments based on literary criticism to strike out the passages referring to the virgin birth from the lukan narrative (1:27 with its two mentions of *parthenos* (= virgin, young woman); 1:34f with its clear assertion of the miraculous conception; 3:23: *hōs enomizeto*) on the grounds that they are secondary additions. In this way he sought to arrive at an account in which the virgin birth was omitted. This attempt, though misguided, has not yet been wholly recognised as obsolete. From the text-critical point of view this approach involves an indefensible arbitrariness with regard to the clear and unambiguous assertion of these passages, but apart from this the erasures which it involves would deprive the narrative of its underlying point and consistency, and would fail to do justice to the significant difference between the proclamation of the birth of Jesus here, and that found in Jn

1:8-25. The very fact that the angel was sent not to Joseph—as might have been expected from his prior apparition to Zechariah—but to Mary, the bride, shows that there is a mystery here which primarily affects Mary. A further point which can be noticed in the narrative of the prediction of the birth of John is that the great age of Zechariah and the barrenness of Elizabeth up to this point is stressed, so that the intervention of God here is brought into line with the Old Testament episodes affecting women such as Sarah, who were favoured by God with the power to conceive naturally even though circumstances had seemed to rule it out. The same point is implicitly conveyed in the story of Zechariah and Elizabeth as told in Lk 1:23f. In Mary, on the other hand, as presented in Lk 1:27, 34, we are confronted with a young, chaste maiden who received a promise and a guarantee that she would conceive a child who was the Messiah by reason of a special intervention on God's part. In this no reference whatever is made to any human father, and in fact it can plainly be seen that any such father is excluded. The evangelist's reserve with regard to the fact of the conception and the miraculous incarnation of the child is palpable, and he says nothing of this.

These considerations, drawn as they are from the intrinsic content of the narrative, tell strongly in favour of the position that the virgin birth was intended from the first to belong to the gospel narrative of Luke. But apart from this we have the witness of Matthew, which is incontestable on either literary or text-critical grounds. And this, as has been said, must derive from the same original tradition as that which lies behind Luke.

The miraculous intervention of God transcending the process of natural generation is described in Lk 1:35: *pneuma hagion epeleusetai epi se kai dunamis hupsistou episkiasei se* ('the Holy Spirit will come upon you, and the power of the Most High will overshadow you'). Again, in Mt 1:18, 20 the words *ek pneumatos hagiou* ('of the Holy Spirit') make God the agent of the virginal conception. 'Holy Spirit' here can hardly be intended in a trinitarian sense, but rather in accordance with Old Testament usage, for which the synoptics show a preference, so that it is used to designate the special intervention of God. It is apparent that the two relevant clauses stand in synonymous parallelism to one another, and from this it can be deduced that the words 'power of the Most High' is an alternative expression of the same idea. The two expressions 'come upon you' and 'overshadow you', which are likewise to be taken as synonymous, are hardly intended as analogous to the natural processes of generation. Such an interpretation cannot be maintained either on grounds of linguistic usage or in terms of the Old Testament and Jewish idea of God. In view of the religious tone of the narrative, characterised as it is throughout by an atmosphere of deep reverence, it is more probable that the term *overshadow* is calculatedly reminiscent of the 'glory of God' descending upon the Tabernacle as described in Ex 40:34f. The term used for this in LXX is *epeskiazen*. The clause in 1:35b can be translated in various ways, but the reference to the 'Son of God' which it contains is certainly not intended to imply that it was only through the virgin birth and by reason of it that the child who was conceived was to be called 'Son of God'. The references to the 'Holy Spirit' and the 'power of the Most High' point rather to the mystery of the Son of God from all eternity, who by means of the virgin birth becomes man. Admittedly this indication is somewhat subtle, and, from a theological point of view, rather vague in the manner of its formulation (see the interpretation of 'Holy Spirit' and 'power of the Most High' in the earlier patristic exegesis of the *Logos*).

For critics of the gospels who have a rationalist approach, and who deny the reality of the supernatural as attested in biblical revelation, the question of how the idea of the virgin birth arose represents a much discussed problem. The passage from Isaiah (7:14) concerning the conception and birth of Immanuel through a 'maiden', which is cited in Mt 1:22f, plays a particularly important part in this discussion. Attention is especially focused upon the term *parthenos*, the LXX translation of the Hebrew *ʿalmâh*. It is held that it is possible to regard this prophetic oracle as the point of departure for the idea of a virgin birth. However the fact must be borne in mind that in LXX *parthenos* is also used to designate a young woman who has attained sufficient maturity to be ready for marriage (Gen 24:43; 34:3; Sir 30:20), so that it cannot be established that when the translator used *parthenos* in this passage of Isaiah he was thinking of a virgin in the strict sense, let alone of a virginal conception and birth. But over and above these considerations it must further be observed that the quotation,

which probably also underlies the lukan narrative, as used by Matthew has chiefly the force of a reflective commentary. He often inserts quotations of this kind by way of commentary in order to establish a connection between the facts which he has received and is handing down (and which are initially quite independent of the Old Testament records) and the salvific history recorded in the Old Testament. In the instance under consideration it should be borne in mind that, according to the present state of our knowledge of pre-christian judaism, Is 7:14 was never interpreted in the sense of a virgin birth, so that to the Jewish reader the account in Mt 1:18-25 must have appeared absolutely new and astonishing. Thus Is 7:14 cannot be taken as the point of departure for the idea of the virgin birth. Moreover the extent to which the contrary opinion was prevalent in judaism can also be gathered from the fact that in the later Greek translations of the Old Testament (second century: Aquila, Theodotian, Symmachus), which emerged in the time of the anti-christian polemic, the neutral word *neanis* (=young woman) was adopted in place of *parthenos* in Is 7:14.

Other attempts at explaining the virgin birth as recorded in the New Testament seek to establish influences of oriental and hellenistic myths according to which famous men such as Plato, Alexander, and Augustus were born of the union of gods with human women. In this connection the birth of a child promised in Virgil's Fourth Eclogue has been the object of special notice, as also have the ideas of the origins of divinised kings as children of the queen and the god Amon-Re, which are to be found especially in Egypt. These variations upon the *hieros gamos* (= 'sacral marriage') theme differ widely one from another, ranging from an extremely realistic and gross idea of sexual union to a sublimisation of the process. But however varied the individual versions may be, the idea always persists of a material union, and in this connection the expression *parthenos*, constantly recurring especially in these myths, is used in a very broad sense. Thus Ishtar, the Babylonian goddess of love (as also her counterparts Aphrodite, Hathor-Isis, or the mother of Helios), is often called 'virgin' although she appears as 'the *hierodoulē* (= temple courtesan) of all the gods'. This description is merely intended to convey the idea of unfading bloom and freshness, or that of the unwavering power of the goddess; it is not meant to contain the implication of being virginally intact. In this connection it should be noticed that in the earliest age of christianity these myths were no longer taken seriously as relating historical facts even among pagans. For this reason it is more than questionable whether the interests of christian preaching would have been served by ascribing virgin birth in this sense to men unless it was supported by the awareness of a revelation which was taken extremely seriously. Moreover such an assumption would utterly fail to do justice to the biblical concept of God, differing essentially as this did from that prevailing in the religions of antiquity. This idea of God as the absolutely spiritual being also falls to the ground if we assume that the conception of *pneuma* in the infancy nar-

rative is nothing else than a substitute for conceptions found in the accounts of 'sacral marriages' in hellenistic mythology. In that case one would be forced to assume that the idea of the spirit in the infancy narrative was different from that in the rest of the gospel. Besides this we should also notice that the infancy narrative emerged from the matrix of Jewish christianity, and this implies that it is the Hebrew word *rûaḥ* which lies behind the word *pneuma* ($\nearrow$ spirit), and this Hebrew word has a feminine, not a masculine, force.

One further point remains to be added. It has sometimes been suggested that the idea of the virgin birth arose from theologising activities within the christian community as it sought to interpret its beliefs. But in what we have said above we have already made it clear that any such hypothesis is wholly superfluous. For the virgin birth is not necessarily postulated by the christian message, however much— once we have received the revealed truth—we may go on to educe ideas from it which are significant in their bearing upon the mystery of the incarnation of the eternal Son of God.

Bibliography: O. Bardenhewer, *Mariä Verkündigung*, Freiburg 1903; A. Steinmann, *Die jungfr. Geburt d. Herrn*, Münster 1926; J. Gresham, *The Virgin Birth of Christ*, New York and London 1930; M. Dibelius, *Jungfrauengeburt und Krippenkind*, Heidelberg 1932; J.-M. Vosté, *De conceptione virginali Jesu Christi*, Rome 1933; K. L. Schmidt, 'Die jungfr. Geburt Jesu Christi', *TB* 14 (1935), 289–97; K. Prümm, 'Empfangen vom Hl. Geiste, geboren aus Maria der Jungfrau', *Der christl. Glaube und die altheidnische Welt* I, 1935, 253–333; D. Edwards, *The Virgin Birth in History and Faith*, London 1943; R. Laurentin, *Structure et théologie de Lc 1–2*, Paris 1957; *R. Laurentin, *Queen of Heaven*, Dublin–London 1961²; E. Nroden,

Die Geburt des Kindes, Darmstadt 1958; E. Pax, *LTK* v², 1210f; G. Delling, *TDNT* v, 826–37; J. Bauer, 'Monstra te esse matrem, virgo singularis', *MTZ* 9 (1958), 124–35; K. H. Schelkle, *Die Mutter des Erlösers*, Düsseldorf 1958; J. Schmid, *Das Ev. nach Lukas (RNT* 3), 1960⁴, 44–50; O. Michel and O. Betz, *Von Gott gezeugt (BZNW* 26), 1960, 3–23; J. Gewiess, 'Lk 1:34', *BZ* 5 (1961), 221–34; A. Strobel, 'Der Gruss an Maria', *ZNW* 53 (1962), 87–111; G. Miegge, *Die Jungfrau Maria*, Göttingen 1962; M. Rehm, 'Almah', *BZ* 8 (1964), 89–101; A. Vögtle, 'Die Genealogie Mt 1:2–11 und die matthäische Kindheitsgeschichte', *BZ* 8 (1964), 45–58 and 239–62; and 9 (1969), 32–49; *L. Hermans, *The Bible on the Childhood of Jesus*, London 1965; *E. Schillebeeckx, *Mary, Mother of the Redemption*, London and New York 1964, 9–47.

Johannes Kürzinger

Virginity

A. The only reasons known to the *Old Testament* for setting a high value on virginity are, first, that maidens should be kept inviolate up to their marriage, and secondly, that virginity constitutes an element in cultic purity (↗ clean and unclean). For instances of the importance attached to maidens being preserved inviolate see Gen 34:7, 31 and also Gen 24:16, Judg 19:24. The loss of her virginity means that the maiden's marriageable value is diminished (Ex 22:15f; Deut 22:14–19). Indeed it entails the penalty of stoning (Deut 22:20f) or at any rate the loss of her honour (2 Sam 13:2–18; Lam 5:11; Sir 7:24; 42:9–11). The High Priest is forbidden to take any but a virgin in marriage (Lev 21:13f. This prescription applies to all priests in Ezek 44:22).

Virginity as a life-long state is unknown. So far from being a desirable condition it is counted as the greatest misfortune to die before marriage (Judg 11:37f. Moving scenes of funeral lamentations are known from Greek vase paintings, especially those appearing upon vessels destined for unmarried women: see K. Schefold, *Griechische Kunst als relig. Phänomen*, Hamburg 1959, 103), or even simply to remain childless when one has been married (Gen 30:23; 1 Sam 1:6, 11, 15). When the menfolk have been decimated by war the women actually decide to enter upon a marriage in which a single husband is shared by seven of them, and in which, moreover, they make themselves responsible for their own food and clothing, simply for the sake of being married and being able to bear the name of a husband (Is 4:1).

There are some indications that the unmarried state was prized in *later judaism*, in that it was considered honourable for a widow to remain unmarried after the death of her husband (Judith 16:22; cf Lk 2:36f). This is in line with the ideal of control of the instincts as pleasing to God, an ideal which finds expression in the prayer of Tobias: 'Not for fleshly lust do I take to wife . . .' (Tob 8:7). In Essene circles one repeatedly encounters a certain disdain for marriage, which is based first and foremost upon a contempt for woman, who is inclined to be dissolute and unfaithful (Josephus, *Bell. Jud.*, 2:8, 2), egotistical and immoderately jealous, shameless and arrogant, one who corrupts men's morals and would actually break up the monastic community of the Essenes (Philo in Euseb. *Praep. Evang.* 8:11). How far these reasons put forward by Philo and Josephus are the correct ones is incertain. Doubtless married

Essenes did occur, and in the Community Rule this is actually presupposed. But against this 1 QS is silent on the subject of marriage. Prohibitions such as that of not appearing naked before fellow-members of the sect or even allowing an involuntary exposure of the private parts (1 QS VII 12–14) visualise a community of men in that they are directed against homosexual tendencies. On the other hand, skeletons of women and children also have been found in the cemetery of Qumran, and celibacy is nowhere enjoined as a matter of precept. Still less is any motive adduced for such a prescription. Probably the solution is to be found in the fact that the members of the community thought of themselves as priests ministering at the true sanctuary, and it would have seemed obvious to them that sexual abstinence was required as a necessary condition for this cultic ministration (↗ clean; see also J. Maier, *Die Texte vom Toten Meer* II, Munich–Basle 1960, 10f).

B. The *New Testament.* Mary, espoused as she was to Joseph, after she had brought the divine child into the world while still remaining a virgin (↗ virgin birth), chose the state of permanent virginity. Contrary to a long-established exegesis of Lk 1:34, however, she did not regard virginity in marriage as praiseworthy, or undertake it right from the first, for otherwise she would not have committed herself to entering upon any marriage at all. Mary's question in Lk 1:34 (in the context of the story of the annunciation the motive behind this is to provide an opening for the divine message) expresses nothing but astonishment at the fact that she is to become a mother at the time of her espousals, before actually being taken into her bridegroom's house (for a detailed exposition, see J. B. Bauer, *MTZ* 9 [1958], 124–35, and *Theologisches Jahrbuch*, Leipzig 1960, 257–70).

Jesus freely chooses the celibate state. We may recall the saying concerning those who disqualify themselves for marriage for the sake of the kingdom of heaven, a saying which it is not given to everyone to understand (Mt 19:10ff). J. Blinzler (*ZNW* 28 [1957], 254–70) is certainly right when he interprets this as Jesus' self-defence before the scribes and pharisees, who are precisely reproaching Jesus with this celibate life that he leads. In any case, the apostles did not take the saying as applying to themselves, as is shown by 1 Cor 9:5; for here we are told that they take their wives with them on their missionary journeys (see J. B. Bauer, *BZ* 3 [1959], 94–102). From this it may be deduced that Jesus' answer to Peter's question (Lk 18:28ff): 'There is no man who has left house or wife etc . . . for the sake of the kingdom of God who will not receive manifold more . . .', in no sense demands that marriage shall be completely given up. What Jesus is really concerned with here, as also in Mt 10:37f, is to define the priority of duties. As for the mention of the four daughters of Philip the evangelist in Acts 21:9, it may reasonably be doubted whether this is intended to imply anything more than simply that these '*virgins* endowed with the spirit of prophecy' were unmarried.

Paul, who is himself celibate (1 Cor 7:7), recommends the celibate state when it is a ↗ charisma (1 Cor 7:7), because then man can give undivided service to Christ (1 Cor 7:32–5), especially in the final age which has already commenced (1 Cor 7:26, 28), for this entails a certain emancipation from all earthly ties. We should keep our eyes fixed upon the ultimate, in which there will be no sexual union (1 Cor 7:29 cp Mk 12:35; Mt 22:30; Lk 20:35f; see further Mt 24:37ff; Lk 17:26f), no tears (1 Cor 7:30; see also Mt 5:4; Lk 6:21; Rev 7:17; 21:4), no earthly joy, no earthly gain, and no more commerce (1 Cor 7:30f; see also Lk 12:15–21; ↗ riches).

The pastoral epistles require that he who undertakes an ecclesiastical office shall not have entered upon in the past, or enter upon in the future, any fresh marriage after the death of his first wife (1 Tim 3:2, 12; Tit 1:6). Again, only widows of one husband were admitted to the official status of widows in the early christian community (1 Tim 5:9). In both instances, proof of a well-balanced personality must be looked for, as manifested precisely by self-mastery in the matter of the instincts (see the conclusion of A above).

The 'virgins' (*parthenoi*) mentioned in Rev 14:4 are to be taken in a metaphorical sense. 'These have not defiled themselves with women, for they are chaste'. What is meant by this is faithful adherence to Christ, just as elsewhere: in the prophets, too, unchastity and adultery mean unfaithfulness to God as covenant partner. It cannot be intended to designate these chosen ones as virgins in the physical sense (as is still obstinately maintained in many commentaries, see Lohmeyer, Schick, etc, *ad loc.*), for in that case Peter himself and the other married apostles would be excluded, and marriage would be stigmatised as 'defilement' (see Bonsirven and Karrer, *ad loc.*). Similarly in 2 Cor 11:2 virginity is an expression of total and exclusive adherence to Christ, to whom Paul has consecrated the community: 'For I betrothed you to Christ to present you as a pure bride to her one husband' (for the linguistic usage, see also Jer 18:13ff).

Bibliography: J. Fischer, *Ehe und Jungfräulichkeit im NT* (*BZF* 9) 1919, 3f; J. Dillersberger, 'Die Jungfräulichkeit nach der Lehre Jesu', *Anima* 7 (1952), 201–7; A. Löhr, 'Die Jungfräulichkeit als christliche Wesenshaltung nach Schrift und Liturgie', *Anima* 7 (1952), 207–20; J. Schneider, *TDNT* II, 765–8; G. Delling, *TDNT* v, 826–37; J. B. Bauer, *BL* 23 (1955/6), 8–13; Haag 875f; J. Michl, *LTK* v², 1213f; J. Leipoldt, *Griechische Philosophie und frühchristliche Askese*, Berlin 1961, esp. 31–8; J. Leal gives an enlightening treatment of 1 Cor VII in *VD* 35 (1957), 97–102, and especially also 1 Cor VII 36ff, where it is certainly a christian man (that is not 'father') and his bride (here *parthenos* manifestly has this meaning, just as in 2 Cor XI 2) that are in question (see also W. G. Kümmel, *Festschrift Bultmann*, (*BZNW* 21), 1957², 275–95; J. B. Bauer, *BL* 22 [1954/5], 143; and J. O'Rourke, *CBQ* 20 [1958], 292–8); L. Legrand, 'Fécondité virginale selon l'Esprit dans le NT', *NRT* 84 (1962), 65–75; L. Legrand, 'The Sacrificial Value of Virginity', *Scripture* 14 (1962), 65–75; L. Legrand, *La virginité dans la Bible*, Paris 1964; E. H. Maly, 'Virginity in the New Testament', *Marian Studies* 13 (1962), 41–61; R. Boon, 'Ontstaan, verbreiding en theologie der virginiteit in de vroeg-christelijke kerk', *TT* 16 (1961/2), 417–49; F. Wulf, *GL* 36 (1963), 341–52; *J.-P. Audet, Structures of Christian Priesthood: Home, Marriage, and Celibacy in the Pastoral Service of the Church*, London and New York 1967, esp. 1–121.

Johannes B. Bauer

Vision of God

A. *The 'vision' of God on earth.* 1. References to 'visions' of God are not infrequent in the *Old Testament*, but extremely varied in meaning. There are passages which are more primitive in outlook, in which God is thought of as present to the physical sight, that is in a divine apparition (theophany). By means of this, it is thought, God has willed to favour certain men with the privilege of holding converse with him and receiving his revelation. At the 'visit of God' to Mamre (Gen 18) Abraham sees three men (v 2). God comes to visit him with two companions (angels) in human form, promises him that a son will be born to him (v 10) and holds a discussion with him about Sodom (vv 20–33). His appearance is not described; instead the one point on which the narrative concentrates exclusively for its meaning is his coming and speaking with Abraham. Still more mysterious is Jacob's nocturnal struggle with God (Gen 32:25–33), after which the patriarch declares: 'I have seen God face to face, and yet my life is preserved' (v 30; see also 33:10), thus expressing the fact that he has had a direct personal encounter with God, who has confronted him as a human contestant of extreme strength, and yet who has remained hidden in the darkness of night and shrouded in mystery. At the same time we already find in the words of Jacob/Israel a hint of a conviction which is to be still more clearly expressed in later passages, namely that no man can see God and still remain alive (see also Ex 24:11; 33:20; Judg 6:22f; 13:22f—in the last two of these passages it is the 'angel of Yahweh' that is spoken of). The apparition imparted to Moses in the burning thornbush (Ex 3) has the sole

purpose of revealing the God of the fathers and laying upon Moses the task of liberating the Israelites from Egypt. The idea of Yahweh making himself visible expressed in v 2 is mitigated—as so often elsewhere in the Old Testament—by the fact that it is the 'angel of Yahweh' who appears in the (or as the) flame of fire; Moses must not come any closer to see the burning thornbush (v 4f), and he veils his face, 'for he was afraid to look at God' (v 6). Again the seventy elders who ascend the mountain of God with Moses 'beheld the God of Israel', and this is regarded as a special proof of grace. Yet God himself is not described, only the flashing and glittering of light 'under his feet' is mentioned (Ex 24:10f). But the intention underlying the still naive language here is to express the close proximity to God of the parties involved. In the 'tent of meeting' where Moses put questions to God, 'the Lord used to speak to Moses face to face as a man speaks to his friend' (Ex 33:11). Yet God accedes to the request of his chosen mediator only to the limited extent of allowing him to see his 'back view' but not his 'face' (Ex 33:18–23). The prophet Elijah experiences the 'passing by of the Lord' without having any kind of vision, only by hearing him, and that too not in the storm, earthquake or fire but in the soft gentle murmuring (1 Kings 19:11f). Thus is expressed the religious conviction of those men who have had an experience of being in immediate proximity to God, or give accounts of this. 'Seeing' is only one of several possible ways of describing their experience. Many turns of phrase in which the 'face of God' is referred to are figurative or even formalised. 'To appear before the face of God' or to 'see' it means to visit the sanctuary (Ex 23:15, 17; 34:20, 23f; Deut 16:16; etc—a courtier's term for an audience). The 'face' of God is his attitude of attention to men, and thus signifies God's help (see Ps 11:7; 17:15; 24:6; 27:8; Job 33:26; Hos 5:15). It can be 'appeased' (literally 'stroked': see Ex 32:11; 1 Sam 13:12; 1 Kings 13:6; etc), and God 'lifts up' his countenance and lets it 'shine' (in the priestly blessing Num 6:25f; see Ps 4:6; 31:16; 67:1; etc). Prayer and cultic veneration in the sanctuary are ways of encountering God on earth, possibilities of 'seeing' him. The possibility of seeing God, supernatural and spiritual as he is, in actual physical fact continues to be denied.

This applies even to the 'visions' of the prophets. In Is 6:1, 5 the prince of the prophets, in speaking of the vision in which he received his vocation, says that he 'saw the Lord' (with his own eyes). But he does not describe his appearance, only that of his surroundings: the throne and seraphim and 'the train of his robe' which 'filled the temple'. For the rest he hears the voice of the Lord (6:8ff), and for all visionaries it is this revelation of the word that is the decisive factor (see 1 Kings 22:19-23, the prophet Micaiah son of Imlah; further on this Amos 9:1). Ezekiel's 'chariot vision' (Ezek 1), which played a major part in later Jewish mysticism for ecstatic experiences, (Merkaba mysticism) likewise mentions only 'something *like* the flashing of polished bronze, which looked *like* fire . . . and brightness shone all round him' (Ezek 1:27). The vision itself is full of similes and comparisons, and the attempt to put it into words is only a stammering and halting one. The description of the 'Ancient of Days' in Dan 7:9 is a figurative and symbolic mode of speaking about God, which is subsequently taken up in the New Testament revelation (see 1:12-17 on the 'one like a son of man'; c 4 on the 'throne'). These are similes and images for the indescribable glory of God in heaven. Right up to christian times judaism adopted an attitude of extreme scepticism towards ecstatic visions. The rabbis issued warning against such presumptuous approaches to God. Of the four rabbis who, according to the Jerusalem Talmud (*ḥagiga* 77a), entered paradise during their lifetime, only Rabbi Akiba survived the ecstatic experience unharmed. It was only later that the demand for a direct mystical experience of God developed.

2. In the *New Testament* complete clarity prevails on the point that a direct vision of God on earth is impossible. When Philip asks for a theophany he receives the reply from Jesus: 'He who has seen me has seen the Father . . . Do you not believe that I am in the Father and the Father in me?' (Jn 14:8-10). It is only in faith that we have the power to 'see' God, that is to attain to union with him. The incarnate Son of God is the perfect image of the Father, and the way to him. In faith the disciples beheld his glory (Jn 1:14), above all in the 'signs' which he performed (see Jn 2:11; 11:40). According to Paul the reason why it is impossible for us to see God is that we are still living in the body; 'we walk by faith, not by sight' (2 Cor 5:7). To believe is still 'to see

darkly in a mirror' (1 Cor 13:12a). Nevertheless in comparison with the old covenant, in which the glory of God was still veiled and limited, 'we behold with unveiled face the glory of the Lord (= Christ), and are being changed into the same image from glory to glory' (2 Cor 3:18). This passage, which has been rendered difficult to understand by Paul's 'midrash', is hardly intended to say more than what follows in 4:4–6, namely, that we can recognise the 'glory of God in the face of Christ' thanks to the fact that we have been endowed with the Holy Spirit and the inner enlightenment from God which illumines our hearts as light illumined darkness at the dawn of creation. Nowhere in the New Testament is any basis to be found for the possibility of a mystical or ecstatic vision of God upon earth. Paul adopts an attitude of extreme reserve towards visions and ecstasies, although he himself has been favoured with them (see 2 Cor 12:1–9). The present is still the time of afflictions and suffering in order that God's 'strength may be made perfect in (human) weakness'. John goes so far as emphatically to reject the idea of any man having seen God at any time (Jn 1:18; 5:37; 6:46; 1 Jn 4:12); only the only-begotten Son has brought us knowledge of God (Jn 1:18), and bears witness to that which he has seen and heard direct (from God) (3:32). It cannot be determined with certainty whether the point of this assertion is directed against the claims of the Jews to the effect that their history contains instances of men seeing God (Moses and the elders? see 1:18; 5:37), or against gnostics' assertions that they have experienced ecstatic visions of God (see 1 Jn 4:12; also 2:3; 3:6; 4:20; 3 Jn 11). In any case the principle of faith is expressed with all possible clarity: only by the revelation of the Son can we attain to knowledge of and communion with God.

B. *The direct vision of God in the world to come and in heaven.* So long as Old Testament religion had no clear light to throw on the possibility of bodily resurrection, and so long as it represented survival after death as a shadowy existence in the underworld (Sheol), it was also incapable of knowing anything of the blessing of a direct vision of God in the age to come. Job 19:26f, which is a difficult passage and textually uncertain, can be interpreted as referring to a vision of God in the next world. More probably, however, what it intends to convey is that God's favour and justification will be restored to Job anew when he has undergone extreme physical chastisement and dereliction of soul (see 14:13; 23:3–7). It is not until resurrection is understood as a participation in the glory of God that we find the idea of the just seeing that glorious world of God in which they themselves are endowed with 'radiance' (see Dan 12:3) and 'clothed with garments of glory' (Enoch [Eth] 62:16; Bar [Syr] 51:3, 5, 10). With loud cries of joy the just behold the 'glory of him who takes them to himself, and enter into rest with sevenfold joy' (4 Ezra 7:91). The seventh and highest joy is that they 'behold the countenance of him whom they have faithfully served in this life' (v 98). The idea of seeing God in heaven could also arise in connection with speculations about Paradise. Thus according to Enoch (Slav) 31:2 God opened heaven to Adam while he was still in Paradise 'so that he should see the angels and the light without darkness'. Reminiscences of the wilderness period also gave rise to the expectation of a direct vision of God: 'Whenever the Israelites saw God they became virtuous. They saw him at the (Red) Sea and became virtuous . . . They saw him at Sinai and became honest . . . They saw him in the tabernacle and became just . . . and if they see him in the world to come then they will be virtuous' (Midr. Ps 149 § 1 [SB I, 213]). Finally the idea of God dwelling in the sanctuary gave rise to the idea of an unveiled vision of his glory in the time of salvation (see Sib v 420–28). In the New Testament description of the heavenly Jerusalem we find: 'They will see his face' (Rev 22:4). In the ApocAbr. 29:20 God promises the virtuous: 'But they see my face and rejoice with my people'. Similarly Jesus praises those men who are pure of heart, 'for they shall see God' (Mt 5:8). In all these passages it is the *eschatological vision* which is being thought of; but since in later Judaism the just were already considered to dwell in a (heavenly) Paradise (and no longer in the underworld), it cannot be excluded that each individual will receive a personal vision of God after his death (see Lk 16:22, 25; 23:42).

Paul and John teach us with all the clarity that could be desired that what is meant by this vision of God in the world to come (or in heaven) is a direct encounter with God, a knowing him, an apprehending him in blessedness, and a becoming one with him in love such as is not yet possible on earth.

Seeing God 'face to face' (1 Cor 13:12a) is contrasted with 'seeing him in a mirror darkly' here on earth. But it is not only our understanding that is affected by this knowledge of him which is no longer 'in part'. For 'knowing God' as conceived of in the bible implies finding union of life with God (see J. Botterweck), and to 'see God' is only one aspect among others of the nearness to God and the blessedness which is to be hoped for in the future kingdom of God (see Mt 5:3–10). 'We shall understand God even as we have been known (by God)' (1 Cor 13:12b), that is as God has embraced us with his gaze, has graciously chosen us and lovingly drawn us to himself. The graciousness of these prior acts on God's part is still more strongly thrown into relief in 1 Jn 3:2: although now we are already children of God in a wholly real sense (by baptism and godliness of life), 'it has not yet been revealed what we shall be, but we know that when it is revealed we shall be like him, for we shall see him as he is'. According to the views of the bible this likeness to God probably consists of glorification, the being adorned with divine and celestial glory (*doxa*), and this enables us too to see God as he is. On the other hand the vision of God assures us of our glorified existence which makes us like God. The promise of paradise is thereby fulfilled, and the longing, unsatisfied ever since paradise, to come near to God as far as any creature can come near to him at all, is brought to rest. But this gracious exaltation to God, in which we are filled and permeated with his nature, and the experience and apprehension of his divine riches which go with this,

951

constitute the blessing of our direct vision of God. We will also see the glory of Christ (Jn 17:24), and Christ will then be able to complete his 'revelation of the name (nature) of God' (17:26). But in 1 Jn 3:2 what John has in mind is not his appearing (at the ↗ parousia, see 2:28), and our likeness to Christ and vision of Christ; for the vision of God and being made like God correspond to the state of being God's children, and these constitute the ultimate fulfilment of that state and its eschatological elevation.

Bibliography: F. Nötscher, *Das Angesicht Gottes schauen, nach biblischer und babylonischer Auffassung,* Würzburg 1924; J. Botterweck, *'Gott erkennen' im Sprachgebrauch des AT,* Bonn 1951; G. Kittel, *Die Religionsgeschichte und das Urchristentum,* Gütersloh 1932, 95–106; J. Dupont, *Gnosis. La connaissance relig. dans les épîtres de s. Paul,* Lyons–Paris 1949; A. Brunner, 'Gott schauen', *ZKT* 73 (1951), 214–22; R. Schnackenburg, *Die Johannesbriefe,* Freiburg 1963², 172f; H. M. Féret, *Connaissance biblique de Dieu,* Paris 1955; W. Michaelis, *TDNT* v, 328–40 and 364–7; A. Wikenhauser, *Die Christusmystik des Apostels Paulus,* Freiburg 1956², 142–56. See also: W. W. Graf Baudissin, 'Gott schauen in der atl. Religion', *ARW* 18 (1915), 173–239; W. Bousset, *Kyrios Christos,* Göttingen 1935⁴, 163–72; R. Bultmann, 'Untersuchungen zum Joh-Ev', *ZNW* 29 (1930), 169–92; N. Hugedé, *La métaphore du miroir dans les épîtres de s. Paul aux Corinthiens,* Neuchâtel–Paris 1937; F. Amiot, 'Deum nemo vidit unquam (Jn 1:18)', *Festschrift A. Robert,* Paris 1957, 470–77.

Rudolf Schnackenburg

Visitation

A. *Old Testament.* English versions of the bible use 'visit' and 'visitation' to translate the term based upon the Hebrew root *pqd*, which in the Greek bible is rendered as *episkopeō* and *episkeptomai*, and in Latin for the most part as *visitare.* Throughout all its various shades of meaning this word retains the basic meaning of 'to prove somebody or something by testing', or 'to see that all is in order'. As predicated of God, visitation is an exercise of his ↗ righteousness, and it implies salvation for the people of God, for the loyal and zealous, and even for repentant sinners, but ruin for the enemies of God and of his people. But whereas in most of the passages in which God's justice is mentioned it imports his faithful fulfilment of his promises of salvation, in most of the passages in which visitation occurs it is the connotation of punishment and misfortune that comes chiefly to the fore. As applied to the individual the visitation of God consists in the fact that he takes an active interest in the man concerned. Thus in Ps 8:5 we find a statement of the part played by God throughout in the fate of man. In passages such as Gen 21:1; 1 Sam 2:21 an individual man experiences the fact that God regards him benevolently and is ever ready to come to his help. In Jer 15:15 and Ps 106:4 it is one who is zealously devoted to Yahweh who experiences this; in Gen 50:24f; Ex 3:16; 4:31; 13:19; Ruth 1:6; Zech 10:3, it is the people of Israel; while in Is 23:17; Jer 27:22; 29:10; Zeph 2:7, it is sinners who have this experience after they have undergone their punishment.

God visits sinners and those who are his enemies, ie, he 'brings them to a reckoning' (Jer 6:15; 49:8; 50:32; Ps 59:5; probably also Job 7:18; Jer 32:5).

In Num 27:16; Is 62:6; Jer 1:10 it is a question of a demonstration of trust on God's part in that he 'entrusts' or commissions a chosen individual with a task of special importance in salvific history. This 'commissioning' can also be applied to the occasions when God uses profane forces as his instruments for punishing the people of God when they have broken the covenant (Lev 26:16; Jer 15:3), the enemies of God (Is 13:4), the enemies of the zealous and devoted (Ps 109:6). Yahweh visits the ↗ way of the sinner, ie, he 'puts him on trial', requites him (Hos 4:9). Above all he visits the sins, ie, he 'takes vengeance' for them, 'exacts a reckoning for transgression' (1 Sam 15:2; Jer 14:10; Hos 9:9; Lam 4:2, 22), as though 'with rod and scourges' (Ps 89:32). Frequently the person to whom God brings home his transgression is named (Ex 32:34; Is 13:11; 26:21; Jer 23:2; 25:12; 36:31; Hos 1:4; 2:15; Amos 3:2).

'The "vengeance" of Yahweh is no blind fury against the individuals or peoples concerned. Rather it always presupposes that their guilt has been established by "examination", or that it is notorious' (Scharbert, p 219). As used in this sense, visitation is closely connected with the ↗ judgement of Yahweh upon sinners and upon the powers which are hostile to God. In the prophets the noun occurs frequently in the sense of 'calling to account' and punishment (Is 10:3; Jer 8:12 etc; Ezek 9:1; Hos 9:7; Mic 7:4).

B. In the *Qumran texts* the verb *pqd* occurs in the sense of testing (1 QS 5:22, 24; 6:21; CD 13:11), of 'the ordination which results from this' (of annihilation 1 QS 2:6, of vindication 1 QS 16:5). God requites the guilt, ie, punishes it (1 QH 14:24); he requites the works of the evil-doer (CD 5:15f;

see also 7:9), visits the earth in order to exact requital from sinners (CD 19:6). He will visit all the members of his covenant who do not hold firm to his commandments, and consign them to destruction at the hands of Belial (CD 8:2; 19:14). CD 1:7 displays an awareness of visitation in the sense that God will pardon and bring help after he has chastised his people. The substantive appears to signify an eschatological visitation (this is numbered among the subjects in which the members must be instructed 1 QS 3:14), the time of which has been established by God (1 QS 3:18; 4:18; 1 QH 1:17; see also CD 8:3; 19:15). It will bring salvation, peace, life, blessing, joy to those who walk according to God's counsels (1 QS 4:6f; see also 1 QH 1:17); but to the obdurate, who walk in the way of darkness, it will bring affliction and destruction (1 QS 4:11ff). Only after this will the true world which is to last for ever emerge (1 QS 4:19). This visitation is to be expected at the end of the days (4 QpIs^b 2:2) by the 'generation of the visitation' (4 QpHos^b 1:10).

C. In the *New Testament* the idea of visitation comes to acquire, to a greater extent than in the Old Testament, the significance of a manifestation of God's benevolence and grace. Thus after Jesus has raised the young man of Nain to life the word goes round among the people 'that God has visited his people' (Lk 7:16), and certain manuscripts add the words 'for good', thereby attesting the fact that the word chiefly bore the significance of 'to punish'. In the Canticle of Zechariah (Lk 1:68, 78) the word

953

under consideration acquires a messianic connotation from its connection with ↗ salvation and ↗ redemption. In Acts 15:14 James declares that Simeon has related how God was solicitous to take from among the Gentiles a people for his name. In this instance the word possesses its full salvific force.

Whereas in the Old Testament the 'day of visitation' (Is 10:3; see also Jer 6:15; 10:15; 11:23; ↗ day of the Lord) is a judgement day, on Jesus' lips the phrase 'time of visitation' is applied to his own coming, the time of the great visitation of grace (Lk 19:44). In 1 Pet 2:12 christians are exhorted to lead exemplary lives in the sight of the gentiles 'so that in case they speak against you as wrongdoers, they may see your good deeds and glorify God on the day of visitation', ie, when God of his grace calls them to the faith (see the exhortation of the Lord in Mt 5:16 and, by way of contrast, Rom 2:24; 1 Tim 6:1).

Bibliography: J. Scharbert, 'Das Verbum PQD in der Theologie des Alten Testaments', *BZ* 4 (1960), 209–26; H. W. Beyer, *TDNT* II, 590–608; J. Boan Hooser, *The Meaning of the Hebrew Root 'pqd' in the Old Testament*, Harvard 1962/3 (dissertation); see also *HTR* 56 (1963), 332.

Johannes B. Bauer

Vocation

Vocation and Election. The verb *qr᾿* ('to call', 'to give a vocation to') is one of the most significant and frequently recurring verbs in the Old Testament. It generally appears in constructions with a simple accusative, but is also found with the preposition *bᵉ* (= 'by'

or 'in'), as for instance in the expression *qr᾿ bᵉšm* (= 'to call by name': Ex 31:2; 35:30; Is 43:1; 45:3–4). Apart from the profane usage, which is richly attested, the word is frequently employed with a religious connotation and in the following specific senses: 1. as a call to repentance and conversion, for instance in Jer 3:12ff; 2. as a personal summons which is at the same time a call to a specific office (Is 44:28; 45:3; 46:11; 48:15; 43:1; 51:2; Gen 12:1–3; Ex 3:1–12; 1 Sam 3:3ff; but also Is 6; Jer 1; Is 42:6; 49:1–9); 3. as a call to salvation, which may be directed to a single individual or to the people of Israel as a whole (Gen 12:1–3; 15:1–6; Is 41:8–9; 43:1; 48:12; 51:2; 54:6). This idea of vocation is often found combined with that of election, for God calls only those whom he has first chosen for a specific office or to have a share in his salvation (eg, Abraham, Moses, David). This appears particularly clearly in Deutero–Isaiah, where 'to call' and 'to choose' frequently occur in parallelism (41:9). However, a clear distinction must be borne in mind between the two acts of God involved. This can be gathered from the very fact that a different verb is used to express election, namely *bḥr* (eg, Deut 7:6; 10:15; 14:2; 18:5; 21:5; Is 7:15; 41:8; 43:10; 44:1–2; 49:7; 65:9, 15, 22; etc). This verb appears 164 times in the Old Testament, ninety-two times with God as subject. In addition to this the verbal substantive *bāḥîr* is also found. By comparison the roots *lqḥ* and *qbts* appear only rarely. *bḥr* is distinguished from *qr᾿* chiefly by the element of election and the act of the will involved.

Election is found throughout the Old

Testament as a key idea which is of decisive importance. Israel perceives God's act of election in episodes as early as his call to the patriarchs (Is 51:2). Indeed in their case it is especially clear that this election proceeds purely from God's sovereign will (Gen 12; 15; 25:22ff). It in no sense presupposes any prior quality on the part of the men concerned or in their relationship with God. Yet Israel is conscious of having been chosen and united to God as a whole in the persons of her patriarchs. From Abraham's time onwards the visible sign of this election is circumcision (Gen 17:9ff). From Sinai onwards it is the covenant relationship (Ex 19:5, etc) by which Israel becomes God's personal possession (Ex 19:5; Deut 7:6)—his people (Deut 4:20; 9:26; Ps 28:9 etc), his vineyard (Is 5:1–7), his firstborn son (Ex 4:22; Jer 31:9), his spouse or bride (Hos 2 etc), his community (Num 20:4; 16:3; Mic 2:4–5; Ps 74:2), his servant (Is 41:8; 42:19; Jer 30:10; Ezek 28:25; etc), as Deutero–Isaiah above all never tires of saying by way of consolation.

Such an election gives those concerned a claim to God's blessing, protection and solicitude, to his *šalôm* (Is 43:3f; 48:15), but at the same time it also entails heightened responsibilities towards him (Amos 2:9ff; 3:1ff). Since the people did not live up to this responsibility as a whole, the circle of the elect narrowed down to the 'holy remnant' (Isaiah, Jeremiah, Ezekiel, Zechariah) or, as it is expressed in the post-exilic literature, to the 'zealous'. As a result election in the strict sense is transferred from the people as a whole to individuals, whereas in earlier times

the election of individuals was only known in the case of kings, priests (Levi and Zadok), and prophets (1 Sam 10:17; 16:10; 2 Sam 16:18; 1 Kings 8:16; 11:34; 89:3; Sir 47:22). Admittedly, consciousness of having been chosen in the persons of the patriarchs continues to predominate in orthodox judaism. The deutero-canonical books display the same attitude as the rest of the post-exilic literature (Sir 46:1; Tob 8:10 [LXX]; Wis 3:9; 4:15). This results on the one hand in a significant narrowing down of the circle comprising the elect, on the other the possibility is opened up of extending it beyond Israel, a fact which is significant for our understanding of vocation and election in the New Testament.

The course marked out by the post-exilic writings of the bible is carried further by the literature of Qumran. References to election in all their various forms are here extraordinarily frequent. 'The elect' is a title of honour by which the community occupying the site from which these documents derive describe themselves (1 QpHab v 4; IX 12; X 13; CD VI 2; the hymns almost throughout; 1 QM III 13; X 9). 1 QpHab speaks of those who depend upon the *moreh tsedeq* as the 'elect of God'. 1 QS III 14ff refers plainly to the fact that the members of the community are chosen by God for the purpose of forming a 'holy community' to enter God's service as followers of the prince of light, and to gain for themselves a share of salvation. In 1 QH *bḥr* is not actually used. Nevertheless, references to the reality which it stands for constantly recur in the hymns, which lead up to the idea of being chosen by

955

God ('bound up in the bundle of life', 'not rejected', 'set upon an even basis', 'placed at the well-spring of life', etc: I 32; II 20; III 22; IV 5; VII 6ff; VIII 3). In CD, too, the word *qr³* occurs repeatedly, and there is a reference to the *qᵉri³ê šm* (2:9), that is, to those whom God has called by name, which in practice is equivalent to election. The 'teacher of righteousness' (I QpHab) and the Zadokite priests (CD VI 2; I QSᵇ III 23) are presented as the elect *par excellence*, while the rest of the members of the community participate in this election only by faith and obedience. The manner in which this election, as well as the possibility of obedience in this sense, applies to them is either not fully thought out or not yet altogether discernible to us in consequence of our knowledge of the distinctive theology of this community up to the present. Whereas in I QS and I QM the holy remnant can only be drawn from Israel, while I QH has nothing to say on this point, CD envisages proselytes as well. But wherever the idea of the remnant is used the Old Testament statements concerning the covenant people are transferred to the community, and indeed to it exclusively. Whoever does not belong to it is a mocker and a recreant. He belongs to the community of Belial, and is destined by God to the judgement.

Already in LXX the Greek word *kaleō* corresponds to the Hebrew *qr³*. It is used both in a profane and a religious sense. It becomes a religious term the moment it is predicated of God. For it means 'to call' (as in Abraham's case), or it can even mean the invitation to share in the blessings of salvation sent out by God. Corresponding to *bḥr* and its derivatives, LXX has *eklegomai* (=to choose, elect) and the words deriving from its root, especially *eklektos* (=*bāḥîr*), which again is used to express God's freedom in choosing and with regard to the medium employed, but also his interest in those who are chosen.

In the *New Testament* John the Baptist appears as a personal summoner (Mk 1:3 and parallels), but the same applies to the apostles also (Mk 1:16–20 and parallels), that is to men who have been given an office, though admittedly this also includes their own call to salvation. They are under God's special protection (Lk 9:1ff; 10:1ff), but they also have a special burden to bear (Lk 9:57ff; Mt 8:19ff). In the New Testament all are called to participate in the blessings of salvation (Rom 8:20; I Cor 1:9; Gal 5:8; I Cor 7:15, 19; I Thess 2:12, 14; I Pet 1:15). But this presupposes repentance, renunciation of self, faithfulness, that is, the co-operation of man (Mk 1:15; Mt 22:12). In the case of the synoptics it is quite evident that they do not regard the call as a *verbum efficax*. Judas too is called (Jn 6:70; 13:18; 15:16), as too are the guests at the royal wedding-feast and the man without a wedding garment Mt 22:1–14). For the call as presented by the synoptics the following conclusions of Daumoser may be taken as established: 1. it is extended to all without restriction, except for the fact that it is so extended only through Jesus; 2. it derives its force from the free will of God himself, without any legal justification; 3. men must not arrogate it to themselves; 4. it confronts them inexorably with the fundamental decision; and 5. when rightly responded to it brings a reward as a direct consequence of this ($\nearrow$ retribution, reward).

Among the synoptics, it is Luke in particular who makes frequent use of *kaleō*, which is less frequent in Matthew and rare in Mark. John likewise rarely employs the idea, while on the contrary Paul, Hebrews, and 1 and 2 Peter use it often. Abraham stands out as the type of the *kaloumenos*, the one who is called. To the extent that Jesus appears as the one who calls, it is precisely a divine function that he exercises when he calls men. Paul again is particularly interested in man's response to the divine call, that is, the act of *pisteuein* ($\nearrow$ faith). In this connection it becomes clear that the call of God through Jesus and his apostles is an act of grace. On the basis of his own experience Paul interprets it as *efficax*, and is thereby brought to making statements of a predestinatory character (Rom). Similarly in Paul *kaleō* (=to call), *klēsis* (=calling), and *klētos* (=one called) have already become theological terms with a definite meaning. For him the *klētoi* are either the apostles (1 Cor 1:1; Rom 1:6) or, still more frequently, christians in general, so that *klētos* and christian become almost synonymous.

So far as *eklegomai* and the idea of election are concerned, they are found throughout the Old and New Testaments alike. It is nowhere denied that Israel is chosen (Mt 2:6; Lk 1:16, 32f; 13:16; Mt 8:12; 12:39; 15:24). Nevertheless Jesus, and with him the whole of the New Testament, decisively rejects those false claims which are based on the sense of election (Mt 3:7ff; Lk 13:23ff; 8:21; 16:19–31;

etc). It neither gives any exclusive rights nor is it a comfortable cushion on which to repose. It demands personal responsibility and obedience in faith in order to become established. Again the New Testament takes up the idea of the remnant, but unlike the Qumran sectarians, it does not take this in the sense of an esoteric group apart, but rather as the new people of God which every man can be called to join. In the New Testament election is always election to an office, whether that of the apostle (this also applies to the traitor), or deacon, missioner or elder (Acts 6; 15:22), or to the universal $\nearrow$ priesthood which glorifies God and proclaims his grace (1 Pet 2:9).

The motifs of free choice, of service, and of selection from a greater number (remnant) appear still more prominently in the substantive *eklogē* (=choice, election) than in the verb. Again it is the eschatological connotation attached to the adjective *eklektos* (=one chosen) that is noticeable throughout the entire New Testament. For the synoptics the *eklektoi* are the fine flower of those chosen by God (Mt 22:14) from Israel and the gentiles, the community of the eschatological age (Lk 18:7; Mt 24: 21–31; Mk 13:19–27). For them God shortens the period of eschatological affliction, guards them from Satan's temptation and redeems them in the new era (similarly too in 1 Pet 2:9). Paul, too, recognises the ultimate goal (1 Cor 1:27–9; Tit 1:1; 1 Tim 5:21). Again, 1 Peter lays the emphasis on the fact that election has already been made before time was (1:2ff). Only in virtue of the fact of having been chosen do the elect proclaim the mercy of God. For this reason they also bear the titles of honour belonging to the Old Testament people of God. The New Testament writings have little to say concerning the rival group of the reprobate, those who are not chosen.

One saying of Jesus in particular deserves special mention, that namely in which *klētoi* and *eklektoi* are set in contrast to each other. It is in Mt 22:14 that this saying is most firmly in place, although perhaps it was once an independent saying. Probably it should be set not merely in the context of the parable of the marriage-feast but in the whole group of parables (21:28–22:14) at the end of which it stands. Whereas in the Old Testament God's call affects those who are chosen, here the called appear as the greater group and the elect as the smaller. The latter are clearly those finally chosen from the circle of the called. Vocation can remain unavailing not only when the one called refuses it, but also when he supposes that he is able to evade the responsibility which it entails. Thus the logion is an emphatic reminder of the importance and urgency of vocation, and a summons to men to show themselves worthy of the ultimate selection which will be made.

Bibliography: K. L. Schmidt, *TDNT* III, 487ff; G. Schrenk, *TDNT* IV, 147ff; E. Egel, *Die Berufungstheologie des Apostels Paulus*, Heidelberg 1939; I. Daumoser, *Berufung und Erwählung bei den Synoptikern*, Meisenheim 1954 (with further copious bibliographical references); H. H. Rowley, *The Biblical Doctrine of Election*, London 1950; T. C. Vriezen, *Die Erwählung Israels nach dem AT*, Zurich 1953; E. Wright, *The Old Testament against its Environment*, 1950; Nötscher, 173–6; Eichrodt I (Index); M. Noth, *Amt und Berufung im AT*, Bonn 1958.

Georg Molin

War

A. *Old Testament*. From the outset it is important to remind ourselves that the Old Testament does not divide life into a religious and a profane sphere. So far from this, life as conceived of in the Old Testament is permeated and interwoven throughout by religion and faith. To one who bears this in mind, an idea which is alien to us of the present day will become comprehensible, namely, that according to the Old Testament even war is a religious event, so that one speaks of the 'holy war' as a religious institution. In this guise it figures in the Old Testament writings from Moses right up to the time of the Maccabees.

1. *Description of the 'holy war'*: the following specific elements can be laid down as characteristic of the holy war: Yahweh's anger is kindled against the enemy of the chosen people (1 Sam 28:18). The trumpets are sounded and the Israelites respond by voluntarily enlisting for military service (Judg 3:27; 6:34f; 1 Sam 13:3). The army thus assembled is called the people (host) of Yahweh (Ex 12:41; Judg 5:11; 20:2; 1 Sam 17:26), and is therefore under a strict obligation to preserve cultic and sexual purity, or alternatively to purify itself (1 Sam 21:6; 2 Sam 11:11). Sacrifices are offered (1 Sam 7:9; 13:9, 12). At a later stage, in the prophets, it is laid upon Israel as a duty to sanctify the war (Jer 6:4; Joel 1:9). Yahweh himself takes command in these wars (Is 13:3; Jer 51:27f). Hence he advances upon the ark at the head of the warriors of Israel (Num 14:42; Deut 20:4; 23:14; Josh 3:11; 10:14; Judg 4:14; 1 Sam

4:6; 2 Sam 5:24). He musters the army (Is 13:4). More than this, Yahweh raises up charismatic leaders to conduct the holy war (Deut 31:7; Judg 6:14). In consequence these wars are called 'Yahweh's wars' (1 Sam 18:17; 25:28). The enemies are Yahweh's enemies (Judg 5:31). It is Yahweh alone who conducts and decides the course of these wars (Ex 14:14, 18; Deut 1:30; Josh 10:42; 11:6; Judg 20:35; 1 Sam 14:23). Israel is required to conduct herself quietly, and to put her trust in Yahweh (Ex 14:13; Deut 20:3; Josh 8:1; 10:25; Judg 7:3; 1 Sam 23:17; 2 Sam 10:12; Is 7:4). The enemy, on the contrary, find their courage failing them (Ex 15:14ff; Josh 2:24; 5:1; 1 Sam 4:7f). Indeed they are filled with a panic that is divinely instilled (Ex 23:27; Deut 7:23; Josh 10:10f; Judg 4:15; 7:22; 1 Sam 5:11; 7:10; 14:15). The booty from the war belongs to Yahweh. It is consecrated to him by being 'put to the ban', and utterly destroyed (Num 21:2f; Josh 6:18f; 1 Sam 15:9). When victory has been achieved Israel renders her thanks to God, and rejoices before him. The laws of war are set forth in detail in Deut 20. Here we find exact directions of how the ban, the total destruction of all that survives, is to be carried out, and what is to be left as booty for the victorious army.

2. *History of the 'holy war'.* After the exodus of the twelve-tribe confederacy from Egypt, Israel was often compelled to engage in wars in the course of executing God's plan for the chosen people. In the episode in which the Egyptian army pursues Israel and is destroyed (Ex 14f) we encounter the earliest instance of the holy war, of which Yahweh himself decides the outcome (Ex 14:14). In the nature of things it must have acquired great importance for the period of the invasion of Canaan and the settlement in the land (Joshua, Judges). The following qualities may be laid down as characteristic of it.

(a) The wars in question are exclusively defensive in character; (b) the entire sacral confederation of tribes took part in the warlike event (at least in spirit). It is united in the consciousness of having Yahweh as its king even in the earthly sphere (Ex 19:5f). Hence it belongs to the exercise of Yahweh's dominion to bestow upon Israel the protection which she needs in wars as well as in peace. The victory which Israel obtains through Yahweh's intervention in her favour is therefore counted as one of the deeds of salvation which God has wrought for his people (Judg 5:11). Thus the holy war in Israel is not the same as the corresponding institution in Islam. For what Israel fights for is not her faith but her existence.

In the period of the Israelite monarchy the institution of the holy war acquires fresh forms. Since the earthly kings were called to be representatives of the divine king, one of the duties which was now laid upon them was the conduct of Israel's wars. The beginnings of a permanent army are already becoming apparent as early as the reign of Saul. It was to become one of the main preoccupations of the future rulers (see especially David's act of numbering the people, 2 Sam 24:1–9). In consequence of this God ceased to intervene directly as he had done hitherto in the waging of war.

Nevertheless certain elements of the holy war do persist and survive, as is to be seen, for instance, in the conduct of Uriah (2 Sam 11:11). It belongs to the ideal of Israelite manhood that it is trained for war (1 Sam 16:18). In David's dialogue with Goliath (1 Sam 17:43–7) the essential traits of the holy war reappear once more, but in a form which has been modified and conditioned by the introduction of earthly kingship. In the preaching of the prophets the idea of the holy war undergoes a fresh transformation. These are conscious of having been appointed guardians of the old sacral institutions, among them that of the holy war. In Samuel's dispute with Saul (1 Sam 15) we see the very first of the Israelite kings confronted with this claim. In the ensuing period this precedent is often followed by the prophets intervening in the warlike projects of the kings (1 Kings 15:13–21; 22:9–17; Is 7:1–9; 30:15; 31:1–3; 37:33–8). Indeed the prophets (Elijah and Elisha) count as the embodiment of God's protection against the enemies of Israel (2 Kings 2:12; 13:14).

The institution of the holy war lives on not merely in virtue of the fact that it has a part to play in the political life of the prophets' own times, but above all because they assign it a prominent place in their prophecies of the future. In their hands revelation as a whole undergoes a development, and with it the idea of the holy war also is transposed on to the new plane which has been attained in the unfolding of revelation, so that it may remain capable of expressing in deeper and more poetic terms the eschatological struggle of the kingdom of God against the forces hostile to him, a struggle which is to take place in the future. In other words, in the prophetic writings the institution of the holy war becomes *eschatologised*. It is transformed into the decisive struggle which is to take place at the end of time, and which is to be brought to its conclusion before the inauguration of God's dominion, which is to take place amid splendour and light, and to pervade the entire universe intensively and extensively. In Isaiah's overall picture of God's intervention in the course of world history he is especially inclined to present this in the form of the holy war. It is in this manner that God will execute his judgement against the people who are hostile to him. In his line of argument he passes on from God's historical intervention to his contest in the future, which gradually assumes meta-historical and typological traits such as appear in a very pronounced form, for instance, in Ezekiel. Not only the gentiles but Israel herself will have experience of this battle of God (Amos 2:4ff). In Mic 4:11–13 Israel is commissioned to conduct this final war against the assembled world of the gentiles as they conspire together to overthrow Zion and frustrate God's plan for Israel. The themes indicated here are projected wholly into the world of eschatology in Ezek 38f. Here we find described in hues that are in part apocalyptic the final onslaught of the gentile powers Gog and Magog, and their definitive destruction. In Ezek 38:19–22 nearly all the traditional traits of the holy war reappear in a form which has been transposed and adapted so as to fit the basic concept of this final contest. Zechariah too, like

Ezekiel, takes up the motifs of the holy war which have been handed down and transposes them so as to make them expressions of the eschatological strife in all its magnitude (4:6; 9:14).

In addition to these instances the holy war also finds an echo in the psalms. Here we find it in its original form, purged of its later developments (for instance, Ps 18; 20; 24:8; 33:16–18; 144). It is actually made the subject of petitionary prayer. Finally the institution of the holy war acquires a new lease of life in the community of the Dead Sea. This, wholly rooted as it is in the Old Testament, is, according to 1 QM (The Scroll of War), summoned as 'the sons of light' (a self-designation) to the historical, or more probably eschatological, struggle against the sons of darkness.

B. *New Testament.* In Lk 14:31; 1 Cor 14:8 the war is taken to be a fact of this present world. Heb 11:34 points back to the heroes of the Old Testament wars. In the apocalyptic sections of the New Testament the war appears to conform to the Old Testament prophecies concerning the final eschatological struggle. In Mt 24:6 and parallels wars are regarded as 'the beginning of afflictions'. They do not inaugurate the end. As events of the intervening period before the *parousia* they merely direct our attention to the fact that the end is coming, and they are intended to remind men of every age of that fact. In Rev 9:7, 9 war and chariots of war serve as images to describe the terrors of the fifth plague, which is expressed in images and motifs drawn from Joel 1–2 (the plague of locusts). The struggle of Michael with the dragon counts as a war (Rev 12:7–17). Again, the beast from the abyss (antichrist) will wage war against the Lamb and the 'saints' (Rev 11:7; see also Dan 7). Similarly with the beast in Rev 13:7. According to Rev 19:19–21 it will be overthrown and consigned to the lake of brimstone. Rev 20:8 takes up the motif of Ezek 38:2: Satan will bring Gog and Magog to wage the final war. But this eschatological enemy will be subjected to total destruction. Then war will be made to cease altogether (Is 2:4; Mic 4:3; Hos 2:18; ↗ peace), and will give place to the eternal peace of the final age in the 'new heaven and the new earth' (Rev 21:1).

Bibliography: A. G. Barrois, *Manuel d'Archéologie biblique* II, Paris 1953; 87–117; O. Bauernfeind, *TDNT* VI, 502–15; Haag 969f; H. Kruse, 'Ethos victoriae in Vetere Testamento', *VD* 30 (1952), 3–13, 65–80, and 143–53; F. Nötscher, *Biblische Altertumskunde*, Bonn 1940, 145–67; J. Pedersen, *Israel. Its Life and Culture* III–IV, Oxford–Copenhagen 1953, 1–32; de Vaux 247–67. See also: H. Fredriksson, *Jahwe als Krieger*, Lund 1945; G. von Rad, *Der Heilige Krieg im Alten Israel*, Göttingen 1958³; *G. von Rad, *Old Testament Theology* I and II (see Index); *G. von Rad, 'Deuteronomy and the Holy War', *Studies in Deuteronomy*, London 1953, 45–59; F. Schwally, *Semitische Kriegsaltertümer* I. *Der heilige Krieg im alten Israel*, Leipzig 1901; J. Comblin, *Theologie des Friedens*, Graz 1963, 84–110.

Heinrich Gross

Water

Beliefs, more or less vigorous in character, in local deities, spirits, and demons thought to inhabit springs, streams, lakes, etc are frequent. But, quite apart from any such beliefs, the findings of ethnology show how prominent a part water plays in the myths, cult, and rituals of peoples by reason of the use to which it is put and the symbolism attached to it. All the fullness of the various forces of life and the possibilities of existence are contained in the meaning of water. (In baptism the act of immersion signifies that one lays aside one's previous form, while to re-emerge from the water signifies to be restored to life.) It is intimately connected with fertility (primarily that of vegetation, but by extension the fertility of beasts and men as well), and as a means of cleansing it also becomes a cultic symbol for the attainment of purity and renewal (the blotting out of sins; ↗ clean and unclean).

As a monotheistic religion, Yahwism does not recognise any water spirits (↗ sea), but nevertheless water does figure prominently in the bible by reason of its importance for life, and also by reason of its manifold symbolic aspects both in the profane and the religious spheres. In the Near East, where water is scarce, it is accounted especially important and precious. Water was offered to strangers who were lodging for the night or passing through (Gen 18:4; 24:32). It was lack of water that brought the people of the Old Testament to murmur against Moses (Ex 15:22–5; 17:1–7; Num 20:1–13). David's bodyguard even put their lives into hazard to bring water for their king (2 Sam 23:16). Numerous miracles are recorded in the Old Testament (Ex 7:17ff; 14:16; 17:6; 2 Kings 2:8) and the New (Mt 8:23–7; 14:22–33; Jn 2:1–11) in which water is either the instrument or the object of miracles. In these God manifests himself as Lord of the elements so that the rituals employed

to obtain rainfall (1 Kings 17:1; 18:42–6; Job 38:34–6) always remain subject to Yahweh's will. Prayers for rain (1 Kings 8:35; 18:36f; Joel 1:20) are directed to God, who punishes the unfaithfulness of the people with drought (Amos 1:2; Joel 1:12; Zech 14:16f). But conversely he rewards faithfulness with fertility and rain (Lev 26:3f; Deut 11:13f; Is 30:23). The libation of water (1 Sam 7:5f) was clearly part of an atonement ceremony (water counted as a symbol of tears Jer 9:17; Ps 119:136), and served as a sign of the blotting out of sins (Ezek 36:25; in the course of the Feast of Tabernacles libations were made in the temple over the altar and the materials of sacrifice in order to entreat for rain, Succoth 4:9; 5:1).

The use of water in the service of the temple—eg 'the molten sea' (1 Kings 7:23–6, and the 'stands' (1 Kings 7:27–39)—had both a practical and a symbolic significance. The temple was accounted the most important manifestation of God's grace. It was the religious centre of the people, from which supernatural life radiated out. Hence in their descriptions of the messianic age the prophets sometimes use images in which God is presented as a 'source of living water' (Jer 2:13). In other passages it is the 'source of the temple waters' that is spoken of (Is 12:3; Ps 36:9; 46:4; see also Rev 22:1f), or the ideas of source and fertility (Joel 3:18), fertility, source, and blotting out of sin (Ezek 47; Zech 13:1; 14:8) appear in combination.

It is the association of water with the idea of purifying that lies behind the numerous ablutions prescribed in the

Old Testament as the means of obtaining cultic purity. 'Living' (ie, flowing) water had greater power and was necessary in cases of leprosy (Lev 14:5–7, 50–52), sexual emissions (Lev 15:13), as well as for the preparation of water of purification (Num 19). Those associated in the cult had to wash themselves before they were ordained (Ex 29:4; Lev 8:6), and also before (Ex 30:17–21; 40:31f; Lev 16:4) or after specific exercises of their office (Lev 16:24, 26, 28; Num 19:7f). Every member of the Old Testament people, for instance, must wash his clothes if he has been suffering from leprosy (Lev 14:8f), eaten carrion (Lev 11:40), experienced an emission due to sickness (Lev 15:5–11), a pollution (Lev 15:16–18) or menstruation (Lev 15:19–24), served in a war (Num 31:24). He must also do this after touching a corpse (Num 19:13, 18f), or the flesh of sin-offerings (Lev 6:20). The practice of washing the hands before meals (Mk 7:2ff) became in the course of time a symbol for interior purity (Ps 26:6; 51:2; 73:13) or innocence (Deut 21:6; Mt 27:24).

The use of water in ordeals as described in the Old Testament must also have originated from the property of water to cleanse in a symbolic as well as in a real sense. A woman who was suspected of adultery had to drink 'bitter water', that is water mingled with dust from the sanctuary, to the accompaniment of a formula of cursing (Num 5:12–31). The prophet Jeremiah recalls this when he announces that the whole of Israel is condemned to drink 'bitter' or 'poisonous' water (Jer 8:14; 9:15; 23:15). In the case of an unsolved murder (Deut 21:1–9) those living near the scene of the crime had to wash their hands over a cow that had been sacrificed in token of their innocence, a practice which was carried out in a manner analogous to that employed in the case of the scapegoat (Lev 16) or the ceremony involving a bird as prescribed for cases of leprosy (Lev 14:1ff).

Water is everywhere symbolically associated with the ideas of purifying, blotting out sins, and renewal, and it is this fact that justifies its use in ↗ baptism, the sacrament of rebirth in the New Testament (Jn 3:1–12; Acts 2:38; Rom 6:3–14; Col 2:8–15; 1 Cor 6:11f).

Bibliography: Art. 'Water' in *Encyclopaedia of Religion and Ethics* XII, 704–19; M. Eliade, *Patterns in Comparative Religion*, London and New York 1958, 188–215 (with extensive bibliography); P. Raymond, *L'eau, sa vie et sa signification dans l'AT* (Supplement to *VT* 6 [1958]); J. Hempel, *RGG* ²*IV*, 1665f; A. A. King, *Holy Water: the use of water for ceremonial and purificatory purposes in pagan, Jewish and Christian times*, London 1926.

Walter Kornfeld

Way

The Hebrew word *derek*, which is usually rendered by *hodos* in Greek, means primarily 'way' in the obvious and literal sense; but often, too, the word is used figuratively, and it is this that we shall be treating of here, even though it is often impossible to perceive the exact extent to which the idea of way as such may still have been conceived of in spatial terms (see Prov 1:31; Is 33:15; 1 Kings 8:32; etc).

In several Old Testament passages, however, *derek* cannot mean way, but must have a force corresponding to the Ugaritic power, exercise of power, or dominion (thus Ps 110:7; Hos 10:13 [Hebrew]; Jer 3:13 AV; Prov 8:22; 31:3; Amos 8:14; Job 40:19; 26:14; see J. B. Bauer, *VD* 35 [1957], 222–7; *VT* 8 [1958], 91f with bibliography).

A. *Old Testament.* 1. The *whole of human life* is described as the way of man (Is 40:27; Job 3:23; 23:10; Ps 37:5): often this also contains the implication that God has the ways of man in his hands (=his power: Dan 5:23; Job 31:4; Jer 10:23; Prov 20:24; this idea is strongly in evidence in 1 QS xi 10ff, 17). Admittedly in this usage many additional shades of meaning may be derived from the context in which it occurs, such as the factor of human decision and purpose.

2. Way can also stand for man's *moral conduct,* how he 'walks' (Ex 18:20; Deut 5:32f; Jer 4:18; Job 21:31; etc).

3. Way in this sense is usually considered in connection with the will of God. The 'way of the Lord' is precisely *the course which God directs man to follow,* and in this sense 'way' is virtually synonymous with 'commandment' (we may notice the parallelism between way and commandment in Jer 7:23 and Ps 119:15). In this sense it can be said that men follow this way of God (as in Job 23:11; Ps 18:21; etc), or they may be reproached with failing to follow or observe or recognise the way of God (Mal 2:9; Jer 5:4f; Wis 5:7; Prov 2:13, 15; etc) and with going their own way (Is 56:11), which they persist in maintaining to be the right one (Prov 12:15; 14:12; 16:25). Hence the demand that they shall turn away from these ways, which God

punishes (Hos 4:9; Ezek 7:5–8 etc), and to turn back (Zech 1:4; Jon 3:8, 10; etc). In this manner it is particularly emphasised that God knows all the ways of men, that he sees them all, and that he scrutinises man's moral conduct (Jer 32:39; Prov 5:21; Sir 17:15).

4. In this connection a certain ambiguity sometimes arises. On the one hand we find reiterated prayers for God's help in showing the petitioner his ways, teaching them to him, leading him by these ways (the numerous turns of phrase with this general import in Ps 119 should be noticed; see also Ps 25:4; 86:11 etc). From this it is clear how much man needs the help of God's grace. On the other hand, entreaties are made again and again for man to be allowed to recognise the ways of God and to walk in, ie, follow them; and requests of this sort leave no possible room for doubt that man alone is answerable for his own way. Still more, the devout man recognises that he is in part responsible for the way of sinners, and he shows them the good way (Ps 51:13; 1 Sam 12:23).

B. *New Testament.* 1. *Access to the sanctuary*: 'The way into the [true] sanctuary was not yet opened as long as the outer tent [of the old covenant?] was still standing' (Heb 9:8; see also 8:2). To this we may attach the difficult passage of Heb 10:19f: 'We have the hope of entering into the sanctuary by the Blood of Jesus. This is the new [*prosphatos* = 'freshly slaughtered', new in this sense] and living way which he opened to us through the curtain, that is, [through] his flesh'. To what should the phrase 'that is, [through] his flesh' be attached? Certainly it cannot be the curtain, as though Jesus' physical nature was a separating element between Christ and God. On the contrary, according to Heb 2:14–18 men are enabled to stand in the relationship of children to God precisely by the human nature assumed by Christ. Philological considerations tell against taking the phrase '[through] his flesh' (ie, through his death) as connected with 'has opened'. In that case one would have expected an instrumental construction. The best course is to take the genitive '[through] his flesh' as epexegetical and so as qualifying 'the . . . way'. The explanation will then be that the new and living way consists precisely in Jesus' humanity. If *prosphatos* is allowed to retain its etymological sense of 'freshly slaughtered', then it can be understood as an oxymoron ('dead and yet living'). The underlying idea would then be similar to that in Rev 5:6, 9, 12; 13:8 (see also 1:18; 2:8). But on these difficult passages see the commentaries (of C. Spicq, and especially J. Héring and P. Teodorico da Castel S. Pietro). What connection can be established with Jn 14 remains obscure.

2. *Jesus as the way.* 'You know the way where I am going' (Jn 14:4). By this Jesus means not the way which leads to God by keeping his commandments, but the way of faithful discipleship. Thomas objects that they, the disciples, know neither the goal of Jesus' journey nor the way by which he is to arrive at it, but Jesus makes use of this objection to make a still deeper pronouncement: 'I am the way, the truth, and the life' (Jn 14:6). Grammatically speaking this sentence belongs to the class of noun clauses with two members (see C. Brockelmann,

Hebr. Syntax, Neukirchen 1956, 10f § 14), as does Ps 19:10: 'The judgements of Yahweh [are] truth' (ie, 'are true', but in a most profound and exclusive sense! see also Ps 109:4: 'I [am] prayer', and 2 Sam 17:3: 'All the people will be peace' [ie, will to a unique extent live in peace and wellbeing]). Jesus' saying, therefore, is to be interpreted as follows: 'Not only do I know the way fully, I am the exemplar of it and manifest it in my own person: this is because I also not merely proclaim the truth, but it is inseparably connected with my person, and it is in my person that truth, and thereby life also, has appeared in the world (see Jn 1:18; 12:44f). Jesus is the life because it is only through him that true life can be obtained (Jn 1:4; 6:33, 51; 11:25).

3. A *figurative* use of way is to be found in Lk 1:79; Rom 3:17; Acts 2:28; 16:17; 1 Cor 12:31. Passages such as Acts 14:16; Rom 3:16; Jas 1:8; 5:20; 2 Pet 2:15, 21 speak of 'walking' (ie, the conduct of one's life). It is certainly the way of 'walking' commanded by God (see A 3 above) that is meant in Mk 12:14 and parallels; Mt 22:16; 1 Cor 4:17, and probably also in Acts 13:10; 2 Pet 2:21; Heb 3:10.

4. In Acts *hodos* has the force of *teaching*, as is shown especially by 24:14, where the reality thus designated is the same as that referred to as *hairesis* or sect (in this passage employed as *abstractum pro concreto*, a self-designation of the christian community; see also 9:2; 19:9, 23; 22:4; 24:22). This absolute use of 'way' in the sense of 'teaching', which in the New Testament appears only in Acts, may to some extent be paralleled in 1 QS IX 17

('to choose the way': notice the singular) and CD ɪɪ 6 ('to depart from the way').

5. *hodos* is used of *the ways which God himself follows*, that is, of his plans for salvation and their accomplishment, in Acts 13:10; 18:25f; Rom 11:33; Rev 15:3.

6. *The teaching on the two ways*, which has its roots in the Old Testament (see Ps 1:6; Prov 4:18f; 15:19; and further TestAsh 1:3–5 etc) is to be found in Matthew's version of the logion concerning the narrow door (Lk 13:24), clearly an addition on the evangelist's part (Mt 7:13f). What is meant here in any case is that the decision for Christ which one is called upon to take costs toil, that the gift of the *basileia* (=kingdom) does not fall into one's lap without effort, and is not to be attained by the easy way. The emphasis is laid upon the earnestness of the decision involved. The saying must not be thought of as containing any element of gloom. Jesus is not answering the question which has been put to him: 'Will only a few be saved?'. Instead he demands: 'Do not ask such useless questions, but make efforts!' Jesus' words are a summons and an invitation, not the solution of a theological problem. In omitting this question (which is original, and which Luke has rightly retained) Matthew has in no sense put a false interpretation upon the logion. In fact it is he who has imparted to the two ways (or doors) that unique characterisation 'narrow or broad', ie, 'easy or difficult', which so powerfully underlines the element which has been mentioned (unless one may suppose that it is an independent though parallel logion of the Lord

which is recorded in this passage in Matthew).

Bibliography: W. Michaelis, *TDNT* v, 42–114; A. Gros, *La thème de la Route dans la Bible*, Lille 1954 (dissertation); J. Schmid, *Das Ev. nach Matthäus* (*RNT* 1) 1956³, 149f; Nötscher (see Index); J. B. Bauer, *VD* 30 (1952), 219–26; J. B. Bauer, *BL* 20 (1952/3), 321–7; F. Nötscher, *Gotteswege und Menschenwege in der Bibel und in Qumran* (*BBB* 15), 1958; P. Nötscher, *Recherches Bibliques* 4, 135–48; P. Nober, *VD* 37 (1959), 176–80 and 362f.

Johannes B. Bauer

Wine

Wine is one of the most ancient cultural benefits known to mankind. The very word for it is common to most languages. In Latin it is *vinum*, from which the Romance-language renderings *vin*, *vino*, etc are derived. In Greek it is *(w)oinos*, in Hebrew *yayin*, in Akkadian *inu*, in Ugaritic *yn*, but it is a non-Semitic word. A Babylonian tradition knows of the vine as the tree of life in the garden of paradise. The planting of the vine by Noah, therefore, may have been an attempt to awaken memories of paradise, and to regard the new beginning after the Flood as a kind of resumption of the creation. Noah began (again?) with vine-growing. . . . The relationship with the earth is no longer quite the same as that in which mankind stood before the Flood, when it was disrupted by a curse (Gen 5:29: 'And he called his name Noah, saying: "Out of the ground which the Lord has cursed this one shall bring us relief from our work, and from the toil of our hands"'). We find the fulfilment of this hope in Gen 9:20. Noah begins with vine-growing, and thereby brings relief to the earth. Through him God has bestowed upon mankind the vine, which, as conceived of in the Old Testament, is the noblest of plants known to nature (see Ps 104:15). To possess a vineyard, to enjoy its fine fruit, and to rest in peace under its shadow was the Israelite's idea of bliss and the object of his messianic longings (Gen 49:11ff; 1 Kings 4:25; 2 Kings 18:31; Hos 2:15; Mic 4:4; Amos 9:13). Utnapishtim, the Babylonian Noah, knows of the vine as the plant which prolongs life. It is understandable that the bible should regard the fruit of the vine as the most precious of all fruits, and one which Yahweh bestows upon his people. The product of the vine is the blessing of God, which Israel must learn by loyalty towards Yahweh (Deut 11:14). A bad harvest counts as punishment from God (Deut 28:39; Hag 1:11; Hos 2:14). When Israel returns once more, God reveals his favour towards the repentant sinners by bestowing afresh the fruit of the vine (Hos 2:22). At the time when Yahweh will restore the fallen booth of David the mountains will drip sweet wine and the hills shall flow with it (Amos 9:13; Joel 3:18). Is 25:6 describes how Yahweh will then prepare a feast for his own of 'fat things' and of wine on the lees. Hence in Mt 9:17 the new wine is the new covenant, and even in Jn 2 the two wines that are mentioned may each represent one of the two covenants. The Jews, drunk as they are on the old wine, can no longer realise the worth of the new, though this is far better than the old. All catholic exegetes are unanimous in holding that the wine at the marriage of Cana has a profound symbolic meaning. Gächter believes

that it can be regarded as a parallel to the miracle of the loaves. The latter foreshadows the bread of the eucharist, the former the blood.

From the outset, therefore, the situation is that bread maintains this present life, whereas wine permits man to gaze, at least momentarily, at another life and opens to him the door which is guarded by the angel with the flaming sword. This is the significance of 'eat, O friends, and drink; drink deeply, O lovers' (Song 5:1). 'What is life to a man who is without wine? It has been created to make men glad' (Sir 31:37).

Wine is also a symbol of the covenant and of the joy arising from it, a sign both of that covenant which men make with each other (such as that between Abraham and Melchizedek; there is no question of a sacrifice here), and also of the covenant which God makes with men. Wine is also found in sacrifices (Ex 29:38ff; Num 15:5). Moreover wine is closely associated with blood. For one thing the very colour is the same, for in Palestine it was for the most part black grapes that were planted. Then, too, wine is frequently described as the blood of the grape. Among the numerous images derived from the vine (Israel, the people of God as a vine, Christ as the true vine) there is hardly any more terrible than that of the treader of the wine-press. When divine retribution and the execution of divine judgement take place it is as though the treader in the wine-press was squeezing the blood from the grapes (Is 63:1–6; Jer 25:30; Lam 1:15; Rev 19:15). In Babylon, and probably also in Canaan, it was believed that the grape, in order to

967

yield wine, has to lay down its life, and that too in a painful manner, so that— such was the belief—the wine of life comes from this painful death (compare Jn 12:24: 'Unless a grain of wheat falls into the earth and dies . . .'). In this way wine, the blood of the vine (Deut 32:14), could be substituted for the blood of sacrificial beasts (Deut 32:38). In Babylon libatior s of wine and blood offerings were identical, and the wine could be mingled with blood.

In spite of wine being so highly prized, however, abstinence from wine was practised. For the priests it was mandatory (Lev 10:9f; Ezek 44:21) to drink no wine when entering upon their sacred duties. Again the Nazarenes were obliged not to take any drink made from grapes (Num 6:3f; Amos 2:12), but only during the time of their novitiate. John the Baptist did the same. (For the Essenes, and the closely related sect of the Dead Sea, this practice was probably extended throughout the whole lifetime.) A sectarian community which totally renounced wine was that of the Rechabites, who continued to practise absolutely rigidly the nomad way of life handed down to them by their ancestor, Jonadab. They were opposed to cultural advances of every kind, and refused to practise cultivation or vine-growing. In Jer 35:12f God speaks through the prophet to the people who have despised his words, and points to the example of the Rechabites: they refuse to drink a single cup of wine (and reading between the lines one can sense how strange and unnecessary this was felt to be) because this has been enjoined upon them by their ancestor. They do this, so unimportant, so idiosyncratic as it is,

because they obey. And Israel does not obey the words of her Father, God, in his wisdom.

We should perhaps draw attention to one further point. Wine figures as one of the chief of the messianic blessings, and in the messianic kingdom it will be drunk in profusion. Anyone who wishes to emphasise that this kingdom is not yet present, such as John the Baptist and his disciples with their asceticism, can demonstrate this fact by abstaining from wine. Jesus too will now drink no more from the fruit of the vine (notice the solemn manner of speaking here in Mt 26:29) until he drinks it once more in the kingdom of the Father.

The bible does not forbid us to enjoy wine. It cheers God and men alike (Judg 9:13). It is created to bring joy to men (Ps 104:15). One should, therefore, give strong drink to him who is perishing, and wine to him who is embittered in soul, so that he may drink and forget his misery (Prov 31:6f).

Warnings are given against excessive enjoyment of wine or drunkenness. With this, as with all other good things, it is a question of moderation. Man's virtue is to be gauged by the fact that he knows how to observe moderation. Thus wine actually becomes a touchstone for testing the hearts of the proud (Sir 31:26). 'Drunkenness increases the anger of a fool to his injury, reducing his strength and adding wounds' (Sir 31:30). 'Wine drunk in season and temperately is rejoicing in heart and gladness of soul' (Sir 31:28).

Bibliography: E. Busse, *Der Wein im Kult des AT*, Freiburg 1922; J. Döller, 'Der Wein in Bibel und Talmud', *Bbl* 4 (1923), 143–67 and 267–99; L. Rost, *Festschrift Alt*, Tübingen 1953, 169ff; G. von Rad, *Genesis: A Commentary*,

London 1963², 132f; A. Maillot, Allmen 307; P. Gächter, *Maria im Erdenleben*, Innsbruck 1955³, 160–63; A. Penna, *Geremia*, Turin 1952, 256–60; G. Closen, *Wege in die Hl. Schrift*, Regensburg 1939, 101–15; H. Seesemann, *TDNT* v, 162–6.

Johannes B. Bauer

Wisdom

A. In the *Old Testament* wisdom is an idea with many shades of meaning, and a great many different qualities are grouped under this head and brought into association with it. For practical reasons we shall draw a distinction in the pages which follow between wisdom as teaching (1), as a human quality (2), and as a divine attribute and power (3).

Like all other peoples Israel too had a practical knowledge of the laws governing human life which was based on her own experience. She observed how many repetitions of an event produced the same or a similar outcome. Specific types of constantly recurring experience made a permanent impression upon her, which she then formulated in proverbs. Practical wisdom of this kind developed from prolonged observation is to be found, for instance, in Prov 16:18: 'Pride goes before destruction, and a haughty spirit before a fall'. It was inevitable that these maxims should have been assembled and handed on as teaching to those under instruction. This empirical and gnomic wisdom in the form of fixed sayings (see Prov 10:1–22:16), as also of counsel (see Prov 22:22–8), is to be found especially in the Book of Proverbs.

In the ancient Near East this wisdom was prized as a benefit of culture. Hence the kings in particular felt themselves responsible for maintaining and encouraging it. The fact that Solomon is mentioned three times in the Book of Proverbs (1:1; 10:1; 25:1) as its author justifies us in concluding that at an early stage the royal court of Jerusalem took over this tradition of the cultivation of wisdom. The wisdom of foreign peoples was known in Israel also: that of the Edomites (Jer 49:7; Obad 8), the Babylonians (Jer 50:35; 51:57) and the Egyptians (1 Kings 4:30), and among the Israelites foreign wisdom was drawn upon without restriction. In Prov 22:17–23:11 the hagiographer follows an Egyptian model (the Book of the Wisdom of Amenemope) and in the case of Prov 30, 31 it can be gathered from the title and the content alike that it presents us with non-Israelite wisdom. Nevertheless Israelite wisdom had a character of its own. Foreign wisdom was given a religious aspect and assimilated to faith in Yahweh. Whereas Egyptian wisdom is addressed only to scribes and officials, that is, is meant for one specific class, Israelite wisdom applies to the covenant people as a whole. This appears clearly in the Book of Proverbs: only a few verses are concerned specifically with court life (see 14:28; 16:12; 19:12), most of them are addressed quite in general to 'everyman'.

While this experiential wisdom also bears specifically Israelite traits, nevertheless when we compare it with the prophetic writings it becomes clear that it does not represent any typical Israelite form of thought. The prophets speak of Yahweh's sovereign *commandment*. The sage, on the other hand, with

969

his *counsel*, intends his message rather for the intelligent consideration of man. Often he adduces motives for it of a utilitarian kind. Man's own interests are central to his message. The message of the prophets can be understood only against the background of salvific history. It is addressed to the covenant people or to individuals as members of the covenant people in their historical situation. The sage, on the other hand, addresses man as man, and thereby abstracts from his historical connections. The earlier experiential wisdom of Israel, therefore, has an international and universally humanist character.

Side by side with this universal and humanist wisdom drawn from experience, and at first not even connected with it, another idea is to be found in Israel, one which envisages wisdom not as acquired knowledge but rather as a gift bestowed by Yahweh. Eliphaz receives his teaching in the form of a nocturnal revelation (Job 4:12–16). For Elihu wisdom is not the fruit of age and experience alone, but an effect of God's spirit (Job 32:6–9), who forces the sage to speak as once he forced the prophets (Job 32:19f). Where wisdom is expected from God in this manner the whole of the Old Testament revelation already in existence could be summed up under the concept of wisdom. This identification of law and wisdom is actually made in Sir 24:23–34: law offers the fullness of wisdom. The wise man no longer forms his teaching on the basis of experience and observance. Now he steeps himself in the holy scriptures of Israel in order himself to become wise, and as one learned in the law to be of service to the uninitiated in speech and in writing (see the prologue of the Greek translator of Sirach).

The author of the Book of Wisdom also incorporates profane knowledge into the wisdom bestowed by revelation. Divine wisdom has imparted all possible knowledge to 'Solomon' (Wis 7:21). He has been instructed by God in all branches of Greek science (7:17–20). 'Solomon', the prototype of the Wisdom teacher, thus owes all his knowledge to God and to the divine wisdom. The experiential wisdom which originally existed as an independent category side by side with religious wisdom is forced to give place increasingly to religious wisdom, until finally it becomes subsumed under it. The fact that Israel summed up religious and profane knowledge as a single whole under the concept of wisdom has its significance for the confrontation between her and the gentiles who surrounded her. Since this concept also occupied an important place in the hellenistic intellectual world, it could serve as a bridge for the encounter with hellenism.

2. Corresponding to the twofold character of wisdom as teaching we also find in the Old Testament a twofold understanding of wisdom as a human quality. It is (a) a gift of God which is imparted to individual men as an act of grace; but it is also (b) a natural quality which is *acquired by experience* and imparted through instruction.

(a) The first idea is to be found especially in the popular writings, in the prophets and in the later wisdom writings (Sir, Wis). There wisdom is the prerogative of God, and for this reason when it is imparted to men it appears in a manner similar to the spirit of God, as a mysterious power equipping the recipient for various kinds of task. Divine wisdom is veiled from man, he does not know the way to it (Job 28:12–27; Bar 3:15–35). To petition for this wisdom would be presumptuous, for it would make man like God (Gen 3:5, 22; see also Ezek 28:1–5). As the possessor of wisdom, however, Yahweh can impart it to men. It endows them with mysterious powers such as the interpretation of dreams (Gen 41:38f; Dan 1:17) and sorcery (Ex 7:11–13; see Wis 10:16), but also artistic skill and the cunning of the craftsman (Ex 28:3; 31:3, 6; 36:1f). But it is above all upon kings, rulers and judges that God bestows wisdom, in order to equip them to discharge their functions rightly. Thus he gives it to Moses (Num 11:17, 25) and his assistants (Num 11:25; Deut 1:13), to the king (Prov 8:15f; 16:10), David (2 Sam 14:17, 20; see 23:1f), Solomon (1 Kings 3:11, 28), and the messianic king of the future (Is 11:2–5).

Whereas in the earlier writings wisdom is imparted chiefly to rulers, later it is offered to all (Prov 2:6; see also 1:20; Ps 32:8; Sir 1:9). Wisdom has become more 'democratic'. Admittedly certain prior conditions are mentioned for the reception of wisdom. Only one who stands in God's favour (Eccles 2:26), who loves God (Sir 1:10), only holy souls (Wis 7:27) obtain wisdom. In the most recent texts Israel is mentioned especially as the possessor of wisdom (Sir 24:8; Bar 3:36; Wis 10:17). Israel reflects upon her long past and realizes the significance of being a chosen people.

Now that the circle of those who receive wisdom is changed, other effects produced by the possession of wisdom are mentioned also: knowledge of God (Job 11:6–9; Wis 9:17), righteousness (Prov 2:6f; Wis 9:17f), wisdom in speech (Job 32:8, 18–20, Sir 39:6; Wis 6:22–5), the spirit of prophecy (Wis 7:27).

(b) Even the most recent of the Old Testament writings recognises a twofold way of arriving at wisdom: prayer (Wis 7:7; 8:21) and instruction (Wis 6:9). Whereas the later writings regard wisdom predominantly as a gift of God, in the earlier stages it was regarded more as a natural quality to be gained through education and experience. For wisdom is first and foremost prudence in the affairs of life, the capacity to guide one's life into happy and prosperous channels. But manual skill is also described as wisdom. The craftsman counts as one who is 'wise of hand' (Sir 9:17). Even the carpenters, goldsmiths and weavers who fashion idolatrous images are called 'wise' (Is 40:20; Jer 10:9). Here wisdom has the force of 'skilfulness'. In a further usage it is the experienced and prudent counsellor who is accounted wise (2 Sam 13:3; 14:2; 20:16), the old man who has been able to accumulate experience throughout a long life (Job 8:8; 12:12; 15:10), the 'scribes' who are well versed in the law (Jer 8:8f). In the period of the monarchy 'scribe' designates the highest of state officials (see 2 Kings 25:19). There seems to have been a special class of 'sages', who enjoyed high repute (Is 3:3; 5:21; 29:14; Jer 8:8; 18:18). This class was probably identical with that of the scribes (Jer 8:8). These sages, together with the prophets and priests, belong to the leading classes of intellectuals in Israel from the eighth century onwards. Probably it is they who assembled the wisdom sayings and employed them in instructing others. In the post-exilic period the sages are no longer royal officials, but those learned in the scriptures who search the law (Sir 39:1) and interpret it in the 'house of instruction' (Sir 39:8; 51:23).

He who possesses knowledge of men, a sound understanding and prudence in managing the affairs of life is accounted wise. The object of behaving wisely is to attain uninterrupted happiness in one's personal life, and this is achieved by regulating one's conduct in accordance with a prudence that is based upon experience (see Prov 10:4, 8, 10, 14, 17). But the wise man also takes into account a higher retribution, one which rewards actions which are morally good in this present age, and punishes evil behaviour (see Prov 10:3, 6, 22, 27, 29). The motive for behaving wisely is to a large extent personal happiness. The wise man does what is morally good not because it is good in itself, but because it obtains a reward and because evil-doing brings punishment upon itself (see Prov 5:1–20). But religious motivations are also to be found, especially in the more recent writings (Sir 7:36; 35:13–24; Wis 9:8). The norms of wise conduct are experience and insight into the consequences of one's actions (see Prov 16:18, 19, 21, 24, 26), the wisdom of the elders and their experiences of life (Prov 1:8; 2:1; 3:1), what is pleasing to God (Prov 11:1; 12:22; 15:9), and in the later wisdom writings the law of Yahweh (Sir 6:37; 17:11; Wis 16:6; 18:4). In cases in which the law of Yahweh is the norm of wise conduct the sinner is accounted a fool, while the righteous is wise and prudent. Sin is then folly, while God's commandments contain the highest wisdom (see Ps 14:1; Sir 1:26f).

(c) Yahweh is the wise. The prophets praise the wisdom of God (Is 28:29; 31:2; 40:13f; Jer 10:12; 51:15; see also Job 9:4; 12:13; 26:12). In other passages wisdom appears less as an attribute of God than as a distinct entity with an existence of its own, the way to which is known to Yahweh alone, and which he has penetrated to its depths (Job 28:23, 27; Bar 3:32). In Prov 1:20–33; 8:1–21; 9:1–6 wisdom is personified in the feminine as a preacher. She extols her prerogatives and exhorts men to pay heed to her instruction. In Prov 8:22–31 wisdom speaks of her own origins. God possessed her from the beginning and she was already born before the beginning of creation. When God created the world she was at his side. A hymn to wisdom of a similar character is to be found in Sir 24:1–22. Wisdom exalts herself because of her origins and the blessings which she confers. She went forth from the mouth of Yahweh, sought for a resting-place throughout the entire world, and finally, at the behest of the Creator, who formed her, pitched her tent in Israel, where she grew and bore rich fruit. In Sir 24:23 this wisdom is identified with the law of Moses. Wisdom appears still more as a subsistent entity in Wis 7:22–8:1. Wisdom is a being who is understanding (7:22), who has come forth from God (7:25) and is God's image (7:26). Special works are ascribed to her. She penetrates and permeates all in a manner similar to the Stoic world reason (7:24; 8:1). She chooses a just one (10:5), leads men in their activities (9:11; 10:10), preserves (10:1, 5) and rescues them (9:18). She loves men (1:6), takes up her abode in them (1:4), and makes them friends of God and of the prophets (7:27). Divine qualities are ascribed to reason. She is immutable (7:27) and all-powerful (7:23, 27). She appears to subsist as a person in her own right, and as distinct from God. She lives with God; God loves her (8:3). She is initiated into God's secret knowledge, and is a chooser of his works (8:4). She is present at the creation of the world (9:9). She directs the course of the world (7:23, 24, 27; 8:1). She sits beside God's throne (9:4). She has come forth from God, and therefore participates in the divine nature (7:25f).

All these statements appear to point to a second divine person, but in view of the strict monotheism of the Old Testament this is extremely improbable. It is significant that in the Book of Wisdom (as also in Proverbs and Sirach) invocations in prayer are never directed to wisdom, but only to God, who can impart wisdom as his gift (Wis 9:4). On the other hand, in the Book of Wisdom wisdom is more than a mere poetic personification of a divine attribute. This appears especially from Wis 7:25f, where wisdom's connection with God is described. It can hardly be said of an attribute or quality that it proceeds from God, or that it is the image of his goodness. Wisdom, therefore, occupies an intermediate position between a subsistent person and a mere attribute of God. The concept of wisdom shares this intermediate position with the concepts of ⌐ word and

⌐ spirit. As dynamic concepts, they stand for a function of God in relation to the world in its concrete essence. These dynamic concepts are in conformity with a specific mode of thought which envisages in plastic and concrete terms a relationship which we are accustomed to represent to ourselves in abstract ones. Wisdom as described in Wis 7:22–8:1, therefore, is in the last analysis God himself in his work in and upon the world.

This representation of the divine activity under the image of wisdom is significant not only from the literary point of view, but also, and chiefly, from the theological one. In presenting divine wisdom in this form the Old Testament hagiographers have paved the way for the New Testament revelation concerning Christ.

B. In the *New Testament* wisdom does not appear to have the same significance which is ascribed to it in the Old. Only rarely do we find human wisdom referred to in commendatory terms (Acts 7:22; 1 Cor 6:5; Lk 16:8). Moral and religious wisdom (Lk 2:40, 52) and the wisdom of the scribes are attributed to Jesus who teaches with power (Mk 6:2; Mt 13:54; see also Lk 2:47). Paul wishes his christians to be 'wise as to what is good' (Rom 16:19). The human wisdom of self-will, which leaves no room for the divine wisdom, is rejected (1 Cor 1:17–29; 2:4ff, 13; 3:19; 2 Cor 1:12; Rom 1:22; Jas 3:15), for it derives from the flesh (2 Cor 1:12), the world (1 Cor 2:6; 3:19), and ultimately from the devil (Jas 3:15). In its self-sufficiency this human wisdom cannot apprehend the wisdom of God which is revealed especially in his mysterious plan of salvation (Rom 11:33). Thus the 'wisdom of the wise' sees in the message of the Cross only folly, whereas it is precisely the power of God that is revealed in it (1 Cor 1:18f). Human wisdom, which holds the wisdom of God for folly, thereby itself becomes folly (1 Cor 3:19). Yet the basic capacity for apprehending the revealed truth is not denied to the wise of this world from the outset. Always conscious that the mission with which he has been entrusted is for the wise and the foolish alike (Rom 1:14), in Corinth Paul actually wins over a few of the wise to faith (1 Cor 1:26). But he who is wise in the human and worldly sense, if he wishes to become truly wise, must first become a fool (1 Cor 3:18), ie, he must first recognise that the wisdom of this world is folly. True wisdom comes from above (Jas 3:17), from God (Jas 1:5), from the Father (Eph 1:17f), from Christ (Lk 21:15; Eph 1:9), from the Spirit (1 Cor 12:8). It explicates the knowledge contained in faith to ever clearer and broader apprehension. It reveals itself in a deep understanding of the event of salvation (1 Cor 2:7-9; Eph 1:8ff, 17-21), but also in the recognition of the divine will and the moral obligations arising from it (Col 1:9f; Jas 3:13, 17). This wisdom, far from consisting in pure and unrestricted speculation, is bound up with moral maturity (1 Cor 3:1-3). Thus there is a wisdom which is reserved to mature christians (1 Cor 2:6).

The explicit statements about wisdom to be found in the New Testament are relatively few in number. The influence of the Old Testament idea of wisdom on the portrayal of Christ in the New Testament is all the more significant on this account. Paul calls Christ the wisdom of God (1 Cor 1:24, 30). A comparison of pauline statements about Christ with the wisdom literature shows that Paul has transferred specific traits, which occur especially in the Book of Wisdom, as attributes of the divine wisdom to Christ. Christ is the image of the invisible God (Col 1:15; see also Wis 7:26), the firstborn of all creation (Col 1:15; see also Prov 8:22; Sir 1:4). Through him all things have come to be, and we too exist through him (1 Cor 8:6; see also Wis 9:1). It is due to him that the cosmos continues to be maintained in existence (Col 1:17; see also Wis 8:1; 7:27). Christ is the reflection of his (God's) glory, and the image of his being (Heb 1:3; see also Wis 7:25f). An approximation between Christ and the divine wisdom is already apparent in the synoptic gospels. In Mt 11:18f the works performed by Christ are compared with the works of wisdom. Mt 11:25-30 is still clearer on this point: in order to give a clear statement of his relationship with the Father and his significance for men Jesus avails himself of the hymnic expressions in which the Old Testament has described the relationship of the divine wisdom to God and to men (see Job 28:25-8; Prov 8:22-35; Sir 1:1-10; 24:18; Bar 3:27-38; Wis 6-9). But the influence which can be recognised most clearly of all is that of the divine wisdom of the Old Testament upon the portrayal of Christ in the fourth gospel. A comparison shows that the author of the prologue lays under contribution ideas which bear the stamp of the wisdom literature. Between the 'word' of the prologue and the divine wisdom of the Old Testament there exists a correspondence which cannot be overlooked (see Prov 1:29; 3:19; 8:22, 30, 35; Sir 24:6, 8; Wis 7:22, 25–30; 8:1). In the gospel itself Christ represents his relationship with the Father and with men in a manner similar to that by which the relationships between wisdom and God and wisdom and men are depicted in the wisdom literature.

Like wisdom Christ too has come forth from God (Jn 8:42; see also Sir 24:3; Wis 7:25). Both have been beloved by God from the very beginning (Jn 3:35; 17:24; see also Prov 8:27–31; Wis 8:3; 9:9). God has given all things into their hand (Jn 3:35; see also Wis 10:1–11:1). As God is at work, so too are the Son and wisdom (Jn 5:17, 19; Wis 11:17; 15:1; 7:22; 8:1; 7:27). In fact both live in intimate union with God (Jn 14:10f; (see also Prov 8:30; Wis 8:3), and are initiated into the knowledge of God (Jn 8:28; 14:24; see also Wis 8:4). Like wisdom, the Son too has been sent into the world in order to redeem it (Jn 3:17; see also Wis 9:17f). Wisdom takes up its abode in men and thereby draws down upon them the love of God (Wis 1:4; 7:27f). Likewise the Son lives in the men who love him and thereby establishes an inner relationship between God and mankind (Jn 14:20–23). In order to come to the Son or to wisdom man first needs God's grace (Jn 6:44; see also Prov 2:6; Sir 39:6; Wis 8:21). Men's destiny is decided according to the attitude which they adopt towards wisdom and to the Son (Jn 5:22, 27; see also Prov 8:35f; Wis 6:18; 10:1–11:1). For these can bestow and maintain life like God himself (Jn 6:27, 51; see also Prov 8:35; Wis 16:26).

He who observes the commandments of wisdom and of the Son thereby obtains eternal life (Jn 8:51; see also Wis 6:18). He who takes these as his guide does not walk in darkness, for wisdom and the Son are light to men (Jn 8:12; see also Wis 7:26; 10:17; 18:3f). Since both derive from God they are free from sin (Jn 8:46; see also Wis 7:25, 30). Because they come from heaven they can bring a heavenly message to men (Jn 3:12; see also Wis 9:16f). Wisdom and Son alike bestow their friendship upon men (Jn 15:15; see also Wis 7:14, 27), preserve and protect them (Jn 17:12; see also Wis 9:11).

Thus the mysterious figure of the divine wisdom has great significance. The New Testament hagiographers found in the Old Testament presentation of wisdom apt concepts in which they could present the generation of Christ by God before the world began, the part he played in the creation of it, and his significance for mankind in a language that was current among the Jews. Surely we are justified in saying that in Christ it was the divine wisdom become man that they were contemplating.

Bibliography: P. Heinisch, *Die persönliche Weisheit des AT in religionsgeschichtlicher Beleuchtung* (*BZF* xi/1–2), Münster 1923; J. Fichtner, *Die altorientalische W. in ihrer israelitisch-jüdischen Ausprägung* (*BZAW* 62), Giessen 1933; C. Spicq, 'La vertu de prudence dans l'AT', *RB* 42 (1933), 187–210; W. Zimmerli, 'Zur Struktur der atl. Weisheit', *ZAW* 51 (1933), 177–204; P. van Imschoot, 'Sagesse et esprit dans l'AT', *RB* 47 (1938), 23–49; A. M. Dubarle, *Les sages d'Israël*, Paris 1946; R. Stecher, 'Die persönliche Weisheit in den Proverbien, Kap 8', *ZKT* 75 (1953), 411–51;

Witness

H. Windisch, 'Die göttliche Weisheit der Juden und die paulinische Christologie', *Ntl. Studien für G. Heinrici*, Leipzig 1914, 220–34; C. H. Dodd, *The Interpretation of the Fourth Gospel*, Cambridge 1953, 274f; A. Feuillet, 'Jésus et la sagesse divine d'après les évangiles synoptiques', *RB* 62 (1955), 161–96; G. Ziener, 'Weisheitsbuch und Johannesevangelium', *Bbl* 38 (1957), 416f; *RGG* 1800–03 and 1804–09; P. van Imschoot, Haag 1701–06; Eichrodt II, 38–45; von Rad I, 418–59; Bultmann I, 326f and II, 129–34; Imschoot I, 59f and 212–23; Heinisch (see Index); *Jerusalem Bible*, London and New York 1966, 723–8, 931f, 978f, 1004f, and 1034f (introductions to the Wisdom books); H. Gese, *Lehre und Wirklichkeit in der alten Weisheit*, Tübingen 1958; G. Fohrer, *TWNT* VII, 476–528.

Georg Ziener

Witness

The expression 'witness', 'to bear witness', 'testimony' are household words in the New Testament. The basic word for witness in Greek is *martus*. It occurs thirty-four times in the New Testament, most frequently in the Acts of the Apostles (thirteen times). In the epistles it occurs nine times in Paul, twice in Hebrews, once in 1 Peter, and five times in Revelation. The synoptics contain four instances of it, but in the johannine gospel and epistles it does not occur at all. The verb *marturein* (=to bear witness) is attested in seventy-six passages. The johannine writings, with forty-seven examples, far outstrip any of the other New Testament writings (John thirty-three times; 1 and 2 John ten times; Revelation four times). Luke has only two instances of it, and it is totally absent from Matthew and Mark. It is found eleven times in Acts, and Paul and Hebrews each have eight instances of it. The same is true of *marturia* (=testi-

mony), which is employed thirty-seven times in the New Testament. In the johannine writings alone it occurs thirty times (fourteen times in John, seven times in 1 and 3 John, nine times in Revelation), in the synoptics only four times (twice in Mark, twice in Luke, not at all in Matthew), in Acts once, and in Paul twice. The word *marturion* (also = testimony) is found twenty times: nine times in the synoptics, twice in Acts, six times in Paul, once each in Hebrews, James, and Revelation. These statistical findings reflect the development in terms of salvation history of the New Testament concept of witness as definitively established in Acts and in the group of writings attributed to John.

I. *Concept.* The word *martus* is derived from the law courts, and is already found in classical Greek and in LXX as a designation for one who has observed an event and can give an account of it, usually in court, by way of proof and to establish where liability does or does not lie (see Lev 5:1; Num 5:13; Deut 17:6f; 1 Sam 20:23; Is 8:2; Mal 3:5; Ps 89:37 [Heb]; Wis 1:6; Mt 26:65; Mk 14:63; Acts 6:13; 7:58; 2 Cor 13:1; 1 Tim 5:19).

Already in classical antiquity, however, the word means not only a witness to fact but also a witness to truth, a man who avows something to be true, that is a man who proclaims truths, stands up for his convictions, expresses his opinions and gives reasons for them (for examples from Greek literature, see *TDNT* IV, 481–4). In the Old Testament the word is found with this meaning only in a few passages (Ex 31:18; Deut 4:45; 6:17; Ps 19:7; 119:14, 24, 31, 46), but it is particularly frequent in the New Testament writings. According to Is 43:9–13 and 44:7–11, Yahweh summons the people of Israel to bear witness on his behalf in his cause against the gods of the gentiles in order that they may declare before all the world that Yahweh alone is the true God who controls the course of history (see, in the New Testament, Rom 1:9; 2 Cor 1:23; Phil 1:8; 1 Thess 2:5f, 10). They are to bear witness to him in this sense on account of his mighty deeds, which they have experienced and acknowledged by faith.

II. *Witness according to the Acts of the Apostles.* A. In the great confrontation which took place between the early church and judaism on the one hand, and the early church and the gentile world on the other, the idea of the *apostle* as witness to fact plays an absolutely primary role.

1. The apostles are first and foremost the eye- and ear-witnesses of the *risen Lord.* In the course of choosing a successor in place of Judas, Peter outlines the chief task of the apostle: 'So one of the men who have accompanied us during all the time that the Lord Jesus went in and out among us, beginning from the baptism of John until the day when he was taken up from us—one of these men must become with us *a witness to his resurrection*' (Acts 1:21f; see also 1:8). With inspiration and 'with great power the apostles gave *testimony of the resurrection of the Lord Jesus*' (Acts 4:33; see also Lk 24:46–8; Acts 2:32; 3:14f; 5:32; 13:31), with whom they had eaten and drunk after his resurrection from the dead (Acts 10:41).

Paul, too, lays claim to the title of 'witness to Christ', even though he has only seen the glorified Lord in a vision (Acts 22:15; 23:11; 26:9–20; Gal 1:11–2:10). Luke, however, draws a subtle distinction by which Paul is primarily 'a minister of the word' and only secondarily a 'witness' to the glorified Lord (Acts 26:16), whereas the converse is true of the eleven, namely that they were primarily 'eyewitnesses', and only secondarily 'ministers of the word' (Lk 1:2). The facts to which the apostles are to bear witness comprise not merely the resurrection and exaltation of Jesus, but also his life: baptism, miracles, healings, castings out of devils, preaching of the joyful message of the gospel. 'You know the word . . . which was proclaimed throughout all Judaea beginning from Galilee after the baptism which John preached: how God anointed Jesus of Nazareth with the Holy Spirit and with power, how he went about doing good and healing all that were oppressed by the devil, for God was with him. And we are *witnesses* to all that he did both in the country of the Jews and in Jerusalem' (Acts 10:37–9; see also 1:22; 5:31–2a; 2:40; 3:13, 18, 26; 10:40a–43; 2 Pet 1:18). But the function of the apostles is not confined merely to bearing witness to the facts. They are also preachers who proclaim the significance of Jesus' resurrection as acknowledged by faith.

2. He alone could be a witness to Christ who was *chosen by God* for this purpose. The seventy-two disciples (see Lk 10:1–17; Acts 1:21–2), the five hundred brethren (1 Cor 15:6–7), and the two pilgrims to Emmaus (Lk 24:13–35) had all equally seen and heard the risen Christ. And yet Acts

recognises only the apostles as 'witnesses of Christ', the 'witnesses *chosen* by God from of old', who, moved by the gift of the Holy Spirit, realised the immense significance of this mighty deed of God (Acts 10:41–2; 13:31; 22:15; 26:16).

3. The apostles bore a *threefold* witness to the ·Lord: (a) It is the witness of the *word* that is primary. They were above all 'ministers of the word', that is of the good news of the risen and glorified Lord. According to the Old Testament a statement had probative force in the law-courts only if it was made by two or three witnesses (see Num 35:30; Deut 17:6; 19:15; Mt 18:16; Jn 8:17; 2 Cor 13:1; 1 Tim 5:19). For this reason, in the great cause for the rehabilitation of Jesus Peter always spoke in the name of the apostolic college when he brought evidence and laid it before the court of the Jews: 'God has raised the author of life from the dead. To this *we* are witnesses' (Acts 3:15; see also 2:32; 5:32; 10:39, 41, 42). Paul, on the contrary, customarily invokes the unique witness of his vision of Christ (see Acts 22:15–18; 23:11; 26:16) to prove his case to his hellenistic hearers.

Although 'unlettered and uneducated' (Acts 4:13), the apostles bore a powerful witness for Christ before a world which was ill-disposed because they had been equipped for the task with the *gift of the Spirit* at Pentecost (Acts 2:4), as had been promised by the Saviour (see Acts 1:8). This gift of the Spirit was a source of light and strength which could not be conquered. Exploring the mine of the Old Testament scriptures, Peter, guided by the Spirit of God, discovered Jesus'

messianic authority prophesied there (Acts 2:34–5 = Ps 110:1; 10:38 = Is 61:1), and also his prophetic mission (3:22–3 = Deut 18:15, 19), his passion under the figure of the mysterious Servant of God (3:13; 4:27, 30 = Is 52:13–53:12; see also Acts 8:32–3), his glorious resurrection (2:25–6 = Ps 16: 8–11), etc, and he found these attested there 'with the certainty of divine truth' (*Summa Theologica* II–II, q 174, a 2 ad 2). The Holy Spirit filled the apostles with power as he had formerly filled the prophets, so that in spite of all difficulties, all dangers, all persecutions, they proclaimed the gospel tidings 'openly': 'For we cannot but speak of what we have seen and heard,' exclaims Peter proudly before the Sanhedrin (Acts 4:20; see also 4:31; 9:27–8; 13:46; 14:3; 18:9–10, 26; 19:8; and see the Old Testament precedents in Is 6:8; Jer 1:18; Ezek 3:8–9; Amos 3:4–8; Mic 3:8).

(b) Like their divine master (Lk 24:19; Acts 2:22), so too the apostles reinforce the witness of the word or of their preaching with 'signs' (*sēmeia*), that is, with miraculous power: 'And many wonders and signs were done through the apostles' (Acts 2:43; 5:12), above all by the hands of Peter (3:1–10; 5:15) and Paul (14:8–10; 19:11–12; see also 4:30; 14:3, 27; 15:4, 12; 21:19).

(c) Finally, the witness of the apostles is only genuine if it carries the stamp of persecutions and suffering, of oppression and the malice of conspirators plain for all to see. The lot of the disciple (Mt 10:17–22; Lk 21:12–15; Jn 16:1–2; 1 Pet 5:1) is the same as the lot of his master (Mt 23:34–5; Lk 11:47–51; Jn 15:20; Acts 3:22–3).

Under the influence of the Holy Spirit, the first christians regarded the condemnation of Jesus by the Roman authorities, the threats of the Sanhedrin and the fetters of the apostles, as the fulfilment of the messianic prophecy of Ps 2:1–2 (=Acts 4:25–6): 'For truly in this city there were gathered together against thy holy servant Jesus, whom thou didst anoint, both Herod and Pontius Pilate, with the gentiles and the peoples of Israel, to do whatever thy hand and thy plan had predestined to take place' (Acts 4:27–8). The power from on high had turned timid men into heroes who trod in the footprints of the servant of God: 'Then they left the presence of the council rejoicing that they were counted worthy to suffer dishonour for the name of Jesus' (Acts 5:41). The message of the beatitudes pronounced by Jesus had come true in their lives (see Mt 5:10–12; Lk 6:22–3). Indeed they were now ready for the ultimate test, to seal their witness to the master with their blood (see Acts 5:29; 6:15; 20:24; 21:13), although Luke in his account has not taken up the tradition of the violent death suffered by the prince of the apostles.

(B) Since the apostles alone were called to be witnesses to the fact of the resurrection, they are the witnesses to Christ *par excellence*. But their inspired witness to Christ has awakened an echo in the primitive community of christians which henceforward will not be silenced until the end of time.

1. If the christians of the early church no longer have any direct experience of the crucified and risen Lord they are none the less called to bear witness to him in word and deed.

This is witness in the broader sense, the indirect witness which is based upon the Easter preaching of the apostles. While, therefore, it does not rest upon the same foundations as that of the apostles, it has the same person as its subject, namely, the risen Lord.

2. The apostles sometimes refer to the fact of this indirect form of witness. Before the Sanhedrin Peter solemnly accounts for his actions in the following terms: 'We are witnesses to these things [the death and resurrection of Christ], and so is *the Holy Spirit whom God has given to those who obey him*' (Acts 5:32; see also 15:28), that is to say that the Holy Spirit also bears witness to the glorified Christ through the mouths of the Jewish and gentile christians who speak and act under his influence (see 2:4; 4:8, 31; 15:28). At Pentecost the Holy Ghost was poured out 'upon all flesh', that is, upon all members of the people of God (see Acts 2:17–21 = Joel 2:28–9, 32). After the liberation of the apostles Peter and Paul a 'miniature Pentecost' took place: 'And when they had prayed the place in which they were gathered together was shaken, and they were all filled with the Holy Spirit and spoke the words of God with boldness' (Acts 4:31).

The gentiles, too, received the gift of the Spirit of God, as, for example, in the case of the household of Cornelius: 'While Peter was still saying this the Holy Spirit fell upon all who heard the word, and the believers from among the circumcised [the Jewish christians] who came with Peter were amazed because the gift of the Holy Spirit had been poured out even upon the gentiles' (Acts 10:44; see also 11:15,

17). At the crucial council of Jerusalem Peter underlined this revolutionary fact of salvation: 'God who knows the heart bore witness to them [the gentiles], giving them the Holy Spirit just as he did to us' (Acts 15:8; see also 8:12, 17; 19:5–6).

Individuals, too, were endowed with the gift of the Holy Spirit, as, for example, Philip (Acts 8:29), Barnabas (Acts 11:24; 13:2), Stephen (Acts 6:5, 10; 7:55), Timothy (2 Tim 1:6).

3. The witness of the community, which was confined to the church at Jerusalem, as well as the witness of individual christians, which was spread through the whole world, brought astonishing effects in its train.

(a) The message of the apostles at Easter, in which they called upon men to become christians, exercised an overwhelming attraction upon the primitive church, in which a glorious spring of christian life sprang up, while unshakeable faith in the resurrection of Christ, the pledge of their own glorification, to be accomplished at the return of the Lord, kindled the spark of christian joy in the hearts of the first christians, a joy which sprang into flame chiefly at the liturgical celebration of the breaking of bread: 'Day by day . . . breaking bread in their homes, they partook of food with glad and generous hearts' (Acts 2:46; see also Eph 5:19), and praised the *magnalia Dei* (see also Acts 2:47; 3:8–9; 4:21; 11:18; 13:48; 21:20; Lk 24:52f). They gave vent to their overflowing joy in inarticulate cries and disconnected gestures according as the gift of tongues prompted them (see also Acts 2:4, 13, 17; 10:46; 19:6; 1 Cor 14; ↗ charisma).

The fiery Easter preaching of the apostles kindled in the hearts of the young communities the spark of an energetic brotherly love, the most winning element in the witness to Christ.

In the course of portraying the life of the early church from three distinct aspects (Acts 2:42–7; 4:32–5; 5:12–16), Luke has occasion to speak of the *koinōnia* (2:42), the 'brotherly fellowship' which welded the hearts and spirits of the believers into a unity: 'The company of those who believed were of one heart and soul' (4:32). In this happy period, in which many hearts beat as one, the faithful held all things in common. They sold property and possessions in order to distribute the proceeds among the starving brethren to each according to his need (Acts 2:44–5; 4:32, 34, 35). The name of Barnabas in particular shines out from the roll of honour of those who performed deeds of the most noble love, for he sold his field and laid the money at the foot of the apostles (Acts 4:37). This evidence of acts of brotherly love is more urgently relevant than ever before in our world, so rent as it is by social conflicts. Abbé Pierre, the apostle of the rag-pickers, testifies to the fact that in his brotherhood of Emmaus the order of the theological virtues is inverted. On their arrival the 'clochards' are given every kind of loving service. By degrees, under the rays of a heartfelt love, the ice of embitterment and cynicism melts. Hope is gradually generated in the hearts of these deprived ones, a hope which is at first purely at the natural level, and which is then directed, as it were spontaneously, towards the higher goods.

Finally faith in Christ is kindled in them.

(b) From Acts 6 onwards, the apostles, together with their disciples, priests and laymen alike, go out into the wide world in order to win over the gentiles to Christ above all by the preaching of the gospel message and by 'martyrdom'.

It was the chief task of the apostle to testify solemnly as in a trial in the law-courts to the fact of Jesus' resurrection, and thereby to his innocence. He was to do this before the Council of the Jews and the populace of Jerusalem. With the sending out of the apostles, the time of the *kērugma*, of the gospel, of the word of God is inaugurated—that is, the time when the good news of salvation in Christ is boldly proclaimed. Thus the function of the herald, the messenger who strives to win over Jewish and gentile hearers alike to Christ, comes to be associated with the task of bearing witness, and to be considered as an element of the highest importance in it.

So far as *believers* were concerned the great missionary campaign was inaugurated outside and beyond the holy city, whence they had been driven and scattered throughout the whole world by persecutions: 'They went from place to place and 'proclaimed' (*euangelizomai*) the 'word' (*logos*) (Acts 8:4; see also vv 12, 25, 35, 40; 11:19). Philip 'preached' Christ resoundingly (*kērussō*: Acts 8:5; see also 21:8). In these and other passages what is meant by *kērugma*, gospel, and word of God is nothing else than the indirect witness to Christ. The preaching of the Easter message awakened an unshakeable faith in the glorified Lord in the hearts of the first christians (see Rom 10:8–9, 14–17). They in their turn bore witness to the glorified Lord with burning inspiration. The modern apostle too, whether he be priest or layman, is called to bear witness to the risen Christ to a world which has grown pagan (see Lk 24:49; Acts 1:4, 5, 8; 2:33). We too ask for the gift of the Spirit, without which we can achieve nothing: when we humbly implore it from God he will open to us the immeasurable depths of holy scripture and will equip us with suprahuman power.

It is in persecutions and in the martyr's death that the christians' witness to their risen saviour shines out in all its purity. The *kērugma*, the message and word of God, represent a kind of preaching which is full of power to win men over to Christ; but they are devoid of any element of the forensic. They are the unalloyed expressions of convictions which are firm as a rock. But when christians stand before the bar of this world's courts they are no longer concerned to make attestations of their faith designed to win others over to it. Their preoccupation in this situation is simply to bear burning witness to Christ. It is witness in the juridical sense. The Holy Spirit will bear witness to the Lord through their mouths (see Lk 12:11; 21:12–15; Mt 10:17–20; Mk 13:11). First in the list of the unending procession of 'martyrs', Stephen the deacon stands out as 'a man full of faith and of the Holy Spirit' (Acts 6:5; see also vv 8, 10); 'But he, full of the Holy Spirit, gazed into heaven and saw the glory of God, and Jesus standing at the right hand of God'

(Acts 7:55-6). The Acts of the Apostles knows only this single one of those who bore witness with their blood: 'When the blood of Stephen thy witness (*martus*) was shed' (Acts 22:20; see also Rev 2:13; 11:3; 17:6). Since the deacon had no personal knowledge of the Lord either during his earthly life or in his risen state, he is not a witness to fact as the apostles were. On the other hand the expression does not signify 'martyr' in the sense which the term has acquired today, even though it is on the way to it. Towards the middle of the second century, when persecution and violent death for the sake of Christ became the daily bread of the church, the word *martus* came to be used solely as the technical term for the act of bearing witness by the shedding of one's blood—that is, martyrdom.

The prosecution of the faithful who remain true to Christ intensifies as the centuries unfold. The christians' witness by blood will be brought to an end only at the parousia by the witness of Jesus himself, the 'reliable and faithful witness' (Rev 1:5; 3:14) which he will then bear to all his own who have been faithful witnesses to him (see Lk 12:8-9).

III. In his gospel and epistles, *John* intentionally avoids the expression *martus*, but uses the verb *marturein* (forty-seven times) and the noun *marturia* (thirty times) all the more frequently on that account. This choice corresponds to the development of the idea of Christ which reached its culmination in John the evangelist. Like the apostles, John too had been a witness of Jesus' resurrection (see Jn 20-21; 1 Jn 1:1-3), but the time for revising the trial of Jesus before the Sanhedrin and the people of Jerusalem through the witness of the apostles was long passed. It was pastoral considerations on a cosmic scale that burned in the soul of John the theologian. What he wanted was to bear witness to the person of Christ by his writings.

Seen through the eyes of the disciple whom Jesus loved, Christ developed his redemptive work in the setting of a hostile world. The hostility already indicated by the synoptics (see Mt 10:18; Mk 13:9; Lk 21:13) is still more powerfully emphasised by him. According to him the entire life of Jesus seems to develop in the form of a great trial at law in which Jesus himself and the world are the contestants. The various witnesses who are summoned to the bar of this court all pass on the word of revelation proceeding from the Father. Viewed in this light the johannine concept of witness acquires a juridical character. Hence John never uses the expression *kērugma*, current and frequent though this was in the tradition of the synoptics and Acts. What he is concerned with is not so much the preaching of the gospel message of divine salvation in Christ as the defence of Christ, the acknowledgement of Christ as Redeemer and Son of God. John's writings are not primarily intended to win over believers. Rather they have an apologetic character. They do not represent an avowal which is propagandist in character, as do the *kērugma*, the gospel or the word of God. Rather these writings constitute an ardent defence of Christ, and it is in this sense that they bear witness to him.

1. *On what is this witness based?* The witness is a statement concerning facts and events which are known from personal experience. In John the 'witness' is very often connected with the verb 'to see' (instances in 1:34; 3:11, 32; 19:35; 1 Jn 1:2; 4:14). The witnesses have seen with their bodily eyes an event which took place in Jesus' life. Therefore it is witness to fact (*martus*) which is meant, in the sense in which we have encountered this in the synoptics and Acts.

But according to John it is not to the facts as such of salvation history that the men who are called bear witness, but rather to the deeper reality hidden behind those facts. The baptist sees an event in the external world which points to the Messiahship of Jesus. He bears witness to this (1:32). John sees water and blood flowing from the side of Jesus; but it is not to the salvific fact as such that he bears witness, but rather to 'water and blood' as sacramental signs of baptism and the eucharist (19:36–7; 1 Jn 1:1–3). Behind the observed fact lies hidden a reality which is invisible, and which the earthly witness can only know through revelation. And it is to this that he bears witness. For this witness bodily vision of the fact in question was indispensable. For without it they would never have been able to bear witness at all (15:27). But their witness points on to that which revelation or faith has disclosed to them concerning the person of Jesus. For John witness is not primarily witness to fact, but witness to belief or to truth. Here, as in other instances, we are confronted with a special quality in the writing of this evangelist by which a given expression is used to signify a sensible experience and a mysterious spiritual reality both at the same time.

2. *To what does the johannine gospel bear witness?* From what has been said it will be clear that it is neither the resurrection of Jesus nor the events of his earthly life that constitute the subject of his witness. In his inmost heart stands the person of Christ (1:7, 8, 15; 5:31, 32, 36, 37, 39; 8:14, 18; 10:25; 1 Jn 5:9). In all these passages the question which the witness is intended to answer for us is: 'Who is Jesus?' The witness penetrates through the words and deeds of Jesus to the mystery of his being, to the spiritual reality of his person. The Baptist testifies to the Messiahship of Jesus, which is visible only to the eyes of faith (1:15, 32; 5:33;). The focal point of the witness is the person and the mission of Christ as revealed to believers alone. It is not the work of redemption that constitutes the central nucleus of the johannine theology but the person of the redeemer himself. It is this that gives his christology its special attraction.

3. *Who bears witness?* The evangelist records a whole series of witnesses. The baptist must bear witness to the light (1:7, 8, 15, 19, 32, 34; 3:26; 5:33, 36), to his messianic dignity (1:15), to the fact that he is the Son of God (1:30). The scriptures, in which God himself speaks, bear witness concerning Christ (5:39); hence one believes the word contained in them as one believes God himself, who speaks to us through his Son (5:24). The disciples bear witness concerning Christ (15:27; 19:35; 21:24); so, too, Jesus himself bears witness concerning himself (5:31; 8:

13). Jesus' witness concerning himself is basically identical with the witness of the Father (5:32) who has sent him (3:34; 14:24). In immediate association with it is the witness of the 'works' which the Father has 'given' the Son power to perform (5:36). They are the works of the Father himself (9:3, 4; 10:37), who lives in Jesus as Jesus lives in him (10:38; 14:10–11). Later the Spirit of truth will bear witness in the church (15:26; 16:13). He will 'recall' to the disciples all that Jesus has said and done, that is he will disclose to them the deeper sense and the full significance of the words and deeds of Christ.

In the last analysis all of these distinct testimonies can be traced back to the single and unique testimony of the Father—to the Father's revelation which finds expression in the various earthly witnesses, is fulfilled in the witness borne by Jesus, and lives on in the witness of the Holy Spirit.

4. *What is the purpose of this witness?* From what has been stated so far it is evident that the witness in John is of its essence aimed at faith. It is meant to arouse and to deepen faith in Christ. The Baptist came to bear witness that all may believe (1:7). The evangelist gives testimony of the events of the crucifixion in order that all may come to believe (19:35).

According to 1 Jn 5:5–12 Jesus Christ constitutes the focal point of faith, and one which is based upon a threefold witness. Jesus Christ has come 'by water and blood', that is in the baptism at the Jordan and through death on the Cross. But there is also a reference to the 'water and blood' which flowed from Jesus' side (v 6ab).

Thus two distinct levels of significance for salvific history are to be found in 'water and blood', making them signs of baptism and the eucharist. To the historical witness of 'water and blood' (v 10 in the perfect) a third witness is added, that namely of the Spirit: the Spirit testifies to the reality and the presence of the Son of God in baptism and the eucharist (v 7: present tense).

According to Old Testament ideas of justice a statement is considered valid in law only if it is confirmed by two or three witnesses. For this reason three witnesses are called to testify that Christ is the Son of God: the Spirit, the water, and the blood. The witness of the Spirit evokes in us faith in Christ as Son of God (vv 5, 10). Baptism and eucharist admit us to a share in this divine life (v 11), life in the Son (v 11).

The witness of God (vv 9–10) combines all three witnesses in itself, the witness of the Spirit, the water and the blood. For through the threefold witness of faith and the two sacraments God himself gives testimony concerning his Son. But this witness of God finds a response only in the heart of the believer. Only for the believer can it become a source of life.

The apostles were called by God to be eye- and ear-witnesses of the risen and glorified Lord. The witnesses of the fourth gospel have plumbed revelation to its depths and there they have discovered the unfathomable mystery of the person of Christ and have borne witness to it. Their witness is a burning summons to believe in Jesus Christ, in the Messiah, in the word, and in the Glory of the Father.

May we, too, enlisted like the first christians in the corps of the risen and glorified Lord, and filled with the power which faith in the resurrection bestows, bear witness to the Lord by a life of true brotherly love and deep resignation to suffering! May the witness of the Father concerning his Son strengthen ever more in us faith in Christ! Pius XII summoned all christians to this task of bearing witness: 'Today more than ever, and as in the first centuries of her existence, the church chiefly needs *witnesses* . . . who by their whole way of life make the true countenance of Christ shine out before a world which has grown pagan' (*AAS* 39 [1947], 312).

Bibliography: General: H. von Campenhausen, *Die Idee des Martyriums in der alten Kirche*, Göttingen 1936; J. Smend, 'Der Zeugnischarakter der christl. Verkündigung', *ZST* 13 (1936), 489–517; E. Peterson, *Zeuge der Wahrheit*, Leipzig 1937; R. Asting, *Die Verkündigung des Wortes im Urchristentum*, Stuttgart 1939; E. Günther, *Martyrs. Die Geschichte eines Wortes*, Hamburg 1941; A. Verheul, 'Apostolaat en Verrijzenis', *Studia Cath.* 26 (1951), 171–84; M. Barth, *Der Augenzeuge*, 1946; E. Günther, 'Zeuge und Märtyrer', *ZNW* 47 (1956), 145–61; M. Lods, *Confesseurs et martyrs*, Neuchâtel-Paris 1948; N. Brox, *Zeuge und Märtyrer*, Munich 1961; H. Strathmann, *TDNT* IV, 474–514; S. de Diétrich, Allmen 456–8; A. Verheul, *DB* 1807f; *HTG* II, 903–11.
On Acts: L. Cerfaux, 'Témoins du Christ d'après les Actes', *Receuil Cerfaux* II, 1954, 157–74; A. Retif, 'Témoignage et prédication missionnaire dans les Actes des Apôtres', *NRT* 73 (1951), 152–65; A. Rétif, *Foi au Christ et Mission*, 1953; R. Koch, 'Témoignage d'après les Actes', *Masses Ouvrières* 129 (1957), 16–33; 131 (1957), 4–25.
On John: B. Trepanier, 'Contribution à une recherche sur l'idée de témoin dans les écrits johanniques', *Revue de l'Univ. d'Ottawa* 15 (1945), 5–63; C. Masson, 'Le témoignage de Jean', *RTP* 38 (1950), 120–27; A. Vanhoye, 'Témoignage et Vie en Dieu selon le quatrième évangile', *Christus* 16 (1955), 155–71; W. Nauck, 'Die Tradition und der Charakter des ersten Johannesbriefes', *Wissenschaftliche Untersuchungen zum NT*, ed. J. Jeremias and O. Michel, 1957; I. de la Potterie, 'La notion de témoignage dans S. Jean', *SP* II (Paris–Gembloux 1959), 193–208.

Robert Koch

Woman

A. *Woman in the Old Testament.* As the primeval history of the bible shows, the first woman was formed from the first man (Gen 2:21f); she was bone of his bone and flesh of his flesh (Gen 2:23). Hence she was called 'wo-man' by Adam since she was taken from man (Gen 2:23b). She was in the image and likeness of God (Gen 1:26f; ↗ likeness). The Hebrew words ʾîš and ʾiššâh are probably derived, etymologically speaking, from the same root, namely ʾenāš. The name in Hebrew designates the essence of a thing. Here it expresses with delicate artistry not only the complete conformity of nature between man and woman, but also the distinction of the sexes. In exploiting the similarity of sound between ʾîš and ʾiššâh in this way the biblical author has to a considerable extent followed the popular etymology based on the sound of words, which regarded the two terms as masculine and feminine forms of the same linguistic root. According to the account in Genesis it is the woman's function to be a helpmeet and, so to say, a complement to man (Gen 2:18), especially by joining with him in an indissoluble marriage (Gen 2:24). For it was not merely that she might be of the same nature that the first woman was formed from the first man—such identity of nature could equally well have been achieved if woman had been formed in the same way as man—but for the sake of unity between them. Woman, then, in spite of the secondary position she occupies in the order of creation, was called to live in a harmonious relationship with man, but not to be subordinate to him. Yet the very fact that woman was the more easily seduced (Gen 3:6) raises the question of whether woman was not considered the weaker partner. Finally we have that much disputed sentence in which a penalty is imposed upon the woman in Gen 3:16: 'He shall rule over you'. Many exegetes have concluded from this that henceforward woman is made subject to man as a penalty for having fallen into sin, and that the initial equality has been replaced by inequality, that is a reduction of woman's status. On the other hand, against this view the following factors may be pointed out: there can have been no intention to suggest that woman was juridically subordinated to man in the strict sense as a punishment for original sin, for man himself had been equally guilty. Likewise it cannot be a question of a subordination which is simply confined to family relationships, for this is already given in virtue of the original order of creation prior to original sin, and cannot therefore be a penalty arising from the first sin. 'He will rule over you' (16b) seems rather to represent a more specific application of the words: 'I shall greatly multiply your pain in childbearing' (16a), which means that in the marriage act woman must submit to the authority of her husband. For the purpose and the deeper meaning of the one being made subordinate to the other can only be that man and woman shall become one in a relationship of 'one flesh'. It cannot have been intended that woman should be abased or enslaved in either a juridical or a social sense (see J. Coppens and G. Reidick).

From the juridical point of view, the Israelite woman is not always accorded equality with man, but her position was probably far freer than that of women in the legal practice of other oriental peoples. The *marriage laws* are dominated by the principle of patriarchy. When she became married the woman passed from the authority of her father into that of her husband (1 Sam 18:17, 19, 27). The will and the inclination of the girl were, however, to a large extent taken into account (Gen 24:39, 58). The married woman and the espoused virgin alike were obliged to be completely faithful to their husbands. The husband only incurred the guilt of adultery if he intruded upon the marriage or espousals of another (Deut 22:22ff), a fact which is to be explained from the widespread practice of polygamy in Israel. The right of divorce belonged to the husband alone (Deut 24:1-4; ↗ marriage). Virginity—that is, the lack of husband and children—carried with it a stigma in the Old Testament (Gen 30:23; Is 54:4; ↗ virginity).

The highest happiness of which the Israelite woman was capable was that of *motherhood* (Gen 24:60; 30:1; 1 Sam 1:6f; Ps 113:9). When she became a mother she constituted the focal point of family life and as such was the object of honour on all sides and was highly prized. Several Hebrew women have won a place in history by reason of their true and immense motherly love: in particular the mother of Moses

(Ex 2:2–9), as well as Hannah, the mother of Samuel (1 Sam 1–2:21), Rizpah (2 Sam 3:7ff), the mother of the Maccabee brothers, who saw her seven sons die in a single day (2 Macc 7:1–41), and above all Mary, the mother of the Messiah. In Israel mother-love was of such great importance that it became a symbol of divine love on the lips of the prophet Isaiah: 'As one whom his mother comforts, so I will comfort you' (Is 66:13). As mother the Israelite woman enjoyed not only great honour but also equal authority with that of the father: 'Honour thy father and thy mother . . .' (Ex 20:12; Deut 5:16). In Lev 19:3 the mother is actually mentioned before the father: 'Every one of you shall revere his mother and his father . . .'. The breaking of the commandment to honour parents entails the severest penalty whether the offence is committed against the father or the mother (Ex 21:15–17; Lev 20:9).

In the sphere of *penal laws*, too, woman is made equal to man. According to Lev 20:10 the death penalty is prescribed for the adulteress as well as for the adulterer. Again in the case of a domestic animal which has killed someone, it makes no difference to the legal penalty which is prescribed whether its victim was a man or a woman. The owner of the beast is equally liable in either case. These juridical estimates show that for purposes of compensation, etc, man and woman were considered absolutely equal, which is not the case in other Oriental codes.

With regard to rights of inheritance the claims of the first-born alone take precedence over those of the wife. Where there are no sons, daughters have the right of inheritance (Num 27:1–11; 36:1–13). Admittedly in such a case they are obliged to marry within their own tribe in order that their family possessions may remain intact. In Job 42:15 on the other hand, a practice is referred to whereby the daughter shared with her brothers the possessions left by the father. In Ruth 4:3 and Judith 8:7 it is presupposed that a childless widow could inherit from her husband.

Women and girls in Israel were not only praised for their competence in household matters (Prov 31:10–31), they were also completely free to engage in daily affairs outside the domestic sphere (Gen 24:13ff; Ex 2:16; etc). At national festivals and also on religious occasions they appeared quite openly (Deut 12:12; Judg 21:21; 2 Sam 6:12ff), and certain Israelite women actually achieved great repute and influence in *political* life. Outstanding figures were: Miriam, the sister of Moses and Aaron, who under prophetic inspiration uttered the song of triumph at the overthrow of the Egyptians (Ex 15:21); Deborah, who in a period of the greatest religious and national decline acted as a judge of Israel in the mountains of Ephraim, and by her inspiring words guided the battle against Sisera to victory (Judg 4, 5); *Huldah* who prophesied in the name of the Lord like the great prophets of the old covenant, and whose counsel was sought by King Josiah (2 Kings 22); Judith, who freed her native city and the whole of Palestine from the enemy (Judith 15:9); and Esther, who, when confronted with the perilous situation in which her people stood, reacted with the words: 'If I must die, then let me die' (Esther 4:15).

With regard to religion, the woman takes second place to the man to the extent that she is excluded from all official acts of the cult. Israel, unlike other ancient peoples, had no priestesses. Nevertheless, women did perform specific services at the sacred tabernacle (Ex 38:8; 1 Sam 2:22). The woman no less than the man is bound to God by covenant (Deut 29:11). Together with her family she observes the great annual festivals, especially Passover (Ex 12:3), and also participates in the sacrificial meal prescribed in the cult (1 Sam 1:4f; Deut 12:12; 15:20). Sacrifices of purification are prescribed for the Israelite woman for various occasions (Lev 12; 15:19-33). Pious parents educated their daughters in accordance with the law of Moses (Dan 13:3). Women had to attend with the rest at the reading of the Book of the Covenant in order that they might learn to observe it exactly (Deut 31:12; Josh 8:35; Neh 8:2). They too are held personally responsible for transgressions (Amos 4:1; Is 3:16f).

Thus the portrayal of women in the Old Testament is on the whole not an unattractive one. It takes on more sombre hues in the period of post-exilic judaism. But this darkness is broken by the light of the day of redemption, in which man and woman appear once more equal in dignity as on the day of the creation.

B. *Woman in the New Testament.* In the course of his daily life Jesus is often occupied with the affairs of women, sick women whom he heals, sinners whom he forgives, woman disciples to whom he reveals himself. But it is chiefly Paul and Peter in their letters, and Luke in the Acts of the Apostles, who show us the official position accorded to woman in the christian way of life.

1. *Jesus and women.* For Jesus woman is just as much a person as man in the sight of God. For this reason he extended his salvific work to women too. He showed his compassion not only to Israelite women but to gentile women too. Even though he has been sent only to the lost sheep of the house of Israel, he fulfils the entreaty of a gentile mother because of her faith, the greatness of which he wonders at and praises. Then he heals her daughter with the words: 'Be it done for you as you desire' (Mt 15:21-8; Mk 7:24-30). He does not shrink from the touch of a woman who is unclean by reason of an issue of blood, but lovingly addresses her as his daughter (Mt 9:20-22; Mk 5:25-34; Lk 8:43-8). He heals the mother-in-law of Simon Peter, in whose house he is staying (Mt 8:14f; Mk 1:29-31; Lk 4:38f), as well as the daughter of Jairus, the leader of the synagogue (Mk 5:21-3 and 35-43). He strives for the soul of the Samaritan woman at the well of Jacob and turns her into a believer and a proclaimer of his name (Jn 4:1-42). He has a word of forgiveness for the unhappy adulteress. Full of compassionate love he bends down to the repentant sinner and forgives all her sins (Jn 8:1-11). In Galilee while at table in the house of a Pharisee, he allows his feet to be anointed by a woman sinner notorious in the city, and pronounces the judgement of divine pity: 'Your faith has saved you. Go in peace' (Lk 7:36-50).

Jesus stays in the house of the sisters of Bethany, and explains the word of God to them (Lk 10:38–42). It is to a woman that he reveals the deepest mystery of the hope of a resurrection, namely, Martha the sister of Lazarus (Jn 11:1–44). He accords the highest praise to the loving act performed by Mary of Bethany: 'Wherever this gospel is preached in the whole world, what she has done will be told in memory of her' (Mt 26:6–13; Mk 14:3–9; Jn 12:1–8). Finally he appears in his risen state to Mary Magdalene *before* appearing to the apostles, and it is to her that he gives the task of bringing the news to the disciples that he is alive: hence the title of honour 'apostola apostolorum' has rightly been bestowed upon her (Jn 20:1–18; Mk 16:9–11).

It can plainly be seen, then, that Jesus fulfilled his vocation as Saviour by helping many women as well as men. Often a section of tradition which has to do with men is counterbalanced by a corresponding parable about a woman: the lost sheep—the lost drachma, the parable of the mustard seed taken from husbandry—the parable of the leaven taken from the domestic sphere.

Women are found among the followers of Jesus (Lk 8:2f; see also Mk 15:40f), and these often minister to him as far as they are able. They follow him right up to his death and watch this from afar (Mt 27:55f; Mk 15:40f; Lk 23:49). They also see the grave and watch while his body is buried.

2. *The official position of woman in the New Testament.* Paul in particular shows in his letters how the early Christian community interpreted Jesus' acts. For those who have become children of God there is no difference between man and woman. 'There is neither male nor female (a reference to Gen 1:27); you are all one in Christ Jesus' (Gal 3:27). Hence woman is made equal to man in the hope of eternal life (1 Pet 3:7). From the outset women belong to the church as fully enfranchised members (Acts 1:14; 12:12). This appears particularly clearly from the lists of those to whom Paul extends greetings in his epistles, where women are addressed as sisters and fellow workers (Rom 16:1, 3; 1 Cor 9:5, etc).

On the other hand, however, Paul does affirm that the wife is subordinate to her husband. In the New Testament too woman is considered subordinate to man in the created order (1 Cor 11:3). Here, however, there is no question of any diminution of her dignity any more than Christ's dignity is diminished in relation to God. What Paul shows, rather, is how the basic law of dependence permeates the whole of the divine order. There is nothing here, therefore, which women could have felt as particularly objectionable. The requirement that women shall wear veils in the communal assemblies (1 Cor 11:5ff) appears to have been an external expression determined by the customs actually prevailing at that time of woman's dependence on man for her very existence. 'Woman was taken from man and created for man: in the presence of the angels she must bear the sign of this dependence...' (F. Prat, *La théologie de Saint Paul*, Paris 1945, 573). In this a clear reference to Gen 2:18, 21 and 23 can be seen.

Whereas in 1 Cor 11 all that is forbidden is for women to take part in the communal assemblies unveiled, 1 Cor 14:34f requires that women shall be absolutely silent. Thus a certain development of ideas can be discerned, reaching its climax in 1 Tim. 1 Cor 11:5 permits charismatic utterances to women provided that they are veiled. 1 Cor 14:34 forbids women natural speech in the public assembly. Finally, 1 Tim 2:12 contains a prohibition of public teaching, and the reasons given for this are domestic in character, and based upon the natural position of women themselves. The pastoral practice of modern catholicism is to this day based upon the position adopted by the early christians. Woman's natural vocation is the bearing of children. It is through this that woman finds her rightful place in the divine order, provided she has faith and love (1 Tim 2:15). Thus with regard to the priesthood she is not simply thrust into the background even though this office is reserved to the male sex alone, but is rather called from the very outset to co-operate in its dissemination in her role as mother.

The pauline letters thus give a clear and consistent picture of women's position in the church and in celebrations of the liturgy. By comparison with those of men, the rights of women are clearly limited. It is fitting for a woman to show her piety in good works (1 Tim 2:10). A widow, if she genuinely remains a widow (1 Tim 5:3), may take up a specific position in the service of the church in connection with works of charity. In this case she is to be entered on a special list and must fulfil three requirements: she must be over sixty, have been only once married, and must lead an authentic christian life, expressed in actions prompted by love of her neighbour, bringing up children, hospitality, 'washing the feet of the saints' (ie, selfless and humble service), relieving the afflicted and 'doing good in every way' (1 Tim 5:9f). Younger widows, on the other hand, ought to marry, to avoid being tempted to break the promise they make to Christ and the church on their entry into the service of the community (1 Tim 5:11–14).

Women are, however, barred from preaching the word in liturgical celebrations, whether in a free and charismatic or an official form. They must conform to the order of the liturgy and leave the preaching of the word to men. This ruling is based on the order of creation; Adam was created first, and then Eve (1 Tim 2:13), and this order remains valid in the liturgy after the redemption as well. The differences between the sexes in the order of creation are not in contradiction to their equality in the order of redemption—as G. Fitzer claims in support of his case for striking out the *mulier taceat* verse as unpauline because of its incompatibility with 1 Cor 11. The differences between men and women arising from the creation and the unity and equality of the sexes as a result of the redemption are two different things, and on different levels. The equality of the sexes, being 'all one in Christ Jesus' (Gal 3:28), does not imply a theological equality, but refers to the status of being children of God, which men and women equally inherit through baptism. The priority established in the order of creation is a fact which remains unchanged. 1 Cor 14:34 cannot therefore be simply an example of a temporally conditioned judgement about the position of women in the liturgy, but must be a conscious decision of fundamental significance. The pauline rule of *mulier taceat* in the liturgy has lost none of its importance, but is still valid today.

The right relation between the order of creation and the order of redemption must be preserved, and the unanimous practice of the whole church, to which Paul refers in 1 Cor 14:33b, should under no circumstances be overlooked. Attempts to give men and women a basically equal position in the liturgy, such as have been undertaken in some protestant communities, should therefore give way before the contrary practice of nearly two thousand years.

Bibliography: H. Zschokke, *Die biblischen Frauen des AT*, Freiburg 1882; P. Tischleder, *Wesen und Stellung der Frau nach der Lehre des heiligen Paulus (NA* 10/3-4), Münster 1932; J. Sickenberger, *Die Briefe des heiligen Paulus an die Korinther und Römer*, Bonn 1932; J. Coppens, 'La soumission de la femme à l'homme d'après Gen 3:16b', *ETL* 14 (1937), 632ff; A. Oepke, *TDNT* I, 776-89; P. Ketter, *Christus und die Frauen* I and II, Stuttgart 1949/50; G. von le Fort, *Die ewige Frau*, Olten 1949[12]; K. Neulinger, *Frauengestalten des NT*, Vienna 1950 (dissertation); N. J. Hommes, 'Taceat mulier in ecclesia', *Arcana Revelata (Festschrift Grosheide)*, 1951, 33-43; A. Adam, *Christus und die Frau*, Ettal 1951; Haag 494; G. Reidick, *Die hierarchische Struktur der Ehe*, Munich 1953; J. Leipold, *Die Frau in der antiken Welt und im Urchristentum*, Berlin 1962; C. Seltmann, *La Femme dans l'antiquité*, Paris 1956; L. Hick, *Die Stellung des heiligen Paulus zur Frau im Ramen unserer Zeit*, Cologne 1957; F. Horst, *RGG* II³, 1067f; H. Greeven, *RGG* II³, 1069f; H. Renckens, *Urgeschichte und Heilsgeschichte*, Mainz 1959; A. Rosenberg, *Die Erhebung des Weiblichen. Ordnung und Austand der Frau in unserer Zeit*, Olten 1959; J. Michl, *LTK* IV², 294ff; E. Kähler, *Die Frau in den paulinischen Briefen*, Zurich 1960; H. Rusch, *Töchter des Glaubens*, Mainz 1960; de Vaux 39f; E. Gössmann, *Die Frau und ihr Auftrag*, Freiburg 1961; E. Gössmann, *Mann und Frau in Familie und Oeffent-lichkeit*, Munich 1964; F. Rienecker, *Lexikon zur Bibel*, 1503ff; P. Morant, *Die Anfänge der Menschheit*, Lucerne 1962²; Georg Richter, *Deutsches Wörterbuch zum NT*, Regensburg 1962, 254-65; G. Heinzelmann, *Frau und Konzil*, Zürich 1962; G. Fitzer, *Das Weib schweige in der Gemeinde*, 1963; G. G. Blum, 'Das Amt der Frau im NT', *NT* 7 (1964), 142-62; M. Rosseels, *Der Frau aber geziemt es zu schweigen*, Vienna 1964; *Die Frau im Aufbruch der Kirche*, Munich 1964.

Elisabeth Koffmahn

Word

A. *Old Testament*. To the Hebrew mind the word is more than the expression of an idea spoken aloud. Hebrew man sees in it something dynamic that presses on towards a further realisation. This applies to human words of blessing and cursing. Once these have been uttered they can no longer be revoked, and their effectiveness extends into the far future (Gen 20:7; Josh 6:26; 1 Kings 16:34). But it is Yahweh's word above all that is powerful in its effects: 'For as the rain and the snow come down from heaven and return not thither but water the earth, making it bring forth and sprout, giving seed to the sower and bread to the eater, so shall my word be that goes forth from my mouth. It shall not return to me empty, but it shall accomplish that which I purpose and prosper in the thing for which I sent it' (Is 55:10f).

The Old Testament knows of Yahweh's word in three forms: 1. as a prophetic utterance; 2. as a legal utterance; and 3. as a creative utterance.

1. Yahweh *puts his words in the mouth of the prophet* (Jer 1:9), and he is

commissioned to proclaim Yahweh's word to the people (Is 6:8). The prophet cannot resist Yahweh's call. Even if he is unwilling to speak in his name the word of God burns in him like burning fire shut up in his bones, so that he cannot endure it (Jer 20:9). The word of God proclaimed by the prophets is the decisive force in the history of Israel (1 Sam 9:27; 15:13–23; 2 Sam 7:4; etc). It is carried out irresistibly (1 Kings 2:27; 2 Kings 1:17; 9:36; 22:16). In contrast to the falsehoods of the lying prophets, it is full of power like a hammer which shatters rocks (Jer 23:29). In itself Yahweh's word signifies *salvation* (Is 2:2–5; Jer 30:1), but when it is despised it takes effect in the form of *punitive judgement* (Jer 26:4–6).

2. The prophetic word is conditioned by the situation in which it is uttered. It is addressed, that is to say, to specific hearers at a specific point in time. The word of the law, on the other hand, applies to the whole people and for all ages. Israel receives her law ('the words' Ex 34:28; see also Ps 147:19) from Yahweh (Ex 20:1, 22). Yahweh expects Israel scrupulously to observe every word with which he has charged her (Deut 12:32). His directing word is not unattainable to Israel. It is present revelation which, handed on by word of mouth, can be taken into the heart and so acted upon (Deut 30:11–14). If Israel follows the word of Yahweh she will remain alive and increase, and Yahweh will bless her in the land of promise (Deut 30:15f). But if Israel does not hearken she will perish (Deut 30:18).

3. 'Word', therefore, stands for the revealed will of Yahweh, who inter-venes again and again in the destiny of his people, but also lays upon them a firm and immutable order. But it is only a short step from this to ascribe to the word of Yahweh the creation considered as a still broader sphere of divine revelation. By his word Yahweh forms the world (Gen 1; Is 48:13; Ps 33:9; Wis 9:1). His word maintains the course of natural events (Ps 147:15–18). The powers of nature hearken to the word of the Lord (Ps 148:8). They do not disobey it (Sir 39:31).

The Old Testament ascribes to the divine word all the works which God has performed, the fashioning and directing of the world, the promise and the demand which he makes to his own people. But in the speculations of later Jewish theologians (insofar as these are available to us in the canonical scriptures) this divine activity is summed up not under the concept of word but under the image of ↗ wisdom. Only in a few passages is a greater degree of subsistence (Is 9:8; 55:11; Ps 107:20) and an activity of its own (Is 55:11; Ps 148:8; Wis 16:12, 26; 18:14–16) ascribed to the divine word. God's word always attains its goal (Is 55:11). It commands the powers of nature (Ps 148:8). It heals all things (Wis 16:12). It preserves the life of the faithful (Wis 16:26). Like a fierce warrior God's almighty word brings death to the enemies of his people (Wis 18:14–16).

B. *New Testament.* In the New Testament 'word' is found chiefly with the following meanings: 1. the word of God in the Old Testament; 2. the particular sayings and the preaching of Jesus as a whole; 3. the early christian preaching about Jesus; and finally,

4. Jesus himself is called the Word.

1. Paul draws a contrast between the word of man, the content of which is merely the foolishness of human wisdom (1 Cor 1:17–21), and the word of God, which is ever powerful to take effect (1 Thess 2:13). It is full of life and power, and sharper than a two-edged sword (Heb 4:12) because it is precisely God's word, and as such penetrates the inmost heart of man so as to compel him to take a decision at that level. Primitive christianity found this significance in the word of God ready to hand in the Old Testament. The word directed to the prophets (Acts 3:25; 7:3, 6, 31f; see also Lk 2:29; 3:2) and the word preached by the prophets (Mk 7:13; Mt 1:22; 2:15; 15:6) is the word of God. The Old Testament word retains its binding character for Christians (Rom 12:19f; 13:8–10; see also Jn 10:35). But the Old Testament word and the New Testament word are not on the same plane. The word of God in the Old Testament is a mysterious pointer to the word of God of the new covenant. The word of God in the New Testament is the fulfilment of the word of God in the old covenant (see Col. 1:25).

2. *Individual sayings of Jesus* are called 'the word (of the Lord)' (Mt 26:75; Lk 22:61; Jn 7:36 [Lit. 'What is this word?']), and are cited as such in the New Testament (Acts 11:16; 20:35; 1 Thess 4:15; see also 1 Cor 7:10, 12, 25). Only in a few instances (Mk 2:2; 4:33; Lk 5:1; Acts 10:36) is Jesus' preaching taken as a whole called 'the word'. It is striking how seldom the word of the Lord is explicitly referred to outside the gospels. Often, however, the word of

Christ is used in a freer form without being explicitly characterised as a word of the Lord (see 1 Cor 13:2—Mt 17:20). It is true in general that those responsible for transmitting the sayings of Jesus do not cling over-anxiously to their exact historical wording (see the beatitudes: Mt 5:3–12; Lk 6:21–6) and the discourse at the last supper (Mt 26:26–9; Mk 14:22–5; Lk 22:15–20; 1 Cor 11:23–5). The first christians had not as yet acquired a book in which the exact wording of these sayings was precisely established. The word of the Lord was made known to them in the preaching of the apostles, who were commissioned by Christ and supported by his authority in order that they might bear witness to him (Mt 28:18–20). The fact that this word of the Lord possessed an unique authority for the first christians is apparent from the very manner in which Paul relies upon the commandments of Christ in deciding his own personal dispositions (1 Cor 7:10, 12, 25).

The synoptics record for us how the words of Jesus were received by those who heard them. The hearers sense the *claim* underlying these words. Some of them take scandal. They say that Jesus is possessed because of his words (Jn 10:20). Others, however, are astonished (Mk 1:27). They are profoundly impressed by the authority which is manifest in his words (Mt 7:28f; Lk 4:32). Jesus does not speak like the scribes, who invoke the support of scripture and tradition (Mt 7:29), but with the authority of the Son (Mt 11:27; Lk 10:22). The Son does not speak of himself; his word comes from the Father who has sent him (Jn 14:10, 24; 17:8). Since the Father is at work in the utterances of Jesus (Jn 14:10), his word is powerful to take effect. It heals the sick (Mt 8:8; Lk 7:7, 15), controls nature (Mk 4:39; Lk 5:5) and drives out devils (Mk 1:25f).

But for all this *the hearer is free to accept or to reject the word of Jesus.* He either receives it and keeps it or fails to keep it (Jn 8:51; 12:47f; 14:24; 15:20). To reject the word of Jesus implies the judgement of God (Jn 12:47f). But he who receives the word of Jesus with faith is 'clean' (Jn 15:3), 'he has eternal life; he does not come into judgement but has passed from death to life' (Jn 5:24). Assuredly only he to whom the Father has given it can receive the words of Jesus rightly (Mt 19:11; Mk 4:11; Lk 9:45; Jn 6:44, 65).

3. Together with prayer the apostles regard the 'ministry of the word' as their essential task (Acts 6:4). The word which the apostles proclaim (Acts 13:5; 15:36) is not the word of Old Testament revelation (see Acts 17:11), nor is it simply a repetition of the teaching of Jesus. Rather it is preaching about Jesus, about his words and deeds (Lk 1:2; Acts 1:1). It is the joyful message (Acts 15:7) of the salvation bestowed in Jesus Christ (Acts 13:26; Rom 5; Eph 1:13). The apostolic preaching is the word of God (Acts 4:31; 6:2, 7) because God himself has spoken the word (1 Thess 2:13). The apostle is anxious to guard against altering it or falsifying it (2 Cor 2:17; 4:2). He is a *minister of the word* (see Lk 1:2). He has to spread the word spoken by God, throughout the earth (Rom 15:9).

Since the apostolic preaching is derived from God, it is guaranteed by him who originates it to be effective. It is by his power that the word increases (Acts 19:20). It is itself the power of God (1 Cor 1:18). Hence it is active (Heb 4:12; 1 Thess 2:13) and sharper than a two-edged sword (Heb 4:12; see also Eph 6:17). Where it is received with faith it brings about redemption (Jas 1:21).

4. In his Son God has uttered his word finally and for all time. The revelation of the Old Testament was ordered to this word and finds its fulfilment in it (Col 1:25-7). The life of Jesus, his words and deeds, constitute a central revelation of God. The revelation in the Son, who says of himself: 'Before Abraham was I am' (Jn 8:58), does not, however, begin only at Jesus' birth. Led by the Spirit (Jn 14:26; 16:13) the first Christians scrutinise the Old Testament scriptures (Acts 8:35; 17:2f, 11), which bear witness to Jesus (Jn 5:39f). They realise that all revelation has been made through the Son. Where the Old Testament scriptures speak of the divine word or the divine wisdom as a medium of revelation, there is Christ already at work in his pre-existent state. Through the Son, the reflection of the glory of God (Heb 1:3; 2 Cor 4:4; Col 1:15—Wis 7:26), the world was formed (Heb 1:2—Wis 9:1). In him all things have their being (Col 1:17—Wis 8:1). In the form of wisdom (Wis 10:15–11:1) and word (Wis 16:12, 26; 18:22) the pre-existent Christ has accompanied Israel through the wilderness and bestowed spiritual food and spiritual drink upon her (1 Cor 10:1-4). In his vocation vision (Is 6:1-13) Isaiah saw the glory of

Christ (Jn 12:41). The revelation in the Son, therefore, is not *one revelation among many*, but *all revelation* has been made through the Son: the Old Testament revelation through the pre-existent Christ, the final revelation of the New Testament through Jesus, the Son of God become man. The pre-existing and the incarnate Christ is *the* revelation in the absolute, or, according to Jn 1:1, *the* word (see 1 Jn 1:1; Rev 19:13). As Jesus allows himself to be known as the bread of life in the distribution of bread (Jn 6), as the resurrection and the life in the raising of Lazarus (Jn 11), and as the light of the world (Jn 8:12; see also 9:39) in the healing of the blind (Jn 9), so too in his word (Jn 14:10, 24) he manifests the fact that he is *the* Word (the *Logos*) (Jn 1:1, 14).

Bibliography: P. Heinisch, *Das 'Wort' im AT und im Alten Orient* (*BZF* x 7–8), 1922; O. Grether, *Name und Wort Gottes im Alten Testament* (*BZAW* 64), 1934; Cullmann 255–75; Heinisch 122–7; Eichrodt II, 32–8; Procksch 468–75; Imschoot I, 188–95; von Rad II, 80–98; Jacob 103–9; Vriezen 74–93 and 214–17; Stauffer 38–42; O. Procksch and G. Kittel, *TDNT* IV, 89–140; Haag 1036–9 and 1718–23. See also: Bultmann (see Index); L. Dürr, *Die Wertung des göttlichen Wortes im AT und im Antiken Orient*, Leipzig 1938; C. Westermann, *Grundformen prophetischer Rede*, Munich 1960; G. Ebeling, *Wort und Glaube*, Tübingen 1962²; H. Schlier, *Wort Gottes*, Würzburg 1962².

Georg Ziener

Work

The conceptual range attached to the word *work* embraces so much material that it is difficult to fix upon any one clear definition. It includes the work of God in the creation as well as the wearisome toil of the slave. Again in the New Testament we encounter a third usage of the word, namely, as applied to the work of Christ and to work for the gospel. Every aspect of this threefold usage will be briefly reviewed in the pages which follow.

The work of God is creative work. No man can act like God, and furthermore none of the gods can act as God acts (Ps 85:8). All that exists is the work of God's hands (Ps 8; 18; 9:1). But these anthropomorphic ideas are to be found only in the more primitive descriptions. Already in the Priestly narrative of Gen 1:1, 2, 3 the sublime idea is inculcated that God has called all things into existence by his word and his will alone. Through the idea of the creative word of God—'He spoke and it took place'—the thought of the bible has given expression in the most effective possible way to its consciousness of the absolute power and transcendence of God in relation to his creation. In all this, however, work is by no means regarded as degrading. The bible does not hesitate constantly to apply anthropomorphic usages to God. Apart from the childlike simplicity of the Yahwist, a simplicity which lives on still in the words of Our Lord concerning God who feeds the sparrows and clothes the lilies of the field, we have only to think of the images of Deutero–Isaiah, such as that of the potter and the clay (Is 45:9). Thus in one way or another the biblical authors have found a way of expressing no less a truth than the absolute power of God as Creator.

The bible never describes the work of man as creative. Indeed it actually shows itself in a certain sense hostile to human creative work, as for instance in the decoration of the sanctuary, for in this the danger of idolatry may lie if images are set up. The second commandment of God is designed to avert this danger. Thus work was never regarded as a participation in the creative work of God. What the biblical authors had in mind was their own daily work in all its toilsomeness: God sets his blessing upon it. Day by day the amount of work done remains constant (Ps 104:19ff). The wisdom books praise industry and diligence (Prov 6:6). Even kings do not consider it beneath their dignity to work (1 Sam 11:5). Work is an element in the divinely ordained structure of the world and of human nature. So much is work an integral part of the divinely willed order of life that the decalogue contains no vestige of any commandment such as: 'Thou shalt not be idle'. On the contrary, a special prescription has to be included in it to make man rest from his work.

Already before the fall work is an integral element in human life (Gen 1:28; 2:15). And yet 'cursed is the ground because of you; in toil you shall eat of it all the days of your life . . .' (Gen 3:17ff). It is not until man rebels against God's wise law that the cosmic order is upset and the curse makes itself felt, particularly in the sphere of work.

The work of Christ. Christ himself is a worker (*tektōn*). This is normally translated as 'carpenter' (Mk 6:3), although the term may have been intended in a more general sense as signifying craftsman, skilled worker in general. The evangelists have no further interest in the fact that Jesus was a worker. John does not mention it at all. Paul does perhaps refer to it when he says that Christ assumed the form of a servant (Phil 2:7). Servant (*doulos* in Greek) was at that time used to designate slaves, the 'workers' of antiquity. But, as has been said, the evangelists take no further notice of this truth, which is assuredly of far-reaching significance for theology. For them the work of Jesus is not his work as a craftsman but his work as Redeemer of the world. John brings out this significance most clearly in his use of the word *work*. 'My food is to do the will of him that sent me, and to accomplish his work' (4:34; 5:17; 6:28f; 9:4). The works of Christ are the ↗ miracles, the signs which manifest to the believers his unique work of ↗ revelation and ↗ redemption. The service which Jesus performs, culminating on the ↗ Cross, is the accomplishment of the work entrusted to him by God (17:4). Hence the fourth gospel actually records the last words of the dying Messiah as the pregnant exclamation: 'It is consummated' (19:30; see also 5:28). The work of Christ, the deed of redemption once and for all consummated on behalf of mankind, has been accomplished.

It follows that *the work of the Christian* consists equally in ↗ faith and in acting in conformity with faith. 'This is the work of God, that you believe in him whom he has sent' (Jn 6:29; Phil 2:13; 2 Thess 1:11). God works in us. Our work is wholly and entirely his work. Thus we are actually 'fellow workmen for God' (1 Cor 3:9; 2 Cor 6:1; Mk 16:20). Properly speaking the work of Christians consists in promoting the gospel and helping to further the salvation willed by God. The Christian is one who works for the harvest, sows the word, plants (1 Cor 3:6ff; Jn 4:35ff), one who works as the ambassador of divine atonement (2 Cor 5:20ff). As a member of the body of Christ everyone has his own special task assigned to him (1 Cor 12). This is the work for which the christian is called; it is for this that he has been empowered with the Holy Spirit. This is his particular 'vocation'. The christian must remain faithful to his calling (1 Cor 7:20ff), for the worldly position in which he finds himself is not decisive. It is not the goal at which he aims, but only the means of attaining that goal. It makes no difference even if he is a slave. It is possible that even the bishops of the early church were slaves (Eucharistos) whose freedom was purchased with money raised by the communities. But by and large the axiom holds good: 'Remain in that state in which you were when you came to the faith'. When God calls a man into his service to do his 'work' it can entail a change in his worldly occupation (Mk 1:18: 'They left their nets and followed him'), but this by no means necessarily follows. All this is not to say that the worldly calling could be a matter of indifference to the christian, but it does mean that it is in some sense secondary (as Paul deliberately carried on the work of tent-making, Acts 18:3).

The *New Testament* attitude on the subject of work is expressed in the 'rules of life' (*Haustafeln*) inserted in the epistles (Col 3:22–4:1; Eph 4:5–9; 1 Tim 6:1ff; Tit 2:9ff; 1 Pet 2:18–25). What it is principally concerned with is the duties of workers, of 'slaves', and the space devoted to them is a clear indication of the social stratum from which the first christians derived (see 1 Cor 1:26: 'For consider your call, brethren; not many of you were wise according to worldly standards, not many were powerful, not many were of noble birth; but God chose what is foolish in the world . . . what is weak in the world . . .').

The authors of the epistles do not altogether omit to mention the responsibilities of slave owners: they must give their workers what is right because they know that they themselves have a Master in heaven (Col 4:1) who is also the Master of their servants, and who is not impressed by personal status (Eph 6:9). No criticism of the social system or of the institution of slavery is to be found in the New Testament. No-one who truly apprehends the nature of the gospel preached by the apostles will be surprised at this. Inevitably it required a long period of time before the Church realised the implications of its own preaching; that when it preached a message which had to do with the setting free of the world—a world, moreover, which was liable to judgement and was already passing away— this entailed certain general consequences with regard to the setting free of those in the world who were fettered by society. Nevertheless, consequences of this sort did take effect in the practical life of the church right from the outset. In the community of the church there was no distinction between poor and rich, slaves and freemen (Jas 2:1–13; Gal 3:28). Furthermore it should be noticed that the kind of slavery involved was not that of galley-slaves or forced labour in the mines, and that it was neither necessarily nor customarily harsh in character. Slaves could attain to high positions in their master's household, and were often held in affection and respect as members of the family (1 Pet 2:18). The 'rules of life' have as the basis of their exhortations the truth that the christian worker does his work, not in the first instance for those who are his masters 'in the flesh', but for Christ himself: 'Slaves, be obedient to those who are your earthly masters, with fear and trembling, in singleness of heart, as to Christ; not in the way of eye-service, as men-pleasers, but as servants of Christ, doing the will of God from the heart, rendering service with a good will as to the Lord and not to men' (Eph 6:5–7). The ultimate motive behind the christian ethic of work is not any natural law, not even a divine dispensation contained in the Old Testament. Rather it is that ⟋obedience which the christian owes to his heavenly Master. The earthly master is the 'type' of Christ. He represents 'our Lord' himself. Such work keeps the name of God from being defamed (1 Tim 6:1).

On this interpretation the fulfilment of God's commandment to work becomes possible for man when he has been redeemed no longer from motives of obedience to the law or from a sense of duty but, like all acts inspired by christian morality, from the motive of thankfulness (⟋thanksgiving) to the heavenly Lord: 'Whatever your task work heartily as serving the Lord and not men' (Col 3:23). The redemption took place 'that he might purify for himself a people of his own who are zealous for good deeds' (Tit 2:11–

14). The first vision of Christ is for those who see in it with the eyes of faith the sign of the coming eschatological Redemption which will be completed at his second coming, and which even now bears its fruit in the christian life and in the daily work of christians (Richardson, 32). A passage of Paul deserves special mention at this point because it affords us a deep insight into the connections between atonement and salvation: 'Yet woman will be saved through bearing children (if, of course, she continues in faith and love and holiness with modesty)' (1 Tim 2:15). From Gen 3:16 onwards the bearing and rearing of children, and a kind of motherhood that is painful, is imposed by God upon woman in expiation for the fault of the first mother. Paul now says that woman can actually achieve her salvation by fulfilling her duties of motherhood, because thereby she is submitting herself to the dispensation of God, always presupposing, of course, that she possesses the basic virtues and attitudes appropriate to the christian life. What applies to a woman surely applies to man also whose situation is in this respect wholly parallel. As the pains of motherhood are imposed on woman as an expiation, so too the hardships, toil and disappointments which man endures in the work of his calling are laid upon him. Now if woman achieves salvation by fulfilling this work of expiation laid upon her, why should the same not apply to man? He too, as he performs his allotted work, and still more if he accepts all the hardships and privations which it entails, will be performing the work of his own salvation.

Christ himself, the fulfiller of the

whole law of God, has also fulfilled the commandment to work. 1 Peter and Titus regard the service of the christian worker as an imitation of Christ. Even though Christ's work was primarily the work of redemption, still as man he has fulfilled the whole law of God, and perhaps the fulfilment of the command to work is integrally bound up with the act of redemption, as it seems legitimate to conclude from a consideration of the passage in 1 Tim 2:15 cited above. Until about his thirtieth year Jesus was a village craftsman. We have perfectly sound evidence for this fact, even though the hagiographers did not choose to dwell upon it. None of the facts concerning the Lord recorded in the gospels can be devoid of significance for the belief and moral conduct of christians. Christian piety has always loved to dwell upon the image of Jesus in the carpenter's workshop. The Master who spoke of his yoke as 'light' was the good workman who knew the difference between a well-made and a badly-made yoke which the poor ox would have to bear at the plough. It is certainly no less justifiable for the church to hold up the example of Christ in the workshop for the edification of christian workers than for Peter or Paul to make use of the example of his patience in suffering as the model for christian love, always provided that we do not treat sentimentally of what our redemption has cost, or entertain any such idea as that Christ redeems us from sin and redeems us in our working life merely by his example (Richardson, 20).

The New Testament teaching on work may already seem unpopular in the eyes of progressives by the very fact that it makes obedience one of the principal virtues of society. The 'rules of life' show that the master–servant relationship is one of the most fundamental relationships which has been established by God and has been sanctioned by God's natural law, in the same way as the relationship between ruler and ruled, husband and wife, parents and child. The structure of the human community is necessarily hierarchical and not egalitarian. The health of society consists in the fact that the individual takes his due responsibility for the duties entailed by his position within the organism as a whole. Even in the immense ramifications of modern industry there will always be a basic *kurios–doulos* (master–servant) relationship, to which these rules of life in the New Testament point. But what this relationship implies will have to be worked out by those whose lives are governed by it.

The bible knows nothing of a 'problem of leisure time'. Man works so long as it is day (Ps 104:22ff; Jn 9:4). A six or eight-hour day never entered into consideration. On the contrary it was counted as folly (sin) to be idle between daybreak and sunset! The free days in antiquity were the holy days: religious festivals brought freedom from the burden of daily work and relaxation. Moreover the sabbath law had its humanitarian aspect (Ex 20:10): to provide rest for man and beast. Its principle purpose, however, was religious in character, the sanctification of the sabbath, for in six days the Lord made heaven and earth and the sea and all that are therein, but on the seventh day he rested. Theological insights are to be found here which go far deeper than our discussion of free time. The meaning and purpose of human life as a whole are entered into here. The author of Hebrews (3:7–4:11) has developed these thoughts in a surprising manner. In the rhythmic alternation of work and rest is to be found a reflection of the image of God in which we were created. The work of man, like that of his Creator, culminates in rest, and his principle goal is not work but that eternal⁷ rest, that eternal joy which is to be found in God. The lukan pericope concerning Mary and Martha (10:42) is also explicit in making clear this order of priorities: Mary has chosen 'the better part', for the highest act which man is capable of on earth is the worship of God. In the last analysis the question is not whether our work results in great achievements and accomplishments on the human level; we must not put our trust in the work of our hands. Ultimately all our work will vanish from heaven and earth. The significance of our work is to be found not here but in the world to come, and the question is whether the Lord will be able to say: 'Well done, good and faithful servant; enter into the joy of your Master' (Mt 25:21; see also 25:34). Thus it is not its worldly value or the profit that accrues to us from our life of toil which gives our work its christian meaning, but its ultimate eschatological bearing on the heavenly goal. 'Therefore, my beloved brethren, be steadfast, immovable, always abounding in the work of the Lord, knowing that in the Lord your labour is not in vain!' (1 Cor 15:58). What is here being spoken of is not in some sense the dissemination of the gospel tidings, but all the work and toil of the christian (see Rev 14:13).

Work as sacrifice. As members of Christ we offer up ourselves, 'our bodies and souls' (see Rom 12:1ff). The eucharist, the church's sacrifice, is the offering of the body of Christ (see Augustine, *The City of God*, x, vi). Bread and wine are symbols of ourselves, our souls and our bodies, but also of our daily work, without which there would be neither bread nor wine. Moreover, the 'elements' with the help of which the miracle of our nourishment is accomplished are 'brought' or 'presented' to the Master himself. Without this 'bringing to' or 'offering' there would have been no sacrifice. It is striking that in John, who speaks with such emphasis of the bread 'which comes from heaven', we should find a unique presentation of the miracle of the loaves. Suddenly the disciples (in contrast to the synoptic accounts) recede into the background. It is Jesus who plays the central role. It is not the disciples who draw his attention to the people's hunger. Instead he acts on his own initiative. It is not, as in the synoptics, the apostles who bring the loaves to the Master, but a boy (*paidarion*). Thus in the version of the fourth gospel the loaves and fishes are the materials presented or offered by the people and not by the apostles. Could it be that even as early as the time of John it was the liturgical custom that the offertory was made, not by the bishop-presbyters (representing the apostles), but by the deacon in the name of the people, and that the evangelist is deliberately trying to underline the significance of the sacrifice of the community in the sacrament of the bread of heaven? But whatever the purpose of the author may have been, one point is clear, namely that the final impression left by his sixth chapter consists in the great emphasis he lays on the truth that there is no gift of the living Bread unless the sacramental elements have first been brought in faith by the liturgical community (Richardson, 51f).

The christian ethic of work, the meaning of work according to New Testament doctrine, applies only to christians. The christian understands the hardships of work as such in a world affected by the fall, and bears them joyfully for the Lord, to whom his service is really given. Every work which the christian performs has an eschatological bearing in that it belongs, so to say, to the dimension of time and space, in which, in the existing state of the divine dispensation, our testing and our redemption are worked out. It is in this dimension of time and space that the good works according to which each individual will be judged are performed in order that he may enter into God's rest. Rest from work comes to stand as an image to remind us of the final purpose and the final goal, which consist precisely in that rest with God. Still more the connection between our work and the liturgy shows that our work is taken up in the liturgy as that which the sacrament presupposes, just as our creaturehood in all its fallen state must be there in order to make its redemption possible (*quod 'mirabiliter condidisti, mirabilius reformasti'*).

Bibliography: A. Richardson, *The Biblical Doctrine of Work*, London 1952. We sometimes follow Richardson's work very closely, occasionally supplementing his presentation. This book meets with our agreement except for the negative judgement on Sirach (pp 14 and 39). See also: N. Peters, *Das Buch Jesus Sirach*, Münster 1913, 318; J. A. Kleist, 'Ergon', *CBQ* 6 (1944), 61–8; G. Bertram, *TDNT* II, 635–52; *BTHW* 35–7; Allmen 463f; A. Steinmann, *Jesus und die soziale Not der Gegenwart*, Paderborn 1929², 49–70 (p 49 for further bibliography); S. Kalischer, 'Die Wertschätzung der Arbeit in Bibel und Talmud', *Festschrift H. Cohens*, Berlin 1912, 579–608; E. Beijer, *Svensk Teologisk Kvartalskrift* 29 (1953), 25–41; H. Weinstock, *Arbeit und Bildung*, Heidelberg 1954; P. Termes Rós, *El trabajo según la Biblia*, Barcelona 1955; H. Rondet, *Die Theologie der Arbeit*, Würzburg 1956; W. Bienert, *Die Arbeit nach der Lehre der Bibel*, Stuttgart 1956²; P. Benoit, *LV* 20 (1955), 73–86; A. Vögtle, *LTK* I², 801–3; J. B. Bauer, *Der Seelsorger* 25 (1955), 344–51; J. B. Bauer, *BL* 24 (1957), 198–201; F. Gryglewicz, *Bbl* 37 (1956), 314–37; B. Prete, *Sacra Doctrina* 2 (1956), 280–309; P. de Haes, *Collectanea Mechlinensia* 43 (1958), 370–73 and 497–500; R. Falconer, *JBL* 60 (1941), 375–9 (on 1 Tim 2:14f); W. Bienert, 'Die Arbeit nach der Lehre der Bibel', *Studium Generale* (1961), 151–62; F. Storni, 'El trabajo en la Biblia', *Ciencia y Fe* 13 (1957), 321–32; E. Testa, *Il lavoro nella Bibbia*, Assisi 1959; F. Vattioni, 'Il lavoro nei primi tre capitoli della Genesi', *Studi Sociali* 1 (Rome 1961), 109–19.

Johannes B. Bauer

World

A. It is illuminating to notice how different the Greek conception of 'world' is from that of the Old Testament. In it God and world are not two entities at opposite poles from one another. Instead the *kosmos* is the 'all-embracing divine'. Both are included in a single order, which is opposed to chaos. Cosmogony is theogony. Thus there is no unbridgeable gulf between God and the world, any more than there is between God and man. The remote origins of cosmology are delineated by Homer, Hesiod, and the Orphics. From the chaos of the beginning emerged the domain of light, from which in turn the theogony develops. For Hesiod the divine element in the world still persists. It is God as the supreme power which has two distinct aspects, the cosmic and the ethical. Other authors point in the same direction. Anaximenes, for example, is responsible for the characterisation of the world as *kosmos*, that is, as 'world-as-order'. For Heraclitus the primordial power becomes *logos*, and so constitutes a unity of human and world intelligence and a world-order that informs all things—unity as a harmony of opposites. Faith in the divine *logos* has a spiritualising effect upon nature religion. The Pythagoreans discover that number is the principle of the cosmos of things, and according to the principle of correspondence this becomes the first law of man and society in ethics and politics. Anaxagoras understands the deity as the *nous* (= mind, intelligence) which governs the world throughout: since *pronoia* (= providence) is absent from it, the world remains a mechanism which can be understood in purely causal terms. On this theory the world is a *unio mystica* in virtue of the divine power which permeates it and controls it. This *unio mystica* is understood as *pneuma* (spirit), the outward manifestations of which are *aretai* (virtues) or *energeiai* (activities), which are understood ontologically, and which constitute the bond which holds all together: *sumpatheia* ('sympathy'). This in turn is the expression of the *hen zōon* ('the single living thing') in which the supreme god conceals himself. He acts

through the *deuteros theos* (lit = 'second god') or demiurge. The basic law of the cosmos is 'the eternal return of the same' (compare Nietzsche). But man does not see himself as blessed in the cosmos because he finds himself in the 'prison of the Heimarmene'—otherworldly longings. The problem, the tension which exists between the transcendent god on the one hand and, on the other, the eternal timeless world permeated and controlled by divine power yet distinct from the deity, also defeated Plato and his school.

But for all this the problem of the *kosmos* has been analysed from so many different points of view that the concept is capable of becoming a vehicle of revelatory language. Here admittedly the question is transposed from the purely philosophical and cosmological plane to that in which the question of supernatural redemption arises. The problem is spiritualised in neoplatonism. Philo expands the concept into *kosmos noētos* (= 'the world of reason') and *kosmos aisthētos* (= 'the world of perception'), Plotinus into that of *kosmos houtos* ('this world') and *kosmos ekeinos* ('that world'). He thereby mitigates the dualism and establishes a bridge between the two opposing principles by means of the concept of the world as *eikōn* (image, likeness). It is this that Augustine takes over and makes the basis of his cosmology. The Gnosis of the Corpus Hermeticum takes cosmos as 'the body of God' (W. Nestle, *Vom Mythos zum Logos. Die Selbstentfaltung des griechischen Denkens,* 1942[2]).

B. The basic characteristics of the Greek concept of *kosmos* are: unity, immanent norm, duty, the interrelationship of cosmos, society, and human nature. These provide a point of contact with the judaism of the Old Testament which separates heaven, earth, and 'the all' in its manner of speaking. In hellenistic thought the cosmos is understood in spatial terms. It is only in the Wisdom books and Maccabees that we find the concept of the universe as consisting of earth and mankind (compare the later anti-Gnostic mysticism of the Merkaba).

C. The use of the concept of *kosmos* in the New Testament is based upon the development described above. In it we must distinguish the following distinct senses:

1. *kosmos* regarded more from the cosmological and speculative point of view, that is from the philosophical aspect, or *kosmos* as interpreted cosmogonically. In this sense it is true to say that scripture has in the first instance nothing to do with it. The ideas which are worked out scientifically, a mixture of neoplatonist and gnostic speculations with an element of stoicism, provide a foil to New Testament interpretation. It is not the function of revelation to develop a cosmology in the true sense, except for recognising that the *kosmos* is a created entity. The New Testament image of the world considered from the aspect of natural science and philosophy remains indefinite. The conception of the world as presented here is simply taken over from philosophy. That is, the world is conceived of as a space divided into three parts: heaven, earth, and the underworld. We have no intention here of examining the influence on the early christian conception of the world exercised by early

cabbalistic or gnostic views entertained by Jewish christians. These combined typically Jewish ideas with mysticism. Here, however, we must confine ourselves to indicating the following expressions which seem to betray this influence: *stoikheia tou kosmou* (= 'the elemental principles of the world': Gal 4:3; Col 2:8, 20); *ek tou kosmou— en tō(i) kosmō(i)* (= 'out of the world— in the world': Jn 15:19; 17:11). (See Jonas, *Gnosis und spätantiker Geist*, 1934, 153 n 1). This world is *the sphere, the arena of human life*, and so from the point of view of intellectual interpretation neutral.

2. In particular cases it is impossible to establish precisely whether *kosmos* is intended to signify the arena in which human action takes place or the human race which enlivens it. In the following passages it is probably to be understood in the first of these senses: 'light of the world' (Jn 8:12); according to Jn 3:17, Christ has been sent into the world as the evangelist too has been sent; according to Jn 8:23, Christ is not of this world, and according to Jn 18:36 neither is his 'kingdom'. According to Jn 3:16 he has been sent by the Father and has come from motives of love for the world; he presides in judgement over the 'prince (*arkhōn*) of this world'. 2 Cor 5:19 provides a typical example in which *kosmos* is used in the sense of the arena in which the drama takes place. The opposition between God and the world becomes wholly apparent only in Christ, but at the same time so does God's atoning activity: *kosmos* = the world of humanity, mankind as a whole. But to the extent that the *kosmos* concept is taken in the sense of the

universe as the arena of salvific history it extends beyond the limits of merely human history. The entire universe is included in the development of this world history, which nevertheless does not cease to remain a truly human history. Christ is precisely 'the first-born of all creation' (Col 1:15). A further idea is that the state of having fallen into evil necessarily follows from man's involvement in the *kosmos*. This idea, which is mentioned by the apostle, has something of the ancient concept of *anaĝkē* (=necessity, inevitability) in it. We shall be returning to treat explicitly of it at a later stage. Imprisonment in the Heimarmene of the sublunar regions and of *anaĝkē* gives way to the redeemed state of the cosmos. But once it is redeemed it loses this sense and becomes instead the 'dominion of God', 'the aeon to come', the 'new heaven' and the 'new earth', so that these concepts of the New Testament must be regarded as the end of the development of the idea of *kosmos* in the history of ideas. Paul takes the concept quite broadly as signifying *the universe as such*, in which he also includes the world of angels, thereby making it analogous to the stoic explanation of cosmos as the system of gods and men taken as a whole, with the aim of contrasting this new cosmos with the world which is totally hostile to God. John takes a similar view when he regards world history as a dramatic struggle.

3. *Kosmos* can only be intended to signify *humanity* in these passages: 'The sin of the world' blotted out by the Lamb according to Jn 1:29; 'Saviour of the world' in Jn 4:42; 'the world knows him not' in Jn 1:10; and, in contrast with this, 'all the world has gone after him' in Jn 12:19. In these cases mankind is always understood *collectively*, and this is also the sense of Jn 14:27; 1 Jn 4:4; 1 Jn 5:19—believers are 'of God', and unbelievers 'in (the power of) the evil one'. By this John intends to give expression to the supreme point in his theology, namely, that salvation history is a duel, but nevertheless a duel the issue of which is in fact already decided: 'I have overcome the world' (Jn 16:33). But when 'the world' is taken in this sense, it is inevitable that it should cease to be regarded as *alien to God*. Apart from this opposition between that which belongs to God and that which is alien to him (compare the concepts of 'inclination' and 'alienation' in Plotinus 1 1:12), 'world' cannot be explained, a fact which applies particularly to the 'supernatural cosmology' in the johannine prologue. This idea is not far removed from what the Mandeans mean when they speak of 'the worlds', the equivalent of the *aiōnes* in hellenistic thought (yet another relationship would be that between 'world' and 'heaven'). (On the effect of this upon early christian times, see J. Ritter, 'Mundus intelligibilis', *Philos. Abhanlungen* VI, 1957, 19.) It is precisely these interpretations of *kosmos* that are carried over as definitions into mysticism on the one hand, and which, on the other hand, in the non-christian sphere are 'demonised', with the result that from the idea 'world=darkness' and 'the whole world lies in the power of the evil one' (1 Jn 5:19), it is only a short step to the rejection of 'the wisdom of this world'—to which, again, is related

the idea of 'the rulers of the world' who are hostile to 'the kingdom (rule) of God'. *Kosmos* as an expression of that which is alien to God cannot, however, have anything to do with the un-redeemed state in the New Testament sense, but is rather derived from a mixture of philosophical, Old Testament, and mystical ideas. The New Testament then takes it over and develops it further.

4. *Kosmos* as 'mankind' contains a special and pregnant shade of meaning in the New Testament when it signifies 'mankind as fallen' and is brought into connection with Christ and the redeeming activity of God. Since, therefore, according to 1 Tim 1:15 Christ has come to redeem sinners, it follows that those who are redeemed constitute his kingdom (Col 1:13), so that the *ekklēsia* (=christian church) does not belong to the world. The 'saints' live in the *kosmos* (1 Cor 5:10) but they honour the Creator (Acts 17:24) and are thankful for God's natural gifts (Acts 14:15). According to 1 Cor 7:31 the saints must 'deal with the world' while at the same time conducting themselves as though they did not 'deal with it' (1 Cor 7:30; 2 Cor 6:10). For *kosmos* connotes of its very nature unregeneracy, hostility to God, a hindrance to true christian living, and it is emphasised again and again that it is the duty of christians to keep themselves uncontaminated by it (Jas 1:27: 'to keep oneself unstained from the world'). See Rom 12:2; 1 Cor 7:31. In Jas 4:4 'friendship with the world is enmity with God'.

In the pauline and johannine theology of redemption the problem of the cosmos is thrust right into the foreground. In John, however, the idea seems to be taken in a still more unequivocal sense than in Paul. The latter understands the 'world' in a narrower sense, in that cosmos only becomes explicable from the fact that there is a 'Saviour of the world' (1 Jn 4:14). This is the sense implicit in *aiōn houtos* (='this age (world)') as contrasted with *aiōn ekeinos* (='that age', 'the other world') (see Eph 1:21). In 1 Cor 1:20 'the wisdom of the world' is equivalent to 'folly with God' (1 Cor 3:19). According to 1 Cor 1:26, other standards apply with God than those prevailing in the world: compare the contrast between 'worldly grief' and 'godly grief' in 2 Cor 7:10. Sin constitutes the basis for the opposition between God and the world: 'the whole world may be held accountable to God' (Rom 3:19) as sinful. This is also the reason why Jn 3:17 and 1 Cor 6:2 speak of 'condemning/judging the world'. The condemnation of the world in 1 Cor 11:32 is similarly motivated. Israel, inasmuch as she has rendered herself liable to judgement, is included in the 'whole world' (Rom 3:19), and thereby set in contrast to the just. Again, in 1 Cor 2:8 it is the world as having fallen under the curse that is meant when the accusation of having crucified the Lord is applied to 'the rulers of this age'.

It can be seen, then, that the idea of *kosmos* is divided up into several different shades of meaning. Nevertheless, while the concept cannot be taken as expressing definitively any one concrete sense, it can be taken to stand in the neoplatonist sense for the unifying concept that lies behind a whole system of ideas which are abstract in character.

This is particularly applicable when it is combined with terms such as 'kingdom' (*basileia*).

5. On the meaning of *kosmos* when Jesus Christ is taken to be its model, measure, and dominant idea, and when it is understood to be analogous on the supernatural plane to the *Logos* of antiquity, ⟋ creation, likeness, word.

Bibliography: W. Kranz, 'Kosmos', *Archiv für Begriffsgesch.* II 1 and 2, ed. E. Rothacker, 1955/7; A. Jenni, *ZAW* 23 (1952), 197–248; 24 (1953), 1–35; H. Sasse, *TDNT* III, 867–98; F. Mussner, *Christus das All und die Kirche*, Trier 1955; E. Walter, *Christus und der Kosmos*, Stuttgart 1948; R. Schnackenburg, *Die Johannesbriefe*, Freiburg 1953, 117–20; G. Kittel, *TDNT* III, 857–98; G. Liddell and R. Scott (ed.), *A Greek–English Lexicon* I, Oxford 1940, 985.

Albert Auer

Wrath

I. *Human anger.* 1. *Holy anger.* Anger is justified and holy when used to vindicate the rights of others and especially God's sovereignty and sanctity (David, 2 Sam 12:5; Nehemiah, Neh 5:6; Moses, Ex 16:20; 32:19, 22; Num 31:14; Lev 10:16; Elisha, 2 Kings 13:19; Jesus, Mk 3:5; see also Jn 11:33, 38; Paul Acts 17:16). 2. *Anger in the sapiential books of the Old Testament.* Anger will result in injustice (Prov 14:17; 29:22) and work disaster; it destroys health, it impedes God's mercy and provokes His divine judgement (Prov 27:4; Sir 28:3–5; 30:24). The wise man is patient, the quick-tempered a fool (Prov 14:29; 15:18; 16:32; 14:17, 29). The incompatibility of anger with ⟋ wisdom is one of the tenets of old Egyptian wisdom: the boisterous cannot be wise (see also

J. Fichner, *Die altorientalische Weisheit in ihrer israelitisch-jüdischen Ausprägung*, 1953, 20f). In particular, anger with God is condemned (Job 18:4; see also 40:6). God even punishes anger at the good fortune of the wicked, for they will be judged by God himself (Prov 24:17f; Ps 37:7–9). 3. *Anger in the New Testament.* The New Testament generally disapproves of anger, although it does not reject it completely. Anger is, above all, an attribute of the devil and his henchmen (Rev 12:17; see also 12:12; of Herod, Mt 2:16). Jesus warns against wilful and unjustified anger with our fellow men, 'for anger is equal to murder' (Mt 5:22), and leads to words and acts which cannot be right in God's eyes (Jas 1:19f). Anger in the opinion of Paul is a sin (Col 3:8; Eph 4:31): love is not angry (1 Cor 13:5). Those who are angry interfere with the rights of God (Rom 12:19): they give way to the devil as sin is impending over those who are angry (Eph 4:26f). Anger is followed by God's judgement (Col 3:8; Rev 11:18). The Christian should, therefore, never be angry or incense others (Eph 6:4). Those who stand close to God must control their passions (those who pray, 1 Tim 2:8; the bishop, Tit 1:7).

II. *The wrath of God.* 1. *In the Old Testament.* The numerous expressions of anger or wrath are much more frequently used for God than for man. They describe the emotion of anger as an inner fire, and its effect as the snorting, foaming, boiling, and bursting of pent-up energy (see Is 30:27f; 34:5–10). God's wrath is very realistically described as flame, fire and storm (Ps 2:11; Is 13:13; Jer 15:14;

30:23; Ps 83:15). This anthropomorphism—ascribing human passions to God—is less strong in later periods. The word 'anger' is then used without the name of God (Is 63:5), and God's anger (2 Sam 24:1) is replaced by 'Satan' (1 Chron 21:1).

Yahweh's wrath is sometimes described as incomprehensible, 'irrational': Gen 32:23-33 (Jacob's struggle); Ex 4:24 (attack on Moses); Ex 33:20; Judg 13:22; Is 6:5 (the fatal effect of seeing God); Ex 19:9-25; 20:18-21; Num 1:51; 1 Sam 6:19. Even in these passages, God's features are not described as 'demoniacal' (P. Volz, *Das Dämonische in Jahweh*, 1924, 7-17): the expression of his displeasure is not arbitrary, but only indicates his incomprehensibility and sanctity (Haag 1754f; Eichrenrodt 1, 170f). God's anger is a reaction against man's offensive actions, and is caused by sin and violation of the covenant. God's wrath falls on Israel as it rebels against the divine dispensation (Num 11:1; 17:6-15; 13:25-14:38; Deut 1:34f), shows contempt for God, falls away from him and turns to strange gods (Ex 32; Num 25; Deut 11:16f; 12:29-13:19; 29:15-17; see also 9:18; Judg 2:14; 3:8; 10:7; 1 Kings 14:15; 16:33 and many other instances). The historical pattern of the period of the judges and kings is apostasy, God's wrath, conversion. The central motive for God's anger in the prophetical sermon is the offended love of God: God's love is despised by his own people (Hos 5:10; 8:5; Is 9:11; Jer 4:4; Ezek 5:13; 7:3 and many other instances; see also Amos 2:9-11; 3:2; Hos 11:1-6; Is 1:2f; 5:1-7; 17:10; Jer 2:1-3; 31:1-3; Ezek 16:4-14).

God has the absolute dominion over all nations. He is angry when in their pride they refuse to acknowledge it (Gen 11), or on their own authority go beyond their commission to chastise his people, the Jews (Is 10:5-15; see also 14:4-6; Ezek 25:15-17; Zech 1:15). The Old Testament makes man the subject of God's wrath because he is sinful. In ancient history (Gen 2-11), the path of mankind goes from the fall of our first parents (Gen 2-3), through fratricide (4) and growing perversion of the generation of the flood (6-8), to the hybris of the Tower of Babel and its punishment. Being guilty (Ps 90:8; Job 14:1-4; see Heinisch 219), man will fade away under God's anger (Ps 90:7).

Man in the Old Testament can perceive God's wrath whenever his existence is being threatened. The law (Deut 7:4; 9:8, 19 and other instances) and the prophets (Is 30:27f; 34:2, 5; 63:1-4; Jer 50:13; Ezek 22:31; 43:8) announce his 'destructive anger'. In historiography and in the preaching of the prophets historical disasters are imputed to God's wrath: drought, famine, epidemics and plagues, pestilence and extradition to the enemy (Num 11:1, 10; 12:9; 17:10; 2 Sam 24); but especially exile is given in prophetical preaching as the result of God's wrath. Here we also find the proclamation of a judgement of wrath at the end of time ('Day of Wrath' Amos 5:18f; Is 2:9-21; Zeph 1:15-18). The effects of God's wrath on the fate of the individual—with whom only later periods are concerned—are illness, affliction caused by personal enemies, premature death and absence of God (Job; Ps 88:16f; 90:7f; 102:9-12 and other instances).

God's wrath is frequently kindled against the sinners (Ex 19:12; Num 11:33; 12:9; 17:6–11; 25:9–11; 2 Sam 6:7), but God often shows patience (Ex 34:6f; Num 14:18; Neh 1:8f; Is 48:9; Ps 103:8). God warns through these blows before he destroys (Amos 4:6–11; Is 9:11; Jer 4:4): in his forbearance he gives time for repentance (Jon 4:2). About the duration of divine wrath Jer 3:12 says, 'I will not be angry for ever'. Yahweh has hidden his face from his people in exile, convulsed with anger, but only for a little while, and he shows mercy with them in his everlasting kindness (Is 54:8–10). The apocalyptists came to understand that the end of God's wrath must come before the time of grace (Dan 8:19; Is 26:20). Yahweh's enemies are struck by his anger for ever (Nahum 1:2; Mal 1:4).

Divine legislation (Deut 6:14), the preaching of the prophets and public worship (Num 1:53) have prevented his destroying wrath. The prayers of those affected by his wrath (Judg 3:8f; Is 64:8; Jer 10:24; Ps 6:2; 38:1) and the intercessory prayers for them (of Moses: Ex 32:11f; Num 11:1f; 14:11–19; Deut 9:18; Ps 106:23; Num 12:13; of Amos: Amos 7:2–6; of Jeremiah: Jer 14:7; 18:20; of Job: Job 42:7f) cry out for the mercy of the angry God. God's wrath is a reaction against sin and violation of his sanctity; therefore he demands expiation as a condition for giving up his anger (Num 25:1–5; 6–11; Jos 7:1, 25). Peace-offerings are also mentioned (Num 16:46; 2 Sam 24). The prophets therefore demand serious conversion and repentance (Jer 4:4, 8; 36:7). God puts an end to 'the judgement of

wrath' of the exile after Israel has drunk 'the cup of "wrath"', paid her debt, and 'received from God's hand double for all her sins' (Is 51:17, 22; 40:2).

Although in the Old Testament God's wrath is frequently mentioned, anger is never (except in Nah 1:2 'the Lord is a revenger and has wrath') given as an essential attribute of God (like holiness in the expression 'the Holy One of Israel', Is 1:4 and other instances). Anger is kept in check by the ↗ righteousness of God (allegiance to the covenant) (Jer 10:24; Ps 6:1; 38:1). God's mercy prevails over his wrath (Is 54:8–10; Ps 30:6; Is 12).

2. *In the New Testament.* The proclamation of God's wrath is not only peculiar to the Old Testament; John the Baptist, Jesus, Paul, and John all mention it. Jesus never ascribes anger to God directly. Most passages give the impression that God's wrath represents something independent, existing outside of God but depending on him; the ↗ judgement, the reckoning. The thought of the effect is stronger than 'the psychic reaction'; theological thinking outweighs psychological appreciation. Nevertheless, God's anger is never dissociated from emotion (Rom 9:22; especially Heb 3:11; 4:3 quoting Ps 95:11).

Anger attributed to God is also part of the picture given of Jesus, most explicitly in Mark where theological reflection is most scarce. Luke tones down the passionate features in Christ (J. Schmid, 'Das Evangelium nach Lukas', *RNT* 3 (1955³), 19). Anger and wrath as such are hardly ever mentioned, but the expression of his anger is frequently related in the gospel.

Jesus is angry with the powers of wickedness and their activities. He inveighs against Satan, who tempts him (Mt 4:10); against Peter, who, failing to understand Christ's passion, 'did not think of the things that are of God, but only of the things that are of men' (Mt 16:23 and parallel passages); he scolds the devils (Mk 1:25; 9:25; Lk 4:41), and is angry at the sight of the lepers (Mk 1:41) as illness is an evil which was not in God's original plan but came into the world through the sin of man. He is indignant at the Pharisees and the devilish behaviour of man (Mt 23; Jn 8:44). Jesus' anger with the Pharisees is mixed with compassion; he is angry at the resistance against the message of God's mercy and is filled with sorrow since this proclamation of love was also meant for them (Mk 3:5; see also 15:28). Jesus' anger springs from despised love (see Lk 15:28; Mt 18:34). He is angry where the honour of his father is offended (when casting the traders out of the temple Mt 21:12 and parallel passages; Jn 2:14–17). For the impenitent he has only words of threatening anger (Mt 11:20–24 and parallel passages; Mk 11:14; see also Lk 13:7). Here already is manifest the anger of the judgement which Jesus will display at the end of time (Mt 25:41).

God's wrath in the preaching of John the Baptist is eschatological in character ('the wrath to come', Mt 3:7). The divine judgement which the Baptist threatens is the unquenchable hell-fire (Mt 3:12). Only 'the worthy fruit of penance' can save (Mt 3:8). This proclamation of God's wrath is the echo of the preaching of the prophets and is taken over by Jesus, even though this has not explicit-ly been reported and the words of Jesus handed down to us do not contain the actual expression 'God's wrath' in this particular sense or context. In the parable of the royal marriage feast and that of the merciless servant, the angry king (or lord) passes judgement (Mt 22:7; 18:34). The punishment is 'destruction' (Lk 19:27; 12:46 and parallel passages; see also Mt 22:7) and merciless imprisonment until the debts have been paid (Mt 18:34), being cast into the hell-fire (Mt 13:42; 25:41).

Pauline theology connects the idea of God's wrath (or in short: wrath) with its fundamental themes. In the eschatological present time, God reveals his justice (Rom 1:17) as well as his wrath (Rom 1:18) which is only known by faith (Rom 1:17). God's wrath is already present. Paul regards the immorality of the heathens, their idolatry, fornication, and heartlessness as the effects of his wrath ('God has given them up', Rom 1:24, 26, 28). Their sinfulness is not regarded as the cause but as the result of the judgement (anger), as such it only becomes manifest in the death and resurrection of Christ (see Rom 3:25f; O. Kuss, *Der Römerbrief*, I, Regensburg 1957, 32–5). In order to punish those who resist his ordinance, God avails himself of the worldly powers which are thought of as the instruments of God's wrath active in the present (Rom 13:4f). According to the 'anti-semitic' passage 1 Thess 2:16, God's wrath falls upon the Jews for their resistance against salvation, for killing the prophets and the Messiah, and for persecuting the apostles (Acts 17:5–9:13); and from this moment 'until the end' God's wrath will manifest itself most severely to the people of Israel (not 'for ever'; see also Rom 11:25–32). God has given them up to their⟋ hardness of heart, through which they not only persist in their unbelief, but even try to prevent the salvation of the gentiles.

God's wrath, already active in this sinful human generation, will only be fully effective in the future; also Paul regards God's wrath as essentially eschatological. God's sanctity and dominion will finally be established with the punishment of all those who oppose him (Rom 2:5; 3:5; 5:9; 9:22; 1 Thess 1:10; 5:9; Col 3:6; Eph 5:6; it is not clear whether reference is made to the present or the future, Rom 4:5; 12:19). For Paul, too, the day of judgement is the 'Day of Wrath' (Rom 2:5). The final judgement will bring 'anger and wrath', 'tribulation and anguish' Rom 2:8); wrath is 'punishment'.

All men are subjected to God's wrath since they are all sinners (Rom 1:18–3:20); they are all 'by nature' ('as far as we ourselves or our own contribution is concerned'; H. Schlier, *Der Brief an die Epheser*, Düsseldorf 1957, 107) 'children of wrath', subject to the divine judgement (Eph 2:3); what in point of fact is mentioned here is the effect of original sin (see H. Schlier, *loc. cit.*; J. Mehlmann, *Natura filii irae*, Rome 1959). Man is a 'vessel of wrath', since God has destined him to fall a victim to his wrath (not without man's own fault). The reasons for this divine wrath are the sin of man, his contempt for the revelation of God himself in the creation of the world (Rom 1:18, 21f), his contempt for God's works in the revelation of his law (Rom 2:17–24; 3:19f), contempt for his holy love

(Rom 2:4; 1 Thess 2:14f), and returning uncharitableness for God's love (Rom 2:5). Obduracy and impenitence 'treasure up wrath against the Day of Judgement' (Rom 2:5). Contention with God and inobedience to the revealed truth bring wrath and indignation (Rom 2:8).

God's wrath is thought to be connected with his mercy and patience (Rom 9:22f). God has shown great patience with the 'vessels of wrath', the guilty men 'fitted for destruction' (damnation) (see Rom 2:4; 3:25f) in order to manifest his wrath (see the demonstration of the power of God's wrath Rom 1:18–3:20) and to reveal his power to defeat sin. God wants to proclaim the abundance of his glory to 'the vessel of his mercy', man, to whom he wants to show his mercy and whom he had predestined to glory. Paul sees in God's tolerance of evil a means to secure good objects; it justifies God's attitude towards the impenitence and obduracy of Israel. God's benignity will lead to penance (Rom 2:4). Man should never impatiently try to anticipate God's wrath, which is waiting in patience (Rom 12:19).

Man seeks salvation from God's wrath, which he won't find through the Law, for the Law is not only powerless but even 'works wrath' (Rom 4:15; see also 3:20; 5:20; 7:7–13; Gal 3:19). The law, according to Pauline theology, is a cause of transgression and therefore of damnation (God's wrath); promise and faith are the only ways of escaping God's wrath. Salvation from this wrath is brought by Jesus Christ. God has not predestined the christian for wrath but for salvation through Jesus Christ our Lord. Jesus has snatched us from the wrath to come (1 Thess 1:10). Through the continued pneumatic activity of Christ's death (or through his intervention in the eschatological judgement) all christians who have been justified and reconciled will be able to stand this eschatological judgement for which also they have to appear (Rom 5:9).

The drama of the eschatological events revealed in the Book of Revelation is the drama of the battle between God's wrath and the anger of Satan (Rev 12:7) and his henchmen (anger of the nations 11:18). The day of judgement, when this battle will take place is 'the great day of their wrath', of the wrath of him who sits on the throne and the wrath of the Lamb (6:16f; 11:18). The battlefield is the church. Satan is thrown down to earth raging with fury (12:12) and persecutes the church in return (12:13). God condemns all the powers of wickedness to death and destruction. He warns against the adoration of the Beast and threatens with the wine of the wrath of God, which has been prepared undiluted in the cup of his wrath (14:9f), with damnation (see 4:11). The great Babylon who has made all nations drink of the wine of her fornication (14:8; 18:3) falls; she has led other nations into apostasy, and this apostasy itself is a punishment ('wine of the wrath of God'; see Rom 1:18–32). God's judgement is compared to a vintage, cast into the great press of God's wrath (Rev 14:19; see also Is 63:1–6). God's wrath finds its completion in the execution of his judgement; seven angels with the seven last plagues are shown (Rev 15:1). One of the four living creatures passes to the seven angels seven golden vials full of the wrath of God to be poured out upon the earth (16:1). The great city of Babylon is given 'the cup of the wine of the indignation of his wrath' (16:19). Christ, the conqueror in this final battle, appears as the one who stamps the wine-press; he treads 'the wine-press of the fierceness of the wrath of God the Almighty' (19:15). God's wrath is victorious after all has been subjected to Christ (1 Cor 15:28).

In the other writings of John, the expression 'wrath of God' appears only once (Jn 3:36). Mankind stands guilty under God's wrath, subject to his judgement. In contradistinction to 'wrath' or 'anger' stands 'life everlasting'. The choice for or against Christ is decisive of whether man will be lost for ever or be saved from divine judgement and attain eternal life (see Jn 3:17f). In the faith in Christ, which is obedience, the eschatological gift of freedom from God's wrath has become a reality already in this present time (johannine eschatology).

Bibliography: Haag, 1754–7; H. Kleinknecht, J. Fichtner, G. Stählin, and others, *TDNT* III, 167f and V, 382–447 (= *Wrath* [BKW XIII], London 1964); Eichrodt I, 258–69; Meinertz II, 33ff; Bultmann, 238ff; G. Schrenk, *Unser Glaube an den Zorn Gottes nach dem Röm*, 1944; A. von Jüchen, *Der Zorn Gottes*, 1948.

Alois Stöger

Supplementary Bibliography

Analytical Index
of Articles
and Cross-References

Index of
Biblical References

Index of
Hebrew and Greek Words

Supplementary Bibliography

This supplement contains the most important books and articles which have appeared since the publication of the third German edition of the *Encyclopedia* in 1967. It has been specially prepared for this edition by the editor of the original, Professor J. B. Bauer, in the hope of thereby increasing the value of the *Encyclopedia* to English-speaking users.

Abraham

H. Werner, 'Abraham. Der Erstling und Repräsentant Israels', *Exempla Biblica* 1, 1965; N. A. Dahl. 'The Story of Abraham in Luke-Acts', *Festschrift P. Schubert*, Nashville/New York 1966, 139–58; K. Berger. 'Abraham in den paulinischen Hauptbriefen (Gal 3; 4, 21–31; Röm 4; 9–11; 2 C 11, 22)', *MTZ* 17 (1966), 47–89; A. González, *Abraham, Father of Believers*, London/New York 1968; H. Gaubert, *Abraham, Loved by God*, New York 1969.

Adam

A. J. Campbell, 'Adam', *Theology* 69 (1966), 216–22; P. Lengsfeld, 'Adam und Christus. Die Adam-Christus-Typologie im NT und ihre dogmatische Verwendung bei M. J. Scheeben u. K. Barth', *Koinonia* . . . 9 (1965); H. Müller, 'Der rabbinische Qal-Waehomer-Schluss in paulin. Typologie. Zur Adam-Christustypologie in Röm 5', *ZNW* 58 (1967), 73–92.

Almsgiving

S. J. Assaf, *La notion de l'aumône chez les Mésopotamiens, les Phéniciens et dans l'AT*, Strasbourg 1967 (dissertation).

Amen

J. C. G. Greig, *Abba and Amen: Their relevance to Christology (Studia Evangelica)* V, 2, *TU* 103 (1968), 3–20.

Angel

M. Takahashi, 'An Oriental's Approach to the Problem of Angelology', *ZAW* 78 (1966), 343–350; J. Quinlan, 'Engelen en duivels', *Tijdschrift voor Theologie*, 7 (1967), 43–61, English summary 62; É. Pascal, *Les anges dans la littérature préexilienne de l'AT*, Rome 1965/6 (dissertation).

Apostle

S. Freyne, 'The Twelve Apostles—An Essay in Redaction Criticism', *ITQ* 34 (1967), 242–53; F. Agnew, 'Vocatio primorum discipulorum in traditione synoptica', *VD* 46 (1968), 129–47; F. Bovon, 'L'origine des récits concernant les apôtres', *RTP* 100 (1967) 345–50; R. P. Meye, *Jesus and the Twelve: Discipleship and Revelation in Mark's Gospel*, Grand Rapids, Michigan 1968.

Ascension

J. Heuschen, *The Bible on The Ascension*, 1965; J. M. Egan, 'Meaning of the Ascension', *CrossCrown* 18 (1966), 164–74.

Asceticism

J. Leipoldt, *Griechische Philosophie und frühchristliche Askese*, Berlin 1961; H. A. Wenning, 'Die Askese im Zeugnis der Bibel', *Zer Bib* 8, 1966; H. A. Wennink, *The Bible on Asceticism*, St Norbert Abbey Series 14, 1966.

Atonement

D. Hill, 'Greek Words and Hebrew Meanings. Studies in the Semantics of Soteriological Terms', London/New York 1967.

Ban

A. Dekkers, *Der Kriegsherem und das Naturrecht. Mit einem religionswissenschaftlichen Vergleich*, Vienna 1964 (dissertation); B. Löbmann, 'Die Exkommunikation im NT', *Theologisches Jahrbuch*, 8 (1965), 446–58; W. Doskocil, 'Exkommunikation', *RAC* 7, 49 (1966), 1–22.

Baptism

D. M. Stanley, 'The NT Doctrine of Baptism', D. M. Stanley, *The Apostolic Church in the NT*, Westminster, Md, 1965, 140–94, 421–28 = *TS*

1015

18 (1957), 169–215; E. C. Whitaker, 'The History of the Baptismal Formula', *JEH* 16 (1965), 1–12; W. Bieder, *Die Verheissung der Taufe im NT*, Zürich 1966; J. Pryke, 'The Sacraments of Holy Baptism and Holy Communion in the Light of the Ritual Washings and Sacred Meals at Qumran', *RQ* 5 (1966), 543–52; D. W. B. Robinson, 'Born of Water and Spirit: Does Jn 3:5 Refer to Baptism?', *Reformed Theological Review*, 25 (1966), 15–23; O. Böcker, *Dämonenfurcht und Dämonenabwehr. Ein Beitrag zur Vorgeschichte der christlichen Taufe*, Stuttgart 1969.

Baptism of Jesus

E. Wehrli, 'Jesus' Baptism and Ours', *TheolLife* 8, 1 (1965), 24–34; S. L. Jr. Johnson, 'The Baptism of Christ', *Bibliotheca Sacra*, 123 (1966), 220–29; M. Sabbe, 'Le baptême de Jésus. Étude sur les origines littéraires du récit des Évangiles synoptiques', *Don. natal. J. Coppens* 2 (Gembloux/Paris 1967), 184–211; J. K. Howard, 'The Baptism of Jesus and its Present Significance', *Evangelical Quarterly*, London 39 (1967), 131–38.

Blessing

W. Bieder, *Segnen und Bekennen; eine biblische und eine historische Studie*, Basle 1965; W. Schenk, *Der Segen im NT (eine begriffsanalytische Studie)*, Jena 1965 (dissertation); F. Asensio, 'Trayectoria histórico-teológica de la "bendición" bíblica de Yahweh en labios del hombre', *Greg* 48 (1967), 253–83.

Blood

G. Kiefer, *Das Blut im Kult des Alten Bundes. Ein Beitrag zur Theologie des alttest. Kultes*, Trier 1966 (dissertation).

Blood of Christ

E. F. Siegman, 'The Blood of Christ in St. Paul's Soteriology', *Contemp. NT Studies* (Collegeville, Minn. 1965), 359–74.

Body

Bo Reicke, 'Body and Soul in the NT', *ST* 19 (1965), 200–12.

Brethren of Jesus

J. Blinzler, *Die Brüder und Schwestern Jesu*, Stuttgart 1967².

Building up

M. E. Thrall, 'The Meaning of oikodomeo in Relation to the Concept of syneidesis (1 Cor 8:10)', *Stud. Ev.* 4, 1 (1968), 468–72.

Charisma

O. Perels, 'Charisma in NT', *Fuldaer Hefte* 15 (1964).

Church

A. Cole, *The Body of Christ. A NT Image of the Church*, Philadelphia 1965; G. S. R. Cox, 'The Emerging Organization of the Church in the NT, and the Limitations Imposed Thereon', *Evangelical Quarterly*, 33 (1966), 22–39; B. F. Meyer, 'The Initial Self-Understanding of the Church', *CBQ* 27 (1965), 35–42; R. Schnackenburg, *The Church in the NT*, London/New York 1965; D. J. O'Connor, 'Is the Church the New Israel?', *ITQ* 33 (1966), 161–64; D. M. Stanley, *The Apostolic Church in the NT*, Westminster, Md, 1965; *Volk Gottes. Zum Kirchenverständnis der kath., evang. und anglikanischen Theologie. Festgabe für Josef Höfer*, ed. R. Bäumer and H. Dolch, Freiburg i. B, 1967; M. J. Le Guillou, *Christ and Church: A Theology of the Mystery*, New York 1966; F. Hahn and P. Rieger (ed.), *Anfänge der Kirche im NT (Ev Forum 8)*, 1957; O. Kuss, 'Hat Jesus die Kirche eigentlich gewollt? Rückblick auf das NT', *Kontexte* 4 (1962), 15–22; W. G. Kümmel, *Kirchenbegriff und Geschichtsbewußtsein in der Urgemeinde und bei Jesus*, Göttingen 1968; R. J. McKelvey, *The New Temple. The Church in the New Testament*, Oxford 1969.

Circumcision

E. Isaac, 'Circumcision as a Covenant Rite', *Anthropos* 59 (1964), 444–56; R. Schwarzenberger, *Bedeutung und Geschichte der Beschneidung im AT mit besonderer Berücksichtigung der Forschungsergebnisse aus Ethnologie und alter Geschichte*, Vienna 1964 (dissertation).

Clean and unclean

W. Kornfeld, 'Reine und unreine Tiere im AT', *Kairos* 7 (1965), 134–47; J. Raasch, 'The Monastic Concept of Purity of Heart and its Sources', *StMonast* 8 (1966), 7–33, 183–213.

Confession

W. Bieder, *Segnen und Bekennen; eine biblische und eine historische Studie*, Basle 1965; F. B. Craddock, 'The Meaning of Confession in the NT', *MidStream* 6, 2 (1967), 17–28.

Conscience

M. E. Thrall, 'The Pauline Use of syneidesis', *NTS* 14 (1967), 118–25.

Consolation

C. J. Bjerkelund, *Parakalô. Form, Funktion und Sinn der parakalô-Sätze in den paulinischen Briefen*,

Oslo 1967; A. Grabner-Haider, 'Paraklese und Eschatologie bei Paulus. Mensch und Welt im Anspruch der Zukunft Gottes', *NA* N.F. 4 (1968); F. W. Danker, '1 Peter 1, 24–2, 17—A Consolatory Pericope', *ZNW* 58 (1967), 93–102.

Contest

V. C. Pfitzner, 'Paul and the Agon Motif. Traditional Athletic Imagery in the Pauline Literature', *Suppl. to NT* 16 (1967).

Conversion

S. Smalley, 'Conversion in the NT', *Churchman* 78 (1964), 193–210; W. Trilling, 'Metanoia also Grundforderung der neutest. Lebenslehre', *Einübung des Glaubens, Festschrift K. Tilman*, Würzburg 1964, 178–90; A. Hulsbosch, *The Bible on Conversion*, St Norbert Abbey Series 18 (1966); B. Prete, 'La conversione nei Vangeli', *Sacra Doctrina* 11 (1966), 173–93; R. Schnackenburg, 'Umkehr-Predigt im NT', R. Schnackenburg, *Christliche Existenz nach dem NT* 1, Munich 1967, 35–60 = *MTZ* 1, 4 (1950), 1–13, considerably revised.

Covenant

D. J. McCarthy, 'Covenant in the OT: The Present State of Inquiry', *CBQ* 27 (1965), 217–41; F. Asensio, 'Teología e historia del pacto: en torno a una interrogación bíblica', *Greg* 47 (1966), 665–84; W. Eichrodt, 'Covenant and Law. Thoughts on Recent Discussion', *Interpretation* 20 (1966), 302–21; G. Fohrer, 'AT—"Amphiktyonie" und "Bund"?', *TLZ* 91 (1966), 801–16, 893–904; M. H. Woudstra, 'The Ark of the Covenant from Conquest to Kingship', *Bibl. & Theol. St.* 1965; A. Deissler, 'Die Bundespartnerschaft des Menschen mit Gott als Hinwendung zur Welt und Mitmenschen', J. B. Metz. (ed.), *Weltverständnis im Glauben*, Mainz 1965, 203–23; J. Swetnam, 'Diatheke in the Septuagint Account of Sinai', *Biblica* 47 (1966), 438–44; P. Altmann, *Erwählungstheologie und Universalismus im AT*, 1965; W. Eichrodt, 'Covenant and Law: Thoughts on Recent Discussion', *Interpretation* 20 (1966), 302–21; F. C. Fensham, 'Covenant, Promise and Expectation in the Bible', *TZ* 23 (1967), 305–22.

Creation

P. Haes, *Die Schöpfung als Heilsmysterium. Erforschung der Quellen*, Mainz 1964; G. Schneider, *Kainē Ktisis. Die Idee der Neuschöpfung beim Apostel Paulus und ihr religionsgeschichtlicher Hintergrund*, Trier 1959 (dissertation); H. F. Weiss, 'Untersuchungen zur Kosmologie des hellenistischen und palästinischen Judentums', *TU* 97 (1966); 'Die Schöpfung im NT', *Ex auditu verbi, Festschrift G. C. Berkouwer*, Kampen 1965, 56–72.

Cross

G. Q. Reijners, 'The Terminology of the Holy Cross in Early Christian Literature as Based upon OT Typology', *Graecitas Christianorum Primaeva* 2, Nijmegen 1965; E. Dinkler, 'Comments on the History of the Symbol of the Cross', *Journal for Theology and the Church*, 1 (1965), 124–45; F. Dölger, 'Beiträge zur Geschichte des Kreuzzeichens VII', *Jahrbuch für Antike und Christentum* 7 (1964, ed. 1966), 5–38; E. Dinkler, *Signum Crucis*, Tübingen 1967.

Cult

A. S. Kapelrud, 'The Role of the Cult in Old Israel', J. P. Hyatt (ed.), *Bible in Mod. Scholarship*, New York 1965, 44–56; response by B. Vawter: 57–64; by H. G. May: 65–73; H. J. Kraus, *Worship in Israel. A Cultic History of the OT*, Oxford/Richmond, Va, 1966; H. H. Rowley, *Worship in Ancient Israel. Its Form and Meaning*, London 1957; S. Herrmann, 'Kultreligion und Buchreligion. Kultische Funktionen in Israel und in Ägypten', *BZAW* 105 (1967), 95–105; A. Z. Idelzohn, *Jewish Liturgy and its Development*, New York 1967; H. H. Rowley, *Worship in Ancient Israel*, Philadelphia 1967; J. G. Trapiello, 'Mito y culto en el AT', *Angelicum* 44 (1967), 449–77.

Cup

G. Braumann, 'Leidenskelch und Todestaufe', *ZNW* 56 (1965) 178–83.

Death

N. Tromp, *Primitive Conceptions of Death and After-Life in the OT with Special Regard to Ugaritic Literature*, Rome 1967 (dissertation); P. Grelot, 'La théologie de la mort dans l'Écriture Sainte', *VS* Suppl. 77 (1966), 143–93; B. van Iersel, 'Vragen naar dood en leven in het NT', *Verbum* 33 (1966), 185–96; P. H. Menoud, *Le sort des trépassés d'après le NT*, Neuchâtel 1966²; N. J. Tromp, 'De conceptionibus primitivis orci et mortis in V.T. occurrentibus, consideratis in luce litteraturae ugariticae', *VD* 45 (1967), 209–17.

Decalogue

K. Kinoshita, *A Study of the Decalogue*, New York 1963 (dissertation); H. Gese, 'Der Dekalog als Ganzheit betrachtet', *ZTK* 64 (1967), 121–38.

Supplementary Bibliography

Demon

P. E. S. Thompson, 'Die Dämonen in der bibl. Theologie', G. Rosenkranz (ed.), Beiträge zur biblischen Theologie, Munich 1967, 148–63; J. E. Bruns, 'Toward a New Understanding of the Demonic', *Ecumenist* 4 (1965), 29–37; O. Böcker, *Dämonenfurcht und Dämonenabwehr. Ein Beitrag zur Vorgeschichte der christlichen Taufe*, Stuttgart 1969.

Demythologising

C. Duncan, 'The Bible and Objectifying Thinking—What Does Bultmann Mean by Demythologizing?', *Australian Biblical Review*, 14 (1966), 24–32; H. Fries, *Bultmann–Barth and Catholic Theology*, Duquesne Studies, Theol. Ser., 8, Pittsburgh, Pa, 1967; E. Hübner, 'Entmythologisierung als theologische Aufgabe', *Festschrift K. Barth*, Zürich 1966, 238–60; J. Knox, *Myth and Truth: An Essay on the Language of Faith*, London 1966; W. H. Schmidt, 'Mythos im AT', *ET*. N.S. 27 (1967), 237–54; K. Ward, 'Myth and Fact in Christianity', *SJT* 20 (1967), 385–96.

Discipline

J. A. Muirhead, *Education in the NT* (Monographs in Christian Education, No. 2), New York 1965; J. N. Sevenster, 'Education or Conversion: Epictetus or the Gospels', *NVT* 8 (1966), 247–62; V. C. Pritzner, *Paul and the Agon Motif. Traditional Athletic Imagery in the Pauline Literature*, Suppl. to *NT* 16, Leiden 1967; J. Gray, 'The Nature and Function of Adult Christian Education in the Church', *SJT* 19 (1966), 457–63.

Dream

F. Schmidtke, 'Träume, Orakel und Totengeister als Künder der Zukunft in Israel und Babylonien', *BZ* 11 (1967), 240–46.

Easter

P. Grelot and J. Pierron, *The Paschal Feast in the Bible*, Baltimore 1966; W. Huber, 'Passa und Ostern. Untersuchungen zur Osterfeier der Alten Kirche', *BZNW* 35 (1969).

Eucharist

N. Hook, *The Eucharist in the NT*, London 1964; E. J. Kilmartin, *The Eucharist in the Primitive Church*, Englewood Cliffs, NJ, 1965; Jr. S. McCormick, *The Lord's Supper. A Biblical Interpretation*, Philadelphia 1966; J. J. von Allmen, 'Essai sur le repas du Seigneur', *Cahiers théologiques* 55 (1966); W. Elert, *Eucharist and Church Fellowship in the First Four Centuries*, St Louis, Mo., 1966; J. Jeremias, *The Eucharistic Words of Jesus*, Rev. ed. London/New York 1966; W. Barclay, *The Lord's Supper*, London 1967; F. Hahn, 'Die alttest. Motive in der urchristlichen Abendmahlsüberlieferung', *ET* N.S. 27 (1967), 337–74; E. Schweizer, *The Lord's Supper acc. to the NT*, Philadelphia 1967; J. Wilkinson, *The Supper and the Eucharist*, London 1965; S. Accame, *L'istituzione dell'Eucaristia*, Naples 1968.

Faith

(S.) J. Heijke, *The Bible on Faith*, St Norbert Abbey Series 22, De Père, Wisc. 1966; A. L. Mulka, '"Fides quae per caritatem operatur" (Gal 5, 6)', *CBQ* 28 (1966), 174–88; H. Ljungman, 'Pistis, a Study of its Presuppositions and its Meaning in Pauline Use', *Acta Reg. Soc. Hum. Lit. Lundensis*, 64 (1964).

Fasting

F. G. Cremer, 'Die Fastenansage Jesu. Mk 2, 20 (u. Parr.) in der Sicht der patristischen und scholastischen Exegese', *BBB* 23 (1965); J. O'Hara, 'Christian Fasting (Mt 5, 15–18)', *Scripture* 19 (1967), 3–18; R. Arbesmann, 'Fasten', 'Fastenspeise', 'Fasttage', *RAC* 7, 447–93, 493–500, and 500–24.

Father

J. Jeremias, 'Die Botschaft Jesu vom Vater', *Calwer Hefte* 92 (1968); P. Gutiérrez, *La paternité spirituelle selon S. Paul, Études Bibliques*, Paris 1968

Fear

J. Becker, 'Gottesfurcht im AT', *AnBib* 25 (1965).

Flesh

A. Sand, 'Der Begriff "Fleisch" in den paulinischen Hauptbriefen', O. Kuss (ed.), *Biblische Untersuchungen* 2, Regensburg 1967.

Freedom

D. Doughty, '"Heiligkeit u. Freiheit"—eine exegetische Untersuchung der Anwendung des paulinischen Freiheitsgedankens in 1 Kor 7', Göttingen 1965 (dissertation); C. Johansson, *Concepts of Freedom in the OT*, New York 1965; G. Moran, 'Freedom in Christian Revelation', *Proc. Soc. Cath. College Teachers of Sacred Doctrine* 11 (1965), 59–77; J. Cambier, 'La liberté chrétienne dans le NT', *Bbl* 48 (1967), 116–27; G. de Ru, *Over Vrijheid*, Wageningen 1967; D. Nestle, *Eleutheria. Studien zum Wesen der Freiheit bei den Griechen und im NT. Teil I. Die*

Griechen (Hermeneut. Unters. z. Theologie 6), Tübingen 1967.

Fulfilment

K. Runia, 'The Interpretation of the OT by the NT', *Vox Reformata* 5 (1965); L. Goppelt, 'Erfüllen', *TWNT* VIII (1966), 246–60; W. Rothfuchs, *Die Erfüllungszitate des Matthäus-Evangeliums*, Stuttgart 1969.

God OT

B. van Iersel, *The Bible on the Living God*, London 1965; J. S. Chesnut, *The OT Understanding of God*, Philadelphia 1968; R. C. Dentan, *The Knowledge of God in Ancient Israel*, New York 1968; A. Jukas, *The Names of God in Holy Scripture*, Grand Rapids, Michigan 1967; H. D. Preuss, *Jahweglaube u. Zukunftserwartung* (*BWANT* 87), 1968.

God NT

A. W. Argyle, *God in the NT*, London 1965; T. Müller, *Gottesbild und Gottesbeziehung im NT*, Zürich/Frankfurt a.M. 1966; R. M. Grant, *The Early Christian Doctrine of God*, Charlottesville, Virginia 1966; J. Pfammatter, 'Eigenschaften und Verhaltensweisen Gottes im NT', Feiner-Löhrer (ed.), *Mysterium Salutis* 2 (Einsiedeln/Köln 1967), 272–90; K. H. Schelkle, 'Gott der Eine u. Dreieine', K. H. Schelkle, *Wort u. Schrift* (Düsseldorf 1966), 81–95; F. J. Schierse, 'Die neutestamentliche Trinitätsoffenbarung', Feiner-Löhrer (ed.), *Mysterium Salutis* 2 (Einsiedeln/Köln 1967), 85–131; R. Schulte, 'Die Vorbereitung der Trinitätsoffenbarung', Feiner-Löhrer (ed.), *Mysterium Salutis* 2 (Einsiedeln/Köln 1967), 55–73 (49–84).

Gospel

O. Michel, 'Evangelium', *RAC* 6, 47 (1965), 1107ff

Government

W. Schneemelcher, *Kirche und Staat im NT: Festschrift H. Kunst*, Berlin 1967; J. M. Paupert, *The Politics of the Gospel*, New York 1969.

Grace

O. J. Thomas, 'Irresistible Grace', *Vox Evangelica* 4 (1965), 55–64.

Holy

D. S. Shapiro, 'The Meaning of Holiness in Judaism', *Tradition* 7, 1 (1965), 46–80.

Hope

W. Zimmerli, *Der Mensch und seine Hoffnung seit den Aussagen des AT*, Göttingen 1968; J. Moltmann, *Theology of Hope*, London/New York 1967; H. Sasse, 'Some Thoughts on Christian Hope', *Reformed Theological Review* 26 (1967), 41–54.

Hour

H. van den Bussche, 'De Betekenis van het Uur in het vierde Evangelie', *Collationes Gandavienses* 2 (1952), 5–16; J. Leal, 'La hora de Jesús, la hora de sa Madre (Joh 2:4)', *Estudios Eccl.* 26 (1952), 147–68; J. Michl, 'Bemerkungen zu Joh 2:4', *Bbl* 36 (1955), 492–509; C. F. Ceroke, 'The Problem of Ambiguity in John 2:4', *CBQ* 21 (1959), 316–40; A. Feuillet, 'L'Heure de Jésus et le Signe de Cana', *ETL* 36 (1960), 5–22; R. Schnackenburg, *Das erste Wunder Jesu*, Leipzig 1960³; W. Thüsing, *Die Erhöhung und Verherrlichung Jesu im Johannesevangelium*, Münster 1960.

Inheritance

A. M. Brown, *The Concept of Inheritance in the OT*, New York 1965 (Columbia dissertation); J. D. Hester, 'The "Heir" and Heilsgeschichte: A Study of Gal 4:1ff', *Oikonomia, Festschrift O. Cullmann* (Hamburg 1967), 118–25.

Intercession

H. Zillikens, 'Segenssprüche und Fürbitten in der Frömmigkeit des Alten Bundes', *LitgJb* 17 (1967), 96–102.

Jerusalem

N. W. Porteous, 'Jerusalem–Zion: The Growth of a Symbol', N. W. Porteous, *Living the Mystery* (Oxford 1967), 93–111.

Jesus Christ

R. H. Fuller, *The Foundations of NT Christology*, London/New York 1965; F. Gogarten, *Jesus Christus. Wende der Welt. Grundfragen zur Christologie*, Tübingen 1966; A. T. Hanson, *Jesus Christ in the OT*, London 1965; A. J. B. Higgins, *Jesus and the Son of Man*, London/Philadelphia 1965; R. Marlow, 'The Son of Man in Recent Journal Literature, *CBQ* 28 (1966), 20–30; M. Kähler, *The So-Called Historical Jesus and the Historic Biblical Christ*, Philadelphia 1964; H. K. McArthur, *The Quest through the Centuries: The Search for the Historical Jesus*, Philadelphia 1966; H. Berkhof, *Christ the Meaning of History*, London/Richmond, Va 1966; L. Sabourin, *The Names and Titles of Jesus. Themes of Biblical Theology*, New York

1967; S. H. Hooke, *The Resurrection of Christ as History and Experience*, London 1967; N. Clark, *Interpreting the Resurrection*, London 1967; G. W. H. Lampe and D. M. MacKinnon, *The Resurrection*, London/Philadelphia 1966; T. Boman, *Die Jesus-Überlieferung im Lichte der neueren Volkskunde*, Göttingen 1967; C. K. Barrett, *Jesus and the Gospel Tradition*, London 1967; R. C. Foster, *Introduction and Early Ministry. Studies in the Life of Christ*, Grand Rapids, Michigan 1966; E. J. Goodspeed, *A Life of Jesus*, New York 1967; W. K. Kümmel, 'Jesusforschung seit 1950', *Theologische Rundschau*, Tübingen 31 (1966) 15–46, 289–315; E. W. Saunders, *Jesus in the Gospels*, Englewood Cliffs NJ, 1967; V. Taylor, *The Life and Mystery of Jesus*, New York 1967; W. Trilling, *Fragen zur Geschichtlichkeit Jesu*, Düsseldorf 1967²; H. R. Balz, 'Methodische Probleme der neutest. Christologie', *WissMonANT* 25 (1967); F. H. Borsch, *The Son of Man in Myth and History*, London/Philadelphia 1967; R. E. Brown, *Jesus God and Man. Modern Biblical Reflections*, Milwaukee 1967; J. Knox, *The Humanity and Divinity of Christ. A Study of Pattern in Christology*, London/New York 1967; W. E. Lynch, *Jesus in the Synoptic Gospels*, Milwaukee 1967; R. Slenczka, 'Geschichtlichkeit und Personsein Jesu Christi', *Forschungen zur systematischen und ökumenischen Theologie* 18 (1967); H. Flender, *Die Botschaft Jesu von der Herrschaft Gottes*, Munich 1968; K. Niederwimmer, *Jesus*, Göttingen 1968; R. Schippers, *Jezus Christus in het historisch Onderzoek*, Kampen 1969; H. Braun, *Jesus*, Stuttgart 1969; G. Strecker, 'Die historische und theologische Problematik der Jesusfrage', *ET* 29 (1969), 453–76.

Joy

A. B. du Toit, *Der Aspekt der Freude im urchristl. Abendmahl*, Winterthur 1965.

Justification

P. Crowley, 'Justification by Faith in St. Paul', *Scripture* 18 (1966), 91–111; K. Kertelge, '*Rechtfertigung*' *bei Paulus. Studien zur Struktur und zum Bedeutungsgehalt des paulinischen Rechtfertigungsbegriffs* (*NA* 3), 1967.

Lamb of God

J. Blenkinsopp, 'The Lamb of God', *Clergy Review* 50 (1965), 868–72; F. Gryglewicz, 'Das Lamm Gottes', *NTS* 13 (1966), 133–46; N. Hillyer, '"The Lamb" in the Apoc.' *Evangelical Quarterly* 39 (1967), 228–36; J. D'Souza, *The Lamb of God in the Johannine Writings*, Allahabad 1968.

Law

O. Kuss, 'Nomos bei Paulus', *MTZ* 17 (1966), 173–227.

Life

S. H. Hooke, 'Israel and the After-Life', *Expository Times*, 76 (1964), 236–39; 'The Extracanonical Literature, ib. 273–76; G. Dautzenberg, *Sein Leben bewahren. Psyché in den Herrenworten der Evangelien*, (*Studien zum Alten und Neuen Testament* 14, 1966); A. J. Feldman. *The Concept of Immortality in Judaism Historically Considered*, New York 1964; M. Carbonara Naddei, 'L'immortalità dell'anima nel pensiero dei Greci', *Sophia* 33 (1966), 272–300; R. Taylor, 'The Eschatological Meaning of Life and Death in the Book of Wisdom I–V', *ETL* 42 (1966), 72–137 = *Analecta Lovaniensia Biblica et Orientalia* 4 (1966).

Lord's day

L. T. Geraty, 'The Pascha and the Origin of Sunday Observance', *Andrews University Seminary Studies* 3 (1965), 85–96; F. A. Regan, 'Dies dominica and dies solis. The Beginnings of the Lord's Day in Christian Antiquity. An Abstract of a Dissertation', *Cath. Univ. of America. St. in S. Theol* 125A (1961); P. Delhaye and J. L. Lecat, 'Dimanche et Sabbat', *Mélanges de Science Religieuse*, 23 (1966), 3–14, 73–93; J. W. Leitch, 'Lord Also of the Sabbath', *Scottish Journal of Theology* 19 (1966), 426–33; W. Rordorf, *Sunday. The History of the Day of Rest and Worship in the Earliest Centuries of the Christian Church*, London/Philadelphia 1968.

Love

T. Barrosse, *Christianity: Mystery of Love. An Essay in Biblical Theology*, Notre Dame, Ind., 1964; C. Spicq, *Agape in the NT*, 3 vols, London/St Louis 1963–1966; J. T. Sanders, 'First Cor. 13. Its Interpretation since the First World War', *Interpretation* 20 (1966), 159–87.

Man

Leo Adler, *Der Mensch in der Sicht der Bibel*, Munich/Basle 1965; W. Zimmerli, 'Der Mensch und seine Hoffnung nach den Aussagen des AT', *Festschrift T. C. Vriezen*, Wageningen 1966, 389–402; W. Mork, *The Biblical Meaning of Man*, Milwaukee 1967; D. Burkhard (ed.), *Man before God: Toward a Theology of Man*, New York 1966.

Marriage

K. H. Schelkle, 'Ehe und Ehelosigkeit im NT', *WW* 29 (1966), 1–15; G. N. Vollebregt, *The*

Bible on Marriage, London 1965; A. Isaksson, *Marriage and Ministry in the New Temple. A Study with Special Reference to Mt 19, 3–12* (!) *and 1 Cor 11, 3–16*, Lund 1965; J. Cambier, 'Le grand mystère concernant le Christ et son Église, Éph 5, 22–33', *Bibl* 47 (1966), 43–90; K. Kahana, *The Theory of Marriage in Jewish Law*, Leiden 1966; H. Crouzel, 'Séparation ou remariage selon les Pères anciens', *Greg* 47 (1966), 472–94; H. Doms, 'Zur biblischen Sicht der Ehe', Feiner-Löhrer (ed.), *Mysterium Salutis* 2, Einsiedeln/Köln 1967, 724–37; V. J. Pospishil, *Divorce and Remarriage*, New York/London 1967; E. Schillebeeckx, *Marriage: Secular Reality & Saving Mystery*: I. *Marriage in OT and NT*, II. *Marriage in the History of the Church*, London 1965; R. Patai, *L'amour et le couple aux temps bibliques*, Tours 1967; R. Yaron, 'The Restoration of Marriage', *Journal of Jewish Studies* 17 (1966), 1–11; H. Baltensweiler, 'Die Ehe im NT. Exegetische Untersuchungen über Ehe, Ehelosigkeit und Ehescheidung', *Abhandlungen zur Theologie des Alten und Neuen Testaments* 32 (1967); W. J. Harrington, *The Bible on Marriage*, Dublin 1963; M. Thurian, *Matrimonio y celibato*, Saragosa 1966; A. Mahoney, 'A New Look at the Divorce Clauses in Mt 5, 32 and 19, 9', *CBQ* 30 (1968), 29–38.

Mary

J. Çantinat, *Mary in the Bible*, Westminster, Md., 1965; J. Galot, *Mary in the Gospel*, Westminster, Md, 1965; J. F. Craghan, *Mary's Vow of Virginity*, Munich 1965 (dissertation); A. Vögtle, 'Mt 1, 25 und die Virginitas B.M. Virginis post partum', *Tübinger Theologische Quartalschrift* 147 (1967), 28–39; B. Rinaldi, *Mary of Nazareth: Myth or History?*, Westminster, Md, 1966; F. M. Braun, *Mother of God's People*, Staten Island 1967; J. F. Craghan, *Mary. The Virginal Wife and the Married Virgin*, *The Problematic of Mary's Vow of Virginity*, Rome 1967; P. de Rosa, 'The Significance of Mary's virginity', *Clergy Review* 51 (1966), 419–29; *Maria in S. Scriptura. Acta Congressus Mariologici-Mariani in Republica Dominicana anno 1965 celebrati*, Rome 1967; H. Räisänen, 'Die Mutter Jesu im NT', *Annales Acad. Scient. Fennicae* Ser. B 158 (1969).

Mediation

H. Langkammer, *Christus als Schöpfungsmittler. Die biblischen Texte und der Ursprung des Glaubens*, Diss. Pont. Inst. Biblici, Rome 1966 (Biblical Institute dissertation); R. Bring, 'Der Mittler und das Gesetz. Eine Studie zu Gal 3, 20', *KD* 12 (1966), 292–309.

Meditation

M. L. Danieli, *Il concetto di contemplazione nell'AT*, Bologna 1965.

Messianism

S. Zeitlin, *The Origin of the Idea of the Messiah: Festschrift A. H. Silver*, New York 1963; P. Zerafa, 'Priestly Messianism in the OT', *Angelicum* 42 (1965), 318–41; S. Herrmann, *Die prophetischen Heilserwartungen im Alten Testament. Ursprung und Gestaltwandel*, Stuttgart 1966; J. Coppens, 'Le prémessianisme vétérotestamentaire', *Recherches Bibliques* 8 (1967), 153–79; *Il Messianismo: Atti della XVIII Settimana Biblica*, Brescia 1966; J. Scharbert, 'Der Messias im AT und im Judentum', *Stud. und Berichte der Katholischen Akademie in Bayern* 33 (1965), 47–78; Martin Rehm, 'Der königliche Messias im Licht der Immanuel-Weissagungen des Buches Jesaja', *Eichstätter Studien* (NF Bd 1) (XII und 432), 1968.

Millenarianism

R. D. Culver, *Daniel and the Latter Days (A Study in Millennialism)*,[2] Chicago 1965; H. Schumacher, *Das tausendjährige Königreich Christi auf Erden. Eine biblische Untersuchung im Lichte des Fortschreitens der göttlichen Heilsoffenbarung und Heilsgeschichte*, Stuttgart 1964.

Miracle

Miracles: Cambridge Studies in their Philosophy and History, ed. C. F. D. Moule, London 1965; J. Scharbert, 'Was versteht das AT unter Wunder?', *Bibel und Kirche* 22 (1967) 37–46; A. de Groot, *The Bible on Miracles*, St Norbert Abbey Series 19, 1966; B. B. Warfield, *Miracles: Yesterday and Today*, Grand Rapids, Mich., 1965; A. Heising, *Multiplicatio panum: Die Botschaft der Brotvermehrung*, Stuttgart 1966; L. Monden, *Signs and Wonders—A Study of the Miraculous Element in Religion*, New York 1966; R. D. Smith, *Comparative Miracles*, St Louis, Mo., 1965; R. H. Fuller, *Interpreting the Miracles*, London 1966; D. Connolly, 'Ad miracula sanationum apud Mt', *VD* 45 (1967), 306–25; K. Tagawa, 'Miracles et Évangile: La pensée personnelle de l'évangéliste Marc', *Ét. d'hist. et phil. rel.* 62 (1966); H. Baltensweiler, 'Wunder und Glaube im NT', *TZ* 23 (1967), 241–56; F. Mussner, *Die Wunder Jesu. Eine Hinführung*, München 1967; G. Schille, 'Die urchristliche Wundertradition. Ein Beitrag zur Frage nach dem irdischen Jesus', *Arb. z. Theol.* 1, 29 (1967).

Moses

I. H. Weisfeld, *This Man Moses*, New York 1966; K. Kastner, *Moses im NT*, Munich 1967 (dissertation); W. A. Meeks, 'The Prophet-King: Moses' Traditions and the Johannine Christology', Suppl. to *NT* 14 (1967); H. Schmid, 'Mose', *BZAW* 110 (1968).

Mystery

F. Gavin, *The Jewish Antecedents of the Christian Sacraments*, New York 1969.

Name

H. H. Rowley, *Dictionary of Bible Personal Names*, London 1968.

Neighbour

F. Mussner, 'Der Begriff des "Nächsten" in der Verkündigung Jesu. Dargelegt am Gleichnis vom barmherzigen Samariter', F. Mussner, *Praesentia Salutis* (Düsseldorf 1967), 125–32 (= *TTZ* 64 (1955), 91–9).

Oath

S. Mayence, *La parole de Jésus sur le serment (Mt 5, 33–37; Jac 5, 12). Tradition et rédaction dans l'Év. de Mt*, Louvain 1965 (dissertation).

Obedience

B. Schwank, '"Gehorsam" im NT: Erbe und Auftrag', *Beuron* 42 (1966), 469–76.

Original Sin

A. M. Dubarle, *The Biblical Doctrine of Original Sin*, London/New York 1964/1965; Z. Alszeghy and M. Flick, 'Il peccato originale in prospettiva personalistica', *Greg* 46 (1965), 705–32; W. T. Bruner, *Children of the Devil: A Fresh Investigation of the Fall of Man and Original Sin*, New York 1966; K. Condon, 'The Biblical Doctrine of Original Sin', *ITQ* 34 (1967), 20–36; P. Grelot, 'Réflexions sur le problème du péché originel', *NRT* 99 (1967), 337–75, 449–84; J. P. Mackey, 'Original Sin and Polygenism: The State of the Question', *ITQ* 34 (1967), 99–114; P. Grelot, 'Réflexions sur le problème du péché originel', *Cah. de l'Act. rel.* 24 (1967); P. De Rosa, *Christ and Original Sin*, London/Milwaukee 1967; J. Scharbert, *Prolegomena eines Alttestamentlers zur Erbsündenlehre*, Freiburg i.B. 1968; K. H. Schelkle, *Schuld als Erbteil*, Einsiedeln/Köln 1968.

Parable

J. Dupont, 'Le chapitre des paraboles', *NRT* 89 (1967), 800–20; C. J. Galloway, 'The Point of Parable', *Bible Today* 28 (1967), 1952–60; D. O. Jr. Via, *The Parables: Their Literary and Existential Dimension*, Philadelphia 1967.

Paradise

B. Hemelsoet, 'Das Paradies im Zeugnis der Bibel', *Zeugnis der Bibel* 6 (1965).

Parousia

A. L. Moore, 'The Parousia in the NT', Suppl. to *NvT* 13 (1966); I. H. Marshall, 'Martyrdom and the Parousia in the Revelation of John', *Studia Evangelica* 4, 1 (1968), 333–9.

Passion of Jesus

E. Best, *The Temptation and the Passion: The Markan Soteriology*, Cambridge/New York 1965; Fr. Normann, *Christos Didaskalos. Die Vorstellung von Christus als Lehrer in der christlichen Literatur des ersten und zweiten Jahrhunderts* (Münsterische Beiträge zur Theologie 32), Münster 1967; H. Conzelmann, 'Historie und Theologie in den synoptischen Passionsberichten', F. Viering (ed.), *Die Bedeutung des Todes Jesu* (Gütersloh 1967), 35–54; A. Vanhoye, *Structure and Theology of the Accounts of the Passion in the Synoptic Gospels* (Bible Today, Suppl. 81. 1), Collegeville, Minn., 1967; C. D. Peddinghaus, *Die Entstehung der Leidensgeschichte. Eine traditionsgeschichtliche und historische Untersuchung des Werdens und Wachsens der erzählenden Passionstradition bis zum Entwurf des Markus*, Heidelberg 1966 (dissertation); *Zur Bedeutung des Todes Jesu. Exegetische Beiträge* (von) H. Conzelmann, E. Käsemann, E. Haenchen, E. Flesseman-van Leer, E. Lohse: Schriftenreihe des Theol. Ausschusses der Ev. Kirche der Union, Gütersloh 1967; J. Knox, *The Death of Christ. The Cross in NT History and Faith*, London 1967; F. W. Bantz (ed.), *Das Wort vorm Kreuz. Evangelische und kath. Theologen verkündigen Christus, den Gekreuzigten*, Cologne 1967; F. Schütz, *Der leidende Christus. Die angefochtene Gemeinde und das Christuskerygma der lukanischen Schriften*, Stuttgart 1969.

Perfection

V. Luck, *Die Vollkommenheitsforderung der Bergpredigt*, München 1968.

Persecution

A. Harr, *The Theme of Jewish Persecution of Christians in the Gospel acc to Mt*, New York 1963 (Union Theological Seminary dissertation).

Poverty

A. Gelin, *The Poor of Yahweh*, Collegeville, Minn., 1964; L. E. Keck, 'The Poor among the Saints in the NT', *ZNW* 56 (1965), 100–29; H. J. Degenhardt, *Besitz und Besitzverzicht nach den lukanischen Schriften*, Stuttgart 1965.

Power

R. Penna, 'La Dynamis Theou; riflessione in margine a 1 Cor 1, 18–25', *Rivista Biblica* ... *Italiana* 15 (1967), 281–94.

Praise

R. J. Ledogar, 'Verbs of Praise in the LXX Translation of the Hebrew Canon', *Bibl* 48 (1967), 29–56.

Prayer

J. de Fraine, *Praying with the Bible*, New York 1964; W. Ott, *Gebet und Heil. Die Bedeutung der Gebetsparänese in der lukanischen Theologie* (Studien zum Alten und Neuen Testament 12), München 1965; J. Gnilka, 'Jesus und das Gebet', *Bibel und Leben* 6 (1965), 79–91; G. Bernini, 'La Preghiera nell'AT', R. Boccassino, *La Preghiera*, ed. R. Boccassino, Milan/Rome 1967, 321–417, 417–46; A. González, *La oracion en la Biblia*, Madrid 1968.

Preaching

D. M. Stanley, 'The Primitive Preaching: The Traditional Schema', *Concilium* 20 (1966), 88–100; R. C. Worly, *Preaching and Teaching in the Earliest Church*, Philadelphia 1967.

Priest(hood)

A. H. J. Gunneweg, *Leviten und Priester. Hauptlinien der Traditionsbildung und Geschichte des israelitisch-jüdischen Kultpersonals* (FRLANT 89), Göttingen 1965; K. H. A. Schelkle, *A Priestly People*, London 1965; J. C. G. Greig, *The Eschatological Ministry* (Essays in Mem. of G. H. C. Macgregor), Oxford 1965, 99–131; J. Baker, 'The Priesthood of All Believers', *Theology* 69 (1966), 60–65; C. (= K.) Romaniuk, *Le Sacerdoce dans le NT*, Le Puy/Lyons 1966; R. A. Stewart, 'The Sinless High-Priest', *NTS* 14 (1967), 126–35; J. Blenkinsopp, 'Presbyter to Priest: Ministry in the Early Church', *Worship* 41 (1967), 428–38; Y. Congar, *Priest and Layman*, London 1967; J. Blank, O. Schreuder, K. Rahner, A. Görres, F. Klostermann, *Weltpriester nach dem Konzil.* (Münchener Akademie-Schriften, ed. F. Henrich, Bd. 46), Munich 1969; A. Cody, *A History of Old Testament Priesthood*, Rome 1969.

Primacy

Il primato di Pietro nel pensiero contemporaneo, Bologna 1965; Š. Porúbčan, 'The Consciousness of Peter's Primacy in the NT', *Archivum Historiae Pontificiae* 5 (1967), 9–39; W. J. Tobin, 'La primauté de Pierre selon les évangiles', *Lumen Vitae* 22 (1967), 629–73; B. Rigaux, 'S. Pierre et l'exégèse contemporaine (bulletin)',

Concilium 3, 27 (1967), 129–52; *San Pietro. Scritti di A. Bea ecc: Atti della XIX Settimana Biblica* (dell')Associazione Biblica Italiana, Brescia 1967.

Principalities and powers

W. Manson, 'Principalities and Powers: The Spiritual Background of the Work of Jesus in the Synoptic Gospels', W. Manson, *Jesus & The Christian* (London 1967), 77–88.

Rebirth

E. Stein, 'Der Begriff der Palingenesie im talmudischen Judentum', *MGWJ* 83 (1939, ed. 1964), 194–205.

Redemption

G. W. Grogan, 'The Experience of Salvation in the Old and NT', *Vox Evangelica* 5 (1967), 4–26; E. M. B. Green, *The Meaning of Salvation*, London 1965; W. G. Most, 'A Biblical Theology of Redemption in a Covenant Framework', *CBQ* 29 (1967), 1–19; M. E. McIver, 'The Cosmic Dimensions of Salvation in the Thought of St. Paul', *Worship* 40 (1966), 156–64; R. Zehnle, 'The Salvific Character of Jesus' Death in Lucan Soteriology', *TS* 30 (1969), 420–44.

Rest

J. Cadet, 'Repos dominical et loisir humain', *MD* 83 (1965), 71–97; M. D. Philippe, 'Le repos du Père et l'Alliance éternelle', *Verbum Caro* 20, 79 (1966), 9–25.

Restoration

S. Rayburn, 'Cosmic Transfiguration', *Church Quarterly Review* 168, London 1967, 162–67.

Resurrection

G. Wied, *Der Auferstehungsglaube im späten Israel in seiner Bedeutung für das Verhältnis von Apokalyptik und Weisheit*, Bonn 1964/65 (dissertation); L. Swain, 'The Resurrection in the OT. Eternal Life in the OT', *Clergy Review* 51 (1966), 949–54, 52 (1967), 104–09; S. K. Aboa, *Die Entstehung der Auferstehungshoffnung im AT*, Hamburg 1966/67 (dissertation); E. Brandenburger, 'Die Auferstehung der Glaubenden als historisches und theologisches Problem', *Wort und Dienst* 9 (1967), 16–33; J. Schmid, 'Auferstehung des Fleisches. I. Biblisch', *Sacramentum Mundi* 1 (Freiburg i.B. 1967), 385–97; J. Comblin, *The Resurrection in the Plan of Salvation*, Notre Dame, Ind., 1966.

Supplementary Bibliography

Revelation

D. Lührmann, *Das Offenbarungsverständnis bei Paulus und in den paulinischen Gemeinden* (*WissMonANT* 16) 1965.

Reward

A. Marmorstein, *The doctrine of merits in old Rabbinical literature*, 2 vols, New York 1968.

Righteousness (justice)

O. Kaiser, 'Dike und Sedaqa. Zur Frage nach der sittlichen Weltordnung. Ein theologisches Präludium', *Neue Zeitschrift für systematische Theologie und Religionsphilosophie* 7 (1965), 251–73; P. Stuhlmacher, 'Gerechtigkeit Gottes bei Paulus', *FRLANT* 87 (1965).

Sabbath

S. T. Jr. Kimbrough, 'The Concept of Sabbath at Qumrân', *RQ* 5 (1966), 483–502; J. H. Meesters, *Op zoek naar de oorsprong van de Sabbat* (Studia Semitica Neerl. 8.), Assen 1966; N. A. Barack, *A History of the Sabbath*, New York 1965.

Satan

M. E. Boismard, 'Satan selon l'Ancien et le NT', *LV* 15, 78 (1966), 61–76; R. S. Kluger, *Satan in the OT*, Evanston, Ill., 1967; C. Duquoc, 'Satan—Symbol oder Person?', *Christus vor uns . . .*, Bergen-Enkheim 1966, 49–57; P. von der Osten-Sacken, *Gott und Belial*, Göttingen 1969.

Scandal

W. Molinski, 'Ärgernis', *Sacramentum Mundi* 1 (Freiburg i.B. 1967), 318–27.

Scripture

J. Bright, *The Authority of the OT*, New York/London 1967; J. C. Wenger, *God's Word Written; Essays on the Nature of Biblical Revelation and Authority*, Scottdale, Pa., 1966.

Shepherd

O. Kiefer, *Die Hirtenrede. Analyse und Deutung von Joh 10, 1–18*, Stuttgart 1967; A. J. Simonis, *Die Hirtenrede im Johannes-Evangelium. Versuch einer Analyse von Joh 10, 1–18 nach Entstehung, Hintergrund und Inhalt* (Analecta Biblica 29), Rome 1967; P. de Robert, *Le Berger d'Israël. Essai sur le thème pastoral dans l'AT* (Cahiers Théologiques 57), Neuchâtel/Paris 1968.

Sin

R. Knierim, *Die Hauptbegriffe für Sünde im AT*, Gütersloh 1965; A. Buechler, *Studies in Sin and Atonement in the Rabbinic Literature of the First Century*, New York 1967; B. F. Malina, 'Some observations on the Origin of Sin in Judaism and St. Paul', *CBQ* 31 (1969), 18–34; L. van den Wijngaert, 'Die Sünde in der Priesterschriftlichen Urgeschichte', *Theologie und Philosophie* 43 (1969), 35–50.

Sonship

P. Wülfing von Martitz, G. Fohrer, E. Schweizer, E. Lohse, W. Schneemelcher, *TWNT* VIII (1967), 334–84.

Spirit

H. Berkhof. *The Doctrine of the Holy Spirit*, Richmond, Va., 1964; K. McNamara, 'The Holy Spirit in the Church', *ITQ* 32 (1965), 281–94; G. H. Davies, 'The Holy Spirit (=HS) in the OT', ibid., 129–34; F. Stagg, 'The HS in the NT', ibid., 135–47; *De Spiritu Sancto. Bijdragen tot de leer van de Heilige Geest bij gelegenheid van het 2e eeuwfeest van het Stipendium Bernardinum*, Utrecht 1964; D. Moody, *Spirit of the Living God. The Biblical Concepts Interpreted in Context*, Philadelphia 1968.

Suffering

A. Bertrangs, *The Bible on Suffering*, St Norbert Abbey Series 11, 1966.

Temple

B. Gärtner, *The Temple and the Community in Qumran and the NT* (SocNTS Monograph Series), Cambridge/New York 1965; R. E. Clements, *God and Temple*, Oxford/Philadelphia 1965; K. Baltzer, 'The Meaning of the Temple in the Lukan Writings', *Harvard Theological Review* 58 (1965), 263–77; L. Gaston, 'The Theology of the Temple. The NT Fulfillment of OT Heilsgeschichte', *Oikonomia, Festschrift O. Cullmann*, Hamburg 1967, 32–41; H. Lignée, *The Temple of Yahweh*, Baltimore 1966; N. Poulssen, *König und Tempel im Glaubenszeugnis des AT*, Stuttgart 1967.

Temptation

B. van Iersel, *The Bible on the Temptations of Man* (St Norbert Abbey Series 12), 1966; C. B. Houk, Peirasmos, 'The Lord's Prayer, and the Massah Tradition', *Scottish Journal of Theology* 19 (1966), 216–25; H. Clavier, 'Tentation et anamartésie dans le NT', *RHPR* 47 (1967), 150–64; J. Dupont, *Les tentations de Jésus au désert* (Studia Neotest., 4), Bruges/Paris 1968; 'The Origin of the Narrative of Jesus' Temptations', *Theology Digest* 15 (1967), 230–35.

Three

G. Delling, 'Drei', *TWNT* VIII (1966), 215–325.

Time

P. Brunner, 'Die Zeit im christlichen Glauben', Brunner, *Pro Ecclesia* II, Berlin/Hamburg 1966, 50–59; J. V. L. Casserley, *Toward a Theology of History*, London 1965; A. E. Willingale, 'Time in the Bible', *Faith & Thought* 96, 1 (1967), 25–53; C. Mugler, 'Le retour éternel et le temps linéaire dans la pensée grecque', *Bulletin de l'Association G. Budé* 25, 4 (1966), 405–19.

Tradition

Y. M. J. Congar, *Tradition and Traditions: An Historical and a Theological Essay*, London/New York 1966/1967; H. T. Mayer, 'Scripture, Tradition, and Authority in the Life of the Early Church', *Concordia Theological Monthly* 38 (1967), 19–23; *Holy Book and Holy Tradition*, Intern. Coll., Manchester, 1968.

Transfiguration

A. M. Ramsey, *The Glory of God and the Transfiguration of Christ*, London 1967; L. F. Rivera, 'Interpretatio Transfigurationis Jesu in redactione evangelii Marci', *VD* 46 (1968), 99–104.

Truth

H. Blocher, 'La notion biblique de vérité', *Ét. Év.* 26, 4 (1966), 145–58; L. Goppelt, 'Wahrheit als Befreiung. Das neutest. Zeugnis von der Wahrheit nach dem Jo.-Ev.', H. R. Muller-Schwefe (ed.), *Was ist Wahrheit?*, Göttingen 1965; R. Schnackenburg, 'Zum Begriff der "Wahrheit" in den beiden kleinen Johannesbriefen', *BZ* 11 (1967), 253–58.

Virgin Birth

H. v. Campenhausen, *The Virgin Birth in the Theology of the Ancient Church*, London/Naperville, Ill., 1964; J. Bligh, 'The Virgin Birth', *Heythrop Journal* 6 (1965), 109–197; J. F. Craghan, *Mary's Vow of Virginity*, Munich 1965 (dissertation); J. Riedl, *Die Vorgeschichte Jesu*, Stuttgart 1968; R. Kilian, *Die Verheißung Immanuels*, Stuttgart 1969; J. Michl, 'Die Jungfrauengeburt im NT', *Mariologische Studien IV* (1969), 145–84.

Virginity

D. W. Trautman, *The Eunuch Logion of Mt 19, 12: Historical and exegetical Dimensions as Related to Celibacy*, Rome 1966 (Angelicum dissertation); L. Swain, 'St. Paul on Celibacy', *Clergy Review* 51 (1966), 785–91; K. H. Schelkle, 'Ehe und Ehelosigkeit im NT', K. H. Schelkle, *Wort und Schrift*, Düsseldorf 1966, 183–98 = *WW* 29 (1966), 1–15; J. Blenkinsopp, *Celibacy, Ministry, Church*, London and New York 1968.

Vocation

J. de Fraine, *The Bible on Vocation and Election*, St Norbert Abbey Series 21, 1966.

Water

L. Goppelt, 'Wasser', *TWNT* VIII (1966), 313–33.

Way

E. Repo, *Der "Weg" als Selbstbezeichnung des Urchristentums. Eine traditionsgeschichtliche und semasiologische Untersuchung* (*Annales Academiae Scientiarum Fennicae* B, 132, 2), Helsinki 1964; N. Brox, *Der Glaube als Weg*, München/Salzburg 1968.

Wine

R. Borig, *Der wahre Weinstock. Untersuchungen zu Jo 15, 1–10* (*Studien zum Alten u. Neuen Testament* 16), Munich 1967; A. Smitmans, *Das Weinwunder von Kana. Die Auslegung von Jo 2, 1–11 bei den Vätern und heute* (*Beiträge zur Geschichte der bibl. Exegese* 6), Tübingen 1966.

Wisdom

B. De Pinto, 'Word and Wisdom in St. John', *Script* 19 (1967), 19–27; M. Conti, 'La Sophia di 2 Petr 3, 15', *Rivista Biblica Italiana* 17 (1969), 121–38.

Witness

J. C. Hindley, 'Witness in the Fourth Gospel', *Scottish Journal of Theology* 18 (1965), 319–37.

Woman

J. Bottéro, 'La femme dans l'ancien Israël', *Hist. mondiale de la femme* 1, Paris 1965, 224–47; R. Loewe, *The Position of Women in Judaism*, London 1966; K. Stendahl, *The Bible and the Role of Women. A Case Study in Hermeneutics*, Philadelphia 1966; T. Maertens, *La promotion de la femme dans la Bible: Points de repère*, Tournai 1967; C. J. Vos, *Woman in Old Worship*, Delft 1968 (dissertation).

Work

J. L. Gómez de Morales, *El trabajo en la Biblia*, Madrid 1966.

World

G. Hierzenberger, *Weltbewertung bei Paulus nach 1 Kor 7, 29–31. Eine exegetisch-kerygmatische Studie* (KomBeitrANT), Düsseldorf 1967; R. Schnackenburg, 'Der Christ und die Zukunft der Welt', R. Schnackenburg, *Christl. Existenz nach dem NT* 2, Munich 1968, 149–85; idem, 'Das Verständnis der Welt nach dem NT', ib., vol. 1, Munich 1967, 157–85.

ANALYTICAL INDEX OF ARTICLES AND CROSS-REFERENCES

This analytical index has been compiled to enable readers to derive maximum benefit from the encyclopedia, and to locate easily and quickly important passages dealing with a given biblical-theological theme.

Words in bold type are the main entries for the articles in the encyclopedia: the italicised words indented below each bold-type entry indicate cross-references to the article in question from other articles. All arrowed cross-references in the text itself are included, and many more besides.

Words in roman type are cognates, synonyms, antonyms, etc. for themes treated in the italicised articles indicated after the arrow.

Abraham 3–6
  Covenant 142
  Father 262
  Justification 453
  Mediation 567
  Spirit 875
  Temptation 903f
  Three 911
  Vision of God 948
  Vocation 955

Absolution ↗ *Goodness, Mercy, Reconciliation*

Abstinence ↗ *Asceticism, Fasting, Self-denial*

Abundance ↗ *Riches*

Abyss ↗ *Creation, Sea*

Acceptance ↗ *Sacrifice*

Accuser ↗ *Satan*

Acknowledgement ↗ *Confession*

Adam 6–9
  Body 81
  Covenant 142
  Light 505
  Likeness 509–13
  Man 542–5
  Marriage 551f
  Messianism 576
  Original sin 620–24
  Paradise 629–33
  Sin 849, 861
  Spirit 871f

Adoption ↗ *Father, Inheritance, Sonship*

Adoration 9–15
  Antichrist 31
  Conversion 138–40
  Flesh 274f
  Hypocrite 390–92
  Prayer 679f, 682f
  Spirit 877–88
  Truth 932

Adultery ↗ *Marriage*

Advent ↗ *Parousia, Visitation*

Adversary ↗ *Enemy, Satan*

Affliction ↗ *Persecution, Sickness*

Agape 15–16
  Church 111
  Eucharist 232, 237
  Goodness 327
  Love 518–41

Ages ↗ *Time*

Allegory ↗ *Parable*

Alliance ↗ *Covenant*

Almsgiving 16–19
  Death 184
  Love 524–7, 529–31, 535–8
  Mercy 574
  Riches 775–80
  Righteousness 784

Altar ↗ *Sacrifice*

Amen 19–20
  Faith 244
  Truth 927

Anathema ↗ *Ban*

Angel 20–28
  Demon 192, 194f
  Glory 298
  Heaven 367f
  Mediation 569, 571f
  Mission 589
  Paradise 629–32
  Principalities 712–16
  Revelation 771
  Satan 808–12
  Scripture 824
  Sonship 863
  Temptation 904

Anger ↗ *Wrath*

Anointing ↗ *Jesus Christ*

Antichrist 28–32
  Adoration 14f
  Hell 370
  Parousia 635
  Scandal 815

Apocalypse ↗ *Revelation*

Apokatastasis ↗ *Restoration*

INDEX OF BIBLICAL REFERENCES

The books of the Bible are listed in the order in which they appear in the Revised Standard Version of the Bible (Catholic Edition). The individual references to a given book of the Bible are listed in their natural order of chapter and verse, but where two or more passages of differing lengths begin with the same verse precedence is taken by the longer or more inclusive reference.

All references to individual verses and chapters and to groups of verses and chapters are included. References to whole books of the Bible are not included, however.

In the synoptic gospel listings certain entries appear in italic type. These represent the references to parallel passages directly implied, but not explicitly cited, by the text. All parallel passages directly implied by textual references to a particular synoptic gospel passage *and parallels* are included, but such parallel passages are only entered in this index if a textual reference calls for them. For example, under Mark the following roman-type entry appears:

9:7   37, 123, 225, 434, 528,
531, 924

This means that there is an explicit reference to Mk 9:7 on each of the seven text pages listed. On two of these pages, however—pp 528 and 531—the reference is in the form 'Mk 9:7 and parallels'. One of the parallels to Mk 9:7 is Lk 9:35, and it will be seen that there are two consecutive entries for this latter reference:

9:35   123, 695
9:35 (|| Mk 9:7)   528, 531

The roman-type entry signifies that explicit references to Lk 9:35 will be found on pp 123 and 695. The italic-type entry signifies that implicit references to Lk 9:35 will be found on pp. 528 and 531 in the form 'Mk 9:7 and parallels'.

This feature is designed to help readers derive full benefit from the encyclopedia, while using it alongside the Bible or a biblical commentary, or while preparing sermons, lectures, etc., based on particular passages of the synoptic gospels.

OLD TESTAMENT

Genesis	page	Genesis—cont.	page	Genesis—cont.	page
1–5	6	1:26	366, 509, 511	2:8–15	339
1	511, 809, 825, 992	1:26b	544	2:8–14	630
1:1–2	504	1:27	93, 509, 511, 545, 989	2:8ff	629
1:1ff	224, 301, 302, 366, 585, 586	1:28	69, 71, 366, 552, 724, 996	2:8	147, 319
1:1	147, 995	1:29	349	2:9–17	316, 317
1:2–9	825	1:30	366	2:10	357
1:2	826, 871, 878, 879, 887, 995	1:31	147, 519	2:15ff	630
		2–11	1007	2:15	319, 629, 897, 996
1:3–30	871	2–3	317, 319, 320, 1007	2:16	319, 629
1:3f	504	2	511, 629, 631	2:17	181, 182, 317, 319, 339, 500, 620
1:3	504, 533, 995	2:1	366	2:18ff	690
1:4	505, 519	2:2f	797, 798, 799	2:18	551, 985, 989
1:6–8	366	2:3	372	2:19–23	319, 366
1:6	533	2:4–3:24	629	2:19	147, 339, 879
1:7	147	2:4–7	630	2:20	319, 551
1:10	519	2:4	147	2:21–4	630
1:11	349	2:5	6, 339, 542	2:21ff	81, 545, 985
1:14–17	366	2:7ff	519	2:21	273, 989
1:14ff	149	2:7	6, 8, 81, 147, 181, 281, 283, 307, 319, 446, 500, 542, 547, 872, 887	2:22	90, 339, 552
1:22	69, 71, 724			2:23–4	261, 274, 319
1:26–7	549			2:23f	9
1:26ff	6, 7, 81, 519, 544, 985	2:8–3:24	620	2:23	551, 983, 989

Isaiah—*cont.*

52:13–53:12	82, 386, 6...
52:13	8...
52:15	79, 80, 155, 168, 29...
53	424, 431, 479, 52... 804, 843, 854, 890, 892, 894
53:1–9	657
53:1–6	656
53:1–4	895
53:1	843
53:3–5	846
53:3	890
53:4–12	569
53:4	537, 842, 843, 847
53:5	650, 831, 841, 843
53:6	234
53:7f	292, 386, 843
53:7	234, 478
53:8	900
53:10–12	237
53:10ff	144, 292, 892
53:10	234, 843
53:10b–12	234
53:11f	570
53:11	144, 899
53:12	229, 234, 239, 293, 663, 842, 843
54f	840
54:1–17	414
54:1ff	837
54:1	103
54:3	579
54:4–10	143
54:4–8	555
54:4	986
54:5–8	217, 522
54:5f	104, 852
54:5	306, 521
54:6	872, 954
54:7–12	413
54:8–10	522, 1008
54:8	521
54:9	614
54:10	144, 234, 579, 649, 728, 752
54:11f	91
54:12	144
54:13f	649
54:13	92
54:16	724
55:3–5	842
55:3	234, 338, 579, 616
55:5	364
55:6f	523
55:6	732, 830
55:7	521
55:8f	724
55:8	303
55:10f	991
55:11	309, 339, 694, 992
56–66	579
56	523
56:1	781, 782, 784

50:.	
56:11	
57:1–2	
57:1f	182
57:13	598, 869, 870
57:14–19	217
57:15	386, 387, 673, 872
57:16	543, 544, 872
57:17	831, 891
57:18f	648
57:20f	219
57:21	649, 841
58:1–5	523
58:2	473, 781, 785
58:3–7	258, 259
58:3	386
58:5ff	851
58:5	386
58:6–12	16, 259
58:6f	525
58:6	590
58:7	274
58:8	504
58:13f	799, 800
59:2	849
59:3	76
59:4	376
59:9	376
59:11	376
59:16	399
59:17	407
59:19ff	633
59:19	611, 871
59:21	616, 708
60ff	457
60	414, 419
60:1–62:12	414
60:1–3	504
60:1ff	226, 634
60:1	831
60:7	708
60:9ff	294
60:10	521
60:11	708
60:13	296
60:14	10
60:15	555
60:16	414
60:19f	504
60:21	350
60:22	651
61	442
61:1–4	876
61:1–3	876
61:1–2	691
61:1f	292, 387, 590, 879
61:1	226, 673, 687, 688, 689, 874, 878, 978

Index of biblical references

page
935
350, 872
294
708
234, 414, 616
71
104, 439, 555

...—*cont.*

	783
	226, 504
	104
62:4	414, 522
62:5	143, 439
62:6f	399
62:6	952
62:8ff	414
62:10–12	103
62:12	739, 744
63:1–6	77, 350, 444, 936, 967, 1011
63:1–4	1007
63:5	1007
63:7–19	874
63:7	521
63:9	521
63:10–14	880
63:10ff	655
63:10	309
63:11f	595
63:11	218, 873
63:16	262, 863
63:17	347
64:1	63, 65, 367
64:4	529
64:5	621
64:8	65, 306, 863, 1008
64:11	65
64:14	65
65:1–4	893
65:1	831, 832
65:2	155
65:3	191
65:6	85
65:8ff	657
65:9	954
65:11	598
65:14	360
65:15	176, 179, 954
65:16	71
65:17	360, 366, 367, 634, 744, 748, 752, 876
65:20–22	582
65:20f	631
65:22	582, 954
65:23	71
65:25	631, 649, 879
66:1f	91
66:1	310, 367, 903
66:2	386, 872
66:3	70
66:9f	872
66:11–13	134
66:12f	893
66:13	303, 306, 521, 987
66:14	771
66:15–17	444

NEW TESTAMENT

Index of biblical references

1. *Hebrew words and roots*

ᵓab, 260, 264
ᶜabad, 930
ᵓabrāhām, 3
ᵓabrām, 3
ᵓādām, 297, 339, 542
ᵃᵈāmâh, 6, 339, 542
ᶜādan, 629
ᵓāḥ, 86, 88, 613
ᵓāhab, 518, 520f, 523, 525f, 540
ᵓaʰᵃbâh, 518, 521, 523
ᵓâhābat, 325
ᵓālâh, 174, 176
ᶜālas, 679
ᶜālāts, 679
ᶜalmāh, 560, 943
ᵓālôth, 174
ᵓam, 652, 674
ᶜām, 363f, 406
ᶜāmāl, 890
ᵓāman, 244, 376, 927
ᵓāmats, 346f
ᵓāmēn, 19f
ᵓāmint, 927
ᵓammîm, 652
ᵓānān, 296
ᵓānaš, 543
ᵓanāšîm, 674
ᵓānāw, 672
ᶜᵃnāwâh, 672
ᵓānāwîm, 386, 673, 876
ᶜānî, 672f
ᵓānîim, 386
ᵓanšê, 928
ᵓānwe, 673
ᵓappayîm, 325
ᵓappîm, 322
ᵓaqnîᵓēm, 406
ᵓārar, 174f
ᶜārēl, 347
ᵓārûr, 174
ᶜāsâh, 147
ᵓāšām, 802, 804
ᵓāsar, 67
ᵓaᶜéreth, 184
ᶜāthar, 398
ᵓāwâh, 206
ᶜāwôn, 850
ᶜᵃzārâh, 51

bāḥar, 695
bāḥîr, 954, 956
bānâh, 90
bārāᵓ, 147, 585
bārak, 69f
bārek, 677

barûk, 69
bāśar, 328, 543, 546, 548
bāṭaḥ, 244, 376f
bātsaᶜ, 146
bᵉ, 831
bᵉᵉmeth, 927
bᵉhēmâh, 544
bᵉkôr, 271
bᵉlôᵓ, 406
bᵉrākâh, 69f, 629
bᵉrîth, 140f, 143
bᵉšm, 954
bᵉśôrâh, 328
betsaᶜ, 146
bḥr, 954–6
bikkûrîm, 271
bîn, 316
biqqēš, 829
Bōᶜaz, 900
bōnê, 93
ᶜbwdt, 930

daᶜath, 317
dābaq, 523
dābar, 687
dal, 672
dām, 75
dāmîm, 75
dāraš, 316, 391, 829
dᵉbārîm, 480f
dᵉbîr, 900
dᵉmûth, 509
dērek, 346, 963

ᵓebed, 522, 674, 839
ᵓēbel, 890
ᵓebyôn, 672
ᵓēdâh, 652
ᵓeden, 629
ᶜēdôth, 481
ᵓēlām, 900
ᵓêlîm, 22
ᵓᵉlōhê, 712
ᵓᵉlōhîm, 191, 509f, 629, 674, 879
ᵓᵉmeth, 244, 519f, 534, 782, 927–31
ᵏᵉnāš, 985
ᵏᵉnôš, 542f
ᵓerek, 322, 325
ᵓeš, 269
ᵉēth, 379f, 912
ᶜēzer, 551

gāᵓal, 739f
gādap, 67
gan, 629

1183

2. *Greek words and prepositional phrases*